FOURTH EUROPEAN CONFERENCE
ON ARTIFICIAL LIFE

Complex Adaptive Systems
John H. Holland, Christopher G. Langton, and Stewart W. Wilson, advisors

FOURTH EUROPEAN CONFERENCE ON ARTIFICIAL LIFE

edited by
Phil Husbands and Inman Harvey

A Bradford Book

The MIT Press
Cambridge, Massachusetts
London, England

CONTENTS

EVOLUTIONARY DYNAMICS

MORPHOGENESIS

EMULATION OF NATURAL BEHAVIOR, AND ROBOTICS

EVOLUTIONARY ROBOTICS, EVOLVABLE HARDWARE AND APPLICATIONS

COMMUNICATION, COOPERATION AND COLLECTIVE BEHAVIOR

ARTIFICIAL WORLDS

Preface

Physiological life is of course not 'Life'. And neither is psychological life. Life is the world.
Ludwig Wittgenstein

Without deviation, progress is not possible.
Frank Zappa

He said it was artificial respiration, but now I find I am to have his child.
Anthony Burgess, *Inside Mr. Enderby*

Since its inception in the late 1980s, the interdisciplinary field of Artificial Life has brought together scientists interested in a formal and general understanding of living systems. At its core are endeavours to synthesize life-like phenomena in artificial media, usually computers or robots, in an attempt to establish such an understanding.

This book contains 63 of the 174 papers submitted for presentation at The Fourth European Conference on Artificial Life (ECAL97), held in Brighton, UK from 28th to 31st July, 1997. The book is divided into sections corresponding to the main conference sessions.

Although the field of Artificial Life is still defining itself, the papers collected here begin to show signs of a maturing discipline. Much of the work described builds on previous research; motivations and foundations are carefully thought about. There is less highly speculative exploratory work than at earlier conferences. While all these things are to be welcomed — progress is unlikely without them — we strongly believe that the most exciting, radical and potentially important research comes out of a concerted interdisciplinary probing and challenging of the mainstream. Because of this we hope that the early vitality of Artificial Life will not diminish, that the field will remain outward looking and that new cross-discipline interfaces are defined and exploited. We believe that the sorts of approaches covered by this volume have great potential, it is up to our community to make sure that this is fulfilled.

ECAL97 could not have taken place without the invaluable help of many people and organizations. We are especially grateful to members of the program committee, listed overleaf. We are also very grateful to the following people for additional reviewing: Ezequiel di Paolo, Jason Noble, Jon Bird, Anil Seth, David Nicholson and Kyran Dale.

We thank the organizing committee, Medeni Fordham, Joseph Faith and Owen Holland, for the very hard work they put into making the conference a success. Various members of Sussex University's School of Cognitive and Computing Sciences and the Sussex Centre for Computational Neuroscience and Robotics provided invaluable help of many kinds at all stages of the organization of ECAL97 — thanks.

We thank the following sponsors for their generous financial support: BT, Cyberlife Technology, Brighton and Hove Council and The Times Higher Education Supplement.

We are indebted to Helen Little for the artistic conception of the conference poster and proceedings cover.

Finally, we hope you enjoy and benefit from the papers in this book.

Phil Husbands and Inman Harvey
ECAL97

Centre for Computational Neuroscience and Robotics
School of Cognitive and Computing Sciences
University of Sussex
Brighton, UK

Program Committee

FOURTH EUROPEAN CONFERENCE ON ARTIFICIAL LIFE

FOUNDATIONS AND EPISTEMOLOGY

Epistemic Autonomy in Models of Living Systems

Erich Prem

The Austrian Research Institute for Artificial Intelligence

Schottengasse 3, A-1010 Wien, Austria

erich@ai.univie.ac.at

Abstract

This paper discusses ontological implications of embodied AI for Artificial Life models. The importance of robotic systems for ALife lies in the fact that they are not purely formal models and thus have to address issues of semantic adaptation and epistemic autonomy, which means the system's own ability to decide upon the validity of measurements. Epistemic autonomy in artificial systems is a difficult problem that poses foundational questions. The proposal is to concentrate on biological transformations of epistemological questions that have lead to the development of modern ethology. Such a view suggests to take a Heideggerian stance and leads to a reformulation of modern ontological conceptions by means of a clear and scientific notion of finality and anticipation. The argument is to take this ontological position as a framework within which ALife models should be developed.

Key words: epistemic autonomy, embodied AI, epistemology, robotics, theoretical biology, finality, teleology, ontology.

1 Introduction

1.1 Artificial Life

Post-modern epistemologists and commentators of science usually regard interdisciplinarity as a distinguishing advantage of the newly founded 20th century disciplines. ALife is one example for such a co-operative field. However, interdisciplinarity does not come without a price to pay. Chemists, biologists, computer scientists, etc. all seem to study very different aspects of living systems by means of similar methods. These methods have been described as [Langton 89]

- the synthesis of life-like behaviors within artificial systems,

- the study of ongoing dynamics rather than a final result,

- and the construction of systems which exhibit emergent phenomena.

What unifies researchers in ALife are their methods rather than their goals. Of course, there is a general interest in "life" as the phenomenon under study. Unfortunately though, life is too vague to ensure a common direction of research. Evidence for this claim can be found in the fact that some are interested in "systems that exhibit phenomena of living systems", others search for the origins of chemical reproduction, again others try to solve the philosophical problems of auto-poiesis. And a completely different set of researchers, namely roboticists, try to construct physical systems which exhibit some behavioral similarities with that of living animals.

This paper aims at a better understanding of differences in the research aims and methods within ALife. We start (and end) our investigation by reconsidering Aristotle's arguments for a primacy of the formal in scientific theories. Aristotle's appreciation is generally shared by scientists in the field of ALife. However, a purely formal approach to living systems was also criticized from within the field. In Sec. 2 some of these positions are explained and compared with the new field of embodied AI. It turns out that many arguments against ALife center around the notion of measurement. Of vital importance for living systems is the correct interpretation of measurements as well as the adaptation of sensory organs to different environments, which is an evolutionary process. An understanding of these processes seems only possible with an understanding of the animal's environment. In Sec. 3 it will be argued that this understanding should be gained from the animal's point of view. This together with the notion of adaptation and anticipation leads us to a formulation of a new ontological framework for the study of autonomous systems.

1.2 Life as a formal property

Many proponents in the field of ALife regard "life" as a property of the *organization* of matter rather than a material phenomenon. Some have even argued that the "material" that realizes life is irrelevant to the study of its properties. Others, mainly epistemologically interested researchers, have argued that "Life is matter with meaning." [Pattee 95] and that living systems are material structures with memory by virtue of which they construct, control and adapt to their environment. The fact that our notion of living systems stems from biological realizations which are physical, i.e. material systems, is obvious. The development of a purely formal account of the phenomenon of life is, historically, paralleled by formal accounts of physical phenomena, of cognition and of intelligence.

The usual argument that is used to support such a methodological approach is based on the fact that the material underlying living phenomena can take on a wide range from single cells to elephants. Matter in these living systems, however, is of a highly individual nature. But a scientist interested in "life" as a general property seeks to describe what is common to all living systems. A clear account of what it means to be alive is one of the basic, still unresolved problems of biology, maybe best described by [Schrödinger 67]. Instead of an explanation that could give a complete description of the "essence" of living systems, of "what it means to be this" ($\tau\grave{o}$ $\tau\acute{\iota}$ $\tilde{\eta}\nu$ $\epsilon\tilde{\iota}\nu\alpha\iota$), computationalists are satisfied with systems that exhibit properties which living systems (or intelligent, or cognitive) also possess. This restriction to formalized properties alone happens through a process of abstraction, in which an I-O behavior of the system interface turns into the center of scientific interest. It has been argued often before that it is generally impossible to reason backwards from the I-O behavior of a system to the system that realizes a function [Rosen 85, Pattee 95, Prem 95a]. Nevertheless, there still is a strong fascination that emanates from the formal dating back to Aristotle.

In the first book of his "physics" Aristotle develops his theory of first principles, most importantly of form and matter. The argument starts with a discussion of the origin of movement and change, for Aristotle the starting point for all scientific explanations. Change is identified by means of some substratum that is able to manifest the change. This substratum can be easily identified with matter. The ability of coming to be something, however, must be based on a specific form of privation. For Aristotle, "pure" matter shows this kind of privation due to its lack of *form*. Formless matter does not identify things properly and cannot explain change completely. Formlessness is a positive deficiency of matter. Although matter is the first substratum of everything, from which something comes, it does not have an ontic or epistemic status of its own. Matter "is" only because of its lack of, and therefore, potential for form. The substratum, in a next step, is not only form-able, it *needs* to be formed. This results in the primacy of form over matter. Knowledge of things must be based on formal principles rather than on material substrates, as the following quote from Aristotle's Metaphysics shows:

> By form I mean the essence of each thing and its primary substance. For even contraries have in a sense the same form; for the substance of a privation is the opposite of substance, e.g. health is the substance of disease... [Aristotle, 7,1032b 1]

Additionally, "form" is one of the four original causes that explain the why of things (formal, material, efficient, and final cause).

> In one of [the four senses] we mean the substance, i.e. the essence (for the 'why' is reducible finally to the definition, and the ultimate 'why' is a cause and principle); in another the matter or substratum, in a third the source of the change, and in a fourth the cause opposed to this, the purpose and the good (for this is the end of all generation and change). [Aristotle, 1, 983b 25].

The success of Aristotle's paradigm of form in ALife is based on the coincidence that computers are excellent in reproducing form. Unfortunately though, computers cannot reproduce matter. This is why a major branch of ALife is busy with the construction of computer simulations of (sometimes over-)simplified physics or chemistry. In fact, as [Rosen 91] has pointed out, computers implement formalisms in perfect analogy to the first three causes of Aristotle. Axioms of a formalisms may be considered material causes, efficient causes can mean production rules and formal causes can be identified with a particular sequence of production rules. Finality is usually omitted, because it does not respect the flow of "formal time", indeed it appears to violate this flow because the cause is later than the effect.

I have argued before that there is evidence that ALife should not be pursued as such a purely formal discipline [Prem 95a]. Instead, there exists a small sub-field of ALife that has the potential of contributing to an understanding of living systems on a basis which is far from being only formal.

2 Embodied Artificial Intelligence

2.1 A departure from formal models

In its short history, embodied Artificial Intelligence has challenged a sizeable number of foes. Among the list of opponents we find classical robotics and Artificial Intelligence (AI) in computer science, cognitivism in psychology, and objectivism in philosophy. The provocation lies in embodied AI's attack on a fundamental assumption of modern Western science. Dating back to medieval philosophy (or to Descartes, if you prefer) this assumption has been the primacy of the mental in the study of human cognition. 'Mental' here does not only refer to the opposite of 'physical' but also means 'rational' which is often considered opposed to emotion and intuition. To the extent that embodied AI tries to replace this predominance of the mental and rational by an emphasized acknowledgement of the bodily basis of cognition [Brooks 91] it threatens the disciplines mentioned above, which have a long tradition in disregarding the human body. In the context of ALife, embodied AI also threatens ALife's appraisal of the formal. Typical research in embodied AI proceeds by constructing physical robots with real-world dynamics. The dynamic behaviors of these robots are studied and generated by complex control systems and high interaction rates of the system and its environment.

It is easy to see that embodied AI proceeds quite differently from conventional robotic research and Artificial Intelligence [Prem 97a, Prem 97b]. Embodied AI has been shown to improve on the dynamical qualities of intelligent embodied systems, i.e. to get the interaction dynamics right. However, the structures of the new embodied control programs are very different from the traditional ones. Robot control tasks are no longer considered to be of a purely formal nature. To the roboticist in embodied AI it is unimportant whether she realizes a function by means of a computational procedure or a physical characteristic of the robot. Getting the interaction dynamics right is more important. Thus the control task is not considered as a purely computational I-O mapping, but as a combination of a physically and informationally transducing process that serves to generate "intelligent" bodily behavior. The realization of these control tasks does not happen by means of functional modules with clearly defined interfaces. It is achieved by dynamically interacting processes that are tightly coupled with the environment and with environmental time rather than with internal state-transition time (cf. [Prem 97b]). The system-environment coupling of robots is based on effectors and measurement devices. The use of meters marks the departure from purely formal models most clearly.

2.2 Measurement: semantic adaptation and epistemic autonomy

Many critics of formal ALife approaches have concentrated on the semantic gap between simulation and measurement [Rosen 91, Pattee 92, Pattee 95]. It was already John von Neumann who pointed out that results of measurements, choices of observables, the construction of measurement devices and the measurement process itself cannot, in principle, be formalized [von Neumann 55, von Neumann 66]. The reason lies in the fact that the process of measurement is not of a purely formal nature. Measurement is a process in which two dynamical systems interact. It is true that the interaction can be interpreted as a mapping of complex situation to simple patterns, but this view disregards the inherently dynamic nature of the measurement process [Rosen 78]. There are two main problems with measurement for roboticists: One is the construction of measurement devices that optimally support the robot.

The other is the interpretation of numbers delivered by some existing meter.

The construction of meters in biological systems is a process of semantic adaptation in which new observables are developed by the system. [Cariani 90] has pointed to the problems that arise from the difficulties of investigating the semantic process of measurement by means of syntactic computer simulations. Either are we forced to take the artificial organism's point of view and neglect the interpretation of the sensor, or our simulation will appear as a large state-determined system. Moreover, semantic adaptation is very hard to be reproduced artificially [Pask 61].

Robot engineers cannot wait for evolution and must design meters that support the dynamical robot behavior. Embodied AI has developed a specific strategy for the design of these meters that can be sharply distinguished from previous approaches. Instead of developing complex sensors with complex interpretation routines, the emphasis is now on quick sensor interpretation. This has lead to an increased use of simple sensors (switches, IR, etc.) with higher rates of sensor readings to support the system dynamics.

These high rates of sensor interpretation are possible, because the meaning of the sensor reading is *physically* highly restricted. Instead of using a camera and searching for constraints on video data that allow the identification of a certain object, robots are now equipped with physically constrained object recognition sensors, e.g. a special "soda-can sensor" [Connell 90]. This strategy emphasizes the physical design and coupling of a system at the cost of formal sophistication (at least with respect to sensor readings). From an epistemological point of view, the truth about the predicate "soda-can in front of gripper" is materialized in physical interaction (especially if we take into account that the robot can also check whether the can is empty by trying to lift it) up. This marks a clear departure from previous approaches in which truth conditions were constructed as formal constraints on streams of numbers.

The deeper reason for this strategy lies in the necessity to equip embodied systems with *epistemic autonomy*. A robot must be able to find out whether its sensor readings are distorted and, even more importantly, exactly when a measurement has occured. The correct *interpretation* of sensor readings is of vital importance for the generation of useful system actions. This epistemic condition on autonomous systems is central to all ALife models, indeed to all living systems. It arises in autonomous embodied models, because no humans are available to interpret the data and a pre-selection of valid data is impossible for practical reasons. (This is in sharp distinction from purely formal domains, in which the interpretation of simulated sensors can always be reduced to formal constraints. The ability for whiskers to break, however, is usually not modeled in any robot simulation.)

While semantic adaptation has been recognized as important for living systems and as very problematic for ALife, epistemic autonomy has not found similar attention so far. (The general importance of meter interpretation has been addressed by many authors, e.g. in the work of H.H. Pattee and R. Rosen. The importance of "system detectable error" has been argued by [Bickhard & Terveen 95, Bickhard 97] from an embodied perspective and is discussed in Sec. 4.2.) It should be emphasized that epistemic autonomy is a phenomenon at the level of the individual, whereas semantic adaptation is usually regarded as an evolutionary phenomenon. Epistemic autonomy has been recognized as important in embodied AI due to the urging need to construct systems that can decide upon the validity of their sensor readings. Let us now take a closer look on the epistemic consequences of such a perspective in relation to theoretical biology.

3 Theoretical biology and functional circuits

I propose a concentration on a view of system epistemics that is more oriented towards biology and has a sensory-motor perspective rather than a merely formal or even evolutionary one. In such a perspective the fundamental building blocks of epistemic conditions are control schemata for motor patterns that arise from perceptual interaction with the system environment. The drives for the system arise from within the system as needs or goals.

As early as 1928 Jakob von Uexküll described a view of biology which bases the study of animals on the animal's view of the world rather than on a scientist's "objective" view of the animal and its environment. This is basically a Kantian turn in producing better predictions of how an animal will behave in a given context.

As an example consider the difference between the two following descriptions of the tick's feeding behavior:

1. The tick attacks warm-blooded animals like humans or deer when they make contact with the trees or grass inhabited by the tick.

2. The tick bites when making contact with anything which has a superficial temperature of 37° C and emits butyric acid.

Both explanations can provide useful insights. The first description is immediately easy to understand and can be interpreted as giving a functional-explanatory answer.[1] From a mere descriptional viewpoint, however, the second version has a higher predictive value. The analysis which is necessary to come up with the second way of describing the tick behavior consists in a careful study

---

[1] I owe this insight to an anonymous reviewer.

of a tick's sensory organs and reflexes. In fact, the second version is more a description of *how the tick sees the world* in human terms.

> The sensations of the mind become properties of things during the construction of the world, or, one could also say, the subjective qualities construct the objective world. [J. v. Uexküll]

For the tick there are no humans, deer, trees, grass, etc. All that governs the tick behavior in the feeding context are specific features of two environmental qualities: temperature and chemical concentration. However, at the point where Kant's considerations lead to a discussion of categories as the final set of tools of reason to bring the "manifoldness of experience into the unity of concepts", von Uexküll develops descriptions of sensor (and actuator) spaces. His intention is to describe, how the

> marking signs of our attention turn into marks of the world. [Ibd.]

The source of this transformation process is formed by goal-driven interaction with the environment. The basic construct for explaining this interaction space is the description of *functional circuits*. Figure 1 depicts Uexküll's view of such a circuit (slightly adapted here). A "thing" in the animal's world is only "effector-" and "receptor-bearer". It can be thought of as a generator for signals to receptor organs and as a receptor of manipulations through effectors.

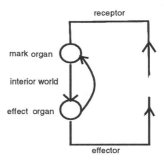

Figure 1: Action circuit as described by von Uexküll.

The formation of sensory experience is not only based on inter-*action*. Even more importantly, the interaction has a specific purpose. Such a purpose turns the encountered object from a collection of merely causally operating parts of physical entities into a meaningful assembly of things which are integrated in a purposeful whole. The essential point is *to understand how the thing is embedded in an action and how this action is embedded in a purposeful interaction with the world*. In order to fully understand the system's world, our task consists in the dissection of the functional world (i.e. the whole of the subject's functional circuits).

Such a point of view is surprisingly close to the credo of embodied AI where the descriptive strategy outlined above is turned into a design method. Starting from functional interaction circuits, the engineer tries to develop a minimalist architecture that fulfills the system requirements. An example for this strategy can be found in [Connell 90].

Summarizing Uexküll's position, there can be no understanding of animals without clarifying how they see the world, or better, what makes up the animal's world. Most notably, no such understanding seems possible without having gained insight into the animal's meaningful whole of functional circuits. To the modern, enlightened scientist such a view is dangerously close to the teleology which has been systematically eliminated from biology in the last century. However, there is a perfectly scientific version of finality that can help in the explanation and construction of embodied AI systems. Such a turn in describing representational elements in embodied AI systems even seems necessary, as will be argued in the next section.

4 Finality

4.1 Anticipation

Consider an adaptive autonomous system that exhibits physical interaction with its environment. A part of such a behavioral system [Brooks 85, Connell 90] is schematically depicted in figure 2.

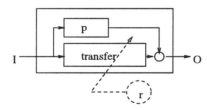

Figure 2: Behavioral module that transfers an input to an output if the applicability predicate p is true. The transfer function is learned based on a training signal r.

In this system, the behavior generated by the transfer function is learned based on a training signal. Let us assume that the training signal serves to optimize some criterion that is of importance to the system. It might, for example, assist in the provision of food. Following a description by [Rosen 85], we realize that the system's input is I, while the adaptation is determined by the optimization criterion r. Of course, it is reasonable to believe that there is a linkage between the "predicate" to be learned and the observables of the system environment I. Two things happen in this picture.

Firstly, the learning mechanism that selects the proper parameters generates a picture of the external linkage (between I and the predicate to be learned) *within* the system. Secondly, the adaptation must on principle be in a certain sense slower than the system-environment in-

teraction. Thus, the system implicitly generates a *model* of the linkage, and also, of the system-environment interaction. (For an extensive treatment of these system-theoretic properties cf. [Rosen 85].)

The result of such a learning or selection mechanism is a transfer function that "predicts" external reinforcement, i.e. it drives the system in a way that fitness is optimized before it is evaluated. This is why Rosen calls such systems *"anticipatory."* Representations (data structures, models) in the transfer functions become shaped based on their predictive value with respect to maximizing fitness. As a further consequence, these representations must be properly explained with reference to the future outcome of the system's interaction with its environment. This results in a finalistic or teleological terminology. (A discussion of this process based on a computational model of symbol grounding can be found in [Prem 95b].)

Note that the selection mechanism itself works perfectly causally. It operates based on inputs and "rewards". But the generation of some kind of internal model (be it symbolic, connectionist, or statistical) makes it necessary to change the merely causal description of the system and the system's "representational" framework to either a finalistic or, probably, intentional one. The physical embodiment of our system is an important fact in this context. Bodily interaction is hard to describe and measure perfectly and complicates a causal description. This implies that an explanation of the robot behavior by means of intentional terms can often be more natural.

4.2 Epistemic Autonomy and Representation

As innocent as this descriptional framework may look, it has a rather strong influence on the system's representational framework. It is now likely that sensory impressions of the system are categorized in classes that form items of the same usefulness to the system. In the same sense that "chairs" are properly described by their function "for sitting" for humans, objects in an embodied system's environment will now be classified due to their functional properties. It is clear that such a representational frame can be conceptually opaque in relation to human concepts.[2]

Additionally, the system will appear to behave depending on future events. This happens, because the actions are chosen so as to maximize reward or fitness that is evaluated later, based on an internalized goal-oriented model of system-environment interaction. This model, however, is based on the system's past experience.

There is evidence at the neurophysiological level that exactly this kind of finalistic indicative representation plays a major role in sensory-motor body-

[2] "And if a lion could speak, we would not understand it." [Wittgenstein 53]

environment interaction [Tanji et al. 94]. The subject centered viewpoint of Uexküll has also been well supported by neurophysiological evidence. Experiments by [Graziano et al. 94] show that premotor neurons play a major role in the coding of visual space. The evidence suggests that the encoding of the spatial location of an object happens in arm-centered coordinates rather than using a retinocentric representation. This again points to the way how system-environment interaction of an embodied architecture creates models that are oriented by the system's functional needs.

Epistemic autonomy in an adaptive, autonomous, embodied agent is based on the kind of interactive representation outlined above. [Bickhard 97] makes the case for this kind of representation in order to allow for "system detectable representational error". As Bickhard rightly points out, this kind of representation is necessary for action selection in agents that operate in insufficiently predictable environments. The detection of representational error in such schemes is based on internal interaction outcomes. The system must anticipate internal system states that indicate the success of the associated interaction. The representational content of such schemes consists in presuppositions about the environment. The indication implicitly stands for those properties of the environment, in which the indicated outcomes occur. Thus the representation can be false, when the anticipated outcome does not occur.

Bickhard's "system detectable representational error" also contributes to a better understanding of epistemic autonomy. The *interpretations* of measurements of the environment in the model presented above amount to anticipations of outcomes of interaction. In this view, measurements are elements of an anticipatory process themselves, because they map a multiplicity of events on few states which are indicative for successful interaction.

Of course, this kind of epistemic autonomy does not mean that all problems for the animal are solved. It is not automatically possible for the individual to tell which of many subsystems is in error when the indicated (anticipated) outcome does not occur. It can still be the interaction that failed, an ungrounded anticipation, or a wrong meter reading. In practice, such a clarification must happen by means of comparisons with other meters and other experiences of the autonomous system.

5 Ontological Aspects

This finalistic view brings with it the development of a rather distinct system ontology. The ontological position outlined below is developed with respect to the existential-ontological philosophy of Martin Heidegger [Heidegger 27]. (A Heideggerian account of aspects of ALife can also be found in [Wheeler 95].) The analysis that has brought us here suggests that this new approach to autonomous system ontology is of primary importance

to the study of living systems. Von Uexküll's and our notion of *things* in the animal's world can be best compared with what Heidegger calls *equipment*. In the human Being's everyday practices things in our world make sense because we can use them.

> We shall call those entities which we encounter in concern *"equipment"*. In our dealings we come across equipment for writing, sewing, working, transportation, measurement. The kind of being which equipment possesses must be exhibited. [Heidegger 27, p.68, taken from [Dreyfus 90]]

The entities that will be encountered this way are not objects in the above sense. We do not simply add a functional predicate to them. *Dealing* with them is our primordial way of having them, not some bare perceptual cognition. To paraphrase Heidegger, "hammering" does not know about this property of being a tool. Instead, the more we are immediately engaged in coping with the problem of fixing something, the less the hammer is taken as an object which can be used in-order-to hammer [Heidegger 27, p.69]. Strictly speaking, for Heidegger nothing like one equipment in this sense exists. This is because anything which we are using is embedded in a whole of multiple references to other tools and purposes. The hammer thereby refers to nails, tables, wood, etc.–i.e. a whole world of equipment and also of meaningful coping with the world. As long as we are engaged in "hammering"–in a purposeful dealing with equipment–and this equipment simply is "available", we do not even think about it. In such a situation the tools are simply "ready-to-hand".

> The world presents itself in the equipmental nexus, in the reference to a previously seen whole. [Heidegger 27, p.75, my translation]

The world does not consist of things which are "ready-to-hand", because it is only in situations of breakdown that the equipment can be recognized as one thing primarily identified by its sensory or physical properties. In these situations the things are deprived of being "ready-to-hand", creating mere *occurrentness*[3].

For Heidegger then, the fact that the world usually does not present itself as a world (in the usual scientific sense of the word) is the

> condition of the possibility of the non-entering of the available from the inconspicuous phenomenal structure of this being-in-itself. [Heidegger 27, p.75, my translation]

This view opposes any tradition which believes that things can be identified with reference to their sensory properties. Basically, this belief is based on the Cartesian

---

[3]This is Dreyfus' translation of "Vorhandenheit", which I find more appropriate than the standard "present-at-hand".

assumption that extension must be essential characteristic of substance.

> [...] *Descartes* is not merely giving an ontological misconception of the world, but that his interpretation and its basis have lead to *skipping* the phenomenon of the world as well as the being of the [...] innerworldly being. [Heidegger 27, p.95, my transl.]

In the end, this is one of the main sources of the problems of traditional robotics. From the idea that sensory and physical properties would be primordial it follows that a physical theory must be used to decide upon (detect, describe, deal with) objects encountered in the world. Moreover, such a theoretical approach must be used to find out whether a table could also be used as a chair. Any usage of tools and any way of dealing with the world therefore have to be explained with respect to those sensory qualities. In a (remotely) existential-ontological view, however, this problem simply does not arise in this way, because dealing with things for a specific purpose is the prevailing mode of encountering them, or rather: to create them. The argument therefore, is not that theoretical objects cannot exist, but that their functional properties must remain inaccessible if functions are not taken as the primordial source of creating things.

Contrary to what people in the field of traditional AI have proposed (perhaps most prominently [Minsky 85]), "functions" may not be some additional property attached to an object, but at the very heart of what things actually are, i.e. of what there is in the world. The conditions of the possibility of object constitution are, of course, constrained by the sensory system. Knowledge about the nature of objects can only be gained by understanding the different actions of the system. The actions, and the related behaviors, must be based on understanding functional circuits. The system engineer must design this functional world and the autonomous system's goals (yielding *hetero*-nomous instead of *auto*-nomous behavior). For the ALife scientist, this implies an increased interest in the analysis of functional circuits and in the circular causation of measurements, representations, and action selection.

Heidegger's approach can also be sharply contrasted with Aristotle's ontological primacy of the formal. In his work on technology he explicitly mentions that Socrates and Plato think of essence as something persistent [Heidegger 54]. This persistence is found in the formal appearance of things ($\epsilon\tilde{\iota}\delta o\sigma$), what Aristotle later called "$\tau\grave{o}\ \tau\acute{\iota}\ \tilde{\eta}\nu\ \epsilon\tilde{\iota}\nu\alpha\iota$'. As opposed to this view, Heidegger argues for a primacy of effect and work[4] (in the sense of "being at work"). The essence of things therefore lies

in their potential or real effects on others, in the induction of changes. Such a view is in close proximity to the practical experiences of roboticists. The first task during the construction of a robot always consists in studying the mutual effects that environment and robot will or must have on each other.

Heideggerian ontology is radically different from the conventional physical view. In my interpretation[5] it acknowledges a teleological element in nature, however, without explicitly mentioning it. This fact is reminiscent of the account that early biologists have given of finality and "entelechie" as well as of Aristotle's discussion of final causation. But in contrast to these accounts, today we need not recur to any kind of divine authority. Instead, the kind of anticipatory adaptation in any autonomous system that physically interacts with the world and has been described in this paper, leads to a most natural account of these teleological ontologies.

6 Conclusion

Embodied Artificial Intelligence is a field of research that can productively contribute to ALife problems in a way that is very different from comparable approaches. The acknowledgement of real physics in embodied AI questions the validity of purely formal accounts of living phenomena on several distinct levels. One of these phenomena is the crossing of the epistemic boundary that lies between a system and its environment. In real life, this boundary is overcome by measurement devices, which introduces the need for epistemic autonomy in such systems. Truth conditions on sensory data are not of a purely formal nature due to the reference to physics and system-environment interaction. Measurement and adaptation in an autonomous embodied system automatically means the development of representation schemes which are based on anticipation and interaction outcome. An understanding of these representations and how they come about lies at the very heart of theoretical biology.

Such an account of autonomy also lends itself nicely to a better understanding of modern ontologies and thus has the potential for changing our understanding of knowledge and the way we humans think about ourselves. Most importantly, an emphasis of embodied AI models of living systems ensures a reacknowledgement of natural elements, be they evolution, biology, ethology, or physiology.

7 Acknowledgments

The Austrian Research Institute for Artificial Intelligence is sponsored by the Austrian Federal Ministry of Science and Transport. The author gratefully acknowledges support from Rodney Brooks and the MIT AI Lab.

---

[4]Originally Heidegger uses the verb "wesen", which is derived from the noun "Wesen", which means "essence". Interestingly, the German word for "creature" is also "Wesen".

[5]in fact, it is the Wittgensteinian interpretation of [Dreyfus 90]

References

[Aristotle] Aristotle. Metaphysics.

[Bickhard & Terveen 95] Bickhard M.H., Terveen L. 1995. *Foundational Issues in Artificial Intelligence and Cognitive Science.* Elsevier Science Publishers.

[Bickhard 97] Bickhard M.H. 1997. The Emergence of Representation in Autonomous Agents, in Prem E. (ed.) *Epistemological Issues of Embodied AI.* Cybernetics & Systems, 28(6), 1997.

[Brooks 85] Brooks R.A. 1985. A Robust Layered Control System for a Mobile Robot. *AI-Memo 864.* Cambridge, MA: AI-Laboratory, Massachusetts Institute of Technology.

[Brooks 91] Brooks R.A. 1991. Intelligence without Representation. In Special Volume: Foundations of Artificial Intelligence, *Artificial Intelligence,* 47(1–3).

[Cariani 90] Cariani P. 1990. Implications from Structural Evolution: Semantic Adaptation, in Caudill M.(ed.), *Proceedings of the International Joint Conference on Neural Networks.* Hillsdale, NJ: Lawrence Erlbaum, pp. 47–50.

[Connell 90] Connell J.H. 1990. *Minimalist Mobile Robotics.* San Diego, C.: Academic Press.

[Dreyfus 90] Dreyfus H.L. 1990. *Being-in-the-world.* Cambridge, MA.: MIT Press.

[Graziano et al. 94] Graziano M.S.A., Yap G.S., and Gross C.G. 1994. Coding of Visual Space by Premotor Neurons. *Science,* 11 November 1994, 266, pp. 1054–1057.

[Heidegger 27] Heidegger M. 1927. *Sein und Zeit.* (Being and Time.) Tübingen: Niemayer.

[Heidegger 54] Heidegger M. 1954. Die Frage nach der Technik. (The question for technology.) *Vorträge u. Aufsätze.* Pfullingen: Neske, pp. 9–40, (6th ed. 1990).

[Langton 89] Langton C.G. (ed.) 1989. *Artificial Life.* Reading, MA: Addison-Wesley.

[von Neumann 55] von Neumann J. 1955. *Mathematical Foundations of Quantum Mechanics.* Priceton, NJ: Princeton University Press.

[von Neumann 66] von Neumann J. 1966. *The Theory of Self-reproducing Automata.* Urbana, IL.: University of Illinois Press.

[Minsky 85] Minsky, M. 1985. *The Society of Mind.* New York, NY: Simon & Schuster.

[Pask 61] Pask G. 1961. *An Approach to Cybernetics.* London: Hutchinson.

[Pattee 92] Pattee H.H. 1992. The Measurement Problem in Physics, Computation, and Brain Theories, in Carvallo M.E.(ed.) *Nature, Cognition and System II.* Dordrecht: Kluwer, pp. 197–192, 1992.

[Pattee 95] Pattee H.H. 1995. Artificial Life Needs a Real Epistemology, in Moran F., et al.(eds.), *Advances in Artif. Life.* Berlin: Springer, pp. 23–38.

[Prem 95a] Prem E. 1995. Grounding and the Entailment Structure in Robots and Artificial Life, in Moran F., et al.(eds.), *Advances in Artificial Life.* Berlin: Springer, pp. 39–51.

[Prem 95b] Prem E. 1995. Dynamic Symbol Grounding, State Construction, and the Problem of Teleology, in Mira J. et al. (eds.), *From Natural to Artif. Neural Computation.* Proc. Int. Workshop on Artif. Neural Networks. Berlin: Springer, pp. 619–626.

[Prem 97a] Prem E. 1997. The behavior-based firm. *Applied Artificial Intelligence.* **11** (3), pp. 173–195.

[Prem 97b] Prem E. 1997. The implications of embodiment for cognitive theories. *Austrian Res. Inst. f. Artif. Intell.* Vienna, TR-97-11. `ftp://www.ai.univie.ac.at/papers/oefai-tr-97-11.ps.Z`

[Rosen 78] Rosen R. 1978. *Fundamentals of Measurement and Representation of Natural Systems.* New York: North-Holland.

[Rosen 85] Rosen, R. 1985. *Anticipatory Systems.* Oxford, UK: Pergamon.

[Rosen 91] Rosen R. 1991. *Life Itself.* New York: Columbia University Press.

[Schrödinger 67] Schrödinger E. 1967. *What is Life... ?* Cambridge, UK: Cambridge University Press.

[Tanji et al. 94] Tanji J., and Shima K. 1994. Role for supplementary motor area cells in planning several movements ahead. *Nature,* 371 (6496), pp. 413–416.

[von Uexküll 28] von Uexküll J. 1928. *Theoretische Biologie.* (Theoretical Biology.) Frankfurt/Main: Suhrkamp.

[Wheeler 95] Wheeler M. 1995. *Escaping from the Cartesian Mind-Set: Heidegger and Artificial Life.* In Moran F., et al.(eds.), Advances in Artificial Life. Berlin: Springer, LNAI 929, pp. 65–76.

[Wittgenstein 53] Wittgenstein L. 1953. *Philosophische Untersuchungen.* (Philosophical Investigations.) Frankfurt/Main: Suhrkamp.

Cognition's Coming Home:
the Reunion of Life and Mind

Michael Wheeler
Department of Experimental Psychology
University of Oxford
South Parks Road, Oxford, OX1 3UD, U.K.
Phone: +44 1865 271417
Fax: +44 1865 310447
E-Mail: michaelw@psy.ox.ac.uk

Abstract

I draw a distinction between *orthodox cognitive science* and *biological cognitive science*. The former tends to ignore biological considerations whilst the latter holds that life and mind share a common set of organizational principles. The suggestion here is that artificial life (A-Life) is (potentially) the intellectual engine of the latter. The goal then becomes to map out the conceptual profile of that A-Life-driven cognitive science. Paying special attention to the relationship between neurobiological/biochemical phenomena and cognition, I argue that the commitment to functionalism in orthodox cognitive science provides compelling evidence that that approach is wedded to a recognizably Cartesian account of the relationship between life and mind. By contrast, the fundamental commitments of a biological cognitive science tell in favour of a radically different, generically Aristotelian framework. I show how the concept of *self-organization* — arguably *the* central theoretical idea in A-Life — might be the keystone of a neo-Aristotelian biological cognitive science.

1 Introduction

First the good news: artificial life (A-Life) is an exciting and fast-developing research endeavour which threatens to revolutionize cognitive science. Now the bad news: there is an enormous amount of theoretical work still to be done before we can claim to have anything approaching a systematic understanding of the conceptual framework within which an A-Life-oriented cognitive science will advance. Such an understanding would be useful not only as an academic exercise in the philosophy of science. It would help to shape the questions asked by, and to clarify the results of, empirical research. In this paper I hope to make a modest contribution to the type of systematic understanding required.[1] My strategy will be to draw a distinction between two sorts of cognitive science (the orthodox and the biological), and to show how these two distinct styles of cognitive-scientific thinking are the heirs to two radically different visions of the place of mind in nature (the Cartesian and the Aristotelian). The take-home-message will be that A-Life has the potential to be the intellectual engine of a biological cognitive science working within a generically Aristotelian conceptual framework.[2]

2 Two Sorts of Cognitive Science

Life in cognitive science used to be simple. It was uncontroversial that artificial intelligence (AI) was the *theoretical core* of the field, in the sense that concepts which had been developed by, or which were typically appealed to within, AI (concepts such as 'algorithm', 'heuristic', and 'information processing') provided cognitive science with its theoretical vocabulary (cf. [4]). However, the emergence of A-Life has made things more complicated.

In practice, 'A-Life' is an umbrella term covering a diverse range of projects, from models of RNA replication and sensory-motor activity to studies of collective intelligence and population dynamics. This diversity makes it hard to state a compact definition of the field. However, in the context of this paper, I think that it will be both accurate and illuminating to define A-Life as the

---

[1] Other contributions include those by Pfeifer [36] (a discussion of design principles for autonomous agents), Varela [43] (the development of a biology of intentionality based on autopoiesis [30]) and Varela *et al.* [44] (the canonical presentation of the enactive approach to cognitive science). My target is more general than autonomous agent research, and although my proposed framework undoubtedly shares some of its characteristics with autopoietic theory and enactivism, it does not depend on the epistemological commitments which shape those paradigms, and is arrived at via a very different route.

[2] The idea that Aristotle's account of life might be in general harmony with a self-organization-based A-Life perspective is tantalizingly aired, but not explored in detail, by Boden [6, pp.21-2].

attempt to understand the systems of life (including, ultimately, the phenomena that we group together with labels such as intelligence, mind, and cognition) through the synthesis and analysis of artifacts (computer models, artificial worlds, and robots). Now, unless one adopts a highly restricted and, in my view, unjustifiably narrow definition of AI (e.g., as fundamentally logic-based, or as interested only in human-level intelligence), there must be an overlap between A-Life and AI, such that some styles of A-Life research (e.g., designing intelligent, autonomous, animal-like robots) are examples of AI too, albeit of a rather unfamiliar kind. So, in order to get things into focus, we need to draw a distinction between (i) A-Life (which includes some forms of AI), and (ii) AI which is *not* also A-Life. I shall call the latter style of research *orthodox AI* (OAI).

OAI can be defined by its commitment to the idea that a healthy science of intelligence can, for the most part, ignore biological considerations, which tend to enter the picture only as 'implementation details' or 'contingent historical particulars', and, in general, do not provide or constrain the concepts and principles used to construct scientific explanations of intelligence. This tendency towards *biological neutrality* expresses itself along a number of different dimensions, such as (a) a disregard for, or an overly simplistic view of, what goes on in biological nervous systems and (more generally) in biological bodies, (b) a neglect of the constraints imposed on biological intelligence by the necessity to act in real-time in an often hostile, unpredictable, and unforgiving environment, and (c) a blindness to the fact that an animal's behaviour will often be highly specific to its ecological niche.[3]

OAI, thus characterized, is the intellectual core of (what I shall call) *orthodox cognitive science* (OCS). Given this relationship, we should expect OCS to display the same stripe and expressions of biological neutrality as OAI, only this time with respect to scientific explanations of mind and cognition. And that is exactly what we find. On the orthodox cognitive-scientific story, to explain the sort of cognition enjoyed by biological cognizers, one can, for the most part, ignore facts about that biological cognizer's biology. (An exception to this rule — the specification of functional normativity via Darwinian selection — will be discussed in section 6.)

Most, although far from all, work in AI and cognitive science has been orthodox (i.e., prone to biological neutrality). This *includes* the *vast majority*, although far from all, of the models developed under the banner of connectionism. (The depressingly common claim that connectionist networks *in general* are 'biologically realistic psychological models' is, I think, bogus. I shall say

why later.) But now imagine a radically different sort of beast: a truly *biological* cognitive science. By this I mean a cognitive science which is committed to what Godfrey-Smith calls *strong continuity*, the claim that "[life] and mind have a common abstract pattern or set of basic organizational properties ... Mind is literally life-*like*" [19, p.83, original emphasis]. Given this commitment, the guiding principle of a biological cognitive science would be that cognition has to be explained using the same fundamental concepts and principles as figure in our best explanations of other biological phenomena. A biological cognitive science would be literally a *life*-science.[4]

Notice four things about strong continuity:

1. Strong continuity entails — although it is not entailed by — a weaker form of continuity, according to which for an entity to have a mind, it must be alive, although in order to be alive, it need not have a mind (cf. [19, p.83]). This form of continuity is not, on its own, enough for a truly biological cognitive science, since it does not guarantee that one has to appeal to the organizational properties of life in order to understand cognition.

2. It does not follow from strong continuity that life and cognition are *the same* (in the sense of 'same' articulated by Varela [43] and Stewart [40]). The claim is continuity, not equivalence.

3. In the context of a biological cognitive science, strong continuity suggests a 'bottom-up' research methodology. First one seeks satisfying explanations of *some of* the 'simple' non-cognitive manifestations of life (in order to establish the appropriate theoretical concepts). Then one confronts its more complex cognitive manifestations.

4. Strong continuity will disturb those who hanker after a truly general cognitive science. Of course, it *might* transpire that the same set of organizational properties explains not only life and mind of the naturally-occurring terrestrial variety, but also their extra-terrestrial counterparts (if such phenomena exist), plus all forms of artificial life and artificial mentality that could conceivably exist (if one believes that artifacts could literally be alive and have minds). If things do turn out this way, then the idea of a general cognitive science will be safe. However, nothing in the idea of strong continuity guarantees this result (cf. [6, 16]). Given that I have raised the spectre of life-as-it-could-be, I should stress that, in this paper, I am interested only in naturally-occurring terrestrial life and, therefore, in naturally-occurring terrestrial minds.

It seems beyond reasonable doubt that a biological cognitive science cannot be built around OAI. But now

---

[3]These sorts of biologically-motivated criticisms of OAI are often made by A-Lifers, and occasionally surfaced prior to the advent of A-Life (e.g., [11, chapter 4]).

[4]Godfrey-Smith glosses strong continuity in terms of shared functional properties. However, as is evident from his own initial appeal to *organizational* properties, it is not essential to the idea of strong continuity that what are shared between life and mind are, strictly speaking, functional properties. And given the fact that, later in this paper, I am critical of functionalism in cognitive science, and sympathetic to positions which place limits on functionalist thinking in biology, I have, at the outset, opted for a characterization of strong continuity in terms of organization.

how about A-Life? I suggested earlier that A-Life can be characterized as the attempt to use artificial media to investigate the phenomena of life. That puts us in the right intellectual ball-park. I also highlighted the fact that explanations of intelligence, mind, and cognition are on the A-Life agenda. This indicates, I think, that the canonical A-Life view is that these phenomena should be treated as essentially linked to (a sub-set of) living systems, which implies, in turn, that A-Lifers do, on the whole, accept the weaker notion of continuity identified earlier. Of course, that acceptance of weak continuity does not oblige A-Lifers to embrace the guiding principle of a biological cognitive science, the strong continuity thesis. Nevertheless, although strong continuity is not strictly entailed by the A-Life ethos, researchers in and around the A-Life movement often buy heavily into the idea. For example, Bedau [2] argues that A-Life models will provide explanations of the "supple emergent dynamics" that are the essence of life *and* mind. And Carneiro and Stewart [10] suggest that a study which, on their analysis, undermines the traditional self-nonself distinction in immunology has implications for 'higher-level' notions of 'self' and 'individual'.[5] The crucial point is that the A-Life ethos not only permits strong continuity, it actively encourages it. Neither of these facts of A-Life are true of OAI.

The stage is now set for us to state explicitly the relationship that exists between A-Life and a biological cognitive science. The explanations of living systems proposed within A-Life are typically formulated in a theoretical vocabulary which is made up of a set of rather distinctive scientific concepts (e.g., 'self-organization', 'autonomy', and 'emergent functionality'). If those very same concepts also provide a biological cognitive science with *its* theoretical vocabulary, then A-Life will be the intellectual core of that cognitive science, in exactly the same way that OAI is the intellectual core of OCS.

3   Still Cartesian After All These Years

It will be useful to concentrate, for a while, on one specific issue over which OCS and biological cognitive science diverge, namely the explanatory relationship which exists between, on the one hand, the neurobiological/biochemical features of living organisms, and, on the other, cognition. (In effect, this issue generates the first dimension of biological neutrality in OCS, as identified in section 2.) The divergence in question can be explained by the fact that the two sorts of cognitive science are shaped by radically different philosophical frameworks. Shortly I shall introduce the idea that a biological cognitive science fits most naturally into a generically Aris-

---

[5]It is also telling that, in the Proceedings of the Third European Conference on A-Life [34], one of the sections (grouping together papers of a similar theoretical content) is called "Adaptive and Cognitive Systems".

totelian framework. But first I shall, once again, unearth the Cartesian roots of OCS. I say "once again" because there are already several different versions of the claim that most of our existing cognitive science is overwhelming Cartesian in spirit (e.g., [15, 23, 44]). Thus whilst my arguments here (and in [46, 47]) reflect my own particular take on the issues, their overall contribution is to add additional fuel to an already burning fire.

Anybody with even a passing interest in philosophy of mind knows that Descartes thought of the mental and the physical as two separate, yet interacting, ontological realms [14]. However, a second contribution which Descartes made to the study of mind is less widely acknowledged. This second contribution was a form of psychological explanation — let's call it *explanatory dualism* — which maintains the following two theses simultaneously: (i) to explain physical phenomena, one need appeal only to specifically physical entities or states, and to specifically physical laws; (ii) to explain psychological phenomena, one need appeal only to specifically mental entities or states, and to specifically mental laws. Explanatory dualism is perfectly consistent with the idea that mental events are, ultimately, physical events. On a physicalist ontology, whether we offer a physical or a psychological style of explanation will depend on the description under which, given our current explanatory goals, we are taking the events of interest to fall.

Significantly, Descartes thought of the cognizer's organic body as just another physical object in the physical world. Given his explanatory dualism, this thought committed him to the view that neurobiological/biochemical explanations of events in the cognizer's body are *irrelevant* to psychological explanations of events in the cognizer's mind, in the sense that psychological explanation can proceed in the absence of any detailed neurobiological/biochemical knowledge of the cognizer's body. This explanatory disembodiment of the mind entails also an explanatory discontinuity, in this context, between life and mind. Scientific explanations of the processes proper to what the Cartesian thinks of as organic, bodily life (processes such as reproduction, digestion, and growth) fall ultimately within a biological domain of explanation which is construed as reducible to the physical sciences. Scientific explanations of mental processes, on the other hand, would need to be couched in a language *altogether different* from that biological language, a language specific to psychology. This amounts to a rejection of the strong continuity thesis. In other words, explanatory dualism is incompatible with a biological cognitive science.

Now, functionalists in the philosophy of mind hold that the defining feature of a type of mental state is the causal role that that state plays in mediating between (i) sensory input, (ii) other types of mental states, and (iii) motor behaviour. Strictly speaking, functionalism makes no commitment to the nature of the substrate in which mental states are ultimately realized, since being in a particular mental state just *is*, we are told, being in a specific functional state, and the very same functional state might, in principle, be realized in carbon-based biochemistry, silicon brains, or Cartesian mind-stuff. Hence, in principle, functionalism is consistent with substance-dualism. This in-principle fact might seem irrelevant, given that functionalism is usually yoked to a token identity theory, according to which every instance of a given type of mental state is one and the very same thing as some physical state of a physical system. But, whatever else it may do, the addition of the token-identity requirement does not make the neurobiological and biochemical details of the biological cognizer's body relevant to the process of psychological *explanation*. According to the functionalist, the process of psychological explanation can be conducted in splendid isolation from those very details. We have met this position already: *functionalism is a form of Cartesian explanatory dualism.*

So how are the explanatory dualist credentials of functionalism relevant to an understanding of OCS? The answer is that OCS is underwritten by functionalism. Indeed, computational states (the sort of states to which OAI and OCS appeal in their explanations) are paradigmatic examples of functionally defined states. Hence it is no accident that, in one of the classic statements of functionalism, Putnam explicates the theory by way of a Turing machine [37]. But now once we acknowledge the functionalist foundations of OCS, and with them the generically Cartesian account of the explanatory relationship between the living body and the mind which those foundations engender, we can see why it is that OCS is committed to the idea that cognition can be explained without essential reference to, or understanding of, the neurobiological and biochemical basis of that cognition. In other words, we can see why it is that OCS adopts an explanatory stance which is anathema to a biological cognitive science.[6]

4   Beyond Cartesianism

It is time to test the water of a biological cognitive science, to see what might be involved in going beyond Cartesianism. Research into connectionist (or artificial neural) networks is a suitable arena for this test, because such research spans OAI and A-Life.

Clark [11] characterizes connectionists as *microfunctionalists*. This is telling, because the standard architectural assumptions made in orthodox (i.e., OCS-style) connectionism follow the functionalist edict to grant min-

imal theoretical weight to the biological basis of cognition. Whilst it is true that the architecture of orthodox connectionist networks resembles the abstract structure of biological nervous systems, there are significant areas of divergence. For example: (i) certain restrictions often placed on connectivity in connectionist networks (e.g. feed-forward activation passes or symmetrical connections) are, generally speaking, not reflected in real nervous systems; (ii) biological networks are inherently noisy; (iii) there is rarely any real correspondence between connectionist units and biological neurons (the latter are far more complex); (iv) mainstream connectionist networks feature units which are uniform in structure and function, whereas biological networks typically feature many distinct types of neuron; (v) timing in connectionist networks has tended to be based either on a global, digital clock which keeps the progressive activity of the units in synchronization or on methods of stochastic update; but there is evidence to suggest that the individual timing of neuronal events could itself be of major significance in understanding the behaviour of biological neural networks (see the discussion of timing in [23]).

These architectural dissimilarities mean that the intrinsic dynamics of standard connectionist networks are positively impoverished when compared to those exhibited by biological networks. *Given strong continuity,* one should expect to find that, for example, oscillatory rhythms and chaotic attractors — phenomena from which mainstream connectionists often shy away, but which are the focus of much neurobiology (e.g., [3, 39]) — will be crucial to an understanding of cognition. A-Life-oriented evolutionary roboticists often allow artificial evolution to design neural network sensory-motor control systems in which at least some of the restrictive architectural assumptions identified above are dropped, and which are, therefore, capable of richer intrinsic dynamical profiles (e.g., [24]). Such dynamical neural networks, which are (in part at least) biologically inspired, undoubtedly represent an important step towards a biological cognitive science. But they are only the beginning. If one looks closely at biological brains, what one sees challenges the idea that what we call cognition can be explained by appealing solely to the idea of signals sent along neatly specifiable connecting pathways. For example, there is experimental evidence that post-synaptic receptors sense presynaptic release of the neurotransmitter glutamate from sites other than 'their own' presynaptic release sites. Because glutamate is released in 'clouds', presynaptic releases can, through spill-over, affect distant post-synaptic receptors [27]. There is no reason to suppose that effects such as glutamate spill-over, which are not conducive to standard neural network modelling, can be treated as 'implementation details' or 'noise', to be ignored when artificial media are employed to investigate the systems underlying cogni-

---

[6]Whilst we are on the subject, it is worth noting that OCS embraces a host of other Cartesianisms which get exposed in the literature, such as that the job of perception is to infer, from sensory data, information about the pre-existing features of an objective world, and that perception, thought, and action are temporally distinct and theoretically separable.

tion. There is every possibility that they are essential features of the 'strategy' by which brains contribute to adaptive behaviour. In short, we should always remember that, whatever else they may be, biological brains are complex *chemical* machines.[7]

In order to integrate such biologically inspired observations into a coherent theoretical framework, we need to find a non-Cartesian conceptual space in which to think about life and mind, a space shaped by strong continuity. Fortunately such a space already exists, courtesy of Aristotle.[8]

5   From Psychology to Psuche-ology

Aristotle's term *psuche* [1] is usually translated as 'soul', but this is misleading. The word 'soul' carries overtones of a spiritual mode of existence which are contrary to the overwhelming tendency in Aristotle's thought. As Wilkes notes, for Aristotle, stinging-nettles have psuche [48, p.109]. A better start is made if one observes that, for Aristotle, *the psuche of an organism is the set of species-typical capacities in virtue of which that organism is alive.* In other words, each species of organism will have associated with it a particular set of (what I shall call) *life-capacities* which will, under normal circumstances, be expressed in individual members of that species; and, under normal circumstances, what it is for an organism of that species to be alive is for that organism to express that species-typical set of life-capacities, i.e., that psuche. The life-capacities making up any particular psuche will be drawn from (something like) the following master-list: self-nourishment, growth and decay, reproduction, appetite, touch, non-tactile forms of perception, self-controlled motion, and intellectual reasoning. Roughly speaking, the later in this master-list a capacity comes, the more sophisticated Aristotle held it to be. This is significant, because a psuche is a *hierarchical* structure in which, generally speaking, the possession of a certain life-capacity presupposes the possession of the less sophisticated life-capacities in the master-list. So, for example, the possession of touch presupposes the possession of appetite, reproduction, growth and decay, and self-nourishment. In addition, there is also a relationship of *explanatory dependence* between life-capacities, such that any individual life-capacity can-

not be fully understood in isolation from the others in the particular psuche in question.[9]

Aristotle's view is that we need the concept of the psuche in order to achieve satisfactory explanations in the life-sciences. To understand his reasoning here, we need to introduce the distinction between *form* and *matter*. To a first approximation (we shall return to this issue later) 'form', for Aristotle, means something like *distinctive mode of organization* (cf. [18]). Thus he tells us that the particular shape of a certain statue is that statue's form, whilst its matter is the physical stuff out of which it is made. The form of an axe is something like its ability to chop, the matter is the wood and iron out of which the axe is made. Moving into the biological world, the form of the eye is the ability to see; the matter, according to Aristotle's ancient biology, consists of water. The form of anger is something like a desire for retaliation; the matter, again according to Aristotle, is a boiling of blood around the heart. When Aristotle applies the form-matter distinction to whole living organisms, we are told that *the form of a living creature is its psuche, its set of life-capacities; the matter is the organic body which underlies those capacities.*

Given this preliminary understanding of the concept of 'form', to give an *explanation in terms of form* is to give an explanation in which the distinctive organization of an entity is, for good explanatory reasons, given priority over the material constitution of that entity. So say that one wished to explain how houseflies achieve real-time, visually guided aerial navigation in cluttered, dynamic environments. Aristotle would be quite at home with the idea that disciplines such as neurobiology and biochemistry might combine to explain the workings of the machinery that enables such behaviour. In fact, whatever science might mean by the term 'material', Aristotle would *expect* there to be a straightforwardly material explanation of visually guided, aerial navigation in houseflies. Such an explanation is far from trivial. Each of the fly's two compound eyes features a panoramic, non-uniform, two-dimensional array of photosensors. These arrays are connected to a parallel network of dedicated image-processors and flight-control processors performing asynchronously in real-time. Via a further network of neurons, this system drives a set of muscles that, together with gyroscopic organs, controls the wings [17]. Nevertheless, any purely material explanation, however

---

[7]For a more detailed philosophical discussion of evolutionary robotics, and its relationship with a dynamical systems approach to cognitive science, see [45]. Studies in which artificial evolution is allowed to operate on reconfigurable hardware provide support for the idea that evolution will produce control systems whose intrinsic physical dynamics are crucial (sometimes in surprising ways) to adaptive success [42].

[8]Previously I have tried to counter Cartesianism by exploring a neo-Heideggerian perspective on cognitive science and A-Life [46, 47]. I see the present investigation of the relevance of Aristotelian ideas as being fundamentally continuous with that project. In presenting my contemporary reading of Aristotle I have, for reasons of space, been forced to forego detailed textual exegesis.

[9]The list of Aristotelian life-capacities which I have given above might be challenged, because Aristotle gives different lists in different places, and there are exegetical disputes about exactly how the various capacities are to be divided-up. Similarly, the relationship of presupposition may not always be as straightforward as I have suggested. These caveats need not be causes for alarm, because the fine-grained details are not crucial for the argument of this paper. For a systematic analysis of the structure of the psuche, see [29]. For an approach to defining life which is both influential in A-Life and opposed to the Aristotelian strategy of appealing to sets of life-capacities, see [30].

complex, would not enable the life-sciences to understand that material process, *as the natural phenomenon that it most properly is.* To construct a complete natural explanation, one would need to understand that process in the context of the particular set of life-capacities which are definitional of housefly-life — the housefly form of life, as one might say. In other words, the specific physical system underlying visually guided, aerial navigation in houseflies needs to be understood as enabling the expression of a species-typical life-capacity, namely the type of self-controlled motion that is characteristic of houseflies.

Individual life-capacities can, of course, be shared by different species, although to say that daffodils and humans share the life-capacity of self-nourishment is not to say that daffodils and humans achieve self-nourishment in the same way; there may be variations between species in the way in which a shared life-capacity is expressed. According to Aristotle, all living things possess the capacities of self-nourishment, growth and decay, and reproduction.[10] Plants possess *only* those life-capacities, whereas animals possess all of those, plus perceptual life-capacities as well. Notice that it is with the introduction of the perceptual life-capacities that one first encounters what we ordinarily think of as mind and cognition. At the top of the psuche-logical hierarchy we find the fanciest of all the life-capacities, that of intellectual reasoning. For Aristotle, the only animal to possess this capacity is the human being. One has to say, I think, that it is just about impossible to square Aristotle's account of intellectual reasoning with the rest of what he says about life-capacities, because although his overwhelming tendency is to reject the idea that the psuche is ontologically distinct from the body, still he claims that the 'active' part of the life-capacity of intellectual reasoning (something like 'intellectual intuition') is immortal and eternal. Given this apparent inconsistency, the modern interpreter is, it seems, entitled to bring the human intellect into line. One way to achieve this is to exploit Aristotle's view that part of the natural developmental process by which we humans come to express our full set of species-typical life-capacities (our distinctive *animal* form) is for us to become, via our upbringing, socialization, and linguistic development, rational users of our intellect (cf. [32]). For this developmental trajectory to qualify as natural (and, therefore, for it to do the job being asked of it), culture and language must be explained as purely biological phenomena — distinctively human perhaps, but purely biological nonetheless. No mean task, and beyond the scope of this paper. Nevertheless, if we assume that it can done, then we have secured an interpretation of the psuche which licences neither an ontological nor an explanatory divide between the living body and the mind.

So, according to Aristotle, in virtue of the fact that a particular living natural body has the psuche characteristic of life in its species, that living natural body will be able to do certain things. Having a mind is simply one of those things, a way in which certain organisms are manifestly alive. And whether we are talking about digestion, reproduction, perception, or thinking, we are talking about an embodied life-capacity, a biological phenomenon which is to be explained in terms of matter and psuche. In other words, Aristotle was a strong continuity theorist. My suggestion, then, is that *the Aristotelian concept of the psuche provides both strong support for, and a useful way of articulating in more detail, the strong continuity thesis that is the central plank of an A-Life-driven, biological cognitive science.* Nice idea, but...

6 Form, Function, and Self-Organization

We are not quite home. Before any celebrations begin I need to resist an interpretation of Aristotle which is at odds with the interpretation favoured here. That competing interpretation takes Aristotle's framework to be the intellectual forerunner of functionalism in the philosophy of mind (see, e.g., [48]). Since I have identified functionalism as a neo-Cartesian theory of mind, and I wish to contrast Aristotle's conceptual framework with Cartesianism, I have to resist the functionalist interpretation. My strategy will take Aristotelian thought into scientific territory which is the natural habitat of A-Lifers.

It is now common for functionalist philosophers of mind within the naturalist tradition to link the idea of cognitive function to the idea of Darwinian evolutionary function (e.g., [33]). On a Darwinian account, the evolutionary function of, for example, part of the frog's visual system is to detect food in the form of flies (rather than to detect the fast-moving black dots to which the sub-system proximally responds), because that's what that sub-system has been selected for during the frog's evolutionary history (rather than to detect fast-moving black dots, some of which are not flies). The idea behind the proposed link is that one can tell a selectionist story across the board, for the functions of, for example, the heart, aggressive signals, perceptual states, and beliefs. It might seem that one doesn't strictly *need* to connect cognitive function with evolutionary function, in order to make functionalism work. However, the functionalist needs a court of appeal in order to rule out seemingly bogus attributions of function (e.g., that the function of that part of the frog's visual system is to track fast-moving black dots). For artifacts, the court of appeal is us. An artifact's function is what we *designed it to do.* But no intelligent hands have been involved in the crafting of biological systems or (for those biological systems that have them) their minds, so another source of functional normativity is required. Darwinian selection

---

[10]Aristotle's inclusion of reproduction may be problematic. Ask any mule. Boden [6] suggests that this oversight might be remedied by appeal to the fact that mules are generated by reproduction.

is the prime candidate, thus making the securing of functional normativity a rare case in which OCS will almost certainly appeal to biological considerations.[11]

The linking of cognitive function to Darwinian function allows us to assess the functionalist interpretation of Aristotle by asking whether or not it is plausible to give evolutionary-functional definitions of the various life-capacities (biological forms). To answer this question we need to return to our preliminary understanding of biological form. We have been working with the idea that life-capacities can be understood as distinctive modes of organization. But now we must take account of the fact that Aristotle characterized biological modes of organization as *internal* to the entities concerned. In other words, the modes of organization in which we are interested, for the purposes of life-scientific explanation, are not externally imposed upon biological systems, but rather are essential aspects of the intrinsic natures of those systems [18]. Amazingly, we can now make sense of this idea, in a contemporary scientific context.

Self-organization is a phenomenon that occurs in energetically open complex systems, where large numbers of the system's components interact with each other in nonlinear ways to produce the autonomous emergence and maintenance of structured order (cf. [6, p.3] and [41, pp.54-6]). The term 'autonomous' is commonly used in characterizations of self-organization to capture the fact that the order observed in a self-organizing system has to be explained by appeal to the intrinsic nature of the system itself. So, in my view, the most natural, satisfying, and consistent way to make sense of Aristotle's framework, in a contemporary scientific context, is to think of biological forms not merely as 'distinctive modes of organization', but as 'distinctive modes of *self*-organization', as *the characteristic modes of order that emerge autonomously in biological self-organizing systems*. The Aristotelian scholars Code and Moravcsik characterize the psuche as an "internal principle ... that counteracts the natural migrations of its material elements" [12, p.139]. Using the contemporary language which I have suggested, one might echo this characterization in the thought that the psuche is a locus of emergent order that counteracts increasing entropy.

In explicating my neo-Aristotelian position in terms

of self-organizing systems, I am simultaneously forging a connection between Aristotle and A-Life, because the concept of 'self-organization' is, at least arguably, *the* key theoretical idea appealed to in A-Life. Having made this claim, I should pause to consider the following response: "To successfully identify a theoretical concept as *the* core idea in A-Life, one must single out a concept which applies only to living things. Self-organization occurs not only in living systems, but also in non-living systems. Thus self-organization is not distinctively biological, and the concept cannot enjoy pride of place in the theoretical vocabulary of A-Life". The next move might be to suggest either (a) that a particular *species* of self-organization, such as *adaptive* self-organization, is what is needed, or (b) that we need to call on the concept of autopoiesis [30]. (An autopoietic system can be thought of, somewhat crudely, as a system which continually creates or self-organizes the conditions for its own continued self-organization.) In fact, strictly speaking, the core argument of this paper requires only that the concept of 'self-organization' be *important* to A-Life thinking, something which the response, as stated, does not deny. However, in my view, the idea that self-organization is the key theoretical term in A-Life survives the response intact. First, from an Aristotelian perspective it is a mistake to think that it is the job of the concept of self-organization to make an explanation distinctively biological. Rather it is the concept of the psuche which performs that role (see section 5). Second, it seems likely that adaptive self-organization *and* autopoiesis will be crucial to the A-Life understanding of living systems, which is consonant with my preferred analysis, since in order to make sense of these notions, one needs the idea of self-organization.

To appreciate how my proposed appeal to self-organization undermines the functionalist interpretation of Aristotle, we need to understand (as far as anyone can at present) the relationship, in evolution, between self-organization and selection (the source of evolutionary function). Here, I think, we can appeal to the work of Kauffman and, in particular, to the lessons of his NK model [25, 26].[12] An example from Burian and Richardson's discussion of Kauffman's work will help to focus the issue [9]. Assume that the generic order of a particular self-organizing system under evolutionary influence is to be blue, but that selection favours red. After many generations of evolution, will blue persist in the population, even though it is being selected against, and to what extent will it be visible? The NK model suggests the following answer: blue (the generic order) will be common, even given strong selection in favour of red.

Let's be a little more specific. If we adopt an inter-

---

[11] For a specific attempt to make functionalism work without selection, see [13]. Then see [33] for a compelling, pro-selectionist, pro-functionalist response which argues that the attempt in question fails to connect function with purpose, thereby having the seemingly unacceptable consequence that a diseased heart which is incapable of pumping blood no longer has the function of pumping blood. In essence, this objection is a version of the argument which I have cast in terms of functional normativity.

It is worth noticing that even if an appropriate alternative source of functional normativity could, in principle, be found, it seems overwhelmingly likely that the functionalist will be strongly disposed to appeal to selection anyway, in order to ensure that her theory is an integrated part of contemporary scientific thought. Many thanks to Maggie Boden for pointing this out to me.

[12] There is, of course, a wider debate over the place occupied by Darwinian selection in evolutionary theory (see, for starters, [21, 22, 31]). Here I am concerned only with the more specific issue of the relationship between self-organization and selection, an issue which is at the heart of Kauffman's work (see also [20]).

pretation of the NK model such that the parameter N is the number of genes in each genotype, and the parameter K is the degree of epistasis, then, as K increases, the fitness landscape becomes increasingly random, such that the fitness values of genotypic neighbours are uncorrelated. Since evolution by mutation and selection will be unlikely to find global optima in this random space, sub-optimal generic forms will persist. If K is low, then the fitness landscape will be smooth and gradual, but may have very shallow inclines (if N is high), in which case only small fitness differences will be available for selection to exploit, or very steep inclines (if N is low), in which case small mutations will tend to have relatively large disruptive effects. In either case, one cannot expect to find populations converged at the fitness peaks, and sub-optimal generic forms will survive. The message is that, for a wide range of parameter values, the results of self-organization rather than selection will be dominant.

If Kauffman is right, then there are profound implications for the scope of functionalist explanation. We have agreed to attribute functions only to traits that have been selected for. Indeed, we have agreed that the function of a trait *is* what it has been selected for. So the conclusion that many persisting biological forms may not have been selected for entails that many biological forms may, strictly speaking, have no function. Of course, there may commonly be scenarios in which generic forms confer fitness benefits, and, therefore, those forms will be maintained by selection and will acquire functions. But notice that even here we have already acknowledged a source of generic form (i.e., self-organization) that acts prior to selection. It seems that it is simply not possible to do as the functionalist interpreter of Aristotle would like, and to explicate biological form *entirely* in terms of biological function. We can summarize the argument here, and highlight its full implications for the key concerns of this paper, in the following way: If we assume (a) strong continuity, (b) a world in which the functionalist about the mind is required to explain cognitive function in terms of biological function, and (c) that Kauffman is right about biological order, then we can conclude that some persisting types of cognitive phenomena (cognitive forms, as one might say) simply do not have functions (because they have not been selected for, indeed they may have persisted despite being selected against); other types of cognitive phenomena that *do* have functions may well have a non-selective source (i.e., self-organization), and hence cannot simply be given functional definitions. The clear implication is that cognitive science, understood as the investigation of the mechanisms that explain cognitive forms, will (at best) be radically incomplete, if it is carried out exclusively within the standard functionalist framework of the orthodox view.

A second argument against the functionalist interpretation of Aristotle also appeals to self-organizing systems, but in a different way, by re-engaging with the relationship between neurobiological/biochemical phenomena and cognition. Earlier I suggested that to give an explanation in terms of the psuche is to give an explanation in which the distinctive (self-)organization of an organism is given priority over its material constitution. From this explanatory perspective, the material (neurobiological/biochemical) aspects of an organism have to be understood in terms of the biological forms (life-capacities, generic forms) which those aspects generate and maintain [18]. To do justice to this demand, one needs an account of organic matter as essentially a dynamic *potentiality* for generating biological form (see [12, pp.138-41]). This is, of course, precisely what one gets if one understands the organic body in terms of a certain sub-class of self-organizing physical systems (cf. [20]). Then, if one looks at things from the opposite direction, one sees that biological forms, including cognitive phenomena, are the inevitable products of those very same physical systems. In this self-organization-based development of a generically Aristotelian position, there is no useful scientific-explanatory stance from which any of the life-capacities — cognitive life-capacities included — can be explained without essential reference to, or understanding of, the neurobiological and biochemical dynamics which generate those capacities in the living body. The functionalist interpretation of Aristotle goes wrong here precisely because it attempts to foist upon Aristotle the Cartesian account according to which the cognitive life-capacities (although not, for example, growth and decay) can be explained without any such reference. The explanatory dualism that the functionalist interpretation requires is not licenced by the account that I have just given. What is licenced, however, is a repeat of the claim that self-organization — a concept from the heartland of A-Life — is likely to be one of the theoretical foundations of a non-Cartesian biological cognitive science.

To round off this section I shall draw attention to some suggestive recent research in which the concept of self-organization is being put to work in a psuche-logical arena. The conceptual reorientation recommended in this paper demands that biological and psychological development are explanatorily continuous. It seems beyond doubt that the concept of self-organization will be crucial to explanations of biological development (see, e.g., [20]). Thus the idea of self-organization ought to be crucial to explanations of psychological development too. It is encouraging, then, that powerful evidence in favour of just such a view can be found in some recent developmental psychology. Embracing strong continuity, Thelen and Smith seek "commonalities across all development, from the first cleavage of the fertilized egg, through the earliest somatic and morphological differentiation, the complex processes of neurogenesis and emerging physiological competences, and their ultimate expression in behavior throughout the life span" [41, introduction, p.xiv]. They proceed to argue, with the support of some elegant mathematical models of the developmental data, that the process by which infants learn to walk is best explained as an example of self-organization, in which complex, nonlinear dynamical systems evolve towards preferred states under certain domain-specific constraints (e.g., anatomy, shared environmental structure). Here is not the place to embark on a detailed commentary on this work. I mention it merely to make two points: first, that a self-organization-based biological cognitive science which confronts human as well as non-human behaviour is not mere speculation; it is already an emerging force; and, second, to stress that, by applying its distinctive resources and methods to the problem of understanding self-organization in biological systems, A-Life is at the intellectual heart of that endeavour.[13]

7 The Homecoming

In *At Home in the Universe*, Kauffman suggests that life is "a natural outgrowth of the world in which we live" [26, p.48]. In this paper I have suggested that cognition is, in turn, a natural outgrowth of life. Moreover I have endorsed the idea that there is a strong explanatory continuity between life and mind. To meet the demands placed upon us by this full-bodied naturalism, we need a cognitive science that is truly biological, one that reunites mind with life by rejecting generically Cartesian explanatory assumptions in favour of a distinctively Aristotelian philosophy. If I am right, A-Life will be the theoretical core of that cognitive science. So break out the champagne because, with the help of A-Life (and Aristotle), cognition is most surely coming home.

Acknowledgements

This work was supported by a Junior Research Fellowship at Christ Church, Oxford, with additional assistance from the McDonnell-Pew Centre for Cognitive Neuroscience. Thanks to Maggie Boden, Seth Bullock, Ron Chrisley, Andy Clark, Phil Husbands, Mick O'Shea, Julie Rutkowska, and Tim Smithers for invaluable discussions, and to four anonymous reviewers for helpful suggestions.

References

[1] Aristotle. *De Anima*. Adolf M. Hakkert, Amsterdam, 1965. Reprint of R.D. Hicks' 1907 translation.

[2] M. Bedau. Emergent supple dynamics in life and mind. Forthcoming in *Brain and Cognition*.

[3] P.R. Benjamin and C.J. Elliot. Snail feeding oscillator: the central pattern generator and its control by modulatory interneurons. In J.W. Jacklet, editor, *Neuronal and Cellular Oscillators*, chapter 7, pages 173–214. Dekker, 1989.

[4] M. A. Boden. Introduction. In [5], 1-21, 1990.

[5] M. A. Boden, editor. *The Philosophy of Artificial Intelligence*. Oxford University Press, Oxford, 1990.

[6] M. A. Boden. Introduction. In [7], 1-35, 1996.

[7] M. A. Boden, editor. *The Philosophy of Artificial Life*. Oxford University Press, Oxford, 1996.

[8] R. Brooks and P. Maes, editors. *Artificial Life IV: Proceedings of the Fourth International Workshop on the Synthesis and Simulation of Living Systems*, Cambridge, Mass. and London, England, 1994. MIT Press / Bradford Books.

[9] R. M. Burian and R. C. Richardson. Form and order in evolutionary biology. In A. Fine, M. Forbes, and L. Wessels, editors, *PSA 1990: Proceedings of the 1990 Biennial Meeting of the Philosophy of Science Association, ii*, pages 267–87, East Lansing, Mich., 1991. Reprinted in [7], 146-72.

[10] J. Carneiro and J. Stewart. Self and nonself revisited: Lessons from modelling the immune network. In [34], 406-420.

[11] A. Clark. *Microcognition: Philosophy, Cognitive Science, and Parallel Distributed Processing*. MIT Press / Bradford Books, Cambridge, Mass. and London, England, 1989.

[12] A. Code and J. Moravcsik. Explaining various forms of living. In [35], 129-45, 1992.

[13] R. Cummins. Functional analysis. *Journal of Philosophy*, 72:741–65, 1975.

[14] R. Descartes. Meditations on the first philosophy. In *Discourse on Method and the Meditations*. Penguin, London, 1641. Translated by F.E. Sutcliffe in 1968.

[15] H. L. Dreyfus. *Being-in-the-World: A Commentary on Heidegger's Being and Time, Divison 1*. MIT Press, Cambridge, Mass. and London, England, 1991.

[16] M. Elton. What *are* you talking about? A-Life and cognitive science. *AISB Quarterly*, 87:47–54, 1994.

[17] N. Franceschini, J. M. Pichon, and C. Blanes. From insect vision to robot vision. *Philosophical Transactions of the Royal Society*, series B, 337:283–94, 1992.

[18] M. Frede. On Aristotle's conception of the soul. In [35], 93-107, 1992.

---

[13]For important additional evidence that concepts from A-Life will help us to understand infant development, see [38].

[19] P. Godfrey-Smith. Spencer and Dewey on life and mind. In [8], 80-9, 1994. Reprinted in [7], 314-31.

[20] B. Goodwin. *How the Leopard Changed its Spots: the Evolution of Complexity.* Phoenix, London, 1994.

[21] S. J. Gould and R. C. Lewontin. The spandrels of San Marco and the Panglossian paradigm: A critique of the adaptationist programme. *Proceedings of the Royal Society of London*, 205:581–98, 1979.

[22] S.J. Gould and E.S. Vrba. Exaptation: A missing term in the science of form. *Paleobiology*, 8(1):4–15, 1982.

[23] I. Harvey. *The Artificial Evolution of Adaptive Behaviour.* PhD thesis, School of Cognitive and Computing Sciences, University of Sussex, 1994.

[24] P. Husbands, I. Harvey, and D. Cliff. Circle in the round: State space attractors for evolved sighted robots. *Robotics and Autonomous Systems*, 15:83–106, 1995.

[25] S. Kauffman. *The Origins or Order: Self-Organization and Selection in Evolution.* Oxford University Press, New York, 1993.

[26] S. Kauffman. *At Home in the Universe: the Search for Laws of Self-Organization and Complexity.* Penguin, London, 1996.

[27] D.M. Kullman, S.A. Siegelbaum, and F. Aszetly. LTP of AMPA and NMDA receptor-mediated signals: Evidence for presynaptic expression and extrasynaptic glutamate spill-over. *Neuron*, 17:461–74, 1996.

[28] P. Maes, M. Mataric, J.-A. Meyer, J. Pollack, and S. W. Wilson, editors. *From Animals to Animats 4: Proceedings of the Fourth International Conference on Simulation of Adaptive Behavior*, Cambridge, Mass. and London, England, 1996. MIT Press / Bradford Books.

[29] G. B. Matthews. *De Anima* 2. 2-4 and the meaning of *life*. In [35]. Reprinted as *Aristotle on Life* in [7], 304-13, 1992.

[30] H. R. Maturana and F. J. Varela. *Autopoiesis and Cognition: the Realization of the Living.* Reidel, Boston, 1980.

[31] J. Maynard Smith. Optimization theory in evolution. *Annual Review of Ecology and Systematics*, 9:31–56, 1978.

[32] J. McDowell. *Mind and World.* Harvard University Press, Cambridge, Mass. and London, England, 1994.

[33] R.G. Millikan. *White Queen Psychology and Other Essays for Alice.* MIT Press / Bradford Books, Cambridge, Mass. and London, England, 1995.

[34] F. Moran, A. Moreno, J.J. Merelo, and P. Chacon, editors. *Advances in Artificial Life: Proceedings of the Third European Conference on Artificial Life*, Berlin and Heidelberg, 1995. Springer-Verlag.

[35] M. C. Nussbaum and A. O. Rorty, editors. *Essays on Aristotle's* De Anima. Clarendon, Oxford, 1992.

[36] R. Pfeifer. Building "fungus eaters": Design principles of autonomous agents. In [28, pp.3-12], 1996.

[37] H. Putnam. The nature of mental states. In W. G. Lycan, editor, *Mind and Cognition: a Reader*, pages 47–56. Basil Blackwell, Oxford, England, and Cambridge, Mass., 1990.

[38] J. C. Rutkowska. Can development be designed? What we may learn from the Cog project. In [34], 383-95, 1995.

[39] C. A. Skarda and W. J. Freeman. How brains make chaos in order to make sense of the world. *Behavioral and Brain Sciences*, 10:161–195, 1987.

[40] J. Stewart. Cognition = life: Implications for higher-level cognition. *Behavioural Processes*, 35:311–26, 1996.

[41] E. Thelen and L. B. Smith. *A Dynamic Systems Approach to the Development of Cognition and Action.* MIT Press, Cambridge, Mass., 1993.

[42] A. Thompson. Evolving electronic robot controllers that exploit hardware resources. In [34], 641-57, 1995.

[43] F. J. Varela. Autopoiesis and a biology of intentionality. In *Proceedings of a workshop on Autopoiesis and Perception, Dublin City University*, 1992.

[44] F. J. Varela, E. Thompson, and E. Rosch. *The Embodied Mind: Cognitive Science and Human Experience.* MIT Press, Cambridge, Mass. and London, England, 1991.

[45] M. Wheeler. From activation to activity: Representation, computation, and the dynamics of neural network control systems. *AISB Quarterly*, 87:36–42, 1994.

[46] M. Wheeler. Escaping from the Cartesian mind-set: Heidegger and artificial life. In [34], 65-76, 1995.

[47] M. Wheeler. From robots to Rothko: the bringing forth of worlds. In [7], 209-36, 1996.

[48] K. V. Wilkes. *Psuche* versus the mind. In [35], 109-27, 1992.

In Defence of Functional Analysis

Joe Faith

School of Cognitive and Computing Sciences, University of Sussex, Brighton, UK

josephf@cogs.susx.ac.uk

Abstract

Computationalism presupposed a modular-functional analysis of cognitive behaviour, and its failure has encouraged the search for alternative analytical techniques, such as behavioural decomposition and dynamical systems theory. This paper argues that these alternatives can be no more than useful heuristics, and that a functional analysis is necessary for an understanding of intentional adaptive behaviour, but that this need not imply the existence of cognitive modules.

1 Mechanism, Explanation and Elimination

The function of most of the interactions between a living thing and its environment are directly metabolic — digestion, respiration, photosynthesis, etc. In the case of the simplest of organisms these are the *only* interactions engaged in. However, more complicated organisms also engage in interactions in which the function is not directly metabolic, but depend upon an objective relationship between that bit of the environment with which it is engaged, and some other bit that may hold some adaptive benefit — what Gibson described as an *affordance* [27]. For example, when an animal reacts to light hitting its retina it does so, not because this reaction in itself helps the animals survival, but because the pattern of light on the retina stands in some objective relationship to some feature of the environment that may be. (In some cases — such as plant phototaxis — the two functions are combined in one behaviour). In other words the function of these interactions is *about* something else in the environment. These interactions are thus necessarily *intentional*: they can only be understood by reference to the distal object. If the organism is to be consistently adaptive then the objective relationship between it and that affordance must be reflected[1] in some way in the organism's nervous system (if not in its psychological experience).

If a behaviour is adaptive in this way then it must display some form of regularity: if there is food available, then the organism must reliably find it; if there is

---

[1] "Reflected" is used, not in the mirror-like sense, but in the sense of "the change in the weather was reflected in people's dress".

a predator, then it must avoid it; and so on. In general, adaptive behaviour presupposes behaviour that is regular, reliable or robust with respect to some *affordance* offered by the environment [27]. Obviously not all such regular behaviours will be adaptive — consider an organism that reliably runs *towards* a predator — nor does the regularity have to perfect. Nonetheless, behavioural regularity is a pre-requisite of behavioural adaptivity.

How can a mechanism produce such behavioural regularities — what is the nature of this "reflection"? One way is for them to be codified in a set of rules that use representations of the state of the environment (such as "if there is some food, then move towards it"), and then to build a system that follows these rules. This is the intuition underlying computationalism, with all its attendant problems [10].

An alternative is described by Daniel Dennett:

> But how *could* the order be there, so visible amidst the noise, if it were not the direct outline of a concrete orderly process in the background? Well, it *could* be there thanks to the statistical effect of very many concrete minutiae producing, as if by a hidden hand, an approximation of the "ideal" order. Philosophers have tended to ignore a variety of regularity intermediate between the regularities of planets and other objects "obeying" the laws of physics and the regularities of rule-following (that is, rule-*consulting*) systems. These intermediate regularities are those which are preserved under selection pressure. [18, p43]

Thus behavioural regularities need not be produced by a corresponding functional entity in the underlying mechanism — a "controlled variable" [48] — rather they can be a collective by-product of many essentially independent processes. Douglas Hofstadter [31, p642] gives the example of a computer system whose performance degrades disastrously when there are more than, say, 35 users on the system. A naive observer may suspect that there is a mechanism that detects the number of users and controls performance accordingly. In fact the drop in performance is due to the system "thrashing" — spending so much time swapping between users, that there is no time left for useful processing. This regular, environmentally-contingent, behaviour is a result of what Hendriks-Jansen calls "interactive emergence" [30] between the mechanism and its environment, and is not caused by any discrete functional entity in the former. These two ways of producing behavioural regularities correspond to Marr's distinction between Type I and Type II mechanisms [37].

A rule-following, Type I, system has at least two levels of organisation: the lower level of the underlying mechanism, and the higher level of the rules that it follows. For example, a digital computer is realised in an electrodynamical system that displays higher-level organisation in the form of the virtual machinery of its software. This higher level of organisation is as real as the lower level, and cannot be reduced to it: the higher level can be *explained* in terms of the lower, but cannot be *explained away*. A full explanation of the system must describe both levels. A Type II system, on the other hand, has no such higher level of organisation. Its behaviour when interacting with an environment may possibly be describable in terms of strict rules, but these rules are purely a property of its behaviour and do not correspond to any entities in (or level of organisation of) the underlying mechanism.

The regularities in adaptive, behaviour are usually described using *intentional* terminology. For example: "the agent turned left because it thought that there was some food over there and it was hungry". If the behaviour were produced by a Type I mechanism that instantiates these rules as a level of organisation, then these descriptions would be true explanations — they would not just describe the behaviour, but also correctly identify features of the mechanism that *produced* that behaviour. In our example, there would be some functional entity in the organism's mechanism that corresponds to the sensing of the position of the food on the various different occasions when the intentional description could be applied.

However, there need be no such correspondence. If the mechanism were of Type II then the intentional interpretation may accurately describe the *behaviour* of the agent even though it bears no relationship to the way in which the underlying mechanism *produces* that behaviour. If this is the case then we would be justified in eliminating the intentional explanation in favour of an analysis purely in terms of the underlying mechanism, understood as a dynamical system [45][12]. The intentional interpretation would be descriptive, but not explanatory.

Consider this analogy. Suppose that a ball were affected by two forces: one pushing north, and one west. We can describe the behaviour of the ball as being due to a single force acting north-west, and this is a perfectly accurate, and predictive, description. However the entities postulated by this description bear no relation to the mechanism that produced the behaviour. It is thus equivalent to an intentional interpretation of a Type II system. A true *explanation* of the behaviour of the ball would eliminate the resultant force in favour of the underlying components, just as the intentional interpretation should be eliminated in favour of a dynamical systems explanation. Note that we cannot distinguish between the descriptions of the behaviour on a purely empirical basis, rather we have to investigate the mechanism that produced the behaviour.

The central problem of naturalising intentionality is in what sense is it true that an agent interracts with a distal object, rather than with proximal stimuli. This paper avoids this problem, and instead asks in what sense is it *useful* to make such claims. The conclusion is that if an ascription of intentionality to an agent is to have explanatory, rather than just descriptive, virtue, then it must be grounded in the functional organisation of the mechanism underlying its behaviour.

2 The Evolution of Adaptive Behaviour

There is no *a priori* reason why natural or artificial adaptive systems should be of either type: both are capable of displaying exactly the same behaviours. However there are practical reasons why Type I mechanisms will be favoured when behaviours emerge through a process of learning, development, or evolution — unlike Hofstadter's example, which was an accidental by-product of a design produced for another purpose.

Recall that adaptive behaviour demands that an agent coordinate its activity with respect to an affordance that the environment offers. To do this the agent must detect it — where "detect" is used in the widest sense of "being influenced by its presence". Given some affordances, and some sensory mechanisms, this can be done very simply. Consider one of the vehicles discussed by Braitenberg [6]: a mobile robot with two driven wheels, a castor to prevent toppling, and two light sensors, both pointing forwards with one to the left and one to the right. If the output from the left sensor is connected to the right motor, and *vice versa*, then the robot will continuously turn and move in the direction of the strongest light source. This reliable behaviour is not due to any internal representations or a rule-following mechanism. The presence of an affordance can also be detected in much more complex sensory input, given a suitable sensory mechanism — such as the tracheal tubes of the female cricket, which are precisely tuned to detect the male's chirp [52][32].

In these cases there is a very simple relationship between the presence of an affordance and a particular sensory input, and a Type II mechanism is capable of using this relationship to produce adaptive behaviour. However organisms often have to use general-purpose mechanisms (such as retinal arrays or olfactory bulbs) rather than specialised detectors (such as tracheal tubes, or pheromone detectors). As the sensory mechanisms become more general, so the presence of particular affordances become less explicit. For example, in olfactory systems that detect pheromones, the presence of the affordance that the pheromone signals is proportional to the activity of a local set of receptor cells. In contrast, when an odour is detected by an olfactory bulb it produces an oscillatory pattern that is distributed across a very wide area [44]. How can neural mechanisms evolve, or learn, to use such general sensory systems to reliably detect the presence of an affordance?

In such cases, the more successful mechanisms will be those that are better able to generalise from one case of a behavioural regularity to another. Consider shift invariance. In this case the regularity required is a similar response to an image that may be presented at different positions on a retina. It would be possible to teach, or evolve, a Type II mechanism to respond suitably to a number of particular image presentations. However, since it is a Type II mechanism then the way in which it achieves these responses may have nothing in common with each other: the behavioural regularity may not be due to a regularity in the underlying mechanism.

This mechanism is likely to be robust against certain changes in input: the addition of noise to the input would only change each input channel by a small amount, and thus we may expect the response of the mechanism to be similar. However other changes, such as moving the image on the retina, result in each input channel changing by a large amount — spots that were dark will now be light, and *vice versa*. There is no reason why a previously successful mechanism would produce similar behaviour given such different novel inputs. By contrast, a Type I solution would, by definition, involve some functional element that responds similarly to the same pattern regardless of its particular position. Such a solution, if it can be found, will generalise more robustly and will thus be favoured by evolution or a learning regime.

For example, one possible (though completely artificial) Type II solution to learning shift invariance would be a look-up table that lists a number of different retinal inputs and their required responses. This solution is completely incapable of generalising beyond the listed inputs, unlike a Type I solution that depended on noticing what the positive cases had in common.

Type I organisation need not be a property of the internal mechanism; it may also be achieved through active perception. For example *Drosophila* solves shift invariance, not through a detector that can recognise a pattern anywhere on the retina, but by moving its eye until a template is matched [19]. A similar strategy is used in [43] to solve the problem of distinguishing small objects from large ones using only a one dimensional array of proximity sensors. If the vehicle "wall-hugs" any object that it comes across, then the size of the object being hugged will be inversely proportional to the rate of turning, which can be detected as a difference in left and right wheel speeds. Both methods achieve affordance-

behaviour regularities by unifying affordance-detection through a single functional unit — whether this unification is done internally or through the agents own activity.

Thus we would expect Type I affordance-detection to be an almost inevitable product of even the most unbiased learning or evolution regimes [49]; and, indeed, this is the case. In [22] Floreano and Mondada describe the artificial evolution of a neural network controller for a Khepera-style robot. Its task is to explore a simple arena, returning to a recharging "base" that is demarcated by a black floor patch, directed by a bright light. The fitness of an individual rises with the total amount of movement, along with avoiding obstacles. Although the need to recharge is not an explicit element in the fitness function, it is a behaviour that obviously must be evolved in order to maximise fitness. Thus the location of the base is a feature of the environment that it would be very useful for the robot to detect (though it could be found by a random search, albeit less efficiently). The most fit individual was found to be using one hidden node of the network in order to do this — its activation corresponded to the distance from the base, reaching a maximum when it was "home". As the authors note:

> In this experience the robot autonomously evolved the ability to use the raw sensor data and built an internal representation of the world in order to find the recharging area and return to this place at a given time. This behaviour is based on an accurate evaluation of the battery residual time and on an internal representation of the environment. In fact some of the hidden nodes displayed activation levels that clearly mapped the environment geometry. [41]

The second example is [29], in which a team from the University of Sussex evolved a neural network to control the movement of a camera-head mounted on a gantry, whose motion is designed to mimic that of a wheeled robot. In this case both the internal network, and the morphology of the visual sensors, was available for selection. The task presented was to approach a white triangular target, whilst avoiding a rectangular one. The successful robot used two sensors, one with a visual field above the other. It locates the triangle by rotating on the spot until just the lower sensor sees white, when it moves straight ahead. This has the effect of fixating the robot on the oblique edge of the triangle. As the triangle looms up such that both sensors go high, or if the motion causes the edge to be lost, then the robot will start to rotate until the edge can be fixated again. The rotate/move-straight distinction is effected by a single unit that takes an inhibitory connection from the upper sensor and an excitatory link from the lower, and is thus only fully activated when the robot is facing towards the triangle's edge. Therefore this robot uses a mixture of active perception, a sensor morphology closely tied to the structure of the environment, and a representational architecture in order to produce adaptive behaviour.

The evolutionary pressure to generalise behaviour thus produces a pressure to localise function. Thus we find that the most robust, stereotyped, behaviours are produced by the most functionally specialised mechanisms. For example, sensory-motor behaviours, such as saccades or fixation movements, that have to be very fast and reliable tend to be produced via very clearly defined topographic cortical maps [39].

It is also worth remembering that not all components are localised, structurally individuated entities like hearts and lungs: in small animals the functions of respiration and circulation can be achieved by diffusion processes. This does not imply that there are no entities — stomata etc — that carry this function, but that they form a distributed, functionally individuated, "component" or subsystem; rather than a localised, structurally indivuated, one. Similarly, componential-functional decomposition in neural networks need not imply the existence of "grandmother" cells, or even of clearly delimited modules. Something can play a well-defined functional role with respect to other components even if it is not topographically localised. For an intuition pump, think of the geographically diffuse functional components of human societies, such as political organisations, classes, companies etc. As was shown above, it is usually only the most stereotyped behaviours that result in localised functional modularisation; and even these do not work in isolation. For example, although only a small number of neurons are directly involved in the gill-withdrawal reflex of *Aplysia*, up to 300 others are simultaneously activated, since siphon stimulation *also* causes many other behaviours: mantle contraction, inking, mucus release, postural changes, respiratory pumping etc. [2]

Functions Without Computations

It must be emphasised that a functional decomposition is relative to a behaviour of the overall system [14]. This is the crucial difference between this approach to functional analysis, and the *modular*-functional analysis of classical computationalism. Fodor [23] argues for the existence of modules that are the prior explanatory atoms of all cognitive behaviour. Modules are general purpose, they play the same role in all behaviour, and so have a fixed function. However, the functional analysis given above *starts* from a particular behaviour, and then asks how it is achieved. Analysing different behaviours may reveal a different functional decomposition with no component playing the same role in each case. It is modularity, rather than functional analysis *per se* that defines a computationalist perspective.

When a single unit is described as representing the presence of a target triangle, this is a description of how

a mechanism achieves a behaviour. Representation is not what an entity *is*, but rather what it *does* in a behavioural context. Representation is not merely a correlation between internal and external state that only exists for an external observer, but a relational, functional property between a mechanism and a particular behaviour that it displays.

3 Functional Analysis and Dynamical Systems Theory

What do we gain by a functional analysis of such simple systems? After all, if a functional analysis is needed in a simple case like the triangle-seeking robot, then there seems no principled reason why it could not be applied in even simpler cases. For example, the neural mechanism of the Braitenberg light-seeking vehicle is actually no more than a pair of crossed wires. However we *could* describe it in functional terms as an input module (comprising the two sensors) that passes a representation of the world (the state of the two wires) to the output module (the motors). Although no principled "bottom line" for functional explanation can be given, this need not invalidate its use. After all, if we consider a vacuum that contains just a few molecules of a gas, then concepts such as "temperature" and "pressure" would seem superfluous compared to a far more precise kinematic description of the molecular motion. However this does not mean that the bulk gas properties are not well-defined; it is only when the number of molecules increases that the explanatory power of these properties becomes essential.

A more principled objection is that functional-intentional explanations should be eliminated in favour of a description of the agent in its environment as a coupled dynamical system (DS) [28][50]. At this point two versions of the DS Theory should be distinguished, depending on what are taken as the state variables of the system. The state variables are the explanatory "atoms" of DST. Once a set of state variables has been identified, then their relationships and effects on each other are described with a set of evolution equations. Factors that are external to, but impact upon, the system are included as parameters to those equations. Two dynamical systems in which the state variables of one system act as the parameters for the other (and *vice versa*) are described as being *coupled*, and together form a new super-system which may, in turn have its own environment and parameters. A dynamical system is analysed by examining the structure and topology of the phase space of the system, and any basins of attraction that underpin any identifiable behavioural modes — what Agre and Chapman call "routines" [1].

The first, weaker, version of DST allows mental and intentional attributes to be used as state variables — such as the motivations, beliefs and decisions modelled in [11]. This approach thus shares the fundamental Cartesian assumption of classical computational psychology, that cognition takes place in a mental "space" built from representations of the world. The only difference is that the rules for the manipulation of these representations are essentially temporal. The weak form of DST therefore stands in the same relation to computationalism as classical connectionism [16]: it shares an explanatory framework, but uses more complicated rules.

The stronger form of DST therefore restricts state variables to be non-mental, i.e. *physical*, properties of the system and its environment [4] [46]. This approach was first used 50 years earlier by Ross Ashby [3]. In the case of agents built from a neural network, the obvious choice of state variables are the activation of single neurons or neural masses [33][24]. However, this restriction has consequences for how DST can be used.

DST is supposed to provide an explanation of how cognitive behaviour is produced, rather than simply describing the dynamics of the internal mechanism. In order to do this a DST model must therefore include not just a whole agent but also its *environment* (though see [34]). Let us assume for the moment that determining the evolution equations for state variables that are internal to the agent is unproblematic. The environment can then be handled in one of three ways. The first is to ignore it by leaving any environmental impact on the system as undetermined parameters: this is obviously no answer for analysing the behaviour of whole agents. The second, as advocated in [46] and [4], is to treat the environment as a dynamical system in its own right, tightly coupled to that of the agent. This, however, is a form of Laplacean reductionism. Consider trying to produce a DST model of a bird trying to land in a tree. The bird must coordinate its body with a swaying branch using its eyes, brain, and muscles. The obvious state variables for the bird will include retinal cell inputs, the activations of the neurons in the visuo-motor system, and muscle nerve outputs. However the retinal inputs to the system will be affected by the most trivial changes in the environment: the wind catching a leaf and causing a shadow to move, for instance. This perturbation of input will, in turn, alter the trajectory in the phase space of the system. If we want to know how the bird lands reliably despite the incidental movement of so many factors in the environment, then it seems as though we will have to model the tree in as much detail as the nervous system of the bird. This is impossible in practise, even if we agree with Laplace that it may be possible in principle. The only case of a full DST analysis of a whole agent-environment system that I am aware of is [33], in which the environment is completely static. In [4] the neural network controller for a hexapod robot is modelled as a dynamical system, but its environment is treated as the body that it controls (the environment external to the body is again assumed to be static), and only a localised 5-neuron subsystem

is *analysed* as such. (This is not meant to detract from the great subtlety of the evolved design. The point is that it is not possible to fully appreciate it from a purely dynamical systems perspective.)

The only alternative for DST is to postulate features of the phase space of the agent-environment system that are immune to the incidental, un-modellable, changes to state variables. This is the way in which Walter Freeman uses DST to model oscillations in the olfactory bulb [25]. Two points should be noted about this model. The first is that it is *not* an attempt to model a whole agent-environment system, rather it is a model of an isolated functional module with a well-defined input and output. Second, the whole point of this model and the experimental *in vivo* work on which it is based [51], is to show how certain characteristics of the phase space of the olfactory bulb are immune to certain changes in input: in particular that the spatial amplitude pattern of the dominant oscillations carries odorant information [26], despite the stochasticity of epithelial receptor activity [35]. In other words, DST is being used to examine how the olfactory bulb fulfills the function of the classification of odorant information; in this case it underpins, rather than undermines, a functional analysis [21].

In general, DST tries to relate particular behaviours to topological features in the phase space of the system. This requires two things. The first is that certain state variables of the agent and environment have to be ignored at certain times: for example if we want to know how an agent is physically negotiating an obstacle, then the olfactory input will not be relevant. This corresponds to taking projections of the phase space in order to reveal topographic regularities. A system could well be in a well-defined limit cycle with respect to 2 state variables, whilst another varies seemingly randomly. The underlying order is only exposed if we consider a 2-variable sensory-motor subsystem, for which the state variables of the larger system act as parameters. Changes to these parameters may well drastically alter the topology of the subspace causing a change in the behavioural mode, and hence they cannot be ignored but, until they do change, the exhibited behaviour must be analysed with respect to a subset of state variables. If we recall that state variables measure physical properties of parts of the system, then dynamical systems analysis requires that a particular behaviour is related to properties of a physical subsystem. Second, the topographic features to which behavioural modes are related are identified with respect to *values* of state variables — i.e., with respect to the internal state of a subsystem. The internal state may not be a *static value*, but rather — as in the case of the olfactory bulb — must be a *stable mode* of activity.

Therefore, contrary to the many claims made for it, if DST is to be used to analyse the adaptive behaviour of whole agents in dynamic environments it will require that the presence of affordances in the environment be related to the functional role of the state of subcomponents of the system. In other words, DST in practise produces a functional, componential, and hence *intentional*, analysis. Adaptive systems, like everything else, may be *modelled* as a dynamical system. The point is that they cannot be *understood* as such.

4 Functional Analysis and Behavioural Decomposition

Another proposed alternative to the componential-functional analysis of adaptive behaviour is behavioural decomposition. Instead of decomposition into simpler *functions*, the overall behaviour should be decomposed into simpler *behavioural capacities*. As Cummins puts it:

> A cook's capacity to bake a cake analyzes into other capacities of the "whole cook". ...My capacity to multiply 27 time 32 analyses into the capacity to multiply 2 times 7, to add 5 and 1, etc. These capacities are not (so far as is known) capacities of my components: indeed, this analysis seems to put no constraints at all on my componential analysis. [15, p29]

Brooks [7][8] has demonstrated how each of these whole-agent capacities may be achieved by a "layer" in a control architecture, connected to the sensors and motors of the system and working semi-independently of each other. (Also see [36] [30] [47].) Contrast this to the normal modular decomposition [23] in which only the sensory and motor modules are connected to the outside world, with all other modules communicating between themselves using representations.

However, given a behavioural decomposition and a corresponding layered control architecture, the problem still remains of *how* each of these layers achieve their, admittedly simpler, intentional behaviours. Brooks *et al* argue that this can be achieved "by using the world as its own best model" — in other words without any complex transformations of sensory input. However, unless "magic sensors" are available which detect the presence of an affordance directly (and pheromone detectors are a common natural example), then this will not be possible. Even the most cited implementation of Brooks' architecture, Mataric's *Toto* [38], uses clearly defined, localised components to indicate states of the agent-environment interaction. As Brooks states:

> My earlier paper [10] is often criticised for advocating absolutely no representation of the world within a behaviour-based robot. This criticism is invalid. I make it clear in the paper that I reject traditional Artificial Intelligence representation schemes. I also made it clear that I reject explicit representations of goals within the machine.
> There can, however, be representations which are partial models of the world — in fact I mentioned that "individual layers extract only those *aspects* of the world which they fund relevant — projections of a representations into a simple subspace". The form these representations take, within the context of the computational model we are using, will depend on the particular task those representations are to be used for. [9, p19]

Behavioural decomposition also often implicitly assumes that adaptive agents have a discrete set of distinct units of behaviour [20] — one for each layer. For example, Hendriks-Jansen describes species-specific fixed action patterns as "natural kinds" — atoms out of which the overall behavioural repertoire is built [30]. The same intuition underlies the use of extrinsic fitness functions to evolve neural network controllers for adaptive agents, scoring each member of the population on their performance on a precisely defined behaviour. This is closely related to Dawkins' genetic determinism, in which the "extended" phenotype of the organism — which includes behavioural properties — is divided into discrete traits, each of which is encoded by a single gene [17].

Beer and Gallagher [5] have tried to avoid this behavioural atomism by advocating the use of *intrinsic* fitness functions, in which the selection is more "natural". Instead of reproductive success being determined by success in a behavioural trial, the members of the population have autonomous metabolic and reproductive cycles. This means that, as in natural selection, the evolved agents are judged on their overall "way of life" rather than performance over a set of atomistic behaviours. (See [42] for a simple example.)

5 Conclusion

If we want to understand how evolved mechanisms produce adaptive behaviour, then there is no philosophical or practical alternative to functional analysis. A dynamical systems analysis, though a useful counterweight to computationalist assumptions, is based on a Laplacean philosophical error and reduces to functional analysis in practise. Behavioural decomposition is a useful heuristic for synthesis, but assumes the existence of behavioural atoms, and begs the question of how those atoms are achieved.

A functional analysis of the adaptive behaviour of an agent must relate how it is coordinated with respect to affordances offered by the environment, to internal functional entities. Therefore the analysis will be necessarily *intentional*. Instead of discarding functional, intentional analyses, we should investigating how they can be used in non-modular, non-computational ways.

Acknowledgements

Thanks to Maggie Boden, Ron Chrisley and Jason Noble for useful comments on earlier drafts of this paper.

References

[1] P.E. Agre and D. Chapman. *Pengi: An implementation of a theory of activity*, pages 196–201. 1987.

[2] J.S. Altman and J. Kien. Highlighting *aplysia*'s networks. *Trends in Neuroscience*, 13(3), 1990.

[3] W.R. Ashby. *Design for a brain: The origin of adaptive behaviour*. Chapman Hall, 1952.

[4] R.D. Beer. A dynamical systems perspective on autonomous agents. Technical Report 92-11, Case Western Reserve University, Cleveland, Ohio, 1992.

[5] R.D. Beer and J.C. Gallagher. Evolving dynamical neural networks for adaptive behaviour. *Adaptive Behaviour*, 1(1), 1992.

[6] V. Braitenberg. *Vehicles : experiments in synthetic psychology*. MIT Press, 1984.

[7] R. Brooks. A robust layered control system for a mobile robot. *IEEE Journal of Robotics and Automation*, (2):14–23, April 1986.

[8] R. Brooks. Challenges for complete creature architectures. In Meyer and Wilson [40], pages 434–443.

[9] R. Brooks. Intelligence without reason. Technical Report 1293, MIT Artificial Intelligence Laboratory, April 1991.

[10] R. Brooks. Intelligence without representation. *Artificial Intelligence*, (47):139–159, 1991.

[11] J.R. Busemeyer and J.T. Townsend. Decision field theory: A dynamic-cognitive approach to decision making in an uncertain environment. *Psychological Review*, (100):432–459, 1993.

[12] P.M. Churchland. Eliminative materialism and the propositional attitudes. *Journal of Philosophy*, (78), 1981.

[13] D. Cliff, P. Husbands, J.A. Meyer, and S.W. Wilson, editors. *From animals to animats 3: Proceedings of the third international conference on the simulation of adaptive behaviour*. MIT Press, 1994.

[14] R. Cummins. Functional analysis. *Journal of Philosophy*, 72:741–765, 1975.

[15] R. Cummins. *The nature of psychological explanation*. MIT Press, 1983.

[16] R. Cummins and G. Schwarz. Radical connectionism. *The Southern Journal of Philosophy*, XXVI - supplement:43–72, 1987.

[17] R. Dawkins. *The Extended Phenotype*. W.H.Freeman, 1982.

[18] D.C. Dennett. Real patterns. *The Journal of Philosophy*, 88(3):27–51, 1991.

[19] M. Dill, R. Wolf, and M. Heisenberg. Visual-pattern recognition in drosophila involves retinotopic matching. *Nature*, 365(6448):751–753, 1993.

[20] B Enc. Units of behaviour. *Philosophy of Science*, (62):523–542, 1995.

[21] J.E. Faith. The role of oscillations in the olfactory bulb. Master's thesis, School of Cognitive and Computing Sciences, University of Sussex, Brighton, 1995.

[22] D. Floreano and F. Mondada. Evolution of homing navigation in a real mobile robot. *IEEE transactions on systems, man and cybernetics*, 26(3), 1996.

[23] J.A. Fodor. *Modularity of mind: an essay on faculty psychology*. MIT Press, 1983.

[24] W.J. Freeman. *Mass Action in the Nervous System*. Academic Press, New York, 1975.

[25] W.J. Freeman. Simulation of chaotic EEG patterns with a dynamic model of the olfactory system. *Biological Cybernetics*, 56:139–150, 1987.

[26] W.J. Freeman and C.A. Skarda. Spatial EEG patterns, non-linear dynamics and perception: the neo-Sherringtonian view. *Brain Research Reviews*, 10:147–175, 1985.

[27] J.J. Gibson. *The Ecological Approach To Visual Perception*. Houghton Mifflin, Boston, Ma, 1979.

[28] M. Giunti. Dynamical models of cognition. In T. Van Gelder and R. Port, editors, *Mind as motion*. MIT Press, 1995.

[29] I. Harvey, P. Husbands, and D. Cliff. Seeing the light: artificial evolution, real vision. In Cliff et al. [13], pages 392–401.

[30] H. Hendriks-Jansen. *Catching ourselves in the act: situated activity, interactive emergence, evolution and human thought*. MIT Press, 1996.

[31] D.R. Hofstadter. Waking up from the Boolean dream, or subcognition as computation. In *Metamagical Themas*. Penguin, Harmondsworth, Middlesex, 1985.

[32] F. Huber and J. Thorson. Cricket auditory communication. *Scientific American*, 253(6):46–54, 1985.

[33] P. Husbands, I. Harvey, and D. Cliff. Circle in the round: State space attractors for evolved sighted robots. *Robotics and Autonomous Systems*, (15), 1995.

[34] N. Jakobi. Half-baked, *ad hoc* and noisy: Minimal simulations for evolutionary robotics. This volume.

[35] J.S. Kauer. Contributions of topography and parallel processing to odor coding in the vertebrate olfactory pathway. *Trends in Neuroscience*, 14(2):79–85, 1991.

[36] P. Maes, editor. *Designing Autonomous Agents: Theory and Practise from Biology to Engineering and Back.* Special Issues of *Robotics and Autonomous Systems*. MIT, 1991.

[37] D. Marr. Artificial intelligence: A personal view. In M. Boden, editor, *The Philosophy of Artificial Intelligence*. Oxford University Press, 1977.

[38] M.J. Matarić. Navigating with a rat brain: A neurologically-inspired model for robot spatial representation. In Meyer and Wilson [40], pages 169–175.

[39] M. Merzenich and J. Kaas. Principles of organization of sensory-perceptual systems in mammals. *Progress in psychobiology and physiological psychology*, (9):1–42, 1980.

[40] J.A. Meyer and S.W. Wilson, editors. *From animals to animats: Proceedings of the first international conference on the simulation of adaptive behaviour (SAB90)*. MIT Press, 1991.

[41] F. Mondada and D. Floreano. Evolution of neural control structures: some experiments on mobile robots. *Robotics and Autonomous Systems*, 16:183–195, 1996.

[42] N.H. Packard. Intrinsic adaption in a simple model for evolution. In C. Langton, editor, *Artificial Life: Proceedings of the workshop on artificial life*, Santa Fe Institute studies in the sciences of complexity. Addison-Wesley, 1988.

[43] C. Scheier and R. Pfeifer. Classification as sensory-motor coordination: A case study on autonomous agents. In F. Moran, A. Moreno, J.J. Merelo, and P. Chacon, editors, *Advances in artificial life: proceedings of the third European Conference on Artificial Life*, number 929 in Lecture notes in artificial intelligence. Springer, 1995.

[44] C.A. Skarda and W.J. Freeman. How brains make chaos in order to make sense of the world. *The Behavioral and Brain Sciences*, 10:161–195, 1987.

[45] T. Smithers. Taking eliminative materialism seriously: A methodology for autonomous systems research. In F.J. Varela and P. Bourgine, editors, *Towards a practise of autonomous systems: proceedings of the first European Conference on Artificial Life*, 1992.

[46] T. Smithers. What the dynamics of adaptive behaviour and cognition might look like in agent-environment interaction systems. In T. Smithers and A. Moreno, editors, *3rd International Workshop on Artificial Life and Artificial Intelligence, The Role of Dynamics and Representation in Adaptive Behaviour and Cognition*, San Sebastian, Spain, 1994.

[47] L. Steels. Towards a theory of emergent functionality. In Meyer and Wilson [40].

[48] L. Steels. The artificial life roots of artificial intelligence. *Artificial Life Journal*, 1, 1994.

[49] C. Thornton. Brave mobots use representation. Cognitive Science Research Paper 401, School of Cognitive and Computing Sciences, University of Sussex, Brighton, 1995.

[50] T. Van Gelder. The dynamical hypothesis in cognitive science. *Behavioral and Brain Sciences*, submitted.

[51] G. Viana Di Prisco and W.J. Freeman. Odour-related bulbar EEG spatial pattern analysis during appetitive conditioning in rabbits. *Behavioural Neuroscience*, 98(5):964–978, 1985.

[52] B. Webb. Robotic experiments in cricket phonotaxis. In Cliff et al. [13].

"Why are there so few biologists here?"

– *Artificial Life as a theoretical biology of artistry*

Lars Risan

Centre for Technology and Culture,
University of Oslo,
Gaustadalléen 21, N-0371 Oslo, Norway
Email: lars.risan@ima.uio.no

The question in the title of this paper was raised at the final discussion at the *Simulation of Adaptive Behavior '94* (SAB 94) conference and was brought up again one year later, at the *European Conference of Artificial Life '95* (ECAL 95) in Granada. In the introduction to the proceedings of the latter conference we read: «It is our opinion, and that of many others, that the future *survival* of ALife is highly related to the presence of *people from biology* in the field.» (Moran et. al. 1995:V, emphasis in original)

A good reason, it seems to me, why the real or possible lack of biologists in the field may be problematic is as follows. We ought (further) to establish Artificial Life as a theoretical biology that, following Waddington, will present broader concepts of what life is than the notions upheld by the leading genetical determinism of molecular biology. As proponents of such a theoretical biology, we would benefit from contacts with biologists, partly to be inspired by them, but perhaps more important; to be able to inspire them. We could call this the *argument of influence*; ALifers have something to say to biologists, so it would be nice if they cared to listen.

Related to this argument is another; we might call it the *argument of legitimacy*. If Artificial Life is going to speak to biologists, then it will have to do so as a legitimate biological science. ALifers will have to address biologists with an authority that biologists accept as legitimate. For this to happen, ALifers and biologists will have to socialise; they will have to develop a common language, as well as common methods and interests; they will have to read each other's papers and attend each other's conferences.

Having authority and influence, Artificial Life will be able to mould our common concepts of what life as such is, and ALife does have something to say about this.

If ALife is not further developed as a theoretical biology, the field may well end up where much of AI has ended; as a purely computer engineering enterprise, devoted entirely to the optimisation of computer performance and devoid of any interest in asking fundamental questions about life or cognition.

Geoffrey Miller expressed these two alternatives with rhetorical clarity at a talk he gave during my visit at the *School of Cognitive and Computing Sciences* (COGS), later published in (Miller 1996): Artificial Life can choose between becoming a «Real Science» aiming at knowledge of nature and marked by good scholarship, or it may become a «Computer Science» searching for speed and money, and marked by technical insight. To put it a bit crudely, the two alternatives of the field of ALife are; to go down the golden road of engineering – and ask questions of economic relevance, or to follow the relatively untrodden path of theoretical biology – and ask questions of theoretical importance. It seems to me that those who worry about the lack of biologists in the field prefer the untrodden path of theoretical biology to the golden road of engineering.

I entirely agree that what makes ALife worthwhile is its aspirations as a theoretical biology. Biologists are indeed needed as part of such a science. I also think that ALife may have important contributions to make to a larger biological, scientific, and contemporary discourse on life and technology. I do not think, however, that too much «engineering» and the real or possible lack of biologists are the only «problems» in ALife research, nor do I think that getting more biologists in the field is the whole «solution».

In this paper I will argue, first, that Artificial Life can be both an engineering endeavour and a theoretical biology. There is a possible bond between these two enterprises. Second, I will argue that by recognising this bond, ALife may become a *powerful* theoretical biology. The theoretical biology of Artificial Life may, as it were, walk down the golden road of its engineering.

As an anthropologist of science I know Artificial Life research a bit from the outside. My subject matter is not any particular topic *within* ALife research, it is ALife research as such. I did my anthropological fieldwork, leading to my degree, at COGS in 1993/94. I also visited several other centres of ALife research and attended a number of conferences. From this fieldwork I learned something about ALife research as a human and technological endeavour. This paper is based on these lessons, but it is not a presentation of cool ethnographical results, of «what I found». Rather, it is my own normative and subjective involvement with my own subject matter – ALife research – a field to which I have never been a totally disinterested witness, even if I have not been a truly immersed insider either.

In the following I will first argue for the potential unity of the engineering and the theoretical biology of ALife, later showing how this may be a powerful unity. To do this I must first present my understanding of what the engineering and theoretical biology of ALife is – and of what it *ought* to be. I will start by looking at ALife as engineering.

ALife as Engineering – and both as Art

The aspect of Artificial Life that most obviously separates it from Real Life (or *life-as-we-know-it*) is that it is technology; it is constructed or engineered by humans. As I think most of you will agree, «engineering» means more than the application of formal, scientific methods to the making of machines. It involves many non-formalised practices, often talked about as skills or intuitions. As the Dreyfus brothers have pointed out (Dreyfus & Dreyfus 1987), to become an expert – for example in making ALife simulations – is to *forget* about the formal, text-book representations. As such an expertise, engineering has a lot in common with what the old Greeks called *techne*, a

word that is normally translated as «art», «craft», «skill» or «technique». Engineering, then, is a form of art, not art in the sense of fine art, but in the sense of a skilled, creative practice. ALife simulations and robots are *expressions*. ALife items express something, and as expressions they have relationship not only to what is expressed, but also to the one who expresses them. As artistic expressions, ALife simulations have aesthetic value.

From what I have said above, we see that to say that life is artificial, is to say that it has a particular relationship to a «creator» or an agent. It is not something given independent of agency. It is not only «sober», dry and objective science. There is a difference then, between the ALifer and the ideal objective scientist. We may speak about this difference in terms of «intimacy» versus «distance». There is a more intimate relationship between the ALifer and his or her Artificial Life than there is between the ideal objective scientist and his or her detached Real Life.

In my thesis I have written at length about the close relationship between the ALife researcher (or «artist») and his or her simulation, in the everyday life of the laboratory as well as in those talks at ALife conferences that have been explicitly called art (Risan 1996). I have sometimes been surprised at an ALife talk to hear the «scientist» call himself an artist as well as calling his presentation art. Moreover, scientific presentations have sometimes been performances of no less artistry than performances explicitly labelled «art». I think Karl Sims' presentations at ALIFE IV and SAB 94 (Sims 1994) are good examples of this.

To recapture Sims' simulation briefly: In this simulation «arm-like» creatures evolve a morphology – a shape – and a *control system* or a *brain*. These creatures may have one or two arms with one or more joints. They live in three-dimensional space, and have to relate to (simulated) gravity, surface friction, and their own materiality; their own weight and inertia. The simulation is presented in a highly realistic way: The ground is a bit lighter in the foreground than in the background and is equipped with rows of squares. This helps us see that the ground disappears into the horizon. The creatures have lighter and darker sides and throw shadows on the ground. The presentation of the simulation was in the form of a video, played on a large screen. In selected video clips the box-creatures moved in real time, and although their shapes were pretty strange, their movements were strikingly lifelike and familiar. During the presentation of the simulation the observer's point of view moved. The observer's «eyes» were like a moving camera, zooming in and following the moving animats.

Sims' simulation was one of the best received ALife presentations in 1994. Arguing that this simulation – the result of an engineering enterprise – should be understood as an artistic expression, a good starting point would be to ask why it became popular. Why did we appreciate it? On a couple of occasions I have told anthropologists who know nothing of ALife, biology or computer science about Sims' simulation. They have not been impressed by the state of art in ALife. Compared to real life, or a Walt Disney animation for that matter, Sims' simulation seems trivial.

I think an important reason for this indifference is the fact that these anthropologists don't know how difficult it is to make such a simulation. They did not see that Sims cleverly used a powerful «Connection Machine®» to do something that no one had thought of or mastered before him. One has to know the techniques required to appreciate the difficulties of a task. That is to say, one has to know the relationship that the created object has to the creator. To appreciate a piece of art includes the appreciation of the agency, skills, and tools of the *artist*.

If we think of Sims' presentation as a *performance*, then it might have been a performance in two senses of the word. According to the Oxford Dictionary «Performance» may mean «the action of performing a play, a part in a play, a piece of music, etc.», or it may mean «the capacities of a machine, especially a motor vehicle or aircraft». We may call these two performances «human-performance» and «machine-performance». Sims presentation, particularly the realism of the simulation, exemplified both of these «performances». We were fascinated with how *both* a powerful Connection Machine® and a skilled Karl Sims had actually been able to produce this «truly astonishing» (Langton 1994:iii) realism.

At this point, however, I seem to have forgotten one important aspect of Sims' simulation. Was not the most impressive feature of this simulation the co-evolution of the species in it? Many expressed such an opinion. This co-evolution, where the tasks as well as the solutions were evolving, exemplified a particular kind of valued performance in ALife research; the performance of autonomous technology. When we say that a car performs well it mainly means that it «obeys» the orders of the driver. It does what he

or she wants it to do, it speeds up, slows down and turns only when the driver wants it to. It is predictable. However, when an ALife program such as a Genetic Algorithm performs well it is *not* predictable. It evolves something that the ALifer had not thought of. The machine-performance of the simulation has some of the properties that we normally associate with human-performances (e.g., a performing musician); a certain degree of creativity and autonomy. This is a central aspect of most ALife research. It is the quest for, as Langton has expressed it, «getting the humans out of the loop».

The performance of Sims' simulation, then, was not only a result of Karl Sims' skilful handling of the latest high-performance computer. There were *two* actors; Karl Sims and the Genetic Algorithm.[1] The artistry was performed by a human being skilfully handling high-tech and a partly autonomous machine. ALifers are in a position where they know how to value the agency, skills, and creativity of both.

A question then arises: How did these two actors interact in order to produce the artistic object, the video-clips presented at the conference? Did they co-operate, compete, love...? The next section suggests some partial answers to this question.

ALife as Theoretical Biology

Let me begin this discussion with some theoretical speculations that illustrate a particular aspect of what ALife as theoretical biology may be.

Many of you have seen Chris Langton's illustration of our possible common future with ALife technology: the double helix where «man» and «machine» – Real Life and Artificial Life – co-evolve as autonomous, yet mutually dependent parts of a larger system. Kevin Kelly verbalises the same image in his book *Out of Control*:

> Until recently, all our artifacts, all our handmade creations have been under our authority. But as we cultivate synthetic life in our artifacts, we cultivate the loss of our command. «Out of control», to be honest, is a great exaggeration of the state that our enlivened machines will take. They will remain indirectly under our

---

[1] Note that the machine-agency is not that of the individual animats in the simulation. The creative process was the artificial evolution as a whole.

influence and guidance, but free of our domination (Kelly 1994:329)

The opposite will also have to be the case, if you initially believed in technological determinism; *We* will remain indirectly under the influence and guidance of our machines, but free of their domination.

To Inman Harvey the co-evolution of human beings and ALife machines is not a condition that may exist sometime in the future. It already exist. Harvey describes his own research in evolutionary robotics as a co-evolution of his own understanding of robotics and the robots' capabilities in adapting to the tasks that he sets up (Harvey 1993:27-28). The robots do not impose their facts upon the passively witnessing researcher, and the researcher does not control, in a «top-down» way, how the robots are to behave.

Philosopher Isabelle Stengers theorised along the same lines at the ECAL '95 conference (Stengers 1995). Her argument is important not only as an example of a specific kind of theoretical biology of ALife, but as a source of inspiration to this paper. In thinking about the relationship between the researcher and the experimental apparatus, she explores the emotional attitudes that different experimental settings may require. The conventional experiment is a highly predictable machine-performance. When Galileo made his slope and his polished balls, the balls could do nothing but roll down the slope, and Galileo could do nothing but witness the facts imposed on him. The performance that Galileo designed had, Stengers writes, «the very strange and unusual power to tell how it should be described.» (1995:4)

The advent of experiments that have the power to tell how they shall be described is the advent of modern science. It is also the advent of the modern scientist. The experimental setting, as it was developed during the 17th century, included a particular role to be enacted by the one who observed the experimental events. Observing an event that he had not created (it has traditionally been a male), the observer had to be a *trustworthy witness*. In order to argue for the validity of statements made by witnesses, Robert Boyle (1627-1691), the founder of Royal Society, referred to a contemporary law that defined the legitimate juridical witness (Shapin and Schaffer 1985:327). The statements of these witnesses were to be valid, even if they did not conform to the geometrical ideal of logically following first principles. (An ideal that early modernity had inherited from the medieval scholastic tradition of building large, coherent systems of thought.) To guarantee this validity, the subjectivity of the witness had to be transparent. The witness merely reported on an external event; he was an uninterested spokesperson, representing the witnessed event; Nature, and not himself. The ideal scientist, then, became what Haraway has described as a *modest witness* (Haraway 1996), describing a scene without being an emotionally engaged participant of that scene.

Isabelle Stengers discusses how this experimental ideal becomes problematic when the experimental subjects are beings who are able to learn and to produce interpretations. This, Stengers writes, is the «curse of experimental psychology». She is worth quoting at length:

> In experimental psychology laboratories the scientist fully intends to be the one asking the question and defining the meaning of the answer, but he or she can never know if the experimental subject truly answered this same question. We face here what I would call, in the most generic sense, the problem of imagination. We cannot have a human being forgetting that he or she is being asked questions in a scientific laboratory. We cannot control the interpretation he or she will give to the situation. This is for example what happened to research in the field of experimental hypnosis. At first sight, hypnosis was an ideal situation for experimentation. The scientist induces hypnosis through a standard, reproducible procedure, and then tests and measures the changes of behavoior which he or she will correlate with this 'state'. Well, it is not that simple. The main result of experimentation in this field is that those measured changes do not testify in a reliable way about hypnosis. Indeed, the experimental subject's behavior cannot be dissociated from their ideas about what hypnosis produces, what it is to be hypnotized, and what it means to be or not to be sensitive to hypnotic induction. Their behavior also incorporates their knowledge that they are in the hands of scientists and their guesses about what the scientist is looking for. In other words, the experimental setting, here, does not purify a common phenomenon in order to produce a reliable witness, defined by well controlled variables. (Stengers, 1995:4)

To sum up Stenger's point; when the experimental subject is a learning and interpreting being – an actor and not a rolling ball – it may refuse to answer the question that the experimental setting is designed to ask.

Things become even more problematic when the experimental setting does not aim at reducing the actor to a trivial machine (as in the case of experimental hypnosis), but at exploring the capabilities of an actor as such. As an example of this, Stengers mentions ethologists who experiment with the abilities of apes to speak a language. When the apes have grown old and the ethologists need new experimental subjects, these researchers find themselves unable to kill their old apes or to send them off to a zoo. They have become fond of their apes (Stengers 1995:7). This, Stengers argues, is probably more than a mere side effect of their research. The researchers work to put on a «human-performance», a performance of some kind of autonomous creature. To achieve this performance, the ethologists cannot control the apes as Galileo controlled the balls. They have to enter into another kind of relationship with their experimental subjects. They have to socialise with the apes. Hence, their emotional involvement is necessary for the socialisation of the apes to be successful.

The relationship the ethologists established, and probably had to establish, between themselves and the apes was based on something like mutual trust, respect, and love. The researchers had to address their experimental subjects with their hearts, not only with the transparent mind of the modest witness.

The reader may have guessed where this argument leads: ALife research aims at making some kind of autonomous agents. These agents, unlike Galileo's polished balls, cannot be controlled «top-down». We may, as Harvey suggests, have to think of our relationship to these agents as a co-evolutionary process. It may however be that we, in practising such a co-evolution, will have to allow for new emotions to emerge. Perhaps these emotions have to do with trust and respect, yes, perhaps even love. Perhaps we need to explore these emotions in order to understand our own research.

There is, admittedly, a big difference between human beings and primates on the one hand and Harvey's triangle-seeking robot on the other. Most ALife technology today is perhaps closer to Galileo's rolling balls than to speaking human beings or primates. So why should my argument carry over from the former context to the latter? My answer to such an objection is that the whole point of ALife – as a technological enterprise – is *not* to make billiard-ball-like-technology. It is to make the new kind of machines that cybernetician Heinz von Foerster called *non-trivial machines*, machines that are synthetically determined and historically dependent, yet analytically *in*determinable and *un*predictable (von Foerster 1991:69). To set up a classical experiment is to make a *trivial machine* (1991:70), a machine that is analytically determinable and predictable. The modesty (i.e., objectivity) of the witness is dependent on this «triviality» because it is the analytical determinism and predictability of such a machine that give it the power to tell how it should be described.

An animat or an animal (for example a psychologist's rat in a maze) may, in an experiment, be set up to perform a trivial-machine-performance. But then the researcher cannot explore the *non-triviality* of that creature. When ALifers attempt to make and explore non-trivial machines they are transgressing the boundaries of the experiment, here included, their own role as modest witnesses.

Now, the speculations above, I will argue, are part of what ought to be the theoretical biology of Artificial Life. They are not the only element in such a theoretical biology, but they are an important part of it. A central premise of most ALife research is that life equals cognition (Stewart 1992). The theoretical biology of ALife is therefore also a cognitive science. Early cyberneticians soon realised that studying cybernetic and biological systems was itself an instance of a cybernetic process (likewise, studying cognition is a cognitive process). So they invented the terms «Cybernetics of cybernetics» and «second order cybernetics» (Mead 1968). The speculations I have outlined above could be called *ALife of ALife*, or perhaps *second order theoretical biology*. This is not be the only kind of theoretical biology. There is plenty of room for a regular, «first order theoretical biology». Sims' creatures co-evolve. To study this process is first order theoretical biology. Sims' simulation co-evolves with Karl Sims. To study this process is second order theoretical biology.

Taking yet another step back, the bond between ALife as art and ALife as theoretical biology becomes clear. To allow that Artificial Life research is artistry is to recognize the creativity, expressions, and performances of a double agency;

the agency of the researcher and that of the simulation or robots. The second order theoretical biology I have outlined above explores precisely that double agency.

Strongholds

Why has molecular biology become Big Science whereas theoretical biology has been confined to a rather marginal position in the public consciousness? Is it because molecular biology, as opposed to theoretical biology, is speaking the truth? Is Nature the ally of molecular biology, giving the latter its stronghold? I do not think so, even if I do not deny the importance of the many discoveries in molecular biology. I think the reason, briefly outlined, is more like thus:

In a modern, technological society, the reductionism of molecular biology promises simple, technologically feasible solutions to what people of this society think of as problems, problems having, among other things, to do with food production for a growing population, and with curing diseases. Ultimately, this «medical problem» is the inescapable fact that we are all dying, and that dying is painful. On the one hand, then, we have people with «problems». On the other hand we have a medical and food industry with «solutions». Between them is molecular biology. Or, put differently, between most people and «health, happiness and a long life» there is molecular biology, between the pharmaceutical industry and «profit» there is molecular biology. In a modern, capitalistic network of people and culturally shaped interests, molecular biology occupies what Michel Callon calls an *obligatory passage point* (Callon 1986). It is due to this strategic position that molecular biology is Big Science. Its stronghold is based on its ability to *interest* (to «be between», from Latin; *inter esse*) consumers (or their representatives) and capital.

Now, a theoretical biologist, in ALife or elsewhere, may question the usefulness of the Human Genome Project on the grounds that it is based on naive assumptions about morphogenesis and development, that «genes» are seen to code for «diseases» in a much too simplified way. That may be true, but such an objection will not solve people's «problems», nor will it provide the pharmaceutical industry with a profitable drug. Failing to interest people, theoretical biology remains marginal.

If the Human Genome Project fails to deliver the goods – cures for genetically determined diseases – it may be that there will be an interested and listening audience available for ALifers with knowledge of morphogenesis, development, and adaptive behaviour. I think, however, that ALife will have to seek strongholds by addressing other interests than people's health. I think the engineering – or artistry – of ALife is a better candidate. ALife is already catching consumers' as well as the capital's interest in art and entertainment, for example in Millennium Interactive's development of the computer game «Creatures».

This should not be taken as an appeal to the ALife community to move collectively to Hollywood. My point is that the stronghold of Artificial Life as art and engineering can also be the stronghold of ALife as theoretical biology. Theoretical biology may become influential. How can this be the case?

First, ALife is not only an artistic enterprise. It is an experimental science characterised by ALifers' practice of scientific rigor. As Dave Cliff (1990) has pointed out, one important way to practise ALife as an experimental science is by making synthetic worlds. In these worlds interaction between animats, etc., can take place without involving the researcher. The researcher can study this interaction from a bird's eye perspective, without taking part in the studied interaction. The researcher has an «objective» perspective on worlds «out there». Hence, problems of regular (first order) theoretical biology can be tested experimentally thus achieving the legitimacy of knowledge produced by experimental science. This, of course, is what many ALifers do today.

Let me make a few comments on this objectivity. First, the objectivity of an ALifer observing a simulation is limited to the period during which the simulation is up and running. If we take a broader perspective, including a larger context and a longer time span, we see that, in the periods between the runs, the researcher is tweaking parameters and rewriting code. Hence, a picture more like *co-evolution* – rather than that of an objective observer witnessing worlds behind screens – emerges.

Second, making worlds to be studied at an objective distance is a way of «getting the humans out of the loop». It is a means by which to make autonomous agents. The success of this endeavour may therefore undermine the very objectivity on which it is based, because the autonomy of the agents means that they may not answer («objectively») the questions that the experimental setting is designed to be ask them.

The second way in which the stronghold of ALife as artistry may become the stronghold of ALife as theoretical biology is through interactive simulations and interactive robotics. Many of you are familiar with Bruce Blumberg's virtual dog, who interacts with a representation of Blumberg himself (presented at ECAL 94, see also http://bruce.www.media.mit.edu/people/bruce). I will here look closer at another example of interactive ALife.

Felix Hess from the Netherlands presented a group of fascinating, interactive robots at the ECAL '93 conference (Hess 1993). Hess showed us 25 small robots that he compared to *frogs*. These «frogs» could produce a sound – they «quacked» – and they reacted to this «quacking» with certain movements and with new «quacking». During the presentation the robots moved around on an enclosed section of the floor, «quacking» to each other and moving in relation to each other. Hess describes the motivation for his work thus:

> Enchanted by the frogs of Australia, I acquired sound recognition equipment and managed to capture many frogs on stereo tape. However, listening to a recording is not the same as listening to live frogs, obviously. A live frog chorus is interactive, it is sensitive to the circumstances and to the behaviour of the listener. This live, interactive quality is lost in a recording. (Hess 1993:453)

Hess recreated this interactivity by letting his robot-frogs react to loud sounds, such as a human voice. When people spoke or made other noises, the robots, like frogs in the night, sat still and became quiet. In order to observe any interactions between the «frogs», the human audience had to tip toe and whisper to each other. This made the atmosphere in the room very different from that of a conventional ALife presentation. *Sound* became important, our own sound. We, the audience, could not distantly watch worlds behind screens, we were – with our noisy bodies – involved in the production of the interaction between the robots. Hess concludes:

> Through actually building machines such as the «sound creatures» one can get a «feel» for the relationship between sensitivity and intelligence. This work has only increased my respect for the frogs, who taught me to sit still in silence and listen. (Hess 1993:457)

These simulations and robots are «second order simulations», directly addressing a second order theoretical biology. They are not only exploring interactions between artificial agents or animats. They are exploring the interaction between artificial agents and the researcher. To theorise around them is necessarily a self-reflexive, «second order» endeavour. They are artistic expressions (or perhaps entertainment) that explicitly explore the boundary between the researcher and the quasi-subjects of the experiment.

The third and perhaps most important way in which ALife as theoretical biology may profit from ALife as artistry has been touched upon in the two former points. Making «autonomous agents» is, as Kelly writes, necessarily to «cultivate the loss of our command». But when we cultivate this loss of command we also explore the limits of traditional experimental science. The paradoxical and amazing feature of the scientific experiment is that by perfectly controlling and *constructing* the context, the results produced will impose themselves on the researcher as external facts that cannot be denied, only observed. Hence, the researcher becomes a distanced witness of an objective event. When we cultivate the loss of our command, we also cultivate the loss of objectivity because we can no longer perfectly control the experimental setting.

Furthermore, if the experimental subject loses its ability to determine how it should be described, then the witness loses his or her modesty and distance (or objectivity). The researcher will then have to enter another kind of relationship with his or her experimental subject. I suggest, following Langton and Harvey, that that relationship may be something like «co-evolution». Hence, the researcher will have to allow for – perhaps even explore – other emotions than those of the ideal distanced witness.

Recognising and exploring ALife as artistry provides us with a science of life where we can explore other relationships with, and other emotions towards, the life that we are studying. If we want to make autonomous agents and understand the stuff of life scientifically, then these explorations may not only be desirable, they may be necessary. We may, in our scientific quest for the creation of life, have to question the traditional role of the scientist.

Recognising ALife as artistry may also be a way to situate ALife as an *obligatory passage point* in a social network of interested actors. The theoretical biology of ALife, I hope I have shown, may be an integrated part of this artistry. Hence, creating this obligatory passage point is a way to bring – a now self-reflexive – theoretical biology out of its marginal position and into Big Science. I suggest that getting more artists into the field is a better way to achieve this than to ask for more biologists.

Acknowledgements

Many thanks to Mary Lee Nielsen and Kari-Anne Ulfsnes for their thorough proof-reading and always valuable comments. This paper has been produced with support from the Norwegian Research Council (117137/530).

References

Callon, Michel (1986) «Some elements of a sociology of translation: domestication of the scallops and the fishermen of St Brieuc Bay» in John Law (ed.) *Power, Action and Belief*, London: Routledge & Kegan.

Cliff, Dave (1990) *Computational Neuroethology: A Provisional Manifesto*, CSRP 163, University of Sussex.

Dreyfus, Hubert, and Stuart Dreyfus (1987) *Mind over Machine. The power of human expertise in the era of the computer*. New York: The Free Press.

Haraway, Donna J. (1996) «Modest Witness; Feminist Diffractions in Science Studies», in Peter Galison and David J. Stump, *The Disunity of Science*, California: Stanford University Press.

Harvey, Inman (1993) *The Artificial Evolution of Adaptive Behaviour*, The University of Sussex.

Hess, Felix (1993) *Electronic sound creatures*, Proceedings to the ECAL '93 conference, Belgium.

Kelly, Kevin (1994) *Out of Control*, Massachusetts: Reading.

Langton, Christopher G. (1994) «Editor's Introduction: Special Issue on highlights of the ALife IV Conference» in *Artificial Life* Volume 1, Number 4, Summer 1994, The MIT Press.

Mead, Margaret (1968) «Cybernetics of Cybernetics», in *Purposive Systems*, Heinz von Foerster et al. (eds.) New York: Spartan Books.

Miller Geoffrey (1996) «Artificial Life as theoretical biology: How to do real science with computer simulation», in Margaret Boden, *Philosophy of Artificial Life*, Oxford Readings in Philosophy, Oxford University Press.

Moran, F. et al. (ed.) (1995) *Advances in Artificial Life, Third European Conference on Artificial Life*, Granada, Spain, June 4-6, 1995 Proceedings, Berlin: Springer.

Risan, Lars (1996) *Artificial Life: A Technoscience Leaving Modernity? An anthropology of subjects and objects* Oslo: Hovedfagsoppgave, Institutt og Museum for Antropologi, Universitetet i Oslo.

Shapin, Steven and Schaffer Simon (1985) *Leviathan and the air-pump*, Princeton: University Press.

Sims, Karl (1994) «Evolving 3D Morphology and Behavior by Competition» in *Artificial Life*, Volume 1, Number 4, 353-372.

Stengers, Isabelle (1995) *God's heart and the stuff of life*, presented at ECAL 95.

Stewart, John (1992) «Life=Cognition The epistemological and ontological significance of Artificial Life», in Francisco Varela and Paul Bourgine: *Toward a Practice of Autonomous Systems, Proceedings of the first European Conference on Artificial Life*, Cambridge, Massachusetts: The MIT Press.

von Foerster, Heinz (1991) «Through the eyes of the Other», in *Research and Reflexivity*, Frederick Steer (ed.). London: Sage.

BASIC MODELS AND RNA
EVOLUTION

Rediscovering Computational Autopoiesis

Barry McMullin
Santa Fe Institute
1399 Hyde Park Road
Santa Fe, NM 87501
USA

mcmullin@eeng.dcu.ie
http://www.eeng.dcu.ie/~mcmullin

Francisco J. Varela
LENA—CNRS URA 654
Hopital del la Salpetriere
47, Blvd. de l'Hopital
75651 Paris cedex 13
France.

fv@ccr.jussieu.fr

Abstract

This paper summarises some initial empirical results from a new computer model (artificial chemistry) which exhibits spontaneous emergence and persistence of *autopoietic* organisation. The model is based on a system originally presented by Varela, Maturana and Uribe [11]. In carrying out this re-implementation it was found that an additional interaction (chain-based bond inhibition), not documented in the original description by Varela et al., is critical to the realisation of the autopoietic phenomena. This required interaction was re-discovered only following careful examination of (unpublished) source code for an early version of the original model. The purpose of the paper is thus twofold: firstly to identify and discuss this previously undocumented, but essential, interaction; and secondly to argue, on the basis of this particular case, for the importance of exploiting the emerging technologies which support publication of completely detailed software models (in addition, of course, to conventional publication of summary experimental results).

Keywords: Autopoiesis, Artificial Life, Artificial Chemistry, Origin of Life.

1 Introduction

The concept of *autopoiesis* [3, 9] occupies a distinctive position in the entire field of biology as one of the very few substantive attempts to give an integrated characterisation of the nature of living systems which is clearly separate from a mere listing of arbitrary "properties" (such as metabolism, growth, reproduction etc.). The concept was originated some twenty-five years ago, by Humberto Maturana and Francisco Varela [10]. Its influence since then has been diverse and sustained—see, for example, [13, 7].[1]

The first widely distributed, and thus seminal, description of the concept of autopoiesis was that of [11], which was illustrated with a computer model of a "minimal" example. Experimental data from this model showed both the spontaneous formation and ongoing repair of an autopoietic system embedded in a two dimensional, discrete space. This was accompanied by a qualitative description of the artificial chemistry realised by the model, and a more detailed algorithmic account of the simulation program.

This computer model has been extremely influential in providing a relatively simple, graphic, exemplar of the concept of autopoiesis. It demonstrated that the idea of autopoietic organisation, although subtle and abstract, could be instantiated in a relatively simple, and concrete, system.

However: a recent reappraisal of the original presentation of this computer model has revealed significant flaws—flaws which, if they were left uncorrected, might tend to undermine its role as a concrete example of autopoiesis.

A number of technical difficulties with even interpreting the original algorithm, and apparent discrepancies between the algorithm and the experimental data, have been discussed in a previously published working paper [5]. That paper also incorporates, as an appendix, the `FORTRAN-IV` code of a version of the original program used by Varela et al. Careful study of this code has now allowed the identification of an additional interaction, present in the code, but omitted from all published descriptions of the model.

---

[1] An excellent, comprehensive, bibliography of the literature on autopoiesis is maintained by Randall Whitaker at:

http://www.informatik.umu.se/~rwhit/AT.html

In this paper we present experimental results from a completely new implementation of the qualitative chemistry described by Varela et al. which suggests that this additional interaction is, indeed, critical to the realisation of the autopoietic phenomena; and that, conversely, provided this additional interaction is included, the autopoietic phenomena are not dependent on any particular details of the original program or algorithm, but may be expected in *any* system sharing the same qualitative chemistry.

2 The Original Qualitative Chemistry

The chemistry takes places in a discrete, two dimensional, space. Each position in the space is either empty or occupied by a single particle. Particles generally move in random walks in the space. There are three distinct particle types, engaging in three distinct reactions:

- Production: Two substrate (S) particles may react, in the presence of a catalyst (K) particle to form a link (L) particle.

- Bonding: L particles may bond to other L particles. Each L particle can form (at most) two bonds, thus allowing the formation of indefinitely long chains, which may close to form membranes. Bonded L particles become immobile.

- Disintegration: An L particle may spontaneously disintegrate, yielding two S particles. When this occurs any bonds associated with the L particle are destroyed also.

Chains of L particles are permeable to S particles but impermeable to K and L particles. Thus a closed chain, or membrane, which encloses K or L particles effectively traps such particles.

3 The Phenomena

The basic autopoietic phenomenon predicted for this system is the possibility of realising dynamic cell-like structures which, on an ongoing basis, produce the conditions for their own maintenance. Such a system would consist of a closed chain (membrane) of L particles enclosing one or more K particles. Because S particles can permeate through the membrane, there can be ongoing production of L particles. Since these cannot escape from the membrane, this will result in the build up of a relatively high concentration of L particles. On an ongoing basis, the membrane will rupture as a result of disintegration of component L particles. Because of the high concentration of L particles inside the membrane, there should be a high probability that one of these will drift to the rupture site and effect a repair, *before* the K particle(s) escape, thus re-establishing precisely the conditions allowing the build up of that high concentration of L particles.

A secondary phenomenon which *may* arise is the spontaneous establishment of an autopoietic system from a randomised initial arrangement of the particles.

Clearly, the issue of spontaneous formation does not arise unless the system actually supports autopoietic organisation. In this sense the phenomenon of autopoietic organisation is *logically* prior to spontaneous formation (though chronologically following from it). For this reason, the phenomenon of spontaneous formation will *not* be considered further in this paper. Instead, in all the experiments reported, a putatively autopoietic entity will be artificially introduced into the system; the question at issue will be whether this entity succeeds in realising the autopoietic reaction network already described.

4 The SCL Program

The newly developed program is called SCL (for Substrate-Catalyst-Link) [6]. This has been implemented using the SWARM[2] simulation system, developed at the Santa Fe Institute[3].

A conscious decision was taken that SCL would *not* be based on the *algorithm* originally published by Varela et al., but should rather reflect an independent implementation of the same *qualitative* chemistry. This stemmed partly from the previously documented problems with the original algorithm [5]; but it also reflected a desire to test the robustness of the autopoietic phenomena—i.e. are they perhaps reliant on some artifact of the original program and/or algorithm, or are they robust outcomes from the given qualitative chemistry.

The version of SCL used to generate the results described in this paper (v0.05.01) differs in minor ways from that described in the previously published documentation (v0.04) [6]. The complete source code relating to SCL v0.05.01 is available as:

```
ftp://ftp.santafe.edu/pub/swarm/
users-contrib/anarchy/scl-0.05.01.tar.gz
```

The SCL data files relating to the experiments described here are available in:

```
ftp://ftp.santafe.edu/pub/swarm/
users-contrib/anarchy/scl-data00.tar.gz
```

A key to the display of the three particle types in SCL is provided in figure 1.

5 Experimental Protocol

This paper will describe the results from two separate experiments with SCL. In each case the same experimental protocol was followed. Each experiment consisted of 5 runs of SCL. The initial configuration was

---

[2] http://www.santafe.edu/projects/swarm
[3] http://www.santafe.edu

- ◘ Substrate
- ▩ Catalyst
- ☐ Link
- ▣ Link with absorbed Substrate

Figure 1: Key to Particle Types.

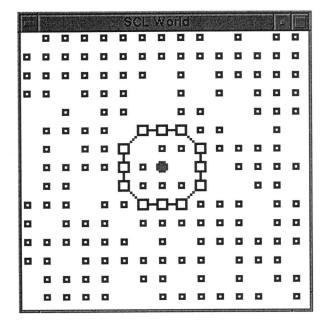

Figure 2: Initial Configuration.

identical in all runs, and is illustrated in figure 2. This comprises a single artificially constructed cell-like entity, being a closed membrane of L particles enclosing a single K particle. This is embedded in a 15 × 15 toroidal space. The five runs in each experiment differed only in the initial state of the underlying pseudo-random number generator. These five distinct initial states are specified in the files `run1.stt` through `run5.stt` in the distributed data file archive (`scl-data00.tar.gz`).

The two experiments differed only in that experiment 1 implemented just the reactions of the qualitative chemistry described in section 2, whereas experiment 2 incorporated the newly rediscovered chain-based bond inhibition interaction (to be discussed in section 7).

SCL supports a variety of parameters controlling reaction rates, mobility parameters, etc. Apart from the parameter controlling the additional interaction just mentioned, these parameters were held constant across all runs and both experiments. These parameter sets for experiments 1 and 2 are specified in the files `exp1.prm`

and `exp2.prm` respectively, in the distributed data file archive.

The `disintegrationProbability` parameter was set at 0.001 in all cases.[4] This is the probability that any given L particle will disintegrate per unit time. The membrane in the initial configuration is composed of 12 L particles. It follows that the expected time to first rupture of the initial membrane is given by:

$$\tau = \frac{1}{1 - (1 - P_d)^{12}} \simeq 84$$

6 Experiment 1

6.1 Run 1-1

As expected, S particles initially permeate through the membrane and, under the influence of the K particle, production of L particles starts. However, instead of these L particles remaining mobile, trapped within the membrane, in readiness to repair any rupture, they begin to spontaneously bond to *each other*. Given that bonded L particles are specified to be immobile, this means that such particles are *not* available to drift to a rupture site. The screenshot of figure 3 was taken at time 110. The membrane has not yet suffered any decay. However, the interior of the membrane is now completely clogged with bonded—and thus immobile—L particles. Only two open positions remain inside the membrane, one occupied by the K particle. Since the production reaction requires two S particles adjacent to each other and to the K particle, there is no longer any available site for further production within the membrane, and further production of L particles is impossible. It follows that, whenever the membrane does eventually rupture, there will be no mobile L particles available to effect a repair.

In fact, the membrane suffers a double rupture at times 234 and 235, yielding the configuration shown in figure 4. The chain which had previously been formed inside the membrane now becomes spliced to one side of the rupture site, forming a folded chain. This no longer encloses the K particle. Indeed, should the folded chain become closed, the K particle would necessarily be *outside* it. Thus, the initial, putatively autopoietic, entity has clearly now irreversibly degenerated, without having undergone even a single episode of self-repair.

6.2 Run 1-2

On this run, the initial rupture of the membrane occurs relatively early, at time 31. Just one L particle has been produced within the membrane by this time. However,

---

[4] This is a factor of 10 smaller than the value originally suggested by Varela et al. This reflects the fact that the *maximum* rate of the production reaction is approximately this much slower in SCL than in the original model, so that 10 timesteps in SCL can be considered roughly comparable to one timestep in the original.

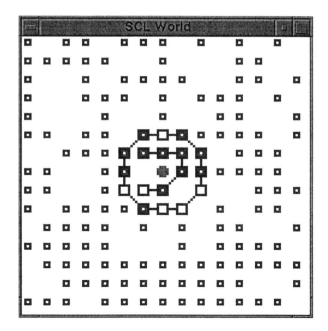

Figure 3: Experiment 1, Run 1, Time 110.

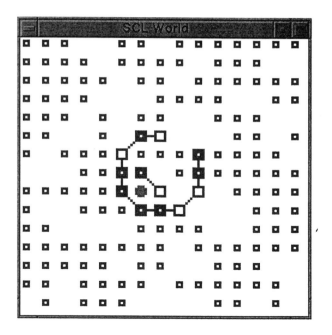

Figure 5: Experiment 1, Run 2, Time 069.

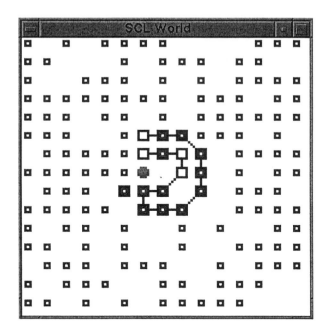

Figure 4: Experiment 1, Run 1, Time 235.

since this means the particle is still mobile, there is at least some possibility that it may drift to the rupture site and effect a repair. A second L particle is produced at time 63, thus improving the possibility of a repair. However, at time 69, these two L particles bond to each other, thus becoming immobile, and unavailable to drift

to the rupture site. Moreover, they are located in such a position that the K particle is blocked in all four directions. This configuration is illustrated in figure 5. Not only is the K particle now also effectively immobile, but, again, there is no space available adjacent to it to permit further production of new L particles. Thus, there is no possibility of repairing the existing rupture. As with run 1, the initial entity has clearly already irreversibly degenerated.

6.3 Runs 1-3 to 1-5

Given the descriptions of runs 1 and 2, only a brief description of the remaining runs is necessary. Precisely the same failure mechanism is again observed: the L particles produced within the membrane spontaneously bond to each other, thus becoming immobile, rather than remaining available to drift to a rupture site when it arises; the interior of the membrane becomes progressively clogged up, until there is no longer space available for further production. At this point, since no L particles are available to repair any rupture, and no more can be produced within the membrane, the original entity has effectively degenerated. In all three runs this occurs without even a single episode of successful repair of the membrane. The times at which this condition is reached are as follows:

Run	Time
3	282
4	126
5	165

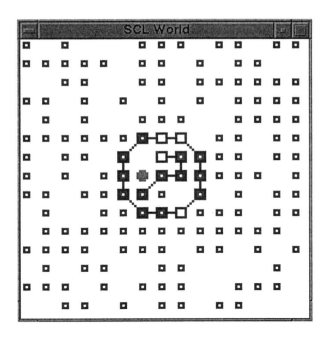

Figure 6: Experiment 1, Run 3, Time 282.

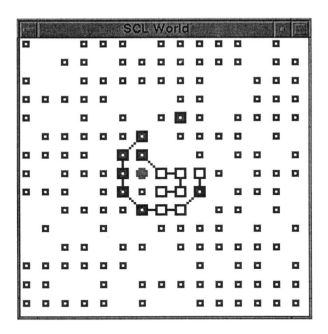

Figure 7: Experiment 1, Run 4, Time 126.

These terminal configurations for runs 3–5 are shown in figures 6, 7 and 8 respectively.

6.4 Discussion 1

In all five runs of experiment 1 a consistent *failure* of the autopoietic process was observed. This is due to the

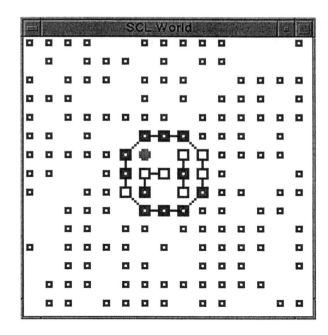

Figure 8: Experiment 1, Run 5, Time 165.

spontaneous and premature bonding of the L particles produced within the membrane, thus making them immobile and unavailable to effect a repair to the membrane. With the benefit of these experimental results, it seems fairly obvious that this failure mode was already implicit in the *qualitative* chemistry described by Varela et al. [11]. It is evidently *not* dependent on any particular details of the implementation, nor on the specific parameters settings.

This conclusion is corroborated by the fact that this same failure mechanism has been observed in previous (unpublished) experiments with two other, *independent*, implementations of this reaction scheme [1, 8], and has also been previously reported by Lizana [2]. This class of failure seems also to have been recognised, at least implicitly, in the re-implementation(s) carried out by Zeleny [12, Figure 4].

Two attempted solutions to this failure mechanism were briefly investigated, before the preferred solution, to be discussed in section 7, was finally identified.

Firstly, the bonding reaction was separated into two cases: bonding between two free L particles, and bonding between a free L particle and an L particle already having one bond. The latter is the case of interest for membrane repair. These were controlled by separate rate parameters. This allowed the "spontaneous" bonding reaction to be made very slow. This should ensure that the free L particles formed within the membrane would not spontaneously bond with each other but would rather be held in reserve for membrane repair.[5] However, this idea proved largely ineffective. The problem is that, once a rupture *does* occur it frequently happens that, instead of a single free L repairing the membrane, *all* of the free L particles become quickly incorporated into an inward spiraling chain fragment.

The second mechanism appears to have been independently suggested by both Zeleny [12] and Lizana [2]. This involves inhibiting bonding to a free L particle in some neighborhood of any K particle. In Lizana's case, this effect seems to have been limited to the *immediate* (Moore) neighborhood of a K particle, whereas Zeleny seems to have used arbitrarily large (and dynamically changing?) neighborhoods. The idea appears to be that the K particle(s) can establish zone(s) of bond inhibition around them. The membrane can then form (roughly) at the edge of such a zone. L particles within these zones will remain free, and ready to drift to a rupture site to effect a repair.

Both Zeleney and Lizana apparently got this mechanism to give somewhat satisfactory results. The mechanism has been investigated to only a limited extent with SCL. Specifically, the use of indefinitely large inhibition zones (as suggested by Zeleny) has *not* been pursued, since it violates an objective that the model should rely only on local (Moore neighborhood) interactions. With this (self-imposed) restriction, the results have generally been mediocre. Two counteracting effects have been noticed. Firstly, even within a relatively small membrane such as illustrated in figure 2, the K particle may transiently drift away from the central position; if free L particles also drift away from this position, then they may still be able to spontaneously bond and become immobile. Even though the K particle may drift back into their vicinity, it is now too late—the bonding has already occurred.[6] Secondly, if a rupture occurs in the neighborhood of the K particle it is now very difficult to effect a repair, even if a free L particle should drift into an appropriate position; worse still, this is precisely the situation in which swift repair is most important, lest the K particle should escape completely. These problems can be overcome, to an extent, by making the K particle immobile (in the center of the cavity). While Lizana's description is not fully detailed, it seems that this may be what she indeed did. The mobility of K particles also seems to have been severely constrained in a number of Zeleny's experiments. In our view, this significantly reduces the generality and interest of the model, and must be considered an unsatisfactory solution.

---

[5]Of course, this would make spontaneous formation of an initial membrane much less probable; but that issue was deferred.

[6]Presumably, the K particle should not be assigned an effect of rupturing these bonds again, because they cannot be distinguished from the bonds making up the membrane; on the other hand, this does seem to have been a mechanism actually used by Zeleny in some experiments [12, Figure 6].

7   Chain-based Bond Inhibition

By far the most troubling aspect of the results discussed above is that they are not consistent with the experimental results originally presented by Varela et al. [11].

In particular, a careful examination of those original results suggests that the model must have had some, unspecified, mechanism to overcome or preempt the class of failure now described here. However, given that the work was done over 25 years ago, it seemed that it would be extremely difficult to gain much further insight into this problem. The current author who was involved in the original work (Varela), no longer had any clear recollection of what additional mechanism was present in the model to account for this discrepancy.

Fortunately, a printout of an early version of the original simulation program, coded in FORTRAN-IV, has recently been rediscovered, and has now been incorporated in a published technical report [5]. As discussed in more detail in that report, this program has been rekeyed, and it has been possible to execute it again. This did not reproduce the precise results of the original publication; most likely it was not exactly the same version, and, in any case, the original pseudo-random number source is no longer available, so the precise execution trajectory is bound to be different. However, this did suffice to show that the program did, indeed, exhibit some mechanism whereby free links, confined within the membrane, tended *not* to spontaneously bond to each other. This motivated a detailed reanalysis of the program code, which finally resulted in the identification of a previously un-reported interaction—*chain-based bond inhibition*.

This is an interaction whereby bonding is inhibited to any free L particle which is in the immediate vicinity of another L particle which is doubly bonded. In effect then, a free L particle cannot form a bond as long as it is alongside (as opposed to at the end of) an existing chain of L particles; but it *can* form bond(s) when it is at the end of a chain; and, especially, when it is positioned at a site where a chain has broken (i.e. a rupture site).[7]

The next section reviews experimental results from SCL when the chain-based bond inhibition reaction is enabled.

8   Experiment 2

8.1   Run 2-1

Between time 0 and time 226 the initial membrane suffers two ruptures which are repaired with no change of membrane morphology. Between time 227 and 444 there

---

[7]This interaction has previously been outlined in the SCL documentation [6]. However, there is an error, or ambiguity, in that earlier description, in that it suggests that bond inhibition applies to both free and singly bonded L particles. In fact, it applies only to free L particles. Applying it to singly bonded L particles would actually *prevent* membrane repair from taking place.

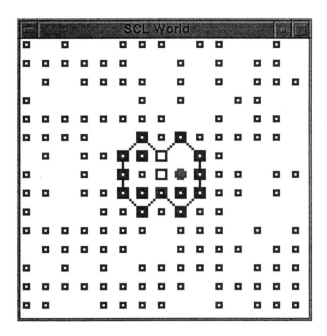

Figure 9: Experiment 2, Run 1, Time 444.

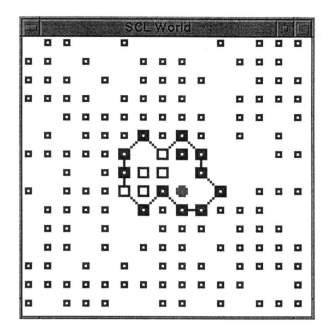

Figure 10: Experiment 2, Run 1, Time 1310.

are four rupture and repair episodes, yielding the new membrane morphology shown in figure 9.

This new morphology appears to be relatively robust. The entity persists in this morphology up to time 1250, in the course of which there are 5 more rupture and (successful) repair episodes. Between time 1250 and time 1310 there are two rupture and repair episodes yielding the new membrane morphology shown in figure 10. The entity survives in this morphology, through two more rupture and repair episodes until time 1741. There are then two ruptures in quick succession, at times 1742 and 1745. At time 1746 the membrane fragments, and partially spirals into the cavity, as shown in figure 11. It is then no longer possible to recover the closed membrane through any simple process of self repair.

8.2 Run 2-2

Between time 0 and time 133 the initial membrane suffers three ruptures which are repaired with no change of membrane morphology. A rupture at time 134 is repaired at time 137, yielding the new membrane morphology shown in figure 12. The entity persists in this morphology up to time 452, in the course of which there is one more rupture and (successful) repair episode. A further rupture at time 453 is eventually repaired at time 555; but in the interim, a second rupture at time 542 leads to a partial spiral into the cavity, as with run 1, and again it is then no longer possible to recover a closed membrane through any simple process of self repair.

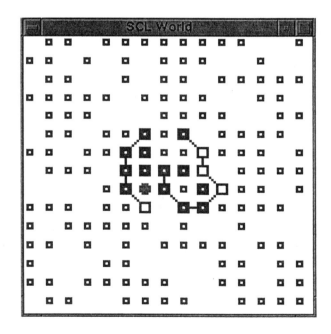

Figure 11: Experiment 2, Run 1, Time 1746.

8.3 Run 2-3

In this run there are two very early ruptures (times 6 and 13), before there has been time for an effective build up in the concentration of free L particles. The K particle almost escapes immediately, but, instead, an extension of the membrane forms around it. There is a further

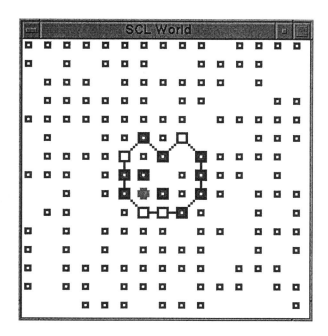

Figure 12: Experiment 2, Run 2, Time 137.

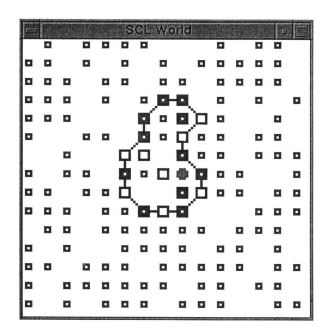

Figure 13: Experiment 2, Run 3, Time 148.

independent rupture at time 139, but at time 148 a closed membrane reforms with the new morphology shown in figure 13

A further rupture at time 171 results again in an inward spiral and it is then no longer possible to recover a closed membrane through any simple process of self repair.

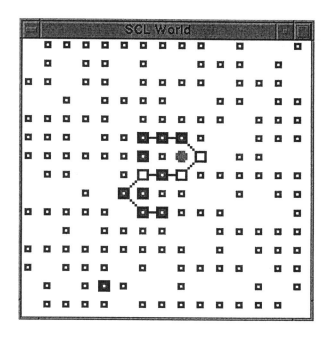

Figure 14: Experiment 2, Run 4, Time 1508.

8.4 Run 2-4

Following three rupture and repair episodes, at time 199 the entity forms into the same morphology encountered in run 1 (figure 9)—albeit, now rotated through 90°. This morphology again appears relatively robust, persisting from time 199 to time 1437, through 12 rupture and self-repair episodes. Between times 1438 and 1500 there are *four* additional ruptures. Of these, one is successfully repaired, but the overall damage to the membrane is now too great, and by time 1508 it has degenerated into a single curved chain as shown in figure 14. Again, it is then no longer possible to recover a closed membrane through any simple process of self repair.

8.5 Run 2-5

In this run there are two early ruptures at time 22 and 119, severely damaging the original membrane. An inward spiral forms. Coincidentally, another rupture allows the inward spiral to close forming a "new" membrane at time 245, with the morphology shown in figure 15. However, the cavity is now linear and thus does not afford *any* reaction sites for production of new L particles. This entity is therefore not capable of re-establishing the autopoietic reaction network.

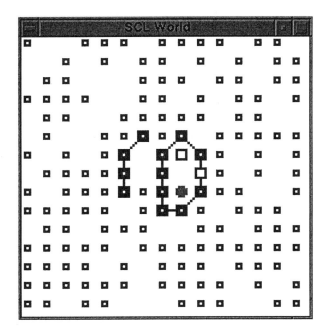

Figure 15: Experiment 2, Run 5, Time 245.

8.6 Discussion 2

There is substantial variation among the five runs comprising experiment 2. In runs 3 and 5, the initial entity effectively fails completely to establish a closed, autopoietic, reaction network. However, in runs 1, 2 and 4, an autopoietic reaction network *is* established, and a succession of successful repair episodes occurs. In runs 1 and 4 a morphology becomes established which is apparently particularly robust, persisting in each case for approximately 1000 time steps of the model.

The work reported here has not involved any extensive or comprehensive investigation of variations in the various reaction rate and mobility parameters available in the SCL model. It might well be possible to find combinations of parameter settings in which the establishment and maintenance of autopoietic reaction networks is more robust, and the autopoietic entities would thus be more stable and longer lived. However, the basic results of experiment 2 clearly show that this model *can* exhibit persistent, self repairing, autopoietic reaction networks, in the form originally described by Varela et al. [11]

Given that the only difference between experiment 1 and experiment 2 is the (re-)introduction of the chain-based bond inhibition interaction, it seems reasonable to conclude that this phenomenon of computational autopoiesis relies critically on the presence of this interaction.

9 Conclusion

The primary conclusion from the work described here is that the original report of computational modelling of autopoiesis [11] was flawed, in that it failed to identify the chain-based bond inhibition interaction as being present and, indeed, as being an essential requirement for the achievement of the described autopoietic phenomena.

Given the lapse of time since the original publication, it is now difficult to suggest any definitive explanation as to how this interaction, actually present in the program code, came to be overlooked in the qualitative and algorithmic descriptions. However, as described elsewhere [10], the work was carried out during a difficult and turbulent time in Chile, and, further, there was a considerable time interval between the actual experiments and eventual publication. These factors together probably provide an adequate explanation for the oversight.

It should be emphasised that the substantive point of this paper is to correct the historical record. This is clearly relevant for anyone who wishes to reproduce, or *extend*, the phenomena of the original model. However, this correction does not add to, or modify, the original conceptual foundation of autopoiesis in any significant way.

In any case, the work described here also raises a more general question about the publication of computationally based ALife research. A key feature of scientific publication is that it should facilitate independent critical testing of whatever phenomena are presented. In this particular case, the defect in the original reporting (*not* a defect in the original model!) was uncovered only when a copy of the original program code was rediscovered by chance. At the time of the original publication, the technological facilities were not generally available to support easy distribution or access to accompanying code—but this is no longer the case. We would suggest therefore that as a general principle, published reports on computer models of ALife should be accompanied by access to the program code for the models on the World Wide Web.

Bare access to program code is, of course, of limited value in itself. Effective critical review would require that it should be "reasonably" feasible that others in the community be able to *execute* (and, indeed, modify) this code. This suggests a need for some degree of standardisation, where that is possible. The Swarm simulation system, with its open licensing for scientific research, offers a candidate platform for such standardisation. Indeed, this was a key reason for adopting Swarm in the development of the SCL system [6]. Our experience of using Swarm in this application suggests that it can provide a stable, efficient, and portable basis for wide dissemination of this kind of ALife research.

Acknowledgments

Initial work on re-implementing a computational model of autopoiesis was carried out by a former student of McMullin, Hyder Aswad. We are also grateful to Francoise Jullien and John Mingers for making available their independent re-implementations of the model of [11]. Ms. Marita Prandoni and Ms. Peggy Jones provided invaluable assistance in translating original documents from Spanish. All errors in the current paper remain, of course, our own responsibility.

This paper was written while McMullin was a visiting researcher (1996/97) with the Swarm Project Group at the Santa Fe Institute. This visit was made possible by generous support from Dublin City University and the Swarm Project. Swarm has been supported by Grant No. N00014-94-1-G014 from the Department of the Navy, Naval Research Laboratory, acting in cooperation with the Advanced Research Projects Agency. Swarm has also benefited from earlier support from The Carol O'Donnell Foundation and from Mr. and Mrs. Michael Grantham.

References

[1] Francois Jullien and Barry McMullin. FRJ's Simple Autopoiesis Program, 1995. Program source in Pascal, for MS-DOS platform.
`ftp://ftp.eeng.dcu.ie/pub/autonomy/frj_sap`

[2] Rosa Lizana. Modelo bidimensional de reproduccion como fractura de una unidad autopoietica. Master's thesis, Universidad De Chile, Facultad de Ciencias, Departamento de Biologia, 1981. In Spanish.

[3] Humberto R. Maturana and Francisco J. Varela. Autopoiesis: The organization of the living. In *Autopoiesis and Cognition: The Realization of the Living* [4], pages 59–138.

[4] Humberto R. Maturana and Francisco J. Varela. *Autopoiesis and Cognition: The Realization of the Living*, volume 42. D. Reidel Publishing Company, Dordrecht, Holland, 1980.

[5] Barry McMullin. Computational autopoiesis: The original algorithm. Working Paper 97-01-001, Santa Fe Institute, Santa Fe, NM 87501, USA, January 1997.
`http://www.santafe.edu/sfi/publications/Working-Papers/97-01-001/`

[6] Barry McMullin. SCL: An artificial chemistry in *Swarm*. Working Paper 97-01-002, Santa Fe Institute, Santa Fe, NM 87501, USA, January 1997.
`http://www.santafe.edu/sfi/publications/Working-Papers/97-01-002/`

[7] John Mingers. *Self-Producing Systems: Implications and Applications of Autopoiesis*. Plenum Publishing, New York, 1994.

[8] John Mingers and Barry McMullin. JM's Simple Autopoiesis Program, 1997. Program source in Pascal, for MS-DOS platform.
`ftp://ftp.eeng.dcu.ie/pub/autonomy/jm_sap`

[9] Francisco J. Varela. *Principles of Biological Autonomy*. North-Holland, New York, 1979.

[10] Francisco J. Varela. The early days of autopoiesis: Heinz and Chile. *Systems Research*, 13(3):407–416, 1996.

[11] Francisco J. Varela, Humberto R. Maturana, and R. Uribe. Autopoiesis: The organization of living systems, its characterization and a model. *BioSystems*, 5:187–196, 1974.

[12] Milan Zeleny. Self-organization of living systems: A formal model of autopoiesis. *International Journal of General Systems*, 4:13–28, 1977.

[13] Milan Zeleny, editor. *Autopoiesis: A Theory of Living Organization*, volume 3 of *North Holland Series in General Systems Research*. North Holland, New York, 1981.

Revision History

The first draft of this paper was published in February 1997, simultaneously as Working Paper No. 97-02-012 of the Santa Fe Institute and as Technical Report No. bmcm9703 of the Dublin City University ALife Laboratory. This is a revised version, presented at ECAL-97, Brighton, UK July 1997, proceedings published by The MIT Press, edited by Phil Husbands and Inman Harvey.

Retrieval

The resources comprising this paper are electronically retrievable, in various formats, via the World Wide Web, from:

`http://www.eeng.dcu.ie/~alife/bmcm-ecal97/`

Copyright

An Attempt for Description of Quasi–Autopoietic Systems Using Metabolism–Repair Systems

Tatsuya Nomura

Evolutionary Systems Department
ATR Human Information Processing Research Laboratories
2-2, Hikaridai, Seika-cho, Soraku-gun, Kyoto 619-02 JAPAN
Phone: +81–774–95–1010, Fax: +81–774–95–1008, E-mail: nomura@hip.atr.co.jp

Abstract

In this paper, we attempt to describe Autopoietic Systems using a mathematical framework of Metabolism–Repair Systems. Our description does not strictly reflect pure autopoiesis, and can only represent quasi–autopoietic systems. However, we believe that this attempt will spur discussions on the formal description of autopoiesis and the relation to mental and social systems, and so on, and we dare to propose a rough model.

1 Introduction

Autopoiesis is a neologism, introduced by Maturana and Varela to designate the organization of a minimal living system [8]. Maturana produced this theory from his research on visual nervous systems, and Varela developed his own system theory based on it. Later, Luhmann applied autopoiesis to the theory of social systems, developing his own interpretation of it [7].

Recently, this theory has been applied to not only sociology but also psychopathology [2]. Moreover, Kawamoto has continued his own development of autopoiesis. In his book, he designated the properties of autopoiesis by comparison with conventional system theories [6].

However, there is still no mathematical model that represents autopoiesis itself. A machine learning model inspired by autopoiesis was proposed to do tasks such as pattern recognition [3], but this model does not represent autopoiesis itself.

There are Metabolism–Repair Systems ((M, R) systems), a mathematical system model introduced by Rosen to formalize the functional activities of a living cell – metabolism, repair, and replication [9]. This system model maintains its metabolic activity through inputs from environments and repair activity.

Fontana and Buss suggested the similarity between their study and these systems [5]. In this paper, we try to describe autopoietic systems using a mathematical framework of (M, R) systems. Our attempt may

be very thoughtless because of the difficulty in interpreting autopoiesis in the framework of the naive set theory. Accordingly, our description does not strictly reflect pure autopoiesis, and can only represent quasi–autopoietic systems. Nevertheless, we believe that this attempt will spur discussions on the formal description of autopoiesis and the relation between autopoiesis, mental systems, and social systems, and so on, which has been a highly controversial point. Based on this belief, we dare to propose a rough model of quasi–autopoietic systems.

We give an aspect of (M, R) systems in section 2, and an aspect of autopoiesis and a discussion on its interpretation in section 3. Then, we propose a description of quasi–autopoietic systems and explain a way of coupling them in section 4. In this paper, we focus our attention on cyclic systems and apply our description of quasi–autopoietic systems to systems of this type in section 5. Finally, we discuss the problems of our framework in section 6.

2 Metabolism–Repair Systems

(M, R) system is a model proposed as one solution to the question of how it is possible for the overall life time of an input–output system to be greater than that of any of its components. Rosen has stated the following [9]: Biological cells are continually repairing themselves. In order to keep the system functioning beyond the lifetimes of its components, it is necessary to replace components before their lifetimes has been exceeded.

The simplest (M, R) systems represent the above aspect in the following diagram:

$$A \xrightarrow{f} B \xrightarrow{\phi_f} H(A,B) \qquad (1)$$

Here, A is a set of inputs from an environment to the system, B is a set of outputs from the system to the environment, f is a component of the system represented as a map from A to B, and ϕ_f is the repair component of f as a map from B to $H(A,B)$ ($H(X,Y)$ is the set of all maps from a set X to a set Y). In biological cells, f

corresponds to the metabolism, and ϕ_f to the repair. If $\phi_f(b) = f$ $(b = f(a))$ is satisfied for the input $a \in A$, we can say that the system self–maintains itself.

Moreover, a replicator component is introduced in the following diagram:

$$B \xrightarrow{\phi_f} H(A, B) \xrightarrow{\Phi_f} H(B, H(A, B)) \qquad (2)$$
$$(\Phi_f \in H(H(A, B), H(B, H(A, B))))$$

Here, the replicator component satisfies $\Phi_f(\phi_f(b)) = \Phi_f(f) = \phi_f$ for the above b and f. Figure 1(a) shows the simplest (M, R) system.

Diagram (2) also represents an (M, R) system. However, Φ_f can be constructed by the preceding (M, R) system in the following way:
For a and b such that $b = f(a)$ and $\phi_f(b) = f$, if $\hat{b} : H(B, H(A, B)) \to H(A, B)$ $(\hat{b}(\phi)(a') = \phi(b)(a')$ $(\phi \in H(B, H(A, B)), a' \in A))$ has the inverse map $\hat{b}^{-1}$, it is easily proved that $\hat{b}^{-1}(f) = \phi_f$. Thus, we can set $\Phi_f = \hat{b}^{-1}$.

General (M, R) systems are represented in the following form:

$$(\hat{A}, \hat{F}, \hat{A}_f, \phi_f) : \qquad (3)$$

$\hat{A}$: a family of sets, $\hat{F}$: a family of maps

$$\forall f \in \hat{F} \ \exists A_1, \ldots, A_m, B \in \hat{A} \ s.t. \ f \in H\left(\prod_{i=1}^{m} A_i, B\right)$$

$$\forall A \in \hat{A} \ \exists f \in \hat{F} \ s.t.$$

A = the domain of f, or the range of f

$$\forall f \in \hat{F} \ \exists \hat{A}_f \subset \hat{A}, \ \phi_f : \prod_{C \in \hat{A}_f} C \to H\left(\prod_{i=1}^{m} A_i, B\right)$$

$$\left(\prod_{i=1}^{m} A_i = \text{domain of } f, \ B = \text{range of } f\right)$$

Here, $A \in \hat{A}$ which are not any of the domains of $f \in \hat{F}$, are input sets from the outside of the system; those which are not any of the ranges of $f \in \hat{F}$ are output sets to the outside of the system. $\hat{F}$ is the set of the metabolism and ϕ_f corresponds to the repair for each $f \in \hat{F}$. Figure 1(b) shows general (M, R) systems. The repair for each metabolism depends on the output of itself or the others.

Casti developed a theory of (M, R) systems assumed as linear systems, to mathematically analyze the conditions for stability in self–maintenance [1]. In this paper, we borrow the framework of metabolism and repair in (M, R) systems and apply it to our description of the dynamical aspect of input–output behaviors, and the framework of replication and apply it to our description of the circular operations.

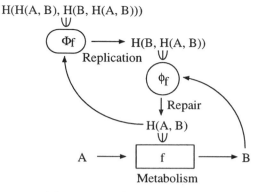

(a) Simplest (M, R) System

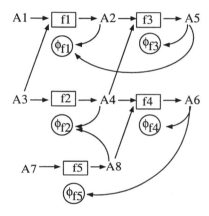

(b) General (M, R) System

Figure 1: (M, R) Systems

3 Autopoiesis

3.1 Aspect of Autopoiesis

Autopoiesis provides a framework in which a system exists as a living organization, based on physical and chemical processes. Maturana declared that living systems are machinery, and then claimed that autopoietic machinery is equivalent to living systems.

An autopoietic system is one that continuously produces the components that specify it, while at the same time realizing itself to be a concrete unity in space and time; this makes the network of production of components possible. An autopoietic system is organized as a network of processes of production of components, where these components:

1. continuously regenerate and realize the network that produces them, and

2. constitute the system as a distinguishable unity in the domain in which they exist.

Maturana gives a car as a representative example of a non–autopoietic system and claims the following [8]: The self–maintenance of a car as itself is realized only when there is a relation between inputs from a driver and outputs of the car. On the other hand, living systems self–maintains themselves by repeatedly reproducing the components and not by actions from others. Although they take nutritious substances from the outside, the organization is not determined corresponding to the substances. The processes for self–reproduction exist firstly and foremost, and the nutritious substances are subordinate to these processes.

The characteristics of autopoietic systems Maturana gives are as follows:

1. Autonomy:
   Autopoietic machinery integrates various changes into the maintenance of its organization. A car, the above example of a non–autopoietic system, does not have any autonomy.

2. Individuality:
   Autopoietic machinery has its identity independent of mutual actions between it and external observers, by repeatedly reproducing and maintaining the organization. The identity of a non–autopoietic system is dependent on external observers and such a system does not have any individuality.

3. Self–Determination of the Boundary of the System:
   Autopoietic machinery determines its boundary through the self–reproduction processes. Since the boundaries of non–autopoietic systems are determined by external observers, self–determination of the boundaries does not apply to them.

4. Absence of Input and Output in the System:
   Even if a stimulus independent of an autopoietic machine causes continuous changes in the machine, these changes are subordinate to the maintenance of the organization which specifies the machine. Thus, the relation between the stimulus and the changes lies in the area of observation, and not in the organization.

Moreover, Kawamoto positions dynamical stable systems which self–maintain themselves through metabolism to the outside, self–organizing systems such as crystals which grow while morphing themselves according to their environment, and autopoietic systems, as the first, the second, and the third generation systems, respectively [6]. Kawamoto particularly focuses on the fourth item among the above characteristics of autopoiesis, i.e., absence of input and output in the system.

Important is the view where the system is understood based on the production processes when we consider the "absence of input and output". Kawamoto claims the following: The view of the relation between inputs and outputs in the system is one from external observers and it does not clarify the organization or the operation of the production in the system. A living cell only reproduces its components and does not produce the components while adjusting itself according to the relation between itself and oxygen in the air. Although the density of oxygen affects the production processes, external observers decide the influence and not the cell. As long as the system is grasped from an internal view of the cell, the system does not have any "inputs and outputs".

The gist in the concept of autopoietic systems Kawamoto gives involves the following:

1. The set of components of a system is determined by the operation of the system.

2. The operation of the system precedes the initial condition.

3. The operation of the system is executed only to succeed itself and does not aim to produce by–products.

4. In the operation of the system, the things that happen in the system clearly differ from the things that external observers discriminate.

3.2 Difficulty in Interpretation for Autopoiesis

How systems are grasped from the view of external observers is interpreted as separating the observers from the environment including the system, distinguishing between the system and the background in the environment, and verifying the relation between the system and the distinguished background, that is, the outside of the system. Autopoiesis forces us to give up this view, that is, to put our view in the system, not in the outside of the environment.

Kawamoto gives the following statement as an example of this shift of view: If a person is fast running on the ground like drawing a circle, the person just continuously reproduces the action of running, although an external observer decides that the person is determining the boundary of the system. When the person stops running, the boundary vanishes.

However, this shift of view is not easily acceptable in the contemporary situation where the view of external observers is still major in natural science. If a person bounded to this view observes an autopoietic system, the view shifts towards the outside of the environment and the system is grasped as a static map or dynamical system in a state space. Even if the view shifts towards the inside of the system, the production processes of the components themselves are grasped as the object of the observation and the view of external observers is not completely given up. In the above example of a running person, the observer produces an image of the relation between the person as the object of the observation and the space where the person is running.

Moreover, as long as the view of external observers is not given up, the above gist of Kawamoto, in particular, the determination of the set of components by the operation and the precedability of the operation with the initial condition in the system cannot be understood. In the conventional system theory, state spaces where the operation is defined firstly exist, the initial condition is determined independent of the operation, and the properties in the state spaces by the operation such as time evolution are discussed.

A person bounded to the view of external observers cannot imagine the situation where the operation determines its domain and initial condition. Thus, such a person can imagine just self–organizing systems such as hyper–circles, which belong to the second generation systems Kawamoto claims.

It cannot be denied that we are bounded to the view of external observers. Yet, we attempt to verify whether there is a form of systems which satisfies the above gist of Kawamoto within the view of external observers.

4 Quasi–Autopoietic Systems

4.1 Description of Quasi–Autopoietic Systems

We cannot describe pure autopoiesis unless we give up the view of external observers. Thus, it is difficult to represent autopoiesis in the framework of the naive set theory, in which no operation is defined unless the domain and range set are defined in advance.

Here, we propose a description of systems which satisfies the gist of Kawamoto for autopoiesis in section 3 within the framework of the naive set theory; the system are called quasi–autopoietic systems. The underlying motivation for quasi–autopoietic systems is to verify whether it is completely impossible to introduce the characteristics of autopoiesis into conventional system theories and represent them as a computational model.

The most basic description of quasi–autopoietic systems is given in the following diagram:

$$A \xrightarrow{f} B \xrightarrow{\phi} H(A, B) \tag{4}$$

$$H(B, H(A, B)) \xrightarrow{F} H(B, H(A, B)) \tag{5}$$

Here, (4) is the same form as (1) which represents the (M, R) systems in section 2. Instead of the replication map from $H(A, B)$ to $H(B, H(A, B))$ in the (M, R) systems shown in (2), the map F on $H(B, H(A, B))$ is given. This map determines the system's self by defining its self as an invariant set with a kind of ergodicity property for the map; that is, its self QAP is defined as follows:

$$QAP \subset H(B, H(A, B)), \ F(QAP) = QAP, \tag{6}$$

$$^{\forall}\phi, \phi' \in QAP, \ ^{\exists}n \in \mathbf{N} \ s.t. \ F^n(\phi') = \phi \tag{7}$$

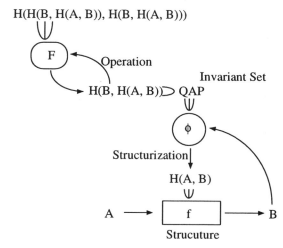

(a) The Most Basic Quasi–Autopoietic System

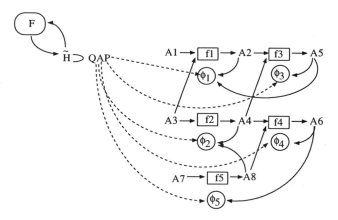

(b) General Quasi–Autopoietic System

Figure 2: Aspect of Quasi–Autopoietic Systems

Figure 2(a) shows an aspect of the most basic quasi–autopoietic systems. The system acts in the following way. The initial state of the system in $H(B, H(A, B))$ is selected within its self $QAP \subset H(B, H(A, B))$, and that in $H(A, B)$ is randomly selected. Next, given an input $a \in A$, the next states f' and ϕ' are determined in the following way:

$$b = f(a), \ (a \in A, \ b \in B)$$

$$f' = \phi(b) = \phi(f(a)), \ (f' \in H(A, B)) \tag{8}$$

$$\phi' = F(\phi) \ (\phi' \in H(B, H(A, B))) \tag{9}$$

Because an (M, R) system's self is the metabolism f and the repair ϕ_f, the main point is to keep f unchanged through self–maintenance by ϕ_f. In the quasi–autopoietic system, f and ϕ are permitted to change within QAP because the system's self that is maintained is QAP. The essential action in the system is not the processing from the input set A to the output set B, but the iteration of F on $H(B, H(A, B))$.

Here, we verify whether this quasi–autopoietic system satisfies the gist of Kawamoto in section 3 by regarding the map F as the operation and ϕ as the components of the system:

1. QAP is an invariant set of F. Moreover, whether an element in $H(B, H(A, B))$ belongs to QAP is determined by F, that is, by the reachability from the initial state of the system through F, because of the ergodicity property in (7). Thus, we can interpret this aspect as the one satisfying the first point in the gist.

2. In order for the system to exist as a quasi–autopoietic system, the initial state must belong to an invariant set for F. Thus, we can regard this aspect as the one satisfying the second point in the gist.

3. The thing the system executes results in a new state being made within QAP by iterating F, and not in the input–output map f being produced. Thus, we can regard this aspect as the one satisfying the third point in the gist.

4. If external observers watch only the input–output relation in the system and the changes in the relation, the thing that happens in the system, that is, the iteration of F within QAP, differs from the things which these observers discriminate in the system, that is, f. Thus, we can regard this aspect as the one satisfying the fourth point in the gist.

In the same way as with (M, R) systems, general quasi–autopoietic systems are represented in the following form:

$$(\hat{A}, \hat{H}, \hat{A}_H, F): \tag{10}$$

$\hat{A}$: a family of sets, $\hat{H}$: a family of sets of maps
$\forall H \in \hat{H}$ $\exists A_1, \dots, A_n, B_1, \dots, B_m \in \hat{A}$ s.t.

$$H = H\left(\prod_{i=1}^{m} A_i, \prod_{j=1}^{m} B_j\right)$$

$\forall A \in \hat{A}$ $\exists H \in \hat{H}$ s.t.

   A = the domain in H, or the range in H
$\forall H \in \hat{H}$ $\exists \hat{A}_H \subset \hat{A}$

$$F : \tilde{H} \to \tilde{H} \quad \left(\tilde{H} := \prod_{H \in \hat{H}} H\left(\prod_{C \in A_H} C, H\right)\right)$$

Figure 2(b) shows an aspect of general quasi–autopoietic systems. In this case, the system's self QAP is an invariant set of $\tilde{H}$ with the ergodicity property for F. F represents the network between the components of the system.

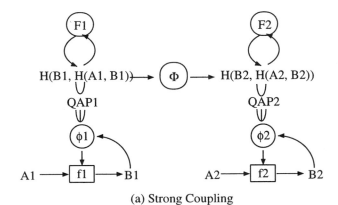

(a) Strong Coupling

(b) Weak Coupling

Figure 3: Coupling of Quasi–Autopoietic Systems

4.2 Coupling of Quasi–Autopoietic Systems

Using the quasi–autopoietic system in section 4.1, we can present a description for coupling them. In this paper, we give two kinds of couplings between quasi–autopoietic systems, called strong coupling and weak coupling.

In strong coupling, for two given quasi–autopoietic systems

$$\left.\begin{array}{l} A_i \xrightarrow{f_i} B_i \xrightarrow{\phi_i} H(A_i, B_i) \\ H(B_i, H(A_i, B_i)) \xrightarrow{F_i} H(B_i, H(A_i, B_i)) \\ QAP_i \subset H(B_i, H(A_i, B_i)) \end{array}\right\} \tag{11}$$

$$(i = 1, 2)$$

we assume that a map Φ from $H(B_1, H(A_1, B_1))$ to $H(B_2, H(A_2, B_2))$ exists such that the following commutative diagram is satisfied:

$$\begin{array}{ccc} H(B_1, H(A_1, B_1)) & \xrightarrow{F_1} & H(B_1, H(A_1, B_1)) \\ \downarrow \Phi & & \downarrow \Phi \\ H(B_2, H(A_2, B_2)) & \xrightarrow{F_2} & H(B_2, H(A_2, B_2)) \end{array} \tag{12}$$

Figure 3(a) shows the form of strong coupling. It is easily proved from the above diagram that $\Phi(QAP_1)$ is an invariant set with the ergodicity property in (7) for F_2. We define that these quasi–autopoietic systems are strongly coupled if $QAP_2 = \Phi(QAP_1)$. In this coupling, the former system determines the latter system. If the inverse map of ϕ exists, both systems mutually specify each other.

In weak coupling, for the given two quasi–autopoietic systems in (11), we assume the following situation:

$$B_1 \;\; = \;\; O \times S, \; A_1 = I \times S \tag{13}$$

that is, a part of the output set of the former system is a part of the input set of the latter system. The latter system acts based on the output from the former system, which is a part of the environment of the latter system. Figure 3(b) shows the form of weak coupling. In this coupling, either the former or the latter system's self is not affected by the other.

5 Cyclic Systems based on Quasi–Autopoietic Systems

In autopoiesis and self–organized systems, a cyclic property is frequently discussed. In order to clarify the concept of quasi–autopoietic systems, we focus our attention on a particular form of systems, cyclic systems. In this paper, we verify the possible form based on the framework of quasi–autopoietic systems.

Now, we consider the following cyclic system:

$$A_i = I_i \times S_i, \; B_i = O_i \times S_{i+1} \tag{14}$$

$$A_i \xrightarrow{f_i} B_i \xrightarrow{\phi_i} H(A_i, B_i) \tag{15}$$

$$(i = 1, \ldots, n, \; S_{n+1} = S_1)$$

In this system, I_i is the set of the i–th inputs from the outside of the cycle, O_i is the set of the i–th outputs to the outside of the cycle, and they construct parts of the input and output sets of the i–th input–output unit. Moreover, another part of the output set of the i–th input–output unit is another part of the input set of the $(i + 1)$–th unit. This cyclic system has a kind of auto–catalytic structure, e.g., a hyper–circle.

The cycle acts in the following way. The initial states of the cycle in $H(A_i, B_i)$ (f_i) and those in S_i (s_i) are randomly selected. Next, given an input $x_i \in I_i$, the next states f_i' and s_i' are determined in the following way:

$$(y_i, s_{i+1}') \;\; = \;\; f_i(x_i, s_i) \tag{16}$$

$$f_i' \;\; = \;\; \phi_i(y_i, s_{i+1}') = \phi_i(f_i(x_i, s_i)) \tag{17}$$

$$(y_i, s_{i+1}') \in O_i \times S_{i+1},$$
$$(x_i, s_i) \in I_i \times S_i$$
$$(i = 1, \ldots, n, \; s_{n+1}' = s_1')$$

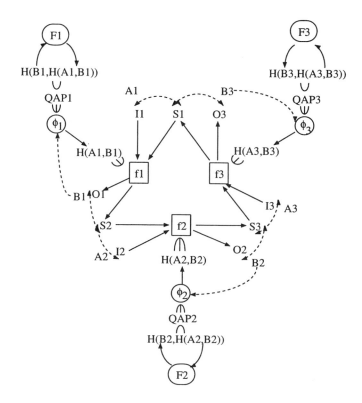

Figure 4: Weakly Coupled Cycle of Quasi–Autopoietic Systems ($n = 3$)

5.1 Coupled Cycles

In the form of the modification for ϕ_i, we can consider three kinds of cycles based on the framework of quasi–autopoietic systems: (1) weakly coupled cycle of quasi–autopoietic systems, (2) strongly coupled cycle of quasi–autopoietic systems, and (3) quasi–autopoietic cycle.

In weakly coupled cycles, the most basic quasi–autopoietic systems are coupled cyclicly and weakly as shown in section 4.2. The modification of ϕ_i to ϕ_i' is done by the following form:

$$H(B_i, H(A_i, B_i)) \xrightarrow{F_i} H(B_i, H(A_i, B_i)) \tag{18}$$

$$\phi_i' = F_i(\phi_i) \tag{19}$$

$$(i = 1, \ldots, n)$$

As shown in (15) and (18), the i–th unit makes a quasi–autopoietic system and it is weakly coupled with the $(i + 1)$–th quasi–autopoietic system, cyclicly. Figure 4 shows an aspect of the weakly coupled cycle. In this cycle, each quasi–autopoietic system has an independent self QAP_i through F_i and it does not affect the others.

In strongly coupled cycles, the most basic quasi–autopoietic systems are coupled cyclicly and strongly as shown in section 4.2. Since the i–th unit makes a quasi–autopoietic system and it is cyclicly coupled with the

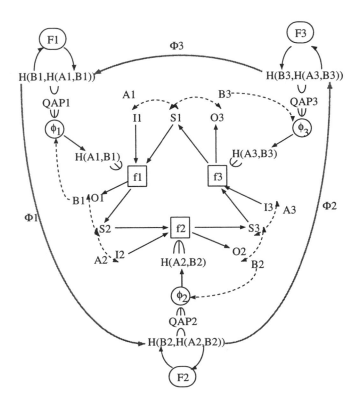

Figure 5: Strongly Coupled Cycle of Quasi–Autopoietic Systems ($n = 3$)

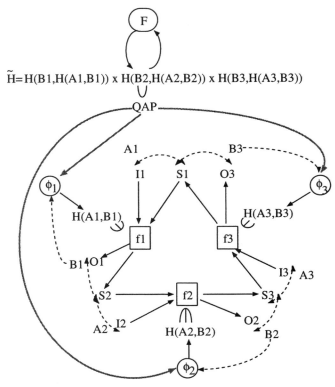

Figure 6: Quasi–Autopoietic Cycle ($n = 3$)

$(i + 1)$–th quasi–autopoietic system in the same way as for the weakly coupled cycle, the modification of ϕ_i to ϕ_i' is done by the same form as (18) and (19). However, the modification of ϕ_i is done while maintaining the following boundary condition for the maps $\{\Phi_i\}_{i=1}^n$ which are associated with strong coupling:

$$
\begin{array}{ccc}
H_i & \overset{F_i}{\rightarrow} & H_i \\
\downarrow \Phi_i & & \downarrow \Phi_i \\
H_{i+1} & \overset{F_{i+1}}{\rightarrow} & H_{i+1}
\end{array}
\qquad (20)
$$

$$\phi_{i+1} = \Phi_i(\phi_i) \qquad (21)$$

$$
\left(
\begin{array}{l}
i = 1, \ldots, n,\ H_i = H(B_i, H(A_i, B_i)) \\
A_{n+1} = A_1,\ B_{n+1} = B_1, \\
F_{n+1} = F_1, \phi_{n+1} = \phi_1
\end{array}
\right)
$$

By the commutative diagram in (20), this boundary condition is maintained through the operation if the initial state of the cycle in H_i satisfies it. Figure 5 shows an aspect of the strongly coupled cycle. In this cycle, although each quasi–autopoietic system has its own self QAP_i through F_i, it does affect the others through the strong coupling by Φ_i.

Quasi–autopoietic cycles are not a system which can be represented as a coupling of quasi–autopoietic systems, but one general quasi–autopoietic system as shown

in section 4.1. Thus, each input–output unit does not correspond to a quasi–autopoietic system, and the cycle has its own self QAP through the map F. The modification of ϕ_i to ϕ_i' is done in the following form:

$$F \ : \ \tilde{H} \to \tilde{H} \qquad (22)$$

$$\left(\tilde{H} = \prod_{i=1}^{n} H(B_i, H(A_i, B_i)) \right)$$

$$(\phi_1', \ldots, \phi_n') = F(\phi_1, \ldots, \phi_n) \qquad (23)$$

Figure 6 shows an aspect of the quasi–autopoietic cycle. Although several systems' selves can exist in coupled cycles, this cycle's self is not divided into subsystems.

5.2 Coupling of Cycles

Based on the forms of cycles shown in the above sections, we can extend the coupling of quasi–autopoietic systems to the coupling of coupled cycles or quasi–autopoietic cycles. Here, we can consider two types of couplings, weak coupling and strong coupling in the same way as section 4.2.

In the weak coupling of cycles, the quasi–autopoietic system in a coupled cycle or the general quasi–autopoietic system corresponding to a quasi–autopoietic cycle is weakly coupled with another. In other words, for a cycle shown in (14) and (15) and another cycle in the following:

$$C_j = P_j \times T_j, \ D_j = Q_j \times T_{j+1} \qquad (24)$$

$$C_j \overset{g_j}{\to} D_j \overset{\varphi_j}{\to} H(C_j, D_j) \qquad (25)$$

$$(j = 1, \ldots, m, \ T_{m+1} = T_1)$$

the i–th input–output unit in the former cycle and the j–th unit in the latter cycle are coupled through $O_i = P_j$. Figure 7 shows a weak coupling of cycles. This coupling is not dependent on the form of cycles shown in the above sections, but only on the level of input–output units.

In the strong coupling of cycles, the quasi–autopoietic system in a coupled cycle or the general quasi–autopoietic system corresponding to a quasi–autopoietic cycle is strongly coupled with another. In other words, the most basic quasi–autopoietic system shown in (18) of a coupled cycle or the general quasi–autopoietic system shown in (22) of a quasi–autopoietic cycle is strongly coupled with the most basic quasi–autopoietic system of another coupled cycle

$$H(D_j, H(C_j, D_j)) \overset{G_j}{\to} H(D_j, H(C_j, D_j)) \qquad (26)$$

$$(j = 1, \ldots, m)$$

or the general quasi–autopoietic system of another quasi–autopoietic cycle

$$G \ : \ \tilde{W} \to \tilde{W} \ \left(\tilde{W} = \prod_{j=1}^{m} H(D_j, H(C_j, D_j)) \right) (27)$$

Figure 8 shows a strong coupling of cycles. This coupling is dependent on the form of cycles, and three forms of couplings are considered: (a) coupling of coupled cycles of quasi–autopoietic systems, (b) coupling of a coupled cycle and a quasi–autopoietic cycle, and (c) coupling of quasi–autopoietic cycles. In case (a), the i–th quasi–autopoietic system's self QAP_i in a coupled cycle specifies the j–th system's self QAP'_j in another cycle. In case (b), a quasi–autopoietic cycle's self QAP specifies the quasi–autopoietic system's self QAP'_j in a coupled cycle, or the opposite specification is done. In case (c) a quasi–autopoietic cycle's self QAP specifies that of another quasi–autopoietic cycle QAP'.

6 Discussion

Through the previous sections, we gave a description for quasi–autopoietic systems using the framework of (M, R) systems, coupling of them, and the representation of cyclic systems based on the description. Although this is an attempt to possibly represent autopoiesis within the naive set theory, many problems remain.

First, we introduced an invariant set with the ergodicity property in the set of repair maps in (M, R) systems to represent the self–determination of the system's

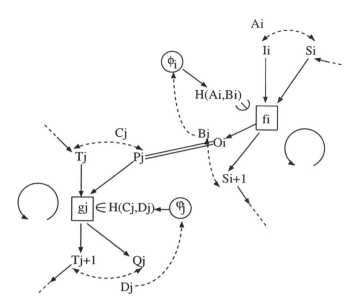

Figure 7: Weak Coupling of Cycles

boundary. However, this is only to give a class for an equivalent relation on the set given in advance by the operator given in advance. In other words, the space where the system's self exists is determined in advance and then the operator is also determined as the map on it. In pure autopoiesis, the set of components must be determined by the operator in the system, that is, the domain and range of the operator must be determined through the operator itself.

Second, we separated the operator and input–output actions in the system to represent the absence of inputs–outputs in the system. This caused the input–output actions to not affect the self–determination of the system's boundary and the operator acted independent of the outside of the system. If we regard the input–output actions as a part of the components, however, what happened was not realistic. Although we introduced coupling of the systems, this is a very provisional idea. Thus, our description does not strictly reflect the properties of pure autopoiesis, and can represent just quasi–systems as mentioned in section 1.

As a solution for these problems, we consider the effectiveness of λ–calculus for the representation of the interaction between the components and operator inspired by the approach which Fontana and Buss have proposed [4], because it can deal with the components and operator in the same level.

Even if our description is narrowly meaningful, there are many problems to be solved. First, we have not done either a comparison of our description with conventional system theories or a verification of the adequacy to the representation of concrete systems such as living cells,

56

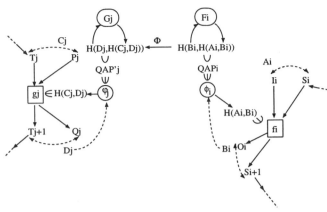

(a) Coupling of Coupled Cycles

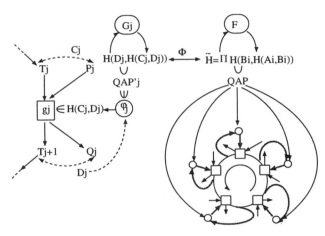

(b) Coupling of a Coupled Cycle and a
Quasi–Autopoietic Cycle

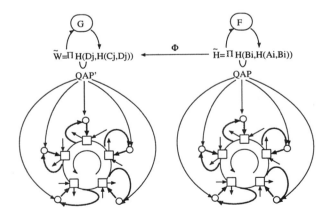

(c) Coupling of Quasi–Autopoietic Cycles

Figure 8: Strong Coupling of Cycles

mental systems, and social systems, yet. This is difficult, but must be done as quickly as possible if we aim to propose a new system theory.

Moreover, we have to clarify mathematical properties within our description, construct a concrete model on a computer, and execute simulations to verify the properties, because our purpose is to represent the characteristics of autopoiesis as a computational model.

These must be solved as future problems.

Acknowledgment

The author would like to thank Dr. Katsunori Shimohara at ATR Human Information Processing Research Laboratories for his support.

References

[1] J. L. Casti. The Theory of Metabolism–Repair Systems. *APPLIED MATHEMATICS AND COMPUTATION*, 28:113–154, 1988.

[2] L. Ciompi. *Affektlogik – Über die Struktur der Psyche und ihre Entwicklung.* Ein Beitrage zur Schizophreneiforschung, 2. Auflage, Klett–cotta, Stuttgart, 1982 (Japanese Edition: Gakuju Shoin, Publishers, Ltd., 1994).

[3] G. Deffuant, T. Fuhs, E. Monneret, P. Nourgine, and F. Varela. Semi–Algebraic Networks: An Attempt to Design Gemometric Autopoietic Models. *Artificial Life*, 2(2):157–177, 1995.

[4] W. Fontana and L. W. Buss. "The Arrival of the Fittest": Toward a Theory of Biological Organization. *Bulletin of Mathmatical Biology*, 56:1–64, 1994.

[5] W. Fontana and L. W. Buss. The barrier of objects: From dynamical systems to bounded organizations. In J. Casti and A. Karlqvist, editors, *Boundaries and Barriers*, pages 56–116. Addison–Wesley, 1996.

[6] H. Kawamoto. *Autopoiesis: The Third Generation System.* Seido–sha Publishers, 1995 (Japanese).

[7] G. Kneer and A. Nassehi. *Niklas Luhmanns Theorie Sozialer Systeme.* Wilhelm Fink Verlag, 1993 (Japanese Edition: Shinsen–sha Publishers, 1995).

[8] H. R. Maturana and F. J. Varela. *AUTOPOIESIS and COGNITION: THE REALIZATION OF THE LIVING.* D. Reidel Publishing Company, 1980 (Japanese Edition: Kokubun–sha Publishers, 1991).

[9] R. Rosen. *FOUNDATIONS OF MATHEMATICAL BIOLOGY*, Vol. 2, chapter 4. Some Relational Cell Models: The Metabolism–Repair Systems, pp. 217–253. Academic Press, 1972.

Symbolic and global dynamics in coupled genetic networks: evolution of artificial cell populations at the edge of and within chaotic transient behaviour

Franco A. Bignone[*,a,c], **Roberto Livi**[b,c], **Marco Propato**[b],

[a]I.S.T., L.go Rosanna Benzi, 10, I-16132 Genova, &
Dip.to Biologia Animale e Genetica, Università di Firenze,
Via Romana 17-19, I-50125 Firenze, Italy.
[b]Dipartimento di Fisica Università di Firenze,
Largo Fermi 2, I-50125 Firenze, Italy.
[c]I.N.F.M.–FORUM, Unità di Firenze,
Largo Fermi 2, I-50125 Firenze, Italy.
FAB: abignone@cisi.unige.it
RL: LIVI@fi.infn.it
MP: marco@roberto.fi.infn.it

Abstract

We investigate the main dynamical features of a Coupled Map Lattice that mimics the evolution in time of genetic networks in regular cellular clusters. Each cell is represented by the same network of genes whose protein products determine mutual interactions both in space and time. The global dynamics – quantified by the mean concentrations of the products on the overall lattice –, and the symbolic dynamics – activity-inactivity patterns of the genes –, have been analyzed in the long-transient regime, shown by the system in certain regions of the parameter space.

Although the system is linearly stable – the maximum Lyapunov exponent is proved to be always negative –, the long transient regime exhibits stationary features proper of chaotic evolution. Moreover, in the other regions of the parameter space the dynamics shows shorter transients and more regular behaviour. The analysis of the global and symbolic dynamics allows the interpretation of these different regimes in biological terms.

The main outcome of this work is the formulation of a novel hypothesis – in respect of the definition by C. Langton of *life at the edge of chaos* based on Cellular Automata – that, upon comparison with experimental data, could have interesting consequences for the understanding of biological evolution mechanisms.

Keywords: Gene expression, Genetic Networks, Coupled map lattices, Evolution, Cellular automata, Signal transduction systems.

* Mailing address: Franco A. Bignone, I.S.T., Viale Benedetto XV 10, I-16132 Genova, Italy.
Fax:+39-10-5600-210,
e-mail: abignone@cisi.unige.it

1 Introduction

A general feature of higher biological systems, most animals and plants, is multicellularity. Such organisms are made of a complex social organization of populations of cells specialized for different tasks. The acquisition of this structure during evolution is in general thought to give an advantage in terms of specialized tasks that different subpopulations can perform. In respect of an isolated cell, such as for bacteria or protista, multicellular organisms can subdivide different specialized functions inside a large population, achieving in this way a much more complex organization.

At the level of tissue organization, in early evolution, one can imagine the possibility of building up complexity through the establishment of message systems, able to convey informations from cell to cell on a local basis. One of the most simple, and most studied, examples of this kind is Dictyostelium discoideum. In the case of this amoeba, the aggregation phase, before sporulation occurs, is driven by signalling through cAMP waves that organize the slug in order to produce the fruiting body when cells enter starvation [1].

The general organization of all multicellular organisms, in biochemical terms, reflects this fact. Cellular biochemistry in higher Eukaryota is made of two main compartments. At a basic level we have an intracellular dynamics characteristic for every cell, or acting as a bulk for a group of them always with some local variations. This is separated from similar dynamics of the surrounding cells by the cell membrane, that acts - except, for instance, in the case of syncitia - as a selective barrier filtering molecular information from the surrounding tissue. In fact, the coupling among cells, i.e. the transmission of information, occurs through the membrane, thanks to a complex machinery of different molecules carrying specific signals. These can be quite diversified in their nature, such as cross-membrane receptors or lipid-soluble molecules. From the evolutionary point of view one can imagine the establishment of very simple systems of interaction in the early cells that started to get organized in the way we see now in higher animals and plants.

It is worth stressing that the possibility of interconnection between different metabolisms has some additional advantages and consequences in respect of simple specialization. These consequences, that are not immediately evident at first sight, can be best understood when considering the dynamical aspects of such organization.

In his early work on boolean-networks S. Kauffman has proposed that the number of steady states attainable by random connected networks should correspond to the different possibilities of organization that multicellular organisms exhibit. In other words, the number of possible differentiative states should be reflected in the complexity of the genome, corresponding roughly to the number of possible steady states that cells can achieve. The relationship, emerging in this case through the study of animal genomes, is close to a power law such as $S^{1/2}$, where S is the size of the genome, calculated as the quantity of DNA. This is true when considering isolated cells. If one considers an isolated boolean network, or any kind of biochemical network with the possibility of multiple steady states, or in turn a neural network, this statement is correct. Different values of the exponent may occur if the mean number of interconnections between elements is varied, but a power-law behaviour is generally obtained [2].

On the other hand, if one considers multicellular organisms, two further factors must be taken into account: global and local coupling. The former represents the influence exerted by the overall organism through circulation – or other means, as it happens in the nervous system –, the latter is the coupling taking place at the level of cell-cell interactions.

This organization has immediately different effects on the possible states that a system can achieve. Steady states that are not possible for the isolated cell become available to the population. This fact is well known for most spatially extended systems but, to our knowledge, it has not been stressed enough for what concern evolution theory. One of the net results that early multicellularity can thus achieve is the possibility to modulate cellular biochemistry in a way unaccessible for isolated individuals. In early evolution this might have been a big advantage for cell populations that kept together as a whole. Establishing linkages between biochemical networks in a cell population, depending on the setting of the coupling strength, provides immediately large advantages in terms of novel possibilities of behaviour. Notice that this can be done without any change in the preexisting internal organization of a cell, except, obviously, for what concerns the new system carrying the signals.

Nonetheless, this is not the end of the story. Another fact emerges from theoretical considerations related to the values that global variables – averages on the overall population – can take by intercellular communication. Actually, such variables have the possibility to evolve maintaining their average value close to some typical and, possibly, optimal level for each isolated individual. In other words, the richness of the variability inside the population determined by the coupling among individuals is counterbalanced by the global features of the dynamics that have a tendency to keep average variables within prescribed range of values.

This can produce additional advantages from an evolutionary point of view. In fact, not only the basic biochemistry of a cell dosen't have to be modified in order to get new dynamical possibilities, but the fact that the global variables stay close to those of the isolated cells implies also a sort of stability with respect to the environment – the surrounding medium where cells live –.

In achieving multicellularity the only immediate need for an unicellular organism is thus the establishment of a communication system, so that the increase in the number of new possible steady states naturally arises from the inner structure of the dynamics. Analogously, there is no immediate need for a different environment, being global variables close to individual levels. Summarizing, the main advantage favouring multicellularity is that cells can acquire a richer spectrum of possible responses, while maintaining global features almost unchanged with respect to individual ones that were selected by the environment of unicellular ancestors.

These hypotheses emerge from the dynamical study of a simple model of coupled genetic networks that has been proposed recently [3, 4, 5, 6], and that we shall describe in Section 2. Nonetheless, it is worth stressing that the above reported remarks apply generically to a whole class of models of biochemical interactions, as long as certain requirements are met in terms of interactions and non-linearities of the system.

The rationale for our investigation has been driven by the consideration that a detailed formal study of the complex signal transduction systems in higher Eukaryota, due to the number of molecular species and to the consequent sophistication of the systems involved, is at present out of reach. Moreover several additional intricacies exist because of phenomena related to the spatial structure of cells and tissues.

Nevertheless, the use of simple models that contain some basic features of the problem at hand may as well provide useful insights on the possible broad spectrum dynamics arising from the general organization of biological systems. In fact, a reductionist attitude revealed fruitful in many research domains, notably in statistical mechanics, where certain universal behaviours characterizing a wide class of phenomena can be ascribed to essential features of the symmetries and of the kind of interactions, irrespectively of the many additional details differentiating the various contexts.

The model is based on Coupled Maps Lattices [CML] methodologies. CML are a class of theoretical tools introduced in recent years as space-time discretized versions of reaction-diffusion systems – see [7, 8] for reviews –. These models have obvious advantages despite the theoretical difficulties introduced by the discretization of space and time. In particular, they allow for an easy implementation in terms of computer algorithms.

An important aspect of CML to be stressed in this context is that they typically display long transient dynamics for some set of values of the parameters. This is an important result yielding a well founded guess in terms of generalization of our results to a larger class of models.

At variance with usual CML, in our model maps are replaced by formal genetic networks whose dynamical evolution is governed by a step function that sets the activation or the deactivation of each gene through a connectivity matrix. The matrix considered here yields periodic dynamics. As in standard CML, spatial coupling is simulated by a diffusive term.

In Section 3 we discuss the coupled dynamics of the system, and briefly report on the results concerning transient regimes. The global and the symbolic dynamics of the model are discussed in section 4. In the last Section we present our interpretation of the results, and compare the behaviour of our model with Cellular Automata [CA]. We also discuss some questions raised by our investigation in respect of the concept of *life at the edge of chaos* introduced by C. Langton [9]. Further considerations on the stability of the dynamical regimes occurring in the model indicate the need for a strict control over the system, that can be obviously envisioned in the DNA. This could be necessary in order to drive the system behaviour in those regions of the parameter space at the boudary of long transient regimes.

2   Model description

The simple model that we are going to consider [3, 4, 5, 6] is made of cells evolving in time according to the following genomic rule

$$x_i(t+1) = x_i(t)(1 - C_i) + v_i(t)P_i \qquad (1)$$

Here x_i represents the concentration of the protein expressed by the i-th gene; P_i and C_i correspond to the production and decay rate of x_i, respectively. The function v_i controls the activity of the i-th gene through a step-like coupling with the other genes , that form the genetic network acting inside the cell:

$$v_i(t) = \begin{cases} 1, & \text{if } \sum_{j=1}^{n} x_j(t)r_{i,j} \geq k_i; \\ 0, & \text{otherwise.} \end{cases} \qquad (2)$$

The index j labels all the n genes of the network, $r_{i,j}$ are real numbers representing the weighted regulatory connections between genes, k_i is the threshold value allowing for switching the i-th gene *on* $\equiv 1$ and *off* $\equiv 0$. This model is similar to the one introduced by L. Glass and S. Kauffman [10], and it could also be considered as the space-time discrete version of previous models introduced by B. C. Goodwin [11] using ordinary differential equations.

The general assumption to simulate gene-expression in a tissue, is that cells are arranged into a predefined space and mutual interactions are set. Accordingly, we consider the cell population on a regular lattice made of N sites, where each individual interacts with its neighbours by a diffusive coupling. The dynamical equation of the i-th gene of the cell located at site m on the lattice reads

$$\begin{aligned} x_i(m, t+1) = {} & (1 - C_i)\, x_i(m, t) \\ & + P_i\, v_i[x_1(m, t), \ldots, x_n(m, t)] \\ & + \gamma_i \left[\left(\sum_{l \in Q} x_i(l, t) \right) - q x_i(m, t) \right] \end{aligned} \qquad (3)$$

In what follows we shall always assume periodic boundary conditions on the lattice; these make the previous expression well defined also for the cells at the lattice boundaries. Nonetheless, most of the results hereafter reported apply to systems where other kinds of boundary conditions (e.g., no-flux or fixed) are chosen. The parameter γ_i is the diffusion constant of the protein expressed by the i-th gene and Q indicates the set of the q neighbours of each cell. In this scheme the spatial coupling is conceptualized as a simple diffusion of proteins among the cells. This has to be considered as the idealization of a real signal transduction mechanism that may involve several intermediate steps.

In order to maintain the x_i's bounded to non-negative values we impose the following condition for all i :

$$1 - C_i - q\,\gamma_i \geq 0 \qquad (4)$$

For the simulations studied in this paper we have chosen a formal genetic network of two genes where the regulatory connections take the values

$$r_{ij} = \begin{cases} +1, & \text{if } i \neq j; \\ -1, & \text{if } i = j \end{cases} \qquad (5)$$

where i, $j = 1$, 2. With this choice each gene activates the other one and inhibits itself. The threshold values in (2) (assumed to be positive) are fixed to $k_1 = k_2 = 1$. (It is worth stressing that this choice is not a prejudice of generality, as discussed in [5]) . The parameters in (1) have been chosen as follows : $C_1 = 0.2$, $C_2 = 0.4$, $P_1 = 2.0$ and $P_2 = 14.0$. Apart a small set of initial conditions yielding the trivial fixed point solution $x_1 = 0$, $x_2 = 0$, the dyamics (1) evolves to a stable period-4 orbit.

3 Coupled dynamics

The evolution equation (3) is proved to be linearly stable [5]. This implies that any initial condition will eventually approach a stable periodic orbit. Nonetheless, quite complex behaviours are observed. In particular, in a wide range of values of the diffusion parameters γ_i the space-time patterns do not exhibit any apparent regularity over a significantly long transient time τ. In practice, τ is defined as the time needed for dynamics (3) to reach the periodic orbit within an accuracy $\Delta = 10^{-6}$ on each $x_i(m, t)$ (we have also verified that the results do not change significantly as soon as $\Delta \leq 10^{-4}$) . We have performed a systematic study of the different dynamical regimes occurring when γ_1, γ_2 and N are varied by measuring the average transient time $\langle \tau \rangle - \langle \bullet \rangle$ is defined over many different random initial conditions – and by identifying the final periodic orbit attained by the dynamics. N has been varied in the range $12 - 40$ (larger values impose extremely lenghty computations); the parameter space spanned by the diffusion parameters γ_1 and γ_2 has been explored in the intervals $(0.0, 0.4)$ and $(0.0, 0.3)$, respectively [5]. The results are summarized in Fig. 1. In the region generally close to the borders of the parameter space, $\langle \tau(N) \rangle$ grows at most linearly with N, with a relatively small rate. For intermediate values of γ_2 different behaviours occur when γ_1 is varied. One can identify a full range of values where $\langle \tau \rangle$ grows exponetially with N (the same kind of behaviour has been observed in [12, 13]) , separated from the region of linear regimes by a narrow boundary, where numerical data are compatible with a power-law behaviour ($\langle \tau(N) \rangle \sim N^\beta$, with $\beta > 1$) [14]. It is worth stressing that the existence of average trasients growing exponetially with N implies that dynamics (3), although linearly stable, is unpredictable in the thermodynamic limit.

For what concerns the kind of final periodic orbits we have observed that in general their number increases with N. For $N \sim 10$ and values of γ_1 and γ_2 extending

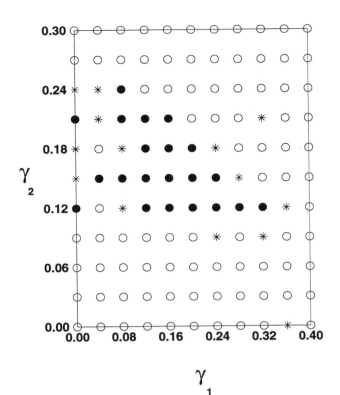

Figure 1: Different transient regimes in the (γ_1, γ_2) space: ($\bullet$) exponential, ($\circ$) linear and ($*$) intermediate – data from [5] –.

from zero up to the region which includes the exponential regime the most frequent periodic orbit corresponds to a spatially homogeneous configuration, where $x_i(m, t)$ is independet of m. We have observed that in this case the whole system evolves synchronously on the period-4 solution of the spatially uncoupled two-gene network, while the homogeneous solution $x_i(m, t) = 0$, $i = 1, 2\ \forall m, t$ is never observed.

For increasing values of N the homogeneous attractor becomes less and less frequent and the final periodic orbits of the linear and exponential regimes exhibit quite different features.

Specifically, in the linear case they are made by extended spatially regular regions evolving with different phases, separated by localized defects that move with the same constant velocity (that, in some cases, vanishes). In general these periods are larger than the one of the homogeneous periodic orbit.

The origin of such periodic orbits can be easily understood by considering that, when starting from random initial conditions, the local nature of the interaction tends to synchronize the phase of cells in some extended domain. Subsequently, these domains extend to other neighbouring cells, until a defect is created to interpolate between domains in different phases. In fact, this process acts in parallel on different zones of the lattice and it is characterized by a typical correlation length extending over ~ 10 cells. A more detailed description is reported in [5] .

4 Global and Symbolic Analysis of the Dynamics

In most biochemical experiments the measured quantities are averaged in space over a large number of cells – in some cases up to 10^8 –. This suggests to take into account in our model global properties of the dynamics by considering the evolution in time of the spatial averages of the concentrations of proteins

$$\langle x_i(t) \rangle = \frac{1}{N} \sum_{m=1}^{N} x_i(m,t) \quad , \qquad i = 1, 2 \quad (6)$$

This analysis allows one for understanding the dynamical mechanisms yielding the final periodic orbit.

section. In the linear regime, due to long range space-time correlations, the state variables are very efficiently synchronized so that $\langle x_i(t) \rangle$ tend smoothly and rapidly to the values of the final periodic orbit (see Fig. 2). In the power-law regime they evolve following a complex pattern – see Fig. 3 –. The evolution towards the final periodic orbit is not stationary and still depends on the initial condition. At variance with the linear regime, the Fourier frequency spectrum of $\langle x_i(t) \rangle$, evaluated over different time intervals, shows an ever-changing intricate structure as time increases, until it collapses to the frequency of the final periodic orbit. In the exponential regime, after a short pretransient (~ 100 time steps), every cell exhibits a sort of "stochastic" evolution close to the values of the period-4 orbit of the uncoupled system, until a sudden transition to the final periodic orbit takes place (see Fig. 2 C and D).

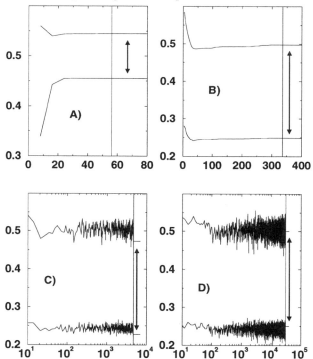

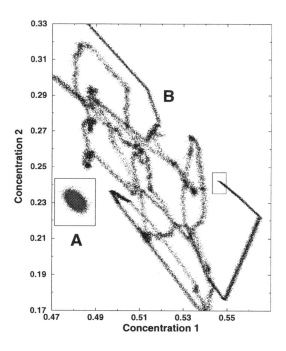

Figure 2: $\langle x_i(t) \rangle$ vs. t. Linear regime: $N = 200$, $\gamma_1 = 0.24$, $\gamma_2 = 0.27$ (A); $\gamma_1 = 0.20$, $\gamma_2 = 0.06$ (B). Exponential regime: $N = 32$, $\gamma_1 = 0.20$, $\gamma_2 = 0.15$, nonhomogeneous orbit (C), homogeneous orbit (D). Vertical lines shows the end of the transient regimes, while arrows indicate the values of $\langle x_i(t) \rangle$ on the different final orbits. Every point is averaged on the period T of the final periodic orbit.

In fact, $\langle x_i(t) \rangle$ behave quite differently in the three regions ot the parameter space singled out in the previous

Figure 3: Average concentrations in time on a lattice with $N = 10^4$. Diffusion constants are: A) exponential regime, $\gamma_1 = 0.24$ and $\gamma_2 = 0.12$ – the values taken by the variables in this case are shown in the boxed area –; B) power-law regime, $\gamma_1 = 0.24$ and $\gamma_2 = 0.09$ – Here the boxed area shows the values taken by the variables while approaching the final orbits –. Each plot contains $5 * 10^4$ points of the transient.

The probability distribution of one of the two average concentrations (see Fig. 4) is a very clean gaussian centered around a non-null mean value.

By varying N, the mean square fluctuations σ^2 of $\langle x_i(t) \rangle$ are found to satisfy the law of large numbers: $\sigma^2 \propto N^{-1}$ [6]. Moreover, the time autocorrelation functions [5] exhibit an exponetial decay. As a consequence, the synchronization mechanism yelding the asymptotic periodic dynamics appears as a stochastic process involving uncorrelated quantities evolving like random independent variables. This provides a rough explanation of the exponential increase of $\langle \tau(N) \rangle$ with N.

In a biological perspective this is quite an interesting result. In the exponential regime cells are able to evolve according to a global average dynamics around a well defined average value of $\langle x_i(t) \rangle$: a hypothetical experiment on a living cellular population could not be able to detect any cyclic behaviour in sampling space-averaged quantities, that would result undistinguishable from stochastic variables showing nice statistical properties – quite an unexpected scenario for an out of equilibrium system.

The main result of our simulations is that a fully deterministic, diffusively coupled and linearly stable dynamics can give rise to a transient (i.e. nonequilibrium) stationary regime exhibiting robust statistical properties. In

vided by the step-like function $v_i(m,t)$. Namely, each spatial configuration of the lattice at any given time can be represented through the values taken by $v_i(m,t)$ as a sequence of 0's and 1's. Notice that in the linear regime, after a transient lasting over a few time steps O(10), the sequence of 0's and 1's is exactly the same characterizing the final periodic orbit; the significance of this kind of analysis in the power-law regime is prevented by the non-stationarity properties of the dynamics.

In the exponential regime these symbolic sequences evolve in time according to a seemingly random process. The main point is to understand if the robust stationarity properties of this regime can be recovered and interpreted in terms of the symbolic dynamics. For this purpose we have considered substring of 40 elements of such sequences on a lattice with $N = 10^4$. As usual, each of these substrings can be associated to the binary representation of a number s in the interval [0,1]. The return map of s corresponding to one of these substrings is plotted in Fig.s 5 and 6 .

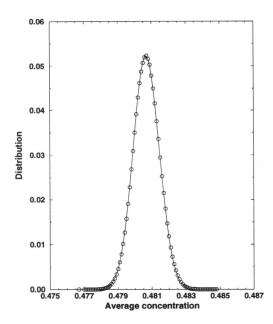

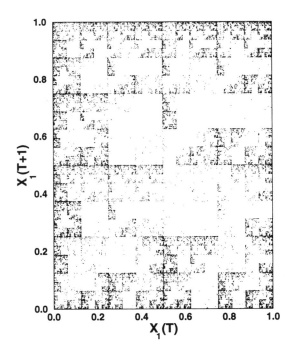

Figure 4: Distribution of $\langle x_1 \rangle$ on a lattice with $N = 5 * 10^4$. Diffusion constants are $\gamma_1 = 0.24$ and $\gamma_2 = 0.12$. Points are numerical results and straight line is the best fit with a gaussian curve with $\langle x \rangle = 0.48067$ and $\sigma^2 = \langle x^2 \rangle - \langle x \rangle^2 = 5.8211 * 10^{-7}$.

Figure 5: Symbolic dynamics of concentration x_1 of a substring of 40 cells in the $t, t+1$ map. Diffusion constants are $\gamma_1 = 0.24$ and $\gamma_2 = 0.12$.

order to characterize in more detail the basic features of the exponential regime one can observe that dynamics (3) implements a natural symbolic representation pro-

It is evident that both patterns seems to be chaotic with a typical fractal structure. This indicates that any symbolic trajectory lies on a "repeller", since we are in a transient state. In order to characterize the fractal structure of such a repeller we have considered substrings of $n = 20$ symbols. We have partioned the interval $[0, 1]$ of the corresponding number s into 2^n boxes and we have measured how many times N_k the trajectory visits the k-th box. According to a standard procedure in dynamical systems, we have sampled $\mathcal{N}$ substrings from a typical space-time symbolic pattern and we have computed the frequency $p_k = N_k/\mathcal{N}$. For large values of $\mathcal{N}$ and of n this is expected to scale with n as follows:

$$p_k \sim 2^{-n\alpha_k} \qquad (7)$$

Here α_k is the scaling exponent, that can take values in a range corresponding to the different regions of the invariant (more precisely, stationary) measure. The number of times that α_k takes a value between α and $\alpha + d\alpha$ is given by

$$N_\alpha \sim 2^{nf(\alpha)} \qquad (8)$$

The continuos function $f(\alpha)$ is the spectrum of dimensions and can be intrepreted as the Hausdorff dimension of the set of points which display the same pointwise dimension α. In other terms $f(\alpha)$ represents the distribution of the α values.

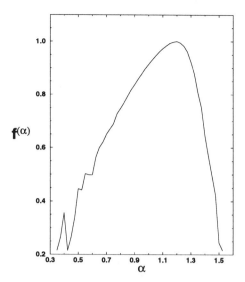

Figure 7: Function $f(\alpha)$ vs. α for protein x_2. Chain length is $N = 10^4$ cells and substring is 20 cells. Diffusion coupling is $\gamma_1 = 0.24$ and $\gamma_2 = 0.12$. Averages have been performed on $\mathcal{N} = 3,994 * 10^9$ substrings.

5   Discussion

Many of the dynamical and statistical properties characterizing the various regimes occurring in the model have been extensively discussed in the previous section. Here we want to add further comments on the relevance of the dynamical regimes of our model in a biological perspective. For instance, in the power-law regime the richness of behaviour emerging from the non-stationarity of the dynamics may provide a relevant interpretative tool in biological terms, presumably more fruitful, for its very features, than the usual dynamical modelling based on systems exhibiting some equilibrium properties. In fact, whatever time scale one considers, biological systems are never set on a true equilibrium state. In a mathematical perspective one might wonder if in the $N \to \infty$ limit the power-law region separating the linear from the exponential regimes shrinks to zero. On the other hand, in biological systems N, even if large, is always finite. Moreover, one should consider also that in the exponential regime our data imply that a lattice with $N = 200$ may give rise to $\langle \tau(N) \rangle \sim 10^{40}$. In other words, even a relatively small system, a long way below Avogadro's number, may produce extremely long trasient behaviours.

All of these results pose several technical questions related to the study of experimental data as we have discussed in previous papers [3, 4, 5, 6]. We refer to the same papers for a discussion about the general applica-

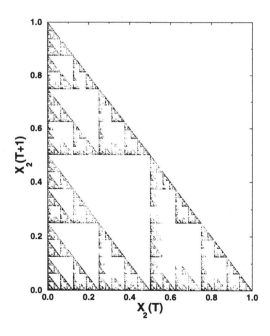

Figure 6: Symbolic dynamics of concentration x_2 of a substring of 40 cells in the $t, t+1$ map. Diffusion constants are $\gamma_1 = 0.24$ and $\gamma_2 = 0.12$.

Looking at the spectrum of dimensions $f(\alpha)$ shown in Fig. 7 one can conclude that in the exponential regime transient dynamics lives on a repeller equipped with a multifractal measure. This accounts for the robustness of this stationary regime.

bility of the model, and for a comparison of its assumptions in relation to other models based on discontinuous approaches. In this context we would like to draw attention to some theoretical aspects related to the interpretation of the dynamics observed from the point of view of development and evolution.

In both these fields there have been discussions centered around the main point of the importance of the nucleic acids – DNA in the case of development, nucleic acids in general in the study of early evolution –, in creating and maintaining biodiversity and specific biological structures, as compared to emergent dynamical phenomena or chemical instabilities. This is a long standing debate in the interpretation of development in biological systems between theoreticians and experimentalists. It can be traced back to the theoretical contributions of C. Heinselwood on multiple steady states in bacteria and of A. Turing [15] on development, and to S. Luria on the experimental side. It has resurged again recently in discussions about development [2, 16].

These two conceptual approaches have been considered in conflict as explanations of the sources for structure and complexity in living forms. One point of view stresses strongly the directing role of DNA in driving development. This view has been shown to be correct in several experimental systems. The other approach has been, instead, called into picture in order to sustain hypotheses linked to the formation of emerging structures, both in early evolution and during development. Also in this second case examples exist that can support this view – D. discoideum, cited already in the introduction, is one of the best known cases –. A similar situation exists for what concerns theories related to prebiotic evolution, but we will not discuss this aspect here.

If one considers the model described in this paper the experimental evidence and theoretical considerations seem less contradictory, expecially for what concerns development. If we set the system on parameter values that keep it inside the exponential transient regime, it can stay there, even in the presence of disturbance, for a very long time. In order to create structures inside it – inhomogeneous and ordered formation of concentration gradients – the possibility exists of a change in parameters that move the population of cells towards the boundary between the exponential and the linear regions. At this point, whatever structure is formed, it is going to be strongly dependent from the status of the system when it enters the new parameter region. Moreover, these structures are going to be sensitive to finite amplitude perturbations [5]. The only possibility of stabilization, in order to obtain a specific pattern, is going to be a strict control of the dynamics, both in terms of initial conditions and parameters. If this happens the large richness of behaviours present in the model can be exploited and an extremely large number of morpholo-

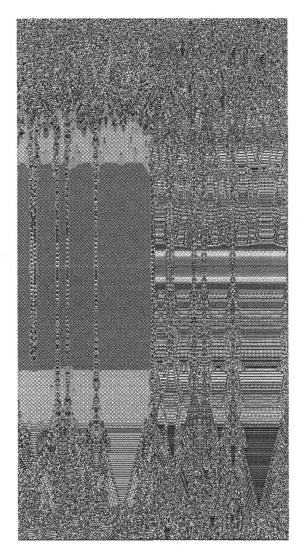

Figure 8: Example of a ring dynamics for the network studied during a continuous variation for γ_i in the (γ_1, γ_2) space. Plots represent a ring of 200 elements, color coding correspond respectively to concentrations for gene products x_1 and x_2 – left to right –, time goes from top to bottom – 1000 time steps –. The path in (γ_1, γ_2) space followed by the parameter is a circle centered around: $\gamma_1 = 0.16$ and $\gamma_2 = 0.19$; with a radius of 0.06, at the beginning the values are: $\gamma_1 = 0.16$ and $\gamma_2 = 0.13$.

gies can be obtained.

This idea is obviously speculative, but it is a nice insight into what could be an interesting possiblity to be studied more in depth. As an example, one should consider a path in the γ_1, γ_2 space, as shown in Fig. 8.

In this case we have simulated the dynamics of a lattice with $N = 200$ cells, starting from random initial conditions for the x_i's. At every time step γ_1 and γ_2 have been changed slightly in order to make a circle in the (γ_1, γ_2) space. The path was started from the region of exponential growth, driven through the intermediate boundary up to the linear region and back.

We know that signal tranduction systems could well drive an eukaryotic cell through a similar path by changing the coupling strength of cell-cell communication. In most real cases the signal transduction system making up γ_i is a complex network of interactions.

It is evident that in the middle region of the plot, while conditions for the dynamics are those for the linear growth, the system settles on a periodic orbit that would kill the resurgence of new chaotic dynamics. The presence of some small regions of instability, where defects persist, allows for the chaotic long transients to start again.

In Fig. 9, to further stress our point, we report the pattern of a simulation with parameters at the boundary between the exponential and the linear regimes. After some finite perturbation has been introduced into one point of the system – we are dealing here again with a ring dynamics as above –, we have compared the unperturbed dynamics with the perturbed one. The middle plot shows the difference between them. The richness of morphologies that can be obtained in the power-law regime is evident.

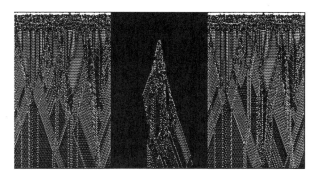

Figure 9: Example of a ring dynamics for the network studied in the presence of a perturbation in one site. Plots represent a ring of 200 elements, color coding correspond to concentration for gene product x_1, time goes from top to bottom, γ_1 and γ_2 are: 0.08, 0.12; In the plot is shown the difference in the dynamics between the unperturbed and the perturbed runs.

The dynamics in this region can be so much diversified that, without a proper control, it could not give rise

spontaneously to any repeatable dynamics. These facts, taken together, pose the question of an efficient control system able to drive such behaviour into a preferential direction.

These considerations bring us to the last point of our discussion, i.e. the relation between CML and CA. This has been discussed already several times [13]. What is particularly interesting in our case is the comparison between the λ parameter of C. Langhton [17] and the subdivision that we obtained of γ_i space. In both cases the intermediate values of the parameters between *chaotic* and *limit point* behaviour are those able to generate patterns and structures of variable complexity. The additional information that we get in our case, in respect of the simulations done with CA, is the quantitative study of the stationary behaviour of spatially averaged observables.

Two important facts emerge in this respect. While in the linear and in the exponential regimes the evolution is stable and practically independent of the initial conditions, this does not hold for the power-law regime. This fact is interesting in respect of another long debated point in biology related to development.

This model makes evident how chance can find in the inner properties of a multicellular organism a wide spectrum of dynamical possibilities, that can be exploited in order to create new life forms. At the same time, the inner instability of such dynamics could make the control system neccessary both during the transient life of the individual and during its development. Moreover, in the latter case, in order to create a specific morphology out of this dynamics, initial conditions have to be set quite carefully.

These conclusions are quite speculative at this level, but the richness of this class of models seems likely to open a new fruitful perspective into the study of the problems discussed above.

Acknowledgements

We want to thank P. Grassberger and A. Politi for the many useful remarks and suggestions. This work has been partially supported by C.N.R. grant # 95.01751.CT14 "Studio analitico della dinamica della regolazione genica e della morfogenesi", and by funds from the National Ministry of Public Health. F.B. and R.L. would like to thank I.S.I., Torino, for the kind hospitality during the workshop of the EEC Network "Complexity and Chaos", contract # ERBCHRX-CT940546, in 1995 and 1996, during which part of this research has been done.

References

[1] Kessin, R.H., Genetics of early Dictyostelium discoideum development, *Mi-*

crob. Rev. **52** (1988) 29-49.

[2] Kauffman, S.A., The origins of order: self-organization and selection in evolution, Oxford University Press, 1993, New York, NY.

[3] Bignone, F.A., Cells-Gene interactions simulation on a coupled map lattice, *Journal of Theoretical Biology* **161** (1993) 231-249.

[4] Bignone, F.A., Coupled maps lattice dynamics on a variable space for the study of development, *ACRI96, Milano*, to appear in Computer Series, Springer Verlag, Berlin.

[5] Bignone, F.A., Livi, R., Propato, M., Dynamical stability and finite amplitude perturbations in coupled genetic networks, *Physica D*, to appear.

[6] Bignone, F.A., Livi, R., Propato, M., Long transients dynamics in biochemical networks, *Proc. IPCAT97* submitted.

[7] Kapral, R., Discrete models for chemically reacting systems, *J. Math. Chem.* **6** (1991) 113-163.

[8] Kaneko, K., Overview of coupled map lattices, *CHAOS* **2** (1992) 279-282.

[9] Langton, C.G., Computation at the edge of chaos: phase transitions and emergent computations, *Physica D* **42** (1990) 12-37.

[10] Glass, L., Kauffman, S.A., The logical analysis of continuous non-linear biochemical control networks, *J. Theor. Biol.*, **39**, 103-129, 1973.

[11] Goodwin, B.C., Temporal organization in cells, Academic Press, London, 1963.

[12] Crutchfield, J.P., Kaneko, K., Are attractors relevant to turbolence ?, *Phys. Rev. Lett.* **60** (1988) 2715-2718.

[13] Politi, A., Livi, R., Oppo, G.L., Kapral, R., Unpredictable behaviour in stable systems, *Europhys. Lett.* **22** (1993) 571-576.

[14] Kaneko, K., Supertransients, spatiotemporal intermittency and stability of fully developed spatiotemporal chaos, *Phys. Lett.* **149 A** (1990) 105-112.

[15] Turing, M.A., The chemical basis of morphogenesis, *Philos. Trans. R. Soc. London B* **237** (1952) 37-72.

[16] Akam, M., Making stripes inelegantly, *Nature* **341** (1989) 282-283.

[17] Langton, C.G., Studying artificial life with cellular automata, *Physica D* **22** (1986) 120-149.

Time Out of Joint: Attractors in Asynchronous Random Boolean Networks

Inman Harvey[1] and Terry Bossomaier[2]
[1]Centre for Computational Neuroscience and Robotics
School of Cognitive and Computing Sciences
and School of Biological Sciences
University of Sussex, Brighton UK
[2]School of Information Technology
Charles Sturt University, Bathurst NSW, Australia
inmanh@cogs.susx.ac.uk tbossomaier@csu.edu.au

Abstract

Random Boolean networks (RBNs) are complex systems composed of many simple components which have been much analysed and shown to have many robust generic properties. Some synchronous versions have been influential as highly abstract models of specific biological systems, but for many biological phenomena asynchronous versions are more plausible models. Though asynchronous RBNs are indeterministic they can be shown to have generic properties that are simpler than, and very different from, the synchronous versions. These properties are demonstrated for the first time here through computer simulation and through analysis.

1 Introduction

Models of complex physical and biological phenomena inevitably ignore much of the detail of the real phenomena and simplify into systems with a small number of concepts. Complex behaviour can be generated from conceptually simple primitive elements if they interconnect and interact in large numbers. Cellular automata (CAs) and Random Boolean Networks (RBNs) are two such classes of models.

With such models any one out of an enormous range of possible initial states for the system can be specified, and the pathway through state space observed as the system is updated. An important result from the theory of RBNs is that under certain conditions the multiplicity of initial states converge onto a small number of attractors [8]. When using an RBN as a model of a genetic regulatory network this result has suggested that with (for instance) 100,000 binary switches, each assumed to be modelling a switching gene regulated by two others, despite the $2^{100,000}$ possible initial states of the system

there will be only of the order of $\sqrt{100,000} \simeq 300$ attractors, or classes of end-states. This is seen as a reasonable correspondence with the number of genes and number of cell-types in the human body, and it is suggested that the behaviour of such RBNs underlies the relationship between these numbers.

In this paper we draw attention to the fact that these RBN models rely on synchronous updating. Such updating will give a deterministic pathway from any given initial state of the system, and this fact is used in the analysis of RBNs with such tools as DDLAB [16]. We here give a first analysis of some aspects of *asynchronous* RBNs and show that their behaviour is radically different from the synchronous versions. There cannot be cyclic attractors though point attractors are still possible. If such point attractors are present then they are usually in very small numbers, typically single figures, regardless of the size of the system.

This casts doubt on the relevance of the (synchronous) RBN results to such biological phenomena as genetic regulatory networks, unless new arguments are presented as to why such networks should update synchronously. For many physical and biological phenomena the assumption of asynchrony seems more plausible.

2 Cellular Automata and Random Boolean Networks

CAs have a regular spatial array of nodes or cells, each of which can take one of a finite set of values; and an update rule whereby the subsequent value of each cell is a function of the present values of itself and its local neighbours. From an initial state of the CA where the value of each cell is specified, the same update rule is applied at each cell simultaneously to generate the subsequent state of the CA. A sequence of such iterations gives rise to a deterministic path through the CA state space, leading to a point attractor or a cyclic attractor in this space (for a CA with a finite number of nodes any path through the finite state space must eventually cycle).

A Boolean Network (BN) is a variation on a CA in which the property of neighbourhood between cells laid out in a spatial array is replaced by directed links between nodes regardless of spatial location. Each of N nodes can take the value 0 or 1, and when updated its new value depends on the current values of those other nodes (possibly including itself) which have links directed onto it. Typically each node has the same number K of links arriving at it, and the update rule is some Boolean function of these K inputs which can be specified with a lookup table of 2^K binary entries — there are a possible 2^{2^K} such lookup tables.

For a Random BN the links between nodes are specified at random, as are the Boolean functions applicable at each node; once specified these links and Boolean functions do not alter. We shall here allow at most one influencing link from one node to another. For each node there are $N!/(N-K)!$ possible ordered choices of K different links, so for the system as a whole there are $(N!/(N-K)!)^N$ possible arrangements of connectivity. It is necessary here to take account of the ordering because most Boolean functions will be affected differently by successive incoming links. Choosing for each of N nodes a possible lookup table gives a total of $(2^{2^K})^N$ possible combinations of N Boolean functions. Thus there are a very large number, say a *gazillion* G RBNs where

$$G = (\frac{2^{2^K} N!}{(N-K)!})^N$$

Many of these RBNs will be identical to each other subject only to relabelling of the nodes or links. The calculations above assume that the nodes/links can be labelled and distinguished from each other. If the different decision had been made to count two RBNs as one when renumbering nodes/links can make them identical, then the number of combinations would be smaller.

Despite this enormous range of possible RBNs for any given values of N and K a number of conclusions can be drawn about their generic behaviour. One interesting result from which many conclusions have been drawn is that as K decreases from N to 1, the generic behaviour of such networks undergoes a phase transition at $K = 2$ 'from chaos to order'. In [8] Kauffman draws the following conclusions for *synchronous* RBNs:

- $K = N$: there are about N/e cyclic attractors with associated basins of attraction — a relatively small number. The median expected length of state cycles is $0.5 \times 2^{N/2}$ — an exponentially large number. The system is unstable to perturbations, in that typically a single flip of a node perturbed from outside moves the whole system into a different basin.

- $K \geq 5$: there are still a modest number of chaotic attractors (in the sense of having very long state cycles susceptible to perturbations) for such values of K, and even perhaps for K as low as 3.

- $K = 2$: such systems exhibit very high order. The expected median state cycle length is about $\sqrt{N}$ — a surprisingly small number. The number of state cycle attractors is also about $\sqrt{N}$. These cycles are generally robust to perturbations, which usually fail to shift the system into a different attractor.

- $K = 1$: the network falls apart into separate loops with tails. This gives separate isolated subsystems, whose product gives the overall behaviour. Median lengths of state cycles are of order $\sqrt{\pi N/2}$, and the number of such attractors is exponential in N.

The particular properties of $K = 2$ has resulted in the suggestion [8] that these can be seen as models of genetic regulatory networks, as discussed in Section 1.

3 The Boolean idealisation

In [8] (pp. 182–183) RBNs are proposed by Kauffman as a means of constructing a statistical mechanics over ensembles of complex dynamical systems which contain a multitude of coupled variables. Such systems include genetic regulatory networks, the immune system and idiotype networks, autocatalytic polymer systems and neural networks.

In fitting such complex systems into a framework such as RBNs, simplifications and abstractions must be made; two of these are the Boolean idealisation and the Synchrony idealisation. The Boolean idealisation assumes that some important features of such systems can be captured if the coupled variables are allowed only the values 0 and 1, instead of a continuous range.

This can be justified in many circumstances. Variables representing physical quantities at a node of a system typically have a floor value of zero (or of saturation in a negative sense), and a maximum ceiling value of positive saturation. This gives some version of a sigmoid response curve of output as a function of inputs. When a number of such nodes with sigmoidal functions are coupled together, then feedback interactions result in values at each node being *quickly* pushed to a maximum or minimum [8, 14, 15].

Hence the Boolean idealisation has some justification and some plausibility in these circumstances; particularly where the time constants implied by *"quickly"* mean that periods spent in transient values are negligible compared to periods when values are at a maximum or minimum.

4 The Synchrony idealisation

The same cannot be said for the idealisation of such complex systems as synchronous. In [8] the only mention of synchrony made by Kauffman is (p. 189):

> The simplest class of Boolean networks is *synchronous*, which means that all elements update their activities at the same moment.

Later in [8] (p. 483) it is pointed out that in the synchronous RBNs modelled, attractors are stable to 'most but not all perturbations' in which the activities of any single 'gene' are altered (read: a single node has its value changed). This is used to suggest that:

> This length [of cycle] does not change dramatically for asynchronous models, as just noted.

However in this quotation the sense of 'asynchronous' appears to be that of occasional perturbations in an otherwise synchronous system. As will be shown below, when there is no synchrony the behaviour of RBNs is very different.

In [3] Boolean networks are used as models of genetic regulatory networks, with a discussion of the issues involved in making simplifying assumptions. Although their aim is to achieve "a biologically defensible model", Dellaert and Beer use synchronous updating, with this justification:

> Discrete time, synchronously updating networks are certainly not biologically defensible: in development the interactions between regulatory elements do not occur in a lock-step fashion. The alternative is to update all nodes asynchronously, each node having a given probability at any time to recompute its value from its inputs at that time. This introduces an element of nondeterminism however, that might render any genetic search in a space of such networks very difficult. In addition, they are less readily analyzed than their synchronous counterparts, for which there are excellent analysis tools available [the authors quote here (Wuensche 1994) [16]].

It appears that reasons for rejecting asynchrony have been a desire for simplicity, and worries about indeterminism. When in an asynchronous RBN (ARBN) nodes are updated in a random order this does indeed introduce indeterminism. We can thus no longer rely on the argument from deterministic pathways through state spaces with a finite number of points to deduce that an attractor (point or cyclic) must eventually be reached from any initial point. It is tempting to assume from this that in ARBNs attractors are non-existent or at any rate are. This assumption we shall show to be false.

With CAs there has been some discussion in recent years of asynchronous updating [1, 13], and a recognition that the behaviour of synchronous and asynchronous versions can vary widely. In [7] it was pointed out by Huberman and Glance that CA simulations by Nowak and May of Prisoner's Dilemma interactions based on synchronous updating [10] lead to conclusions which cannot be justified when more realistic assumptions of asynchrony are tested out. This led to a response at the Third European Conference on Artificial Life by Nowak and May [9]:

> There are, however, some situations where it may be more appropriate to work in continuous time, choosing individual sites at random, evaluating all the scores, and updating immediately. Huberman and Glance [7], indeed suggest that "if a computer simulation is to mimic a real world system ... it should contain procedures that ensure that the updating of the interacting entities is continuous and asynchronous". We strongly disagree with this extreme view, believing that discrete time is appropriate for many biological situations, and continuous time for others.

Whilst concurring with this last sentence, the view we take is that when modelling physical or biological systems of many interacting parts, asynchronous models should be the default version unless there are good reasons advanced for considering discrete time versions. Hopfield makes a similar point [6] in the context of Hopfield networks as models of brain processes, in contrast to Perceptron models:

> ...Perceptron modelling required synchronous neurons like a conventional digital computer. There is no evidence for such global synchrony and, given the delays of nerve signal propagation, there would be no way to use global synchrony effectively. Chiefly computational properties which can exist in spite of asynchrony have interesting implications in biology.

Adrian Thompson points out (personal communication) that the Synchrony idealisation is perhaps made most dangerous exactly when it is associated with the Boolean idealisation. It is a common technique when producing a computational simulation of a continuous analogue system to approximate the differential equations which govern the interdependent changes of variables by fine time-slicing. With this technique, all the variables are updated synchronously, and *in the absence of discontinuities* arbitrary precision can be achieved by making the time-slices fine enough. However the Boolean idealisation introduces just the kind of discontinuities that can make the Synchrony idealisation misleading — except in those cases where it can genuinely be shown

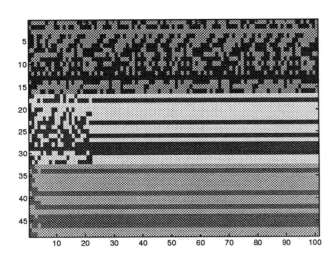

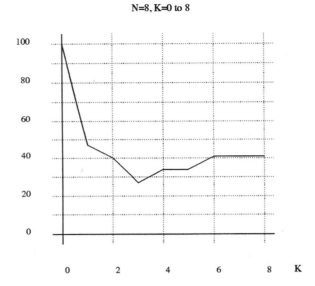

N=8, K=0 to 8

Figure 1: *Plots of the three methods of iterating an RBN (N = K = 16) with the same connectivity, Boolean functions and initial state. Rows 1–16, method 1; rows 17–32, method 2; rows 33–48, method 3. The same initial position is shown on the left, and the state is plotted after N updates in each case; in the first case this is N simultaneous updates. It can be seen that the synchronous version appears to have reached a cyclic attractor of period 38 after 10N updates, the second has converged to a point attractor by 22N updates, the last version reached a point attractor after just 4N updates. In the latter two asynchronous cases the same attractor was reached.*

Figure 2: *Here is shown the number of runs out of 100 where a point attractor is reached within 10000N updates; for N = 8 and different values of K.*

that numerous discontinuous changes should indeed be modelled as simultaneous.

Though synchronous RBNs have been used as biological models, there seems to be a surprising lack of discussion, either of an experimental or analytic nature, of ARBNs in the literature. The remainder of this paper is a first attempt at repairing this omission.

5   Experiments with ARBNs

A number of RBNs were simulated with different values for N and K. In initial experiments the same RBN was iterated from the same arbitrary initial position using three alternative methods for updating.

1. Conventional synchronous updating of all N nodes simultaneously.

2. The N nodes were updated in a randomly ordered sequence; before each sequence a new random ordering of the N nodes was made. This implies that after each sequence of N, every node had been updated exactly once.

3. For each update a node was selected at random. in practice, a sequence of N updates was drawn with replacement from the numbers 1 to N.

By projecting the evolving patterns on the monitor as the simulation ran it was seen that frequently the second and third methods arrived fairly quickly at an unchanging pattern, a point attractor in state space; an example is given in Figure 1. This was contrary to the tempting assumption that such attractors in ARBNs were rare, and made it feasible to automate a search for them. The test for reaching such a point attractor was to check every possible update in turn, and verify that none of them changed the value of any node. It was observed that in general when the third method arrived at an attractor it did so earlier than the second method, so in further experiments only the third method was used.

In this search, for all update methods a maximum of $10000N$ node updates was made from a random initial state, equivalent to 10000 synchronous updates by the first method. For reasons of speed, checks were made at intervals to see whether any of the methods had already reached a point attractor, in which case that part of the run was discontinued. A record was made for each N, K of how often out of 100 trials a point attractor was reached within this maximum timespan, with random choices of connections, Boolean functions, and initial states.

The results shown in Figures 2 and 3 were that point attractors were frequently found for all K, but with *least* probability around $K = 3$. In order to get a picture of typical sizes of basins of attraction for a point attractor, a number of ARBNs which reached a PA were iterated

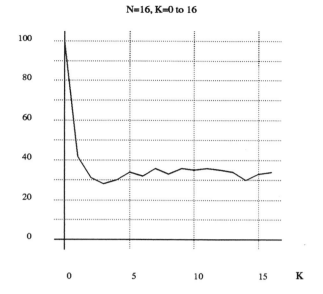

N=16, K=0 to 16

Figure 3: *As the previous figure, but for N = 16 and different values of K.*

K:	1	3	6	16
Reached PA	63	38	53	43
1 PA	42	18	27	1
2 PAs	17	11	18	10
3 PAs	1	2	5	10
4 PAs	2	2	-	1
5 PAs	-	1	-	-
6 PAs	1	-	-	-
7 PAs	-	1	-	-
1 PA or noncv	-	3	3	11
2 PAs or noncv	-	-	-	7
3 PAs or noncv	-	-	-	3

Table 1: *For $N = 16$ and each of the various values of K listed, 100 new runs were done on different ARBNs. For those ARBNS that reached a PA on the first run, a further 9 runs (making 10 in all) were done from different randomly chosen initial states. The number of different PAs reached were noted, together with those that sometimes did not reach a PA on later runs before $10000N$ iterations — nonconverged or 'noncv'.*

for a maximum of $10000N$ updates from a number of randomly chosen different initial states. Results are shown in Table 1 and indicate that for these values of N, when point attractors are found their basins of attraction generally include most of state space. It should be noticed that for $K \leq 6$ it is more common to have a single PA than 2 or more, but for the maximum value of K 2 or 3 PAs (or 1 PA plus failure to converge) are more common than having a single PA that is reliably reached.

This suggests that although for all K there are skewed distributions of PAs (with, we shall show later, a mean of one per ARBN), the nature of the skewed distribution varies with K. For low K there will be a small number of ARBNs with a large number of PAs, and a large number with either zero or one. For large K, when there are PAs there tend to be, in these examples, 2 or 3 of them.

6 Loose Attractors and Point Attractors in ARBNs

The indeterminacy of ARBNs means that attractors and basins of attraction can be somewhat different from their counterparts in deterministic systems. Point attractors, where the network settles into a state from which no possible update can shift it, are the only clear case where the counterparts can be considered identical.

When the network passes indefinitely through a subset of its possible states, this is generally neither strictly a cyclic attractor nor a strange attractor, in the deterministic sense of these words. We shall call $\mathcal{A}$ a *loose attractor* if for all possible states S of the network such that $S \in \mathcal{A}$ and for all possible successor states (through one or more updates) S' of S, $S' \in \mathcal{A}$. The *definite basin*

$B_d(\mathcal{A})$ of such a loose attractor $\mathcal{A}$ is the set of states from which *all possible paths* lead (in the long term) into states of $\mathcal{A}$. The *possible basin* $B_p(\mathcal{A})$ is the set of states from which at least *one possible path* leads into $B_d(\mathcal{A})$. Those states in $B_p(\mathcal{A})$ which do not feature in $B_d(\mathcal{A})$ can be considered as $R(\mathcal{A})$, the 'rim of potential access' to the definite basin $B_d(\mathcal{A})$. There is no comparable concept in the deterministic world of synchronous RBNs, but with ARBNs a state can lie in the possible basins of more than one attractor (point or loose attractor). This is demonstrated with a simple example in Figure 4.

In the language of digraphs, or directed graphs, a set of points such that there is a directed pathway between any two is termed a *strongly directed component* (SDC). Our definition of loose attractor corresponds to such a SDC; the trajectory through state space is ergodic wandering though all the states within it. There are well known results concerning similar components in *undirected* random graphs [4, 2]. As connectivity between points in a random graph increases, there is a threshold after which a 'giant component' emerges, which contains a majority of the points. The threshold is when there are $N/2$ edges in an undirected graph of N nodes. At a further threshold of $0.5Nlog(N)$ edges the graph becomes fully connected, and Hamiltonian cycles start to appear.

There seems to be a shortage of comparable results for digraphs. In [12, 11] experimental results for simulated random digraphs suggest that the threshold for the emergence of a giant SDC basin of attraction is when there are about $N\pi/2$ edges.

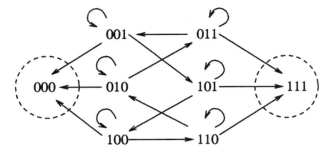

Figure 4: *The possible paths through state space of a specific ARBN with N = 3, K = 1. Each node when updated has a Boolean function which makes that node copy the value of the node to the left (with wrap-round). Each state has 3 possible paths leading from it, depending on which node is updated; the states 000 and 111 are point attractors from which all paths return to the same state. All states except these two lie in the possible basins, and rims of potential access, to both PAs.*

7 An Energy Measure for ARBNs

There are interesting analogies between ARBNs and Hopfield networks [6]. In such networks there are a number of nodes or neurons which can take values 0 or 1, which are updated asynchronously; each node has a threshold and weighted links from the other ones, and when updated changes its value according to whether the weighted sum of inputs is above or below the threshold. The universal connectivity of Hopfield networks is comparable to RBNs where $K = N$, but the threshold functions of Hopfield networks are equivalent to a subset of the Boolean functions of RBNs.

The particular properties of Hopfield networks with symmetric weights allowed the definition of an 'energy function' which successive updates tend to minimise. Hence the network converges to local minima of this function, the attractors of state space. There is no obvious comparable energy function for ARBNs.

One function for ARBNs which updates do not in general tend to minimise is 'volatility'. For any particular state of the N nodes this can be defined as the number of nodes which, if chosen for update, will change value. When the volatility is zero we have reached a point attractor, but the volatility fitness landscape is in general complex with many local non-zero minima.

Our initial technique for attempting to find point attractors was to use simulated annealing over the volatility landscape in a manner comparable to Boltzmann machines [5]. This method proved unsuccessful, until the simple strategy of just letting the ARBNs run freely was adopted, with the results reported above.

8 Analysis of ARBNs

For some fixed values of N and K, let us consider the ensemble of all possible different ARBNs of N nodes each with K links. As before, we are assuming that nodes can be distinguished, and hence two ARBNs which are identical bar different ordering of the nodes do indeed count as two different members of this ensemble. The number of members G was calculated above (Section 2) in terms of N and K.

From a randomly chosen state S of an ARBN randomly selected from this ensemble, there are N possibilities for the choice of which node is next to be updated — depending on the random order of updating. Any such choice of node i will result in all other nodes remaining the same, while node i either flips or remains the same depending on its associated Boolean function. As the Boolean functions are randomly set up, we can assume in the absence of other information a probability of 0.5 that there is no change and the system remains in state S when the ith node is updated. Given N possibilities for i, the probability that S remains unchanged whichever node is updated is $0.5^N = 1/2^N$ — the probability that S is a point attractor. We can here multiply together these N probabilities of $1/2$; provided we are considering the ensemble as a whole, these probabilities are independent.

This probability $1/2^N$ of being a point attractor holds true for all 2^N possible states of each of the G members of the ensemble. Hence if we consider all $G \times 2^N$ possible states of members of the ensemble, precisely G of them will be point attractors. Hence the expected number of point attractors in any randomly drawn member of the ensemble — any randomly chosen ARBN — is precisely one. It should be noted that this is *independent* of the values of N and K.

Of course this does not mean that each ARBN has exactly one point attractor (PA); the average of one per ARBN is distributed otherwise. If it was the case that for *each* ARBN from the ensemble, the probabilities of each state being a point attractor were independently $1/2^N$, then we would have a Poisson distribution. Using the approximation $(1 - 1/2^N)^{2^N} \simeq 1/e$ for large N, we would calculate probabilities of $0, 1, 2 \ldots n \ldots$ point attractors as respectively $1/e, 1/e, 1/e^2 \ldots 1/e^n \ldots (1/e \simeq 0.3679)$. This Poisson distribution gives the mean number of PAs as one, and the probability that an arbitrary ARBN has at least one PA as $1 - 1/e \simeq 0.6321$.

However the distribution does not follow this pattern, because for any one ARBN the probability of one state being a PA is *not independent* of the probability of another state also being so. Only within the ensemble as a whole, where we can vary Boolean functions and connecting links, can we treat the probabilities as independent for each state. Between ARBNs the distribution is in fact highly skewed. We can identify specific ARBNs

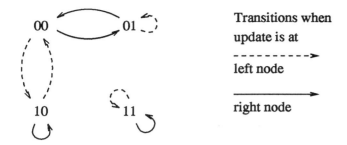

Figure 5: *State space of a particular ARBN with N = K = 2 with Boolean functions as shown in the following table. There are 4 possible states for the pair of nodes to have, and at any time there are 2 equally likely possibilities for the next node which happens to be updated.*

Node being updated	self	other	new value
First	0	0	1
	0	1	0
	1	0	0
	1	1	1
Second	0	0	1
	0	1	0
	1	0	0
	1	1	1

Table 2: *Lookup table showing the Boolean functions for the particular N = 2, K = 2 ARBN of the previous figure.*

from the ensemble which have every one of their possible 2^N states a PA; consider the case where the Boolean functions at every node specify that the node retains its value on update, regardless of the values of any linked nodes. Due to the skewed distribution, we can expect the probability that an arbitrary ARBN has at least one PA will be less than that calculated for the Poisson distribution; the experimental results confirm this.

ARBNs have loose attractors rather than the cyclic attractors of RBNs, because of the indeterminism in order of update. The loose and cyclic attractors can only be one and the same for the special case where $N = 1$ and the Boolean is such that the system cycles between values 0 and 1 at this single node. For $N = 2$ we can construct an example with a single point attractor plus a loose attractor, as seen in Figure 5. Here $N = 2$ and $K = 2$, and the update rules in Table 2 can be summarised as: for whichever node is chosen to be updated, if the *other* node has value 0 the update node should be flipped, otherwise it should stay the same.

This raises the possibility that there may in a large system be one or more point attractors, but their basins of attraction may be insignificant. So we should analyse the probability of a point, or a subset of points, being disconnected from the rest of state space.

Consider first the probability of a point in state space being a 'Garden of Eden' (GoE) state which has no possible ancestors (other than itself[1]). There are N possible neighbours in state space which each *could* (with 50% probability) have been an ancestor, if their Boolean functions had given appropriate values; we are temporarily ignoring the additional possibility that it could be its own ancestor. As with the calculations for the expected number of point attractors, we consider the ensemble of all G possible ARBNs with specific values of N and K. The probability of any one point being a GoE point for

any one member of this ensemble is $1/2^N$, the reciprocal of the number of points in state space, giving a total of G GoE points to be shared amongst the G ARBNs; the mean number of GoE states per ARBN is one, again independent of N and K.

For point attractors we argued above that the distribution is skewed, by demonstrating how individual ARBNs with a very large number of PAs can be found. Those very same ARBNs specified above also have every point in state space a GoE state with no possible (different) ancestor. So once again it appears that the distribution is highly skewed. However, outside these abnormal special cases, it would appear that the probability that a point attractor should also happen to be a Garden of Eden point is vanishingly small for large N; so the example shown for $N = 2$ should be considered an aberration.

9 Special cases: K=0, 1

For very small values of K we can analyse the evolution of an ARBN. Setting $K = 0$ implies that the Boolean function at each node depends on no other values, and gives a fixed result (either 0 or 1). Hence from any initial values for the nodes, after each has been updated once they will all have come to rest at their final values, a point attractor in state space; there is always exactly one such attractor.

When $K = 1$ the update rule at each node depends on the value of one other node, and on the Boolean function used. There are 4 possible Boolean functions of one input I, which can be classified as output = 0, 1, I (copy) and Ĩ (differ). In the first two cases the value of I is irrelevant. So we can expect some (on average 50%) of the nodes to be 'volatile' or subject to influence from exactly one other node; and the other nodes will have settled on their final fixed value by the time they have been updated once.

If a volatile node is influenced by another node which itself is (or becomes) frozen in value, this in turn freezes this volatile node. However if there is a Hamiltonian directed cycle of volatile nodes each influencing the next,

---

[1]There is a further category of Garden of Eden states which do not have themself as a possible ancestor; this category excludes point attractors.

then such a cycle has the potential to stay volatile for-ever. To check whether such a cycle keeps altering nodes indefinitely one should classify each Boolean function in the chain into 'copy' or 'differ'. If the number of 'differs' in the chain is odd the cycle can never terminate, and the system will not reach a point attractor; indeed there will not be a point attractor for it to reach.

If the number of 'differs' is even then that particular cycle will settle down into one of two possible fixed point attractors, depending on the initial state and the order of updating. For example, as shown in Figure 4 a cycle of 3 nodes each influencing the next with a 'copy' function will remain for ever unchanged if all 3 nodes start off with value 0, or all 3 with value 1; from any other initial values the conclusion will depend on the (random) order of updating. If all such cycles are of this 'even' form (or there are no such cycles) then the system will settle down into a point attractor *from any initial state*; otherwise it will never settle down.

Thus for $K = 1$ we expect that for those ARBNs which have point attractors, their basins of attraction include every possible initial point This is consistent with the experimental results shown in Table 1.

10 Increasing K: 2, 3 . . .

If we increase K to 2 or 3, then it is still true that ARBNS have an expected one point attractor each (with a skewed distribution), but in such cases there is now a real chance that many initial positions fall outside their basin of attraction. The example shown in Figure 5 shows one such case for $K = 2$ and $N = 2$; though there is a point at-tractor, from 75% of possible initial states it is never reached.

The experimental evidence (Table 1) indicates that $K = 3$ gives the smallest chance of arriving at a point attractor. The number of cases where the system some-times failed to converge to a PA though one was known to exist was 3 out of 38. This still leaves open the possi-bility that some of the 62 runs which were aborted after failing to reach a PA on the first run did in fact contain PAs that were not found. As K gets larger it becomes in-creasingly unlikely that a point attractor (and its basin of attraction) should remain isolated from the rest of state space. Although analytical calculations have not been made, this should be expected from consideration of the increase in connectivity of a digraph as the number of edges per node increases.

11 Summarising ARBNs

We are now in a position to draw up a list of properties of ARBNs which can be compared with that given for synchronous RBNs in Section 2.

- $K = N$: the expected number of point attractors for any ARBN is one, though with a skewed dis-

tribution. The limited experimental evidence sug-gests that when a PA exists, there are frequently 2 or 3 of them. When there are such attractors then their basin of attraction generally covers most of state space. When there is no such attractor the system will continue changing ergodically, in a loose attrac-tor.

- $K \geq 5$: the expected number of attractors is the same as when $K = N$; it seems to be more common to have just one or two PAs.

- $K = 3, 2$: the number of attractors still obeys the same law. The skewed distribution includes a small number of ARBNs which have a large number of PAs.

- $K = 1$: the numbers of attractors obeys the same law, but now any such attractors have basins of attraction covering all of state space — there is no chance of 'missing' an attractor if one exists.

- $K = 0$: in this limiting case there is exactly one attractor which is reached from all initial states.

The two lists have such widely different characteris-tics that there is no sense in which the behaviour of syn-chronous RBNs gives any clue towards the behaviour of ARBNs.

12 Conclusions

Synchronous RBNs have been much analysed, and their properties have been used as models of biological phe-nomena such as genetic regulatory networks. They are models at a high level of abstraction, where significant simplifying idealisations have been made. The assump-tion has been made that despite such idealisations the generic properties of these complex systems is largely ro-bust to those properties that have been ignored.

The Boolean idealisation is one such simplification, and arguments have been presented to justify this as plausible for many classes of biological systems. The Synchrony idealisation is a common practical one to make when approximating continuous systems with fine time-slicing — but this in general falls down when deal-ing with discontinuous systems such as those produced through the Boolean idealisation. It follows that results from synchronous RBNs may only be applicable to bio-logical systems where there are special reasons to believe that some synchronising mechanism exists.

One might assume that ARBNs have similar behaviour to the synchronous version — the main thrust of this pa-per is that on the present evidence this would be very mistaken. The non-deterministic nature of ARBNs has prevented the application of methods used to analyse the synchronous version, and it seems some have been deterred from using ARBNs because of their assumed in-tractability. However it turned out to be remarkably easy to obtain these very preliminary results for the generic behaviour of ARBNs, both through computer simulations and through analysis.

The indeterminism means that there are no cyclic attractors, only point or loose attractors; the expected number of point attractors in an ARBN is one, independent of the value of K. When such point attractors exist, their basins generally drain most of state space — all of state space in the case of $K = 1$. These characteristics of point attractors differs enormously from those of synchronous RBNs, and there is as yet no evidence of any relationship between loose attractors in ARBNs and cyclic attractors in synchronous RBNs.

In the absence of justifications for the assumption of synchrony, these results cast doubt on the value of synchronous RBNs as models for many biological phenomena, including genetic regulatory networks.

Acknowledgments

This work has been supported with funding from the authors' Universities, and in particular IH acknowledges funding from CSU for a Visiting Research Fellowship to Bathurst where this work was done.

References

[1] A. I. Adamatsky. Complexity of identifying asynchronous nonstationary cellular automata. *Journal of Computer and Systems Science International*, 31(3):127–130, 1993.

[2] B. Bollobas. *Random Graphs*. Academic Press, London, 1985.

[3] F. Dellaert and R. Beer. Toward an evolvable model of development for autonomous agent synthesis. In P. Maes and R. Brooks, editors, *Proceedings of Alife 4*, pages 246–257, Cambridge MA, 1994. MIT Press.

[4] P. Erdos and A. Renyi. *On the Evolution of Random Graphs*. Institute of Mathematics, Hungarian Academy of Sciences, 1960.

[5] G. E. Hinton and T. J. Sejnowski. Learning and relearning in Boltzmann machines. In D. E. Rumelhart and J.L. McClelland, editors, *Parallel Distributed Processing, Explorations in the Microstructure of Cognition, Vol. 1*, pages 282–317. MIT Press, 1986.

[6] J. J. Hopfield. Neural networks and physical systems with emergent collective computational abilities. *Proceedings of the National Academy of Sciences*, 79:2554–2558, 1982.

[7] B. A. Huberman and N. S. Glance. Evolutionary games and computer simulations. *Proc. of the National Academy of Sciences*, 90(16):7716–7718, 1993.

[8] S. A. Kauffman. *The Origins of Order*. Oxford University Press, 1993.

[9] R. M. May, S. Bonhoeffer, and M. A. Nowak. Spatial games and evolution of cooperation. In F. Morán, A. Moreno, J. J. Merelo, and P. Chacón, editors, *Advances in Artificial Life*, pages 749–759, 1995.

[10] M. A. Nowak and R. M. May. Evolutionary games and spatial chaos. *Nature*, 359:826–829, 1992.

[11] D. Seeley. Network evolution and the emergence of structure. In T. Bossomaier and D. Green, editors, *Complex Systems*. Cambridge University Press, 1997.

[12] D. Seeley and S. Ronald. The emergence of connectivity and fractal time in the evolution of random digraphs. In T. Bossomaier and D. Green, editors, *Complex Systems: from Biology to Computation*. IOS Press, Amsterdam, 1992.

[13] M. Sipper, M. Tomassini, and M.S. Capcarrere. Evolving asynchronous and scalable non-uniform cellular automata. In *Proc. of Intl. Conf. on Artificial Neural Networks and Genetic Algorithms (ICANNGA97)*. Springer-Verlag, 1997.

[14] D. Thieffry and R. Thomas. Logical synthesis of regulatory models. In *Self-Organization and Life: From Simple Rules to Global Complexity, European Conference on Artificial Life (ECAL-93)*. Brussels, Belgium, 1993.

[15] R. Thomas. Boolean formalisation of genetic control circuits. *Journal of Theoretical Biology*, 42:563–585, 1973.

[16] A. Wuensche. The ghost in the machine: Basins of attraction of random boolean networks. In C. G. Langton, editor, *Artificial Life III*, pages 465–501, Reading, MA, 1994. Addison-Wesley.

Insights Into Evolution of RNA-Structures

Stephan Kopp[a], Christian M. Reidys[b], Peter Schuster[a]

[a]Inst. f. Theoretical Chemistry, University of Vienna
Währingerstr. 17, A-1090 Vienna, Austria

[b]Los Alamos National Laboratory
TSA-DO/SA, Los Alamos, NM 87545, USA

E-Mail: robo@tbi.univie.ac.at

Abstract

A mathematical model for the relation of ribonucleic acid (RNA) sequences and coarse grained three dimensional structures of these RNA molecules is used to investigate optimization processes as they occur in RNA evolution. The basic features of the theory are that sequences must be compatible with the structure. This yields connected and dense networks in the sequence space. Computational results of the sequence to structure mappings by Monte Carlo methods demonstrate that the tertiary structures cannot have intramolecular bonds of arbitrary number if this molecule shall have a significance during the optimization process.

1 Introduction

Molecules of RNA-sequences hold within themselves an enormous variety of chemical facilities. Where the sequence is destined to contain information about several characteristics of the molecule, the spatial conformation of these molecules is essential for their actual enzymatic activities. Due to these properties, RNA might have been one of the first molecules related to life [2]. To elucidate the relation between sequence and conformation we use a simplified model to represent 3D-RNA structures.

In a coarse grained approximation the structure can be considered as a random contact graph. The nucleotides are represented by the vertices of this graph, chemical bonds between two nucleotides are represented by edges. These structures can also be considered as contact matrices, meaning that the matrix element c_{ij} is unequal to zero if the nucleotides i and j have a chemical bond. To study 3D-structure optimization contact matrices are generated by Monte Carlo Methods instead of using data obtained from crystallography or NMR spectra. Nevertheless they are subjected to certain constraints, such as minimum sizes of loops and stacks.

We focus on statistical properties of the sequence to structure relation and therefore we use random mapping rather than trying to predict RNA-structures by means of energy calculation. Random mapping means that RNA sequences are randomly mapped to one matrix (i.e. one structure) if they fulfill certain compatibility criteria (see def. 2.1 and def. 2.4). These criteria contain Watson-Crick and wobble base-pairs for instance, but also include 3D-contacts.

Inspired by investigations of secondary structure landscapes by Fontana et al. [1] and Reidys et al. [8] we study generic properties of the mapping such as the number of sequences mapped to one structure i.e., the size of the preimage. We further examine the organization of the preimages: how many components is a preimage composed of, does a threshold value for the number of tertiary contacts exist, before the nets decompose in many small ones? As demonstrated for RNA secondary structures, the mapping yields the same generic properties as folding algorithms do (see [5]).

2 Theory

An RNA sequence is regarded as a molecule consisting of n residues which are taken from a finite set $\mathcal{A}$. This *alphabet* $\mathcal{A}$ has α elements. Therefore a sequence can be interpreted as a vertex $V = \{P_1, \ldots, P_n\} \in \mathcal{Q}_\alpha^n$, the generalized hypercube. A secondary structure with a rule for the base pairs can be defined as:

Definition 2.1
A secondary structure s with m base pairs is a 1-regular random graph on $2m < n$ residues $\{P_{i_1}, \ldots, P_{i_{2m}}\}$. The base pairs are described by a symmetric relation $\mathcal{R}_* \subset \mathcal{A} \times \mathcal{A}$ for all m edges.

This means, the origin o and the terminus t of an edge (= base pair) fulfill the relation $o \, \mathcal{R}_* \, t$. This relation is motivated by the standard base pairs such as Watson-Crick or wobble base pairs. A sequence is called to be *compatible* with a structure, if the $2m$ residues of matter fulfill this relation. The *set of compatibles* $\mathcal{C}[s]$ is the set

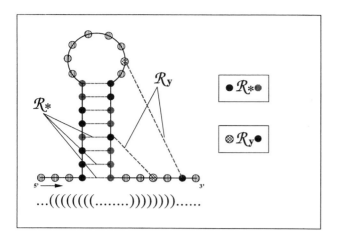

Figure 1: Schematic presentation of an RNA structure. The contacts setting up the secondary structure are marked by dotted lines. The residues involved in these contacts must be in the symmetrical relation $\mathcal{R}_*$. Residues forming tertiary contacts (dashed lines) must fulfill the relation $\mathcal{R}_y$ (also symmetrical). In general the circles in this figure do not represent a specific type of nucleic acid. The different shapes and textures indicate that the position fulfills the relations as shown or can be chosen arbitrarily, as in the unpaired positions. The presented sequence is only one of $\alpha^{14} \times \rho_*^7 \times \rho_y$ possible sequences. The secondary structure is also presented in the bracket-dot notation. Since RNA molecules have chemically different ends the bracket-dot notation is to be read from left to right (which is different from the structure starting at the right hand side).

of all sequences, where the appropriate residues fulfill $\mathcal{R}_*$. The number of elements in $\mathcal{R}_*$ is denoted by ρ_*. Figure 1 illustrates this idea: The circles may be substituted by one of the nucleotides in the alphabet $\mathcal{A}$. Those being involved in a base pair have to fulfill the relation $\mathcal{R}_*$ or $\mathcal{R}_y$, respectively, i.e., only one position can be chosen arbitrarily.

To simulate an algorithm which folds RNA sequences into secondary structures, which makes use of thermodynamical parameters, we map the sequences $\in \mathcal{C}[s]$ by random. Nevertheless one sequence is mapped to exactly one structure. These sequence to structure mapping yields so called *neutral nets* for every structure. If the mapping is done with a random parameter $p > p^*$ ($p^* = 1 - 1/\sqrt[\alpha-1]{\alpha}$), the neutral nets are connected and dense in $\mathcal{C}[s]$.

Definition 2.2

Any two sequneces v_i and v_j of one net are connected if sequence i can be reached from any other sequence j by appropriate mutations and every sequence along this way also belongs to the net i.e., there exists a path. All the sequences which are connected, belong to the same component. A net can constist of more than one component.

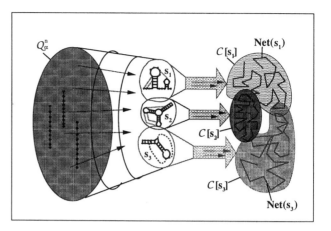

Figure 2: Draft of the sequence to structure mapping. The sequences (plotted as chains) are vertices in the generalized hypercube $\mathcal{Q}_\alpha^n$. The structures s_i filter out those sequences which belong to the associated set of compatible sequences $\mathcal{C}[s_i]$ (large arrows). From every $\mathcal{C}[s]$ sequences are chosen randomly yielding the neutral net (small arrows). Note that for two different structures the sets $\mathcal{C}[s_i]$ and $\mathcal{C}[s_j]$ have a nonempty intersection. The neutral nets are represented by the lines within the sets. The doted lines in the structure represent tertiary interactions.

Definition 2.3

A net of one structure is dense in $\mathcal{C}[s]$ for every sequence $v \in \mathcal{C}[s]$ not belonging to the neutral net there exists a sequence v' in the neutral net so that v can be transformed into v' by one mutation (see [8]).

See fig. 2 for an illustration of the mapping procedure and the idea of neutral nets.

It was proven mathematically by Reidys [7] and shown by means of computer simulations, that a neutral net has a *giant component* i.e., the component which contains at least 2/3 of the sequences of the net. Sorting the components according to their size we obtain the sequence of components (SoC). Comparison of data obtained from folding and random mapping shows that main features such as preimage distribution and sequence of components are nearly identical. These results encourage us to investigate optimization processes of structures.

Given two structures s_i and s_j it holds that the intersection $\mathcal{C}[s_i] \cap \mathcal{C}[s_j] \neq \emptyset$. This fact in combination with the characteristic of a mapping that a sequence can be mapped to one structure only, has the result that the number of sequences belonging to the neutral net of one structure i usually is smaller than the size the according $\mathcal{C}[s_i]$. This yields a distribution of the sizes which can be described by Zipf's law i.e., $f(x) = a(b + x)^{-c}$. The structures can be grouped into common structures and rare structures. A convenient criterion for being common is: size of net$> \alpha^n/$(number structures). Under a

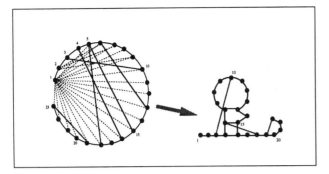

Figure 3: Construction of random structures for a sequence of length $n = 23$. Left part: For the construction of a random structure the circle representation is an appropriate presentation [6]. The 3 secondary structure contacts are drawn by the black lines. Dashed lines show all possible edges for residues #1 and some for #2. With respect to transparency not all possible $\binom{23}{2} - 3$ connections are shown. Dashed edges are chosen with probability c_2/n. The accepted ones are printed as solid gray lines. Right part: the resulting structure is shown as familiar plot, where the tertiary interactions are drawn schematically. The real geometry cannot be pictured here.

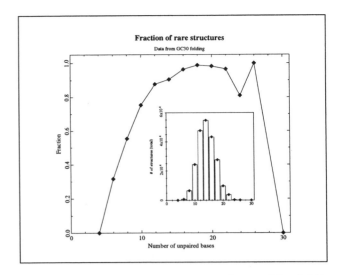

Figure 4: The secondary structures obtained by folding all sequences in $\mathcal{Q}_{GC}^{30}$ with an algorithm, calculating the minimum free energy structure. The structures are classified by the number of unpaired residues. For each class of structures with the same number of unpaired bases the fraction of those being rare is plotted. The inner graph shows the total number of structures per class.

mapping above the threshold p^* the neutral nets of two common structures are both dense in the intersection. This allows optimization. Walking on the neutral net of a common structure one finds almost all other common structures, if the n point mutations of the actual sequence are mapped.

We now investigate mapping from sequence space to tertiary structures. According to the model proposed in [9] a tertiary structure is a coarse grained representation of a structure. The tertiary interactions are considered as edges on some vertices of the sequence, which are not subjected to geometrical constraints. We can define this as follows:

Definition 2.4

A tertiary structure is considered as a random contact graph i.e., the secondary structure as defined in 2.1 plus a random graph G_p on all the n vertices. The base pairs in this graph are described by the symmetric relation $\mathcal{R}_y$, which analogously to $\mathcal{R}_*$ determines the type of the pair.

The graph G_p is obtained by assigning each of the remaining $\binom{n}{2} - m$ 'free edges' with probability $p = c_2/n$ to G_p (see fig. 3). The number of elements in $\mathcal{R}_y$ is denoted by ρ_y. Using an open circle as representation of the sequence one can easily draw all allowed edges. For the contacts being involved in the secondary structure, the edges must not cross. This restriction is nullified for contacts of the tertiary type.

From biology one obtains the the following sets, serving as alphabet and pairing relation: $\mathcal{A} = \{A, C, G, U\}$,

and $\mathcal{R}_* = \{(AU), (CG), (GC), (GU), (UA), (UG)\}$ (i.e., $\alpha = 4\, \rho_* = 6$). The relation $\mathcal{R}_y$ is arbitrary since rules for tertiary interactions are not well known.

3 Computational results and Conclusion

In our simulation we restrict the length of the sequences to 30, the alphabet to $\mathcal{A} = \{C, G\}$ yielding the relation $\mathcal{R}_* = \{(CG), (GC)\}$ for the base pairs in the secondary structure. We choose the tertiary relation to be binary too, i.e. $\mathcal{R}_y = \mathcal{R}_*$. Results from complete folding of the $\mathcal{Q}_{GC}^{30}$ reveals, that most of the common secondary structures consist of not more than 50 % unpaired bases (see fig. 4). The folding was done with the RNAfold program [4]. The average number of sequences folding into one structure is determined by $\alpha^n/(\#\text{secondary structures}) = 2^{30}/218\,820 \sim 4907$. Structures being realized by less than this number are called rare structure. The plot in fig. 4 shows that more than 95 % of the structures with 16 to 26 unpaired bases are rare. Structures with 24 and 26 unpaired bases are even absolutely of no importance.

Since we need an *a priory* set of structures to perform the mapping process, we create an certain number of random secondary structures. From the folding experiment we see, that 20000 structures are sufficient to cover all common ones. According to the results from the minimum free energy folding experiment, we create the random secondary structures with the constraint that they must have not more than 16 unpaired residues. This is also rational since structures having too many unpaired residues would cover a part of the sequence space $\mathcal{Q}_{GC}^{30}$, whereas structures with more than 50 % base pairs are energetically more stabel and favorized. i Therefore the secondary structures used in our experiments consist of at most 16 unpaired residues.

The mapping itself is done in a hierarchical way. At first, the mapping from $\mathcal{Q}_{GC}^{30}$ into secondary structures is performed: We assign numbers arbitrarily to the structures. We than take the structure with number 1 to perform the random mapping. From all sequences $\in \mathcal{C}[s_1]$ we select with random parameter p those which shall belong to the neutral net. Next we proceed with structure $i = 2, 3 \ldots$, doing the same. Here we have to check if a sequence is not yet mapped to a structure $j < i$.

We now investigate the nets. Evaluating the sizes yields a ranking of the structures which is in general different from the initial numbering. Of interest are the sequence of components. Table 1 shows the result for the 20 most common structures (see appendix). The nets all consist of only one component which is in good agreement with the results from complete folding experiments [3]. The nets start to decay in many small components when the random parameter p becomes less than 0.5 [5]. We now focus on a parameter which provides large nets without decomposing to investigate the preimages of a mapping into tertiary structures.

For the 20 most common structures of the previous mapping into secondary structures we superimpose 3d contacts with different probability parameters c_2 (see fig. 3). Any sequences belonging to the net of the secondary structure s_i are mapped to the according tertiary structure, if the sequence is compatible with this 3d-structure i.e., there is no random mapping from the neutral nets into these 3d-structures. The results of the sequence of components decomposition (SoC) are shown in table 2-6. The number of tertiary contacts (#3d) varies due to the random process of generating the structures.

Although the neutral nets become smaller, when the parameter for random contacts c_2 increases, these nets still consist of only one component. Clearly, when the net sizes become to small, the neutral nets of the tertiary structures of this type are not able to percolate through sequence space. We see, that the average number of neutral sequences is below the number of a common structure (in our example 51540 sequences/structure), as soon as c_2 exceeds a value of 0.40. We conclude that a graph may not have an arbitrary number of 3d contacts. Otherwise the concept of *neutral mutation* cannot be executed successfully.

References

[1] Walter Fontana, Wolfgang Schnabl, and Peter Schuster. Physical aspects of evolutionary optimization and adaption. *Physical Review A*, 40(6):3301–3321, 1989.

[2] Walter Gilbert. The RNA world. *Nature*, 319:618, 1986.

[3] Walter Gruener, Robert Giegerich, Dirk Strothmann, Christian Reidys, Jacqueline Weber, Ivo L. Hofacker, Peter F. Stadler, and Peter Schuster. Analysis of RNA Sequence Structure Maps by Exhaustive Enumeration. II. Structures of Neutral Networks and Shape Space Covering. *Monath. Chem.*, 127:375–389, 1996.

[4] Ivo L. Hofacker, Walter Fontana, Peter F. Stadler, L.Sebastian Bonhoeffer, Manfred Tacker, and Peter Schuster. Fast Folding and Comparison of RNA Secondary Structures (the Vienna RNA Package). *Monatshefte f. Chemie*, 125(2):167–188, 1994.

[5] Stephan Kopp, Christian Reidys, and Peter Schuster. Exploration of Artificial Landscapes Based on Random Graphs. In F. Schweitzer, editor, *Self-Organisation of Complex Structures: From Individual to Collective Dynamics*, London, U.K., 1997. Gordon and Breach Science Publ.

[6] Ruth Nussinov, George Piecznik, Jerrold R. Griggs, and Daniel J. Kleitmann. Algorithms for loop matching. *SIAM J. Appl. Math.*, 35(1):68–82, 1978.

[7] Christian Reidys. *Neutral Networks of RNA Secondary Structures*. PhD thesis, Friedrich Schiller Universtät Jena, 1995.

[8] Christian Reidys, Perter F. Stadler, and Peter Schuster. Generic Properties of Combinatory Maps and Neutral Networks of RNA Secondary Structures. *Bull. Math. Biol.*, 1996. acceptet.

[9] Christian M. Reidys. Mapping in random structures. *SIAM J. Disc. Math.*, 1996. submitted.

A Sequence of Components

Rank	|Net|	Structure	SoC
1	2804188	(((((((...))...))..((......))))	2804188
2	2697855	...((((((.((...))....))).)).))	2697855
3	2682809	.((..((.(((......))..)))).)).	2682809
4	2648435	..(((.((.......))(((...)))))).	2648435
5	2647515	((((((.((.....))...)))).))....	2647515
6	2633441	((((...((.((.))))...))))....	2633441
7	2629265	...((..((((((....)))).)).)).)...	2629265
8	2603470	.((((.....))((.((..))...)))).	2603470
9	2588026	.((...((((...)).)))((......))	2588026
10	2587464	.((.((...((...)).)))..((...))	2587464
11	2570058	((((...((....))))))((.....))..	2570058
12	2549611	((((.((.....))..))((...))..))	2549611
13	2540477	((.((....))((...((...))))..)).	2540477
14	2528530	((.((..((.((......)).)).)))).	2528530
15	2517178	....((.(((((...))...))...))))	2517178
16	2516578	((((.((..((...))..)).)).))..	2516578
17	2478934	((.(((((...)))).)).....((.....))	2478934
18	2470577	.(((.....)))(((.((....))..)))	2470577
19	2461398	..((.(((...)))(((...)))).))....	2461398
20	2449467	.((.(((((........((....))))))))	2449467

Table 1: The 20 biggest nets of a random mapping of the $\mathcal{Q}_{GC}^{30}$ into secondary structures. The random parameter is $p = 0.8$. The nets do not decompose into many disjunct components.

Rank	|Net|	Structure	#3d	SoC
1	1410315	(((((((...))...))..((......))))	1	1410315
2	1349159	...((((((.((...))....))).)).))	1	1349159
3	2682809	.((..((.(((......))..)))).)).	0	2682809
4	653865	..(((.((.......))(((...)))))).	2	653865
5	1303819	((((((.((.....))...)))).))....	1	1303819
6	1316992	((((...((.((.))))...))))....	1	1316992
7	1312075	...((..((((((....)))).)).)).)...	1	1312075
8	1264635	.((((.....))((.((...))...)))).	1	1264635
9	651103	.((...((((...)).)))((......))	2	651103
10	666468	.((.((...((...)).)))..((...))	2	666468
11	1285744	((((...((....))))))((.....))..	1	1285744
12	2549611	((((.((.....))..))((...))..))	0	2549611
13	2540477	((.((....))((...((...))))..)).	0	2540477
14	2528530	((.((..((.((......)).)).)))).	0	2528530
15	2517178	....((.(((((...))...))...))))	0	2517178
16	1261573	((((.((..((...))..)).)).))..	1	1261573
17	1241538	((.(((((...)))).)).....((.....))	1	1241538
18	1232087	.(((.....)))(((.((....))..)))	1	1232087
19	1167323	..((.(((...)))(((...)))).))....	1	1167323
20	2449467	.((.(((((........((....))))))))	0	2449467

Table 2: The nets for tertiary parameter $c_2 = 0.05$. The number of tertiary contacts is small (0-2).

Rank	|Net|	Structure	#3d	SoC
1	85299	(((((((...))...))..((......))))	5	85299
2	659139	...((((((.((...))......)).)).))	2	659139
3	1340820	.((..((.(((.(......)).))))).)).	1	1340820
4	649433	..(((.((.......))(((...)))))).	2	649433
5	1325663	((((((.((.....))...)))).))....	1	1325663
6	658335	((((...((.((...))))...))))....	2	658335
7	1316474	...((..((((((....)))).)).))....	1	1316474
8	2603470	.(((((.....))((.((...))...)))).	0	2603470
9	644047	.((...(((...))..))))((......))	2	644047
10	1319868	.((.((...((...)).))))..((...))	1	1319868
11	641396	((((...((....))))))((.....))..	2	641396
12	1247267	((((.((......))..))((...))..))	1	1247267
13	1270217	((.((....))((...((...))))..)).	1	1270217
14	2528530	((.((...((.((......)).)).)))).	0	2528530
15	627723	....((.(((((((...))...))..))))	2	627723
16	629039	((((.((...((...))..)).))..).)..	2	629039
17	618416	((.(((((...)))).))....((.....))	2	618416
18	1216503	.(((......)))(((.((.....))..)))	1	1216503
19	2461398	..((.(((...)))(((...)))).))....	0	2461398
20	2449467	.((.((((.......((....)))))))))	0	2449467

Table 3: Sequence of components for tertiary structures created with parameter $c_2 = 0.15$.

Rank	|Net|	Structure	#3d	SoC	
1	175115	(((((((...))...))..((......))))	4	175115	
2	2697855	...((((((.((...)).....)).)).))	0	2697855	
3	670665	.((..((.(((((......))..))))).)).	2	670665	
4	162672	..(((.((.......))(((...)))))).	4	162672	
5	661908	((((((.((.....))...)))).))....	2	661908	
6	637952	((((...((.((...))))...))))....	2	637952	
7	0	...((.(((((((....)))).)).))....	2	0	
8	651944	.((((.....))((.((...))...)))).	2	651944	
9	1295842	.((...(((((...)).))))((......))	1	1295842	
10	40640	.((.((...((...)).)))).. ((...))	6	39020,	1620
11	148318	((((...((....))))))((.....))..	4	148318	
12	635907	((((.((......))..))((...))..))	2	635907	
13	312888	((.((....))((...((...))))..)).	3	312888	
14	2528530	((.((...((.((......)).)).)))).	0	2528530	
15	304161	....((.(((((((...))...))..))))	3	304161	

Table 4: Sequence of components for tertiary structures created with parameter $c_2 = 0.25$. Only one net decomposes into 2 subnets. Another has no sequence being compatible with the 3d-struture.

Rank	|Net|	Structure	#3d	SoC
1	43623	(((((.(...))...)).((......))))	6	43623
2	150488	...((((((.((...)).....)).)).))	4	150488
3	331455	.((..((.(((((......)).)))).)).	3	331455
5	331964	((((((.((.....))...)))).))...	3	331964
6	88249	((((...((.((...))))...))))....	5	88249
7	658725	...((..(((((((....)))).)).)).)...	2	658725
8	656408	.((((.....))((.((...))...)))).	2	656408
9	335758	.((...(((((...)).))))((......))	3	335758
10	153614	.((.((...((...)).)))).((...))	4	153614
11	163433	((((...((....))))))((.....))..	4	163433
12	20332	((((.((......))..))((...))..))	7	20332
13	312818	((.((....))((...((...)))).)).	3	312818
15	23693	....((.(((((((...))...))...)))))	7	23693
16	170607	(((((.((...((...))..)).)).))..	4	170607
17	138550	((.((((...)))).)))....((.....))	4	138550
18	312947	.(((......)))(((.((....))..)))	3	312947
19	77346	..((.(((...)))((...))).))....	5	77346
20	18385	.((.((((........((....))))))))	7	18385

Table 5: Sequence of components for tertiary structures created with parameter $c_2 = 0.40$

Rank	|Net|	Structure	#3d	SoC
1	20778	(((((((...))...))..((......))))	7	20778
2	332625	...((((((.((...)).....)).)).))	3	332625
3	329703	.((..((.(((((......)).)))).)).	3	329703
4	166108	..(((.((......))(((...)))))).	4	166108
5	35250	((((((.((.....))...)))).))...	6	35250
6	20189	((((...((.((...))))...))))....	7	20189
7	152094	...((..(((((((....)))).)).)).)...	5	152094
8	40201	.((((.....))((.((...))...)))).	6	40201
9	2211	.((...(((((...)).))))((......))	10	2211
10	40129	.((.((...((...)).)))).((...))	6	40129
11	0	((((...((....))))))((.....))..	7	0
12	79929	((((.((......))..))((...))..))	5	79929
13	10481	((.((....))((...((...)))).)).	8	10481
14	40215	((.((...((.((......)).)).)))).	6	40215
15	76188	....((.(((((((...))...))...)))))	5	76188
16	1211	((((.((...((...))..)).)).))..	11	1211
17	19246	((.((((...)))).)))....((.....))	7	19246
18	2367	.(((......)))(((.((....))..)))	10	2367
19	77862	..((.(((...)))((...))).))....	5	77862
20	18789	.((.((((........((....))))))))..	7	18789
21	2454	(((((((....))).))...)).((...))..	10	2454

Table 6: Sequence of components decomposition for tertiary structures created with parameter $c_2 = 0.50$.

Molecular Evolution of Catalysis

Christian V. Forst
IMB Jena
Beutenbergstr. 11
07745 Jena
Germany
E-mail: `chris @ imb-jena.de`

Abstract

In this paper we consider evolutionary dynamics of catalytically active species with a distinct genotype – phenotype relationship. Folding landscapes of RNA-molecules serve as a paradigm for this relationship with essential neutral properties. This landscape itself is partitioned by phenotypes (realized as secondary structures). To each genotype (represented as sequence) a structure is assigned in a unique way. The set of all sequences which map into a particular structure is modeled as random graph in sequence space (the so-called *neutral network*). A catalytic network is realized as a random digraph with maximal out-degree 2 and secondary structures as vertex set. Studying a population of catalytic RNA-molecules shows significantly different behavior compared to a deterministic description: hypercycles are able to co-exist and survive resp. a parasite with superior catalytic support. A "switching" between different dynamical organizations of the network can be observed, dynamical stability of a hypercyclic organization against errors and the existence of an error-threshold of catalysis can be reported.

1 Introduction

Todays biology heads towards a grand synthesis of combining knowledge from three different disciplines: molecular biology, developmental biology, and evolutionary biology. Initialized by the epochal discoveries made by Francis Crick and James Watson in the year 1953 molecular biology came into being. First steps in the direction of a *molecular evolutionary biology* were already taken in the late sixties by the pioneer work of Sol Spiegelman [23] who developed *serial transfer experiments* as a new method of molecular evolution in the test tube. Manfred Eigen [4] at about the same time formulated a kinetic theory of molecular evolution. Since then studying evolution of molecules in laboratory systems has become a research area of its own. Nowadays these experiments in the test tube indicate that evolution in the sense of

Charles Darwin – by selection and variation – is not uniquely granted to cellular life only: optimization of replicating biopolymers by properties related to *fitness* is readily observed *in vitro* with *naked* RNA molecules in evolutionary experiments.

Darwinian dynamics is understood as a hill climbing process on a *fitness landscape* where fitness-values are assigned to genotypes (i.e. DNA or RNA sequences). Interpreted in terms of the theory of dynamical systems this dynamic is simple in the sense of following a gradient and finding a (local or global) fitness maximum. Even at this level of description controversy approaches have been discussed in history. Not only climbing to an optimum but genetic drift is seen as playing an important role for improving the *evolutionary search capacity* of a whole population [26, 27]. This *neutral theory* which often has been understood as antipole to Darwin's theory was proposed by Motoo Kimura in the late sixties [15, 14]. In the contrary he does not assume that selection plays *no* role but denies that any appreciable fraction of molecular change is caused by selective forces. He is saying in his theory that the *majority of changes* in evolution at the molecular level were the results of random drift of genotypes. Genetic drift and gradient walk are not the only feature of evolutionary systems. Interactions through catalysis, predator-prey or host-parasite behavior suppresses optimization of individual fitness. Formulating molecular evolution in terms of evolutionary dynamics has to take into consideration not only approaching a steady state but also complex dynamical phenomena like oscillations or chaotic behavior in space and time.

Evolutionary dynamics itself is a highly complex process. Therefore we omit additional difficulties in considering spatiotemporal patterns and introduce a comprehensive model which tries to account for most of the relevant features of molecular evolution. Peter Schuster proposed an interaction of three processes described in three different abstract metric spaces [22]:

- the *sequence space* of genotypes being DNA or RNA sequences,

- the *shape space* of phenotypes, and

- the *concentration space* of biochemical reaction kinetics.

The sequence space $\mathcal{Q}_\alpha^n$ is a metric space containing all sequences of chain-length n with alphabet-length α (i.e. the number of letters used in an alphabet $\mathcal{A}$). For DNA or RNA sequences α is 4, for peptides α would be 20 due to 4 distinct nucleotides common in DNA or RNA and 20 aminoacids in peptides and proteins resp. As a metric serves the Hamming metric [11]. The shape space covers all possible structures considered. The definition of structures itself is highly context dependent. Clearly two biopolymers with different sequences will form different spatial conformations at atomic resolution. This descriptions is, no question, adequate for comparison of active sites of enzymes (or ribozymes). In contrast, stating that all tRNAs have the same shape refers to a different understanding of structure on a coarse-grained level. Secondary structures may serve as one example which is suitable for our purpose of developing a mathematical model of molecular evolution. Similarities and dissimilarities of RNA structures can be expressed by means of mathematical measures with metric properties. Finally concentration space is the conventional space in which chemical reaction kinetics is described. Martin Feinberg formalized this concept in mathematical terms [6]. The conceptual cycle which is formed by a projection

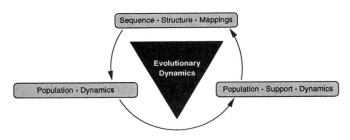

Figure 1: Evolutionary dynamics in sequence-, shape-, and concentration-space.

of evolutionary dynamics upon the three abstract spaces is sketched in Fig. 1.

Question raised in this papers deal with all three aspects of evolutionary dynamics. We give a mathematical description of a generic genotype – phenotype relation which maps RNA sequences to secondary structures. The topology of preimages in sequence-space with respect to this mapping is analyzed by graph theory. This preimage forms a so called *neutral network*. By subsequent mapping a complete folding landscape is constructed. A dynamical system is presented where the time evolution of a finite population of RNA molecules is described by stochastic point processes. By error-prone replication and unspecific elution the population moves in sequence space "guided" by evolutionary dynamics.

We present a chemical reaction network which implies complex dynamical behavior and which is explored by this population. One critical parameter is the error-rate which determines the dynamics significantly. The occurrence of an *error-threshold of catalysis* can be reported.

2 Neutral Networks of RNA Structures

2.1 Secondary Structures and Compatible Sets

RNA secondary structures and the induced sequence – structure relationship are a suitable and generic description for genotype – phenotype mapping which is important in molecular evolutionary biology. RNA secondary structures represent a type of coarse-graining of biopolymer structures. They commonly are understood as list of Watson-Crick ($\mathbf{A{=}U}$ and $\mathbf{G{\equiv}C}$) and Wobble ($\mathbf{G{-}U}$) base-pairs which are compatible with unknotted and pseudoknot-free two-dimensional graphs (for a precise formal definition we refer to Waterman [24]).

Defining secondary structures independently of chemical or physical restrictions yields a general description based on contacts with respect to arbitrary alphabets $\mathcal{A}$ with arbitrary pairing rules Π. A *pairing rule* Π on $\mathcal{A}$ is given as a set of pairs of letters from the given alphabet (i.e. $\mathbf{AU}$, $\mathbf{UA}$, $\mathbf{GC}$, $\mathbf{CG}$, $\mathbf{GU}$, $\mathbf{UG}$ for natural RNA-molecules with alphabet $\mathbf{A}$, $\mathbf{U}$, $\mathbf{G}$, $\mathbf{C}$). This concept can easily be extended to a general description of biopolymer structures via contact maps [16]. Similar to secondary structures a general *contact structure c* is determined by a *set of contacts* of c omitting the trivial contacts due to adjacent letters in the succession of the sequence.

A relevant concept in studying sequence – structure relation is how sequences has to be composed to fulfill necessary conditions for folding into a desired structure. In the following we define *compatibility* of a sequence to a given structure: A sequence x is said to be *compatible* to a structure s if all basepairs required by s can be provided by x_i and $x_j \in x$ with respect to the pairing rule Π for each base pair. $\mathbf{C}(s)$ is the set of all sequences which are compatible to structure s. The number of compatible sequences is readily computed for secondary structures (with n_u unpaired bases and n_p base pairs this evaluates to $4^{n_u} \cdot 6^{n_p}$).

2.2 Preimages and Complete Mappings

The relation between RNA sequences and secondary structures is understood as a (non-necessarily invertible) mapping f_n from sequence space $\mathcal{Q}_\alpha^n$ into shape space $\mathcal{S}_n$. The set of all sequences folding into a given structure is denoted as *neutral network* $\Gamma_n(s)$ with respect to s. $\mathcal{Q}_\alpha^n$ denotes the generalized hypercube of dimension n over an alphabet $\mathcal{A}$ of size α (i.e. the number of letters in $\mathcal{A}$ is α), and $s \in \mathcal{S}_n$ is a fixed secondary structure. Mathematically $\Gamma_n(s)$ refers to the induced subgraph of

$f_n^{-1}(s)$ in $\mathbf{C}(s)$ ($f_n^{-1}(s)$ indicates the *preimage* of a fixed structure s w.r.t the mapping f_n). A scetch of these embeddings is shown in Fig. 2.

Remark: The graph of compatible sequences $\mathcal{C}(s)$ to a fixed secondary structure s is

$$\mathcal{C}(s) = \mathcal{Q}_\alpha^{n_u} \times \mathcal{Q}_\beta^{n_p}$$

α is the number of different nucleotides, and β is the number of different *types* of base pairs that can be formed by α different nucleotides.

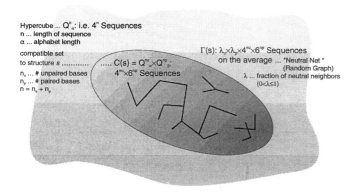

Figure 2: Sketch of a neutral network $\Gamma(s)$ (shown as solid line graph) embedded in the set of sequences compatible to structure s (i.e. $\mathbf{C}(s)$ – indicated as oval) which itself is embedded in sequence space $\mathcal{Q}_\alpha^n$ (realized as shaded background).

Sequences folding into the same structure are thus represented by a subgraph that is *randomly* induced on the set of compatible sequences corresponding to this structure [20]. Accordingly this model is of probabilistic nature and properties of random subgraphs are studied as functions of a single parameter – a probability measure over all possible induced subgraphs in a given sub-hypercube with a *choosing parameter* λ. This parameter represents the mean fraction of neighbors that are neutral with respect to the structure. – the *fraction of neutrality* with $0 \leq \lambda \leq 1$. Considering paired and unpaired regions we are dealing with two independent assignments for each corresponding choosing probability λ_p and λ_u resp. are used. Now vertices in both subcubes $\mathcal{Q}_\alpha^{n_u}$ and $\mathcal{Q}_\beta^{n_p}$ are chosen independently with these probabilities λ_u and λ_p resp. This is equivalent to choosing pairs of vertices in $\mathcal{C}(s)$ and yields exactly the desired neutral network $\Gamma_n(s)$ as probability space with its corresponding probability measure.

Two remarkable results are assertions about *density* and *connectivity* of subgraphs. In analogy to percolation theory these propererties are fulfilled almost sure if λ

exceeds the threshold value

$$\lambda^* = 1 - \sqrt[1-\alpha]{\alpha}$$

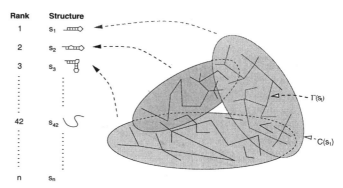

Figure 3: Complete sequence to structure mapping: neutral networks are constructed by subsequent (random) mapping of sequences to an ordered set of structures. Note that any pair of compatible sets have a non-empty intersection (for a proof see [20]).

Once we know how to construct a neutral network $\Gamma_n(s)$ we order the set of secondary structures $\mathcal{S}_n$ and define a complete mapping by iterating the construction process of the corresponding neutral network w.r.t. the ordering. The preimage for the structure with highest rank s_1 is assigned independently. For all other structures s_i, $i > 1$ the mapping depends on all previous assignments. A visualization of this process is shown in Fig. 3.

3 Dynamics of Catalytic Reaction Networks

3.1 Replication-Deletion Process

Let $\mathbf{P}$ be a (finite) population of size N defined as family of vertices $(P_i \,|\, i \in N)$ with $\{ P_i \,|\, i \in N \} \subset \mathrm{v}(\mathcal{Q}_\alpha^n)$ and $N \geq 2$. The theory of point processes provides a powerful tool by identifying such a family $(v_i \,|\, i \in N)$ with an integer valued measure $\phi: \mathcal{Q}_\alpha^n \to \mathbb{R}$:

$$\mathbf{P} = (P_i \,|\, i \in N) \quad \longleftrightarrow \quad \phi \stackrel{def}{=} \sum_{i=1}^{N} g_{P_i}, \qquad (1)$$

where $g_{P_i}(v) \stackrel{def}{=} \begin{cases} 1 & \text{for } v \neq P_i \\ 0 & \text{otherwise} \end{cases}$.

The set of sequences where ϕ is nonzero is referred to as *support* of ϕ. Thus the *restriction* of ϕ to a subgraph $Y \subset \mathcal{Q}_\alpha^n$ is tantamount to characterize subpopulations on $\mathrm{v}(Y)$.

The time evolution of ϕ is obtained by a mapping from $(P_i \,|\, i \in N)$ to the family $(P_i' \,|\, i \in N)$ as follows: we select an ordered pair (P_l, P_k) where $P_l, P_k \in \{ P_i \,|\, i \in N \}$. For this purpose let $\mathcal{F}_s$ be a "fitness" of s in a generalized sense which will be outlined in section 3.2. Accordingly the average "fitness" of ϕ reads

$$\mathcal{F}_\phi = \sum_s \phi(\mathrm{v}(\Gamma_n(s)))\mathcal{F}_s.$$

Now the first coordinate P_l of this ordered pair is chosen with probability $\mathcal{F}_s/\mathcal{F}_\phi$ among the elements of $\mathbf{P}$. The second coordinate of the above pair is selected with uniform probability on $(P_i \neq P_l \,|\, i \in N)$ i.e. $1/(N-1)$. We assume the times $\hat{T}$ between these mappings to be exponentially distributed (scaled by the mean fitness)

$$\mu\{\hat{T} \leq t\} = e^{-\mathcal{F}_\phi t}.$$

We map $P_l = (x_1, ..., x_n)$ randomly into the vertex $P^* = (x'_1, ..., x'_n)$. This is done by mapping each coordinate x_i to a $x'_i \neq x_i$ with probability $\wp$ where all $x'_i \neq x_i$ are equally distributed and leave the coordinate fixed otherwise. This random mapping $v_l \mapsto v^*$ is called "replication". Finally, we delete the second coordinate of the pair (v_l, v_k), that is v_k and have a mapping $(P_l, P_k) \mapsto (P_l, P^*)$. Thereby we obtain a "new" family by substituting the P_k by the P^*. This process is referred to as *replication-deletion process*.

3.2 Exploring Catalytic Nets

The aim of this paper is to analyze the behavior of a population exploring a given (large) catalytic network. In terms of graph-theory we understand a *catalytic network* as digraph $\mathcal{N}$ with $\mathrm{v}(\mathcal{N}) \subseteq \mathcal{S}_n$ and an edge-set as follows: edges are valued by a function $g: \mathrm{e}(\mathcal{N}) \to \mathbb{R}_0^+$ which corresponds to a reaction-rate of catalysis. I.e. fixing an edge ϵ then we define $g(\epsilon)$ as reaction-rate for the catalysis of phenotype $s_i = t(\epsilon)$ by phenotype $s_k = o(\epsilon)$. We call $o(\epsilon)$ *catalyst* and $t(\epsilon)$ *template*. If $o(\epsilon) = t(\epsilon)$ then ϵ describes an *autocatalytic reaction*.

In our model we consider a maximal out-degree of $\mathcal{N} \leq 2$. In addition to catalysis there exists an uncatalyzed replication with rate $f: \mathrm{v}(\mathcal{N}) \to \mathbb{R}_0^+$

The generalized "fitness" introduced in section 3.1 corresponds directly with above defined reaction-rates f and g. Thus the "fitness" of an individual phenotype s is

$$\begin{aligned} \mathcal{F}_s =\ & \phi\{\mathrm{v}(\Gamma_n[s])\}f(s) \\ & + \sum_{s=t(\epsilon)} \phi\{\mathrm{v}(\Gamma_n(s))\}\phi\{\mathrm{v}(\Gamma_n[o(\epsilon)])\}g(\epsilon). \end{aligned} \quad (2)$$

Translated to chemical reaction equation the dynamical behavior of the above system can be described as follows: We denote I_i, $i = 1, ..., n$ as reacting species with a fixed phenotype $s(I_i)$, W_{ij} indicates the probability of reproducing I_j by replicating I_i.:

$$I_i \xrightarrow{f[s(I_i)] \cdot W_{ij}} I_i + I_j$$

$$I_i + I_k \xrightarrow{g[s(I_i), s(I_k)] \cdot W_{ij}} I_i + I_j + I_k \quad (3)$$

$$I_i \xrightarrow{\Phi} \emptyset$$

Thus the $f[s(I_i)]$'s refer to the level of phenotypes whereas the W_{ij}'s indicate the genotypes dynamic. The $g[s(I_i), s(I_k)]$'s denote the rate of the catalyzed reaction. By decoupling both levels from each other yields following schema (Fig. 4):

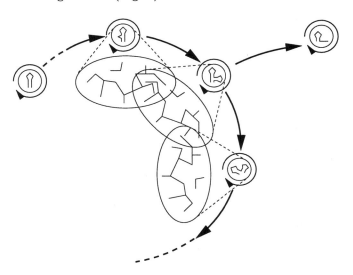

Figure 4: Hypercyclic reaction-network with a parasite including a genotype – phenotype mapping. Each phenotype — sketched by secondary structures — induce a corresponding compatible set and an embedded neutral net. The parasitic phenotype profits by a hypercyclic phenotype only without providing support.

Important for the dynamical characteristics of the system are the reaction-graphs of phenotypes and the error-prone replications on the level of genotypes. The topologies of the underlying neutral nets assure that there are couplings between each two of them. Parts of the population can switch from one net to the other and thereby cause a stabilizing effect for the hypercycle.

3.2.1 Hypercycles and Parasites

Considering stability of a hypercyclic organization one has to consider to what extend this stability can be maintained in drastic scenarios. One of these drastic scenarios is the competition of a hypercycle with a parasite (Fig. 4). The results known by stability analysis of this system in case of infinite populations let us expect the following [12]: depending on the ratio of the reaction rates of the competitors and of the initial concentrations either the hypercycle or the parasite will survive at the expense of the other.

Different approaches has been pursued by Boerlijst and Hogeweg [3] who studied hypercycles and parasites in an two-dimensional spatial system. They observed formation of spirals and a "cleaning"-capacity of the system against attacks of parasites.

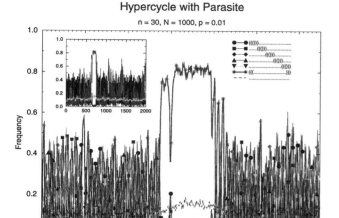

Figure 5: Fife-member Hypercycle with parasite. Starting with one member of the hypercycle the parasite becomes dominant at generation 600. The hypercycle is still able to coexist with the parasite and out-competes the latter at a later generation. Parameters are: population size = 1000, chain length = 30, catalyzed reactions are the same for hypercyclic members as for the parasite.

Similar effects can be noticed in our stochastic formulation of a homogeneous system with the above defined partly neutral genotype – phenotype mapping (equation 3): in contrast to homogeneous models with infinite population size the competition between parasite and hypercycle is not a 0-1 behavior. Both competitors can coexist for a long time and can over-populate but not extinguish each other. A characteristic time evolution is shown in Fig. 5.

3.2.2   Voyaging large Catalytic Nets

In order to study *formation*, structural *stabilization* against hostile environment, and *evolution* of catalytic active entities (i.e. hypercycles) we have to establish an artificial world of interacting catalytic networks. In contrast to approaches made by various people [1, 2, 7, 13, 18] where autocatalytic sets emerge automatically we setup a system with fixed but very large catalytic network which has to be explored by the population:

Using an ordered set of 1000 secondary structures as phenotypes, a catalytic network of about 420 random hypercycles of size 3 to 7, and about 18 additional random reaction paths is constructed. This yields a total of about 2000 possible reaction-paths. By an initial population of $N = 1000$ individual with phenotype of rank 1 the catalytic network is explored. For the corresponding

reaction-rates we are dealing with two distinct scenarios:

- **equal opportunity:** function g is constant on $e(\mathcal{N})$ (Fig. 6.) therefore neutral evolution of catalytic units can be observed.

- **optimization:** g has a random distribution with distinct expectation- value and variance (Fig. 7). The population explores the catalytic network in search for better support.

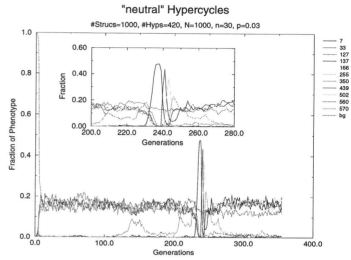

Figure 6: Neutral evolution of hypercycles: embedded in an artificial secondary-structure landscape of 1000 phenotypes 420 randomly chosen hypercycles of length three to seven are assigned. In addition 27 reaction paths between randomly chosen phenotypes are defined. Due to the constant function g no optimization is possible but "switching" from one hypercycle to another can be observed. In general only those phenotypes are displayed whichever reached the global, maximal concentration in the simulation at least once.

This still quite simple model gives deep insight how new catalytic active units can be formed, how they can re-organize by neutral drift and how optimization to more efficient units take place. Important for this purpose is the error-rate on genotype level which is contained in the stochastic mutation matrices W_{ij}. This leads us to the next section.

3.3   Error-Threshold

One essential question one may ask is, what is the influence of the error-rate on the dynamical behavior of the system. Well known is the quasi-species concept of Eigen *et al.*[4, 5] which has been described by an birth-death ansatz by Nowak & Schuster [17]. The critical error rate p_* of the genotypic error-threshold is determined by following expression:

$$(1 - p_*)^n = \frac{1}{\sigma} \qquad (4)$$

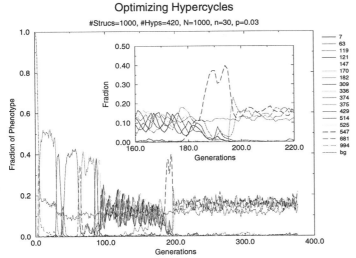

Figure 7: Voyaging large catalytic networks: similar to Fig. 6 420 randomly chosen hypercycles of length three to seven are assigned. In addition 18 reaction paths between randomly chosen phenotypes are defined. In this figure an optimization from one catalytic organization (four-member hypercycle) to a three-member hypercycle is shown. Analogue to Fig. 6 only those phenotypes are displayed whichever reached the global, maximal concentration in the simulation at least once.

where n is the chain-length and σ is the superiority of the master.

3.3.1 Phenotypic Error-Threshold

Extending the mean-field approach of Eigen *et al.* of an evolving population by a biologically motivated genotype – phenotype relationship yields the following system [8]: consider a single fixed secondary structure s and the preimage $f^{-1}(s)$ as subgraph $\Gamma(s)$ of the sequence-space. This induces in a natural way a *fitness landscape* f_Γ on the complete sequence space $\mathcal{Q}_\alpha^n$:

$$f(x) = \left\{ \begin{array}{ll} 1 & \text{if } x \notin \Gamma \\ \sigma & \text{if } x \in \Gamma \end{array} \right\}. \qquad (5)$$

with $\sigma > 1$. We call f a *single shape* landscape in contrast to the single peak landscape of Eigen *et al.*. We used this landscape and applied a birth-death process of replicating RNA-molecules in a constant environment characterized in section 3.1. One significant result of this model is the existence of a so called *phenotypic error-threshold*. Beyond a critical error-rate p_* the information of a fit phenotype is lost for the population and is replaced by random drift. Fig. 8 shows a density plot for a single shape landscape with $\lambda_u = \lambda_p = 0.5$ and $N = 1000$.

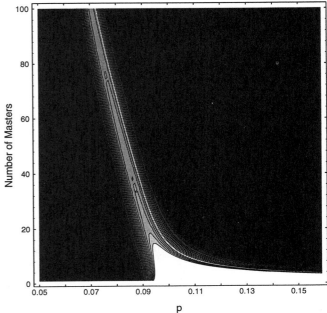

Figure 8: Density plot of the stationary distribution for a single-shape landscape with $\lambda_u = \lambda_p = 0.5$ and $N = 1000$. Light area denote high probability. Note that 0 is binding state beyond the error-threshold.

3.3.2 Error-Threshold of Catalysis

Extending the concept of the importance of a single phenotype for the evolving population to the maintenance of cooperative behavior of a set of phenotypes leads to a general understanding: Assume the importance of a hypercyclic organization. Then one may ask how stable is this catalytic network against mutational influences?

We are starting with a five-member hypercycle with population size $N = 1000$ and error-rate $p = 0$ (other parameters of the simulations are: chain-length $n = 30$, $n_u = n_p = 10$, catalytic support between members of hypercycle $h = 10$, all other reaction rates $r = 1$). By subsequently increasing p by 0.02 and "relaxation" of the system for 500 generations per new p-value we record the number of individuals which have the phenotype of the hypercycle (i.e. which are on the corresponding neutral networks). Fig. 9 shows the result of this simulation. One can notice that phases of organized hypercyclic dynamics alternates with aperiodicity where the hypercycle has to self-reorganize in sequence-space due to diffusion of its members (not shown). Beyond a critical error-rate $p_* = 0.11$ the information of the hypercycle is lost for the population. Comparing p_*-values between this system and the single-shape landscape with simple birth-death dynamics one observes a larger "buffering" capacity for the hypercyclic reaction-network. I.e. similar p_*-values are detected for $\lambda_u = \lambda_p = 0.5$ for the reaction-network and for $\lambda_u = \lambda_p = 0.8$ for the simple single-shape model.

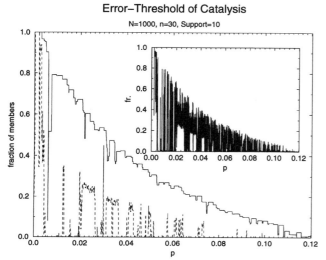

Figure 9: Error-Threshold of catalysis: the fraction of hypercyclic members depending on the error rate p is shown. The small plot refers to the member with maximal fraction per p-value. The large diagram show running averages of this data: the solid line denotes a running average over 500 samples of the maximum, the dashed line refers to a running average over 50 datapoints of the minimum. Hypercyclic "activity" occur at extended maxima of the dashed line.

There is a second effect of the error-rate on the stability of the periodic phases of the reaction-network. For higher p-values the observed lifetime of these phases become shorter. This can be understood by "mixing" properties of the mutation. Analogue studies of mutational influences on small deterministic autocatalytic reaction nets show a phase transition of the periodic and chaotic behavior of the system to a stable fixed point [21, 24]. Due to neutral properties of the underlying sequence – structure relationship the reaction-network is highly tolerant against these destabilizing effects. Although a significant change at $p_h = 0.04$ can be observed between long-living hypercyclic dynamics for $p < p_h$ and short lifetime for $p > p_h$ the existence of these dynamics itself persists up to high error-rates. Fig. 10 shows the life-time of the periodic behavior of the hypercycle depending on the error-rate p. The line refers to a linear regression for data-points at $p > p_h$ with $intercept = 374$ and $slope = -3449$. The linear regression function becomes 0 at $p = 0.108$ – the error threshold.

4 Conclusion

Evolutionary dynamics interpreted as an adaptive walk in an high-dimensional fitness landscape implies several assumptions which are crucial for the validity of the model: (i) constant environment and (ii) independent reproduction. In nature neither the first nor the second assumptions are realized even on a rudimentary scale.

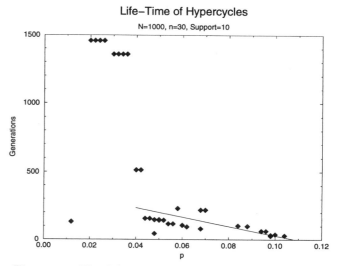

Figure 10: The life time of the periodic behavior of the hypercycle is shown depending on the error rate p. A "phase-transition" at $p \approx 0.04$ can be observed. The drawn solid line indicates a linear approximation of the data beyond this phase-transition. This line crosses the x-axes at $p = 0.108$ – the error-threshold.

Constant environment can be interpreted that environmental changes shall occur on a slower time-scale than the adaption of the population. Coevolving species may influence the environment of a population. But this influence may take place on the same time-scale as adaption due to the same adaptive mechanism. Therefore landscape models of coevolution could easily fail and should be considered with special care. The second assumption of independent reproduction is dealt with similar care. Independent production implies independence of replication-rates from the concentration of the respective individual. Host-parasite systems, predator-prey scenarios and symbiotic interactions are examples of such dependencies and are impossible to be described by walks on complex landscapes. Experiments of directed molecular evolution performed in laboratories are almost always dealing with constant environments and the replication rate are commonly independent of the concentrations. In nature, however, neither the first nor the second assumptions are realized even on a rudimentary scale.

Recent experimental studies of quasi-viral amplification systems give a different picture [9, 10]. Utilizing even simple regulatory systems like quasi-viral amplification and understanding infectious cycles of Viridae depends crucially on insights of complex dynamical correlations. The model presented here is a first step in this direction: the neutral property of the underlying genotype – phenotype mapping both stabilizes the system and enables "save" optimization. Due to this property of the landscape catalytically organized entities (such as a hypercycle) become tolerant against parasites with even higher fitness. If the reaction rates of parasite and hypercycle are in the same order of magnitude an alternating revival and repression is observed. Hypercycles are capable for evolutionary optimization and reorganize accordingly (e.g. the periodicity can change with adaption). Not only the tolerance against competing systems but also tolerance against mutations has been observed. A catalytically organized entity maintains its organization up to high error rates. Before the dynamic behavior breaks down at the error-threshold of catalysis a phase transition occurs where short-living hypercycles follow hypercycles with long life time.

Evolutionary dynamics in its full capability of describing interacting evolving species provides a powerful tool for molecular evolutionary biology. Not only evolutionary experiments yield better models but also these models are capable for the design of optimal experimental strategies. This synthesis between theoretical model and experimental setup is the key of a comprehensive and complete description of molecular evolution.

Acknowledgments

I would like to thank Peter Schuster for fruitful discussions. Special thanks are directed to Christian Reidys for helpful hints especially by formulating graph-theoretical problems. Proof-reading of the manuscript by Ulrike Göbel and Janos Palinkas is gratefully acknowledged.

References

[1] Richard J. Bagley and J. Doyne Farmer. Spontaneous emergence of a metabolism. In Christopher G. Langton, Charles Taylor, J. Doyne Farmer, and Steen Rasmussen, editors, *Artificial Life II*, volume X of *Santa Fe Institute Studies in the Science of Complexity*, chapter Origin/Self-Organization, pages 93–141. Addison Wesley, Redwood City, 1992.

[2] Richard J. Bagley, J. Doyne Farmer, and Walter Fontana. Evolution of a metabolism. In Christopher G. Langton, Charles Taylor, J. Doyne Farmer, and Steen Rasmussen, editors, *Artificial Life II*, volume X of *Santa Fe Institute Studies in the Science of Complexity*, chapter Origin/Self-Organization, pages 141–158. Addison Wesley, Redwood City, 1992.

[3] M. C. Boerlijst and P. Hogeweg. Spiral wave structure in pre-biotic evolution: Hypercycles stable against parasites. *Physica D*, 48:17 – 28, 1991.

[4] M. Eigen. Selforganization of matter and the evolution of biological macromolecules. *Die Naturwissenschaften*, 10:465–523, 1971.

[5] M. Eigen, J. McCaskill, and P. Schuster. The molecular Quasispecies. *Adv. Chem. Phys.*, 75:149 – 263, 1989.

[6] Martin Feinberg. Mathematical aspects of mass action kinetics. In L. Lapidus and N.R. Amundson, editors, *Chemical Reactor Theory, A Review*, pages 1–78, Englewood Cliffs, NJ, 1977. Prentice-Hall Inc.

[7] Walter Fontana and Leo W. Buss. "The Arrival of the Fittest": Towards a theory of biological organization. *Bull. Math. Biol.*, 56:1–64, 1994.

[8] Christian V. Forst, Christian Reidys, and Jacqueline Weber. Evolutionary dynamics and optimization: Neutral Networks as model-landscape for RNA secondary-structure folding-landscapes. In F. Morán, A. Moreno, J.J. Merelo, and P. Chacón, editors, *Advances in Artificial Life*, volume 929 of *Lecture Notes in Artificial Intelligence*, Berlin, Heidelberg, New York, 1995. ECAL '95, Springer. Santa Fe Preprint 95-10-094.

[9] Michael Gebinoga. Hypercycles in biological systems. *J. Endocyt.*, 1995. submitted.

[10] Michael Gebinoga and Frank Oehlenschläger. Comparison of self-sustained sequence replication reaction systems. *Eur. J. Biochem.*, 235:256–261, 1996.

[11] R. W. Hamming. *Coding and Information Theory*. Prentice Hall, Englewood Cliffs, 1986.

[12] J. Hofbauer and K. Sigmund. *The Theory of Evolution and Dynamical Systems*. Cambridge University Press (Cambridge), 1988.

[13] Stuart A. Kauffman. Autocatalytic sets of proteins. *J. Theoret. Biol.*, 119(1):1–24, 1986.

[14] M. Kimura. *The Neutral Theory of Molecular Evolution*. Cambridge Univ. Press, Cambridge, UK, 1983.

[15] Motoo Kimura. Evolutionary rate at the molecular level. *Nature*, 217:624 – 626, 1968.

[16] Stephan Kopp, Christian M. Reidys, and Peter Schuster. Exploration of artificial landscapes based on random graphs. In Frank Schweitzer, editor, *Self-Organization of Complex Structures: From Individual to Collective Behavior*, London, UK, 1996. Gordon and Breach.

[17] Martin Nowak and Peter Schuster. Error tresholds of replication in finite populations, mutation frequencies and the onset of Muller's ratchet. *Journal of theoretical Biology*, 137:375–395, 1989.

[18] Steen Rasmussen, Carsten Knudsen, and Rasmus Feldberg. Dynamics of programmable matter. In Christopher G. Langton, Charles Taylor, J. Doyne Farmer, and Steen Rasmussen, editors, *Artificial Life II*, volume X of *Santa Fe Institute Studies in the Sciences of Complexity*, pages 211–254, Redwood City, 1991. Addison Wesley.

[19] Christian Reidys, Peter F. Stadler, and Peter Schuster. Generic properties of combinatory maps and neutral networks of RNA secondary structures. *Bull. Math. Biol.*, 59(2):339–397, 1997.

[20] Wolfgang Schnabl, Peter F. Stadler, Christian Forst, and Peter Schuster. Full characterization of a strange attractor: Chaotic dynamics in low dimensional replicator systems. *Physica D*, 48:65 – 90, 1991.

[21] Peter Schuster. Artificial life and molecular evolutionary biology. In F. Morán, A. Moreno, J.J. Merelo, and P. Chacón, editors, *Advances in Artificial Life*, Lecture Notes in Artificial Intelligence, Berlin, Heidelberg, New York, 1995. ECAL '95, Springer.

[22] S. Spiegelman. An approach to the experimental analysis of precellular evolution. *Quart. Rev. Biophys.*, 17:213, 1971.

[23] Peter F. Stadler, Wolfgang Schnabl, Christian V. Forst, and Peter Schuster. Dynamic of small autocatalytic reaction networks – II. Replication, mutation and catalysis. *Bull. Math. Biol.*, 57(1):21–61, 1995.

[24] M. S. Waterman. Secondary structure of single - stranded nucleic acids. *Studies on foundations and combinatorics, Advances in mathematics supplementary studies, Academic Press N.Y.*, 1:167 – 212, 1978.

[25] Sewall Wright. Evolution in mendelian populations. *Genetics*, 16:97–159, 1931.

[26] Sewall Wright. The roles of mutation, inbreeding, crossbreeeding and selection in evolution. In D. F. Jones, editor, *int. Proceedings of the Sixth International Congress on Genetics*, volume 1, pages 356–366, 1932.

Evolution of Random Catalytic Networks

S.M. Fraser[a] and C.M. Reidys[a,b]
[a] Santa Fe Institute, 1399 Hyde Park Rd., Santa Fe, NM 87501, USA
[b] Los Alamos National Laboratory, TSA/DO-SA, Los Alamos, NM 87548, USA
{smfr, duck}@santafe.edu

Abstract

In this paper we investigate the evolution of populations of sequences realising structures which form a random catalytic network. Sequences are mapped into structures, between which are catalytic interactions that determine their instantaneous fitness. The catalytic network is constructed as a directed random graph. Populations evolving under point mutations realise a comparatively small induced subgraph of the complete catalytic network. We prove that at certain parameter values, the probability of occurrence of some relevant subgraphs, on which the population can stabilise, is maximized. We present results which show that populations reliably discover and persist on directed cycles in the catalytic graph, though these may be lost because of stochastic effects, and we study the effect of population size on this behavior.

1 Introduction

Understanding evolutionary dynamics requires an understanding at a number of different levels—the population dynamics which results from selection, the mechanisms underlying the exploration of sequence space by an evolving population (population support dynamics), and the sequence to structure mapping [24]. Many of the intriguing properties of the mapping between RNA sequences and their secondary structures are being elucidated [26, 24], and these show that there exist in sequence space so-called neutral networks [22, 12, 13]: largely connected sets of sequences, all of which map into the same structure, and on which populations of sequences can move by point mutations while keeping their structure constant. Neutral networks allow populations to explore structure space by neutral mutations, while "testing" those structures encountered by the mutant relatives of the master sequence which form a cloud around the sequences on the neutral network. A high proportion of the structures in the space can be encountered in this way [25]. As well as being of interest to the molecular evolution community and those interested in neutral evolution [17], these properties of the sequence to structure mapping are essential for the evolutionary optimization of biopolymers.

The sequence to structure mapping used in our analysis has been introduced in [20]. It maps sequences into so-called *random structures*, and exhibits many of the above properties. In these structures, secondary and tertiary bonds are selected independently, whereas RNA secondary structures consist mainly of stacks and loops and have knot-free contact graphs. In this paper we study evolution on random metabolic networks, formed by random structures, taking into account this sequence to structure map. We consider such a chemistry to be composed of simple catalytic interactions which have the effect of increasing the fitness of catalyzed structures. In so doing, we have a system in which the three dynamical processes outlined above, which contribute to the evolutionary dynamics, are realized.

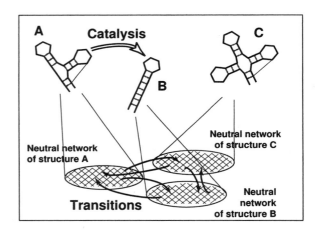

Figure 1: This figure illustrates the two main processes that drive the dynamics. Here molecule **A** catalyses molecule **B**, whereas molecule **C** is an isolated vertex in the catalytic network. The neutral networks of all three molecules come close in sequence space, allowing populations to make transitions between them.

A number of previous studies have investigated the emergence of autocatalytic sets and metabolic networks. Kauffman [15, 16] discusses the emergence of catalytic closure in a chemistry of polymers undergoing cleavage and condensation reactions. As the length of the largest polymer in the system increases, the number of reactions grows faster than the number of chemical species. A kinetic model of this system [8] shows formation of autocatalytic sets under some conditions, which is refined [1] to describe the metadynamics using a set of continuous differential equations with a concentration threshold. Unlike these studies, we model the dynamics with what is termed [1] a *stochastic molecular collisions* approach. In fact, the dynamics in our systems is determined on two levels (Figure 1); first, the stochastic molecular collisions model which determines fitness, and second, a stochastic phenomenon on finite populations which is induced by the sequence to structure mapping—below certain population sizes, the entire population performs transitions between neutral networks. This phenomenon is described in more detail below.

We will consider molecules as *random structures* which consist of *graphs* and *multi-sets of relations* imposed on the extremities of their edges [20]. The graph represents the molecule at a level of coarse-graining where molecular structure is encoded in the list of edges (bonds) in the graph. Note that backbone bonds are not considered as edges in contact graphs. The relations imposed on the edges then represent the bonding rules of the molecule, for example the formation of Watson–Crick base pairs by the nucleotides of an RNA sequence. This view of molecular structure suggests that molecules can be studied from a rather new point of view: they are correlation schemes that induce landscapes that can be searched effectively by point mutations. Systematic experiments [21] have shown how structural properties and optimization performance are related.

In order to specify a chemistry of interactions between molecules, we now consider random structures as the vertices of a new graph, the *random chemistry*. In this directed graph of catalytic activity, an edge from one vertex (structure) to another specifies that the structure at the origin of the edge catalyses the production of the structure at the terminus. Note that here, structures catalyze each other directly. This is unlike some previous models of autocatalytic systems. In Kauffman [15, 16, 14] polymers catalyze the formation of other polymers by increasing reaction rates, giving rise to a hypergraph of catalytic activity. Our direct catalysis is more similar to the model of Rasmussen [18], and makes for a simpler, more tractable system. In Eigen *et al.* [4] there is a linear relation between the concentration of the catalyst and the replication rate, which is not the case in our model.

After a formal description of random structures and the mapping of sequences into structures, we describe the graph theoretic properties of the metabolic network, and show an interesting result relating to the frequency of "stable" cycles. We then analyse the time evolution

of populations of sequences on the landscape formed by these catalytic sets of structures. In particular, we study the effects of population size on the dynamics, and determine whether populations stabilize on certain substructure in the metabolic graph. Some of the counterintuitive features of the system are explained in terms of transition phenomena between neutral networks.

2   Sequence to Structure Maps

Let us first review some terminology of graph theory. A *graph* X consists of a tuple (vX, eX) and a map $o \otimes t : eX \longrightarrow vX \times vX$. vX is called the *vertex set* and eX the *edge set*. An element $P \in X$ is called a *vertex* of X; an element $y \in X$ is called an *edge*. The vertex $o(y)$ is called the *origin* of y and the vertex $t(y)$ is called the *terminus* of y; $o(y), t(y)$ are called the *extremities* of some edge y. There is an obvious notion of Y being a *subgraph* of X. We call a subgraph Y *induced*, if for any $P, P' \in Y$ being extremities of an edge $y \in X$, it follows $y \in Y$. A *path* in X is a sequence $(Q_1, y_1, Q_2, y_2, \ldots, y_n, Q_{n+1})$, where $Q_i \in X$, $y_i \in X$, $o(y_i) = Q_i$ and $t(y_i) = Q_{i+1}$. A path such that $Q_1 = Q_{n+1}$ is called a *cycle*. X is called *connected* if any two vertices are vertices of a path of X. A connected graph without cycles is called a *tree*.

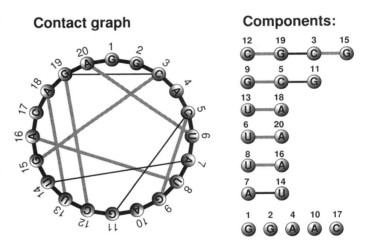

Contact graph   **Components:**

Figure 2: A contact graph, consisting of an ordered set of vertices (numbered), between which there can be either secondary (gray) or tertiary (thin black) edges, together with its set of components.

In general, contact graphs of structures contain two types of edges: secondary and tertiary bonds. A nucleotide can have at most one secondary bond; for tertiary bonds there is no such restriction. We will take this fact into account by modeling secondary bonds as a partial 1-factor graph and tertiary bonds as a pure random graph. More formally, let m be the number of secondary bonds in the molecule, and c_2 the fraction of nucleotides involved in tertiary bonds. Then the contact graph is a graph on the n indices of the coordinates of a sequence, whose edge set is the union of the edge sets of two random graphs (Figure 2). The first is a 1-regular graph on $2m$ vertices, obtained by picking m pairs of indices without replacement. The second one is a random graph on n vertices, obtained by selecting the remaining $\binom{n}{2} - m$ edges with independent probability $p = \frac{c_2}{n}$. Here, c_2 is the probability of a specific nucleotide being involved in a tertiary interaction. It has been shown in [20] that in the limit of long sequences almost all vertices of the random contact graphs are contained in tree components of logarithmic size (relative to sequence length). This means that such structures are robust under point mutations— since most mutations will hit nucleotides in isolated or small components, sequences are quite likely to remain compatible with a structure after replication.

A *random structure*, s_n, on n nucleotides of a finite alphabet $\mathcal{A}$ consists of:

- a contact graph $X_1 \otimes X_2$

- a family of symmetric relations $(\mathcal{R}_*, \mathcal{R}_y)_{y \in X_2}$, where $\mathcal{R}_*, \mathcal{R}_y \subset \mathcal{A} \times \mathcal{A}$.

Each $\mathcal{R}_y$ is supposed to have the property: for all $a \in \mathcal{A}$ there exists one $b \in \mathcal{A}$ with the property: $a \mathcal{R}_y b$. The relation $\mathcal{R}_*$ is motivated by Watson–Crick *base-pairing rules* observed in RNA secondary structures. For $y \in X_2$ the relation $\mathcal{R}_y$ corresponds to a specific (tertiary) interaction rule that might be context dependent. Little is known about the nature of tertiary interactions; for the simulations described below, Watson–Crick base-pairing rules are used for these also.

Let $\mathcal{Q}_\alpha^n$ be the generalized hypercube whose vertex set is the set of all sequences of length n over an alphabet $\mathcal{A}$ with α members. A sequence $V \in \mathcal{Q}_\alpha^n$ is called *compatible* to a random structure s_n if and only if, for each edge in the contact graph, the nucleotides at the extremities of that edge fulfill the base pairing rules (Figure 3):

- for all bonds y of the partial 1-factor graph X_1 its nucleotides indexed by the extremities $\{o(y), t(y)\}$ have the property $P_{o(y)} \mathcal{R}_* P_{t(y)}$ (note that since $\mathcal{R}_*$ is symmetric we also have $P_{t(y)} \mathcal{R}_* P_{o(y)}$)

- its nucleotides fulfill for all tertiary bonds $y \in X_2$: $P_{o(y)} \mathcal{R}_y P_{t(y)}$.

We obtain mappings of sequences into structures $f : \mathcal{Q}_\alpha^n \longrightarrow \{s_n\}$ by constructing the corresponding preimages as random graphs in sequence space, as follows: we fix a mapping $r : \{s_n\} \to \mathbb{N}$ having the property $j \leq i \implies r(s_j) \geq r(s_i)$ and set

$$f_r^{-1}(s_0) = \Gamma_n[s_0]$$
$$f_r^{-1}(s_i) = \Gamma_n[s_i] \setminus \bigcup_{j < i} [\Gamma_n[s_i] \cap \Gamma_n[s_j]] . \quad (1)$$

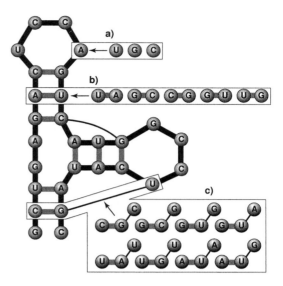

Figure 3: This figure illustrates the notion of *compatibility* of a sequence with respect to a structure. For three types of components (single nucleotides **a**, nucleotides in secondary interactions **b**, and those in secondary and tertiary interactions **c**), compatible sets of vertices are shown.

The *preimage* of a structure (being the set of sequences which actually realise the structure) is thus an induced subgraph of the set of compatible sequences (those which are capable of realising the structure). Using some theorems on the properties of random induced subgraphs, it has been shown [19, 20], that the preimages of random structures form *neutral networks*, i.e. vastly extended, percolating networks in sequence space. Explicitly it has been shown [22, 19, 21] that $\lambda^* = 1 - \sqrt[\alpha-1]{\alpha^{-1}}$ is a threshold value for density and connectivity of these neutral networks, λ being the proportion of neutral neighbors of a sequence, that is, the probability that, after a point mutation, the sequence is still mapped into the same structure:

$$\lim_{n \to \infty} \mu_n \{\Gamma_n \text{ is dense and connected}\} = \begin{cases} 1 \text{ for } \lambda > \lambda^* \\ 0 \text{ for } \lambda < \lambda^* . \end{cases}$$

The above results suggest that the preimage of a random structure consists of large connected subgraphs in sequence space.

3   Random Chemistries

We will define a *random chemistry* as a directed graph with the following relation associated to its directed edges y: *the structure located at the origin of y catalyses the formation of the structure located at the terminus.*

By no means do all random chemistries exhibit catalytic cycles. Their existence is heavily dependent on the maximal allowed number of molecules that *could* be catalyzed. To demonstrate that cycles are rare in some chemistries, we first discuss a random chemistry in which the number of molecules that can be catalyzed by a particular molecule is bounded by 2 [20]. The analysis proceeds by considering the union of two partial 1-factor graphs.

Let K_n be the complete graph on the n vertices $\{1, \ldots, n\}$. We fix a subset of $2m$ vertices $\{i_1, \ldots, i_{2m}\} \subset \{1, \ldots, n\}$ and define a graph $X_{m,n}$ having vertex set $\{1, \ldots, n\}$ as a directed 1-regular graph on $\{i_1, \ldots, i_{2m}\}$ (which are the vertices incident to exactly one edge). Clearly, there are

$$L(m,n) = \frac{1}{m!} \prod_{k=0}^{m-1} [(n-2k)(n-(2k+1))]$$

different graphs $X_{m,n}$. These form a finite probability space by assigning uniform probability i.e. $\mu_1(X) = 1/L(m,n)$. Two graphs, $X_{m,n}$ and $X'_{m,n}$, induce the graph $X_{m,n} \cup X'_{m,n}$ whose vertex set is $\{1, \ldots, n\}$ and whose edge set is $eX_{m,n} \cup eX'_{m,n}$. Obviously there are different pairs $X_{m,n}, X'_{m,n}$, leading to $X_{m,n} \cup X'_{m,n}$.

We now introduce our basic random graph model. It consists of subgraphs of K_n of the form $X_{m,n} \cup X'_{m,n}$ with the underlying probability measure

$$\mu_2\{Y\} = \sum_{(X_{m,n}, X'_{m,n}) : X_{m,n} \cup X'_{m,n} = Y} \mu_1\{X\} \mu_1\{X'\}.$$

This probability space will be referred to as $\Gamma_{m,n}$. It is easily verified that for a real number $\epsilon > 0$ a random graph $\Gamma_{m,n}$ has asymptotically $2m$ edges, and we can choose $m(n)$ and n big enough such that the average vertex degree is $\geq 1 - \epsilon$. As a first illustration, the expectation value for cycles of length 2 in $X_{m,n} \cup X'_{m,n}$ is, for $2m \leq n$:

$$\binom{n}{2} 2 \left[\frac{m}{n(n-1)}\right]^2 < \frac{1}{4} \frac{n}{n-1},$$

Lemma 1. *[20] Suppose $m, n \in N$ such that $2m \leq n$. Then for the random graph $\Gamma_{m,n}$ the following two assertions hold:*
(i) almost all vertices are contained in tree components,
(ii) there exists a constant $C > 0$ with the property that almost surely all components in Γ_m^n have sizes $\leq C \ln(n)$.

The above result proves that autocatalytic cycles are very rare in this type of random chemistry.

We next introduce a random chemistry that consists of subgraphs of a complete graph on n vertices, K_n, and is referred to as G_p. A subgraph here is obtained by selecting an edge of K_n with independent probability $p = c/n$, $c > 0$ a constant, and vK_n as vertex set. Hence a subgraph $Y < G_p$ with ℓ edges has probability $\mu_{c/n}(Y) = [c/n]^\ell [1 - c/n]^{n(n-1)-\ell}$. For $G_{c/n}$, $p_n = 1/n$ is a well known threshold function [2]:

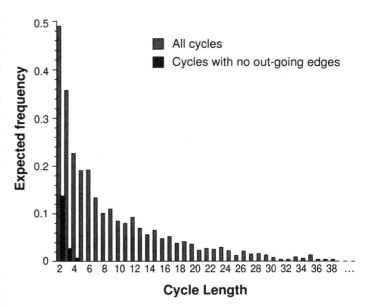

Figure 4: Frequency distribution of cycles in a random graph $G_{1/1000}$ on $n = 1000$ vertices, averaged over a sample of 1000 random graphs.

- for $0 < c < 1$ $G_{c/n}$ asymptotically almost surely all paths in $G_{c/n}$ have size $\leq O(\ln(n))$ and almost all vertices are contained in paths without backtracking

- for $c > 1$ $G_{c/n}$ a constant fraction of vertices is contained in paths with backtracking.

However, for any $c > 0$ there is a constant probability for the existence of cycles. For the expectation value of the numbers of cycles of length ℓ, we derive

$$\frac{1}{\ell}(n)_\ell \left[\frac{c}{n}\right]^\ell.$$

The above result implies that for finite ℓ, $\frac{1}{\ell}(n)_\ell \left[\frac{c}{n}\right]^\ell \sim c^\ell/\ell$, where $(n)_\ell = n(n-1)\ldots(n-\ell+1)$. Experimentally obtained distributions of cycle lengths, which verify this result, are shown in Figure 4.

For $0 < c < 1$ the probability of picking a vertex *not* contained in a tree-component tends to 0 for increasing n. For $c = 1$ a distinct change occurs in the structure of the random graph: a constant fraction of vertices is contained in components with cycles, and a giant component emerges in the graph. Changes in graph properties with increasing connectivity are well known [23], and have previously been discussed in the context of catalytic networks by Kauffman [16, 14] and Rasmussen [18].

We now suppose the following relation associated with a directed edge y of $G_{c/n}$: *the origin of y catalyses the terminus.* With this interpretation a random digraph becomes a catalytic network. The basic parameter c can be viewed as the mean number of structures that can be catalyzed by a given structure. In this context, it is of interest to determine the existence of certain induced subgraphs in $G_{c/n}$ that represent "cooperative" substructures in the catalytic graph. In particular, we are interested in finding cycles that have no outgoing edges, since such edges are "parasitic" on the stability of the cycle:

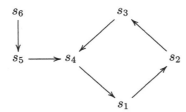

Lemma 2. *Let H_ℓ be the random variable counting the number of cycles in the probability space $G_{c/n}$ that have no outgoing edges. Then*

$$\mathbf{E}_c(H_\ell) = (n)_\ell \frac{1}{\ell} \left[\frac{c}{n}\right]^\ell \left[1 - \frac{c}{n}\right]^{(n-2)\ell},$$

and $\lim_{n\to\infty} \mathbf{E}_c(H_\ell) \sim \frac{1}{\ell} c^\ell e^{-c\ell}$. For an arbitrary natural number ℓ, $\mathbf{E}_c(H_\ell)$ is maximal for $c = 1$.

Proof: We apply linearity of expectation and first compute the probability of the occurrence of a cycle of length ℓ with no outgoing edges on ℓ fixed vertices (i.e. random structures) $s_1, \ldots, s_\ell$. This probability is given by

$$\left[\frac{c}{n}\right]^\ell \left[1 - \frac{c}{n}\right]^{(n-2)\ell},$$

since ℓ directed edges have to be selected among the ℓ vertices in a unique way and each of the vertices s_i has $n-2$ further out-edges none of which can be chosen. Now there are $(n)_\ell = n(n-1)\ldots(n-\ell+1)$ ways to select an ordered ℓ-tuple of vertices, and so doing we have counted each cycle-subgraph ℓ times, since we have started in every vertex s_i, $i = 1, \ldots, \ell$. Linearity of expectation implies now

$$\mathbf{E}_c(H_\ell) = (n)_\ell \frac{1}{\ell} \left[\frac{c}{n}\right]^\ell \left[1 - \frac{c}{n}\right]^{(n-2)\ell}.$$

The asymptotic results follows immediately. Finally,

$$\begin{aligned}
\frac{d}{dc}\left[\lim_{n\to\infty} \mathbf{E}_c(H_\ell)\right] &= \frac{1}{\ell}\left[\ell c^{(\ell-1)}e^{-c\ell} - c^\ell \ell e^{-c\ell}\right] \\
&= c^{\ell-1}e^{-c\ell}[1-c]
\end{aligned}$$

from which we conclude that for $c = 1$ $\lim_{n\to\infty} \mathbf{E}_c(H_\ell)$ is maximal, and the lemma is proved. $\square$

This result is important for the existence of stable cycles in the metabolic network, and shows that each structure should catalyze on average one other structure to maximize the probability of finding cycles with no outgoing edges.

4 Evolution in a random chemistry

We now fix a random chemistry $G_{1/n}$ (i.e. $c = 1$) as a random digraph over the set of structures, which are realized by members of a population of sequences. The time evolution of the population is obtained as a birth-death process with fixed population size N. This is a replication-deletion process similar to a discrete version of flow-reactor dynamics, with fixed population size.

A *population* $\mathbf{V}$, of size N, is a (finite) multi-set of sequences $(V_i \mid i \in N)$, where $\{V_i \mid i \in N\} \subset \mathcal{Q}_\alpha^n$ and $N > 1$. The time evolution of $\mathbf{V}$ is obtained by a mapping from $(V_i \mid i \in N)$ to the family $(V_i' \mid i \in N)$ as follows: we select an ordered pair (V_l, V_k) where $V_l, V_k \in \{V_i \mid i \in N\}$. The first coordinate of the pair V_l is chosen with a probability that is its fitness, relative to the mean fitness in the population. The second coordinate is selected with uniform probability on $(V_i \neq V_l \mid i \in N)$, i.e. $1/(N-1)$. Next we map the first sequence, $V_l = (x_1, \ldots, x_n)$, into the sequence $V^* = (x_1', \ldots, x_n')$; in other words we replicate the sequence in an error-prone fashion. This is performed by assigning to each coordinate x_i a $x_i' \neq x_i$ with probability p where all $x_i' \neq x_i$ are equally distributed, and leaving the coordinate fixed otherwise. This random mapping $V_l \mapsto V^*$ is called *replication*. Finally, we delete the second coordinate of the pair (V_l, V_k), that is V_k, and have a mapping $(V_l, V_k) \mapsto (V_l, V^*)$. The new sequence V^* is mapped into a structure by an iterated test for compatibility with each structure in an array of predefined structures, in which a λ-biased coin toss determines whether the sequence is mapped into each structure with which it is compatible. This is the realization of the iteration described in Equation (1). We perform such replication-deletion events at equidistant time steps, and for a population of size N we refer to a *generation* as N such time steps.

This replication-deletion process induces a dynamics on the population of sequences that should be contrasted with the dynamics induced by random search. The replication-deletion process maintains relatedness among the individuals in the population, meaning that the population is clustered in one or more regions of sequence space. Moves in that space are local only, mediated by point mutations. Given a population on the neutral network of a structure with high fitness, some proportion of that population will persist on that neutral network, and be responsible for the majority of replication events. Their offspring may either be mapped onto the same structure, or onto a different structure, in which case they "fall off" the neutral network. The population thus consists of a replicating core, and a cloud of offspring which "explore" nearby sequence space for higher fitness structures.

The dynamics of finite populations on neutral networks induced by sequence to structure maps exhibits

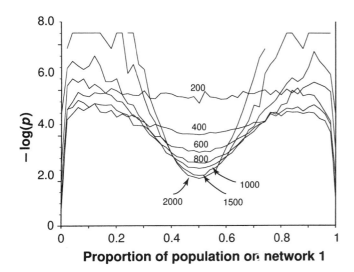

Figure 5: The probability distribution $-log(p)$ of the state of a population of sequences in a two-structure landscape, with increasing population size. At low N the population spends most of its time on one or other of the neutral networks, and can only span both networks simultaneously with $N > 1000$. State sampled every 10 generations from runs of 5000 generations, with $n = 30$.

distinct stochastic effects described in [19, 10, 27]. In a flat landscape, populations perform so-called *transitions* between neutral networks; a critical minimal population size can be characterized by the landscape and the neutral network [11]. Below this critical size, populations are unable to persist on two networks simultaneously; above it, they can (Figure 5). These phenomena determine much of the behavior of the experiments with random chemistries described below.

We now introduce the dynamical fitness assignment. At a time t, an arbitrary element of the population $V \in \mathbf{V}$ realizes a structure $s(V)$ from the mapping described above. This structure $s(V)$ is now a vertex in the corresponding random chemistry. We then identify all structures that are origins of edges which have $s(V)$ as terminus—the set of potential catalysts for $s(V)$, call it $\kappa[s(V)] = \{s_1, \ldots, s_r\}$.

For example, in the following subgraph of a random chemistry:

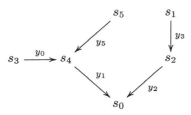

a sequence that was mapped into s_0 can be potentially catalyzed by sequences mapped into s_4 and s_2.

Next we determine how many sequences exist in our population at time t which are mapped into the set of catalysts $\kappa[s(V)]$. We assume the probability that within a single time-step a given molecule collides with $s(V)$ to be $\wp$ (independent of the structure of the molecules), which can be thought of as a function of the temperature of the system. The probability that at least one molecule from the set $\kappa[s(V)]$ collides with $s(V)$ is $1 - [1 - \wp]^{|\kappa[s(V)]|}$. Once a collision happens a duplex, consisting of $s(V)$ and the catalyzing molecule, forms with probability β, which is thus a binding affinity parameter. Note that β is normally a function of $s(V)$ and the catalysing molecule, though in our simulations β is kept constant for simplicity. With duplex formation, we consider $s(V)$ to be catalyzed by a specific element of $\kappa[s(V)]$, and assign to V the high fitness $\mathcal{K}$, otherwise it receives a low fitness of 1. A catalysis thus happens with probability

$$1 - [1 - \wp]^{\beta|\kappa[s(V)]|} .$$

This duplex is assumed to be short-lived, with the fitness of $s(V)$ returning to its normal level in the next time step unless catalyzed again. Iterating this procedure we assign fitness values to all elements of the population $\mathbf{V}$.

5   Computational Results

Experiments described here generally study the time evolution of populations of sequences with $n = 30$, population sizes N between 2000 and 8000, and the error rate p set such that the mean number of mutations per sequence on replication is one: $pn = 1$. The fitness of sequences realising catalyzed structures $\mathcal{K} = 100$, and uncatalyzed structures are assigned fitness 1. Sequences here are evolving in a landscape of 1000 structures, which are generated at random at the start of the run, and over which the catalytic network with $c = 1$ (see Lemma 2) is constructed, again at random. Runs are initialized with a population of randomly-generated sequences. Results from such runs are shown in Figures 6–8.

As is apparent from Figure 6, showing which structures are realized by the majority of the population, there are periods when the identity of this most common structure changes rapidly (suggesting that the population is continually realising different sets of structures) and periods of "stasis" when the most realised structures remain the same for a time. Examination of the metabolic graph reveals that these periods of stasis occur when the population finds a cycle (Figure 8). This they do with surprising consistency, despite the low proportion of structures involved in cycles which are short enough to support autocatalysis. However, populations on cycles inevitably leave the cycle, as one would expect from the stochastic nature of transitions between neutral networks (see Figure 5).

The experimental results also show the dramatic effect of population size on the subgraph of the metabolic

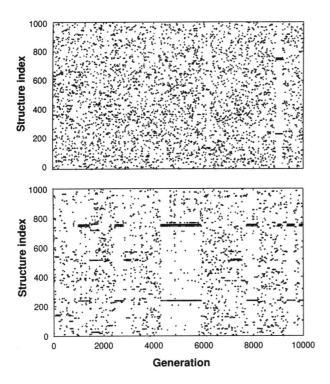

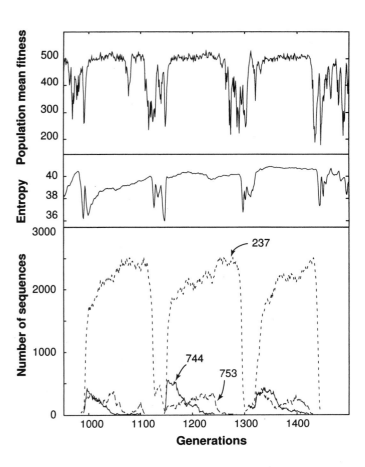

Figure 6: Time evolution of populations of a $N = 2000$ (upper) and a $N = 5000$ (lower) sequences of length 30, displayed in terms of the identities of the three most frequent structures realized by the population, on the same catalytic network. This catalytic network contains 5 cycles; the periods when the larger population inhabit the shortest, a 3-cycle, are evident. The structure of the catalytic graph around this 3-cycle is shown in Figure 8.

Figure 7: A close-up of the $N = 5000$ run shown in Figure 6, showing mean fitness (top), population entropy (middle) and (bottom) frequencies of sequences realising the members of the 3-cycle. Numbers correspond to structures which form a catalytic network displayed in Figure 8. Evidence for cycling of the population around the cycle is clear.

graph which is occupied at any one time, which can be understood in terms of the effects of N on the persistence of populations on one or more neutral networks (Figure 5). Smaller populations can be thought of as being "smeared" over a large number of structures, unable to maintain populations on more than one neutral network at a time and thus incapable of exploiting the catalytic effects of spanning the neutral networks of several catalyzing structures. As population size increases, the actual number of structures realised as the most frequent structure *decreases* because the population "condenses" onto substructures of the catalytic network that provide support, such as nodes with a higher in-degree. In addition, cycle persistence is longer, and the population spends more time on cycles.

Examination of the behavior of the population on a 3-cycle (Figures 7 and 8) shows that mean fitness is consistently high, as would be expected when a large proportion of the population are realising structures which are being reliably catalyzed. There is also evidence of flow around this cycle. The entropy plot reveals clearly when transitions are taking place, which are marked by sud-

den drops in entropy as the population is taken over by the offspring of sequences which are realising a new, fitter structure. Once such a structure is found (and while it remains fit) the population spreads out on its neutral network, increasing the entropy measure.

6 Discussion

In this paper we have shown that finite populations of sequences replicating with mutation and being mapped via a sequence to structure map into random structures, realize specific induced subgraphs of their underlying random chemistry. In our random chemistries all catalytic activities are equal, whence small cycles without outgoing edges are singled out to be the attractors of the evolutionary dynamics. Clearly, more detailed models of metabolic networks with, for example, Gaussian distributed catalytic activities, will exhibit different features. However, the emergence of cycles is a non-trivial fact and heavily depends on the random chemistry model, though is a generic feature of all models of metabolic networks. Unlike some other models intended to show the emergence of autocatalysis, the random chemistry graph in the current implementation stays fixed for the length of the run. The edges of this underlying graph should be interpreted as the chemical rules of the system; it is the subgraph induced by members of the population realising certain structures that is of interest, and it is this that reflects the emergent "metabolism" of the system. As the results show, populations inevitably exploit cycles when N is large enough.

Auto-catalytic networks have been studied by Eigen and Schuster [3, 4, 5, 7, 6], Kauffman [15] and others [10]. In the case of the Eigen-Schuster hypercycle the underlying equations were ODEs of the form

$$\frac{d}{dt}x_i = k_{i-1}x_{i-1}[\sum a_{k,i}x_i - \Phi(t)] \quad k_{i-1} > 0, \quad (2)$$

where x_{i-1}, x_i are the concentrations of molecules of type $i-1, i$ such that $i-1$ catalyses i and $\Phi(t)$ is the dilution flux. The catalytic activity here is essentially additive. Based on the Eigen-Schuster dynamics, Forst [9] has studied hypercycles incorporating sequence to structure mappings in RNA secondary structures, comparing nonlinear differential equation and finite population size results. The current model differs from these previous models in several respects. First, our basic assumption is that the replication of a sequence is catalyzed by exactly 1 other molecule. During the replication event the catalyst and target molecules form a duplex. Hence, doubling of the number of possible catalysts does not double the replication rate. The basic term here is $1 - [1 - \wp]^{|\kappa[s(V)]|}$ which is the probability that the molecule collides with a catalyst. Moreover we do not assume a cycle to be given. In our random chemistries the population establishes on certain classes of cycles singled out as a kind of attractor type. The resulting time evolution, i.e. the series of realized metabolic sub-networks

$$\{\mathbf{V}_t \,|\, t = 1, \ldots, n\} \longrightarrow \{M_t < G_{1/n}\} \quad (3)$$

where M_t is the metabolic network at t, is thence driven by two phenomena. First the topology induced by the sequence to structure mapping, which induces the capacity for neutral evolution, and second the dynamic fitness assignment. Neutral evolution is exactly the reason why cycles with outgoing edges go extinct after a certain time, even if the cycle has no out-going edges. This occurs by a random fixation of a "parasitic" structure that is may be catalyzed by a structure contained in the cycle, or may be some other high-fitness structure. As a consequence, the autocatalytic network collapses.

It is important to realise that transitions are not restricted to taking place between structures joined by a catalytic edge. Such an edge increases the likelihood that

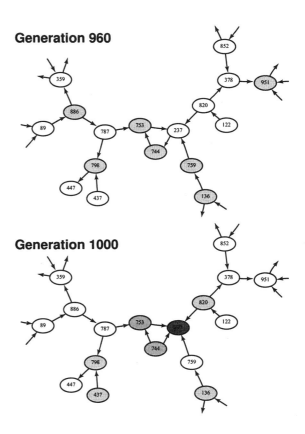

Generation 960

Generation 1000

Figure 8: Graphical illustration of population movement around the 3-cycle realised in Figure 7. Vertices of the graph are labelled with the index of the structure, arrows show catalytic edges of the random chemistry. Gray shades reflect the proportion of the population realising each structure. For more details see Figure 7, where actual numbers of sequences realising those structures are displayed.

the terminus will be the destination for a transition, because the target structure's fitness is maintained at a high level by the population on the origin of the edge. However, almost any high-fitness structure is a potential destination for a transition, since the neutral networks of most structures come close in sequence space [22, 24], and the majority of structures have neutral networks which are large enough to make them searchable [26].

In summary, we have introduced a model of the evolution of populations of sequences which are mapped into structures which form a catalytic network, in which both the structures and the catalytic digraph can be understood in graph theoretic terms. As in [18, 14], we identify $c = 1$ to be a critical threshold for the emergence of cycles in the graph of catalysis, though we also show that this value maximizes the probability of finding cycles with no out-going edges, which are important for the persistence of autocatalytic sets. The model presented here differs from previous models of autocatalysis by including a sequence to structure mapping, and being modeled by a stochastic collision process with finite population size. Preliminary results show how readily populations discover stabilizing sub-structures in the catalytic graph, and the effect of population size on this process.

Acknowledgments We thank Christopher L. Barrett for stimulating discussions, and William Tozier for his comments on the manuscript. Special thanks to Darrell Morgeson for his support. SF is funded by DARPA under grant ONR N0014-95-1-1000.

References

[1] Bagley, R.J. and Farmer, J.D. (1990) Spontaneous emergence of a metabolism. In C.G. Langton, C. Taylor, J.D. Farmer, and S. Rasmussen, editors, *Artificial Life II*, pages 93–140. Santa Fe Institute Studies in the Sciences of Complexity.

[2] Bollobás, B. (1985) *Random Graphs*. Academic Press, New York.

[3] Eigen, M. (1971) Selforganization of matter and the evolution of biological macromolecules. *Die Naturwissenschaften*, 10:465–523.

[4] Eigen, M. and Schuster, P.K. (1977) The hypercycle A: A principle of natural self-organization: Emergence of the hypercycle. *Naturwissenschaften*, 64:541–565.

[5] Eigen, M. and Schuster, P.K. (1979) *The Hypercycle: a principle of natural self-organization*. Springer, Berlin.

[6] Eigen, M. and Schuster, P.K. (1982) Stages of emerging life—five principles of early organization. *J. Mol. Evol.*, 19:47–61.

[7] Eigen, M., Schuster, P.K., Sigmund, K. and Wolff, R. (1980) Elementary step dynamics of catalytic hypercycles. *BioSystems*, 13:1–22.

[8] Farmer, J. D., Kauffman, S.A., and Packard, N. (1986) Autocatalytic replication of polymers. *Physica*, 22 D:50–67.

[9] Forst, C.V. and Reidys, C.M. (1996) On evolutionary dynamics. In *Proceedings of ALife V*. ALife V, Japan.

[10] Forst, C.V., Reidys, C.M., and Weber, J. (1995) Evolutionary dynamics and optimization: Neutral networks as model landscape for RNA secondary structure folding landscapes. In F. Morán, A. Moreno, J.J. Merelo, and P. Chacón, editors, *Advances in Artificial Life*, Lecture Notes in Artificial Intelligence, Springer, Berlin.

[11] Fraser, S.M. and Reidys, C.M. (1997) Evolutionary dynamics on random structures. In *Proceedings of the First Conference on Simulation and Optimization*, accepted.

[12] Grüner, W., Giegerich, R., Strothmann, D., Reidys, C.M., Weber, J., Hofacker, I.L., Stadler, P.F. and Schuster, P.K. (1996) Analysis of RNA sequence structure maps by exhaustive enumeration I. Neutral networks. *Monatshefte fuer Chemie*, 127:355–374.

[13] Grüner, W., Giegerich, R., Strothmann, D., Reidys, C.M., Weber, J., Hofacker, I.L., Stadler, P.F. and Schuster, P.K. (1996) Analysis of RNA sequence structure maps by exhaustive enumeration II. Structures of neutral networks and shape space covering. *Monatshefte fuer Chemie*, 127:375–389.

[14] Kauffman, S.A. (1993) *The Origins of Order*. Oxford University Press, Oxford, UK.

[15] Kauffman, S.A. (1971) Cellular Homoeostasis, epigenesis and replication in randomly aggregated macromolecular systems. *J. Cybernetics*, 1:71–96.

[16] Kauffman, S.A. (1986) Autocatalytic sets of proteins. *J. Theor. Biol.*, 119:1–24.

[17] Kimura, M. (1983) *The Neutral Theory of Molecular Evolution*. Cambridge University Press, Cambridge, UK.

[18] Rasmussen, S. (1987) Towards a quantitative theory of the origin of life. In C.G. Langton, editor, *Artificial Life I*, pages 79–104. Santa Fe Institute Studies in the Sciences of Complexity.

[19] Reidys, C.M. (1995) *Neutral Networks of RNA Secondary Structures*. PhD thesis, Friedrich Schiller Universität, IMB Jena.

[20] Reidys, C.M. (1996) Mapping in random structures. *SIAM Journal of Discrete Mathematics and Optimization*. submitted.

[21] Reidys, C.M. (1997) Random induced subgraphs of generalized n-cubes. *Advances in Applied Mathematics*, in press.

[22] Reidys, C.M., Stadler, P.F., and Schuster, P.K. (1997) Generic properties of combinatory maps and neutral networks of RNA secondary structures. *Bull. Math. Biol.*, 59(2):339–397.

[23] Erdős, P. and Rényi, A. (1960) On the evolution of random graphs. *Publ. Math. Inst. Hung. Acad. Sci.*, 5:17–61.

[24] Schuster, P.K. (1996) How does complexity arise in evolution? *Complexity*, 1:22–30.

[25] Schuster, P.K. (1995) Artificial life and molecular evolutionary biology. In F. Morán, A. Moreno, J.J. Merelo, and P. Chacón, editors, *Advances in Artificial Life*, Lecture Notes in Artificial Intelligence, Springer, Berlin.

[26] Schuster, P.K., Fontana, W., Stadler, P.F. and Hofacker, I.L. (1994) From sequences to shapes and back: a case study in RNA secondary structures. *Proc.Roy.Soc.*, B 255:279–284.

[27] Weber, J. (1997) *Dynamics on Neutral Evolution*. PhD thesis, Friedrich Schiller University, Jena.

Optimization Criteria for Design of Serial Transfer Evolution Experiments

Klausdieter Weller

Institut für Molekulare Biotechnologie, Jena, Germany

Beutenbergstraße 11, PF 100 813, D-07708 Jena, Germany

Phone: **49 (3641) 65 6455   Fax: **49 (3641) 65 6335

E-Mail: kweller@imb-jena.de

Key words:

RNA Systems, Fitness Landscapes, Natural Selection, Sexual Selection, Ecosystem Evolution, Evolutionary Optimization, Evolutionary Computation, Simulations of Ecological and Evolving Systems, Collective Behaviour, Cooperation, Evolution of Social Behaviour

Stochastic Modeling, Molecular Evolution, Evolution Reactor, Serial Transfer as Selection Pressure, Artificial Evolution, Optimization Criteria, Experiment Design, Population Dynamics, Quasispecies, Kinetic Fitness, Replication Kinetics, RNA Secondary Structure Prediction from Sequence, Structure-Function Mapping, Emergent Behaviour

Contents

Abstract

As opposed to rational design of biomolecular functions, using data base search, molecular modeling, and Quantitative Structure-Activity Relations, evolutionary design is based on molecular diversity and uses artificial evolution to obtain desired functions in growing biomolecule populations, subject to mutation and selection under well-designed selection pressure. Artificial evolution is directed evolution to obtain the desired species through survival of the fittest by designing environmental conditions.

Optimization of evolution experiments, therefore, is optimization of a criterion of evolution success in the space of experimental conditions. They are given by the parameters of the simulation model of molecular evolution under the selection pressure of the particular evolution reactor regime.

Two mutually complementary optimization criteria of evolution success are suggested. The criterion of evolution speed aims at obtaining the fittest species fastest. The criterion of quality control aims at obtaining the fittest species purest.

1 RNA, the Primary Target to both Natural and Artificial Life

Biological macromolecules are the result of eons of evolution. In order to understand these macromolecules, it is necessary to understand the evolutionary pressures that determined their current form. Conversely, the properties of these macromolecules encode this heritage, and can provide insight into the process of evolution. The effort to understand, reconstruct and simulate the evolution of biopolymers, including their structure and function, has become a key task involving such diverse fields as evolutionary biology, molecular biology, structural biology, biophysical chemistry, and bio-informatics.

Among molecular evolutionists it is common belief that molecular life started by using RNA as both an autocatalytically reproducing molecule and a first carrier of genetic information [1].

Arguments in favour of this so-called RNA world are both chemical and genetic. RNA rather than DNA is chemically simple enough to have been produced by known processes of polymer chemistry at the end of the prebiotic phase of the evolution of life, and RNA is able to evolve catalytic functions (ribozymes). RNA is able to be subject to Darwinian evolution since it represents simultaneously a genotype by its sequence, which is subject to mutation, and a phenotype by its secondary structure, which is subject to selection. Both length and replication accuracy of RNA are sufficient to encode the gene products required for early life. Although recent RNA is a messenger rather than a carrier of genetic information (apart from RNA viruses) it is striking that even in its recent role in cellular division of labour, RNA's function is determined by its secondary structure. Indeed, its secondary structure determines both its replication rate and its translation rate.

Due to these properties, RNA is not only an appropriate target for natural but also for artificial molecular evolution. Nucleic acid synthesis provides the RNA populations that are exposed to well-designed selection pressure to do directed evolution of RNA species with desired functions in evolution automata.

An evolution automaton is an integrated system for synthesizing and screening molecules using silicon wafers with numerous microscopic reaction vessels on their surfaces, subject to serial transfer of replicating RNA aliquots towards fresh supply of monomers and replicase enzyme [2] Error-prone replication under serial transfer leads to selection of fast growing species, since only those species have some chance to survive repetitive dilution.

2 Animal versus Molecule Breeding

Imagine to be a rural breeder. Your aim is breeding high performance domestic animals. Space of stables is limited. You have to do some random decimation at constant time intervals. You want to save time and money for food. Each successor race is higher in performance than its precessor race.

What would you consider a breeding success? High evolution speed where highest possible performance is reached as soon as possible or rather medium term prevalence of medium performance races?

High evolution speed requires a lot of attempts with their risk of failure by producing low performance animals who nevertheless consume food. You save time but not money.

Medium term prevalence of medium performance races means metastable establishment of rather purebred races of good performance. However, even if transition periods towards higher performance races are relatively short, you have to wait long for the appearance of the highest possible performance race. You save money but not time.

These optimization criteria seem to be mutually exclusive or at least complementary to each other. Therefore, for evolution experiment design we shall compute separate optimization criteria, either a measure of evolution speed or a measure of molecular quality control. Each of these criteria will require different parameter constellations of experimental conditions.

3 Stochastic Simulation Model of Molecular Evolution

3.1 Deterministic versus Stochastic Evolution Models

There are several types of evolution reactors, distinct by their regime of selection pressure.

Deterministic selection theory considers two types of selection pressure, constant population size (constant organization), as realized experimentally in (dilution) flow reactor and constant flow (of monomers), as realized experimentally in continuously stirred tank reactor (CSTR) [3] [4].

However, deterministic models of evolution reactors are inappropriate for the design of artificial evolution for several reasons.

In simulation for experimental design of molecular evolutionary systems, realistic replication kinetics must be used, which is intractable by deterministic models. Realistic replication kinetics can be treated analytically only in special cases and in an approximative manner. Further, the approximation implies the assumption of monomer bases in excess with constant concentrations incorporated into rate constants, enzyme and polymer being the only reactants. [5]

The deterministic theory of molecular evolution ignores molecular details (of mutation and selection) and reaction intermediates in enzymatic RNA replication (enzyme-nucleic acid complexes).

In macroscopic phenomenological reaction kinetics the rate constants are model parameters without any explicit relation to properties of reactants. In evolutionary processes, however, replication and degradation rates, A and D [6, 7] of RNA species are functions of structural properties of RNA secondary structures.

Therefore, one has to resort to a numerical algorithm for the simulation of stochastic time evolution of coupled (bio)chemical reaction networks [8].

In this framework, the structure of the RNA molecules is the carrier of their kinetic fitness both for replication (A) and for degradation (D). However, the system suffers from frustration, since secondary structure stability is negatively correlated to both replication and degradation reactivity, A and D.

In this framework, any number of coupled chemical reactions may be treated, even the extended reaction scheme of enzymatic replication [9]. However, the present model does not yet treat the enzyme as a reactant.

The development of the stochastic simulation model of serial transfer experiments, as a C program, was based on a C program FlowReactor [10] using a comparative fitness model of RNA replication where the replication rate of evolving RNA species increases at decreasing structural distance of their secondary structure from some predefined target structure considered fittest.

RNA secondary structure prediction was done by means of FOLD inside the Vienna RNA Package [11] which is implemented into the simulation program.

The selection pressure regime in this stochastic simulation model of serial transfer corresponds to that of constant population size (constant organization) , as realized experimentally in (dilution) flow reactor, apart from replacement of continuous with discontinuous dilution regime. Nevertheless, it is E = A - D, the effective rate of replication, that is optimized in serial transfer evolution.

The main modifications done to develop the stochastic simulation model of serial transfer experiments, as a C program STReactor, concern transition from continuous to discontinuous dilution regime, and substitution of the comparative fitness model with some absolute fitness model evaluating intrinsic structural features to compute replication and degradation rates A and D, as well as involvement of monomeric reactants into both model and optimization.

3.2 Computerized Simulation Model of Serial Transfer Reactor

Elements and parameters of a simplified model of serial transfer experiments are as follows

- n reaction vessels for serial transfer

- n concentrations (of enzyme replicase), of ATP, UTP, GTP and CTP, and RNA (number of monomer or polymer molecules, respectively)

- mechanism of (enzymatic) RNA replication

- mutation rate or instead single digit accuracy of RNA replication

- time interval Δt between serial tranfers

- aliquot $\Delta V/V$ of serial transfer or dilution factor

- model assumption on the fitness landscape of RNA mutants

In stochastic simulation models of molecular evolution, a tree data structure keeps track of the mutatively replicating polymer population. In its nodes there are stored the sequences, their copy numbers, their secondary structures, and some associated information.

The algorithm by Gillespie for numerical simulation of the stochastics of coupled chemical reactions treats replication and degradation as these coupled reactions. They take place as stochastic events at stochastic moments and in stochastic order.

Replication and degradation reactivities of population members are the main part of the associated information stored in the tree nodes. In the context of Gillespie's algorithm it is called channel reactivity of replication or degradation, respectively, since in general there are several reaction channels.

In striking contrast to conventional chemical kinetics, the stochastic model allows for relating the channel reactivity to properties of the reactants. An equivalent term for channel reactivity is kinetic fitness.

The adequate choice of the fitness model is a decisive element in model development. To design a realistic evolution model, fitness must be taken to be a measure of replication or degradation reactivity, respectively. Structural details of RNA secondary structure are judged with respect to their promotion of replication and their resistance to degradation in order to compute some score for kinetic fitness, A and D.

Mutative replication is modelled as a single reaction. The role of the enzyme replicase is treated implicitly only, in terms of its overall monomer-unspecific replication accuracy. Based on this replication accuracy at each sequence site a stochastic decision is met on whether or not to mutate this site.

The serial transfer reactor regime is defined by discontinuous dilution at fixed time intervals as a selection pressure. Small aliquots of the replication mixture are transferred into the next test tube containing a fresh solution of monomers (and an enzyme for RNA replication). Most mutants of small copy numbers are discarded at dilution; only mutants of high copy number will be transferred, in copy numbers reduced according to the dilution factor.

In striking contrast to the stochastic simulation model of continuous dilution flow reactor (FlowReactor), in the stochastic simulation model of serial transfer reactor (STReactor), dilution is not any more a stochastic event i.e. a quasireaction besides replication. Rather, replications are the single reactions in the sense of stochastic simulation of coupled (bio)chemical reactions, unless a degradation reaction is added explicitly.

Dilution is now an extrinsic rather than an intrinsic process. Dilution is not any more a part of the routine react(), containing the numerical algorithm for the simulation of stochastic time evolution of coupled chemical reaction networks, but is performed by one hierarchical level higher in the main program.

The former numerical simulation by react() in the main program of FlowReactor is now embedded into a cycle of dimension n running across the n test tubes of serial transfer experiments in STReactor. In each of the test tubes a simulation is now running until the user-defined stop time is reached. Dilution is performed at each transition into the next test tube in this n-dimensional cycle.

Dilution is performed by traversing the tree representing the mutatively replicating polymer population. Based on the dilution factor at each node a stochastic decision is met on whether or not to reduce the copy number of the current node. As a result, a corresponding fraction of single copy sequences will remain in the tree together with an appropriately reduced copy number of frequent sequences.

By appropriate reinitiation, after each dilution the monomer particle numbers for the next test tube are read by the program and the total reactivity is calculated anew. Time parameters are reinitiated to zero.

In contrast to the former case of FlowReactor, the program STReactor considers explicitly the monomer particle numbers in its simulation algorithm. The introduction of monomer particle numbers affects the model of replication, the computation of replication channel reactivities and hence the computation of total reactivity. Most importantly, the replication channel reactivities based on structural fitness measures alone must be replaced with monomer-dependent channel reactivities everywhere in the C code, in particular in the visit functions of tree traversal, to account for proper weights in replication node selection at random.

Gillespie's algorithm introduces channel reactivities as composed from two factors, c and h, a structural factor as a measure of the reaction probability, and a combinatorial factor of reactant configurations according to the reaction stoichiometry (of A,U,G,C), which counts the number of realizations of that reaction. In FlowReactor, the combinatorial factor was reduced to the copy number of a particular sequence. What has to be supplemented is a combinatorial factor of monomer configurations in a replication reaction.

The computation of this combinatorial factor of monomer configurations requires a stoichiometric analysis of each sequence selected. This factor is not computed as a binomial coefficient that would apply to parallel reactions where any serial order of reactant incorporation into the reaction product is irrelevant. Instead, the serial character of replication reactions was modelled by counting different orders of monomer incorporation as different realizations.

In contrast to replication, degradation (without degrading agents) is modelled as hydrolysis reaction of first order. Therefore, the combinatorial factor of degradation channel reactivities is just the copy number of a particular sequence.

The model of replication was changed in comparison with FlowReactor. Mutative sites according to the replication accuracy were found as before. However, the wrong monomer for incorporation is selected according to its current relative supply. Most importantly, monomer consumption during replication is balanced and monomer particle numbers are updated regularly so as to provide their current values for any computation of combinatorial factor of monomer configurations in a replication reaction.

The mean time interval between stochastic events is inversely proportional to the total reactivity of the reaction mixture, which is the sum of replication and degradation channel reactivities over all nodes.

Two cases of simulation interruptions have been taken into account which may be identified by their corresponding error messages: "abortive replication due to missing monomers" and "no sequence transferred, abort of serial transfer"

Two different replication models, i.e. mechanism of non-enzymatic RNA replication, were investigated in detail: single strand replication as a simplified model and complementary PLUS and MINUS strand replication as a more realistic model. The latter was derived from the former by first constructing the complementary sequence of each replication sequence selected and taking subsequently the complementary sequence to be subject to mutation. The results presented (Figures 1, 2 and Figures 3, 4, 5, 6) refer to the second model of replication. They show the common evolution of quasispecies pairs with comparable copy numbers.

4 Results and Discussion

4.1 Result Files

There are two types of result files, monitor files (Figures 1, 2) and snapshot files (Figures 3, 4, 5, 6).

At the end of the simulation run, these result files or protocol records may be inspected. The monitor file presents a short description of the simulation run across several test tubes in terms of average quantities. Snapshot files are detailed descriptions of the current evolutionary state of the population in the container. They are provided by the program at dump time intervals.

The columns of the monitor file refering to Gillespie's algorithm are as follows

- current time in arbitrary units, reinitialized in every subsequent test tube
- current number of foldings performed on sequences resulting from mutative replication
- current number of sequence individuals in the evolution container
- current number of structure individuals in the evolution container
- current average sequence diversity (number of species per sequence)
- current average structure diversity (number of species per structure)
- current average replication reactivity (reactivity per sequence)
- current average degradation reactivity (reactivity per sequence)
- current average structural distance from target (distance per sequence)
- current number of monomers A

- current number of monomers U
- current number of monomers G
- current number of monomers C
- current total reactivity of reaction mixture
- current total reactivity divided by current sequence number

The columns of the monitor file referring to the evolution model are as follows (Figures 1, 2, discussed in the next section)

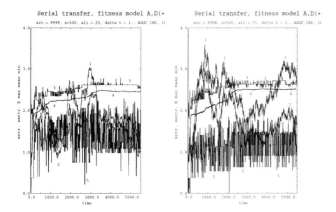

Figure 1: conservative evolution

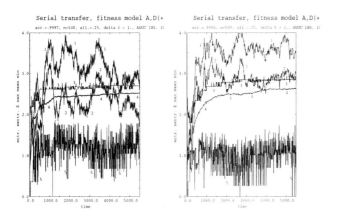

Figure 2: progressive evolution

- current entropic diversity of sequences, entr (1)
- current entropic diversity of structures, sentr (2)
- current maximum excess productivity, E max (3)
- current mean excess productivity, E mean (4)
- current minimum excess productivity, E min (5)

Snapshot files contain two head lines indicating the number (label) of the particular test tube and the time of population dump of that test tube. Next, the sequences in that population are listed together with some numerical characteristics and their secondary structure. These numerical characteristics of individuals in the population

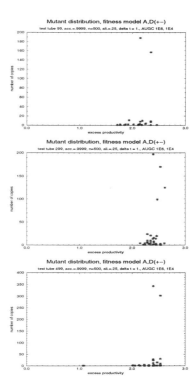

Figure 3: conservative evolution, mutant distribution

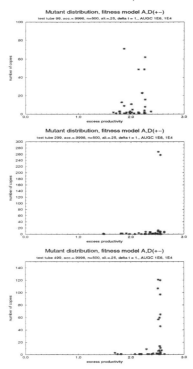

Figure 4: conservative evolution, mutant distribution

are their index, their number of copies, their structural replication rate A, their structural degradation rate D, their excess productivity E = A - D, and their structural distance from target (just as a label, not used in this fitness model).

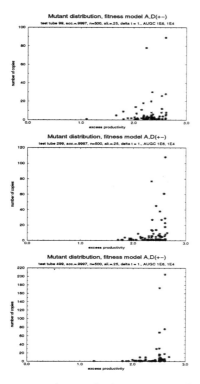

Figure 5: progressive evolution, mutant distribution

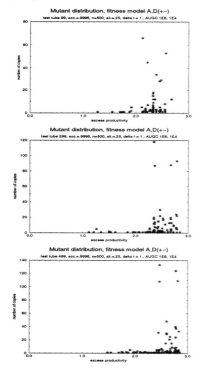

Figure 6: progressive evolution, mutant distribution

Snapshot files provide current mutant distributions, i.e. plots of their number of copies versus their kinetic fitness values E (Figures 3, 4, 5, 6).

Snapshot files present even more details not shown by the corresponding plot, such as sequences and structures of population members and current population size.

Population analysis finds in each snapshot file the master pair of quasispecies, by looking for the species of maximum copy number and its complementary sequence, and it finds the best and the worst individual.

4.2 Definition of Optimization Criteria

Comparison of four simulation runs was done, run for the same parameters of serial transfers n, Δt, $\Delta V/V$, but different values of replication accuracy (Figures 1, 2 and Figures 3, 4, 5, 6). The present case study, therefore, is not an attempt to design selection pressure but, instead, an attempt to define optimization criteria of evolution success, either evolution speed or quality control.

As predicted by deterministic selection theory for continuous dilution at constant organization, the evolution optimizes the mean value of excess productivity E = A - D. This result is independent of the composition of the population in terms of individual E values.

From deterministic selection theory the phenomenon of error threshold is well known. In stochastic evolution models, the composition of the population will become less and less distinct in terms of quasispecies if the replication accuracy decreases.

Conservative evolution (Figure 1, Figure 3, 4) at relatively high replication accuracy enables metastable stationary states of quasispecies characterized by low enough values of entropic population diversity. Only successively the system finds better molecule races keeping good races in predominant copy numbers for long periods. Only a few bad species can be tolerated.

Progressive evolution (Figure 2, Figure 5, 6) at relatively low replication accuracy enables more attempts to check candidates for the function looked for. Mean excess productivity will enhance immediately and find its optimum soon in the evolution run. However, at the same time the system will encounter more failure. It finds nearly instantaneously enough good species so as to tolerate more bad species.

Consider the curves of mean excess productivity and of entropic diversity. Transitions to higher evolutionary levels are associated with diversity maxima. Since the function looked for is related to structure rather than to sequence, structural diversity is more relevant than sequence diversity [12]. Structural diversity is lower than sequence diversity. A multitude of alternative sequences fold up to the same structure. The evolutionary pressure limits the number of possible structures, but not the number of sequences which make up these structures.

The conclusion of greatest impact on evolutionary experiments from the theory of sequence-structure mapping is the statement that a multitude of sequences may give rise to a particular structure with particular functionality or fitness, rather than a single sequence. This fact ensures that the probability of the evolutionary synthesis of a predefined RNA species with predefined functionality is not practically zero [13].

Entropic diversity takes on characteristic numerical values for particular compositions of the population. If the population is uniform this measure is zero. If the population consists of two species exactly equal in copy number, this measure is ln 2. If the population consists of n species exactly equal in copy number, this measure is ln n.

In conclusion, the following optimization criteria are suggested.

A measure of evolution speed should be the fraction of the evolution run period in which the system already lives at its optimum value of mean excess productivity.

A measure of quality control should be the number of incidences per serial transfer, where the entropic diversity of structures takes on values less than ln 3.

From an experimental point of view, these measures of success might seem not to be very satisfactory. Note, however, that a serial transfer regime can favour only species of rapid growth, rather than of specific interaction or enzyme functionality. In serial transfer simulation you have to initiate the population with a library of almost functional molecules. The simulation model will then find fast replicating variants of library members in preparative amounts.

This simulation model might be useful for prerunning a number of experimental conditions and exploring evolutionary scenarios. To more closely approach experimental design, more sophisticated information management and decision support seem necessary for validation of simulation with experimental and archival data.

Acknowledgements

The author would like to thank Peter Schuster for discussion and encouragement, and Christian Forst, Jacqueline Weber, and Ulrike Goebel (IMB Jena) for helpful comments and suggestions. This work is based on the BMB+F Project 9502.

References

[1] Raymond F. Gesteland and John F. Atkins (eds.), The RNA World, The Nature of Modern RNA Suggests a Prebiotic RNA World, Cold Spring Harbor Laboratory Press, 1993

[2] A. Schober, Strategien einer evolutiven Biotechnologie, Theses, Verlag Shaker, Aachen 1994 (Berichte aus der Physik)

[3] B.-O. Küppers, Molecular Theory of Evolution, Springer 1983

[4] Peter Schuster and Karl Sigmund, Dynamics of Evolutionary Optimization, Berichte der Bunsen-Gesellschaft für physikalische Chemie, 89, 668-682, 1985

[5] B. Gassner and P. Schuster, Model Studies on RNA-Replication, Monatshefte für Chemie 113, 237-263, 1982

[6] Walter Fontana and Wolfgang Schnabl and Peter Schuster, Physical aspects of evolutionary optimization and adaption, Physical Review A, 40, 3301-3321, 1989

[7] W. Fontana and T. Griesmacher and W. Schnabl and P.F. Stadler and P. Schuster, Statistics of landscapes based on free energies, Replication and Degredation Rate Constants of RNA Secondary Structures, Monatshefte der Chemie, 122, 795-819, 1991

[8] D.T. Gillespie, A General Method for Numerically Simulating the Stochastic Time Evolution of Coupled Chemical Reactions, J. Comput. Phys. 22, 403-434, 1976

[9] C. K. Biebricher and M. Eigen and W. C. Gardiner Jr. Kinetics of RNA replication, Biochemistry, 22, 2544-2559, 1983

[10] W. Fontana, Ein Computermodell der evolutionären Optimierung, Theses 1987, Inst. of Theoretical Chemistry, Uni. Vienna, Austria

[11] I.L. Hofacker, W. Fontana, P.F.Stadler, L.S. Bonhoeffer, M. Tacker, and P. Schuster, Fast Folding and Comparison of RNA Secondary Structure (The Vienna RNA Package) Monatshefte für Chemie (Chemical Monthly) 125, 167-188, 1994

[12] Peter Schuster and Walter Fontana and Peter F. Stadler and Ivo L. Hofacker, From Sequences to Shapes and Back: A Case Study in RNA Secondary Structures, Proc.Roy.Soc.(London)B, 255, 279-284, 1994

[13] Peter Schuster, Artificial Life and Molecular Evolutionary Biology, Lecture Notes in Artificial Intelligence 929, Subseries of Lecture Notes in Computer Science, F. Moran, A. Moreno, J.J. Merelo, P. Chacon (eds.), Advances in Artificial Life, Third European Conference on Artificial Life Granada, Spain, June 1995, Springer

EVOLUTIONARY DYNAMICS

Competition in a Fitness Landscape

Franco Bagnoli[(1)]*and **Michele Bezzi**[(2)]†

(1) Dipartimento di Matematica Applicata, Università di Firenze,
via S. Marta, 3 I-50139, Firenze, Italy; e-mail: bagnoli@dma.unifi.it.
(2) Dipartimento di Fisica, Università di Bologna,
Via Irnerio 46, I-40126 Bologna, Italy; e-mail: bezzi@ing.unifi.it.

Abstract

We present an extension of Eigen's model for quasi-species including the competition among individuals, proposed as the simplest mechanism for the formation of new species in a smooth fitness landscape. The evolution equation for the probability distribution of species has the form of a nonlinear reaction-diffusion equation. We are able to obtain analytically an approximation of the critical threshold for the species formation. The comparison with the numerical resolution of the original equation is very good.

1 Introduction

In this paper we address the problem of formation of species in simple ecosystems, possibly mirroring some aspects of bacterial and viral evolution. Our model can be considered as an extension of Eigen's model [1, 2]. With respect to the latter, we introduce the interactions among individuals.

The correspondence of this kind of models with real biological systems is rather schematic: the (haploid) organisms are only represented by their genetic information (the genotype), and we do not consider sexuality nor age structure or polymorphism. Moreover, a spatial mean field approximation is applied, so that the relevant dynamical quantity is the distribution of genotypes. This distribution evolves under the combined effects of selection and mutations. Selection is represented by the concept of fitness landscape [3, 4], a function of the genotype that represents the average fraction of survivors per unit of time, and includes the effects of reproductive efficiency, survival and foraging strategies, predation and parassitism, etc. In other words, the fitness function is the evolutive landscape seen by a given individual. Only point mutations are considered, and these are assumed to be generated by independent Poisson processes. The presence of mutations allows the definition of the distance between two genotypes, given by the minimum number of mutations required to connect them. Assuming only point mutations, the genotypic space is a hypercube, each direction being spanned by the possible values of each symbol in the sequence. In the Boolean case, which is the one considered here, each point mutation connects two vertices along the axis corresponding to the locus where the mutation has taken place.

In the original work, Eigen and Schuster [2] showed that a landscape with a single maximum of the fitness allows for a phase transition from a bell-shaped distribution of the population centered at the location of the maximum of the fitness function (the *master sequence*) to a flatter distribution. This *error transition* is triggered by the mutation rate.

It has been shown [5, 6] that Eigen's model is equivalent to an equilibrium statistical mechanical model of interacting spins, the latter being the elements of the genome. In this way several evolutionary concepts can be mapped to a statistical mechanics language. In particular, for a static fitness landscape, the evolution becomes the process of optimization of an "energy" function (the logarithm of the fitness), balanced by the entropy. The genealogy of a particular genome can be represented as a two-dimensional spin system. We refer to the two directions as the time and the genotypic one, respectively. The coupling in the time direction is ferromagnetic and is given by the mutations. The coupling in the genotypic direction is given by the fitness function and is in general long range. While this mapping is suggestive and allows a precise characterization of vaguely defined terms, from

*also INFN and INFM sez. di Firenze; DRECAM-SPEC, CEA Saclay, 91191 Gif-Sur-Yvette Cedex, France
†INFN, sez. di Bologna

the point of view of numerical and analytical treatments of the equations, the original differential equation approach is more effective.

Borrowing the language of statistical mechanics, the single sharp maximum case (the one studied originally by Eigen and Schuster [2]) can be defined as a degenerate genotypic space, since all individuals but the master sequence have the same fitness, and we consider it as a particular case of the more general class of genotypic spaces in which the fitness depends only on the genotypic distance from the master sequence.

The degenerate landscape can be represented as a linear one by introducing the appropriate multiplicity factor. Using this approach, one implicitly assumes that all degenerate strains are evenly populated, i.e., that there exist high transition rates among these strains. This assumption has been exploited in the study of the phase diagram of the single sharp maximum case [7].

Finally, assuming a hierarchy for the relevance of mutations, one can have a pure linear genotypic space. For instance, let us consider Boolean sequences of length L and assume that $000\ldots$ is the master sequence. Deleterious mutations $0 \to 1$ are assumed to be non-lethal only if they accumulate at the ends of the sequence, as (for $L = 3$)

$$111 \leftrightarrow 110 \leftrightarrow 100 \leftrightarrow 000 \leftrightarrow 001 \leftrightarrow 011 \leftrightarrow 111, \quad (1)$$

where the arrows denote the mutations. One can introduce a genotypic index $-3 \le x \le 3$ and rewrite eq. (1) as

$$-3 \leftrightarrow -2 \leftrightarrow -1 \leftrightarrow 0 \leftrightarrow 1 \leftrightarrow 2 \leftrightarrow 3 \equiv -3,$$

i.e., we have a linear genotypic space with periodic boundary conditions.

An hypothetical example of such a hierarchical space is that of a series of genes that code for enzymes involved in a metabolic pathway. A mutation in the first enzyme of the sequence is more likely lethal, while a mutation that lowers the affinity of the last enzyme with its substrate could be easily retained even if the fitness of the individual is lowered. This mutation reduce also the specificity of the last enzyme with its substrate (which is the product of the previous metabolic step), allowing a mutation in the previous enzyme and so on.

Almost all the works dealt with abstract landscapes (mainly RNA world). The difficulty in applying these concepts to real biological systems concerns the definition of the fitness function, that relates the genotype to the phenotype. In particular, the difficulty resides in predicting the stability or the efficiency of a protein given its sequence of amino acids. One can circumvent this difficulty taking into consideration only the subclass of all possible mutations that do not change the protein structure. One example of an explicit definition of the fitness function is given by the variation of the reproductive rate of bacteria due to synonymous mutations and tRNA usage [8, 9]. This study can be considered an example of a degenerate smooth maximum fitness landscape. Another explicit biological application concerns the evolution of RNA viruses on HeLa cultures [10]. In this case the fitness landscape was assumed to be linear (without multiplicity).

While in general the fitness landscape depends on the presence of others individuals and changes with time, it is much simpler to study the problem for a given (static) landscape, that can be thought as an approximation for diluted, rapidly evolving organisms or self-catalytic molecules (RNA world), while all other species remain constant. In these static landscapes, all strains are coupled by the normalization of the probability distribution, and for small values of the mutation rate (a situation fulfilled in the real case) and smooth landscapes, the fittest quasi-species always eliminates all others [6]. The global coupling given by the normalization of probability corresponds to the case of finite population size or the alternative phases of exponential growth followed by starvation and death. For of a rugged static landscape (for instance generated by an Hopfield Hamiltonian [5, 6]), the distribution of species can reflect the distribution of the peaks of fitness. In these cases the interesting question concerns the error transition.

In this work we address the problem of species formation in presence of competition. The idea of our approach is the following: we look for a stable probability distribution formed by separated quasi-species, and for each of them we compute the effective fitness landscape due to the competition with individuals of the same and all other species. Then, the parameters of the distribution (position and weight of quasi-species) are obtained in a self-consistent way. In this way we are able to compute analytically the threshold for species formation transition in a linear landscape.

We shall deal with coupled differential and finite difference equations, that can be thought as a mean field approximation of a true microscopic model. The effect of the finiteness of population, however, should imply a cutoff on the tail of the distribution, due to the discreteness of the individuals, and thus the dependence of evolution on the initial condition (for an application of the cutoff effect, see Ref. [10]). We do not consider here these effects.

The sketch of this paper is the following: first of all, we formalize the model in section 2, then we work out the distribution of a quasi-species near a maximum of the effective fitness landscape in section 3, and finally we apply the self-consistency condition in section 4, comparing the analytical approximation with the numerical resolution. Conclusions and perspectives are drawn in the last section.

2 The model

We describe in detail the approximations that lead to our model. An individual is identified by its genome, represented by an integer index x (no polymorphism nor age structure). We study the case of a linear genotypic space (hierarchical relevance of mutations).

We shall not consider here age structure nor the effects of polymorphism in the phenotype. For the sake of simplicity, we shall deal only with haploid organisms. Moreover, we do not consider the spatial structure (spatial mean field). The experimental setup of reference is that of an bacterial population that grows in a stirred liquid medium, with constant supply of food and removal of solution, so that the average size of the population is constant. Another possible experiment concerns RNA viruses [10].

We consider the distribution $p(x, t)$, that gives the probability of observing the strain x at time t within the population. We shall denote the whole distribution as $\boldsymbol{p}(t)$. At each time step we have

$$\sum_x p(x, t) = 1. \qquad (2)$$

Organisms undergo selection, reproduction and mutation. The reproduction and death rates are represented by a fitness function $A\big(x, \boldsymbol{p}(t)\big)$, that represents the average fraction of individual of a given strain x surviving after a time step in absence of mutation for a given probability distribution $\boldsymbol{p}(t)$.

As usual, we consider only point mutations, and we factorize the probability of multiple mutations (i.e., they are considered independent events). The rate of mutation per time step of a single element of the genome is μ; each point mutation connects the strain x to $x + 1$ or $x - 1$.

Since we want to model existing populations, we deal with small mutation rates. In this limit, only one point mutation can occur at most during a time step. This is the main difference with previous works, in which the main goal was to study a mutation-induced phase transition (error threshold).

With these assumptions, the generic evolution equation (master equation) for the probability distribution is

$$\alpha(t)p(x, t+1) = \left(1 + \mu\frac{\delta^2}{\delta x^2}\right) A\big(x, \boldsymbol{p}(t)\big)p(x, t); \qquad (3)$$

where the discrete second derivative $\delta^2/\delta x^2$ is defined as

$$\frac{\delta f(x)}{\delta x^2} = f(x+1) + f(x-1) - 2f(x),$$

and $\alpha(t)$ maintains the normalization of $\boldsymbol{p}(t)$. In the following we shall mix freely the continuous and discrete formulations of the problem.

The numerical resolution of eq. (3) shows that a stable asymptotic distribution exists for almost all initial conditions. In the asymptotic limit $t \to \infty$, $\boldsymbol{p}(t+1) = \boldsymbol{p}(t) \equiv \boldsymbol{p}(x)$. Summing over x in eq. (3) and using the normalization condition, eq. (2), we have:

$$\alpha = \sum_x A(x, \boldsymbol{p})p(x) = \overline{A}. \qquad (4)$$

The normalization factor α thus corresponds to the average fitness. The quantities A and α are defined up to an arbitrary constant.

In general the fitness A depends on x and on the probability distribution $\boldsymbol{p}$. The dependence on x includes the structural stability of proteins, the efficiency of enzymes, etc. This corresponds to the fitness of the individual x if grown in isolation. On the other hand, the effective fitness seen by an individual depends also on the composition of the environment, i.e., on $\boldsymbol{p}$. This $\boldsymbol{p}$-dependence can be further split into two parts: the competition with other clones of the same strain, (intra-strain competition) and that with different strains (inter-strains competition), disregarding more complex patterns as the group structure (colonies). The intra-strain term has the effect of broadening the curve of a quasi-species and of lowering its fitness, while the inter-strains part can induce the formation of distinct quasi-species.

Since A is strictly positive, it can be written as

$$A(x, \boldsymbol{p}) = \exp\big(H(x, \boldsymbol{p})\big).$$

If A is sufficiently smooth (including the dependence on $\boldsymbol{p}$), one can rewrite eq. (3) in the asymptotic limit, using a continuous approximation for x as

$$\alpha p = Ap + \mu\frac{\partial^2}{\partial x^2}(Ap), \qquad (5)$$

Where we have neglected to indicate the genotype index x and the explicit dependence on $\boldsymbol{p}$. Eq. (5) has the form of a nonlinear diffusion-reaction equation. Since we want to investigate the phenomenon of species formation, we look for an asymptotic distribution $\boldsymbol{p}$ formed by a superposition of several non-overlapping bell-shaped curves, where the term non-overlapping means almost uncoupled by mutations. Let us number these curves using the index i, and denote each of them as $p_i(x)$, with $p(x) = \sum_i p_i(x)$. Each $p_i(x)$ is centered around $\overline{x}_i$ and its weight is $\int p_i(x)dx = \gamma_i$, with $\sum_i \gamma_i = 1$. We further assume that each $p_i(x)$ obeys the same asymptotic condition, eq. (5) (this is a sufficient but not necessary condition). Defining

$$\overline{A}_i = \frac{1}{\gamma_i}\int A(x)p_i(x)dx = \alpha, \qquad (6)$$

we see that in a stable ecosystem all quasi-species have the same average fitness.

3 Evolution near a maximum

We need the expression of p if a given static fitness $A(x)$ has a smooth, isolated maximum for $x = 0$ (*smooth maximum* approximation). Let us assume that

$$A(x) \simeq A_0(1 - ax^2), \qquad (7)$$

where $A_0 = A(0)$. Substituting $q = Ap$ in eq. (5) we have (neglecting to indicate the genotype index x, and using primes to denote differentiation with respect to it):

$$\frac{\alpha}{A}q = q + \mu q''.$$

Looking for $q = \exp(w)$,

$$\frac{\alpha}{A} = 1 + \mu(w'^2 + w''),$$

and approximating $A^{-1} = A_0^{-1}(1 + ax^2)$, we have

$$\frac{\alpha}{A_0}(1 + ax^2) = 1 + \mu(w'^2 + w''). \qquad (8)$$

A possible solution is

$$w(x) = -\frac{x^2}{2\sigma^2}.$$

Substituting into eq. (8) we finally get

$$\frac{\alpha}{A_0} = \frac{2 + a\mu - \sqrt{4a\mu + a^2\mu^2}}{2}. \qquad (9)$$

Since $\alpha = \overline{A}$, α/A_0 is less than one we have chosen the minus sign. In the limit $a\mu \to 0$ (small mutation rate and smooth maximum), we have

$$\frac{\alpha}{A_0} \simeq 1 - \sqrt{a\mu}$$

and

$$\sigma^2 \simeq \sqrt{\frac{\mu}{a}}. \qquad (10)$$

The asymptotic solution is

$$p(x) = \gamma \frac{1 + ax^2}{\sqrt{2\pi}\sigma(1 + a\sigma^2)} \exp\left(-\frac{x^2}{2\sigma^2}\right),$$

so that $\int p(x)dx = \gamma$. The solution is a bell-shaped curve, its width σ being determined by the combined effects of the curvature a of maximum and the mutation rate μ.. In the next section, we shall apply these results to a quasi-species i. In this case one should substitute $p \to p_i$, $\gamma \to \gamma_i$ and $x \to x - \overline{x}_i$.

For completeness, we study also the case of a *sharp maximum*, for which $A(x)$ varies considerably with x. In this case the growth rate of less fit strains has a large

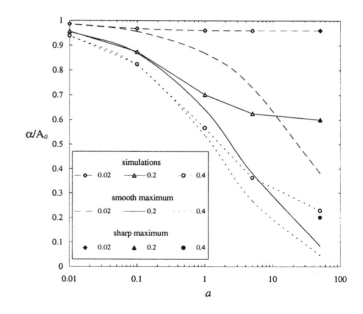

Figure 1: Average fitness α/A_0 versus the coefficient a, of the fitness function, eq. (7), for some values of the mutation rate μ. Legend: *numerical resolution* corresponds to the numerical solution of eq. (3), *smooth maximum* refers to eq. (9) and *sharp maximum* to eq. (11)

contribution from the mutations of fittest strains, while the reverse flow is negligible, thus

$$p(x - 1)A(x - 1) \gg p(x)A(x) \gg p(x + 1)A(x + 1)$$

neglecting last term, and substituting $q(x) = A(x)p(x)$ in eq. (3) we get:

$$\frac{\alpha}{A_0} = 1 - 2\mu \qquad \text{for } x = 0 \quad (11)$$

$$q(x) = \frac{\mu}{(\alpha A(x) - 1 + 2\mu)}q(x - 1) \qquad \text{for } x > 0 \quad (12)$$

Near $x = 0$, combining eq. (11), eq. (12) and eq. (7)), we have

$$q(x) = \frac{\mu}{(1 - 2\mu)ax^2}q(x - 1).$$

In this approximation the solution is

$$q(x) = \left(\frac{\mu}{1 - 2\mu a}\right)^x \frac{1}{(x!)^2},$$

and

$$y(x) = A(x)q(x) \simeq \frac{1}{A_0}(1 + ax^2)\left(\frac{\mu A_0}{\alpha a}\right)^x \frac{1}{x!^2}.$$

We have checked the validity of these approximations numerically solving eq. (3); the comparisons are shown in Figure (1). We observe that the *smooth maximum* approximation agrees with the numerics for for small values of a, when $A(x)$ varies slowly with x, while the *sharp maximum* approximation agrees with the numerical results for large values of a, when small variations of x correspond to large variations of $A(x)$.

4 Speciation

Let us now study the stable quasi-species distribution for a simple interacting fitness landscape. The fitness $A(x, \boldsymbol{p}) = \exp(H(x, \boldsymbol{p}))$ is given by

$$H(x, \boldsymbol{p}) = H_0 + H_1(x) + H_2(x, \boldsymbol{p}) + \ldots$$

where H_0 is an arbitrary constant, $H_1(x)$ is the static landscape, i.e., the fitness seen by an individual in isolation (it includes the interaction with all other slowly varying species) and $H_2(x, \boldsymbol{p})$ is the interaction landscape. We examine the case of a single quadratic maximum of H_1, using the explicit form:

$$H_1(x) = b \left(1 - \frac{|x|}{r} - \frac{1}{1 + \frac{|x|}{r}} \right),$$

where r gives the amplitude of the quadratic maximum, and b is the curvature. For $x \to \infty$, $H_1(x) \simeq b(1 - |x|/r)$, while for $x \to 0$, $H_1(x) \simeq -bx^2/r^2$. We have checked numerically that other similar smooth potentials give the same results of this one.

We assume that the interactions among individuals are always negative (competition) and decrease exponentially with the distance:

$$H_2(x, \boldsymbol{p}) = -J \int \exp\left(-\frac{(x-y)^2}{2R^2} \right) p(y) dy.$$

Numerically solving eq. (3) we obtain the asymptotic probability distribution showed in Figure 2. One can observe the presence of several non-overlapping quasi-species. For $R \to \infty$, substituting $p(x) = \sum_i p_i(x)$, one has

$$H_2(x, \boldsymbol{p}) = -J \sum_i \gamma_i \exp\left(-\frac{(x - \overline{x}_i)^2}{2R^2} \right).$$

The location $\overline{x}_k$ of the maximum of the quasi-species k is given by:

$$\left. \frac{dA}{dx} \right|_{\overline{x}_k} = 0.$$

The species 0 occupies the fittest position $\overline{x}_0 = 0$. For $k \neq 0$ we have (using the large x approximation for H_1):

$$-\frac{b}{r} + J \sum_i \gamma_i \frac{\overline{x}_k - \overline{x}_i}{R^2} \exp\left(-\frac{(\overline{x}_k - \overline{x}_i)^2}{2R^2} \right) = 0.$$

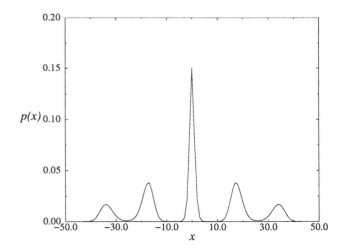

Figure 2: Probability distribution with five quasi-species. Numerical values are $\mu = 0.01$, $H_0 = 1.0$, $b = 0.2$, $J = 7.0$, $R = 10$ and $r = 3$.

We consider now the case of three species, two of which are symmetric with respect to the dominant one. We have $\overline{x}_0 = 0$, $\overline{x}_1 = -\overline{x}_2 = \overline{x}$. In the limit $\mu \to 0$, we can consider $\alpha = A_0(1 - \sqrt{a\mu}) = A_0$, and thus $\alpha = A(0) = A(\overline{x})$ (this is a strong approximation which simplifies the computation), and

$$-b + \frac{b\overline{x}}{r} + J\gamma_1 + \frac{R^2 b}{r\overline{x}} = J\gamma_0 + 2\frac{\gamma_1}{\gamma_0}\frac{R^2 b}{r\overline{x}}.$$

Finally, we have the following system

$$z^2 - G(\gamma_0 - \gamma_1)z + 1 - 2\frac{\gamma_1}{\gamma_0} - z\frac{r}{R} = 0, \qquad (13)$$

$$\gamma_0 + 2\gamma_1 = 1, \qquad (14)$$

$$G\gamma_0 z \exp(-z^2/2) = 1, \qquad (15)$$

where $z = \overline{x}/R$ and $G = Jr/Rb$.

The limit of coexistence for the three species is given by $\gamma_0 = 1$ (and thus $\gamma_1 = 0$). We compute the critical value G_c of G for the coexistence of three species, in the limit $r/R \to 0$. The first order term $G_c^{(0)}$ is obtained computing z from eq. (14)

$$z = \frac{G_c^{(0)} + \sqrt{G_c^{(0)^2} - 4}}{2},$$

and inserting this value into eq. (15). Solving numerically this equation, we have $G_c^{(0)} \simeq 2.2160$. The first correction $G_c^{(1)}(r/R)$ is obtained from eq. (14), and is simply $G_c^{(1)} = -r/R$. So finally we have for the critical threshold of species formation G_c

$$G_c = 2.216 - \frac{r}{R}. \qquad (16)$$

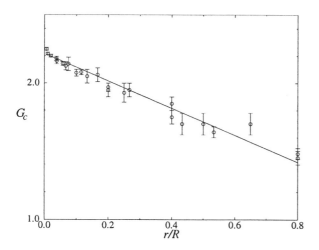

Figure 3: Behavior of G_c versus r/R. The continuous line represents the analytical approximation, eq. (16), the circles are obtained from numerical resolution. The error bars represent the maximum error.

We have solved numerically eq. (3) for different values of the parameters, and we have checked that the threshold of coexistence of the three species depends only on G. In particular, this threshold does not depends on the mutation rate μ, at least for $\mu < 0.1$, which is a very high mutation rate for real organisms. The most important effect of μ is the broadening of quasi-species curves, that can eventually merge. In the range of parameters used, G depends only on ratio r/R. Both these results are in agreement with the analytical predictions obtained above. In Figure 3 we compare the numerical and analytical results, plotting the different threshold value G_c as function of r/R.

5   Discussion and conclusions

We have studied a simple model for species formation. This model can be considered an extension of Eigen's one [1, 2], with the inclusion of competition, which if the fundamental ingredient for species formation in smooth landscapes. On the other hand, from an individual's point of view and disregarding complex structures such as the colonial organization, the more similar the phenotype the more important the sharing of resources and thus the competition. Since we assumed a smooth dependence of phenotype on genotype, we simply modeled the competition $J(x,y)$ between the two strains x and y by means of a smooth function of the distance between two genotypes: $J(x,y) = -J \exp(-(x-y)^2/2R^2)$. In this way the strongest competition occurs with other instances of the same strain, which is reasonable. One can interpret our interaction terms as a cluster expansion of a long-range potential, in which we retained single and two bodies contributions. From the point of view of population dynamics, our form of modeling the competition is

equivalent to the Verlhust damping term (logistic equation).

In a real ecosystem, however, there could be positive contributions to the interaction term J. In particular, it can happen that $J(x,y) > 0$ and $J(y,x) < 0$ (predation or parassitism), or $J(x,y) > 0$ and $J(y,x) > 0$ (cooperation). An investigation on the origin of complexity in random ecosystems is in progress. In particular we want to study the effects of time fluctuation of fitness (say due to human interaction) on the number of coexisting species.

We have studied the effects of competition in a linear (i.e., hierarchic) genotypic space. Our results synthesize in Figure 3. The dependence of the threshold for the formation of quasi-species obtained analytically from our approximations reflects very well the numerical results. We also checked that the latter does not depend on the mutation rate μ, up to $\mu = 0.1$.

Acknowledgements

We wish to thank G. Guasti, G. Cocho, R. Rechtman, G. Martinez-Mekler and P.Lió for fruitful discussions. M.B. thanks the Dipartimento di Matematica Applicata "G. Sansone" for friendly hospitality. Part of this work was done during the workshop *Chaos and Complexity* at ISI-Villa Gualino (Torino, Italy) under CE contract ERBCHBGCT930295.

References

[1] W. Eigen, *Naturwissenshaften* **58** 465 (1971).

[2] W. Eigen and P. Schuster, *Naturwissenshaften* **64**, 541 (1977).

[3] S. Wright, *The Roles of Mutation, Inbreeding, Crossbreeding, and Selection in Evolution*, Proc. 6th Int. Cong. Genetics, Ithaca, **1**, 356 (1932).

[4] L. Peliti, *Fitness Landscapes and evolution* http://xxx.lanl.gov/abs/cond-mat/9505003

[5] I. Leuthäusser, *J. Stat. Phys* **48** 343 (1987).

[6] P. Tarazona, *Phys. Rev. A* **45** 6038 (1992).

[7] D. Alves and J. F. Fontanari, *Phys. Rev. E* **54** 4048 (1996).

[8] F. Bagnoli and P. Lió, *J. Theor. Biol.* **173** 271 (1995).

[9] F. Bagnoli, G. Guasti, P. Lió, *Translation optimization in bacteria: statistical models*, in Nonlinear Excitations in Biomolecules, M. Peyrard, Editor (Les Editions de Phisique-Springer, 1995).

[10] L.S. Tsimring, H. Levine and D.A. Kessler, *Phys. Rev. Lett.* **76** 4440 (1996).

Information Analysis of Fitness Landscapes

Vesselin K. Vassilev

Information Technologies Lab
New Bulgarian University
Acad. G. Bonchev Str., bl. 8,
Sofia 1113, Bulgaria
E-mail: vesselin@inf.nbu.acad.bg

Abstract

This paper introduces a method for analysis of fitness landscapes. The underlying idea is to consider a fitness landscape as an ensemble of objects with different information characteristics, namely the information content, the entropy of the ensemble, and the information stability that is obtained by filtering the information content out. The information characteristics of a range of landscapes with known correlation features are analyzed in an attempt to determine the influence of the landscape ruggedness on the information characteristics of the landscape. We show that the proposed analysis is accurate measure of landscape ruggedness, and a suitable tool for investigating the modality of the landscapes. Using the information analysis, we study a smoothing landscape technique that is inspired by the idea that a landscape could be considered as a superposition of smoother landscapes. The analysis reveals why smoothing is achieved and what actually decrease the landscape ruggedness when the smoothing landscape technique is used.

1 Introduction

The notion of a *fitness landscape*, introduced by Wright [21], has become an important concept in evolutionary computation. The relationship between genotypes, determined by an evolutionary operator, and the fitness values assigned to each genotype via some mapping, known as a fitness function, constitutes the fitness landscape [8]. Recently, the landscapes of a range of problems of known difficulty have been analyzed in an attempt to determine the relation between the structure of the landscapes and the performance of the Evolutionary Algorithms (EAs) [2, 3, 12, 13, 14]. In this paper, a method for analysis of the structure of the landscapes is proposed. The analysis is used to explore a smoothing landscape technique.

The analysis of the structure of the fitness landscapes allows us to examine the difficulty of the task that has to be solved. A number of techniques for analysis of the structure of the landscapes exists [20, 12, 13, 17, 6]. Weinberger has investigated how the autocorrelation function of the fitness values of points along the steps of a random walk relates to the ruggedness of the examined landscape [20]. The autocorrelation function of random walks for various landscapes has been also explored by Manderick, Weger, and Spiessens [13]. Together with the autocorrelation function, they have examined the correlation length of the landscapes and the fitness correlation of the corresponding evolutionary operators. Lipsitch has applied the correlation analysis to landscapes generated by iterations of elementary cellular automata to explore the relationship between the nature of the local interactions of neighboring genes, characteristics of the generated landscapes, and the adaptive capabilities of the populations on these landscapes [12]. Another landscape analysis method, based on the described correlation techniques, has been proposed by Hordijk [6]. He has used the Box-Jenkins approach to statistical time series in order to extend the correlation analysis.

The work, reported here, proposes a different method for analysis of the structure of the landscapes. It is inspired by the information dimension, that is a measure of rugged systems [18], and is called an *information analysis*. The method is based on the assumption that each fitness landscape can be presented as an ensemble of various information objects, which are characterized by their size, form, and distribution. To analyze these characteristics, we explore two information features of the landscapes. These are first, the information content or the degree of diversity of the local optima, and second, the information stability or the expressiveness of the optima. These features allow us to obtain information about the structure of the landscapes that can not be given by the other analysis methods.

Using the information analysis we explore a smoothing landscape technique inspired by the assumption that a rugged landscape can be presented by a superposition of smoother landscapes [16]. To smooth a landscape, we replace the landscape structures by one of the smoother landscape substructures. The replacement is implemented by changing the fitness function, so that the information about the global optima that could be obtained by the original landscape to be preserved.

Similarly to the autocorrelation function, the information analysis is applicable to the fitness values of individuals along the steps of a random walk. That is why an important assumption made here is that the fitness landscapes are statistically isotropic.

The paper includes in section two a brief description of the landscape model and several important notes about the landscape ruggedness. Section three offers the information analysis. The analysis is examined in section four. Having the information analysis, a landscape smoothing is studied in section five. At the end, discussion is made and some conclusions are derived.

2 Fitness Landscapes

The fitness landscapes are search spaces which elements are *phenotypes*, represented by their *genotype*. A *fitness value* is assigned to each genotype and it reflects the phenotype ability to survive and reproduce. This process of evaluating of a genotype is implemented by a *fitness function* that specifies how *good* the encoded phenotype is. Usually, the better genotype has a higher fitness value. There is a relation between the points on the landscape and it is defined by the evolutionary operator that is used to search on the landscape. By applying this operator, a move is made from one point to another. This defines connections between the genotypes. A pair of genotypes will be connected, when the genotypes is reached from one another by applying the evolutionary operator exactly once. So, the fitness landscapes are search spaces obtained by applying the evolutionary operators to the elements of the search space of an evolutionary algorithm. In its most general form a landscape is a directed graph whose vertices are genotypes, labelled with fitnesses, and whose edges are connections among genotypes, defined by the evolutionary operator [8]. The described model has two important advantages: first, easily can be defined such notions as local and global optimum, neighbor, basin of attraction, etc; and second, the different evolutionary operators construct different fitness landscapes.

The adaptive capabilities of the Evolutionary Algorithms strongly depend on the structure of the fitness landscapes. If the landscape is rugged, it is difficult for the population to adapt. Hence, the landscape is hard for the EA. The degree of ruggedness of the landscapes is determined by the fitness differences between neighboring points. In other words, the landscape ruggedness depends mainly on the characteristics of the global and local optima. These are the altitude of each optimum, the size of the basin of attraction that is determined by the optimum, and the diversity of the optima. A landscape will be rugged, when the diversity and the altitude of the local optima is very high, and the basin of attraction of each optimum is very small.

The most popular way to examine the landscape ruggedness is to measure the degree of correlation between points of the landscape [20, 13, 12]. The degree of correlation between the individuals depends on the difference between their fitness values. The smooth landscapes are highly correlated because the landscape points have similar fitnesses. If the fitness difference is very large, the landscape is very rugged and the correlation is low.

The correlation measures provide some generalized information about the ruggedness of fitness landscapes. Unfortunately, this information is often insufficient to examine the structure of the landscapes precisely. Several types of features specify the landscape ruggedness. To analyze them, we consider that the fitness landscape can be defined as an ensemble of objects where each object is presented by a vertex and the possible outcomes that may be produced by the corresponding evolutionary operator of the vertex. Notice, that there are several types of vertices which can be classified into three class: flat points (each vertex together with its neighbors belongs to a plain), isolated points (each vertex is higher/lower then all neighbors), and the third class that is constituted by the vertices which are not flat or isolated points. We use two information features to specify the degree of ruggedness of an ensemble of objects. These features are the *information content* of the ensemble, that can be specified by Shannon entropy, and the *information stability*, the expressiveness of the objects. The information content of a landscape will be specified by the diversity of local optima which form the landscape. Respectively, the information stability of a landscape depends on the differences of the vertices' fitnesses.

3 A Fitness Landscape Analysis

In this section, we define a landscapes analysis that reflects the described above information characteristics.

3.1 The Information Characteristics of Landscapes

We evaluate the information content of the landscape, where the accuracy of the estimation is determined by a special parameter. This parameter allows us to analyze the structure and to determine the information stability of the examined landscape.

Let $F = \{f_0, f_1, ..., f_n\}$ be a sequence of fitnesses, which are real numbers from the interval $\mathcal{I}$, obtained by a random walk on the landscape $\mathcal{L}$. Therefore they correspond to a path in $\mathcal{L}$ and contain information about the structure of the landscape. If $\mathcal{L}$ is rugged, we will expect that the interpolated sequence F will be a rugged curve. The interpolated sequence will be a straight line, when the landscape is flat. In order to measure the information content of the sequence F, we estimate the information entropy of a string $Q(\varepsilon) = q_0 q_1 q_2 ... q_{n-1}$, where each element $q_i \in \{-1, 0, 1\}$ is determined by the function

$$\sigma_F(i, \varepsilon) = \begin{cases} -1, & \text{if } f_{i+1} - f_i < -\varepsilon \\ 0, & \text{if } |f_{i+1} - f_i| \leq \varepsilon \\ 1, & \text{if } f_{i+1} - f_i > \varepsilon \end{cases} \qquad (1)$$

in the following way:

$$q_i = \sigma_F(i, \varepsilon). \qquad (2)$$

The parameter ε is a fixed real number from the interval $[0, l_\mathcal{I}]$, where $l_\mathcal{I}$ is the length of the interval $\mathcal{I}$. This parameter determines the accuracy of the calculation of the string $Q(\varepsilon)$. If $\varepsilon = 0$, the function σ_F will be very sensitive to the differences between fitnesses and $Q(\varepsilon)$ will be determined as precisely as possible. When the parameter ε is $l_\mathcal{I}$, the string $Q(\varepsilon)$ will be a string of 0's.

The string $Q(\varepsilon)$ contains information about the structure of the landscape. Note that the function σ_F associates each edge of the path, constituted by F, with an element from the set $\{-1, 0, 1\}$. Therefore each string $q_i q_{i+1}$ presents one vertex from the path F. In order to estimate the information entropy of $Q(\varepsilon)$, we use the function:

$$H(\varepsilon) = -\sum_{p \neq q} P_{\{pq\}} \log P_{\{pq\}}, \qquad (3)$$

where $P_{\{pq\}}$ are the probabilities of the possible substrings pq of different elements from the set $\{-1, 0, 1\}$.

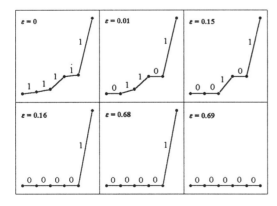

Figure 1: The string $Q(\varepsilon)$ of a sample landscape path $F = \{0, 0.01, 0.05, 0.2, 0.21, 0.9\}$ for several ε parameters. The parameter ε changes the information that corresponds to the landscape structure.

By calculating the information entropy of the string $Q(\varepsilon)$, we measure the information content of F where the accuracy of the estimation is tuned by the parameter ε. Note that the parameter ε is like a glasses through which we observe the corresponding landscape (Figure 1). For

small values of ε, the function σ_F of the equation 1 will be very sensitive to the difference between fitnesses, i.e. our glasses allow us to see each element of the landscape. If ε is zero then the accuracy of the estimation, given by $H(\varepsilon)$, is high. In contrast, for $\varepsilon = l_\mathcal{I}$, the information content of $Q(\varepsilon)$ will be zero, i.e. the landscape will be determined as relatively smooth. We use the parameter ε in order to filter the information content out. Therefore this parameter can be used to specify the information stability of the landscape.

Consider for example the fitness sequence $F = \{0, 0.01, 0.05, 0.2, 0.21, 0.9\}$ from the interval $[0, 1]$. To calculate the function $H(\varepsilon)$ we have to derive the string $Q(\varepsilon) = q_1 q_2 q_3 q_4$ (see Figure 1). The information char-

ε	$Q(\varepsilon)$	$H(\varepsilon)$
0	11111	0
0.01	01101	0.4091
0.15	00101	0.4091
0.16	00001	0.3593
0.68	00001	0.3593
0.69	00000	0
1	00000	0

Table 1: Information characteristics of the landscape path $F = \{0, 0.01, 0.05, 0.2, 0.21, 0.9\}$.

acteristics of the example landscape path are presented in Table 1. This is a special case of *irregular* climbing on the landscape, i.e. the moving steps are not uniform. Although the information stability is comparatively high (approximately 0.69), since the information content $H(0)$ is zero, we can conclude that the landscape is smooth. The landscape, however, is not flat as $H(0) < H(0.01)$.

3.2 Properties of the Information Characteristics

The information characteristics have four important properties. First, for each sequence of fitnesses the information stability $\varepsilon^\star$ can be derived. It follows from the definition of the string $Q(\varepsilon)$. Since $Q(l_\mathcal{I})$ is a string of 0's, we conclude that $\varepsilon^\star \leq l_\mathcal{I}$.

Second, if $\varepsilon^\star$ is the information stability then $H(\varepsilon)$ will be zero for each ε greater than $\varepsilon^\star$, i.e. $\varepsilon^\star \leq \varepsilon \leq l_\mathcal{I}$. Therefore, it is unnecessary to calculate the information content for values of the parameter ε, higher than the information stability.

Third, the information content $H(\varepsilon)$ for landscapes generated by *regular* climbing or descending steps is a positive constant for each $\varepsilon \in [0, \varepsilon^\star)$, where $\varepsilon^\star$ is the information stability. We say that a given landscape will be generated by *regular* moving steps when the condition

$$f_{i+1} = f_i \pm const$$

is fulfilled for each landscape path (fitness sequence)

$$...f_i, f_{i+1}, ..., f_{i+k}, ...$$

This class is interesting because it generalizes the maximally multimodal landscapes (it has been shown that the maximally multimodal landscapes can be easy for EAs [7]). Unfortunately, various types of landscapes are presented in this class. In order to specify when a given landscape is maximally multimodal, together with the information content $H(\varepsilon)$, we have to calculate the coefficient:

$$h(\varepsilon) = - \sum_{q \in \{-1,0,1\}} P_{\{qq\}} \log P_{\{qq\}}, \qquad (4)$$

where $P_{\{qq\}}$ are the probabilities of the possible substrings qq in $Q(\varepsilon)$. This coefficient is an estimate of the variety of *straight parts* of the corresponding landscape path. When the coefficient $h(0)$ is approximately zero then the investigated landscape, that is determined by regular moving steps, could be maximally rugged. Certainly, this will depend mainly on the information content $H(\varepsilon)$. Using these notes, we propose the following assertion:

If $H(\varepsilon) = \log 2$ and $h(\varepsilon) = 0$ for each $\varepsilon \in [0, \varepsilon^\star)$, where $\varepsilon^\star$ is the information stability, then the explored landscape path will be maximally multimodal or an increasing/decreasing step function.

Since $h(\varepsilon) = 0$ and $H(\varepsilon) > 0$ for each $\varepsilon \in [0, \varepsilon^\star)$, it follows that each substring $q_i q_{i+1}$ in the string $Q(\varepsilon) = q_0 q_1 q_2 ... q_{n-1}$, where $q_i \in \{-1, 0, 1\}$, is nonhomogeneous, i.e. there are not *straight parts* in the landscape path. Furthermore, when $h(\varepsilon)$ is zero, the minimal entropy of the string $Q(\varepsilon)$ will be $\log 2$. It is due to the fact that the entropy of $Q(\varepsilon)$ will be minimal, when $q_i = q_{i+2}$ and $q_i \neq q_{i+1}$. Hence, $Q(\varepsilon)$ is the string $pqpq...pq$ for each $\varepsilon \in [0, \varepsilon^\star)$, where $p, q \in \{-1, 0, 1\}$ and $p \neq q$, since

$$
\begin{aligned}
H(\varepsilon) &= -P_{\{pq\}} \log P_{\{pq\}} - P_{\{qp\}} \log P_{\{qp\}} \\
&= -\frac{n/2}{n} \log \frac{n/2}{n} - \frac{n/2}{n} \log \frac{n/2}{n} \\
&= -\log \frac{1}{2} \\
&= \log 2
\end{aligned}
$$

where n is the length of $Q(\varepsilon)$. It is evident that the explored path will be:

- maximally multimodal, when p is -1 and q is 1 (p is 1 and q is -1);

- an increasing step function, when p is 0 and q is 1 (p is 1 and q is 0);

- a decreasing step function, when p is 0 and q is -1 (p is -1 and q is 0).

Fourth, there is a sequence of fitnesses and parameters ε_1, ε_2 such that

$$H(\varepsilon_1) < H(\varepsilon_2),$$

where $0 \leq \varepsilon_1 < \varepsilon_2 \leq l_\mathcal{I}$. At first sight it seems that $H(\varepsilon)$ will decrease when the parameter ε increases. However, there are exceptions which are related to the landscapes, generated by irregular moving steps. We demonstrate that such sequence exists. Let $a \in \mathcal{I}$, and let c be a positive constant such that $a + \frac{3}{2}c \in \mathcal{I}$. Hence, we can define a sequence of fitnesses in the following way:

$$
\begin{aligned}
f_1 &= a \\
f_2 &= f_1 + \frac{c}{2} \\
f_3 &= f_2 + c \\
f_4 &= f_2 \\
&... \\
f_k &= f_{k-4} \ , \ k > 4 \ .
\end{aligned}
$$

If $\varepsilon_2 = \frac{c}{2}$ and $\varepsilon_1 = \frac{\varepsilon_2}{2}$ then $H(\varepsilon_1) < H(\varepsilon_2)$. A typical example of such landscapes is presented in Table 1, where $\varepsilon_1 = 0$ and $\varepsilon_2 = 0.01$.

3.3 The Information Analysis of Landscapes

Having the definition of the information characteristics, a landscape analysis technique can now be proposed. First, using the landscape model as given in section 2, we use a particular evolutionary operator to perform a random walk on the landscape. Applying the operator to m genotypes, we generate m sequences of fitness values. Second, for each sequence of fitness values, the information content is calculated for several values of the parameter ε. Note, however, that the parameter ε has to cover the interval $[0, l_\mathcal{I}]$. So, we obtain m functions $H_1(\varepsilon), H_2(\varepsilon), ..., H_m(\varepsilon)$ that represent the information characteristics of the corresponding landscape paths. Third, having the information characteristics of each sequence of fitnesses, an *information function* is constructed as means of the information contents, i.e.

$$H(\varepsilon) = \frac{1}{m} \sum_{i=1}^{m} H_i(\varepsilon).$$

The information function is the average information content $H(\varepsilon)$ of the investigated landscape.

4 The Information Characteristics and Fitness Landscape Ruggedness

In this section, several landscapes with tunable ruggedness [9, 12] are examined by using the proposed information analysis. The goal is to show that the information analysis is reliable and does not contradict the conclusions, suggested by the degree of correlation between the points of the landscapes.

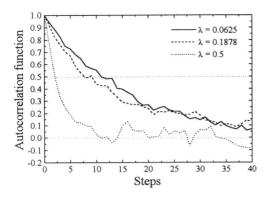

Figure 2: Autocorrelation of random walks on landscapes generated by iterations of elementary cellular automata with λ parameters 0.0625, 0.1878, and 0.5.

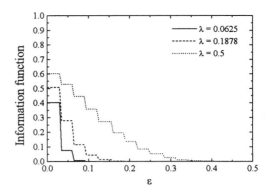

Figure 3: Information function of landscapes generated by iterations of elementary cellular automata with λ parameters 0.0625, 0.1878, and 0.5.

4.1 Cellular Automata Landscapes

Fitness landscapes with tunable ruggedness can be generated by elementary cellular automata [4]. Briefly, the landscapes are constructed by estimating the phenotypes, created through k iterations of cellular automata, initialized with genotypes [12]. The ruggedness can be tuned by a special parameter λ that determines the rate of information entropy in the automata transition rule [10]. Using this parameter Li, Packard, and Langton divide the elementary cellular automata rules into six classes [11]. These classifications are based on the differences in the behavior of elementary cellular automata. Lipsitch has shown that fitness landscapes can be classified according to the classification of cellular automata rules that generate them. Roughly, three classes of landscapes, generated by cellular automata, exist. The highest correlated landscapes, which form the first class, correspond to automata rule classes 1 and 2 (homogeneous and nonhomogeneous fixed points). The next class is constituted by landscapes which are generated by automata rules of class 3 (periodic attractor). And the third class of lowest correlated landscapes corresponds to classes 4, 5 and 6 (chaotic and complex behavior).

According to the above classification, in order to compare the information and the autocorrelation functions, we investigate several landscapes which are constructed by rules with λ parameters 0.0625, 0.1878, and 0.5. We use uniform mutation with a probability 0.01 to perform the random walks on the landscapes. The results of our experiments are presented in Figures 2 and 3.

Several conclusions can be derived from the presented results. The information characteristics of the landscapes (Figure 3) agree with the degree of correlation, determined from the plots shown in Figure 2. For example, the highest correlated landscape, which is generated by automata rule with the parameter $\lambda = 0.0625$, provides lowest information characteristics. The informa-

tion stability of the corresponding curve, shown in Figure 3, suggests that there are not peaks on the explored paths, which are higher than 0.1 (note that $\varepsilon \in [0, 1]$). The information content of the ensemble of the highest peaks falls to 0.0006. This indicates that the ruggedness of the paths is determined mainly of the lowest peaks whose entropy is approximately 0.4. Comparing these values to the corresponding ones, obtained by the curves which are generated by rules with λ parameters 0.1878 and 0.5, we can make the conclusion that the landscape is relatively smooth. The conclusion is based on the assumption that the constructed landscapes are statistically isotropic.

The results from the experiments, shown in Figures 2 and 3, suggest that there is a reverse relation between the correlation and the information characteristics. This fact can be accepted as a proof that the measures have similar behavior. For instance, the steepest autocorrelation function corresponds to the information function with highest information characteristics. Notice, however, that using the information analysis, we obtain additional information about the structure of the fitness landscapes that could not be obtained by the autocorrelation function.

4.2 NK-landscapes

The NK-model of landscapes, introduced by Kauffman [9], defines a family of fitness landscapes (NK-landscapes) with tunable ruggedness. They are defined with two parameters - the length of the genotype, N, and the number of genes that epistatically influence each gene, K $(0 < K \leq N)$. The fitness of each genotype is the mean of the fitness contributions of the genes, where the fitness contribution of the i^{-th} gene is formed by the i^{-th} allele and its $K - 1$ neighbors. Therefore the parameter K determines the degree of interaction between genes in the genotype.

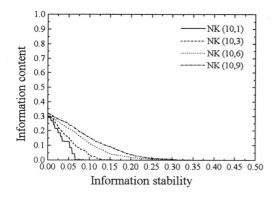

Figure 4: Information function of the NK(10,K) landscapes ($K = 1, 3, 6, 9$), generated by uniform mutation with probability 0.01.

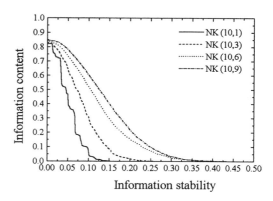

Figure 5: Information function of the NK(10,K) landscapes ($K = 1, 3, 6, 9$), generated by uniform mutation with probability 0.1.

It has been demonstrated that when the parameter K is increased towards N, the fitness landscape ruggedness will be increased too [9, 13]. Having this fact, we examine several landscapes, generated by uniform mutation with probabilities 0.01 and 0.1. The results of the experiments are presented in Figures 4 and 5, respectively. These Figures show the information characteristics of landscapes with parameters $N = 10$ and $K = 1, 3, 6, 9$.

The information function $H(\varepsilon)$ is sensitive to the parameter K, hence, to the landscape ruggedness. The plots in Figures 4 and 5 show that when the degree of interaction between genes, K, is changed from 1 to 9, then the information characteristics increase following the increases of the ruggedness of the generated landscapes. It is clear that

$$H_{10,1}(\varepsilon) \leq H_{10,3}(\varepsilon) \leq H_{10,6}(\varepsilon) \leq H_{10,9}(\varepsilon)$$

for each $\varepsilon \in [0, 1]$, where $H_{n,k}(\varepsilon)$ is the information function of the NK-landscape with parameters $N = n$ and $K = k$ (note that $\varepsilon \in [0, 1]$). The steepest information function, $H_{n,k}(\varepsilon)$, presents the information characteristics of the smoothest landscape NK(10,1), while the less steep information functions correspond to more rugged landscapes.

The ruggedness of the landscapes depends also on the mutation probability. The landscapes, generated by mutation with probability 0.1 (Figure 5), provide higher values for $H(\varepsilon)$ than the other, whose information characteristics are presented in Figure 4. For example, the information content $H(0)$ of the landscapes, generated by mutation with probability 0.01, is approximately 0.3, while the information content $H(0)$ of the mutation landscapes with probability 0.1 is approximately 0.82.

An interesting result of the experiments that demonstrates the effectiveness of the proposed analysis is that the information content $H(0)$ is almost unchangeable for

all values of the parameter K, i.e.

$$H_{10,k}(0) \approx H_{10,l}(0),$$

where $0 < k, l \leq 10$. Therefore the expressiveness of the optima will be increased, when the parameter K is increased. The presented Figures 4 and 5 suggest that the information content $H(0)$ of NK-landscapes, generated by a mutation operator, depends mainly on the mutation rate. Notice that such conclusion could not be obtained by the other measures of landscapes.

5 Fitness Landscape Smoothing

The evolutionary search is often hindered by the fitness landscape ruggedness [12, 13, 14]. This specifies the importance of the problem of landscape smoothing. It is clear that the landscape ruggedness depends on three components of EAs:

- the search space and its structure;

- the evolutionary operators;

- the fitness function.

The search space is defined by the problem that has to be solved. In this sense we could not change it and hence, to smooth the corresponding landscapes. When the coding scheme is changed, a new kind of genotypes will be obtained, and a new search space will be constructed. However, we could not know whether this landscape will be smoother then the previous one.

The evolutionary operators are the next important tools for tuning the landscape characteristics [13, 15]. Usually, by changing the parameters of the evolutionary operators, we tune the landscape ruggedness, however, it could lead to ineffective evolutionary search. For example, when the genotypes have a length 10, it would be senselessly to use uniform mutation with probability

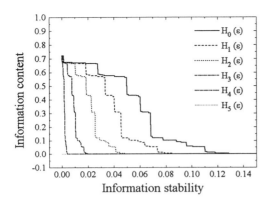

Figure 6: The information functions H_0, H_1,..., H_5 of NK(5,1) landscapes, generated by uniform mutation with probability 0.1, and fitness functions f_0, f_1, ..., f_5, respectively.

0.00001, although the generated landscape will be very smooth.

A simple way to decrease the landscape ruggedness is to change the fitness function [16] so that the information that could be obtained by the landscape to be unchanged. The idea is that the landscape contains a "noisy" information about the global optima. The noise is specified by little peaks placed on the landscape hills, plateaus, and valleys. So, we need a changed fitness function that can decrease the noise.

Let f be a fitness function. It assigns a fitness value to each point of the landscape. We assume that each point is represented by a genotype. If ϕ is a genotype, its fitness value will be $f(\phi)$, determined by the fitness function f.

We denote the set of neighbors of a genotype ϕ with $\mathcal{N}_\phi(k)$, where k is a radius of the set. In other words, $\mathcal{N}_\phi(k)$ includes the genotype ϕ, and all neighbors on distance 1, 2, ..., k. The neighbors are genotypes reachable from ϕ by 1, 2, ..., k applying of the evolutionary operator to ϕ. Having these notes, we define a function

$$f_k(\phi) = \frac{1}{n(\mathcal{N}_\phi(k))} \sum_{\forall \psi \in \mathcal{N}_\phi(k)} f(\psi),$$

where $n(\mathcal{N}_\phi(k))$ is the number of all neighbors. The function assigns the genotypes with the average fitness values from their neighbors. If f_k is used as a fitness function, the evolutionary search must lead to a higher area of the landscape. The largeness of the area is determined by the parameter k. Evidently, when k is zero, the function f_k will be the fitness function f. Using the information analysis, we show that the function f_k, constructed above, decreases the landscape ruggedness. Since the function f_k decreases the fitness differences, we have to expect that it will decrease the landscape ruggedness, too. It is demonstrated in Figure 6 which represents

the information characteristics of several NK-landscapes where the genotype length is 5, and the degree of interaction between genes, K, is 1. We investigated landscapes that correspond to the fitness functions f_0, f_1, ..., f_5. The operator that is used in the experiments is uniform mutation with probability 0.1. The presented results demonstrate that the information stability decreases as the largeness of the neighborhood increases. For example, the information stability of the landscape, generated by f_5, is zero. Consequently, it is flat. By increasing the neighborhood radius k, we decrease the fitness differences, however, the differences remain. It specifies the constant level on the information contents $H(0)$ of the landscapes (except the landscape that corresponds to the fitness function f_5). An important result of the experiments is that the investigated landscapes, generated by f_0, f_1, ..., f_4, have a similar information structure. It is revealed by the information functions, plotted in Figure 6.

6 Discussion

The previous sections enable us to determine the introduced fitness landscape analysis as an useful tool for investigating the structure of the landscapes. This technique is simple, elegant and has the following advantages. First, it is a highly accurate measure of landscape ruggedness. To reveal this important property of the measure, we have examined several landscapes with tunable ruggedness. We have seen that the information function $H(\varepsilon)$ is sensitive to the changes in the landscape ruggedness. The information characteristics, presented by the information function $H(\varepsilon)$, increase when a landscape is tuned from smooth to rugged. Note, however, that we estimate two information characteristics that correspond to the diversity and the expressiveness of the landscape optima. This allows us to analyze exactly what makes one landscape more rugged than others, and why two landscapes with equal correlation characteristics are differently hard for the EAs. Second, it can be used to explore the modality of the landscapes. This advantage is a consequence of the definition of the proposed analysis. We have noted that when the information content $H(\varepsilon)$ is a constant log 2 and the function $h(\varepsilon)$ is zero for each $\varepsilon \in [0, \varepsilon^\star)$, where $\varepsilon^\star$ is the information stability, the investigated landscape is maximally multimodal or an increasing/decreasing step function. Consequently, the landscape could be easy for the corresponding EA [7, 19]. Finally, it can be effortlessly implemented. This follows from the definition of the analysis method.

A method for smoothing landscape ruggedness has been investigated in this paper. It is based on the idea that the fitness function can be changed so that the landscape ruggedness to be decreased. Using the proposed landscape analysis, we have revealed what make the smoothed landscape smoother then the original landscape. It has been shown that the smoothing method decreases the information stability of the landscape, however, the information content remains unchanged. Also, an important result of the experiments is that the smoothed landscapes have a similar information structure (see Figure 6). In other words, landscape smoothing decreases the differences between the fitnesses, however, a difference remains. Consequently, the landscape smoothing could be used to perform a global search (search for the highest landscape area) on the landscape.

7   Conclusion

A novel method for analysis of fitness landscapes has been proposed in this paper and it has been called an information analysis. The development of the method includes an investigation of two information features that characterize the landscape ruggedness. This idea arised from the opinion that the ruggedness of the fitness landscapes is not only dependent on the number of local optima, but also on the diversity and expressiveness of these optima. The proposed method identifies the diversity of the optima using the information content as a characteristic of the optima. The information about the optima is augmented by the information stability of the landscape, which is an estimate of the expressiveness of the optima. The information analysis has been used to explore a smoothing landscape technique. The analysis helped us to reveal what make the smoothed landscape smoother then the original one.

The approach raises several important questions. We have seen that using the information analysis, we obtain additional information that could not be obtained by the autocorrelation function. However, how we can use this information? How it can help us to develop effective evolutionary algorithms? Is there a mechanism that connects the information characteristics of landscapes with the elements, and the parameters of the EAs? These are open questions for further research.

References

[1] D. Goldberg. *Genetic Algorithms in Search, Optimization and Machine Learning*. Addison-Wesley, 1989.

[2] D. Goldberg. Genetic Algorithms and Walsh Functions: Part II, Deception and Its Analysis. *Complex Systems*, 3, pp. 153-171, 1989.

[3] J. J. Grefenstette, and J. E. Baker. How Genetic Algorithms Work: A Critical Look at Implicit Parallelism. In J. D. Schaffer (ed.), *Proceedings of the Third International Conference on Genetic Algorithms*, pp. 20-27. San Francisc, CA: Morgan Kaufmann, 1989.

[4] H. A. Gutowitz. *Cellular Automata*. Cambridge, MA: MIT Press, 1990.

[5] J. Holland. *Adaptation in Natural and Artificial Systems* (second edition). Cambridge, MA: MIT Press, 1992.

[6] W. Hordijk. A Measure of Landscapes. SFI Report No. 95-05-049, 1995.

[7] J. Horn, and D. Goldberg. Genetic Algorithm Difficulty and the Modality of Fitness Landscapes. IlliGAL Report No. 94006, 1994.

[8] T. Jones. *Evolutionary Algorithms, Fitness Landscapes and Search*. PhD thesis, University of New Mexico, Albuquergue, NM, 1995.

[9] S. Kauffman. Adaptation on Rugged Fitness Landscapes. In D. Stein (ed.), *Lectures in the Sciences of Complexity*, pp. 527-618. Addison-Wesley, 1989.

[10] C. G. Langton. Computation at the Edge of Chaos: Phase Transitions and Emergent Computation. *Physica D 42*, pp. 12-37, 1990.

[11] W. Li, N. H. Packard, and C. G. Langton. Transition Phenomena in Cellular Automata Rule Space. *Physica D 45*, pp. 77-94, 1990.

[12] M. Lipsitch. Adaptation on Rugged Landscapes Generated by Iterated Local Interactions of Neighboring Genes. In R. K. Belew, and L. B. Booker (ed.), *Proceedings of the Fourth International Conference on Genetic Algorithms*, pp. 128-135. San Francisco, CA: Morgan Kaufmann, 1991.

[13] B. Manderick, M. De Weger, and P. Spiessens. The Genetic Algorithm and the Structure of the Fitness Landscape. In R. K. Belew, and L. B. Booker (ed.), *Proceedings of the Fourth International Conference on Genetic Algorithms*, pp. 143-150. San Francisco, CA: Morgan Kaufmann, 1991.

[14] M. Mitchell, S. Forrest, and J. Holland. The Royal Road for Genetic Algorithms: Fitness Landscapes and GA Performance. In J. Varela, and P. Bourgine (ed.), *Proceedings of the First European Conference on Artificial Life*, pp. 245-254. Cambridge, MA: MIT Press, 1991.

[15] V. Slavov, and N. Nikolaev. Fitness Landscapes and Inductive Genetic Programming. In *Proceedings of the Third International Conference on Artificial NNs and GAs*. Norwich, UK, 1997.

[16] V. Slavov, and N. Nikolaev. Inductive Genetic Programming and the Superposition of Fitness Landscapes. In Th. Baeck (ed.), *Proceedings of the Seventh International Conference on Genetic Algorithms*. San Francisco, CA: Morgan Kaufmann, 1997.

[17] P. F. Stadler. Landscapes and Their Correlation Functions. SFI Report No. 95-07-067, 1995.

[18] J. Theiler. Estimating Fractal Dimension. *J. Opt. Soc. Am. A*, 7(6), pp. 1055-1073, 1990.

[19] V. Vassilev. *Evolutionary Algorithms and Adaptation*. MSc thesis, New Bulgarian University, Sofia, 1996.

[20] E. D. Weinberger. Correlated and Uncorrelated Fitness Landscapes and How to Tell the Difference. *Biological Cybernetics*, 63, pp. 325-336. Springer-Verlag, 1990.

[21] S. Wright. The Roles of Mutation, Inbreeding, Crossbreeding and Selection in Evolution. In D. F. Jones (ed.), *Proceedings of the Sixth International Congress on Genetics*, 1, pp. 356-366, 1932.

A Comparison of Evolutionary Activity
in Artificial Evolving Systems and in the Biosphere

Mark A. Bedau, Emile Snyder, C. Titus Brown
Reed College, 3203 SE Woodstock Blvd., Portland, OR 97202, USA
Email: {mab, emile, brown}@reed.edu

Norman H. Packard
Prediction Company, 236 Montezuma St., Santa Fe, NM 87501, USA
Email: n@predict.com

Abstract

Bedau and Packard [7] devised an approach to quantifying the adaptive phenomena in artificial systems. We use this approach to define two statistics: cumulative evolutionary activity and mean cumulative evolutionary activity. Then we measure the dynamics of cumulative evolutionary activity, mean cumulative evolutionary activity and diversity, on an evolutionary time scale, in two artificial systems and in the biosphere as reflected in the fossil record. We also measure these statistics in selectively-neutral analogues of the artificial models. Comparing these data prompts us to draw three conclusions: (i) evolutionary activity statistics do measure continual adaptive success, (ii) evolutionary activity statistics can be compared in artificial systems and in the biosphere, and (iii) there is an arrow of increasing cumulative evolutionary activity in the biosphere but not in the artificial models of evolution. The third conclusion is quantitative evidence that the artificial evolving systems are qualitatively different from the biosphere.

1 Evolutionary Activity Trends

We propose a way to quantify certain long-term trends involving adaptation in evolving systems, and we compare such trends in the fossil record and in data from two artificial evolving systems. Long-term patterns in the history of life on Earth have been actively discussed ever since evolution theory originated with Lamark and Darwin. This is no surprise for those, like ourselves, who agree with McKinney ([22], p. 28) that "[t]he concept of 'trend' is arguably the single most important in the study of evolution."

This discussion of evolutionary trends has become connected with myriad issues, including the role of adaptation in evolution, the directionality of evolution—especially with respect to various kinds of complexity or organization—and the allied general notion of progress. Recent work on long-term trends in the history of life on Earth spans the gamut from (i) studies of transitions in the evolution that suggest directionality related to taxonomic diversity [33], taxonomic survivorship [27], or structural and functional complexity of organisms [21]; to (ii) decrial of any suggestion of "progressive" trends [12, 10, 13, 31], including those involving complexity and adaptation; to (iii) an intermediate insistence on "emphatic agnosticism" based on the difficulties of quantifying and measuring complexity [25]. Controversy about the adaptive significance of long-term evolutionary trends partly reflects a broader controversy about the role of adaptation in biotic evolution in general; work on this topic spans another broad gamut, ranging from a rejection of the notion that adaptation is quantifiable or measurable [14] to experimental tests of adaptation in evolving populations of bacteria [36]. And similar themes are now surfacing in studies of artificial evolving systems, in which one finds claims to have observed long-term trends of "open-ended evolution" or "perpetual novelty" [19, 29, 17].

Our concern in this paper is with trends involving adaptation rather than complexity, and our primary aim is to make a quantitative comparison of such trends in model systems and in the biosphere. We think that adaptation is indeed quantifiable and measurable, using *evolutionary activity*, an approach first introduced in the context of model evolving systems [7] and here slightly modified so that it applies to both model evolving systems and to data from the fossil record. Our procedure will be to compare the dynamics of evolutionary activity displayed in the fossil record with that displayed in two artificial evolving systems—the Evita model and the Bugs model. We hope our comparison of evolutionary activity in artificial and natural systems will lead to a better understanding of whether and, if so, why evolving systems exhibit long-term trends involving adaptation.

Evolutionary activity (or "activity", as we will sometimes say for simplicity) is computed from data obtained by observing an evolving system. In our view an evolving system consists of a population of components, all of which participate in a cycle of birth, life and death, with each component largely determined by inherited traits. (We use this "component" terminology to maintain generality.) Birth, however, allows for the possibility of innovations being introduced into the population. If the innovation is adaptive, it persists in the population with a beneficial effect on the survival potential of the components that have it. It persists not only in the component which first receives the innovation, but in all subsequent components that inherit the innovation, i.e., in an entire lineage. If the innovation is not adaptive, it either disappears or persists passively.

The idea of evolutionary activity is to identify innovations that make a difference. Generally we consider an innovation to "make a difference" if it persists and continues to be used. Counters are attached to components for bookkeeping purposes, to update each components' current activity as the component persists and is used. If the components are passed along during reproduction, the corresponding counters are inherited with the components, maintaining an increasing count for an entire lineage. Two large issues immediately arise:

1. What should be counted as an innovation? In fact, innovations may be identified on many levels in most evolving systems. We define an innovation as the introduction of a new component into the system. In the case of Evita, the components are entire genotypes. In the case of Bugs, they are also genotypes, though in previous studies, innovations on the level of individual alleles have been measured [7, 4]. For the fossil record, components will be taxonomic families; an innovation is the appearance of a family in the fossil record.

2. How should a given innovation contribute to the evolutionary activity of the system? We measure activity contributions by attaching a counter to each component of the system. In all the work we present here a component's activity counter is incremented each time step if the component simply exists at that time step. Though there are ways to refine this simple counting method, and we discuss some of them below, we use this version because it is directly applicable to the fossil data.

More formally, let $f_i(t)$ indicate whether the ith component is present in the record at time t:

$$f_i(t) = \begin{cases} 1 & \text{if component } i \text{ exists at } t \\ 0 & \text{otherwise} \end{cases} \qquad (1)$$

Then we define the evolutionary activity $a_i(t)$ of the ith component at time t as its presence integrated over the time period from its origin up to t, provided it exists:

$$a_i(t) = \begin{cases} \int_0^t f_i(t)dt & \text{if component } i \text{ exists at } t \\ 0 & \text{otherwise} \end{cases} \qquad (2)$$

Thus, a_i is the ith component's activity counter. Note that a different resolution of the second issue above would result in a different formula for incrementing the activity counters (as in reference [7]). The *cumulative evolutionary activity*, $A(t)$, at time t (which we will often call just "cumulative activity") is simply the sum of the evolutionary activity of all components:

$$A(t) = \sum_i a_i(t). \qquad (3)$$

The *diversity*, $D(t)$, is simply the number of components present at t,

$$D(t) = \#\{i : a_i(t) > 0\}, \qquad (4)$$

where $\#\{\cdot\}$ denotes set cardinality. Then, the *mean cumulative evolutionary activity*, $\bar{A}(t)$, (which we will often call simply "mean activity") is the cumulative evolutionary activity $A(t)$ divided by the diversity $D(t)$:

$$\bar{A}(t) = \frac{A(t)}{D(t)}. \qquad (5)$$

Note that the cumulative activity is the product of a measure of diversity (the number of components $D(t)$) with a measure of duration or persistence (the mean evolutionary activity $\bar{A}(t)$). These two aspects have already been noted as characteristic of evolution [15]; we have simply formed a measurable statistic with them.

A system could show significant diversity increase over time but *not* show significant activity increase over time. An example is an evolutionary system with a high mutation rate. Diversity will be high compared to similar systems with lower mutation rates, but activity will be low compared to the same reference group.

The cumulative activity defined by equation 3 is only one of a host of statistics that may be computed from the activity counters $\{a_i\}$ defined in equation 2. In reference [7], for example, we argue for a different statistic to capture what we might intuitively identify with "adaptive evolutionary innovation". The cumulative activity does not support such an interpretation; we use it here for its computational ease and because we feel it broadly reflects continual adaptive success in the evolutionary processes we consider here.

As we have mentioned, evolutionary activity was first developed and applied in the context of a model evolutionary system [7]. The motivation for viewing evolutionary activity as a measure of adaptation during evolution is particularly strong for such model systems, in large part because of intuition obtained by the experimental control they offer. In particular, as we illustrate for the Evita and Bugs models below, it is possible to "turn off" adaptation in a simulation, while leaving reproduction and death, resulting in a random sampling of components in the population, with no connection between the components and the survivability of the components. This sort of neutral analogue can then be compared with the normal situation, in which specific properties of components can have a very strong effect on their survivability. The introduction of a new component that has a positive effect on survivability is strongly reflected in the evolutionary activity.

The neutral analogue essentially produces a random walk in the space of possible components, analogous to other models of random evolution [28, 15]. Such models are relevant to biological evolution not necessarily because they are plausible models in themselves but because they highlight those aspects of an evolving system, if any, which are due to adaptation as against those which are due merely to random processes and historical accident.

2   The Evita Model

The Evita model is a limited-interaction system consisting of self-replicating strings of code, akin to Tierra [29] and Avida [1]. As in Tierra and Avida, programs in a customized assembly language replicate while subject to "cosmic-ray" mutation. Unlike Tierra but like Avida, these programs are limited in interaction to their nearest neighbors on a two dimensional grid. And unlike both Tierra and Avida, no code parasitism is allowed in Evita.

The differences between Tierra, Avida and Evita, while not profound in outlook, are significant. The 2-D interaction ensures that the spread of information throughout the population is dependent on the size of the system; whereas Tierra allows instantaneous interaction between widely disparate areas, this cannot happen in Avida or Evita. Blocking parasitism and more complicated interactions (e.g. hyperparasitism and code pirating) allows us to study the root dynamics of these systems.

The system is initialized with a single human-written program placed randomly on an N by M grid. This program then executes and reproduces; each offspring is placed within a small radius of the parent program on the grid, and they then also start executing. When a parent program can find no unoccupied grid locations nearby, the system chooses randomly from the oldest of its neighbors, "kills" that neighbor, and places the offspring there. No other interaction between programs is permitted.

During each "timestep" in this system the program at each occupied grid spot receives a fixed amount of the processor time. This time is allocated in a way that is unbiased by position; hence, no organism can gain an advantage in its placement. In fact, the only real advantage position can give is the relative fitness of the surrounding population: it may be that the nearby creatures are less fit, e.g. reproduce more slowly, than the creature placed onto their edge.

Mutation rate is specified in terms of the probability per timestep that each given "codon" or assembly language instruction in a genotype is mutated. Thus, the probability that a given program suffers a mutation somewhere is proportional to its length; longer programs are more likely to suffer a mutation. While the probability that a given program is mutated is independent of the size of the population of programs, the probability that a mutation occurs somewhere in the population is clearly proportional to the population size. Typically, mutation rates are specified in terms of 10^{-5} mutations per timestep: that is, a mutation rate of m would mean that a given codon would mutate on average once every $\frac{10^5}{m}$ timesteps. This means, for example, that in a run with 1600 creatures with an average length of 30 instructions, a mutation rate of 1 would cause one mutation somewhere in the population approximately every other timestep.

The model has a clear biological analogy. The system represents a biological "soup", full of self-replicating strands of code (similar to RNA). Survival is governed primarily by reproductive speed, and evolution towards faster programs is the behavior usually exhibited. This kind of system, while extremely simple, shows interesting evolutionary behavior. Many people have used Tierra, Avida, and similar simple systems to examine a variety of issues in evolutionary dynamics [29, 30, 1, 20, 35, 2].

Evita is explicitly designed so that the only way the programs interact is through reproduction. On average, programs that reproduce faster will supplant their more slowly reproducing neighbors. A program's rate of reproduction or "gestation time" depends only on its genotype, and a genotype's gestation time is the sole determinant of the expected rate at which programs with that genotype will produce offspring. Thus, all significant adaptive events in Evita are changes in gestation time.

We also define a neutral analogue of Evita, which differs from Evita only in that there is no chance that a genotype's presence or concentration in the population is due to its adaptive significance. Nominal "programs" exist at grid locations, reproduce and die. The neutral model has two parameters: the number of mutations in the population per timestep (possibly a vector), and the number of "programs" that reproduce per timestep (possibly a vector). When the neutral model is due to have a reproduction event, the self-reproducing "program" is chosen at random from the population (with equal probability). When a "program" reproduces, its oldest neighboring "program" dies and the new child occupies the newly emptied grid location. Each "program" has a nominal "genotype" which it's children inherit. Whenever a mutation strikes a "program" it is assigned a new "genotype". The evolutionary dynamics in this neutral analogue is reduced to a simple random walk in genotype space [2]. Genotypes arise and go extinct, and their concentrations change over time, but the genotype dynamics is only weakly linked to adaptation through the reproduction rate parameter determined by the normal model. None of the dynamic of a genotype in the neutral analogue is due to that genotype's adaptive significance for the genotypes have no adaptive significance whatsoever.

By recording mutation rates and reproduction rates from an actual Evita run, the neutral analogue can then be run with these vectors as parameters. The behavior of this neutral analogue allows us to determine which aspects of the behavior of our original Evita run were due to adaptation and which can be attributed to the underlying non-adaptive architecture of the system.

3 The Bugs Model

The Bugs model consist of many agents that exist in a spatial grid, sensing the resources in their local environment, moving as a function of what they sense, ingesting the resources they find, and reproducing or dying as a function of their internal resource levels. The Bugs model is in a line of models that originated with Packard [26] and has subsequently been evolving in various hands [7, 8, 3, 5, 4, 6, 11]

The Bugs model's spatial structure is a grid of sites with periodic boundary conditions, i.e., a toroidal lattice. Besides the agents, all that exists in the world are 50 tiny (3×3 sites) square blocks of resources, which are spread over the lattice of sites and replenished as needed from an external source. The resource distribution is static in space and time because resources are immediately replenished at a site whenever they are consumed. Nevertheless, since the agents constantly extract resources and expend them by living and reproducing, the agents function as the system's resource sinks and the whole system is dissipative.

Adaptation is resource driven since the agents need a steady supply of resources in order to survive and reproduce. Agents interact with the resource field at each time step by ingesting all of the resources (if any) found at their current location and storing it in their internal resource reservoir. Agents must continually replenish this reservoir to survive for they must expend resources at each time step to cover their (constant) "existence taxes" and "movement taxes" (variable, proportional to distance moved). If an agent's internal resource supply drops to zero, it dies and disappears from the world.

Each agent moves each time step as dictated by its ge-

netically encoded sensorimotor map: a table of behavior rules of the form IF (environment j sensed) THEN (do behavior k). Only one agent can reside at a given site at a given time, so an agent randomly walks to the first free site if its sensorimotor map sends it to a site which is already occupied. An agent receives sensory information about the resources (but not the other agents) in the von Neumann neighborhood of five sites centered on its present location in the lattice. An agent can discriminate whether or not resources are present at each site in its von Neumann neighborhood. Thus, each sensory state j corresponds to one of the different detectable local environments (there are about 15 of these in the model studied here). Each behavior k is either a jump vector between one and fifteen sites in any one of the eight compass directions (north, northeast, east, etc.), or it is a random walk to the first unoccupied site. This yields a finite behavioral repertoire consisting of $(8 \times 15)+1 = 121$ different possible behaviors. Thus, an agent's genotype, i.e., its sensorimotor map, consist of a movement genetically hardwired for each detectable environmental condition. These genotypes are extremely simple, amounting to nothing more than a lookup table of sensorimotor rules. On the other hand, the space in which adaptation occurs is vast, consisting of up to $121^{15} \approx 10^{32}$ distinct possible genotypes.

An agent reproduces (asexually—without recombination) if its resource reservoir exceeds a certain threshold. The parent produces one child, which starts life with half of its parent's resource supply. The child also inherits its parent's sensorimotor map, except that mutations may replace the behaviors linked to some sensory states with randomly chosen behaviors. The mutation rate parameter determines the probability of a mutation at a single locus, i.e., the probability that the behavior associated with a given sensory state changes. At the extreme case in which the mutation rate is set to one, a child's entire sensorimotor map is chosen at random. The results presented here were all produced with the mutation rate set to 0.05.

A time step in the simulation cycles through the entire population and has each agent, in turn, complete the following sequence of events: sense its present von Neumann neighborhood, move to the new location dictated by its sensorimotor map unless that site is already occupied, in which case randomly walk to the first unoccupied site, consume any resources found at its new location, expend enough resources to cover existence and movement taxes, and then, if its resource reservoir is high enough or empty, either reproduce or die.

Sensorimotor strategies evolve over generations. A given simulation starts with randomly distributed agents containing randomly chosen sensorimotor strategies. The model contains no *a priori* fitness function, as Packard (1989) has emphasized, so the population's size and genetic constitution fluctuates with the contingencies of extracting resources. Agents with maladaptive strategies tend to find few resources and thus to die, taking their sensorimotor genes with them; by contrast, agents with adaptive strategies tend to find sufficient resources to reproduce, spreading their sensorimotor strategies (with some mutations) through the population.

In resource-driven and space-limited models like the Bugs model observed population size is a good measure of the fitness of the genotypes in the population. Significant adaptive events typically create notable population rises. Populations with behaviorally heterogeneous strategies have a hard time surviving on the tiny 3×3 blocks. Agents following different behavioral strategies will tend to collide, which will tend to bump one of them off the block into the resource desert. Thus, typically all agents on a given 3×3 block follow exactly the same behavioral strategy. All the agents are in a holding pattern continually cycling over a subset of the resource sites on the tiny block. The strategies are typically simple behavioral cycles which jump through a short sequence of sites on the block. The simplest cycles (period 2) consist of jumping back and forth between two sites. The next simplest strategy (period 3) cycles through a triple of sites.

Behavioral strategies with higher periods have a selective advantage (every thing else being equal). Since a 3×3 block contains 9 distinct sites, it can support at most a period 9 strategy. A period n strategy has room for at most n agents. Thus, longer period strategies can support larger populations because they can exploit more of the available energetic resources. All agents on blocks reproduce at the same rate, so a block with a larger population will produce offspring at a higher rate. Thus, blocks with populations with larger period strategies will exert greater migration pressure and, thus, will enjoy a selective advantage throughout the hundreds of tiny resource islands.

Thus, the main kind of adaptation that occurs in the present Bugs model involves extending the period of an existing strategy, which allows the population to exploit more of the available resource sites. Thus, evolution in a random field of 3×3 blocks tends to create populations with higher period strategies.

As we did with Evita, we also create a neutral analogue of the Bugs model, which differs from the Bugs only in that a genotype's persistence is no reflection of its adaptive significance. Nominal "agents" are born, live, reproduce, and die at rates determined exactly by the values of those variables measured in a particular run of the normal Bugs model. (For this reason, the population time series in fig. 3 for the normal Bug model and the neutral analogue are exactly the same.) The distinctive feature of the neutral analogue is that birth, reproduction and

death events happen to "agents" chosen at random from among those present in the population. Each "agent" has a nominal "genotype" which it inherited from its parent unless it suffered a mutation at birth (mutation rate is another model parameter). The evolutionary dynamics of the neutral analogue of the Bugs model is a random walk in genotype space. As with Evita's neutral analogue, none of the dynamic of a given genotypes in this neutral analogue of the Bugs model is due to that genotype's adaptive significance for it has no adaptive significance.

4   The Fossil Data

The fossil data sets indicate the geological stages or epochs with the first and last appearance of taxonomic families. The Benton data [9] covers all families in all kingdoms found in the fossil record, for a total of 7111 families. The Sepkoski data [32] indicates the fossil record for 3358 marine animal families. The duration of different stages and epochs varies widely, ranging over three orders of magnitude. In order to assign a uniform time scale to the fossil data, we converted stages and epochs into time indications expressed in units of millions of years ago using Harland's time scale [16].

We are most interested in analyzing long-term trends among fossil species, but we study fossil families because much more complete data is available at this level of analysis [37, 34]. Although fossil family data is certainly no precise predictor of fossil species data, there is evidence that species-level trends in the fossil record are reflected at the family level (see [37] and the references cited therein). Sepkoski and Hulver ([34], p. 14) summarize the situation thus: "Although families do not display all of the detail of the fossil record, they should be sufficiently sensitive to show major evolutionary trends and patterns with characteristic timescales of fives to tens of millions of years". The trends we discuss in this paper occur on time scales at least that long.

5   Results

We computed the cumulative activity $A(t)$, mean activity $\bar{A}(t)$, and diversity $D(t)$ in both the Benton and Sepkoski fossil data sets (fig. 1). We also computed these statistics from data produced by numerous simulations of the Evita and Bugs models and chose representative examples of the behavior of the statistics in Evita (fig. 2, above) and Bugs (fig. 3, above). Finally, we computed the same statistics from data produced by the neutral analogue of Evita (fig. 2, below) and the neutral analogue of the Bugs (fig. 3, below). In each case, the neutral analogues were given parameters that exactly corresponded to those that governed the normal Evita and Bugs runs.

We start the fossil data at the Cambrian explosion, due

to the relative crudeness of the preceding data. Visible in the data are the major extinction events, such as the largest one of all which ends the Permian period, and the famous "K/T" extinction which involved the final demise of the dinosaurs and is thought to have been caused by a meteorite impact.

The Evita simulation shows the single ancestral program quickly replicating enough to fill up the 40×40 grid. Most of the significant improvements in reproduction rate occur at the very beginning of the simulation. The local peaks in cumulative and mean activity during the course of the simulation correspond to the introduction of new genotypes that are neutral variants, that is, they have the same adaptive significance as the other major genotypes in the population. In other words, the bulk of this simulation consists of a random drift among genotypes that are selectively neutral, along the lines of the neutral theory of evolution [18]. Note that these selectively-neutral variants are highly adaptive—they are remarkably effective at the task of survival and reproduction—but they just do this job equally well.

The first fifth of the Bugs simulation shows the population adapting to the tiny blocks by increasing the cycle size of their behavioral strategy. At least three major innovations are recognizable in the population size dynamics. After the third major innovation, the evolutionary dynamics settles down into a random drift among selectively-neutral variant genotypes, as in the Evita simulation.

Notice that there is a striking difference in the behavior of the artificial models and their neutral analogues. The neutral analogues do not produce anything like the same statistics as the normal models (except for the population size in the Bug neutral analogue, of course, and its shadow in the diversity and cumulative activity time series). In particular, the cumulative and mean activity values in the neutral analogues are negligible, by comparison, while their diversity values are significantly higher. Evidently, adaptation has a dramatic effect when it is allowed to affect the persistence of genotypes.

When we compare the evolutionary activity in these three figures, we see another striking difference. The fossil data shows a long-term trend of cumulative activity and diversity increasing more than linearly; fossil mean activity increases roughly linearly into the Permian period but then shows no further trend. But there is no long-term trend in any statistic in the Evita and Bugs data.

6   Discussion

We draw three main conclusions from our comparison of evolutionary activity in artificial systems and in the biosphere:

Conclusion 1: Cumulative evolutionary activity measures continual adaptive success for the evolutionary pro-

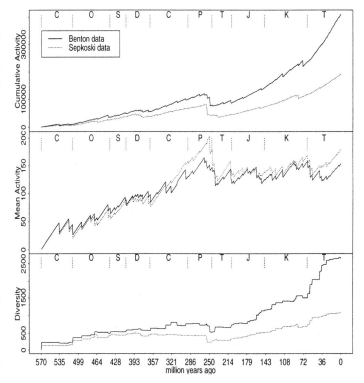

Figure 1: Cumulative activity (top), mean activity (middle), and diversity (bottom) in the fossil data of Benton and Sepkoski. The labels at the top of each graph show the boundaries between the standard geological periods, thus: Cambrian, Ordovician, Silurian, Devonian, Carboniferous, Permian, Triassic, Jurassic, Cretaceous, Tertiary.

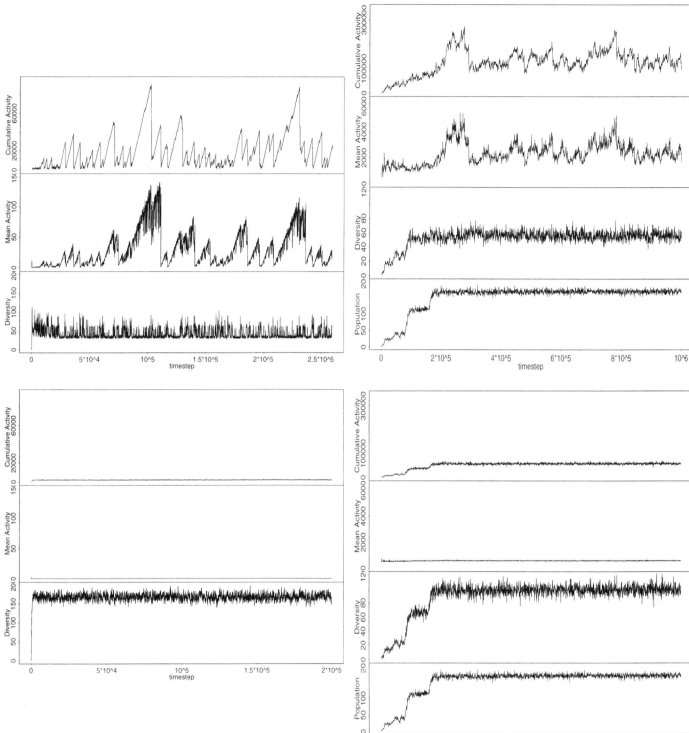

Figure 2: Above: cumulative activity (top), mean activity (middle), and diversity (bottom) in an Evita simulation. Below: the same statistics for a neutral analogue of the Evita simulation above.

Figure 3: Above: cumulative activity (top), mean activity (upper middle), diversity (lower middle) and population (bottom) in a Bugs simulation. Below: the same statistics for a neutral analogue of the Bugs simulation above. Note that the population size time series in the neutral analogue is taken directly from the population data generated in the normal Bug simulation above.

cesses we consider. This is clear for the two model systems primarily from the comparison provided by the neutral analogues.

Conclusion 2: Cumulative evolutionary activity, along with mean activity and diversity, are statistics that enable artificial evolutionary models to be compared quantitatively with evolution in the biosphere. It is clearly possible to measure these statistics in artificial and natural systems. The proof of this pudding (conclusion 2) comes in the eating.

Conclusion 3: If we accept conclusions 1 and 2, then comparison of evolutionary activity in the data from the fossil record and from the artificial evolving systems reveals that long-term trends involving adaptation are present in the biosphere but missing in the artificial models.

Our statistics show that the Evita and Bugs models do not show comparable evolutionary activity to the evolutionary activity of the biosphere indicated in the fossil record. The primary difference is that cumulative evolutionary activity and diversity of the biosphere shows a strong increase on an evolutionary time scale, but the Evita and Bugs models do not. Furthermore, the trends shown in the biosphere are unlikely to be "accidental" products of anything like the artificial models, for to our knowledge the artificial models *never* exhibit such trends. These strong increasing trends imply a directionality in biological evolution that is missing in the artificial evolutionary systems. Specifically, the biosphere shows an arrow of increasing cumulative activity as well as an arrow of increasing diversity. These are directly related since the post-Permian increase in cumulative activity is driven mainly by the increase in diversity. (Recall that cumulative activity is the product of diversity and mean activity.) But the arrow of cumulative activity is especially interesting because of its implications about the directionality of *adaptation* in biological evolution.

We view conclusion 3 as quantitative evidence that the artificial models are qualitatively different from the biosphere. We suspect that *no* existing artificial system is qualitatively like the biosphere. If this is right, then an objective of the first importance is to devise an artificial model that captures the qualitative behavior of the biosphere.

We should note that the Evita and Bugs models disallow any interesting interactions between organisms; no predator-prey connections, no cooperation, no communication, nothing. But other artificial evolving models do permit such interactions; e.g., Echo [17] and Tierra [29]. We purposely focused this first study on especially simple and well understood artificial models, to make it easier to understand our results. An obvious next step is to extend this study to more complex artificial models, and this is part of current work. However, we conjecture that the conclusions of this pilot study will hold for Echo

and Tierra as well.

The spatial and temporal scales of the Evita and Bugs models are vastly smaller than the spatial and temporal scale of the biosphere; and the same applies to the general complexity of the systems. So perhaps these models should not be expected to show evolutionary activity comparable to the biosphere. But we are confident that scaling up space and time in the Evita and Bugs models will not change the qualitative character of their activity curves. This confidence comes in part from observations besides those reported here, but the conjecture is subject to further direct empirical test. We similarly doubt that simply making the models more "complex" will make the quality of their behavior like that of the biosphere. We think that the primary reason behind the biosphere's arrow of cumulative activity is that the dynamics of the biosphere constantly create new niches and new evolutionary possibilities through interactions between diverse organisms. This aspect of biological evolution dramatically amplifies both diversity and evolutionary activity, and it is an aspect not evident in these models.

The cumulative activity curve from the fossils is qualitatively similar to the initial transient of the Bugs cumulative activity curve. So, the explanation of the qualitative difference in the long-term cumulative activity shown in the fossils and in the artificial models might be that the biosphere has been on some kind of "transient" during the period reflected in the fossil record. The eventual statistical stabilization of the artificial evolving systems might be caused by the systems hitting their resource "ceilings"; in this case, growth in activity would be limited by the finite spatial and energetic resources available to support adaptive innovations.

Evolution in the biosphere seems to have been free from any inexorable resource ceilings, but we suspect that this is largely because the biosphere's evolution continues to make new resources available when it creates new niches. In fact, organisms occupying new niches seem to create the possibility for yet newer niches; i.e., the space of innovations available to evolution is constantly growing. We believe that this aspect of biological evolution is the most important aspect missing from artificial models; simply increasing resources to the artificial models studied here does not seem to significantly affect observed patterns of evolution. This suggests it would be interesting to make a more careful comparison of the fossil record data with initial transients of artificial systems, before the systems have exhausted the possibilities for significant adaptation. This will be a topic of future work.

There are problems and pitfalls inherent in using the fossil record to study long-term trends [27]. In particular, the "pull of the present" is a well-known sampling bias due to the fact that there are simply more recent fossils to study than older fossils. Future work will investigate the extent to which our analysis of fossil record trends can be supported more rigorously.

We have tried to illustrate the value of studying evolutionary trends by devising statistics that apply both to data from the fossil record and to data generated by artificial systems. Such statistics provide a normal form for expressing conclusions about the behavior of artificial models and about how those models are relevant to understanding biological evolution. Our work here has focussed on the cumulative evolutionary activity statistic, but this is not the only interesting statistic. As we mentioned in section 1 above, other statistics defined in terms of evolutionary activity highlight other kinds of comparisons among systems, which might provide additional kinds of insights into evolutionary trends. Perhaps yet further statistics unconnected with evolutionary activity might find a similar use.

Comparing cumulative evolutionary activity in artificial systems and in the biosphere has lead to a negative result (Conclusion 3): present artificial models of evolution apparently lack some important characteristic of the biosphere—whatever it is that is responsible for its arrow of increasing cumulative activity. However, this conclusion crystalizes an important constructive and creative challenge: to devise an artificial model of evolution that succeeds where the present models fail. Here, again, statistics like evolutionary activity show their value, for they provide a quantitative test for whether an artificial evolutionary model and a natural evolving system like the biosphere exhibit the same kind of long-term trends in adaptation.

Acknowledgements. Thanks to M. J. Benton and J. J. Sepkoski, Jr., for making their fossil data available. For helpful discussion, thanks to Bob French, Tim Keitt, Dan McShea, Richard Smith, Peter Todd, the anonymous ECAL97 reviewers, the audience at the Santa Fe Institute when MAB discussed some of these results in July 1996, and the audience at the Cascade Systems Society meeting when MAB presented this material in March 1997.

References

[1] Adami, C., Brown, C. T. 1994. Evolutionary learning in the 2D artificial life system "avida". In R. Brooks and P. Maes, (Eds.), *Artificial Life IV* (pp. 377-381). Cambridge, MA: Bradford/MIT Press.

[2] Adami, C., Brown, C.T., Haggerty, M.R. 1995. Abundance-distributions in artificial life and stochastic models: "age and area" revisited. In F. Morán, A. Moreno, J.J. Merelo, P. Chacón, (Eds.), *Advances in Artificial Life* (pp. 503–514). Berlin: Springer.

[3] Bedau, M. A. 1994. The evolution of sensorimotor functionality. In P. Gaussier and J. D. Nicoud (Eds.), *From Perception to Action* (pp. 134–145). New York: IEEE Press.

[4] Bedau, M. A. 1995. Three illustrations of artificial life's working hypothesis. In W. Banzhaf and F. Eeckman (Eds.), *Evolution and Biocomputation—Computational Models of Evolution* (pp. 53–68). Berlin: Springer.

[5] Bedau, M. A., Bahm, A. 1994. Bifurcation structure in diversity dynamics. In R. Brooks and P. Maes, (Eds.), *Artificial Life IV* (pp. 258–268). Cambridge, MA: Bradford/MIT Press.

[6] Bedau, M. A., Giger, M., Zwick, M. 1995. Adaptive diversity dynamics in static resource models. *Advances in Systems Science and Applications* 1, 1–6.

[7] Bedau, M. A., Packard, N. H. 1992. Measurement of evolutionary activity, teleology, and life. In C. G. Langton, C. E. Taylor, J. D. Farmer, S. Rasmussen, (Eds.), *Artificial Life II* (pp. 431–461). Redwood City, Calif.: Addison-Wesley.

[8] Bedau, M. A., Ronneburg, F., Zwick, M. 1992. Dynamics of diversity in an evolving population. In R. Männer and B. Manderick, (Eds.), *Parallel Problem Solving from Nature, 2* (pp. 94–104). Amsterdam: North-Holland.

[9] Benton, M. J., ed. 1993. *The Fossil Record 2*. London: Chapman and Hall.

[10] Dawkins, R. 1992. Progress. In W. F. Keller and E. Lloyd, (Eds.), *Keywords in Evolutionary Biology* (pp. 263–272). Cambridge, MA: Harvard University Press.

[11] Fletcher, J., Zwick, M., Bedau, M. A. 1996. Dependence of adaptability on environmental structure in a simple evolutionary model. *Adaptive Behavior* 4, 283-315.

[12] Gould, S. J. 1989. *Wonderful Life: The Burgess Shale and the Nature of History*. New York: Norton.

[13] Gould, S. J. 1996. *Full House*, New York: Harmony Books.

[14] Gould, S. J., Lewontin, R.C. 1979. The spandrels of San Marco and the Panglossian paradigm: a critique of the adaptationist programme. *Proceedings of the Royal Society of London Series B* 205, 581–598.

[15] Gould, S. J., Raup, D. M., Sepkoski, Jr., J. J. 1977. The shape of evolution: a comparison of real and random clades. *Paleobiology* 3, 23–40.

[16] Harland, W. B., Armstrong, R. L., Cox, A. V., Craig, L. E., Smith, A. G., Smith, D. G., 1990. *A Geological Time Scale 1989*. Cambridge: Cambridge University Press.

[17] Holland, J. H. 1992. *Adaptation in Natural and Artificial Systems: An introductory analysis with applications to biology, control, and artificial intelligence*, 2nd edition. Cambridge: MIT Press/Bradford Books.

[18] Kimura, M. 1983. *The Neutral Theory of Molecular Evolution*. Cambridge: Cambridge University Press.

[19] Lindgren, L. 1992. Evolutionary phenomena in simple dynamics. In C. G. Langton, C. E. Taylor, J. D. Farmer, S. Rasmussen, (Eds.), *Artificial Life II* (pp. 295–312). Redwood City, Calif.: Addison-Wesley.

[20] Maley, C. C. 1994. The computational completeness of Ray's Tierran assembly language. In C. G. Langton, (Ed.), *Artificial Life III* (pp. 503–514). Redwood City, Calif.: Addison-Wesley.

[21] Maynard Smith, J., Szathmary, E. 1995. *The Major Transitions in Evolution*. Oxford: Freeman.

[22] McKinney, M. L. Classifying and analysing evolutionary trends. In K. J. McNamara, (Ed.), *Evolutionary Trends* (pp. 28–58). Tucson: The University of Arizona Press.

[23] McNamara, K. J. 1990. Preface. In K. J. McNamara, (Ed.), *Evolutionary Trends* (pp. xv–xviii). Tucson: The University of Arizona Press.

[24] McNamara, K. J., ed. 1990. *Evolutionary Trends*. Tucson: The University of Arizona Press.

[25] McShea, D. W. 1996. Metazoan complexity and evolution: is there a trend? *Evolution* 50, 477–492.

[26] Packard, N. H. 1989. Intrinsic adaptation in a simple model for evolution. In C. G. Langton, (Ed.), *Artificial Life* (pp. 141–155). Redwood City, Calif.: Addison-Wesley.

[27] Raup, D. M. 1988. Testing the fossil record for evolutionary progress. In M. H. Nitecki, (Ed.), *Evolutionary Progress*. Chicago: The University of Chicago Press.

[28] Raup, D. M., Gould, S. J. 1974. Stochastic simulation and evolution of morphology—towards a nomothetic paleontology. *Systematic Zoology* 23, 305–322.

[29] Ray, T. S. 1992. An approach to the synthesis of life. In C. G. Langton, C. E. Taylor, J. D. Farmer, S. Rasmussen, (Eds.), *Artificial Life II* (pp. 371–408). Redwood City, Calif.: Addison-Wesley.

[30] Ray, T. S. 1993/1994. An evolutionary approach to synthetic biology: zen and the art of creating life. *Artificial Life* 1, 179–209.

[31] Ruse, M. 1996. *Monad to Man: The Concept of Progress in Evolutionary Biology*. Cambridge, MA: Harvard University Press.

[32] Sepkoski, Jr., J.J. 1992. *A Compendium of Fossil Marine Animal Families*, 2nd ed. Milwaukee Public Museum Contributions in Biology and Geology, Vol. 61.

[33] Sepkoski, J. J., Bambach, R. K., Raup, D. M., Valentine, J. W. 1981. Phanerozoic marine diversity and the fossil record. *Nature* 293, 435–437.

[34] Sepkoski, J. J., Hulver, M. L. 1985. An atlas of phanerozoic clade diversity diagrams. In J. W. Valentine, (Ed.), *Phanerozoic Diversity Patterns: Profiles in Macroevolution* (pp. 11–39). Princeton: Princeton University Press.

[35] Thearling, K., Ray, T. 1994. Evolving multi-cellular artificial life. In R. Brooks and P. Maes, (Eds.), *Artificial Life IV* (pp. 283–288). Cambridge, MA: Bradford/MIT Press.

[36] Travisano, M., J.A. Mongold, A.F. Bennet, R.E. Lenski. 1995. Experimental tests of the roles of adaptation, chance, and history in evolution. *Science* 267, 87–90.

[37] Valentine, J. W. 1985. Diversity as data. In J. W. Valentine, (Ed.), *Phanerozoic Diversity Patterns: Profiles in Macroevolution* (pp. 3–8). Princeton: Princeton University Press.

Guiding or Hiding:
Explorations into the Effects of Learning on the Rate of Evolution.

Giles Mayley

School of Cognitive and Computing Sciences,
University of Sussex, Brighton, BN1 9QH, England.
email: gilesm@cogs.susx.ac.uk

Abstract

Individual lifetime learning can 'guide' an evolving population to areas of high fitness in genotype space through an evolutionary phenomenon known as the Baldwin effect (Baldwin, 1896; Hinton & Nowlan, 1987). It is the accepted wisdom that this guiding speeds up the rate of evolution. By highlighting another interaction between learning and evolution, that will be termed the *Hiding effect*, it will be argued here that this depends on the measure of evolutionary speed one adopts. The Hiding effect shows that learning can reduce the selection pressure between individuals by 'hiding' their genetic differences. There is thus a trade-off between the Baldwin effect and the Hiding effect to determine learning's influence on evolution and two factors that contribute to this trade-off, the cost of learning and landscape epistasis, are investigated experimentally.

1 Introduction

In recent years there has been a renewed interest in the Artificial Life and Adaptive Behaviour communities in an evolutionary phenomenon known as the Baldwin Effect (Baldwin, 1896; Hinton & Nowlan, 1987; Gruau & Whitley, 1993; Belew, 1989; Belew & Mitchell, 1996; Whitley, Scott Gordon, & Mathias, 1994). It has become the accepted wisdom that, through the Baldwin Effect, the inclusion of learning 'guides' an evolutionary system to fit solutions and therefore 'speeds up' the evolutionary process. The emphasis in this body of work has been on the rate at which fit phenotypes can be produced by a genetic algorithm (G.A.) in what are largely function optimisation experiments. However, there are many evolutionary scenarios that cannot be described as function optimisation; for example, the Species Adaptive Genetic Algorithms (SAGA) of Harvey (1992) or co-evolutionary systems that are prone to Red-Queen effects (Cliff & Miller, 1995). In these cases, measures of evolutionary speed, rate or progress that simply involve the number of generations until a fit phenotype is produced

are meaningless since there will always be evolutionary driven movement in genotype space that may not lead to fitness increases.

The purpose of this paper is to show that the view concerning the speeding up of evolutionary progress afforded by the inclusion of learning depends on the measure of evolutionary speed one adopts. As an aid to this I will highlight a second evolutionary phenomenon which occurs when learning is included in an evolutionary system that, under some measures, slows down evolution. I will call this effect the 'Hiding effect'.

I will first describe the Baldwin effect and how it's effect on the dynamics of an evolving population on a fitness landscape is generally viewed. I will then describe the Hiding effect and how the evolutionary dynamics are different to the Baldwin effect. Section 4 discusses the trade-off between the two effects, suggesting conditions under which one would dominate the other. Section 5 describes the simulation experiments that were run to investigate the topics discussed, Section 6 defines the measures used to assess the rate of evolution and the results are presented in Section 7.

2 The Baldwin Effect

The Baldwin effect is an evolutionary phenomenon that has been discussed, on and off, for the past 100 years. Introduced independently by Baldwin (1896) and Lloyd Morgan (1896) it was a means of explaining cases of apparent inheritance of acquired characteristics without recourse to Lamarckianism. It was first tested empirically on *drosophila* by Waddington in the 1950's (Waddington, 1953, 1956) and was finally brought to the attention of the A-life/Adaptive Behaviour communities by Hinton and Nowlan (1987). The Baldwin effect deals with a specific interaction between the two adaptive processes of evolution and learning. Here, learning is taken to be any environmentally-driven phenotypic change that increases an individual's survival chances (fitness). The two processes are arranged thus: a population of individuals are evolving to perform a specific task (in artificial evolution with a G.A.). Their phenotypes are generated from their

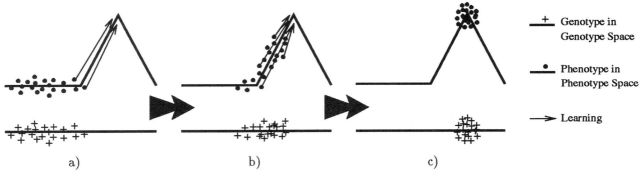

Figure 1: *The Baldwin Effect: The one dimensional genotypes are translated to phenotypes which can then modify themselves in phenotype space. The heights of the phenotypes represent relative fitness. a) Some individuals in the population are able to achieve a fit trait through learning and will therefore be selected; b) Differing levels of learning among individuals in the population leads to the genetic assimilation of the trait. (Note: for clarity only a few arrows are shown — in fact the majority of phenotypes are learning); c) The trait is now innate. Learning has guided evolution to the fitness peak.*

genotypes at the beginning of a generation and are then modified by learning *on the same task* (Menczer & Belew, 1994) and given a fitness score. The fitness score of the *modified individual* is used for the purposes of selection among conspecifics but no information about the structure or behaviour of the modified individual is translated back into the genotype. Despite this non-Lamarckian framework, the learning process can still effect the course of evolution through the Baldwin effect.

Referring to Figure 1, we can see that within a population of non-identical individuals, some will be 'closer' in genotype space than others to areas of increased fitness. If these individuals are able to learn the appropriate phenotypic trait that corresponds to the increased fitness they will, therefore, be selected for (Figure 1a). The 'centre of gravity' of the population thus moves in genotype space towards the area of increased fitness (Figure 1b) and the initially learned trait may become innate in subsequent generations (Figure 1c) in a process known as *genetic assimilation* (Waddington, 1942). It can be said that learning is 'guiding' evolution (Hinton & Nowlan, 1987; Maynard Smith, 1987). This process is subject to a few conditions, though. First, once the entire population is learning the fitter trait, there must be further selection pressure for the reduction in the level of learning to occur. This is supplied by a cost for learning. That is, there are certain evolutionary costs to be paid by a learning individual over a non-learning one for displaying a particular phenotypic trait (see Johnston (1982) for biological review and Turney (1996), Anderson (1995), Mayley (1996a, 1996b) for examples from the A-Life/S.A.B. literature). Assuming these costs become reduced the 'more innate' a trait becomes, then they provide the selection pressure for the reduction in the level of learning that is necessary for genetic assimilation to occur. Another condition that has been discussed in (Mayley, 1996b) is that the genotypic space and the phenotypic space must have

the property of *neighbourhood correlation* with respect to the genetic operators and the learning rule for genetic assimilation of a learned trait to be guaranteed. That is, the small changes in the phenotype that are a result of learning must correlate to possible small changes in the genotype using the genetic operators available.

Now that I have described the Baldwin effect, we can look at it in terms of its influence on the speed or rate of evolution. In Figure 1a, those individuals that are learning the fitter trait will achieve an increased fitness score. An experimenter monitoring the average fitness of the population will notice an increase in this measure. However, at this stage, there has been no movement of the population in genotype space and therefore no evolution. Learning is increasing the fitness scores additively. It is in the transition from Figure 1a to Figure 1b that a learning-directed movement in the population's position in genotype space occurs and so it is only at this stage that we can say learning is guiding evolution. With respect to the Baldwin effect, the question is: How can we be sure that evolution and learning are not producing a fitness increase in a purely additive fashion rather than through learning guiding evolution? That is, in comparing a graph of average fitness over generations in a learning and evolution experiment with that from an evolution alone experiment, if we were to remove that aspect of the fitness scores that was attributable to learning, how can we be sure we wouldn't have identical graphs? Evolution implies genotypic change, and an increased level of average population fitness in an experiment combining learning and evolution is not necessarily a good indication of increased evolutionary progress. So what is? Well, this will be dealt with in Section 6 but for now I just want to emphasise that the Baldwin effect implies that learning produces (directed) population movement through *genotype* space that would not be there if evolution were applied alone (as was most definitely the case in Hinton and Nowlan (1987)).

3   The Hiding Effect

This phenomenon, that I will call the Hiding effect of learning on evolution, is by no means a new idea. It has been described in several reviews of the effects of learning on evolution in the biology literature (Johnston, 1982; Gordon, 1992) and is mentioned in the Artificial Life/Adaptive Behaviour literature in the introduction to Belew and Mitchell (1996). However, unlike the Baldwin effect, I have not see any investigation into the nature or conditions of this effect.

The Hiding effect can be considered as one of the costs or selective disadvantages of learning (intro. Belew & Mitchell, 1996). It occurs like this: Members of an evolving population with different genotypes are selected for according to their phenotypic traits. The differences between the genotypes produce differences between their associated phenotypes that allow selection to get a hold and make a discrimination. Therefore, individuals with differing genotypes that learn to perform the same trait, or modify their phenotypes so that they are the same, reduce selection's ability to discriminate between them. Genetic differences are hidden from selection by learning. This is illustrated in Figure 2. Conceptually, each

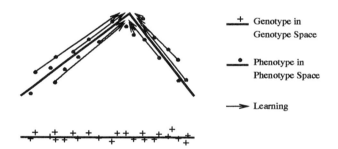

Figure 2: *The Hiding Effect: The one dimensional genotypes are translated to phenotypes which can then modify themselves in phenotype space. (Note: again, only a few arrows are shown). The heights of the phenotypes represent relative fitness. The differences between individual's genotypes are hidden to selection by their phenotypes learning the same trait.*

genotype in genotype space, represented by the black crosses in Figure 2, can be thought of as having an innate phenotype in phenotypic space, represented by the black blobs. The distances between the blobs indicate differences in the innately specified trait and translate directly to their associated genetic differences. If these individuals were unable to learn, then selection would have these phenotypic differences to work on and, because of the fitness differentials indicated by the height of the phenotypic landscape and the fact that the phenotypic differences are a good indicator of genetic dif-

ferences, evolution would move the population towards areas of increased fitness. However, with each individual possessing the ability to learn, as indicated by the arrows, (i.e. change their phenotype to one situated in an area of increased fitness in phenotype space) then the differences between the individuals' phenotypes are reduced. Since their phenotypes are now identical, each member of the population will achieve the same fitness and so the selection pressure between them is reduced by the learning over a non-learning population in the same position. We would expect this decrease in the selection pressure to lead to a reduction in the rate of movement of the population through genotype space, i.e. the rate of evolution would be reduced by the inclusion of learning in this case.

4   The Baldwin/Hiding Trade-off

The previous two sections have described how evolution can be both speeded up and slowed down by the inclusion of learning. There must, therefore be some sort of trade-off between the Baldwin effect and the Hiding effect or a set of conditions that determine whether one dominates the other in the determination of the actual rate of evolution. This section will describe two possible conditions which will then be tested in the experiments presented in Section 5. The first factor that influences the trade-off between the Baldwin effect and the Hiding effect is the cost of learning. It has already been stated in Section 2 that the ability to learn a specific trait can cost an individual over a non-learning conspecific. This cost is what supplies the selection pressure for the genetic assimilation of a learned trait, as in Figure 1b. It was also stated that the Hiding effect itself can be considered a learning cost or a selective disadvantage. However, the Hiding effect is of a fundamentally different nature to the costs which provide the selection pressure for genetic assimilation. Instead of being paid by the individual relative to its conspecifics, it is borne by the population as a whole[1]. It is the slowing-down of the rate of evolution that is the penalty that the Hiding effect bestows on the whole population relative to a non-learning one (or indeed a different population that is competing for resources may be able to 'out-evolve' the population that is experiencing the Hiding effect). Although the Hiding effect is itself a selective disadvantage against learning, for it to be sustained and genetic assimilation of the learned trait prevented, the individual-specific learning costs must be minimal. That is, to show this effect, we want to avoid the situation in Figure 1b in which the costs provide the selection pressure for the population to reduce the level of learning and climb to the area of

---

[1] In the classification of the various costs that have to be paid in an evolutionary system for learning, presented by Mayley (1996b), the Hiding effect falls into category 4 — individual non-specific costs.

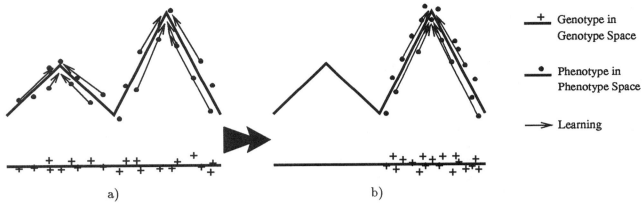

Figure 3: *The Trade-off Between the Baldwin Effect and the Hiding Effect Brought about by Epistasis: The one dimensional genotypes are translated to phenotypes which can then modify themselves in phenotype space. The heights of the phenotypes represent relative fitness. a) Members of the population are learning their local fitness maxima. (Note: again, only a few arrows are shown); b) Differences in the heights of the local fitness maxima lead to the selection of individuals that achieve the highest maximum. This maximum is then hidden from selection by the individuals' learning.*

increased fitness in genotype space. In natural systems it is very difficult for organisms to avoid the costs of learning since their fitness is effectively continuously assessed throughout their lifetime and any mistakes made or time wasted whilst learning will cost them over a non-learning individual. However, it is possible to avoid individual specific costs in artificial evolution by awarding individuals their fitness depending on their performance achieved at the end of any learning trials as in Chalmers (1990) (see Mayley (1996a) for greater discussion of this point).

The second condition that influences the trade-off between the Baldwin effect and the Hiding effect is epistasis. We can see this if we refer to Figure 3. Members of a learning population that are spread over several peaks will each be able to learn their local peak (Figure 3a). Those that learn the highest peak will be selected for and so come to dominate the population (Figure 3b). Thus we have a directed movement of the population in genotype space towards an area of high fitness that is driven by traits that have been learnt by the individuals during their lifetime (Baldwin effect). However, once all the members of the population are learning the high peak, the genetic differences between them are no longer available for selection and, in the absence of any individual-specific learning cost, the learned trait(s) cannot be genetically assimilated (Hiding effect). This illustrates the trade-off between the Baldwin effect and the Hiding effect and we can have situations where there is a mixture of the two phenomenon. We would therefore expect the Hiding effect to dominate in evolutionary situations where there is low individual-specific learning costs and low epistasis but as epistasis increases the Baldwin effect gains more and more influence and as costs increase it should come to dominate the Hiding effect.

5 Simulation Experiments

A set of experiments is described that make explicit the cost of learning and landscape epistasis as parameters. Section 6 will describe the techniques used to monitor the rates of evolution in these experiments.

5.1 Genotypes, Phenotypes and Fitness

Each individual has a genotype and a phenotype that both consist of a binary string of length N. The goals of evolution and learning are to produce phenotypes with the highest fitness according to Kauffman's NK fitness landscape model (Kauffman, 1993). It is expected that

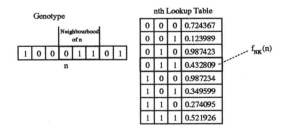

Figure 4: *Illustration of the calculation of $f_{NK}(n)$ on Kauffman's NK fitness model with $N = 8$, $K = 2$.*

the majority of the readership is familiar with NK fitness landscapes but for those who are not, here is the briefest of descriptions. N refers to the length of a binary string and the value of K sets the level of epistasis by determining the dependence the partial fitness of a bit at location n has on the bits in a neighbourhood of K other locations. The neighbourhood may be the K locations nearest to n in the string or a set of K locations randomly picked from anywhere on the string.

A series of N lookup tables are generated, one for each location. Each table has 2^{K+1} random entries in the interval $(0,1)$. The fitness, F_{NK}, of a particular string is calculated by $F_{NK} = \frac{1}{N} \sum_{n=1}^{N} f_{NK}(n)$ where the partial fitness $f_{NK}(n)$ is obtained from the nth lookup table using the values of the bits in location n and its neighbourhood as the lookup key (Figure 4). Thus when $K = 0$, each location contributes independently to the overall fitness of the string and the landscape is smooth; when $K = (N-1)$ the fitness landscape is maximally rugged.

5.2 Learning

Lifetime learning is implemented as a steepest-ascent hill-climb by the phenotype on the NK landscape. The bits in an individual's phenotype are initially set to be the same as those in its genotype, giving the individual a definite innate phenotype and a starting point from which to begin its learning search. The fitness of this innate *phenotype* is tested using the NK fitness model. Learning then proceeds as a set of learning trials. Each bit is flipped, the fitness of the resulting phenotype tested and the bit flipped back again. When all N bits have been tested, the bit that produced the best fitness increase is flipped permanently. This process of testing each bit and selecting the best, called a learning operation, continues until no further fitness increase is achieved. We thus have the phenotype performing a local hill-climb to its nearest local optima, in accordance that with the view that learning is a local search whilst evolution is a population based one. To make the learning cost an explicit parameter, it is incorporated into the fitness function (Section 5.3).

5.3 Experiment Overview

A population of random genotypes of size 100 is generated with $N = 20$. Each individual's genotype is copied to its phenotype and learning takes place as described in Section 5.2. The fitness is evaluated using the equation:

$$F(g_i) = F_{NK}(p'_i) - cx \qquad (1)$$

where $F(g_i)$ is the fitness awarded to genotype g_i, $F_{NK}(p'_i)$ is the NK fitness of the best string found by learning, c is the cost of each learning operation and x is the number of learning operations it took find p'_i. The cx term in Equation 1 is used to provide a cost for learning. The individual is penalised a fixed amount for each learning operation that actually takes place. Once the fitnesses of all the individuals in the population have been evaluated, they are bred to form the next generation using fitness-proportional selection with $0.99 \times$ the fitness of the worst as the base, a crossover probability of 0.7 and an average mutation rate of 0.3 bits per genotype $(0.3/N$ per bit).

6 Measuring the Rate of Evolution

In the above discussion we have been considering the influence of learning on the rate of evolution, but what exactly is meant by this term?

It was stated in Section 2 that monitoring the average fitness of the population in a non-Lamarckian framework could lead to a false idea of the rate of evolution. The average fitness of the population is an indication of the rate at which the system is able to produce fit phenotypes. If the experimenter's motivation is an engineering one, where the requirement is to produce a good, working solution to a problem, then this is sufficient. However, that is not the motivation here. We are interested in the effect learning has on the movement of the population through genotype space: The Baldwin effect promotes that movement; the Hiding effect suppresses it. A similar situation was encountered by Cliff and Miller (1995) in which problems of assessing continued evolutionary activity in co-evolutionary scenarios were considered. Here, tracking average fitness is meaningless since the fitness of one population depends on the other. Cliff and Miller used image-processing techniques to look at patterns of genetic change and persistence over generations in bitmap images of elite and consensus sequences[2]. Although giving a good indicator of genetic activity, their results were largely qualitative making checking the rate of evolution in any given system difficult. Bedau and Packard (1991) monitored evolutionary activity in a different way. All of the phenotypic traits of the members of the population were monitored for their lifetime usage and therefore their contribution to fitness[3] could be individually assessed. The genes that directly coded for those traits that persisted population-wise over generations were thus considered evolutionarily favourable and the rate at which new, favourable genes were created was considered a measure of evolutionary activity. The problem with the approach as a general method of measuring evolutionary activity is that once the direct mapping between genotype and phenotypic traits is lost (e.g. some sort of morphogenesis scheme is used to construct a phenotype from a genotype) then the decision as to which gene contributes to which phenotypic trait is a hard one. More specifically, when dealing with learning and evolution, if the phenotype changes during its lifetime through learning then the decision is impossible.

One of the biggest problems encountered by both Cliff and Miller (1995) and Bedau and Packard (1991) in tracking evolutionary movement in genotype space is that of distinguishing between useful, directed population movement and random drift. Harvey and Thomp-

---

[2] Other techniques were also described that only apply to co-evolutionary scenarios.

[3] Bedau and Packard actually used an energetic model where an individual's fitness was implicit but that distinction is not important here.

son (1996) have developed methods to try and accomplish this and the techniques described here draw on this work. I will describe a collection of measures of evolutionary activity that together are sufficient to give us a picture of the different effects that learning has on evolution when influenced by the Baldwin effect and the Hiding effect.

Centroid Movement: The centroid of a population at any given generation is its center of gravity in genotype space. Each genotype is treated as a vector of 0.0's and 1.0's and the centroid is average of these vectors: $C_i = \frac{1}{P} \sum_{j=1}^{P} g_{ij}$. Where C_i is the centroid at generation i; P is the population size and g_{ij} is the jth genotypic vector at generation i. We can thus plot the distance moved by the centroid from generation $i - 1$ to i: $|C_i - C_{i-1}|$.

Centroid Direction Correlation (C.D.C.): A population under no selection pressure that is performing a random walk will show a large centroid movement each generation. We want to capture a more directed form of movement; a movement that is sustained over generations as new genetic material takes over the population. This is done by taking the cosine of the angle between the vectors of the motion of the centroid between two generations:

$$C.D.C._i = \frac{(C_i - C_{i-1}) \cdot (C_{i-1} - C_{i-2})}{|C_i - C_{i-1}||C_{i-1} - C_{i-2}|} \qquad (2)$$

Thus, when the centroid moves in a similar direction through genotype space over two generations, this measure will be close to 1.0; in opposite directions it will be close to -1.0 and orthogonally, close to 0.0 (most likely with random movement in high dimensional space).

Principal Component Analysis: Harvey and Thompson (1996) use a technique to visualise the movement of their evolving population through genotype space that reduces the dimensionality of their genotypes from 1800 to 2. This is done by projecting the centroids of the population over generations onto the first and second principal components of the trace they made through genotype space. The direct genotype to phenotype mapping and the one to one relationship between evolutionary task and the learning task in the particular experiments above, allow us to go further. As well as projecting the genotypic centroids onto the principal components, we can also project the phenotypic centroids. This will effectively lay phenotype space on top of genotype space, viewed from the angle of most movement in genotype space, and should allow us to see if learning is indeed guiding evolution.

Innate Phenotype Fitness: Since the above experiment was designed such that each individual has an innate phenotype on which learning acts, we can remove the components of the fitness scores that are attributable to learning. We can then plot the average of this across the population; it should indicate whether the population has moved to areas in genotype space that are innately fitter.

7 Results

The experiment was run with parameter values $c = 0.00$ (individual-specific cost-free learning), $c = 0.03$ (costly learning), and $K = 0$ (non-epistatic), $K = 5$ (epistatic). The results presented in this section are the average of 50 runs of the simulation unless otherwise stated.

7.1 Cost-Free Learning

Figure 5 shows the results for when $c = 0.00$. In the case where $K = 0$, the first thing to note is that the average fitness graph and the fitness of the best individual (Figure 5a) are constant and equal throughout the evolutionary run (the two graphs are laid over each other so there appears to be only one line). All members of the population have been able to find the globally optimal phenotype from the first generation, regardless of their genetic make-up. This continues for the entire simulation run. Because their phenotypes are all achieving the same score, there is no selection between the genotypes, and the average fitness scored by the innate phenotypes remains at 0.5, the average score that a randomly generated string would achieve on an NK fitness landscape. That is, there is no selection pressure for the genotypes to move to areas of increased fitness in genotype space that are achievable without learning. Each individual obtains it's fitness score purely through learning. With $c = 0.00$ and $K = 0$ we are seeing the Hiding effect at its most prominent: Each individual obtains its fitness score purely through learning and there is no evolution.

However, this is not to say that there is no movement of the genotypes in genotype space at all, as we can see if we look at Figure 5b, the graph of distance moved by the centroid of the population each generation. We notice that there is in fact a consistent level of movement throughout the simulation run (average over generations $= 0.208$). Since there is no evolution, i.e. no selection resulting in directed population movement, this motion is due to random drift[4]. Confirmation of this is given by the C.D.C. graph (Figure 5c). Remembering that this is a measure of directed centroid movement over generations and will be positive for a correlated direction, negative for anti-correlated and zero for uncorrelated, we can see that during this experiment there was very little directed movement within genotype space (average over generations $= -0.0064$). We can get strong qual-

---

[4] The level in Figure 5b is the same as that produced in a separate experiment where members of population were each awarded a random fitness with all other experimental conditions identical (not shown).

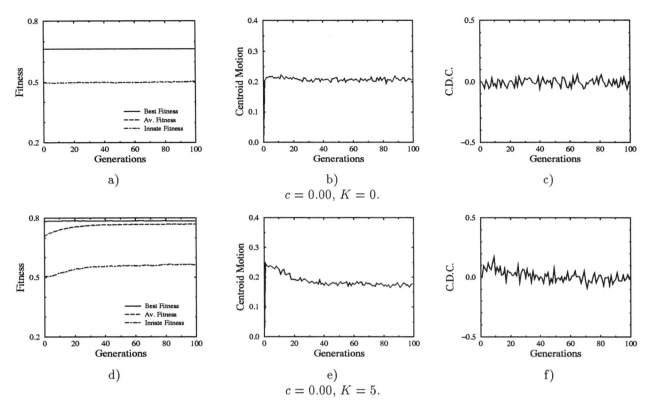

Figure 5: *Results from experimental runs with $c = 0.00$ and $K = 0$, $K = 5$: a), d) Fitness of the best member in the population, average fitness of members in the population and average innate fitness of members in the population, all over generations, plotted on the same axes; b), e) Distance moved by the centroid of the population in genotype space; c), f) Centroid Direction Correlation — indication of the correlation in the direction of movement of the genotypic centroid each generation.*

itative confirmation of this picture from the Principal Component Analysis shown in Figure 7a. The crosses represent the projection of the genotypic centroids on the first two principal components of the genotypic centroids over generations, the circles, the learnt phenotypic centroids from the same perspective and the lines connect genotypic centroids with phenotypic centroids from the same generation, representing learning. All the phenoytpic centroids are positioned on top of each other at the top of the Figure. This is because the phenotypes all learn the global optima throughout the evolutionary run. However, the genotypic centroids move around genotype space in a random way — there is no selection pressure for them to move in any particular direction.

Moving on to the case where $c = 0.00$ and $K = 5$ — a more epistatic fitness landscape — we can see a marked difference in the fitness graphs in Figure 5d when compared with 5a. First of all, the best fitness remains high for the entire run as in the case with $K = 0$ but the average fitness is no longer constant over generations. It starts off high, well above the 0.5 random average, and climbs steadily in the first 40 generations or so, until it is near the best fitness. We can see why this happens from the other three lines. The population starts off spread

out all over genotype space. Their phenotypes all learn their local fitness peaks, which will vary in size, and the ones that achieve the higher fitness scores will be selected for. The phenotypic selection has the effect of moving the population in *genotype space* so that they are near the area corresponding to increased fitness in phenotype space. The graph of innate fitness thus starts off at the random average of 0.5 and increases steadily in the same period to reach a level of 0.56 as the population moves to the fitter area. Figure 5e show the magnitude of this movement in genotype space indicated by the increased level (above 0.208) of this line in the first 20 generations or so. Confirmation that this is *directed* movement is given in Figure 5f where the C.D.C. is beginning to show consistent levels above zero in the same period. The fact that the innate fitness graph doesn't climb any further indicates that there is still a large level of learning occurring once the population has settled around a peak; the peak now being hidden from selection by that learning.

The P.C.A. in figure 7b shows the movement in genotype space in this case. The genotypic centroids start off in the bottom righthand corner of the Figure with the centroids of their learned phenotypes to the northwest of them. The population then moves in genotype

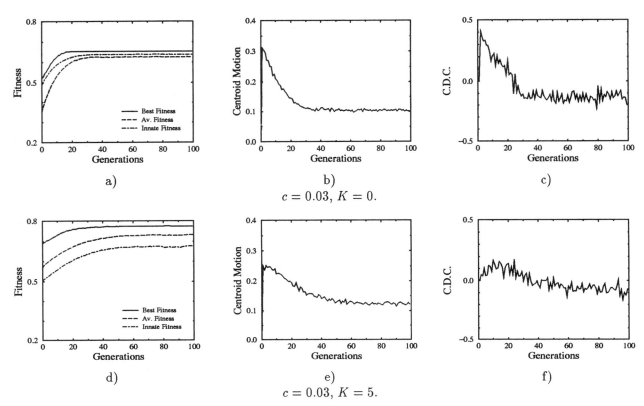

$c = 0.03, K = 0.$

$c = 0.03, K = 5.$

Figure 6: *Results from experimental runs with $c = 0.03$ and $K = 0$, $K = 5$: a), d) Fitness of the best member in the population, average fitness of members in the population and average innate fitness of members in the population, all over generations, plotted on the same axes; b), e) Distance moved by the centroid of the population in genotype space; c), f) Centroid Direction Correlation — indication of the correlation in the direction of movement of the genotypic centroid each generation.*

space in this same direction, following the phenotypes. In the latter generations, the genotypic centroids never quite 'catch up' with the phenotypic centroids indicating that full genetic assimilation has not occurred. The population has moved to an area in genotype space that innately produces fitter that random phenotyes, through fitness scores that were achieved through learning. It is fairly clear that the situation described in Section 4 has occurred here in which there has been a trade-off between the Baldwin effect and the Hiding effect.

7.2 Costly Learning

We now turn to Figure 6 which shows the results from simulation runs where learning costs the individuals 0.03 fitness points for each learning operation performed. Firstly, when $K = 0$, it is noticeable from Figure 6a that both the best fitness and the average fitness start off appreciably lower than in the cost-free cases and then climb up to a similar value after about 30 generations. The reason for these lower levels of fitness is that, although the individuals are learning the global optima, they are being penalised for that learning. The increasing fitness levels

over generations then comes about through the selection pressure to reduce these costs which can only be done by the population moving in genotype space towards the area that produces innate, globally-optimal phenotypes to reduce the level of learning. This is shown by the innate fitness graph in Figure 6a. It climbs to a level similar to the other two lines indicating that the majority of an individual's fitness is a result of the position of its innate phenotype in phenotypic space and only minimally as a result of learning. This shows strongly that the global optima has been genetically assimilated[5]. Figure 6b and c show the strong movement across genotype space as this assimilation takes place. In the early generations the levels are well above their baselines of 0.208 and 0.0 respectively, but it is interesting to note what happens to them after the genotypes reach the global optimum at about generation 30 — Figure 6b falls well

---

[5] One point to note in passing with these graphs is that the innate fitness graph is higher that the average fitness graph. This is because the individuals are being penalised heavily for their learning but, because we are imposing learning on them, can only evolve to areas in genotype space that require less learning rather than to not learn at all. This is of little consequence to the arguments presented here since we are dealing only with learning individuals.

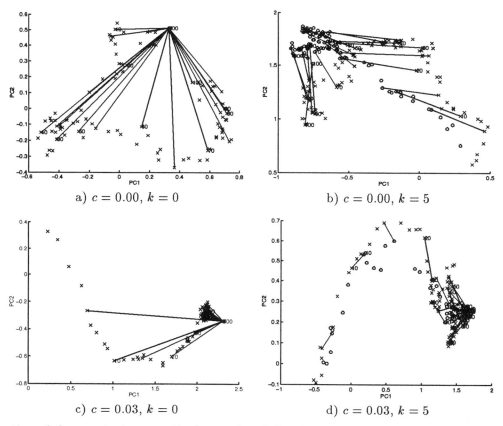

Figure 7: *Projection of the genotypic centroids (crosses) and the phenotypic centroids (circles) on the first two principal components of the genotypic centroids over generations. The lines connect genotypic and phenotypic centroids from the same generation to represent learning (for clarity they are only shown for every fifth generation) and the numbered labels indicate generation (every 10). These plots are each from a single simulation run with the parameter settings as shown.*

below 0.208 and the C.D.C. becomes negative. This is because the population is converged on the global optimum with little selection pressure in any direction. Mutation will cause individuals to fall off the optimum and any imbalance in the direction that individuals fall will cause the centroid to slowly shift away from the optimum. The fallen individuals will then have to learn the optimal phenotype and therefore incur a cost of learning. These individuals will then be selected against and the centroid will move back towards the optimum — the opposite direction from which it moved previously. We therefore get small, frequent movements of the centroid that are negatively correlated with the previous direction.

The P.C.A. for costly learning on a non-epistatic landscape is shown in Figure 7c and is rather different from the cost-free case in Figure 7a. Once again, all the centroids of the learned phenotypes are situated on the global optimum (to the right of the Figure) throughout the evolutionary run but in the first 30 generations the genotypic centroids quickly arrive in the same area as the learning becomes genetically assimilated, in contrast

with Figure 7a. Subsequent to that, the genotypic centroids remain very close to the optimum, confirming the picture of a population continually falling off the peak and then being pushed back.

We look now at costly learning with $K = 5$. In this case the fitness, centroid movement and C.D.C. graphs indicate a less severe but more prolonged movement of the centroid across genotype space than in the $K = 0$ case. This is because there are more fitness peaks across phenotype space for the learning individuals to explore, reducing the selection pressure between them. This is born out by the P.C.A. shown in Figure 7d where the phenotypic centroids progress across the projection in contrast to Figure 7c where they were firmly fixed to the global optimum. The genotypic centroids follow the phenotypic centroids in their associated space in a similar manner to Figure 7b but at a faster rate because of the selection pressure of reducing the cost of learning. Notably also is that, in the later generations, the genotypic centroids are packed more tightly around the area of genotype space that innately corresponds to the fitness peak in phenotype space that the population eventually settles on. This is because the selection pressure from the cost of learning overcomes the Hiding effect that was seen in Figure 7b.

8 Conclusion

I started with a discussion of the Baldwin effect and stated that the accepted wisdom is that the inclusion of learning in a evolutionary scenario speeded up the rate of evolution. It was noted that this is usually assumed from an increased production of fit phenotypes as indicated by an average or best fitness measure. I then suggested that these measures may not be appropriate, highlighting the Hiding effect as a phenomenon that slowed the progress of an evolving population through genotype space, whilst still producing fit phenotypes. Factors governing whether the Baldwin effect or the Hiding effect dominates in any given evolutionary scenario were suggested and it was shown experimentally that the Hiding effect dominates when epistasis and the cost of learning are low, the Baldwin effect dominates when the cost of learning is high, but when the costs are low and the epistasis is high there is a mixture of the two.

One note concerning C.D.C. measurement of evolutionary rate used here: On the NK fitness landscapes it was a good indicator of directed genotypic movement. However, on more realistic landscapes in which there is significant levels of 'junk D.N.A.' and neutral networks, hitchhiking may lead to some problems.

Acknowledgments

I would like to thank Dave Cliff, Inman Harvey, Phil Husbands and Adrian Thompson for their kind help.

References

Anderson, R. (1995). Learning and evolution: A quantitative genetics approach. *Journal of Theoretical Biology*, *175*, 89–101.

Baldwin, J. (1896). A new factor in evolution. *The American Naturalist*, *30*, 441–451.

Bedau, M., & Packard, N. (1991). Measurement of evolutionary activity, teleology, and life. In Langton, C., Taylor, C., Farmer, J., & Rasmussen, S. (Eds.), *Artificial Life II: Proceedings of the Workshop on Artificial Life*. Addison-Wesley.

Belew, R., & Mitchell, M. (Eds.). (1996). *Adaptive Individuals in Evolving Populations: Models snd Algorithms*. Addison-Wesley.

Belew, R. K. (1989). When both individuals and populations search: Adding simple learning to the genetic algorithm. In Schaffer, J. D. (Ed.), *Proceedings of the Third International Conference on Genetic Algorithms*, pp. 34–41 San Matteo, CA. Morgan Kauffmann.

Chalmers, D. J. (1990). The evolution of learning: An experiment in genetic connectionism. In Touretzky, D. S., Elman, J. L., Sejnowski, T. J., & Hinton, G. E. (Eds.), *Proceedings of the 1990 Connectionist Models Summer School* San Matteo, CA. Morgan Kaufmann, San Matteo, CA.

Cliff, D., & Miller, G. (1995). Tracking the Red Queen: Measurements of adaptive progress in co-evolutionary simulations.

In Moran, F., Moreno, A., Merelo, J., & Cachon, P. (Eds.), *Advances in Artificial Life: Proceedings of the Third European Conference on Artificial Life (ECAL95)*, pp. 200–218. Springer Verlag.

Gordon, D. (1992). Phenotypic plasticity. In Fox Feller, E., & Lloyd, E. (Eds.), *keywords in Evolutionary Biology*. Harvard University Press.

Gruau, F., & Whitley, D. (1993). The cellular developmental of neural networks: the interaction of learning and evolution. Research report 93-04, Laboratoire de l'Informatique du Parallélisme, Ecole Normale Supérieure de Lyon.

Harvey, I. (1992). Species adaptation genetic algorithms: A basis for a continuing SAGA. In Varela, F., & Bourgine, P. (Eds.), *Towards a Practice of Autonomous Systems: Proceedings of first European Conference on Artificial Life*. MIT Press/Bradford Books.

Harvey, I., & Thompson, A. (1996). Through the labyrinth, evolution finds a way: A silicon ridge.. In *Proceedings of The First International Conference on Evolvable Systems: from Biology to Hardware (ICES96)*. Springer-Verlag.

Hinton, G. E., & Nowlan, S. J. (1987). How learning can guide evolution. *Complex Systems*, *1*, 495 – 502.

Johnston, T. (1982). Selective costs and benefits in the evolution of learning. In Rosenblatt, J., Hinde, R., Beer, C., & Busnel, M. (Eds.), *Advances in the Study of Behavior.*, Vol. 12, pp. 65–106. Academic Press.

Kauffman, S. (1993). *The Origins of Order: Self-Organization and Selection in Evolution*. Oxford University Press.

Lloyd Morgan, C. (1896). On modification and variation. *Science*, *4*, 733–740.

Mayley, G. (1996a). The evolutionary cost of learning. In Maes, P., Mataric, M., Meyer, J., Pollack, J., & Wilson, S. (Eds.), *From Animals to Animats 4: Proceedings of the Fourth International Conference on Simulation of Adaptive Behavior*, pp. 458–467. MIT Press.

Mayley, G. (1996b). Landscapes, learning costs and genetic assimilation. *Evolution, Learning and Instinct: 100 Years of the Baldwin Effect. A Special Edition of Evolutionary Computation*, *4*(3), 213–234.

Maynard Smith, J. (1987). When learning guides evolution. *Nature*, *329*, 761–762.

Menczer, F., & Belew, R. (1994). Evolving sensors in environments of controlled complexity. In Brooks, R., & Maes, P. (Eds.), *Artificial Life IV*, pp. 210–221.

Turney, P. (1996). Myths and legends of the Baldwin Effect. In Fogarty, T., & Venturini, G. (Eds.), *Proceedings of the ICML-96 (13th International Conference on Machine Learning)*, pp. 135–142 Bari, Italy. Workshop proceedings not published.

Waddington, C. (1942). Canalization of development and the inheritance of acquired characters. *Nature*, *150*, 563–565.

Waddington, C. (1953). Genetic assimilation of an acquired character. *Evolution*, *7*, 118–126.

Waddington, C. (1956). Genetic assimilation of the *bithorax* phenotype. *Evolution*, *10*, 1–13.

Whitley, D., Scott Gordon, V., & Mathias, K. (1994). Lamarckian evolution, the Baldwin Effect and functional optimization. In Davidor, Y., Schwefel, H. P., & Manner, R. (Eds.), *Parallel Problem Solving from Nature-PPSN III*, pp. 6–15. Springer-Verlag.

Adaptation toward Changing Environments:
Why Darwinian in Nature?

Takahiro Sasaki *and **Mario Tokoro**†
Department of Computer Science,
Faculty of Science and Technology, Keio University
3-14-1 Hiyoshi, Kohoku-ku, Yokohama 223, Japan
{*sasaki,mario*} *@mt.cs.keio.ac.jp*

Abstract

The processes of adaptation in a multi-agent system consist of two complementary phases: 1) *learning*, occurring within each agent's individual lifetime, and 2) *evolution*, occurring over successive generations of the population. In this paper, we observe the dynamics of such adaptive processes in a simple abstract model, where each neural network is regarded as an individual capable of learning, and genetic algorithms are applied as the evolutionary processes for the population of such agents. By evaluating the characteristics of two different mechanisms of genetic inheritance, i.e *Darwinian* and *Lamarckian*, we show the following results. While the Lamarckian mechanism is far more effective than the Darwinian one under static environments, it is found to be unstable and performs quite poorly under dynamic environments. In contrast, even under dynamic environments, a Darwinian population is not only more stable than a Lamarckian one, but also maintains its adaptability with respect to such dynamic environments.

1 Introduction

Conventional artificial systems are usually defined strictly in a *top-down* manner so as to function precisely and effectively for certain purposes, under specifically closed domains. Therefore, those systems lack the adaptiveness to any uncertain or unexpected situations. On the other hand, for natural systems (ranging from swarms of cells to human societies) in the real world, not only their designs but also their entire behaviours emerge through *bottom-up* processes. However, these natural systems do adapt themselves quite well to

the real-world environment that exhibits dynamic and unpredictable characteristics, and also, somehow, cope with a variety of difficulties. Therefore, the underlying mechanisms in nature or human societies may be relevant when we consider, for example, novel information processing mechanisms for artificial intelligence systems or software agents that are to be used in an open environment. A research area called *Artificial Life* [7], which analyses mathematical aspects of the dynamics residing in life by synthesis and simulation, has recently received much attention, and considerable advances have been made in using principles of nature as models for possible methods of adaptive information processing.

Any natural system can be regarded, to some extent, as a *Multi-agent system*, which is a kind of environment populated by multiple (semi-)autonomous subjects referred to as agents. Natural ecosystems or human societies are undoubtedly typical examples of the multi-agent system. In such systems, where each agent possesses a certain degree of autonomy, we should consider the processes of adaptation that have taken place, not only at the population level, but also at an individual level. For example, in the world of natural organisms, the adaptation of the system can be viewed as a process consisting of two complementary phases, each taking place at different spatio-temporal levels: 1) *learning*, occurring within each individual lifetime, and 2) *evolution*, occurring over successive generations of the population. We can also observe these kinds of hierarchical adaptive processes in the human economic world, where an agent may be either an individual or a company. Here arises a naive question: "How should these processes of adaptation at the different levels be connected with each other for a higher advantage?" The main goal of this paper is to provide a possible direction for answers to this question.

1.1 Lamarckism and Darwinism

In the following, we consider a world populated by natural organisms as a typical example of multi-agent systems and focus attention on the processes of adaptation

---

*Also with "Research for the Future" Project, Faculty of Science and Technology, Keio University, Shin-Kawasaki-Mitsui Building West 3F, 890-12 Kashimada, Saiwai-ku, Kawasaki 221, Japan

†Also with Sony Computer Science Laboratory Inc., 3-14-13 Higashigotanda, Shinagawa-ku, Tokyo 141, Japan

in such system. First of all, the behaviour of an organism is not fixed through its lifetime. It develops a tendency to repeat the actions that produce pleasure or benefit, and to avoid those that cause danger or pain. For basic survival, each organism becomes adapted to the environment through its interactions with the environment, by processes called "learning." On the other hand, organisms are not born in a blank state. The basic structure of the brain, which determines the organism's behaviour, as well as its entire body, is developed according to genetic information that is inherited from its ancestors. Such genetic mechanisms, through which features can be inherited in succeeding generations, may not produce exactly the same features in offspring as in parents, because of genetic mutation and recombination. In general, the genes that succeed in constructing an individual better at survival than others in the population, tend to have more copies of themselves reproduced. The cumulative process consisting of genetic mutation and natural selection, leading to improved adaptation of organisms to their environment, is called "evolution."

In the history of evolutionary theory, there have been two major ideas that give different explanations for the motive force of natural evolution and the phenomenon of genetic inheritance. These ideas are called *Lamarckism* and *Darwinism*. The main point of the former is that the motive force of evolution is the effect of "inheritance of acquired characters." Through interactions with the environment or learning, individuals may undergo some adaptive changes, that will then somehow be put in their genes and direct the evolutionary process. On the other hand, the central dogma of the latter is that the motive force of evolution is "(non-random) natural selection following on random mutation"; mutation itself has no direction, but some individuals with advantageous mutations will have more chance of survival through natural selection. It claims that evolution is nothing but these cumulative processes of natural selection. To summarize in other words, while the Lamarckian idea assumes the direct connection between the adaptation at the individual level and that at the population level, the Darwinian idea clearly divides them from each other. As we know, the mainstream of today's evolutionary theory is Darwinian, and Lamarckism is regarded as wrong or as a heresy.

1.2 Adaptation toward Dynamic Environments

Due to the biological background, most of the studies on the issues of learning and evolution have been based on the mechanism of Darwinian genetic inheritance [3, 1, 9]. On the other hand, especially from a pure viewpoint of constructing practical applications, where there is no need to persist in holding the Darwinian model, some studies have attained significant improvements in the system's performance by introducing

a Lamarckian mechanism [2, 5]. However, few investigations have attempted a thorough comparison between the Lamarckian mechanism and the Darwinian one, since the advantage of Lamarckian over Darwinian seems rather obvious. As we are going to mention in the following, however, neither of the opinions are satisfactory, not only biologically but also from engineering viewpoint.

With regard to biology, we should be aware that processes that must be regarded as Lamarckian inheritance actually do take place in nature, albeit rarely. For example, a certain kind of water flea develops thorns on its body surface in an environment where many predators exist, and these thorns are transmitted to the offspring through the ovum once this adaptive change occurs [11]. It has been proven that this inheritance is not caused by changes in DNA itself, which are typically involved in what is called evolution, but by changes in the mechanism of genetic switching. However, this Lamarckian process should not be neglected even from the biological viewpoint. With regard to engineering, we would like to point out that most of the previous studies on the application of evolutionary computing took only static environments into consideration, and few observations and discussions have been made on dynamic environments. While it is natural for us to suppose that the Lamarckian mechanism is far more effective than the Darwinian one under static environments, it would not be true under dynamic environments. In such environments, in addition to the requirement of "how well agents can adapt themselves to a certain environment", another requirement arises of "*how well agents can follow the changes in the environment.*"

In response to our motivation mentioned above, the following pages focus attention on the adaptive processes of evolutionary agents under dynamic environments. In order to observe its evolutionary dynamics, we construct a simple abstract model, where each *neural network* [10] is regarded as an agent capable of learning, and *genetic algorithms* (GAs) [4] are applied as the evolutionary processes for the population of such agents. Two mechanisms of genetic inheritance are considered, *Darwinian* and *Lamarckian*. We evaluate the adaptability and robustness of the evolutionary agents, and try to clarify the characteristics of mechanisms required for the adaptation toward dynamic environments.

2 Model: A World of Agents

Here, we will describe our experimental framework with a concrete scenario in order to make our discussion more easily understandable.

A hundred agents come into the "world", with 500 units of initial "life energy" for each. In our simulation, each agent is an individual which has a feed-forward neural network that serves as its "brain", meaning that the agent takes action based on the network outputs (Figure

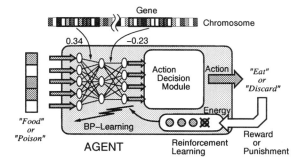

Figure 1: An architecture of an agent

1). The neural network has three layers, each of which contains five or six input neurons, three hidden neurons, and eight output neurons. Each neuron is fully connected to all neurons of the next layer. We take an array of real numbers as a "chromosome" from which the neural network is developed. The chromosome directly encodes all the connective weights of the network [8, 12]. Each value of the chromosomes in the initial generation is initialized randomly (between $-0.30 \sim 0.30$), and the better combinations are passed on genetically. It hardly needs to be said that not every neuronal connection of natural organisms can be determined directly from genes. Models closer to the real mechanism of embryogenesis do exist; for example, a grammatical method that applies graph rewriting rules recursively for the development of a network [6]. However, we can still focus on issues of learning and evolution even without such sophisticated models.

The world contains two groups of materials both of which have distinctive features (patterns of bits): "edible" materials and "poisonous" materials. When an agent is given any material, the agent inputs the pattern of the material into its neural network and stochastically determines whether to "eat" or "discard" it according to the outputs of the network. If what the agent ate was a food, the agent receives 10 units of energy and tries to train itself to produce the "eat" action with a higher probability for that pattern. Conversely, if the agent ate a poison, the agent loses a comparable amount of energy and tries to train itself to produce the "discard" action with a higher probability for that pattern. When the agent discards the material, no learning is conducted. The aim of each agent is to maximize its energy by learning a *rule* that discriminates food and poison through its experiences. We use the *Back Propagation Learning Algorithm*, in combination with a *Reinforcement Learning* framework, to train each agent. Connective weights of the network are modified by applying the expression typically used in various research on neural networks:

$$w(t+1) = w(t) - \eta \left. \frac{\partial E(w)}{\partial w} \right|_{w=w(t)} + \alpha \Delta w(t) \quad (1)$$

Here, two constants η and α are the coefficients of learning and inertia, respectively. In this paper, we set these values as $\eta = 0.75$ and $\alpha = 0.8$. The vector of connective weights at learning step t is represented as $w(t)$, and the error function of a network is represented as $E(w)$.

When an agent selects an action based on the network outputs, the action is not mapped directly from the pattern of outputs itself. The network outputs are fed once as signals to an "Action Decision Module" (Figure 1), which then finally determines the action of the agent stochastically according to the signals. As shown in the following, a Boltzmann distribution is used by the action decision module to determine the agent's action.

$$p(a_i|s) = \frac{\exp(o_i/T)}{\sum_{j \in possible\_actions} exp(o_j/T)} \quad (2)$$

Here, $p(a_i|s)$ represents the probability that an agent takes an action a_i in a situation s, and o_i represents the total value of the network outputs which corresponds to the action a_i. The degree of "adventurousness" of the agent is controlled by the temperature value T. When T is low, the agent tends to determine its own action by faithfully obeying the network outputs, which reflect its own experience of the past, and shows conservative behaviours. On the other hand, as T takes a higher value, the agent becomes more adventurous and its decisions are less affected by the network outputs. We set the value T to 0.3. This kind of stochastic mechanism is necessary to maintain the possibility of seeking more advantageous behaviours, even if an agent has already acquired a certain appropriate behavioural pattern.

Each agent is repeatedly offered a certain number of materials and learning occurs. We regard this number of repeated events as the length of an agent's "lifetime." At the end of each generation, some of the agents are selected as parents by a stochastic criterion proportional to the level of their energy, which is thus regarded as their fitness. Chromosomes of the selected agents undergo the genetic processes of crossing-over and mutation. Thus the selected parents reproduce new offspring, which then undergo lifetime learning in the following generation. The connective weights of the agents' neural networks must have been modified through their lifetime learning, but Darwinian agents do not transmit the results of the modification to the next generation. They just transmit their chromosomes which they inherited from their parents in the process of GAs (Figure 2a). On the other hand, Lamarckian agents re-encode the connection weights that suffered modification into their chromosomes, and transmit them in the process of GAs (Figure 2b). Here, the number of crossing-over points is set randomly from the range $0 \sim 4$, and positions of the points are also determined randomly. A mutation occurs at the rate of 5%, and its value ranges randomly between ± 0.5. Although the values used in this paper

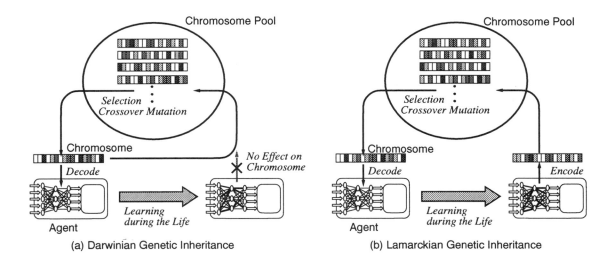

Figure 2: The mechanisms of Darwinian and Lamarckian genetic inheritance

are set heuristically according to some preliminary experiments, we have confirmed that changing these values within a moderate range results in qualitatively similar outcomes.

The flow of our experiments is summarized as follows.

1. A population of the first generation is generated ($g = 1$).

2. Each agent of the g-th generation conducts learning by taking actions during a certain period defined as its lifetime.

3. Fitness of each agent is calculated from the energy which it possesses.

4. Based on their fitness, some agents are selected stochastically as the parents and reproduce offspring of $(g+1)$-*th* generation through genetic processes such as crossing-over and mutation.

5. Increment g by unity ($g = g + 1$), and return to 2.

3 Experimental Evaluations: Darwinian vs. Lamarckian under Dynamic Environments

We have confirmed from the preliminary experiments that the Lamarckian mechanism is far more effective than the Darwinian one under static environments. These results are intuitively understandable, since Lamarckian agents can continue the learning process that their parents have suspended halfway in the previous generation, while Darwinian agents must make a fresh start in each generation.

However, a real-world agent such as a natural organism should cope adaptively with dynamic and complex changes in the environment. In such environments, the most advantageous rule for an agent to learn may change accordingly.

3.1 Experiment 1 – An environment where only partial information is available

First, we consider a situation with a dynamic characteristic in a low degree, where the discrimination rule between food and poison itself does not change, but not all the information necessary to learn the complete rule is available at one time. Moreover, an available piece of information changes with time. This corresponds to a situation where some kinds of unknown materials suddenly appear and other kinds of materials disappear from the world.

Now, let us consider a world where food and poison are characterized by arrays of six bits, as shown in Figure 3. White and black cells represent "0" and "1", respectively. The symbol "∗" means *don't care* whether it is "0" or "1". That is to say, food and poison are discriminated by the upper three bits, and the lower three are noise bits. Note that each agent does not "know" of the existence of noise, nor which bits are noise. The agent tries to maximize the chance of its own survival by acquiring the discrimination rule that corresponds to a parity problem of three bits. However, not all the information necessary for the agents to learn the complete rule is supplied at one time. The world considered here contains only four types of materials at one time, where two are food and the other two are poison (Figure 3), and where the constituent materials of the world change with time. We consider a situation where constituent materials of the world change at intervals of 20 generations.

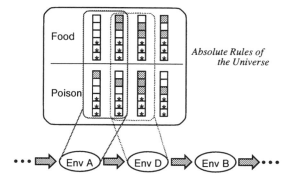

An Environment as a Partial View of the Universe

	Food				Poison			
Env A	O	O	X	X	O	O	X	X
Env B	X	X	O	O	X	X	O	O
Env C	O	X	O	X	O	X	O	X
Env D	X	O	X	O	X	O	X	O
Env E	O	X	X	O	X	O	O	X
Env F	X	O	O	X	O	X	X	O

Figure 3: Experiment 1 – An environment where only partial information is available

Both Figures 4a and 4b show the change in the average fitness of the populations. While Figure 4a shows the range from initial generation to 1000*th* generation with a magnified scale, Figure 4b shows the results for the longer span. As is evident from these figures, the fitness of Lamarckian agents oscillates violently as constituent materials change, while the fitness of Darwinian agents oscillates less and is more stable. These results indicate that the mechanism of Darwinian inheritance is superior to that of Lamarckian with regard to robustness against changes in the environment.

The point we would like to especially emphasize here, is that each time the environment changes, the fitness of Darwinian agents does not make a fresh start but gradually increases as the generation proceeds. That is to say, even though only a partial piece of information is available at a time, Darwinian agents seem to be gradually acquiring the complete rule by integrating those pieces of partial information through successive generations. To confirm this practically, we carried out a further experiment. In the first place, agents of the initial generation, 2000*th* generation, 4000*th* generation, and 6000*th* generation were preserved while conducting the experiment whose results are shown in Figure 4. Next, each of the four groups of agents was trained in an environment with the complete set of the rule. That is to say, all the eight patterns shown in Figure 3 were presented to agents,

and their learning abilities were evaluated. The learning curves of each generation are shown in Figure 5. Each of the figures shows the average output error curves for the discrimination ability learned during their lifetime. The mean squared error is used to measure the difference between the actual outputs and the ideal outputs. As shown in Figure 5a, neither the initial generation of Lamarckian agents nor that of Darwinian agents can learn an appropriate discrimination rule. As the generation reaches 2000 (Figure 5b), Lamarckian agents come to output innately somewhat better values, yet the errors are not reduced much through their lifetime learning. Conversely, Darwinian agents tend to output innately somewhat worse values than that of Lamarckian agents, yet they reduce their errors during their lifetime learning. As the generations proceed further (4000*th* generation in Figure 5c and 6000*th* generation in 5d), we can see that a population of agents which appropriately learn the complete rule can be formed through the Darwinian mechanism. On the other hand, the Lamarckian mechanism still produces populations of agents that cannot appropriately learn the complete rule.

The explanation for the Lamarckian agents' unstable behaviour is as follows. For example, with regard to "Env A" shown in Figure 3, agents do not need to learn the perfect rule of the three-bits parity problem, but that of the two-bits parity problem (the XOR problem) is sufficient for discriminating between food and poison, since the third bit of any material takes the same value which in this case is "0". However, let us consider a situation where the world suddenly changes its condition from "Env A" to "Env B". The knowledge of the two-bits parity problem which agents have acquired in "Env A" now becomes not only useless, but also even harmful for their survival, since the acquired knowledge will have the opposite meaning in "Env B". Through the Lamarckian mechanism, agents directly transmit to their offspring the modification of network connections caused by their lifetime learning, thus adapting themselves too deeply to a specific situation. It is difficult for a population to escape from this deep adaptation. In contrast, through the Darwinian mechanism, while each agent can quickly adapt itself to specific situations in the short term with learning at an individual level, agents do not commit to the specific situations, but gradually approach universality in the long term through evolution at the population level.

3.2 Experiment 2 – An environment where the rule changes

In an environment with a dynamic characteristic in a higher degree, the discrimination rule itself may change. Here, we consider a situation where the rules are reversed, so that food and poison swap their roles repeatedly at each particular interval (Figure 6). Although a

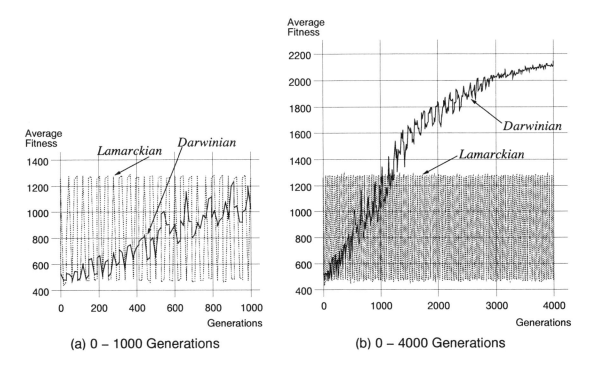

Figure 4: Experiment 1 – The average fitness

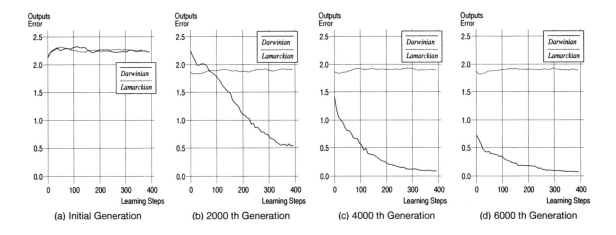

Figure 5: Experiment 1 – The changes in learning curves through generations

situation where conditions advantageous to survival are overturned, as considered here, may seem to be rather arbitrary, it can actually happen. A well-known example is the *industrial melanism* of certain moths, which occurred in the Industrial Revolution era in England [11]. Although details of the example are omitted in this paper due to limitations of space, it indicates that rules which affect survival chances are not eternal but fluid, and may sometimes suffer drastic changes.

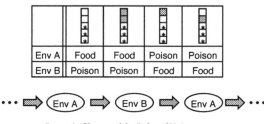

Figure 6: Experiment 2 – An environment where the rule changes

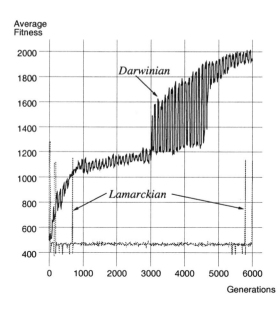

Figure 7: Experiment 2 – The average fitness

As shown in Figure 6, let us consider here a situation where each material is represented as a pattern of five bits. Neglecting the three noise bits, agents can discriminate between food and poison based on the rule of the XOR problem, yet the semantics of the patterns change with time. We consider a situation where the discrimination rule is overturned at intervals of 50 generations.

Figure 7 shows the change in the average fitness of the populations. As one can intuitively imagine, Lamarckian agents cannot adapt themselves to the environment. On the other hand, the point that we should especially emphasize is that the fitness of Darwinian agents rises over successive generations, although oscillation is observed. This seems counterintuitive, since here the discrimination rule itself suffers changes.

This result shows that a population of agents which can cope with both rules of "Env A" and "Env B" is formed through the Darwinian mechanism. To confirm this practically, we let four populations (an initial generation, 2000*th*, 4000*th*, and 6000*th* generation), which were preserved in the experiment, conduct learning under each of the two rules, and observed their learning curves. Figure 8 shows the results. Neither the initial population of Lamarckian agents nor of Darwinian agents can conduct appropriate learning (Figure 8a). However, by the 2000*th* generation, the difference between the two populations becomes apparent (Figure 8b). As shown in the figure, we can confirm that the Darwinian mechanism forms a population of agents that learns both rules to some extent. As the generations proceed further and reach the 6000*th*, Darwinian agents come to learn each of the two rules more appropriately (Figure 8d). In

contrast, Lamarckian agents cannot appropriately learn either rule. The two learning curves for Lamarckian agents in the 6000*th* generation differ from each other, since agents cope with one rule better than the other. However, even if the preferred rule is given, Lamarckian agents cannot learn it better than Darwinian agents.

A possible explanation for the surprising behaviour of the Darwinian population is that they may have gradually grasped something common to both rules through the generations. In the environment considered here (Figure 6), materials can at least be grouped into two sets according to the pattern of first and second bits, although the rule of which group corresponds to food and which corresponds to poison changes with time. Agents may acquire the abstract "grouping rule" genetically at a population level, and then learn the details of the discrimination rule that differs from generation to generation at an individual level.

4   Summary

The mechanism of Lamarckian genetic inheritance is far more effective than that of Darwinian agents under static environments, since it merges both processes of learning and evolution in a direct manner, and thus enables agents to adapt quickly toward a given situation. However, since Lamarckian agents adapt themselves to the situation too greedily, they have difficulty in leaving the specific state of adaptation once it has taken place. Therefore, under dynamic environments where rules may suffer changes, the Lamarckian mechanism performs poorly and turns out to behave quite unstably. On the other hand, the Darwinian mechanism maintains stability. In

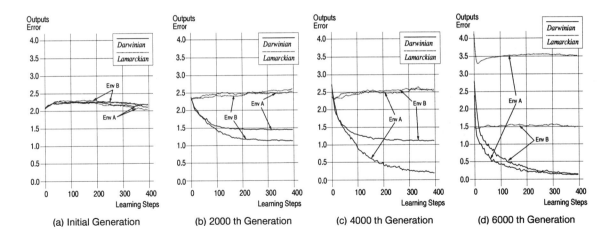

Figure 8: Experiment 2 – The change of learning curves through generations

such environments, the Darwinian mechanism, where the processes of learning and evolution are kept clearly divided, realizes more stable and better behaviour compared to the Lamarckian one. Darwinian agents cope with the detailed changes of rules at an individual level of learning, while to some extent keeping the generality. Moreover, Darwinian agents shows not only stability but also gradual improvements in their fitness over successive generations, even under dynamic environments. That is to say, Darwinian agents have adaptability toward dynamic environments.

Related to the above, there is one thing that we would like to point out concerning the Darwinian mechanism, from the learning ability curves shown in Figure 5 and 8. In Experiment 1, where the rule itself did not change, output errors of innate neural networks decreased in later generations (Figure 5). In short, individuals came to behave appropriately from their birth. On the other hand, in Experiment 2, where the rule itself changed with time, output errors of innate neural networks increased instead (Figures 8). This indicates that, under environments with dynamic characteristics to a higher degree, the ability to behave appropriately from the beginning is not so important; but, to have possibilities for learning to cope with a variety of situations becomes much more important. That is to say, rather than the "ability to *perform* something", the "ability to *learn* something" plays a more important role under the dynamic environments. Since the Lamarckian mechanism transmits the former ability too greedily, it does not work well under the dynamic environments.

5   Discussion

Although the model used in this paper has taken some ideas from the mechanisms of real life, it is an extremely abstract one that simplifies a number of biologically im-

portant factors. Therefore, our results may not have a direct impact, for example, on biology. Nevertheless, we may be able to find a number of important suggestions even from the results on our simple model used here.

For example, it is an evident fact that most organisms evolve in the Darwinian manner, although it is reported that processes that can be regarded as Lamarckian inheritance also take place in nature, as we have mentioned in section 1. While a *phenotype* is developed through quite complex processes according to the information of a *genotype* which is encoded on the *DNA*, it is very difficult to determine and compose "in reverse" the corresponding formation of the genotype for a certain phenotype. It is often said that these facts have made Lamarckian inheritance impossible (or strictly speaking, quite rare). However, from our experimental results, we may suggest another explanation for the essential reason why creatures would select the Darwinian strategy of genetic inheritance in the earlier stages of their evolution. Needless to say, the real world is an environment with strong dynamic characteristics; therefore the Darwinian inheritance itself has been an advantageous strategy for the adaptation to the real world.

We can go further with our discussion in connection with this point of view. The immortality of artificial intelligent systems is often considered to be one of their greatest merits, yet our experimental results urge us to reconsider this naive assumption. The Lamarckian mechanism can be regarded in a sense as a mechanism that enables never-ending learning, since the agents can continue the learning process that their parents suspended halfway[1]. The experimental results indicate that, under dynamic environments, the immortality of

---

[1] Although the Lamarckian mechanism considered here suffers natural selection, chromosomal crossing-over, and gene mutation, we can consider it as a mechanism for never-ending learning, in a rough sense.

artificial systems will turn out to be a flaw. Rather than living forever, the alternation of generations with appropriate intervals will play an important role, and the mechanism of genetic inheritance should be of a Darwinian style, where successive generations conduct learning independently of their parents.

6 Conclusions

Through some simulations using neural networks and genetic algorithms, we evaluated how learning at the individual level with two different inheritance mechanisms affects the evolutionary processes at the population level. The experimental results are summarized as follows:

1. Under a dynamic environment, agents with the Darwinian mechanism are more robust and show more stable behaviour than Lamarckian agents.

2. Moreover, agents with the Darwinian mechanism not only possess stability but also maintain adaptability even toward the dynamic environment itself.

We have clarified the fundamental characteristics which are required for the adaptation toward dynamic environments by using a model of an artificial organisms' world. Although we have used a number of biological terms in this paper, the essential processes concerned are the *collection, exploitation, modification and transmission* of information. Therefore, the results obtained here may give helpful suggestions in, for example, designing artificial intelligence systems or software agents that will be brought into play under dynamic environments.

Acknowledgments

The authors wish to thank everyone in the Sony Computer Science Laboratory for the fruitful discussions that helped shape our work. Special thanks are due to Dr. Hiroaki Kitano, Dr. Eiichi Osawa, Dr. Jun Tani, and Dr. Toru Ohira for their helpful suggestions with respect to the direction of this work.

References

[1] David H. Ackley and Michael L. Littman. Interactions between Learning and Evolution. In Christphor G. Langton, Charles Taylor, J. Doyne Farmer, and Steen Rasmussen, editors, *Artificial Life II, SFI Studies in the Sciences of Complexity, vol.X*, pages 487–509. Addison-Wesley, 1992.

[2] John J. Grefenstette. Lamarckian Learning in Multi-agent Environments. In *Proceedings of 4th International Conference on Genetic Algorithms and their applications (ICGA-91)*, pages 303–310, 1991.

[3] G. E. Hinton and S. J. Nowlan. How Learning Can Guide Evolution. *Complex Systems*, 1:495–502, 1987.

[4] J. H. Holland. *Adaptation in Natural and Artificial Systems*. The University of Michigan Press, 1975.

[5] Akira Imada and Keijiro Araki. Lamarckian evolution of associative memory. In *Proceedings of 1996 IEEE The Third International Conference on Evolutionary Computation (ICEC-96)*, pages 676–680, 1996.

[6] Hiroaki Kitano. Designing Neural Networks using Genetic Algorithms with Graph Generation System. *Complex System*, 4(4):461–476, 1990.

[7] Christopher G. Langton, editor. *Artificial Life: An Overview*. MIT Press, 1995.

[8] David J. Montana and Lawrence Davis. Training Feedforward Neural Networks Using Genetic Algorithms. In *Proceedings of the 11th International Conference on Artificial Intelligence (IJCAI-89)*, pages 762–767, 1989.

[9] Domenico Parisi, Stefano Nolfi, and Federico Cecconi. Learning, Behavior and Evolution. In *Toward a Practice of Autonomous Systems: Proceedings of the First European Conference on Artificial Life*, pages 207–216. MIT Press, 1991.

[10] David E. Rumelhart, James L. McClelland, and the PDP Research Group. *Parallel Distributed Processing: Explorations in the Microstructure of Cognition. (Volume 1: Foundations, Volume 2: Psychological and Biological Models)*. MIT Press, 1986.

[11] John Maynard Smith. *Evolutionary Genetics*. Oxford University Press, 1989.

[12] Darrell Whitley and Thomas Hanson. Optimizing Neural Networks Using Faster, More Accurate Genetic Search. In *Proceedings of 3rd International Conference on Genetic Algorithms and their applications (ICGA-89)*, pages 391–396, 1989.

Models for Interacting Populations of Memes:
Competition and Niche Behavior

Michael L. Best
Media Laboratory
Massachustes Institute of Technology
E15-320F
Cambridge, Massachustes 02139
USA

mikeb@media.mit.edu
http://www.media.mit.edu/~mikeb

Abstract

We make use of a set of text analysis tools, primarily based on Latent Semantic Indexing, to study the dynamics of memes on the Net. Our analysis discovers replicating memes within posts to the USENET News (or NetNews) system. We cluster the posts to NetNews into clouds within a conceptual sequence space; these clusters describe quasi-species. We then go on to study the pairwise interactions between these quasi-species by computing the cross-correlation between the interacting population's level of post activity. We analyze a particular corpus of posts to the soc.women newsgroup and argue that strong negative cross-correlations are examples of competition between the quasi-species. We find that high levels of competition occur more frequently among quasi-species who exist within a narrow ecological niche. We note that this phenomena also occurs in natural ecologies.

1 Introduction

Ideas do not exist in a vacuum. Neither does discourse, the interconnected ideas which make up conversation and texts. In this research we investigate the pairwise interaction between populations of ideas within discourse: Are our text populations in competition with each other? Do they mutually benefit each other? Do they prey on one another?

This work attempts to build models of *population memetics* by bringing together two disciplines: Alife and text analysis. Through techniques of text analysis we determine the salient co-occurring word sets, texts, and text clusters, and track their temporal dynamics. We then study the life-like properties of this human-made system by considering its behavior in terms of replicators, organisms, and species.

Richard Dawkins coined the term *meme* to describe replicating conceptual units (Dawkins 1976). In studying the population dynamics of ideas we consider the meme to be the largest reliably replicating unit within our text corpus (Pocklington & Best 1996, Pocklington 1996). Through text analy-

sis we identify memes within a corpus and cluster together those texts which make use of a common set of memes. These clusters describe species-like relationships among the texts.

The particular texts we study are posts to the popular USENET News (or NetNews) system. These posts form the basis of a new Alife environment, the *corporal ecology* (Best 1996, 1997). In this ecology texts are the organisms, the digital system defined by NetNews describes an environment, and human authors operating within some culturally defined parameters are the scarce resource.

At the core of our study sits a large text analysis software system based primarily on Latent Semantic Indexing (LSI) (Furnas, *et.al* 1988; Deerwester, *et.al.* 1990; Dumais 1992, 1993). This system reads each post and computes the frequency with which each word appears. These word counts are then used in computing a vector representation for each text. A principal component analysis is performed on this collection of vectors to discover re-occurring word sets; these are our memes. Each post is then re-represented in terms of these memes. By grouping texts which are close to one another within this meme-space we cluster semantically similar texts into species-like categories or *quasi-species* (Eigen, *et.al.* 1988).

We proceed to study the interactions between those populations which coincide temporally. For each cluster we compute a series which represents its volume of post activity over time, for instance how many texts of a given cluster were posted on a given day. Cross-correlations between each pair of time series are then determined. We find that some pairs have strong negative correlations and argue that these are examples of texts in competition. A number of examples of such competition are explored in depth. We argue that high competition is correlated with those text clusters which exist within a narrow ecological niche; this phenomena is also observed in natural ecologies (Pianka 1981).

Note that this is an unusual shift from the typical Alife environment. We are not synthesizing replicators, embodying them into agents, and observing their life-like interactions.

Instead we are studying a pre-existing artifact. Through our analysis we *discover* replicators within organisms, and use theory-neutral techniques to observe their dynamics.

In this paper we first briefly overview the NetNews environment and describe the LSI based text analysis system. Next we describe the mechanism used to determine the temporal dynamics and cross-correlations given a corpus of posts. We then relate the cross-correlations to models of interacting populations. In Section 6 we examine in depth a couple pairs of post clusters with strong interactions. We then describe a theory of niches within the corporal ecology and note that narrow ecological niches are correlated with significant competition. We end with our conclusions.

2 The NetNews Corpus

Understanding our corpus requires a basic knowledge of the NetNews system. NetNews is an electronic discussion system developed for and supported on the Internet (Kantor & Lapsley 1986). Discussion groups have formed along subjects ranging from science to politics to literature to various hobbies. The collections of messages are organized into particular subject groups called *newsgroups*. The newsgroups themselves are organized in a tree-like hierarchy which has general top-level categories at the root and moves to more specific topics as you progress towards the leaves. A newsgroup name is defined as the entire path from the top-level category through any subsequent refining categories down to the name of the group itself. Category and group names are delimited by the period symbol. Thus, "soc.relgion" is the name of a newsgroup concerned with social issues around the world's religions and "soc.religion.hindu" is a more specific group devoted to Hinduism.

Texts sent to NetNews, the *posts*, are composed of a number of fields only a few of which are relevant here. The user creating the post is responsible for the post body (that is, the actual text of the message) as well as a subject line. The subject line is composed of a few words which describe what the post is about. NetNews software will attach a number of additional fields to posted messages including a timestamp and the user name of the person who created the post.

Posts can be either an independent message or a follow-up to a previous message. A follow-up, or "in-reply-to" message, will have special threading information in its header linking it to the previous posts to which it is a reply. This header information allows news readers to reconstruct the discussion thread.

NetNews today has grown considerably from its beginnings in the late 70's and 80's. With over 80,000 posts arriving each day, it provides an excellent dataset for the study of cultural microevolution.

```
From: mikeb@media.mit.edu
Newsgroups: soc.religion.hindu
Subject: Angkor Wat
Date: 26 Jan 1997 02:17:05 -0700

Is Angkor Wat, the magnificent tem-
ple complex in the jungles of Cambo-
dia, considered a Buddhist or Hindu
shrine?
```

FIGURE 1. A fictitious example post sent to the soc.religion.hindu newsgroup along with some of its header information.

3 The Text Analysis Method

We analyze a corpus of posts to NetNews to distill their salient replicating unit or memes, and to cluster together posts which make common use of those memes. We do this by employing a large system of text analysis software we have built. The techniques employed are based on the vector space model of text retrieval and Latent Semantic Indexing (LSI).

3.1 Vector Space Representation

We begin with a corpus composed of the full-text of a group of posts. We analyze the corpus and identify a high-dimensioned space which describes the conceptual elements within the texts. For each post we identify a point within this space which captures it semantically. This technique is known as a vector space representation (Salton & Buckley 1988; Frakes & Baeza-Yates 1992). Each dimension in this space will represent a *term* from the corpus where a term is a word that occurs with some frequency (e.g. in at least three posts) but not with too much frequency (e.g. the word "not" is dropped from the term list). The goal is to arrive at a set of terms which semantically capture the texts within the corpus.

Given the conceptual space described by this set of terms each post can be represented as a point within this space. We score each document according to the frequency each term occurs within its text, and assign each term/document pairing this *term weight*. The weighting we use for each term/document pair is a function of the *term frequency* (simply the number of times the term occurs in the post) and the *inverse document frequency (IDF)*. Consider a corpus of m posts and a particular term, j, within a list of n terms. Then the IDF is given by,

$$IDF_j = \log\left(\left\lfloor \frac{m - m_j}{m_j} \right\rfloor\right),$$

where m_j is the number of posts across the entire corpus in which term j appears. The term weight for a document, i, and term, j, is then defined by,

$$TermWeight_{ij} = w_{ij} = \log(TermFrequency_{ij}) \cdot IDF_j.$$

Each term weight, then, is a function of the inter- and intra-document term frequencies.

Each post, i, is now represented by a particular term vector,

$$r_i = (w_{i1}, w_{i2}, ..., w_{in}).$$

The entire collection of m term vectors, one for each post, define the *term/document matrix, A,*

$$A = \begin{bmatrix} r_1 \\ r_2 \\ ... \\ r_m \end{bmatrix} = \begin{bmatrix} w_{11} & w_{12} & ... & w_{1n} \\ w_{21} & w_{22} & ... & w_{2n} \\ ... & ... & ... & ... \\ w_{m1} & w_{m2} & ... & w_{mn} \end{bmatrix}.$$

This set of steps, culminating in the term/document matrix, form the basis for much of modern text retrieval or filtering and are at the core of most Web search engines.

3.2 Latent Semantic Indexing

LSI is a technique used to distill high-order structures from a term/document matrix, consisting of sets of terms which re-occur together through the corpus with appreciable frequency. The re-occurring term sets are discovered through a principal component method called Singular Value Decomposition (SVD). While LSI was primarily developed to improve text retrieval, we are interested in its ability to find replicating term sets which act as memes. We will first overview the LSI technique and then discuss how it discovers memes.

LSI was originally proposed and has been extensively studied by Susan Dumais of Bell Communications Research and her colleagues (Furnas, *et.al.* 1988; Deerwester, *et.al.* 1990; Dumais 1992, 1993). Peter Foltz investigated the use of LSI in clustering NetNews articles for information filtering (Foltz 1990). Michael Berry and co-authors researched a variety of numerical approaches to efficiently perform SVD on large sparse matrices such as those found in text retrieval (Berry 1992; Berry, *et.al.* 1993; Berry & Fierro 1995).

The SVD technique decomposes the term/document matrix into a left and right orthonormal matrix of eigenvectors and a diagonal matrix of eigenvalues. The decomposition is formulized as,

$$A \approx A_k = U \Sigma V^T = \sum_{i=1}^{k} u_i \cdot \sigma_i \cdot v_i^T.$$

The term/document matrix, A, is approximated by a rank-k decomposition, A_k; in fact the SVD technique is known to produce the *best* rank-k approximation to a low-rank matrix (Berry 1992).

We are interested in only the right orthonormal matrix of eigenvectors, V^T. Each row of this matrix defines a set of terms whose co-occurrences have some statistically salient re-occurrences throughout the corpus. That is, each eigenvector describes a subspace of the term vector space for which the terms are frequently found together. These *term-subspaces* describe a set of semantically significant associative patterns in the words of the underlying corpus of documents; we can think of each subspace as a *conceptual index* into the corpus (Furnas *et.al.* 1988).

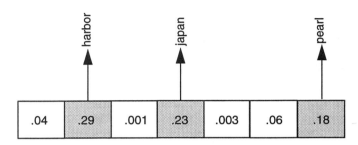

FIGURE 2. Most significant weights in the vector (shaded) represent the salient terms.

For instance, Figure 2 depicts a term-subspace which marks three words as having significant re-occurrences, and therefore replicating together with success: "harbor", "japan", and "pearl". (Note that this term-subspace was the result of analyzing a collection of military posts.) These term-subspaces make up our replicators and are our putative memes.

Our final text analysis step is to "compress" the original term/document matrix by multiplying it with this right orthonormal matrix of eigenvectors (in other words we perform a projection). This, in effect, produces a *term-subspace/document* matrix. Each post is represented by a collection of weights where each weight now describes the degree to which a term-subspace is expressed within its post's text.

4 Meme and Quasi-species

4.1 Term-subspace as Putative Meme

We are looking for replicators within the corpus which are subject to natural selection. Elsewhere we have argued at length as to why the term-subspace captures the requirements of a true meme because its word sets act as a unit of selection within the corpus (Best 1996, 1997; Pocklington & Best 1997). The strengths of this term-set as a replicating unit of selection are due to it meeting the following conditions:

- it is subject to replication by copying,

- it has strong copying fidelity,

- but not perfect fidelity, it is subject to mutation,

- it has a strong covariance with replicative success (Lewontin 1970; Eigen 1992).

We will quickly review each of these points in turn.

SVD techniques exploit structure within the term/document matrix by locating co-occurring sets of terms. Clearly these term sets are replicating through the corpus since that is the precise statistical phenomena the SVD analysis detects. However it is not obvious this replication is generally due to copying. Instances of precise copying occur when an in-reply-to thread includes elements of a previous post's text via the copying mechanism provided by the software system. Other instances of copying occur within a particular context or discussion thread when authors copy by hand words or phrases from previous posts into their new texts. More abstractly, replication occurs because certain memes are traveling outside of the NetNews environment (and thus outside of our means of analysis) and authors again act as copying agents injecting them into the corporal ecology. But, clearly, some re-occurrences are not due to copying but are a chance process where unrelated texts bring together similar words. The likelihood of such chance re-occurrences will be a function of the size and quality of our replicating unit. In summary, term-subspaces are instances of replication often due to copying.

The copying fidelity of a term-subspace is also a direct outcome of the SVD statistical analysis. But importantly, the copying fidelity of re-occurring term sets is not perfect across the entire corpus; the term sets will co-occur with some variation. Some of this variation is due to random mutations caused by the copying errors of human authors. These mutations work "backwards" into the actual term-subspace representation for a post organism. That is, a random mutation at the post level will actually result in a random mutation in the vector subspace representation (the memotype) for the post organism. In this way, the memes as represented in the memotype are subject to mutation.

Finally, we have elsewhere shown there can be a strong covariance between the replicative success of a cluster or thread of posts and the degree to which they express certain term-subspaces (Pocklington & Best 1997). In other words, a group of posts can increase its volume of activity over time by increasing the degree to which it expresses certain term sets within its post's text. This, then, is a covariance between the *fitness* of a population of posts and the expression of a particular *trait* as defined by a term-subspace. The demonstration of this covariance is critical to establishing that a replicator is subject to natural selection.

4.2 Quasi-species

If the term-subspace is a reasonable model for the meme then the term-subspace vector representation of a post is a good model of the post's *memotype*. Much as a genotype describes a point within genetic sequence-space for each organism, the memotype describes a point within conceptual sequence-space. By *sequence-space* we mean any of the search spaces defined by a replicator undergoing selection. Examples of sequence-spaces include the gene space, protein spaces under molecular evolution, and the meme space defined within a corporal ecology.

The notion of a *quasi-species* is due primarily to Manfred Eigen (Eigen, *et.al.* 1988; Eigen 1992). He states that the "quasi-species represents a weighted distribution of mutants centered around one or several master sequences. It is the target of selection in a system of replicating individuals that replicate without co-operating with one another (RNA molecules, viruses, bacteria)," (Eigen 1992). One organism is a *mutant* of another if it is particularly close to the other in sequence-space.

We wish to group our posts into quasi-species. This requires finding groups of memotypes which are centered together within the conceptual sequence space. To do so we employ a simple clustering algorithm, the Nearest Neighbor Algorithm (Jain & Dubes 1988). We first normalize each post memotype to unit length; this amounts to discarding text length information and representing only the *relative* strength of each meme within a text. The clustering algorithm then considers each post memotype in turn. The current memotype is compared to each memotype which has already been assigned to a cluster. If the closest of such vectors is not farther than a threshold distance, then the current vector is assigned to that cluster. Otherwise the current vector is assigned to a new cluster. This continues until each and every vector is assigned to a cluster.

This process assigns each post to a quasi-species defined as those posts which are close to one another in conceptual sequence-space.

4.3 Comparison to Natural Ecologies

We are describing phenomena within a corpus of texts in terms of population ecology and population genetics. This is not simply a metaphorical device; we believe that interacting populations of texts and their constituent memes are evolving ecologies quite exactly. However there are clearly a number of interesting differences between genes and memes (as here operationally defined), natural organisms and texts, ecologies and corpora. Important differences include the driving forces behind mutation within the texts and the role of self-replication and lineage within the corpora. We leave to future work a more complete analysis of these differences.

5 Models for Interacting Populations

We now turn to studying the interaction between quasi-species of posts. We have so far only studied the pairwise interactions between post quasi-species. Similar pairwise interactions have been widely studied within theoretical ecology. Consider two interacting populations: one population can either have a positive effect (+) on another by increasing the other's chance for survival and reproduction, a negative effect (-) by decreasing the other population's survival chances, or a neutral (0) effect. The ecological community has assigned terms to the most prevalent forms of pairwise interaction, in particular:

- Mutualism (+, +)
- Competition (-, -)
- Neutralism (0, 0)
- Predator/prey (+, -)
  (Pielou 1969; May 1981B).

Our goal is to study the pairwise interactions of quasi-species within the corporal ecology with the hope of discovering some of these interaction types.

5.1 Time Series

To study how the interactions of populations affects growth rates we must define a method to measure a quasi-species' growth over time. Recall that a quasi-species describes a collection of posts which are close to one another in sequence-space. Each of these posts has associated with it a *timestamp* identifying when that text was posted to the system; in effect, its birth time and date. (Note that a post organism has something of a zero-length life-span; it comes into existence when posted but has no clear time of death.)

A histogram of the timestamp data is created with a 24 hour bucket size. That is, for each quasi-species we count how many member texts where posted on one day, how many on the next, and so forth through the entire population of texts. The datasets currently used span on the order of two weeks and consist of thousands of posts. So for each day a quasi-species has a volume of activity which can range from zero to 10's of posts. This rather course unit, the day, has been chosen to neutralize the strong daily patterns of post activities (e.g. activity may concentrate in the afternoons and drop off late at night, different timezones will shift this behavior and thus encode geographic biases). Thus the patterns of rise and fall in the volume of posts within a quasi-species when measured at the day level will, hopefully, reflect true changes in interest level and authorship activity rather then other external or systemic factors

5.2 The Test Corpus

Figure 3 is a typical graph for the volume of posts within a particular quasi-species over a period of ten days. This cluster was found within a corpus of all posts sent to the soc.women newsgroup between January 8, 1997 (the far left of the graph) and January 28, 1997 (the far right). In the figure the number of posts in a day is represented by the height of the graph. This particular cluster of texts exhibited an initial set of posts, a few days worth of silence, then a rapid building up of activity which then declined precipitously at the end of the dataset. The entire corpus used consisted of 1,793 posts over the same

ten day period. The clustering mechanism arrived at 292 quasi-species the largest of which contained 103 posts.

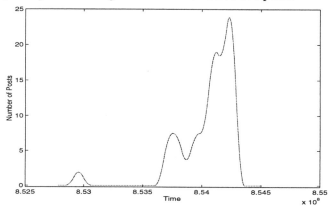

FIGURE 3. Typical time series of posts to quasi-species. Time axis is measured in seconds since Jan. 1 1970.

5.3 Time Series Cross-correlation

To study the relationship between the time series of two populations of posts we use the cross-correlation function. The use of the cross-correlation to study bivariate processes, and time series in particular, is well known (Chatfield 1989). Each time series is normalized to be of zero mean and unit standard deviation; that is, we subtract off the mean and divide by the standard deviation. In this way, the cross-correlations will not be dominated by the absolute volume of post activity within some cluster and instead will be sensitive to both large and small sized clusters.

We assume the readers are familiar with the regular covariance and correlation functions. Then the cross-correlation for two time series, X and Y, is given by,

$$\rho_{xy} = \frac{\gamma_{xy}}{\sqrt{\gamma_{xx}\gamma_{yy}}}.$$

Here $\gamma_{xy} = \text{Cov}(X, Y)$ and γ_{xx} and γ_{yy} are the variance of X and Y respectively. Note this formulation only considers the cross-correlation for a zero time lag. That is, it considers how the two time series are correlated for identically matching points in time. With a nonzero lag the cross-correlation would study cases when the two series might have correlations offset by some fixed amount of time. Since we group our time data into day-long chunks the zero-lag cross-correlation will be sensitive to covariances which have a time offset as large as 24 hours; this builds into the time series an adequate time lag.

When the cross-correlation between two sets of data is significantly different than zero it suggests the two sets of data have some relationship between them. A positive value means an increase in one series is likely to co-occur with an increase in the other series. A negative value means an increase in one series is likely to co-occur with a decrease in the other series.

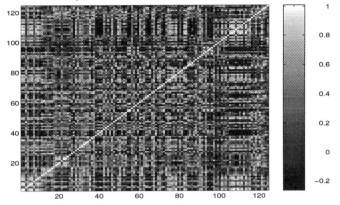

FIGURE 4. The pairwise time series cross-correlation for 125 largest quasi-species clusters.

Figure 4 shows the pairwise cross-correlations for the 125 largest quasi-species clusters within our corpus. The diagonal represents the cross-correlation between a time series and itself which, as expected, is identically one. Note that the matrix is symmetric about the diagonal. The off-diagonal values range from near one to -0.26. The mean cross-correlation is 0.3. This value is quite high, indicating that most of these post clusters are somehow positively related. We suspect this high average cross-correlation is at least partially due to external or systemic affects which were not removed by the day-long bucket size. For instance, our analysis would be sensitive to patterns due to the Monday-Friday work week common in the West. Further, some of this correlation may be due to a high level of mutualistic interactions amongst the posts. Clearly, the ideas conveyed within the soc.women newsgroup often share behaviors.

In our analysis this overall high correlation does not particularly matter since we are concerned with the *relative* cross-correlation -- that is, those that are the largest and those that are the smallest.

6 Negative Cross-correlations: Competition versus Predator/Prey

We have primarily studied those pairs of quasi-species with relatively strong negative cross-correlations; to wit, those where $\rho_{xy} \leq -0.2$. Note that in all such cases (there are 42) $P < .001$ suggesting that with extremely high probability the correlations are not due to chance. Figure 5 and Figure 6 plot

two such interactions, both fairly characteristic of this population.

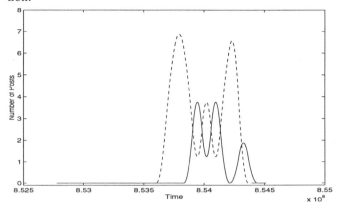

FIGURE 5. Volume of activity for two quasi-species. The cross-correlation between these two series is -0.26.

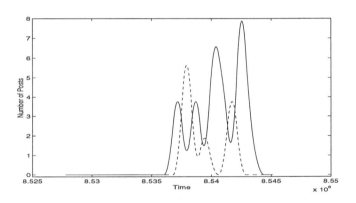

FIGURE 6. Volume of activity for a different set of two quasi-species. The cross-correlation between these two series is -0.23

Both of these figures demonstrate a clear negative covariance between the volume of activity of the two post clusters. This negative covariance is both statistically significant and visually compelling. But what do these graphs signify and can it be interpreted within the rubric of ecological interactions?

At first glance the interactions appear to be of a predator/prey variety; they have a (+, -) relationship to them. However, competition might also produce similar interaction phenomena if the competitors are operating close to some limitation or environmental carrying capacity. In such instances the relationship between population sizes will be a zero-sum game, when one goes up the other must come down. To be able to classify the interactions of Figure 5 and 6 we need to consider the qualitative details of these two interactions through direct study of the texts.

Recall that in the case of a predator/prey relationship one population enjoys an increased growth rate at the *expense* of another population (e.g. one population feeds on the other). The presence of a relatively large population of predators will result in a diminished level of success for the prey (they get eaten up). Conversely, the relative absence of prey will result in diminished success for the predator (they have nothing to eat).

Now consider the case of competition. In competition two interacting populations inhibit each other in some way, reducing each other's level of success. This often occurs when the two populations rely on the same limited resource. Unlike the predator/prey relationship where the predator requires the prey for success, with competition the two populations would just as soon avoid each other all together.

This pressure towards avoidance is the source of much ecological diversity since it propels populations to explore new and therefore competition-free niches (Pianka 1981). An ecological *niche*, for some particular species, is simply that collection of resources the species relies on. Interspecific niche overlap occurs when two or more species share one, some, or perhaps all of their resources. When those resources are scarce, interspecific competition will result. The *width* of a niche is simply a qualitative sense of the variety and number of resources which a population makes use of.

6.1 Competition and Niche Behavior

We have studied the set of posts which make up the four quasi-species shown in Figures 5 and 6 in an attempt to qualitatively classify their interactions. The quasi-species of Figure 5 are made up of posts within a single thread. The subject line for these posts reads, "Men's Reproductive Rights". In general, these posts are concerned with the responsibilities and rights of men towards their unborn children. The quasi-species displayed with a dashed line in the figure is centered around the use of contraceptives. It consists of a collection of posts wherein the authors debate who is most responsible, the women or the man, when using contraception. The quasi-species with a solid line deals instead with the use of abortion and whether the father has any intrinsic rights in deciding whether or not to abort an unborn child.

In Figure 6 these two quasi-species are also from a single thread. The subject line here reads, "Unequal distribution of wealth?". This particular thread of discussion was rather large. In fact there was a total of 365 posts to this thread which our text analysis tools broke up into a number of quasi-species due to the significant bifurcations of topic. In other words, many parallel discussions occurred all within a single in-reply-to thread. The cluster of discussion shown with the solid line in Figure 6 centered around a debate as to whether the US military was a "socialist collective". The quasi-species with the dashed line was a debate on the value of releasing the mentally ill from hospitals. Clearly, these two debates are quite dissimilar even though they span the same set of days and are posts to the same discussion thread.

The quasi-species of Figure 5 are different but related discussions. Those of Figure 6 are different and not clearly related. Still, we believe that both of these sets of interactions demonstrate elements of competition. Within the texts there is no evidence of predator memes; in Figure 6, in fact, the memes seem entirely orthogonal to one another. However, in both examples the memes are competing for the same collection of human authors who must act as their agents if they are to propagate and succeed. This seems even more likely when we consider that all these posts are to the same newsgroup which due to its narrow subject area supports only a limited supply of human posters. Moreover, each pair of interactions are confined to a single thread of discussion, which again has an even more limited set of potential human authors since users of the NetNews system often zero-in on particular threads they find interesting and ignore others. After inspecting most of the interactions which demonstrated strong negative correlations we observed no examples of predator/prey interactions but many instances which appeared to be examples of competition.

6.1.1 Statistical Artifacts

We computed the cross-correlation between 125 different clusters, arriving at 15,625 different correlations. It is possible, therefore, that the cross-correlations with large negative values exist simply by chance; they represent the tail of the distribution of correlations.

However, we believe that our qualitative analysis provides strong evidence that these negative correlations are *not* artifacts but are indeed due to an interaction phenomena between the two quasi-species. The two pairs of quasi-species described in detail above demonstrate this point. The likelihood that two quasi-species be brought together by mere chance *and* both be from the same thread (out of 324 threads within the corpus) seems vanishingly small.

6.1.2 Competition

We now will test our theory that these interactions are of a competitive nature. Again recall that competition is often caused by populations existing within the same (narrow) ecological niche. What makes up an ecological niche for a meme within NetNews? We argue that the newsgroups themselves make up spatially distributed ecological niches. Since there is relatively little interaction between newsgroups (save the phenomena of cross-posting) we would expect these niches to behave something like island ecologies -- they remain relatively isolated from each other. Within a single newsgroup (which is all we have studied so far) niches might be described by threads of discussions. As previously stated, we have found that individual posters to the system tend to become involved in particular in-reply-to threads which interest them. Thus the memes within a particular thread make use of a set of human resources which is smaller then the entire set of potential human resources available to the newsgroup. These resources define the niche.

We theorize that cross-correlations which approach -1 in our corpus are examples of competition, and competition will be more likely between populations which are posted to the same threads and thus have overlapping niches. The most direct way to test this theory is to see if negative cross-correlations between two quasi-species correlates with the degree to which they post to the same threads. For each of the 125x125 pairwise interactions we computed the number of threads each of the quasi-species pairs had in common and divided that by the total number of threads posted to by each quasi-species. For example, one quasi-species may contain posts which went to two different in-reply-to threads. Another quasi-species may have posts which span three different threads one of which is identical to a thread within the first group. So this pair of quasi-species would have posted to a total of four different groups one of which was shared. Their relative niche overlap would therefore be 0.25.

We calculated the correlation coefficient between the negative cross-correlations of Figure 4 and the percentage of thread overlap between these quasi-species pairs. We found this correlation to be -0.04. While this correlation is statistically significant (P < .001), it is not very pronounced. The negative sign, though, does indicate that as the level of competition increases (a negative cross-correlation) the percent of overlap of their niche also increases (a larger positive shared thread percentage).

This small correlation coefficient may be due to a small signal/noise ratio. Since most pairwise interactions result in small correlations, the relative number of large negative correlations is quite small. The number of interactions grows with the square of the number of quasi-species. We suspect that a simpler experiment which grows linearly with the number of quasi-species will have a better signal/noise ratio.

We've studied the correlations between the absolute number of in-reply-to threads a quasi-species is posted to and the average degree to which the quasi-species finds itself correlated with other clusters. Our hypothesis is that the absolute number of threads a quasi-species is posted to will be related to the average degree of competition the quasi-species experiences in its interactions. Since the variety of resources used by an entity defines it niche, if a quasi-species is posted to a relatively small number of threads then it exists in a narrow ecological niche. Should there subsequently be any interspecific overlap of these narrow niches, scarcity will result in competitive encounters. We computed the correlation coefficient between the total number of threads within a quasi-species and its *average* cross-correlation value. The correlation coefficient here is 0.25. Thus, as the number of threads within a quasi-species increases (the set of available resources is widened) the average level of competition diminishes (the mean

pairwise cross-correlation also increases). This correlation is statistically significant (P < .001) and rather pronounced.

We further computed the correlation coefficient when the absolute number of threads was normalized by the size of the quasi-species. We might expect that the number of threads employed by a quasi-species would grow with the number of posts within that quasi-species. In other words, as a quasi-species gets larger the number of threads increases too. This might effect the analysis above such that instead of measuring niche width we were simply measuring quasi-species size. Dividing out the size amounts to computing the *average* number of threads employed by a post for a given quasi-species. When this set of values was correlated with the mean cross-correlation we arrived at a nearly identical coefficient as above and again clear statistical significance. Thus quasi-species size is not a major factor in level of competition.

7 Conclusions

We have described a set of text analysis tools, based primarily on Latent Semantic Indexing, which distill replicating memes from a corpus of text. We have trained this analysis system on a corpus of posts to NetNews. This makes up a corporal ecology where the posts are organisms, NetNews is the environment, and human authors are a scarce resource. We argue that this represents an important bridging of text analysis and the Alife research program. Further, it amounts to a novel shift for Alife research -- rather then synthesizing life-like agents we are analyzing a pre-existing environment and discovering life-like behaviors.

In results reported here we group together posts which make use of similar sets of memes. These groups, clouds within a conceptual sequence-space, describe quasi-species. For each quasi-species we compute its time-wise volume of activity by histogramming its daily post levels. We then study the pairwise interaction between quasi-species by computing the cross-correlations between their time series. In our corpus, strong negative cross-correlations signify conditions of competition between the interacting populations where the quasi-species are competing for a limited set of human authors. Furthermore, quasi-species with relatively narrow ecological niches, those which make use of a small number of in-reply-to threads, are more likely to be in competition with other quasi-species. This behavior is analogous to what is found in natural ecologies (Pianka 1981).

Why do these quasi-species compete? Qualitative analysis of the posts, such as those described in Section 6, shows that many competing quasi-species are posts sent to the same or similar threads. Competition is over the scarce authorship resources within these specific thread niches. Over time a particular thread of discussion may bifurcate into two or more internal themes which then proceed to compete for "air-time" within the thread.

Acknowledgments

We thank the two anonymous reviewers for their helpful critique of this paper. We gratefully acknowledge the significant input of Richard Pocklington to this work and his careful reading of a draft of this paper. Laurie Hiyakumoto also gave very helpful comments on a draft of this paper. We thank Bernd Schoner and Michael Patrick Johnson. Finally, the author is pleased to thank the sponsors of the MIT Media Laboratory for their financial support.

References

Berry, M.W. (1992) Large-scale Sparse Singular Value Computations. *The International Journal of Supercomputer Applications.* Vol. 6, No. 1.

Berry, M., T. Do, G. O'Brien, V. Krishna, & S. Varadhan (1993). SVDPACKC (Version 1.0) User's Guide. University of Tennessee Computer Science Department Technical Report, CS-93-194.

Berry, M.W. & R.D. Fierro (1995). Low-Rank Orthogonal Decompositions for Information Retrieval Applications. University of Tennessee Computer Science Department Technical Report, CS-95-284.

Best, M.L (1996). An Ecology of the Net: Message Morphology and Evolution in NetNews. Massachustes Institute of Technology, Media Laboratory, Machine Understanding Technical Report, 96-001.

Best, M.L. (1997). An Ecology of Text: Using Text Retrieval to Study Alife on the Net. Submitted to *Journal of Artificial Life.*

Chatfield, C. (1989). *The Analysis of Time Series An Introduction.* London: Chapman and Hall.

Dawkins, R. (1976). *The Selfish Gene.* New York, Oxford University Press.

Dawkins, R. (1982). *The Extended Phenotype.* San Francisco, WH Freeman.

Deerwester, S. S.T. Dumais, G.W. Furnas, T.K Landauer, and R. Harshman (1990). Indexing by Latent Semantic Analysis. *Journal of the American Society for Information Science.* 41(6): 391-407.

Dumais, S.T. (1992). LSI meets TREC: A status report. In *The First Text REtrieval Conference (TREC-1),* ed. D. Harman. NIST Special Publication 500-207.

Dumais, S.T. (1993). Latent semantic indexing (LSI) and TREC-2. In *The Second Text REtrieval Conference (TREC-2),* ed. D. Harman. NIST Special Publication 500-215.

Eigen, M.J, J. McCaskill, & P. Schuster (1988). Molecular Quasi-Species. *Journal of Physical Chemistry,* Vol. 92, No. 24.

Eigen, M. (1992). *Steps Towards Life: A Perspective on Evolution.* Oxford: Oxford University Press.

Foltz, P.W. (1990). Using Latent Semantic Indexing for Information Filtering. *Proceedings of the 5th Conference on Office Information Systems.* ACM SIGOIS Bulletin vol. 11, issues 2,3.

Frakes, W.B. & R. Baeza-Yates, eds. (1992). *Information Retrieval: Data Structures and Algorithms.* Englewood Cliffs, New Jersey: Prentice Hall.

Furnas, G.W., S. Deerwester, S.T. Dumais, T.K. Landauer, R.A. Harshman, L.A. Streeter, & K.E. Lochbaum (1988). Information Retrieval using a Singular Value Decomposition Model of Latent Semantic Structure. *Proceedings of the 11th International Conference on Research and Development in Information Retrieval (SIGIR).* New York: Association for Computing Machinery.

Jain, A.K. & R.C. Dubes (1988). *Algorithms for Clustering Data.* Englewood Cliffs, New Jersey: Prentice Hall.

Kantor, B. & P. Lapsley (1986). *Network News Transfer Protocol: A Proposed Standard for the Stream-Based Transmission of News.* Internet RFC-977.

Lewontin, R.C. (1970). The Units of Selection. *Annual Review of Ecology and Systematics,* Vol. 1.

Lewontin, R.C. (1974). *The Genetic Basis of Evolutionary Change.* New York, Columbia University Press.

May, R.M. ed. (1981A). *Theoretical Ecology Principles and Applications.* Oxford: Blackwell Scientific Publications.

May, R.M. ed (1981B). Models for Two Interacting Populations. In May 1981A.

Pianka, E.,R. (1981). Competition and Niche Theory. In May 1981A.

Pielou, E.C. (1969). *An Introduction to Mathematical Ecology.* New York: Wiley-Interscience.

Pocklington, R. (1996). *Population Genetics and Cultural History,* Msc Thesis, Simon Fraser University, Burnaby.

Pocklington, R. & M.L. Best (1997). Cultural Evolution and Units of Selection in Replicating Text. To appear *Journal of Theoretical Biology.*

Salton, G. & C. Buckley (1988). Term-weighting Approaches in Automatic Text Retrieval. *Information Processing & Management.* 24: 5, 513-523.

N-Sex Reproduction in Dynamic Environments.

Paul Coker and Chris Winter

Applied Research and Technology
BT Laboratories
Martlesham Heath
Ipswich IP5 7RE

paul.coker@bt-sys.bt.co.uk

chris.winter@bt-sys.bt.co.uk

Abstract

By examining the success of various adaptive strategies in a complex and dynamic environment, it is demonstrated that the optimal number of sexes required for mating is related to the dynamics of the underlying environment. A simulation involving various species of flowers (or telecom companies) attracting bees (or users) to facilitate reproduction, was created. The fitness of an organism was based around the ability to attract a large proportion of good pollen carriers. Following the 'possible worlds' view of artificial life, each species requires a different number of parents/sexes to reproduce. A number of key issues emerge about interpreting learning and evolution in dynamic environments including the advantage that a dominant starting position imposes, and the effect of complex landscapes on the underlying dynamics.

1. Introduction

Artificial Life has been described as studying 'life as it could be' rather than 'life as it is'. It is equally interesting to consider that biology has long inspired developments in computer science from artificial intelligence with its expert systems, case based reasoning and similar supposed models of human functions, through neural networks and genetic algorithms and programs. Turing was fascinated with morphogenesis. Could 'life as it could be' inspire computer science with yet more intellectual and application tools? Certainly, for those in the computing and communication industries there are perceived to be immense problems with the current systems. They are unreliable, prone to fraudulent attack, expensive to maintain etc. And whilst hardware has improved in productivity at something like 55% per annum over 50 years, software productivity is down at the 5% per annum figure. Could we evolve instead of program our systems? Could we make them self-healing and self-

optimising? Could we get complexity from simplicity, rather than the reverse?

The goal of much of our research is tackle these issues. As a consequence of this desire to both produce evolutionary software and understand the dynamics of learning systems, we became interested in an apparently simple question: 'Why do most species only have two sexes?'. There is a logical follow on from this which is that slavishly mimicking biology may not be the most useful way of building non-biological artificial life systems. All forms of evolution can be viewed as dynamic searches to find an acceptable solution to the problem of survival. Such searches are not aimed at some general optimal solution, but one which is good enough to survive as the world changes. The effects of the number of sexual partners and the crossover operator used is likely to have a large impact on how quickly and efficiently the space of solutions is searched. Although the question apparently relates to sexual evolution, the information gained about a system that learns in a dynamic environment may be applicable to much wider technical arenas. Applications already under consideration include network management using adaptive elements, business modelling, dynamic workforce scheduling and distributed societies of learning intelligent agents. In each case better understanding of the nature of the search processes and how they relate to the dynamics of the environment are very useful.

In nature, multi-cellular organisms have evolved, for the most part, to use both two sexes and two parents for reproduction. Asexual reproduction is still common, however, for prokaryotes and some slime moulds use a multi-sex system. The evolution to using specifically three or more parents and sexes has not occurred in nature. This may be due to some specific evolutionary reasons for preferring one or two sexes: such as the practicality of finding sufficient partners at the right time and space; or to the disadvantage of passing less of ones' genome to the next generation; or to some other, more complex, reason.

Artificial Life techniques allow us to investigate various biological scenarios that have never been, or are no longer, present in the world. However, whilst interesting for tackling non-biological issues, interpretation in terms of real biological systems needs to proceed with care. The Alife system described below has none of the mating problems faced by animals in the real world: finding the required number of parents to reproduce is not controlled by the physical world they live in; nor are there any great overheads to mating and producing offspring. Under these unusual artificial conditions could more complex sexual strategies prove to be a better way to evolve?

1.1 Biological Background

Understanding why sexual reproduction should have evolved at all has taxed biologists for the greater part of this century. Many examinations have been made into the costs of sexual reproduction as compared to any gain [1]. Typical advantages cited have included the ability to fight off parasites by keeping pace with their evolving behaviours [2]; the advantages of shared parentage among some species; and the effect it has on the likelihood of offspring surviving [3]. There are many sexual species that do not co-operate as parents though, and many abandon their eggs to survive on their own as with fish and turtles.

Although many species have passed through a period of asexual type behaviour most eukaryotes have changed to using two sexes [4]. This has mainly been attributed to the problems of genetic loading of detrimental genes in asexual populations [5]. Many species seem to have passed through a dual phase of asexual and two sex behaviour, with two sex gaining enough of an advantage to take over. Many other asexual species are thought to have not made the transition to sexual behaviour and subsequently died out.

There is a perceived cost to sexual reproduction - only half of an organisms genes are passed on to the offspring. This seems to go against the 'selfish' driving influence of evolution. The structure and life-style of an organism can be seen as just a very complex way of passing on its genes to the next generation. The body being merely a vehicle for the genes that are really in control [6]. There at least needs to be a two fold advantage to the organisms to participate in sexual reproduction just to break even. There is an advantage to the population as a whole to conduct in sexual reproduction to avoid genetic bottlenecks occurring and to share new improved genetic solutions. Evolution is driven, however, by individuals intent on passing on their own genes and for whom wider considerations only apply when they confer individual benefits.

The combination of advantages that sexual reproduction gives must outweigh the disadvantage of lower genetic transmission for it to have dominated the higher species sexual strategies.

1.2 Artificial Life Simulations

Much Alife research has used either asexual or two parent sex as a way of evolving their system. This is illustrated by the work on genetic algorithms [7] (even in the advanced versions such as Saga [8]) and genetic programs [9]. Most of the variation has gone into the cross-over operator.

GAs and GPs are used to search for optimal solutions to specific problems within artificial environments. The environment is static, in the sense that changes in other members of the population only indirectly affect an individuals success. The actual fitness function does not depend on the individuals present. A degree of dynamism is brought about in co-evolving prey-predator models [10], and there the dynamics does appear to speed the evolutionary process. However, the great majority of evolutionary systems are optimisation oriented, environmentally static and competition is only indirect.

Evolution via asexual reproduction is often seen as a way of introducing some random variation into a converging set of solutions, while two parent sex is used to share better genes and recombine them into hopefully more useful combinations. The techniques are largely based on trial and error with no clear guidelines available to work from. If two sex mating improves upon asexual systems then it is worth investigating if, and when, higher levels of sexual interaction may bring about even greater evolutionary benefits.

2. Methodology

The simulation chosen here was based around the idea of evolving flowers, that succeed by attracting bees to come to them. It was also designed to map onto a business model of a multi-service network where companies offer various services to attract users. In both cases the flowers, or companies, want to expend the minimum cost to attract sufficient bees or users. Their measure of success could be the number of ' users' attracted; the profit made in total from all their visitors; or the profit per visitor (which is a measure of efficiency). The reward for efficiently attracting more ' users' is higher reproduction rates, expressed as growth in the size and number of packages/products that can be offered. Those organisms with the lowest attraction rate at the end of a cycle, are replaced with children selected via a biased roulette wheel from the surviving population of potential parents.

In this simulation the starting point was to have six species of attractors and one species of users. Each species used a different sexual reproduction method: either asexual or 2-6 parents. Each organism is born into one gender type which it maintains throughout its life.

Two models were developed using either scent/colour/cost of flying/nectar gain/pollen transferred etc. or Telecoms services and users. There are only minor differences between these and the sections below are largely described in terms of a Telecoms business model.

2.1 Species Behaviours

The users start life as a pool of six thousand randomly generated individuals. In nature many flowers have evolved to attract one particular species that in turn has evolved to serve only that type of plant, as in the case of figs and wasps [11]. This provides the plant with greater assurance that any deposited pollen is likely to reach the required target and the user with constant food. Often the plant hides the food in such a way that only the required species can access it via a proboscis or some other access method. Here it is possible for a species of attractors to evolve and compete by attracting some subset of the users.

The user organisms are attracted to an attractor via a set of personal criteria that each holds. A state of "satisfaction" is held by each user of its current situation. Once a user is sufficiently unhappy it picks another attractor to use.

The user organisms can either keep their criteria for choosing a provider for the length of the simulation or can change as time passes. This allows the system to either try to evolve towards a moving target or towards a more stable world.

There is a finite set of resources in the size of the population of users. They have varying types of activity built into them from heavy to light (equivalent to call making rates or alternatively viewed as flying and nectar gathering activity). An organism attracting a greater numbers of heavy users will therefore be at an obvious advantage.

The implicit target for the attractor organisms is to encourage enough user organisms to join them so that they will reproduce at a faster rate than their neighbours.

2.2 Genome

The genetic coding and mapping are described here in terms of telecommunications features. The genome is a string of binary symbols. These encode the prices of different types of calls, the percentage of different discounts and the kinds of extra services offered. (i.e. 'local call rate' = 1000 {8 pence}, 'rental' = 001010 {10p a day}, 'business discount' = 000101 {5 %}, 'rating periods' = 0010 {2 price rates a day}, 'answer phone' = 1 or 0 {Yes/No}, 'Friends & Family' = 1010 {Number of cheep connections provided.}) This allowed the genome to be easier to build and made the simulation applicable to a real world problem. Biased selection, crossover and point mutation of the binary encoded data, allow the organisms to evolve.

All organisms are haploid. This was mainly chosen due to the inherent problems of building in dominance and recessive factors in n-ploid organisms. N-ploid systems require building in rules of behaviour to govern how gene selection will occur and could adversely effect the outcome of the n-sex research at this stage. Future work in this area will be important as the use of n-ploid dominance may be a very critical component for effective evolution in nature.

The mapping of the genes to the organisms behaviour is such that several genes code for the price charged to a user for the different types of calls offered. Another set of genes control the discounts offered and a further set select the types of addition services provided. This equates to the quality of nectar on offer or the ability of a flower to deposit pollen on the best or preferred type of animal.

2.3 Fitness Function

Each user has a set of their own needs and the rate of calls they will make. This leads to a bill being generated at the end of each period by applying pricing data held in the genes of the organism they are using, to the call usage. Other genes encode for discounts offered and services provided. The billing data is then used to calculate the profit gained from each user. There is an associated cost of providing connections when calls are made, which is deducted from the bill to ascertain the profit attained.

The total profit produced by each organism is then used to rank it within its species. A proportion of the lowest ranked organisms are finally removed. Some are taken from all the organisms with the lowest attraction of each species and the rest from the lowest ranked remaining organisms in the whole world.

2.4 Selection

A species is selected to gain a new member via a biased roulette wheel of the total profit obtained by the whole population. This gives all the species the chance to reproduce but favours those with the highest number of busy users attracted. The organisms are unaware of the needs of the users in their world but can only offer their current set of attractants and determine what response has been attained by the amount of resulting attention.

In this simulation attracting the largest number of users is not enough to be the best species in the world and therefore reproduce at a higher rate. The organisms are actually judged on the average profit obtained from each user. This is also true in nature, where it is not simply good enough to have the largest number of visitors (taking the precious pollen), attracted to a plant. What is required is to have a large number of insects that are likely to transport pollen to a female plant of the same species and not just visit any other plant wasting the precious genes entrusted to them. Therefore attracting a large number of busy and helpful users will gain a plant a marked advantage over plants that have a large percentage of their pollen lost (users contributing low profits through low activity).

The various species cannot interfere with each other but can surpass the others by reproducing at a high enough rate. Once a species has gained enough of an advantage over its neighbours it is unlikely that they will be able to fight back. Gaining an early evolutionary advantage will bring great benefits. Therefore the reproductive strategy that brings about quick enough results is likely to succeed in this world.

There are no predators in the world or random forces that can interfere with the pure evolutionary race. We have endeavoured to set up a purely Red Queen [12] genetic race to determine which species performs the best.

2.5 Reproduction

Once a species has been selected, the required number of parents, each of a different sex, is selected proportionally to the individual profits of each organism. If there are not members of all the sex's present in the population reproduction will not take place. Two different forms of sexual reproduction were tried. The 'two parent' version used in GAs where the sexes are not discrete but equivalent; and a discrete sex version as occurs in most natural species. The former allows mating with any other member of the population, the latter only with a subset.

The selected parents then supply pre-determined genes to the child. (The genes are held on one chromosome. To achieve crossover between the parents all the chromosomes of the selected parents are split into equal sections. Each parent then passes one section of the chromosome to the child. i.e. For 3 parent sex the chromosomes are split into 3 parts and the first gender type passes the first section to the child, the second parent the next section and so on until the child's chromosome is complete.) This equates in biology to females always supplying the cell body including the genes in the mitochondria while male genes control the sex of the offspring and any additional functions supplied on the sex designating chromosome.

The newly created chromosome in the child is subjected to a 1% rate of point mutation. The child is assumed to reach active status and reproductive fitness at the start of the next cycle in the system. Each child is allowed to exist in the system for a short period to start attracting users to itself

before selection pressures are brought upon the population as a whole again.

2.6 Customer Satisfaction

A users satisfaction level is directly connected to the size of the bill and services received from the attracting organism. If during each cycle a user becomes unhappy with some aspect of the service offered its state of satisfaction will decrease and the likelihood of moving on therefore increases. The whole of the attractors genome leads to the profitability (reproduction rate) of an organism, by attracting and keeping a user.

2.7 Simulation Cycle

At the start there are 6 species each containing 100 organisms (with equal proportions of gender types) with 10 users attracted to them. Each species is given a different reproductive strategy to employ. Organisms start with a randomly generated genome set within certain limits (i.e. Local calls cannot be more expensive than USA calls). All users start with a randomly selected set of requirements (Prices expecting to pay, types of services required etc.).

A bill is generated for each user and the total profit of each organism and species calculated. The organisms are then sorted in order of average profit per user, for each species. The lowest 10% are selected for death. 5% is deleted across all the species and 5% from that lowest rated remaining organisms.

To replace these deleted organisms, species are probabilistically selected via their total profit and thence the required number of different sex parents. A child is created with multi sex crossover and the genes allowed to mutate at a rate of 1% per generation. Therefore better performing species and potential parents are more likely to mate but all organisms have some chance of reproducing.

The users satisfaction level changes by comparing the bill given to them and the price they want to pay, along with the quality of service offered. If the users are sufficiently unhappy they are allowed to choose another service or company to join. Before settling on a new attractor/service the unhappy user investigates one organism from each species and picks the one that best fits its own requirements (i.e. Which service offers the size of business discount required. Which attractor has the most additional services. Which rental rate fits that required by the user.) often settling on the best compromise. This migration continues until a number equal to the population size of users has moved. This means that unhappy users are likely to move around a lot until they are attracted strongly to a new provider. This process allows the children time to attract new users and the chance to reproduce themselves.

The system continues to cycle for 100 generations. 2000 runs of 100 generations were made for each set up and the sex strategy of the winners analysed. Eight simulations were run with different combinations of parents or discrete sexes; customer satisfaction done on cost only or by a more general measure; and static or changing users.

3. Results and Discussion

The winning species can be seen as either the one with the largest population of users attracted to it, or in purely business terms, the one with the highest profit or average profit per user. In reality as long as a species or a company is growing in size or at least sustaining its present foothold in relation to the whole world/marketplace, the survival strategy is immaterial. After conducting the 16000 trials, some measure was needed of success. It was decided as a first attempt to judge a species by its energy reaping abilities (total profit) and by its efficiency (profit per user). For each of the 8 different trials the success of each of the 6 attractor species in coming first under these criteria was measured. It was found that varying the users criteria had no overall effect.

Table 1 below summarises the distribution of winners when the users selected the attractor species based on a variety of parameters; it shows the effect of discrete sexes against all members being one sex and a number of parents of identical sex being chosen. At the end of 100 generations for each of the 2000 runs, the company with the highest profit and the one with the highest average profit was noted. At the end of the 2000 runs the number of times the species had the highest score was calculated.

Table 1: Distribution of winners for 2000 runs for cases either of discrete sex or parent numbers were varied. Users' satisfaction was based on pricing levels and the quality of services provided.

Parameters	Best	Number of Parents					
		1	2	3	4	5	6
Sex	Total	155	118	138	300	535	**754**
Sex	Eff	249	186	294	**510**	480	281
Parents	Total	27	103	63	188	431	**1188**
Parents	Eff	140	121	377	**505**	470	387

Notes: 'Best' means the criteria used to select the winner after 100 generations. Sex, refers to where each of the parents was of a different gender type. Parents, refers to where a number of parents were selected without regard to their gender classification. Total means it was based on the total profit made by all the members of that species. Eff means it was based on the average efficiency of the members of that species (efficiency = profit/users).

Clearly there is a bimodal split as to the most successful strategy. If we consider just the main selection criteria - efficiency - by which failing individuals are eliminated from the population, then four sex is best, with five sex running close. Surprisingly if we consider what happens when it comes to the criteria of total profitability then six sex wins handsomely. Why? It turns out that a part of the selection criteria for producing the replacement offspring used total profitability as the success measure. This gives a complex bi-modal fitness function with two different survival possibilities. Either you grow big and use total profit or you remain small and use efficiency. This can be seen by looking at Figs 1-3 which shows a typical time evolution of three of the species.

Further work investigating higher numbers of sexes in a species (seven and above) will be required to find the optimum number for producing the highest total profit, via attracting larger numbers of users. Four sexes here gives the optimum average score per user.

Six sex clearly gets to gather all the users - taking over from two sexes early success. This rapidly translates into the most profit (Fig 2), again eclipsing two sex.

Users Aquired

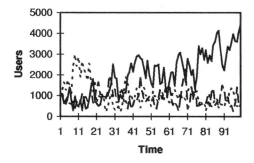

Figure 1: A typical plot showing the number of individuals in three species (solid = 6 sex, dashes = 4 sexes, dots = 2 sexes) over 100 generations.

Total Profit

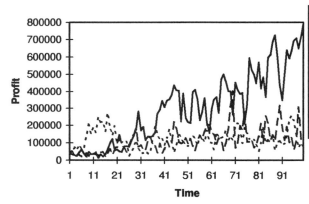

Fig 2: Success based on total profit - six sex comes out best due to the number of users

Efficiency

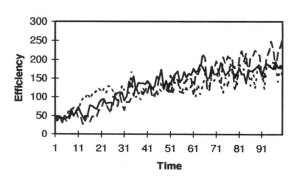

Fig 3: Success based on efficiency, where four sex wins.

However, two and four sex manage to maintain their overall efficiency, with four sex beating the six sex rival at the end. The two approaches give divergent behaviours. The question is why does six sex succeed so well?

Imagine that the problem is to climb a (static) fitness hill. The trouble with sex is that the crossover continuously disrupts successful genotypes, broadening the search. Asexual reproduction climbs steadily upwards. Now the disruptive effects of 3 or more sexes is much greater. If you want to continuously hunt around exploiting many niches in a dynamic environment clearly breadth of search may be most important. Six sex finds optima rapidly and is dispersed off them - speed, rather than convergence, may be the key criteria. So what happens if we change the world to a simple one where the users do not have a multi-variable selection criteria but only use cost.

Table 2: Results of 2000 runs for cases either of discrete sex or parent numbers were varied. Users' satisfaction was

based solely on the prices offered by the telecoms companies alone.

Parameters	Best	Number of Parents					
		1	2	3	4	5	6
Sex	Total	**490**	273	251	**401**	314	271
Sex	Eff	388	330	324	**411**	348	198
Parents	Total	43	279	282	**736**	307	352
Parents	Eff	43	300	377	**757**	293	229

Now something quite different happens. The difference between discrete sex and having many parents but one sex appears for the first time. Also either asexual or four sexes wins! The change in the landscape has changed the nature of the implicit fitness function, but not the dynamics.

Additional results and analysis of the data gathered reinforces this idea that the number of sexes that is best is a function of the dynamics. First when an early, simpler system was built three sexes won (simpler dynamics); and also there was a 'bug' which meant that in early versions the starting points were not randomly assigned but that they were heavily weighted in favour of certain positions. This enabled us to play around and discover that if the starting advantage was large enough, and the advantaged party sufficiently adaptive then no amount of sexual advantage in the chasing groups could prevent it overcoming them. It is often claimed that in evolution the better will always win. Not so, the dynamics of chance in the environment may often enable a less efficient but still dominant player to suppress his rival.

We believe this is the first dynamic competitive environment to explore the issue of higher numbers of genders for sexual reproduction. Some surprising results have been observed that suggest that simple thought experiments may not give the right answers. Clearly in natural systems the life-cycle time varies as well as the type of sexual reproduction, which creates another dynamic as well. This may explain the failure of asexual reproduction here but its natural success in prokaryotes.

More widely though, the results are a warning about applying lessons learnt in simple static environments about learning systems to real systems controlling noisy, dynamic environments. Two sexes may be the best for genetic algorithms, but not for evolution in this environment. How many other learning techniques are not matched to the dynamics of the environments they are designed for?

4. Conclusions

Initial discussions came down firmly on the accepted belief that two sexes is best. A large number of reasons were advanced for this. But successive experiments have been very clear: depending on the precise dynamics 3 or 4 sexes (or parents) did better; and where there was a bimodal implicit fitness function six sexes appeared to win.

The rational behind this is discussed above. The conclusion is simple (and in retrospect obvious) - the optimum strategy is the one which most closely matches the rate of change in the environment, *i.e.* the dynamics of the system. These dynamics would be very different if individuals had to spend time finding suitable partners (the mating dynamics), so in that sense they are different to biological systems. However in extrapolating from 'life as it is' to 'life as it could be' or, more importantly, 'life as it could be applied' lessons from biology needed to be applied with great care. Just because the dynamics of a biological system may prove that two sexes is optimal for biological adaptation, this may not be the case elsewhere. Evolutionary optimisers such as Genetic Algorithms run in a bloodless, static world where the fitness function is explicit and unchanging. The optimal search algorithm will have a cross-over function related to the shape of the search space and not the dynamics and thus is much less relevant to the dynamic learning we were interested in, or to real biological systems.

Understanding adaptation in complex dynamic systems has only just begun. The n-sex problem is an interesting and instructive starting point.

5. References

1. Crow, J.F.; Developmental Genetics **15** (1994) 205.

2. Hamilton W.D., Axelrod R. Tanese R.; Proc. Natl. Acad. Sci USA **87** (1990) 3566.

3. Jones, S. ;"The Language of the Genes" Harper Collins, London (1993).

4. Dawkins, R.; "Climbing Mount Improbable" Penguin, London (1996)

5. Kondrashov, A.S.; Nature **336** (1988) 435.

6. Van Valen, L.; Evol.Theor. **1** (1973) 1.

7. Holland, J.H.; "Adaptation in Natural and Artificial Systems" University of Michigan, Michigan (1975).

8. Harvey, I.; "Artificial Life III" ed. Langton, C.G., Addison-Wesley, Reading, (1994) 299.

9. Koza, J.; "Genetic Programming" MIT Press, Cambridge (1993).

10. Hillis, D.; "Artificial Life II" eds. Langton, C.G., Taylor, C., Farmer, J.D. and Rasmussen, S., Addison-Wesley, Reading, (1992) 313.

11. Grafen, A. and Godfrey, H.C.J.; Proc. Roy. Soc. Lond. B **245** (1991) 73

12. Ray, T.; "Artificial Life II" eds. Langton, C.G., Taylor, C., Farmer, J.D. and Rasmussen, S., Addison-Wesley, Reading, (1992) 371.

MORPHOGENESIS

Emergence of Differentiation Rules leading to Hierarchy and Diversity

Chikara Furusawa and Kunihiko Kaneko

Department of Pure and Applied Sciences
University of Tokyo, Komaba, Meguro-ku, Tokyo 153, JAPAN

Abstract

An abstract model for cell differentiation is studied, where cells with oscillatory internal dynamics interact through environment. The cells are found to differentiate based on dynamical instability, as is discussed in the isologous diversification theory. These differentiations obey specific hierarchical rules which emerge from dynamics without sophisticated programs implemented in advance. The rate of cell differentiation is modulated, depending on the distribution of cell types, which lead to a higher-level population dynamics. The global stability and the diversity of cell society appear as a result of this dynamics. The results provide a novel viewpoint on the origin of complex cell society, while relevance to some biological problems is also discussed.

1 Introduction

Cell differentiation is a general phenomenon in the course of development of a multicellular organism. Although all the cells contain the same genome set but they become specialized in different ways through the developmental process. In molecular biology, the emergence of different cell types is determined rather precisely, by a set of specified instructions, given by on-off switching processes. The switch depends on inputs by signal molecules, which leads to a variety of cell types as outputs. In fact, some molecular signals which cause the differentiations are identified experimentally. However, these relations between cause and effect are not so simply one-to-one. These relations include a large number of reactions, and each substrate in these reactions plays a different role in a different context. In this standpoint, it is an important question how such rules, which determine the differentiations and maintain the cell society, emerge from complex chemical reaction network.

As for the on-off switching network of genes, Kaufmann[1] demonstrated that the abstract Boolean network model leads to a variety of final states, depending on the initial conditions. He concluded that each final state corresponds to each cell type. However, these initial conditions themselves are selected so that corresponding cell types appear suitably in the course of development. To deal with this selection processes, it is necessary to take account of cellular interactions which are not included the gene network picture.

Thus, it is important to consider a system of internal dynamics with suitable interactions. One of the authors (KK) and Yomo have performed several simulations of interacting cells with internal biochemical networks and cell divisions that lead to the change of degrees of freedom. The "isologous diversification theory" is proposed as a general mechanism of spontaneous differentiation of replicating biological units[2,3,4]. In isologous diversification theory, the cells, which have oscillatory chemical reactions within, differentiate through interaction with other cells, as their number increases through divisions. This differentiation is provided by the separation of orbits in the phase space, which is not attributed to a specific chemical substance, but is triggered by the instability of a nonlinear system.

In the present paper we extend these previous studies[4] to incorporate the formation of cell society with complex internal dynamics in each cell[5]. From several simulations of a model with internal reaction dynamics, three novel features are observed; **emergence of hierarchical rules of differentiation, sta-**

bility in cell society through modulation of the rate of differentiation, and diversity of cell groups. It will be shown that the differentiation processes corresponds to the transition of attracting states of internal dynamics in each cell. The rules of differentiation emerges as a constraint of this transition, which depends on the interaction among cells. Indeed the rate of differentiation is modulated by the distribution of each cell type in the cell society. As a result of this modulation, the population dynamics of each cell type emerges as higher level, from which stability and diversity of cell groups are explained.

2 Model for Differentiation

Our model for the differentiation consists of

- Internal biochemical reaction dynamics in each cell

- Cell-to-cell interaction through media

- Cell division

The basic strategy of the modeling follows the previous works[4], although we take different dynamics for each of the above three processes. In essence we assume a network of catalytic reactions for internal dynamics that also allows chaotic oscillations of chemical concentrations, while the interaction process is just a diffusion of chemicals through media.

We represent the internal state of a cell by k chemicals' concentrations as dynamical variables. Cells are assumed to be in surrounding media, where the same set of chemicals is given. Hence the dynamics of the internal state is represented by a set of variables $x_i^{(m)}(t)$, the concentration of the m-th chemical species at the i-th cell, at time t. The corresponding concentration of the species in the medium is represented by a set of variables $X^{(m)}(t)$. We assume that the medium is well stirred by neglecting the spatial variation of the concentration.

2.1 Internal reaction dynamics

As internal chemical reaction dynamics we choose a catalytic network among the k chemicals. Each reaction from the chemical i to j is assumed to be catalyzed by some chemical ℓ, determined by a matrix (i, j, ℓ). To represent this reaction-matrix we adopt the notation

$Con(i, j, \ell)$ which takes unity when the reaction from the chemical i to j is catalyzed by ℓ, and takes 0 otherwise. Each chemical has several paths to other chemicals, which act as a substrate to create several enzymes for other reactions. Thus these reactions form a complicated network. This matrix $Con(i, j, \ell)$ is generated randomly and is fixed throughout the simulation.

Still there can be a variety of choices in the enzymatic chemical kinetics. In this paper, we assume quadratic effect of enzymes. Thus the reaction from the chemical m to ℓ aided by the chemical j leads to the term $e_1 x_i^{(m)}(t)(x_i^{(j)}(t))^2$, where e_1 is a coefficient for chemical reactions, which is taken identical for all paths.

Of course, the biochemical mechanisms of cells are very much complicated. We do not take into account of the details here, since our purpose is to show the differentiation process as a general consequence of interacting cells with internal nonlinear dynamics. What we need here is essentially the biochemical reaction that allows for nonlinear oscillation, which is generally expected as long as there is a positive feedback process. In our model, we choose a simple network with a small number of chemical substances ($k = 16$), to capture the essence of such dynamical behavior. Although a specific reaction network of the quadratic form is adopted to construct the scenario to be presented, we should note that our results are rather generally observed in a wide variety of models, as long as complex oscillation is allowed by the internal dynamics. It should be noted that in the real biological systems, oscillations are observed in some chemical substrates as Ca, cyclic AMP, and so on[6,7,8].

Besides the change of chemical concentrations, we take into account the change of volume of a cell. The volume is now treated as a dynamical variable, which increases as a result of transportation of chemicals into the cell from the environment. As a first approximation, it is reasonable to assume that the volume of cell is proportional to the sum of chemicals in the cell. We note that the concentrations of chemicals are diluted as a result of increase of the volume of the cell. With the above assumption, this dilution effect is identical to impose the restriction $\sum_\ell x_i^{(\ell)} = 1$, that is, the normalization of chemical concentrations at each step of the calculation, while the volume change is calculated from the transport as will be given later.

2.2 Cell-to-cell interaction through diffusion to media

Each cell communicates with its environment through transport of chemicals. Thus cells interact with each other through the environment. Here we consider only diffusion process through the cell membrane, and omit another complex transport mechanisms such as channel proteins for simplicity. Thus, the rates of chemicals transported into a cell are proportional to differences of chemical concentrations between the inside and the outside of the cell.

The transportation or diffusion coefficient should be different by chemicals. Here we assume that there are two types of chemicals, which can penetrate the membrane and which can not. We use the notation σ_m, which takes the value 1 if the chemical $x_i^{(m)}$ is penetrable, and takes 0 otherwise.

To sum up all these process, the dynamics of chemical concentration in each cell are represented as follows:

$$dx_i^{(\ell)}(t)/dt = \delta x_i^{(\ell)}(t) - (1/k)\sum_{l=1}^{k}\delta x_i^{(\ell)}(t) \quad (1)$$

with

$$\delta x_i^\ell(t) = \sum_{m,j} Con(m,\ell,j)\, e_1\, x_i^{(m)}(t)\,(x_i^{(j)}(t))^2$$
$$- \sum_{m',j'} Con(\ell,m',j')\, e_1\, x_i^{(\ell)}(t)\,(x_i^{(j')}(t))^2$$
$$+ \sigma_\ell D(X^{(\ell)}(t) - x_i^{(\ell)}(t)) \quad (2)$$

where the term with $\sum Con(\cdots)$ represents paths coming into, and out of, ℓ respectively. The term $\delta x_i^{(\ell)}$ gives the increment of chemical ℓ, while the second term in eq.(1) gives the constraint of $\sum_\ell x_i^{(\ell)}(t) = 1$ due to the growth of the volume. The third term in eq.(2) represents the transportation between the medium, where D denotes the diffusion constant, which we assume to be identical for all chemicals. Since the penetrable chemicals in the medium can be consumed with the flow to the cells, we need some flow of chemicals(nutrition) into the medium from the outside. By denoting the external concentration of these chemicals by $\overline{X}$ and its flow rate per volume of the medium by f, the dynamics of

penetrable chemicals in the media is written as

$$dX^{(\ell)}(t)/dt = f\sigma_\ell(\overline{X^{(\ell)}} - X^{(\ell)}(t))$$
$$- (1/V)\sum_{i=1}^{N}\sigma_\ell D(X^{(\ell)}(t) - x_i^{(\ell)}(t)) \quad (3)$$

where N is the total number of the cells in the environment, while V denotes the volume ratio of the medium to a cell.

2.3 Cell division process

Each cell takes penetrable chemicals from the medium as the nutrient, while the reactions in the cell transform them to unpenetrable chemicals which construct the body of the cell such as membrane and DNA. As the result of these reactions, the volume of the cell is increased by the factor $(1 + \sum_\ell \delta x_i^\ell(t))$ per dt. In the this paper, the cell is assumed to divide into two almost identical cells when the volume of the cell is doubled.

Chemical compositions of the two divided cells are almost identical with their mother's but slight differences between them are also assumed. In other words, each cell has $(1 + \epsilon)x^{(l)}$ and $(1 - \epsilon)x^{(l)}$ respectively with a small "noise" ϵ, a random number with a small amplitude, say over $[-10^{-6}, 10^{-6}]$. Although the existence of this imbalance is essential to the differentiation in our model and in nature, the mechanism or the degree of imbalance is not important for the differentiation itself. The important feature of our model is the amplification of microscopic differences between the cells through the instability of the internal dynamics.

3 Differentiation Process

Starting from a single cell with randomly chosen chemical concentrations $x_i^{(\ell)}$ (satisfying $\sum_\ell x_i^{(\ell)} = 1$), we have performed several simulations of the model. In Fig.1, a time series of concentration of the chemicals in a cell is plotted, when only a single cell is in the medium. We call this state "type-0" or "0" in this paper. This is the only attractor of the single cell dynamics, which is detected from randomly chosen initial conditions. (As will be seen later, another attractor is found, which, however, is detected only by choosing a special initial condition). Starting from this single cell, the differentiation proceeds as follows.

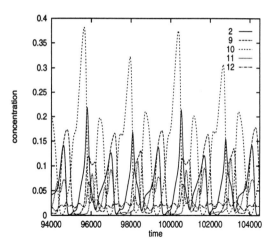

Figure 1: Overlaid time series of $x^{(m)}(t)$ of a single cell in medium, obtained form a network with 16 chemicals and three connections in each chemical. We have plotted only the time series of 5 chemicals out of 16 internal chemicals to avoid indistinct figure. Each line with the number m=2,9,10,11,12 gives the time series of the concentrations of the corresponding chemical $x^{(m)}(t)$. This oscillatory behavior is a limit cycle, whose period T is longer than the plotted range of the figure(about $T = 16000$ time steps). The parameters are set as $e_1 = 1$, $D = 0.01$, $f = 0.01, \overline{X^{(\ell)}} = 0.1$ for all ℓ, $V = 100$, chemicals $x^{(\ell)}(t)$ for $m < 3$ are penetrable(i.e., $\sigma_\ell = 1$), and others are not. The reaction network $Con(i, j, \ell)$ is randomly chosen, and is fixed throughout the simulation results of the present paper.

synchronous division of identical cell type

With the diffusion term, external chemicals flow into the cell, which leads to the increase of the volume of the cell. Hence the cell is divided into two with almost identical chemical concentrations. Chemicals of the two daughter cells oscillate coherently, with the same dynamical behavior as their mother cell. As the number of cells increase by power of two (i.e., $1-2-4-8\cdots$) with further divisions, the coherence of oscillations is easily lost. Such loss of synchrony is expected from the studies of coupled nonlinear oscillations. The microscopic differences introduced at each cell division are amplified to a macroscopic level through interaction, which destroys the phase coherence. We note, however, at this stage,

internal dynamics of cells still belong to the same attractor, and the divisions occur synchronously.

differentiation

When the number of cells exceeds some threshold value, some cells start to show a different type of dynamics. In the present example, 2 cells start to show a different dynamical behavior (as plotted in Fig.2(a)), when the total cell number becomes 16. In Fig.2(a), the time series of the chemicals in this cell are plotted. We call the state as "type-1" cell. Note that this state is not an attractor of internal dynamics of a single cell. The state is stabilized only by the coexistence of cells with a different type. In Fig.3, orbits of chemical concentrations at the transition form type-0 to type-1 are plotted in the phase space. It shows that each attractor occupies distinct regimes in the phase space. These two types of cells are clearly distinguishable as digitally distinct states. Hence this phenomenon is regarded as differentiation.

As the cell number further increases, another type of cell appears, which we call "type-2". Its chemical dynamics is plotted in Fig.2(b). This type-2 cell is again differentiated from the type-0 cell. The type-0 cells have potentiality to differentiate to either "1" and "2", while some of the type-0 cells remain to be of the same type by the division. At this stage, cells of the types "1" and "2" reproduce themselves, but the offsprings never go back to the type-0 cell.

hierarchical differentiation

For some simulations (i.e., for some initial conditions), the differentiation process stops at this stage, and only three types of cells coexist. In many other simulations, however, the differentiation process continues. At this stage, hierarchical differentiation occurs. The cell type "1" further differentiates into either of three groups represented as "3", "4", or "5". The time series of these three types are shown in Fig.2(c)-(e). The appearance of these types 3,4,5 depends on the composition of chemicals of the first cell.

At this stage the differentiation is determined, and cellular memory is formed as is first discussed in [4]. Accordingly we can draw the cell lineage diagram as shown in Fig.4, where the division process with time is represented by the connected line between mother and daughter cells while the type of each line in the figure shows the cell type.

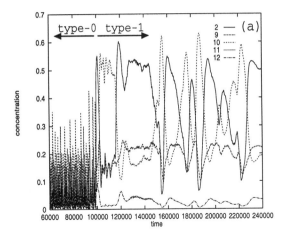

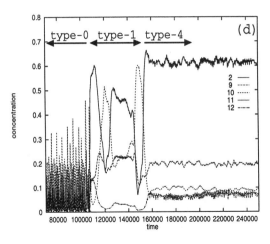

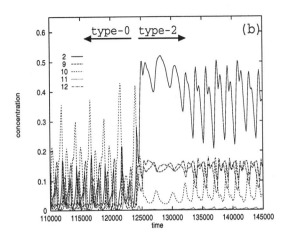

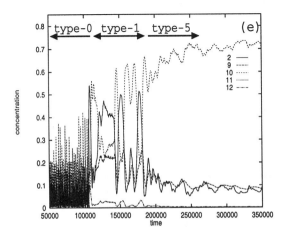

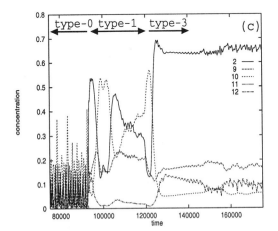

Figure 2: Time series of $x^{(m)}(t)$, overlaid for the 5 chemicals (as given in Fig.1)in a cell. (a)-(e) represent the course of differentiation to type1-type5 cells respectively. The differentiation to type-3, 4, and 5 cells always occurs from type-1 cells.

emergence of rules for differentiation

The switch of types by differentiations follows a specific rule. In Fig.5, we write down an automaton-like representation of the rule of differentiation. The cell-type "0" has three possibilities; one to make itself, and the others to produce "1" and "2" cell types. The type-1 cell has potentiality of further differentiation and self replication, while this cell type never goes back to the type-0 cell. The cell types-3, 4, and 5 reproduce themselves without any further differentiation. Among these three types, the cell type-5 is an attractor by itself, while others replicate only under the presence of other types of cells. The type-5 is rather special, whose appearance destabilizes the cell society consisting of "0", "1", and "2". Once the type-5 cell appears, all the cells will finally be transformed to this type.

amplification of difference and global stability

Note that this differentiation is not induced directly by the tiny differences introduced at the division. The switch from one cell-type to another does not occur simultaneously with the division, but later occurs through the interaction among the cells. The tiny difference between two daughter cells is amplified to yield macroscopic difference through the interaction. This phenomenon is caused by dynamical instability in the total system consisting of all cells and medium.

As the number of cells increases, initial dynamical state starts to be destabilized. When the instability exceeds some threshold, the differentiation starts. Then, the emergence of other cell types stabilizes the dynamics of destabilized cell type (type-0) again. The cell differentiation process in our model is due to the amplification of tiny differences by orbital instability (transient chaos) due to the cell-to-cell interaction, while the coexistence of different cell types stabilizes the system.

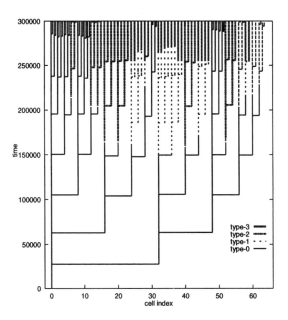

Figure 4: Cell lineage diagram. Differentiation of cells (whose indices are given by the horizontal axis) is plotted with time as the vertical axis. In this diagram, each bifurcation of lines through the horizontal segments corresponds to the division of the cell, while the type of each line indicates the cell type.

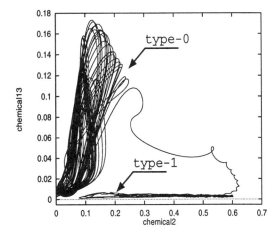

Figure 3: Orbit of internal chemical dynamics in the phase space. The orbit of chemical concentrations at a transient process from type-0 to type-1 cells is plotted in the projected space $(x^{(2)}(t), x^{(13)}(t))$. Each cell type is clearly distinct in the phase space.

4 Interaction dependent rules and stability of cell society

In Fig.5, we have shown that the automaton-like rule has emerged without explicit implementation. All differentiation processes follow this rule, while the choice of each arrow depends on distribution of cell types. When there are multiple choices of differentiation process (as in "0" → "0", or "0" → "1", and "0" → "2") the rate of the choice of each path is neither fixed nor random, but is governed by the distribution of coexisting cell types in the system.

It should be noted that the information on the distribution of cell types in the cell society is embedded in each internal dynamics. In other words, each attracting state of internal dynamics is gradually modified with the change of distribution of other cells. This modification of internal dynamics is much smaller than the differences between different cell types. Thus, there are two types of information in internal dynamics, the analogue one which embeds the global distribution of cell types and the digital information to give each cell type.

This analogue information controls the occurrence of the differentiation, because the transition between the types depends on their modification. On the other hand, change of the distribution of distinct cell types is embedded again as analogue information. For example, the orbit of type-0 cell in Fig.3 is shifted towards the direction of that of type-1, as the number of type-1 cell is reduced. With this shift, the differentiation from the type-0 to the type-1 is increased.

As a result of this interplay between two types of information, the higher level dynamics emerges, which controls the rate of the division and differentiation depending on the number of each cell type. This dynamics can be represented by the population dynamics of the number of the type-k cells n_k ($k = 0, \cdots, 5$). The behavior of this dynamics should be stochastic, because only the information on the number of cell types is extracted, by neglecting the lower-level information on the internal state (of chemical concentrations).

This dynamics of differentiation allows for the stability at the level of ensemble of cells. The variety and the population distribution of cell types are robust against the perturbations. As an example, let us consider the stage with three cell types ("0" ,"1" ,"2" in Fig.5). When the type-2 cells are removed to decrease the population, events of differentiations from "0" to "2" are enhanced, and the original distribution is recovered, with the mechanism of the shift of the orbits mentioned already. In this case, the stability is sustained by controlling the rate of differentiation from "0" to other types, and this behavior of type-0 cell can be regarded as a stem cell. Note that this type of regulation system is often adopted in the real multicellular organism (e.g. in the hemopoietic system)[9].

This kind of robustness at an ensemble level is expected from our isologous diversification theory, since the stability of macroscopic characteristics is attained in coupled dynamical systems[10,11]. An important point of our result is that this robustness always emerges from dynamical differentiation process, without sophisticated programs. This result provides a novel viewpoint to understand how the stability of the cell society is maintained in the multicellular organism.

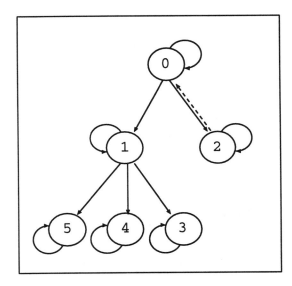

Figure 5: Automaton-like representation of the rule of differentiation. The path to the own node itself represents the reproduction of its type, while the paths to other nodes represent the potentiality to differentiation to the corresponding cell types. The dotted line from type-2 to type-0 gives an exceptional case: Indeed the differentiation from "2" to "0" never occurs when several types of cells such as "0","1" and "2" coexist. It occurs exceptionally only if "5" cells dominate the system, when all cells are finally differentiated to type-"5". In this case the type-"2" cells de-differentiate to "0" (and finally to "5").

5 Differentiation of Colonies

In the diagram of Fig.5 there are six types of cells. However, this does not necessarily mean that all of these cell types coexist in a cell society emerged in the course of the development. Cell colonies consisting only of two or three cell types can appear: For example, a cell colony only of "0","1", and "2" types and that of "0", "2", and "4" types exist.

This implies that the dynamics on the number of cells of each type, which controls the rate of differentiation, has also several stable attractors. These attractors correspond to stable distributions of cell types in the cell colonies. In other words, there are several possible distributions of cell types in each cell colony even if it is developed from a single type-0 cell. To confirm it, we have performed the following simulations. As an initial condition, we put one cell whose internal chem-

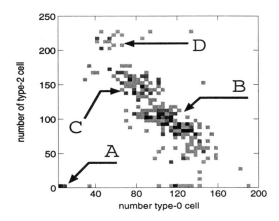

Figure 6: Density-plot of the number of type-0 and type-2 cells. Starting from a single cell with randomly chosen chemical concentrations, the simulation is carried out until the total cell number reaches 300, when the distribution of each types of cell is measured. Repeating 347 runs, the density-plot in (n_0, n_2) space is obtained by counting the number of initial conditions that lead to the corresponding distribution. There are several distinct peaks which correspond to the possible distribution of cell society.

ical concentrations are chosen randomly, and perform our dynamics with the chemical reactions and the divisions, until the total number of cells reaches a given threshold value (N=300 in the present simulation), when we stop the simulation to count the number of each type of cells. We have repeated this course of simulation over a hundred times with different initial conditions (i.e., internal chemical concentrations of the first cell).

Fig.6 gives a density-plot of the number of type-0 and type-2 cells, where the number of such initial configurations that lead to the distribution (n_0, n_2) is represented with a grayscale at the corresponding site. There are several peaks (dark-spots) denoted in the figure as "A" ~ "D", which correspond to distinct sets of cell colonies. Each dark-spot has a peculiar combination of cell types: The spot at $(n_0, n_2) = (0, 0)$ ("A" in the figure) corresponds to a colony consisting only of cell type-5, while the spot "B" denotes the colony of 0,1,2, "C" of 0,2,3, and "D" of 0,2,4, respectively. As is mentioned, the course of development at the first stage is independent of

the initial conditions (for example, it is common that the type-0 cell appears first, and then type-1 and type-2 cells are differentiated). However, at a later stage, several types of colonies emerge depending on the initial conditions.

Fig.6 implies that there are several attractors on the higher-level dynamics on the number of cell types n_k. As mentioned, the attractor of this dynamics is stable against small perturbations on the number of cells of each type. To understand this dynamics clearly, we have also performed the simulations without developmental processes, to focus on the stability of each colony without referring to the developmental process with the increase of cell numbers.

In this simulation, as initial condition, N cells are placed in the medium, where the concentration of chemicals in each cell is selected so that they give type-0,1,or 2 cells. The division rule is removed and the total number of cells in the medium is fixed (to N=100 in the present case). We continue the dynamics until the system settles down through the differentiation processes to a stable distribution of cell types, when the final cell-type distribution is counted. In this way, we have obtained the flow chart of the change of (n_0, n_1, n_2), as is plotted in Fig.7, where the direction of change of n_0 and n_2 is represented by the arrow, starting from the initial distribution given by (n_0, n_1, n_2). (Note that the number of cells of types 1,3,4, and 5 are given by $100 - n_0 - n_2$.) This chart shows that there are at least 6 stable cell colonies with distinct cell-type distribution $\{n_0, \cdots n_5\}$, given by $(n_0, n_2) =(0,0)$, (38,32), (30,50), (18,58), and (0,78) respectively. All of these cell colonies have basin of attractions, and the corresponding cell-type distribution is stable against external perturbation, as is supported by the higher-level dynamics on $\{n_0, \cdots n_5\}$. One can see that these compositions of cell types for the colony "A" ~ "D" correspond to the dark-spots in Fig.6, respectively. On the other hand, "E" in Fig.7 does not have a correspondence in Fig.6. This cell colony consisting only of type-2 and type-4 cells never appears through the development from a single cell. Also, the volume ratio of the basin of the attraction into each cell colony is often highly deviated from the rate of initial conditions for the corresponding colony in Fig.6. Furthermore, there are slight differences between the locations of stable distributions between Fig.6 and Fig.7. These discrepancies are caused by the additional developmental process underlying in the simulation of Fig.6. The developmental process enhances or reduces the appearance of colonies selectively.

Summing up, the coexistence of several stable cell colonies is clear. Depending on the initial cell condition, different cell colonies are obtained. The result here means that several types of tissues can appear through the interactions among cells. This kind of diversity is often observed in a cultivation system of a colony of blood cells starting from a single stem cell[12]. Our result provides not only an explanation to these experiments, but also sheds light on the emergence of diverse organisms in the evolutionary process.

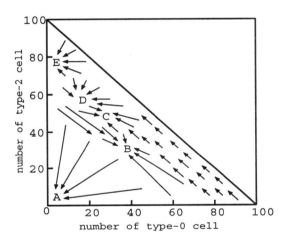

Figure 7: Flow chart of the change of (n_0, n_1, n_2). The simulations starting from the initial condition at each $(n_0, 100 - n_0 - n_2, n_2)$ are carried out under fixing the total cell number to 100 (without cell division). Change of the number of cell types is measured from simulations, from which the direction of changes of (n_0, n_2) is shown as an arrow in the (n_0, n_2) space. As is seen, there are six fixed points, which correspond to the stable population distribution of cell types.

6 Discussion

In the present paper, we have studied differentiation process which is induced by dynamical instability of the whole cell society.

Let us summarize the consequences of our simulations. First, cells are differentiated through the interplay between internal dynamics of each cell and the interaction among cells through media. The differentiations are caused by dynamical instability of an internal cellular state that appears when the cell number exceeds some threshold value. The destabilized state of some of cells is changed into some other state. Thus a group of cells with different stable dynamics appears, and the whole cellular dynamics is stabilized again because of the coexistence of different types of cells. The differentiated states are discrete, which are transmitted to their daughter cells as a digital memory. We note the stability of such states is maintained by appropriate distribution of cell types, which, on the other hand, is formed from the cell-level dynamics.

These differentiations obey a hierarchical rule written in Fig.5, which emerges without any sophisticated programs implemented in advance. In addition, the rate of differentiations is modulated by the distribution of cells of different types. The information of this distribution is embedded into each cell, as a slight (analogue) modulation of the cell dynamics for each type. Thus there emerge two types of information, digital one which gives the cell-type and the analogue one in which the global information of cell society is embedded. The latter controls the rate of the appearance of differentiated cell types. The interplay between the two types of informations sustains a higher level dynamics of differentiation, which is represented by the stochastic population dynamics on the number of each cell type $n_0, n_1, .., $ and n_5. As a result of this dynamics, the cell society maintains stability and diversity.

We should stress that in our system, the rules to maintain the complex cell society emerge from the mechanism of dynamical system, which includes the inter- and intra- dynamics of the cell. It is often believed that these rules, which determine when, where and what type of a cell appears in a multicellular organism, should be pre-specified as the information on DNA. We do not deny the importance of DNA as information processing mechanism, but, rather, we propose a novel mechanism about the emergence of rules from several regulation mechanisms, including those associated with DNA molecules. Our results clearly show the importance of dynamical aspect of these regulation mechanisms.

Several simulations are performed with different chemical networks and different number of chemicals, and the results of them support that the above process of differentiation is a general feature of cell society when oscillatory internal dynamics of the cell and cell-to-cell interaction are taken into account.

Application to biological problems

Although our model reaction process does not have one-to-one correspondence to any existing biochemical network, the present scenario sheds a new light on biological phenomena, and is useful to elucidate some open questions in biology. Let us discuss some of them.

First consider a hemopoietic system[13]. The blood contains many types of cells with different functions, while a pluripotent stem cell in the bone marrow gives rise to all classes of blood cells. Most of blood cells have limited lifespans, and it is important to control the differentiation and proliferation of the hemopoietic stem cell to maintain this system. The experimental results in vitro show that the differentiation of hemopoietic stem cell is not deterministic but stochastic, and stability of blood system is sustained by regulation of probability of differentiations[9]. In addition, various cell colonies with different cell types and distribution appear as a result of cultivation of the same type of stem cell[12]. The mechanism of stochastic differentiation and these regulation are still unknown. Our results provide a novel interpretation of this system. We have shown that, without any random event or external regulation system, the stochastic differentiation of each cell, the stability through the regulation of probability of the differentiation, and diversity of cell colonies naturally appear. Indeed, in the hemopoietic system, the complex network of signal molecules is observed, and it is plausible to assume the dynamical interaction which is adopted in our theory.

Second, it is interesting to discuss the evolution of a multicellular organism from our viewpoint. In the present multicellular organisms, the differentiations are controlled elaborately. However, it is hard to imagine that such mechanism appeared at the same time with the emergence of the multicellular organisms. According to our results, the appearance of rules to govern the differentiation processes is rather natural, as long as nonlinear oscillatory dynamics and interactions are included.

acknowledgements

The authors are grateful to T. Yomo, T. Ikegami, S. Sasa, and T. Yamamoto for stimulating discussions. The work is partially supported by Grant-in-Aids for Scientific Research from the Ministry of Education, Science, and Culture of Japan.

References

1. S.A. Kauffman, J. Theo. Biol. 22 (1969), 437
2. K. Kaneko and T. Yomo, Physica 75 D (1994), 89-102
3. K. Kaneko and T. Yomo, *Advances in Artificial Life*, F. Moran et al. eds., Springer, 1995, pp. 329-340
4. K. Kaneko and T. Yomo, Bull. Math. Biol. 59, (1997), 139
5. K. Kaneko, Physica 41 D (1990), 137
6. K. Kaneko, Physica 54 D (1991), 5
7. K. Kaneko, Physica 55 D (1992), 368
8. C. Furusawa and K. Kaneko, submitted to J. Theo. Biol.
9. B. Hess and A. Boiteux Ann. Rev. Biochem. 40 (1971), 237
10. J. J. Tyson, et al., TIBS 21 (1996), 89
11. B. Goodwin, "Temporal Organization in Cells", Academic Press, London (1963)
12. J. E. Till and E. A. McCulloch, Radiat. Res. 14 (1961) 213
13. T. Nakahata, et. al., J. Cell.Phy. 113 (1982), 455
14. M. Ogawa, Blood 81 (1993), 2844

Recursive Mappings and the Complexity Catastrophes

Stephen Hill
Centre for Neural and Adaptive Systems,
School of Computing,
University of Plymouth,
PLYMOUTH,
PL4 8AA
stevehi@soc.plym.ac.uk

Abstract

Recursive mappings such as Lindenmeyer systems have been proposed as a model of some aspects of the morphogenic process. In this paper one such mapping, the M-system, is introduced and compared with an iterative system, the Random Boolean Networks described by Kauffman. There are fundamental differences in the statistical properties of these two systems, especially in their behaviour as system complexity increases.

1 Introduction

In an extended body of work (summarised in [5]), Kauffman has demonstrated the existence of spontaneous order in a class of iterative systems known as Random Boolean Nets (RBN's). Such systems are a simplification of systems of coupled difference equations; each parameter being reduced to a boolean value, and the mapping between parameters restricted to the set of boolean functions. In each system the number of parameters is set at N and the coupling of each parameter is restricted to a given number $K \leq N$. At time t each parameter is thus some boolean function of K other parameters at time $t - 1$. When such a system is followed over repeated iterations, the system relaxes into either a single state (an attracting fixed point) or a cycle (an attracting limit cycle).

The most interesting feature of such systems is that their behaviour seems solely dependent on the coupling parameter K. As K increases a net will cross over from an ordered regime, where systems under initially similar conditions will tend to converge over time, to a disordered (indeed chaotic) regime where initially similar systems diverge in state. The transition occurs at between $K = 2$ and $K = 3$. Kauffman has postulated that this may be an example of the 'edge of chaos' phase transition [7].

Whilst Kauffman's original motivation was the study of the genomic regulatory system, and in particular how

a system of such incredible complexity could evolve; RBN type systems (sometimes known as NK systems) have since been proposed to model a variety of phenomena in different fields, e.g. immune system networks [4], polymer auotcatalysis[2], and neural interactions [11]. These systems may all be described by coupled difference or differential equations; RBN systems offer a means to investigate the statistical mechanics and general properties of such complex coupled iterative systems.

RBN's provide a suitable model for systems consisting of a stable number of interacting parts, in which the interactions are iterated. There are however systems for which this form of analysis is inadequate. The class of systems whose dimensionality[1] is not fixed do not appear, at first sight, to be amenable to this form of analysis. This class includes the class of recursive finite state automata(RFSA), described below.

Recursive finite state automata are recursive systems whose evolution through time is controlled by a finite set of rules, each consisting of a precondition and an transformation. At time t, each elementary part of the system (which will be described as a cell or node) is in one of a finite number of states s. Each elementary part of the system which matches a precondition will undergo the transformation contained in the appropriate rule. These transformations may include splitting the elementary part into two or more parts, removing the part, changing the state of the part, or a combination thereof. Such systems include Lindenmeyer Systems [9] and Context-Sensitive Cell Systems [8].

These systems are important because they are believed to model some aspects of the morphogenic process. Such systems have been used to model the development of plants (Lindenmeyer systems), and to encode Neural Network architectures within a genetic algorithm [1][3] [6]. This paper sets out to explore the statistical mechanics of such systems. In sections 2 and 3 one such

---

[1] For the present I would wish to consider only those systems with an integral Hausendorf Dimension, i.e. to exclude fractal systems

system, the M-system, is introduced and implementational details discussed. In section 4 I present a series of experiments designed to explore the properties of the M-system. In sections 5 and 6 the results are discussed and comparisons drawn between recursive and iterative systems. Finally, in section 7 the two complexity catastrophes introduced by Kauffman[5] are discussed with reference to the results obtained for M-systems.

2 M-systems

The system described is a formal system analogous to a Lindenmeyer, or L-system. The main difference is that whilst an L-system considers rule-based systems acting on one or more dimensional arrays, this system (which I have termed a Morphogenic or M-system) acts upon a graph structure[2], where the number of neighbours to any node is not fixed. This system is designed as a minimal formal analogue of a biological morphogenic system. Intercell communication is possible, a cell can affect its local environment by the release or absorption of the morphogens which mediate development. [10]

The elementary parts of an M-system are the nodes of a directed graph, each node may be in one of a number of possible states. The nodes of the graph are connected by (directed) edges. Every edge carries a number of *morphogens* on it; these morphogens are released (and absorbed) by the nodes during productions. The development of each node in the system is controlled by a combination of its state and the morphogen levels in its neighbourhood (defined as the set of edges that touch it).

In each state, there is a threshold level defined for every morphogen. The set of thresholds partition the morphogen space (the space of all possible combinations of morphogen levels around a given node) into a number of regions. The production rule that is implemented on a given node is dependent upon which region in the morphogen space the mean morphogen levels in the neighbourhood of that node lie. Hence the development is controlled by both the state, which which controls the partition of the morphogen space, and the morphogen levels, which (given the partition) control which production rule is implemented. Figure 1 illustrates the manner in which the morphogen space partition is controlled by the state.

Each production rule may be complex, consisting of a number of lower-level instructions which may involve various types of splitting behaviour, a state change in any new vertices produced, as well as morphogen release or absorption by the original (and maybe the new) cell. In the case where cell-splitting results in the creation of a new cell, the state of the new cell is determined by comparison of the morphogen levels in the new cell with

---
[2]In this case a directed graph

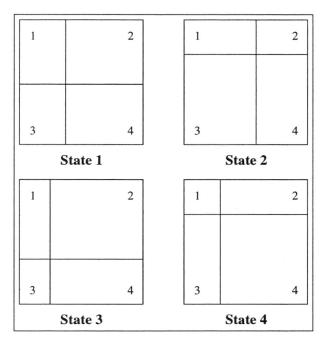

Figure 1: Example of the distribution of morphogen level thresholds within a 2M system. Depending on the state that the node is in, any given point in the morphogen space might implement one of a number differing production rules (labelled 1-4 above).

the threshold levels in the state of the parent cell before splitting.

Formally, an n-morphogen morphogenic system (or nM system) is an ordered quintuple $< M, I, K, G, P >$ where M is an ordered list of n morphogens, I is an ordered list of the 2^n possible node states, K is an ordered list of their respective threshold levels in each of the node states $i \epsilon I$, G is the initial state of the system. P is a set of 2^{2n} production rules each of the form:

$$p : (A, \{l_A(m) \mid m \epsilon M\}, i) \rightarrow (B, \{l_b(m) \mid m \epsilon M, b \epsilon B\}, J \epsilon I) \tag{1}$$

where A is a trivial subgraph consisting of a single node in one of the node states $i \epsilon I$, $l_k(m)$ is the level of morphogen m in the neighbourhood of node k, B is a subgraph formed from A by the transformation, and J in an ordered list of node states, one corresponding to each node in B under some (given) ordering of the nodes in B.

It should be noted that, from the definition given above, every node is a finite state automaton analogous to a Turing machine and subject to similar constraints concerning halting behaviour. In particular, there is no a-priori method of determining whether the development of any particular phenotype will halt in finite time. There is thus no simple relationship between the complexity of a system and phenotype size (i.e. number of nodes and connections); a system with any number of rules can give rise to non-halting phenotype development.

3 M-system implementation

This system was designed as a coding for neural neural network architectures. The production rule set has been chosen to include a variety of cell-split types which produce structures approprriate to this implementation. The directed graph produced by the M-system is interpreted as a neural network. Each node in the graph is interpreted as a simple neuron, and each directed edge as a connection between the neurons corresponding to the nodes at either end of the directed edge. The direction of the connection is the same as the direction of the connected edge.

One of the harder problems found in the use of morphogenic GA codings is to ensure that the resulting networks have the correct number of inputs and outputs. This is overcome by choosing the initial graph G carefully in order to maximise the probability that the resulting phenotype has appropriate structure. In the experiments described, G was a graph consisting of three nodes connected in series. The first node (with a single output) being identifiable as an input node, and the last node (with a single input) being identifiable as an output node. Development was restricted to the remaining unidentified node and its descendants, to try to ensure a resulting single input, single output network as desired[3].

The following scheme was used to code M-systems into a binary genome:

For each state:

- 4 Bits: Cell transformation rule. There are 9 possible transformation rules under the schema implemented. The mapping between these 4 bits and the 9 possible rules (henceforth the *transformation mapping*) is of paramount importance in determining the effectiveness of the system. The transformation mapping was optimised using a genetic algorithm in order to maximise entropy. [4]

- 4 Bits: Each morphogen absorbtion/release. This was coded in the range ±7.

- 8 bits: Each morphogen threshold, lying in the range 0–255. This proved initially problematic: Given the Central Limit Theorem of statistics, the sum of a number of independent identical random variables has an approximately normal distribution. This results in the distribution of morphogen levels within

a developing network becoming biased towards the centre of the morphogen level range, because each absorption or release is taken from a uniform distribution of possible values. By using a decoding mapping of the form

$$y = A \tanh^{-1} Bx \qquad (2)$$

on the coded threshold, the threshold levels are also biased towards the centre of the morphogen level range to match the expected morphogen level distribution. This results in a far more diverse range of phenotypes.

As stated above, the number of states within the system is 2^n where n is the number of morphogens. From the above list, it can be seen that the genome length, L is of the form

$$L = (4 + 12n)2^n \qquad (3)$$

since the length of each state description is also linearly dependent upon the number of morphogens, n.

Due to the detail of system implementation, I have restricted the implementation of M-systems to those systems involving an odd number of morphogens, as this avoids redundant bits within the genome. Direct comparisons can therefore meaningfully be made between implemented systems with differing numbers of morphogens.

4 Experimentation

The experimentation described is designed to elucidate general and statistical properties of M-systems. The coding of the rule-based system into a binary genome is helpful, since it presents an easy characterisation of the space of all possible nM-systems, for any given n. It is thus possible to describe the statistical properties of the mapping from the genotype space, to the resulting phenotype space. Indeed, due to the huge numbers of points in the spaces under consideration, this is the only way that the general properties of such a mapping may be described. The mapping from points in the space of M-systems coded by the scheme presented above (the genotype space) to the space of directed graphs (the phenotype space) will henceforth be referred to as the *M-system mapping*.

4.1 Method

The mapping from the genotype space S to the phenotype space P is a partitioning of S into a number of disjoint sets, $A_1, \ldots, A_d$, each corresponding to a different[5]

---

[3]The system is being used for evolving neural network players of iterated 2 player games, where a single input, single output network with (possible) recurrancies is required

[4]Whilst this genetic algorithm is not of primary interest, it did yield data on the relationship between entropy and diversity, which is discussed in section 4.

[5]The notion of what makes 2 graphs different is quite tricky from a practical point of view, as graph isomorphism is an $\mathcal{NP}$-hard problem. For the purposes of this paper, we consider two graphs *equal* if there exists an invertable mapping between nodes in each graph with equal numbers of connections in each direction.

graph. Note that the sets do not necessarily have to consist of points connected via a sequence of one-mutant neighbours. A one-mutant neighbour of a point x in the genotype space is a point tranformable into x by flipping a single bit. The following measures of the statistical properties of the partitioning mapping are of interest:

Diversity. The interval between the discovery of sucessive new phenotypes may be analysed via regression or curve fitting techniques in order to estimate the total number of phenotypes within the genotype space. In these systems we find that the least squares error on the observed data is minimised by using an exponential regression. The diversity, d, of the space is thus estimated on this basis.

Entropy. This is the Shannon entropy of the partitioning function:

$$H = \sum_{i=1}^{i=d} p(A_i) \log_2 p(A_i) \qquad (4)$$

The entropy of the mapping indicates its *bias*. If two mappings give rise to the same number of phenotypes, then the partition with the more unifom probability function between phenotypes will have the higher entropy. The entropy also indicates the number of typical phenotypes in the space. The entropy may be shown experimentally to converge towards a well defined value as the number of points sampled increases (see figure 2).

It was found during the optimisation of the transformation mapping (see section 3 above) that it was possible to gain higher diversity at the expense of lower entropy, in this case there were one or two extremely probable phenotypes and a large number of highly improbable phenotypes (see figures 3 and 4). This was felt to be undesirable, as it effectively increased the redundancy of the genome. Note the approximately linear relationship between entropy and diversity observed during the oprimisation of the transformation mapping (figure 3). The reason for this is still unexplained.

Stability. This is the probability that a system that has been perturbed by having a single bit flipped will map to the same phenotype, i.e. the probability that a one-mutant neighbour to a given sample point in the genotype space lies in the same set under the partitioning function.

Note that the first two items are global measures, and the last item a local measure at a point in the space S. It is also possible to construct local measures of diversity and entropy (H_l and d_l respectively), by considering these two measures in the set of one-mutant neighbours of any point. These are also important measures; they

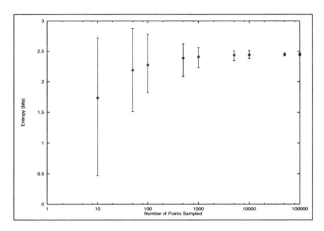

Figure 2: Convergence of the entropy of the 3M-system mapping as the number of points sampled increases. This sequence was taken during the optimisation of the transformation mapping. Error bars indicate the range of values recorded over 1000 runs.

indicate the degree to which local areas around particular points in the space are similar to the space as a whole.

In the results that follow, the global measures (entropy and diversity) are base upon consideration of 10,000 randomly picked points in the space. The local measures are obtained by exhaustively considering all one-mutant neighbours of a given point; in each case 1000 points were considered.

4.2   Results

Statistics for the M-systems used are presented below in Table 1. Note that for the purposes of comparison we also present k_{10000}, the number of partitions found in the first 10,000 sampled points, and k_{2^n}, the number of partitions found in the first 2^n points, which indicates the approximate number of phenotypes we should expect to find in a one-mutant neighbourhood of a point, if that neighbourhood is typical of the space as a whole. The genome length L, which indicates the size of the space is also presented. In figures 4 and 5 data generated for the 3M-system is shown (results for the 5M and 7M systems show no significant differences). Figure 4 shows the probability distribution across the various phenotypes found, whilst figure 5 shows the times between sucessive new phenotypes being found.

5   Statistical Properties of the M-System Mapping

Table 1 gives a lot of information about M-systems. First, these are very stable systems under pertubation. Most single mutations either have no effect on the mor-

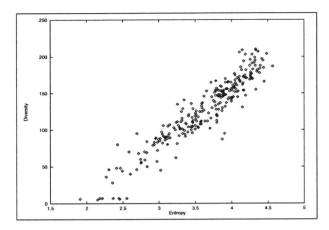

Figure 3: Observed relationship between entropy and diversity in the 3M-system during the optimisation of the transformation mapping using a genetic algorithm

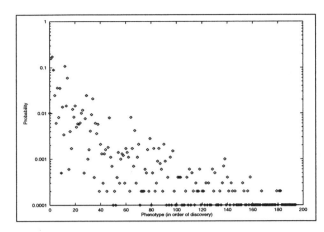

Figure 4: Probability distribution across phenotypes in the 3M-system mapping.

n		3	5	7
Gene length		320	2048	11,624
H		4.578	4.741	4.636
k_{10000}		196	272	206
k_{2^n}		48	131	216
d (estimated)		2,740	8,100	100,000
Stability		0.97	0.99	0.99
H_l	$\overline{x}$	0.217	0.080	0.026
	σ	0.150	0.070	0.023
d_l	$\overline{x}$	6.59	9.57	13.31
	σ	3.50	6.57	10.62

Table 1: Statistical measures of the partition of the genotype space under 3, 5 and 7 morphogen M-system mappings.

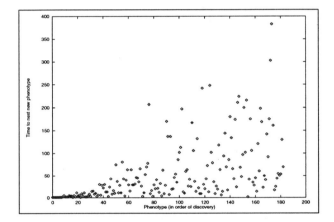

Figure 5: Time to the find next new phenotype as a function of the number of phenotypes found in the 3M-system mapping.

phogenic process, or (less likely) alter the process in a manner which does not affect the final state of the system. This is important if an M-system coding is used under a genetic algorithm for two reasons. First, the stability implies that any fitness function imposed on the phenotype will result in a well correlated fitness landscape (which is important if the genetic algorithm is to work efficiently). Secondly, it is important in that it allows a population of homogeneous individuals to maintain a degree of diversity within their genetic material. This may prove important in allowing continued evolution if the environment changes for any reason.

The low expected local entropy H_l and low expected local diversity d_l in comparison with H and k_{2^n} respectively also confirm that this mapping is stable and well correlated. Small areas of the space (i.e. the one-mutant boxes around sampled points) are not typical of the space as a whole, even for 7M-systems, they are far more or-

dered than the space as a whole.

It may be noted that whilst as n increases, the estimated diversity d increases rapidly, the number of partitions found in the first 10,000 sampled points, $k_{10,000}$ does not follow this trend. Indeed, the method used to estimate the diversity, by an exponential curve fitting:

$$| S | = \int_1^d e^{Cx} dx \qquad (5)$$

results in d being linear in the genome length l. Because any node can only be in one state at a time, there may be reason to believe that a linear relationship between the number of states in the system and the diversity of the system actually exists[6]. This would indicate that

---

[6]I am presently endeavouring to formally demonstrate such a relationship

Connect-ivity	No of Attractors	Homeostatic Stability	Reachability of cycles after Permutation
$K = N$	$2^{N/2-1}$	low	high
$K > 5$	$\sim N(\frac{\log \frac{1}{0.5 \pm \alpha}}{2})$	low	high
$K = 1$	Exponential in N	low	high
$K = 2$	$\sqrt{N}$	high	low

Table 2: Properties of random boolean nets for different values of K. Homeostatic stability refers to the tendancy to return to the same attractor after a transient reversal of any one element. Reachability amongst other state cycles refers to the number of other attractor cycles reachable by single pertubations. α is a constant dependent on K referred to in the original text. Taken from [5]

the relationship between the diversity and the genome length should be approximately linear.

Finally, one may note that the entropy of the system is not greatly effected by increasing the number of morphogens, despite the increase in the number of states that results. Figure 4 shows that the relative sizes of the partitions appears to be bounded from above by a negative exponential distribution.

6 Comparison with RBN Systems

The statistics that have been gathered on M-systems should allow a comparison between M-systems and RBN's. Table 2 presents the salient features of the statistics of RBN systems (after Kauffman [5]).

Whilst M-systems and RBN systems do not give rise to completely identical statistics, due to their different natures, meaningful comparisons may certainly be made. It is possible to compare the homeostatic stability of an RBN system with the stability of an M-system. If a permenant mutation of a single bit is unlikely to change the partition (in RBN terms the attractor) that a point falls into, then clearly a transient mutation is at least equally unlikely to effect a change in the resulting phenotype.

One may thus compare the number of attractors in an RBN system with the diversity of an M-system, the homeostaic stability with the stability, and the reachability of attractors after permutation with the local diversity d_l.

Such a comparison shows that the M-system statistics do not appear consistant with the statistics for RBN's. M-systems appear most consistant with $K = 2$ RBN's, but there is no evidence that the number of phenotypes scales with the square root of the genome length, L.

I believe that the reason is that M-systems are members of a fundamentally different class of systems, the recursive systems. RBN systems are essentially parallel

systems; the state of the system at time t is determined in parallel for all elements of the system, and is dependent on the state of all elements at time $t-1$. Such parallelism is not found in recursive systems; the state of any node is determined only by its own state (and in some systems, such as M-systems and parametric Lindenmeyer systems, by the local environment), which activates a single rule coded within the genome. Different elements of the developing phenotype may invoke different rules simultaneously, but the process is effectively a serial process, albeit one that is being enacted independently on a number of sites.

7 M-systems and the Complexity Catastrophes

The practical use of an M-system mapping is the coding of some form of directed graph structure into a genome, so that directed graphs can be evolved under a selective process, for example a genetic algorithm. More generally, recursive finite state automata might be coded using a similar mapping. Adaptive evolution automatically raises the question of fitness: Here we consider the effects of an arbitary fitness function which maps from the phenotype space P to a real value, for instance in the range $[0, 1]$. Such a landscape will necessarily be a plateau landscape, each plateau corresponding to a partcular phenotype.

The results shown above indicate that M-system mappings retain their well-ordered properties across a wide range of genome lengths. This is not the case with RBN systems. Assuming M-systems as a typical subclass of recursive finite state automata, I now wish to consider why such RFSA's might scale well with increasing complexity. It may be thought that complexity might be measured in terms of genome length L, or in terms of the maximum number of developmental stages allowed. Since each node of the system is a finite state automata, the question of halting behaviour is relevent; I wish only to consider complexity in terms of genome length at this point, as complexity in terms of the maximum number of developmental stages adds issues of halting behaviour into the notion of complexity.

Kauffman [5] has claimed that all systems must ultimately fall prey to one of two complexity catastrophes under natural selection. If the elements of the system are sufficiently independent, then as complexity increases, they will become relatively less important in determining the final state of the system. In this case selection pressure will become weaker than mutational pressure, and the population will be unable to maintain a position clustered around a fitness peak (i.e. the individuals in the population will no longer show a homogeneity of advantageous features).

Alternatively, if the elements of the system are highly coupled, Kauffman claims that as complexity increases, more and more of the features that the overall system exhibits will be due to the interaction of the elements. In most cases these features will be weakly expressed, because the elements of the system are acting in opposition to each other. Hence (from an adaptive viewpoint) it becomes harder and harder to find populations in which advantageous features are prevelant, because the complexity of the system usually works aginst the strong expression of any particular features.

A recursive system has certain intrinsic invariant properties . These properties ensure that the system remains well-ordered as complexity increases. Consider how a recursive mapping works: The first rule acts on a single element of the developing phenome; and depending on which rule it is, and how it is expressed, will lead to one of a number of (possibly incomplete) phenotypes. Suppose the first rule splits the initial element in some way. Then at the second stage of development, each of the two elements will independently invoke a rule, and maybe perform some transformation. This process may then continue through additional stages of development until the finished phenotype is produced.

The important point to note is that at each stage of development, the total number of rules invoked during that stage will increase[7] monotonically throughout development. The first rule consulted can influence the development of the entire phenotype, each of the second two rules consulted can influence the development of half the phenotype etc. The earliest rules to be consulted have the most effect over the final form of the phenome, the later rules progressively less influence.

Now consider the first complexity crisis. Increasing the complexity of the system does not change the fact that only one rule can be invoked at the first stage of development, or that the earliest rules to be consulted have the most influence on the final form of the phenotype. Increasing complexity cannot change the relative interdependence of parts of the system; the recursive nature of the system keeps this invariant. In a population of systems under a selection pressure, mutations which affect the expression of earlier rules will have a greater effect that mutations which affect the expression of later rules. In the former case, selection pressure will exceed mutation pressure, keeping the early development of the organism stable. In the latter case, mutational drift will occur, allowing the population to flow from peak to peak, while keeping the sites which have the most effect on development intact.

The second complexity catastrophe is similarly affected by the recursive nature of the system. Only one rule can be expressed first, and this will have the most effect on the final features of the phenome. It follows that most rules will only affect the later development of the phenotype. Increasing complexity can add extra levels of detail to the picture, but will not affect the broad brush strokes that have already been laid down. In terms of adaptive systems, one might envisage a fractal landscape (for example a Koch curve), where increasing the number of stages of development increases the detail in the system, whilst having very little effect on the overall shape. Effectively, the landscape is moving as close as possible to a situation where (in the limit) every point on the landscape is a local optima. Increasing complexity does not alter the basic structure of the landscape, it just adds finer and finer levels of detail.

8 Conclusion

Recursive mappings, of which M-systems are but one example, are a fundamentally different family of mapping to iterative systems such as Random Boolean Networks. The underlying mechanisms of this class of mappings have important consequences for the stability of these mappings aginst pertubation, and against increasing complexity. In particular, recursive mappings appear not to be prone to the complexity catastrophes noted by Kauffman.

9 Acknowledgements

Stephen Hill is supported by EPSRC Grant No. 95303083. Thanks to Professor Peter Saunders of King's College London for his help and encouragement, and to the members of CNAS and the two anonymous reviewers for their helpful comments.

References

[1] Angelo Cangelosi, Dominico Parisi, and Stefano Nolfi. Cell division and migration in a 'genotype' for neural networks. *Network*, 5:497–515, 1994.

[2] J.D. Farmer, S.A. Kauffman, and N.H. Packard. The immune system, adaptation and machine learning. *Physica D*, page 50, 1986.

[3] Nick Jakobi. Harnessing morphogenesis. In *Proceedings of Information Processing in Cells and Tissues*, pages 29–41. University of Liverpool, 1995.

[4] Stuart A. Kauffman. The evolution of economic webs. In P.W. Anderson, J. Arrow, and D. Pines, editors, *The Economy as an Evolving Complex System*, volume 5 of *Santa Fe Institute Studies in the Sciences of Complexity*. Addison-Wesley, Reading, Mass, 1988.

[5] Stuart A. Kauffman. *The Origins of Order: Self-Organization and Selection in Evolution*. Oxford University Press, New York, 1993.

---

[7]This, of course, is a simplification: There are some atypical circumstances where the number of elements may decrease during a stage of development. This fact does not affect the thrust of the argument

[6] Hiroaki Kitano. Neurogenetic learning: An integrated method of designing and training neural networks using genetic algorithms. *Physica D*, August 1994.

[7] Christopher G. Langton. Computation to the edge of chaos: Phase transitions and emergent computation. *Physica D*, 42:120, 1990.

[8] Martin Lantin and F. David Fracchia. Generalized context-sensitive cell systems. In *Proceedings of Information Processing in Cells and Tissues*, pages 42–54. University of Liverpool, 1995.

[9] Aristid Lindenmeyer. Developmental systems without cellular interactions, their languages and grammars. *Journal of Theoretical Biology*, 50:455–464, 1971.

[10] Alan M.Turing. The chemical basis of morphogenesis. *Philosophical Transactions of the Royal Society. London*, B237:37–72, 1952.

[11] D.E. Rummelhart and J.L. McClelland. *Parallel Distributed Processing: Explorations in the Microstructure of Cognition*, volume 1 and 2. Bradford, Cambridge, Mass., 1986.

On The Evolution of Multicellularity

Larry Bull

Faculty of Computer Studies and Mathematics
University of the West of England,
Bristol, BS16 1QY, U.K.
larry@ics.uwe.ac.uk

Abstract

In this paper the initial conditions for the emergence of multicellular organisms are examined. Using the tuneable abstract NKC model of evolution comparisons in evolutionary performance are made between unicellular organisms and very simple multicellular organisms, under varying conditions. The results show that multicellularity without differentiation appears selectively neutral, but that differentiation to soma proves beneficial as the amount of epistasis in the fitness landscape increases. This is explained by considering mutations in the generation of daughter cells and their subsequent effect on the propagule's fitness. This is interpreted as a simple example of the Baldwin effect.

1. Introduction

Approximately 550 million years ago the Cambrian explosion brought forth all the major phyla of multicellular animals. However multicellularity is thought to have evolved up to 200 million years before that and has occurred at least three times - in fungi, plants and animals. In this paper the conditions under which simple multicellularity proves beneficial in comparison to unicellularity are examined. Kauffman and Johnsen's [1989] genetics-based NKC model, which allows the systematic alteration of various aspects of an evolving environment, is used to show that multicellularity proves beneficial when the amount of organism epistasis is increased. It is shown that multicellularity without differentiation appears to be selectively neutral [Kimura 1983] in comparison to equivalent unicellular organisms, but that simple differentiation to non-reproducing cells (soma) can prove beneficial in terms of mean performance. One explanation for these results may be found by considering the Baldwin effect [Baldwin 1896]. If the multicellular organism is considered as a selective whole reproducing cells (gametes) can have their "true" genetic fitness altered by producing daughter cells which are slightly different to them, via the background mutation. In this way natural selection can be guided towards better genetic combinations than those which already exist in the reproducing population - the Baldwin effect. That is, less fit mothers connected to fitter daughters can stand a higher chance of selection than equivalent mothers on their own when the differences between mother and daughter are produced by unavoidable mutations.

The paper is arranged as follows: the next section describes the NKC model. Section 3 describes the first population-based version of the model used here and presents some results. Section 4 introduces a version of the model which considers aggregates of unicellular organisms and presents the results from its use. All findings are discussed in Sections 5 and 6.

2. The NKC Model

Kauffman and Johnsen [1989] introduced the NKC model to allow the systematic study of various aspects of ecological evolution. In the model an individual is represented by a haploid genome of N (binary) genes, each of which depends upon K other genes in its genome. Thus increasing K, with respect to N, increases the epistatic linkage. This increases the ruggedness of the fitness landscapes by increasing the number of fitness peaks, which in turn increases the steepness of their sides and decreases their typical heights. Each gene is also said to depend upon C traits in the other organisms with which it interacts. The adaptive moves by one organism may deform the fitness landscape(s) of its partner(s). Altering C, with respect to N, changes how dramatically adaptive moves by each organism deform the landscape(s) of its partner(s). It is shown that as C increases mean performance drops and the time taken to reach an equilibrium point increases, along with an associated decrease in the equilibrium fitness level.

The model assumes all intergenome (C) and intragenome (K) interactions are so complex that it is only appropriate to assign random values to their effects on fitness. Therefore for each of the possible K+C interactions, a table of $2^{(K+C+1)}$ fitnesses is created, with all entries in the range 0.0 to 1.0, such that there is one fitness value for each combination of traits (Figure 1). The fitness contribution of each gene is found from its individual table. These fitnesses are then summed and normalised by N to give the selective fitness of the total genome (the reader is referred to [Kauffman 1993] for full details of the model).

Kauffman and Johnsen used populations of one individual (said to represent a converged species) and mutation to evolve them asynchronously. In this paper a standard generational genetic algorithm (GA) [Holland 1975] is applied to a population-based synchronous version of the model.

3. The Evolution of Multicellularity

In this paper the evolutionary performance of three types of organism are compared: unicellular organisms, multicellular organisms without differentiation and multicellular

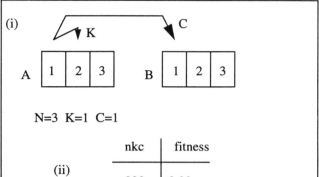

(i)

A | 1 | 2 | 3
B | 1 | 2 | 3

N=3 K=1 C=1

(ii)

nkc	fitness
000	0.32
001	0.41
010	0.52
011	0.29
100	0.75
101	0.47
110	0.36
111	0.58

Figure 1: Showing an example NKC function. (i) Shows each gene depends on one gene locally (K) and one gene in another genome (C). Therefore there are eight possible allele configurations, each of which is assigned a random fitness, as shown in (ii). Total fitness is the normalised sum of these values.

organisms with simple differentiation. Each organism which survives the selection process is assumed able to divide once. In this way multicellular organisms consisting of two cells are compared to unicellular organisms.

Unicellular organisms: A population (size P) of unicellular organisms consists of P/2 individuals which are the offspring of the previous evolutionary generation (via selection and mutation) and P/2 individuals which are their offspring (via mutation); selection works over P individuals to produce P/2 offspring, each of which divides to create a population of P separate individuals. Each individual is evaluated on the given NKC function.

Non-differentiated multicellular organisms: A population of non-differentiated multicellular organisms consists of P/2 offspring from the last generation (via selection and mutation), where each of these produces a connected daughter cell (via mutation), i.e. P genomes exist in total. At the end of a generation *all* cells, both propagules and daughters, are able to reproduce; again selection works over P genomes to produce P/2 offspring for the next generation.

Both the mother and daughter are evaluated on the given NKC function.

Differentiated multicellular organisms: A population of differentiated multicellular organisms also consists of P/2 offspring from the previous generation, where each of these produces a connected daughter cell. At the end of each generation selection works only on the initial P/2 propagules and *not* the daughter cells; the daughter cells are said to have differentiated to soma. Therefore selection works over P/2 individuals to produce P/2 offspring, but again P evaluations occur at each generation since the daughters are evaluated on the given NKC function.

3.1 Genetic Algorithm Model

A standard GA is applied to Kauffman and Johnsen's NKC model, using fitness proportionate selection (roulette wheel) and mutation (recombination is not used). There is one population for each type of organism. The parameter C here refers to the organisms' environment (C_e), represented by an extra evolving population of unicellular organisms. In this way the effects of increased environmental interdependence (pressure) can be examined ($C_e > 1$) by picking an individual from the environmental population (size 3P) to be evaluated with the current organism. Various values of N have been tried with no significant difference in results being found. N=12 and/or 24 are used throughout this paper.

Multicellular organisms are formed by a number of binding mechanisms. In higher plants the cells are connected via cytoplasmic bridges and exist within a rigid honeycomb of cellulose chambers. The cells of most animals are bound together by a relatively loose meshwork of large extracellular organic molecules (the extracellular matrix) and by adhesion between their plasma membranes. In all cases the cells exist as a larger whole during their lifetime. To take this into account for the multicellular organisms modeled here an *average* of the two cells' fitnesses is assigned to the reproductive cell(s). That is, it is assumed that the daughter and propagule affect each others' fitnesses and hence the average of their combined fitness is used for selection (this point will be returned to later since it is important). In the case of the bad mother/good daughter example mentioned in the introduction, they would represent a moderately fit single organism for selection.

Three important aspects of multicellular origins are not considered here, that of the possible conflict between the mother and daughter (e.g.[Buss 1987]), details of the mechanism by which the first cells joined (e.g.[Szathmary 1994]) and how a mother distinguishes between producing a propagule or daughter cell (e.g.[Wolpert 1990]). These aspects are presumed to be resolved here. This paper is concerned with the conditions under which multicellularity could have emerged in a unicellular environment before functional differentiation evolved (most traditional models assume differentiation in the daughter, e.g. feeding [Wolpert 1990]).

All experiments consist of running a generational GA over

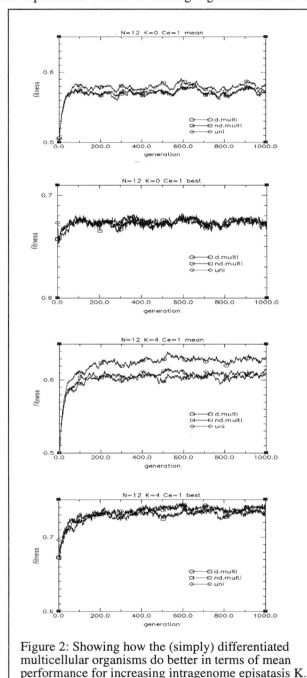

Figure 2: Showing how the (simply) differentiated multicellular organisms do better in terms of mean performance for increasing intragenome episatasis K.

2000 generations, for 100 trials (10 runs on each of 10 NKC functions), for various parameters.

3.2 Results

Table 1 and Figure 2 show the general result for P=100, mutation rate set at 0.01 per bit and $C_e=1$, for various K. It can be seen that as the amount of intragenome epistasis (K) increases the differentiated multicellular (d.multi) organisms

Table 1: Showing the effects of varying the amount of epistasis with regards which cell configuration performs best terms of finding optima (**b**) and mean population performance (**m**). Differentiated multicellular denoted d.multi.

K	1	4	7	10
b	all=	all=	all=	all=
m	all=	d.multi	d.multi	d.multi

$N=12\ C_e=1$

K	1	4	7	10
b	all=	all=	all=	all=
m	all=	all=	d.multi	d.multi

$N=12\ C_e=3$

K	1	4	7	10	13	16
b	all=	all=	all=	all=	all=	all=
m	all=	d.multi	d.multi	d.multi	d.multi	d.multi

$N=24\ C_e=1$

K	1	4	7	10	13	16
b	all=	all=	all=	all=	all=	X
m	all=	all=	d.multi	d.multi	d.multi	X

$N=24\ C_e=3$

do better in terms of mean fitness than both the unicellular (uni) and non-differentiated multicellular (nd.multi) organisms. That is, the emergence of differentiated multicellularity, a phenomenon which may itself increase complexity (next section), appears to benefit evolution on complex landscapes. It can also be seen that there is no significant difference between the best and mean performances of the other two types of organism. That is, the evolution of what is perhaps the first step in the process of becoming a differentiated multicellular organism, that of the propagule staying joined to the daughter cell, appears to be selectively neutral here.

Table 1 also shows the general result for the same model when the amount of dependence with the environment is increased ($C_e = 3$). It can be seen that the amount of intragenome epistasis must increase (K>4) before the differentiated multicellular organisms again do better than the others.

The effects of altering the population size and mutation rate have also been examined. Increasing (e.g. P=200) and decreasing (e.g. P=50) the population size does not appear to have any effect on the general result reported above (results not shown). However, the unicellular and non-differentiated organisms often do better when the mutation rate is decreased

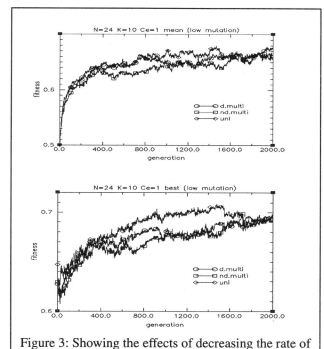

Figure 3: Showing the effects of decreasing the rate of mutation on the different organisms.

(e.g. 0.001 per bit), doing as well as the differentiated organisms in terms of mean performance and often better in terms of optima found (Figure 3). Results (not shown) are the same as those above for larger rates of mutation (e.g. 0.02 per bit).

A second aspect of the evolution of multicellularity is now considered.

4. Multicellularity From the Aggregation of Unicellular Organisms

Multicellularity is not strictly a eukaryotic phenomenon - it is also seen in prokaryotes through the aggregation of (unicellular) organisms. For example, the rod-shaped Myxobacteria usually live together in loose colonies pooling their digestive enzymes. When food supplies are exhausted or scarce they aggregate into a fruiting body, within which they differentiate, to produce spores that can survive hostile

conditions. Unicellular eukaryotes, such as Myxomycota, have similar life-cycles. Green algae range from single-celled organisms (e.g. Chlamydomonas) to aggregates of a few cells (e.g. of the genus Gonium) to fully multicellular organisms with differentiation (e.g. Volvox), prompting the suggestion that multicellularity has evolved from unicellular aggregates.

In the previous model the effects on fitness of two cells being joined together during their lifetime was considered by giving the propagule(s) an average of the two "true" fitnesses. However, the NKC model allows inter-genome epistasis to be modeled explicitly (as it was with the parameter C_e). It is therefore possible to add a second C parameter to the model which considers the unavoidable epistasis between the two cells (C_d). Once this is done it no longer becomes possible to compare the two forms of multicellularity with their equivalent unicellular ancestors since the fitness functions will be different - unicellular would have tables of $2^{(K+Ce+1)}$ whereas multicellular would have tables of size $2^{(K+Ce+Cd+1)}$. Comparing multicellular organisms at various levels of inter-cellular epistasis to equivalent unicellular organisms is possible, however, if the latter are assumed to exist in a colonial form; the interdependence between the individuals in the aggregate is modeled as the interdependence between the cells of the multicellular organism (C_d). A unicellular aggregate consists of the initial individual and its offspring here, which is how many are formed in nature.

4.1 Genetic Algorithm Model

As stated above, the parameter C considers the effects of others on a given individual's fitness. However, for individuals which spend a significant amount of their life-cycle in very close proximity, the effects of the given individual on the others' fitnesses should also still be considered in *its* fitness. That is, such a collective of individuals, whether multicellular or an aggregate, should be viewed as a functional whole for selection; a combined fitness measure of all parts should be assigned to the reproductive individual(s). This reasoning is similar to that used in the discussion of close interspecies symbioses [Allee et al. 1949] [Margulis 1992].

Here, as in the above section, the reproductive cells of multicellular organisms are given a combined fitness measure. For the equivalent aggregates of unicellular organisms both possible cases are considered; aggregate models using individual fitnesses and combined fitnesses are examined. Note that unicellular aggregates with a combined fitness measure are equivalent to multicellular organisms without differentiation here.

4.2 Results

Table 2 and Figure 4 show the general result for P=100,

mutation rate set at 0.01 per bit and $C_e=1$, for various K and C_d, for both types of aggregate. It can again be seen that the differentiated multicellular organisms do better in terms of mean performance under most conditions. Again the difference between the unicellular organisms and non-

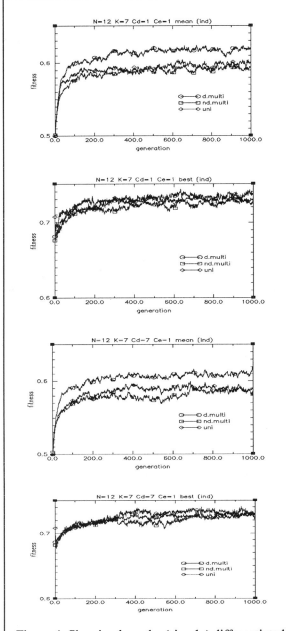

Figure 4: Showing how the (simply) differentiated multicellular organisms do better in terms of mean performance for increasing intergenome epistasis in comparison to non-differentiated organisms and unicellular aggregates (using individual fitnesses).

differentiated organisms is not significant. Increasing C_e also causes the advantages of multicellular differentiation to be lost for lower K, as before (not shown).

The effects of altering the population size and mutation rate have also been examined for these two models. Increasing (e.g. P=200) and decreasing (e.g. P=50) the population size does not appear to have any effect on the general result reported above, except that for higher K (K>10) both forms of unicellular aggregate sometimes do better in terms of optima

Table 2: Showing the effects of varying the amount of epistasis with regards which cell configuration performs best in terms of finding optima (**b**) and mean population performance (**m**) using aggregates of unicells. Differentiated multicelular denoted d.multi or d. Unicellular denoted uni. Non-differentiated multicellular denoted nd.

C	K	1	4	7	10
1	**b**	all=	all=	all=	all=
	m	d=nd	d.multi	d.multi	d.multi
3	**b**	uni=d	all=	all=	all=
	m	d	d.multi	d.multi	d.multi
5	**b**	all=	uni=d	uni=d	all=
	m	d	d.multi	d.multi	d.multi

N=12 $C_e=1$ Aggregate: individual

C	K	1	4	7	10
1	**b**	all=	all=	all=	all=
	m	d.mu	d.mult	d.mult	d.mult
3	**b**	all=	all=	all=	all=
	m	d.mul	d.mult	d.mult	d.mult
5	**b**	all=	all=	all=	all=
	m	d.mul	d.mult	d.mult	d.mult

N=12 $C_e=1$ Aggregate: combined

found (results not shown). The unicellular and non-differentiated organisms again often do better than before (results not shown) when the mutation rate is decreased (e.g. 0.001), particularly the unicellular aggregates. Results (not shown) are the same as those above for larger rates of mutation (e.g. 0.02).

The use of recombination in all of the above models does not alter the general result (not shown).

5. Discussion

In the above models it has been found that multicellularity with a simple form of differentiation (to soma) proves beneficial when the fitness landscape is rugged. With the division error rate set low a few selection-generated genomes are evaluated in an environment in which their daughter is slightly different from them. The original genome receives the average of their combined fitnesses; the generated genome gets the average of its "true" fitness and a slightly different one. The effect of this is to alter the shape of the underlying fitness landscape for selection since a genome can do better, or worse, than it would on its own. That is, if a given genome can be mutated into a better daughter genome, it must be near a good combination of traits for the function/niche and so the search is guided toward that region since the original genome operated on by selection gets a higher than expected fitness.

Previously Hinton and Nowlan [1987] (and many others since) have shown how life-time learning can achieve the same effect. They showed that a "needle in a haystack" problem can be solved more easily when individuals are given the ability to learn, since the learning can guide evolution to good gene combinations by altering the shape of the fitness landscape; evolution generated genomes receive different (better) fitnesses than they would without learning since they are able to do local (random) search. They describe how learning can turn a difficult problem into a smooth unimodal function because genomes closer to the needle-like optimum are, on average, increasingly able to find it via random learning. This phenomenon is known as the "Baldwin effect" [Baldwin 1896]. Mayley [1996] has recently applied Hinton and Nowlan's model to a version of the NK model used here and found that learning becomes increasingly beneficial with increasing K. Therefore the simple form of cell differentiation in multicellular organisms can be seen as an example of the Baldwin effect. The fact that considerably decreasing the mutation rate led to a loss of advantage supports this since less learning is possible in an effectively smaller gene pool; the differentiated organisms often did worse in terms of optima found.

The same fitness altering effect also occurs in both the non-differentiated multicellular case and in the aggregate unicellular case where a combined fitness is used. However, here if a low fitness individual is paired with a good one both receive an average fitness. This means that low fitness genomes look better for selection and will stand a higher chance of producing offspring than expected. The fitness landscape altering effect hinders the search process. Conversely, under multicellular differentiation, even when a good genome creates a less fit daughter, the genome which goes back into the population for selection is better than its fitness implies (although the search may be hindered/delayed somewhat by this phenomenon).

Therefore results here indicate that the evolution of multicellularity appears no more likely to have occurred via unicellular organisms living in aggregates (section 4) than those which lived alone (section 3); the Baldwin effect is caused by the same phenomenon under both conditions and gives the same advantage.

6. Conclusions

In this paper the conditions under which simple multicellularity could have emerged have been examined. It has been found that multicellularity without differentiation to soma appears selectively neutral in comparison to equivalent unicellularity. However, for fitness landscapes of higher epistasis it has been found that the differentiation of daughter cells to soma proves beneficial in terms of mean performance. The Baldwin effect has been proposed as an explanation of this phenomenon. It has recently been suggested that a similar effect occurs in the immune system [Hightower et al. 1996] and in eusocial colonies [Bull & Holland 1997].

It was also found that increasing the amount of landscape oscillation due to the environment negated the effects of the random form of learning until the ruggedness of the landscape was increased - until $K > C_e$. The relationship between K and C is known to be important within the model [Kauffman & Johnsen 1989], with the region $K > C$ said to represent the stable or "ordered" regime. That is, the results indicate that learning is only beneficial in a coevolutionary context when the amount of intragenome epistasis is greater than the amount of intergenome epistasis. This is now being examined.

The two-celled organisms considered here are more like the early animals (Metazoa) than plants in that differentiation of the germ-line is assumed to have occurred immediately. For early plant-like multicellular organisms it must have been possible for either the propagule or the daughter to become reproductive. A version of the model presented in section 3 has been used in which either cell randomly becomes the gamete (results not shown). It was found that the Baldwin effect advantage is lost and that this form of multicellularity is also selectively neutral; plant-like differentiation did no better or worse than the unicellular and non-differentiated multi-cellular organisms. The consequences of simple organisms, like sponges, reproducing by budding off portions of their bodies has not been examined.

The fact that the multicellular organisms did no better in terms of locating optima may, in part, be due to the characteristics of the NKC model (the previously noted other work on the Baldwin effect using it [Mayley 1996] found similar results). In light of this a version of the model has been used in which the three types of organism compete for population space in a finite environment (as in [Bull &

Fogarty 1996]). Starting from equal sizes, selection works over all three sub-populations of organism types such that the most beneficial comes to dominate the space. It is found that the improvement in mean performance is enough to make the differentiated multicellular organisms take over (results not shown).

Finally, the fact that only epistatic/complex organisms appear to benefit from multicellularity is potentially significant. Previously [Bull et al. 1995] it has been shown how the uptake of hereditary endosymbionts (organelles) reduces environmental instabilities and *increases* the epistasis of the host. This suggests that early (organelle carrying) unicellular eukaryotes were exactly the kind of organisms which would be able to take advantage of the type of differentiated multicellularity modeled here. Indeed, Maynard-Smith and Szathmary [1995, p223] note that since the capacities for gene regulation and cell hereditary were already present in (the genetically less complex) bacteria enabling, for example, the distinction between producing propagules and daughters, the evolution of multicellularity may have been limited by a lack of organelles. They suggest that the possibilities due to the cytoskeleton, the comparably more efficient photosynthesis/respiratory of plasmids/mitochondria and that there are no multicellular archaezoans (eukaryotes without mitichondria) are all key factors.

7. Acknowledgments

Thanks to A G Pipe for his comments on the first draft of this manuscript. This work was supported by Hewlett Packard Laboratories.

8. References

Allee W C, Emerson A E, Schmidt K P, Park T & Park O (1949)(eds.), *Principles in Animal Ecology*, Saunders Company.

Baldwin J M (1896), "A New Factor in Evolution", *American Naturalist*, 30:441-451.

Bull L & Fogarty T C (1996), "Artificial Symbiogenesis", *Journal of Artificial Life*, Vol 2, No3:269-292.

Bull L, Fogarty T C & Pipe A G (1995), "Artificial Endosymbiosis", in F Moran, A Mereno, J J Merelo & P Chacon (eds.) *Advances in Artificial Life - Proceedings of the Third European Conference on Artificial Life*, Springer-Verlag, pp273-289.

Bull L & Holland O (1997), "Evolutionary Computing in Multi-agent Environments: Eusociality", in J R Koza, K Deb, M Dorigo, D B Fogel, M Garzon, H Iba & R Riolo (eds.) *Proceedings of the Second Annual Conference on Genetic Programming*, MIT Press, to appear.

Buss L W (1987)(ed.), *The Evolution of Individuality*, Prnceton University Press, Princeton.

Hightower R, Forrest S, Perelson A S (1996), "The Baldwin Effect in the Immune System: Learning by Somatic Mutation", in R K Belew & M Mitchell (eds.) *Adaptive Individuals in Evolving Populations*, Addison-Wesley, Redwood City, pp159-167.

Hinton G E & Nowlan S J (1987), "How Learning Can Guide Evolution", *Complex Systems* 1:495-502.

Holland J H (1975)(ed.), *Adaptation in Natural and Artificial Systems*, University of Michigan Press, Ann Arbor.

Kauffman S A (1993)(ed.), *The Origins of Order: Self-organisation and Selection in Evolution,* Oxford University Press, New York.

Kauffman S A & Johnsen S (1989), "Coevolution to the Edge of Chaos: Coupled Fitness Landscapes, Poised States and Coevolutionary Avalanches", in C G Langton, C Taylor, J D Farmer & S Rasmussen (eds.) *Artificial Life II*, Addison-Wesley, Redwood City, pp325-370.

Kimura M (1983)(ed.), *The Neutral Theory of Molecular Evolution*, Cambridge University Press, New York.

Margulis L (1992)(ed.), *Symbiosis in Cell Evolution*, W H Freeman, New York.

Mayley G (1996), "The Evolutionary Cost of Learning", in P Maes, M Mataric, J-A Meyer, J Pollack & S W Wilson (eds.) *From Animals to Animats 4*, MIT Press, MA, pp458-467.

Maynard-Smith J & Szathmary E (1995)(eds.), *The Major Transitions in Evolution*, W H Freeman, Oxford.

Szathmary E (1994), "Toy Models for Simple Forms of Multicellularity", *Journal of Theoretical Biology* No. 169:125-132.

Wolpert L (1990), "The Evolution of Developement", *Biological Journal of the Linnean Society* 39:109-124.

Emergence of Structure and Function in Evolutionary Modular Neural Networks*

Sung-Bae Cho[1,2] and Katsunori Shimohara[2]

[1] Dept. of Computer Science, Yonsei University
134 Shinchon-dong, Sudaemoon-ku, Seoul 120-749, Korea
E-mail: sbcho@csai.yonsei.ac.kr

[2] ATR Human Information Processing Research Laboratories
2-2 Hikaridai, Seika-cho, Soraku-gun, Kyoto 619-02, Japan
E-mail: [sbcho, katsu]@hip.atr.co.jp

Abstract

The concept of emergence takes an important role in the study of Artificial Life, but there is not so much work to exploit this concept in the design of neural networks. Moreover, many evolutionary neural networks have paid little attention to the fact that they can evolve from modules. This paper investigates the emergence of structure and functionality of modular neural networks through evolution. The model presented at this paper might not only develop new functionality spontaneously but also grow and evolve its own structure autonomously. We show the potential of the model by applying to a visual categorization task with handwritten digits. Sophisticated network architectures as well as functional subsystems emerge from an initial set of randomly-connected networks. Moreover, the evolved neural network has reproduced some of the characteristics of natural visual system, such as the organization of coarse and fine processing of stimuli in separate pathways.

1 Introduction

Evolutionary design of the optimal neural networks has shown a great possibility to develop adaptive systems that can change the architectures and learning rules according to the environments. There are more than hundred publications that report a new evolutionary design method of neural networks [1, 2, 3, 4, 5, 6, 7]. One of the important advantages of evolutionary neural networks is their adaptability to a dynamic environment, and this adaptive process is achieved through the evolution of connection weights, architectures and learning rules [5].

Designing the optimal architecture of neural networks can be formulated as searching in the space in which each point represents an architecture. The performance level of all the architectures forms a surface in the space. There are several characteristics in such a surface which make evolutionary algorithms to be a promising candidate than the conventional ones [8].

Most of the previous evolutionary neural networks, however, show little structural constraints. Some networks assume total connectivity between all nodes. Others assume a hierarchical, multi-layered structure where each node in a layer is connected to all nodes in neighboring layers. However, there is a large body of neuropsychological evidence showing that the human information processing system consists of modules, which are subdivisions in identifiable parts, each with its own purpose or function.

Question may then be raised at how to design the neural networks with various modules. There have also been extensive works to design efficient architectures in engineering point of view, which has produced some success in several problems. However, we still know of no comprehensive analytical solution to the problem of relating architecture to function. The architecture of the brain results from a long evolutionary process in which a large set of specialized subsystems emerged interactively carrying out the tasks necessary for survival and reproduction, but it appears that learning a large-scale task from scratch in such networks may take a very long time.

This paper takes a module as a building block for designing neural networks, which was originally proposed by [9], and investigates the emergent properties of the structure and function through evolutionary algorithm similar to genetic programming [10]. Each module has

*This work was supported in part by a grant no. 961-0901-009-2 from the Korea Science and Engineering Foundation (KOSEF) and a grant from the Ministry of Science and Technology in Korea.

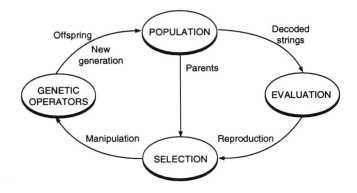

Figure 1: A typical procedure for evolutionary algorithm.

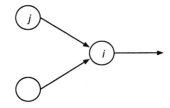

Figure 2: Interconnection between nodes.

the ability to autonomously categorize input activation patterns into discrete categories, and representations are distributed over modules rather than over individual nodes. Among the general principles are modularity, locality, self-induced noise, and self-induced learning. The proposed model of evolutionary neural networks is able not only to develop new functionality spontaneously but also to grow and evolve its own structure autonomously.

2 Evolutionary Neural Networks

2.1 Overview

In order to give autonomy and creativity to a neural processing system, it is vital that the system itself should have some mechanism to spontaneously generate change in its function and structure [11]. The basic idea is to consider a module as a building block resulting in local representations by competition, and develop complex intermodule connections with evolutionary mechanism.

In computing terms, an evolutionary algorithm maps a problem onto a set of strings, each string representing a potential solution. In the problem at hand, a string encodes the network architecture and learning parameters in tree structure. The evolutionary algorithm then manipulates the most promising strings in its search for improved solutions. This process operates through a simple cycle of stages:

1. creation of a population of tree-structured strings,

2. evaluation of each string,

3. selection of good strings, and

4. genetic manipulation to create the new population of strings.

Figure 1 shows these four stages using the biologically inspired terminology. In our work to date, we have used an evolutionary algorithm similar to genetic programming with rank-based selection scheme [12].

2.2 Modular Neural Networks

The activation value of each node is calculated as follows (see Figure 2):

$$e_i = \sum_j w_{ij} a_j(t), \qquad (1)$$

where w_{ij} denotes the weight of a connection from node j to node i. The effective input to node i, e_i, is the weighted sum of the individual activations of all nodes connected to the input side of the node. The input may be either positive (excitatory) or negative (inhibitory).

A module based on such nodes is designed to model neocortical minicolumns, as first proposed by J.M.J. Murre [9]. The constraints embodied in the model include:

1. Dale's principle (that individual neurons emit only one type of transmitter),

2. learning as a local phenomenon that does not require knowledge of the correct response, and

3. the capacity to differentiate between novel and familiar input and behave differently on that basis.

The internal structure of each module is fixed and the weights of all intramodular connections are non-modifiable during learning process (see Figure 3(a)). In a module, R-node represents a particular pattern of input activations to a module, V-node inhibits all other nodes in a module, A-node activates a positive function of the amount of competition in a module, and E-node activation is a measure of the level of competition going on in a module. The most important feature of a module is to autonomously categorize input activation patterns into discrete categories, which is facilitated as the association of an input pattern with a unique R-node.

The process goes with the resolution of a winner-take-all competition between all R-nodes activated by input. In the first presentation of a pattern to a module, all R-nodes are activated equally, which results in a state of maximal competition. It is resolved by the inhibitory V-nodes and a state-dependent noise mechanism. The noise is proportional to the amount of competition, as measured through the number of active R-nodes by the A-

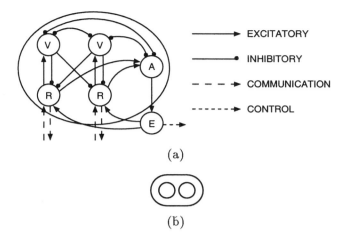

(a)

(b)

Figure 3: (a) Schematic diagram of the internal structure of a module; (b) Simplified diagram of the module (a).

node and E-node. Evolutionary mechanism gives a possibility of change to the phenotype of a module through the genetic operators.

The interconnection between two modules means that all R-nodes in one module are connected to all R-nodes in the other module. These intermodule connections are modifiable by Hebb rule with the following equation:

$$\Delta w_{ij}(t+1)$$

$$= \mu_t a_i \left([K - w_{ij}(t)] a_j - L w_{ij}(t) \sum_{f \neq j} w_{if}(t) a_f \right), \quad (2)$$

$$\mu_t = d + w_{\mu_E} a_E, \quad (3)$$

where a_i, a_j and a_f are activations of the corresponding nodes, respectively: $w_{ij}(t)$ is the interweight between R-nodes j and i, $w_{if}(t)$ indicates an interweight from a neighboring R-node f (of j) to R-node i, and $\Delta w_{ij}(t+1)$ is the change in weight from j to i at time $t+1$. Note that L and K (K determines the maximum value of an interweight) are positive constants, d is a constant with a small value, and a_E is the activation of the E-node. As a mechanism for generating change and integrating the changes into the whole system, we use evolutionary algorithm to determine the parameters in the above learning rule and structure of intermodule connections.

2.3 Gene Representation

Three kinds of information should be encoded in the genotype representation: the structure of intermodule connection, the number of nodes in each module, and the parameters of learning and activation rules. The intermodule weights are determined by the Hebb rule mentioned at the previous section. In order to represent

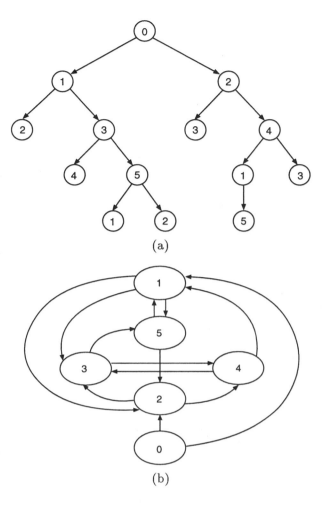

(a)

(b)

Figure 4: (a) Genetic code encoded by tree structure; (b) A modular neural network architecture developed by the gene of diagram (a).

the information appropriately, a tree-like structure has been adopted. An arc in a tree expresses an intermodule connection, and each node represents a specific module and the number of nodes therein.

An example of the genotype is shown in Figure 4. Each node has a number representing a specific module. In this figure other information such as the number of nodes and parameters of the learning and activation rules are omitted. The root of the tree is the input module that replaces the start symbol. A child node has a module number to be applied to the symbols which represent the modules connected by its mother module. In the course of decoding, the connections from a module to itself and the ones to the input module are ignored. This representation has some redundant connections as well as some meaningless ones, which might define some module that is not in the path from input to output modules.

By performing a number of genetic operators in the

gene pool, the interconnection between modules as well as the number of them are changed. Designing the gene to represent the interconnectivity makes it possible to generate a variety of offsprings and to evolve them.

2.4 Genetic Operators

The following genetic operators are used in our approach.

- **Selection**: Rank-based selection [13] is used. In this selection scheme, each individual survives to the next generation in proportion to the rank of its performance. Elite preserving strategy [10] is also applied to the selection. Some of the best individuals in the population are made to remain to the next generation. This prevents all of the best individuals from being eliminated by stochastic genetic drifts.

- **Crossover**: Crossover exchanges subtrees between two genes. It is similar to the operator used in genetic programming [10]. By performing crossover, many useful interconnection parts are gathered, and the intermodule connectivity evolves. An example of the crossover is shown in Figure 5(a).

- **Deletion**: Deletion deletes a subtree from the gene. This operator is expected to cause the deletion of useless parts in the gene. As a result, a more compact individual with the same functions might be generated (see Figure 5(b)).

- **Mutation**: Mutation changes each tree node to a new node in proportion to the mutation rate. This operator plays the role of changing the internal parameters of the selected node, such as the number of nodes in the module. An important role of the mutation is to enforce local search and make slight modifications to the connectivity parts obtained by crossover and duplication. An example of mutation is shown in Figure 5(c).

- **Insertion**: Insertion is similar to duplication except that it inserts subtrees or nodes from another gene below the selected node (see Figure 5(d)).

- **Duplication**: Duplication imitates the gene duplication [14] in living creatures and makes it possible to evolve the gene from a simple structure to a complex one. It also increases the complexity of functions and expands the network scale.

Duplication inserts a copy of a subtree within the same gene. The subtree is the part of the gene where the nodes with the same category appear in a list. Duplication leads to a functionally correct interconnection. Just after duplication is performed, the inserted subtree does not affect the individual's behavior and is neutral. Therefore, duplication does not change the functionality for

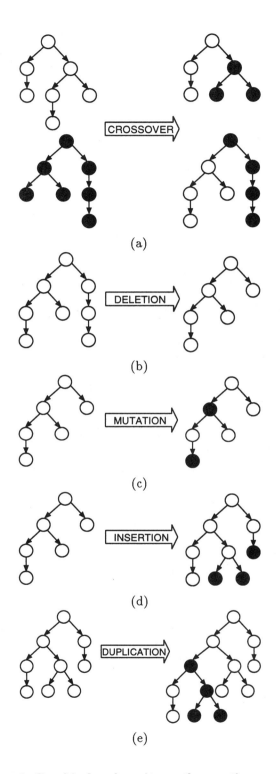

(a)

(b)

(c)

(d)

(e)

Figure 5: Graphical explanation on the genetic operators used.

Figure 6: Sample data.

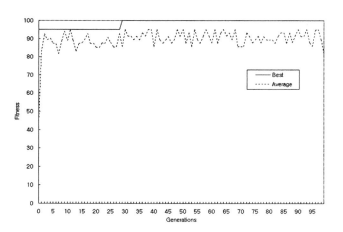

Figure 7: Best and average fitness changes as generation goes.

Table 1: The result of generalization rates with relevant information.

	Gen.	Correct	#Module	#Node	#Link
1	5	91.25%	2	17	7
2	21	93.75%	2	8	7
3	35	95.00%	4	16	13
4	65	95.00%	4	16	14
5	178	95.00%	4	16	15
6	179	96.25%	4	14	16
7	203	97.50%	4	17	15

the individual. The inserted subtree may be modified by mutations and a new function might emerge. The other parts of the gene also change and the inserted subtree is incorporated into the whole behavior. Figure 5(e) shows an example of duplication.

3 Simulation Results

3.1 Environments

In order to confirm the possibility of the proposed model, we have used the handwritten digit database of Concordia University of Canada, which consists of 6000 unconstrained digits originally collected from dead letter envelopes by the U.S. Postal Services at different locations in the U.S. The digits of this database were digitized in bilevel on a 64×224 grid of 0.153mm square elements, giving a resolution of approximately 166 PPI. Among the data, 300 digits were used for training and another 300 digits for testing. Figure 6 shows some representative samples taken from the database. We can see that many different writing styles are apparent, as well as digits of different sizes and stroke widths.

The size of a pattern was normalized by fitting a coarse, 10×10 grid over each digit. The proportion of blackness in each square of the grid provided 100 continuous activation values for each pattern. Network architectures generated by the evolutionary mechanism were trained with 300 patterns in two rounds of subsequent presentations. A single presentation lasted for 60 cycles (i.e., iterative updates of all activations and learning weights). A fitness value was assigned to a solution by testing the performance of a trained network with the 300 training digits, and the recognition performance was tested on the other 300 digits. Initial population consisted of 50 neural networks of having random connections. Each network contains one input module of size 100, one output module of size 10, and different number of hidden modules. Every module can be connected to every other module.

3.2 Evolution of Networks

Figure 7 shows the best and average fitness changes in the course of evolution. As the figure depicts, it is clear that the performance increases as the generation goes, and after the initial radical improvements the overall fitness settles down soon. Nearly all the best solutions present in the population after a few number of generations scored over 90% correct recognition for the training data set. However, the generalization rates were gradually improved as the generation goes.

Table 1 picks up some of the best results obtained during evolution, and Figure 8 shows some of the corresponding networks evolved. As can be seen, the evolution led to the increase of complexity, and new structures as well as new functionality emerged in the course of evolution: In general, the early networks have simple structures. In the early stages of the evolution some complicated architectures emerged, but they were disappeared as the search of the optimal solution matured. The earlier good specific solutions probably overfitted some of the peculiar training set with lack of generality.

The last network (c) is the final architecture producing

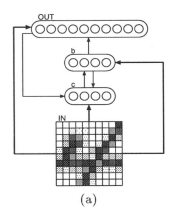

(a)

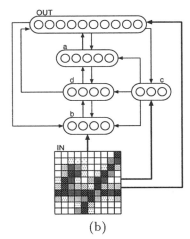

(b)

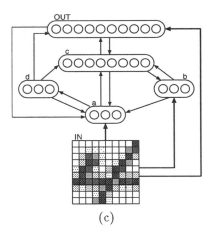

(c)

Figure 8: Some of the modular neural networks evolved; (a) 21st generation; (b) 178th generation; (c) 203rd generation (final network).

Table 2: The basic subsystems in the final network.

Subsystem	Pathways
1	IN → OUT
2	IN → a ↔ c ↔ OUT, OUT → a
3	IN → a ↔ d → OUT, OUT → a
4	IN → a ↔ d → c ↔ OUT, OUT → a
5	IN → b ↔ c ↔ OUT

Table 3: The performance of subsystems in the final network.

Index	Performance	Index	Performance
1	17.33%	1+2+3	96.00%
2	9.67%	1+2+4	96.00%
3	7.33%	1+2+5	18.67%
4	9.67%	1+3+4	95.67%
5	10.00 %	1+3+5	96.00%
1+2	18.67%	1+4+5	18.67%
1+3	27.33%	2+3+4	10.00%
1+4	18.67%	2+3+5	11.67%
1+5	18.67%	3+4+5	10.33%
2+3	10.00%	1+2+3+4	96.00%
2+4	10.00%	1+2+3+5	96.00%
2+5	9.67%	1+3+4+5	96.00%
3+4	9.67%	2+3+4+5	11.67%
3+5	10.33%	1+2+3+4+5	96.33%
4+5	10.00%		

the best result. This contains four hidden modules of size 3, 3, 8 and 3, implementing different subsystems that cooperatively process input at different resolutions. The direct connection from the input module to the output module forms the most fine-grained processing stream. It is supplemented by a sophisticated modular structure in which two modules are globally connected with the input. A sort of hierarchical structure (IN → a → c → OUT) with feedback connections has emerged, and two coarser processing streams as well as local feedback projections support the main processing stream.

3.3 Emergent Properties

In order to observe how the cooperative subsystems emerged during evolution, a thorough analysis on the final network has been conducted. The network of Figure 8(c) consists of the five basic subsystems as shown in Table 2. These lead to 31 combinations of subsystems which may be redundant. Table 3 shows the performance of these subsystems.

This table indicates that the subsystems of combining 1 and 3 play an important role with the support from one of the other subsystems: 2, 4, or 5. Furthermore, a

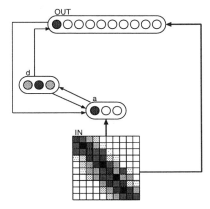

Figure 9: The subnetwork of 1+3 in the final network.

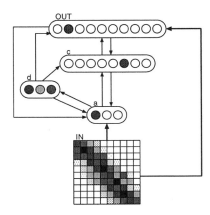

Figure 10: The subnetwork of 1+2+3 in the final network.

deeper analysis on the results implies that each subsystem emerged with its own functionality. For example, the subsystem 1 mainly works for classifying the classes 0 and 7, the subsystem 2 for the class 6, the subsystem 3 for the classes 5 and 8, and so on. As the network gets sophisticated by combining several subsystems, they act as one of the following behaviors: cooperation, competition, or separation. For an instance of separation, in the combination of 1 and 3, each subsystem behaves independently, which leads to the total performance as close to sum of subsystems 1 and 3.

It is quite difficult to fully analyze the neural behaviors because they concern with the oscillatory activation dynamics. To make the analysis simpler, we have presented a sample of the class 1 to two subnetworks respectively and obtained a series of snapshots of the internal activations. The first network is the subsystem of 1+3 as shown in Figure 9. This system has produced the answer as the class 0, which is wrong:

	(OUT 0123456789	a 012	d *)
→	(OUT 0123456789	a 012	d 012)
→	(OUT 0123456789	a 01	d 012)
→	(OUT 012345789	a 0	d 012)
→	(OUT 01279	a 0	d 012)
→	(OUT 017	a 0	d 012)
→	(OUT 07	a 0	d 012)
→	(OUT 0	a 0	d 012)

where the numbers represent the activated nodes and * means that there is no node activated in the module. As mentioned above, the subsystem of 1+3 acts an important role as a fundamental network, but it does not perform good by itself and needs the support from the other subsystem.

The second network is the subsystem of 1+2+3 as shown in Figure 10. This system has turned out to produce the correct result with respect to the same input as

follows:

	(OUT 0123456789	a 012	c *	d *)
→	(OUT 0123456789	a 012	c 01234567	d 012)
→	(OUT 0123456789	a 012	c 0234567	d 012)
→	(OUT 0123456789	a 0	c 023456	d 012)
→	(OUT 0123456789	a 0	c 03456	d 012)
→	(OUT 012345789	a 0	c 3456	d 012)
→	(OUT 12345789	a 0	c 456	d 012)
→	(OUT 178	a 0	c 5	d 012)
→	(OUT 1	a 0	c 5	d 012)

In this network, the coupled oscillatory circuit between c and OUT modules resolves the competition and induces the correct classification. This shows how the oscillatory dynamics finds out the category structure:

	c	OUT
	(5463027189)	(1782345906)
→	(54630)	(178234590)
→	(5463)	(17823459)
→	(5)	(178)
→	(5)	(1)

In the test of generalization capability, for the patterns that are similar to the trained, the network produced the direct activation through a specific pathway. On the contrary, the network oscillated among several pathways to make a consensus for the strange patterns. The basic processing pathways in this case complemented each other to result in an improved overall categorization. Furthermore, the recurrent connections utilized bottom-up and top-down information that interactively influenced categorization at both directions.

Table 4 reports the confusion matrix of the recognition of the final network with the test data of 300 digits. This is not competable to a practical pattern recognizer,

Table 4: Confusion matrix for the final network.

	0	1	2	3	4	5	6	7	8	9
0	30	0	0	0	0	0	0	0	0	0
1	0	30	0	0	0	0	0	0	0	0
2	0	0	30	0	0	0	0	0	0	0
3	0	0	0	30	0	0	0	0	0	0
4	0	0	0	0	30	0	0	0	0	0
5	0	0	0	0	0	30	0	0	0	0
6	0	0	0	0	0	0	30	0	0	0
7	0	1	0	0	0	0	0	29	0	0
8	0	5	2	1	0	2	0	0	20	0
9	0	0	0	0	0	0	0	0	0	30

but we can assure that the proposed evolutionary neural network works. We can appreciate the power of evolution to design complex structures with some sophisticated network architectures autonomously. Inherently, the proposed evolutionary neural networks can learn incrementally with new data sets, which demonstrates the relative superiority compared with the conventional neural networks such as backpropagation neural network.

4   Concluding Remarks

We have described a preliminary design of the modular neural networks developed by evolutionary algorithm, and investigated the emergent properties of the structure and function through evolution. It has a modular structure with intramodular competition, and intermodular excitatory connections. This sort of network has a potential to take an important part in several engineering tasks exhibiting adaptive behaviors. We are attempting to make the evolutionary mechanism sophisticated by incorporating the concept of co-evolution and some developmental process like Lyndenmayer system into the evolutionary process.

Acknowledgements

The authors would like to thank Dr. Y. Tohkura at ATR HIP laboratories for continuous encouragement, and Mr. S.-I. Lee at Yonsei University for supporting the experiments.

References

[1] S.A. Harp, "Towards the genetic synthesis of neural networks," in *Proc. Genetic Algorithms*, pp. 360–369, 1989.

[2] D. Whitley and T. Hanson, "Optimizing neural networks using faster, more accurate genetic search," in *Proc. Genetic Algorithms*, pp. 391–396, 1989.

[3] H. Kitano, "Designing neural networks using genetic algorithms with graph generation system," *Complex Systems*, vol. 4, no. 4, pp. 461–476, 1990.

[4] D.T. Cliff, I. Harvey and P. Husbands, "Incremental evolution of neural network architectures for adaptive behavior," *Technical Report CSRP 256*, University of Sussex School of Cognitive and Computing Science, 1992.

[5] X. Yao, "Evolutionary artificial neural networks," *Int. Journal of Neural Systems*, vol. 4, no. 3, pp. 203–222, 1993.

[6] S. Nolfi, O. Miglino and D. Parisi, "Phenotypic plasticity in evolving neural networks: Evolving the control system for an autonomous agent," *Technical Report PCIA-94-04*, Institute of Psychology, C.N.R., Rome, 1994.

[7] S.-B. Cho and K. Shimohara, "An evolutionary synthesis of autonomous agents with modular neural networks," *Proc. Int. Workshop on Artificial Life V*, Vol. Poster Presentations, pp. 200–204, Nara, May 1996.

[8] G.F. Miller, P.M. Todd and S.U. Hedge, "Designing neural networks using genetic algorithms," in *Proc. Third Int. Conf. on Genetic Algorithms and Their Applications*, pp. 379–384, Morgan Kaufmann, San Mateo, CA, 1989.

[9] J.M.J. Murre, R.H. Phaf and G. Wolters, "CALM: Categorizing and learning module," *Neural Networks*, vol. 5, pp. 55–82, 1992.

[10] J.R. Koza, *Genetic Programming on the Programming of Computers by means of Natural Selection*, The MIT Press, 1992.

[11] K. Shimohara, "Evolutionary systems for brain communications–Towards an artificial brain," in *Artificial Life IV*, edited by R. Brooks and P. Maes, The MIT Press, 1994.

[12] D. Whitley, "The GENITOR algorithm and selective pressure: why rank-based allocation of reproductive trials is best," in *Proc. Third Int. Conf. on Genetic Algorithms and Their Applications*, pp. 116–121, Morgan Kaufmann, San Mateo, CA, 1989.

[13] D.E. Goldberg, *Genetic Algorithms in Search, Optimization, and Machine Learning*, Addison-Wesley, 1989.

[14] K. Wada and S. Tanaka, "Can GAs survive?," *Journal of the Society of Instrument and Control Engineers*, vol. 32, no. 1, pp. 17–23, 1993.

Evolving Morphologies of Simulated 3d Organisms Based on Differential Gene Expression

Peter Eggenberger

AILab and Software Engineering, Department of Computer Science
University of Zurich
Winterthurerstrasse 190, 8057 Zurich, Switzerland
FAX: +41-1-363 00 35; Email: eggen@ifi.unizh.ch

Abstract

Most simulations of biological evolution depend on a rather restricted set of properties. In this paper a richer model, based on differential gene expression is introduced to control developmental processes in an artificial evolutionary system. Differential gene expression is used to get different cell types and to modulate cell division and cell death. One of the advantages using developmental processes in evolutionary systems is the reduction of the information needed in the genome to encode e.g. shapes or cell types which results in better scaling behavior of the system. My result showed that the shaping of multicellular organisms in 3d is possible with the proposed system.

1 Introduction

In the field of artificial evolution, current research tries to imitate biological concepts of evolution and development to simulate or build artificial organisms. This paper reports on a biologically inspired model that has been used to evolve 3d shapes of simulated, multicellular organisms. The model is based on cell-cell interactions which allow the regulation of gene expression in a specific and concentration dependent way.

As biological organisms are the product of the interplay of genetics, developmental processes and evolution [10, 13], I included several developmental processes, such as cell division, cell death and cell differentiation in the proposed artificial evolutionary system (AES). Even though this makes the whole approach more complex, there are several good reasons to include developmental processes in the AES:

First of all, developmental processes can reduce the information in the genome which is needed to encode a body shape or a neural network. This allows for example to make the length of the genome independent of the number of the cells in an organisms which results in a better scaling behavior, when the number of cells increases. This is especially important in three dimensional system. Second, developmental processes can take advantage of the possibilities of self-organization of a multicomponent system. In our case, the type of the artificial cells is such an emergent property. Cell types are not pre-specified, but a result of intercellular communication. Third, as every cell contains the same genome, an approach with developmental processes is conceptually much closer to the principle of parallel distributed information processing (in this case on the level of genes). This is important, if one wants to distribute the simulation on several computers or processors. Fourth, systems with developmental processes have an inherent stability. An example of this is cell growth: although every cell has the possibility to choose randomly a free place around the six next neighboring places, the emerging shapes are rather similar (see 8). Fifth, from a biological point of view, AES with developmental processes have much more biological appeal and allow therefore a comparison with biological data, which can often be very useful and inspiring.

In the next section I discuss the related

work on combining developmental processes with evolutionary computing methods to evolve simulated or real world autonomous agents. In section three the used biological concepts are explained and in section four the implementation of these concepts are described. Results are presented in section five and in the last section I discuss the advantages and disadvantages of the proposed approach.

2 Related Work

Babloyantz and Hiernaux [1] made a model of gene regulation and cell differentiation which was based on the operon model of gene regulation. They implemented the chemical reactions as ordinary differential equation and chose the parameters of these equations from the biological data of the bacteria Escherichia coli. The model was restricted to one cell. Fleischer and Barr [12] used a genetic encoding (hand coded) to specify the developmental processes by means of ordinary differential equations which were coupled with if-clauses to allow for differential gene expression. While from a biological perspective this approach is highly fruitful it is not suitable for autonomous agents because of the high computational costs. Stork et al. [28] developed a system to evolve artificial networks. They introduced a structured genome which consists of two types of genes, control genes (also called enhancers) and structural genes. The activities of the different genes are directly encoded in an activity table where the state of each gene is determined genetically. Belew [2] used a grammar to simulate developmental processes. His scheme is context sensitive, but it is restricted to pre-specified neural network topologies. Gruau and Whitley [14] encoded the developmental process as a grammar tree. In this approach the cells inherit their connections and no context sensitive development is possible. Vaario [29] proposed a grammar-based simulation tool, in which the developmental process is described by a set of rules. A rule-based system bears the danger that certain properties of the system are defined by the designer rather than being emergent from the developmental process. Nolfi [24] and Cangelosi et al. [4] proposed a developmental model for neural networks based on cell division and cell migration. The major flaw of

this approach is that the number of the genes in the genome grows with the number of neurons which leads to a bad scaling behavior. Kitano [17, 18] developed a model based on a genetic algorithm to simulate the metabolism of cells, cell division and neurogenesis. The genome encodes metabolic rules which describe chemical reactions in a cell. These rules are linked to ordinary differential equations to calculate the changes of all the possible substances. Also diffusion and active transport of these substances are implemented. In addition a model of neurogenesis is included which is based on special growth factors. Simple cell differentiation of cells were reported (at least two different types of cells), where different substances are marks for the cell's state. Even neural networks were evolved, but to which no function could be assigned. In contrast to our approach, Kitano used no differential gene expression and in his system no forms of cell clusters evolved. Michel and Biondi [23] introduced a developmental model which uses morphogenetic mechanisms to evolve neural control structures for autonomous agents. As this model does not describe any mechanisms about cell differentiation, it is not clear how different cells can result. Sims [27] described a system for the evolution of artificial creatures that compete in a physically realistic simulation of a three-dimensional artificial world. Dellaert and Beer [9] proposed a model based on Boolean networks to evolve autonomous agents in two dimensions. They use a genetic algorithm to specify boolean functions which depend on different cell products which are able to activate a gene. If a gene is activated one or two different substances are produced. Mechanisms of cell differentiation like cell induction and symmetry breaking are included. Their system was able to evolve simple autonomous agents. In this approach the developmental process was not modulated by specific and concentration dependent gene regulation mechanisms.

3 The Used Biological Concepts

The study of developmental biology has led to the identification of many mechanisms for morphogenesis and development. The following mechanisms are generally accepted to be important for development in biological systems:

- cell differentiation (cell lineage and cell-cell interactions)

- cell division [10, 13]

- cell death [10, 13]

- positional information by morphogenetic gradients [33]

These mechanisms will be shortly described in the next section.

3.1 Gene Regulation

In living organisms all somatic cells contain the same genome (with a few exceptions, e.g. as some blood cells (lymphocytes)). The differences between the cells are emergent and due to regulatory mechanisms which can turn genes on or off. Two cells are different, if they have different subsets of active genes. In other words, one can define a cell type as a set of cells with the same gene activity pattern [20, 13].

The activity of a gene is regulated by special regions in the genome, the regulatory units [21, 26]. Two types of regulatory elements affect the activity of a gene. The first group consists of the so-called regulatory units or cis-regulators which represent specific DNA regions. The other group are the transcription factors or trans-regulators which are soluble and affect the activity of a gene by binding on a cis-element of that gene. (See Figure 1).

Figure 1: Cis and trans regulatory units are schematically shown. The concentration of the trans regulators (transcription factors) at the cis regulators (regulatory units) and the affinity between the regulators determine the activity of the gene.

In prokaryotes (simple unicellular organisms such as bacteria) several genes can be under the control of one single cis regulator. In cells of eukaryotes (more complicated organisms such as plants or vertebrates) typically several cis regulators regulate one single gene.

The activity of a gene depends on the following factors

1. the affinity of the cis- and trans regulators [26]

2. the concentration of trans-regulators at the genome [13]

3. the interactions of all the proteins which are necessary for the transcription of a gene by polymerases [13][p.380]

4. autocatalytic regulation of the gene once it is activated

3.2 Cell division and Cell Death

The duration of cell division varies among different cell types: Neurons and muscle cells do not divide anymore, whereas gut or blood cells divide all the time. These differences are due to different regulatory mechanisms which control cell division. In cell cultures cells stop to divide, if they have contact with each other (contact inhibition). Another mechanism is the regulation of cell proliferation by growth factors. To these belong several hormones like steroid hormones (such as progesteron which has an effect on nuclear receptors), protein hormones like insuline, nerve growth factors which influence the cell via a surface receptor on the cell membrane or mediators like prostaglandines. An overview on how cells division is regulated, is given in figure 2 [13].

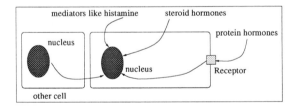

Figure 2: Overview of the possible influences on how cell division by different substances.

There exist physiological mechanisms in the cell which can cause programmed cell death by activating special genes [10, 13]. Programmed cell death is seen during many biological processes as development of the neural system [10], the gut, the limb buds, bones or lymphocytes. A well known example is the worm Caenorhabditis elegans in which many cells will die. In vertebrates cell death is used to shape certain body parts. Examples are the limbs in which cell death shapes the joints and separates fingers and toes [13][p.712]. But also in the nervous systems of mammals up to 70 percent of the cells die [10].

3.3 Cell Differentiation

Two cells are different, if they express different subsets of active genes in their genomes. Studies of biological cell differentiation are based on identification and characterization of differentiation markers, which often correspond to certain gene expressions [20].

Cell differentiation is based on two different mechanisms: cell lineage and cell induction. The first is an autonomous mechanism where cell differentiation depends on intracellular factors, which are unequally distributed in different cells [13].

With the second mechanism, cell induction, cells become different because they get different signaling from other cells. Developmental biologists talk of induction, if one embryonic region sends a signal to a a second embryonic region, which determines the fate of this second region [13][p.591].

3.4 Positional Information

Wolpert [31, 32, 33] proposed a mechanism, how cells are informed about their positions during development. An example of such a mechanism is a concentration gradient of a morphogen which every cell is able to read. The effect of a morphogen depends on the type of substance and the affinity between the substance and the cis-regulators. If these effects exceed a certain threshold, genes can be turned on or off. The existence of such morphogens is been established[20, 25]. Developmentally important substances from the mother are placed in the egg at the beginning of the development of the embryo. These substances are used to guide development in the early stages and are often also the base of symmetry breaking mechanisms to determine e.g. the body axis. These so called maternal effects are especially well studied in Drosophila [20]. An example of a morphogen is bicoid RNA, which is used in Drosophila to determine the anterior-posterior axe of the body during the very first stages of development [20, 25].

4 Implementation

4.1 Gene Regulation

To obtain cells which are able to differentiate, I introduced a set of regulatory mechanisms of gene expression in an artificial genome.

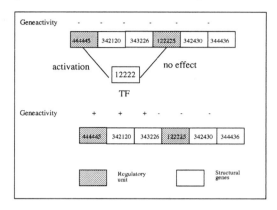

Figure 3: A transcription factor (TF) is compared to two regulatory units and the TF is only able to activate one if the affinity and the concentration are high enough.

In contrast to the usal genetic algorithms, a structured genome was used that contain two classes of genes: regulatory units and structural genes (See figure 1). The regulatory units are some kind of switches to turn on or off the genes they control. Structural genes encode for specific substances which are used to modulate developmental processes.

Every gene has the same length of n integers of which the last integer (in the following called marker) is used to indicate to which of the two gene classes a specific gene belongs. The possible values of the integers are taken from the set {0,1,2,3,4,5,6}. The first gene of the genome is assumed to be a regulatory unit. The following genes between the first gene and the marker 5 are per definition also regulatory units. All the genes between the marker 5 and the marker 6 are structural genes. The activity of the (these) structural gene(s) depend on the regulatory unit(s) directly adjacent to them. After the marker 6 is encountered the next marker 5 is searched and all genes between them are regulatory units which control the structural genes between the 5 and the next 6. This reading continues until all genes are classified. Several regulatory units can determine the activity of one or several structural genes. Figure 4 illustrates an example of a typical genome which is used in the AES.

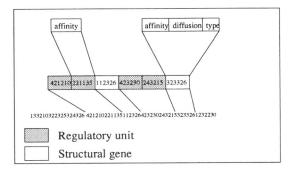

Figure 4: Some integers of the genes are used to encode substance classes and properties like the diffusion coefficient and the region where the affinity is calculated. Type is used to specify to which class a gene product belongs.

The activity of a structural gene is regulated in the following way. Every cell contains a list of transcription factors (TF) which influence its genome. The TF's as well as the regulatory units are implemented as strings of integers. The two strings are then compared: The first n (typically 6-8) integers of the string are used to calculate the affinity. As every string contains numbers out of the set $\{1,2,3,4\}$, the affinity is calculated in base 4. The total difference between the integers of the TF- and the regulator string represents the degree of affinity. As the difference can be negative as well as positive, the sign is used to determine the effect. A negative sign represents an inhibitory effect whereas a positive sign represents an activating effect. In a second step, also the concentration of the TF's is taken into account. A concentration is assigned to every TF. The product of the affinity and the concentration of every TF at a regulatory unit is calculated and the products summed. The same is repeated for every regulatory unit of a gene. The total sum is then put in a sigmoidal function and if a fixed threshold is exceeded, the gene is activated or inhibited (See equations 1,2,3).

$$r_j = \sum_{i=1}^{n} aff_i * conc_i \qquad (1)$$

$$a_k = \frac{1}{1 + exp^- (\sum_{j=1} r_j)} \qquad (2)$$

$$g_k = \begin{cases} -1.0 & : & a_k < 0.2 \\ 1.0 & : & a_k > 0.8 \\ 0.0 & : & otherwise \end{cases} \qquad (3)$$

- aff_i = affinity of the ith TF with the jth regulatory unit gene
- $conc_i$ = concentration of the ith TF
- r_j = activity of the jth regulatory unit of a structural gene
- a_k = total sum of the activities of all regulatory units of the kth gene
- g_k = activity of kth gene

4.2 Classes of Gene products

Depending on which structural gene is active, one of the following possibilities can occur:

1. A transcription factor is produced to regulate the gene activities.

2. A cell adhesion molecule (CAM) is produced to connect cells to each other, if on the other cell's surface is a CAM with a high enough affinity

3. A receptor is produced to regulate the communication between the cells.

4. A artificial function like cell division, cell death or searching can occur.

Which of these activities occur is determined by the first three integers of a structural gene (see fig 4).

4.3 Cell Differentiation

To simulate cell differentiation I implemented three different possible pathways to exchange information between cells. First, there are substances which do not leave the cell and which regulate the activity of its own gene. Second, there are substances which penetrate the cell wall and can reach all cells that are nearby. Third, there are specific receptors on the cell surface which can be stimulated by substances.

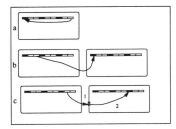

Figure 5: Intercellular gene regulation by activators and repressors.The following regulation scheme is implemented: a. intracellular regulation b. intercellular regulation c. The intercellular communication depends on a receptor (1), which sends an activating signal to a regulatory site (2), if the affinity between the receptor and the transcription factor is high enough.

If a transcription factor has a high enough affinity to the receptor, a gene or a group of genes is influenced as if the transcription factor would be at the genome. Only those cells which have a specific receptor on the cell surface will respond to a certain substance (Figure 5).

4.4 Positional Information

The mechanism of positional information is already implemented by the regulatory mechanisms mentioned above. TFs produced by a cell can diffuse to nearby cells. In this case, they could be called morphogens that may induce a change of the state of some genes in cells which can read this message. In my implementation a morphogen is just a kind of TF which is also represented as an integer string with an associated concentration. Note, that this is not a biologically realistic implementation, because TFs can usually not pass the cell membrane. One should note that this mechanism is not just a simple signaling, because the reading mechanism (the cis-regulators) is also controlled by the AES. Therefore the same gradient (same concentrations and the same substance) can have very different effects on different cells (See illustration in figure 7). Some examples of such effects are changes in cell type, cell division rate or motility. These basic developmental processes are in principle implemented the same way.

4.5 Classes of Gene Products and Functions of a Cell

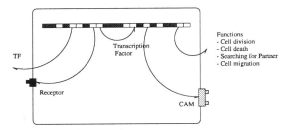

Figure 6: Overview on the products and functions of a cell in the AES.(The functions of the different substances are explained in the text).

The different active genes will determine which substances are produced in a cell. These substances are stored in lists for further use.

At this point of the development the artificial cells have a structured genome, a list which holds the activity of the genes (which can change dynamically) and different lists which represent different substance classes that are contained in the cell.

4.6 Evolution

The base of my AES is a genetic algorithm which changes randomly a population of 120 genomes. In our experiments I used n (usually 8) units which contained 2 regulatory units for 2 structural genes to control the shaping of the multicellular organisms. As genetic operators I used one-point cross over and mutation.

5   Results

5.1 Cell Differentiation

In our AES the concentrations of the morphogens are read by the cells. Depending on which regulatory units are activated, the same morphogen can have different effects. In figure 7 some examples of different effects of the same morphogen are shown. The reading mechanisms (the regulatory units) vary in their affinity, which explains the different effects on the different cells.

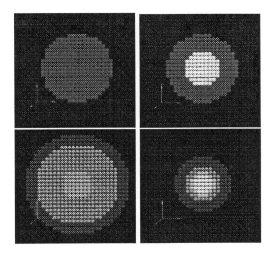

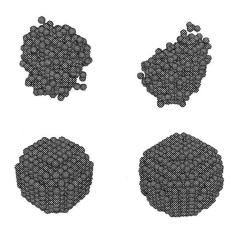

Figure 7: In the middle of a plane of cells a morphogenetic source is put and the cells read the concentration of the morphogen. Different cells have different gene activity patterns. Note that depending on the cell, the same morphogen can have different effects.

Figure 8: The two upper cell clusters are the result of random cell growth. The two lower cell clusters emerged if in addition one morphogen is allowed to modulate the growth (See text for more details).

5.2 Growth and Forms

In Drosophila the substance bicoid RNA acts as a morphogen to determine the anterior-posterior axis of the body. The genomes are reading the concentration of this morphogen and genes are activated in a specific and concentration dependent way. In analogy to these facts the AES has the possibility to put morphogens at different places in a grid. The different gradients which are possibly built up are a sort of chemical coordinate system which is read by the cells and will inform them of their position by activating different genes. In this way it is possible to guide the growth of cells, because once the concentration of a substance which activates the cell division gene drops below a certain threshold , growth will stop. In figure 8 the modulating effect of morphogen gradients on a random growth process with contact inhibition is illustrated. During the implemented cell growth, each cell looks for a free place in the next 6 neighbors and chooses one randomly. If there is no empty neighbor hood around a cell, its division is inhibited (contact inhibition). Note that during a random growth process the emergent forms are rather different (See upper part of figure 8). A morphogen producing cell is positioned in the middle of the grid, which activates cell division. If the influence of the concentration of the morphogen and the affinity goes below a threshold, the cells stop to divide. Now, the structure of the cell cluster is smoothed out and becomes independent of the randomness of the cell division. The size of the balls is the result of the different concentration and the different diffusion properties of the morphogen, as well as the properties of the reading mechanism of the genes (cis-regulators).

5.3 Development of bilateral shapes

First, the program generates the environment and a population of genomes. One cell is positioned in the middle of a 3d grid of typically 30x30x30 sites. This grid represents the environment of the cells and is used to position cells and cell products in the environment. Three sources of different morphogens are positioned on 3 different axes in space with varying distances to the first cell. These sources produce morphogens which diffuse into the environment. The cells are able to read and interpret these gradients with the effect that possibly different genes are expressed. Also cell induction as another mechanism of cell differentiation is used. The cells can synthesize transcription factors, which influence the gene activities of other cells.

The fitness function was depended on the number of cells and their position with respect to the x-axis.

1.

$$\text{fitness} = \max - |(\max - n)| \qquad (4)$$

max = cell number which is assumed optimal

n = actual cell number after the cell divisions have stopped

2. for every existing cell the fitness was increased, if the cell had a symmetrical counterpart at the other side of the x-axis. After the number of cells stopped to increase, the fitness of the organisms was evaluated. If the number of cells was bigger than a predefined number of cells, the fitness was put to 0.0.

Figure 9: Several examples of evolved forms. The fitness functions only evaluated the number of cells and the bilaterality of the found organisms.

6   Discussion

As the number of genes in the genome is insufficient to specify precisely every cell, epigenetic processes with their combinatorial expression of sets of genes are used in Nature to specify the cells [15]. Therefore, I proposed in this work that biological ideas are useful and applicable to the field of artificial evolution. Implementing important developmental processes we showed that cell growth, cell differentiation and the development of shapes of simple organisms are in the reach of this AES.

In contrast to less biological approaches the following points are noteworthy:

- as in real cells every artificial cell contains the same genetic information

- differential gene expression allows the modulation of developmental processes such as cell division, cell death and shaping of an organism.

- epigenetic processes allow to reduce the length of the genome. Especially important is the fact that the genome will not necessarily grow, if the number of cells is larger.

- no direct encoding of genetic information for cell types, cell position or links to other cells, because these things are emergent properties of epigenetic processes

The proposed AES was able to evolve three dimensional shapes for simulated, multicellular organisms. With the proposed AES a step towards the following scientific goals is made:

- the AES evolves plans of three dimensional robots which can be used to produce real world robots

- the investigation of the co-evolution of the morphology (shape) and its neural control structures for 3d, multicellular organisms. It was shown that also neural networks for real world robots can be evolved by the same type of AES [11].

- if one investigates complex systems one tries to understand how simple parts are able to build more complex wholes. In our specific case we ask: What should a singele cell be able to do, if many cells should be able to develop a more complex organism?

- one of the main problems of every artificial evolutionary system is the evolvability.

Which capabilities have to be introduced in an AES that systems of increasing complexity can be evolved? (Chaitin[5] gives a definition of complexity).

- analysis of the simulator to explore its limits. We will analyze statistically our AES and test the different results with different initializations of the random generator and the different possibilities of the genetic operators which can be introduced if one uses structured genomes. Interchanging and duplicating genetic material seems very promising to us, especially as these operators change possible interactions between cells.

7 Acknowledgements

References

[1] Agnesa Babloyantz and J. Hiernaux. Models for positional information and positional differentiation. *Proceedings of the National Academy of Science, USA*, 71(4):1530–1533, 1974.

[2] Richard K. Belew. Interposing an ontogenic model between genetic algorithms and neural networks. In *Advances in neural Information Processing Systems (NIPS),S.J. Hanson and J.D. Cowan and C.L.Giles,Morgan Kauffman:San Mate,1993*, 1993.

[3] Rodney Brooks and Pattie Maes, editors. *Artificial Life IV: Proceedings of the Workshop on Artificial Life*, Cambridge, MA, 1994. MIT Press. Workshop held at the MIT.

[4] Angelo Cangelosi, Domenico Parisi, and Stefano Nolfi. Cell division and migration in a 'genotype' for neural networks. *Network*, 5:497–515, 1994.

[5] Gregory J. Chaitin. Randomness and mathematical proof. *Scientific Americain*, 232(5):47–58, 1975.

[6] Frank Dellaert and Randall D. Beer. A developmental model for the evolution of complete autonomous agents. In [22], pages 393–401, 1996.

[7] Gerald M. Edelman. *Topobiology:An Introduction to Molecular Embryology*. New York:Basic Books, 1989.

[8] Peter Eggenberger. Cell interactions for development in evolutionary robotics. In [22], pages 440–448, 1996.

[9] Kurt Fleischer and Alan H. Barr. A simulation testbed for the study of multicellular development: The multiple mechanisms of morphogenesis. In [19], pages 389–416, 1992.

[10] Scott F. Gilbert. *Developmental Biology*. Massachusetts: Sinauer Associates, Inc, 1994.

[11] Frederic Gruau and D. Whitley. The cellular developmental of neural networks: the interaction of learning and evolution. Technical Report 93-04, Laboratoire de l'Informatique du Parallélisme, Ecole Normale Supérieure de Lyon, France, 1993.

[12] Eric R. Kandel, James H. Schwartz, and Thomas M. Jessell. *Essentials of Neural Science and Behavior*. Appleton & Lange, 1995.

[13] Hiroaki Kitano. Evolution of metabolism for morphogenesis. In Rodney A. Brooks and Pattie Maes, editors, [3], pages 49–58, 1994.

[14] Hiroaki Kitano. A simple model of neurogenesis and cell differentiation based on evolutionary large-scale chaos. *Artificial Life*, 2:79–99, 1995.

[15] Christopher G. Langton, editor. *Artificial Life III: Proceedings of the Workshop on Artificial Life*, Reading, MA, 1994. Addison-Wesley. Workshop held June, 1992 in Santa Fe, New Mexico.

[16] Peter A. Lawrence. *The making of a fly: The genetics of animal design*. Blackwell Scientific Publications, 1992.

[17] Benjamin Lewin. *Genes V*. Oxford University Press, 1994.

[18] Pattie Maes, Maja J. Mataric, Jean-Arcady Meyer, Jordan Pollack, and Stewart W. Wilson, editors. *From animals to animats 4: Proceedings of the fourth international conference on simulation of adaptive behavior*. MIT Press, 1996.

[19] Olivier Michel and Joelle Bondi. From the chromosome to the neural network. In *Proceedings of the interantioal conference on artificial Neural Networks and Genetic Algorithms (ICANNA'95)*, 1995.

[20] Stefano Nolfi, Dario Floreano, Orazio Miglino, and Francesco Mondada. How to evolve autonomous robots: Different approaches in evolutionary robotics. In P. Meas R. A. Brooks, editor, *Artificial Life IV*. Cambridge, MA: MIT Press, 1994.

[21] Christiane Nüsslein-Volhard. Gradients that organize embryo development. *Scientific Americain*, 275:38–43, August 1996.

[22] Mark Ptashne. *A Genetic Switch. Phage lambda and Higher Organisms*. Cell Press and Blackwell Scientific Publications, 1992.

[23] Karl Sims. Evolving 3d morphology and behavior by competition. *Artificial Life*, 1:353–372, 1995.

[24] David G. Stork, Bernie Jackson, and Scott Walter. Non-optimality via pre-adaptation in simple neural systems. In *Paper presented at the Artifical Life II,Santa Fe, Mexico*, 1992.

[25] Jari Vaario. Modelling adaptive self-organization. In *Proceedings of the Fourth International Workshop on the Synthesis of Living Systems*, 1994.

[26] Lewis Wolpert. Positional information and pattern formation. *Curr. Top. Dev. Biol.*, 6:183–224, 1971.

[27] Lewis Wolpert. Pattern formation in biological development. *Sci. Am.*, 239(4):124–137, 1978.

[28] Lewis Wolpert. Positional information revisited. *Development*, (suppl.):3–12, 1989.

Formation of Neural Structures

Jari Vaario,* Akira Onitsuka,† and Katsuo Shimohara
ATR Human Information Processing Laboratories
2-2 Hikari-dai, Seika-cho, Soraku-gun, Kyoto 619-02, JAPAN
E-mail: {jari,xoni,katsu}@hip.atr.co.jp

Abstract

In this paper a new method for modeling the growth of neural structures is proposed. The motive of this research is to explore the possibilities for biologically plausible neural growth, and to study how neural based systems could be closely embodied into the environment where they exist. As a result of this research we have found a simple method based on diffusion field modeling to be able to control neural growth together with genetic factors. The simulation results show how neural structures are capable of creating a meaningful network to control the simple behaviors of an artificial creature in a simulated world. The environment control reduces the need for genetic control factors thereby providing faster evolution with a simple genetic coding.

1 Introduction

The modeling of growing neural structures has long been a subject of interest for biologists [3, 2]. However, the growth models of neural structures could also make interesting contributions to the engineering field.

In this paper we explore the possibilities for modelling biologically inspired neural structures through growth for engineering applications. Thus the motive is twofold: contributing to biological neural models, and contributing to the engineering field. As it is shown, the problem faced here, in the first step, is to be sufficiently detailed to contribute something to the former goal, and on the other hand to have an engineering application where the merit of the method is clearly visible.

In the paper we first describe the modeling method based on modeling diffusion field directed growth. This method is extended into three-dimensional neural structures with the capability of propagating signals. This far the results are biologically oriented. In the next step these structures are used for modeling a whole robot nervous system to direct simple behaviors in the environment. From the engineering point of view the created

behaviors could have been done much more easily by some other method, but from the research perspective the method used is unique for creating biologically plausible control structures.

This is believed to be the first research of its kind to model neural structures in sufficient biological detail to control in real-time the behavior of artificial creatures. In fact, as it is shown, one must model a whole creature in order to grow meaningful neural structures [15]. An organism, and especially its neural structure, is an assimilation to the environment in which it is living [10].

The first preliminary results were reported in [8] for general tree dimensional structures and in [7] for neural structures to control light seeking behavior. Here the new results include the avoidance behavior as well as behaviorial evolution. The earlier work [13, 12] reports similar behavior generation by using a production rule approach.

First the background of the research is explained with a discussion of the merits of modeling the growth process, and this is followed by a detailed description of the modeling method itself. The behavior generated by the neural structures is the result of evolution. The growth of neural structures and the propagation of neural signals are described in detail within an example environment. The final conclusion summarizes the future direction of the research.

2 Background

2.1 Diffusion Limited Aggregation

Diffusion based modeling has been used mainly for bacteria modeling. One of these models is called Diffusion Limited Aggregation (DLA) [11].

In aggregation simulation a cell is placed on a two-dimensional grid of chemical concentrations ($C_{(x,y)}$) occupying one site (●). The probability that this cell will be divided to another cell surrounding this cell (○) is calculated as follows (illustrated in Figure 1).

$$p((x,y) \in \circ \to \bullet) = \frac{(C_{x,y})^\eta}{\sum_{(i,j) \in \circ}(C_{i,j})^\eta} \qquad (1)$$

where '$(x,y) \in \circ \to \bullet$' represents the condition that an

---

*Also Nara Women's University, Department of Information and Computer Sciences, jari@ics.nara-wu.ac.jp
†Also Kobe University, Graduate School

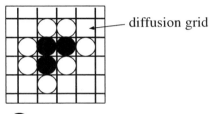

: an existing cell

: a possible location of a new cell

Figure 1: An illustration of the two-dimensional DLA model. The propabilities of $p(x, y) \in \circ \rightarrow \bullet$ are calculated by Eq. 1.

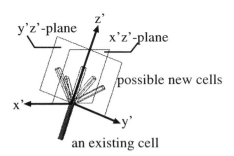

Figure 2: An illustration of the three-dimensional DLA model. Now new cells (represented by stripes instead of boxes) can have five possible locations with probabilities calculated similar to the two-dimensional DLA model.

unoccupied site at the point (x, y) is changed to a cell of the organism, and η represents the relation between the local environment and the growth probability.

This is extended into a three-dimensional DLA model as shown in Figure 2.

2.1.1 Diffusion simulation

Generally it is assumed that the speed of the diffusion process in the environment, described by Eq.(2), is very fast compared to that of the growth process of an organism. According to the assumption, the environment (concentration field) will become a steady state, *i.e.*, the left side of Eq.(2) is equal to zero. Thus, the distribution of the concentration is described by Eq.(3) , which is called the homogeneous Laplace equation [1].

$$\frac{dC}{dt} = D \nabla^2 C \tag{2}$$

$$\nabla^2 C = \frac{\partial^2 C}{\partial x^2} + \frac{\partial^2 C}{\partial y^2} + \frac{\partial^2 C}{\partial z^2} = 0 \tag{3}$$

where D represents the diffusion coefficient, and $C = C(t, x, y, z)$ represents the concentration value of a substance at the point (x, y, z) of the environment at time t.

The algorithm for calculating the concentration value is approximated as follows.

$$
\begin{aligned}
C_{i,j,k} &= (C_{i-1,j,k} + C_{i+1,j,k} + C_{i,j-1,k} + C_{i,j+1,k} + \\
&\quad C_{i,j,k-1} + C_{i,j,k+1})/6 \tag{4}
\end{aligned}
$$

The diffusion is calculated as a simple average value of surrounding cells, and this calculation is repeated until the difference with the previous value is less than ε (Eq 5).

$$\max_{i,j,k} |C_{i,j,k}^{t+1} - C_{i,j,k}^t| < \varepsilon \tag{5}$$

2.1.2 Properties

The DLA model is most suitable for modeling unicellular organisms. There is no direct concept for appling this to multicellular organisms. However, it is obvious that the same principle of deciding the growth direction could easily be used for modeling various growth patterns.

An interesting feature of DLA models is the capability of controlling the branching structure by a single parameter (η in Eq. 1). This is illustrated in Figure 3 in a 2D and 3D space.

2.2 Growing Neural Network Models

The interest in modeling growing neural networks has mainly been based on biological motivations: to imitate and model the biological growth of neural structures. Several methods have been proposed [6, 9]. Most of them are based on plain genetic controllability, which is not so biologically plausible.

We, however, would like to argue here that there might be an engineering advantage in modeling the growth process as a function of environment. This merit comes from reducing the genetic factors and letting the environmental factors direct the growth.

This could be considered in two parts: first, the environment is stable, but the genetic information changes, and, second, the genetic information is stable, but the environment changes.

In the former case, it is obvious that some common control factors could be taken care of by the environment. These factors should always be the same in spite of the genetic information that is used. Thus including these into the genetic information could only be counterproductive, because they are not evolvable information, but part of the physical environment. We have to make a clear distinction between what is evolvable matter, and what should be considered as physical laws.

The latter case indicates the situation where the same genetic information produces different neural structures when the environment changes. In other words, if this kind of neural structure is viable, it indicates that the

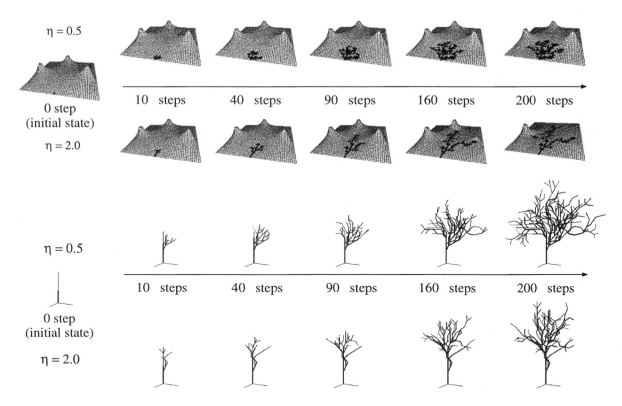

Figure 3: The effect of the η parameter for the branching of DLA structures in a 2D and 3D space.

structure is capable of adapting during the growth process, ie., to adapt without genetic modifications. This leads to the evolution of adaptable neural structures, compared to a system where a genetic adaptation is always required for any environmental change.

Thus, by modeling the growth process, we will have a simpler genetic code to be evolved, and we will have the evolution of adaptable neural structures. In addition, one can consider the situation of mutual competition between neural connections and a repairing mechanism for damaged connections.

3 Modeling Method

In the following the neural, creature, and evolution models are explained in detail.

3.1 Neural dynamics

Neural dynamics are divided into the growth of connections, signal propagation through connections, and learnability.

3.1.1 Connection growth

The fundamental feature of the modeling method is to grow the connection in the diffusion field. The growth is modeled based on the previously described DLA method. The location of the next cellular element is determined

by the probabilities. The probability to create a new element around the ($k = \{Ri = Right, L = Left, T = Top, B = Bottom, F = Front, Re = Rear\}$) ith element will be calculated by Eq. 6 with various diffusion sources ($j = \{c_0, ..., c_n\}$).

$$p_k = \frac{\sum_j^{\{c_0,...,c_n\}} (\mid \alpha_i^j \mid (C_k^j)^\eta}{\sum_l^{\{Ri,L,T,B,F,Re\}} (\sum_j^{\{c_0,...,c_n\}} \mid \alpha_i^j \mid C_l^j)^\eta} \qquad (6)$$

The α^j value is used to control the growth for a particular diffusion source. This is like determining how much sensitivity it has for each diffusion source. The value itself is modified by the enforcement mechanism explained later in connection with learning.

The method also implies that the location of the cellular element is set to zero value. This provides the competition between several cellular elements, that is connections, for the diffusion matter. A connection receiving more diffusion matter will be enforced to grow, and a connection not receiving matter will be depressed. In order to create biologically plausible growth patterns, the connections not capable of receiving diffusion matter will starve (controlled by α^j), and will gradually be removed (if $\sum_j^{\{c_0,....,c_n\}} < \alpha_{remove}$). This gives more space for other connections to grow and modify themselves later.

The first connections are targeting the same diffusion sources. The result is a very dense network of connections. However, when the network becomes capable of controlling the behavior of the whole creature, some connections will be enforced while others will be de-enforced (controlled by modifying the α^j value). The details of this mechanism will be explained later with a simulation example.

3.1.2 Signal propagation

Figure 4 gives an overview of neurons consisting of several cellular elements. The signal propagation is illustrated as dendrites receiving chemicals at their tip to be propagated toward the nucleus, and furthermore via axons out as chemicals. Thus the neural structure forms a 'short cut' for chemicals to be diffused (called propagation) from place 'A' to place 'B'.

The actual signal is calculated according to Eq. 7.

$$S_i = \sum_{j}^{\{sen_0,\ldots,sen_n\}} (\text{sign}(\alpha_i^j) \times \sum_{1}^{\{Ri,L,T,B,F,Re\}} (C_1^j)) \quad (7)$$

Thus the signal is either negative or positive depending on the sign of α_i^j ($j = \{sensor_0, ..., sensor_n\}$). The strength of the signal is not modified at the dendrite side, but at the axon side.

$$S_k = \sum_i (\alpha_i^k \times S_i \times \frac{C_i^k}{C_{source}^k}) \quad (8)$$

This signal is used to calculate the motor activity. The value is over all neuron tips (i) depending on the α_i^k value ($k = \{motor_0, motor_1\}$). The latter part ($\frac{C_i^k}{C_{source}^k}$) causes the signal to become greater when the distance to the motor source is smaller, ie., when the distance is zero then $C_i^k = C_{source}^k$, and zero if the distance is too long.

The speed of the signal propagation is thought to be fast, but accompanied by a slight reduction of the signal strength. The reduction is 1% per one cellular element in the axon path. This signal dumping effect was introduced for biological plausibility and it resulted in a penalty for longer connections.

The excitory and inhibitory dendrites are modeled so as to give each neuron two initial dendrites with each separately defined as an excitory or inhibitory dendrite (controlled by $\text{sign}(\alpha) = \{+, -\}$, respectively). This default assignment as an excitory or inhibitory type is assumed to come from genetic information.

The signals are summed by dendrites at each joining element. For the nucleus two kinds of function are used (once again assumed to be determined by genetic information): the *transparency* function ($S = S'$) and *inversion* function ($S = S' / | S' | \times 100/e^{(|S'|/10)}$). The shape of the functions is visible in Figure 4.

The former simply passes the signal as it is without doing any processing on it. The latter inverts low signals to

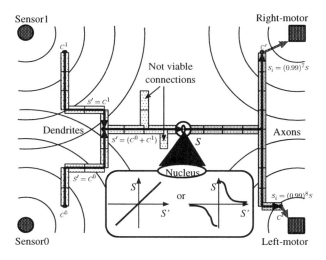

Figure 4: A model of neurons consisting of cellular elements.

high signals, and vice versa high signals to low signals. It would be easy to modify the simulation to have a more biologically plausible function here, but these were considered to be sufficient.

3.1.3 Learnability

The learnability of the structures is partly determined by the number and the length of the connections (signal dump). In addition, a local reinforcement learning is used. This reinforcement ($\alpha_i^{\{j,k\}} = \alpha_i^{\{j,k\}} + \Delta_i$) is calculated according to Eq. 9.

This also affects the possibility of the connection growing further and the viability of the connection. Only at the axon side the signal propagation is affected by increasing or decreasing the signal throughput.

$$\Delta_i = \beta \frac{C_i^{\{j,k\}}}{C_{source}^{\{j,k\}}} \quad (9)$$

The β value is determined for each neuron by its genetic information. Table 1 summarizes the β values used. The basic idea is to let evolution select one type, and then to use these values.

For example, let's take a neuron with evaluation type 1-1. If the signal increases from the previous value, this is interpreted by the neuron as a positive result and a reward is given. However, if the signal decreases, a penalty is given because the Δ value becomes negative. Note that it is impossible to say how these values are mapped to the global behaviors because this depends also on where the connections are formed.

| signal | β reinforcement | | | |
change	$1-1$	$1-2$	$2-1$	$2-2$
increase	β_1	$\frac{1}{2}\beta_1$	$-\frac{1}{4}\beta_1$	$-\beta_1$
equal	$\frac{1}{2}\beta_1$	0	0	$-\frac{1}{2}\beta_1$
decrease	$-\beta_1$	$-\frac{1}{4}\beta_1$	$\frac{1}{2}\beta_1$	$-\beta_1$

Table 1: The possible reinforcement parameters.

3.2 Creature: Between Internal and External Worlds

Figure 5 gives an overview of a model consisting of the internal world of a creature ('brain') and the external world ('environment') mapped through the physical dimensions ('body'). The mapping happens through sensors and motors, so the locations are given in this research.

3.2.1 Sensor model

The stimulus at each sensor (j) from the light sources (m) is calculated by Eq. 10.

$$Stimulus_j = \sum_m (I_m \times cos\Theta_{jm} \times \frac{D_{max} - D_{jm}}{D_{max}}) \quad (10)$$

The angle between sensor and light source (Θ_{jm}) is restricted to the sensing angle ($-\Theta_{max}\ldots\Theta_{max}$), and the distance ($D_{jm}$) is restricted to the maximum sensing distance (D_{max}). The light insensitivity ($I_m = 100$) will give $Stimulus_j\ approx 100$ in front of the light and after the distance D_{max} a zero value.

The second possible sensor was for obstacles. This proximity sensor (a whisker) was calculated by exploring a set of 21 points placed in a triangle in front of it [5]. The $Stimulus_j$ value varies between 0 and 100 with 0 meaning no obstacles, and 100 meaning an obstacle occupying all 21 points.

The $Stimulus_j$ value is used to generate the diffusion source inside the internal world (Eq. 11).

$$C^j = A_1(1 + A_2 \times Stimulus_j) \quad (11)$$

where A_1 and A_2 are constant. Note that each sensor generates its own diffusion matter. Thus the diffusion calculation should be done for each type.

3.2.2 Motor model

The motor ($k = \{motor_0, motor_1\}$) generates a velocity based on the signal it receives.

$$V_k = A \times S_k, \quad (12)$$

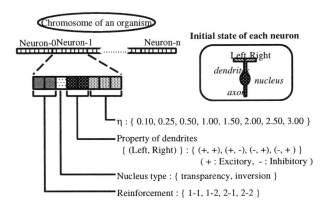

Figure 6: The summary of genetic information used.

where A is a scaling constant and S_k is the propagated signal by Eq. 8. The direction of the creature is determined by the difference of the velocity of the two motors used.

The motor also generates a diffusion field independent to the environment. This is defined as $C^k = A_1$. This is used to attract axons.

3.3 Evolution parameters

In relation to the creature model, the genetic code and fitness calculation must be given for the evolution.

3.3.1 Genetic coding

The genetic code was compressed into five neurons with each having eight bits of code. The necessary information for the neural structures was defined as follows.

1. Reinforcement: the set of β values shown in Table 1.

2. Nucleus type: whether the nucleus processing is according to the transparency or inversion function.

3. Type of dendrites: what are the dendrite types (excitory + or inhibitory −).

4. Connectivity parameter: the degree of 'hairiness' of the neuron.

Figure 6 summarizes the information included in code.

3.3.2 Fitness calculation

Fitness for the creatures is evaluated by

$$f = \sum_{step}^{end} (\mid V_{step} \mid \times(1 - \sqrt{\mid \Delta v_{step} \mid})) \quad (13)$$

where V is a measure of the average rotation speed of the two wheels, and Δv is the algebraic difference between the signed speed values of the wheels [4].

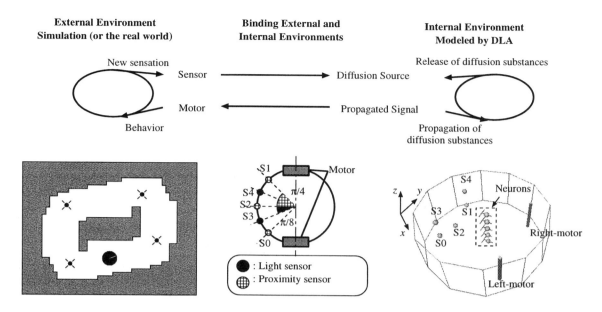

Figure 5: The relation between external and internal worlds.

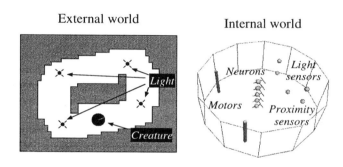

Figure 7: The initial settings of external and internal environments.

4 Results

The simulations were done with an internal world set to consist of five initial neurons, five sensors (two for light and three for avoidance), and two motors. The size of the diffusion grid was $16 \times 26 \times 12$. The external world was set to consist of four lights and several walls capable of restricting the visibility of lights. These settings are visualized in Figure 7.

The aim was to find a neural structure capable of navigating from one light to the other and to avoid walls. Although the task sounds moderate, the challenge is to grow a proper neural structure to go toward lights and at the same time to avoid obstacles.

4.1 Evolution

The evolution of creatures was done using a population of 12 creatures. The roulette selection mechanism was used for two point cross-over operations. Teh mutation rate was set to one bit per generation. The task was defined so that reaching a light was rewarded by 100 units for survival and collisions were penalized by 10 units.

In 12 generations, the evolution produced the optimum creature for navigating in the given environment from one light to the other while avoiding the walls. The parameters for the neurons are summarized in Table 2.

neuron	nucleus	dendrites	η	β
n_0	transparency	+ & +	0.1	1-1
n_1	transparency	− & +	3.0	1-1
n_2	transparency	+ & +	3.0	1-1
n_3	transparency	− & +	3.0	1-1
n_4	transparency	+ & +	3.0	1-1

Table 2: Summary of the evolutionary found neuron parameters.

The result was surprisingly similar neuron parameters. All nucleus functions became transparent, and all reinforcement styles were the same. Although this result requires further analysis, in the following the neural dynamics for these formed neural structures are given.

4.2 Growth of connections

The growth of connections is shown in Figure 8. Each connection is given separately.

4.3 Generated behavior

The above described neural structure is capable of directing the behavior shown in Figure 9. Note that when

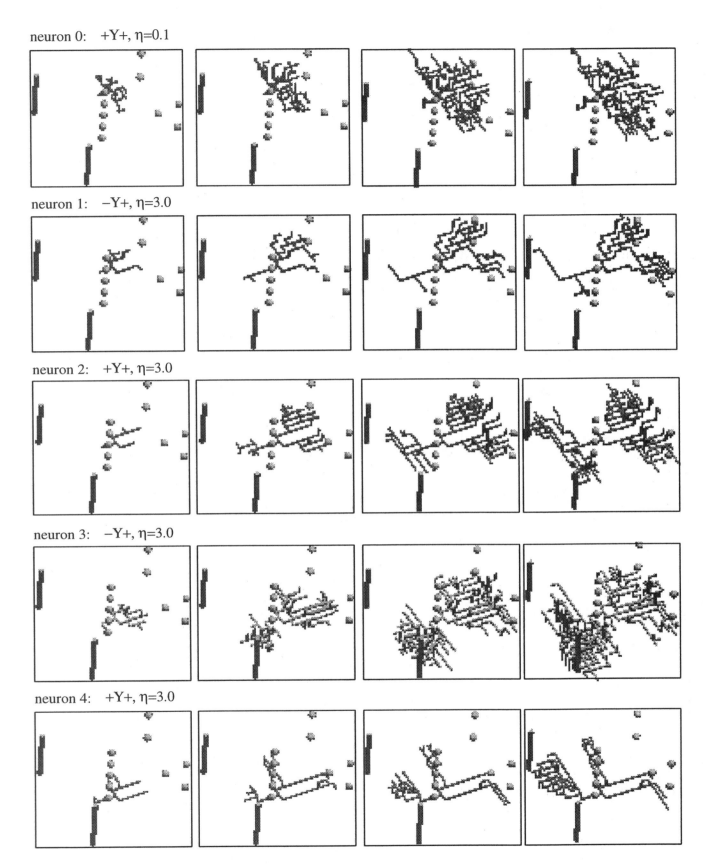

neuron 0:   +Y+, η=0.1

neuron 1:   −Y+, η=3.0

neuron 2:   +Y+, η=3.0

neuron 3:   −Y+, η=3.0

neuron 4:   +Y+, η=3.0

Figure 8: The growth of connections for five neurons.

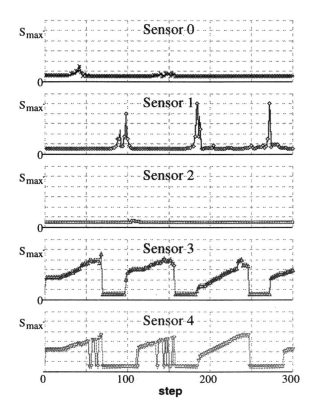

Figure 10: The sensor activity. Sensors from zero to two are proximity sensors, and three and four are light sensors.

the light is reached it will turn off. Thus the next light will start to attract the creature.

4.4 Analysis of signal activities

In the following a detailed analysis of signal activity in the neural structure is given.

First, the sensor activity is shown in Figure 10. The sensors from zero to two are proximity sensors (whiskers), and three and four are light sensors. The activity is plotted with a time scale. Compared to the created behavior shown in Figure 9 one can easily observe the change of light activity and time when the creature is approaching the walls.

To understand the generated neuron activity one should follow the connections from sensors to neurons. The logical network is shown in Figure 11 to help in this task (cf. to the genetic information for the neurons shown in Table 2).

In this particular case the neural structure didn't change for this logical connectivity, although in some other case this could have happened. Once formed, the structure was quite stable.

One can observe that neuron n_0 has no connections to motors. Thus it does not participate in controlling the creature.

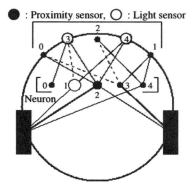

Figure 11: The logical connectivity. The inhibitorial connections are plotted with dashed lines, and excitorial connections with solid lines. The α value is shown by the thickness of the line The signal strength is shown by the size of the neuron. The sign of the signal is indicated by a filled circle for positive signals and a plain circle for negative signals. The shape of neural representation describes the type of neuron: circle for a transparency and box (not shown here) for an inversion nucleus.

Figure 12 shows the input signals at each of the dendrite tips, and the generated output signal. One can observe that neuron n_1 does the main work for controlling light approaching, while neuron n_3 does the main work for controlling avoidance. Observing that neuron n_1 is connected only for the left side motor, and neuron n_3 is connected only for the right side motor, one can say that the left side motor was used for controlling light approaching and the right side motor for obstacle avoidance. This result is quite obvious for the given environment.

The motor activity charts show the signals arriving at each motor. The role of neuron n_2 becomes clear here. It is used mainly to generate the forward movement, and, as above mentioned, signals from neurons n_1 and n_3 modify this movement.

4.4.1 Discussion

Concerning the modeling method, the results were very interesting. A neural structure capable of creating the aimed behavior was achieved. The initially given five neurons were more than enough to control the behavior. An interesting specialization of neurons emerged.

The results suggest that in the early evolution of neural systems, a small number of neurons is capable of creating meaningful behavior. Also the emerged specialization of neurons might be a clue for defining the modularity of neural systems. In further research this would be an approach to create modular neural systems capable of more complex behaviors.

One has to say that the evolution of the above neural structures does not always convert. Depending on the

Generated behavior

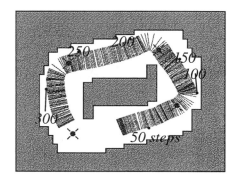

Propagating connections

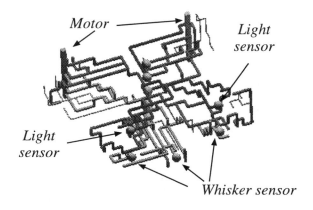

Figure 9: The resulting behavior with propagating connections.

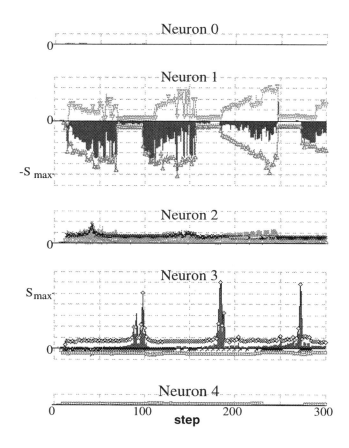

Figure 12: The neuron activity. The lines represent the signals at each of the dendrites, and the bars represent the output signal.

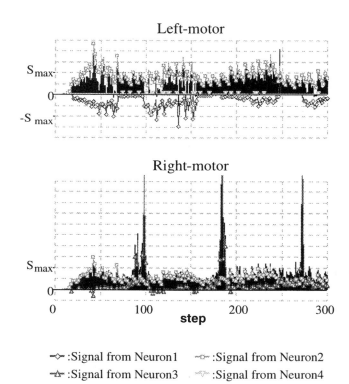

-◇-:Signal from Neuron1   -○-:Signal from Neuron2
-△-:Signal from Neuron3   -×-:Signal from Neuron4

Figure 13: The motor activity. The lines represent the input signals from each of the axons connected to the motors, and the bar represents the generated activity.

initial conditions, the required behavior sometimes did not evolve. Also, the current neural growth is controlled solely by the diffusion fields so that the created structures are specialized for the particular environment in which they grow. A more general approach is to increase the genetic factors, as it has been discussed in [14].

5 Conclusion

Research has shown that diffusion field control is capable of directing the growth of neural networks. Simulation provides a real-time, three-dimensional visualization of the growth process. It would be relatively easy to include other controlling factors for this growth, such as mechanical space. At the moment, biological plausibility is restricted to chemical diffusion.

As it was shown, with a simple parametric change one can select the type of neuron, from a 'hairy' neuron to a 'long reaching arm' neuron. This factor is strictly based on the local behavior of the neuron, and thus could be part of the genetic information. In the current research, all neural structures were simple, from sensors to motors. This was considered the first step in simulating neural based behavior. In the next step, more complicated structures with neuron to neuron connections, and recurrent connections should be considered.

The environment used was a simple simulation of light and obstacles. More realistic simulations should be tested and, finally, the method should be tested in the real world. This approach is thought to be realistic, because the aim is to move the whole growing process to the real world, not only the resulting network.

Currently, only one creature is used. This will be extended to several creatures with some kind of communication mechanisms. This direction is thought to offer a lot of new challenges, such as how the communication mechanisms (generation and receiving) are able to evolve, how the communication protocol is able to evolve, and how some kind collaboration based on this communication is able to evolve. A new research branch has been established to study these problems.

In general, the method has provided an interesting starting point by reducing the needed genetic information and letting the environment take care of some of the control. With a careful balance of these two factors, it may be possible not only to achieve interesting applications, but also to better understand the fundamental concepts of evolution.

References

[1] Robert B. Banks. *Growth and Diffusion Phenomena*. Springer-Verlag, 1994.

[2] Gerald M. Edelman. *Neural Darwinism - The Theory of Neuronal Group Selection*. Basic Books, New York, 1987.

[3] Gerald M. Edelman. *Topobiology*. Basic Books, 1988.

[4] D. Floreano and F. Mondada. Evolution of plastic neurocontrollers for situated agents. In *From Animals to Animat IV*. The MIT Press, 1996.

[5] Oliver Michel. Khepera simulator version 2.0 user manual. Web: http://wwwi3s.unice.fr/ om, 1996.

[6] Eric Mjolsness, David H. Shapr, and John Reinitz. A connectionist model of development. *Journal of Theorethical Biology*, 152:429–453, 1991.

[7] Akira Onitsuka, Jari Vaario, Katsunori Shimohara, and Kanji Ueda. Behavior generation based on enhanced dla model at neural network. In Jong-Hwan Kim and Xin Yao, editors, *Simulated Evolution and Learning*. Springer-Verlag, 1996.

[8] Akira Onitsuka, Jari Vaario, and Kanji Ueda. Structural formation by enhanced diffusion limited aggregation model. In *Artificial Life V*. May 14-16, 1996, Nara, Japan, 1996.

[9] Domenico Parisi, Stefano Nolfi, and Federico Cecconi. Learning, behavior, and evolution. In Francisco J. Varela and Paul Bourgine, editors, *Towards a Practice of Autonomous Systems: Proceedings of the First European Conference on Artificial Life*, pages 207–216. A Bradford Book, MIT Press, 1992.

[10] Jean Piaget. *Adaptation and Intelligence — Organic Selection and Phenocopy*. The University of Chicago Press, 1974. (reprint 1980).

[11] L. M. Sander. Fractal growth processes. *Nature*, 322:789–793, 1986.

[12] Jari Vaario. From evolutionary computation to computational evolution. *Informatica*, 18(4):417—434, 1994.

[13] Jari Vaario, Koichi Hori, and Setsuo Ohsuga. Toward evolutionary design of autonomous systems. *The International Journal in Computer Simulation*, 5:187—206, 1995.

[14] Jari Vaario, Naoko Ogata, and Katsunori Shimohara. Synthesis of environment directed and genetic growth. In *Artificial Life V*. May 14-16, 1996, Nara, Japan, 1996.

[15] Francisco J. Varela, Evan Thompson, and Eleanor Rosch. *The Embodied Mind*. The MIT Press, 1993.

Activity-based Pruning in Developmental Artificial Neural Networks

Alistair G Rust[1,2], Rod Adams[1], Stella George[1] and Hamid Bolouri[2,3]
[1] Department of Computer Science, University of Hertfordshire, UK
[2] Engineering Research and Development Centre, University of Hertfordshire, UK
[3] Biology 216-76, California Institute of Technology, USA
E-mail : a.g.rust@herts.ac.uk

Abstract

The expression of development programmes encoded in genes leads to the wide range of structures and functionality found in biology. Neural development is a highly adaptive form of self-organisation. This arises from the ability of neural systems to *fine-tune* their structure to both internal and external environments after an initial over-production of neural elements. Such structural refinement is a necessary part of self-organisation. This paper reports a biologically motivated model that regulates and refines the growth of neuron-to-neuron interconnections in a 3D artificial neural network. Our inspiration is spontaneous neural activity and the multiple roles of neurotrophic factors in biological systems. The model implements self-regulating growth of neurons, and competitive mechanisms which remove complete neuronal trees and differentiate between individual synapses.

1 Developmental Self-Organisation and Artificial Evolution

The rich variety of neural systems seen in nature are produced by the programmes of development that are encoded in genes. The programmes operate across different levels of scale. For example, they govern the assembly of neurons, the growth of neuron interconnections to form networks and the integration of networks to create modular, hierarchical neural systems. It is thought that although the behaviours of such programmes are complex they are expressed in terms of imprecise rules [36].

Development programmes do not contain exact *blueprints* of neural systems but are highly adaptable self-organising processes. The mapping from genotype to phenotype is highly non-linear and interactions with the chemical environment, within which development occurs, are crucial in shaping neural structure. During initial development a neural system generally over-produces many structural elements such as neurons, dendrites, axons and synapses: known as the Overshoot Phenomenon [39]. This enables the system to subsequently *fine-tune* itself to account for variations in rule-interactions and environmental factors, where the refinement of structure is often governed by competitive processes [13]. For example, refinement can occur through the death of inappropriately connected neurons and through the reduction of the number of synapses maintained by an individual neuron.

Evolution shapes development through modifications to genomes by the processes of gene duplication and point mutation. Therefore, the processes of evolutionary adaption and genetic encoding are inherently interlinked.

Thus efficient artificial evolution of neural systems requires appropriately coded developmental processes.

2 Developmental Artificial Neural Networks

Designing artificial neural networks (ANNs) using models analogous to biological development has received recent attention in the ALife community [22]. The usefulness of Developmental ANNs (DANNs) has been demonstrated in a number of applications, the most widespread being the design of autonomous robot controllers [9, 18, 27]. DANNs use a number of algorithmic methods to encode development rules and the environment within which the rules are expressed. These range from highly abstract implementations [2, 3, 12, 15] through to those which closely model biological processes [9, 10]. A number of these models require networks to be structurally regulated before being used functionally. This regulation includes removing unconnected neurons [27], removing duplicated, redundant connections [14] or withdrawing axons [38].

A set of development rules should be designed to enable the development of a variety of neuron and network structures. The larger the range, the greater the number of potentially useful structures for different applications. If rules are too strictly defined then development is limited to a narrow set of programmes, restricting the usefulness of the method. However, rules that span wide ranges of development may evolve redundant structural elements which must be regulated and refined. Regulation is therefore a necessary part of adaption. This paper presents the search for biologically-inspired rules that provide self-regulation and self-refining of artificial neural structures and is organised as follows.

Section 3 briefly reviews the previous work on our DANN. Sections 4 introduces neuro-biological processes from which refinement and regulation rules were identified. The implementation is described in Section 5 followed by a selection of results in Section 6. The results and future work are discussed in Section 7.

3 Previous Work

The aim of our work is to identify a minimally complex rule set for the development of morphologically and functionally distinct ANNs. Our method is to abstract and model neural development rules within a three stage framework [31]:

Phase 1 Growth. The creation of neuron-to-neuron connectivity.

Phase 2 Spontaneous activity. Refinement of the initial structure using internal, spontaneous neural activity to determine redundant structural features suitable for pruning.

Phase 3 Learning. Refinement of functionality based on external stimuli.

We have previously implemented a DANN to investigate Phase 1 of the framework: the growth of neuron-to-neuron interconnections [31,32]. Generic growth rules mimic the 3D development of axons and dendrites, collectively termed neurites. Development occurs in an artificial chemical environment, with an underlying, background chemical gradient which guides initial growth.

Cell differentiation and migration [28] are assumed to have previously occurred so that neurons are fixed in approximately planar layers. (Modelling cell migration prior to connection formation introduces further complexity which was deemed unnecessary in our approach [4, 9]). Neurons and their neurites emit local chemical gradients of artificial neurotrophin [16, 28]. The diffusion characteristics are determined by the parameters; strength, range and diffusion law (e.g. $1/distance^n$). These local gradients influence the growth of other neurites.

Each neuron has a set of intrinsic growth rules and growth parameters which determine how it extends axons and dendrites, or whether it acts as a stationary 'target'. Neurons in the same layer possess the same set of rules and parameters. In the current implementation growth occurs between two layers at any one time, where each layer of neurons emit chemicals opposite to the other growing layer.

The design of the growth rules is motivated by the idea that development uses imprecise rules [36] and aims

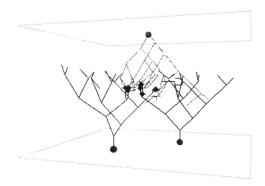

Figure 1: A simple 3D structure showing an over-development of neural outgrowth. Cell bodies are represented as spheres, while synapses are the central triangles.

to capture emergent behaviour such as that exhibited by Reynold's *boids* rules [30]. Inexact rule descriptions are intentionally used since exact rules tend to be less robust. Neurite tips obey the following growth rules:

- Follow the path of the steepest increase in the appropriate artificial neurotrophin.

- Maintain the same path unless attracted by a larger gradient.

- Branch if intrinsically programmed or if there are two strong local gradients.

- Form a synapse once an opposite neurite is encountered.

Hence, connections are formed by neurites searching for their target cells by following chemical gradients emitted from neurites of the opposite type. The tips of growing neurites perform hill-climbing amongst the chemical gradients produced by other neurites. Neurites may branch at pre-defined times (intrinsic splitting) or based on the state of local chemical gradients (environmental splitting).

Figure 1 is an example of the type of 3D structure which emerges from the rules. The development of 3D networks is novel in itself as the majority of other proposed models are 2D [2,4,9,18,27].

Through the selection of different parameter values, the rules are capable of producing a wide-range of development programmes allowing a similarly wide selection of structures to develop. In this way the DANN is not bound to producing a restricted range of stereo-typed network morphologies, as occurs in other models [27,38].

The simultaneous growth of axons and dendrites, along with their ability to establish local chemical gradients, creates an 'active' environment. This results in a great variety of neuron-to-neuron interactions and types of morphologies grown. Other models do use the concept of gradients to guide growth but these gradient sources are usually static [9,18,38].

We mimic natural selection by using a genetic algorithm (GA) to obtain an optimal set of developmental rule parameters for any given application [32].

One consequence of the growth phase is an overproduction of axon and dendrite outgrowths together with multiple synapse connections. (See Figure 1). This occurs in biological systems and also in other DANNs, as noted in Section 2. The remainder of this paper concentrates on modelling mechanisms of spontaneous neural activity and the pruning of extraneous connections.

4 Biological Mechanisms of Regulation

Evolution has developed a number of elegant methods with which to regulate and refine the structure of neural systems. This section provides an overview of the mechanisms abstracted from neural development that have been used in our model.

Much of the following discussion focuses on the family of proteins found in the developing nervous system called neurotrophins (NTs) [16]. NTs are secreted by neurons and are sensed by specific receptors on in-growing axons. Currently 6 NTs have been identified of which nerve growth factor (NGF) is the most characterised family member [16,25]. NTs have multi-functional roles in development including axon guidance [28], axon and dendrite branching [1,6,24], synapse modification [20,37], and neural regulation [16]. NTs are known to be regulated by neural activity [23,37].

4.1 Neural Regulation and the Neurotrophic Hypothesis

Up to 50% of many types of neurons die during the development of the vertebrate nervous system, where death occurs shortly after synapse connections are made with target neurons [1,29]. The percentage of neurons dying varies from neural region to region and between species [16]. It is thought that an excess production of neurons provides a means for future evolutionary changes [16].

One mechanism suggested to account for such widespread neuronal death is the Neurotrophic Hypothesis. The hypothesis relies on two major suppositions. Firstly, that developing neurons depend on obtaining specific NT factors produced by the target neurons they innervate. If a neuron is unable to obtain a sufficient supply of NT an intrinsic program causes it to die [7,29]. Secondly, NT is produced in limited amounts causing competition for supply between innervating axons [13,16].

Neurotrophin induced death is believed to aid development by:

- Automatically eliminating neurons that have made connections to inappropriate targets.

- Providing an elegant means of matching the numbers of pre- and post-synaptic neurons [7]. Often pre- and post-synaptic groups of neurons are generated independently, separated by some distance. Neural regulation is a mechanism to adjust the ratio of neurons [16].

- Increasing the likelihood that target cells become innervated.

Some classes of neurons are dependent on multiple NT factors which act concurrently or sequentially during development [8]. An intrinsic programme in the presynaptic neurons determines the on-set and duration of dependency on NTs [8,29]. Therefore, the neurotrophic hypothesis is not limited to a neuron being dependent upon a single type of NT.

In mammalian sensory neurons the initial axon outgrowth is independent of NT supply, [1,8]. (This suggests that NTs provide localised and not long range chemical effects [1].) NTs are produced once axons arrive in the target area and axons become NT dependent [1,8]. Axonal branching is encouraged by some types of NT [6] whereby post-synaptic neurons can influence their own innervation [1]: high NT levels result in densely connected regions, whilst low levels result in sparsely connected regions [8]. NT supplied to axons in the target area is retrogradely transported back to the cell body where its regulatory effect is determined [1].

NT is present in limited supply causing competition between axons. Experiments have shown that neurons which are normally eliminated during development will survive if the level of NT is artificially increased, suggesting that neurons are not intrinsically programmed to die during development [1,8,16].

4.2 Pre-natal Neural Activity and Synapse Reinforcement

Neural activity is crucial in the formation of connections within the central nervous system. Initial connections form in the absence of neural activity but the fine-tuning of structure is activity-dependent [13]. Pre-natal neural activity has an important role in shaping neural circuitry before external stimuli are present. The effects of pre-natal activity on the visual system has been extensively studied, in particular the segregation of input from the eyes to the lateral geniculate nucleus (LGN) [34,41]. Although the discussion is related to the visual system, the general mechanisms are of interest.

Recordings from developing retinas have shown ganglion neurons spontaneously emitting bursts of action potentials [11,34]. Activity is mediated through a tangential network of ganglion cells and amacrine cells, connected via gap junctions [42]. The patterns of spontaneous activity in neighbouring cells are more highly correlated than with distant cells. The spatial firing pat-

Figure 2: A simplified example of waves of pre-natal activity traversing the developing retina. The hexagonal grid defines the array of retinal ganglion cells being measured. The dots represent neurons with the highest firing rates. The direction of travel is indicated by the arrow. Modified from [34].

terns of the neurons causes waves of activity to sweep across the retina as idealised in Figure 2. These waves are generated at regular intervals in between periods of no-activity and traverse the retina in different and random directions. The waves disappear prior to birth [34].

It is thought that spontaneous neural activity may spatially and temporally correlate visual input [34]. This has lead to the suggestion that Hebbian learning [17] may underlie the refinement of initial connections made between the retina and the LGN [34]. The signals from neighbouring ganglion cells will arrive at synapses in the LGN with near synchrony and may cause these synapses to be strengthened. Signals arriving asynchronously at synapses may cause them be weakened, ie. 'cells that fire together, wire together' [34].

There is still doubt over the molecular mechanisms underlying activity-dependent synapse enhancement [34]. NTs may offer a possible link since they are released from dendrites in an activity-dependent mechanism [37]. When an NT producing neuron receives input from a pre-synaptic neuron, NT is released across the synapse junction. If the pre-synaptic connection is NT sensitive, the NT release has a positive feedback effect and reinforces the efficacy (strength) of the synapse.

Hebbian learning requires synapse-specific modifications between pre- and post-synaptic neurons. There is little experimental data on the mechanisms of synapse-specific reinforcement [35]. However, Sossin has proposed a model of long term memory development incorporating synapse-specific modification [35]. The method proposes that a form of activation causes a pre-synaptic neuron to *mark* all of its synapses as 'activated' in a tree-wide process. When a post-synaptic cell is activated it only reinforces those synapses which are *mark*ed as 'activated'.

4.3 Neural Activity and Neural Outgrowth

One mechanism to reduce the degree of overproduction of neural structure is to regulate neurite growth. Neurite outgrowth can be controlled by changes in calcium concentrations in growth cones [39]. The calcium theory of neurite outgrowth proposes that low intra-cellular

calcium concentrations stimulate growth, higher concentrations inhibit growth and even higher concentrations lead to regression of neurites.

Neurite outgrowth can potentially therefore be affected by any factors that change the levels of intra-cellular calcium. NTs cause an increase in calcium concentrations [37], providing NTs with another role in development. Action potentials are also known to cause modifications to calcium levels [5, 33].

5   Sculpting Structure

Our model was implemented using the same design methodology employed for the growth rules [31]. Namely the key mechanisms of biological neural development were identified and expressed in terms of imprecise rules [36]. The aim of the model is to refine structure using Hebbian learning [17].

The model provides 2 levels of regulation: Global and Local. Global regulation removes neurons and their associated neurite trees if they are poorly connected with their target neurons, ie. a comparison is made between the connections of a neuron and the rest of the neuron population. Local regulation occurs at the level of synapses, where it is possible to differentiate between individual synapses on neurite trees. This requires synapse-specific modification as opposed to tree-wide modification.

The following assumptions have been made:

- Regulation occurs between two layers of neurons at any one time. Activity events are initiated by axon growing neurons (pre-synaptic) forcing responses in dendritic (post-synaptic) neurons.

- Growth and activity steps are interspersed. Spontaneous activity occurs once connections have been made and takes place between subsequent growth steps.

- Neurites are modelled as being unmyelinated ie lossy. (Dendrites along with 67% of axons are unmyelinated. The remaining 33% of axons do not become myelinated until they have finished developing [19].)

5.1   Entwining Spontaneous Activity and NT

Regulation is modelled by activity signals travelling from neurons in a pre-synaptic layer to neurons in a post-synaptic layer. If the level of activity that a post-synaptic neuron receives is above a *firing_threshold* NT is returned. This causes active synapses to be reinforced and supplies pre-synaptic neurons with NT. After some pre-defined period growth and activity steps are stopped. Pruning then occurs and the method is as follows.

A pre-synaptic neuron is selected at random and emits an activity signal into its axonal tree. The other neurons

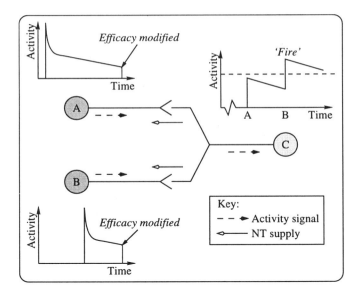

Figure 3: A simple example demonstrating the modelled interactions between activity and NT. A and B are pre-synaptic neurons, whilst C is a post-synaptic neuron.

in the layer relay this activity signal at time intervals determined by their distance from the triggering neuron. In this way a wave of activity is initiated which radiates across the pre-synaptic layer. Randomly choosing a neuron at each activity step causes waves to travel in different directions across the layer.

An activity signal travels through the axonal arbour towards synapses and actively-growing neurite tips. The strength of the signal decreases as 1/distance (ie. the curved sections of A and B's activity/time graphs in Figure 3) and at each branch point its value is halved. A signal arriving at a growing tip has no effect.

When a signal encounters a synapse, the synapse is marked as *active* and the current value of the signal sets a *sensitivity_level*. This level decays (currently implemented as linear) with time (ie. the linear sections of A and B's activity/time graphs in Figure 3) such that after some period it will have dropped to zero whereby the synapse becomes *inactive*.

The original activity signal is multiplied by the synapse's *efficacy* value and is transmitted into the connecting dendritic tree. *Efficacy* is initialised to 1 when a synapse first forms. The modified signal travels through the dendrite paths towards the soma of the connecting post-synaptic neuron. The signal again decreases as 1/distance.

Post-synaptic neurons sum activity signals as they arrive at the soma. The strength of this *activity_sum* also decays (again currently linear) over time (see activity/time graph of neuron C in Figure 3).

The level of the *activity_sum* is assessed at discrete times. If it is greater than the *firing_threshold* the neuron

initiates the production of a signal, otherwise the neuron takes no action. This is illustrated in Figure 3. The signal from A alone was insufficient to cause C to fire. However, with the arrival of signal B combined with the decaying level of A, the *firing_threshold* is exceeded and C triggers a signal, which when received by its synapses, will cause the release of NT. A post-synaptic neuron can 'fire' more than once during an activity phase.

The soma emits a non-decaying signal which travels along all dendrite paths halving at branches. The value of this signal when it arrives at a synapse determines the strength of NT produced.

When NT is emitted from the post-synaptic side of a synapse it crosses the junction modifying the *efficacy* value :

$$\Delta efficacy = sensitivity\_level * \text{NT}$$

Synapses that have yet to become *active* or those that were previously *active* but where the *sensitivity level* has decayed to zero, receive no reinforcement. In Figure 3 differential reinforcement of the synapses occurs. A by itself did not cause C to fire. When C does fire, both A and B's synapses are modified but B's synapse receives the stronger reinforcement since the *sensitivity_level* of A's synapse has decayed further as it has been *active* for longer.

NT present at the synapses of a pre-synaptic neuron are transported back to the soma and summed. Arrival times of NT at the soma are not important.

Once all activity has subsided the next growth step begins.

5.2 Self-regulating Growth

High firing activity at the post-synaptic neuron and high NT supply at the pre-synaptic neuron indicate that the neurons involved are making 'good' connections and therefore have less need for new growth. Here we implemented a level of growth retardation for those neurons that are successfully forming synapses, motivated by the regulatory effect that changes in intra-cellular calcium has on neurite growth. Inhibiting growth affects the whole neuritic tree of a neuron and not just single tips. Although a neuron may suspend growth, it will still participate in any activity steps that may occur.

The growth of a post-synaptic neuron is modulated by the number of times it fires during an activity step. As the frequency of firing increases, growth is halted for longer. The growth of the pre-synaptic layer is regulated by the difference in NT supply between activity steps. The larger the difference, the longer growth is suspended.

For both classes of neuron a sigmoid function is used to determine the length of time for which growth is prevented.

The use of neural activity to regulate growth has previously been modelled by Van Ooyen et al where they advocated the use of a non-linear growth-regulating function [39, 40]. Their model differs from our approach in that they investigated the 2D growth of dendritic trees for a single layer of neurons. The degree of overlap between dendritic fields resulted in an increase in activity between neurons causing them to reduce, stop or retract growth.

5.3 Regulation

The process of interleaving growth and spontaneous activity is repeated until the whole growth phase is complete. Regulation then begins based on the cumulative effects of the previous activity-driven events.

Global regulation operates on the pre-synaptic neurons but has knock-on effects to post-synaptic neurons. We mimic competition between neurons by a simple dynamic threshold. The NT levels of all the pre-synaptic neurons are summed and a threshold equal to the average value is calculated. Neurons with NT levels below this threshold are removed from the network together with their axonal arborisation. The post-synaptic neurons' connections are modified accordingly.

Post-synaptic neurons regulate the process of synapse refinement, which occurs after global regulation. Two competitive strategies have been implemented, only one of which is used at any one time:

- Tree-wide. All the efficacies of the synapses on a dendritic tree are summed and a threshold equal to the average is calculated. Synapses with efficacies falling below this threshold are removed.

- Neuron specific. In this case, an efficacy threshold value is calculated for each individual pre-synaptic neuron that connects to a dendritic tree. A post-synaptic neuron thereby remains connected to the same number of pre-synaptic neurons as before pruning occurred, except that the number of synapses maintained decreases.

6 Results

A two layer DANN was initialised with a 24 neuron lower layer that projected axons towards a single neuron producing dendrites. A single neuron was chosen simply to illustrate the principles of the model. Regulation of multiple neurons in multiple layers has also been implemented. The dendrites of the top layer neuron were set to split immediately and then regularly thereafter. This was to encourage the dendritic neuron to connect with as many axons as possible such that the effectiveness of the regulatory mechanisms could be analysed. Both methods of synapse regulation were investigated.

The results after growth and regulation are illustrated in Figure 4 and summarised in Table 1. The area of the dendritic tree of the single neuron is superimposed on Figures 4 (b) and (c) as the shaded polygon. (Dendritic

Measure	Post-regulation Phase			
	None	Global	Tree	Specific
No tips	35	28	22	19
No branches	34	27	21	18
No segments	69	55	43	37
Mean segment length	3.70	4.05	4.16	5.03
No neurons contacted	17	12	9	12
No synapses	75	60	35	28
Dendritic field area	551	497	474	509
Synapse density	0.14	0.12	0.07	0.06

Table 1: A summary of structural changes to the dendritic neuron.

field area is calculated by finding the smallest convex polygon that includes all the tips of the tree.) With both stages of regulation (global and local) the structure of the DANN is refined.

The complexity of the interconnections pre-regulation is illustrated in Figure 4(a) where the dendrite has formed 75 synapse connections with 17 out of the 24 axonal neurons. Neurons on the periphery of the layer have wide-spreading axon growth since portions of their trees did not sense the chemical gradients emitted by the dendrites and were therefore not attracted to grow towards them. (The number of synapses that the dendritic tree has does not equal the number of its tips as synapses can form along the length of a dendrite and not just at tips.) After global regulation, the area that the dendritic tree covers has reduced, connections now being maintained by 50% of axonal neurons. Figure 4(b) shows the 12 axonal neurons that remain. They maintain, on average, 5 synapses with the dendritic neuron.

A graphical comparison between pre- and post-regulation (tree-wide) for the dendritic neuron is shown in Figure 5. (The view is side-on compared to Figure 4 so as to better illustrate the number and positions of synapses.) Clearly the dendritic tree is structurally less complex and the number of synapses has been rationalised.

The final two columns of Table 1 compare the two methods of synapse regulation: tree-wide and neuron-specific. Tree-wide refinement results in a focusing of a neuron's dendritic tree into a smaller area (see Figure 4(c)). Only 9 of the axonal neurons formed strong enough connections to remain after synapse regulation and subsequently the average number of synapses per neuron decreased from 5 to about 4. This method along with neuron-specific refinement, results in an increase in the average segment length.

Neuron-specific refinement allows a neuron to maintain connections with all of the neurons it contacts. Therefore, the number of different neurons contacted pre- and post-synapse regulation remains the same whilst there is a slight increase in the area covered by the dendritic tree. This is because the area is calculated using the tips of the dendritic tree which, due to branching, may not be the points of furthest spread. For example, see the right-hand side of Figure 5(b). After pruning new tips may be formed from synapses on segments which although at higher depths within the tree, have a larger spread. Therefore, the calculated dendritic field area increases. Long-distance neurite paths remain whilst the number of connections with local neurons is pared down, with an average of just over 2 synapses per neuron. Both methods, tree-wide and neuron-specific, result in an increase in the average segment length. However, this increase is greater for the neuron-specific method since fewer long-distance connections are removed.

Figure 6 shows differential axon growth in the DANN, due to the effects of NT supply. The left-most axon was on the periphery of the DANN and did not connect to the dendritic tree. As a result no NT was supplied to indicate the successful formation of synapses and so growth was not inhibited. The right-most neuron, however, did make a number of synapses on the dendritic tree and was supplied with NT which suspended growth. This resulted in a less extensive development of its axonal tree. Axon tips also remained unconnected at the end of growth since the synapses that were made, supplied a sufficient level of NT halting the growth of the whole axonal tree.

The frequency with which the dendritic neuron fired during an activity phase also increased over time and is illustrated in Figure 7. This caused the dendritic neuron to stop growing and act as a static target for growing axons. The dendritic neuron does not stop firing since it is still in receipt of activity signals. For example, the number of new synapses formed by in-growing axons at time 31 increased the potential number of firing stimuli, accounting for the increase in the firing rate of the dendritic neuron.

7 Discussion

Multiple synapses between two neurons are often maintained in our model in contrast to other DANNs where one-to-one connections are the norm [15,27]. These multiple connections are retained since in biological neural systems the position of synapses on a neuron's dendritic tree greatly affect its function [21,26]. Variations in dendritic position of synapses from the same pre-synaptic neuron result in varying phase responses and increased emphasis being placed on signals. This has functional significance [19].

Our model provides reinforcement of connections but as yet no means to discriminate between excitatory and inhibitory inputs to a neuron. We have yet to implement inhibitory connections. The *efficacy* value will, however, provide a guide to the significance of a synapse which may then determine the 'strength' that the junction will

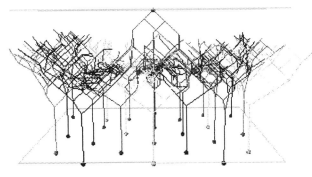

(a) Pre-neuron regulation

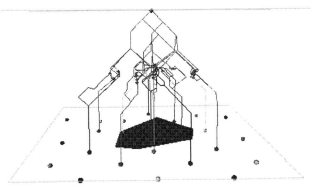

(b) After removing poorly connected neurons

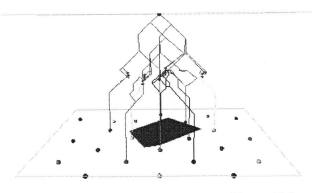

(c) After removing weak synapses (Tree-wide)

Figure 4: Various stages in the growth and regulation of two layer network.

have when it is used functionally.

Figure 8 is an example of pre-synaptic neurons mutually reinforcing each other's synapses, thereby 'wiring' their responses to a post-synaptic neuron. Neuron A causes C to fire, releasing NT at both synapses, where B's *efficacy* actually receives the greatest reinforcement since it's synapse has been active for a shorter time (see dashed lines in A and B's activity/time graphs in Figure

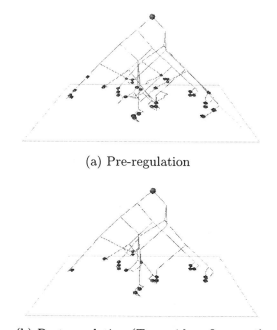

(a) Pre-regulation

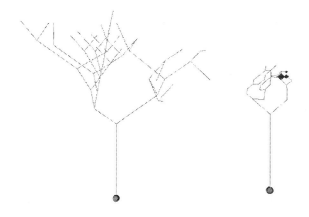

(b) Post-regulation (Tree-wide refinement)

Figure 5: Structural changes to the dendritic neuron.

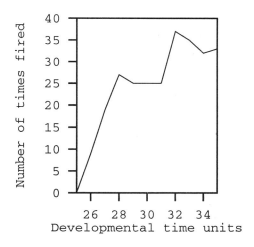

Figure 7: The firing events of the dendritic neuron.

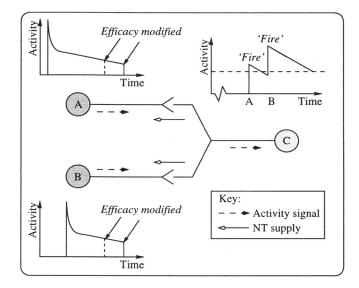

Figure 8: The correlation between firing sequences and connectivity. A and B are pre-synaptic neurons. C is post-synaptic.

8). However, B also causes C to fire and A's synapse receives further reinforcement since it is still active. In the example it appears that A is penalised for firing first because it receives a lower degree of reinforcement. However, if the firing events are subsequently reversed because the wave of activity travels across the layer in the opposite direction, such that B fires before A, then with reinforcement occurring as before, both neurons will have been modified in the same way. Biological evidence suggests that the random directions taken by spontaneous neural activity correlates the development of connections

(in the pre-natal visual system [34]). This seems to be the case in our model.

Our primary intent of future work is to add functionality to the networks. Modelling the development of a biological retina is the current testbed application. Our aim is to grow networks which are quantitatively similar to their biological counterparts and then to impose function. The development rules provide a number of opportunities to study the relationship between structure and function. For example, tree-wide synapse refinement may cause the receptive fields of neurons to focus onto particular input connections by reducing the area that a dendritic tree covers.

The parameters of the model require further investiga-

Figure 6: Two axonal neurons exhibiting differential growth.

tion to determine their significance and sensitivity. The growth rules have previously been investigated using a genetic algorithm to determine optimal parameter values. The combination of growth and refinement rules will be investigated in a similar manner.

8 Conclusion

Our goal is to specify a methodology to evolve biologically plausible ANNs. Biological neural development and its self-organising abilities are the inspiration for our approach. Exhaustively simulating biological systems is not however our aim. This requires an appreciation of numerous and complex interactions of chemical and biological processes. The general method adopted is to identify and abstract the key principles of neural development to form candidate rules for modelling.

Rule design has been incremental. A set of generic growth rules has been specified that is able to create a range of neural structures via a variety of programmes of development. Refinement and regulatory rules have since been added to allow these structures to be *fine-tuned* and adapted, prior to being used functionally. Refinement and regulation are necessary processes of adaptive modelling.

Both the growth and refinement rule sets provide the basic mechanisms for further investigations into ANN design. The DANN that we have implemented is however general enough to be able to simulate the development of other neural circuits and systems. The next phase of work is to add functionality to the DANN. Mimicking the development of the structures and function of biological retinas is currently being studied.

References

[1] Yves-Alain Barde. Trophic factors and neuronal survival. *Neuron*, 2:1525–1534, June 1989.

[2] Richard K Belew. Interposing an ontogenetic model between genetic algorithms and neural networks. In J Cowan, editor, *Advances in Neural Information Processing Systems 5 (NIPS5)*, pages 99–106, San Mateo, CA, 1993. Morgan Kaufman.

[3] Egbert J W Boers, Herman Kuiper, Bart L M Happel, and Ida G Sprinkhuizen-Kuyper. Designing modular artificial neural networks. Technical Report 93-24, Leiden University, September 1993.

[4] Angelo Cangelosi, Domenico Parisi, and Stefano Nolfi. Cell division and migration in a 'genotype' for neural networks. *Network*, 5:497–515, 1994.

[5] Christopher S Cohan, John A Connor, and Stanley B Kater. Electrically and chemically mediated increases in intracellular calcium in neuronal growth cones. *The Journal of Neuroscience*, 7(11):3588–3599, November 1987.

[6] Susana Cohen-Cory and Scott E Fraser. Effects of brain-derived neurotrophic factor on optic axon branching and remodelling in vivo. *Nature*, 378:192–196, 9 November 1995.

[7] Alun M Davies. Intrinsic programmes of growth and survival in developing vertebrate neurons. *Trends in Neurosciences*, Vol.17 No.5:195–198, 1994.

[8] Alun M Davies. The neurotrophic hypothesis: Where does it stand? *Philosophical Transactions of the Royal Society of London: Series B*, 351(1338):389–394, 29 March 1996.

[9] Frank Dellaert and Randall D Beer. Co-evolving body and brain in autonomous agents using a developmental model. Technical Report CES-94-16, Case Western Reserve University, August 1994.

[10] Kurt Fleischer. *A Multiple-Mechanism Developmental Model for Defining Self-Organizing Geometric Structures*. PhD dissertation, California Institute of Technology, May 1995.

[11] Lucia Galli and Maffei Lamberto. Spontaneous impulse activity of rat retinal ganglion cells in prenatal life. *Science*, 242:90–91, 7 October 1988.

[12] Felix Gers and Hugo deGaris. CAM-Brain: A new model for ATR's cellular automata based artificial brain project. In *To appear in proceedings of 1st International Conference on Evolvable Systems: from Biology to Hardware*, 1996.

[13] Corey S Goodman and Carla J Shatz. Developmental mechanisims that generate precise patterns of neuronal connectivity. *Cell*, 72(Review Suppl):77–98, January 1993.

[14] Frederic Gruau. Efficient computer morphogenesis: A pictorial demonstration. Working Paper 94-04-027, Santa Fe, Santa Fe, New Mexico, April 1994.

[15] Frederic Gruau. *Neural Network Synthesis Using Cellular Encoding and the Genetic Algorithm*. Thesis, Ecole Normale Superieure de Lyon, January 1994.

[16] Zach W Hall. *An Introduction to Molecular Neurobiology*. Sinauer Associates, Sunderland, MA, 1st edition, 1992.

[17] Donald O Hebb. *The Organization of Behaviour*. John Wiley and Sons, London, 1st edition, 1949.

[18] Nick Jakobi. Harnessing morphogenesis. In *To Appear in Proceedings of International Conference on Information Processing in Cells and Tissues*, 1995.

[19] Eric R Kandel, James H Schwartz, and Thomas M Jessell. *Essentials of Neural Science and Behaviour: International Edition*. Prentice Hall, London, 1st edition, 1995.

[20] Hyejin Kang and Erin M Schuman. Long-lasting neurotrophin-induced enhancement of synaptic transmission in the adult hippocampus. *Science*, 267:1658–1662, 17 March 1995.

[21] C Koch, T Poggio, and V Torre. Nonlinear interactions in a dendritic tree: Localization, timing and role in information processing. *Proceedings of the National Academy of Sciences of the USA*, 80(9):2799–2802, May 1983.

[22] Jerome Kodjabachian and Jean-Arcady Meyer. Evolution and development of control architectures in animats. *Robotics and Autonomous Systems*, 16:161–182, 1995.

[23] Bai Lu, Midori Yokoyama, Cheryl F Dreyfus, and Ira B Black. Depolarizing stimuli regulate nerve growth factor gene expression in cultured hippocampal neurons. *Proceedings of the National Academy of Science of the USA*, 88:6289–6292, July 1991.

[24] A Kimberley McAllister, Donald C Lo, and Lawrence C Katz. Neurotrophins regulate dendritic growth in developing visual cortex. *Neuron*, 15:791–803, October 1995.

[25] Stephen B McMahon. Neurotrophins and sensory neurons: Role in development, maintenance and injury: Preface. *Philosophical Transactions of the Royal Society of London: Series B*, 351(1338):363–364, 29 March 1996.

[26] B W Mel. NDMA-based pattern-discrimination in a modelled cortical neuron. *Neural Computation*, 4(4):502–517, July 1992.

[27] Stefano Nolfi and Domenico Parisi. Growing neural networks. Technical Report PCIA-91-15, Institiute of Pyschology, Rome, December 1991.

[28] Dale Purves and Jeff W Lichtman. *Principles of Neural Development*. Sinauer Associates, Sunderland, MA, 1st edition, 1985.

[29] Martin C Raff, Barbara A Barres, Julia F Burne, Harriet S Coles, Yasuki Ishizaki, and Michael D Jacobsen. Programmed cell death and the control of cell survival: Lessons from the nervous system. *Science*, 262:695–700, 29 October 1993.

[30] Craig W Reynolds. Flocks, herds, and schools: A distributed behavioral model. *Computer Graphics*, 21:25–34, July 1987.

[31] Alistair G Rust, Rod Adams, Stella George, and Hamid Bolouri. Artificial evolution: Modelling the development of the retina. Technical Memorandum ERDC/1996/0015, ERDC, University of Hertfordshire, UK, September 1996.

[32] Alistair G Rust, Rod Adams, Stella George, and Hamid Bolouri. Designing development rules for artificial evolution. In *Proceedings of 3rd International Conference on Artificial Neural Networks and Genetic Algorithms (ICANNGA97)*, 1997.

[33] Karl Schilling, Michael H Dickinson, John A Connor, and James I Morgan. Electrical activity in cerebellar cultures and determines Purkinje cell dendritic growth patterns. *Neuron*, 7:891–902, December 1991.

[34] Carla J Shatz. Role for spontaneous neural activity in the patterning of connections between retina and LGN during visual system development. *International Journal of Developmental Neuroscience*, 12(6):531–546, 1994.

[35] Wayne S Sossin. Mechanisms for the generation of synapse specificity in long-term memory: the implications of a requirement for transcription. *Trends in Neurosciences*, 19(6):215–218, 1996.

[36] Michael P Stryker. Precise development from imprecise rules. *Science*, 263:1244–1245, 4 March 1994.

[37] Hans Thoenen. Neurotrophins and neuronal plasticity. *Science*, 270:593–598, 27 October 1995.

[38] Jari Vaario. Modeling adaptive self-organization. In Rodney A Brooks and Pattie Maes, editors, *Artificial Life IV : Proceedings of the Fourth International Workshop on the Synthesis and Simulation of Living Systems*, pages 313–318, London, 1994. MIT Press.

[39] A van Ooyen and J van Pelt. Activity-dependent outgrowth of neurons and overshoot phenomena in developing neural networks. *Journal of Theoretical Biology*, 167:27–43, 1994.

[40] A van Ooyen, J van Pelt, and M A Corner. Implications of activity dependent neurite outgrowth for neuronal morphology and network development. *Journal of Theoretical Biology*, 172:63–82, 1995.

[41] R O L Wong, A Chernjavsky, S J Smith, and C J Shatz. Early functional neural networks in the developing retina. *Nature*, 374:716–718, 20 April 1995.

[42] Rachel O L Wong, Markus Meister, and Carla J Shatz. Transient period of correlated bursting activity during development of the mammalian retina. *Neuron*, 11:923–938, November 1993.

EMULATION OF NATURAL BEHAVIOR, AND ROBOTICS

Homing by Parameterized Scene Matching

Matthias O. Franz   Bernhard Schölkopf   Heinrich H. Bülthoff

Max–Planck–Institut für biologische Kybernetik
Spemannstraße 38, D-72076 Tübingen, Germany
franz/bs/hhb@mpik-tueb.mpg.de

Abstract

In visual homing tasks, animals as well as robots can compute their movements from the current view and a snapshot taken at a home position. Solving this problem exactly would require knowledge about the distances to visible landmarks, information, which is not directly available to passive vision systems. We propose a homing scheme that dispenses with accurate distance information by using parameterized disparity fields. These are obtained from an approximation that incorporates prior knowledge about perspective distortions of the visual environment. A mathematical analysis proves that the approximation does not prevent the scheme from approaching the goal with arbitrary accuracy. Mobile robot experiments are used to demonstrate the practical feasibility of the approach.

1   Introduction

For many animal species it is vital to be able to find their way back to a shelter or to a rewarding food source. In particular, flying animals cannot rely on idiothetic information for this task, as they are subject to drift. Thus they have to use external information, often provided by *vision*. A location may be identified visually using one of two methods: first, by association with an image *of* the location (recorded while approaching or leaving it), or second, by association with an image of the panorama as seen *from* the location. These two methods depend on the visual characteristics of the location, and determine how such a snapshot can be used to recover its associated spatial position: if the location itself is marked by salient optical features, these can be *tracked* until the goal is reached (e.g. Collett 1996). If there are no such features, the goal direction after a displacement has to be inferred by comparing the current visual input to the snapshot: image regions in the direction of the displacement are expanded while the image in the goal direction is contracted. Driving into the direction of maximal image contraction finally leads to the goal position (cf. Figure 1).

Note that even though neither of the two possible approaches necessarily requires recognition mechanisms, our distinction already foreshadows another distinction which is known in the domain of recognition, namely the one between object recognition and scene recognition (see e.g. Tarr & Bülthoff, 1996). As in our case, these two domains differ in that the former deals with something localized in space that the observer is not part of, whereas the latter deals with something non–local, surrounding the observer. Inspired by this distinction, we shall use the term *scene–based homing* to refer to visual homing strategies which make use of the whole scene, rather than tracking single objects.

A number of experiments have shown that invertebrates such as bees or ants are able to pinpoint a location defined by an array of nearby landmarks (see Collett 1992 for a review). Apparently, these insects search for their goal at places where the retinal image forms the best match to a memorized snapshot. Cartwright and Collett (1983) have put forward the hypothesis that bees might be able to actively extract the goal direction by a mechanism using the azimuth and size change of visible objects after a displacement.

In the present work, we want to approach homing from a different viewpoint: Rather than proposing a model or mechanisms underlying actual insect behaviour we will focus in this study on the problems that any agent has to face when using perspective distortion to infer the goal direction from a snapshot. To that end we use real robots to avoid the idealizations one necessarily has to accept when simulating an agent and its environment. We limit ourselves to mechanisms that are computationally inexpensive, both to afford robotic implementation and to avoid overly complex explanations.

In the next section, we give a mathematical description of the basic task, followed by the introduction of a new algorithm (Section 3) that is able to cope with some of the shortfalls of previous approaches. Section 4 describes our implementation on a mobile robot and presents experimental results. We conclude our study with a discussion of the results and relate them to previous approaches taken by researchers in biology and robotics.

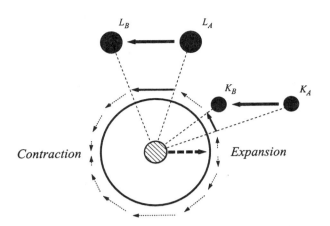

Figure 1: By displacing the sensor ring along the dashed arrow, the landmarks L_A and K_A are shifted to new positions L_B and K_B relative to the sensor. The image region in the direction of displacement expands, while the opposite region contracts. If the landmarks are isotropically distributed, then the vector sum of the disparities always points towards the starting point.

2 Inferring the home direction from perspective distortion

To characterize the basic task mathematically, we start by giving some definitions which will be used throughout the paper. As an idealized model of an agent we choose a mobile sensor ring measuring the surrounding light intensity. If the allowed movements of the sensor ring are restricted to two dimensions then a ring parallel to the movement plane suffices in principle, to determine the relevant motion parameters. The agent is able to record a 360° view of the surrounding panorama as a snapshot. The position of an image point on the sensor ring is denoted by the angle θ. All points in the environment giving rise to identifiable points in the image are called landmarks. This should not be confused with the usual notion of a landmark as a physical object. In our terminology, a visible object may contain several landmarks.

Suppose we displace the sensor ring in direction α at position A by a distance d to point B and change its orientation by the angle ψ (see Fig.2). As a consequence, the image of landmark L at distance r is shifted from θ to a new position $\theta + \delta$ (assuming a static environment). From the triangle ALB in Fig.2 we obtain

$$\frac{r}{d} = \frac{\sin(\theta - \alpha + \psi + \delta)}{\sin(\psi + \delta)}. \tag{1}$$

This relation can be used to compute the direction $\beta = \alpha + \pi$ back to the starting position A from the change δ in the landmark position (the *disparity*), if r/d and ψ are known.

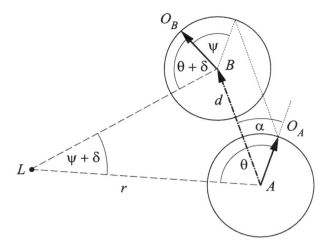

Figure 2: Displacing a ring sensor from A to B in direction α (with respect to sensor's initial orientation O_A) and rotating it by ψ leads to a change δ of the viewing angle of a landmark L.

Before relation Eq. (1) can be applied for homing tasks, two basic problems have to be solved:

1. In order to compute the disparity δ, a correspondence between image points in the snapshot and in the current view must be established. Since the displacement is the result of an arbitrary movement, we are not allowed to assume that image points belonging to the same landmark occur at similar locations in both the snapshot and current view.

2. A visually navigating agent has no access to the actual distance r of the landmark at L. Therefore, this lack of knowledge must be compensated by some additional assumption about the distance distribution of possible landmarks in the environment.

The computation of disparities requires techniques used for optical flow analysis, or mechanisms for object recognition that allow to identify regions in different images as belonging to the same object. The problem can be alleviated if the agent either knows its orientation with respect to an external reference (Cartwright & Collett 1983, Wittmann 1995) or always keeps a constant orientation (Hong et al. 1991, Röfer 1995).

In previous approaches, two basic assumptions have been used to compensate for the lack of distance knowledge:

Isotropic landmark distribution. If the surrounding landmarks are distributed isotropically (i.e. frequency and distance of landmarks does not depend on the viewing direction), one obtains the correct goal direction by summing over all disparity vectors along the sensor ring, since all disparity components orthogonal to direction of the displacement cancel each other (see Figure 1).

Weak perspective. The weak perspective projection approach is based on the assumption that the projected objects are sufficiently far away from the sensor, so that the distance differences of the individual landmarks belonging to a single object become negligible.[1] The individual disparities of the landmarks can be measured while the unknowns α, ψ and r/d in Eq. (1) remain the same all over the object. Thus, an object containing at least three landmarks suffices to determine the home direction. To use this approximation, the agent must be able to segment image regions belonging to an object from the background, and to identify the object in different images.

In the following section, we will introduce an algorithm based on an approximation which we call *equal distance assumption*. The surrounding landmarks are assumed to have approximately identical distances from the location of the snapshot. Similar to the approximation of an isotropic landmark distribution, a homing algorithm based on this assumption does not need any object recognition mechanisms and can rely on optical flow techniques. Additionally, this approach provides constraints for the computation of the disparity field which will be used in our algorithm. As the equal distance assumption is, in the strictest sense, unrealistic, we will show in Section 3.2 that the effect of the resulting errors on homing performance remain small.

3 Homing with parameterized disparity fields

3.1 A matched filter based on the equal distance assumption

Before applying the equal distance assumption we will convert Eq. (1) into a suitable form for the subsequent analysis. Solving Eq. (1) for ψ, we have

$$\tan(\psi + \delta) = \frac{d\sin(\theta - \alpha)}{r - d\cos(\theta - \alpha)}. \tag{2}$$

We assume a typical landmark distance R and denote the deviation from it by r' so that $r = R + r'$. This leads to

$$\tan(\psi + \delta) = \frac{\frac{d}{R}\sin(\theta - \alpha)}{1 + \frac{r'}{R} - \frac{d}{R}\cos(\theta - \alpha)}. \tag{3}$$

By setting $\epsilon = r'/R$, $\nu = d/R$ and $\gamma = \theta - \alpha$ to simplify the notation, we obtain from Eq. (3)

$$\delta = \arctan\left(\frac{\nu\sin\gamma}{1 + \epsilon - \nu\cos\gamma}\right) - \psi. \tag{4}$$

The cases $\nu = 0$, $\epsilon = -1$ and $\gamma = 0, \pi$, $\nu = 1 + \epsilon$ have to be excluded which means that the agent is not allowed to occupy the same position as a landmark while homing or taking a snapshot.

We now apply the equal distance assumption by neglecting the individual distance differences ϵ of the surrounding landmarks. The resulting expression

$$\delta = \arctan\left(\frac{\nu\sin\gamma}{1 - \nu\cos\gamma}\right) - \psi. \tag{5}$$

describes the disparity field when all landmarks are located at a distance R from the starting position. The disparity field is completely determined by only three parameters α, ψ and ν. This allows us to estimate the real disparity field and the home direction using the following algorithm:

1. For all parameter values of α, ψ and ν the current view is distorted by shifting the image positions θ of the single pixels according to Eq. (5). The result of this procedure are new images that would have been obtained if the sensor was displaced in an environment where the constant distance assumption was perfectly valid.

2. The generated images are compared to a snapshot taken at the home position. To measure the degree of match between both images we use the Euclidian distance between the grey values at each pixel. The best match is produced by a disparity field which reconstructs the home view as accurately as possible.

3. In a final step, the parameter value of α leading to the best match is selected as an estimate $\beta = \alpha + \pi$ of the home direction.[2]

Note that in order to determine Eq. (5) completely, at least three landmarks must be visible. Otherwise, the home direction can only be estimated if additional information sources such as compasses or odometers are available. The parameterized disparity field $\delta(\theta)|_{\epsilon=0}$ can be interpreted as a matched filter in the sense that the parameter set that reproduces best the actual disparity field can be assumed to approximate the real one. Since the direction of the displacement α is one of the parameters, the best matching disparity immediately gives the goal direction. Similar motion templates for determining egomotion parameters from given optical flow fields have been described for the visual system of the blowfly *Calliphora* (Krapp & Hengstenberg 1996), and theoretically by Nelson & Aloimonos (1988).

Although the equal distance assumption is hardly ever valid in its strictest sense, the estimate of the disparity field is quite robust as will be demonstrated in the next section.

---

[1]Note that the second assumption of weak perspective is automatically satisfied for a sensor ring: the object is always near the optical axis of some sensors.

[2]The relative distance ν obtained by this matching process is generally not the mean relative distance of the surrounding landmarks, but a weighted average according to the disparity caused by each individual landmark.

3.2 Error due to the equal distance assumption

Let

$$E(\epsilon, \nu) := \delta(\epsilon, \nu) - \delta(0, \nu) \qquad (6)$$

denote the error in the disparity δ due to neglecting the deviation of the landmark distance r' from the averaged distance R. We want to show that for each $\epsilon > -1$, fixed γ, and any desired accuracy bound $E_0 > 0$, there exists a ν_0 such that $\nu < \nu_0$ implies $|E(\epsilon, \nu)| < E_0$. In other words, even if the equal distance approximation does not hold, we can reach any desired accuracy level, provided that we are close enough to the goal.

For the proof, we use the Taylor expansion of E (cf. Eqs. (6), (5)) in ϵ,

$$
\begin{aligned}
E(\epsilon, \nu) &= \frac{-\nu \sin \gamma}{1 + \nu^2 - 2\nu \cos \gamma} \cdot \epsilon \\
&+ \frac{(1 + \vartheta\epsilon - \nu \cos \gamma)\nu \sin \gamma}{\left(\nu^2 \sin^2 \gamma + (1 + \vartheta\epsilon - \nu \cos \gamma)^2\right)^2} \cdot \epsilon^2, (7)
\end{aligned}
$$

where $0 < \vartheta < 1$. Clearly, the first term tends to 0 as ν tends to 0. If $\epsilon \geq 0$, then the second term can also easily be seen to tend to 0: its denominator will not tend to zero, while the denumerator always does. If $\epsilon < 0$, we need to take a closer look at the denominator: First note that even though ϑ might depend on ν, we know that for all γ,

$$1 + \vartheta\epsilon > 1 + \epsilon > 0. \qquad (8)$$

Thus we can choose $\nu_0 > 0$ such that for $\nu < \nu_0$,

$$
\begin{aligned}
1 + \vartheta\epsilon - \nu \cos \gamma &> 1 + \epsilon - \nu \cos \gamma \\
&\geq \kappa > 0 \qquad (9)
\end{aligned}
$$

for some suitable κ. Hence for $\nu < \nu_0$ the denominator is bounded from below by κ^4, whereas the numerator approaches 0, which completes the proof.

Therefore, for every snapshot containing at least three landmarks, there exists a catchment area in which the location of the snapshot can be approached arbitrarily closely. In practise, the catchment areas tend to be larger than one might expect from the equal distance approximation, as there are several factors which effectively select a ring–shaped area for the matching procedure. First, the error induced by an infinitely distant point is relatively small, compared to disparities generated by nearby landmarks. Second, very close points will not have an effect as adverse as might be expected from their large disparities, since commonly used obstacle avoidance systems make them less likely to occur. In addition, the vision system's limited depth of field will cause both very close and very distant landmarks to be blurred and reduced in contrast, which decreases their effect on the matching procedure. This serendipitous bonus makes our approximation all the more suitable for real world applications.

3.3 Limitation of accuracy by sensor noise

As we have shown in the previous section, the equal distance assumption does not influence the spatial accuracy of the homing scheme. Therefore, the primary limiting factor is the pixel and quantization noise of the sensor ring. In the following, we will determine the influence of noise on the spatial accuracy, namely the smallest achievable relative distance from the goal $\Delta\nu$.

We assume that the intensity distribution $h(\theta)$ sampled by the sensor ring is low-pass filtered in a subsequent processing stage so that the derivative of the intensity distribution $h'(\theta)$ is well defined for all sensor coordinates θ and spatial aliasing effects are eliminated.

The variance of the noise in the intensity distribution is given by $\Delta h_{noise}^2 = \sigma_{sensor} + \Delta^2/12$, where σ_{sensor} is the sensor noise and the second term results from the quantization error (here, Δ is the step size of the quantizer, cf. Oppenheim & Schafer 1989). As a consequence, the maximally resolvable intensity change is $2\Delta h_{noise}$ according to the usual reliability criterion for communication systems which is analogous to assuming that the threshold signal to noise ratio is unity (Goldman 1953).

A small displacement of the sensor ring from the location of the snapshot induces a small change $\Delta\theta$ in the position of the image features. The resulting change of the detected intensity distribution at θ is, to a first order approximation,

$$\Delta h(\theta) = h'(\theta) \cdot \Delta\theta. \qquad (10)$$

From (10), we find that the maximally resolvable image displacement is

$$\Delta\theta = \frac{2}{h'(\theta)} \Delta h_{noise}. \qquad (11)$$

From Eq. (5), we obtain the expression

$$\frac{\partial\nu}{\partial\delta} = \frac{(1 + \epsilon)\sin\gamma}{\sin^2(\gamma + \psi + \delta)}, \qquad (12)$$

so that the maximal spatial accuracy is given by

$$
\begin{aligned}
\Delta\nu &= \nu(\delta + \Delta\theta) - \nu(\delta) \\
&\approx \frac{\partial\nu}{\partial\delta} \cdot \Delta\theta \\
&= \frac{2(1 + \epsilon)\sin\gamma}{h'(\theta)\sin^2(\gamma + \psi + \delta)} \Delta h_{noise}. \qquad (13)
\end{aligned}
$$

This shows that for extreme noise levels, low contrast and sensor positions very close to landmarks, $\Delta\nu$ may become larger than the catchment area, so that in these cases the described homing scheme is not applicable. Note, that the above limitation is derived for only one landmark. When more landmarks are visible, the spatial accuracy becomes higher due to the effect of statistical averaging.

4 Results

4.1 Experimental setup

Most experiments were conducted in an arena with dimensions 118×102 cm. Visual cues were provided by model houses and landmarks surrounding the arena (see Fig. 3). In these experiments, we used a modified Khepera miniature robot (Fig. 4) connected to an SGI Indy workstation via a serial and video transmission cable. Our scheme was also tested in a real office environment on a six-wheeled platform with wireless modem and video transmission.

The imaging system on the robot comprises a conical mirror mounted above a small video camera which points up to the center of the cone (Fig. 4). This configuration allows for a 360° horizontal field of view extending from 10° below to 10° above the horizon. A similar imaging technique was used by Chahl and Srinivasan (1996) and Yagi, Nishizawa, & Yachida (1995). The video image was sampled on four circles along the horizon with a resolution of 2.5° and averaged vertically to provide robustness against inaccuracies in the imaging system and tilt of the robot platform. In a subsequent processing stage, a spatiotemporal Wiener lowpass filter (e.g. Goldman, 1953) was applied to the resulting one-dimensional array. To remove changes in the illumination, the average background component was subtracted and, in a final step, the contrast of the array was maximized via histogram equalization. The movement commands calculated from this data were transmitted back to the robot using a serial data link with a maximal transmission rate of 12 commands per second for the Khepera (5 for the wireless modem).

The Khepera's position was tracked with a colour camera mounted above the arena, tuned to a red marker attached to the robot. Position and image data were

Figure 4: Khepera^{TM} robot with camera module and custom made conical mirror, which permits sampling of the environment over 360°, in a range of ±10° about the horizon.

recorded with a time stamp and synchronized offline.

4.2 Performance of the homing scheme

The viability of our approach was tested in an experiment with the Khepera robot in the "toy house" arena. During the homing runs, the robot computed the home direction every 83 ms relative to the current driving direction. The home vector was used to set the new driving direction. For 20 different home positions, the robot was displaced relative to each home position by distances in the range of 5 to 25 cm in random directions. A trial was counted as a success if the robot reached the home position within a radius of 1 cm without colliding with an obstacle or exceeding a search time limit of 30 sec-

Figure 3: Test arena with toy houses, used in the homing experiments (see Sec. 4.1).

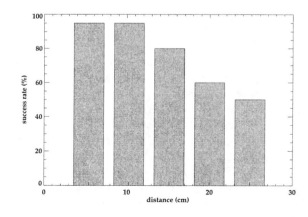

Figure 5: Success rate for 100 homing runs, with starting distances between 5 and 25 cm.

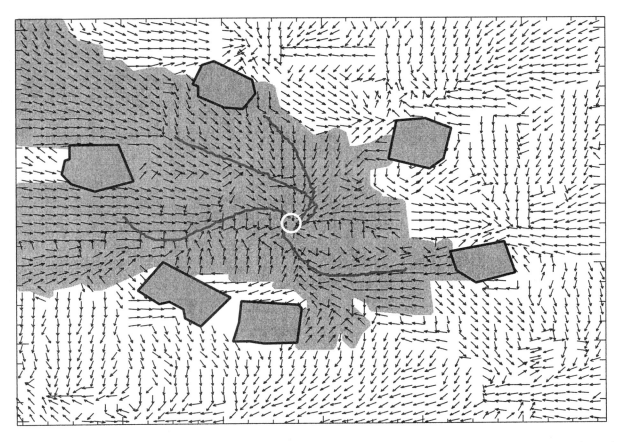

Figure 6: Home vector field for a central view in the arena (118 × 102 cm) shown in Fig. 3, with sample trajectories of a homing Khepera robot. The catchment area is depicted in grey, and the home position is marked by a circle.

onds. The success rates in Fig. 5 show that the algorithm performs robustly up to an average distance of 15 cm from the home position. For larger distances, the start position was often outside the open space around the home position, so that occlusions affected the performance. Sample trajectories from the homing runs are shown in Fig. 6. In the office environment, homing was successful up to 2 m away from the home position.

With the help of the tracking device the size of the *catchment area* can be visualized (Fig. 6) using the following procedure: During a test run, the robot covered the whole arena with 10000 snapshots thus approximating the entire set of possible views (the view manifold) of this environment. For a selected home view, we calculated the corresponding home vector at all possible positions which lead to the map in Fig. 6. A point is considered part of the catchment area, if there is a path along the goal vectors leading to the goal. As can be seen from Fig. 6, the catchment area can cover the entire open space around the goal position. If the goal is placed nearer to an object, the catchment area decreases in size only moderately, which allows the effective use of

the homing scheme in all areas of the arena where the robot does not collide with objects.

To assess the directional *accuracy* of the computed home vectors, we recorded 450 pairs of views during a random walk and computed the respective home vectors for each pair (Fig. 7). The pairs were required to be connected by a direct line of sight, and no snapshots were taken within ≈ 2 *cm* reach of the obstacles. To evaluate the accuracy of our method, we calculated the average homeward component for distances in the range of 1 to 15 cm in 1 cm bins, each containing 30 samples. This measure characterizes both the accuracy and the angular dispersion of the computed home vectors and is often applied in homing experiments (Batschelet, 1981). As long as the homeward component stays significantly above zero, the robot moves nearer to the goal; if it is close to one, the robot moves directly homeward. The decrease in accuracy for distances smaller than 2 cm is due to sensor noise as predicted by Eq. (13). At distances larger than 15 cm the data base was too small, because pairs with larger distances fulfilling the imposed conditions occurred very rarely during the random walk, due to the cluttered structure of the arena. Other experiments indicate that the accuracy decreases rapidly due to occlusions beyond this value. This should not be considered a limitation of the homing scheme, but a characteristic of the environment.

4.3 Improvements by independent parameter estimation

The function over which the optimization in the three parameters α, ψ and ν has to be performed, has multiple local minima, thus standard gradient descent methods cannot be used. Since a global search is very time consuming it is convenient if ψ or ν can be estimated independently. A possible solution would be the use of an external compass to estimate ψ, but it can also be extracted from image data alone, as described below.

Spatial distance from image distance Due to the occurence of multiple local minima, the Euclidean image distance cannot be used to home by direct gradient descent. Nevertheless, the image distance between snapshot and current view correlates well with the relative distance ν, as can be seen from Fig. 8. The map was calculated from the view manifold data described in Sec. 4.2. In fact, up to a certain distance, spatial distance may be inferred from measured image distance. As the estimate of the other two parameters α and ψ is very robust to variations in ν (in particular, at large distances, cf. Sec. 3.2), we use a linear approximation for the relationship between spatial and image distance. This speeds up the algorithm considerably, so that home vectors can be computed in our $C++$ implementation at a frame rate of 25 Hz on the SGI Indy workstation (R4400 Processor at 100 MHz).

Orientation estimation Similarly, the change of orientation ψ may be estimated by shifting snapshot and cur-

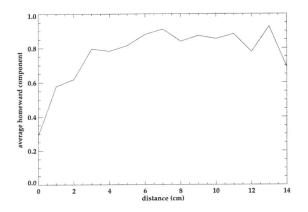

Figure 7: Average homeward component of computed home vector.

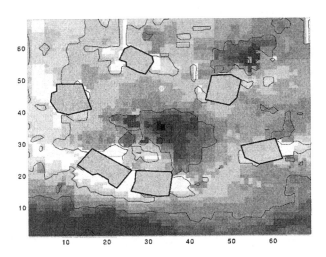

Figure 8: Euclidean image distance map for the home in Fig. 6. The displayed grey values correspond to the minimum distance which can be obtained by rotating the respective views. Darker areas represent smaller image distances.

rent view until a minimal image distance is reached. Unfortunately, this only works well near the goal. Since the algorithm does not tolerate large errors in the estimate of ψ, this method is not directly applicable in our scheme. A different approach, however, which we have successfully tested in other experiments, involves using previously acquired information to speed up the estimation of ψ. In particular, restricting the search space for ψ to the neighbourhood of previous estimates of ψ did not decrease accuracy.

5 Discussion

Previous approaches to scene–based homing. In the following, we will relate our approach to previously published approaches by briefly discussing a number of scene–based homing schemes and pointing out some differences to the present approach. In doing so, we will mainly focus on the type of approximations and the correspondence mechanisms utilized (summarized in Table 1).

Most approaches use a 360° field of view, greatly reducing computational cost: for limited fields of view, invisible parts must be kept in some internal representation, whereas for an omnidirectional sensor, all non-occluded landmarks are permanently visible. As Nelson & Aloimonos (1988) pointed out, there is an additional advantage: In a 360° field of view, the rotatory and translatory part of the disparity field can easily be separated, while in the case of limited fields of view, there is no unique decomposition. Therefore, considerable effort has gone into technical implementations, including a camera pointing at a spherical mirror (Hong et al. 1991), and a rotating intensity sensor (Röfer 1995).

Author	Approx-imation	Correspon-dence	Input	Constant orientation	Implemen-tation
Cartwright & Collett 1983	Isotropic landmark distribution	Region matching	Binary, one-dim., 360°.	yes	Computer simulation
Hong et al. 1991	Isotropic landmark distribution	Feature matching	Grey value, one-dim., 360°.	yes	Mobile robot
Röfer 1995	Isotropic landmark distribution	Kohonen network	Grey value, one-dim., 360°.	yes	Mobile robot
Wittmann 1995	Isotropic landmark distribution	Correlation on resolution pyramid	Grey value, one-dim., 360°.	yes	Computer simulation
Basri & Rivli 1995	Weak perspective	Linear com-bination of model images	Video images	no	Computer simulation
Franz et al. 1997	Equal distance	Parameterized disparity fields	Grey value, one-dim., 360°.	no	Mobile robot

Table 1: Overview of scene–based homing schemes (cf. Sec. 5)

Cartwright & Collett (1983) and Wittmann (1995) proposed models for honey bee landmark navigation. Both assume that the bee stores its orientation with respect to an external compass reference provided by the sun or the earth's magnetic field. This allows the bee to keep the orientation of snapshots constant, either by "mental" counterrotation or appropriate body orientation. Similarly, the camera platforms of the robot used by Hong et al. and Röfer do not rotate when the robot changes direction, so that all views have constant orientation. As pointed out in Sec. 4.3, this has the advantage of greatly reducing computational cost. The schemes of Cartwright & Collett and Wittmann are implemented in idealized computer models, so they do not have to provide solutions on how to deal with noisy orientation estimates. Since these errors may result in large deviations in the estimation of the home direction, small rotatory deviations are compensated for in the robotic implementations of Hong et al. and Röfer. However, the orientation of the platforms is subject to cumulative errors, thus their schemes may fail in large scale environments.

It should be noted that although the above approaches differ in the way they establish correspondences between views, they all rely on constant orientation and the approximation of isotropic landmark distribution. Apart from the fact that the latter is rarely realized, the error in the computed home direction due to this approximation may be very large, even close to the goal (e.g., if all landmarks were concentrated near K_A in Figure 1). Thus, these schemes may converge very slowly in strongly non-

isotropic environments, and even fail for higher noise levels. Cartwright & Collett included therefore an additional feature in their scheme to reproduce the experimental data: The vector sum for the computation of the home direction contains not only the tangential disparity vectors but also radial vectors which act to lessen the size discrepancy of the visible objects. This makes their scheme less sensitive to non-isotropic landmark distributions (and even works if only one single object is visible), but requires mechanisms for object recognition.

The scheme of Basri & Rivli (1995), unlike the above approaches, operates with a limited field of view. It uses images of objects with identifiable features, taken from different view points, as model images. Under weak perspective conditions any other view of the object can be generated by a linear combination of the model views. The goal direction is computed from the transformation coefficients of the current view and the snapshot. In addition to the mathematical discussion, Basri & Rivli validate their method on real–world test images; however, they do not give results obtained for simulated vehicles or robots.

The present approach: parameterized disparity fields. In this paper, we have proposed a novel approach to scene–based homing, based on the equal distance assumption described in Sec. 2. The accuracy with which the algorithm can approach a goal was shown to be limited only by sensor noise, not by the approximation, and that every snapshot is surrounded by a catchment area. Robot experiments demonstrated the validity of our method for real world applications and provided a quantitative assessment of its performance.

As the computation of disparity fields is an ill-posed problem, some additional assumption about the field had to be included. Our scheme makes explicit use of the underlying geometry of the task. Together with the equal distance assumption, this yields a low–dimensional parameterization of the possible disparity fields. The low-dimensionality leads to an optimization problem solvable in real time. All disparity fields defined by the parameterization, in particular the result of the optimization, are such that they can occur in real–world situations. This, however, is not guaranteed for general optical flow methods such as feature matching or correlation.

Clearly, our homing scheme is limited to the immediately accessible surroundings of a snapshot. Elsewhere, we have described how to deal with navigation in large-scale environments by combining several snapshots into a graph-like structure (Schölkopf & Mallot 1995, Franz et al. 1997).

Since this work was largely inspired by biology we want to conclude with a few remarks concerning the biological relevance of our scheme. The proposed algorithm could be implemented with matched filters in very simple neural circuitry. As Krapp & Hengstenberg (1996) have recently shown, flies use matched filters for complex stimuli such as generic optical flow fields. Moreover, we note that in our approach, 3–D information is only present implicitly, in the use of perspective distortion, and in the geometrical parameterization of disparity fields. Previous studies have shown that a variety of visual tasks (e.g. object recognition, see Bülthoff & Edelman, 1992) can be accomplished by biological systems without using explicit 3–D representations. Although these observations support our approach, we emphasize that it is not an explicit model of animal behaviour. It rather aims at understanding possible solutions to a general problem which robots as well as animals have to solve.

Acknowledgements. The present work has profited from discussions and technical support by Hanspeter Mallot, Philipp Georg, Susanne Huber, and Titus Neumann. We thank Ralf Möller and Guy Wallis for helpful comments on the manuscript. Financial support was provided by the Max–Planck–Gesellschaft and the Studienstiftung des deutschen Volkes.

References

[1] R. Basri and E. Rivlin. Localization and homing using combinations of model views. *Artificial Intelligence*, 78:327 – 354, 1995.

[2] E. Batschelet. *Circular statistics in biology*. Academic Press, London, 1981.

[3] H. H. Bülthoff and S. Edelman. Psychophysical support for a 2–D view interpolation theory of object recognition. *Proceedings of the National Academy of Science*, 89:60 – 64, 1992.

[4] B. A. Cartwright and T. S. Collett. Landmark learning in bees. *J. comp. Physiol. A*, 151:521 – 543, 1983.

[5] J. S. Chahl and M. V. Srinivasan. Visual computation of egomotion using an image interpolation technique. *Biol. Cybern.*, 74:405 – 411, 1996.

[6] T. S. Collett. Landmark learning and guidance in insects. *Phil. Trans. R. Soc. Lond. B*, 337:295 – 303, 1992.

[7] T. S. Collett. Insect navigation en route to the goal: Multiple strategies for the use of landmarks. *J. exp. Biol.*, 199:227 – 235, 1996.

[8] M. O. Franz, B. Schölkopf, P. Georg, H. A. Mallot, and H. H. Bülthoff. Learning view graphs for robot navigation. In W. L. Johnson, editor, *Proc. 1. Intl. Conf. on Autonomous Agents*, pages 138 – 147, New York, 1997. ACM Press.

[9] S. Goldman. *Information theory*. Dover, New York, 1953.

[10] J. Hong, X. Tan, B. Pinette, R. Weiss, and E. M. Riseman. Image-based homing. In *Proc. IEEE Intl. Conf. on Robotics and Automation 1991*, pages 620 – 625, 1991.

[11] H. G. Krapp and R. Hengstenberg. Estimation of self–motion by optic flow processing in single visual interneurons. *Nature*, 384:463 – 466, 1996.

[12] R. C. Nelson and J. Aloimonos. Finding motion parameters from spherical motion fields (or the advantages of having eyes in the back of you head). *Biol. Cybern.*, 1988:261 – 273, 1988.

[13] A. V. Oppenheim and R. W. Schafer. *Discrete–time signal processing*. Prentice Hall, Englewood Cliffs, NJ, 1989.

[14] T. Röfer. Controlling a robot with image-based homing. In B. Krieg-Brückner and C. Herwig, editors, *Kognitive Robotik (ZKW Bericht Nr. 3)*, Zentrum für Kognitionswissenschaften, Universität Bremen, 1995.

[15] B. Schölkopf and H. A. Mallot. View–based cognitive mapping and path planning. *Adaptive Behavior*, 3:311 – 348, 1995.

[16] M. J. Tarr and H. H. Bülthoff (eds.). Abstracts of the scene recognition workshop Tübingen. Technical Report 30, Max–Planck–Institut für biologische Kybernetik, 1996. Available as /pub/mpi-memos/TR-30.ps.Z via anonymous ftp from ftp.mpik-tueb.mpg.de.

[17] T. Wittmann. Modeling landmark navigation. In B. Krieg-Brückner and C. Herwig, editors, *Kognitive Robotik (ZKW Bericht Nr. 3)*, Zentrum für Kognitionswissenschaften, Universität Bremen, 1995.

[18] Y. Yagi, Y. Nishizawa, and M. Yachida. Map-based navigation for a mobile robot with omnidirectional image sensor COPIS. *IEEE Trans. Robotics Automat.*, 11:634 – 648, 1995.

A Robot Attracted to the Cricket Species *Gryllus bimaculatus*

Henrik Hautop Lund[1]   **Barbara Webb[2]**   **John Hallam[1]**

[1] Department of Artificial Intelligence
University of Edinburgh
5 Forrest Hill, Edinburgh EH1 2QL, Scotland, UK

[2] Department of Psychology
University of Nottingham
Nottingham NG7 2RD, UK

henrikl@dai.ed.ac.uk   Barbara.Webb@nottingham.ac.uk   john@dai.ed.ac.uk
http://www.dai.ed.ac.uk/staff/personal_pages/henrikl/

Abstract

Unlike most Artificial Life studies, we use biological data to verify a hypothesis about control mechanisms. We recorded male cricket *Gryllus bimaculatus* calling song, built a robot with the hypothesised control mechanism for phonotaxis behaviour and verified that it could account for the behaviour by observing the robot doing phonotaxis to the *real* cricket song. Further, we present a set of robot experiments that show how frequency dependence of the ear directionality in crickets can account for frequency selectivity in phonotaxis. Further, the results suggest that this mechanism also might account for part of the female choice behaviour.

1   Introduction

In the last decade or so, most Artificial Life experiments have been used to study behaviours, ecosystem dynamics, evolutionary processes, etc. A principal goal has been to use these experiments to underline the new paradigm that states that we have to study both "life as we know it" and "life as it could be" in order to obtain a general theory about life [5]. However, the distinction between "life as we know it" and "life as it could be" has resulted in nearly all Artificial Life researchers studying the latter, because this is what distinguishes the new paradigm from more traditional approaches toward the understanding of life. It seems quite peculiar that, where possible, the mainstream Artificial Life research has not tried to verify its hypotheses on natural life. This fact raises the serious question of whether many Artificial Life experiments are more than mere thought experiments or computer games.

There have been some Artificial Life studies that make use of biological data (for a recent review, see [15]), and recently, a few groups have started to use artificial agents or robots to verify hypotheses about control mechanisms of specific living animals.

Saito and Fukuda [12] made a robot of the same structure and size as a 7-8 years old female siamang ape in order to study brachiation. Grasso et al. [3] have made a robot lobster in order to test chemical orientation strategies that real lobsters might use to locate odour sources. We [8] used the Khepera robot in an experimental setup equal to the rats open field box experiment setup to show that one cannot conclude the construction of Euclidean cognitive maps in rats solely based on evidence from open field box experiments. Lambrinos et al. [4] built a robot with polarized light sensors in order to study how insect (desert ant, honey bee, cricket) nervous systems might extract compass information and do dead reckoning, which is unclear in neurophysiology/biology. It is significant, that these experiments were performed in the same environments as where biological experiments were performed, so the collected data is directly comparable with biological data.

Most modelling studies need to impose some artificial constraints to get a simulator or robot to work at all. But these constraints should not be such as to severely limit the potential for verifying the hypothesis against biological data, else the model tells us little. In this paper, our artificial organism (a robot) can be put under the same conditions as the living animal it models. Thus we can examine how the hypothesised control mechanism, implemented on the robot, can account for the animal's behaviour.

---

[0] The first author made the experiments and analysis described in the paper and wrote sections 1, 4, 6, and parts of 3. The second author provided the hypotheses tested and wrote sections 2 and 5. The third author designed the auditory circuit and wrote section 3.

Previously, we used a LEGO robot to show how a simple control mechanism could account for phonotaxis behaviour in crickets [17]. That is, the ability of a female cricket to locate the calling song of a male was reproduced. In particular the robot showed "preference" for certain songs in a manner that matched the female cricket, but using a much simpler decision mechanism than had previously been thought necessary.

However there were a number of limitations on that model that prevented a full evaluation against cricket behavioural data:

- It had a limited auditory processing speed that meant that the songs used were 10-20 times slower than real crickets (eg. *Gryllus bimaculatus* song consists of chirps with three syllables, each about 20ms long and separated by 20ms, with 200ms pauses between chirps; the robot song was 300ms syllables with 300ms gaps, and no chirp structure).

- a lower carrier frequency was used (2kHz vs. 4.7kHz) and it was not possible with that circuit to look at the effects of varying the carrier frequency although this is known to be an important factor in phonotaxis preferences (see below).

- the size of the robot restricted the experiments to be performed in an arena of size 200:1 with respect to the robot, where cricket experiments are normally performed in arenas of size 1000:1 relative to the animal.

In the current experiments we have re-implemented the circuitry and control mechanism on a Khepera robot. This has a faster processing speed so we can now use real cricket songs in testing the behaviour. We also have an arena that is almost 2500:1 the size of the robot. And the characteristics of the ear circuit allow us to test the previously unexplored assumption that characteristics of the *directionality* of peripheral auditory system of the cricket might be sufficient to explain some of the apparent preference for certain frequencies of song.

2 Cricket Phonotaxis and Frequency Selectivity

2.1 Calling song

Calling songs (CS) of most cricket species have a small bandwidth carrier frequency. The actual frequency varies with species from about 2 to 8 kHz. The most commonly studied species for phonotaxis experiments have carrier frequencies between 4.5kHz and 5.5kHz; *Gryllus bimaculatus* has a typical carrier of 4.7-4.8kHz. Individuals may vary by +/- 100Hz. However as Popov and Shuvalov [11] noted "it cannot be used as a basic [i.e. single] cue for recognition [of conspecifics] ...because, in most cases studied, the spectra of the CSs of sympatric species of crickets often overlap to a degree that cannot be resolved by their auditory system" (p. 114).

Sound is produced by the movement of a 'plectrum' over a 'file' as the cricket closes its wings. The rate of tripping of the teeth of the file is determined by the resonant properties of the harp, a specialised area on the wing that radiates the sound. This produces a pure and fairly constant carrier frequency [1].

It has been argued that these relatively low frequencies are advantageous for the propagation of sound over long distances, especially through vegetation which acts as a low-pass filter. However low frequency sounds pose difficulties for receptor directionality, particularly for small animals such as crickets. Michelsen (pers. comm.) suggests that the evolutionary discovery of the unique auditory apparatus of the cricket was a critical breakthrough in enabling these animals to use pure low frequencies for communication.

2.2 Auditory Apparatus

The cricket's auditory equipment comprises a pair of tympani, one on each front foreleg, a pair of auditory spiricles on either side of the front part of the body, and a set of tracheal tubes connecting these organs. Sound reaches each tympanum directly through the air, but also from the other auditory ports after delay and filtering in the tracheal tubes.

The vibrations of the tympani, which are transduced by auditory receptors, are thus determined by a combination of filtered delayed and direct sounds. The effect of the combination is as follows. Consider a sound impinging on the right tympanum from a source directly to the cricket's left. Sound also arrives via the right tympanum and spiricles after a certain delay. If the sound is of the correct frequency, the delayed version of the sound will arrive in phase with the direct sound and, since they affect opposite sides of the tympanum they will interact to cancel each other out. If this situation obtains, the delayed sound arriving at the left tympanum via the tracheal tubes will be in anti-phase to the directly arriving sound, and will reinforce the vibrations of that tympanum. In other words, provided the sound frequency matches the properties of the delay and filtering system implemented by the positioning of the acoustic ports and the structure of the internal tubes, the effect of the auditory morphology is to enhance the difference in perceived amplitude between the two tympani.

The simplest form of this model is when we assume that the internal delay between the tympani is equal to the time taken for sound to travel through the air between them. In that case, the two sound paths to the tympanum directly opposite the sound source always contribute in phase, and the response at that tympanum is minimal independent of frequency. For a maximal response from the tympanum closest to the source, the delay must then equal one quarter of the period of the incoming sound[1].

---

[1] Plus any number of whole periods, of course.

Arriving sounds will then produce a tympanal response that depends strongly on the direction to the source, even though the amplitudes of the sounds arriving at each tympanum by the direct path will differ relatively little for a distant source.

2.3 *Effects of varying the carrier frequency*

A number of studies have shown frequency selectivity in the approach of female crickets to otherwise identical songs. Most commonly reported is the threshold intensity required to drive a phonotaxis response. Thus Popov and Shuvalov [11] reported that *G. bimaculatus* tested in a Y-maze reacted to 4.5kHz songs at 10dB lower intensity than 3 or 7kHz tones and no positive taxis occurred above 12kHz. Segejeva and Popov [13] testing flight reactions found signals of 5kHz had 15-20dB lower thresholds than those of 4 or 6 kHz. Moiseff et al. [9] showed for *Teleogryllus* a similarly shaped threshold curve centred on 5-5.5kHz. Stout et al. [14] report sharp tuning to 4-5kHz in arena tests of *Acheta domestica*.

Many of these studies assume the frequency selectivity in behaviour reflects frequency-dependent differences in sensitivity in auditory receptors, and this undoubtedly forms part of the explanation. However as Stout et al. [14] point out, the behavioural curves appear more sharply tuned than the acoustic inter-neuron response curves. An additional factor could be the observation that most crickets show negative phonotaxis to high frequency sounds (escaping from bats): perhaps the decreased response at frequencies higher than 6 kHz represents a conflict between positive and negative taxis?

A third factor may be that the *directionality* of the cricket's ears is highly frequency dependent (see below for an explanation of why this is so). If the cricket cannot detect a difference between its ears it may not respond phonotactically even though the sound is 'audible'. For example Boyd and Lewis [2] report that "an appreciable L-R difference was usually evident between about 4-6kHz but differences of more than 10dB were restricted to frequencies within a band of some 300Hz either side of the best frequency" (p.530). Michelsen et al. [7] showed that at different frequencies of sound (1-20kHz), the direction of the sound had a great or lesser effect on amplitude at the tympanum, with the biggest directional effect occurring at the calling song frequency.

Two behavioural studies emphasise this possibility. Oldfield [10] considered the accuracy of turns made during taxis to signals varying in frequency and found that (i) for 2.5 or 12kHz only chance levels of turns were made in the right direction (ii) the angle relative to the midline at which significantly more turns were made in the correct direction increased as the frequency increased, from 13 degrees for 4.5 kHz to 30 degrees for 5.5kHz, and 50 degrees for 6.5kHz or 9kHz.

Thorson et al. [16] note that in earlier arena stud-

ies crickets responding to songs of abnormal carrier frequencies "display behaviour similar to scanning without responding phonotactically" (Hill (1972) quoted in [16], op cit). They suggest this may be related to the effect they demonstrate on the treadmill whereby high intensity sound of abnormal carrier frequency causes "tracking phonotactically ...in systematically wrong directions" with angular error increasing with the frequency of carrier used. This systematic bias was also revealed in some arena experiments.

In the experiments described below we are investigating to what extent the frequency dependence of the ear directionality *alone* can contribute to frequency selectivity in phonotactic behaviour.

3 Auditory circuit

The hypothesised effect of the cricket's auditory morphology is modelled using the programmable electronic circuitry whose block structure is shown in figure 1. Microphones 1 and 4 model the two tympani, while 2 and 3 model the auditory spiricles. Wideband (3–18kHz) preamplifiers buffer the microphone outputs, which are then fed to a set of delay lines that synthesise the two relative delays (τ_1 and τ_2) shown in solid lines[2] in the figure. The delayed spiricle signals are weighted and summed with each tympanal signal to generate the composite response to the sound field at each tympanum, then the amplitude of the latter is made available to the control software.

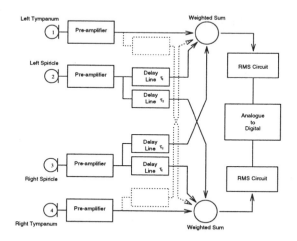

Figure 1: Block Diagram of the Peripheral Auditory Model. (©The authors, 1997.)

---

[2]Research [7] shows that the main contributions to the tympanal signal in the cricket are due to the tympanum itself and the two auditory spiricles — the contralateral tympanum makes only a small contribution to the signal. The dotted lines in the figure show the extra circuitry necessary to model a contralateral tympanal contribution. The system described here implements a simplified version of Michelsen and colleagues' findings [7], in that the tracheal tubes are modelled by wideband channels and lateral symmetry is assumed.

The electronic circuitry allows a number of parameters to be adjusted in order to model known properties of the cricket auditory morphology. The gains of the pre-amplifiers are individually controllable over the range 6-120; the two relative delays are programmable up to $160\mu s$ (1 bit corresponds to 625ns, in which time sound at room temperature propagates about 0.2mm); and the contribution of each component of the weighted sum is programmable in the range ± 1. All of these can be set within their respective ranges with 8 bit precision.

The electronics comprises two types of custom printed circuit board — *channel boards* which perform the signal processing, and a *clock board* which comprises the programming interface, delay synthesis circuitry, and bus decoding logic for connection to the Khepera robot. The latter board is round and plugs into the Khepera, while two channel boards are 55mm square and stand vertically above the clock board (see figure 2). Each channel board handles the signals from two microphones.

Figure 2: The Khepera robot with the auditory circuit. (©The authors, 1997.)

For the experiments described here, the circuitry is used in a somewhat simpler mode of operation. Spiricle contributions are neglected, and the model implemented assumes that only the tympani contribute — as noted above, this is not strictly accurate, but in fact is a reasonable and simple approximation for our purposes here. To operate the circuitry in this mode, microphones 1 and 4 are omitted and the τ_2 delay is used to model the effect of the inter-aural tracheal tube. Note in particular that there are no narrow band filtering steps in the signal processing: frequency dependence and directional response both arise from the composition of multiple signal paths.

The microphones are placed on the front of the robot pointing forward (see figure 2). We set them so that there is a spacing of approximately 18mm in between them, since 18mm corresponds to approximately 1/4 wavelength of a 4.7kHz sound (the carrier frequency of male *Gryllus bimaculatus* song). Dependent on the microphones, we empirically set the pre-amplifiers to get an equal response as output from the pre-amplifiers when giving equal input to the two microphones. The microphones might be more or less responsive, so this empirical setting of the pre-amplifiers is necessary. We place the robot with the microphones directly toward one loud speaker at a distance of 100cm. By emitting sound from the loud speaker and looking at the output from the two pre-amplifiers, we can then adjust the gain to get an equal response on both sides. The two relative delays (τ_2) are set to the time sound propagates the length of 1/4 wavelength of 4.7kHz. This corresponds to $53\mu s$ or approximately 85 bits as one bit corresponds to 625ns. On each side, the direct signal from the pre-amplifier and the delayed signal from the opposite side are fed into the mixer that, in our case, performs $1.0*\tau_1 - 1.0*\tau_2$. Each side's mixed signal is then sent through an RMS and an A/D converter to one of the Khepera's input channels.

As is shown on figure 3, this hardware processing of the auditory signal results in phase cancellation, when the input signal is of right carrier frequency (4.7 kHz). When the robot faces 90 degrees away from the loud speaker and the left microphone is nearest to the sound source, there will be an increased output from the left channel and very low output from the right channel (figure 3 (1)). The opposite happens if the robot is turned another 180 degrees, so that the right microphone is closer to the sound source (figure 3 (3)).

In our hypothesised control mechanism, the output from the circuit is fed into a comparator mechanism similar to that described in [17]. That is, for each side the output is fed into a leaky integrator, and whichever side reaches threshold first causes a small turn to be made in that direction. The default movement of the robot is a forward movement.

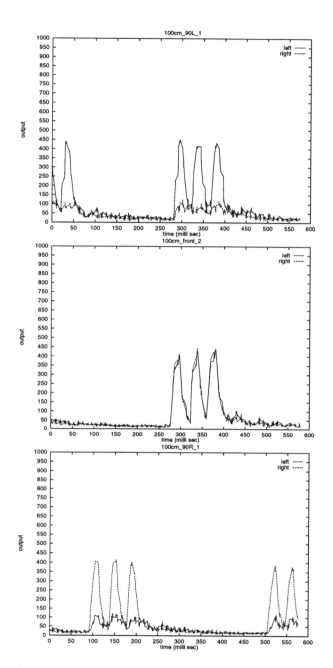

Figure 3: The output of the ears circuit's left and right channel when the robot is 100 cm away from the loud speaker that emits recordings of male cricket *Gryllus bimaculatus* song. The three figures show the output when the robot has the speaker at (1) 90 degrees left; (2) front; (3) 90 degrees right. (©The authors, 1997.)

4   Robot phonotaxis and frequency selectivity

4.1   Taxis to Real Sound

We made recordings of male *Gryllus bimaculatus* calling song at Life Science Department, University of Nottingham. The adult male cricket was sitting in a sand-floored arena and was recorded using a Maplin uni-directional dynamic microphone (YU-34) on a Marantz Stereo cassette recorder (CP230) from a distance of about 20cm. A 30s part of these recordings is played through a host Pentium computer with SB AWE32 sound card and was repeated twice for each experiment. The sound was fed through an amplifier to a loud speaker that was placed on a 240*240cm arena in our robot lab. It should be noted that we did nothing to control echos from the surrounding environment.

For each experiment, we placed the Khepera robot in the arena 150 cm away from the loud speaker. We alternated between two starting positions with the robot facing approximately 45 degrees away from the loud speaker either to the left or to the right.

In order to record the movements of the robot, we have built a simple video-tracking system [6]. We place a CCD camera approximately 2m above the arena, put a LED on top of the robot, and then use a Matrox Meteor framegrabber with our software to collect data.

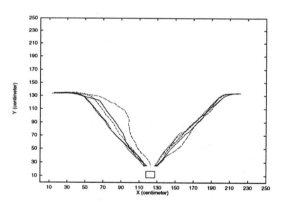

Figure 4: The robot's behaviour when recorded song of a male *Gryllus bimaculatus* is emitted from the loud speaker. (©The authors, 1997.)

Figure 4 shows the trajectories of the robot when the male *Gryllus bimaculatus* calling song was emitted from the loud speaker at the bottom. The experiment was repeated ten times. It is evident that the robot succesfully responded to the real cricket song, and navigated toward it. Initially, the robot moved forward a small amount of time before it reacted to the cricket calling song that was emitted from the loud speaker. Then, it turned toward the sound and navigated very directly toward the sound. At the scale of this figure, it is difficult to notice all the small turns that the robot performed in response to the calling song. In fact, in a distance of approximately 1m away from the sound source, the robot responded to most of the syllables (of a length of approximately 20 ms). On average, the robot made 7 turns/second, but most of them were around the midline toward the speaker and the trajectories appear very straight on the scale of figure 4. This result shows that the robot with the simple control mechanism based on comparison of signals on each side does phonotaxis very well when put under exactly the same condition as crickets in arena experiments. Hence, the simple control mechanism is enough to account for the female cricket's behaviour under these conditions.

4.2 Taxis to Different Frequencies

To test whether the frequency dependence of the ear directionality might contribute to frequency selectivity in crickets, we made another set of experiments, in which we played song with different carrier frequencies, namely of 2.35kHz, 4.7kHz, and 9.4kHz. 4.7kHz is the carrier frequency of the *Gryllus bimaculatus* calling song (wavelength λ_1), while 2.35kHz has a wavelength (λ_2) twice the size of 4.7kHz, and 9.4kHz has a wavelength (λ_3) of half the size of 4.7kHz. For 4.7kHz, sound at the near ear arrives in antiphase (it is delayed by $\lambda_1/2$) and gives a net amplitude of 2 at that ear, roughly. For 9.4kHz it is delayed by λ_3 and arrives in phase, giving a low amplitude; and for 2.35kHz it arives delayed $\lambda_2/4$ and gives a 1.4 amplitude. Therefore, we would expect the robot to be less responsive to 2.35kHz, and not to respond to 9.4kHz at all (if the signals were perfect, which they are not).

As in biological experiments with varying carrier frequency (see section 2.3), we did not use recordings of cricket song in this case. Instead, we generated artificial songs ourselves with chirps of three syllables with 200ms in between chirps. The syllables were of 20ms, and pauses in between syllables were 20ms. That is, the pattern of sound was as in the real cricket calling song.

Because the individual microphones might be more or less responsive to different frequencies, we once again calibrated the sound input via the programmable pre-amplifiers so that the output of the pre-amplifiers were at equal levels for sound of the different frequencies. This means that we cancel out any frequency-dependent differences in auditory receptors, and effectively can test whether frequency dependence of ear directionality alone can account for frequency selectivity in phonotaxis.

Figure 5, 6, and 7 show the results of the experiments with the songs with three different carrier frequencies. We allowed the robot to move ten times for 60 seconds with starting positions alternating between facing approximately 45 degrees left or right away from the loud speaker at a distance of 150cm. This was done for all three carrier frequencies.

As hypothesised, the robot would not respond to song of 9.4kHz, but just move in a straight line, since forward movement was the default movement (see figure 7). On the other hand, the robot performed phonotaxis to both 4.7kHz (see figure 5) and 2.35kHz (see figure

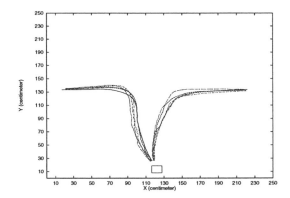

Figure 5: The robot's behaviour when computer generated song of 2.35 kHz is emitted from the loud speaker. (©The authors, 1997.)

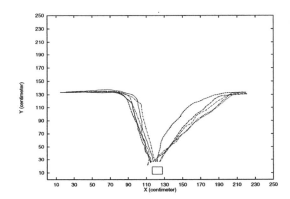

Figure 6: The robot's behaviour when computer generated song of 4.7 kHz is emitted from the loud speaker. (©The authors, 1997.)

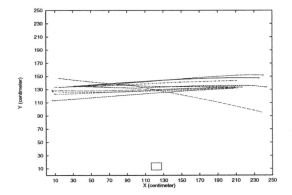

Figure 7: The robot's behaviour when computer generated song of 9.4 kHz is emitted from the loud speaker. (©The authors, 1997.)

6). However, the movements seemed more straight toward the loud speaker at 4.7kHz, especially at the right side of figure 5, while the robot seemed to move very close toward the middle of the arena before turning when presented with song of 2.35kHz. This suggests, that the

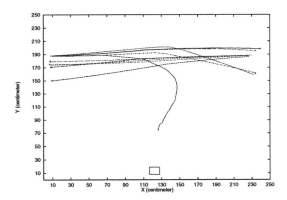

Figure 8: The robot's behaviour when starting further away as computer generated song of 2.35 kHz is emitted from the loud speaker. (©The authors, 1997.)

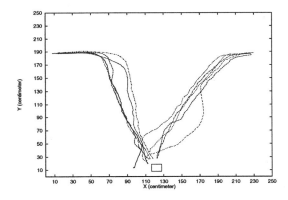

Figure 9: The robot's behaviour when starting further away as computer generated song of 4.7 kHz is emitted from the loud speaker. (©The authors, 1997.)

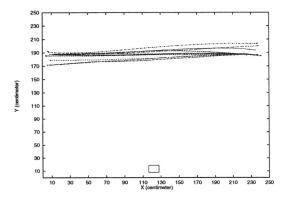

Figure 10: The robot's behaviour when starting further away as computer generated song of 9.4 kHz is emitted from the loud speaker. (©The authors, 1997.)

robot was more responsive to 4.7kHz, since it was able to turn at a smaller angle toward the speaker when presented with 4.7kHz — when moving straight toward the centre, the angle between loud speaker and microphones increases toward 90 degrees, at which point, an ideal signal would produce the highest output from the auditory circuit according to the hardware settings.

To further investigate whether selectivity of carrier frequency of 4.7kHz was the case, we did an additional set of experiments, in which the starting position of the robot was increased to 200cm away from the loud speaker. The robot was still able to perform quite succesful phonotaxis to 4.7kHz, even though it seemed to make a slight miss once out of the ten runs[3] (see figure 9). Not surprisingly, the robot still did not perform phonotaxis at 9.4kHz (see figure 10). However, the behaviour at 2.35kHz changed dramatically (see figure 8). Where the robot did phonotaxis when started closer to the sound source, it did not respond to the sound of 2.35kHz at this distance. Rather, it simply performed the default movement of moving forward. However, in one case out of the ten runs it responded to the sound, but made a very slow turn, so that it could not reach the sound source within the 60 seconds, and in a couple of other runs it responded once or twice which changed the movement only slightly. Hence, this distance seemed to be just above the maximum distance at which the robot could do phonotaxis to a song with carrier frequency of 2.35kHz.

Phonotaxis at 2.35kHz only occurs when the robot is close enough to the sound, and if we place the robot even closer to the sound source, phonotaxis at 9.4kHz can occur (data not shown here). These results can be interpreted as the robot being responsive to song of different carrier frequencies down to specific intensities. We have not measured the intensities of the song at different distances from the loud speaker, but obviously the intensity drops when further away from the loud speaker. The experiments show that frequency dependence of the ear directionality *alone* can contribute to frequency selectivity in phonotaxis, and the obtained results are comparable with the behavioural studies on crickets. Indeed, both behavioural studies with crickets [9, 11, 13, 14] and the present experiments with the robot show that the crickets react to songs with the ideal carrier frequency at lower intensity than to songs with carrier frequencies away from the ideal.

4.3 Taxis to Two Songs

To further investigate frequency selectivity, we did a number of experiments with two different sound sources.

---

[3]However, the reason for this miss seemed to be interference from the Khepera motors on the auditory circuit, so that the interaural delays changed. In the new circuit that we are producing there will be a 3.3V regulator that should isolate the auditory circuit from interference from the Khepera motors.

We placed two loud speakers in the arena and emitted computer generated song with carrier frequency of 4.7kHz from one loud speaker, and computer generated song with carrier frequency of 6.7kHz from the other loud speaker. The songs had the same pattern as the songs used in the previous experiments, and they were played in synchrony. With two different sound sources, it is difficult to calibrate the auditory system to ensure no frequency-dependent differences in sensitivity. Hence, the pre-amplifiers were set to an intermediate level. Regardless of this, the robot showed selectivity toward the song with the *Gryllus bimaculatus* carrier frequency of 4.7kHz, as shown on figure 11. Indeed, in nine out of the ten runs with different starting positions, the robot would navigate toward the 4.7kHz song, while it would move toward the 6.7kHz song only when placed very close to the loud speaker that emitted this song.

On the other hand, when the robot was placed at a starting position equidistant from the two sources, as shown on figure 12, the robot showed selectivity toward the song with 4.7kHz carrier frequency in all cases. It should be noted that we did not have a decibel meter or other equipment available to determine the output level from the two loud speakers. Hence, in order to obtain equal volume levels, we used the robot's auditory circuit to empirically set the outputs from the loud speakers' amplifier.

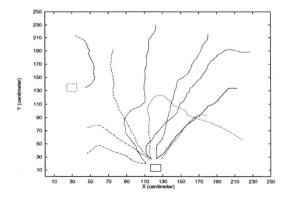

Figure 11: The robot's behaviour when computer generated song of 4.7 kHz is emitted from the loud speaker at the bottom and computer generated song of 6.7 kHz is emitted from the loud speaker to the left. The robot is placed at ten different starting positions. (©The authors, 1997.)

Where the previous results could be interpreted as interspecies choice/selectivity for the conspecific song, we made an extra set of experiments to test for intraspecies choice. Hence, we emitted the 4.7kHz song from two loud speakers in the arena. Again, the songs were played in synchrony. This would model two crickets sitting a bit more than 1m apart and singing (even though that they most often do not sing in synchrony). As is shown

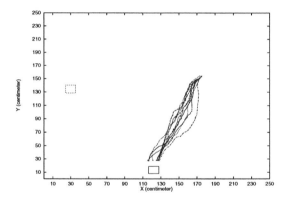

Figure 12: The robot's behaviour when computer generated song of 4.7 kHz is emitted from the loud speaker at the bottom and computer generated song of 6.7 kHz is emitted from the loud speaker to the left. The robot is placed at a starting position equidistant from the two sources in all ten runs. (©The authors, 1997.)

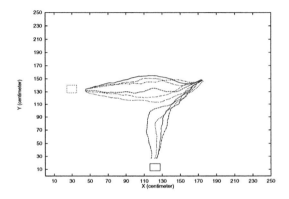

Figure 13: The robot's behaviour when computer generated song of 4.7 kHz is emitted from the two loud speakers in stereo. (©The authors, 1997.)

on figure 13, the robot would "choose" one of the sound sources and move fairly straight toward that one.

5 Discussion

These experiments show that at least a certain amount of frequency selectivity in phonotaxis behaviour can be derived from the properties of the directionality of the ears. That is, the robot, and presumably the cricket, have difficulty approaching songs of the wrong frequency simply because their ears cannot provide accurate directionality at those frequencies.

As discussed in section 2 this is probably not the whole explanation of frequency selectivity. Crickets do have a certain degree of frequency tuning in their auditory receptors and are most sensitive to the calling song frequency. Nevertheless the current results show that the directional effects are likely to play a significant additional role, even under complex conditions such as choosing a song of one frequency over another.

6   Conclusion

With this work, we have shown that our hypothesised control mechanism can account for phonotaxis behaviour not only under artificial experimental settings, but also when tested under biologically true conditions: the robot with the newly developed auditory circuit does phonotaxis to *real* cricket song. Hence, we can conclude that the hypothesised control mechanism can account for the female cricket's phonotaxis behaviour, even though that these experiments cannot tell whether this is the cricket control mechanism — only neurophysiological evidence can tell that. However, this simple control mechanism has been verified to be a possibility.

In future experiments, we will use the Khepera with the newly developed auditory circuit to make syllable rate experiments, in which we want to determine at what range of syllable lengths and at what syllable repetition rates taxis is performed. Further, we will investigate the female choice behaviour more thoroughly, for example by playing syllables of an ideal song alternately in each speaker and by investigating what the minimum pitch difference is for statistical consistent choice of the ideal song.

Acknowledgements

Henrik Hautop Lund is supported by EPSRC grant nr. GR/K 78942 and The Danish National Research Councils. The development of the auditory circuit has been done together with Andrew Haston. Facilities were provided by the Universities of Edinburgh and Nottingham.

References

[1] H. C. Bennet-Clark. Songs and the Physics of Sound Production. In F. Huber, T. E. Moore, and W. Loher, editors, *Cricket Behaviour and Neurobiology*, pages 227–261, Ithaca, New York, 1989. Cornell University Press.

[2] P. Boyd and B. Lewis. Peripheral auditory directionality in the cricket (*Gryllus campestris L., Teleogryllus oceanicus Le Guillou*). *J. comp. physiol.*, 153:523–532, 1983.

[3] F. Grasso, T. Consi, D. Mountain, and J. Atema. Locating Odor Sources in Turbulence with a Lobster Inspired Robot. In P. Maes, M. J. Mataric, J. Meyer, J. Pollack, and S. W. Wilson, editors, *From Animals to Animats 4: Proceedings of the Fourth International Conference on Simulation of Adaptive Behavior*, Cambridge, MA, 1996. MIT Press.

[4] D. Lambrinos, M. Maris, H. Kobayashi, T. Labhart, R. Pfeifer, and R. Wehner. An autonomous agent navigating with a polarized light compass. Technical report, Computer Science Department, University of Zurich, 1997. Submitted to Adaptive Behavior.

[5] C. G. Langton. Artificial life. In L. Nadel and D. Stein, editors, *Lectures in Complex Systems*, Reading, MA, 1992. Addison-Wesley.

[6] H. H. Lund, E. d. V. Cuenca, and J. Hallam. A Simple Real-Time Mobile Robot Tracking System. Technical Paper 41, Department of Artificial Intelligence, University of Edinburgh, 1996.

[7] A. Michelsen, A. V. Popov, and B. Lewis. Physics of directional hearing in the cricket *Gryllus bimaculatus. J. comp. physiol.*, 175:153–164, 1994.

[8] O. Miglino and H. H. Lund. Open Field Box Experiments with Rats and Robots. Technical report, C.N.R., Rome, 1996.

[9] A. Moiseff, G. S. Pollack, and R. R. Hoy. Steering responses of flying crickets to sound and ultrasound: Mate attraction and predator avoidance. *Proc. Natl. Acad. Sci. USA*, 75:4052–4056, 1978.

[10] B. P. Oldfield. Accuracy of Orientation of Female Crickets, *Teleogryllus oceanicus (Gryllidae)*: Dependence on song spectrum. *J. comp. physiol.*, 141:93–99, 1980.

[11] A. V. Popov and V. F. Shuvalov. Phonotactic behaviour of crickets. *J. comp. physiol.*, 119:111–128, 1977.

[12] F. Saito and T. Fukuda. A First Result of The Brachiator III — A New Brachiation Robot Modeled on a Siamang. In C. Langton and K. Shimohara, editors, *Proceedings of ALIFE V*, Cambridge, MA, 1996. MIT Press.

[13] M. V. Segejeva and A. V. Popov. Ontogeny of positive phonotaxis in female crickets, *Gryllus bimaculatus De Geer*: dynamics of sensitivity, frequency-intensity domain and selectivity to the temporal pattern of male calling song. *J. comp. physiol. A*, 174:381–389, 1994.

[14] J. F. Stout, C. H. De Haan, and R. W. McGhee. Attractiveness of the male *Acheta domesticus* calling song to females I. Dependence on each of the calling song features. *J. comp. physiol.*, 153:509–521, 1983.

[15] C. E. Taylor and D. Jefferson. Artificial life as a tool for biological inquiry. *Artificial Life*, 1(1-2):1–13, 1994.

[16] J. Thorson, T. Weber, and F. Huber. Auditory Behaviour of the Cricket II. Simplicity of Calling Song recognition in *Gryllus* and Anomalous Phonotaxis

at Abnormal Carrier Frequencies. *J. comp. physiol.*, 146:361–378, 1982.

[17] B. Webb. Using robots to model animals: a cricket test. *Robotics and Autonomous Systems*, 16:117–134, 1995.

Artificial Lampreys: Comparing Naturally and Artificially Evolved Swimming Controllers

Auke Jan Ijspeert*, **John Hallam***, **David Willshaw**[†]
*Dept. of Artificial Intelligence, U. of Edinburgh, 5 Forrest Hill, Edinburgh EH1 2QL
[†]Centre for Cognitive Science, U. of Edinburgh, 2 Buccleuch Place, Edinburgh EH8 9LW
{aukei,john}@dai.ed.ac.uk david@cns.ed.ac.uk

Abstract

This paper studies and compares naturally and artificially evolved neural networks controlling the motion of an animal: the anguilliform swimming of a lamprey. The swimming controller of the lamprey, extensively studied and modeled by Grillner and Ekeberg [8, 5], is reproduced. A real number Genetic Algorithm is used to develop alternative artificial controllers composed of neurons similar to those of the biological model. We examine the feasibility of using Genetic Algorithms to evolve neural controllers and evaluate the quality of the evolved networks by comparing them with the biological controller. Results show that artificial controllers can be obtained with architectures other than the biological one, and which, in some ways, are more efficient.

1 Introduction

Interactions between Neuroscience and Artificial Intelligence (AI) are currently growing as inspirations from Neuroscience become frequent in AI and models and techniques from AI are increasingly used in Neuroscience. Our research is particularly interested in neural locomotion controllers for autonomous agents which are biologically inspired and how to develop controllers using Evolutionary Algorithms.

Nature has developed a diversity of very effective motion controllers which are able to create the oscillatory activity necessary for motion as well as to adapt, using sensory information, to dynamic environments. These controllers are generally distributed and present remarkable robustness and flexibility. These interesting features have led roboticists to create biologically inspired neural locomotion controllers for robots or simulated agents [1]. Models of walking controllers in stick insects have, for instance, been used to control hexapod robots [3].

In return, AI techniques can be used to give some insights on Neuroscience measurements and give some hints about the computation performed. In the case of locomotion control, the local bending reflex of the leech has, for instance, been reproduced by a biologically plausible recurrent neural network optimised with an adapted backpropagation algorithm [9].

A recent AI technique to develop adapted controllers is evolving neural configurations using an Evolutionary Algorithm. This technique has been used successfully to develop walking controllers for hexapod agents [2] or biped agents [4], for instance.

This paper examines the lamprey's swimming controller which has been studied extensively by Grillner and his colleagues [8]. The mathematical model of the biological controller given in [5] is reproduced. Artificial controllers are created by using a Genetic Algorithm (GA) to evolve neural networks composed of neurons similar to those of the biological model. There is a double motivation for evolving artificial solutions. The first one is to study the alternative possibilities which Nature could have chosen to obtain controllers with an adapted behaviour, the second one is to evaluate how good a GA is as a tool for creating neural controllers for a specific task. Comparing the new solutions with the biological model will determine the quality of the evolved solutions.

2 Biological Controller

The lamprey is a fish without paired fins which swims by creating an undulation along its body. The corresponding neural activity is created by a Central Pattern Generator (CPG) situated in the spinal cord. The CPG is composed of segments capable of generating oscillatory signals which are coupled together in a way that propagates waves of motoneuron activity from head to tail [8]. Several mathematical models have been developed which are able to reproduce the neural activity measured on real lampreys [8, 5].

The mathematical model of the biological controller given in [5] is simulated, using MATLAB. The model simulates two-dimensional swimming and is based on two simplifications. Firstly, populations of similar real neurons are represented by single neuron units; secondly the output of a neuron unit is not spiking but corresponds to the mean firing frequency of the population ($\in [0, 1]$).

The model presented here corresponds to that model except that stretch sensitive edge cells (EC) are not included. These cells are not necessary for the creation of oscillations and play a role only when the lamprey swims in unstable water where they coordinate the neural activity with actual movements of the body [6].

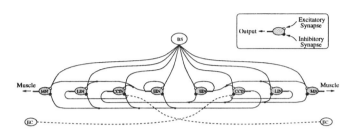

Figure 1: Biological segmental network. A segmental network is made of 8 neurons of 4 different types (see text). The biological model in this paper corresponds to the model described in [5], except that edge cells (EC) are not included. A dash means no connection.

$$\dot{\xi}_+ = \frac{1}{\tau_D}(\sum_{i \in \Psi_+} u_i w_i - \xi_+) \tag{1}$$

$$\dot{\xi}_- = \frac{1}{\tau_D}(\sum_{i \in \Psi_-} u_i w_i - \xi_-) \tag{2}$$

$$\dot{\vartheta} = \frac{1}{\tau_A}(u - \vartheta) \tag{3}$$

$$u = \begin{cases} 1 - \exp\{(\Theta - \xi_+)\Gamma\} - \xi_- - \mu\vartheta & (u > 0) \\ 0 & (u \leq 0) \end{cases} \tag{4}$$

where Ψ_+ and Ψ_- represent the groups of pre-synaptic excitatory and inhibitory neurons respectively, ξ_+ and ξ_- are the delayed 'reactions' to excitatory and inhibitory input and ϑ represents the frequency adaptation observed in some real neurons. The parameters of each type of neuron are given in Table 2. Neuron types have different times of reaction, thresholds and frequency adaptation. These parameters as well as the connection weights of Table 1 have been defined so that the simulation of the model fits physiological observations [5].

	EINl	CCINl	LINl	EINr	CCINr	LINr	BS
EINl	0.4	-	-	-	-2.0	-	2.0
CCINl	3.0	-	-1.0	-	-2.0	-	7.0
LINl	13.0	-	-	-	-1.0	-	5.0
MNl	1.0	-	-	-	-2.0	-	5.0
EINr	-	-2.0	-	0.4	-	-	2.0
CCINr	-	-2.0	-	3.0	-	-1.0	7.0
LINr	-	-1.0	-	13.0	-	-	5.0
MNr	-	-2.0	-	1.0	-	-	5.0

Table 1: Biological connection weights, as given in [5]. A row corresponds to the weights of the pre-synaptic connections. Excitatory and inhibitory connections are represented by positive and negative weights respectively. Left and right neurons are indicated by l and r.

Neuron type	Θ	Γ	τ_D	μ	τ_A
EIN	-0.2	1.8	30 ms	0.3	400 ms
CCIN	0.5	1.0	20 ms	0.3	200 ms
LIN	8.0	0.5	50 ms	0.0	-
MN	0.1	0.3	20 ms	0.0	-

Table 2: Neuron parameters, as given in [5]. Θ is the threshold, Γ the gain, τ_D the time constant of the dendritic sums, μ the coefficient of frequency adaptation and τ_A, the time constant of the frequency adaptation.

Segmental oscillators (Figure 1) are made of 8 neurons of 4 different types: excitatory interneurons (EIN), contralateral inhibitory interneurons (CCIN), lateral inhibitory interneurons (LIN) and motoneurons (MN). All receive excitation from the brainstem (BS). The output of the motoneurons is connected to lateral muscles and waves of motoneuron activity are transformed into waves of muscular contraction and thus undulations of the body. The connection weights between the neuron units are given in Table 1. The self-connections of the EIN neurons express the mutual excitation which happens among the population of neurons represented by the single EIN unit.

A neuron unit is a leaky integrator with a saturating transfer function defined by three differential equations. The output u of such a neuron is calculated as follows:

Oscillatory activity appears in segmental networks when an adequate level of excitation is applied from the brainstem. There are no oscillations if the excitation level is too low, and, when the level is too high, the neurons saturate after a few oscillations. In between, the system oscillates with a frequency proportional to the excitation. Our simulations[1] show that frequencies between 1.7 Hz and 5.6 Hz can be obtained, which does not cover the observed range on real lampreys completely (between 0.25Hz and 10Hz [10][2]). A typical oscillation is shown in Figure 2. The frequency of the oscillations in the segmental networks directly determines the speed of the fish in the water. The ability to change frequency is thus an important aspect of the model as it allows the lamprey to control its speed and adapt it to the environment.

---

[1]The differential equations are solved using a fourth order Runge-Kutta method with adaptive step size.

[2]It has been shown that voltage-sensitive N-Methyl-D-Aspartate receptors play an important role in slow oscillations[10]. As these are not included in this model, the lowest frequencies of the biological range can not be reproduced.

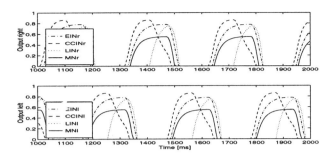

Figure 2: Typical activity of the 8 neurons of the biological segmental network.

A complete controller is composed of approximately 100 interconnected segments. Interconnections are extensions of the segmental connections to (up to ten) neighbour segments. The extent of each connection is given in [5]. Travelling waves of oscillations are created due to an asymmetry of the extensions favouring the caudal direction. Extra excitation on the five segments closest to the head increases the lag between segments and reduces the undulation wavelength. Wavelengths as small as approximately 50% of a 100-segment body can be obtained. The most efficient swimming is obtained with undulations whose wavelength corresponds to the length of the body, and indeed this is what is observed in many fishes [7]. Interestingly, the frequency of the oscillation and the wavelength of the undulation can be changed nearly independently.

This model can also perform turning or even backward swimming. Turning is obtained by exciting one side more than the other over the whole spinal cord, which results in higher amplitudes of signal going to the muscles of one side. Backward swimming is possible by giving some extra excitation to the most caudal (rather than rostral) segments, which causes the travelling wave to go backwards.

3 Evolving controllers

Artificial controllers are developed using a GA. The development of solutions is done in two stages. First segmental oscillators are evolved, then complete controllers are created by evolving the interconnections between fixed segmental networks. The GA encodes the connectivity of potential solutions and solutions are evaluated by simulating their neural activity over a fixed time and rewarding specific behaviours. There is no mechanical simulation of the lamprey's swimming. To evaluate controllers without mechanical simulation is possible, firstly, because no sensory feedback is necessary for the creation of oscillations and, secondly, because the body and muscular structure of the lamprey are suf-

ficiently simple that good and bad controllers can be distinguished by evaluating their neural activity. The main features of controllers on which we will concentrate are the possibilities of varying the frequency of oscillations and the wavelength of spatial undulations. The frequency of oscillations in each segment directly determines the speed of swimming and therefore control of the frequency of oscillations means control of speed. The control of the wavelength of the undulation allows variation of the 'type' of swimming in order to adapt it to the environment and, for instance, to find the most efficient swimming for different external conditions.

3.1 Segmental oscillators

3.1.1 Genetic Algorithm implementation

The same basic GA is used for both design stages. Solutions are encoded in fixed-length chromosomes made of real number genes $\in [0, 1]$. Parents are chosen with a rank-based probability for breeding, and children are created either by a two-point crossover operator (probability $Prob\_Xover$) or by simply copying the two parents (probability $1 - Prob\_Xover$). Genes are mutated with a probability $Prob\_Mut$ and given a new value:
$$new\_value = old\_value + Mut\_Range \cdot rand$$
where $rand$ is a random number $\in [-0.5, 0.5]$. If a new value is outside the range $[0, 1]$, it is set to the closest limit. A selective pressure is created by keeping the size of the population constant and rejecting the worst solutions at each generation. The GA and the simulations are implemented with MATLAB for this design stage.

3.1.2 Encoding Assumptions

Artificial segmental oscillators are created by evolving the connectivity between neurons similar to the biological model. The problem of evolving segmental oscillators is defined by several assumptions:

1. Only the connectivity (i.e. the weights of all the possible connections between neurons) is evolved.

2. The number of neurons is fixed to 8.

3. The types of neurons (parameters of eq. 1–4) are fixed. There are two neurons of each type as in the biological model[3].

4. Weights are bounded between two fixed values, one negative, one positive.

5. Symmetry of the connections between left and right neurons is imposed.

---

[3]Note that the names of the neuron types EIN, CCIN and LIN describe the function of these neurons in the biological model and this function may change in other configurations. We will keep them only to describe the corresponding neuron parameters.

6. Segmental oscillators have no sensory feedback (no edge cells and no mechanical simulation).

The weight bounds are chosen to include the biological range of weights. The symmetry between left and right neurons reduces the dimension of the search space by a factor of 2.

A segmental oscillator is represented by a chromosome through a direct encoding of each connection weight into a gene, a real number between 0 and 1. A chromosome is translated into a configuration by linearly transforming the gene's value into a value between the two fixed weight bounds and transforming the rescaled vector into the matrix giving the weights of all the possible connections.

3.1.3 Fitness function

The evaluation of the fitness of a segmental network is based on qualitative features of the neural activity of motoneurons. Only these neurons are considered as their signals determine the muscular activity along the body. An evaluation consists of fixed-length simulations with asymmetric initial conditions[4].

A fitness function is developed which rewards the following behaviour for the motoneurons activity:

1. regular oscillations,

2. periods corresponding to an alternation of an active and a resting phase, with a single peak of activity per period,

3. opposite behaviour between left and right motoneurons,

4. monotonic relation between excitation and oscillation frequency,

5. large range of frequencies.

As already mentioned, controllers with a large range of frequencies are rewarded because the frequency of oscillations determines the speed of swimming and therefore large ranges of frequency offer more flexibility in the control of speed. Note that because the activity in the interneurons (neurons other than the motoneurons) is not considered, oscillators with fewer than 8 active neurons can be developed.

The mathematical definition of the fitness is as follows:

$$fitness = \begin{cases} fit\_oscil \cdot (1 + freq\_range) \\ \qquad \text{if } fit\_oscil > 0.5 \\ fit\_oscil \quad \text{otherwise} \end{cases}$$

where

$$fit\_oscil = fit1 \cdot fit2 \cdot fit3 \in [(0.05)^3, 1]$$

[4]All the left neurons of a segment are excited.

The function *fit_oscil* rewards the three first points of the desired behaviour of a solution, with the functions *fit1*, *fit2* and *fit3* rewarding respectively varying outputs, regularity and opposite behaviour between left and right motoneurons. These three functions are bounded between 0.05 (bad behaviour) and 1 (good behaviour), and vary linearly between these values for one or several variables. The bounds for each variable, determining when the value of the variable is bad, good or in between, have been determined by hand on 40 examples of different behaviours from initial experiments. It is possible to fix these bounds such that *fit_oscil* clearly makes the difference between interesting solutions and the others. A limit of 0.5 is thus determined above which a solution is certain to oscillate regularly with opposite behaviour between left and right motoneurons[5].

The value *freq_range* corresponds to the range of frequency (in Hz) in which the solutions oscillate regularly (*fit_oscil* higher than 0.5) with a frequency increasing with the excitation level. An evaluation consists thus of a first simulation at a fixed level of excitation (equal to 1) which determines *fit_oscil*, followed, if *fit_oscil* is higher than 0.5, by a set of simulations at different excitation levels (0.1 steps) in order to determine *freq_range*.

3.1.4 Results

As first tests showed that there existed many different solutions with similar fitness values, three experiments were done with different encodings in order to study different neural configurations: encoding all the possible connections between the 8 neurons; encoding all the possible connections except feedback from motoneurons; and encoding only the biological connections. For each experiment, five evolutions are performed with different initial populations of 100 chromosomes. The number of generations for each experiment is chosen so that frequency ranges higher than 7Hz are reached in all runs. An *elite population* is then created, made of the 20 best solutions of each initial evolution. This new population is then further evolved until frequency ranges higher than 14Hz are reached. The basic GA parameters for each experiment are given in Table 3.

Experiment 1, fully connected network: All the possible connections between the 8 neurons and the brainstem (without feedback from neurons to the brainstem) are encoded, resulting in 72 possible connections[6]. Due to the left/right symmetry assumption, a chromosome has thus 36 genes. This encoding allows feedback

[5]On the 40 examples of neural activities, 17 correspond to interesting behaviours. With the chosen fixed bounds of *fit1*, *fit2* and *fit3*, all the good behaviours have a *fit_oscil* value higher than 0.6 and all the others have a value lower than 0.25, with most lower than 0.1.

[6]Each neuron can have a self-connection.

Population size	100
Number of children	30
Weight bounds	[-5,15]
Crossover probability	0.5
Mutation probability	0.4
Mutation range	0.4

Table 3: GA parameters for evolving segmental oscillators

from the motoneurons to the other neurons, which is not the case in the biological model where the only output connection from motoneurons goes to muscles.

As mentioned, the evolutions all started with different initial populations. Within these 500 randomly generated configurations, only 4 produce varying outputs (of which one could be a potential controller, i.e. a solution with regular asymmetric oscillations and variable frequency). This means that approximately 1% of the 36-dimension variable space sampled here corresponds to configurations with varying outputs among which the GA must find interesting controllers.

After 200 generations, all evolutions successfully converged to potential controllers, which produce regular oscillations, opposite behaviour between left and right motoneurons and variable frequency. There exists a large diversity of controller configurations and behaviours within the final populations. Configurations vary in terms of weight values, connection types and number of active neurons; none is similar to the biological configuration nor to the biological configuration with a swap of function between the neurons types. The number of neurons participating in the oscillations varies between 4,6 and 8. The signal shapes of the neurons other than motoneurons (the interneurons) can be very different, with for instance, signals that have more than one peak per period, or that oscillate without resting phases.

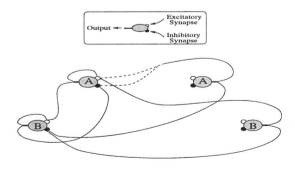

Figure 3: Four-neuron oscillator. Variations (broken lines) of a 4-neuron structure (2 neurons A and 2 neurons B) found in several evolved segmental oscillators. Only the input connections of the 2 left neurons are given, the others can be found by symmetry.

The frequency ranges of the best solutions of each evolution after 200 generations lay between 7.1 Hz and 9.6 Hz. These results are summarised in Table 7. These five best solutions are able to create the oscillations with fewer than 8 neurons (either 6 or 4 neurons) for most of the frequencies in the frequency range. Some neurons are active at low frequencies and do not participate (they stay at zero) in the oscillations at higher frequencies. These neurons can be removed and the solutions still oscillate at most of the frequencies except the lowest. Interestingly, the resulting 4-neuron configurations of runs 1, 2 and 3 present a similar structure (when the left/right symmetry is taken in account and the type of neuron is ignored), having the same type of connections, excitatory or inhibitory, for all the connections, except one for the solution of run1. These runs seem thus to have converged to solutions built on a similar 4-neuron oscillator structure (Figure 3).

The best solution after evolving the *elite population* for 150 generations, has a very large frequency range, 16.4Hz (from 2.8Hz to 19.2Hz), which is thus more than 4 times larger then the frequency range of the biological model (3.9Hz). The behaviour and the connectivity of that solution are given in Figure 4 and Table 4.

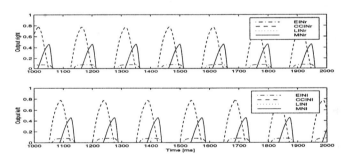

Figure 4: Fully connected network: Simulation of the best solution of exp.1. Frequency=6.7Hz. At higher frequencies, only the MN and CCIN neurons are active.

	EINl	CCINl	LINl	MNl	EINr	CCINr	LINr	MNr	BS
EINl	-5.0	3.2	11.2	8.3	-0.7	-1.4	-5.0	7.0	-2.7
CCINl	10.0	14.7	10.4	-3.2	-3.0	-1.7	0.7	3.6	10.2
LINl	5.0	2.0	5.9	8.0	12.3	8.3	-3.2	-3.9	4.7
MNL	-5.0	1.9	10.3	15.0	2.3	-4.9	7.3	-0.7	9.2
EINr	-0.7	-1.4	-5.0	7.0	-5.0	3.2	11.2	8.3	-2.7
CCINr	-3.0	-1.7	0.7	3.6	10.0	14.7	10.4	-3.2	10.2
LINr	12.3	8.3	-3.2	-3.9	5.0	2.0	5.9	8.0	4.7
MNr	2.3	-4.9	7.3	-0.7	-5.0	1.9	10.3	15.0	9.2

Table 4: Fully connected network: Connection weights of the best solution of exp.1. A row corresponds to the weights of the pre-synaptic connections. This solution is based on a four-neuron oscillator made of MN and CCIN neurons.

The oscillations of this solution are mainly due to the interaction between CCIN neurons and motoneurons. By removing the other neurons, it is possible to create a solution which presents identical behaviour, except at low frequencies, and which oscillates at frequencies between 6.9Hz and 19.2Hz[7]. Note that such a controller with only 4 neurons is only possible because of the feedback from motoneurons. This 4-neuron structure is identical to that of the best solution of run1 in terms of connection types (excitatory or inhibitory).

Experiment2, fully connected network without MN feedback: Here all the possible connections are encoded except that feedback from motoneurons to the other neurons is not allowed. This situation is thus closer to the biological model in which there is no such feedback and in which the motoneurons do not participate in the creation of oscillations. 56 connections are thus encoded in 28-gene chromosomes. Within the initial 500 randomly generated configurations, only 3 produce varying outputs (less than 1% of the 28-dimension variable space) of which none could be a potential controller.

All evolutions, except one, successfully converged, within 150 generations, to potential controllers, which produce regular oscillations, opposite behaviour between left and right motoneurons and variable frequency. The failed evolution converged prematurely to a local maximum corresponding to a non-oscillating solution and did not manage to improve it within 150 generations. Again a diversity of neural configurations has been found.

The frequency ranges of the best solutions of the four other evolutions after 150 generations lay between 10.3 Hz and 17.5 Hz (See summary in Table 7). The oscillations of the best solution of run 5 are created by the EIN and CCIN neurons (LIN neurons stay inactive, at all frequencies). The corresponding 4-neuron structure is similar in terms of connection types (excitatory or inhibitory) to that underlying the oscillations of the best solutions of run1 and the evolved elite population of the first experiment (Figure 3).

The elite population is evolved for 80 extra generations. A best solution is thus created whose frequency range is 21.0Hz (from 2.8Hz to 23.8Hz) which is more than 5 times larger then the frequency range of the biological model. The behaviour and the connectivity of that solution are given in Figure 5 and Table 5. The complete controllers evolved in the second design stage will be based on this segmental network.

Experiment3, biological connections: In this experiment only the biological connections are encoded (the others are set to zero) and the bounds are fixed

---

[7]This shows that, in these fully connected solutions, some connections or even some neurons are not necessary for creating oscillations. One possibility to create solutions with only the necessary connections (results not shown) is to add a mutation which randomly sets some connections to zero and to add a factor to the fitness function rewarding solutions with reduced connectivity.

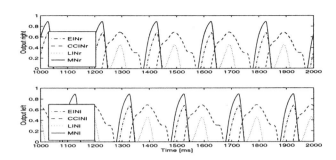

Figure 5: Fully connected network without MN feedback: Simulation of the best solution of exp.2. Frequency=5.0Hz.

	EINl	CCINl	LINl	EINr	CCINr	LINr	BS
EINl	12.5	-5.0	-4.4	6.9	10.8	14.1	9.1
CCINl	7.6	2.7	12.8	-0.5	0.9	-5.0	-0.2
LINl	10.3	9.6	2.7	-1.3	-3.1	14.4	
MNL	14.8	-5.0	-3.4	-1.6	14.9	1.1	14.2
EINr	6.9	10.8	14.1	12.5	-5.0	-4.4	9.1
CCINr	-0.5	0.9	-5.0	7.6	2.7	12.8	-0.2
LINr	-5.0	-1.3	-3.1	10.3	9.6	2.7	14.4
MNr	-1.6	14.9	1.1	14.8	-5.0	-3.4	14.2

Table 5: Fully connected network without MN feedback: Connection weights of the best solution of exp.2. A row corresponds to the weights of the pre-synaptic connections.

such that the types of connection, excitatory or inhibitory, are identical to the biological model. The 26 connections are encoded in 13-gene chromosomes. Within the initial 500 randomly generated configurations, 76 (13% of the sampled variable space) produce varying outputs of which 64 could be potential controllers (regular asymmetric oscillations and variable frequency). Having only the biological connections and fixing their type, excitatory or inhibitory, thus restricts the variable space to a much more favourable search space than having the complete connectivity encoded.

Within only 50 generations, all evolutions converged to interesting solutions. The shapes of the signals are very similar to those of the biological simulations, except for their amplitudes. The frequency range of the best solutions lay between 8.5Hz and 10.7Hz. This means that the range of frequencies of the biological model can be improved by changing the values of its connections a little and using a fitness function which optimises the frequency range. A general observation is that this improvement is obtained by increasing the strengths of the connections. Interestingly, the best solutions have all very similar weights for the inhibitory connections and have converged to a common underlying inhibitory structure.

After evolving the *elite population* for 50 extra generations, a best solution is created (Figure 6 and Table 6)

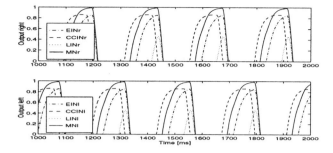

Figure 6: Biological connections: Simulation of the best solution of exp.3. Frequency=4.2Hz.

	EINl	CCINl	LINl	EINr	CCINr	LINr	BS
EINl	2.8	-	-	-	-4.5	-	1.7
CCINl	1.5	-	-4.3	-	-1.4	-	15.0
LINl	10.5	-	-	-	-4.4	-	11.5
MNL	14.7	-	-	-	-3.4	-	13.8
EINr	-	-4.5	-	2.8	-	-	1.7
CCINr	-	-1.4	-	1.5	-	-4.3	15.0
LINr	-	-4.4	-	10.5	-	-	11.5
MNr	-	-3.4	-	14.7	-	-	13.8

Table 6: Biological connections: Connection weights of the best solution of exp.3. A row corresponds to the weights of the pre-synaptic connections. The runs 1 to 5 converged to solutions whose inhibitory weights are very similar to this solution. There seems to be a common underlying inhibitory structure which optimises the frequency range.

whose frequency range is 11.9Hz (from 2.1Hz to 14.0Hz), which is approximately three times the range of the biological model and covers better the range of frequency observed in real lampreys, from 0.25Hz to 10Hz approximately. As observed before, the connections are stronger than in the biological model (absolute value of the weights on average 88% larger than the biological values).

Note that the weights of the biological model (in [5]) have been set by hand in order to fit the biological data (Ekeberg, personal communication). As the model is based on two important simplifications (a whole population of neurons is represented by one mathematical neuron unit and the output of a neuron unit is not a spiking action potential but the mean firing frequency), the weights of the biological model have no biological meaning except for showing that the model is able to reproduce the observed physiological behaviour of the CPG. Results shown here may give some insights into the strengths of the connections relative to each other in order to create oscillations which cover a range of frequencies which is closer to that observed in real lampreys.

Exp.	Run	N. of gen.	Range in Hz	from [Hz]	to [Hz]	Not oscil.
1	1	200	7.7	5.5	13.2	EIN,LIN
	2	200	8.4	1.9	10.3	EIN,CCIN
	3	200	7.1	2.4	9.5	EIN,CCIN
	4	200	9.6	4.2	13.8	CCIN
	5	200	7.9	3.0	10.9	CCIN
	elite	150	16.4	2.8	19.2	EIN,LIN
2	1	150	12.9	2.6	15.5	-
	2	150	-	-	-	-
	3	150	16.0	3.7	19.7	-
	4	150	10.3	2.7	13.0	-
	5	150	17.5	2.5	20.0	LIN
	elite	80	21.0	2.8	23.8	-
3	1	50	10.7	2.3	13.0	-
	2	50	10.2	1.7	11.9	-
	3	50	8.5	2.0	10.5	-
	4	50	8.8	2.1	10.9	-
	5	50	9.4	1.7	11.1	-
	elite	50	14.1	2.0	16.1	-

Table 7: Evolved segmental networks, summary of results. This table gives the range of frequency of the solutions with highest fitness value of each evolution. The neurons which do not oscillate for some of the excitation levels (usually the highest) are indicated.

3.2 Complete controllers

Multi-segmental controllers are developed by evolving the interconnections between fixed segmental oscillators. Two preliminary evolutions are realised, one with an evolved segmental network and one with the segmental network of the biological model. The first evolution will create a complete artificial controller. The evolved segmental network with the largest frequency range is chosen (best solution of experiment 2). The aim of the second evolution is to study the interconnectivity of the biological model. Because the physiological interconnections are not perfectly known [5], evolving the interconnections of the biological model may show whether there are several possibilities for interconnecting the biological segmental networks and creating travelling waves.

3.2.1 Genetic Algorithm implementation

The same basic GA as in the segmental oscillator design stage is used here, except that genes are transformed into integers representing the extent of an interconnection and that the GA and the simulations are implemented in C code.

3.2.2 Encoding assumptions

As in the biological model, segmental networks are interconnected through extensions of connections within a segmental network to neighbour segments. This means that a neuron which is connected to (rather, whose output is sent to) another neuron in one segment, can also have extensions to the corresponding neuron in neighbouring segments. The extent of these interconnections varies with each segmental connection. A connection weight is rescaled by dividing the weight of the connection in the segmental network by the number of neighbour segments it receives input from[8].

The encoding of a complete controller is based on the following assumptions:

1. The weights of the segmental network are fixed, except for the rescaling mentioned above.

2. Only the extents (in the rostral and caudal directions) of the interconnections are evolved.

3. These extents vary between zero and a fixed limit.

4. Symmetry of the interconnections between left and right neurons is imposed.

A complete controller is decoded from a chromosome by transforming and rounding a gene's value into an integer between 0 and the fixed maximum extent and transforming the resulting vector into the two matrixes giving the extent of each segmental connection in the rostral and caudal directions. The maximum extension is chosen to permit the maximum biological extension (10 segments).

3.2.3 *Fitness function*

As for the development for segmental oscillators, the evaluation of the fitness function is based on qualitative features of the neural activity of motoneurons.

We would like the complete controller to be such that

1. each segment oscillates regularly,

2. waves of neural activity propagate from head to tail,

3. the wavelength of the undulation can be varied by changing the amount of extra excitation on the segments closest to the head.

An evaluation consists of two simulations of a 100-segment controller with two different amounts of extra excitation on the five first segments, 0% and 100% of the level of excitation of the other segments (excitation equal to 1.0). The fitness is calculated as follows:

$$
fitness = \begin{cases} oscil\_behav \cdot \ (1 + Lag(100\%) - Lag(0\%)) \\ \quad\quad \text{if } oscil\_behav > 0.5 \\ \quad\quad \text{and both } Lag() \geq 0 \\ oscil\_behav \quad \text{otherwise} \end{cases}
$$

where *oscil_behav* is calculated by measuring *fit_oscil* in segments 1,10,20,...,100 for both evaluations (with and without extra excitation) and taking the minimum measured value. The lag values correspond to the lag per

segment relative to the period of oscillation, in percent (values typically vary between 0% and 2.5%). Note that the range of lags is not explicitly rewarded, but only the range between two fixed levels of extra excitation.

3.2.4 *Results*

The GA parameters of both experiments are given in Table 8. The evolutions of each experiment are stopped when wavelength ranges larger than that of the biological model are reached.

Population size	20
Number of children	6
Extensions bounds	[0,12]
Crossover probability	1.0
Mutation probability	0.4
Mutation range	0.4

Table 8: GA parameters for evolving complete controllers

Complete controller with evolved segmental network A complete artificial controller is created by evolving the interconnections between an evolved segmental network. The best solution of experiment 2 (Table 5), the solution with the largest frequency range of the three experiments, is chosen. As this segmental network has 48 connections between the 8 neurons, the dimension of the search space[9] for both rostral and caudal extensions is 48.

An evolution of a population of 20 chromosomes is realised for 10 generations. Within the initial randomly generated population, 17 of the 20 configurations have regular oscillations in all segments for both levels of extra excitation showing that such a segmental network can be interconnected in different ways and still oscillate regularly. However, most of these solutions present only very small lags, some of them going from the tail to the head. Others create travelling waves whose wavelength is not changed by the level of extra excitation. Only six solutions have a reasonable range of lags per segment (higher than 0.2% of the period).

After 10 generations only, the best solutions have ranges of lags per segment up to 2.3% of the period of oscillation, which is a little bit larger than the range of the biological model. All the solutions except one have extensions favouring the caudal direction on average, as is the case for the biological model. The best solution (Table 9) has lags per segment varying almost linearly with the amount of extra excitation on the first segments and lying between 0.1%(no extra excitation) and

---

[8]This rescaling compensates the weights for the neurons in the first and last segments which receive less input because they have fewer rostral and caudal extensions respectively.

[9]There are 48 possible extensions in both directions, and these are encoded in 48-gene chromosomes because of the symmetry assumption.

2.4%(100% extra excitation) of the period. Wavelengths as small as 42% of a 100-segment body can thus be obtained. The shortest wavelength of the biological model is approximately 50% of the body length. Figure 7 shows an example of the neural activity of the best evolved controller.

	EINl	CCINl	LINl	EINr	CCINr	LINr
EINl	6:10	0:2	4:1	4:10	0:9	6:6
CCINL	11:5	6:9	4:3	4:10	7:1	8:9
LINl	8:8	10:4	7:3	11:5	2:10	0:11
MNl	10:4	12:9	6:8	9:9	12:11	0:9
EINr	4:10	0:9	6:6	6:10	0:2	4:1
CCINr	4:10	7:1	8:9	11:5	6:9	4:3
LINr	11:5	2:10	0:11	8:8	10:4	7:3
MNr	9:9	12:11	0:9	10:4	12:9	6:8

Table 9: Complete evolved controller: rostral:caudal extensions of the best solution. There is an average asymmetry of the interconnections favouring the caudal direction.

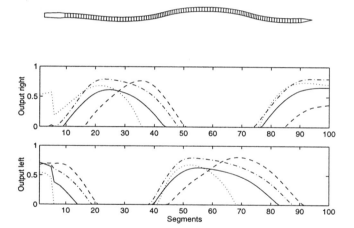

Figure 7: Complete evolved controller: Simulation of the best solution. A snapshot of the neural activity in a 100-segment body (800 neurons) is represented. A wave of neural activity, and therefore an undulation of the body, is created because of time lags between each segment. As in the biological model, these lags are due to the extra excitation on the five first segments and to the average asymmetry of the interconnections favouring the caudal direction. The body represented here is simply a set of trapezia whose parallel lengths are inversely proportional to the signal of the left and right motoneurons of each segment.

This preliminary experiment has shown that it is possible to evolve complete artificial controllers using a GA. The efficiency of swimming with this controller should be checked with a mechanical simulation of the body. Initial tests show that this artificial model is able to induce turning when one side of the spinal cord is more excited than the other, leading to different amplitudes of motoneuron signal, as with the biological model.

Complete controller with biological segmental network   The extensions of the 18 connections between the 8 neurons of the biological segmental network are encoded into a 18-gene chromosome. An evolution of a population of 20 chromosomes is realised for 40 generations.

Again, there seem to be many possibilities for interconnecting the biological segmental network which result in regular oscillations in all segments. After 40 generations the population evolved to solutions with ranges of lags per segment similar to the biological model. The solutions all present an average asymmetry of interconnections favouring the caudal direction. There is a variety of different solutions among the final population, but none is similar to the complete biological controller, mainly because they have asymmetric extension for all connections, not only the connections going from the CCIN neurons as in the biological model (see [5]).

In summary, there are several possibilities for interconnecting the segmental network to obtain travelling waves with variable wavelengths for similar wavelength ranges. The interconnectivity of the biological model is only one of them.

4   Discussion

We have shown that a GA can be successfully used to develop artificial swimming controllers, in a relatively limited number of generations. GAs have thus proved to be an interesting design technique.

A first observation is that there exist many possible solutions other than just variations of the biological controller. Potential segmental oscillators vary in terms of weight values, connection types and even number of active neurons. This results in different kind of behaviours which have in common that the motoneurons present regular oscillations with asymmetric behaviour, but show differences in the activity of the other neurons (the interneurons), with different sequences of activity and signal shapes. The EIN, CCIN and LIN neurons have thus taken other functions than in the biological model where they were respectively excitatory interneurons, contralateral inhibitory interneurons and lateral inhibitory interneurons. None of the evolved solutions corresponds simply to the biological configuration with a swap of function between the neuron types. The only common structure which has been found in several solutions is the 4-neuron oscillator mentioned above (Figure 3). Preliminary results have also shown that there exists a variety of ways in which segmental oscillators can be interconnected in order to form complete controllers. The variety of different potential solutions was also observed for the leech bending reflex by Lockery who found that many different networks, with different sets of connections, could produce a physiologically accurate local bending input-output function [9].

The evolved controllers can be considered as more efficient in terms of frequency range than the biological model, as solutions have been found with frequency ranges several times larger than the frequency range of the biological model, and with the same range of wavelengths for the undulation. We have concentrated on the ability to vary the frequency of the oscillations and on large frequency ranges, because the frequency determines the speed of swimming and a large range of frequency means a greater flexibility of the controller. However, there is probably an upper limit for the frequency at which muscles can contract and mechanical simulations should be made to determine which highest frequencies can actually be performed. The upper limit observed for swimming lampreys is approximately 10Hz[10].

The fitness function could be extended in order to include aspects we have chosen not to consider in this first approach, such as the relation between the excitation level and the amplitude of the motoneuron signals, the shape of these signals, the inclusion of sensory feedback. The next step should in fact evaluate the mechanical behaviour rather than the neural behaviour in order to reward a controller by directly rewarding the effectiveness of swimming.

Our principal interest is to define a methodology for developing locomotion controllers for autonomous agents. But can this research be useful for Neuroscience? The results presented here are probably of limited interest for neuroscientists and the main points we showed are that a variety of potential solutions exists and that the frequency range of the biological model can be optimized by changing the weights of the connections of that model, resulting in a better coverage of the observed physiologically frequency range. But we believe that GAs can prove to be very useful in helping neuroscientists to model a system, by including knowledge from physiological measurements as constraints on the encoding and the fitness functions, and using a GA to determine unknown variables. The experiment in which we fix the biological types of connection and evolve the connection weights is an example of such a methodology.

5   Conclusion

This paper has examined the swimming controller of lampreys and developed alternative artificial solutions using a real number Genetic Algorithm. Artificial controllers composed of neurons similar to those of Ekeberg's biological model [5] have been created in two stages. Many different neural configurations for potential controllers have been shown to exist; the biological network is only one of them. Artificial controllers have been created which are more efficient, in terms of frequency range, than the biological model, with frequency ranges

up to five times larger. We have also shown that the biological weights can be modified in order to increase the frequency range of the biological model and better match the physiological measurements. GAs have proved to be an interesting tool for developing adapted artificial controllers and for optimising the biological network.

References

[1] R.D. Beer. *Intelligence as Adaptive Behavior, an Experiment in Computational Neuroethology*. Academic Press, 1990.

[2] R.D. Beer and J.C. Gallagher. Evolving dynamical neural networks for adaptive behavior. *Adaptive Behavior*, 1(1):91–122, 1991.

[3] H. Cruse, D.E. Brunn, Ch. Bartling, J. Dean, M. Dreifert, T. Kindermann, and J. Schmitz. Walking: A complex behavior controlled by simple networks. *Adaptive Behavior*, 3(4):385–418, 1995.

[4] H. de Garis. Genetic programming: Building artificial nervous systems using genetically programmed neural network modules. In B.W. Porter and R.J. Mooney, editors, *Proceedings of the seventh international conference on machine learning*, pages 132–139. Morgan Kaufmann, 1990.

[5] O. Ekeberg. A combined neuronal and mechanical model of fish swimming. *Biol. Cybern.*, 69:363–374, 1993.

[6] O. Ekeberg, A. Lansner, and S. Grillner. The neural control of fish swimming studied through numerical simulations. *Adaptive Behavior*, 3(4):363–384, 1995.

[7] S. Grillner, Buchanan J.T., P. Wallen, and L. Brodin. Neural control of locomotion in lower vertebrates. In A. H. Cohen, S. Rossignol, and S. Grillner, editors, *Neural control of rhythmic movements in vertebrates*, pages 1–40. Jon Wiley & Sons, 1988.

[8] S. Grillner, P. Wallen, and L. Brodin. Neuronal network generating locomotor behavior in lamprey: Circuitry, transmitters, membrane properties, and simulation. *Annu. Rev. Neurosci.*, 14:169–199, 1991.

[9] S.R. Lockery and T.J. Sejnowski. The computational leech. *Trends in Neuroscience*, 16(7):283–290, 1993.

[10] P. Wallen, O. Ekeberg, A. Lansner, L. Brodin, H. Traven, and S. Grillner. A computer-based model for realistic simulations of neural networks ii: The segmental network generating locomotor rhythmicity in the lamprey. *J. of Neurophysiology*, 6:1939–1950, December 1992.

---

[10]It is not clear if this limit is due to neural or mechanical limitations.

Real Botany with Artifical Plants: A Dynamic, Self-Assembling, Plant Model for Individuals and Populations.

R.L.Colasanti & R. Hunt *

School of Cognitive & Computing Sciences, University of Sussex, Brighton BN1 9QH, U.K.
* Unit of Comparative Plant Ecology, University of Sheffield, Sheffield, S10 2TN, UK
ricardoc@cogs.susx.ac.uk

Abstract

This paper aims to reverse the more usual flow of information from the real biological world to the artificial one, by outlining work performed at the Unit of Comparative Plant Ecology at Sheffield University on computer generated artificial plants. By taking on board the well known A-life mission statement of 'complex behaviour emerging out of simple rules', established A-life techniques of cellular automata and L systems have been adapted and used to produced a whole plant model, that is constructed from a simple set of physiological rules. The purpose of the model is to investigate the extent to which the whole plant's morphology and function can be determined by resource acquisition and utilisation on the part of its components. The emergent behaviour of the whole plant system is such, that the model behaves as a real plant for number of key experiments, and does so in the absence of any description of the whole plant.

The simulation is a two-dimensional section, showing the plant in its above- and below-ground environments. The whole plant is represented by a branching structure made up from standard 'modules'. The behaviour of the complete plant is determined exclusively by a rule set that acts only at the level of the individual module.

At the level of the whole plant, the model displays a classic S-shaped growth curve, plasticity in root-shoot allocation, and foraging in heterogeneous environments.

At the level of the plant population, the model exhibits self thinning along a -2/1 self-thinning line. This accords with the behaviour expected of a two-dimensional system and also adds weight to the 'geometric' interpretation of the -3/2 self thinning line commonly seen in crowded populations of real plants.

1 Introduction

Modular plants

One of the simplest general views of vascular plant form is that individuals are fabricated from iterations of a basic structural module which is continually re-expressed. Plant morphology can thus be interpreted as the result of repeated branching during the decentralised production of new modules. It is the response of such modules to their immediate physical environment, whether this is of biological or physical origin, which informs plant morphology (Horn 1971).

Independent action at the modular level can permit the capture of resources from many different locations by a single individual. The sum of all locally-determined, modular growth represents the whole plant's response to its environment (Silvertown & Lovett Doust 1993).

Modular models

One of the first formalizations of plant growth rules which were used in a computer simulation was that produced by Lindenmayer (1974). L-systems show that a wide range of plant morphologies can be explained by a very small set of rules of spatial development acting on an even smaller set of simple 'constructs'. The latter are the irreducible elements of the structure; in the context of a L-system model, the branching units themselves.

Over the last twenty years the increasing availability of powerful personal computers has given an impetus to rule-based morphology simulation by biologists. (Honda,H 1971; Harper,J.L.. & Bell, A.D. 1979; Harper, L.J. 1985; Waller & Steingraber 1985; Bell 1986; Sutherland & Stillman 1990; Room, Maillette & Hanan 1994; Room & Prusinkiewicz 1996)

Current objectives

We have devised a new model the purpose of which is to investigate the extent to which the whole plant's morphology and function can be determined by resource acquisition and utilisation on the part of its individual modules.

Like the other individual-based models, the behaviour of the whole organism is determined exclusively by a rule set that acts only at the level of the module. However, the model differs from others because it simulates the growth of the individual in terms of the number and position of its modules in the above- and below-ground environments. The other innovative feature of the model is the inclusion of a return effect of the plant on the environment which is achieved by prescribing resource capture and utilisation as the main feature of the rule base. The aim has thus been to see whether, starting from a very simple rule set, an individual-based model of this type is capable of reproducing the most fundamental properties of plant behaviour at several levels of organization simultaneously. Specifically, a selected number of properties which any realistic growth model should possess: an S-shaped individual growth curve (e.g. Evans 1972; Hunt 1982), functional equilibria between root and shoot allocation (e.g. Davidson 1969, Hunt & Burnett 1973), plasticity in root and shoot foraging (e.g. Hutchings 1988; Campbell & Grime 1989a,b), self thinning according to geometric power laws (e.g. Yoda *et al.* 1963; Hutchings, M.J. 1979; Westoby 1984; Sackville Hamilton 1995) .

2 The modular model

The model mimics the form and function of a whole, individual plant through the behaviour of fundamental, indivisible, subcomponents of the plant, a binary branching *module*. A collection of such modules linked together in a branched network forms a whole *root system* or *shoot system*. These networks are analogous to a *binary tree*. Within each whole plant system, every module has a link to one parent module and, potentially, to two offspring modules. The links allow a module to 'know' the identity and the state both of its parent module and of its offspring modules (if any), but no module has 'knowledge' of the state of the whole plant. A *base module* is a module that has no parent module, and an *end module* is a module that has no offspring modules. There is a continuous link from the base module of a binary tree, to any of its end modules via the offspring modules, and from the end module there is a continuous link back to the base module via the parent modules. In the model , a whole plant is described by two binary trees, one representing the above-ground 'shoot'

system, the other representing the below-ground 'root' system. Figure 1 illustrates these principal elements of the model.

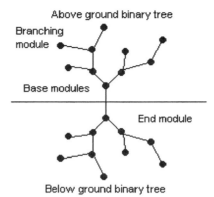

Figure 1 The main components of the modular model described in this paper.

The growth simulation uses a gas lattice cellular automata, and as with other cellular automata models, the spatial area within the simulation is divided into an array of cells. The cell is the indivisible unit of model space and represents the environment potentially occupied by a single plant module. As well as containing (or not) a plant module, each cell in the array can also contain any number of *resource units*. In our simulation, the above-ground resource is represented by *light units* and the below-ground resource by *mineral nutrient units*. There is movement of these resource units between cells. In the below-ground array, a diffusion algorithm causes the flow of resources from high concentrations to low. In the above-ground array, the resources flow from the top of the array to the bottom; new resource units are added at each iteration to the top of the array and removed from the bottom. The below-ground array is a closed system with no new resources added to the system during the simulation.

The outcome of any simulation is controlled by the distribution of resources within the cells of the two arrays, and by the subsequent uptake and utilisation of the resources by the model plant .

3 Rule base description
(a) Resource uptake and transport

Any module which occupies a cell in either the above-ground or the below-ground array is capable of capturing resource from that cell. The captured resource held within an end module can then be moved to its immediate parent module. That module can then transport the resource to its own parent module. By such recursion, resources eventually arrive at the base module. In the above-ground array, any captured light units are transferred as *photosynthate units*. In the below-ground array, any captured mineral nutrient units are transferred as *plant nutrient units*.

The above-ground and below-ground binary trees are linked at their base nodes. This allows resources accumulated at either base node to pass upwards or downwards as appropriate into the other binary tree. Resources that have

been obtained by the modules of a binary tree from their own cellular array are referred to as *captured resources*, whereas resources that have been obtained from the other binary tree via the link between base nodes are referred to as *transported resources*. Thus, in the above-ground binary tree, photosynthate is the captured resource and plant nutrients are the transported resource, and vice-versa in the below-ground binary tree.

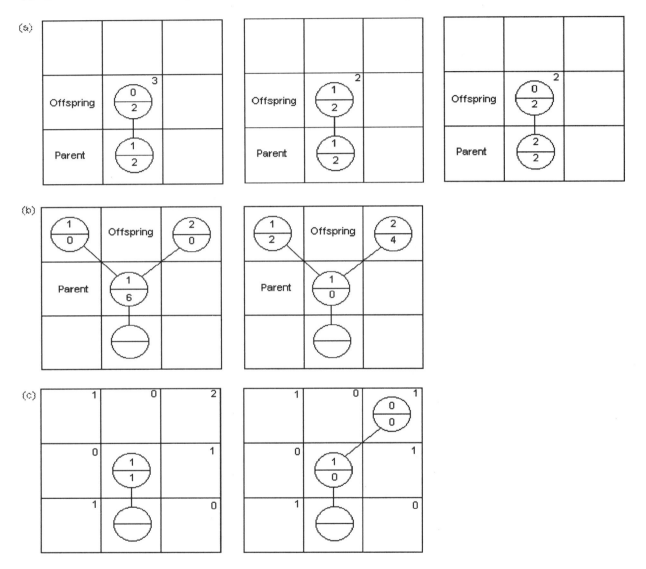

Figure. 2. The method of functioning of the modular model. Numerals indicate the number of units of resource present inside or outside individual models, which are represented by circles. Sequence (a) shows the basics of resource capture and transfer, with captured resources accounted in the upper compartments of each module and transported resources in the lower compartment. Sequence (b) shows resources being transferred from a parent model and shared between two offspring models. Sequence (c) shows the branching of a new end module from a previous end model.

The movement of any transferred resource from a base module to one of its end modules is more problematic than movement of captured resource from an end module to the base module. Whereas movement down a binary tree is a 'reduced decision procedure' (because each module only has one parent to pass the resource to), any movement of transferred resource *up* the tree is an 'increased decision procedure'. At each module, during up-tree movement, a decision often has to be made as to how the transferred resource should be split (if at all) between two offspring. If the whole plant's form and function is to be determined solely by the behaviour of individual modules, then each module can 'know' only its own state and that of its immediately related modules: no global knowledge of the complete state of the plant can exist. This means that no single module may have any direct knowledge of the number of distant offspring modules when deciding how to divide transferred resource between its two immediate offspring. So, the method we have used is to partition any resources which are to be transferred to immediate offspring in direct proportion to the amount of captured resource that these offspring already hold. This amount of resource is an indirect measure of the number of active modules that lie beyond each offspring. The more numerous such modules are, the more resource they will have captured, and the more captured resource will have been passed by them back down the binary tree.

(b) Growth of new modules

Primary growth occurs at an end node where new offspring modules derived from the end module invade vacant cells. As the prerequisite for growth is that any new module must be constructed from a unit of both captured resource and transported resource, if the end module contains at least one unit of transported resource then a new offspring module can be created by combining the(se) unit(s) of transported resource with captured resource(s) from the invaded vacant cell. A vacant cell is chosen from among the (potentially seven) vacant neighbouring cells by selecting the cell containing the most resource.

(c)The model iteration

The model runs in discrete time steps which process resource uptake, growth and resource redistribution in that order.

4 Simulations of individual growth

For all of the simulations of individual plant growth, the array structure consisted of a column of 60 cells (abscissa x) in each of 60 rows (ordinate y). The above-ground array occupied rows 1-30 of this two-dimensional matrix, and the below-ground array rows 31-60. The basal module of the above-ground binary tree was placed in the cell located at $x,y = 30,30$, and the basal module of the below-ground binary tree was placed the in cell at location $x,y = 30,31$. In a first set of simulations, each of the cells in the above-ground array was supplied with one unit of light and, further, each cell in the top row of this array was also replenished with one unit of light at each iteration. Each cell in the below- ground array was supplied with six units of nutrient; the below-ground diffusion algorithm was active.

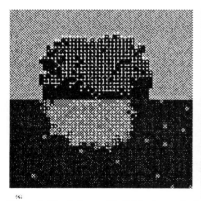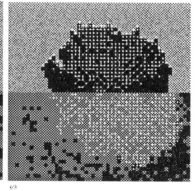

Figure3 Simulations of individual growth. (a) Shows a frame at 80 iterations where each cell in the top row of the above ground array was replenished with one unit of light at each iteration and each cell of the below-ground array was initially supplied with six units of nutrient. In the above ground array, the darker tone represents wholly light-depleted cells and in the below-ground array the lighter tone represents cells containing two or fewer units of nutrient. (b) shows a low-nutrient variant and is exhibiting root shoot allocation to the below ground. (c) represents an initial gradient of below ground resources from right to left.

The simulation was run for 150 iterations. Figure 3a shows an output illustration in the form of a vertical profile, with different colours indicating different resource concentrations. The frame is at 80 iterations, and demonstrates that the morphology of the above- and below-ground binary trees resemble those of the shoot and root structures found in simple real plants. Under the conditions of this simulation, both binary trees are very similar in size, and both show an approximately bilateral (left-right) symmetry. The above-ground binary tree exhibits the property of self shading, where the higher shoots prevent light from reaching the lower shoots. The below-ground binary tree has produced a region of nutrient depletion. With this simulation repeated for two different levels of light and for two different levels of nutrient (combined factorially), and then replicated twenty times, growth curves for a mean number of modules present at each iteration can be presented, as in Fig. 4. These show, for all treatment combinations, that the model exhibits the classical S-shaped curve found in real plants grown as spaced individuals (Hunt & Evans 1980; Hunt 1982).

For a second set of simulations of individual-plant growth, the relative resource levels in the above and below-ground arrays were manipulated. The light units supplied to each cell in the above-ground array were held at one, while the nutrient units supplied to each cell in the below-ground array were reduced to two, with diffusion again active. The simulation was allowed to run for 150 iterations. The output illustration of the simulation can be seen in Fig. 3b

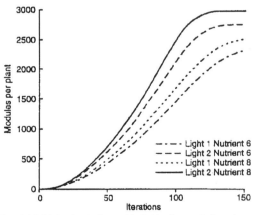

Fig. 4. *Multiple simulations of individual growth, based upon the conditions shown in Fig . 3 a . Graph shows standard S shaped growth curves.*

The first frame of this figure again shows the growth achieved after 5 iterations, and the second frame, at 80 iterations. The second frame shows clearly that the below-ground binary tree is larger than the above-ground tree, and that both are smaller than the equivalent binary trees in the

previous simulation (Fig. 3a). The ability of the model to simulate plasticity in root-shoot partitioning was then confirmed by multiple simulations at two light levels and a wide range of nutrient levels. Each combination was replicated ten times and the results presented as a graph of allometric coefficients plotted against nutrient level (Fig.5). The allometric coefficient, the linear regression coefficient of ln mean root size on ln mean shoot size, is an integrated measure of differential root/shoot partitioning (Hunt 1990). At the higher level of light, and the lower levels of nutrients there is a relatively larger below-ground binary tree, and vice versa. These results entirely concur with much experimental data for real plants (for references see Hunt & Burnett 1973, Hunt & Lloyd 1987).

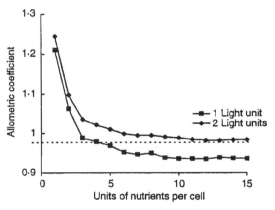

Fig 5. *Multiple simulations of individual growth, based upon the conditions shown in Fig . 3 b Graph shows root-shoot allometeric coefficient.*

A third set of simulations was concerned with heterogeneity in the distribution of below-ground resources. In the simulation illustrated in Fig. 3c, the initial distribution of nutrients in the below-ground array was biased positively to the right. The second frame of Fig. 3c shows the morphology of above-ground and below-ground binary trees after 80 iterations in such an environmentThe below-ground binary tree shows lateral asymmetry, with many more modules to the right of the base module than to the left. The above-ground binary tree, however, is laterally symmetrical (the light resource was homogeneous). The model's ability to place modules preferentially in high-nutrient cells was confirmed by twenty replicate simulations, mean results of which are shown in Fig. 6. This bar diagram presents mean numbers of modules in each of four quadrants of the simulation: the above- or below-ground halves of the binary trees, and the left or right sides of the basal nodes. There is significant asymmetry in the below-ground binary tree ($p<0.01$), though not in the above-ground one, and this difference favours the richer side of the below-ground environment. This nutrient-driven, morphological plasticity mimics the foraging demonstrated in nutrient-patch experiments conducted with real plants (Campbell & Grime 1989a,b, Campbell, Grime & Mackey 1991; Birch & Hutchings 1994).

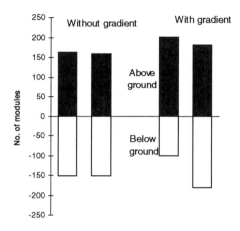

Fig. 6. Multiple simulations of individual growth, based upon the conditions shown in Fig . 3 c Graph shows data for foraging.

5 Simulations of population growth

A well known property of plant populations is self thinning. Self thinning occurs as a plant population matures, an initial population of many small plants, will over the course of time change into a smaller population of larger plants. The pattern of change in real plant populations generally follows the so-called -3/2 power law (Yoda *et al.* 1963; Hutchings 1979; Westoby 1984; Sackville Hamilton 1995), in which the logarithm of individual size is related to the logarithm of population density by a line of that slope. The -3/2 power law arises ultimately from the underlying geometry of the growth process. In any successful two-dimensional model this process ought also to emerge, except that a self-thinning line of slope -2/1 is to be expected. This numerator and denominator should arise simply from the reduced dimensionality of the model system relative to the real world because, in the model, plant 'income' is an approximate function of linear size and plant 'expenditure' a function of area.

The simulations depicted in Fig. 6 display self-thinning across a series of two-dimensional model populations. At the lowest simulated population density, two plants were initiated equidistantly within a 64-column toroidal array (the array was wrapped into a mathematical torus in which column 64 adjoined and preceded column 1). The

simulation was run for 150 iterations and the number of nodes existing in each plant at each time step was logged. This simulation was replicated ten times and the results averaged. Further simulations were then performed at population densities of 4, 6, 8, 16, 32 or 64 plants per 64-column array. When the mean results of these simulations were plotted in the usual way as ln number of modules per individual (i.e. plant size) as a function of ln number of

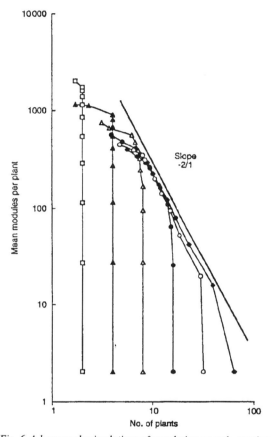

Fig. 6. A large scale simulations of population growth, starting from initial population entities of 2, 4, 8,... 64 equally spaced, identical plants per simulation. All results were averaged over Pinner simulations, for which every tenth iteration has been plotted on a double logarithmic scale. On reaching full interaction between individuals, the denser populations undergo self- thinning along a line of slope -2/1 .

plants per array (i.e. population density), each population, on reaching full interaction between its component individuals, did indeed undergo self-thinning along a line of slope -2/1, as Fig. 8 clearly demonstrates

6 Discussion

Credibility of the model

The central assumption that guided the construction of this model is that the morphology and behaviour of the whole plant could, to an acceptable degree, be derived solely from the functioning of modular components. Our aim was to see whether, starting from the simplest possible rule set, a module-based model was capable of reproducing the most fundamental properties of plant behaviour at several levels of organisation. To test whether or not the model successfully reproduces plant-like characteristics, we restricted our choice of yield attributes to total number of modules per plant, or to plants per population, but were generous in our choice of test simulations (encompassing a wide range of individual, population and community processes). Within the criteria we set ourselves, we feel that the results from the simulations allow us to conclude that there is a direct analogue between the dynamics of our model and those of real plants. This supports the belief that several fundamental aspects of plant form and function, including morphology and interactions with the environment and with other plants, can be described simply and adequately in terms of modular self-assembly and resource capture and utilisation.

At the level of the individual plant, the model mirrors real plant growth in respect of S-shaped growth curves, self shading and morphological plasticity. More interestingly, the model also exhibits a plant growth property that is not immediately predictable: differential root-shoot allocation is an emergent property of the model which could not be anticipated from the rule base governing modular behaviour. This demonstrates the unusual power of this type of modelling approach.

Another emergent property of the model is its capacity for self thinning within crowded stands. The fact that this occurs in a manner which is exactly predictable by geometric reasoning is another impressive demonstration of the extent to which a simple rule base can encapsulate plant behaviour. This result also adds weight to the -3/2 self thinning law itself, indicating that this is also likely to be based upon broadly geometric properties (Westoby 1984; Sackville Hamilton 1995). (It even implies that a hypothetical four-dimensional plant population would thin along a trajectory of slope -4/3.).

Future developments

This model has already been used to investigate the physiological properties involved in plant- plant competition, by changing one aspect of the rule base in a competing plant. (Colasanti & Hunt 1997).

Further improvements could be made to the already realistic morphology of the simulated plants, one possible development would be to include a coding of geometric branching patterns, similar to Lindenmayer's L-system grammar, into behavior of the modules. Any requirement for a meta-level knowledge of plant structure, e.g. the identification of apical nodes, could be conveyed to the constituent modules by a the flow of 'virtual hormones'. Other resources could be introduced both above- and below-ground, e.g. CO_2 and water. These would be different from the existing light and nutrient resources, both in the manner in which they were represented within the environment and in way in which they were handled within a plant module. For example, water could be made to transpire from the end modules of the above-ground shoot system and also to flow under the influence of 'virtual gravity' in the below-ground array. The CO_2 resource, on the other hand, could behave in a similar way to the present below-ground resource, but do so within the above-ground array.

Management processes such as grazing or mowing regimes could also be superimposed

In conclusion we believe that this work has highlighted the undoubted benefit of evolutionary and adaptive systems techniques to the " field " of real plant ecology.

A working version of the model that runs under Microsoft® Windows™ is available at the URL http://www.shef.ac.uk/uni/academic/N-Q/nuocpe

Referances

Bell, A.D. (1986) The simulation of branching patterns in modular organisms. *Philosophical Transactions of the Royal Society, Series B* **313,** 143-159.

Birch, C.P.D. & Hutchings, M.J.(1994) Exploitation of patchily distributed soil resources by the clonal herb *Glechoma hederacea. Journal of Ecology* **82,** 653-664

Campbcll, B.D. & Grime, J.P. (1989) A comparative study of plant responsiveness to the duration of episodes of mineral nutrient enrichment. *New Phytologist* 112, 261267.

Campbell, B.D. & Grime, J.P. (1989a) A new method of exposing developing root systems to controlled patchiness in mineral nutrient supply. *Annals of Botany* **63,** 395-400.

Campbell, B.D. & Grime, J.P. (1989b) A comparative study of plant responsiveness to the duration of episodes of mineral nutrient enrichment. *New Phytologist* **112,** 261-267.

Campbell, B.D., Grime, J.P. & Mackey, J.M.L. (1991) A trade-off between scale and precision in resource foraging. *Oecologia* **87,** 532-538.

Colasanti, R.L. & Grime, J.P. (1993) Resource dynamics and vegetation processes: a deterministic model using two-dimensional cellular automata. *Functional Ecology* **7,** 169-176.

Colasanti, R.L & Hunt, R. (1997) Rssource dynamics and plant growth: a self-assembling model for individuals, populations and communities. *Functional Ecology* **11,**.

Davidson, R.L. (1969) Effect of root/leaf temperature differentials on root/shoot ratios in some pasture grasses and clover. *Annals of Botany* **33,** 561-69

Evans, G.C. (1972) *The Quantitative Analysis of Plant Growth.* Blackwell Scientific Publications, Oxford

Fitter, A.H. (1986) Acquisition and utilization of resources. *Plant Ecology* (ed M.J. Crawley), pp. 375-405. Blackwell Scientific Publications, Oxford.

Grime, J.P. (1979) *Plant Strategies and Vegetation Processes.* John Wiley & Sons Ltd., Chichester.

Harper, J.L. & Bell, A.D. (1979) The population dynamics of growth form in organisms with modular construction. *Population Dynamics* (eds R.M. Anderson, B.D. Turner and L.R. Taylor), pp. 29-52. Blackwell Scientific Publications, Oxford.

Harper, L.J. (1985) Modules, Baranches and the capture of resources. *Population Biology and Evolution of Clonal Organisams* (eds J.B.C. Jackson, R.E. Buss & R.E. Cook), pp. 225-257. Yale University Press, New Haven.

Honda, H (1971) Description of the form of trees by the parameters of the tree-like body. *Journal of Theoretical Biology 31,* 331-338.

Horn, H.S. (1971) *Adaptive Geometry of Trees.* Princeton University Press, New Jersey.

Hunt, R. (1982) *Plant Growth Curves: the Functional Approach to Plant Growth Analysis.* Edward Arnold, London.

Hunt, R. (1990) *Basic Growth Analysis.* Unwin Hyman, London.

Hutchings, M.J. & de Kroon, H. (1994) Foraging in plants : the role of morphological plasticity in resource aquisition. *Advances in Ecological Research* **25,** 159-237.

Hutchings, M.J. (1979) Weight-density relationships in ramet populations of clonal perennal herbs, with special

reference to the -3/2 power law. *Journal of Ecology* **67,** 21-33.

Hutchings, M.J. (1988) Differential foraging for resources and structural plasticity in plants. *Trends in Ecology and Evolution* **3,** 200-204.

Lindenmayer, A. (1974). Adding continuous components to L-systems. *Lecture Notes in Computer Science, Volume 15* (eds Rozenberg, G. & Salomaa, A.), pp.53-68. Springer-Verlag, Berlin.

Room, P.M, Maillette, L. & Hanan, J.S. (1994) Module and metamer dynamics and virtual plants. *Advances in Ecological Research* **25,** 105-157

Room, P.M. & Prusinkiewicz, P. (1996) Virtual plants: new perspectives for ecologists, pathologists and agricultural scientists. *Trends in Plant Science* **1,** 33-38.

Sackville Hamilton, N.R., Matthew, C. & Lemaire, G. (1995) In defence of the -3/2 boundary rule: a re-evaluation of self-thinning concepts and status. *Annals of Botany* **76,** 569-577.

Shugart, H.H. & West, D.C. (1979) Size and pattern of simulated forest stands. *Forest Science* **25,** 120-122.

Silvertown J.W. & Lovett Doust J (1993) *Introduction to Plant Population Ecology (3rd edn.).* Longman, London.

Sutherland, W.J. & Stillman, R.A. (1990) Clonal growth: insights from models. *Clonal Growth in Plants: Regulation and Function* (eds J. van Groenendale & K. de Kroon), pp. 95-11. SPB Academic Publishing, The Hague.

Waller, D.M (1986) The structure of plant communities. *Plant Ecology* (ed M.J. Crawley), pp. 291-320. Blackwell Scientific Publications, Oxford.

Waller, D.M. & Steingraber, D.A (1985) Branching and modular growth: theoretical models and empirical patterns. *Population Biology and Evolution of Clonal Organisms* (eds J.B.C. Jackson, R.E. Buss & R.E. Cook), pp. 225-257. Yale University Press, New Haven.

Westoby, M. (1984) The self thinning rule. *Advances in Ecological Research 14, 167-225.*

Yoda, K, Kira, T. Ogawa, H. & Hozumi, K. (1963). Self-thinning in overcrowded pure stands under cultivated and natural conditions. *Journal of Biology of Osaka City University* **14,** 107-129

The Virtual Biology Laboratories:
A New Approach of Computational Biology

Hiroaki Kitano
Sony Computer Science Laboratory
3-14-13 Higashi-Gotanda, Shinagawa
Tokyo 141, Japan
kitano@csl.sony.co.jp

Shugo Hamahashi
Dept. of Electrical Engineering
Keio University
Yokohama 223, Japan
shugo@mt.cs.keio.ac.jp

Jun Kitazawa
School of Media and Governance
Keio University
Fujisawa 252, Japan
kitazawa@mag.keio.ac.jp

Koji Takao
School of Medicine
Keio University
35 Shinanomachi, Shinjuku
Tokyo 160, Japan
cozy@sun.microb.med.keio.ac.jp

Shin-ichirou Imai
School of Medicine
Keio University
35 Shinanomachi, Shinjuku
Tokyo 160, Japan
imai@sun.microb.med.keio.ac.jp

Abstract

The Virtual Biology Laboratories is an attempt
to create detailed biological models which can be
used for research in molecular biology, developmental biology, and neuro-science. The goal is
to create detailed models of specific model animals, so that various virtual biological experiments (such as gene knock out, microscopic manipulations, site direct mutagenesis) can be performed, and the results compared with actual biological experiments. Currently, we are working
on three specific projects — Perfect C. elegans
Project, Virtual Drosophila Project, and Virtual
Cell Laboratory Project. These projects aim at
detailed modeling of *C. elegans, Drosophila,* and
the aging mechanism of human fibroblast, and
Yeast *saccharomyces cerevisiae.* This paper describes the basic approach and some early results
of the project.

1 Introduction

Modern biology as represented by molecular biology
started when Watson and Click discovered DNA structure in 1953 [Watson and Click, 53]. Coincidently, the
modern form of the computer, a stored program computer or the von Neumann architecture, was invented
only a few years prior to the discovery of DNA. Perhaps,
these are two most significant scientific breakthroughs in
the mid-20th century. Computational biology, or computer aided biology, is where these two areas merge. Although there are substantial efforts to use computer systems in the area of genome data-base, motif extraction,
and structure prediction, no systematic effort has been
made to create a comprehensive model of an entire living
system. We believe that it is a time to start an initiative

to create complete detailed models of biologically significant model animals on computer. The goal of this paper
is to provide a perspective on how computers can be used
more actively in biology and in the way they will change
how biology is performed. This paper describes what is
envisioned, and discusses new ways in which biology is
carried out.

1.1 *From Reductionist to Integrationist*

The fundermental scientific approach of the 20th century
can be characterized as reductionist. Particle physics is
a typical example. It made an ultimate challenge to subdivide this universe into subatomic particles as small as
quark; and the space-time continuum and matter were
reduced to super-strings. In spirit, the approach was applied to biology, which lead to the discovery of DNA as a
basic information carrying component in the living system. Although there is no doubt that science clearly advanced by seeking fundamental components, it does not
necessary enhance our understanding of this universe at
a more macroscopic level. Identification of DNA does not
mean that we understand the dynamics which give rise
to the various phenomena inherent in life. Understanding of phenomena, which consists of many interacting
components, is a important task. While most phenomena involve population dynamics and non-linear interactions, these phenomena often exhibit counter-intuitive
behaviors. Even if the behavior of the system is not
counter-intuitive, tracking the behavior of components
in the system and emerged behavior of an entire system
is almost impossible without the use of computers. This
approach can be characterized as a synthetic understanding of biological system.

1.2 The Model of Scientific Success

Given that the synthetic approach can be a powerful means to help understanding living systems, how should the computational approach be used in biology? Lessons can be learned from the major achievements in science. One of the most successful areas in modern natural science is particle physics. Although the ultimate theory – the theory of everything – is yet to be found, particle physics has discovered a set of basic principles which explain the fundamental mechanisms of matter and force. For example, one of the symbolic success stories involves the standard theory and the discovery of the intermediate vector boson. Glashow, Salam, and Weinberg proposed the electro-weak theory, which is now called "the standard theory", as a unified theory of electromagnetic and weak force. The theory predicted hypothetical particles called intermediate vector bosons (IVB), which had not been discovered at that time. Teams of experimental physicists at CERN tried to discover the IVB, and finally the UV-I team led by Carlo Rubia discovered the predicted particles called W and Z. By the discovery of these particles, the theory was confirmed, and the frontier of research was pushed to quantum color dynamics, which tries to explain the strong force responsible for interaction between quarks.

This story signifies how a new fundamental mechanism in nature can be discovered. In physics, particularly in modern particle physics, prediction using a promising theory has a decisive influence on the course of scientific inquiry. For a theory to be seriously considered, it must be able to explain a set of data which is already available. However, the truly powerful theory should be able to make significant and precise predictions which can be verified. The power of the theory lies in the prediction.

1.3 The Research Cycle of Computer Aided Biology

How can we translate this model into the field of biology? Unlike particle physics, biology inherently deals with a large number of interacting complements. This essential nature of a biological system makes it difficult for the conventional mathematical approach to construct theories which are powerful enough to describe observed phenomena and to predict undiscovered mechanisms. While we do not deny the value of conventional mathematical analysis, we argue that for very complex and heterogeneous systems, the use of computer simulation should be considered as the central methodology.

Therefore, we propose that computer simulation which models mechanisms of biological processes should be used together with actual biological experiments, instead of using abstract mathematics describing average behavior of the system, so that results of simulation (which are virtual experiments) can be verified by tangible experi-

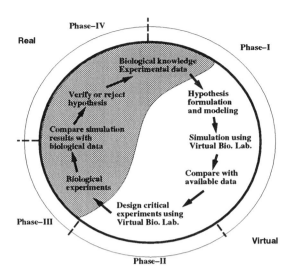

Figure 1: Computer Aided Biological Assay Cycle

ments. The actual procedure is illustrated in Figure 1. First, based on available biological knowledge and data, we create a detailed simulation model and carry out simulation. Once the simulation is performed, the results are compared with available biological data to check the validity of the simulation. Generally, the simulation results are compared with biological data from wild-type of the model animals. This is phase-I of the cycle.

Once the validity of the simulation is confirmed, another set of simulation will be done to identify a set of critical experiments which can provide us decisive evidence on specific biological mechanisms. In this process, several hypotheses on possible mechanisms will be implemented and compared with biological data. As a result, a set of critical experiments will be designed. This is the phase-II.

In Phase-III, actual biological experiments will be conducted based on the experimental design using the simulation system.

Finally, in the phase-IV, results of the experiments will be compared with the results of the simulation, so that the hypothesis can be verified or rejected. Whether the hypothesis is verified or rejected, it will add new knowledge on biological systems. A new cycle begins reflecting the results of the previous cycle.

The goal of this research program is to establish a new paradigm of biological research, and to promote understanding of living systems actually exist, rather than artificial life. It is important that we should be able to promote understanding of existing life, because it is the only instance of life we can agree on.

2 Overall Perspectives

Virtual Biology Laboratories is a research program consisting of several specific research projects under the unified goal of creating a new paradigm of biology using computers. In order to make a case for the proposed approach, and to make major breakthroughs, comprehensive research programs using selected high impact model animals and focusing on the modeling of biologically significant phenomena are needed. Therefore, we have started following projects;

Perfect C. elegans project: This project aims at detailed modeling of *Caenorhabditis elegans (C. elegans)*. The advantage of using *C. elegans* for modeling is the abundance of available data. Complete cell lineage and neural circuit topology is known, and DNA sequencing is expect to be completed within a year or so. Expression patterns of all genes will be made available within a few years.

Virtual Drosophila project:
> *Drosophila melanogaster* is yet another extensively studied animal. Specifically, significant amount of data is available for early embryogenesis, such as gap genes, segment polarity genes, and homeotic genes. Various mutants have been identified, and detailed expression patterns have been studied. In addition, *Drosophila* has a much more complex morphogenesis than *C. elegans* and a substantial central nervous system. Formation of eyes and legs are also well studied. These conditions make *Drosophila* a most ideal subject for computational modeling.

Virtual Cell Laboratory Project: Virtual Cell Laboratory emphasizes simulation of the cell itself and *in vitro* cell culture. Specific targets are aging related mechanisms of human fibroblast, and Yeast *saccharomyces cerevisiae*. Cell aging was selected because it is one of the most significant issues in recent molecular cell biology, and it may involve heterochromatin and other novel regulatory mechanisms. Yeast is a natural choice as a model system for computer simulation, due to the abundance of available data. Mechanisms for cell cycle control are the most well investigated and significant parts of Yeast research.

In this paper, these projects are described using a set of initial accomplishments. While details of each project will be described elsewhere, it is important that the entire research program be described, even though rather sketchily, so that our intentions and approach can be made clear from various perspectives.

3   Perfect C. elegans Project

The Perfect C. elegans project aims at a detailed replication of *C. elegans*. When Sydney Brenner proposed a new project to investigate *C. elegans* to the Medical Research Council, he chose it because it is the simplest possible differentiated organism [Brenner, 63]. The decision was right, and a number of fruitful results were generated, including complete identification of the cell lineage [Sulston and Horvitz, 77; Kimble and Hirsh, 79; Sulston et al., 83], and neural circuits [White et al., 86]. The complete DNA sequencing and expression pattern mapping using whole mount *in situ* hybridization are now within our reach [Sulston et al., 92; Tabara et al., 96]. These investigations clarify what constitutes *C. elegans* and how each components operate. However, understanding the components and their isolated functions does not lead to an understanding of the dynamics behind the development and behavior of this organism. Despite the fact it is the simplest possible differentiated organism, it is still too complex to understand the dynamics and interactions taking place. It is obvious that a synthetic approach needs to be undertaken for better understanding of this intensively studied animal.

Thus, the goal of the Perfect C. elegans project is the creation of a detailed model of *C. elegans*. We intend to implement models for the embryogenesis process, genetic interactions, and neural circuits.

3.1   The Nematode Caenorhabditis elegans

C. elegans is a small worm ubiquitously observed in the soil. It composes the largest biomass on earth. It has a life span of about 3 days and feeds on bacteria. The adult male *C. elegans* has 1031 somatic nuclei, while the adult hermaphrodite has 959 somatic nuclei. The cell lineage of these cells have been fully identified by the extensive work of a group of researchers, notably by [Sulston et al., 83].

The nervous system of *C. elegans* is relatively simple. Its hermaphrodites have only 302 neurons, 56 glial and associated support cells. This accounts for 37% of all somatic cells. In the adult male, the number of neurons are 381, and there are 92 glial and supporting cells, which is 46% of the somatic cells. White classified these neurons into 118 classes, and reported that there are about 5,000 chemical synapses, 2,000 neuromuscular junctions, and 600 gap junctions.

The size of the haploid genome is 8×10^7 nucleotide pairs. The *C. elegans* genome project is being done by the Sanger Center and Washington University, which have already sequenced more than 25% of the genome. Current progress suggests that all genes, which is estimated to be about 13,000, will be identified within a few years.

The mechanism of fate determination involving maternal genes has been intensively investigated. However, subsequent fate determination is largely unknown because downstream genes have not been identified. In order to investigate genetic interactions for fate determination, a project to identify genes that are expressed in specific cell lineage was initiated [Tabara et al., 96]. Kohara's project at the National Institute for Genetics uses *in situ* hybridization on whole mount embryos to identify expression of genes at specific cells and specific times during the embryogenesis.

Many mutants have been isolated which can be used for genetic analysis. For example, the *ced* family affects programmed cell death, and mutations in the *lin* family genes cause cell lineage abnormality. There is a large list of genes and their phenotypical disorders. In addition, a series of manipulations are possible during embryogenesis through laser ablation or direct micro-manipulation.

3.2 Embryogenesis Visualization and Simulation

Given these biological accomplishments and on-going efforts, the perfect C. elegans project aims at creating a detailed simulation model, one that promotes our understanding of life, particularly *C. elegans*.

As the first step toward this goal, we have developed a computer graphics system which visualizes the developmental process of *C. elegans*. The system is based on the cell lineage and cell location data investigated by Sulston et al., along with various other literature. The system generates computer graphics images from the division of the first cell to around 600 minutes after the first cell division.

3.2.1 Data Resource

It is a non-trivial task to create a reasonably accurate computer graphics image based on the available data because information necessary to create three dimensional models is missing. The following information is available:

- the complete cell lineage chart

- hand-drawn pictures in 2-1/2 dimension

  - all 28 cells at 100 minutes
  - 55 out of 180 cells at 200 minutes
  - 137 out of more than 350 cells at 260 minutes
  - 156 out of more than 350 cells at 270 minutes
  - most cells at 430 minutes

- qualitative descriptions of the shape of embryo

- qualitative description of disparity in the size of divided cells

- general information on migration

However, much essential information is missing. For instance, the three-dimensional position of the cells is only given for a subset of cells at only a few time points. In addition, the lineage chart only indicates the approximate time of the divisions and the rough direction of division, such as anterior-posterior, dorsal-ventral, or left-right. For example, the cell lineage of two ring inter-neurons (ADAL and ADAR) are shown as **ADAL AB.plapaaaapp** and **ADAR AB.prapaaaapp**. This means that an **ADAL** cell was derived from the founder cell **AB**, and was created after a series of divisions in the order of posterior (**p**), left (**l**), anterior (**a**), posterior (**p**), four anterior (**aaaa**) divisions, and two posterior divisions (**pp**). **ADAR**, which is a symmet ric counter part has a similar lineage, but made a division to be a right cell after the posterior division. However, in reality, the direction of cell divisions are not necessarily aligned with these axis. A new technique must be develop to understand about the approximate direction of divisions.

By the same token, the locations of cells are drawn as a series of two-dimensional figures. While the approximate two-dimensional location of cells can be estimated from these figures, it only provides crude position for depth (or vertical position) of cells. The vertical position of cells are shown only by using circles with three levels of thickness. Again, a new simulation method needs to be developed to estimate 3D locations of cells.

Obviously, a straightforward way would be to collect three-dimensional position and shape data one step at a time, so that computer graphics could be created based on these data without problems. However, this approach is very labor intensive because each cells at every time step must be manually identified and the position data collected. In order to collect such data, researchers need a crude 3D visualization tool to assist in the identification of cells and their positions. In addition, such an approach cannot be applied to visualize the development of organisms having only a limited amount of position information. Therefore, we need to develop a system which can generate reasonably accurate 3D computer graphics based on limited data sets.

3.2.2 Merging Simulation with Data

Our strategy to overcome this problem is to merge simulation with data. First, in order to assure the accuracy of the computer graphics image, cells must be in the position given in the observed data.

A set of data obtained from actual observation must be represented in machine readable form. Table 1 shows a part of a data record representing cell lineage and cell positions taken from the Sulston data. R is a record type (**f** and **p** mean a full record, **x** means a terminal record), and d_1 and d_2 are the names of daughter cells. When a '*' is attached in front of a symbol, such as '*a', it is concatenated to the name of the mother cell to create the name of the daughter cell. For example, **AB** cell's daughters are labeled '*a' and '*p' in the table. The full name of these daughter cells are **ABa** and **ABp**. x, y, and z indicate the direction of division. The relative volume of the d_1 cell is shown as 'vol'. The time of division is indicated in 'time'. x_1, y_1, z_1, r_1 are the x, y, z positions and the radius of the cell at time point t_1,

R	Cell name	d_1	d_2	x	y	z	vol	time	x_1	y_1	z_1	r_1	t_1	x_2	y_2	z_2	r_2	t_2
f	Egg	AB	P1	0	1	0	.6	0	0	0	0	5.4	0					
p	AB	*a	*p	0	1	-1	.5	18										
p	ABa	*l	*r	-1	0	0	.5	35										
p	ABp	*l	*r	-1	0	0	.5	35										
p	P1	EMS	P2	0	1	-1	.6	19										
p	EMS	MS	E	0	1	0	.6	38										
p	P2	C	P3	0	1	1	.6	44										
								⋮										
p	ABalaaappr	l	r	-1	0	0	.5	287	5.0	15.8	-2	1.8	260	-3.9	15.3	-5	1.7	270

Table 1: Data Record for Cell Lineage and Cell Positions

respectively. A set of data can be repeated for different time points. Basically, this data-base contains most of the information provided in [Sulston et al., 83]. Even when we obtain more accurate data, we can continued to use this data record by making minor changes. One point which needs to be changed is the way the direction of cell division is specified. In the current data structure, it is represented as a three-dimension vector where each dimension has only three values (1, 0, and -1). This will be changed to represent a continuous number. The polar coordinate system will be used. Cell shape information is not included in the current version. This needs to be added in the future.

Second, various simulation techniques are used to fill in missing information, such as the location of cells not given in the data. Essentially, this part of the system computes the dynamics between cells, such as the force to push back colliding cells (equations not shown). However, if only dynamics simulation is used to decide the position of cells, some cells will not be in the position described in the observed data, because of cell movement. In order to compensate for this discrepancy, a force that a cell is supposed to generate for its movement is estimated using the inverse kinematic technique, and added to the cell's force vector.

The shape of an embryo changes after 200 minutes creating the so called "comma" and "2-fold" shape. While the driving force bending the embryo's shape is not identified biologically, computer simulation impose a top-down kinematics. At 200 minutes, a cylindrical coordinate system is imposed to describe cell locations. The cylindrical coordinate system itself slowly bend to agree with the observed shape, so that the cells change their absolute position according to the bending of the cylindrical coordinate. As a result, we have successfully created a computer graphics visualization of embryogenesis of *C. elegans* (fig. 2).

Coloring of cells can be selected to suit the purpose of the visualization. This information is held in the cell color assignment map in the system. The default assignment map is based on the cell fate, as shown in A. An alternative color map assigns colors to each cell based

Color	Cell Fate
Red	Dermal cells
Green	Neural cells
Blue	Digestive system cells
Cyan	Body muscle cells
Magenta	Germ cells
Yellow	Excretory system cells
White	Miscellaneous blast cells (also mixed lineage cells)
Dark Green	Tail spike cells
Dark Grey	Cells which will die
Black	Dead cells (not yet absorbed by other cells)

(A)

Color	Precursor Cell
Red	AB
Green	MS
Blue	E
Cyan	P,Z
Magenta	D
Yellow	C
White	Early generation (ex. Egg)

(B)

Table 2: Color Maps

on the cell precursor (shown in B). All images shown in figure 1 uses the default color map. If 'transparent' is assigned to a cell, the cell will not be visible on the image, although it exists for computing dynamics, making it possible to display only certain cells.

Current implementation uses C++ programming language, an OpenGL graphics library, and a SGI sphere library on a Silicon Graphics workstation. The cell coloring can be selected either by cell fate or by their mother cells (Table 1). The system enables zooming in and out, and rotation around any X-, Y-, Z-axis. Simulation can

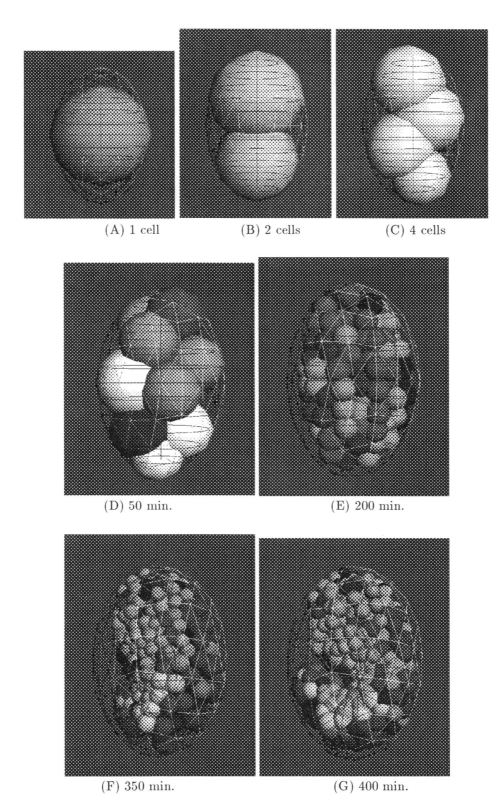

Figure 2: Snapshots of computer graphics images of C. elegans embryogenesis

Computer graphics (CG) images of the development of *C. elegans*. Colors assigned to cells based on the cell fate color map. A, B, and C are snapshots of the CG image at the initial stage (egg), two cells stage, and four cells stage, respectively. D, E, F, and G are snapshots at 50 minutes, 200 minutes, 350 minutes, and 400 minutes after the first cell division, respectively. F and G show the gradual bending of the embryo into the "comma" state.

be paused at any time step during the execution allowing users to closely examine the visualized image as in a still picture.

Implementation of the model can be an extremely useful tool for biologists working on *C. elegans*. It can be a comprehensive visual data-base of C. elegans, as well as being an assistant system for cell identification. Currently, the most widely used computer assisted system for *C. elegans* is the Angler system, also called the 4D system, developed by the Sanger Center. Basically, it is a collection of tagged images taken by Nomarski confocal microscopy. However, the Angler system does not provide the capability to rotate images, or to animate the embryogenesis process. Our system, viewed as a visualization system, compliments the Angler system by providing computer graphics images and simulations linked with a set of optical images.

However, the system is not merely a visualization and data-base interface. It implements a physical model which also computes the dynamics between cells. Modeled as continuous elastic body, it can be augmented as a virtual laboratory in which we can conduct microscopic operations such as shifting cell location and laser ablation. We are currently working on the implementation of a genetic interaction simulator which can be integrated with the physical simulation system already developed. The new genetic components specifically model cell fate determination until the 46 cells stage, where major cell fate determinations are made.

In addition, we have already implemented a simulator for a thermotaxis neural subsystem [Mori and Ohshima, 95]. The implementation of simulator for a complete neural circuit is underway. Overall, the Perfect C. elegans project is at the phase-I level and is quickly moving toward phase-II.

4 Virtual Drosophila Project

The Virtual Drosophila projects aims at the detailed modeling of *Drosophila*, which is yet another extremely well-investigated model animal.

The embryogenesis of *Drosophila* differs from that of *C. elegans* in that it does not form cells at the earliest stages. After 13 successive nuclear divisions, about 6,000 nuclei form a syncytial blastoderm. Cellular membrane do not form until the thirteenth nuclear divisions. Thus, until this stage, gene products can spread freely in the embryo. The major part of the axis and body segment formation takes place during this period. This is a complementary subject to *C. elegans* where cell-cell interaction plays a major role in cell fate determination. By investigating these two model animals which have different embryogenetic mechanisms, we can better understand the essence of development.

As a first stage of the Virtual Drosophila project, we have implemented simulation for body axis and body seg-

Class	Gene
Maternal Effect Genes	bicoid (bcd)
	nanos (nos)
	troso (tor)
Gap Genes	hunchback (hb)
	Kruppel (Kr)
	knirps (kni)
	giant (gt)
	tailless (tll)
	hackebein (hkb)
Pair-Rule Genes	even-skipped (eve)

Table 3: A list of genes implemented in a current version of simulator

ment determination. This is an early embryogenesis process, and involves maternal effect genes, gap genes, pair-rule genes, and segment polarity genes. Table 3 shows the set of genes which have been modeled at present.

The simulator should be able to model such processes as gene transcription, translation, and diffusion. First, gene transcription can be modeled by a stochastic process where activators and repressors compete for a binding site. When two components compete for one binding site, a simple way to approximate the probability on which a component binds to the site can be described as:

$$P = \frac{U_a}{U_a + U_b} \tag{1}$$

where U_a and U_b are the levels of protein a and b concentration near the binding site. However, this assumes that the binding affinity is equal, which is not necessary the case. Thus, by incorporating binding affinity, the above equation can be rewritten as:

$$P = \frac{\alpha_a U_a}{\alpha_a U_a + \alpha_b U_b} \tag{2}$$

where α_a and α_b are the binding affinity of the activator or the repressor a and b, respectively. In a simple model, the amount of transcription directly corelates with the probability that the activator binds to the binding site. There are, however, much more complex situations, which would require more elaborate simulation. The model for such a case will be described elsewhere.

Transcription of a gene results in mRNA. In the simulation, mRNA is created as a product of gene transcription, and protein is created by translating mRNA. Some maternal effects gene products such as *nanos* binds to *hunchback* at translation process, not at the transcriptional process. Products of most other genes involved in this simulation can be assumed to act directly on the promotor region as an activator or as a repressor. The

	bcd	nos	tor	hb	Kr	kni	gt	tll	hkb
bcd				(+)	+				
nos				-					
tor							-		
hb					+	-	-		
Kr						+	-		
kni					-		-		
gt					-	-			
tll					-	-	-		
hkb					-	-	-		

Table 4: Transcriptional Regulation Table

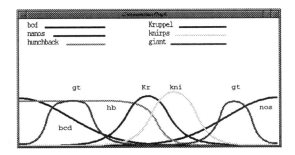

Figure 3: Simulated Expression Pattern of Gap Genes

regulatory relationship between genes and their products are shown in Table 4. In Table 4, + means that the protein acts as transcriptional activator of the target gene. (+) means that it promotes the translation process by acting on mRNA. − shows that it acts as a repressor. For example, *bcd* acts as a promotor of translation for *hb* and as a transcriptional activator for *Kr*.

Once the protein is created, it diffuses throughout the egg. As a crude approximation, we use a cylindrical coordinate system, instead of the exact oval shaped embryo. Currently, we are developing a more accurate 3D, oval egg so that a slight increase in concentration level at the anterior or posterior ends can be modeled. A simple equation for diffusion can be written as:

$$\frac{\partial U_i}{\partial t} \;=\; D_i \frac{\partial^2 U_i}{\partial x^2} \qquad (3)$$

where U_i is concentration of protein i, and D_i is diffusion constant for i.

Figure 3 shows teh simulation result for expression patterns of gap genes for the wild type *Drosophila*. This is highly consistent with actual expression patterns of *Drosophila* wild types.

A pioneering study on simulation of *Drosophila* early embryognesis can be found in [Reinitz and Sharp, 95; Reinitz, et al., 95]. Our simulation system extends such a study by enabling creation of various mutants, such as the *giant* knock out, and the *bcd* knock out, which result in a loss-of-function type mutant, and the overexpresion

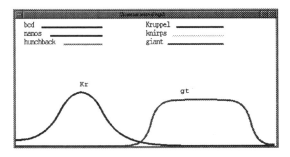

Figure 4: Simulated Expression Pattern of *bcd*- mutant

of specific genes. There are three major ways to carry out mutant analysis using the system.

The first method is the loss-of-function knock out, where a specific gene is knocked out so that no product can be created from that gene. Such experiments can be replicated by simply disabling the transcription of the target gene in the simulator. For example, Figure 4 shows a simulated gene expression pattern of the *bcd*-, *bicoid* knock out mutant. Only *Kr* and *gt* are expressed. Because no *bcd* exists, *hb* is not translated, and therefore is not expressed.

The second method is the overexpression of a gene, where the dosage of product from the target gene is artificially increased. This can be replicated by increasing a parameter which determines transcriptional efficiency, or by imposing a constant level of products to be present in the system.

The third method is site directed mutagenesis, in which a sequence of the specific binding site is altered disabling the activator or the repressor binding capability. For those promotor regions where a detailed model is implemented, this method can be reproduced by changing the binding affinity of specific products at a specific site.

Using these methods, the Virtual Drosophila system can replicate most of the mutation analysis actually carried out by molecular biologists. Thus, we can confirm the accuracy of the simulation. as it predicts possible molecular mechanisms of the embryogenesis process.

Currently, the Virtual Drosophila project is moving from Phase-II to the Phase-III level with regards to prediction on some specific gene regulation mechanisms, such as stripe 2 of *eve*.

5 Virtual Cell Laboratory Project

5.1 Overview

Virtual Cell Laboratory (VCL) is a computer simulation system which implements abstract models of molecular dynamics on gene regulation for each cell. Contrary to previous projects which focused on *in vivo*, VCL targets *in vitro* biological experiments. For many biological systems which have complex population dynamics and nonlinear features, discreteness, and cell-cell interaction, attempts to draw a set of equations often fail to capture the essential dynamics of the system, and they often generate misleading data. Cellular senescence is one of many biological phenomenon, and embodies characteristics where average analysis face difficulties. Thus, our simulation system takes into account following issues:

Cell-based model: In our simulation, virtual cells are created, each of which represents an actual cell in a corresponding biological experiment. This feature enable us to precisely model behaviors of the heterogeneous cell population.

Modeling mechanisms and interactions: We simulate the internal mechanisms and the cell-cell interactions of each cell. Complex dynamics of histon complex, nucleosome, repressor, and cell-cell interactions are generally too complicated to describe using equations without losing essential characteristics. Instead of using equations, we create computer programs to simulate mechanisms inside the cells and their interactions. Each virtual cell is assigned an independent memory space in the main memory of a computer. Features such as, state of nucleosome binding sites, transcription, concentration of regulators and promoters are represented as a set of data structures and variables assigned to each cell. In the current, simulation we can create up to 10^5 virtual cells.

The level of abstraction: We simulate abstract molecular mechanisms, rather than detailed dynamics of each molecule. For investigating phenomenon at the cell population level, modeling from molecular dynamics itself is too detailed and computationally expensive. Instead, we simulate the state of chromatin structure, such as the binding of nucleosome, or telomere shortening.

5.2 VCL Applied to Cellular Senescence

As the first target of the VCL system, we have applied our approach to investigate the mechanisms of cellular senescence. Cultured diploid cells have a limited proliferative potential. This is known as the Hayflick limit [Hayflick and Moorhead, 1961]. This phenomenon has been confirmed by various experiments, and the age of the donor inversely corelates with the doubling potential of the fibroblasts. Numbers of genes associated with cellular senescence have been reported, and numbers of hypotheses have been proposed. However, none explain a comprehensive body of data which includes data that appear to be contradictory. Among many experimental observations, there are two major observations which a correct theory of cellular senescence must ac-

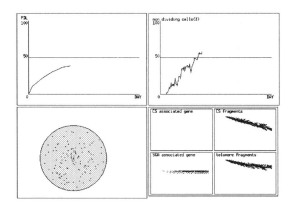

Figure 5: VCL Applied for Cell Aging Simulation

count for. These are growth kinetics data, proportion of non-dividing cells in the culture, and gene expression data. VCL was used to test various hypotheses with regards to cellular senescence. Figure 5 demonstrates the VCL screen applied to cellular senescence. It shows simulated data on growth kinetics, proportion of non-dividing cells in the culture, the physical location of cells with simulated reporter genes, and a simulated continuous northern blotting.

As a result of extensive simulations, we have come to the conclusion that heterochromatin structures control silencing of the genes related to the aging of the human fibroblast [Kitano and Imai, 1996]. The hypothesis not only explains all existing data on normal human fibroblasts, but also explains the data for Simian Virus 40 T Antigen-Transformed Fibroblasts (cells that are transformed by SV-40 T-antigen, which significantly extends their life-span), measured in terms of PDL, and Werner's Syndrome Fibroblasts. These fibroblasts taken from Werner's Syndrome (WS) patients, show significantly shorter life-span. In addition, predictions made by the simulation have been confirmed recently in actual cells [Imai et al., 1996].

The cellular senescence part of the VCL project have completed the first cycle of the computer-aided biological assay. Formulation of a more a detailed hypothesis will be stage-I of the second cycle. The yeast part of the project has just started and is still at the stage-I level.

6 Discussions

These projects are designed to complement the strengths and weaknesses of each project. These are inherent when choosing certain model animals. If, for example, *Drosophila* is chosen, it is not possible to use its cell lineage, because the number of cells is too large. *Drosophila*'s strength is in extensive analysis of the developmental process; also, their body structure is much more complex than *C. elegans*. *C. elegans* has a particular advantage in the existence of a complete cell lineage,

DNA sequence and neural circuit data. However, its neural system and developmental process are too simple; therefore, knowledge obtained by using *C. elegans* cannot be directly applied to other, more complex animals. However, it is an extremely good subject for establishing methodologies and for understanding the basic behavior of developmental and neural systems. In addition, although major differences exist between *C. elegans*, humans, mice, and *Drosophila*, there are substantial commonalities. Extensive studies are now being made on the neurogenesis of central nerve system. VCL focuses on *in vitro* simulation, and tries to model more details of cell itself.

By combining the simulation skills developed for these model animals, we are able to design a generalized software system which can be used for a broad range of computer-aided biological studies. We are currently developing a physical simulation module, a genetic interaction module, and a neural system module. These modules are defined using a class library which defines teh behaviors of genes, cells, cell-cell interactions, and physical interactions. The level of details in the simulation can be adjusted, once the package is completed, by selecting the functions to be used from the class library.

7 Conclusion

In this paper, a trong argument for a new approach to be taken for more powerful usage of computer systems in computational biology, or computer-aided biology, is presented. The three projects described in this paper exemplify this approach. While it is not possible, due to space limitations, to explain the details of each project or to discuss significant predictions enabled by the approach, the activities of our biological counter-parts have been significantly reinforced and empowered. This is mainly because the modeling and simulations provide a clearer picture of possible hypotheses and scenarios which may actually be happening in the living systems. We hope that this paper contributes to the artificial life community in bridging the gap between artificial life and the natural life.

References

[Achacoso and Yamamoto, 92] Achacoso, T., and Yamamoto, W. (1992). *AY's neuroanatomy of C. elegans for computation*, Boca Raton, FL: CRC.

[Brenner, 63] Brenner, S. (1963). *A letter to Max Perutz*, 5, June. Up loaded on http://eatworm.swmed.edu/Sydney.html

[Brenner, 74] Brenner, S. (1974). "Genetics of *Caenorhabditis elegans*," *Genetics*, **77**, 71-94.

[Hayflick and Moorhead, 1961] L. Hayflick and P. S. Moorhead. (1961). "The Serial Cultivation of Human Diploid Cell Strains," *Exp. Cell Res.* 25, 585.

[Kitano and Imai, 1997] Kitano, H., and Imai, S., "A Computer Simulation of Cellular Senescence," in preparation.

[Kitano and Imai, 1996] Kitano, H., and Imai, S., (1996). "The Virtual Cell Laboratory Predicts The Molecular Mechanism of Cellular Senescence — A Computer-Aided Approach to Biology of Aging," *Molecular Biology of the Cell*, Vol. 7, Supplement, 533a.

[Imai et al., 1996] Imai, S., et al. (1996). "OCT-1 Mediated Transcriptional Repressive Machinery Controls Cellular Senescence and Immortalization Associated Gene Transcription," *Molecular Biology of the Cell*, Vol. 7, Supplement, 533a.

[Sulston and Horvitz, 77] Sulston, J. E. & Horvitz, H. R. (1977). "Post-embryonic Cell Lineage of the Nematode, *Caenorhabditis elegans*" *Devl Biol.* **56**, 110-156.

[Kimble and Hirsh, 79] Kimble, J. E. & Hirsh, D. I. (1979). "The Post-Embryonic Cell Lineage of The Hermaphrodite and Male Gonad of *Caenorhadbitis elegans*," *Devl Biol.* **70**, 396-417.

[Mori and Ohshima, 95] Mori, I. and Ohshima, Y. (1995). "Neural regulation of thermotaxis in *Caenorhabditis elegans*", *Nature*, 376, 27.

[Priess and Thomson, 87] Priess, J. and Thomson, J. N. (1987). "Cellular Interactions in Early C. elegans Embryos", *Cell*, 48, 241-250.

[Reinitz and Sharp, 95] Reinitz, J. and Sharp, D. (1995). "Mechanism of *eve* stripe formation", *Mech. Dev.*, 49, 133-158.

[Reinitz, et al., 95] Reinitz, J., Mjolsness, and Sharp, D. (1995). "Model for Cooperative Control of Positional Information in *Drosophila* by Bicoid and Maternal Hunchback", *J. Exp. Zool.*, 271: 47-56.

[Sulston et al., 83] Sulston, J. E., Schierenberg, E., White, J. G. & Thomson, J. N. (1983). "The Embryonic Cell Lineage of the Nematode *Caenohabditis elegans*," *Dev. Biol.* **100**, 64-119.

[Sulston et al., 92] Sulston, J. E. *et al.* (1992). "The C. elegans genome sequencing project: a begining," *Nature* **356**, 37-41.

[Tabara et al., 96] Tabara, H., Motohashi, T. & Kohara, Y. (1996). "A Multi-Well Version of *in situ* Hybridization on Whole Mount Embryos of *Caenorhabditis elegans*," *Nucleic Acids Res.*, **24** 2119-2124.

[Waterston and Sulston, 95] Waterston, R. and Sulston, J. E. (1995). "The genome of *Caenorhabditis elegans*," *Proc Natl Acad Sci USA* 92:24, 10836-40.

[Watson and Click, 53] Watson, J. D., and Click, F. H. (1953). "Molecular Structure of Nucleic Acids: A Structure for Deoxyribose Nucleic Acid," *Nature*, 171: 737-738.

[White et al., 86] White, J. G., Southgate, E., Thomson, J. N. & Brenner, S. (1986). "The Structure of the Nervous System of the Nematode *Caenorhabditis elegans*," *Phil. Trans. R. Soc.* **314**, 1-340.

Constructing Amoeba-Like Behavior System:
Mobile Automata in Vibrating Field

Masanori Kudo, Hiroshi Yokoi, and Yukinori Kakazu

Autonomous Systems Engineering Laboratory

Hokkaido University

North-13 West-8, Kita-ku, Sapporo, Hokkaido 060, Japan

{kudo, yokoi, kakazu}@complex.hokudai.ac.jp

Abstract

This paper reports simulation study on amoeba-like behavior with flexible deformation. Flexible motion of amoeba is so complex that requires high degree of freedom for mathematical design. Features of amoeba like behavior system should be autonomous to perform adaptive behavior, such as free transforming, plastic, and dividable body in the aspect of body structure. Typical example of amoeba that deforms to move is cellular slime mold slug. The slug consists of many cells. To formalize the slug, our approach proposes Mobile Automata (MA) and vibrating field. MA is a mathematical description of a group of motor schema-based mobile agents. Besides, vibrating field as medium of information is introduced to model field mechanism of the slug. In the biology, Cell behavior for the slug crawling is not clear, however automatons' behavior was virtually set to see the macro-level behavior of the system. In this paper, computer simulation imitates MA behavior, such as pushing a food, wrapping a food, dividing in two parts, and transforming its shape to pass through a narrow corridor. Further, thermo-taxis of the slug were modeled by MA, learning mechanism of automata on the vibrating field.

1   Introduction

The purpose of this study is modeling amoeba-like flexible behavior by mathematical design. The flexible deformable creatures are widely adapted in the world, for example, an octopus, a sea slug, and microorganism. Dictiostelium is also one creature that deforms its own body to adapt and to live, it is classified into mycetozoa. The remarkable characteristic of slime mold is that transforms from unicellular period to multicellular period according to the state of environment.

This paper describes model of the amoeba-like behavior of cellular slime mold slug rather than amoeboid movement of a single cell, because single cell's units of behavior is molecular level, while the slug's units of behavior are cells. However, anyway the behavior has emergent functionality. In construction of an amoeba-like behavior model, we are faced following problems. First, it is a subject of complex systems simulation.

Then, it should be analyzed about the individual behavior of units at, for example, crawling. Finally, the characteristics of the emergent functionality may be applied to real robotics systems. However, it is beyond the scope of this paper to analyze and apply the simulated system, although it should be done in future.

We propose formal model, Mobile Automata (MA), for amoeba-like behavior system. Also, we propose field technique for the control of the MA as a whole.

Decentralized control for coordinated amoeba-like behavior on MA is the main problem. Actually, we worked at examining cell level behavior to end up some macro level behavior. That is, amoeboid crawling to a goal, passing through narrow and long corridor, wrapping a food, pushing a food, and thermotaxis as collective behavior.

The organization of this paper is as follows. Section 2 provides related work. Section 3 shows real slugs' features to be modeled. In section 4, we propose our modeling framework; The structure of MA and the control method of field technique. However, the contents of this section rather have tendency to ideal discussions. In section 5, we try to construct basic model of robotics-oriented application problems; amoeboid movement to a goal by MA and locomotion through narrow and long corridor by MA. In section 6, we discuss the previous results. In the last section, we close with conclusions.

2   Related Work

Unit-based approach taken here also can be called cell-based or individual-based approach. Cell-based approaches in modeling the systematic multi-celled organisms are based on cell theory by Schleiden, M. J. and Schwann, T.. That is, "Cells are unit of the structure and functionality of all organisms, and, in a sense, are first-order elements of organisms." (Fleischer & Barr 1994) made developmental models that can represent some characteristic behaviors of cells. (Agarwal 1995) made the Cell Programming Language (CPL) to model and simulate the biological phenomena, e.g., slime mold aggregation and so on. A kind of movable cellular automata, MFA (Movable Finite Automata) (Goel & Thompson 1988), is a very basic idea that can represent physically movable phenomena of cells.

For the field technique, the theory of cellular automata (CA) is a basic model to generate or calculate field pattern from local interactions among cells. Turing's morphogen model is also a more basic model of the field technique. Ueda's work concerned with a model of intelligence of Physarum concluded that self-organizing chemical patterns at chemical molecular level cause the intelligent behaviors (Ueda 1993). As for the systems with emergent functionality, (Steels 1991) discussed theoretically in a form of dynamical systems.

The field technique and movable phenomena of particles deribed VPM (vibrating potential method) proposed by (Yokoi 1992). VPM is applied to imitating cell movement and engineering problem.

3 Aspects of Real Slug to be Modeled

Slime mold is a kind of colony of unicellular amoebae. The slug is one period in slime mold amoebae's life cycle. Slime mold amoebae are rather shapeless one-celled organisms that move by extending contractile portions of themselves (pseudopod). If the food supply becomes exhausted the amoebae begin to aggregate into a number of collection points. After aggregation has been completed, the amoebae that have collected at a given point form a multi-celled slug. Cells constituting the slug come into contact with each other retaining individuality and avoiding fusing, moreover, moves as a unit so that it is not mere cell population, and differentiate a region responding to some stimulation. This moves as a unit, although the formerly free living amoebae retain their cell walls within the slug.

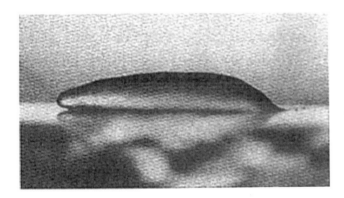

Figure 1: A migrating slug of *Dictyostelium discoideum*

The cellular slime mold slug have such features as phototaxis, thermotaxis, and ability of faster migration. Therefore, the slug can more correctly approach to the spot where will likely be rich of nutrition in future. To sum up features of the slug:
- The slug is multicellular constitution.
- Slime mold amoebae have mobility.
- Slime mold amoebae are in chemical field, and percept the chemical as input.

Automaton corresponds each cell in our model of slug, and MA is regarded as a cellular slime mold slug.

4 Mobile Automata (MA)

Cellular slime mold slug is made from cells. Cells are minimal unit of information processing system. The model of amoeba-like mobility is referred to as a mobile automata, because each automaton has mobility. The mobile behavior is modeled by motor schema-based system using potential field method (Arkin, 1989). Because behavioral schema set of automata is depends on specific domain of simulation, here, we formalize structure and behavioral form of MA. MA should be merely a group of individual units at initial state, and self-organize, for example, by differentiation. However, in this paper differentiation mechanism is not implemented yet, though it is possible in our formal model.

4.1 Automaton

Individual automata should have following specifications.
- It can move physically.
- It is physical entity, so they are subject to some physical laws.
- It acts according to only its schema.
- It directly observes its local environment and reacts to it also directly.
- The desired ends of MA are achieved as emergent property.

Mobile automata consists of six elements, state vector Q, input vector Σ, transition function δ, output vector O, Behavior function B, and initial state vector Q_{init}.

$$MA = (Q, \Sigma, \delta, O, B, Q_{init})$$

where $Q = (q_1, q_2, \ldots, q_n)$, $\quad q_i \in \mathbf{R}$, $\quad i = 1, 2, \ldots, n$
$\Sigma = (\sigma_1, \sigma_2, \ldots, \sigma_m)$, $\quad \sigma_i \in \mathbf{R}$, $\quad i = 1, 2, \ldots, m$
$\delta : Q \times \Sigma \to Q$
$O : (o_1, o_2, \ldots, o_l)$, $\quad o_i \in \mathbf{R}$, $\quad i = 1, 2, \ldots, l$
$B : Q \to O$

4.2 Motor Schema Processing

Each schema produces potential field, and arbitration function calculates final potential. Let $\mathbf{Potential}_u(s)$ be Potential function, so the potential variable is

$$y_1 = \mathbf{Potential}_u(s) \tag{1}$$

Then, arbitration function is

$$G(y_1, \ldots, y_s) = \sum_{i=1}^{i=s} \lambda_i y_i \tag{2}$$

4.3 Field

In nature, interactions between objects are conducted through medium. However, usually in some models, the interactions are represented by some expressions between the two objects. However, if field is to process information rather intelligently, the field mechanism should be modeled like other objects.

Field is a mechanism for controlling the MA to coordinate. The field can be equal to the cellular space consisted of units or extracellular space. The calculations by field are independent from the calculations of unit, but influenced in the boundary condition by the cellular space geometric change and unit's inner states. Then each unit act by some schema, taking an amount of field at its position as local environmental input.

The calculations in the field are like reaction-diffusion process by Turing's morphogen model.

Ueda's hypothesis of chemical self-organization, "Cell movements are caused by rearranging cytoskeleton according to self-organizing chemical pattern," attempts to explain the whole of cell activities (Ueda 1993). Turing's morphogen model is also basically the same model in point of the mechanism for leading many units of a system to show some united activity pattern by information calculated in field.

We also introduce such a field mechanism for unity of MA. One idea is that in cellular automata of MA, some pattern formation should be formed according to some external information (Figure 2).

$$\frac{M\phi}{M^2} = v^2 L^2 \phi - c \frac{M\phi}{M} \qquad (3)$$

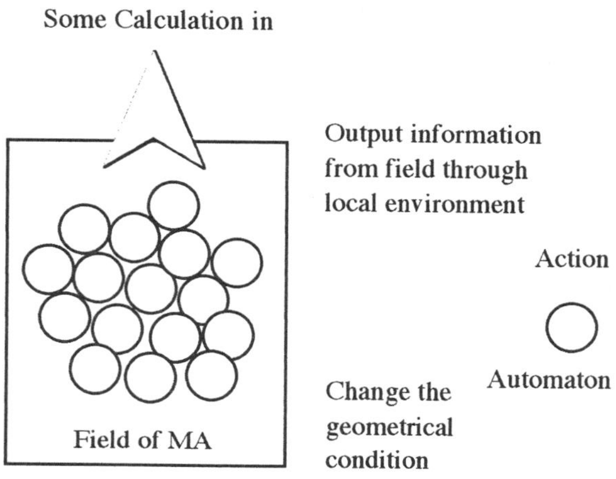

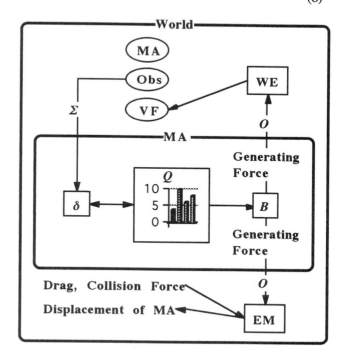

Figure 2: A conceptional schema of field mechanism.

This technique of field control has some merits in (1) understanding the amoeba-like motility from calculations in field, and in (2) designing amoeba-like mobile multi-agent systems with emergent functionalities. However, this idea is not yet implemented faithfully. In one application below, we implemented the field in all environment space.

4.4 World Model

In simulated world, there are physical objects including automata, physical barrier, and field of wave.
- Physical variables of objects {Positions $r_u(x_u, y_u)$, Velocities $v_u(v_{x,u}, v_{y,u})$, Power of migration $p_u(p_{x,u}, p_{y,u})$, effective Size u, Number of bond b_u, Number of units within neighbor $n_{n,u}$}

$$\dot{r}_u = v_u \qquad (4)$$

$$p_u - k_d v_u = 0 \qquad (5)$$

Expression (5): We assume that units are in viscous fluids with low Reynolds number. Therefore drag force kdvu will be operated to units, and units migrate with speed determined by making resultant force equal to 0.

$$DragF_b = k V_b \qquad (6)$$

$$ColF_b = \sum_{c \in 0 \text{ bodies}, \ddot{O} b}^{3} k (\mathbf{d}(b, c) - offset)^2 p \qquad (7)$$

$$DragF_b = ColF_b + AdhF_b + MotF_b \qquad (8)$$

Figure 3: Block diagram of MA and the world. Obs: An Obstacle, VF: Vibrating field, WE: Wave equation, EM: Equation of motion.

5 Leading MA by Vibrating Field

To see the leadability of MA by vibrating field, here, we set food automata as goals of MA.

5.1 Food Behavior

Food vibrates field. If food's position is $r_f(x_f, y_f)$,

$$\phi(r_f, t) = \mathbf{Vibrate}_f(t) \qquad (9)$$

5.2 Automaton's Motor-Schema

Each MA have two motor-schema, **Go-to-wavesource**, and **Adhere-to-neighbor**. **Go-to-wavesource** is for generating potential field to go to the wave source (Figure 4).
- **Go-to-wavesource**: Let k be constant. Then,

$$y_{gtw} = \text{IF } (\dot{\phi} > 0) \text{ THEN } (-k L \phi / |L \phi|)$$
$$\text{ELSE } (k L \phi / |L \phi|) \qquad (10)$$

Figure 4: Attractive potential y_{gtw}

- **Adhere-to-neighbor**: Let β, γ be constant, and r be distance between two automata. Then,

$$y_{atn}(r) = -\frac{\beta}{2}r^2 + \frac{\gamma}{4}r^4 \qquad (11)$$

Figure 5: Adhesion potential y_{atn}

5.3 Parameters

Number of units 60

Vibrate$_f(t)$ 100 Sin (400 t)

6 Simulation Results of Leaded MA

In this section, we set goal automaton vibrating field to lead MA to it. There are four different settings. First, attracting automaton called, here, food is set in the center of the square world. The stable distance between two automata is set smaller than the diameter of a food. MA reached at the food, and pushed it (Figure 6).

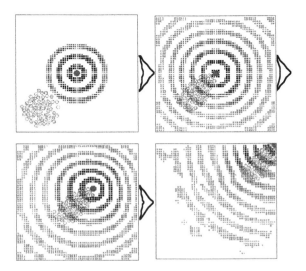

Figure 6: One food is in the center of the picture. MA pushed the food to the upper-right corner.

Then, the setting is similar to the previous one, but the stable distance between two automata is greater than the diameter of the food. MA reached at the food preserving aggregation state, and wrapped it (Figure 7).

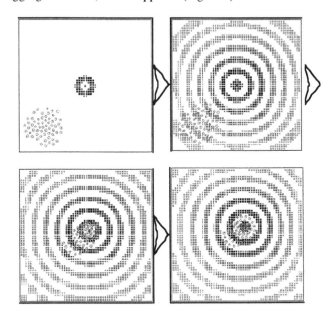

Figure 7: One food is in the center of the world. MA wrapped the food.

Next, there are two foods. MA were positioned initially at the same distance both from the two foods. MA divided in two parts (Figure 8).

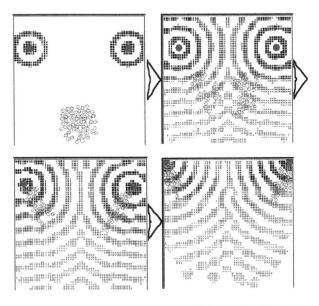

Figure 8: Two foods are in top part of the world. MA divided in two parts, and reached each foods respectively. This result is due to the initial position of MA.

Finally, narrow and long corridor was set between a food and MA. MA transformed its shape though passively, and passed through it to the food (Figure 9).

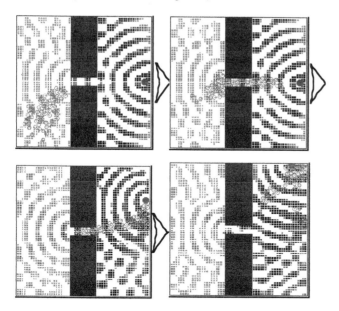

Figure 9: There is the narrow corridor between the food and MA in the initial state. MA could deform its own body to pass through it.

7 Thermotaxis as Emergent Functionality

In this section, MA's purpose is climbing up temperature gradient in the world.

7.1 Thermotaxis of the Slug

Generally, thermotaxis is taxis stimulated by temperature difference in medium. Moreover, taxis is directional movement of creature having ability of free movement responding to external stimulation.

The features of slug's thermotaxis to be modeled are as follows.

- Individual cells can not percept the temperature difference, but by forming multi-celled constitution.
- External factor like heat is merely modifies moving direction of the slug, while the mechanism of polar movement is in the slug.
- The role of organizer region of the slug. The tip of the slug secretes chemotactic attractive substance, and attracts cells constituting the slug.

7.2 Temperature Gradient Setting

Temperature gradient to be percepted by MA is shown in Figure 10.

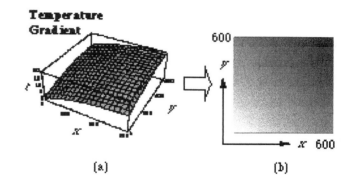

Figure 10: Temperature gradient

7.3 Schema Setting

We assumed that each automaton can store observed temperature in inner state pt. Let k is constant, t is observed temperature, then

$$pt = k \times t$$

Then we assumed motor schema **Climb-inner-gradient** shown in Figure.

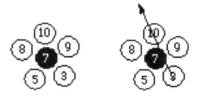

Figure 11: Variable pt in each automaton, i.e. the number. Besides, motor schema **Climb-inner-gradient** is shown by the arrow.

Expected effect is shown in Figure.

Expected Effect

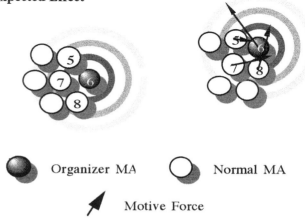

Figure 12: Expected effect of three schema.

8 Simulation Results of Thermotaxis

This section shows two experimental results of MA thermotaxis.

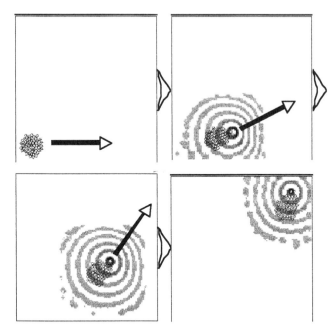

Figure 13: Initial heading of MA is right. As MA moves the heading modifies to upper.

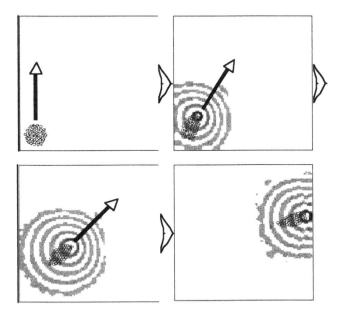

Figure 14: The initial heading of MA is up. As MA moves the heading modifies to right.

9 Discussion

In thermotaxis experiment, what is the difference between percepting directory the local temperature gradient and indirect *pt* gradient of the slug field of *pt*? It seems that cells at edge are tend to move along to the slug shape. This affects MA to move unitedly.

10 Conclusions

The purpose of this study was to realize amoeba-like behaving system by computer simulation. So far we have outlined MA, the model of amoeba-like behavior. In the way of constructing the model, we described it formally. For the united control of MA, we introduced field mechanism as vibrating field. MA could be attracted by food automaton, while they adhered each other. MA showed behavior of passing through a narrow and long corridor, pushing a food, wrapping a food, and dividing in two parts.

By incrementing the number of automaton, and setting automaton's schema more realistically, environments to which it is applicable are computer analysis of movement of each cell at cellular slime mold migration. Moreover, it is expected to apply to real robotics needing to realize the main functionality as emergent behavior with great degree of freedom.

References

Agarwal, P. (1995), "The Cell Programming Language," *Artificial Life*, 2:1, pp.37-77.

Arkin, R. C. (1989), "Motor Schema-Based Mobile Robot Navigation," *International Journal of Robotics Research*, 8:4, pp.92-112.

Fleischer, K. and H. A. Barr (1994), "A Simulation Test bed for the Study of Multicellular Development: The Multiple Mechanisms of Morphogenesis," in C. G. Langton (ed.) (1994), *Artificial Life III*, Reading, MA: Addison-Wesley, pp.389-416.

Goel, N. S. and R. L. Thompson (1988), "Movable Finite Automata (MFA): A New Tool for Computer Modeling of Living Systems," in C. G. Langton (ed.) (1988), *Artificial Life*, Redwood City, CA: Addison-Wesley, pp.317-40.

Kamiya, R. and K. Maruyama (1992), *Saibou no Undou* [*Movement of Cell*], Tokyo: Baifukan.

Maeda, M. and Y. Maeda (1978), *Nenkin no Seibutugaku* [*Biology of Slime Mold*], Tokyo: Tokyo Daigaku Syuppankai.

Ota, J. (1989), *Saibou ha Dono You ni Ugoku ka* [*How to Move the Cell*], Tokyo: Tokyo Kagaku Doujin Kai.

Steels, L. (1991), "Towards a Theory of Emergent Functionality," in J.-A. Meyer and S. W. Wilson (eds.) (1991), *From Animals to Animats: Proceedings of the First International Conference on the Simulation of Adaptive Behavior*, Cambridge, MA: MIT Press, pp.451-61.

Stossel, T. P. (1994), "The Machinery of Cell Crawling," *Scientific American*, September.

Ueda, T. (1993), "Saibou no Tikaku to Koudou wo Seigyo suru [Controlling Perception and Behavior of the Cell]," *Nikkei Science*, pp.32-39.

Yokoi, H. and Kakazu K., "The Behavior of Artificial Worms in a narrow path by the Bionic Model", *Intelligent Engineering System Through Artificial Neural Network*, ASME Press, 33 - 39, (1992)

What's Value Worth?
Constraining Unsupervised Behaviour Acquisition

Julie C. Rutkowska

Cognitive & Computing Sciences
University of Sussex
Brighton, BN1 9QH, UK.

email: julier@cogs.susx.ac.uk

Abstract

Novel architectures for behaviour focus on self-organization and the possibilities of environmentally situated sensory-motor systems. How well does this perspective extend to understanding development? Two approaches to unsupervised behavioural acquisition that are of current interest to roboticists are considered: selection from the system's own activities, based on bias by evolutionarily determined value schemes; and imitation through observation of the behaviour of more competent others. Work with robots is compared with studies of naturally intelligent primates, including human infants, demonstrating the primacy of 'learning by doing' to both accounts of behavioural acquisition.

1   Goals for changing systems

For many traditional domains of inquiry, work in artificial life is offering a radically new view of problems and potential solutions, unified by revealing how complex phenomena can emerge from interaction of many simple processes when an appropriate scale of analysis is adopted for the system in question. In this vein, novel architectures for behaviour increasingly attempt to avoid the programs, plans and goals that underlie the brittle intelligence of traditional computational systems. However, despite their limitations when embodied, embedded agent–environment systems become the focus of interest, traditional notions nevertheless offer an internally coherent view of some essential dimensions of adaptive behaviour. Of particular concern here, they support straightforward ways of talking about *behavioural decomposition*: Recurrent functional patterns that an observer abstracts from an agent's seamless flow of activity can be attributed to operation of permanent components of its program (procedures, sub-routines and so forth); and goals supply explicit 'stop rules' that specify when activity has achieved a more or less stable end-state that is deemed advantageous for the agent.

Very different mechanisms become plausible if we shift focus to action-based knowing that relies for its efficacy on an ongoing process of sensory-motor interaction between agent and environment. Often these mechanisms appear counterintuitive, with little match between tasks that the agent is deemed able to do and mechanism components that are believed necessary for it to do them that is typical of more 'between the ears' accounts of knowing and acting. Novel robotics proposals for agent design, such as the subsumption architecture instantiation of emergent functionality (Brooks, 1991), share the aim of clarifying how intelligent systems can recurrently exhibit context-appropriate patterns of action without being programmed to know what ends they are going to attain, let alone using such knowledge to select behaviours to try to attain those ends.

How well does this perspective extend to systems whose adaptive potential lies in their ability to change their organization? We might hope that it would do so in so far as the common defining property of such systems can be characterized as 'coping with the unknown', whether this takes the form of circumstances that are novel for the species (evolution) or the individual (learning; development).

As far as evolutionary notions are concerned, a relatively clear demarcation is emerging between their pragmatic and theoretical applications (Harvey, Husbands & Cliff, 1992). The use of genetic algorithms to automate the design of sensory-motor controllers in artificial neural networks has relied on using explicit, externally prescribed fitness functions to evaluate the success or otherwise of 'genotypes' in generating robot behaviour that attains whatever specific end(s) the experimenters have in mind. But when it comes to understanding real evolution, valid reservations are expressed about considering it as a process of optimization. Short-term species adaptation might usefully be viewed as solving particular problems, but contemporary animals are not simply solutions to problems posed in their species' long-past evolutionary history.

Despite being more accessible to observation than evolution, individuals' lifetime change presents a murkier picture. Any attempt to characterize this development in terms of the novelty of its acquisitions must confront the fact that numerous natural behavioural and cognitive abilities seem to appear so predictably that they attract invocations of task–behaviour specific genetic programming of precisely the type that has just been questioned (e.g. Parker & Gibson, 1979).

This paper brings together developmental work on robots and primates, including human infants, to assess the prospects for an account of where novel behaviour patterns come from that does not rely on pre-specification of stable patterns of organization that will be acquired. To facilitate comparison, examples focus primarily on a single crucial ability: prehension or use of the body to get hold of things, which serves as the foundation for object manipulation and tool use. Two approaches are considered that may be characterized in terms of unsupervised learning, though through very different mechanisms: *selection* from the system's own activities; and *imitation* of the activities of others.

2   Evaluating value

Work on synthetic neural modelling (a.k.a. neural Darwinism) that has given rise to the Darwin III system offers a significant starting point, aiming to establish the power of self-organization as a developmental framework (Reeke, Finkel, Sporns & Edelman, 1990; Sporns & Edelman, 1993). Implementations of Darwin III concentrate on simulation, but aim to incorporate consideration of neural, morphological, environmental and behavioural constraints. Similar organizational principles have been extended to construction of real robots (Scheier & Lambrinos, 1996; Scheier & Pfeifer, 1995) and to explanations of human infant development (Thelen, Corbetta, Kamm, Spencer, Schneider & Zernicke, 1993; Thelen & Smith, 1994).

Edelman's theory of neuronal group selection proposes that a successful adaptive system will start out with evolutionarily determined neuronal groups underlying sensory and motor processes (simple gestures), but unbiased connectivity with respect to goal-directed sensory-motor co-ordinations. Individual history grounded in variation in experience can then give rise to ontogenetically determined 'wiring', from which emerge action-based categorization and knowing.

Consider a simulation of Darwin III's oculomotor system, reach system (a multi-jointed arm), tactile system and an embedding environment that contains (initially only from an observer's perspective) an object that could be manipulated. Initially, Darwin III's arm movements are appropriately described as random flailing; there are no recurrent sequences of movement that we, as observers, would identify with behaviour patterns. Af-

ter interacting with its environment, however, such sequences are clearly evident. While precise movements vary from trial to trial, they converge on what looks like a behaviour pattern of reaching to the object. A category along the lines of 'graspable thing' has been constructed. Recordings of early prehension in human infants show interesting similarities with these data. Initially variable arm–hand movements distinctive to the individual converge, along individualized paths, to smooth movements readily described as reaching towards and grasping seen objects (Thelen et al., 1993). Robustness of this convergent process in the face of physical–morphological variation can be compared to Darwin III's capacity to 'acquire reaching' from a range of different initial states, e.g. different numbers of arm joints (Sporns & Edelman, 1993).

Darwin III's key achievement can be characterized as discrimination between its adaptive and chance activity. Some patterns of 'neuronal' connectivity get strengthened, i.e. selected for their adaptive potential, by analogy with Darwinian evolutionary theory; others do not. Crucial to this success is the fact that certain sensory-motor configurations are the focus of inbuilt *value schemes* that are assumed to be a product of evolutionary experience. In the case of reaching, the system incorporates a value scheme that treats the hand being in proximity to the object as 'good'; sensory-motor configurations that arrive at this state are strengthened in a version of positive reinforcement. Unlike reinforcement learning, however, there is no corresponding negative reinforcement; sensory-motor configurations that do not result in movements leading to 'hand by object' are simply ignored. We are to "sharply distinguish value schemes from the instructive agents and error feedback employed in most learning algorithms" (Sporns & Edelman, 1993, p.969). In a real *Khepera* robot, employing a value scheme for grasping (getting an object inside its wire 'collecting' loop) enables it to take the further step of discriminating between multiple objects in its environment (Scheier & Pfeifer, 1995).

Both conceptual and pragmatic advances are attained by this approach. Simulated and real robot mechanisms of categorization succeed in diverging from long-problematic views of perceiving as detecting properties of a pre-given, objective external environment prior to action selection. An integrated sensory-motor process is shown to operate, making categorization 'a behavioural act' (Edelman, 1992). This supports the notion that sensors may not function by detecting environmental invariants but depend on sensory-motor covariation, varying in ways that depend on the dynamics of the agent-environment interaction (Rutkowska, 1997; Smithers, 1995). Effective illustration of embedded and embodied knowing is further provided through the way physical–morphological constraints on behavioural acquisition operate; e.g. different environmental objects permit different activities on the part of the *Khepera* robot, and the diameter of its collection wire contributes to determining what are graspable and non-graspable things, providing the robot with a 'body-scaled' notion of object size (Scheier & Pfeifer, 1995).

Pragmatically, value schemes work. Disconnecting a system's value scheme(s) does not result in it acquiring behaviour patterns like reaching or grasping more slowly or more uncertainly, it simply does not acquire them at all. Superficially, it may look as if this approach suffers from a version of connectionism's restricted-input problem. In the case of Darwin III, for instance, agent and environment are modelled so restrictively that it might seem surprising if reaching to the object did not get established. In fact, even in this limited, 2-D version of a whole world, no behaviour pattern of any kind gets set up at all without the value scheme.

Can value schemes of this kind be considered flexible enough to offer a valid account of natural self-organization? Modulo absence of error feedback, their role seems akin to experimenter-determined feedback on the outputs of connectionist learning networks, such as back propagation, and to designer-specified fitness functions used in genetic algorithms research. Do they constitute a vestigial 'ghost in the machine'? Their dominant role raises a number of related issues:

Inbuilt goals? Such value schemes share properties of the goals of traditional artificial intelligence. An observer's description of the task that the system solves is incorporated as a functional component of the agent's mechanisms. Unlike a goal, the value scheme does not play a role in selecting and planning the activities that will lead to the outcome it specifies. Like a goal, however, it provides a 'stop rule' that specifies when activity has 'succeeded' on a specific task. This looks a lot like predetermination of developmental outcomes.

Buck passing to evolution? The approach emphasises individual history, but evolution, in the form of the preadapted value scheme, may be doing more of the work than an epigenetic perspective might hope for. How could value schemes of this kind evolve? They are attributed to evolutionary selection pressures operating on the phenotype, which could be taken as viewing today's animal as a solution to particular tasks confronted by its distant ancestors.

Acquisition or tuning? Darwin III's designers accept that the system is not exhibiting development in the sense of radical qualitative restructuring, or possibly too much by way of learning, in so far as new values for behaviour cannot be acquired. They stress, however, that it is being trained (e.g. Reeke et al., 1990). But how different is this acquisition of sensory-motor co-ordination from a system that starts out with (evolutionarily) biased sensory-motor connectivity then requires individual experience primarily for improvement on initially imper-

fect movement execution? We might almost say that the system's 'central nervous system' comes ready equipped with a behavioural program procedure but needs some practice with the muscle–body machinery in which it is to be implemented for it to run successfully.

Records of Darwin III's training are not unlike those of changing pecking patterns in chicks (Hess, 1956). Initially, chicks' pecking is widely distributed, rarely making contact with grain; over the course of a couple of weeks, their ability to achieve sensory-motor concordance improves, so that their pecks converge to a point on/about the 'target' grain. If, however, chicks are equipped with displacing optical prisms shortly after birth, their pecking still shows increasing convergence, but before and after this refinement the locus of pecking is laterally displaced in relation to the actual position of grain. Like Hess's chicks, human infants equipped with prisms initially reveal misplaced ballistic/reflex reaching to the displaced position at which the object appears. By way of contrast, however, the human infant subsequently becomes capable of ongoing adjustment of hand position until physical contact with the object is made (McDonnell, 1975). This suggests greater sensory-motor flexibility than Darwin III's current value scheme could support.

Restrictive semantics? Potential flexibility in outcome behaviours and tasks that can be successfully tackled would seem to be an important advantage of initially unbiased as opposed to biased sensory-motor connectivity. Chances of novel or unexpected acquisitions are, however, overly restricted by value schemes that have a clear semantics in terms of behaviour patterns, and which go as far as specifying the body parts involved in cases like the reaching value scheme outlined above. While value schemes of some kind may be essential for the developmental process, can they be as behaviourally and morphologically transparent as these examples? Even in arm–hand prehension, not only reaching but numerous behaviours like slapping and shaking readily come to be part of human infants' object-directed repertoire, not to mention complementary and bimanual hand use. A specific value scheme for every such behaviour pattern, e.g. to strengthen connections that achieve proximity of both hands to large objects hence ensuring acquisition of bimanual prehension, seems implausible. That kind of notion nevertheless underlies the success of *Khepera* robot studies that were noted above, which employed grasping and pushing value schemes to ensure acquisition of these forms of manipulation with appropriate objects.

Increased flexibility requires some more general purpose style of value, hence a new take on the task or problem being tackled from the viewpoint of the system itself rather than that of the observer. If we consider value-based accounts of infant prehension, the young infant's mechanisms have been characterized in terms of 'wanting' or 'desiring' a seen object (Thelen et al., 1993). Special significance is attributed to wanting to grab the object and to getting it to the mouth (Thelen & Smith, 1994) (which is certainly where it almost invariably goes, irrespective of its size, if and when contact with it is attained (Rutkowska, 1994a)). For infants this is considered to present a problem of raising the arm and guiding it to the desired object; its developmental solution involves arriving at the motor processes that will "transduce their intentions into a reach movement" (Thelen et al., 1993, p.1060).

How might these task–mechanism assumptions be read, if not in traditional goal-like terms, to clarify how arm–hand prehension might initially get off the ground? Like prehension, locomotion has often been viewed in terms of motor milestones whose outcome forms are strongly prescribed by evolutionary–genetic processes. However, Goldfield (1994) provides excellent analysis of how crawling may develop without any crawling-specific intention or mechanism (or a crawling-specific value scheme). Instead, this behaviour pattern may emerge from a combination of interacting abilities that have independent rates of development, in particular from constraints on reaching, kicking and maintaining orientation to a supporting surface. The behaviour pattern we call crawling can be considered as one of many ways infants establish contact with things they see, in this case involving temporal alteration between support and transport functions of the hands. Hence, lateral asymmetry in head orientation and preferred hand use are crucial constraints on motor pattern selection. Reaching with one hand enables the infant simultaneously to move forward and to not fall over. By way of contrast, reaching with neither hand when both are used to support the body means the infant gets nowhere, no matter how active their legs may be; and reaching with both hands means they fall flat.

What may be underestimated in the previous sketch of 'reaching motivation' is the significance of earlier experience of the hand–object and mouth–object contact that are considered to contribute to the infant's motivation to reach and grasp (Thelen et al., 1993). The developmental basis for a privileged role of arm–hand in prehension is not as straightforward as similarities to Darwin III's 'object–hand' value scheme implies. Rather than selection over arm–hand reaching movements being motivated by wanting objects and intending to reach them, the infant's wants, intentions and goals may emerge from less morphologically dedicated mechanisms that establish object contact, including but not limited to arm–hand movements (Rutkowska, 1994b). It may be only after this initial organizational stage that task–behaviour specific learning might come into play to 'tune' motor patterning, e.g. repetition of moving the (specific) part(s) of the body that achieved a (generally) 'valued' contact outcome.

Acquisition of arm–hand reaching is not, therefore, a good model for natural self-organizing prehension; better is emergence of arm–hand reaching under normal (physical–morphological and environmental) conditions, from a range of alternative 'solutions' possible under altered circumstances. Sporns and Edelman's (1993) suggestion that one-to-one correspondence between value and a specific motor system should not be expected across different species may well apply within species too. For example, it seems obvious that leg–foot prehesnion is normally ruled out by its destabilizing effect on posture. Nevertheless, young infants' earliest movements towards objects often more like whole-body launching than like arm–hand reaching; armless 'thalidomide' subjects acquire prehension, object manipulation and tool use, e.g. writing, through this bodily medium; and other primates come to show more foot prehension than humans, with close to hand–foot equipotentiality in certain primarily tree-dwelling species.

These suggestions are in the spirit of arguments that value systems should respond in terms of "simple criteria of saliency or adaptiveness" (Sporns and Edelman,1993, p.969) since they are "basic evolutionary adaptations that define broad behavioural goals" (Reeke et al., 1990, 613). Indeed Sporns and Edelman (1993) suggest sensory inputs from cutaneous tactile receptors as plausible candidates for an evolutionarily derived value scheme. While this diverges from the robot prehension value schemes discussed above, it is more compatible with proposals for visual value schemes that strengthen 'eye' movements leading to visual stimulation or fixation of bright spots (Reeke et al., 1990; Scheier & Lambrinos, 1995). In terms of the preceding discussion, it is also worth noting that the mouth rather than the hand appears to be the 'ideal' tactile stimulation source for infants, which may contribute to explaining its privileged status as far as developing prehension is concerned.

It is interesting to speculate how far a developing prehension system could get with a general value scheme directed at strengthening sensory-motor configurations in the light of levels of contact/stimulation, say, that they achieve, allied with environmental and physical-morphological constraints on sensation and motion (including form, size and relative location of body parts). Such speculation might, however, most profitably be clarified and tested by informing the architecture of a robot capable of transforming its movements into acquired object-directed behaviour. A real robot for such an experiment would require morphology with more flexible movement–behaviour possibilities than most currently employed designs allow, suggesting that simulation might be an advantageous first step. In particular, more than a single body part potentially capable of object capture seems necessary. Robot grippers may offer a close analog to natural arm–hand systems, but robots generally lack any other morphological components that could subserve a prehension function; whole 'body' pushing currently seems closest. Robot wheels, for instance, are unlike natural leg–foot systems in so far as their movement possibilities are restricted to implementing a single form of behaviour, locomotion.

This perspective diverges from the selectionist approach by moving onto Piagetian territory, where the development of action is a process of construction not just selection. For Piaget (1953), adaptation through initially independent sensory and motor systems began with simple action schemes, such as looking, grasping and sucking, striving to function, i.e. to obtain stimulation under any possible circumstances. What might look to an observer as task- or goal-based activity was simply evidence of this 'functional assimilation' operating in parallel. Hence, infants will grasp or suck anything that comes within range. And infants moving a hand, say, towards a fixated object while making mouthing movements are not trying to retrieve a seen object to the mouth in order to suck it; initially, they are simply trying to see, grasp and suck (anything at all) at the same time.

In summary, the particular type of value scheme discussed above, in particular its behavioural transparency, generates reservations about the general power of the selectionist approach. However, this does not undermine the core notion that 'learning by doing', whose significance was much underplayed in centralized, traditionally representational views of mind, offers excellent prospects for understanding development. Paradoxically, this conclusion also emerges from considering a quite different approach to behavioural acquisition: imitation or learning by watching an expert model.

3 Bridging watching, moving and behaving

Attempts to design robots that can develop their own behaviours in interaction with an environment are increasingly interested in the phenomenon of imitation (e.g. Aitken, 1994; Dautenhahn, 1995; Hayes & Demiris, 1995). Imitation comes in many varieties, but most interesting in this context is the possibility of an agent acquiring novel behaviour through observing the behaviour of another agent who has greater competence in the domain concerned (a model). Unlike more common artificial life notions of collective intelligence, where complex patterns of interaction emerge from environmental constraints on independent or parallel activities of group members with comparable competence (e.g. stigmergic building algorithms), the imitation approach is characterized by learner–model asymmetry. If it can be made to work, the approach looks like novel behaviour almost for free. The model provides a task-specific behavioural decomposition for the learner, who can become able to

do the task themselves through a general-purpose mechanism that supports acquisition of a wide range of particular behaviours. Imitation is internally motivated and supervision is not essential. Nor, contra the selectionist accounts discussed above, is a great deal by way of training or practical experience deemed to be required. This picture seems to me to be more than a little overoptimistic, but considering why this is so helps clarify how learning by seeing and doing may work in naturally intelligent systems.

A key problem with proposing behaviour acquisition through model imitation is that over-complex internal mechanisms are generally deemed necessary on the part of the learner. For example, the developmental literature features a range of mentalistic proposals that mesh with traditional, centralized accounts of mind and action, but are difficult to reconcile with more recent artificial life approaches that are attempting to shed light on self-organization.

In neonates and very young infants, imitation of an adult model's facial movements, such as eye-widening, mouth opening and tongue protrusion, has been attributed to representational mechanisms of the type that Piaget viewed as the outcome of developmental learning and that are typical of traditional cognitivist approaches to mind and behaviour. According to Meltzoff (e.g. 1990), the infant must be able to mentally model and retain in memory a representation of the adult's movements, in order for their own 'copy' behaviour to occur some time after the model gesture has been completed. Cross-modal mapping and considerable abstractness of perception are likewise required: the infant must match something seen (e.g. the model's tongue movement) with movements of their own body that they can feel but cannot see; and adult body parts must be matched with those of the infant despite differences in size, colour, texture and so forth.

Tomasello, Kruger and Ratner (1993) argue that observation-driven imitation is the earliest form of cultural learning, preceding learning by instruction, and assess its potential significance in learning by human infants and children and chimpanzees. Mechanisms of traditionally cognitivist form are deemed essential for true imitative learning of novel actions. The learner must display perspective taking, matching behaviour and function through understanding the adult model's (unseen) intentions and goals behind the (seen) outcomes they generated. Human infants who attain the same outcomes through their own behavioural means may be learning about object affordances, according to Tomasello et al., but they consider this to be neither true imitation nor cultural learning; rather, this is a process of emulation that is typical of chimpanzee behaviour sometimes (wrongly) attributed to imitation.

Such explanations might be viewed as proposing that

incompletely understood complex phenomena emerge out of equally complex phenomena that are no better understood, and as offering relatively little insight into imitation. However, even if less mentalistic mechanisms are proposed (e.g. Heyes, 1993), there are grounds to be cautious about the role that imitation may play in natural learning contexts. Assumptions about imitation may be comparable to Wolfgang Köhler's seminal analysis of problem-solving through insight. As Chance (1960) noted, Köhler's observations of his ape subjects were so dominated by the assumption that a form of mental recombination preceded their solutions to now-classic problems such as the cage–bananas–stick/rake situation that he ignored a good deal of behaviour that did not fit his assumptions. Among this was the fact that young chimpanzees normally spend a non-trivial amount of time playing with sticks, and that only those who have had this practical experience are able to join sticks to construct a rake in solution of the Köhler task. Insight learning may not involve insight in the way that mechanism was meant to be understood. Correspondingly, we may ask to what extent learning in natural contexts really is based on watching and repeating behaviours of an observed model. Is imitation either reliable or significant as a route to novel behavioural acquisitions?

If we first consider human infants, we find that neonatal imitation is reliably demonstrated only for behaviours that are already in the subject's repertoire. In fact, there is evidence from empirical studies that only tongue protrusion may be reliably imitated; and some interpretations question whether this involves model–infantbehavioural mapping. Linking to the earlier discussion of prehension, Jones (1992) has suggested that neonatal tongue protrusion could be a case of mouth opening triggered by sight of the adult face with moving tongue (cf. 'wanting to get a seen object to the mouth').

Studies of older human infants show that, even with behaviours that are in their repertoire, no clear picture emerges of their application to novel objects following maternal demonstration. The most that can be concluded is that observation of an adult model sometimes increases infants' tendency to perform modelled behaviours on selected objects. However, why some behaviour–object pairings achieve this and others do not is unclear. For example, a study in which mothers modelled banging, shaking, moving and rubbing on a toy fish, ball, doll and rattle found a significant increase among 6-month-olds in banging and moving the ball and rattle, whereas with the doll only rubbing it against their body increased (von Hofsten and Siddiqui, 1993). By way of contrast, 12-month-olds increased banging the ball and moving the rattle, but none of the modelled behaviours with the doll. The suggestion that infants may be influenced by the way the mother models what seem to her more appropriate behaviours, and by her enthusiasm in

doing so, seems unconvincing. It may prove more relevant to note that this approach fails to take account of the reciprocity of sensory and motor aspects of action, and their inseparable role in object categorization, that is clearly featured in the selectionist framework. For example, body-scaled properties such as hand size partly determine whether an object is manipulable by adults and infants of different ages. Strictly speaking, it is only possible to imitate the behaviour of a model whose sensory-motor and physical capabilities are in concordance with your own.

This kind of infancy research suggests caution about the role learning by watching a model might play as far as acquisition of novel behaviour is concerned, or even existing behaviour in a new context. The latter form of acquisition is interestingly illustrated in robotics work with the SAM (Sensory–Association–Motor) architecture (Aitken, 1994), which aims to clarify how complex behavioural sequences might be acquired by watching and imitating a model. SAM explores the possibilities for an imitation mechanism in this context to clarify how watching a model can constrain an otherwise intractable random search of motor patterns. Two aspects of the system are significant here. First is SAM's requirement that a repertoire of sensory-motor pairings must have been established prior to the more complex behaviour sequence learning. Second is the way SAM's learning by watching is driven by a sensory reinstatement mechanism. The learning system watches sequences of sensory inputs, which are generated as outcomes of the model's behaviours. Since prior learning has associated sensory and motor processes, repeatedly experiencing a model-generated sensory sequence leads the system to generate the sequence of motor processes that would be needed to produce them. It is notable that this 'imitation' system works for novel chaining of familiar behaviours, but its success does not rely on either watching the model's behaviour or trying to match it. We might conclude that this is not 'real' imitation but, at best, emulation. On the other hand, as we shall see below, the sensory reinstatment notion may successfully highlight an important aspect of interactive learning.

Imitation's reliability and significance as far as learning by watching others' behaviour is concerned are further questioned by studies of wild chimpanzees, such as van Lawick-Goodall's description of developing termiting skills, which retains relative neutrality as far as proposing mechanisms is concerned:

Infants under 2 years of age were not observed to poke grasses, etc., into holes in termite heaps; although I frequently saw them playing with discarded tools whilst their mothers fed there. In addition, from about 9 months of age they sometimes watched their mothers or other individuals closely and picked up and ate an occasional termite. Slightly older infants between 1 and 2 years of age often 'prepare' grasses etc., stripping them lengthwise or biting pieces from the ends, apparently as a form of play. One infant of 1 year and 7 months once picked up a small length of vine and, holding it with the 'power grip'.....jabbed it twice at the surface of the termite mound (there was no sign of a hole) and then dropped it.

The youngest chimpanzee of known age that I watched using a tool in a termite hole was 2 years old. From this age to about 3 years old, the tool using behaviour of an infant at a termite heap was characterized by the selection of inappropriate materials and clumsy technique. In addition, no infant under 3 years was seen to persist at a tool-using bout for longer than 5 minutes — as compared with 15 minutes during the fourth year and several hours during maturity.

.....between 2 and 2.5 years.....infants generally tried to use tools that were far too short to be effective.....Usually these tiny tools were bitten or broken by hand from a tool discarded by an adult.....typically, after prodding a tool into a hole (often one just vacated by another chimpanzee) the infant pulled it out immediately with a quick jerking movement (unlike the slow careful withdrawl made by an adult). Only on two occasions were infants of this age group observed to 'catch' a termite from a total of twenty-two bouts, ranging from a few seconds to five minutes. (van Lawick-Goodall, 1968/76, pp.222-223)

These brief yet typical extracts highlight two points. The first is that acquisition is almost painfully slow, despite continual proximity to competent adults. If this is learning novel behaviours by imitation, it is an awful lot slower than its common 'watch behaviour – match it with your own' definition leads one to expect. To the extent that watching an adult model constrains the behaviour of the learner, it appears do so in a relatively weak sense. In the wild, chimpanzees are taking around five years to become proficient termiters. Yet those reared in human laboratories acquire tool-using abilities like employing a lexeme board to obtain food/objects, operating door handles and so forth in a matter of weeks. As it is unlikely that chimpanzees imitate humans more readily than their conspecifics, such acceleration appears to lie in some other aspect of human learning environments.

Secondly, it is clear that dependence on adults ensures some noticeable constraints on the composition of the environment that will be experienced by the young chimpanzee. What the young can see, and the manipulable objects to which they have practical access, are unintentionally restricted as a by product of adult activity. On the sensory side, 'interesting' outcomes of adult activity, such as sudden availability of choice termites, may play

a more important role in the acquisition process than observation of the model's behaviour *per se*. In the quotation above, and in contemporary films of termiting in the wild, infants' initial close watching of an adult seems readily interpretable as serious interest in termites rather than in the behaviours of termiting. On the motor side, while chimpanzee adults do not appear to engage in explicit training, there is no need for the young to learn to fashion tools from scratch, since numerous discards with which to 'play' are available (cf. Chance's observations the developmental history of chimpanzee stick use).

The acquisition process here may be so slow precisely because it cannot be simply grounded in watching then matching the adult's behaviour(s). Instead, rediscovery of what adults previously discovered in a similar environment may be operating. This would fit with cultural transmission of novel behaviours in chimpanzees (e.g. using chewed leaves as a sponge in rain-filled tree holes) being equally slow, unreliable and predominantly a feature of the still-playful young. Additionally, it is compatible with adult models having acquired the behaviour in question, without raising the 'chicken and egg' question of how they could do so without some original adult whose competence was not itself the outcome of prior imitation.

This phenomenon has commonalities with processes typical of intentional human social scaffolding of behaviour acquisition, especially as far as reducing the number of degrees of freedom in a task is concerned and playing a role in constraining the learner's attention (which has been shown on quite different systems to improve acquisition of sensory-motor mappings (Foner & Maes, 1994; Scheier & Lambrinos, 1995)). There is, however, a significant difference: direct intervention on the motor side. Human scaffolding operates to ensure that infants experience the outcome of a novel behaviour directly, as a consequence of their own activities, not vicariously as is the case with (optional) viewing of chimpanzee adults or the SAM system's attention to sequences of model-generated sensory outcomes. A common feature is enforced repetition of movements that generate the outcome in question, which provides a most forceful route to marking a task's critical attributes. Zukow-Goldring's (in preparation) detailed observations confirm how physical and more reliable are the human adult's scaffolding interventions in infant activity. Demonstrations of activities such as waving goodbye, clapping hands, pressing a lever to release a toy or peeling an orange often focus on repeatedly forcing infants' close attention to attributes of context and materials that are relevant to the task. Equally, they are frequently supplemented by physical interventions such as moving the infant's arm up and down, raising an infant arm to a clapping position, placing an infant hand hand on the lever and pushing, or placing the adult's hands over the infant's while pulling peel off the orange. This is not so much 'learning by doing' as 'learning by being made to do', and it works to provide strong determination of acquired behaviours without employing mechanisms that require their predetermination.

Similar phenomena feature in the robotics literature under the heading of imitation. For example, Dautenhahn (1995) describes an experiment in 'teaching by showing' in which a learner robot acquires competence in navigating about a terrain by copying the movements of a more competent agent. Rather than watching then analyzing movements of the model robot, the learner adopts the strategy of gaining and maintaining physical proximity to the demonstrator, keeping in contact with it as it traverses the terrain. Then, the learner analyses its own preceding movements, to classify how it achieved the navigation task. What is described as deferred imitation of the model is actually repetition of the learner's own previously successful movement pattern to achieve alone the outcome previously obtained with physical support of the 'model' robot. This mechanism is considerably closer to the 'learning by doing' that characterizes social scaffolding than it is to 'learning by watching.'

An interesting property of this 'follow and then repeat your own movements' mechanism is that the learner robot's recognition and classification of its leader's behaviour is a consequence rather than a cause of learning. This is compatible with the infant developmental perspective being developed here. The conclusion of the developmental view on imitation and scaffolding proposes the opposite of Tomasello et al.'s position on imitation. From the infant's perspective, serendipity — unplanned, accidental but fortunate discovery — is the primary form of learning in scaffolding contexts. Infants do not need their own pre-specified intentions and goals in order to acquire novel forms of behaviour for attaining them. Nor do they need to perceive the intentions and goals of adults. Rather, it is through acting in ways that achieve comparable outcomes that infants — and, by analogy, future robots — may construct these goals for themselves and may thus become able to appreciate commonalities between their own behaviours and those of others.

In summary, a type of 'learning by doing' that appears in its strongest incarnation under the guise of scaffolding may prove more commonplace and robust than imitation as a means of acquiring behaviour that is new for the subject concerned. Indeed, some assumed instances of imitation may be better characterized in terms of scaffolding. This does not imply that all learning must be supervised, but it does illustrate key ways in which supervision may accelerate the acquisition process. This form of 'learning by doing' differs from that generated by selectionist value schemes, in so far as value schemes can only select from spontaneously generated movement sequences but cannot prescribe movements in the kind of 'instruction mode' typical of scaffolding. Nevertheless, there is a key similarity between these two approaches: each forefronts learning through 'success' — in attaining evolutionarily determined values and adult determined goals/outcomes respectively — rather than error correction or positive–negative reinforcement. Beyond this, analyses of scaffolding rarely address the 'value' question: why should the learner continue to repeat the scaffolded behaviour once enforcement/support are removed? Two broad directions suggest themselves. One addresses the way scaffolding may exploit general values; the other considers how social interaction itself may be a source of such value. As Sporns and Edelman argue, "the issue of value constraints and their number presents one of the greatest future challenges to selectional theories of brain function" (1993, p.969). What initially may look like very different approaches to the mind may likewise benefit from critical analysis of this issue.

Acknowledgements

I am indebted to Esther Thelen, Pat Zukow-Goldring and members of the Zurich AI Laboratory for helpful discussions on issues addressed in this paper. Thanks to the ECAL97 referees for their valuable comments on an earlier draft.

References

[1] Aitken, A.M. (1994) An architecture for learning to behave. In D. Cliff, P. Husbands, J.-A. Meyer & S.W. Wilson (eds.) *From Animals to Animats 3. Proceedings of the Third International Conference on Simulation of Adaptive Behavior.* MIT Press/Bradford Books.

[2] Brooks, R.A. (1991) Intelligence without representation. *Artificial Intelligence, 47,* 139-160.

[3] Chance, M.R.A. (1960) Köhler's chimpanzees: How did they perform? *Man, 60,* 130-135.

[4] Dautenhahn, K. (1995) Getting to know each other: Artificial social intelligence for autonomous robots. Arbeitspapiere de GMD No. 900.

[5] Edelman, G.M. (1992) *Bright Air, Brilliant Fire: On the Matter of the Mind.* Allen Lane: Penguin Press.

[6] Foner, L.N. & Maes, P. (1994) Paying attention to what's important: Using focus of attention to improve unsupervised learning. In D. Cliff, P. Husbands, J.-A. Meyer & S.W. Wilson (eds.) *From Animals to Animats 3. Proceedings of the Third International Conference on Simulation of Adaptive Behavior.* MIT Press/Bradford Books.

[7] Goldfield, E.C. (1994) Dynamical systems in development: Action systems. In L.B. Smith & E. Thelen (eds.) *A Dynamic Systems Approach to Development: Applications.* MIT Press/Bradford Books.

[8] Lawick-Goodall, J. von (1968) Early tool using in wild chimpanzees. *Animal Behaviour Monographs, 1,* Part 3. Reprinted in: J.S. Bruner, A. Jolly & K. Sylva (eds.) *Play: Its Role in Development and Evolution.* Harmondsworth: Penguin Books.

[9] Harvey, I., Husbands, P. & Cliff, D. (1992) Issues in Evolutionary Robotics. University of Sussex, Cognitive Science Research Paper, Serial No.219.

[10] Hayes, G.M. & Demiris, J. (1995) Towards robot learning by imitation. In: F. Moran, A. Moreno, P.Chacon and J.J. Merelo (eds.) *Advances in Artificial Life: Proceedings of the Third European Conference on Artificial Life.* LNAI/LNCS Series Number 696. Berlin, Heidelberg: Springer Verlag.

[11] Heyes, C.M. (1993) Imitation without perspective-taking. *Behavioral and Brain Sciences, 16,* 524-525.

[12] Hess, E.H. (1956) Space perception in the chick. *Scientific American, 195,* (July), 71-80.

[13] Hofsten, C. von & Siddiqui, A. (1993) Using the mother's actions as a reference for object exploration in 6- and 12-month-old infants. *British Journal of Developmental Psychology, 11,* 61-74.

[14] McDonnell, P.M. (1975) The development of visually guided reaching. *Perception and Psychophysics, 18,* 181-185.

[15] Meltzoff, A.N. (1990) Towards a developmental cognitive science: The implications of cross-modal matching and imitation for the development of representation and memory in infancy. *Annals of the New York Academy of Sciences.* Vol. 608: The Development and Neural Bases of Higher Cognitive Function.

[16] Parker S.T. & Gibson, K.R. (1979) A developmental model for the evolution of language and intelligence in early hominids. *Behavioral and Brain Sciences, 2,* 367-407.

[17] Piaget (1953) *The Origin of Intelligence in the Child.* London: Routledge and Kegan Paul.

[18] Reeke, G.N., Finkel, L.H., Sporns, O. and Edelman, G.M. (1990) Synthetic neural modeling: A multi-level approach to the analysis of brain complexity. In G.M. Edelman, W.E. Gall & W.M. Cowan (eds.) *Signal and Sense: Local and Global Order in Perceptual Maps.* Wiley-Liss.

[19] Rutkowska, J.C. (1994a) Prehension intention from 12 to 22 weeks. *Infant Behavior and Development, 17,* 919.

[20] Rutkowska, J.C. (1994b) Scaling up sensorimotor systems: Constraints from human infancy." *Adaptive Behavior, 2,* 349-373.

[21] Rutkowska, J.C. (1997) Computation, dynamics and sensory-motor development. University of Sussex, Cognitive Science Research Paper Serial No. 460.

[22] Scheier, C. & Pfeifer, R. (1995) Classification as sensorimotor co-ordination: A case study on autonomous agents. In: F. Moran, A. Moreno, P.Chacon & J.J. Merelo (eds.) *Advances in Artificial Life: Proceedings of the Third European Conference on Artificial Life.* LNAI/LNCS Series Number 696. Berlin, Heidelberg: Springer Verlag.

[23] Scheier & Lambrinos, 1996; In: F. Moran, A. Moreno, P.Chacon and J.J. Merelo (eds.) *Advances in Artificial Life: Proceedings of the Third European Conference on Artificial Life.* LNAI/LNCS Series Number 696. Berlin, Heidelberg: Springer Verlag.

[24] Smithers, T. (1995) Are autonomous agents information-processing systems? In L. Steels & R.A. Brooks *The Artificial Life Route to 'Artificial Intelligence': Building Situated Embodied Agents.* Hove: Lawrence Erlbaum.

[25] Sporns, O. & Edelman, G.M. (1993) Solving Bernstein's problem: A proposal for the development of coordinated movement by selection. *Child Development, 64,* 960-981.

[26] Thelen, E., Corbetta, D., Kamm, K., Spencer, J.P., Schneider K. & Zernicke, R.F. (1993) The transition to reaching: Mapping intention and intrinsic dynamics. *Child Development, 64,* 1058-1098.

[27] Thelen, E. & Smith, L.B. (1994) *A Dynamic Systems Approach to the Development of Cognition and Action.* Cambridge, Mass.: Bradford/MIT Press.

[28] Tomasello, M., Kruger, A.C. & Ratner, H.H. (1993) Cultural learning. *Behavioral and Brain Sciences, 16,* no. 3, 495-510.

[29] Zukow-Goldring, P.G. (in press) A social ecological realist approach to the emergence of the lexicon: Educating attention to amodal invariants in gesture and speech. In C. Dent-Read and P. Zukow-Goldring (eds.) *Evolving Explanations of Development: Ecological Approaches to Organism-Environment Systems.* Washington, DC: American Psychological Association.

Building grounded symbols for localization using motivations

Stephane Zrehen, Philippe Gaussier*

Center for Neural Engineering, Autonomous Robotics Laboratory

University of Southern California, USA

*ETIS-ENSEA, Universite de Cergy-Pontoise, France

Email: zrehen@rana.usc.edu, gaussier@ensea.fr

Abstract

This paper presents a neural architecture that allows an animat to find places where it can satisfy drives, and learn how to retrieve them from any place where they cannot be perceived. This system builds on an existing landmark-based target retrieval system (Gaussier and Zrehen 1995). We give insights on the design of a neural motivational system rich enough to give account of real conditions in which animals have to learn. These developments also lead to the construction of a "symbolic" level that is inherently grounded in the animat sensory-motor associations.

1.   Introduction

The animat approach to Artificial Intelligence aims at shifting the emphasis from symbolic representation of the world coupled with logical inferences mechanisms, in the view of solving a particular task, to the design of a set of behaviors adapted to "survival" of an autonomous system in its "natural" environment. Since survival requires several abilities such as feeding, homing, mating or fleeing predators, the animat approach explicitly requires an ability to choose the most appropriate action in order to satisfy either one or a combination of its most important needs at a given moment of its life cycle. In other words, a control architecture for an animat should contain mechanisms that select behavior in response to a set of several possible motivations.

Let us consider an adult dog that has spent some time in a house. When it was first introduced in that particular house, it first had to discover *where* the supper dish and the kennel were, and learn that its eating motivation could be satisfied at the supper dish, and that its sleeping motivation could be satisfied at the kennel.

The purpose of this paper is to model a simplified version of the problem of this dog, i.e., learning at what locations two different drives can be reduced, and to integrate this learning system to a control system that takes into account the correct association of perceptions to actions as they occur through the interactions of an animat with its environment. Thus, we set two targets, a food source and home, in an environment where several landmarks can be identified. We "equip" our animat with two drives: "hunger" and "tiredness." The only knowledge we provide to our animat is that food is the thing to look for when it is hungry, and home when it is tired. Learning concerns the *location* of these different targets, which will only take place if the drive corresponding to a target is active when this target is first encountered. When the two locations of the target are discovered and learned, the lone activation of one of the drives should lead the animat to move towards the location where the drive reduction previously took place.

The motivational system we devise here is intended to be added to our existing landmark-based navigation system (Gaussier and Zrehen 1995) which allows an animat to discover the location of a single target and learn how to retrieve it from any place where it cannot be perceived, with the help of visual landmarks. Our system is meant to be modular, and to use a very limited set of processing tools, in the form of structured neural networks. The motivational system we add in this paper is also made of the same tools. Obviously, the motivational complexity we propose here is very limited, since there is no real dynamics between drives. We will assume that the onset of hunger inhibits tiredness and vice versa. However, we suppose that learning to integrate simple motivations is a necessary step in the direction of making more realistic models of motivationally autonomous agents such as proposed in (McFarland and Gosser 1983).

The paper is divided as follows. In the first part, we offer a review of the relevant litterature addressing learning and motivational systems in the framework of animats. In the second part, we propose a brief explanation of our existing landmark-based target retrieval architecture. In the third part, we explain in detail the required add-ons to that system for motivated target retrieval, and the necessary modification of the neural networks. And finally, we present our implementation and experimental results in the fourth part.

2. Relevant material on learning and motivations in animats.

The first approach to the switching of behaviors on autonomous robots, as proposed by Brooks with the subsumption architecture (Brooks 1986) and later followed on by authors as (Mataric 1990), consists of establishing priorities between these behaviors at design time. For instance, obstacle avoidance should have priority over any behavior such as target following. This approach is limited in its scope, since there is no adaptation to external or internal circumstances. The appropriate response to external cues has to be known and programmed in advance, and behaviors never change. Interestingly, this work shows that it is nevertheless possible to have a limited "motivated" behavior without using an explicit module dedicated to motivations.

Lots of research on animats incorporates some degree of learning. However, it is common to limit the learning to a particular task, even when several behaviors are present. For instance, the DAC architecture (Verschure, Krose et al. 1992) allows an animat to avoid obstacles, and also to try to reach a goal. In that system, learning is confined to the obstacle avoidance. The choice of behaviors between reaching the target or avoiding obstacles is defined in advance, by a rule similar to subsumption in Brook's architectures. (Floreano and Mondada, 1996) solve a more complex problem by learning at the same time how to retrieve a target, and how to avoid obstacles. However, their use of genetic algorithms makes learning fairly long and unrealistic as a model of actual animal learning: the animats thus produced could only live in a single home, and could not afford to move.

Until now, there have been, to our knowledge, few attempts to associate on-line a drive state to the behavior that reduces that drive. Arbib and Lieblich (1977) have proposed a theoretical model for the formation of cognitive maps in the form of a graph where the nodes coding views of a place are explicitly associated to drives. However, there has yet been no full implementation of that model, which provides no precise guidelines about the learning mechanisms and their timing.

More recent work on an explicit motivational system addresses some issues in common with this paper (Donnart and Meyer 1995). The MonaLysa system allows an animat to plan its actions in function of a predefined goal. The main interest is the ability to generate on-line subplans, and to deduce the optimal plan of actions to get to the goal location. In a sense, this system goes a step further than our own concern in that it allows for the explicit coding of intermediate locations between the starting point and the goal. But the ability to do so is due to a heuristic mechanism similar to a hard-wired switch that lets the animat "forget" momentarily its goal in order to avoid obstacles. In our approach, we would like to see the animat learn that particular behavior and when to use it.

3. The PerAc target retrieval system

In this part, we present the intuitive navigational scheme of the PerAc approach navigation, then present briefly its neural network implementation. More details can be found in (Gaussier and Zrehen 1994), (Gaussier and Zrehen 1995), (Zrehen 1995).

3.1. The PerAc approach to landmark-based navigation

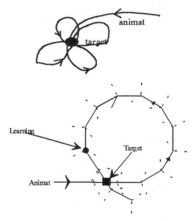

Figure 1. A typical exploration trajectory around the target. The visual angle is limited (dotted lines). Learning takes place when the target is in sight.

The PerAc target retrieval system functions as follows: a target is first encountered, which triggers an exploration reflex in the form of consecutive loops (see (Figure 1) At the extremity of each loop, the target is in sight while it was not at the previous time step. This signal is used to induce learning of a) the landmark azimuths set on a place cell, and b) the association of this place cell to the direction of movement leading to the target. Later on, from a place where the landmarks can be perceived but not the target, a competition among place cells elicits the choice of the movement associated to the most active place cell, which results in bringing the animat closer to the target (see Figure 2.) Details about this target retrieval architecture (Figure 3) can be found in (Gaussier and Zrehen 1995).

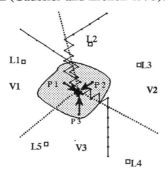

Figure 2. Principle of place retrieval using a few reference points. The choice of the locations coded by the place cells Pis divides the surrounding space in zones Vi. In each Vi, there is a single place cell Pi, and a direction of movement associated with it. In Vi, the landmark scene is more similar at a point P to the scene at Pi than at all the other Pjs. Frontiers between these areas are depicted by dotted lines. If the animat starts from any position in space, it moves a step length in the direction associated with that Vi, until it crosses the boundary to another Vj. The trajectories lead necessarily to the location of the target, indicated by the cross.

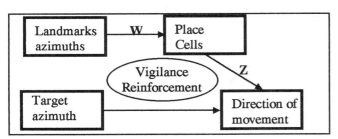

Figure 3: the structure for landmark-based navigation. Plces are coded as a set of landmarks azimuths. At each position in space, a competition among place cells is performed, which elicits a movement in direction of the target.

3.2.   The PerAc neural implementation of navigation

The mechanism described above for target discovery and retrieval can be implemented with a structured neural network. This requires four different groups of neurons (Figure 3 and

Figure 4):

1. The Landmarks Azimuths group (LA). This is an array of neurons where each line represents one landmark. The position of the active neuron on any line gives the measured azimuth of the corresponding

landmark. Neurons are horizontally topologically ordered: two successive neurons on a line represent two successive values of measured azimuth, according to the chosen resolution.

2. The Target Azimuth group (TA). This group is structured as LA, but with a single row. A neuron is active for the corresponding target azimuth only when the target is in sight.

3. The place cells group (PC). This is a competitive neuronal group of the ART-1 type (Carpenter and Grossberg 1987). Cells of that group are called place cells owing to their similarity to the hippocampal pyramidal cells (O'Keefe and Nadel 1978). Indeed, these neurons have to learn to respond to a place. Each neuron in PC receives input from all the cells in LA. When learning occurs, the present pattern in LA is learned by the most active K neuron in PC: we set

$$W(K) = LA$$

Finding the most active neuron in PC amounts to finding the point Pi (Figure 2) closest to the present position in terms of landmark azimuth configuration. In the following, we will call place cells the neurons of that group, whether they are already committed (they have learned a pattern) or not.

4. The Direction of Movement group (DM). This is also a Winner Take All (WTA) group, whose neurons code directions of movement. Each neuron in DM receives one input from the neuron in register in TA. This link is the neuronal translation of the reflex of moving towards the target when it is in sight. In addition, each cell in DM receives input from all the place cells. Thus, when there is a neuron active in TA, the neuron N coding the movement towards the target is elicited in DM. At the same time, a Hebbian learning mechanism is used to raise the Z synaptic weight between the winning neuron K in PC and N: we set

$$Z(TA,N) = 1$$

Such a change amounts to associating the landmark configuration coded by K with the direction of movement coded by N. Thus, if the target is not in sight, finding K as the PC neuron that best matches the measured landmark configuration will elicit the choice of N as the direction of movement. This is the direct translation of the mechanism represented on Figure 2.

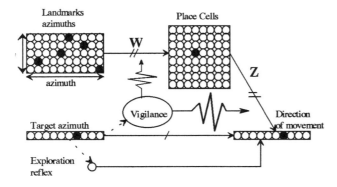

Figure 4. The structure of the PerAc navigation network. When the vigilance is high, the landmarks azimuths configuration is learned on a neuron in the place cell group, and that neuron is associated through Hebbian learning to the direction proposed by the target azimuth. The vigilance rises when there is *one* neuron active in the "Target azimuth" group and there was *none* at the previous time step. The exploration reflex is triggered when there was an active neuron in the "Target azimuth" group at the previous time step and not at the present time. The activation of that neuron forces the activation of a neuron corresponding to a predefined angle of rotation in the "Direction of Movement" group.

Learning is controlled by a global parameter called vigilance V (similar to the parameter of the same name in ART networks (Carpenter and Grossberg 1987), whose function is the following: when V is maximal (equal to 1,) learning takes place in PC and in DM. Otherwise, nothing is learned in these two groups. V takes its maximal value at time t only if the target is in sight at time t and was not at time t-1. This information is obtained by measuring the difference of global activity in TA between successice time steps. Details about the learning mechanisms and activation rules in all the depicted groups can be found in (Gaussier and Zrehen 1995; Zrehen 1995).

In addition to these four groups of neurons, the exploration reflex represented in Figure 2 must be implemented in a neuronal form. The simplest solution consists of using a Exploration Reflex input group of a single neuron which fires when the target is not in sight while it was at the previous time step. This neuron is linked to the neuron in DM coding the chosen rotation angle. A low value for this synaptic link ensures that when the target will be in sight again, the animat will move towards it instead of continuing its rotation.

After exploration has been performed a few times, all the necessary knowledge for retrieval of the target has been recorded. Indeed, from any location where the landmarks are visible but not the target, the neurons in the place cells group will be activated by the measured

landmark scene. The most active neuron in the place cell group will be the one closest to the location of the animat, whose choice will lead to a movement in the same direction as the one previously associated to that neuron, that is, in the direction of the target.

4. Adding a Motivational System

The animat described in the previous section can only learn a single target. Actually, once it has reached it, it cannot leave its vicinity, since all its movements are triggered by the activation of place cells, which in turn choose the movement that lead to the target.

Therefore, in order to let the animat first leave the vicinity of a target it has learned to retrieve, some inhibition mechanism must preclude that inevitable choice of movements towards the target. In a symbolic implementation, any means to accomplish that inhibition would be acceptable, but in a neural framework, the only cells that can be inhibited are either in the group coding movements, or in that containing the place cells.

It is tempting to inhibit the movement cells, since they directly control the direction of the animat. However, this is not a satisfying solution, for the following reason. Let us suppose that the new target is located behind the one that has already been learned, as in Figure 5. Inhibiting the motor cells that would direct the animat to the previous target would also prevent it from heading to the new one. Since there is nothing intrinsically repulsive in the previous target, there is no reason to devise a contouring strategy. Furthermore, in a fundamental sense, the directions bear no meaning in themselves, and should not be seen as the essential information recorded about a target:The choice of the directions that end up being used to retrieve a given target is mostly due to chance, the main factor being the angle under which the animat first perceived the target.

Figure 5. The first target has already been learned. The arrows represent the directions of movement that have been associated with that target. The second target that the animat must reach is right behind the first one. In order to reach it from its present location, the animat must take one of these directions.

Therefore, the simplest remaining choice consists of adding an inhibition mechanism to the place cells that have been allocated during the exploration of the first target. This inhibition should appear when the animat has "lost interest" in this target, due to either the extinction of the drive that was associated to it, or the appearance of a stronger drive requiring another target. Our model thus points to the necessity of having a separate set of place cells for different targets.

The nicest aspect of the modeling we propose here is its simplicity: in order to allow the animat to first leave the first target and learn the necessary information about the next one it will encounter, one single inhibition signal is needed. As we have seen above, inhibiting the activation of the place cells is sufficient to let the animat leave its vicinity. Actually, the resulting trajectory, if no additional factors come into play, is a completely random walk, which is due to the noise on the neurons on the place cells. In addition, since learning among neurons in the group of place cells follows a competition mechanism, the inhibited cells will not participate in the competition, therefore letting the other, uncommitted, cells to win, and learn the new landmarks configurations.

Once admitted this principle, the two remaining problems are a) the coding and regulation of inhibition, as a function of the drives, and b) the learning of the proper associations between the drive state and the place cells. The two next paragraphs explain our solution.

4.1. Coding drives

As was mentioned in the introduction, we admit that basic drives exist a priori in the system. We also admit that the drive and the behavioral response that will lead to its decrease are not the same signal, but that their link is hardwired.

	Hunger	Tiredness	Look for food	Look for home
hungry	1	-1	1	-1
tired	-1	1	-1	1
neutral	0	0	0	0

Table 1. The values the drives can take for a given drive state, and the response of the Planner neurons. We use two neurons for drives which can take three values. The activation of one drives inhibits the other one.

We assimilate the group of cells responsible for the choice of the target to look for, that is, the appropriate behavioral response to the most active drive, to a planner.

In later versions, the role of that planner will be to elicit sequences of actions that lead to the satisfaction of the goal.

We model the drives by ternary functions with strong inhibition between themselves, yielding the value table (Table 1) where rows represents the possible drive states.

In this paper, we model the dynamics of these drives by simple sinusoidal functions, which is equivalent to having the experimenter set the active drive himself. The structure of the complete model is given in Figure 6.

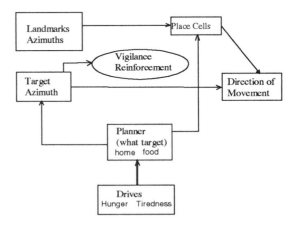

Figure 6. The structure of the neural network for motivated landmark-based navigation. The drives state elicits the choice of the target to look for in the planner. The planner sends an inhibiting signal to the place cells associated to the other targets than the desired one.

Let us admit that the animat has already discovered the two targets and learned all the necessary information. Now let us set the drive to "hunger." The functioning of the system is the following: the "hunger" neuron is set to 1, the "tiredness" neuron to -1. This yields the "food" neuron's activation to be one, and that of the "home" neuron to be -1. This causes the neurons in the Target Azimuth group to respond only to the sight of food and not to the sight of home. In the place cells group, the neurons receive information from the Planner in addition to the landmarks azimuths: the place cells associated to the food all receive the same amount of excitation from the "food" neuron in the planner, and the other place cells do not, which gives them too strong a handicap to win the competition. Therefore, the competition only takes place among the place cells associated to food, and the place cell coding the place closest to the animat wins. This elicits the choice of a movement that will bring the animat closer to the food. In order for the right place cells to receive the additional excitation from the planner, to the exclusion of the others, the synaptic weights linking the "food" Planner neuron and these place cells must have been set to a high value during learning of the target. How this learning takes place is the subject of the next paragraph.

4.2. On-line learning of the association of drives to the location of a target

In the scheme of Figure 6, the synaptic links between the Planner and the place cells group are adaptive: the system cannot know in advance which place cells should correspond to which target. This needs to be learned on-line, while the animat first discovers the target chosen by the planner.

In our modeling, we set the initial value of these synaptic weights to a random value small enough to play no significant role in the first competitions. Then, we use a Hebbian learning rule between the most active neurons in the two groups, which will set the weight linking the "home" neuron to the most active place cell to one. At the same time, the same place cell will learn the set of landmarks azimuths, because the vigilance is set to 1 each time the desired target is perceived.

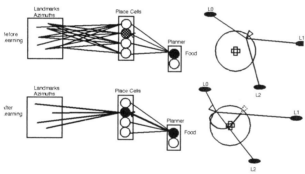

Figure 7. The learning sequence. Place cells receive input from the landmarks azimuths and from the planner. In the upper picture, the weights are all very small, and are represented by thin lines. Nevertheless, one of the place cells wins over the other in response to the landmarks azimuths pattern, and learns it. At the same time, the food neuron is active in the planner. Hebbian learning sets the link between them to 1. In the lower picture, the weight linking the food neuron and the previously winning place cell has value 1. Thus, this place cell receives an additional input of value 1, which is enough to ensure its winning over all the other place cells, in response to any new landmarks configuration.

However, this learning scheme presents a major problem: as a result of the Hebbian learning, the same place cell will always win the competition for all the new locations the exploration reflex will take the animat to. This will happen at the end of the first exploration loop, when the animat should learn a new place cell (see Figure 7.) This is due to the fact that the first place cell to

win the competition will always get the excitation from the active neuron in the Planner, as long as the drive remains active.

As appears from the navigation scheme presented in Paragraph 3, this problem would preclude learning of the minimum necessary information to retrieve the target: one needs to learn at least three different place cells corresponding to three locations well dispersed around the target.

Our solution to this problem is to separate learning in the place cells group in two stages, and to introduce a delay in the link between the Drives group and the Planner. If learning takes place as follows, the problem described above no longer exists:

1. The place cells receive the input from the landmarks azimuths. The competition is performed among place cells according to that sole input.

2. The most active place cell learns the landmarks azimuths.

3. The place cells receive input from the Planner. At this stage the winner found for the landmarks azimuths is still active.

4. The link between the active neuron in the planner and the winner place cell is set to 1 as a result of Hebbian learning.

This learning schedule ensures that at subsequent times when the animat should learn a new set of landmarks azimuths, the first winner will not receive the bias from the planner before the new winner is found and learns the new configuration.

4.3. A more realistic architecture for the motivational system: construction of a symbolic level

In the previous paragraph, we proposed the simplest system that would give rise to the desired motivated behavior of target learning and searching in response to the most active drive. However, the scheme we proposed directly uses the activation of several place cells to "choose" a target. If we think in more human terms, we refer to places by their name, and not directly by the precise set of movements to get there. Also, in view of constructing symbols for places of interest that are grounded in the animat's experience, the set of nodes that represent a particular place should be extremely limited. Since the previously described system makes it difficult to control the set of place cells that will be associated to a given target (a place), it is desirable to allow for a more abstract level of representation. If we can construct a group of neurons that each represent a place through links to a set of place cells associated to a given targets, we in fact obtain a symbolic level representation of places. The obvious advantage of the construction of such neurons is that it avoids the symbol grounding problem (Harnad 1990). The ability to construct the correct input to these nodes also represents a progress in animat neural control architectures, in that is illustrates the ability to learn across several levels: drives, high-level representation of places, recognition of objects and landmarks, and low-level behaviors implemented in the form of learned sensory-motor associations.

We propose to use a group of neurons called "Place" whose main input should be the set of place cells (Figure 8.) Thus, the most active neuron in the Place group should be associated to the active place cells neurons through Hebbian learning, as proposed earlier. In order to ensure separation between these nodes, we also provide them with unconditional links from the set of targets: each neuron in the Place group receives afferences from a complete line in the "Target Azimuth" group. In the proposed implementation, we allow the recognition of four potential targets, hence four lines in the Targets Azimuth group, and four neurons in the Place group.

In addition, we use another input group whose function is to detect the presence of an "interesting place" as one where there is a discovery of an interesting object in the visual field, in conjunction with the presence of a given Drives pattern. The Interesting Place group is a WTA that receives input from the Drives group, thus allowing each one of its node to learn to respond to a possibly complex drive pattern. However, a winner can be elicited in Interesting Place only if the additional input from the "Discover a Target" is active. This happens when some salient object, in other words, a potential target, is in sight. This single neuron group is semantically non-committed a priori: it should respond to any perceived object in a given range. For the time being, having no satisfying object recognition mechanism, we have to simulate its activation.

Thus, the learning scheme becomes the following:

• The physiological state of the animat sets the Drives pattern (in the present modeling, at most one drive is active while the other is inhibited.)

• When a close object is in sight, the neuron is active in "Discover a Target."

• A winner is elicited in "Interesting Place"

• If the object is a target corresponding to the present drive state, one neuron is active on the corresponding line in the Targets Azimuth group. This elicits the choice of the winner in Place as the neuron that gets its input

from the active line in Targets Azimuth. At the same time a neuron is active in the place cells group. Because the object in sight is a target, the vigilance and reinforcement signal are set to 1, which enables learning of the following links:

• The winner in Interesting Place learns the Drives pattern

• The link between the winner in Interesting Place and the Place winner is set to 1

• The bidirectional links between the active place cell and the Place winner are set to their maximal value

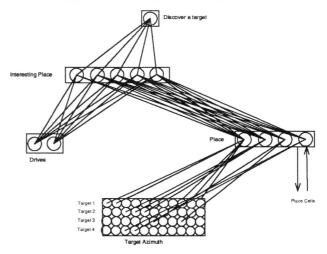

Figure 8. The complete structure of the motivational system. The Drives group provides input to the Interesting Place. The latter is a WTA that can only be activated if an interesting target is in sight, which is signaled by the "Discover a Target" single neuron group. Place neurons each get an input from the corresponding Target Position group. Place is a WTA that can only be activated if it receives positive input from Interesting Place. Thus, learning of a Place only occurs when the animat discovers an interesting target.

5. Implementation

5.1. Experimental Results

The set of experiments we must provide to illustrate the functioning of the network comes naturally. We first "place" the animat in sight of the food source, and set all drives to 0. We expect the animat not to pay attention to the presence of the food target, and therefore to perform a random walk. We see on Figure 9 that it is the case. The animat does not start by moving towards the food source (T1) because there is no neuron active in the Target Azimuth group. Indeed, the symbolic link between the Place and the Drives group prevents all the Target Azimuth neurons to respond to the sight of a target which cannot satisfy the present drive. In other words, the food source is not seen by the system as a target. However, an object is perceived, which causes one neuron in the Interesting Place group to be active. But this information will not be used by the system due to hardwired inhibition of the Targets Azimuth neurons.

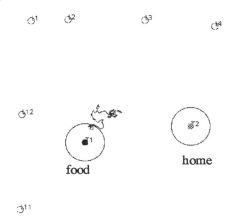

Figure 9. The animat is placed in the vicinity of the food source, and its drive is set to "tired." Therefore, the animat not being hungry does not direct itself towards the target nor learns any information. On the contrary, it performs a random walk due to the noise on the uncommitted place cells. T1 and T2 represent the location of particular places where the targets responding to the drive can be placed.

In this model, there is no need for an explicit exploration drive. The mere absence of a significantly active drive triggers the exploration.

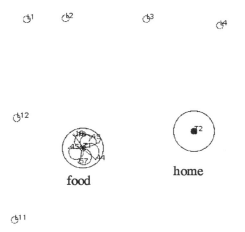

Figure 10. The animat is now placed in the vicinity of the food source while it is hungry. This triggers the usual exploration behavior and the learning of the relevant information to retrieve that target. Numbers represent the index of the committed place cells in their group.

Leaving the animat at the same position, we can now set its drive to "hunger." We see now that it first starts by moving towards the target, then performs the exploration (Figure 10.) Now, when the food source is in sight, one neuron is active in the Target Azimuths group. This in turn allows the animat to move towards the target when it is in sight. The choice of the movement and the presence of an active neuron in the Targets Azimuths group allows the vigilance of the system to increase to 1, which results in learning by uncommitted place cells of the landmarks azimuths. At the same time, each place cell that learns during that exploration sees its synaptic link coming from the active Place set to 1. On Figure 10, the numbers represent the index of the place cells neurons that code that particular location. Their choice is a result of the competition and cannot be known in advance, due to the small noise added to their activity.

If we now set the drive to tiredness, we see on Figure 11 the exploration performed around home. This, as described in Table 1, sets the "hunger" Drive neuron to -1, and the corresponding "Look for food" Planner neuron to have negative activity. Due to the previous Hebbian learning between the "Look for food" neuron and the place cells associated to the food target, the negative activity of the Planner neuron sends a negative signal to these place cells. This negative bias excludes them for the competition, letting uncommitted place cells neurons to code for the new landmarks azimuths. This is illustrated by the difference of place cell indexes between Figure 10 and Figure 11.

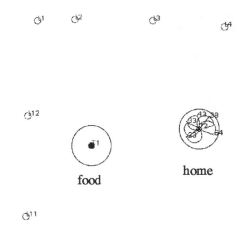

Figure 11. The drive is "tiredness." This setting sends a negative signal to the place cells previously associated to the food target, and lets new uncommitted place cells to win and code the new landmarks azimuths during the exploration.

Now, the necessary information has been learned. The parallel with the dog mentioned in the introduction is that it has now learned where the interesting things are in its new home: its kennel and its supper dish. What is desired at this stage is that the onset of the hunger drive will take our animat to the food source, and the onset of the tiredness drive to home. This is illustrated on Figure 12, which represents the directions the animat would take from several point in the environment in response to its active drive.

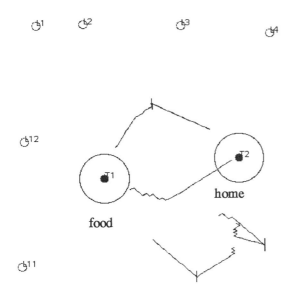

Figure 12. The trajectories of the animat after learning of both targets has taken place. At each starting point indicated by a vertical straight line, the drives were set to the two different possible states. We see on each case that the animat moves towards the target where it has learned to reduce its present drive.

6. Conclusion and future work.

We have presented a completely neural system that allows motivated navigation behavior, in the form of the following experiment: the animat is first placed in sight of a food target while it is hungry, then in sight of its home when it is tired. The adequacy of the present target to the drive state of the animat leads it to learn the location of both targets. Later onset of each of the drive will lead the animat to move to the location of the target corresponding to its drive. In that system, all the necessary information for coding the location of the place is learned while a given drive is more active than others. This took place with the help of high-level symbolic nodes representing places, whose grounding in the animat's experience is granted by the interactions of this animat with the environment.

This set of experiments shows that the proposed architecture allows learning to take place on-line, across several hierarchically distinct levels: drives, recognition of objects through vision, low-level sensory-motor associations for target retrieval, and high-level coding of

place, and their associations to drive reduction. These results give hope for seeing the animat approach get to the level of processing that serves as input to traditional Artificial Intelligence systems.

In our system, learning the location of a target only takes place if the target is the one whose finding should reduce the drive. Thus, there is no latent learning in this system. This is evidently a partial model for having a sufficiently autonomous animat, in the sense of a "motivationally autonomous agent" in McFarland's typology. However, several major problems have been addressed and solved. There was no need to displace the animat to all the locations in the environment and let it try every possible direction of movement, as is usually proposed in reinforcement learning (see (Barto and Sutton 1981; Klopf, Morgan-James et al. 1993; Schmajuk and Blair 1993)). Obviously, the system we propose is fairly complex, and could be simplified by using higher-level operations such as vector addition. However, this cannot easily be done using neural networks, and the result is a homogeneous type of processing across the complete network. In addition, the complex input we simulate in this paper by computing the location of the landmarks and their representations in terms of azimuths, could actually be obtained directly as the output of an active vision system. We showed in (Gaussier and Zrehen 1995) that the structure of a neural network performing recognition of visual scenes by incorporating the ocular saccades they provoke has exactly the same structure as the navigation neural network.

The main addition of this paper concerned the "motivation module" that is a simple "plug-in" to the already existing navigation network, which remains unaltered. With the exception of the necessary delay between the Drives group and the Planner, all the operations needed in the motivation module are of the standard neural form. These findings illustrate the genericity of the PerAc approach as a systematic tool to tackle complex association tasks on-line.

From the cognitive science point of view, the presentation of the motivation as a plug-in to another system could be seen as misleading, since motivations generally seem to influence all aspects of behavior. Actually, one should see the system presented in this paper as an attempt to create the simplest learning animat architecture. In other words, a mobile robot equipped with the mere navigation system without the motivational module should not be seen as an animat since it could only perform one task, and therefore would not be able to ensure a proper life cycle. With the simple architecture proposed here, we have the following behavior. If one drive is active, the animat will move towards the location where it has learned that the drive can be reduced. If no drive is active, then random exploration ensues. This implies that purposeful behavior has been previously associated to the satisfaction of a drive.

The system proposed here should evolve in several directions in order to give account of a completely autonomous animat that behaves more like an animal:

1. We oversimplified the association of the Planner to the Target Azimuth group by "hardwiring" the inhibiting connection, thus letting the animat only pay attention to the target corresponding to its current drive. Future work should tackle this problem from a learning perspective, and let the animat learn what targets satisfy what drives.

2. Learning is immediate. There is no ability with the reinforcement learning algorithm we used here to learn with a delay. This also precludes learning intermediate steps, such as would be required in a maze environment, where some junctions would contain no interesting targets. However, we have devised a modified version of the algorithm that allows learning with a delay in maze environments (Gaussier, Revel et al. 1996). Further study will aim at implementing the proposed motivational module to a maze environment.

3. Learning is directly linked to the satisfaction of an active drive. A more realistic system should allow a form of latent learning, that varies with the intensity of the drives.

4. The interactions of drives we proposed in this paper is extremely simplified, since the activation of one drive automatically inhibits the other. Further development should give a more precise account of the actual interactions between drives as they take place in animals. There should also be a reciprocal influence between drives and the events encountered by the animat, in order to change drive priorities according to particular opportunities.

7.   Bibliography

Barto, A. G. and R. S. Sutton (1981). "Landmark learning: an illustration of associative search." Biological Cybernetics 42: 1-8.

Brooks, R. A. (1986). " A robust layered control system for a mobile robot." IEEE Journal of Robotics and Automation RA-2: 14-23.

Carpenter, G. and S. Grossberg (1987). "A massively parallel architecture for a self-organizing neural pattern recognition machine." Computer Vision, Graphics, and Image Processing 37: 54-115.

Donnart, J.-Y. and J.-A. Meyer (1995). "Learning reactive and planning rules in a motivationally autonomous animat." IEEE Transactions on Systems, Man and Cybernetics.

Floreano, D. and F. Mondada (1996). "Evolution of Homing Navigation in a Real Mobile Robot." IEEE Transactions on Systems, Man, and Cybernetics--Part B: Cybernetics 26(3): 396-407.

Gaussier, P., A. Revel, et al. (1996). "Living in a partially structured environment: how to bypass the limitations of classical reinforcement techniques." to appear in Robotics and Autonomous Systems.

Gaussier, P. and S. Zrehen (1994). A Topological Neural Map for On-Line Learning: Emergence of Obstacle Avoidance. SAB, From Animals to Animats 94, Brighton, MIT Press.

Gaussier, P. and S. Zrehen (1995). "PerAc: A neural architecture to control artificial animals." Robotics and Autonomous Systems 16(2-4): 291-320.

Harnad, S. (1990). "The symbol grounding problem." Physica D 42: 335-346.

Klopf, A. H., S. Morgan-James, et al. (1993). "A hierarchical network of control systems that learn: Modeling nervous system function during classical and instrumental conditioning." Adaptive Behavior 1(3): 263-319.

Mataric, M. (1990). Navigating with a rat brain: A Neurobiologically-Inspired Model for Robot Spatial Representations. First International Conference on Simulation of Adaptive Behavior, MIT Press.

McFarland, D. and T. Gosser (1983). Intelligent Behavior in Animal and Robots. Cambridge, MIT Press / Bradford Books.

O'Keefe, J. and L. Nadel (1978). Hippocampus as a Cognitive Map. Oxford, Clarendon Press Publishers.

Schmajuk, N. A. and H. T. Blair (1993). "Place learning and the dynamics of spatial navigation: A neural network approach." Adaptive Behavior 1(3): 353-385.

Verschure, P. F. M. J., B. Krose, et al. (1992). "Distributed Adaptive Control: The self-organization of structured behavior. Robotics and Autonomous Agents." Robotics and Autonomous Agents 9: 181-196.

Zrehen, S. (1995). Elements of Brain Design for Autonomous Agents. Computer Science Dept. Lausanne, Swiss Federal Institute of Technology: 190.

Dynamical Interactions between Learning, Visual Attention, and Behavior:
An Experiment with a Vision-Based Mobile Robot

Jun Tani, Jun Yamamoto and Hiro Nishi
Sony Computer Science Laboratory Inc.
Takanawa Muse Building, 3-14-13 Higashi-gotanda,
Shinagawa-ku,Tokyo, 141 JAPAN
email: tani@csl.sony.co.jp

Abstract

We investigate how a vision-based robot can learn an analogical model of the environment dynamically through its behavior. We propose a cognitive architecture consisting of multiple neural network modules. The recurrent neural network (RNN) learns the sequence of events encountered incrementally as episodic memories so that the RNN can make prediction based on such sequences in the future. The visual module has two task processes to execute, namely object recognition and wall-following. Attention between these two tasks is switched by means of the topdown prediction made by the RNN. The effect of the topdown prediction to the vision processes is modulated dynamically using the measurement of learning status of the RNN. We have conducted experiments involving learning both static and dynamic environments using a real vision-based mobile robot. It was shown that the robot adapts to the environment in the course of dynamical interactions between its learning, attention and behavioral functions. We show an interpretation of the results from the view of Matsuno's *the internal observer*.

1 Introduction

We speculate that cognitive robots may need to have internal descriptions or analogical models of the world so that they can simulate mentally their own behavioral sequences. In addressing the issues of the description, it is, however, crucial to consider how such a description can be grounded in the physical world and how the mental processes manipulating the description can be situated in the behavioral context[8].

Recently, the dynamical systems approach has been actively studied in the domain of adaptive behavior [3, 19]. We have hypothesized that its language may

best represent cognitive aspects of robots and may provide insight into the above problems of the description. Our previous work[22, 21, 23] concerning robot navigation learning showed that an analogical model of the environment can be successfully embedded in the internal dynamical structure of a neural network model through the learning process, and that mental processes, such as look-ahead prediction or planning, can be situated naturally in the behavioral context as coherence is achieved between the internal and the environmental dynamics. The dynamical systems approach enables robots to attain descriptions which are intrinsic to their behavior.

Our experiments, however, were still limited in their scope. Firstly, due to the simplicity of the robot itself and of its environment, the complexity of their interactions was quite limited and therefore the robot's behavioral became highly deterministic and predictable. (The mobile robot had only a simple sensing device consisting of a laser range finder and two motors on the left and right wheels.) Secondly, our experiments were successful only in the case of learning of static environments. The actual learning was conducted in an off-line manner. These limitations may obscure the essential problems of robot cognition. We speculate that the very problems of cognitions commence in the moment when a robot attempts to interact with an unknown environment and tries to extract a certain structure of the behavioral causalities hidden in the non-deterministic sequences from its interaction experiences.

This paper introduces our new project in which we investigate the above problems. We built a new robot for which the primary sensory input was visual images by a video camera. The robot has to control camera orientation, both horizontally and vertically, in addition to maneuvering of its wheels. During navigation, the robot moves avoiding collisions with obstacle walls and simultaneously tries to recognize passing objects using the vision. This task is not so simple considering the range of its visual field is physically limited and its recogni-

Figure 1: The vision-based mobile robot used in the experiments.

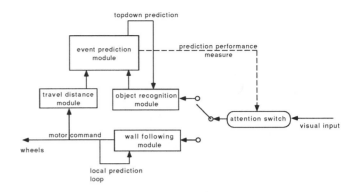

Figure 2: The proposed architecture consisting of multiple modules.

tion process is limited by its real time requirements. The robot has to switch its visual attention dynamically from the wall it is following to the objects it is trying to recognize. The dynamics of its visual attention are observed to affect enormously the ways the robot interacts with its environment.

Our robot attempts to learn incrementally what it experiences and the visual attention dynamics are adapted in real time. A neural network (NN) model consisting of multiple modules learns to categorize the visual images of objects and also learns to predict the sequence of events, such as encountering the objects or the corners of the walls, while the robot moves around the environment. Regarding visual attention, the timing of the attention switching between wall following and object recognition are modulated based on the performance of the NN predictions. Complexity arises when dynamics of the neural learning and the adaptation of the visual attention as well as robot's behavior interact each other. Modulation of the attention dynamics affects the behavior of the robot, which results in further neural learning based on the newly obtained experiences. This learning causes an alteration in the performance of the neural network, which results in further modulations of the attention dynamics.

In the following, we will describe our models and show preliminary results from our experiments.

2   The Robot and Its learning Task

Fig 1. shows our vision-based robot. The robot maneuvers by modulating the rotational speed of its two wheels. The video camera, which is mounted on top of the body, captures color images; the range of its visual field is 60 degrees horizontally and 40 degrees vertically. The camera head can rotate 150 degrees horizontally and 70 de-

grees vertically. 16 touch sensors are mounted around the body. In conjunction with the torque measured by the wheel motors, these touch sensors can detect collisions with obstacles.

The task of the robot is to learn an analogical model of its environment through its travel. When the robot navigates by following a wall in its environment, it will eventually detect an object or a corner in the wall. The robot learns the sequences of what it sees and how far it travels between one corner and the next corner. Once the robot learns the sequence of such events, it becomes able to predict coming events.

The landmark-based navigation approach has been studied by many other researchers [15, 14]. In those investigations, it was proposed that the topological map of the environment can be represented in the form of a finite state machine (FSM). However, only a few investigations studied qualitatively how the robots behave if the detection of landmarks is nondeterministic or how the learning processes evolve if the environment dynamically changes. (Yamauchi and Beer discussed these problems in their formulation using the so-called Adaptive Place Network [26].) We would like to discuss these problems qualitatively by using the dynamical systems approach.

3   Models

3.1   Overview of the model

Fig 2. shows a schematic diagram of our model. The visual image flows into the attention switch module where its flow is switched either to the wall following module or to the object recognition module based on the visual attention dynamics. The wall following module detects the edge of the nearby wall on the left-hand side of the robot and generates the motor commands for the wheels in order for the robot to follow the wall. This module has a local prediction loop so that it can predict how the perceived edge of the nearby wall changes as the robot moves even when the flow of the visual image is interrupted for some seconds due to the attention switch. The motor commands are also sent to the travel distance module for integration with respect to time in order to determine the travel vector from one corner to the next corner. When the object recognition module identifies an object, it sends a categorical signal to the event prediction module. The event prediction module functions when the robot passes a corner. The module receives a travel vector from the previous encountered corner or a categorical identification of an object which the robot found during its travel from the previous corner. The event prediction module then predicts the next event. The prediction of the next object to be encountered is fed back to the object recognition module in the form of the top-down signal. The recognition of an object involves cooperative dynamics between the bottom-up and top-down processes. A measurement of the prediction performance is sent to the attention switch module in order to modulate its dynamics.

3.2 The visual processes

As we have described briefly in the previous section, the robot has to switch its attention between two visual tasks: wall edge following and object recognition. These two tasks are alternated between during the travel.

First, the camera head turns maximally to the left and focuses on the edge between the wall and the floor. The camera head then turns gradually to the forward direction, following the perceived edge line as foveated in the center of the visual field. The measured trajectories of the head's rotation in the horizontal and vertical directions $(\theta_h(i), \theta_v(i))$ represent the shape of the wall edge. This single movement of the camera head from the extreme left to the forward direction takes about 2 seconds. The current motor commands for the wheels wh^t are determined by a pre-determined mapping with respect to $(\theta_h(i), \theta_v(i))^t$. This mapping function is tailored to ensure that the trajectory the robot travels is smooth and avoids collisions with the walls. Since the relative location of the wall gradually changes as the robot moves, it is necessary to predict how the shape of the edge changes as a function of maneuvering. This is necessary because the visual attention can be switched to the other task for a relatively long period. The prediction is done using a simple forward model [12] implemented on a three-layered perceptron-type NN. A trajectory sampled at time t: $(\theta_h(i), \theta_v(i))^t$ is fed into the input of the forward model in addition to the motor commands for the wheels wh^t. The output: $(\theta_h(i), \theta_v(i))^{t+1}$ is the predicted shape at time $t+1$. Although it is mathematically true that the robot can predict a long time ahead through the recursive usage of the forward model, in practice the accuracy of the prediction decays substantially a few seconds into the future. It is important to note that there is a high

risk of collision if the robot travels for more than several seconds relying on this prediction. During the wall following task, corners are detected by means of identifying the shape of the wall edge in addition to the rotation differential between the left and right wheels.

After the camera head turns to the forward direction, it then turns gradually to the right, searching for objects. In our experimental setup, objects are painted with colored patterns; floors and walls are painted grey and white. The search for objects is conducted using the color information. Many researchers [1, 5, 10] in the AI or robotics fields have worked on biologically inspired systems of visual routines and visual searches using color information. We have utilized ideas from their research. In the visual search process, a region consisting of a certain number of color pixels in the visual field "pops-up" [2]. Then, the center of the "pop-up" region is foveated– i.e. the camera head moves so that the region is relocated in the center of the visual field. Van Essen [6] proposed a model of dynamic routing between an attended region in retina and the visual cortical field which is modeled roughly using an associative memory. We used this idea. The attended region of the color image is routed up to the Hopfield [9] type associative memory network where memories of objects are stored as they were learned in the object-centered framework. The Hopfield network consists of 10x10x3 neurons corresponding to the color image of 10x10 pixels. In the routing process, the image of the attended region is scaled so as to match with this pixel size. Three neurons are allocated for each pixel in order to represent its color information. The color of each pixel is categorized into one of three categories in the Hue-Saturation space and only its corresponding neuron is activated. There is an array of winner-take-all neurons which is connected bi-directionariry with the Hopfield network (see Fig 3.). The neurons also receive top-down prediction input from the event prediction module. The strength of this top-down prediction is modulated based on the performance of the prediction module. The recognition proceeds dynamically involving cooperation between these two networks as they receive both the bottom-up visual signals and the top-down prediction signals. The final winner of winner-take-all neurons represents the identified category of the visual image. (The combination of winner-take-all neurons and associative memories has also been studied in the so-called PATON architecture by Omori [18] using a simple numerical analysis.) The dynamics of a neuron in the Hopfield network is given by:

$$u_i(t+1) = \gamma \cdot u_i(t) + k_1 \sum_n w_{i,j}{}^H a_j(t) \quad (1)$$

$$+ k_2 \sum_n w_{i,k}{}^w a_k(t) + k_3 \cdot in_i$$

$$a_i(t+1) = sigmoid(u_i(t+1)/T)$$

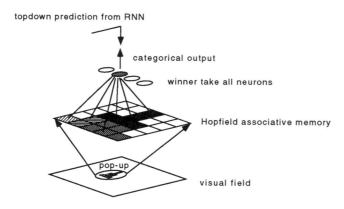

topdown prediction from RNN

categorical output

winner take all neurons

Hopfield associative memory

pop-up

visual field

Figure 3: The object recognition module consisting of the visual field, the Hopfield associative memory and the winner-take-all neurons.

Here, u_i and a_i are the internal state and the activation state of the i-th neuron, respectively, γ is a decay parameter, the $w_{i,j}{}^H$ are the intra-connective weights of the Hopfield network, the $w_{i,j}{}^w$ are the inter-connective weights of the winner-take-all neurons and in_i is the input from the visual field. The dynamics of the winner-take-all neurons are given by:

$$
\begin{aligned}
u_i(t+1) &= \gamma \cdot u_i(t) + h_1 \sum_n w_{i,j}{}^W a_j(t) \qquad (2) \\
&\quad + h_2 \sum_n w_{i,k}{}^h a_k(t) + \eta \cdot pred_i \\
a_i(t+1) &= sigmoid(u_i(t+1)/T)
\end{aligned}
$$

Here, the $w_{i,j}{}^W$ are the intra-connective weights of the winner-take-all neurons, the $w_{i,k}{}^h$ are the interconnective weights from the Hopfield network, $pred_i$ is the input from the top-down prediction and η is a parameter to regulate the strength of this top-down prediction.

The learning takes place after each recognition process (i.e. after the network dynamics are terminated). The intra-connections of the Hopfield network are updated based on Hebb's rule implemented with a constant decay mechanism. The decay is necessary to prevent the weights from diverging in the process of incremental learning. The learning rule is:

$$
\Delta w_{i,j} = -\zeta \cdot w_{i,j} + \epsilon(a_i - 0.5)(a_j - 0.5) \cdot 4.0 \qquad (3)
$$

Here, ζ is a decay parameter. For updating the interconnective weights between the Hopfield network and the winner-take-all neurons, only the winning neuron is set as being activated to 1.0; the others are set as being deactivated to 0.0. Following this process, the same Hebb's learning rule is applied.

3.3 Attention and self-referential processes

The problem with the visual attention arises because the visual process is resource-bounded in both time and space [1]. If our robot spends a longer time in recognizing objects, there is a high risk of collision. On the other hand, if the robot spends a shorter time on the recognition process, the identification results may be in error as the answer is required before the NN dynamics converge. Clearly, a good strategy for determining the timing of the attention switch is required. The time required for convergence depends on the learning status of the NN modules. In the early stages of learning, the attractor of the Hopfield network is shallow and the top-down prediction is inaccurate. Therefore, the Hopfield network dynamics take a long time to converge. In such cases, they likely oscillate because contradictions between the top-down prediction and the bottom-up signals. On the other hand, when the learning converges, the top-down prediction and the bottom-up signals agree quite well, which cause the Hopfield network dynamics to converges rapidly. For this reason, the performance of the prediction module is monitored so that the current learning status can be used to determine when to terminate the iteration of the network dynamics and also to evaluate the validity of the topdown prediction. Here, $steps^{max}$, the maximum steps allowed for iterations of the Hopfield network, is defined by

$$
steps^{max} = l_0 + l_1 \cdot error^{pred} \qquad (4)
$$

where $error^{pred}$ is the current prediction error measure (PEM) of the prediction module (an average of the prediction error among the previous 5 predictions); l_0 and l_1 are constants. In addition to this adaptation strategy, η is defined by

$$
\eta = \eta_0 \cdot (1.0 - error^{pred}) \qquad (5)
$$

where η_0 is a constant. This equation implies that the validity of the top-down prediction increased as the predictability by means of learning is improved.

What we have proposed here is a modeling of self-referential processes in which the robot can be aware of the validity of its own mental processes which is fed back to the attention processes in an unconscious way. These models of the adaptation process of visual attention are also based on the ideas of Koch and Crick [4] in the physiocicical side. They have hypothesized that the neurons in the visual cortical areas whose responses are changed by attentions are the ones that receive inputs from the prefrontal cortex.

3.4 Prediction by recurrent neural net

The event prediction module is implemented with a standard recurrent neural network (RNN) [19, 11] as shown

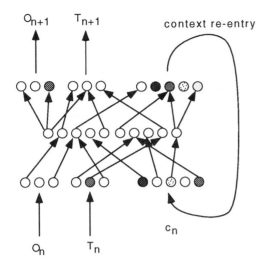

Figure 4: The RNN implemented for the event prediction module.

in Fig 4. The RNN may correspond to the prefrontal cortex, as a number of studies have suggested that the prefrontal cortex performs the function of a working memory or of planning events (see Ref. [7].) The RNN receives input from two different sensory sources. One is a visual image of colored objects; the other is the travel vector from one corner to the next corner. This part of the modeling is based on the well-known fact about "where and what pathways" [24] of visual processing in the human brain. The RNN does not receive direct sensory images of those, but receives categorical signals for them instead. The visual image is categorized by the combination of the Hopfield network and the winner-take-all neurons, as we have described above. The travel vector is categorized using the standard Kohonen network [13] in the travel distance module. The travel vector is entered into the Kohonen network, after which the winner neuron represents the category of the travel vector. The Kohonen net is self-organized in an on-line manner. The output of the RNN is the prediction of the categorical signals for the two sensory sources. In the figure, T_n represents the travel vector category and O_n represents the object category. The RNN process in this figure is one in which the travel vector from the previous corner to the current corner is identified as being in the second category, resulting in a prediction that an object of the third category will be encountered at the next. We employ Jordan's idea of context re-entry which enables the network to represent the internal memory [12]. The current context input c_n (a vector) is a copy of the previous context output: by this means the context units remember the previous internal state. The navigation problem is an example of a so-called "hidden state problem" in

that a given sensory input does not always correspond to a unique situation or position of the robot. Therefore, the current situation or position is identifiable, not by the current sensory input, but by the memory of the sensory sequences stored during travel. Such a memory structure is self-organized through the learning process. The context self-organized in these units is likely to have a rather distributed fuzzy representation. The RNN used in our experiment has 9 input nodes, 9 output nodes, 25 context nodes and 25 hidden units.

3.5 Incremental learning and consolidation process

It is difficult for RNNs to learn the received information incrementally. It is generally observed that the contents of the current memory are severely damaged if the RNN attempts to learn a new teaching sequence. One way to avoid this problem is to save all the past teaching data in a database. When new data is received, it is added to the former date in the database, and all the data is then used to re-train the network. Although this procedure may work well, it is not biologically plausible.

Observations in biology show that some animals and humans may use the hippocampus for a temporary storage of episodic memories [20]. Some theories of memory consolidation postulate that the episodic memories stored in the hippocampus are transferred into some regions of the neocortical systems during sleep. Recent experiments [25] on the hippocampal place cells of rats show evidence that those cells reinstate the information acquired during daytime active behavior. McClelland [17] further assumes that the hippocampus is involved in the reinstatement of the neocortical patterns in long term memory and that the hippocampus plays a teaching role in training the neocortical systems.

We apply these hypotheses to our model of RNN learning. In our system, an experienced sequence of events, which may correspond to a temporary episodic memory, are stored in the hippocampal database. In the consolidation process, the RNN which corresponds to the prefrontal cortex rehearses the stored memory patterns. The rehearsal can be done by recursively activating the RNN using the closed feedback loop from the outputs of the sensory prediction to the sensory inputs. The generated sequential patterns are sent to the hippocampal database. The RNN can be trained using both the rehearsed sequential patterns and the newly experienced ones. In our experiment, the robot stores up to 14 steps of previously encountered events in the hippocampal database. In the consolidation process, the RNN rehearses for 14 iterations to generate a sequence, then 28 steps of the sequential patterns in total are used to re-train the RNN. The re-training of the RNN is conducted by updating the connective weights obtained in the previous training.

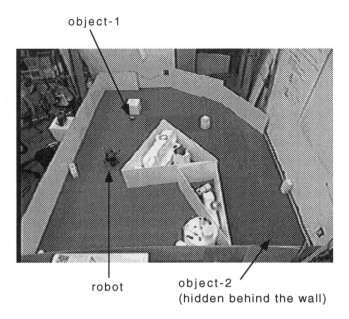

object-1

robot

object-2
(hidden behind the wall)

Figure 5: Workspace adopted for the robot learning experiments.

object-1   object-2

Figure 6: The two objects placed in the workspace which are painted with different color patterns.

4 Experiments

The learning experiments were conducted in the workspace shown in Fig 5., in which two different shapes of objects were located (see Fig 6).

The experiments were conducted in two successive phases; these were learning in the original environment followed by learning in a modified environment.

4.1 Adaptation to the original environment

We will now describe the results for the case of learning in the original environment. Fig 7. shows the observed history of the prediction error measurement (PEM) at each event step in the learning phase. The learning of the RNN is initiated after the RNN experienced 14 steps of the event sequence. During the first period of learning, the PEM gradually decreases. The PEM almost

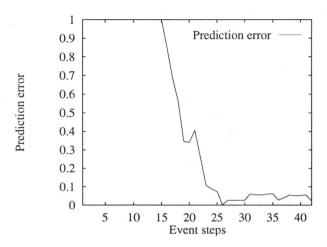

Figure 7: The history of the prediction error as measured for learning in the original environment.

converges in the second period of learning which starts at the 28th step.

Fig 8 shows the prediction sequence, its actual outcome and the associated activation pattern of context units for each step. The steps proceed upwardly in this figure. The number shown to left denotes the event step; the two adjacent rows show the prediction of the sensory category, where the upper row represents the five categories of the visual image and the lower row the four categories of the travel vector. Black squares represent activated categories and their strength is indicated by their size. The next two rows to the right indicate the actual sensory categorical inputs. The upper and the lower rows represent the visual image and the travel vector, respectively. The large square to the right shows the activation pattern of the 25 context units. Fig 8 (a) shows the sequence obtained during the first period of the learning and Fig 8. (b) corresponds to the second period of learning. Fig 8. shows that the prediction fails frequently in the earliest stage, from the 15th to the 21st step. Prediction is, however, improved during the second period of learning, as is also seen also in the history of PEM in Fig 7. We observe a stable periodicity of six steps in the sequence of Fig 8 (b), but, we do not observe such a periodicity in the earlier stage of Fig 8 (a). We examined the dynamical structure of the RNN obtained at the end of the learning process. The RNN was activated recursively by closing the open loop from the sensory prediction to the sensory inputs. We are confident that we have identified an attractor of the limit cycling with the periodicity six in the phase space of the RNN.

We will now illustrate how the visual attention dynamics interact with the behavior of the robot. In Fig 9, we compare two trajectories of robot's travel, one from the

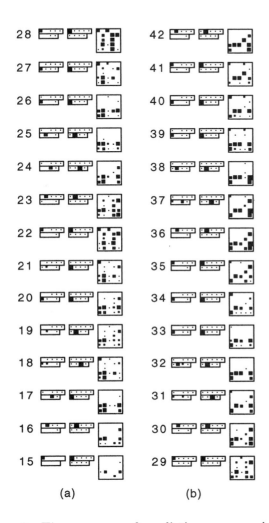

(a)   (b)

Figure 8: The sequence of prediction, sensory inputs, and context activation pattern of the RNN in the first period of the learning (a) and that of the second period (b).

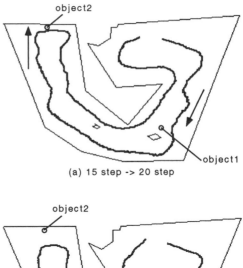

(a) 15 step -> 20 step

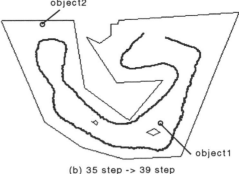

(b) 35 step -> 39 step

Figure 9: Comparison of the robot trajectories corresponding to two different learning statuses. (a) from the first period of learning shows a more winding trajectory than (b) in the second period.

15th to the 20th step in the first period of learning and the other from 35th to 39th step in the second period of learning; these are shown in Fig 9 (a) and (b) respectively. It is seen that the trajectory winds more in (a) than in (b) especially in the way objects are approached. We infer that the maneuvering of the robot became more unstable because the robot spent a greater time on the visual recognition of objects in the first period of learning due to the higher value of the PEM. Therefore, the robot took a higher risk of the mis-detection of events as its trajectory oscillate. In Fig 9 (a) we note that the robot mis-detected a corner immediately after its recognition of object 2 causing it to take for a while until its prediction to recover. Such a nondeterministic phenomenon in the detection of events affects the RNN's learning. In Fig 8., it is frequently seen that the RNN attempts to predict two categories at the same time. The previous experience of a nondeterministic phenomenon in the sequence of experiences caused the generation of such expressions by the RNN.

When the robot happened to predict the correct sequence for some steps, the PEM as well as the time required for the visual recognition were observed to de-

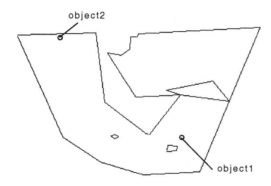

Figure 10: The modified workspace.

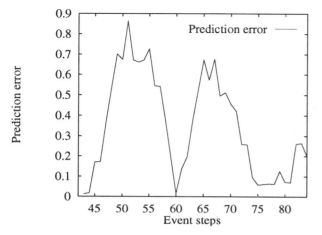

Figure 11: The history of the PEM obtained during learning in the modified environment.

crease. Thereafter a stable regime emerged in which a quasi-coherence was achieved between the dynamics of learning, attention, and behavior. However we speculate that this regime is only marginally stable, as we have observed that the regime could be disrupted by certain catastrophic changes even after a long period of stability. We need to conduct further experiments to investigate more carefully the stability criteria.

4.2 Re-adaptation to a modified environment

After performing the previous experiment, we modified the workspace partially and restarted the robot. The conditions such as the NN weights and the attention parameters were retained from the previous experiment. The geometry of the modified workspace is shown in Fig 10. Fig 11. shows the associated history of the PEM. We observed that the PEM increased when the robot traveled towards the modified region, but the PEM decreased when the robot traveled otherwise in the un-

modified region. This PEM increase decayed as the incremental learning was proceeded. We infer that the former memories were preserved to some extent, but their part in contradiction with the modified environment was gradually altered as a result of the new experiences. However, we need to wait for further experiments to be performed before we can confirm that the observed characteristics are more general.

5 Discussion

We observed dynamical interactions taking place between learning, attention, and behavior, which might be one of crucial points needing to be considered when building cognitive robots. It is important to note that when a robot observes the world, such observations inevitably lead to actions of the robot which change the original relation between the robot and the world. This effect was well illustrated in our experiments, which showed that visual attention affects the maneuvering trajectory. According to Matsuno, the observer is included in the internal loop of actions: the observer is an *internal observer* [16]. The internal observer never maintains descriptions as completely static properties, but instead iteratively generates new descriptions, as the interactions proceed between the observer and the environment.

Someone may ask if there exist any phisical entities which correspond to *the internal observer* in animals or animats. Fact is that all there exist are only dynamical structure in which no separable entities of descriptions and observers are seen.

References

[1] P.E. Agre and D. Chapman. Pengi: an implementation of theory of activity. In *Proc. of the Sixth National Conf. of Aritificial Intelligence*, pp. 268–272, 1987.

[2] A.M.Treisman and G.Gelade. A feature integration theory of attention. *Cognitive Psychology*, Vol. 12, pp. 97–136, 1980.

[3] R.D. Beer. A dynamical systems perspective on agent-environment interaction. *Artificial Intelligence*, Vol. 72, No. 1, pp. 173–215, 1995.

[4] F. Crick and C. Koch. The problem of consciousness. *Scientific American*, Vol. 267, pp. 152–158, 1992.

[5] D.H.Ballard. Animate vision. *Artificial Intelligence*, Vol. 48, pp. 57–86, 1991.

[6] D.C. Van Essen, C.H. Anderson, and B.A. Olshausen. *Dynamic routing strategies in sensory motor, and cognitive processing*. Cambridge, MA: MIT press, 1994.

[7] S.E. Gathercole. Neuropsychology and working memory: a review. *Neuropsychology*, Vol. 8, pp. 494–505, 1994.

[8] S. Harnad. The symbol grounding problem. *Physica D*, Vol. 42, pp. 335–346, 1990.

[9] J.J. Hopfield and D.W. Tank. Neural computation of decision in optimization problems. *Biological Cybernetics*, Vol. 52, pp. 141–152, 1985.

[10] I. Horswill. Visual routines and visual search: a real time implementation and an automata-theoretic analysis. In *Proc. of the Int. Joint National Conf. of Aritificial Intelligence, (IJCAI'95)*, pp. 56–61, 1995.

[11] M.I. Jordan. Attractor dynamics and parallelism in a connectionist sequential machine. In *Proc. of Eighth Annual Conference of Cognitive Science Society*, pp. 531–546. Hillsdale, NJ: Erlbaum, 1986.

[12] M.I. Jordan and D.E. Rumelhart. Forward models: supervised learning with a distal teacher. *Cognitive Science*, Vol. 16, pp. 307–354, 1992.

[13] T. Kohonen. Self-organized formation of topographically correct feature maps. *Biological Cybernetics*, Vol. 43, pp. 59–69, 1982.

[14] B. Kuipers. A qualitative approach to robot exploration and map learning. In *AAAI Workshop Spatial Reasoning and Multi-Sensor Fusion (Chicago)*, pp. 774–779, 1987.

[15] M. Mataric. Integration of representation into goal-driven behavior-based robot. *IEEE Trans. Robotics and Automation*, Vol. 8, No. 3, pp. 304–312, 1992.

[16] K. Matsuno. *Physical Basis of Biology*. CRC Press, Boca Raton, FL., 1989.

[17] J.L. McClelland, B.L. McNaughton, and R. O'Reilly. Why there are complementary learning systems in the Hippocampus and Neocortex. Technical Report PDO.CNS.94.1, Carnegie Mellon University, 1994.

[18] T. Omori and A. Mochizuki. PATON: A Model of Context Dependent Memory Access with an Attention Mechanism. In *Proc. of Int. Conf. on Brain Ppocesses Theories and Models*, 1995.

[19] J.B. Pollack. The induction of dynamical recognizers. *Machine Learning*, Vol. 7, pp. 227–252, 1991.

[20] L.R. Squire, N.J. Cohen, and L. Nadel. The medial temporal region and memory consolidation: A new hypothesis. In H. Weingartner and E. Parker, editors, *Memory consolidation*, pp. 185–210. Erlbaum, Hillsdale, N.J., 1984.

[21] J. Tani. Essential Dynamical Structure in a Learnable Autonomous Robot. In *Proc. of the Third European Conf. of Artificial Life (ECAL'95)*, 1995.

[22] J. Tani. Model-Based Learning for Mobile Robot Navigation from the Dynamical Systems Perspective. *IEEE Trans. System, Man and Cybernetics Part B, Special issue on learning autonomous robots*, Vol. 26, No. 3, pp. 421–436, 1996.

[23] J. Tani and N. Fukumura. Self-organizing internal representation in learning of navigation: a physical experiment by the mobile robot YAMABICO. *Neural Networks*, Vol. 10, No. 1,, 1997.

[24] L.G. Ungerleider and M. Mishkin. Two cortical visual systems. In D.G. Ingle, M.A. Goodale, and R.J. Mansfield, editors, *Analysis of Visual Behavior*. Cambridge, MA: MIT Press, 1982.

[25] M. Wilson. Reactivation of hippocampal ensemble memories during sleep. *Science*, Vol. 265, pp. 676–679, 1994.

[26] B. M. Yamauchi and R. D. Beer. Spatial learning for navigation in dynamic environment. *IEEE Trans. Syst. Man Cybern.*, Vol. 26, No. 3,, 1996.

Emergent Construction of Immune Networks for Autonomous Mobile Robots Through the Metadynamics Function

A. Ishiguro   Y. Shirai   Y. Watanabe   Y. Uchikawa

Dept. of Computational Science and Engineering, Graduate School of Eng., Nagoya University

Furo-cho, Chikusa-ku, Nagoya 464–01, JAPAN

E–mail address: ishiguro@bioele.nuee.nagoya-u.ac.jp

Abstract

In the behavior–based artificial intelligence(AI) approach, there are the following problems that have to be resolved: how do we construct an appropriate arbitration mechanism, and how do we prepare appropriate competence modules. We have been investigating a new behavior arbitration mechanism based on the biological immune system. In this paper, we apply our proposed method to behavior arbitration for an autonomous mobile robot, particularly garbage collecting problem that takes into account of the concept of self–sufficiency. To confirm the feasibility, we carry out some simulations and experiments using a real robot. In addition, we investigate two types of adaptation mechanisms to construct an appropriate artificial immune network without human intervention.

1   Introduction

In recent years much attention has been focused on *behavior–based AI*, which has already demonstrated its robustness and flexibility against dynamically changing world. In this approach, intelligence is expected to result from both mutual interactions among competence modules (i.e. simple behaviors/actions) and interaction between the robot and environment. However, there are still open questions: 1) how do we construct a mechanism that realizes appropriate arbitration among multiple competence modules, and 2) how do we prepare appropriate competence modules.

Brooks has showed a solution to the former problem with the use of the *subsumption architecture*[1][2]. Although this method demonstrates highly robustness, it should be noted that this architecture arbitrates the prepared competence modules on a *fixed priority* basis. It would be quite natural to vary the priorities of the prepared competence modules according to the situation.

Maes proposed an another flexible mechanism called the *behavior network system*[3][4]. In this method, agents (i.e. competence modules) form a network using their cause–effect relationship, and an agent suitable for the current situation and the given goals emerges as the result of activation propagation among agents. This method, however, is difficult to apply to a problem where it is hard to find the cause–effect relationship among agents.

One of the promising approaches to tackle the above mentioned problems is a biologically–inspired approach. Among biological systems, we particularly focus on the *immune system*, since it has various interesting features such as *immunological memory, immunological tolerance, pattern recognition*, and so on viewed from the engineering standpoint.

Recent studies on immunology have clarified that the immune system does not just detect and eliminate the non–self materials called *antigen* such as virus, cancer cells and so on, rather plays important roles to maintain its own system against dynamically changing environments through the interaction among *lymphocytes and/or antibodies*. Therefore, the immune system would be expected to provide a new methodology suitable for dynamic problems dealing with unknown/hostile environments rather than static problems.

Based on the above facts, we have been trying to engineer methods inspired by the biological immune system and the application to robotics[5][6][7]. We expect that there would be an interesting AI technique suitable for dynamically changing environments by imitating the immune system in living organisms.

In this paper, we propose a new decentralized consensus–making system inspired by the biological immune system. We then apply our proposed method to behavior arbitration for an autonomous mobile robot, particularly to the *garbage collecting problem* that takes into account of the concept of *self–sufficiency*. In order to verify our method, we perform some simulations and experiments. In addition, we try to incorporate adaptation mechanisms into the proposed artificial immune network based on *adjustment* and *innovation* mechanisms to autonomously construct appropriate immune networks.

2 Biological immune system

2.1 Overview

The basic components of the biological immune system are *macrophages*, *antibodies* and *lymphocytes* that are mainly classified into two types, that is *B–lymphocytes* and *T–lymphocytes*.

B–lymphocytes are the cells stemming from the *bone marrow*. Roughly 10^7 distinct types of B–lymphocytes are contained in a human body, each of which has distinct molecular structure and produces "Y" shaped antibodies from its surfaces. The antibody recognizes specific antigens, which are the foreign substances that invade living creature, such as virus, cancer cells and so on. This reaction is often likened to a *key and keyhole relationship* (see Figure 1). To cope with continuously changing environment, living systems possess enormous repertoire of antibodies in advance.

On the other hand, T–lymphocytes are the cells maturing in thymus, and they generally perform to kill infected cells and regulate the production of antibodies from B–lymphocytes as outside circuits of B–lymphocyte network (idiotypic network) discussed later.

For the sake of convenience in the following explanation, we introduce several terminology from immunology. The key portion on the antigen recognized by the antibody is called an *epitope* (antigen determinant), and the keyhole portion on the corresponding antibody that recognizes the antigen determinant is called a *paratope*. Recent studies in immunology have clarified that each type of antibody also has its specific antigen determinant called an *idiotope* (see Figure 1).

2.2 Jerne's idiotypic network hypothesis

Based on this fact, Jerne proposed a remarkable hypothesis which he has called the *idiotypic network hypothesis* sometimes called the *immune network hypothesis*[8][9][10][11][12]. This network hypothesis is the concept that antibodies/lymphocytes are not just isolated, namely they are communicating to each other among different species of antibodies/lymphocytes. This idea of Jerne's is schematically shown in Figure 1.

The idiotope **Id1** of antibody 1 (**Ab1**) stimulates the B–lymphocyte 2, which attaches the antibody 2 (**Ab2**) to its surface, through the paratope **P2**. Viewed from the standpoint of **Ab2**, the idiotope **Id1** of **Ab1** works simultaneously as an antigen. As a result, the B–lymphocytes 1 with **Ab1** are suppressed by **Ab2**.

On the other hand, antibody 3 (**Ab3**) stimulates **Ab1** since the idiotope **Id3** of **Ab3** works as an antigen in view of **Ab1**. In this way, the stimulation and suppression chains among antibodies form a large–scaled network and works as a self and not–self recognizer. Therefore, the immune system is expected to provide a new

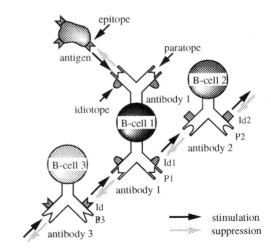

Figure 1: Jerne's idiotypic network hypothesis.

parallel distributed processing mechanism.

2.3 Metadynamics

In the biological immune system, the structure of the network is not fixed, rather variable continuously. It flexibly self–organizes according to dynamic changes of environment. This remarkable function, called the *metadynamics function*[13][14][15], is mainly realized by incorporating newly–generated cells/antibodies and/or removing useless ones. Figure 2 schematically illustrates the metadynamics function.

The new cells are generated by both gene recombination in bone marrow and mutation in the proliferation process of activated cells (the mutant is called *quasi-species*). Although many cells are newly generated every day, most of them have no effect on the existing network and soon die away without any stimulation. Due to such enormous loss, the metadynamics function works to maintain appropriate repertoire of cells so that the system could cope with environmental changes. The metadynamics function would be expected to provide feasible ideas to engineering field as an emergent mechanism.

Furthermore, new types of T–cell, which are also generated by gene recombination, undergo the selection in the thymus before they are incorporated into the body. In the selection mechanism, over 95% of them would be eliminated (*apoptosis*). The eliminated T–cells would strongly respond to self or not respond to self at all. In other word, the selection mechanism accelerate the system to incorporate new types effectively.

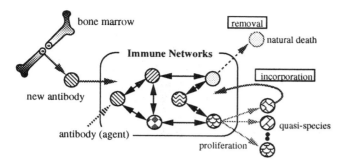

Figure 2: Metadynamics function.

3 Proposed consensus-making network based on the biological immune system

3.1 Action selection problem and the immune network

As described earlier, in the behavior–based AI, how to construct a mechanism that realizes appropriate arbitration among the prepared competence modules must be solved. We approach to this problem from the immunological standpoint, more concretely with use of immune network architecture. Figure 3 schematically shows the action selection system for an autonomous mobile robot and the immune network architecture.

As shown in this figure, current situations, (e.g. distance and direction to the obstacle, etc.) detected by installed sensors, work as multiple antigens, and a prepared competence module (i.e. simple behavior) is regarded as an antibody (or B–lymphocyte), while the interaction between modules is replaced by stimulation and suppression between antibodies. The basic concept of our method is that the immune system equipped with the autonomous mobile robot selects a competence module (antibody) suitable for the detected current situation (antigens) in a bottom-up manner.

3.2 The problem

For the ease of the following explanation, we firstly describe the problem used to confirm the ability of an autonomous mobile robot with our proposed immune network–based action selection mechanism (for convenience, we dub the robot *immunoid*). To make immunoid really autonomous, as Pfeifer et al. advocated, it must not only accomplish the given task, but also be self–sufficient[17][16].

Inspired by their works, we adopt the following garbage collecting problem that takes into account of the concept of self–sufficiency. Figure 4 shows the environment. As can be seen in the figure, this environment, surrounded by walls, has a lot of garbage to be collected. And there exist garbage cans and a battery charger in

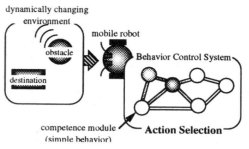

(a) An autonomous mobile robot with an action selection mechanism.

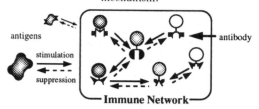

(b) Immune network architecture.

Figure 3: Basic concept of our proposed method.

the home base. The task of immunoid is to collect the garbage into the garbage can without running out of its internal energy (i.e. battery level). Note that immunoid consumes some energy as it moves around the environment. This is similar to the *metabolism* in the biological system.

In this study, we assume that prespecified quantity of initial energy is given to immunoid, and the current energy level can be detected by the simulated internal sensor installed in immunoid. For quantitative evaluation, we also use the following assumptions:

1. Immunoid consumes energy E_m with every step.

2. Immunoid loses additional energy E'_m when it carries garbage.

3. If immunoid collides with garbage or a wall, it loses some energy E_c.

4. If immunoid reaches the home base, it gains full energy.

5. If the energy level of immunoid is high, `go to home base` behavior might not emerge to avoid overcharging.

Based on the above assumptions, we calculate current energy level as:

$$E(t) = E(t - 1) - E_m - E'_m - E_c \quad , \qquad (1)$$

where $E(t)$ denotes the energy level at time t.

For ease of understanding, we explain why this problem is suitable for the behavior arbitration problem in detail using the following situations. Assume that immunoid is in the far distance from the home base, and its energy level is low. In this situation, if immunoid carries the garbage, it will run out of its energy due to the term E'_m in equation (1). Therefore, immunoid should select the `go to home base` behavior to fulfill its energy. In other word, the priority of the `go to home base` behavior should be higher than that of the `garbage collecting` behavior.

On the other hand, if immunoid is in the near distance from the home base. In this situation, unlike the above situation, it would be preferable to select the `garbage collecting` behavior. From these examples, it is understood that immunoid should select an appropriate competence module by flexibly varying the priorities of the prepared competence modules according to the internal/external situations.

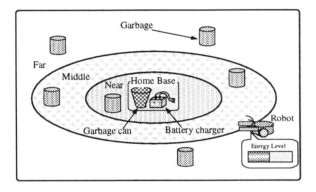

Figure 4: Environment.

3.3 Definition of the antigens and antibodies

As described earlier, the detected current internal/external situation and the prepared simple behavior work as an antigen and an antibody, respectively. In this study, each antigen informs the existence of garbage (direction), obstacle (direction) and home base (direction and distance), and also current internal energy level. For simplicity, we categorize direction and distance of the detected objects and the detected internal energy level as:

- · direction → front, right, left, back
- · distance → far, middle, near
- · energy level → high, low.

Next, we explain how we describe an antibody in detail. To make immunoid select a suitable antibody against the current antigen, we must look carefully into the definition of the antibodies. Moreover, we should notice that our immunological arbitration mechanism selects an antibody in a bottom-up manner through interacting among antibodies.

To realize the above requirements, we defined the description of antibodies as follows. As mentioned in the previous section, the identity of each antibody is generally determined by the structure (e.g. molecular shape) of its paratope and idiotope. Figure 5 depicts our proposed definition of antibodies. As depicted in the figure, we assign a pair of precondition and action to the paratope, and the ID-number of the stimulating antibody and the degree of stimuli to the idiotope, respectively. The structure of the precondition is the same as the antigen described above.

We prepare the following actions for immunoid: `move forward`, `turn right`, `turn left`, `turn backward`, `explore`, `catch garbage` and `search for home base`.

In addition, for the appropriate selection of antibodies, we assign one state variable called *concentration* to each antibody.

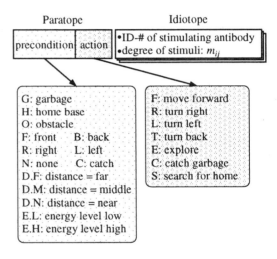

Figure 5: Description of the antibodies.

3.4 Interaction between antibodies

Next, we explain the interaction among antibodies, that is, the basic principle of our immunological consensus-making networks in detail. For the ease of understanding, we assume that immunoid is placed in the situation shown in Figure 6 as an example. In this situation, three antigens listed in the figure possibly invade immunoids interior.

Suppose that the listed four antibodies are prepared in advance that respond to these antigens. For example, **antibody 1** means that if immunoid detects the home base in the right direction, this antibody can be activated and would cause `turn right` action. However, if the current energy level is high, this antibody would give way to other antibodies represented by its idiotope (in this case, **antibody 4**) to prevent over-charging.

Now assume that immunoid has enough energy, in this case **antibodies 1, 2** and **4** are stimulated by the antigens. As a result, the concentration of these antibodies increases. However, due to the interactions indicated by the arrows among the antibodies through their paratopes and idiotopes, the concentration of each antibody varies. Finally, **antibody 2** will have the highest concentration, and then is allowed to be selected. This means that immunoid catches the garbage. In the case where immunoid has not enough energy, **antibody 1** tends to be selected in the same way. This means that immunoid ignores the garbage and tries to recharge its energy. As observed in this example, the interactions among the antibodies work as a priority adjustment mechanism.

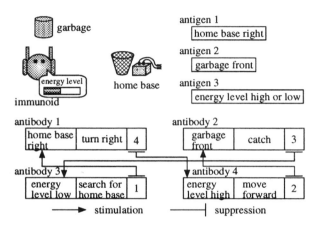

Figure 6: An example of consensus-making network by interacting among antibodies.

3.5 Dynamics

The concentration of i-th antibody, which is denoted by a_i, is calculated as follows:

$$\frac{dA_i(t)}{dt} = \left\{ \sum_{j=1}^{N} m_{ji} a_j(t) - \sum_{k=1}^{N} m_{ik} a_k(t) + m_i - k_i \right\} a_i(t) \quad (2)$$

$$a_i(t+1) = \frac{1}{1 + \exp(0.5 - A_i(t))} \quad , \quad (3)$$

where, in equation (2), N is the number of antibodies. m_{ji} and m_i denote affinities between antibody j and antibody i (i.e. the degree of disallowance), and antibody i and the detected antigen, respectively. The first and second terms of the right hand side denote the stimulation and suppression from other antibodies, respectively. The third term represents the stimulation from the antigen,

and the forth term the dissipation factor (i.e. natural death). Equation (3) is a squashing function used to ensure the stability of the concentration. In this study, selection of antibodies is simply carried out on a *roulette-wheel manner* basis according to the magnitude of concentrations of the antibodies. Note that only one antibody is allowed to activate and act its corresponding behavior to the world.

3.6 Experimental results

To verify the feasibility of our proposed method, we carried out some simulations and experiments. In the experiments, we used the *Khepera* robot, which is widely-used for experiments, as immunoid. The robot has a gripper to catch the garbage and it is equipped with 8 infrared proximity sensors, 8 photo sensors, and one color CCD camera. Each infrared sensor detects garbage or a wall of its corresponding direction. The photo sensors recognize the direction of the electric-light bulb(i.e. the home base). The CCD camera detects the color (red(far), green(middle), blue(near)) at the current position and this in turn tells immunoid the current distance to the home base.

As a rudimentary stage of investigation, we prepared 22 antibodies of which the paratope and the idiotope are described a priori (Figure 7). In the figure, note that the degrees of stimuli in each idiotope are omitted for lack of space. At the beginning, we equipped

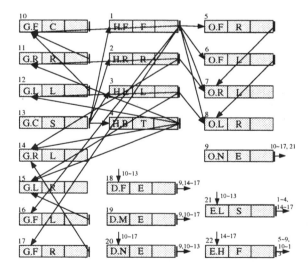

Figure 7: Prepared immune network.

immunoid with the maximum energy level (i.e. 1000). Typical results obtained in the experiments are as follows: while the energy level is enough, immunoid tries to collect garbage into the home base. As the remaining energy runs out, immunoid tends to select an antibodies concerned with go to home base and/or search for home base behaviors. After successful reaching the home base, immunoid starts to explore again. Such a regular behavior could be frequently observed in the experiments.

In order to evaluate the ability of our proposed arbitration mechanism, we furthermore carried out simple experiments by varying the initial energy level. Figure 8(a) and (b) are the resultant trajectories of immunoid in the case where the initial energy level is set to 1000 (maximum) and 300, respectively. In case 1, due to the enough energy level, immunoid collects the garbage B and successfully reach the home base. On the other hand, in case 2, due to the critical energy level immunoid ignores the garbage B and then collects the garbage A. From these figures, it is understood that immunoid selects an appropriate antibodies according to both the internal and external situations by flexibly changing the priorities among the antibodies.

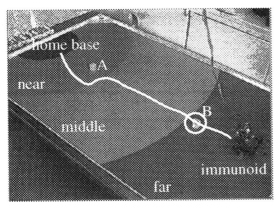

(a) Case 1 (initial energy level = 1000).

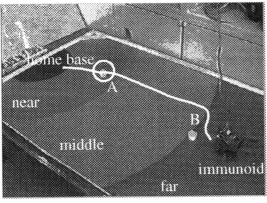

(b) Case 2 (initial energy level = 300).

Figure 8: Resultant trajectories.

4 Adaptation mechanisms

For more usefulness, as some researchers have been pointed out, the introduction of some adaptation mechanisms is highly indispensable. The adaptation mechanism is usually classified into two types: *adjustment* and *innovation*[18][19].

The adjustment can be considered as the adaptation by changing parameters in systems, e.g. modification of synaptic weights in neural networks, while the innovation as the adaptation by selection mechanisms.

In the above experiments, we should notice that we have to appropriately describe the possible antibodies in advance. To overcome such difficulties, we introduce some adaptation mechanisms. In the followings, we propose two types of adaptation mechanisms based on the adjustment and the innovation mechanisms.

4.1 Adjustment mechanism

For an appropriate consensus–making, it is necessary to appropriately determine the ID–number of the stimulating antibody and its degree of stimuli m_{ij}, i.e. priorities among antibodies. To realize this aim, we propose the on–line adjustment mechanism that initially starts from the situation where the idiotopes of the prepared antibodies are undefined, and then obtains the idiotopes using reinforcement signals.

For the following explanation, we assume that antigen 1 and 2 invade immunoids interior (see Figure 9). In this example, antibody 1 (**Ab1**) and 2 (**Ab2**) are simultaneously stimulated by each antigen. Consequently, the concentration of each antibody increases. However, since the priority between **Ab1** and **Ab2** is unknown (because idiotopes are initially undefined, there are no stimulation/suppression chain), in this case either of them can be selected randomly.

Now, assuming that immunoid randomly selects **Ab2** and then receives a positive reinforcement signals as a reward. To make immunoid tend to select **Ab2** under the same or similar antigens(situation), we record the ID–number of **Ab2** (i.e. 2) in the idiotope of **Ab1** and increase a degree of stimuli m_{12}. In this study, we simply modify the degree of stimuli as:

$$m_{12} = \frac{T_p^{Ab_1} + T_r^{Ab_2}}{T_{Ab_2}^{Ab_1}} \quad (4)$$

$$m_{21} = \frac{T_r^{Ab_1} + T_p^{Ab_2}}{T_{Ab_2}^{Ab_1}} \quad , \quad (5)$$

where $T_p^{Ab_1}$ and $T_r^{Ab_1}$ represents the number of times of receiving penalty and reward signal when **Ab1** is selected. $T_{Ab_2}^{Ab_1}$ denotes the number of times when both **Ab1** and **Ab2** are activated by their specific antigens.

We should notice that this procedure works to raise the relative priority of **Ab2** over **Ab1**. In the case where immunoid receives a penalty signal, we record the ID–number of **Ab1** (i.e. 1) in the idiotope of **Ab2** and modify m_{21} in the same way. This works to decrease the relative priority of **Ab2** over **Ab1**. To confirm the valid-

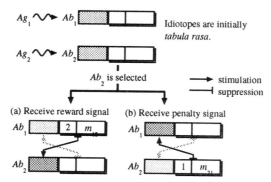

Figure 9: Proposed adjustment mechanism.

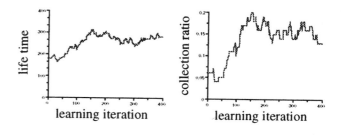

Figure 10: Transition of life time and collection ratio.

ity of this adjustment mechanism, we carried out some simulations. In the simulations, the following reward and penalty signals are used:

Reward

- Immunoid recharges with low energy level.

- Immunoid catches garbage with high energy level.

Penalty

- Immunoid catches garbage with low energy level.

- Immunoid collides with garbage or a wall.

Figure 10 denotes the transitions of the resultant life time and collection ratio. From these results, it is understood that both are improved gradually as iterated.

Figure 11 illustrates an example of the obtained immune networks through our proposed learning process. Note that in this figure only the connections with high affinities are shown. From this figure, this network makes immunoid to search for the charging station when the current energy level is low. And it is also comprehended from this network that if the energy level is high, immunoid tends to select an garbage collecting behavior. Moreover if the distance to the charging station is far, then immunoid tends to search charging station, however if the distance is near, it tends to collect garbage. We are currently implementing this mechanism into the real experimental system.

4.2 Innovation mechanism

In the above adjustment mechanism, we should notice that we must still describe the paratope of each antibody in a top–down manner. One obvious candidate to avoid such difficulties is to incorporate an innovation mechanism. As described in subsection 2.3, in the biological immune system, the metadynamics function can be instantiated as an innovation mechanism. Therefore, we propose the following innovation mechanism inspired by the biological immune system.

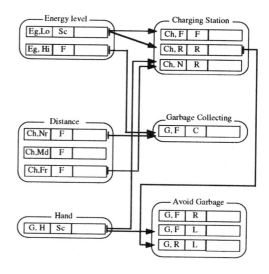

Figure 11: An example of the obtained immune network.

Figure 12 schematically depicts the proposed innovation mechanism. Initially, the immune network consists of N antibodies, each of them is generated by gene recombination and given one state variable named concentration of B–cell. In order to relate this variable to the action selection process, we modify the equation (2) as follows:

$$\frac{dA_i}{dt} = \left\{ \sum_{j=1}^{N} m_{ji}a_j - \sum_{k=1}^{N} m_{ik}a_k + m_i - k_i \right\} a_i b_i(T) \quad , \qquad (6)$$

where $b_i(T)$ is the concentration of B–cell i in the T-th time step. If an antibody receives a reinforcement signal as a result of its action, the corresponding concentration of B–cell is varied as:

$$b_i(T+1) = b_i(T) + r_i \Delta b - K \quad , \qquad (7)$$

where $r_i = 1$ if the antibody i is selected and receives a reward signal, $r_i = -1$ if the antibody i receives a penalty signal, and $r_i = 0$ if the antibody i is not selected. K is the dissipation factor of the B–cell. If $b_i(T)$ becomes below 0, the corresponding antibody is removed, then a new antibody is incorporated through the selection mechanism.

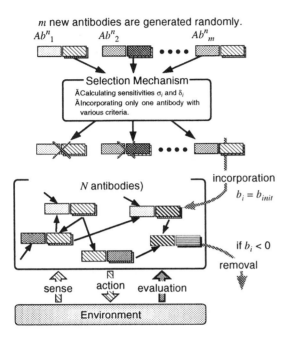

Figure 12: Proposed innovation mechanism.

Next, we explain the selection mechanism inspired by the biological immune system in more detail. First, we randomly generate m candidates for antibodies by gene recombination process. Then we calculate their sensitivities σ_i and δ_i between each new antibody and the existing immune network. σ_i and δ_i are obtained as:

$$\sigma_i = \sum_{j=1}^{N} m_{ji} a_j \qquad (8)$$

$$\delta_i = \sum_{j=1}^{N} m_{ij} a_j \qquad (9)$$

As described earlier, each antibody has the interactions, i.e. stimulation and suppression. Sensitivity σ_i represents the sum of stimulation from the existing network, while sensitivity δ_i is the sum of suppression. Finally, only one antibody is allowed to be incorporated based on the predetermined criterion. To accelerate performance improvement, this criterion in the selection mechanism is highly important. In this study, we used $max\sigma_i$ and $max|\sigma_i - \delta_i|$ as criteria.

To confirm the ability of the proposed innovation mechanism, we applied to a simple example, i.e. obstacle avoiding problem. The simulated environment contains immunoid, multiple obstacles and one charging station. The aim of immunoid is to reach the charging station regularly in order to fulfill its energy level while at the same time avoiding collisions. In the simulations, the following reward and penalty signals are used:

Reward

- Immunoid approaches near the charging station with low energy level.

- Immunoid moves forward without collisions.

Penalty

- Immunoid collides with an obstacle or a wall.

- Immunoid does not move forward when there is no obstacle around it.

Additionally, we assume that the number of antibody N is set to 50, and the number of new antibody m to 20. Figure 13 denotes the transitions of the resultant life time, the number of move–forward actions and the number of collisions in three cases. In case (a), the selection mechanism is not used, namely one randomly generated antibody is incorporated, while in case (b) and (c), the selection mechanism is used with the criterion $max\sigma_i$ and $max|\sigma_i - \delta_i|$, respectively. From these results, the selection mechanisms (particularly the criterion $max\sigma_i$) improve the adaptation performance more rapidly than that without the selection mechanism. We are currently analyzing these results in detail.

5 Conclusions and Further work

In this paper, we proposed a new decentralized consensus-making mechanism based on the biological immune system and confirmed the validity of our proposed system by applying to an behavior arbitration for an autonomous mobile robot. And we proposed two types of adaptation mechanism for an appropriate arbitration using reinforcement signals. For more usefulness, we must clarify how to combine the proposed adjustment and innovation mechanisms. This is currently under investigation.

Acknowledgments

This research was supported in part by Grant–in–Aid for Science Research on Priority Areas from the Japanese Ministry of Education, Science, Sports and Culture (No. 08233208), and Mechatronics Technology Promotion Foundation.

References

[1] R.Brooks, "A Robust Layered Control System for a Mobile Robot", *IEEE Journal of R&A*, Vol.2, No.1, pp.14–23 (1986)

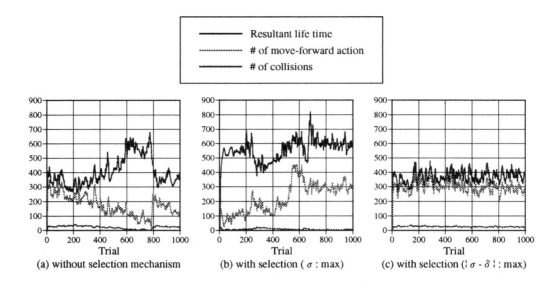

Figure 13: Simulation results under three different selection criteria.

[2] R.Brooks, "Intelligence without reason", *Proc. of IJCAI-91*, pp.569–595 (1991)

[3] P.Maes, "The dynamic action selection", *Proc. of IJCAI-89*, pp.991–997 (1989)

[4] P.Maes, "Situated agent can have goals", *Designing Autonomous Agents*, pp.49–70, MIT Press (1991)

[5] A. Ishiguro, S. Ichikawa and Y. Uchikawa, "A Gait Acquisition of 6–Legged Walking Robot Using Immune Networks", *Journal of Robotics Society of Japan*, Vol.13, No.3, pp.125–128, 1995 (in Japanese), also in *Proc. of IROS'94*, Vol.2, pp.1034–1041 (1994)

[6] A. Ishiguro, Y. Watanabe and Y. Uchikawa, "An Immunological Approach to Dynamic Behavior Control for Autonomous Mobile Robots", in *Proc. of IROS'95*, Vol.1, pp.495–500 (1995)

[7] A. Ishiguro, T.Kondo, Y. Watanabe and Y. Uchikawa, "Dynamic Behavior Arbitration of Autonomous Mobile Robots Using Immune Networks", in *Proc. of ICEC'95*, Vol.2, pp. 722–727 (1995)

[8] N.K.Jerne, "The immune system", *Scientific American*, Vol.229, No.1, pp.52–60 (1973)

[9] N.K.Jerne, "The generative grammar of the immune system", *EMBO Journal*, Vol.4, No.4 (1985)

[10] N.K.Jerne, "Idiotypic networks and other preconceived ideas", *Immunological Rev.*, Vol.79, pp.5–24 (1984)

[11] H.Fujita and K.Aihara, "A distributed surveillance and protection system in living organisms", *Trans. on IEE Japan*, Vol. 107–C, No.11, pp.1042–1048 (1987) (in Japanese)

[12] J.D.Farmer, N.H.Packard and A.S.Perelson, "The immune system, adaptation, and machine learning", *Physica 22D*, pp.187–204 (1986)

[13] F.J.Valera, A. Coutinho, B.Dupire and N.N.Vaz., "Cognitive Networks: Immune, Neural, and Otherwise", *Theoretical Immunology*, Vol.2, pp.359–375 (1988)

[14] J.Stewart, "The Immune System: Emergent Self–Assertion in an Autonomous Network", in *Proceedings of ECAL-93*, pp.1012–1018 (1993)

[15] H.Bersini and F.J.Valera, "The Immune Learning Mechanisms: Reinforcement, Recruitment and their Applications", *Computing with Biological Metaphors*, Ed. R.Paton, Chapman & Hall, pp.166–192 (1994)

[16] R.Pfeifer, "The Fungus Eater Approach to Emotion –A View from Artificial Intelligence", *Technical Report, AI Lab, No. IFIAI95.04*, Computer Science Department, University of Zurich (1995)

[17] D.Lambrinos and C.Scheier, "Extended Braitenberg Architecture", *Technical Report, AI Lab, No. IFIAI95.10*, Computer Science Department, University of Zurich (1995)

[18] B.Manderick, "The importance of selectionist systems for cognition", *Computing with Biological Metaphors*, Ed. R.Paton, Chapman & Hall (1994)

[19] J.D.Farmer, S.A.Kauffman, N.H.Packard and A.S.Perelson, "Adaptive Dynamic Networks as Models for the Immune System and Autocatalytic Sets", *Technical Report LA–UR–86–3287*, Los Alamos National Laboratory, Los Alamos, NM (1986)

The Dynamics of Photo-Taxis: Applying the Agent Environment Interaction System to a Simple Braitenberg Robot

D.L.Bisset
R.C.Vandenbergh
University of Kent at Canterbury Kent. CT2 7NT UK
D.L.Bisset@ukc.ac.uk
rcv@ukc.ac.uk

Abstract

This paper describes a dynamic system used to model the behaviour of α-Photon, a simple Braitenberg robot designed to achieve photo-taxis with a single, stationary light source.

The model is based on the Agent Environment Interaction System described in [Smithers 1994]. The equations detailed in this paper model both the robot and the environment so as to allow a full analysis of the completed agent-environment interaction system.

Finally, a numeric simulation system is developed and used to solve the coupled agent-environment interaction system. Graphical simulation results are presented in the form of the agent's absolute track in a 2D Cartesian space.

1. Introduction

The purpose of this paper is to explore the use of the agent-environment interaction system, Æ-system, as described in [Smithers 1994] to model a simple Braitenberg mobile robot called α-photon. The aim of this exploration is to discover:

- how well the real robot fits the Æ model,
- how difficult it is to construct Æ systems for real robots.
- if it is possible to use the model to investigate aspects of the robot's behaviour.

The purpose of the Æ-system is to provide a generic means of describing the behaviour of an autonomous agent. The assumption is that a description based on dynamics provides a more effective means of describing the behaviour of the agent. This improved modelling of the agent-environment interaction dynamics should then allow the construction of controllers that account for; and make use of, the inherent dynamics of the agent.

The Æ system does not attempt to model any specific robot or environment, but provides a framework for describing the two in terms of their interaction dynamics.

In order to demonstrate that this theoretical framework is sufficient it must be applied to real embodied and situated agents, like α-photon, and shown to be capable of supporting an efficient and effective description of the agent. Ultimately such a description might provide the basis for a controller specification that yields specific behaviours. In order for this to occur it must be possible to analyse the general behaviour of an agent in terms of the Æ-system that describes it. This paper sets out to show what is involved in trying to carry this out.

Although the paper presents simulations that illustrate the equations produced the main results presented in this paper stem from the form of the equations themselves, rather than from the graphical results.

1.1 Agent-Environment Interaction Systems: An Overview

Figure 1 presents a graphical representation of the general Æ system structure and clearly shows how the controller consists of three shells, each held within the other.

The outer shell (infrastructure processes) performs energy transduction either from the world to the agent or vice versa. Inward energy transduction takes place from sensors of external physical properties, such as light, into typically, electrical signals. Outward energy transduction is typically from electrical energy into a physical parameter such as a force acting on the environment.

The central core, the interaction processes, convert between input and output signals and create the vehicle behaviour. The interface parameters for these processes are most readily expressed in terms of normalised parameters (e.g. the minimum and maximum speeds of a motor can be expressed as real number values between 0 and 1, or between -1 and +1). This is because the values available from sensors, and those required by actuators, may not be of the same order or scale and so by

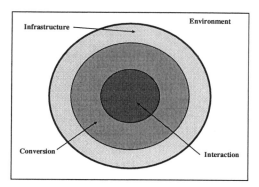

• Figure 1: Agent Environment Interaction System structure.

providing scale independence in the interaction processes their formulation may become more general.

This scale independence is provided by an intermediate layer of processes, the conversion processes, these are in addition to the set of processes originally proposed by [Smithers 1994]. In addition if the computation of the interaction processes are carried out by digital computer, which is highly likely, then these conversion processes will also have to model the conversion of continuous infrastructure parameters to and from data items and handle the finite bounds of the conversion and data representation process. In the limit a robot may be designed with a well matched set of interaction processes in which cased the conversion processes reduce to a set of unity gain functions.

[Smithers, 1994] presents the Agent-Environment equations in terms of a set of coupled 1st order differential equation. The intention of the analysis presented in this paper is to see if the dynamic model of a real robot can be made to fit this particular formalism.

2. α-Photon

In accordance with the proposed layered agent structure, α-Photon is described in stages. Each stage in the analysis corresponds to a single shell in Figure 1, from infrastructure processes to interaction processes via conversion processes.

2.1 Infrastructure Processes: Physical Properties

α-Photon is a very simple Braitenberg robot designed to locate and approach a single stationary light source. Figure 2 shows the physical properties used in the model. It is assumed that α-Photon's centre of gravity is located on the line of the wheel axles. This assumption simplifies the force calculations by ensuring that the forces generated by the wheels are parallel to both each other and the instantaneous velocity vector.

The positions of the light sensors are relative to α-Photon's centre of gravity rather than its geometric centre. In addition α-Photon also has two independently driven motors and two gear boxes. Physical stability is achieved through the use of two castors, which are assumed to be frictionless.

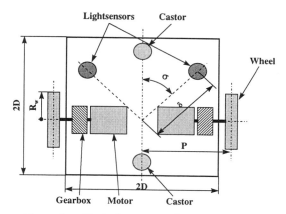

• Figure 3: α-Photon's motor and sensor geometry.

2.1.1 Sensors

As an initial approximation α-Photon's sensors are assumed to respond instantaneously and be omni-directional point sensors. In essence, these assumptions state that the output voltage is solely a function of the sensor's position in the ambient light field and that α-Photon's orientation relative to the light source does not influence the sensor output. In addition, the model also assumes that the sensor's photo-receptors exhibit a linear response to the input luminosity as specified in equation [1] where a is the light intensity to voltage conversion constant of the sensor.

$$S_0(l) = al \qquad [1]$$

$$f(x) = N_s \frac{1 - e^{-b \cdot x}}{1 + e^{-b \cdot x}} \qquad [2]$$

Equation [1] implies that the output voltage, s_o, is unbounded. Clearly this is not the case for real sensors, in which saturation will occur for large light field values. Figure 3 shows a block diagram of the model of the internal sensor structure and how the sigmoid given by equation [2] is used to limit the output range to $[-N_s, N_s]$. The maximal value N_s, represents the sensor's dynamic range (for α-Photon this is 6 Volts). In a sensor, the dynamic range is determined by the physical properties of the sensor component and the circuitry that is used to produce the sensor output voltage. The slope of the sigmoid is determined by the parameter b which must be determined experimentally together with the gradient of the linear response. (Typically the gradient at the middle of the sigmoid is equal to a.).

Figure 4 shows how both the input light field and the corresponding sensor output vary with increasing distance to the

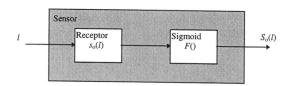

• Figure 2: Sensor block diagram

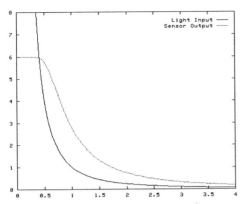

• Figure 4: light intensity and sensor output against distance from source.

light source. See section 3.3 for an analysis of the light field. For now it suffices to know that the light field is inversely proportional to the square of the distance to the source.

It is important to note that even though the light field is unbounded at the origin, the sensor output is not. This is due to the saturation of the physical components of the sensor. This region is important as an agent equipped with a sensor fitting this description cannot distinguish between the actual light source (at the origin) and any other point within the saturation region (this is analysed further in section 3.3).

$$S_0(l) = N_s \frac{1 - e^{-a.b.l}}{1 + e^{-a.b.l}} \qquad [3]$$

Equation [3] represents the fully expanded characteristic equation for the sensor. It expresses the sensor output voltage as a function of the input luminosity. The product of the two sensor parameters (a and b) determines both the saturation region and the response of the output. These constants must be determined from the physical characteristics of the sensors used.

2.1.2 Gearbox

The model assumes the gearbox has neither inertial nor frictional losses associated with it. As expressed in equations [4] and [5], this assumption reduces the gearbox to a simple scaling function. In [4] and [5] N_g represents the gear ratio of the gearbox. α-Photon uses a 32:1 reduction ratio.

$$\omega_w = \frac{\omega}{N_g} \qquad [4]$$

$$M_f = N_g \cdot M_l \qquad [5]$$

In the equations, ω_w denotes the angular velocity of the wheel, while ω is the velocity of the motor. Similarly, M_f represents the torque acting on the wheel, while M_l acts upon the motor. Figure 5 illustrates these physical parameters. In addition, Figure 5 also shows M_m, the torque generated by the motor, and M_r, the internal motor friction torque.

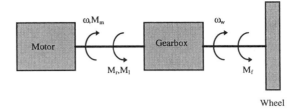

• Figure 5: α-Photon's motor drive chain.

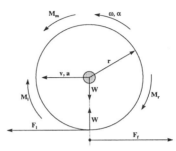

• Figure 6: Forces and torques acting on the wheel and motor

2.1.3 Motors

Since the main objective of this work is to more full understand the interaction dynamics of this robot, it is important to incorporate into the model parameters associated with real motors. α-Photon uses two independently driven Escap 22N28-216E D.C. motors, each fitted with a 32:1 reduction gearbox. In order to simplify the equations involved, the model currently ignores the effect of ambient temperature on motor output.

Figure 6 shows the various forces, torques and physical parameters involved in the analysis of the motor output. F_f is the friction force exerted by the wheel on the floor. According to Newton's Laws, an equal but opposite reaction force is exerted on the wheel. F_l represents the effect of this reaction force on the motor and therefore takes the gearbox into account (see section 2.1.2). The acceleration a and the velocity v are both properties of the wheel rather than the motor. As such, neither are immediately required in the analysis of the motor output, but have been included in the figure for completeness. W represents the weight of the vehicle and r is the wheel radius. Note that ω and α represent properties of the motor, not of the wheel.

Equation [6], which relates the motor's acceleration to inertia and torque, is derived from first principles. The load torque produced by the motor M_l, aims to accelerate the inertial load of both wheel J_l and rotor J_r, while the rotor friction torque M_r opposes this acceleration (see Figure 6). The model assumes that the gearbox connecting wheel and rotor has neither inertia J_g nor friction M_g associated with it. Should this assumption be invalid, an extra term would appear in both the summations.

$$\dot{\omega} = \frac{M_l - M_r}{J_l + J_r} \qquad [6]$$

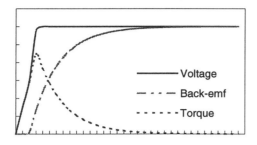

● Figure 7: Motor voltages and their relation to produced torque during start up for zero load.

In order to obtain a solution to the motor velocity equation [6], the two torque components must be analysed further. The inertia of the load J_l, and the rotor J_r, are both constant physical properties of the system.

$$M_l = \frac{k}{R_m}(V - k \cdot \omega) \qquad [7]$$

The load torque is given by equation [7] and is derived by analysing the voltages in the motor [Jucker, 1989] and consists of two competing components, the input voltage V, which increases the output torque, and the induced back-emf (proportional to ω) which acts to decrease the output torque. Both the torque constant k and terminal resistance R_m are motor dependant parameters, whose values are supplied by the manufacturer (in α-Photon's case k has the value 10.1mNm/A and R_m equals 5.8Ω). The model assumes that the rotor resistance R_m is constant even though R_m is a function of temperature (α-Photon's motors have an R_m of 5.8Ω at 22°C while at 100°C, the rated maximum, this increases by 5.4% to 6.1Ω).

Figure 7 plots input voltage, back-emf (proportional to the angular velocity) and motor torque as a function of time for an unloaded motor at start up. The input voltage is limited to ensure the motor specifications are not exceeded. This means that the output torque must also be limited, which explains the spike in the output torque. The input voltage increases much faster than the induced back-emf and dominates the output early on. Due to the upper limit on the voltage the influence of the back-emf increases with time, which results in an exponential decay in the output torque. This characteristic is easily related to the motor's physical properties. As time progresses the torque required to overcome the back-emf increases. This increase reduces the net useful torque which accelerates the motor. Eventually, the resultant torque becomes zero and the velocity stabilises.

Before equation [6] can be used the rotor friction torque M_r needs to be analysed. M_r is a result of friction internal to the motor and as such has characteristics similar to those of friction forces. This implies that M_r is bounded and exhibits hysteresis. The limiting value for the rotor torque is easily derived from the documentation provided by the manufacturer. It is proportional

to the no load current I_o and the motor constant k as expressed in equation [8]. For α-Photon this value is 0.1212mNm.

$$M_r \leq k \cdot I_o \qquad [8]$$

Substitution of [7] into [6] and reordering of the terms gives the differential form of the motor velocity equation [9]

$$\dot{\omega} = \frac{-k^2}{R_m \cdot (J_l + J_r)}\omega + \frac{k}{R_m \cdot (J_l + J_r)}V - \frac{M_r}{J_l + J_r} \qquad [9]$$

The symbolic solution to [9] can be obtained and is given by [10] in which

$$c = \frac{k^2}{R_m}$$

$$J = J_l + J_r$$

$$\omega(t) = \frac{k \cdot e^{-\left(\frac{c \cdot t}{J}\right)} \cdot \int_0^t e^{\left(\frac{c \cdot u}{J}\right)} \cdot V(u) \cdot du}{R_m \cdot J} - \frac{e^{-\left(\frac{c \cdot t}{J}\right)} \cdot \int_0^t e^{\left(\frac{c \cdot u}{J}\right)} \cdot M_r(u) \cdot du}{R_m \cdot J} \qquad [10]$$

Equation [10] is the integral form of the motor equation. It is important to note that [10] is an expression for the angular velocity of the motor and not of the wheel, and that as such, all working forces must be relative to the rotor.

2.2 Conversion Processes

2.2.1 Overview

As depicted in Figure 1, the conversion processes form an interface layer between the infrastructure and interaction processes. They convert the physical properties of the environment, sensed by the infrastructure processes, into data items which are acted upon by the interaction processes. Figure 8 shows the data flow associated with this structure.

For continuous valued sensor data and a digital controller, the conversion processes can be seen to represent analogue to digital and digital to analogue conversions respectively. The conversion processes isolate the core controller from the sensors and actuators.

This structure can best be represented by transformations between vector spaces, one transformation per interface between the process types. Such transforms can be characterised in terms of matrix operations. This notation corresponds to the formalism

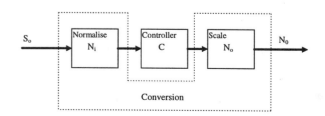

● Figure 8: Converter structure

proposed by Smithers [Smithers, 1994].

$$V_o = S_o \cdot N_i \cdot C \cdot N_o \qquad [11]$$

The conversion transform equation is shown in Equation [11] where S_o and V_o represent the sensor output vector and the actuator input vector respectively.

2.2.2 Normalisation

Equation [12] shows the general form of the normalisation matrix. In the general case shown here, each component of the input vector $\mathbf{S_o}$ has its own dynamic range and must therefore be scaled independently.

$$\mathbf{N_i} = \begin{bmatrix} \dfrac{1}{N_{s1}} & \cdots & 0 & \cdots & 0 \\ \vdots & \ddots & \vdots & & \vdots \\ 0 & \cdots & \dfrac{1}{N_{si}} & \cdots & 0 \\ \vdots & & \vdots & \ddots & \vdots \\ 0 & \cdots & 0 & \cdots & \dfrac{1}{N_{sn}} \end{bmatrix} \qquad [12]$$

α-Photon only has two light sensors so the vector space formed by the sensors is two dimensional. Because of this, the corresponding normalisation matrix must also be two dimensional. Equation [13] represents α-Photon's normalisation transform, in which N_s corresponds to the sensor output range.

$$\mathbf{N_i} = \begin{bmatrix} \dfrac{1}{N_s} & 0 \\ 0 & \dfrac{1}{N_s} \end{bmatrix} \qquad [13]$$

2.2.3 Scaling

The matrix shown in [14] is the general form of the scaling transform matrix. In the general case, not all of the driven motors need have the same input range, so each of the components must again be scaled separately.

$$\mathbf{N_o} = \begin{bmatrix} N_{o1} & \cdots & 0 & \cdots & 0 \\ \vdots & \ddots & \vdots & & \vdots \\ 0 & \cdots & N_{oi} & \cdots & 0 \\ \vdots & & \vdots & \ddots & \vdots \\ 0 & \cdots & 0 & \cdots & N_{om} \end{bmatrix} \qquad [14]$$

As with the normalisation process, α-Photon's scaling matrix (see equation [15]) is two dimensional due to the fact that α-Photon has two actuators. N_m represents the maximum input voltage to the motors.

$$\mathbf{N_o} = \begin{bmatrix} N_m & 0 \\ 0 & N_m \end{bmatrix} \qquad [15]$$

2.3 Interaction Processes: Core Controller

The central core of the controller is the main component of the system and as such predominately determines its behaviour. α-

Photon's core controller matrix is given by equation [16], which corresponds to simply cross-connecting the inputs to the outputs, thus making a-Photon a 3a vehicle in Braitenberg notation.

$$\mathbf{C} = \begin{bmatrix} 0 & 1 \\ 1 & 0 \end{bmatrix} \qquad [16]$$

On a vehicle level, this results in the motor furthest away from the light being driven fastest. The vehicle therefore turns towards the light source due to the imbalance between the forces generated by the motors.

3. Environment

The main aim of this paper is to investigate α-Photon's behaviour, which consists of the interactions between α-Photon and its environment. In order to model these interactions, a suitable analysis of the environment itself is required. This description and analysis is not part of α-Photon's dynamic system. Nor is it part of the dynamic systems description as proposed by Smithers [Smithers, 1994], in which the interactions with the environment and not the environment itself, are important. However in order to complete a full numerical analysis it is necessary to explicitly model the environment.

α-Photon achieves photo-taxis using just two interactions: the agent senses the light field and generates a torque on the wheels. The implications of these interactions on α-Photon have been described earlier (see section 1). This section analyses the effects of these interactions on the environment and its model.

The environment is assumed to be devoid of objects so that α-Photon's motion through 2-space is unobstructed. In addition, the lack of objects means that the light field can easily be calculated given α-Photon's position relative to the light source. This greatly simplifies the ambient light field as no form of ray-tracing is required.

3.1 Agent-Environment Boundary

Beer's dynamic system model [Beer, in press] argues that the boundary between the agent and the environment can be placed arbitrarily, implying that the wheel-floor contact point is not special in any way. One result of the work presented in this paper is to show that there is a good reason for placing the boundary at the wheel-floor contact point. This is because the modelling of the dynamics is made significantly more complex if the boundary is placed at other arbitrary locations (e.g. between the stator and rotor of the motor) because of the mutual interaction mechanisms that exist at these points.

In the course of this work various boundary points have been tested (e.g. the wheel axles and between the motor stator and rotor) and in each case they yield a more complex equation set for the mobility equations. It is somehow intuitively satisfying that the simplest equation set corresponds to the most 'natural'

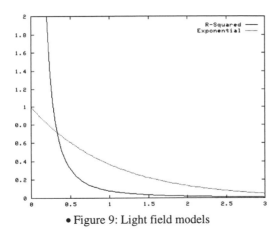

• Figure 9: Light field models

$$r(x,y) = \sqrt{(x_s - x)^2 + (y_s - y)^2} \qquad [17]$$

The first method [18], uses exponential decay where τ determines the rate of decay. The alternative method [19], states that the light value is inversely proportional to the square of the distance. This square law is physically accurate and is derived from the assumption that the source is at the centre of a sphere with radius r.

$$l(x,y) = L \cdot e^{-\frac{r(x,y)}{\tau}} \qquad [18]$$

$$l(x,y) = \frac{L}{4 \cdot \pi \cdot r(x,y)^2} \qquad [19]$$

Figure 9 clearly shows the different characteristics of the two functions. Both graphs assume a unity source intensity (L) and decay rate (τ), where appropriate. Using an exponential function to model the ambient light field has two distinct advantages over the square law. First of all, the light value does not tend to infinity at the origin, and secondly, the exponential model has a lower decay rate. It can be argued that environment factors such as floor or ceiling reflectance might mean that the exponential function provides a more accurate model. This is why the exponential model is used in the simulation results presented later.

solution. This is an important point, as it shows that the system models the intuitive boundary between agent and environment.

3.2 Reference Frame

α-Photon does not require a frame of reference, as neither its sensors nor its motors have (or require) knowledge of the vehicle's absolute position in world space. The sensors detect light levels and the motors generate a torque on the wheels (see sections 3.4 and 3.5). The effect of the produced torque, i.e. the force on the agent, is position dependent, but the force itself is a property of the agent's environment (see section 3.1).

The environment requires a reference system to position objects. Ideally, an agent-centred perspective would be used, as this corresponds to the way that the agent detects the world. This approach although desirable, is impractical as the expressions required to position objects become unnecessarily complex. A practical solution is to use an absolute world based co-ordinate system to describe objects in the world. Such a reference system has the advantage of simplifying the model, but more importantly, it also clearly distinguishes between properties of the environment (such as position and velocity which are expressed in a world centric form) and of the agent (such as produced torque which is robot centric) by providing them with a separate co-ordinate system. This means that transformations have to be explicitly applied to convert from one to the other, thus forcing a clear distinction to be made.

3.3 Light Field

As stated earlier, the environment is free of objects and the light source is stationary. Both these assumptions simplify the light field model and imply that the generated field is inversely proportional to distance.

Two separate models for the field are used, both of which are expressed in terms of the Euclidean distance $r(x,y)$ to the light source positioned at (x_s, y_s) (see [17]). The light intensity of the source is represented by L (expressed in candella).

3.4 Friction

α-Photon's motors produce a torque on the two wheels. This torque itself is not sufficient to produce α-Photon's forward motion. In order to obtain motion, the torque must be converted into forces acting upon the agent. This conversion is only achieved in the presence of friction at the wheel-ground contact point. In the absence of friction, the wheels simply slip over the surface without generating forward motion.

$$F_f \leq \mu(x,y) \cdot W \qquad [20]$$

Equation [20] determines the maximal friction force as a function of the vehicle's weight W and the friction coefficient μ. By making μ position dependant, differential friction (e.g. smooth-rough surface transitions) this will be undertaken in future work. Currently, the model assumes a uniform friction coefficient.

In equation [21] the generated motor output torque is expressed as a function of the gear ratio N_g, the produced load torque M_l and the rotor friction torque M_r (see section 2.1, Figure 5 and Figure 6 for details).

$$M_f = N_g \cdot (M_l - M_r) \qquad [21]$$

$$F = \frac{M_f}{r} \qquad [22]$$

The relationship between torque and the force is expressed by equation [22]. Note that the friction reaction force cannot exceed

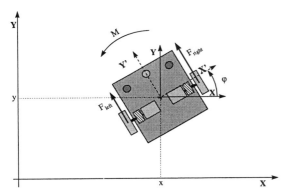

• Figure 10: Relationship between robot centred and world centred positioning.

the maximal value as calculated by equation [20]. Any excess torque or force results in wheel slippage.

3.5 Motion

In the previous section the forces acting upon the agent are derived. This section combines these forces to calculate the resulting motion.

Figure 10 shows the forces acting upon α-Photon and the reference frame in which these forces and accelerations are calculated. In order to uniquely position α-Photon in 2-space, three parameters are required. These are the agent's position (defined as x and y) and its orientation (given by φ). The motion equations derived in this section provide a means of calculating these parameters at each instance in time given suitable starting conditions.

Equation [23] is the fundamental motion equation, which relates the sum of the forces acting on the agent and its momentum to the acceleration of the vehicle, where m is the agent's mass.

$$\sum_i \vec{F}_i + m \cdot \vec{v} = m \cdot \vec{a} \qquad [23]$$

Projection of the terms onto the X-Y reference frame, leads to equations [24] and [25], which are used to obtain both x an y as a function of time.

$$\ddot{x} + \dot{x} = \frac{\left(F_{left} + F_{right}\right)}{m} \cos\left(\varphi + \frac{\pi}{2}\right) \qquad [24]$$

$$\ddot{y} + \dot{y} = \frac{\left(F_{left} + F_{right}\right)}{m} \sin\left(\varphi + \frac{\pi}{2}\right) \qquad [25]$$

In the motion equations the driving forces, F_{right} and F_{left}, are calculated by means of equation [22] with the restriction imposed by equation [20].

Again using basic principles an equation for the angular component of the velocity and acceleration can be derived. The result of this is given by equation [26], where P is the distance between centre of gravity to wheel-floor contact point (see Figure 2).

$$\ddot{\varphi} + \dot{\varphi} = \frac{3}{2} \frac{\left(F_{right} - F_{left}\right)}{m \cdot P} \qquad [26]$$

The three second order differential equations [24], [25] and [26] form an initial value problem. To uniquely identify a solution, a set of six initial conditions are required. This set is formed by α-Photon's position and orientation at time t=0 and the assumption that α-Photon starts out at rest (i.e. the first derivatives of x, y and φ with respect to time, are zero). A numerical solution of this system of differential equations is used to obtain the simulation results.

4. Simulation

4.1 Method

As stated in the previous section, the coupled equations for α-Photon and its environment form an initial value problem, which implies, as should be expected, that the initial conditions are important to differentiate between the various possible solutions. The initial conditions are derived from α-Photon's starting position and orientation together with the fact that α-Photon starts out at rest.

An often used mechanism for solving systems of differential equations is based on the reduction of the order of the system. Each of α-Photon's second order equations is replaced by two new first order equations in new (suitably chosen) variables. While this increases the number of equations from three to six, it reduces the complexity of the overall system. This new system of six equations can be solved using a variety of mechanisms.

The solution used here is a fifth-order Runge-Kutta. The implementation algorithm is based on an algorithm found in [Press, 1993]. This implementation uses adaptive step-size control to increase numerical stability.

4.2 Assumptions and Restrictions

The simulation uses an arbitrary set of physical parameters for both the agent and its environment. But any consistent values could be inserted into the simulation to represent a particular robot.

α-Photon's mass is 0.5kg, wheel base (2P) is 0.10m, body size (2D) is 0.10m. The sensors are mounted symmetrically at π/4 radians (α) at a distance of 0.05m (δ). The wheels have a radius (r) of 0.02m and a mass of 0.01kg. Finally, the gearbox ratio is 32:1 (see Figure 2).

The vehicle's trajectory is plotted in an absolute co-ordinate system as this makes the graphs easier to read and interpret. Orientation increases anti-clockwise, with zero degrees being parallel to the Y-axis, pointing in the Y direction. These three co-ordinates are specified as a triplet in the form (x, y, φ).

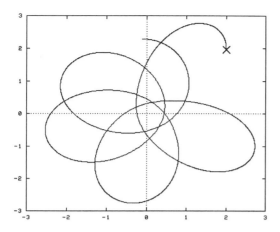

• Figure 11: Trajectory starting at (2.0, 2.0, 0.0)

The simulation runs can be terminated by one of two events. Either α-Photon approaches the light source to within a set distance (10cm) or a predetermined time is reached. In most cases, the latter of the two conditions was used to terminate the simulation.

It should be noted that the simulation does not currently deal with wheel slippage accurately. In particular the hysteresis involved is ignored and the assumption is inherently made that the wheel speed can always be related directly to the vehicle velocity.

4.3 Results

The various graphs show the trajectory for a given environment as the properties of the vehicle are kept constant throughout. The aim is to investigate the effects of both light and friction on α-Photon's photo-taxis.

Initially the vehicle was placed at (2.0, 2.0, 0.0) and the simulation started. To avoid overloading the graph only the initial segment is plotted (see Figure 11). Complete trajectories are presented further on.

Note that the trajectory exhibits *petalling* (this is the rather distinctive pattern formed as the agent overshoots, turns back and overshoots again). This pattern is typical for this type of controller and behaviour, see [Beer, in press] and [Holland & Melhuish, 1996].

Near the light source, the tangential component of α-Photon's velocity dominates the trajectory, while at larger distances the auto-rotation becomes the more important factor.

Figure 12 shows the evolution of the distance between agent and light source over time. The vehicle started from the same initial position as in Figure 11 (at (2.0, 2.0, 0.0)), but this time the simulation is left running until terminated after 10000 seconds.

The plot clearly shows how the agent's trajectory stabilises at a fixed distance from the light source. As the vehicle is still in motion at this point, α-Photon must be circling the light source.

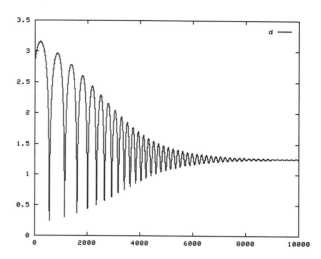

• Figure 12: Distance of robot from light source over time.

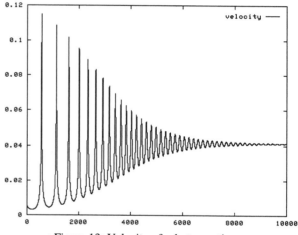

• Figure 13: Velocity of robot over time.

Note the resemblance to the trajectory of an asteroid in a gravitational field. The various forces acting on α-Photon (friction and wheel torque) combine to reduce the amplitude of the oscillation in the velocity each time an orbit is completed (see Figure 13). This decrease in velocity results in a decrease in the overshoot, until eventually all forces compensate each other and a stable trajectory is reached. These figures display a characteristic which is typical of a chaotic system with a fixed point attractor.

Now that α-Photon's trajectory has been analysed, the effects of changes in the environment can be investigated. The influence of changing the light field strength, while keeping the friction coefficient constant, is investigated first. This is then followed by changing the friction coefficient under constant lighting conditions. In each case, the vehicle's initial position is given by (2.0, 2.0, 90.0) and the results plotted on the same scale so that meaningful comparisons can be made.

Figure 14 shows a light source intensity of 1 candella. The evolution towards a stable circular orbit can clearly be seen in

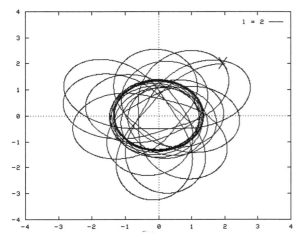

Figure 14: Trajectory with light field value of 2.

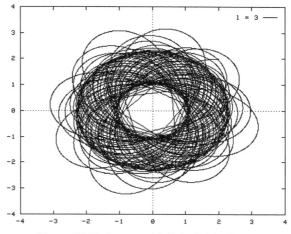

• Figure 15: Trajectory with light field value of 3.

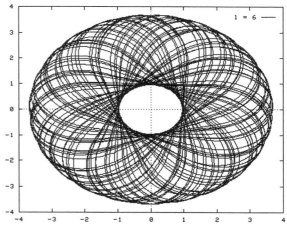

Figure 16: Trajectory with light field value of 6.

both Figure 14. The larger overshoot is caused by the stronger light field. A stronger light field corresponds to a higher maximal velocity, and thus to larger overshoots. Also note that due to the increased light field, the saturation region of the sensors has a larger radius (see section 2.1.1). Once both sensors saturate the vehicle moves in a straight line as the difference between the motor torque on the wheels is now zero. This can be seen as the straight line motion in the centre of Figure 14. In general this behaviour is similar to that found with limit cycle attractor dynamics

Increasing the light source intensity further causes a radical change in behaviour. In this case it is no longer possible to identify a single stable orbit, instead a region of stable radii is formed.

Figure 15 show Photon's trajectory given a light source intensity of 3 candella. In the centre of the graph, the effects of the increased saturation radius can clearly be seen, where the vehicle exhibits straight line motion.

In Figure 16 the light source has been increased to 6 candella. Due to the large saturation region, the vehicle's orbits are shaped rather like squashed rectangles with rounded ends. Each orbit is slightly rotated with regards to the previous, which causes the distinctive toroid pattern. The vehicle oscillates between the outer and inner edge of the region of stable radii, without preference for any particular value. This behaviour can be characterised as limit cycle attractor dynamics of two frequencies, this significant change in dynamics has been brought about by a simple increase in light field intensity.

The above analysis keeps the friction constant and changes the light source intensity. The next stage of the analysis is to investigate the effect of friction on α-Photon's motion. Once again α-Photon is started from (2.0, 2.0, 90) and the simulation left to run for a fixed number of steps. The friction coefficient is kept constant throughout each separate simulation, but varied between runs. Some of the more interesting results are shown here.

Figure 17 plots the followed trajectory for a friction coefficient half that of the one used in Figure 15. Note how each orbit is much longer and narrower. This is due to the fact that reducing the friction reduces the maximal useful torque produced by the motors. This results in more wheel slippage. In essence, wheel slippage extends the sensor saturation region, which explains the long and straight nature of the orbits. Once again this result can be interpreted in terms of a chaotic attractor with a quasi-periodic cycle of three frequencies

It is interesting to note that in both the above cases, the maximal distance to the light source decreases gradually. It is not clear from the simulations if the eventual radius depends on the friction value or not.

5. Conclusions

This paper has shown that Smither's Æ system can be successfully used to encapsulate a dynamic systems description of a real robot. In carrying this out an extra type of process has been added to the Æ system, the conversion processes. These processes interface between the infrastructure and interaction processes to model the process of converting electrical signals into data quantities suitable for processing by a computer based controller.

In observing the relationship between the real robot and the Æ-system it is clear that all of the infrastructure processes carry out some form of energy transduction. Typically infrastructure processes convert form physical forms of energy to electrical forms, or vice-versa, conversion processes convert from electrical forms into data, and interaction processes process data. These three different types of process have a close relationship to the physical form of the robot and its controller. Where the interface electronics corresponds to the infrastructure processes, the data converters correspond to the conversion processes, and the computation carried out in the controller corresponds to the interaction process.

By studying the equations of these three processes the exact representation of the external world, as sensed by the robot can be identified. For example the infrastructure processes do not contain any reference to the absolute position or velocity of the vehicle.

One conclusion from the analysis of this system is that it is important to include the wheel as a part of the robot. Not to do so makes it difficult to fit the equations into the Æ-system, and results in an over complex model. Since this is an intuitive choice it indicates that the divisions imposed on the model by the Æ-system are well founded and justifiable not only from an intuitive perspective but also from a mathematical point of view.

The Æ-system can also be seen to provide a viable framework for the generation of simulation based models that need to include the dynamics of the agent. In particular the ability to identify different modes of behaviour (e.g. changes from limit cycle to quasi-limit cycle dynamics) with simple linear increases in light field intensity show that the model captures the character of the interaction dynamics between the robot and its environment, and in doing so demonstrates the complexity of this interaction. Future work will be needed to see if these dynamic characteristics can be observed in the real robot.

The difficulty in producing simulation results, even for such a simple vehicle, clearly highlights the need for interactive experimentation with the real world in order to carry out analysis on more complex robots or environments.

If the Æ-system is to be of use to the designers of autonomous agents then clearly further investigations are required. In particular the formulation of more complex interaction processes needs to be explored, as does the mechanism for making use of the system to design dynamic controllers.

6. Future Work

The next stage in this work is to carry out measurements of the real robot in its constrained environment to see if the simulation plots represent accurate traces of the behaviour of the robot. Of particular interest is the effect of small scale changes in various

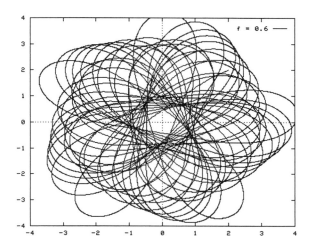

● Figure 17: Trajectory with friction value of 0.6 and light field value of 3.

physical parameters, in particular surface friction, on the motion of the robot. If these results show that the simulations presented in this paper are only an approximation to the real behaviour then this will be concrete proof that agents that interact with the real world must be embodied and not simulated if dynamic interactions with the environment are considered to be important.

7. References

[Braitenberg 1984] Braitenberg. V. *Vehicles* MIT Press.

[Beer, in press] Randall D. Beer, in press, The Dynamics Of Adaptive Behavior: A Research Program. To appear in *Robotics and Autonomous Systems*.

[Holland & Melhuish, 1996] Owen Holland and Chris Melhuish, 1996, Some Adaptive Movements Of Animats With Single Symmetrical Sensors, in *From Animals To Animats 4*, Proceedings Of The Fourth International Conference On Simulation Of Adaptive Behavior, MIT Press

[Jucker, 1989] Erich Jucker, *Physical Properties of Small DC Motors Using an Ironless Rotor*

[Press, 1993] William H. Press, 1993, *Numerical Recipes in C*, Cambridge University Press

[Smithers, 1994] Tim Smithers, 1994, What the Dynamics of Adaptive Behaviour and Cognition Might Look Like in Agent-Environment Interaction Systems, in *On the Role of Dynamics and Representation in Adaptive Behaviour and Cognition*, Workshop Notes of the Third International Workshop on Artificial Life and Artificial Intelligence, University of the Basque Country, Donostia.

A Comparison of Robot Implementations of Explicit and Implicit Activity Selection Schemes

Olatz Arbelaitz Gallego, Elena Lazkano Ortega, & Tim Smithers

Euskal Herriko Unibertsitatea, Informatika Fakultatea
649 Postakutxa, 20080 Donostia, Espaina

Email: [acbargao][ccplaore][ccpsmsmt]@si.ehu.es

Abstract

Activity selection is an important problem in adaptive behaviour in robots and animals. This paper reports the results of a first experiment designed to compare robot implementations of an explicit activity selection mechanism and an implicit activity selection mechanism, a Subsumption Architecture scheme. The objective was to identify what, if any, important differences could be found in the implementations of the two different activity selection schemes. The method was to build two programs, experimentally test that they produce essentially the same behaviour in the same robot, and then to compare these programs and the processes of implementing and testing them. Our conclusions are that the implementation of implicit activity selection leads to a natural localisation and encapsulation of the code, and that this results in an easily tested and extended program. The explicit activity selection program, on the other hand, necessarily contains significant distributed code dependencies and does not preserve the clarity of the selection scheme when presented at an abstract level.

1 Introduction

Activity selection, or action selection or behaviour selection, as it is also sometimes called in the literature, is an important problem in adaptive behaviour in animals and robots, see: [Meyer & Wilson, 92]; [Meyer, et al., 93]; [Cliff, et al., 94], for example. In this literature we see two fundamentally different approaches to this problem, which we call *explicit activity selection* (EAS) and *implicit activity selection* (IAS), respectively. In explicit activity selection mechanisms the activity to be executed at any time is explicitly chosen from the outputs of a number of active, and thus possible, activities. There thus appears, in the architecture of such schemes, a centralised selection function (or box) which takes as input all the possible activity commands and outputs one of them. In implicit activity selection there is no explicit selection made, rather the relationships between the different activity generating components of the architecture are arranged so that only the appropriate activity is generating commands at any one time.

This paper reports on a first experiment designed to compare robot implementations of an explicit activity selection mechanism and an implicit activity selection mechanism. In the next section we briefly review the relevant literature and introduce the particular types of explicit and implicit activity selection schemes we tested. In section three we describe the robots used, the experiment design, and procedure adopted. In section four we present the results and analysis, and in a final section we present a discussion and conclusions.

2 Review

A review of the relevant literature shows that numerous activity selection schemes and mechanisms have been proposed and investigated, but very little of this research has involved robot implementations, and hardly any have attempted a comparative study.

One important and long running line of research on behaviour selection mechanisms and their organisation and neuronal implementation is Arbib's *Schema Theory*, see: [Arbib, 92] for a recent review; and [Arbib & Cobas, 92], [Arbib & Lee, 93], [Liaw & Arbib, 93], for some detailed examples. In robotics, Schema Theory forms the basis for Arkin's work on navigation behaviour in robots, see [Arkin, 89] and [Arkin, 92], for example, and underlies Lyons' work on the robot programming language *RS*, [Lyons, 86] and [Lyons & Hendriks, 95]. In Arkin's implementation, behaviour is the result of an explicit weighted summation of the outputs of active behaviour schemas, [Arkin, 92].

Another important line of work is Brooks' *Subsumption Architecture*, [Brooks, 86]. This has been used on a range of different robots at MIT, see [Brooks, 95] for a review. Subsumption Architecture has also formed the basis of much other robotics work involving variants on the same basic idea, see [Connell, 90], [Payton, 86], [Anderson & Donath, 91], for example. Maes, [Maes, 89] and [Maes, 92], also investigated (computationally) a behaviour selection scheme inspired by the Subsumption Architecture which was tested in a robot implementation by Pebody, [Pebody, 91]. Tyrrell, [Tyrrell, 93], critically compared Maes' distributed scheme with a hierarchical scheme by Rosenblatt and Payton, [Rosenblatt & Payton, 89], but this did not involve any robotic implementations, only further computational investigations. In Subsumption Architecture, the behaviour selection is implicit (in the subsumption relations) and distributed (across the subsumption links).

Nehmzow *et al.*, investigated another architecture for activity selection in robots designed to support learning activity selection, see: [Nehmzow, *et al.*, 89]; [Nemzow & Smithers, 92]; [Nehmzow *et al.*, 93]. This scheme also uses explicit activity selection, in which the output of one behaviour is selected, rather than summing all outputs. Two variants of another simple explicit action selection mechanism were compared by Snaith and Holland, [Snaith & Holland, 92], one of the very few comparative studies involving robot implementations. A robot implementation of a selection scheme based upon inter-behaviour bidding is reported by Sahota, [Sahota, 94], but not compared with other schemes. Hallam *et al.*, [Hallam, *et al.*, 94], report on a robot implementation based on a selection algorithm developed by Halperin and Dunham to model the behaviour of Siamese fighting fish, [Halperin & Dunham, 92]. Both these latter schemes can be understood as different types of implicit activity selection schemes: there is no explicit or centralised behaviour selection process involved. But, again, no comparison was reported with related work.

We can see from this brief review that there is no shortage of proposals for activity selection schemes, and that a variety of these have been implemented in robots. What we do not currently have is much understanding about the differences, similarities, and relative merits of these different schemes. In particular, it is not clear what works best, when, why, and what scales best in systems with many behaviours, and why. One quite reasonable explanation for this lack of comparative understanding is that it is hard enough to design, implement, debug, test, and investigate one selection scheme on a robot, let alone two or more.

Here we report the results of a first experiment designed to compare robot implementations of an explicit behaviour mechanism, based upon the architecture of Nehmzow *et.* *al.*, and a Subsumption Architecture scheme, an implicit selection scheme. In attempting this work we have had two aims: first to try to compare two different types of robot implementations of activity selection; and secondly, to see if such comparative investigation can be done using small and simple robots which are relatively cheap to design, build, debug, test, and use in experiments. The objective of the experiment was to identify what, if any, important differences exist between implementations of the two different action selection schemes. The method was to build the two programs to produce (nominally) the same behaviour in the same robot, experimentally test to see if it is the same, and then to compare the behaviour generated by these programs and the processes of implementing and testing them.

3 Comparison Experiment

The aim of this experiment was to make a first attempt at a comparison of implementations of two different action selection schemes for mobile robots: (i) an explicit action selection scheme after the Nehmzow *et.* *al.* architecture; and (ii) a Brooks' Subsumption Architecture scheme. To make this a practical possibility we used Lego robots based upon the MIT Media Lab' 6.270 microprocessor board, programmed in Interactive C, [Martin, 92]. The objective was to identify, if we could, important differences between the structure and organisation of the two programs, and the processes of their implementation and testing. To do this we attempted to implement nominally the same behaviours in the same robots using the two different action selection schemes. The behaviours used were a *wall-following with obstacle avoidance behaviour* and a *phototaxis behaviour*, together with *stop* (at light) and *forward motion* behaviours. We used a set of four different maze-like test environments, each with a single light source, to assess the similarity of the behaviour of the same robot running the two programs during different trials.

3.1 *Robot Design and Construction*

The design of the robot used follows that of Braintenberg's *Vehicles*, [Braitenberg, 84]. This is a well tried and tested design in our laboratory, and elsewhere. It has two independently driven wheels and one (undriven) fixed direction wheel at the front (not a caster). Two Lego 4.5V motors, both supplied by one 7.2v NiCad. battery, drive the two main wheels. Two channels of Pulse-Width-Modulation control, on the 6.270 board, are used to control the power output of the two motors, and a 1:75 reduction gearbox, built using Lego spur-gears, is used between each motor and drive wheel. This design gives the robot differential steering, as used on many mobile robots today.

The chassis, gearboxes, and superstructure are all built from Lego Technic Ⓣ and are designed so that the center of mass of the complete robot is just forward of the line through the axes of the two drive wheels. This design gives us a compact (250mm by 150mm), manoeuvrable, and relatively fast (up to 0.6m/s) small mobile robot.

The robot is equipped with a three state front bumper: no contact; left side contact; and right side contact. It uses two microswitches each connected to a binary input channel on the processor board. Two light sensors are mounted, one facing front-left and the other front-right. These use light-dependent resistors. Each light sensor is connected to an analog input, and is read, by the program, as an integer value between 0 (high light level) to 255 (low light level). The robot is also equipped with two easily buttons to easily *stop* and *(re)start* the robot. These also use microswitches built into the Lego structure. The clock (internal to the microprocessor) is also used by the robot as a sensor: to detect that specified periods of time have passed, see the specifications of the Behaviours below.

The robot was programmed in Interactive C. This provides an interpreted execution and multi-tasking version of the C language. The multi-tasking allows different processes to be time-sliced quickly and efficiently to give an effect of parallel execution. (See [Martin, 92] Chapter 7, for details.)

3.2 Experimental Setup

To keep the over all experiment practical, the behaviour straightforwardly assessable, and the programs relatively simple, we selected a kind of phototaxis behaviour as the behavioural task to be realised by the robot. The robot is supposed to do phototaxis in an environment containing at least one bright light source and other objects that block the light and possibly prevent straight line paths to the light source by the robot. The strategy employed is to try to wall-follow around objects until there is enough light to do phototaxis and to stop when the light source is very near. To give the robots this competence, four behaviours were specified and implemented in both types of program: stop; wall-follow; phototaxis; and forward. It is this set of four behaviours that the two different activity selection mechanisms operate over in the two programs.

3.3 Behaviours

Each behaviour is specified and implemented as a finite-state machine (FSM) with transitions triggered by changes in appropriate sensor states.

• **Stop**: This behaviour has two states, state-1, in which both motors are set to STOP, and state-0, in which the motor states are undefined, see figure 1(a). The transition from state-1 to state-0 is triggered by pressing the (RE)START button on the robot. The transition from

state-0 to state-1 is triggered either by pressing the STOP button, or when one or both values of the two light sensors are below a specified threshold, signifying AT-LIGHT. This threshold was set to 10 and occurs when the robot is at or near to a light source.

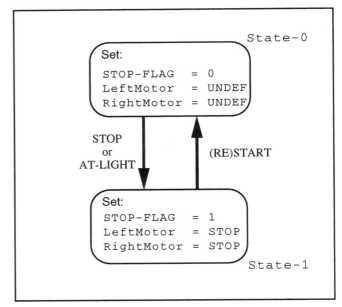

Figure 1(a): The Finite State Machine for the **Stop** Behaviour.

• **Wall-following**: This behaviour is initiated when the robot detects a contact with its bumper sensor. After a contact, the robot moves backwards in a tight arc for a short (variable) period of time and then moves forward in a more gentle arc that is intended to take it towards the obstacle again, but a bit further on. The directions of these curved motions depend upon on which side the contact was detected. If, after going forward for the specified (fixed) period of time, no further contact is detected the robot stops trying to do Wall-following. This behaviour is specified as a three-state FSM. State-0 sets the two motor channels as undefined. State-1 sets the motor states to generate the tight reverse arc motion (REV-L and REV-R), and state-2 sets the motor states to generate the forward arc motion (FWD-L and FWD-R. The transition from state-0 to state-1 is triggered by the bumper sensors detecting a left or right side CONTACT. State-1 can transit back to state-0 if one or both light sensor values are below a threshold value, set to 50 for the experiments reported here (ENOUGH LIGHT). This is used to indicate that there is *enough* light to stop generating wall-following actions. Also, state-1 can transit to state-2 if its REVERSE TIME is up. State-2 can transit to state-0 if there is ENOUGH LIGHT to stop generating wall-following actions (again detected by one or both light sensor values being below 50) or, state-2 can transit to state-0 if the time period for trying to remake contact ends (FORWARD TIME UP). State-2 can also transit to state-1 if a *contact* is detected before FORWARD TIME UP becomes true. See figure 1(b). To help prevent the robot getting stuck, the amount of time it spends reversing is made to depend on the rate of left *and* right contacts it has been detecting. If the rate of left and right contacts are similar this time constant is incremented, up to a fixed maximum. If not, then the time is set to a fixed minimum value.

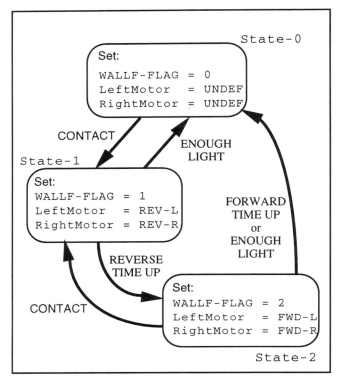

Figure 1(b): The Finite State Machine for the **Wall-following** Behaviour. Note that not all the details are included: the REVERSE TIME modification mechanism is not shown, for example.

We note here that this FSM uses time to trigger some transitions. In Brooks' terminology, this is called an *Augmented* FSM, (AFSM). We prefer to think of the clock as a kind of sensor used to trigger state transitions in behaviours, just as the bumper and light sensors, so we do not use the AFSM terminology.

• **Phototaxis**: This behaviour is defined as a two-state FSM. State-0, leaves the two motors undefined. State-1 defines the motor states to set the robot turning in the direction of the locally detected brightest light level. The transition from state-0 to state-1 occurs when there is a significant difference between the values of the two light sensors. For the experiment described here, this difference was set as more than 15. The state-1 to state-0 transition occurs when the difference between the two

light sensor values is equal to or less than this threshold of 15. See figure 1(c).

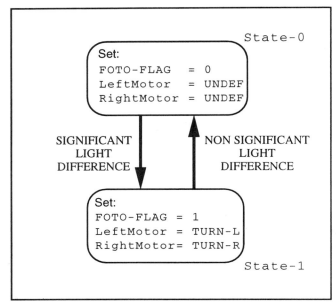

Figure 1(c): The Finite State Machine for the **Phototaxis** Behaviour.

• **Forward**: This behaviour is simply defined as a one-state FSM which sets both motor states to produce forward motion in a straight line at a constant velocity. See figure 1(d).

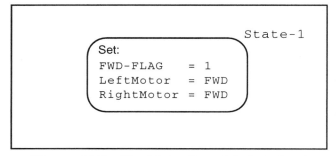

Figure 1(d): The Finite State Machine for the **Forward** Behaviour.

3.4 Actions Selection Schemes and Programs

In the two programs built to implement the two types of activity selection, each behaviour is implemented as a (time-sliced) Interactive C process. In this sense, they are continuously executed when the programs run. Each behaviour is therefore always in one of its defined states, and thus always producing a motor output, undefined in certain states.

In implementing these behaviours we explicitly attempted to keep the programs as similar as seemed reasonable and not too unnatural. We also explicitly attempted to produce (nominally) the same robot behaviour in the same robot when running each program. There are, of course, some important differences between the programs.

In the case of the **Explicit Activity Selection** (EAS) program, the four behaviour processes are augmented by a fifth *Activity Selection* process. This reads all the sensor input channels and decides which behaviour output should go to the motor control channels, see figure 2(a).

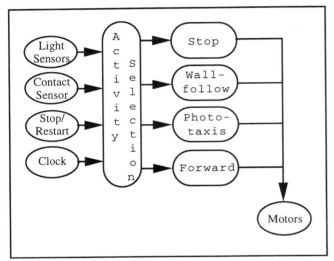

Figure 2(a): The Explicit Activity Selection architecture.

All the sensor values read by this process are made available to the other behaviour processes via globally defined program variables. Thus, in this program the behaviour processes do not read the sensor input channels directly. The explicit selection procedure, implemented by the activity selection process, defines a fixed ordering over the behaviours such that, at any time, the motor output of the program is defined by the `Stop` behaviour if it is not in state-0, or (if it is) by `Wall-follow` if it is not in state-0, or (if it is) by `Phototaxis` if it is not in state-0, or (if it is) by `Forward`. This means that only one of the time-sliced processes in the program actually changes the states of the motor output channels at any one time, thus avoiding possibly confusing interactions arising from the time-slicing mechanism.

In the case of the **Subsumption Architecture** (SA) program, each behaviour process reads the sensor input channels (of the sensors it needs), see figure 2(b). The 'wiring' of the subsumption links is implemented by some extra lines of code in the `Forward` behaviour process. (This again means that only one of the four time-sliced processes actually changes the motor states.) Here a behaviour can subsume another behaviour if it defines

motor states, and not if they are undefined.

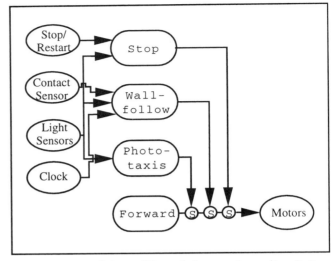

Figure 2(b): The Subsumption (Implicit Activity Selection) architecture.

Both programs were built, tested, and debugged incrementally starting with the `forward` behaviour, followed by the `phototaxis`, `wall-following`, and `stop` behaviours, in this order. In the case of the EAS program, the control process was also implemented with the `forward` behaviour and subsequently extended with the addition of each subsequent behaviour. In the case of the SA program, the `forward` process had to be extended with the addition of each subsequent behaviour since implemented the subsumption links from the other behaviours in this process.

It should be noted that this set of behaviours is not the only decomposition possible for this task. Also, the relationship between the `phototaxis` and `wall-following` behaviours could be reversed, so that, in the EAS program, phototaxis comes before wall-following, or, in the SA program, `phototaxis` subsumes `wall-following`.

3.5 Experimental Environments

Our objective was to identify important implementation differences between these two programs under the condition that they produce nominally the same behaviour in the same robot interacting with the same environment. As we have seen above, there are some necessary differences between these programs, but before assessing these differences, and the processes of building, testing, and debugging them we first had to establish that they *do* produce the same behaviour in the same robot-environment interaction system. It does not necessarily follow that they do just because this is what we intended!

Behaviour, in robots and animals, is notoriously

difficult to define in the sense of specifying the necessary and sufficient conditions for uniquely identifying it. Phototaxis, for example comes in many different forms and varieties. What is phototaxis in one robot or animal might look and be quite different from what is phototaxis in another robot or animal. We can call both phototaxis because both types of behaviour are well characterised by, but not uniquely defined by, a tendency to move in the direction of the brightest local light level. The operationalisation of a measure of some aspect of the behaviour cannot therefore (usually) be based upon a definition of it. We cannot, for example, operationalise a measure of *sameness*, that we need here, using some definition of the phototaxis behaviour we set out to realise. We therefore use an empirical test of sameness based upon a set of four experimental test environments which are, collectively, intended to be representative of the kinds of environments in which our robot is supposed to be able to do phototaxis, see figure 3. Each test environment, or MAZE as we called them, contains an arrangement of objects (formed from house bricks covered in mat paper) that form walls of different geometries, and one light source, a 15W fluorescent light bulb. Each environment is designed to present a different type of phototaxis problem to the robot.

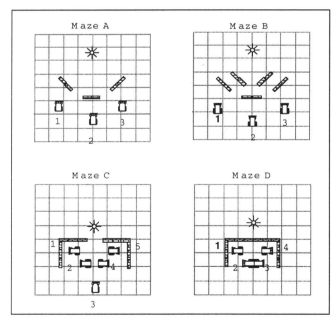

Figure 3: The four different MAZE environments used in the experiment, showing the position of the light source in each case, together with the positons and formations of the obstacles, and the 3, 4, or 5 initial positions and orientations of the robot at the start of each run.

3.6 Experimental Procedure

The two programs were first implemented, tested, and debugged separately and independently, with the EAS program being built first. The program testing was done by putting the robot on the floor of the laboratory in reduced ambient light conditions (i.e., the window shutters down). The robot was allowed to go anywhere in the lab. and to interact with anything it came across, including some of the house bricks used to form the experimental environments. When the phototaxis behaviour was being tested, alone, or in combination with other behaviours, a single stationary light was used. (Some testing was also done with two light sources and with light sources moved by hand.) When both programs were judged to be working correctly (i.e., as specified) and effectively producing what appeared to be the same form of phototaxis behaviour, their behaviour was explicitly tested using the four experimental environments.

For each test environment we specified a number of different starting positions and orientations for the robot, 3, 4, or 5, see figure 3. The robot was also equipped with a marker pen so that it traced out a visible path on the floor as it moved. We then made several runs from each starting position in each test environment (typically 5), alternating the two programs each time. For each run we recorded the time taken for the robot to reach the light source and stop, and made a copy (by hand) of the path traced out by the robot. If the robot failed to reach and stop at the light in 120 seconds, the run was declared a failure. This happened three times in the experiment reported here. The threshold of 120 seconds was an arbitrary value chosen to be much more than a successful run could take. There were two types of failure mode: 1) the robot continued doing wall-following indefinitely—it did not detect enough light to to stop doing wall-following, and 2) when the robot attempted to go straight towards the light but encountered an obstacle with its face perpendicular to its line of motion. In this situation it is possible for the front bumper not to be activated, so the robot does not detect the contact, but nor can it move.

4 Experimental Results and Analysis

A review of the recorded paths for each trial (not presented here) showed a lot of detailed variation between trials for the same starting position and orientation, test environment, and robot program. These variations are reflected in the paths followed and also in the time taken to reach the light, which are presented in figure 4. Even small changes in the initial conditions or environment can greatly affect the subsequent behaviour of the robot. The next step was to compare the collected data to see if, despite all these variations, we could

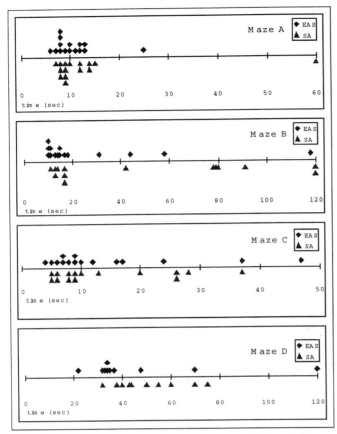

Figure 4: The run time data for the EAS and SA prgrams obtained for each maze type. The run times for the EAS program are presented *above* the time line in the graphs, and the run times for the SA program are presented *below* the time line, in each case.

establish that there was *no* significant difference between the behaviour generated by the two different programs.

First we observed (from the recorded paths) that there was a difference between the trajectories typically produced by the robot when executing each of the two programs. In section 3.3 we described the wall-following movement as consisting of two phases: move backward in a tight arc and then move forward in a more gentle arc. In spite of the two programs having the same values for the backward-time and forward-time constants, and the same motor settings, these steps took longer to execute in the EAS program. As a result, the robot moved further during the backwards phase. The distance to the wall was thus usually larger on starting the forward movement. As a result, the robot tended to advance further along a wall (an obstacle) with the EAS program than with the SA program. The reason for the execution taking longer in the EAS program was because this program has five processes to time-slice over, whereas the SA program has four, and the extra activity

selection process in the EAS program has a relatively long execution cycle. The dynamics of execution of the two programs is thus importantly different, see figure 5.

This difference of detail in wall-following behaviour was reflected in the time needed to reach the light when there was not a straight path to the light, so that the robot had to do some wall-following to get around the obstacle or obstacles. In runs involving small amounts of wall-following there tended to be little difference between the times generated by the two programs, but in runs which involved a lot of wall-following the SA program tended to generate longer run times than the EAS program. This effect can be seen in figure 4, and is most pronounced in the times for **Maze B** and **D**.

Given the variation and this difference in the actual behaviour generated by the two programs, we decided to compare the data from each maze, rather than consider the data for all the mazes as one sample. To do this requires a statistical test, and in this case we chose the Mann-Whitney test, as presented in [Conover, 80], which is a test to see if two random samples can be considered to be taken from the same distribution, in other words, that the two samples have identical distributions. This is a non-parametric version of Student's T-test, [Canavos, 88], and is essentially the same as Wilcoxon's rank sum test and Kendall's S-test, [Bailey, 1981]. Its applicaton depends upon four assumptions: (1) that both samles are random samples from their respective populations, in other words, that the run times for the trials using each program in a given maze are ramdomly selected from the population of possible run times for each program and maze; (2) that the run times are independent both within each sample and between the two samples; (3) that the measurement scale is at least ordinal, which it clearly is, in this case; and (4) that if there is a difference between the population distribution functions, that difference is a difference of location of the distribution, an offset. This last assumption thus requires us to presume that the difference in run times caused by the different wall-following behaviour has the effect of shifting the position of the sample distribution, of one program against the other, but does not otherwise change it.

The procedure for applying this test to two random samples, is as follows. Let $X_1, X_2, X_3, ..., X_n$ denote the random sample of size n from population 1, and let $Y_1, Y_2, Y_3, ..., Y_m$ denote the random sample of size m from population 2. Assign ranks 1 to $n + m$ to the combined samples, where $R(X_i)$ and $R(Y_j)$ denote the rank assigned to X_i and Y_j for all i and j, and let $N = n + m$, for convenience. If several sample values are equale to each other (*tied* in the ranking), assign to each the average of the ranks that would have been assigned to them had there been no ties.

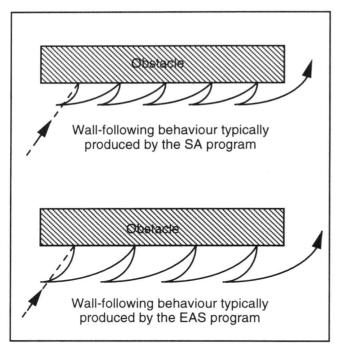

Figure 5: The difference in the wall-following behaviour typically generated by the two programs for the same obstacle.

If there are no ties in the ranking, or just a few, the sum, T, of the ranks assigned to population 1 can be used as a test statistic.

(1)
$$T = \sum_{i=1}^{n} R(X_i)$$

If there are many ties, subtract the mean from T and divide by the standard deviation to get:

(2)
$$T_1 = \frac{T - n \times \frac{N+1}{2}}{\sqrt{\frac{n \times m}{N \times (N-1)} \times \sum_{i=1}^{n} R_i^2 - \frac{n \times m \times (N+1)^2}{4 \times (N-1)}}}$$

where $\sum R_i^2$ refers to the sum of the squares of all N of the ranks or average ranks actually used in both samples.

The hypotheses to be tested in this case are:

$$H_0: P(X < Y) = \tfrac{1}{2},$$
$$H_1: P(X < Y) \neq \tfrac{1}{2},$$

which define a Two-Tailed test.

Given that there are a large number of ties in the ranking of the data in all four cases, we use the value of T_1 as the test statistic. The values for n, m, T, and T_1 obtained from the data for each maze is presented

in table 1, where population 1 is the EAS data and population 2 is the SA data.

Maze	n	m	T	T_1
A	15	15	229.5	-0.126
B	15	15	190.5	-1.886
C	15	15	229.0	-0.147
D	10	10	84.0	-1.589

Table 1: The values of n, m, T, and T_1 for each maze, **A**, **B**, **C**, and **D** calculated using equations (1) and (2) above.

From normal distribution tables we see that a critical region of 0.05 correspondes to values of T_1 greater than -1.645 and less than 1.645, and we see from table 1 that hypothesis H_0 is confirmed for the mazes **A**, **C**, and **D**, and *not* confirmed in the case of maze **B**. In other words, we can say that with 95% confidence that the behaviour generated by the two different programs is the same for the mazes **A**, **C**, and **D**, and is *not* the same in the case of maze **B**. That the behaviour for maze **B** is not the same is perhaps not surprising given the run time data presented in figure 4. Here we see that the run times for the SA programs are more spread out towards longer times than the run times for the EAS program.

5 Discussion and Conclusions

The results of the statistical analysis presented in the previous section allow us to conclude that the behaviour produced by the two programs is essentially the same in three of the four test environments. The difference in the case of maze **B**, it would seem, is due to the effect of the different wall-following behaviour produced by the two programs. We could test this hypothesis by attempting to change the time constants used in one or other of the programs so that both programs tend to produced wall-following behaviour that is much more similar. This would not be difficult to do, and is thus an obvious direction for future work in this investigation.

To try to understand this difference in the wall-following behaviour we can consider the organisation of the processes which implement this behaviour. In the SA program, all processes take similar time to compute one cycle. Things are, however, different in the EAS program, where the activity selection process is responsible for all sensor readings and the updating of the global variables used in the program to communicate the current sensor values to the other Behaviour processes. Having this extra activity selection process in the time-slicing cycle means that the interval of time between the time checks made by the wall-following Behaviour, to see if the reverse time or forward time has been completed, is larger than in the SA program. As a result it can often be the case that these time periods are exceeded, thus giving rise to longer reverse and forward arc motions. Any change made to the activity selection process, due to the addition of another behaviour, for example, will further influence this aspect of the programs execution dynamics. A consequence of this is that modifications may need to be made to the Wall-following Behaviour each time the activity selection process is changed for any reason, if the same wall-following behaviour is to be maintained. So, in this case, we have a strong implicit dependency between different parts of the program.

This is not the only weakness of the EAS program, as far as its development, debugging, and extension, is concerned. The need to centralise all sensor readings, and the use of global variables to communicate these to the other Behaviour processes, also results in distributed code dependeces in the EAS program. These tended to dilute the clarity of the Behavioural decomposition adopted, and which remains much more clear in the SA program. In other words, in the SA program there is an evident greater and more secure degree of encapsulation of the code, associated with the generation of each Behaviour, in the respective processes.

From this relatively simple and limited attempt to compare implementations of these two activity selection schemes, we conclude: (1) that the implementation of the Subsumption Architecture scheme better preserves the logic of the its activity selection mechanism in a natural way, and results in an easier program to test and debug, and incrementally develop; and (2) that the explicit activity selection scheme result in an implementation having higher communication loads, between processes, distributed dependencies, and thus less well encapsulated code. There is, however, an evident need to futher test these aspects, both using different robots and programming languages and real-time execution systems, and with different types of explicit activity selection schemes. There is thus still much to do to pursue this comparative investigation until we reach some reasonably conclusive results. It is however a start.

6 Acknowledgments

We thank Yosu Yurramendi for help in applying the statistical test to our data, Leslie Kaelbling for help in devising and designing the experiment, and Fred Martin for help and advice on the 6.270 system and Interactive C. Partial financial support was provided by the project **UPV 003.230-HA203/95**, funded by the University of the Basque Country, and a NATO Collaborative Research Grant, with Leslie Kaelbling, at Brown University, grant number **CRG 920807**. We also thank two anonymous referees for useful comments on the submitted version of this paper.

References

[Anderson & Donath, 91] Anderson, T. and Donath, M., 1991: Animal behaviour as a paradigm for developing robot autonomy, in, Maes, P. (Ed.), *Designing Autonomous Agents*, Cambridge, M.A.: MIT Press, pp. 145–168.

[Arbib, 92] Arbib, M. A., 1992: Schema theory, in Shapiro, S (Ed.), *The encyclopedia of artificial intelligence* (2nd. edn.), New York: Wiley Interscience.

[Arbib & Cobas, 92] Arbib, M. A. and Cobas, A., 1992: Schemas for prey-catching in frog and toad, in [Meyer & Wilson, 1992], pp. 142–151.

[Arbib & Lee, 93] Arbib, M. A. and Lee, H. B., 1993: Anuran visuomotor coordination for detour behaviour: from retina to motor schemas, in [Meyer, *et al.*, 1993], pp. 42–51.

[Arkin, 89] Arkin, R.C., 1989: Motor schema-based mobile robot navigation, *Int. J. Robotics Research*, **8**(4), pp. 92-112.

[Arkin, 92] Arkin, R.C., 1992: Behaviour-based robot navigation for extended domains, *Adaptive Behavior*, **1**(2), pp. 201–225.

[Bailey, 1981] Bailey, N. T. J., 1981: *Statistical methods in biology*, Second Edition, Edward Arnold.

[Braitenberg, 84] Braitenberg, V., 1984: *Vehicles, experiments in synthetic psychology*, Cambridge, M.A.: MIT Press.

[Brooks, 86] Brooks, R. A., 1986: A robust layered control system for a mobile robot, *IEEE J. Robotics and Automation*, **2**(1), pp. 14–23.

[Brooks, 95] Brooks, R. A., 1995: Intelligence without reason, in Steels, L. and Brooks, R. A. (Eds.), The artificial life route to artificial intelligence, New Jersey: Lawerence Erlbaum, pp. 25–81.

[Canavos, 88] Canavos G. C., 1988: *Probabilidad y estadística*, Madrid: McGraw Hill.

[Cliff, *et al.*, 94] Cliff, D, Husbands, P., Meyer, J.-A., and Wilson S. W. (Eds.), 1994: *From animals to animats 3*, Cambridge, M.A.: MIT Press.

[Connell, 90] Connell, J. H., 1990: *Minimalist mobile robotics*, San Diego, C.A.: Academic Press.

[Conover, 80] Conover, W. J., 1980: *Practical nonparametric statistics, 2nd edition.*, John Wiley and Sons.

[Hallam, *et al.*, 94] Hallam, B. E., Halperin, J. R. P., and Hallam, J. C. T., 1994: An ethological model for implementation in mobile robots, *Adaptive Behavior*, **3**(1), pp. 51–79.

[Halperin & Dunham, 92] Halperin, J. R. P. and Dunham, D. W., 1992: Postponed conditioning: testing a hypothesis about synaptic strengthening, *Adaptive Behavior*, **1**(1), pp. 39–64.

[Liaw & Arbib, 93] Liaw, J.-S., and Arbib, M. A., 1993: Neural mechanisms underlying direction-selective avoidance behavior, *Adaptive Behavior*, **1**(3), pp. 227–262.

[Lyons, 86] Lyons, D. M., 1986: *RS:A formal model of distributed computation for sensory-based robot control*, PhD. Thesis, Department of Computer and Information Sciences, University of Massachusetts.

[Lyons & Hendriks, 95] Lyons, D. M. and Hendriks, A. J., 1995: Planning as incremental adaptation of a reactive system, *Robotics ad Autonomous Systems*, **14**(4), pp 255–288.

[Maes, 89] Maes, P., 1989: The dynamics of action selection, *Proc. IJCAI-89 Conf.*, Detroit.

[Maes, 92] Maes, P, 1992: A bottom-up mechanism for behavior selection in an artificial creature, **in** [Meyer & Wilson, 1992], pp. 238–246.

[Martin, 92]

Martin, F., 1992: The 6.270 robot builder's guide for the 1992 MIT LEGO robot design competition, available from ftp://cherupakha.media.mit.edu/pub/projects/6270, and ftp://cherupakha.media.mit.edu/pub/projects/interactive-c.

[Meyer & Wilson, 92] Meyer, J.-A., and Wilson S. W. (Eds.), 1992: *From animals to animats*, Cambridge, M.A.: MIT Press.

[Meyer, *et al.*, 93] Meyer, J.-A., Roitblat, H. L., and Wilson S. W. (Eds.), 1993: *From animals to animats 2*, Cambridge, M.A.: MIT Press.

[Nehmzow, *et al.*, 89] Nehmzow, U., Hallam, J., and Smithers T., 1989: Really useful robots, **in** Kanade, T., Groen, F. C. A., and Hertzberger, O. L., (Eds.), *Intelligent Autonomous Systems*, Proc. of IAS Conf., Amsterdam.

[Nemzow & Smithers, 92] Nehmzow, U. and Smithers, T., 1992: Learning multiple competences: some initial experimental results, *Neural Networks and a New AI*, ECAI Workshop Notes, Vienna, 1992.

[Nehmzow *et al.*, 93] Nehmzow, U., Smithers, T., and McGonigle, B., 1993: Increasing behavioural repertoire in a mobile robot, **in** [Meyer, *et al.*, 1993], pp. 291–297.

[Payton, 86] Payton, D., 1986: An architecture for reflexive autonomous vehicle control, *Proc. IEEE Conf. Robotics and Automation*, 1986, pp. 1838.

[Pebody, 91] Pebody, M., 1991: *How to make a lego vehicle do the right thing*, M.Sc. Thesis, Department of Artificial Intelligence, University of Edinburgh.

[Rosenblatt & Payton, 89] Rosenblatt. K. J. and Payton, D. W., 1989: A fine-grained alternative to the subsumption architecture for mobile robot control, *Proc. IEEE/INNS Int. joint Conf on Neural Networks*, Washington, DC.

[Sahota, 94] Sahota, M. K., 1994: Action selection for robots in dynamic environments through inter-behaviour bidding, **in** [Cliff, *et al.*, 1994], pp. 138–142.

[Snaith & Holland, 92] Snaith, M. and Holland, O., 1992: An investigation of two mediation strategies suitable for behaviour control in animals and animats, **in** [Meyer & Wilson, 1992], pp. 255–262.

[Tyrrell, 93] Tyrrell, T., 1993: The use of hierarchies for action selection, *Adaptive Behavior*, **1**(3), pp. 387–420.

EVOLUTIONARY ROBOTICS, EVOLVABLE HARDWARE AND APPLICATIONS

Half-baked, Ad-hoc and Noisy:
Minimal Simulations for Evolutionary Robotics

Nick Jakobi

School of Cognitive and Computing Sciences
University of Sussex, Brighton BN1 9QH, England
email: nickja@cogs.susx.ac.uk
tel: (UK) 01273 678061
fax: (UK) 01273 671320

Abstract

This paper puts forward a theoretical framework and formal language for understanding how simple, fast simulations can be used to artificially evolve controllers for real robots. It begins by putting forward a general set of equations that describe the way in which an agent-environment system changes over time, and analyses what it means for an agent to exhibit a particular behaviour within such a system. A minimally sufficient set of conditions are then formally established under which a controller that reliably displays a particular behaviour in simulation will continue to display the same behaviour when transplanted into reality. From this, techniques are derived for ensuring that controllers which evolve to be reliably fit within a simulation will transfer into the real world, and two sets of experiments are briefly described in which controllers that evolved in extremely minimal simulations were able to perform non-trivial and robust behaviours when downloaded onto real robots.

1 Introduction

Several experimenters including [6, 9, 2, 10] have shown that it *is* possible to evolve control architectures in simulation for a real robot. Now this is no longer in doubt the question becomes one of whether the technique will scale up. As Mataric and Cliff point out in [8], if robot controllers evolved in simulation can only be guaranteed to work in reality when a carefully constructed empirically validated simulation is used, then as robots and the behaviours we want to evolve for them become more and more complex, so will the simulations. The worry is that the necessary simulations will be either so computationally expensive that all speed advantages over real-world evolution will be lost, or so hard to design that the time taken in development will outweigh the time saved in evolution. Clearly the main challenge for the simu-

lation approach to evolutionary robotics is to establish that it is possible to evolve control architectures for real robots using simulations that are much simpler than the carefully constructed empirically validated models of the world that Mataric and Cliff talk about.

This paper sets out to meet this challenge. However, it provides much more than just a few examples of controllers that have evolved in simple simulations transferring into reality. It introduces a formalism for reasoning about agents performing behaviours in environments, and *derives* a minimal set of conditions for successful behavioural transference. This provides a sound theoretical basis for a practical simulation-building methodology. As we shall see, it *is* possible to construct minimal simulations for the evolution of complex behaviours on complex robots that run fast and are easy to build.

In Section 2 the formalism is introduced that describes the way in which the coupled dynamical system that is an agent and its environment changes over time, and in Section 3 we put forward a formal notation for the behaviour of an agent in such a system. Section 4 is the backbone of the paper in which a minimal set of conditions for behavioural transference are formally derived. These conditions are listed in section 5, and in section 6 we show how they can be practically applied and used to build minimal simulations for evolutionary robotics. Section 7 outlines two sets of experiments involving a minimal simulation of a Khepera robot and a minimal simulation of the Sussex University gantry robot. Finally section 8 offers some conclusions.

2 State-space equations for a general agent-environment system

Various researchers have discussed the interactions between an agent and its environment in terms of coupled dynamical systems [11, 1]. This section introduces a formalism that can be used to describe these interactions, and puts forward general equations for the way in which an agent-environment system changes over time. Before we do this, however, some basic notation for a generic dynamical system is introduced so that we all know what we're talking about.

Let G be a generic dynamical system. The state of G at time t will be referred to as the state vector g_t. The set of possible initial states g_0 that G can start from at time $t = 0$ will be referred to as G_{init}. The possibly non-deterministic function which describes the way in which the value of g_{t+1} depends on g_t and any external inputs or controls i_t will be referred to as G_{diff}. Thus the behaviour of the dynamical system G from time $t = 0$ is completely captured by the equations

$$g_0 \in G_{init} \quad \text{and} \quad g_{t+1} = G_{diff}(g_t, i_t) \qquad (1)$$

The distinction between agent and environment in an agent-environment system is a hard one to define and can be done in a number of ways. For the purposes of this paper, when the agents we are talking about are robots (simulated or real), we draw the line around the agent's controller. This should be kept in mind as the formalism is put forward below. The software or hardware that receives input signals (in the form of an input vector) from the sensors and sends output signals (in the form of an output vector) to the motors is treated as the agent, and everything else including the actual sensors, motors and the agent's embodied form is treated as the environment. When defined thus, both agent and environment constitute separate dynamic systems, each with their own state, that are linked through the agent's input and output vectors. A way in which this can be captured mathematically is put forward below.

The agent's controller

The agent's controller constitutes a dynamical system in its own right whose trajectory through state space can be perturbed by the environment by way of the controller's sensor input signals i_t. If we call this dynamical system C, then c_t is the state vector of the controller at time t, C_{init} is the set of possible initial states c_0 and C_{diff} is the function that describes the way in which c_{t+1} depends on c_t and i_t. Thus the equations

$$c_0 \in C_{init} \quad \text{and} \quad c_{t+1} = C_{diff}(c_t, i_t) \qquad (2)$$

completely describe how the controller's state changes over time in response to input signals.

The agent's environment

The agent's environment is also regarded as a dynamical system in its own right whose trajectory through state space can be perturbed by the output signals of the controller o_t. If we call this dynamical system E, then e_t is the state vector of the environment at time t, E_{init} is the set of possible initial states e_0 and E_{diff} is the function

that describes the way in which e_{t+1} depends on e_t and o_t. Thus the equations

$$e_0 \in E_{init} \quad \text{and} \quad e_{t+1} = E_{diff}(e_t, o_t) \qquad (3)$$

completely describe how the environment's state changes over time in response to the controller's output signals.

Agent-environment interaction equations

In order to completely describe the way in which a particular agent-environment system changes over time, we need to introduce two new functions that describe the way in which the input signals i_t to the controller C are a function of the state of the environment E at time t, and the way in which the output signals o_t to the environment E are a function of the state of the controller C at time t. We will call these functions E_{out} and C_{out} respectively. These functions effectively couple the dynamical system E to the dynamical system C resulting in a coupled agent-environment dynamical system. Such a system shall be referred to throughout the rest of the paper using the notation E $\rightleftarrows$ C. Thus,

The equations that completely describe how the dynamical system E $\rightleftarrows$ C changes over time are

$$
\begin{aligned}
e_0 &\in E_{init} & c_0 &\in C_{init} \\
i_t &= E_{out}(e_t) & o_t &= C_{out}(c_t) \\
e_{t+1} &= E_{diff}(e_t, o_t) & c_{t+1} &= C_{diff}(c_t, i_t)
\end{aligned} \qquad (4)
$$

Substituting the second line into the third line we define a trajectory T_{EC} of E $\rightleftarrows$ C to be a sequence of pairs of states $< e_i, c_i >$ such that

$$
\begin{aligned}
e_0 &\in E_{init} \quad c_0 \in C_{init} \\
e_{t+1} &= E_{diff}(e_t, C_{out}(c_t)) \\
c_{t+1} &= C_{diff}(c_t, E_{out}(e_t))
\end{aligned} \qquad (5)
$$

In the next sections we will look at what it means for an agent to display a particular behaviour within such a system, and go on to ask what the conditions are under which an agent that displays a behaviour in one system will continue to display it in another.

3 What does it mean for an agent to perform a particular behaviour within an agent-environment system

In most cases, whether or not we say an agent displays a particular behaviour is a function of how the agent *acts* within its environment . Thus, although the current state of the agent's controller and its sensor inputs are, in general, central to the generation and maintenance of a particular behaviour, it is the controller's output and the effects this has on the state of the environment that determines whether or not the agent is actually performing the behaviour at any given time. To illustrate this, consider the behaviour that consists of driving a car down a road. If someone sits in a car and steers it down the road with a blindfold on, then we will still say they are driving the car (blindfolded) down the road. However, if someone receives visual input as if they were driving the car, but they are not in the driver's seat and are not touching the steering wheel, then we will say they are not driving the car down the road. In general, whether or not an agent performs a particular behaviour within a particular agent-environment system depends on the state of the environment rather than the state of the controller.

The way in which the state of the environment changes over time is obviously a function of the controller's motor output, but it is also a function of the environment itself and the ways in which the agent may interact with it. For instance, if a person makes breast-stroke motions with their arms and kicks their legs, then they are producing the correct motor output for swimming. However, it is not until they are immersed in water or something equivalent that they actually *are* swimming[1]. As another example, consider corridor-following behaviour in a small mobile robot. It does not matter what motor output the controller generates: unless the environment includes something that behaves like a corridor, it cannot display the behaviour. The same goes for driving a car down a road (blind-folded or otherwise): without something equivalent to a car or a road, the behaviour is simply not possible.

Every behaviour necessitates a particular base set of environmental features that the agent must be able to interact with in certain ways defined by that behaviour. Unless such features exist, we can never come onto the question of whether the agent is producing appropriate motor output to actually perform that behaviour. In the swimming example, there must be a base set of features that the agent can interact with *as if it were* immersed in a liquid. In the corridor example, there must be a base set of features that the agent can interact with *as if it were* moving about in a corridor, and in the driving example there must be a base set of features that the agent can interact with *as if it were* driving a car down a road. The point is that whether or not the agent *actually is* immersed in a liquid, or moving about in a corridor, or driving a car down a road is immaterial. To decide whether or not the environment is capable of supporting the particular behaviour, we just need to know that it contains a base set of features that the agent can interact with *as if it were*.

The obvious way of describing how an agent interacts with a base set of environmental features to produce future states of that base set is as a dynamical system of the same form as in (1). In fact, we can say that each behaviour defines a whole class of potential dynamical systems that are each minimally sufficient to support that

behaviour. In order to be sufficient in turn, the environment must contain some base set of features that change over time and respond to output signals in the same way as at least one of these behaviour defined dynamical systems. Such a behaviour defined class might include all the dynamic systems that behave like agents in liquids, or all the dynamic systems that behave like agents in corridors, or all the dynamic systems that behave like agents driving cars. To put this more formally,

Let R_e be a reduction operator over state vector $\mathbf{e_t}$ of dynamical system E such that the vector $R_e(\mathbf{e_t})$ consists of an ordered subset of the variables that make up $\mathbf{e_t}$. Let β_{env} be the class of minimally specified dynamical systems B that are each sufficient to support behaviour β. Environment E can support behaviour β if and only if

$$\exists R_e \quad \text{and} \quad \exists B \in \beta_{\mathbf{env}} \quad \text{s.t.}$$
$$\begin{aligned}
&1. \quad \forall \mathbf{e_0} \in E_{init} \quad R_e(\mathbf{e_0}) \in B_{init} \\
&2. \quad R_e(\mathbf{e_t}) = \mathbf{b_t} \quad \Rightarrow \\
&\qquad R_e(E_{diff}(\mathbf{e_t}, \mathbf{o_t})) \sim B_{diff}(\mathbf{b_t}, \mathbf{o_t})
\end{aligned} \tag{6}$$

where the symbol $\sim$ is defined to mean 'can equal', or 'has the same extension as'; the point being that both E and B may be non-deterministic, in which case $\sim$ means that the set of possible values of $\mathbf{b_{t+1}}$ is the same as the set of possible values of $R_e(\mathbf{e_{t+1}})$.

If we *can* find a suitable R_e such that (6) is satisfied, then whether or not the agent actually *does* perform the behaviour within a given time interval is a function of how the variables that R_e picks out change over time. In other words, if $T_{EC} = < \mathbf{e_0}, \mathbf{c_0} >, < \mathbf{e_1}, \mathbf{c_1} > \ldots < \mathbf{e_\tau}, \mathbf{c_\tau} >$ is a trajectory of the system $E \rightleftarrows C$, then whether this trajectory constitutes an instance of behaviour β or not will be a behaviour defined function of the sequence $R_e(\mathbf{e_0}), R_e(\mathbf{e_1}) \ldots, R_e(\mathbf{e_\tau})$ obtained by applying R_e to every $\mathbf{e_t}$ in T_{EC} in turn. We will slightly bend the notation to refer to a sequence of $R_e(\mathbf{e_t})$ obtained in this manner as the projection $R_e(T_{EC})$. We define the behaviour-defined function β_{act}, which returns true or false, to be such that for any particular trajectory T_{EC},

$$\beta_{act}(R_e(T_{EC})) \quad \Leftrightarrow \quad \text{the agent exhibits behaviour } \beta$$

Recapping, we now state the conditions under which an agent can be said to *reliably* perform a particular behaviour β within a particular agent-environment system $E \rightleftarrows C$.

An agent is said to *reliably* perform the behaviour β in $E \rightleftarrows C$ if and only if

$$\exists R_e \quad \text{s.t.}$$

$$\begin{aligned}
&1. \quad \exists B \in \beta_{\mathbf{env}} \quad s.t. \\
&\quad (a) \quad \forall \mathbf{e_0} \in E_{init} \quad R_e(\mathbf{e_0}) \in B_{init} \\
&\quad (b) \quad R_e(\mathbf{e_t}) = \mathbf{b_t} \quad \Rightarrow \\
&\qquad\qquad R_e(E_{diff}(\mathbf{e_t}, \mathbf{o_t})) \sim B_{diff}(\mathbf{b_t}, \mathbf{o_t})
\end{aligned} \tag{7}$$

$$2. \quad \forall T_{EC} \quad \beta_{act}(R_e(T_{EC}))$$

---

[1] Thanks to Joe Faith for this example.

4 What are the conditions under which an agent's behaviour in simulation implies its reliable behaviour in reality?

In this section we formally derive a minimal set of conditions that must be true of a controller and a simulation if the controller's reliable behaviour in simulation is to guarantee its reliable behaviour in reality. The derivation precedes in three stages: from a completely hypothetical and idealized simulation to one that is realizable. This section is the most mathematical of the paper, and as such makes very little reference to real-world examples. In section 6 ways of turning theory into practice are discussed.

In the first stage of the derivation we consider a real world agent-environment system $E \rightleftarrows C$ and a simulation that consists of a single agent-environment system $S \rightleftarrows C$. We show that if S is identical to E, then any behaviour β that the controller reliably performs in simulation, it will also reliably perform in reality.

In the second stage of the derivation we again consider a real world agent-environment system $E \rightleftarrows C$ and a simulation that consists of a single agent-environment system $S \rightleftarrows C$. In this scenario, however, all that E and S have in common is that they both support the same behaviour β, and in so doing, both 'track' the same dynamical system $B \in \beta_{\text{env}}$. We derive conditions on the simulation and controller under which the fact that the controller reliably performs β in simulation implies that it will reliably perform it in reality.

In the third stage we again consider a real world agent-environment system $E \rightleftarrows C$, but our simulation consists of a whole set of different agent-environment systems $\{S^i \rightleftarrows C\}$. In this scenario, all S^i support behaviour β but only one $S^j \in \{S^i\}$ tracks the *same* dynamical system $B \in \beta_{\text{env}}$ as E. We extend the conditions derived in the previous stage under which the fact that the controller reliably performs β in simulation implies that it will reliably perform it in reality.

4.1   S = E

In this subsection we look at a hypothetical simulation consisting of a single agent-environment system $S \rightleftarrows C$ that is identical to a real-world agent-environment interaction system $E \rightleftarrows C$ and show that any behaviour that the agent reliably performs in $S \rightleftarrows C$ it will also reliably perform in $E \rightleftarrows C$.

From Section 2, we can write agent-environment interaction equations for two systems, $E \rightleftarrows C$ and $S \rightleftarrows C$. Note however that the controller dynamical systems C are the same for both systems, so to avoid confusion the symbols for the state of each controller c_t include superscript symbols corresponding to the names of their environment dynamical systems.

$$
\begin{aligned}
\mathbf{e_0} &\in E_{init} \quad \mathbf{c_0^E} \in C_{init} \\
\mathbf{e_{t+1}} &= E_{diff}(\mathbf{e_t}, C_{out}(\mathbf{c_t^E})) \\
\mathbf{c_{t+1}^E} &= C_{diff}(\mathbf{c_t^E}, E_{out}(\mathbf{e_t}))
\end{aligned}
\tag{8}
$$

and

$$
\begin{aligned}
\mathbf{s_0} &\in S_{init} \quad \mathbf{c_0^S} \in C_{init} \\
\mathbf{s_{t+1}} &= S_{diff}(\mathbf{s_t}, C_{out}(\mathbf{c_t^S})) \\
\mathbf{c_{t+1}^S} &= C_{diff}(\mathbf{c_t^S}, S_{out}(\mathbf{s_t}))
\end{aligned}
\tag{9}
$$

Now if S = E then it is evident that every trajectory T_{EC} of $E \rightleftarrows C$ is a *possible* trajectory T_{SC} of $S \rightleftarrows C$. So if something is true of all *possible* trajectories T_{SC} of $S \rightleftarrows C$, it is also true of all possible trajectories T_{EC} of $E \rightleftarrows C$. Therefore

$$
\beta_{act}(R(T_{SC})) \ \forall R(T_{SC}) \ \Rightarrow \ \beta_{act}(R(T_{EC})) \ \forall R(T_{EC})
$$

4.2   S and E track the same $B \in \beta_e nv$

In this scenario, our simulation again consists of a single agent-environment system $S \rightleftarrows C$ and a real-world agent-environment interaction system $E \rightleftarrows C$. All that S and E have in common, however, is that we can define reduction operators R_s and R_e for both systems such that for some dynamical system $B \in \beta_{env}$,

$$
\begin{aligned}
&1. \quad \forall \mathbf{e_0} \in E_{init} \quad R_e(\mathbf{e_0}) \in B_{init} \\
&2. \quad R_e(\mathbf{e_t}) = \mathbf{b_t} \quad \Rightarrow \\
&\qquad R_e(E_{diff}(\mathbf{e_t}, \mathbf{o_t})) \sim B_{diff}(\mathbf{b_t}, \mathbf{o_t})
\end{aligned}
\tag{10}
$$

and

$$
\begin{aligned}
&1. \quad \forall \mathbf{s_0} \in S_{init} \quad R_s(\mathbf{s_0}) \in B_{init} \\
&2. \quad R_s(\mathbf{s_t}) = \mathbf{b_t} \quad \Rightarrow \\
&\qquad R_s(S_{diff}(\mathbf{s_t}, \mathbf{o_t})) \sim B_{diff}(\mathbf{b_t}, \mathbf{o_t})
\end{aligned}
\tag{11}
$$

This is a much looser constraint on the two agent-environment system than identity. In particular it means that the simulation does not need to model the whole of E, which is the entire universe when taken to its logical conclusion, but only the behaviourally relevant features. We shall now derive two conditions on the simulation and controller that must be fulfilled if the fact that the agent reliably performs β in simulation is to imply that it reliably performs β in reality.

Applying the relevant reduction operators to (8) and (9) we get

$$
\begin{aligned}
\mathbf{e_0} &\in E_{init} \quad \mathbf{c_0^E} \in C_{init} \\
R_e(\mathbf{e_{t+1}}) &= R_e(E_{diff}(\mathbf{e_t}, C_{out}(\mathbf{c_t^E}))) \\
\mathbf{c_{t+1}^E} &= C_{diff}(\mathbf{c_t^E}, E_{out}(\mathbf{e_t}))
\end{aligned}
$$

and

$$
\begin{aligned}
\mathbf{s_0} &\in S_{init} \quad \mathbf{c_0^S} \in C_{init} \\
R_s(\mathbf{s_{t+1}}) &= R_s(S_{diff}(\mathbf{s_t}, C_{out}(\mathbf{c_t^S}))) \\
\mathbf{c_{t+1}^S} &= C_{diff}(\mathbf{c_t^S}, S_{out}(\mathbf{s_t}))
\end{aligned}
$$

And we can deduce from (10) and (11) that

$$R_e(e_t) = R_s(s_t)$$
$$\Rightarrow$$
$$R_e(E_{diff}(e_t, o_t)) \sim$$
$$R_s(S_{diff}(s_t, o_t)) \qquad \forall o_t$$

therefore if we introduce the condition on C and S_{out} that

$$R_e(e_t) = R_s(s_t)$$
$$\Rightarrow$$
$$C_{diff}(c_t, E_{out}(e_t)) \sim \qquad (12)$$
$$C_{diff}(c_t, S_{out}(s_t)) \qquad \forall c_t$$

then

$$R_e(e_t) = R_s(s_t) \text{ and } c_t^E = c_t^S$$
$$\Rightarrow$$
$$R_e(E_{diff}(e_t, C_{out}(c_t^E))) \sim$$
$$R_s(S_{diff}(s_t, C_{out}(c_t^S)))$$

$$C_{diff}(c_t^E, E_{out}(e_t)) \sim$$
$$C_{diff}(c_t^S, S_{out}(s_t))$$

which is the same as saying that

$$R_e(e_t) = R_s(s_t) \text{ and } c_t^E = c_t^S$$
$$\Rightarrow$$
$$R_e(e_{t+1}) \sim R_s(s_{t+1})$$
$$c_{t+1}^E \sim c_t^S$$

and if we introduce a further condition on S that

$$\forall e_0 \in E_{init} \quad \exists s_0 \in S_{init}$$
$$s.t. \quad R_e(e_0) = R_s(s_0) \qquad (13)$$

then we can say by induction that

$$\forall e_0 \in E_{init} \quad \exists s_0 \in S_{init}$$
$$s.t. \ R_e(e_0) = R_s(s_0)$$
$$\text{and}$$
$$R_e(e_t) \sim R_s(s_t) \quad \forall t$$

In words, this means that provided condition (12) and (13) are true then every projection $R(T_{EC})$ of E $\rightleftarrows$ C is a *possible* projection $R(T_{SC})$ of S $\rightleftarrows$ C. Therefore if $\beta_{act}(R(T_{SC}))$ for all possible $R(T_{SC})$ of S $\rightleftarrows$ C then $\beta_{act}(R(T_{EC}))$ for all possible $R(T_{EC})$ of E $\rightleftarrows$ C.

At first sight, condition (12) seems contrived and unlikely. However, it can be explained in words simply as the condition that all aspects of the input signals that can effect the controller's internal state must derive exclusively, and in the same way for both systems, from the base sets of environmental features that are picked out by R_e and R_s. We shall refer to controllers that fulfill this condition within an appropriate simulation as being *base set exclusive*.

Condition (13) is much easier to reach an intuitive understanding of: for every possible start state in reality, there must be a possible start state in simulation which is identical with respect to the base sets of environmental features that are picked out by R_e and R_s.

4.3 $S^j \in \{S^i\}$ *and* E *track the same* B $\in \beta_e nv$

In practice, a simulation rarely models even a small portion of the real world 100% accurately. The situation in which S and E track the same dynamical system is, therefore, for the most part hypothetical. However, even if it is impossible to specify exactly a single S that tracks the same dynamical system as the real world environment E, a simulation builder may be able to define *a set* of dynamical systems $\{S^i\}$ (possibly by specifying parameter ranges rather than values) that *contains* an $S^j \in \{S^i\}$ that tracks the same dynamical system as the real world environment E. If the controller then reliably performs behaviour β in *all* $S^j \rightleftarrows$ C, and condition (12) and (13) of section 4.2 are fulfilled, then the controller will reliably perform behaviour β in reality.

More formally,

If the set $\{S^i\}$ is such that

$$\exists S^j \in \{S^i\} \ s.t.$$

1. $R_e(e_t) = R_{sj}(s_t^j)$
$$\Rightarrow$$
$$R_e(E_{diff}(e_t, o_t)) \sim \qquad (14)$$
$$R_{sj}(S_{diff}^j(s_t^j, o_t)) \qquad \forall o_t$$

2. $\forall e_0 \in E_{init} \quad \exists s_0^j \in S_{init}^j$
$$s.t. \quad R_e(e_0) = R_{sj}(s_0^j)$$

and if the controller is base set exclusive for all $\{S^i\}$ such that

$$\forall S^j \in \{S^i\}$$
$$R_e(e_t) = R_{sj}(s_t^j)$$
$$\Rightarrow \qquad (15)$$
$$C_{diff}(c_t, E_{out}(e_t)) \sim$$
$$C_{diff}(c_t, S_{out}^j(s_t^j)) \qquad \forall c_t$$

then the proof of section 4.2 goes through: every projection $R(T_{EC})$ of E $\rightleftarrows$ C is a *possible* projection $R(T_{SjC})$ of $S^j \rightleftarrows$ C.

Therefore since *for all possible* $S^j \in \{S^i\}$, $\beta_{act}(R(T_{SjC}))$ for all possible $R(T_{SjC})$, we know that $\beta_{act}(R(T_{EC}))$ for all possible $R(T_{EC})$ of E $\rightleftarrows$ C.

Note that this requires that

$$\forall S^j \in \{S^i\} \quad \forall T_{SjC} \quad \beta_{act}(R_{sj}(T_{SjC})) \qquad (16)$$

which is a stronger condition on the controller's behaviour than that it just reliably performs behaviour β in one single agent-environment system S $\rightleftarrows$ C. If condition (16) is fulfilled then the controller must be able to perform behaviour β robustly with respect to variations in the way in which the behaviourally relevant base set of environmental features changes over time and responds to output signals. Because of this, we say that a controller that fulfills condition (16) is *base set robust*.

5 Minimal conditions for ensuring reliable behaviour in reality

We are now in a position where we can sum up the last section and put forward a general set of conditions on both controller and simulation that are minimally sufficient to ensure the controller's reliable behaviour in reality. The conditions have been roughly divided in half, two for the controller C and two for the set of simulation environments $\{S^i\}$.

Let β be a behaviour that defines a set β_{env} of dynamical systems B and a function β_{act} that returns true or false when applied to a sequence of the form $R_e(e_0), R_e(e_1) \ldots, R_e(e_\tau)$.

Let $E \rightleftarrows C$ be a real-world agent-environment interaction system that supports behaviour β such that (6) is satisfied.

Let $\{S^i \rightleftarrows C\}$ be a set of agent-environment interaction systems that together constitute a simulation, and each of which supports behaviour β such that (6) is satisfied.

Now if

$\exists S^j \in \{S^i\}$ s.t.

1. $\forall e_0 \in E_{init} \quad \exists s_0^j \in S_{init}^j$
   s.t. $R_e(e_0) = R_{sj}(s_0^j)$

2. $\forall < s_t^j, c_t^{s^j} > \in T_{SjC}$ s.t. $\beta_{act}(R_{sj}(T_{SjC}))$
   $R_e(e_t) = R_{sj}(s_t^j)$ and $c_t^E = c_t^{s^j}$
   $\Rightarrow$
   $R_e(E_{diff}(e_t, C_{out}(c_t^E))) \sim$
   $\quad R_{sj}(S_{diff}^j(s_t^j, C_{out}(c_t^{s^j})))$

$$(17)$$

and

$\forall S^j \in \{S^i\}$

1. $\forall T_{SjC} \quad \beta_{act}(R_{sj}(T_{SjC}))$

2. $\forall < s_t^j, c_t > \in T_{SjC}$ s.t. $\beta_{act}(R_{sj}(T_{SjC}))$
   $R_e(e_t) = R_{sj}(s_t^j)$
   $\Rightarrow$
   $C_{diff}(c_t, E_{out}(e_t)) \sim$
   $\quad C_{diff}(c_t, S_{out}^j(s_t^j))$

$$(18)$$

then

$\forall T_{EC} \quad \beta_{act}(R_E(T_{EC}))$

Conditions (17.1) and (18.1) are versions of conditions (14.2) and (16) respectively. Note however that conditions (17.2) and (18.2) are scoped differently to conditions (14.1) and (15) from which they are respectively derived. The qualification

$\forall < s_t^j, c_t^{s^j} > \in T_{SjC}$ s.t. $\beta_{act}(R_{sj}(T_{SjC}))$

means that these conditions are only required to hold true for those trajectories of the simulation that constitute instances of the agent actually performing behaviour β. But this is all we need, since if condition (18.1) is true, then this will be the only sort of trajectory that the simulation is capable of anyway.

6 Turning theory into practice

In this section we take a brief look at how the conditions we have derived theoretically can be applied in practice to build minimal simulations for evolutionary robotics. Since this paper is primarily concerned with developing the theory behind the practice rather than the practice itself, the reader is directed to [5] where they will find a fuller explication of the issues touched upon here. Below, we look in turn at each of the conditions on simulation and controller put forwards in section 5 and offer suggestions as to how each one can be implemented in a practical minimal simulation.

Once we have come up with a behaviour β which we want to perform and an agent-environment system $E \rightleftarrows C$ which is capable of supporting it, we are ready to start building a minimal simulation. The first thing to do is to distinguish those features of the world that are behaviourally relevant from those that are not, and to work out roughly how this base set of features changes over time and responds to the controller's output signals. In so doing we identify, if only in a rough way, the dynamic system $B \in \beta_{env}$ that is tracked by $R_e(e_t)$.

The next thing to do is to make some sort of model of this dynamic system to act as a basis for our minimal simulation. Using our knowledge of the *inaccuracy* involved in our modelling process, we must ensure that the nature of the model is automatically variable to the extent that the exhaustive set formed by its variations *contains* the original real-world dynamic system. In other words we want the variations to form a set $\{S^i\}$ such that conditions (17.1) and (17.2) are satisfied.

Condition (17.1) is easy to satisfy, in most cases, since we can normally just place the constraint on the real world agent-environment system that there are only a small number of states we will allow it to start in. If we are strict, however, then we must recognise that condition (17.2) is much harder to fulfill, since most modelling of a real-world dynamical system will involve a simplification (and thus a difference) which no amount of parameter-twiddling will render more complex. Nevertheless, even if the simulation involves a simplified model, the fact that a controller is base set robust and fulfills condition (18.1) in the simulation means that it will be robust to small changes in the underlying dynamics of its world. If the set $\{S^i\}$ is large and varied enough, therefore, it is extremely unlikely that the mechanisms employed by reliably fit controllers to cope with all the various $\{S^i \rightleftarrows C\}$ will not also be sufficient to cope with the differences between the closest $S^j \rightleftarrows C$ and $E \rightleftarrows C$. For a discussion of what these mechanisms might look like see [5].

It should also be noted that, from condition (17.2), it is evident that we do not need to build the simulation so that some $S^j \in \{S^i\}$ tracks the same $B \in \beta_{env}$ as E for *all* trajectories of the two systems. The dynamics need only be the same or similar for those states of the simulation that occur when the agent is actually performing behaviour β. Thus, if we are evolving corridor following behaviour, the dynamics of the simulation might differ wildly from those of reality if the controller hits a wall or goes round in circles. Similarly, if we are evolving walking behaviour in an insect-like robot, the dynamics of the simulation might differ wildly from those of reality when the robot's legs clash or drag. This is important when we consider that the hardest aspects of some of these situations to simulate, especially in the latter example, are often those involved in the robot *not* performing the behaviour rather than performing it.

6.1 How to ensure that reliably fit controllers are base set robust and base set exclusive

Let us imagine that we have built a basic simulation according to the methodology outlined above, and that we have therefore defined a suitable set $\{S^i \rightleftarrows C\}$ that satisfactorily fulfills conditions (17.1) and (17.2). How can we then ensure that controllers that evolve to be reliably fit in such a simulation will be both base set robust and base set exclusive to fulfill conditions (18.1) and (18.2)?

The answer is that we must rely on the evolutionary machinery. If a single fitness test consists of several independent trials, each involving an S^j picked at random from $\{S^i\}$, then the only way for a controller to be reliably fit from trial to trial, fitness test after fitness test, generation after generation, is by being able to reliably perform behaviour β in all $\{S^i \leftrightarrows C\}$. Reliably fit controllers will therefore automatically be base set robust and fulfill condition (18.1). In practice, of course, even a reliably fit individual will eventually be displaced from the population by a combination of genetic drift and noise. This usually takes many generations, however, which is sufficient to extensively (if not exhaustively) test the individual in a wide variety of $\{S^i \leftrightarrows C\}$. In most cases this is all that is required.

The method we put forward for ensuring that reliably fit controllers are base set exclusive and fulfill condition (18.2) is similar to that which ensures that they are base set robust. A controller that is base set exclusive is one whose behaviour depends exclusively on the aspects of its input that derive from the base sets of behaviourally relevant environmental features picked out by the reduction operators R_{sj} and R_e. If a controller is reliably fit trial after trial, then those aspects of its input that contribute to its behaviour must in turn be reliable trial after trial. By ensuring that all those aspects of a controller's input that *do not* derive from the behaviourally relevant base sets of environmental features are *unreliable*, from trial to trial, we can ensure that the controller's behaviour will not depend on these aspects if it is to be reliably fit. In other words, by ensuring that *the only* aspects of a controller's input that *are* reliable, trial after trial, derive from the behaviourally relevant environmental features, we can ensure that reliably fit controllers will be base set exclusive.

Note that if a controller is base set exclusive, this does not mean that its behaviour necessarily depends on *all* aspects of the input that derive from the base sets of behaviourally relevant environmental features. Just as we can prevent the behaviour of reliably fit controllers from depending on those aspects of the input that do not derive from these base sets, so we can prevent the behaviour of reliably fit controllers from depending on certain aspects of the input that *do*. We might want to do this for several reasons: certain aspects of the controller's input might derive from the behaviourally relevant environmental features in the simulation in ways that they cannot in reality, or our model might be incomplete or inaccurate in certain respects. In fact, as we shall see, we only need to model *enough* of the way in which the real world base set of behaviourally relevant environmental features contributes to controller inputs for the behaviour to be possible, all other aspects of the input can be made unreliable.

6.2 The potential power of minimal simulations

In the methodology outlined in this section it should be noted that there is no emphasis on the model being either particularly complex or particularly accurate: the main reasons why simulations can become overly computationally expensive and prohibitively time-consuming to build. This is where the potential power of these techniques lie. A reliably fit controller that evolves in an inaccurate and simple minimal simulation is just as likely as any other to cross the reality gap *provided* that a large enough amount of random variation is included in the simulation in the right way. What *is* much more unlikely in this situation, is that reliably fit controllers will evolve at all. There will always be limits to the amount of randomness that the evolutionary machinery can find ways of coping with, no matter how this machinery is set up. If the amount of variation necessary to ensure that reliably fit controllers cross the reality gap surpasses this limit, then reliably fit controllers will just fail to evolve.

However, if the evolutionary machinery *is* sufficiently powerful we can evolve complex control architectures, capable of performing non-trivial real world tasks, using surprisingly inaccurate and simple simulations. In such a situation, one's choice of how to model the robot in its environment can be based on considerations of computational expense and ease of design rather than those of fidelity.

7 Experiments

In this section two sets of experiments are briefly outlined, both involving the evolution of non-trivial behaviours for real robots using minimal simulations. There is not enough room, unfortunately, to provide anything more than a flavour of these practical examples; see [5] for a much fuller account. In the first set of experiments controllers were evolved for the small mobile Khepera robot [7] that were able to solve a T-maze in response to a light signal. In the second set of experiments, controllers were evolved for the Sussex University gantry robot [3] that were able to visually distinguish a triangle from a square, and steer the robot towards it. We will look at each minimal simulation in turn.

7.1 A minimal simulation of a Khepera robot

The aim of the experiments was to evolve a behaviour for the Khepera robot that was at least one step up from the simple reactive behaviours that have been prevalent in the Evolutionary Robotics literature so far. The behaviour that was chosen is shown diagrammatically on the left of figure 1. As a Khepera robot begins to negotiate a T-maze, it passes through a beam of light shining from one of the two sides, chosen at random. To score maximum fitness points the control architecture must 'remember' on which side of the corridor the light went on and, on reaching the junction, turn down the corresponding arm of the T-maze. The minimal simulation used in the experiments was designed with low computational overheads firmly in mind. To give some idea of its simplicity, it contained two look-up-tables, one containing 72 values and one containing 80, and about 300 lines of commented C code that employed nothing more mathematically complicated than floating point arithmetic.

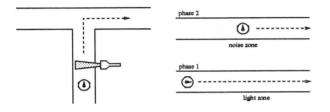

Figure 1: The task in reality and in simulation.

The two phases of the T-maze simulation are shown in figure 1. The basic dynamical system that it models consists simply of the way in which the relative positions

of the robot, the light signal and the walls of the T-maze environment change in response to motor signals. In the first phase, the virtual robot travels down a simple corridor where it receives a light signal from either one side or the other. After it has travelled a predetermined distance, it is suddenly popped out of the first corridor, rotated through ninety degrees, and popped into the middle of a second corridor for phase two. It then has to chose whether to turn left or right, depending on which side the light signal was on, in order to gain maximum fitness points.

The model of the way in which the Khepera moves in response to motor signals, and the model of the way in which the infra-red sensors and ambient light sensors return values as a function of position were all extremely simple yet near enough to reality that a suitable set of agent-environment systems $\{S^i \leftrightarrows C\}$ could be generated just by varying their parameters. However, where *every* member of this set failed completely to correspond to reality (e.g. around the area marked 'noise zone' in figure 1), these aspects were made so unreliable within the simulation that reliably fit controllers were forced to employ strategies that in no way depended upon them. Thus all possible trajectories that the simulation could follow when the controller was reliably fit were forced to exclude these obvious differences between the model and the real world; for reliably fit controllers, the way in which the position of the khepera and the sensor values changed over time within the simulation corresponded roughly to what went on in reality. Therefore, since every real-world start position corresponded to a possible start position within the simulation, (condition 17.1) and (condition 17.2) were satisfied in an approximate way by some $S^j \in \{S^i\}$. Reliably fit control architectures were forced to be base set robust (condition 18.1) just through the act of varying the parameters of the simulation from trial to trial. The sensor models were accurate enough that no special action was required to ensure that reliably fit controllers were base set exclusive (condition 18.2).

Using this minimal simulation, reliably fit recurrent neural network controllers consistently evolved within around 1000 generations, the simulated equivalent of over 17 months of continuous real-world evolution. This took around 4 hours to run as a single user on a SPARC Ultra. In order to see whether it would successfully transfer across the reality gap, one of the first reliably fit networks to evolve was downloaded onto a Khepera robot, and its ability to perform the task in the real world was tested. Sixty different trials were performed one after another, twenty in each of three different widths of corridors (11cm, 18cm and 23cm), with the light on the left for ten trials and the light on the right for the other ten. On all sixty occasions the Khepera performed the task satisfactorily and efficiently, navigating to the end of the correct arm of the T-maze without colliding with the walls.

7.2 A minimal simulation of the gantry robot

In [3], the authors report experiments in which both neural network control architectures and the visual morphologies of their inputs were evolved side by side to perform a simple shape discrimination task for the Sussex University gantry robot[2]. Starting from several different positions and orientations, evolving individuals steered the robot, using visual input, around an all-black rectangular arena with a white triangle and a white square stuck upon one of the long walls. Maximum fitness points were awarded to those controllers that could visually discriminate the triangle from the square and steer the robot towards it. In the experiments reported here, both neural network controllers and their visual morphologies were again evolved to perform the same triangle-square discrimination task, the difference being that they were evolved to perform it under extreme real world noise provided by a set of lights, each turning on and off at different frequencies, known at Sussex as the 'disco lights'.

The simulation was based upon two simple look up table based models: one for the way in which the position of the robot within the rectangular arena changes in response to motor signals, and one for the way in which the location in the arena that each individual pixel projects onto is a function of the position of the robot within its environment. Pixel values, however, were not just a simple function of the location they projected onto since under the 'disco lights' suspended above the gantry, the values returned by pixels of the camera-image vary widely both with respect to time, and with respect to the direction of the camera. Even if we know the exact location within the arena that a particular pixel projects onto, therefore, there is not that much we can say about exactly what the value of that pixel might be. However, there are some general things that hold true except in exceptional circumstances: if a pixel projects onto a wall but not onto a shape then it returns a value within the range 0 to 13, if a pixel projects onto either the triangle or the square then it returns a value between 14 and 15, and if a pixel projects onto either the floor or the ceiling of the arena it returns a value between 0 and 15 (see figure 2). Since these facts about the intervals that pixel values fall into under full 'disco lighting' are almost always the case, and since they are enough to distinguish the white triangle and square from the black walls of the arena, they were the only aspects of the controller's input that we needed to model.

Having done this, all other aspects of the input, including *the way in which* pixel values were assigned within

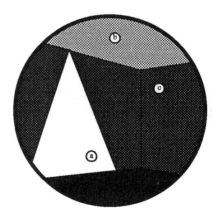

Figure 2: A typical image returned by the camera of the gantry robot. The robot is facing the corner of the arena and the triangle can be seen on the left. The white circles labelled a, b and c are examples of pixels that project onto the triangle, ceiling and wall respectively. Pixel a will return a value between 14 and 15, pixel b will return a value between 0 and 15 and pixel c will return a value between 0 and 13.

these intervals, were varied from trial to trial in a way that made them totally unreliable. In this way, reliably fit individuals were forced to depend solely on the fact that pixel values that projected onto certain surfaces fell within certain intervals, and not on how or where they fell within these intervals. They were therefore forced to be base set exclusive satisfying condition (18.2).

Both models were again near enough to the real situation that a suitable set of agent-environment systems $\{S^i \leftrightarrows C\}$ which satisfactorily fulfilled conditions (17.1) and (17.2) could be generated just by varying their parameters. Reliably fit controllers were again forced to be base set robust and satisfy condition (18.1) as a direct consequence of randomly varying these parameters from trial to trial.

Controllers (and their visual morphologies) that were reliably fit within the simulation consistently evolved within 6000 generations, which is the simulated equivalent of over 3 years worth of continuous real-world evolution. This took around 12 hours to run as a single user on a SPARC Ultra. One of the most efficient networks was chosen for testing: when placed in one of the four starting positions in the arena, the network initially caused the robot to turn in a tight circle clockwise. If the square came into the view of the camera, the rotational speed of the robot would actually increase until the square was out of view. When the triangle came into view, the robot would then 'lock on' and move directly towards it, adjusting its course as it went.

In order to see whether it would cross the reality gap, the network was downloaded onto the gantry, and tested continuously[3] and automatically on the triangle/square task in the real world under full disco lighting. In total, 200 trials were performed: 100 for the triangle on the left and the square on the right, and 100 for the triangle on the right and the square on the left. At the beginning of each trial the robot was started in one of four different starting positions and these were run through in cycle from trial to trial. On each trial, the robot was automatically judged to have successfully achieved the task if, by the end of the trial, it was stationed within a small radius extending out from the centre of the triangle. In total the robot achieved the task 195 times out of 200: 98 with the triangle on the right and 97 with the triangle on the left. As a comparison, the authors of [3] report that the fittest controller they managed to evolve for the same task was at best successful only 80% of the time, and this was under extremely constrained static lighting conditions [4].

8 Conclusions

In the first few sections of this paper a theoretical and notational framework was developed that allowed us to formally state the circumstances under which an agent performs a behaviour within an environment. This framework was then used to prove how the fact that an agent reliably performs a certain behaviour within a simulation can imply that it will continue to reliably perform the same behaviour within the real world, providing that certain conditions are fulfilled by both the controller and the simulation. The next section outlined how this minimal set of conditions for behavioural transfer could be practically applied to the building of minimal simulations for evolutionary robotics, and techniques were put forward for ensuring that controllers which evolved to be reliably fit within such simulations would continue to be reliably fit when downloaded into reality. Finally, two sets of experiments were sketched in which minimal simulations were used to evolve controllers for non-trivial real world tasks. In both sets of experiments, controllers evolved in a matter of hours that were able to perform the behaviours reliably and robustly when downloaded onto the real robots. It *is* therefore possible to evolve complex behaviours for real robots using minimal simulations that run fast and are easy to build.

Acknowledgements

Special thanks to Joe Faith for much discussion, Adam Bockrath for importing rigour, and to Phil Husbands and Jon Bird for proof reading. Thanks also to COGS for the bursary that allows me to undertake this work.

---

[3]In practice, because of the propensity of the mechanics of the gantry robot to seize and the software controlling it to crash, the testing procedure had to be watched continuously, and restarted (from where it had crashed) on a number of occasions.

References

[1] R.D. Beer. A dynamical systems perspective on agent environment interaction. *Artificial Intelligence*, 72(1-2):173–215, 1995.

[2] R.D. Beer and J.C. Gallagher. Evolving dynamic neural networks for adaptive behavior. *Adaptive Behavior*, 1:91–122, 1992.

[3] I. Harvey, P. Husbands, and D. Cliff. Seeing the light: Artificial evolution, real vision. In D. Cliff, P. Husbands, J.A. Meyer, and S. Wilson, editors, *From Animals to Animats 3: Proceedings of the Third International Conference on Simulation of Adaptive Behavior*, volume 3. MIT Press/Bradford Books, 1994.

[4] P. Husbands. Personal communication. 1997.

[5] N. Jakobi. Evolutionary robotics and the radical envelope of noise hypothesis. Cognitive Science Research Paper CSRP457, University of Sussex, 1997.

[6] N. Jakobi, P. Husbands, and I. Harvey. Noise and the reality gap: The use of simulation in evolutionary robotics. In F. Moran, A. Moreno, J.J. Merelo, and P. Chacon, editors, *Advances in Artificial Life: Proc. 3rd European Conference on Artificial Life*. Springer-Verlag, 1995.

[7] K-Team. Khepera users manual. EPFL,Lausanne, June 1993.

[8] M.J. Mataric and D. Cliff. Challenges in evolving controllers for physical robots. *Robot and Autonomous Systems*, 19(1):67–83, 1996.

[9] Olivier Michel. An artificial life approach for the synthesis of autonomous agents. In J.M. Alliot, E. Lutton, E. Ronald, M. Schoenauer, and D. Snyers, editors, *Proceedings of the European Conference on Artificial Evolution*. Springer-Verlag, 1995.

[10] O. Miglino, H.H. Lund, and S. Nolfi. Evolving mobile robots in simulated and real environments. *Artifical Life*, 2(4), 1995.

[11] T. Smithers. What the dynamics of adaptive behaviour and cognition might look like in agent-environment interaction systems. In T. Smithers and A. Moreno, editors, *3rd International Workshop on Artificial Life and Artificial Intelligence, The Role of Dynamics and Representation in Adaptive Behaviour and Cognition*, San Sebastian, Spain, 1994.

Computer Evolution of Buildable Objects

Pablo Funes and Jordan Pollack
Computer Science Department
Volen Center for Complex Systems
Brandeis University
Waltham, MA 02254-9110
{pablo,pollack}@cs.brandeis.edu

Abstract

Creating artificial life forms through evolutionary robotics faces a "chicken and egg" problem: learning to control a complex body is dominated by inductive biases specific to its sensors and effectors, while building a body which is controllable is conditioned on the pre-existence of a brain.

The idea of co-evolution of bodies and brains is becoming popular, but little work has been done in evolution of physical structure because of the lack of a general framework for doing it. Evolution of creatures in simulation has been constrained by the "reality gap" which implies that resultant objects are usually not buildable.

The work we present takes a step in the problem of body evolution by applying evolutionary techniques to the design of structures assembled out of parts. Evolution takes place in a simulator we designed, which computes forces and stresses and predicts failure for 2-dimensional Lego structures. The final printout of our program is a schematic assembly, which can then be built physically. We demonstrate its functionality in several different evolved entities.

1 Introduction

In this paper we report our work in evolution of buildable designs using Lego[1] bricks. Legos are well known for their flexibility when it comes to creating low cost, handy designs of vehicles and structures (see [22], for example). Because of these properties and general availability, Legos constitute a good ground for one of the first experiments involving evolution of computer simulated structures which can be built and deployed.

Instead of incorporating an expert system of engineering

---

1. Lego is a registered trademark of the Lego group.

knowledge into the program, which would result in familiar structures, we provided the algorithm with a model of the physical reality and a purely utilitarian fitness function, thus supplying measures of feasibility and functionality. In this way the evolutionary process runs in an environment that has not been unnecessarily constrained. We added, however, a requirement of computability to reject overly complex structures when they took too long for our simulations to evaluate.

The results are encouraging. The evolved structures had a surprisingly alien look: they are not based in common knowledge on how to build with brick toys; instead, the computer found ways of its own through the evolutionary search process. We were able to assemble the final designs manually and confirm that they accomplish the objectives introduced with our fitness functions.

After some background on related problems, we describe our physical simulation model for two-dimensional Lego structures, and the representation for encoding them and applying evolution. We demonstrate the feasibility of our work with photos of actual objects which were the result of particular optimizations. Finally, we discuss future work and draw some conclusions.

2 Background

In order to evolve both the morphology and behavior of autonomous mechanical devices which can be manufactured, one must have a simulator which operates under several constraints, and a resultant controller which is adaptive enough to cover the gap between simulated and real world.

Features of a simulator for evolving morphology are:

- **Universal** - the simulator should cover an infinite general space of mechanisms.
- **Conservative** - because simulation is never perfect, it should preserve a margin of safety.
- **Efficient** - it should be quicker to test in simulation than through physical production and test.
- **Buildable** - results should be convertible from a simulation to a real object

There are several fields which bear on this question of physical simulation, including qualitative physics and structural mechanics, computer graphics, evolutionary design and robotics.

2.1 Qualitative Physics

Qualitative Physics is the subfield of AI which deals with mechanical and physical knowledge representation. It starts with a logical representation of a mechanism, such as a Heat Pump [7] or a String [8], and produces simulations, or envisionments, of the future behavior of the mechanism. QP has not to our knowledge been used as the simulator in an evolutionary design system.

2.2 Computer Graphics.

The work of Karl Sims [19], [20] was seminal in the fields of evolutionary computation and artificial life. Following the work of Ngo and Marks [16], Sims evolved virtual creatures that have both physical architecture and control programs created by an evolutionary computation process.

Despite their beautiful realism, Sims' organisms are far from real. His simulations do not consider the mechanical feasibility of the articulations between different parts, which in fact overlap each other at the joints, nor the existence of real world mechanisms that could produce the forces responsible for their movements.

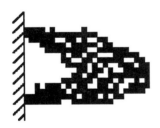

fig. 1. Distribution of material for a piece that optimizes weight and stiffness. From Chapman, Saitou and Jakiela [3]. (Reproduced with permission). This strange shape looks like a distant relative of our evolved Lego objects.

2.3 Structural Mechanics/Structural Topology

The engineering field of structural mechanics is based on methods, such as finite element modelling [23] to construct computable models of continuous materials by approximating them with discrete networks. These tools are in broad use in the engineering community, carefully supervised and oriented towards particular product designs, and are often quite computationally intensive. Applications of genetic algorithms to structural topology optimization ([3], [18]) are

related to our work. This type of application uses genetic algorithms as a search tool to optimize a shape under clearly defined preconditions. The GA is required, for example, to simultaneously maximize the stiffness and minimize the weight of a piece subject to external loads (fig. 1.).

2.4 Evolutionary Design

Evolutionary Design, that is, the utilization of evolutionary computation techniques for industrial design, is a new research area where Peter Bentley's Ph.D. Thesis [2] is ground-breaking work. Bentley uses a GA to evolve shapes for solid objects directed by multiple fitness measures. His evolved designs include tables, prisms, even vehicle profiles.

Bentley's search algorithms use combinations of fitness measures ("Size", "Mass", "No Fragmentation", "Flat Upper Surface", "Supportiveness", etc.) that include some physical constraints, like center of mass positioning or total weight. Lacking a more complete physical model, he relies on specific measures to guide evolution in each case.

2.5 Evolutionary Robotics

Many researchers are working today on the evolution of control software for real robots. Evolutionary Robotics has become a field on its own [15]. Some rely on carefully designed simulations [4], while others apply evolution directly in the real robot [6]. Hybrid techniques [13] are a mixture of the two.

Lund, Hallam and Lee [11], [14] have evolved in simulation both a robot control program and some parameters of its physical body (sensor number and positioning, body size, etc.). Their last paper [14] addresses the possibility of co-evolving a robot controller and auditory morphology for the task of (cricket) phonotaxis. They contemplate the possibility of designing a Lego robot simulator.

3 The Physical Model

The resistance of the plastic material (ABS-acrylonitrile butadiene styrene) of Lego bricks far surpasses the force necessary to either join two of them together or break their unions. This makes it possible to design a model that ignores the resistance of the material and evaluates the strain forces over a group of bricks only at their union areas. If a Lego structure fails, it will generally do so at the joints, but the actual bricks will not be damaged.

This characteristic of Lego structures makes their discretization for modelling an obvious step. Instead of imposing an artificial mesh for simulation purposes only —as in finite elements, for example— these structures are already made of relatively large discrete units.

3.1 Description of the model

Based on elementary statics of rigid bodies, our model considers the union between two bricks as a rigid joint between the centers of mass of each one, located at the center of the actual area of contact between them (fig. 2.). This joint has a measurable torque capacity. That is, more than a certain amount of force applied at a certain distance from the joint will break the two bricks apart. The fundamental assumption of our model is this idealization of the union of two Lego bricks together.

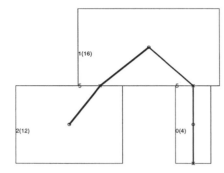

fig. 2. A support model for three Lego bricks.

fig. 3. The family of Lego bricks used in our experiments: Sizes 1x4, 1x6, 1x8, 1x10, 1x12 and 1x16.

Only two-dimensional systems of forces have been considered so far. Using the family of Lego bricks of width 1 available in our lab (fig. 3.) we can consider complex 2-dimensional combinations of bricks and model them as a superimposed system of point masses joined together with a network of rigid joints (fig. 9.).

We have measured the resistance of such joints to external forces and torques and simplified the model to consider only rotational forces being applied at the joint. The resistance to forces other than torques is considered infinite. Our measurements indicate that even the weakest type of joint

can support a relatively big load when it is applied radially only, with zero torque. Our next generation simulator will probably incorporate these forces for an improved model.

Table 1. summarizes our measures of the torque capacities of the Lego joints we use.

Joint size(knobs)	Approximate torque capacity $(N\text{-}m \times 10^{-6})$
1	10.4
2	50.2
3	89.6
4	157.3
5	281.6
6	339.2
7	364.5

Table 1. Estimated minimal torque capacities of the basic types of joints

These measures are relative: They vary from one brick to another, and by undetermined factors such as temperature, humidity, aging, etc. The table shown reflects an attempt at taking a conservative measure: The number we need to use is the minimum that any Lego union of certain characteristics is guaranteed to support and not, for example, the average.

In our simulations we used the conservative figures above and additionally set the gravitational constant to 1.2 times its actual value – thus allowing for an extra 20% error margin.

Our model of 'rigid' joint means it will exert any reaction torque necessary to avoid breaking, up to a certain limit. All we are using is this concept of a *maximum* load. In a stable system, the actual torque being exerted by certain body at any given joint is underdetermined.

This means for example that if two bricks are supporting the weight of a third one between them (fig. 2.), the load could be considered to be distributed among each of the two joints in any legal combination. Since only one joint is enough in this case, we could consider that all the weight is on the left joint, and none on the right one. This can be verified by removing the right supporting brick: The middle one will not fall, because the union with the leftmost brick is strong enough to support its weight.

Our model is thus based on the following principle: *As long as there is a way to distribute the weights among the network of bricks such that no joint is stressed beyond its maximum capacity, the structure will not break.*

3.2 A Greedy Generalized Network Flow Algorithm

The algorithmic rendering of our model is still under development. However, even in its initial state, it worked well enough to use as a basis for fitness testing of structures which were indeed buildable.

This algorithm must find whether or not there exists a distribution of the combined gravitational forces generated by the center of mass of each brick, such that no joint is stressed beyond its maximum capacity.

For each given brick we consider the network of all the joints in the structure as a flow network that will absorb this weight and transmit it to the ground. Each joint can support a certain fraction α of such a force, given by the formula

$$\alpha_{j,b} = \frac{K_j}{d_x(j,b)\, w_b} \qquad (1)$$

for each body b and joint j, where K_j is the maximum capacity of the joint, $d_x(j,b)$ is the distance between the body and the joint along the horizontal axis, and w_b the weight of the body.

If a given body b is fixed and each edge on the graph on fig. 9. is labeled with the corresponding $a_{j,b}$ according to (1), a network flow problem ([5], chapter 27) is obtained where a net flow of 1.0 between a source b and the two sinks at (5,0) and (20,0) represents a valid distribution of the weight of b in the structure.

The complete problem is not reducible, however, to a network flow algorithm, due to the fact that there are multiple forces to be applied at different points, and the capacity of each joint relative to each body varies with the mass of the body and the x-distance between body and joint.

Leaving aside the study of better algorithmic implementations, we are using a greedy algorithm: once a solution has been found for the distribution of the first mass, it is fixed, and a remaining capacity for each joint is computed that will conform a reduced network that must support the weight of the next body, and so on.

While there may in fact should be a single solution to the weight distribution for a static Lego structure which might have a simpler algorithm, our ultimate focus is to be able to manage changes under stress loads, and dynamically predict how legos will break. Any structure that is approved as "gravitationally correct" by our simulation possesses a load distribution that does not overstress any joint, and thus will not fall under its own weight. Our evolutionary algorithm might be limited by the simulation when it fails to approve a structure that was physically valid, but still may succeed by working only in the space of 'provable' solutions.

3.3 Time complexity

A second compromise in our simulation will come from the fact that our initial implementation of the simulation algorithm does not scale well. Its worst case running time would be $O(3^n)$, where n is the number of bricks. Fortunately, in the actual examples, many bricks are connected only to one or two others, thus reducing the number of combinations.

Again this combinatorial explosion problem will ultimately constrain the search space. Only the solutions that can be found by our algorithm in a reasonable time are useful to our evolutionary runs.

We inserted an *ad hoc* limiting parameter into our code to cut off the simulation when it has failed to find a solution after a certain maximum number of iterations.

4 Representation

Our initial representation to perform evolutionary computation over these structures borrows the standard tree mutation and crossover operators from genetic programming [10]. We have implemented a tree notation for two-dimensional Lego structures. Each node on the tree represents a brick and has one size parameter (either 4, 6, 8, 10, 12 or 16 for the available brick sizes) and four potential sons, each one representing a new brick linked at one of its four corners. When a union is present, a joint size parameter determines the number of overlapping knobs in the union.

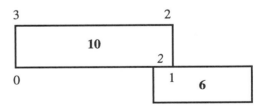

fig. 4. Example of genetic encoding of bricks

The diagram on fig. 4. represents a 10-brick with its 4 joint sites labeled 0, 1, 2, 3, that is linked to a 6-brick by two overlapping knobs. The corresponding tree could be written in pseudo-Lisp notation as

$$\text{(10 nil (2 (6 nil nil nil)) nil nil)} \qquad (2)$$

A problem with this representation, similar in origin to the problem of valid function parameters in genetic programming, is that it is underconstrained: Only some trees will encode valid Lego structures. No more than one brick can be at each corner, so every son node can have at most three descendants, because one of its corners is already accounted for. Joint sizes must also be compatible with each other and in general, two bricks cannot overlap each other. The following extension to (2), for example, is illegal because both 10-bricks would share the same physical space

$$(10 \text{ nil } (2 \ (6 \text{ nil nil nil } (4 \ (10 \text{ nil nil nil})))) \text{ nil nil}) \quad (3)$$

4.1 Mutation and Crossover

There are two possible mutations:

1. Mutation of the joint and brick sizes at any random point

2. Addition of a single brick at a random empty joint

To implement mutation, a random joint in the tree (or the root) is selected, and, if NIL, mutation 2 is applied, otherwise mutation 1.

The basic crossover operator involves two parent trees out of which random subtrees are selected. The offspring generated has the first subtree removed and replaced by the second.

After mutation or crossover operators are applied, a new, possibly invalid specification tree is formed. The result is expanded one node at a time and overlapping is checked. Whenever an overlap is found the tree is truncated at that site.

With this procedure, a maximum spatially valid subtree is built as the result of crossover or mutation.

Once a valid tree has been obtained, the physical model is constructed and the structure tested for gravitational correctness. If approved, fitness is evaluated and the new individual is added to the population.

4.2 Steady State GA with low evolutionary pressure.

Our goal is not to optimize the evolutionary algorithm, but to show that evolution is indeed possible and our models are physically sound. We use a straightforward steady-state genetic algorithm:

```
1. While maximum fitness < Target fitness
2. Do Randomly select mutation or crossover.
3.     Select 1 (2 for crossover) random indi-
       vidual(s) with fitness proportional
       probability.
4.     Apply mutation or crossover operator
5.     Generate physical model and test for
       gravitational load
6.     If the new model will support its own
       weight.
7.         Then replace a random individual
```

with it.(chosen with inverse fitness proportional probability)

We have set the population size to 1000 in all experiments.

4.3 Parallel Asynchronous GA

We are using a parallel version of this algorithm that runs on an SGI Onyx, a 16 processor MIMD machine. Our parallel GA is asynchronous, that is, each processor iterates independently over steps 1 through 7, without any synchronization states.

Fitness evaluations are the interface between a learning evolutionary algorithm and its environment. In complex, dynamic scenarios, fitness evaluations are time consuming. In many cases —imagine a GA having to generate a control program for obstacle avoidance in a robot— a fitness evaluation can be several orders of magnitude slower than the underlaying GA. Algorithms are then required that may run hundreds of parallel fitness assays independently, without synchronizing before the next round.

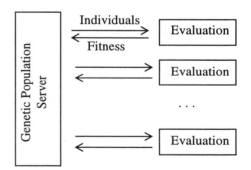

fig. 5. Our parallel GA works as a population server, under the assumption that fitness evaluations are slow and asynchronous.

Our algorithm conceives the population as a genetic server (fig. 5.) that feeds individuals to all available evaluators and receives fitness values from them. This type of algorithm can run on parallel MIMD machines as well as computer networks where different machines evaluate data for a central genetic engine.

5 Results

5.1 Fitness functions

For each experiment below we prepare a custom fitness function that will serve both as a measure for the evolutionary selection process and as a tag that reflects our interest in a computer generated structure. When our algorithm finds a new maximum fitness, it saves this 'champion' and offers it as a new and improved candidate solution for the problem.

Throughout the experiments reported in this paper, fitness values have been a combination of three measures:

1. *Length* (in a certain direction). We use this fitness measure when the desired structure has to be as long or as big as possible.
2. *Normalized distance to a target point.* To avoid an inverse (the smaller the better) fitness, when the algorithm is trying to reach a fixed point we use

$$Nd(S, T) = 1 - \frac{d(S, T)}{d(0, T)} \qquad (4)$$

(where $d(S,T)$ is the distance between the structure and the target and $d(0,T)$ the distance between the target and the origin) as a normalized measure in the range (0,1).
3. *Supportiveness*. To maximize the external weight that a structure can support, we divide the maximum load supported by a candidate by the target supportiveness we are trying to obtain. This is a fitness measure in the interval (0,1)

We demonstrate the effectiveness of our evolutionary structure and Lego simulator on a set of fitness cases resulting in useful computer designed structures.

5.2 The Bridge

The goal of our first experiment was to evolve a structure to go over from one table to another in our lab.

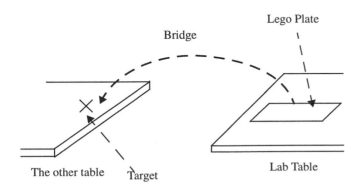

fig. 6. Our 'Lego Bridge' is an evolutionary algorithm that will attempt to create a self-supporting Lego structure that, attached to a base plate fixed at one table, reaches another table without any support outside the plate.

Consider a big Lego square plate fixed to the edge of a table in our lab. Our simulation will permit us to predict whether or not a linear structure made of our family of Lego bricks, which starts at the edge of the table and projects itself without any additional support towards the table on the opposite side of the lab, will collapse under its own weight or not.

Our fitness function was set to be the normalized distance from the object to the target point, at Lego coordinates (-150,0).

fig. 7. The 'Lego bridge' defined by the scheme of fig. 8. is sitting on our lab table.

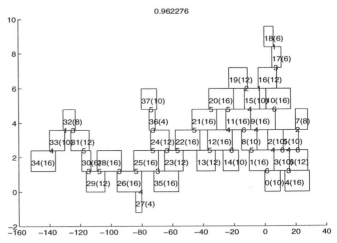

fig. 8. Brick Structure evolved for a Lego 'bridge' spanning 1.20m over the edge of the table. In all our brick diagrams, the spacial coordinates x, y are expressed in "Lego width units", 1 lwu = 8 mm. Note that the *x* scale is compressed at a variable rate for visualization of the entire schematic. The number on top is the fitness value.

Our initial results were encouraging. The genetic algorithm reliably builds a structure that goes up and away from the launching base and then has to lower the tip of the structure to get to the target point.

An example successful run is presented in fig. 8., fig. 9. and the picture of the resulting built Lego bridge in fig. 7. The target fitness of 0.96 was reached after 133,000 iterations.

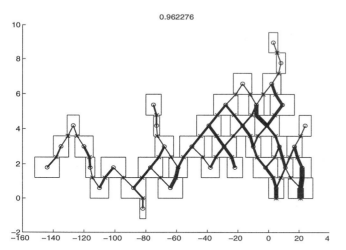

fig. 9. Physical model for the structure on fig. 8. Centers of mass have been marked with circles. Each star is a joint between two of them, and line thickness is proportional to the capacity of each joint.

5.3 Long Bridge

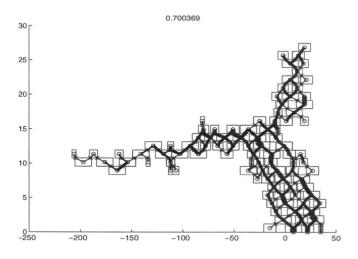

fig. 10. Scheme evolved for the 'Long Bridge' experiment.

Bouyed by our initial success, in our second experiment we removed the 150 unit goal, and simply evolved as long a bridge as possible.

The fitness measure for this experiment is just the length, or stretch over the table measured along the x axis. We had to use an iteration cutout to prevent overly complex designs

from slowing down our network flow algorithm. Our program thus rejects potentially correct structures when the fitness evaluation takes too long.

After 3,240,000 iterations the structure evolved was 1.67 meters long (207 Lego units), made out of 97 bricks.

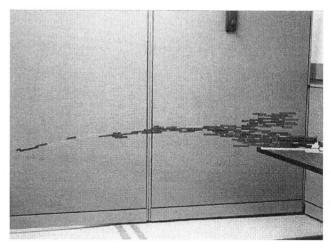

fig. 11. Long Bridge

This experiment reveals one of the limitations of the model. The structure shows an appreciable downwards bending that was not considered in it.

5.4 Scaffold

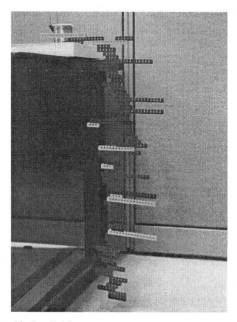

fig. 12. Scaffold.

After working with bridges, we decided we might need a scaffold: evolve a structure growing along the y axis instead of x, from the top of the table down to the floor.

The fitness measure was set to be the normalized distance from the object to a target point in the floor, 0.76 m below the table surface.

The answer was found very quickly; the structure has an alien look but does the job. It evolved in 40,000 iterations.

5.5 Crane Arm

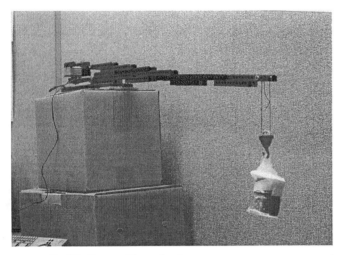

fig. 13. Crane with evolved crane arm.

In the 'crane' experiments we applied our evolutionary environment to a practical problem: To build the arm of a crane which could carry a load. This is our first experiment in designing a structure which would withstand some dynamics of Lego movement when actually built.

A general crane base was designed providing a motor and a stand base for the arm. Two identical parallel arms are needed to hold an axle at the tip from which the hook will hang.

The algorithm should try to find an arm as strong as possible, given the imposed restrictions. To build the crane we use two arms, with the added benefit of doubling the maximum load.

The fitness function was designed to reward having a brick in the right place (.5 m from the base), and for carrying as much weight at the tip before breaking:

$$F(S) = \begin{cases} Nd(S, T) & \text{if } Nd(S, T) < 1 \\ 1 + \dfrac{\text{max load}}{0.5 \text{kg}} & \text{otherwise} \end{cases} \quad (5)$$

A crane arm was found that supports a cargo of 148g. Combining two arms we obtained a crane (fig. 13.) that supports a maximum weight of 295 grams at the tip.

The arm obtained here is optimal: it exploits the maximum torque provided by the base on which we wanted it to attach.

5.6 Rotating Crane Arm

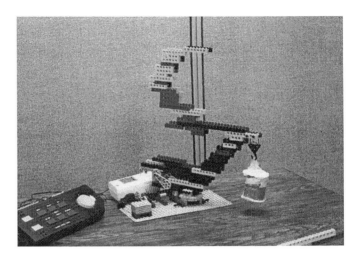

fig. 14. Rotating crane from iteration 220000

In the same spirit as the previous experiment, we added a degree of freedom making our first "3d" design. The rotating crane also consists of a human design that provides the evolutionary algorithm with a sufficient set of constraints so as to guarantee that the evolved structure will be useful.

In this case we designed a rotating base with a motor to pull from a hook. A diagonal arm has to be evolved, providing height and strength for lifting heavy loads.

The fitness measure used was a combination of the length of the arm and the maximum load supported at the tip:

$$F(S) = 1 + \text{length}(S) \frac{\text{max load}}{0.25 \text{kg}} \quad (6)$$

Restrictions were imposed to match the base we designed and to force the arm to grow diagonally.

fig. 15. Rotating crane from iteration 390000.

We obtained a crane that supports a weight of 500 grams at a height of 19.2 cm. and a distance of 16 cm.

It was interesting to observe how a counterweight structure was evolved, but located at the top, not the base as in real cranes. This is the structure built for the crane shown in fig. 14. Subsequently a stronger and much bigger structure was found in which the counterweight "touched down" and attached itself to the base (fig. 15.).

The graph in fig. 16. shows maximum fitness values averaged over 10 runs of this experiment. Error bars indicate standard deviation.

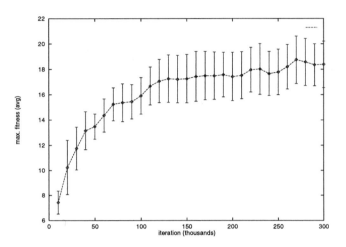

fig. 16. Maximum fitness values over 10 runs of the rotating crane experiment.

6   Future Work

The greedy algorithm that we are using to calculate our models does not find all possible solutions. The existence of a global solution appears to be reducible to a generalized multi-commodity network flow problem, which is treated with approximation algorithms ([9], [12]). Both greedy and approximation algorithms can be improved through the use of heuristics.

The tree representation for Lego structures is a limiting factor. An improved description will open the third dimension, consider a greater variety of block shapes, and bring genotype and phenotype closer, providing a better ground for evolution of objects of higher complexity. A better representation would also allow composite block structures —such as the well-known bricklayers pattern which holds increased stress —to be discovered and replicated as new basic components [1].

By considering three-dimensional forces and torques — and enhancing our modeling of the physical properties of lego structures— a larger universe of buildable objects will be possible. We believe that we can reach some understanding of the dynamic stresses which would be involved in basic Lego mechanisms driven by Lego motors. This would open

the field for evolving active pieces of machinery, including vehicles.

Finally, our basic steady-state GA and our parallel model are elementary approaches which do not take into account many of the advances in the fields of evolutionary computation. An evolutionary algorithm properly tuned for this family of problems can yield improved performance.

7   Conclusions

We have shown that under some constraints, a simulator for objects can be used in an evolutionary computation, and then the objects can be built. This is a little different from evolving controllers for existing robots, and is a step on the way to the full co-evolution of morphology and behavior we believe is necessary for the development of robots and brains of higher complexity than humans can engineer.

Our belief is that in machine learning/evolving systems, more interesting results, such as Sims' creatures or expert backgammon players ([21], [17]), are due more to features of the learning environment than to any sophistication in the learning algorithm itself. By keeping inductive biases and *ad hoc* ingredients to a minimum, we have also demonstrated that interesting real-world behavior can come from a simple virtual model of physics and a basic adaptive algorithm.

Finally, we have only scratched the surface of what is achievable. If we can make a 3-D version of our simulator, and also provide limited dynamics then, besides obvious applications in educational software, we will open the door to a new and fertile area of research in artificial life.

References

[1]   Angeline, P. J. & Pollack, J. B. (1994). Coevolving High-Level Representations. In C. Langton, (ed.) *Proceedings of the Third Artificial Life Meeting.*

[2]   Bentley, P. J. (1996) *Generic Evolutionary Design of Solid Objects using a Genetic Algorithm.* Ph.D. thesis, Division of Computing and Control Systems, School of Engineering, The University of Huddersfield.

[3]   Chapman, C. D., Saitou, K. and Jakiela, M. J. (1993) Genetic Algorithms as an Approach to Configuration and Topology Design, in *Proceedings of the 1993 Design Automation Conference*, DE-Vol. 65-1. Published by the A.S.M.E., Albuquerque, New Mexico, p. 485-498.

[4]   Cliff, D., Harvey, I., Husbands, P. (1996). Artificial Evolution of Visual Control Systems for Robots. To appear in *From Living Eyes to Seeing Machines* M. Srinivisan and S. Venkatesh (eds.), Oxford University Press.

[5] Cormen, T. H., Leiserson, C. E. and Rivest, R. L. (1989). *Introduction to Algorithms*. MIT press - McGraw Hill.

[6] Floreano, D. and Mondada, F. (1994). Automatic Creation of an Autonomous Agent: Genetic Evolution of a Neural Network Driven Robot. In D. Cliff, P. Husbands, J.-A. Meyer, and S. Wilson (Eds.), *From Animals to Animats III*, Cambridge, MA. MIT Press.

[7] Forbus, K. (1984). Qualitative process theory. In *Artificial Intelligence* 24, 85-168.

[8] Gardin, F. and Meltzer, B. (1989). Analogical Representations of Naive Physics. *Artificial Life* 38, pp 139-159.

[9] Iusem, A. and Zenios, S. (1995). Interval Underrelaxed Bregman's method with an application. In *Optimization*, vol. 35, iss. 3, p. 227.

[10] Koza, John R. (1992). *Genetic Programming: On the Programming of Computers by Means of Natural Selection*. Cambridge, MA: The MIT Press.

[11] Lee, W., Hallam, J. and Lund, H. (1996). A Hybrid GP/GA Approach for Co-evolving Controllers and Robot Bodies to Achieve Fitness-Specified Tasks. In *Proceedings of IEEE 3rd International Conference on Evolutionary Computation*. IEEE Press.

[12] Leighton, T., Makedon, F., Plotkin, S., Stein, C., Tardos, E. and Tragoudas, S. (1995). Fast Approximation Algorithms for Muticommodity Flow Problems. *Journal of Computer and Syst. Sciences* 50. p. 228-243.

[13] Lund, H., (1995). Evolving Robot Control Systems. In J. T. Alander (ed.) *Proceedings of 1NWGA*, University of Vaasa, Vaasa.

[14] Lund, H., Hallam, J and Lee, W. (1997). Evolving Robot Morphology. Invited paper in *Proceedings of IEEE Fourth International Conference on Evolutionary Computation*. IEEE Press, NJ.

[15] Mataric, M and Cliff, D. (1996). Challenges In Evolving Controllers for Physical Robots. In *Evolutional Robotics*, special issue of *Robotics and Autonomous Systems*, Vol. 19, No. 1. pp 67-83.

[16] Ngo, J.T., and Marks, J. (1993). Spacetime Constraints Revisited. In *Computer Graphics*, Annual Conference Series. p. 335-342.

[17] Pollack, J. B., Blair, A. and Land, M.(1996). Coevolution of A Backgammon Player. *Proceedings Artificial Life V*, C. Langton, (Ed), MIT Press.

[18] Shoenauer, M. (1996). Shape Representations and Evolution Schemes. In L. J. Fogel, P. J. Angeline and T. Back, Editors, *Proceedings of the 5th Annual Conference on Evolutionary Programming*, MIT Press, to appear.

[19] Sims, K. (1994) Evolving Virtual Creatures. In *Computer Graphics,* Annual Conference Series.

[20] Sims, K. (1994) Evolving 3D Morphology and Behavior by Competition. In *Artificial Life IV Proceedings*, MIT Press.

[21] Tesauro, G. (1995) Temporal difference learning and TD-Gammon. *Communications of the ACM,* 38(3): 58-68.

[22] Webb, B. (1995). Using robots to model animals: a cricket test. *Robotics and Autonomous Systems*, 16.

[23] Zienkiewicz, O.C. *The Finite Element Method in Engineering Science*. McGraw-Hill, New York, 3rd edition, 1977.

Cellular Encoding for Interactive Evolutionary Robotics

Frédéric Gruau and Kameel Quatramaran

University of Sussex, COGS, Falmer, Brighton, BN1 9QH UK
and CWI, INS 4, P.O. Box 94079, NL-1090 GB Amsterdam
gruau@cwi.nl, http://www.cwi.nl/˜ gruau/gruau/gruau.html

Abstract

Research in robotics programming is divided in two camps. The direct hand programmming approach uses an explicit model or a behavioral model (subsumption architecture). The machine learning community uses neural network and/or genetic algorithm. We claim that hand programming and learning are complementary. The two approaches used together can be orders of magnitude more powerful than each approach taken separately. We propose a method to combine them both. It includes three concepts : syntactic constraints to restrict the search space, hand-made problem decomposition, hand given fitness. We use this method to solve a complex problem (eight-legged locomotion). It needs 5000 less evaluations compared to when genetic algorithm are used alone.

1 Introduction

1.1 The motivation for Interactive Evolutionary Algorithm

In [3] Dave Cliff, Inman Harvey and Phil Husband from the university of Sussex lay down a chart for the development of cognitive architectures, or control systems, for situated autonomous agent. They claim that the design by hand of control systems capable of complex sensori-motor processing is likely to become prohibitively difficult as the complexity increases, and they advocate the use of Evolutionary Algorithm (EA) to evolve recurrent dynamic Artificial Neural Networks (ANN) as a potentially efficient engineering method. Our goal is to try to present a concrete proof of this claim by showing an example of big (> 16 units ANN) control system generated using EA. The difference between our work and what we call the "Sussex" approach is that we consider EAs as only one element of the ANN design process. An engineering method is something which is used to help problem solving, that may be combined with any additional symbolic knowledge one can have about a given problem. Our view is that EA should be used interactively in the process of ANN design, but not as a magic wand that will solve all the problems. In contrast with this point of view, Cliff Harvey and Husband seem to rely more on EAs. In [3] they use a direct coding of the ANN. They find ANN without particular regularities, although they acknowledge the fact that a coding which could generate repeated structure would be more appropriate. The advantage of the Sussex approach is that it is pure machine learning, without human intervention. In contrast, we use EA interactively in the ANN design. This is similar to supervised machine learning.

1.2 How do we supervise the evolutionary algorithm?

The key element that enables us to help the EA with symbolic knowledge is the way we encode ANNs. What is coded is a developmental process: how a cell divides and divides again and generates a graph of interconnected cells that finally become an ANN. The development is coded on a tree.

We help the EA using three technics :

- syntactic constraints We provide the EA with syntactic constraints, a "grammar" which restrict the number of possible trees to those having the right syntax. This is similar to program in C needing to satisfy the C-syntax. Syntactic constraints impose a prior probability on the distribution of ANN. We can study the structure of our ANN, identify some regularities, and help the emergence of them by choosing the appropriate syntactic constraints.

- problem decomposition We decompose a problem into subproblems and develop a library of ANNs of increasing complexity.

- interactive fitness We give the fitness by hand and specify intermediate stages in the evolution.

Instead of using neurons in a sort of densely connected neural soup, we want to build a sparsely connected structure, with hierarchy and symmetries, that can be analyzed. We think one needs a lot of faith to believe that EAs can quickly generate complex highly structured ANNs, from scratch. Perhaps nature has proven it is possible, but it took a lot of time and a huge number of individuals. Our approach is to use symbolic knowledge whenever it is easy and simple. By symbolic we mean things which can be expressed by syntactic constraints which are formally BNF grammars or through problem decomposition. By easy we mean symmetries that anybody can perceive. We see symbols as a general format that can define the symmetries of the problem or decompose a problem into sub-problems, or else provide building blocks. The discovery of such things is time-expensive to automate with evolutionary computation, but easily perceived by the human eye. Any non-scientific person can point out the symmetries of the 8-legged robot, and thus build the "symmetry format". We view Evolutionary Computation of ANN as a "desing amplifier" that can "ground" this symmetry format on the real world. This is may be another way to address the well known symbol grounding problem.

1.3 The challenge of this work

In [6] we show that the EA could alone decompose the 6-legged locomotion problem into the sub-problem of generating a sub-ANN for controlling one leg and put together six copies of the sub-ANN. We needed however a powerful IPSC860 32 processors parallel machine, and over 1,000,000 evaluation. We are now working with a real robot (see figure 1), and each fitness evaluation takes a few minutes, and is done by hand. The challenge of the paper was to solve the same problem with only a few hundreds of evaluations using interactive evolution.

What is hand specified in our work is only the fact that there is a symmetry, not the precise ANN architecture. Other researchers have tried to evolved ANNs for legged-locomotion, but they all give more information than we do : they use expert information about the architecture. In the work of Beer and Gallagher [2] the precise Beer architecture is given. This 6-legged architecture described by Beer in [1] has the shape of the number 8, in which all the sub-ANN controlling adjacent legs are connected, the controller of the legs that are symmetric between the two sides are also connected.

In the work of Lewis, Fagg and Solidum [10] not only is the general architecture given but also the precise wiring of all the neurons. This work is the first historic work where the fitness was given interactively by hand, and they also used a decomposition into sub-problem by hand. But the way it is done leaves the EA with only the task of finding four real values. They first generate a leg oscillator using 2 neurons, they only have to find 4 weights to obtain a correct rotation. Then they build the Beer archtitecture by connectiong 6 copies of this 2 neurons oscillator, with some precise links, and weight sharing between similar links. As a result, they once more have only four weights to genetically optimize.

Figure 1: The OCT1 8-legged robot

2 Review of Cellular Encoding

Cellular encoding is a language for local graph transformations that controls the division of cells which grow into an Artificial Neural Network (ANN) [5]. Other kind of developmental process have been proposed in the literature, a good review can be found in [8]. Many schemes have been proposed with partly the goal of modeling biological reality. Cellular encoding has been created with the sole purpose of computer problem solving, and its efficiency has been shown on a range of different problem, a review can be found in [4]. We explain the basic version of Cellular Encoding in this section. Extensive litterature on cellular encoding can be found at Gruau's homepage or PhD thesis [5]. A cell has an input site and an output site and can be linked to other cells with directed and ordered links. A cell or a link also possesses a list of internal registers that represent local memory. The registers are initialized with a default value, and are duplicated when a cell division occurs. The registers contain neuron attributes such as weights and the threshold value. The graph transformations can be classified into cell divisions and modifications of cell and link registers.

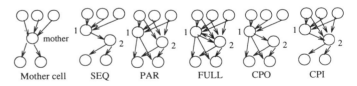

Figure 2: Illustration of main type of division: SEQ, PAR, FULL, CPO, CPI.

A cell division replaces one cell called the parent cell by two cells called child cells. A cell division must specify how the two child cells will be linked. For practical purposes, we give a name to each graph transformation; these names in turn are manipulated by the genetic algorithm. In the *sequential* division denoted SEQ the first child cell inherits the input links, the second child cell inherits the output links and the first child cell is connected to the second child cell. In the *parallel* division denoted PAR both child cells inherit both the input and output links from the parent cell. Hence, each link is duplicated. The child cells are not connected. In general, a particular cell division is specified by indicating for each child cell which link is inherited from the mother cell. The FULL division is the sequential and the parallel division combined. All the links are duplicated, and the two child cells are interconnected with two links, one for each directions. This division can generate completely connected sub-ANNs. The CPO division (CoPy Output) is a sequential division, plus the output links are duplicated in both child cells. Similarly, the CPI division (CoPy Input) is a sequential division, plus the input links are duplicated. Before describing the instructions used to modify cell registers it is useful to describe how an ANN unit performs a computation. The default value of the weights is 1, and the bias is 0. The default transfer function is the identity. Each neuron computes the weighted sum of its inputs, applies the transfer function and obtain s and updates the activity a using the equation $a = a + (s - a)/\tau$ where τ is the time constant of the neuron. See the figures 5 for examples of neural networks. The ANNs computation is performed with integers; the activity is coded using 12 bits so that 4096 corresponds to activity 1. The instruction SBIAS x sets the bias to $x/4096$. The instruction DELTAT sets the time constant of the neuron. SACT sets the initial activity of the neuron. The instruction STEP (resp LINEAR) sets the transfer function to the clipped linear function between -1 and $+1$ (resp to the identity function). The instruction PI sets the sigmoid to multiply all its input together. The WEIGHT instruction is used to modify link registers. It has k integer parameters, each one specifying a real number in floating point notation: the real is equal to the integer between -255 and 256 divided by 256. The parameters are used to set the k weights of the first input links. If a neuron happens to have more than k input links, the weights of the supernumerary input links will be set by default to the value 256 (i.e., $\frac{256}{256} = 1$).

The cellular code is a *grammar-tree* with nodes labeled by names of graph transformations. Each cell carries a duplicate copy of the grammar tree and has an internal register called a reading head that points to a particular position of the grammar tree. At each step of development, each cell executes the graph transformation pointed to by its reading head and then advances the reading head to the left or to the right subtree. After cells terminate development they lose their reading-heads and become neurons.

The order in which cells execute graph transformations is determined as follows: once a cell has executed its graph transformation, it enters a First In First Out (FIFO) queue. The next cell to execute is the head of the FIFO queue. If the cell divides, the child which reads the left subtree enters the FIFO queue first. This order of execution tries to model what would happen if cells were active in parallel. It ensures that a cell cannot be active twice while another cell has not been active at all. The WAIT instruction makes a cell wait for a specified number of steps, and makes it possible to also encode a particular order of execution.

We also used the control program symbol PROGN. It has an arbitrary number of subtrees, and all the subtrees are executed one after the other, starting from the subtree number one.

Consider a control problem where the number of control variables is n and the number of sensors is p. We want to solve this control problem using an ANN with p input units and n output units. There are two possibilities to generate those i/o units. The first method is to impose the i/o units using appropriate syntactic constraints. At the beginning of the development the initial graph of cells consists of p input units connected to a reading cell which is connected to n output units. The input and output units do not read any code, they are fixed during all the development. In effective these cells are pointers or place-holders for the inputs and outputs. The initial reading cell reads at the root of the grammar tree. It will divide according to what it reads and generate all the cells that will eventually generate the final decoded ANN. The second method, called *forcing method*, is to have the EA find itself the right number of i/o units. The development starts with a single cell connected to the input pointer cell and the output pointer cell. At the end of the development, the input (resp. output) units are those which are connected to the input (resp. output) pointer cell. We let the evolutionary algorithm find the right number of input and output unit, by putting a term in the fitness to reward the network which have a correct number of i/o units. The problem with the first method is that we can easily generate an ANN where all the output units output the same signals, and all the inputs are just systematically summed in a weighted sum. The second method works usually better, because the EA is forced to generate a specific cellular code for each i/o unit, that will specify how it is to be connected to the rest of the ANN, and with which weights. To implement the second method we will use the instruction BLOC which blocs the development of a cell until all its input neurons are neurons, and the instruction TESTIO which compares the number of inputs to a specified integer value, and sets a flag accordingly. The flag is later used to compute the fitness.

Last, the instruction CYC is used to add a recurrent link to a unit, from the output site to the input site. That unit can then perform other divisions, duplicate the recurrent link, and generates recurrent connections everywhere.

3 Enhancement of Cellular Encoding

We had to enhance cellular encoding with cloning division, and the use of types. We also implemented another way to obtain recurrent links. All these new elements are reported in this section.

The cloning operation is useful to generate symetric structure. It is really easy to implement, it is done by encapsulating a division instruction into a PROGN instruction. After the division, the two child cells only modify some registers and cut some links, then they simply go to execute the next instruction of the PROGN, and since they both execute the same instruction, it generates a highly symmetric ANN. Figure 3 represent a simple example of clone.

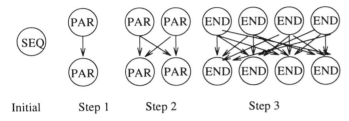

Figure 3: The cloning operation, the above ANN is developed from the code PROGN(SEQ)(PAR)(PAR)(END) which contains three clone division. The development takes three steps, one for each clone.

The use of types allows to code and therefore evolve the cell division itself. It is useful in this study because the target ANN architecture is complex and we do not know a priori which cell division can generate it.

The instruction that we are now presenting have a version for the input unit which ends by the letter 'I' and one for the output units which ends by the letter 'O'. We are now going to use another link register called the type register, which will be initialized when a link is created between two child cells, and that is later used to select links for cutting, reversing, or setting the weight. We also introduce two sets of generic instruction one to select links, and another one to set link register.

The instructions beginning by 'C' and continuing by the name of a register r are used to select links. This instruction selects the links whose register is equal to the value of the argument. For example CTYPEI(1) selects all the input links for which the type register is equal to 1. There is another register called NEW which is a flag that is set each time a new link is created between two child cells, or a recurrent link is added. CNEWO(1) selects all the newly created links, going out of the output site.

The instructions beginning by 'S' and continuing by the name of a register are used to set the value of a register, in some previously selected links. For example the sequence PROGN(CNEWI(1))(STYPEI(2)) sets the type register of newly created links from the input site,

to the value 2. In this work, we only use this instruction for the weights, and for the type.

We also use the instruction RESTRICTI and RESTRICTO which has two arguments x and d_x. It is used to reduce a list of preselected links. Let say there are 10 input links whose type is 2. We can select the 5th and the 6th using the sequence PROGN(CTYPEI (2))(RESTRICTI(5)(2)).

The type register together with the select and the set instructions can be used to encode the connections from the neurons to the input and output pointer cell. Those connection are crucial, since they determine which are the input and the output units. Using type registers, we can let each neuron individually encode whether it is or it is not an input or an output unit. We assign two different types, say 0 and 1, to the link that links the ancestor cell to respectively the input pointer cell and the output pointer cell. Each time a cell divides, the links get duplicated, so that at the near end of the development, all the cells are connected to both the input and the output pointer cell. Each cell can potentially cut the links whose type are 0 or 1, and choose to be an I/O unit.

Last, the instructions REVERSEI and REVERSEO duplicates a previously selected link from cell a to cell b, and make it go from cell b to cell a.

4 Syntactic Constraints

We used a BNF grammar as a general technique to specify both a subset of syntactically correct grammar-trees and the underlying data structure. The default data structure is a tree. When the data structure is not a tree, it can be list, set or integer. By using syntactic constraints on the trees produced by the BNF grammar, a recursive nonterminal of the type tree can be associated with a range that specifies a lower and upper bound on the number of recursive rewritings. In our experiments, this is used to set a lower bound m and an upper bound M on the number of neurons in the final neural network architecture. For the list and set data structure we set a range for the number of elements in these structures. For the integer data structure we set a lower bound and an upper bound of a random integer value. The list and set data structures are described by a set of subtrees called the "elements." The list data structure is used to store a vector of subtrees. Each of the subtrees is derived using one of the elements. Two subtrees may be derived using the same element. The set data structure is like the list data structure, except that each of the subtrees must be derived using a different element.

Figure 4 shows a simple example of syntactic constraints used to restrict the space of possible solutions. First, we impose a clone division, thus the ANN will consist of two identical subANNs. The nonterminal <nn> is recursive. It can be rewritten recursively between 0

```
<nn>[0..8];
<axiom> ::= PROGN(FULL)(<nn>)
<nn>   ::= ( PAR(<nn>)(<nn>) ) | ( CPO(<nn>)(<nn>) ) |
           ( SEQ(<nn>)(<nn>) ) | ( <attribute> )
<attribute> ::=
    (PROGN : set[0..4] of
        (WEIGHT: list[8..8] of (integer[-255..+255]))
        (DELTAT(integer[1..+40]))
        (SBIAS(integer[-4096..+4096])) (STEP) )
```

Figure 4: Tutorial example of syntactic constraints

and 8 times. Each time is it rewritten recursively, it generate a division and adds a new ANN unit. Thus the final number of ANN units will be between 1 and 9. Note that in this particular case, the size of the ANN is proportional to the size of the genome, therefore constraints of the grammar in fig. 4 which controls the size of genome result directly in constraints on ANN growth which controls the ANN size.

The nonterminal <attribute> is used to implement a subset of four possible specializations of the ANN units. The first 8 weights can be set to values between −1 and +1. The time constant can be set to a value that ranges from 1 to 40, and the bias is set to a value between −1 and +1. The transfer function can be set to the STEP function instead of the default transfer function. Since the lower bound on the set range is 0, there can be 0 specializations generated, in which case the ANN unit will compute the sum of its inputs and apply the identity function. Because the upper bound on the set is 4, all the 4 specializations can be generated. In this case, the neuron will make a weighted sum, subtract the bias, apply the clipped linear function. If the lower and the upper bound had been both 1, then exactly one of the features would be generated. This can be used to select an instruction with a given probability. For example, the sequence PROGN: set [1..1] of (WAIT) (WAIT) (WAIT) (CYC) generates a recurrent link with a probability of 0.25.

Crossover. Crossover is implemented such that two cellular codes that are syntactically correct produce an offspring that is also syntactically correct (i.e. that can be parsed by the BNF grammar). Crossover between two **trees** is the classic crossover used in Genetic Programming as advocated by Koza [9], where two subtrees are exchanged. Crossover between two **integers** is disabled. Crossover between two **lists**, or two **sets** is implemented like crossover between bit strings, since the underlying arrangement of all these data structures is a string.

Mutation. To mutate one node of a tree labeled by a terminal t, we replace the subtree beginning at this node by a single node labeled with the nonterminal parent of t. Then we rewrite the tree using the BNF grammar. To mutate a **list**, **set** or **array** data structure, we randomly add or suppress an element. To mutate an integer, we add a random value uniformly distributed between $\pm max(2, (M - n)/8)$. M and m are the upper and lower bounds of the specified integer range.

Each time an offspring is created, all the nodes are mutated with a small probability. For **tree**, **list** and **set** nodes the mutation rate is 0.05, while for the **integer** node it is 0.5. Those probability may be reset at run time of the EA.

5 Experiment and results

To help evolution we decompose the problem by hand: we first evolve the leg controller and then include 8 copies of it to evolve the locomotion controller.

5.1 The leg controller

The challenge for evolution The leg does a **power stroke** when it pushes on the ground to pull the body forward, and the **return stroke** when it lifts the leg and takes it forward. The challenge in this first experiment was to build a good leg controller, one that does not drag the leg on the return stroke, and that starts to push on the ground right at the beginning of the power stroke. The ANN had one single input. The input of 4096 on the input unit must trigger the power stroke, and the input of 0 must trigger the return stroke That implies the right scheduling of four different actions: when exactly the neuron responsible for the lifting and the swinging lift up and down, swing forward and backward. The ANN had 2 outputs: one for each angle.

General setting The command of return stroke or power stroke was hand generated during the genetic run, so as to be able to reproduce the movement whenever and as many times as desired. The EA used 20 individuals, the fitness was given according to a set of features: the highest and the lowest leg position had to be correct, the movement of the leg must start exactly when the signal is received, there must not be dragging of the leg on the return stroke, so the leg must first be lifted and then brought forward. Second the leg must rest on the floor at once on the power stroke, therefore the leg must be first put on the floor and then moved backward.

Syntactic constraints The number of neurons will be between 7 and 21. The division instructions are classic, except for the SHARI1 where the input links are shared between the two child cells, the first child gets the first input, and the second child gets the other inputs. The neuron specializes either as a temporal unit or as a spatial unit. The temporal units have a threshold sigmoid and a time constant that is genetically determined. They are used to introduce a delay in a signal, and the spatial units have a linear sigmoid, and a bias that is genetically determined. They are used to translate and multiply a signal by genetically specified constants. Those two types of units are the building blocks needed to generate a fixed length sequence of signals of different intensities and duration. The duration is controlled by the temporal units, and the intensity by the spatial units.

Results We found a solution the first run in 20 generations. Initially we wanted to terminate the return stroke with the leg up, and to bring it down on the power stroke, the controller evolved in another way, it terminates the return stroke with the leg down, and we thought it would be acceptable. We realized later, that it is actually much better this way, because the robot has always his leg on the ground, except when it is in the middle of a return stroke. So it does not loose balance often.

5.2 The locomotion controller

The Challenge We want to put together 8 copies of the previously evolved leg controller, generate 8 oscillators with correct frequency, coupling, and synchronization, and obtain a fast and smooth locomotion controller.

General setting There are some settings which were constant over the successful run 2, and run 4, and we report them here. The way we give the fitness was highly subjective, and changed during the run depending on how we felt the population had converged or not. We realized that the role of the fitness is not only to reward good individuals, but also to control genetic diversity. Since there is a bit of noise when two individuals are compared, the selective pressure can be controlled by the fitness. The rewarding must be done very cautiously, otherwise newly fit individual will quickly dominate the population. The fitness was a sum of three terms varying between 0.01 and 0.03: To reward oscillations and correct frequencies, the number of legs which oscillate, and the correct phase and coupling. Programming an automatic fitness should be possible but not trivial, and will imply the tuning of many constants to fit the robots. We believe direct evaluation on the robot is quicker.

We started with a population of 32 individuals so as to be able to sample building blocks, and reduce it to 16 after 5 generations. At the same time as we reduced the population, we lowered all the mutation rates (set list and tree) to 0.01 except the integer mutation rate which was increased to 0.4, the idea was to assume that the EA had gotten the right architecture, and to concentrate the genetic search on the weights. The weights were mutated almost one time out of two. The selective pressure was also augmented: the number of individual participating in Boltzmann tournament was increased from 3 to 5.

Those tournaments are used to delete individuals or to select mates. We no longer wanted genetic diversity, but rather genetic convergence of the architecture, similar to tuning an already working solution. We got the idea to use genetic convergence from the SAGA paradigm of Inman Harvey [7]. We threw away the motionless individuals, and those who had not the right number of input/output units. As a results, to generate the first 32 individual in the initial population, we go over one hundred evalutations.

Syntactic constraints constant over the five runs Using fixed cellular code, we specify a general structure including 8 copies of the previously evolved leg controller. The evolved controller is forced to have 8 output units using the forcing method described in section 2. Those output units are bound to the 8 input units of the leg controllers.

Results We did only five runs. The first two runs were done with only seven legs. Run 0: after hours of breeding we input accidentally a fitness of 23, which had the effect to stop the EA, the success predicate being that the fitness is greater than 1. Run 1 gave a not so bad quadripod, but we realized there was a bug in the way we used the link types.

Run 2 and 3: Syntactic constraints: the core of the controller is developed by a cell executing exactly 3 clones, therefore an ANN with an 8-fold symmetries will be generated. The 8 cells generated by these clones will generate the same sub-ANN having between one and seven units. Because of the preceding 3 clones, this sub-ANN will be duplicated 8 times, however, one of those 8 sub-ANNs can potentially control more than one leg.

The clone division and the normal cell division are specified in a similar way. The general type of the division is to be chosen between FULL, PAR, SEQ, CPI and CPO. Right after dividing, the two cells execute a different sequence of cutting operators. We adjust the probability of cutting links by first specifying how often and how many links of a given type are cut. The second child sets the type of the newly created link between the two child cells, if there are some. When a cell stops to divide, it sets all its neuron attributes. First we reverse some links or/and add a recurrent link. We adjust the "amount of recurrence" by setting the probability with which recurrent links are created. We then generate a time constant, some weights, a threshold, an initial activity, and finally the sigmoid type.

During run 2 we got a good solution but not optimal. We realized that it was not possible to mutate the general architecture without destroying the whole genetic code. That would imply replacing a division by another. We think it explains the fact that the general architecture did not change throughout run 2.

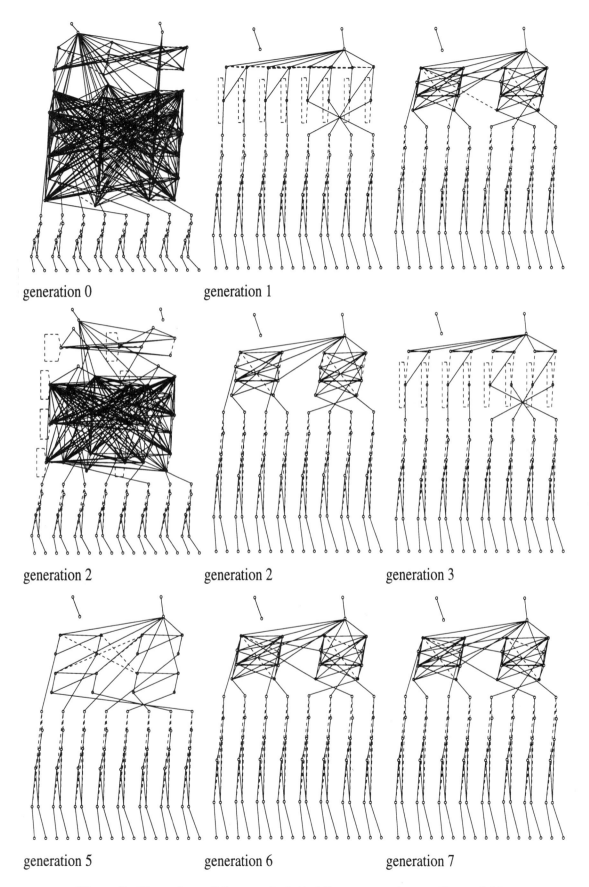

Figure 5: Champions of the run 4, dotted line represents negative weights.

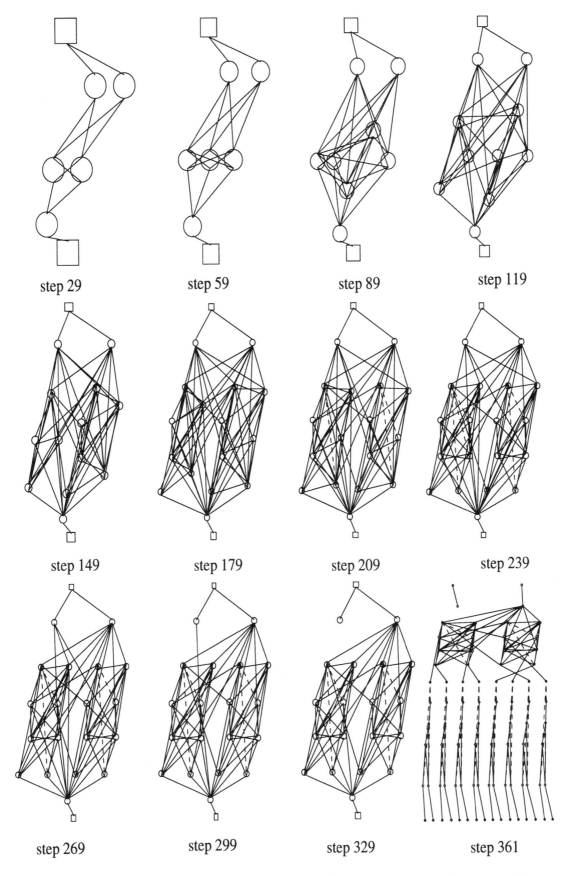

step 29   step 59   step 89   step 119

step 149   step 179   step 209   step 239

step 269   step 299   step 329   step 361

Figure 6: Steps of the development of the Champion, squares represent pointer cells

Run 3 lasted only 5 hours, because we typed a high fitness on the keyboard, for a bad individual who kept reproducing all the time.

Run 4: To enable mutation of the general structure we used only the FULL division for the clone, and force the EA to entirely determine type by type, which links are inherited. This can be mutated independently, and may result in making possible " soft mutation" that modify a small part of the division. Whereas if we mutate a division from CPI to PAR, for example, all the division has to be re-generated from scratch. Also, we felt it was better to encode individually for each neuron if the neuron is an input or an output unit. Those two modifications resulted in producing ANNs whose number of input was always a multiple of 8, and each of the sub ANN is now forced to control one and exactly one leg, unlike the preceding run.

champion analysis Run 4 gave good results in seven generations. A selection of the champions of run 4 are reported in figure 5. This detailed analysis gives the feeling of breeding, of which neural structure we obtained and of how some of them can be directly analyzed to guess their functionality. We use a representation where information flows from top to bottom. The 2 input units were intended for later use. The 16 output units correspond to the 16 motors. On the figure, it is very clear that all the ANNs contain the 8 copies of the previously evolved leg controller. They are like an output layer between the 8 oscillators and the 16 effectors. At generation 0 an ANN produced oscillation on one leg. At generation 1, an ANN had a correct oscillation on all the legs. It used 8 oscillator neurons with a recurrent connection, and 8 neurons that implement a weak coupling. The oscillators loose synchronisation. In generation 1, another ANN produced oscillation, and coupling between the two sides but not within one side. That means that the two front legs for example, or the two right legs are synchronous, but not the left front leg with the left rear leg. At generation 2 an ANN moved the two front legs two times quicker. You can see figure 5, that the part that controls the two front legs is much more sparsely connected. Generation 2 produced another champion: a slow but correct quadripod gait. Generation 3 produces a funny gait with for pairs of two coupled oscillators and inside each pair, one oscillator has a twice bigger frequency. Generation 5 produced a quadripod gait, not too slow, but there still lacks some coupling between the ANNs controlling the legs of one side. There are diagonal connections between the four groups, which implement coupling between the two sides, but there are no connections from top to bottom. At generation 6 we had a nice ANN with all the connection needed for coupling, but the frequency on the right side was slightly greater than on the left side, as a result the robot was constantly turning

right. We got a number of individuals which were always turning right. Generation 7, we finally got success, a perfect quadripod, smooth and fast. We had the robot run for 20 minutes to check the phase lock. The robot walks at 7.5 cm. per second faster than the handcoded controller provided with the robot (6.4 cm. per second at 50 ms. per leg update). Some steps of the development of this ultimate Champion are reported in figure 6. The leg controllers are developped at the very end, in the last picture.

Here is the code of the solution in run 4.

```
LABBL(SBQ(SBQ(PAR(PROGN(WAIT(200))(DBLTAT(1))(SBIAS(0))(PROGN
(CTYPBO(0))(SWBIGHTO(318)(319)(128)(148)(485)(228)(154)(49)(333)(7)
(314)(444)(171)(448))(PROGN(CTYPBO(1))(SWBIGHTO(268)(185)(424)(113)
(54)(357)(316)(259)(102)(90)(43)(299)(367)(477)(78)))(LINBAR)
(PROGN(WAIT(200))(DBLTAT(1))(SBIAS(0))(PROGN(CTYPBO(0))(
SWBIGHTO(453)(461)(82)(56)(283)(111)(385)(43)(409)(312)(391)
(171)(238)))(PROGN(CTYPBO(1))(SWBIGHTO(67)(403)(483)(458)(104)(219)
(505)(323)(234)(94)(291)(330)(154)(198)(355)(324)))(LINBAR)))
(PROGN(WAIT(4))(CTYPBI(-1))(RBSTRICTI(0)(1))(STYPBI(0))(CTYPBI
(-1))(STYPBI(1))(CTYPBI(-1))(STYPBO(0))(FULL(PROGN(PROGN
(PROGN(PROGN(CTYPBI(2))(PROGN(RBSTRICTI(2)(18))(RMI)))(PROGN
(CTYPBI(2))(PROGN(WAIT)(RMI)))(PROGN(CTYPBI(4))(PROGN
(WAIT)(RMI))))(PROGN(PROGN(CTYPBI(3))(PROGN(WAIT)(RMO
)))(PROGN(CTYPBI(3))(PROGN(RBSTRICTO(0)(17))(RMO)))(PROGN
(PROGN(CTYPBI(5))(PROGN(WAIT)(RMO)))))(WAIT(18))(PROGN
(PROGN(PROGN(PROGN(CTYPBI(3))(PROGN(WAIT)(RMI))))(PROGN
(PROGN(CTYPBI(5))(PROGN(WAIT)(RMI)))(PROGN(CTYPBI(5))(PROGN
(WAIT)(RMI))))(PROGN)(PROGN(PROGN(PROGN(CNBWI)(STYPBI(2))
)(CNBWO)(STYPBO(2)))(WAIT(2)))(FULL(PROGN(PROGN(PROGN(
PROGN(PROGN(CTYPBI(5))(PROGN(RBSTRICTI(2)(16))(RMI)))(PROGN(
CTYPBI(5))(PROGN(WAIT)(RMI)))(PROGN))(WAIT(14)))(PROGN(
PROGN(PROGN(PROGN(PROGN(CTYPBI(2))(PROGN(RBSTRICTI(1)(3))(
RMI)))(PROGN(CTYPBI(2))(PROGN(WAIT)(RMI))))(PROGN(PROGN(
CTYPBI(3))(PROGN(RBSTRICTI(1)(31))(RMI)))(PROGN(CTYPBI(3))
(PROGN(WAIT)(RMI))))(PROGN(PROGN(CTYPBI(4))(PROGN(RBSTRICTI
(2)(12))(RMI)))(PROGN(CTYPBI(4))(PROGN(WAIT)(RMI))))(PROGN
(PROGN(CTYPBI(5))(PROGN(WAIT)(RMI))))(PROGN(PROGN(PROGN
(CTYPBO(2))(PROGN(WAIT)(RMO)))(PROGN(CTYPBO(3))(PROGN
(WAIT)(RMO)))(PROGN(CTYPBO(3))(PROGN(WAIT)(RMO)))(PROGN(
PROGN(CTYPBO(4))(PROGN(WAIT)(RMO)))(PROGN(CTYPBO(4))(PROGN
(RBSTRICTO(0)(9))(RMO)))(PROGN(PROGN(CTYPBO(5))(PROGN
(RBSTRICTO(0)(15))(RMO)))(PROGN(CTYPBO(5))(PROGN(RBSTRICTO
(1)(21))(RMO))))(PROGN(PROGN(PROGN(CNBWI)(STYPBI(2))(CNBWO)
(STYPBO(2))))(WAIT(0)))(FULL(PROGN(PROGN(PROGN(PROGN(
PROGN(CTYPBI(5))(PROGN(WAIT)(RMI)))(PROGN(CTYPBI(5))(PROGN
(WAIT)(RMI)))(PROGN))(WAIT(16)))(PROGN(PROGN(PROGN(PROGN
(PROGN(CTYPBI(2))(PROGN(WAIT)(RMI)))(PROGN(CTYPBI(3)
)(PROGN(WAIT)(RMI)))(PROGN(CTYPBI(3))(PROGN(RBSTRICTI(2)(6))
(RMI))))(PROGN(PROGN(CTYPBI(5))(PROGN(RBSTRICTI(0)(2))(RMI)))
(PROGN(CTYPBI(5))(PROGN(RBSTRICTI(2)(7))(RMI))))(PROGN(PROGN
(PROGN(CTYPBO(2))(PROGN(RBSTRICTI(1)(2))(RMO)))(PROGN(PROGN
(CTYPBO(3))(PROGN(RBSTRICTO(2)(9))(RMO)))(PROGN(PROGN(CTYPBO
(5))(PROGN(RBSTRICTO(0)(12))(RMO)))(PROGN(CTYPBO(5))(PROGN
(WAIT)(RMO)))))(PROGN(PROGN(PROGN(CNBWI)(STYPBI(4))(CNBWO)
(STYPBO(4)))))(WAIT(2)))(CPO(PROGN(PROGN(PROGN(PROGN(PROGN
(PROGN(PROGN(CTYPBO(2))(PROGN(WAIT)(RMO))))(PROGN(CTYPBO
(3))(PROGN(WAIT)(RMO)))(PROGN(PROGN(CTYPBO(4))(PROGN(WAIT)
(RMO)))(PROGN(CTYPBO(4))(PROGN(RBSTRICTO(0)(6))(RMO))))(PROGN
(PROGN(CTYPBO(5))(PROGN(WAIT)(RMO))))(WAIT(18))(PROGN
(PROGN(PROGN(CNBWI)(STYPBI(4))(CNBWO(STYPBO(4)))))(PROGN
(WAIT))(PROGN(DBLTAT(4))(PROGN(CTYPBI(2))(SWBIGHT(254)(212)
(170)(-63)(-181)(158)))(PROGN(CTYPBI(3))(SWBIGHT(242)(73)
(103)(56)(9)(226)(48)))(PROGN(CTYPBI(4))(SWBIGHT(4003)(1411)
(-3628)(3953)(1248)(-1062)(1202)))(PROGN(CTYPBI(5))(SWBIGHT
(-2642)(-1926)(2968)(-4094)(-217)(-577)(-2340)))(SBIAS(1896))
(SACT(989)))(PROGN(PROGN(CTYPBO(0))(RMI)))(PROGN(WAIT))
(PROGN(CTYPBO(0))(RMO)))(LINBAR)(BND))))(PROGN(PROGN(PROGN
(PROGN(PROGN(CTYPBI(2))(PROGN(WAIT)(RMI)))(PROGN(CTYPBI(3))
(PROGN(RBSTRICTI(2)(24))(RMI))))(PROGN(CTYPBI(4))(PROGN(WAIT)
(RMI)))(PROGN(CTYPBI(4))(PROGN(WAIT)(RMI))))(PROGN(PROGN
(CTYPBO(2))(PROGN(RBSTRICTO(1)(24))(RMO)))(PROGN(CTYPBO(
4))(PROGN(RBSTRICTO(2)(20))(RMO))))(PROGN(CTYPBO(5))(PROGN
(WAIT)(RMO)))(PROGN(CTYPBO(5))(PROGN(RBSTRICTO(2)(9))(RMO))))
(PROGN(PROGN(CNBWI)(STYPBI(5))(CNBWO)(STYPBO(5)))))(WAIT(3)))
(PROGN(PROGN(PROGN(CNBWI)(STYPBI(3))(CNBWO)(STYPBO(3))))
(PROGN(PROGN(DBLTAT(27))(PROGN(PROGN(CTYPBI(2))(SWBIGHT
(-3469)(-1379)(-3329)(-2945)(296)(-1376)))(PROGN(CTYPBI(3))
(SWBIGHT(196)(3165)(-1501)(-3442)(2994)(-2912)))(PROGN(CTYPBI
(4))(SWBIGHT(2875)(-575)(3329)(-770)(-402)(-793)))(PROGN
(CTYPBI(5))(SWBIGHT(-118)(-179)(-25)(-220)(110)(-240)(170))))
(SBIAS(-1697))(SACT(-1746)))(PROGN(WAIT))(PROGN(WAIT))
(PROGN(WAIT))(LINBAR)(BND)))))))(PROGN(BLOC)(TBSTIO8)
(SHARI(JMP12)(SHARI(JMP12)(SHARI(JMP12)(SHARI(JMP12)
(PROGN(SWITCH)(SHARI(JMP12)(PROGN(SWITCH)(SHARI(JMP12)
(PROGN(SWITCH)(SHARI(JMP12)(JMP12)(1))(1)))(1))(1))(1))
(1))(1)(1)))
```

6 Conclusion

In this work we succeeded to evolve an ANN for controlling an 8-legged robot. Experiments were done without a simulator, and the fitness was determined interactively by hand. We believe that generating an ANN for locomotion controller is not a trivial task, because it needs at least 16 hidden units, unlike most applications that can be found in the literature. This difficult problem has been solved using an enhancement of cellular encoding and helping the EA with symbolic knowledge.

The enhancement includes cell cloning which generate highly symmetric ANNs, and link typing which makes it possible to evolve the cell division itself. Helping the EA is done using 3 technics :

1- With problem decomposition, we first find an ANN for the leg controller and use it as a building block for the locomotion controller.

2- Syntactic constraints specify that there are exactly a three fold symmetry that exploit the fact that $8 = 2^3$ legs are used. It is quite easy to say that the development must begin with three clone division, it is more difficult to say how exactly the division must be done. What's hand specified in our work is only the fact that there is a symmetry, not the precise architecture. The EA alone is able to decompose the problem of locomotion into the subproblem of generating an oscillator, and then makes 8 copies of the oscillator, and combine them with additional links so as to provide the adequate coupling. Other researchers have tried to evolved ANNs for legged-locomotion, but they all use expert information about the architecture.

3- Maybe the most unexpected thing out of this work, is that the breeding is worth its pain. We are not sure that an automatic fitness evaluation that would have just measured the distance walked by the robot would had been successful, even in one week of simulation. There are some precise facts that support this view. First, right at the initial generation, we often got an individual which was just randomly moving its legs, but still managed to get forward quite a bit. Using automatic fitness, the solution would quickly dominate. Vice versa, there are some very nice features which do not make the robot go forward, like oscillation or coupling. Typically, we first track oscillatory behavior, then tune the frequency, get the signal on all the 8 legs, and last, we evolve coupling between the legs, with the right phase delay. That would be a difficult fitness to program because it would involve a lot of parameters.

In short, we developed in this work a new paradigm for using Evolutionary Computation in an interactive way. Syntactic Constraints exploit symmetries to provide a prior probability (machine learning terminology) on the distribution of ANNs. Modular decomposition allow to replace one big problem by two simpler problems. Interactive fitness evaluation can steer the EA towards the solution by specifying intermediate stages. Interactive operation of the Evolutionary Algorithm (EA) appears faster and easier than hand-programing the robot. It takes a few trial and errors if we are to generate the

ANNs by hand.

Acknowledgment

This paper reports on work partially done by Dominique Quatravaux in fullfillment of the master's thesis requirements under supervision of Michel Cosnard and Frédéric Gruau, on Frédéric Gruau's project at CWI in Amsterdam. Dominique declined to be coauthor. F. Gruau was suppported by a postdoctoral TMR grant from the European community within the EASY group at the COGS department in Sussex University.

References

[1] Randall Beer. *Intelligence as adaptive behavior.* Academic Press, 1990.

[2] Randall Beer and John Gallagher. Evolving dynamical neural networks for adaptive behavior. *Adaptive Behavior*, 1:92–122, 1992.

[3] Dave Cliff, Inman Harvey, and Cliff Husband. Exploration in evolutionary robotics. *Adaptive Behavior*, 1:73–110, 1993.

[4] F.Gruau. Artificial cellular development in optimization and compilation. In Sanchez and Tomassini, editors, *Towards Evolvable Hardware.* Springer Verlag, LNCS, 1996.

[5] F. Gruau. *Neural Network Synthesis using Cellular Encoding and the Genetic Algorithm.* PhD Thesis, Ecole Normale Supérieure de Lyon, 1994. ftp: lip.ens-lyon.fr pub/Rapports/PhD/PhD94-01-E.ps.Z (english) PhD94-01-F.ps.Z (french).

[6] F. Gruau. Automatic definition of modular neural networks. *Adaptive Behavior V3N2*, pages 151–183, 1995.

[7] Inman Harvey. Species adaptation genetic algorithm: a basis for continuing saga. Cogs csrp 221, The Evolutionary Robotics Lab, 1995.

[8] J.Kodjabachian and J. Meyer. Development, learning and evolution in animates. In *PerAc'94.* IEEE computer society press, 1994.

[9] John R. Koza. *Genetic programming* MIT press, 1992.

[10] Lewis, Fagg, and Solidum. Genetic programming aprroach to the construction of a neural network for control of a walking robot. In *Proceedings of the IEEE International Conference on Robotics and Automation*, 1993.

Adaptive Behavior in Competing Co-Evolving Species

Dario Floreano
Center for Neuro-Mimetic Systems
Laboratory of Microcomputing
Swiss Federal Institute of Technology
EPFL, Lausanne, Switzerland
floreano@di.epfl.ch

Stefano Nolfi
Department of Neural Systems
and Artificial Life
National Research Council
Viale Marx 15, Roma, Italy
stefano@kant.irmkant.rm.cnr.it

Abstract

Co-evolution of competitive species provides an interesting testbed to study the role of adaptive behavior because it provides unpredictable and dynamic environments. In this paper we experimentally investigate some arguments for the co-evolution of different adaptive protean behaviors in competing species of predators and preys. Both species are implemented as simulated mobile robots (Kheperas) with infrared proximity sensors, but the predator has an additional vision module whereas the prey has a maximum speed set to twice that of the predator. Different types of variability during life for neurocontrollers with the same architecture and genetic length are compared. It is shown that simple forms of proteanism affect co-evolutionary dynamics and that preys rather exploit noisy controllers to generate random trajectories, whereas predators benefit from directional-change controllers to improve pursuit behavior.

1 Introduction

Adaptive behavior –as compared to innate and fixed behavior– might represent an advantage in unpredictable and dynamic environments. In this respect, co-evolution of competitive species provides an interesting testbed to study the role of adaptive behavior. In the simplest scenario of two competing species, such as a predator and a prey, the behavior of each individual is tightly related to the behavior of the competitor both on the evolutionary and on the ontogenetic time scale. On the evolutionary time scale, the coupled dynamics of the system give rise to the "Red Queen effect" whereby the fitness landscape of each population is continuously modified by the competing population [3]. Given the ubiquity of co-evolution in nature, the relative lack of bio-historical evidence for its role in adaptive progress, and the strong assumptions underlying simple mathematical models developed so far, Artificial Life techniques, such as computer simulations of artificial evolution, are a suitable method to study this phenomenon [1].

On the ontogenetic time-scale, it has been argued that pursuit-evasion contests might favor the emergence of "protean behaviors", that is behaviors which are adaptively unpredictable [4]. For example, preys could take advantage of unpredictable escape behaviors based on short sequences of stochastic motor actions. Similarly, predators could take advantage of enhanced perceptual characteristics and/or adaptive sensory-motor intelligence which could enable predictive tracking strategies. Miller and Cliff provided an excellent review of the biological significance of pursuit-evasion contests and several arguments for its relevance in the study of protean adaptive behavior [11]. Recently, they also described initial results from computer simulations of artificial co-evolution of competing agents controlled by continuous-time recurrent neural networks [2], and developed a set of techniques for analyzing and assessing adaptive progress of both populations [1]. Artificial co-evolution of competitive species has been studied also by other researchers using similar methods, such as Ray's "Tierra" system [13], Sim's creatures [15], and Reynolds' pursuer-evader systems [14]. In very recent work, which will be briefly summarized below, we have investigated the potentiality of the Red Queen effect for evolutionary robotics, and showed that, with a suitable combination of realistic simulations and measuring techniques, competitive co-evolution can develop a variety of efficient behaviors without effort in fitness design [7].

However, none of these experimental researches systematically explored the role of ontogenetic adaptive behavior in co-evolution of competing species. Although most of the evolved systems include some form of noise, it is difficult to say whether this plays an important role on the specific dynamics of co-evolving species or it is simply exploited for smoothing the fitness landscape. In general, all the results presented so far are based on single-run studies and do not include comparisons between different adaptation techniques.

The aim of this paper is that of presenting initial re-

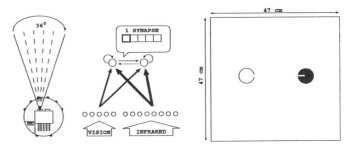

Figure 1: **Right**: The Predator is equipped with the vision module (1D-array of photo-receptors, visual angle of 36°). **Left**: The Prey has a black protuberance which can be detected by the predator everywhere in the environment, but its maximum speed is twice that of the predator. Both Predator and Prey are equipped with 8 Infrared proximity sensors (max detection range was 3 cm in our environment). Evolutionary runs have been conducted in simulation.

Figure 2: **Left and center**: Details of simulation of vision, of neural network architecture, and of genetic encoding. The prey differs from the predator in that it does not have 5 input units for vision. Each synapse in the network is coded by five bits, the first bit determining the sign of the synapse and the remaining four the other synaptic parameters. **Right**: Initial starting position for Prey (left, empty disk with small opening corresponding to frontal direction) and Predator (right, black disk with line corresponding to frontal direction) in the arena. For each competition, the initial orientation is random.

sults on the effect of adaptive protean behavior in co-evolving competing species. In particular, we want to address the following questions: Does protean behavior affect evolutionary dynamics? Do competing species exploit different types of protean strategies, and how does this affect the competitor's behavior? In the attempt to investigate these issues in very simple settings, we have compared co-evolution of competing species equipped with different types of simple adaptive controllers with results from previous experiments where the controllers were genetically determined [7].

2   Method

As often happens in nature, predators and preys belong to different species with different sensory and motor characteristics. Thus, we employed two Khepera robots, one of which (the *Predator*) was equipped with a vision module while the other (the *Prey*) had a maximum available speed set to twice that of the predator (Figure 1). Both individuals were also provided with eight infrared proximity sensors (six on the front side and two on the back) which had a maximum detection range of 3 cm in our environment. The two species evolved in a square arena of size 47 x 47 cm with high white walls so that the predator could always see the prey (if within the visual angle) as a black spot on a white background.

Since co-evolutionary experiments with real robots would require two separate cables for powering the units for several hours, *ad hoc* solutions must be devised to avoid that the cables twist on each other. Instead of building additional hardware, we have resorted to real-

istic computer simulations of the two Kheperas. It has been shown elsewhere that for geometrically-simple environments one can have small discrepancies between behaviors in simulation and on the real robot by sampling sensor activity at different distances and angles of the robot from the objects of the world (see [10] for details). We have thus employed this methodology and sampled infrared sensor activity of each robot in front of a wall and in front of another robot. These values were then separately stored away and accessed through a look-up table depending on the faced object.

Simulation of the visual input required different considerations. The vision module K213 of Khepera is an additional turret which can be plugged-in directly on top of the basic platform. It consists of a 1D-array of 64 photo-receptors which provide a linear image composed of 64 pixel of 256 gray-levels each, sub-tending a view-angle of 36°. The optics are designed to bring into focus objects situated at distances between 5cm and 50cm while an additional sensor of light intensity automatically adapts the scanning speed of the chip to keep the image stable and exploit at best the sensitivity of receptors under a large variety of illumination intensities. The K213 vision turret incorporates a private 68HC11 processor which is used for optional low-level processing of the scanned image before passing it to the robot controller. One of these options is position detection of the pixel with minimal activation in the image which in this case corresponds to the position of the prey in the visual field. Therefore, instead of simulating the response of the 1D-array of receptors resorting to complex and time-consuming ray-tracing techniques, we exploited the built-in facility for position detection of pixel with minimal intensity, and divided the visual angle in five sectors corresponding to five simulated photo-receptors (Figure 2, left). If the pixel with minimal intensity was within the first sector, then the first simulated photo-receptor would become active, if the pixel was within the second sector, then the second photo-receptor would become active, etc. We made sure in a set of preliminary measurements that this type of input reduction was largely sufficient to reliably capture and represent all the relevant visual information available to the predator.

Displacement of the robots was computed by passing to the simulator a vector of wheel velocities (positive and negative values standing for rotation in different directions) and calculating the new x, y position using a set of simple trigonometric equations which gave a maximum estimation error of $0.008mm$ for the predator and $0.016mm$ for the prey, absolutely negligible values with respect to the sensor characteristics (for more details, see [7]).

In line with some of our previous work (e.g., [5]), the robot controller was a simple perceptron of two sigmoid units with recurrent connections at the output layer. The activation of each output unit was used to update the speed value of the corresponding wheel every $100ms$. In the case of the predator, each output unit received connections from five photo-receptors and from eight infrared proximity sensors (Figure 2, center); in the case of the prey, each output unit received input only from 8 infrared proximity sensors, but its activation value was multiplied by 2 before setting the wheel speed. This structure, which is well-suited for evolution of Braitenberg-like obstacle avoidance, was chosen for being a minimally sufficient architecture to evolve something interesting while maintaining system complexity at a manageable level; for the same reason, the architecture was kept fixed, and only synaptic parameters were evolved.

In order to keep things as simple as possible and given the small size of the parameter set, we used direct genetic encoding [16]: each parameter (including recurrent connections and threshold values of output units) was encoded on five bits, the first bit determining the sign of the synapse and the remaining four bits different characteristics of the synapses, depending on the controller type under investigation. Therefore, the genotype of the predator was 5 x (30 synapses + 2 thresholds) bits long while that of the prey was 5 x (20 synapses + 2 thresholds) bits long. Two populations of 100 individuals each were co-evolved for 100 generations. Each individual was tested against the best competitors of the ten previous generations (a similar procedure was used in [15, 14, 1]) in order to improve co-evolutionary stability. For each competition, the prey and predator were always posi-

Condition	Bits for one synapse				
	1	2	3	4	5
1	sign	strength			
2	sign	strength		noise	
3	sign	Hebb rule			rate

Table 1: Genetic encoding of synaptic parameters for each co-evolutionary condition. 1: Genetically-determined controllers; 2: Adaptive-noise controllers; 3: Directional-change controllers.

tioned on a horizontal line in the middle of the environment at a distance corresponding to half the environment width (Figure 2, right), but always at a new random orientation. The competition ended either when the predator touched the prey or after 500 motor updates (corresponding to 50 seconds at maximum on the real robot).

The fitness function Φ_c for each tournament did not require complex and/or global measures; it was simply *TimetoContact* normalized by the maximum number of motor updates (500) TtC for the predator pr, and $1 - TtC$ for the prey py, further averaged over the number of tournaments (10). Therefore the fitness values were always between 0 and 1, where 0 means worst. Individuals were ranked after fitness performance in descending order and the best 20 were allowed to reproduce. One-point crossover was applied on all randomly paired strings with constant probability $pc = 0.1$, and random mutation (bit switching) was applied to each bit with constant probability $pm = 0.05$.[1]

2.1 Protean controllers

Being the definition of protean behavior only qualitative in the literature, we decided to provide the organisms with "protean controllers", that is neural networks which could potentially display forms of adaptive unpredictability or directional change and compare them with neural networks whose behavior was fixed and genetically evolved. For sake of comparison, all the neural networks had the same architecture, the same genotype length (5 bits per synapse), and used a comparable encoding technique. Here we describe three evolutionary conditions, each one corresponding to a different controller type (Table 1). In all conditions, the first bit of each synapse coded its sign (whether excitatory or inhibitory).

In the first condition, the remaining four bits coded the synaptic strength as a value in the range [0, 1]: since no changes take place during the life of the individuals,

---

[1] In preliminary experiments, we compared various evolutionary runs with different pc, and a less severe selection scheme (50 parents out of 100 individuals), but none of these changes affected evolutionary dynamics and outcomes.

let us call them *genetically-determined controllers*.

In the second condition, only two bits coded the synaptic strength (again, in the range [0, 1]), and the remaining two bits coded the level of random noise applied to the synaptic value. Each level corresponded to the lower and upper bounds of a uniform noise distribution: 0.0 (no noise), ±0.337, ±0.667, and ±1.0. At every network activation, each synapse had its own newly-computed noise value added to its strength (with a final check to level out sums below 0.0 or above 1.0). We shall call this condition *adaptive-noise controllers* because each species can evolve the most appropriate noise level for each synapse.

In the third condition, two bits coded four hebbian rules and the remaining two bits the learning rate (0.0, 0.337, 0.667, and 1.0). Four variations of the Hebb rule were used: "pure Hebb" whereby the synaptic strength can only increase when both presynaptic and postsynaptic units are active, "presynaptic" whereby the synapse changes only when the presynaptic unit is active (strengthened when the postsynaptic unit is active, and weakened when the postsynaptic unit is inactive), "postsynaptic" whereby the synapse changes only when the postsynaptic unit is active (strengthened when the presynaptic unit is active, and weakened when the presynaptic unit is inactive), and "covariance" whereby the synapse is strengthened if the difference between pre- and post-synaptic activations is smaller than a threshold (half the activation level, that is 0.5) and is weakened if the difference is larger than such threshold. After decoding a genotype into the corresponding controller, each synapse was randomly initialised to a value in the range [0, 1] and modified at each time step according to the corresponding hebbian rule and learning rate. In a previous paper, we have shown that this evolutionary scheme in a single-agent static environment can develop stable controllers which quickly develop navigation strategies starting from small random synaptic strengths [6]; interested readers will find more details in that paper. Flotzinger has recently replicated those results and studied in more detail the synaptic dynamics, showing that the continuously changing synaptic values reflect (to a certain approximation) input and output values of the network [8]. Therefore, let us call this condition *directional-change controllers*, simply indicating that synaptic changes depend on sensory activation and motor actions.

3 Results

For each condition, 6 different evolutionary runs were performed, each starting with a different seed for initializing the computer random functions. A set of pairwise two-tail t-tests of the average fitness and best fitness along generations among all the six runs, performed to check whether different seeds significantly affected the experimental outcomes, gave negative results at significance level 0.05. Therefore, for each condition below,

we shall plot only data referring to seed 1 (arbitrarily chosen), but the statistical tests reported will be based on all the runs. Each run was carried out separately on a Sun SparcStation 20, lasting approximately 8 to 10 hours (time varied depending on the different controllers and on the performance of the competitors). For the first condition, we briefly summarize the basic results already described in a recent paper where we also presented additional analyses and considerations for robotic applications [7].

As we shall see below, the changing fitness landscape due to the "Red Queen effect" demands novel measuring techniques to monitor the dynamics of co-evolutionary systems. For example, a stationary fitness value over several generations could hide to the observer a set of coupled and rapid changes in both populations. Therefore, for all conditions we show the average fitness of the two competing species along with two types of analysis developed by Cliff and Miller to measure progress in co-evolutionary competitive systems [1]. The first, which they dubbed "CIAO data" (Current Individual vs. Ancestral Opponents), shows the performance of the best individuals of each generation against the best competing ancestors; in applying this technique to our populations after co-evolutionary training, we test each individual ten times (that is ten different individual tournaments) against each best competing ancestor, and plot the average fitness as darker squares for higher values. The second, which they dubbed "Ancestral Hamming Maps", shows the normalized Hamming distance between the genotypes of best individuals along generations (darker squares for higher distance). Both these measures reveal some of the underlying dynamics, such as continuous or instantaneous progress, genetic change, cycling through strategies, etc.

3.1 Genetically-determined controllers

When both controllers were genetically determined, a set of oscillations in fitness values emerged after an initial short period (figure 3, left center), as in [15, p. 36]. The onset and amplitude of these oscillations varied across different seeds, but the general pattern was always the same and it kept repeating for several hundred generations, as we could observe in a continuation of this run up to 500 generations (data not shown). However, continuing a run for more than one hundred generations does not reveal anything new with respect to the analyses reported below. We never observed dominance of one species over the other in any of the evolutionary runs, although the preys tended to display higher peaks due to the initial position advantage.

A *relational measure* of performance gives us additional information on the coupled dynamics of such a co-evolved system: for example, one can derive an index of *relative performance* r_i^c by counting how often one

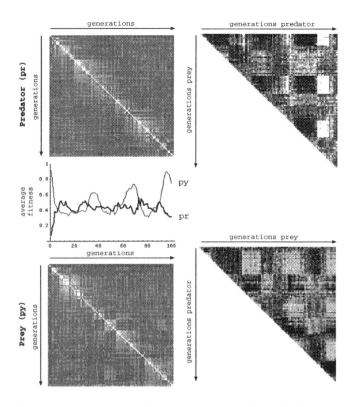

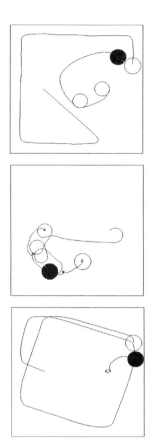

Figure 3: *Genetically-determined controllers.* **Left, center**: Average fitness across generations for predator (pr) and prey (py). **Left, top and bottom**: Ancestral Hamming Maps for predator and prey, respectively: see section 3 for explanation. **Right, top and bottom**: CIAO graphs for predator and prey. respectively: see section 3 for explanation.

Figure 4: Behaviors of *genetically-determined controllers.* Black disk is predator, white is prey. **Top**. Generation 20: The predator has developed good visual tracking strategies. The prey is a wall-follower with obstacle avoidance. **Center**. Generation 70: The prey turns on place quickly backing whenever the predator attacks. **Bottom**. Generation 90. The predator develops a "spider-strategy" slowly backing against a wall and waiting for the fast-approaching prey.

species reports higher fitness than the competing species at each generation for each separate run i in a specific condition c. In our co-evolutionary runs which lasted 100 generations, such index will be in the range $[-100, 100]$, where -100 means that the preys always outperformed the predators, 0 means that both species were equally better or worse than the competitors, and 100 means that the predators always outperformed the preys. In this condition ($c = 1$), the average value over different runs is $\overline{R^1} = 16.67$ with standard deviation of the sample mean $\sigma = 38$, indicating that both species reported similar performances. The development of a better strategies by one of the species corresponded to a decrement in performance of the competing species.

Major changes in behavioral strategies are reflected by the genotype of the best individuals selected for reproduction. The Ancestral Hamming Maps reported on top and bottom left of figure 3 show how each individual differs from the other individuals of its own population. The white diagonal line (Hamming distance zero) is the

identity comparison. Small white areas, which indicate almost identical genotypes, correspond to periods of similar fitness in the performance graph. Since these areas appear in the neighborhood of the matrix diagonal, only best individuals which are close in evolutionary time have similar genotypes. It also means that individuals that report similar fitness, but are distant in time, do not have the same genotype. Small dark lines between white zones indicate an abrupt change of behavioral strategy, whereas a gradual fading of white into gray indicates gradual genetic change (which is quite rare here).

Whether genetic change implies real progress (that is increasingly more complex and efficient pursuit and evasion strategies) or not, is revealed by the CIAO graphs displayed on top and bottom right of figure 3. These graphs show that individuals in later generations do not necessarily score well against competitors of much earlier generations. For example, best predators around generation 90 can hardly catch best preys of generations 0-10, 35-50, and 70-80, despite the fact that the average population fitness is relatively high. This indicates that around generation 90 the predators developed a behavioral strategy tuned to their preceding ten best competitors (during co-evolutionary training, each individual is tested against the best competitors of the preceding ten generations). By carefully comparing the fitness graphs with the CIAO graphs, one can find several indications for the development of behavioral strategies specifically tuned to competitors' behaviors. Another case is shown by the performance of the best preys in the final generations which is quite high in the instantaneous fitness graph, but does not compare so well in the CIAO graphs when the competitors are taken from much earlier generations. Finally, the the Scottish tartan pattern of the CIAO graphs, together with the Ancestral Hamming Maps, indicate periods of relative stasis and fast evolutionary changes in both species (a method for picking out best individuals of each species for efficiency and/or fun purposes has been indicated in a previous paper [7]).

Figure 4 shows some behaviors recorded at interesting points of evolution. At generation 20 we already have challenging tournaments for both species. The prey has developed a good wall-following and obstacle-avoidance behavior, and the predator displays good pursuit strategies. Later, at generation 70, the prey turns in place until it perceives the approaching predator; it then quickly backs (faster than the predator) and starts again rotating. Anytime the prey escapes, the predator performs a half turn on one wheel and re-attacks. The prey is caught when, by chance, the predator attacks it on the side with the motor (where there are no infrared sensors). Finally, at generation 90 the prey has resumed a very fast wall-following strategy. Since high speed combined with a short-range sensor resolution for the prey[2] is such that it cannot avoid an incoming predator, the predator adopts a spider-strategy: it slowly backs towards a wall and there it waits for the fast-approaching prey. However, this predator strategy does not pay off for all the other prey strategies described before, as it can also be seen by the CIAO graph of figure 3.

3.2 Adaptive-noise controllers

The condition with evolutionary adaptive noise ($c = 2$) displayed an average relative performance $\overline{R^2} = 11.66$ with standard deviation of the sample mean $\sigma = 32.5$ which was not statistically different from that of the condition of genetically-determined controllers (probability

value was 0.83 for t-test of the difference of the means between the two conditions, i.e. much bigger than significance level 0.05 typically used for rejecting the equality hypothesis). However, in all runs predator and prey performance did not display the high oscillations observed in condition 1 (except for one run with a small counterphase oscillation in both populations around generation 80); rather, both species displayed similar fitness values, or either the prey or the predator was slightly better than the other, as shown in the center left of figure 5. Furthermore, in all cases the fitness value of the two species required roughly twice the number of initial generations –as compared to condition 1– to reach the intersection point (20 against 10) which marks the establishment of challenging pursuit-evasion tournaments.

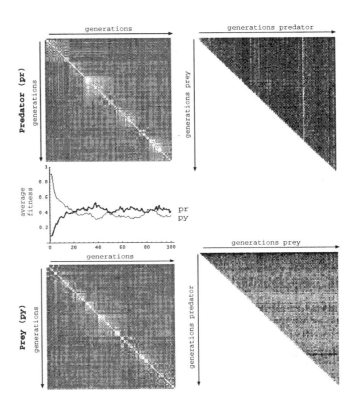

Figure 5: *Adaptive-noise controllers*. **Left, center**: Average fitness across generations for predator (pr) and prey (py). **Left, top and bottom**: Ancestral Hamming Maps for predator and prey, respectively: see section 3 for explanation. **Right, top and bottom**: CIAO graphs for predator and prey, respectively: see section 3 for explanation.

The CIAO graphs revealed a smooth grey texture indicating almost equal performance for all tournaments, except for the initial generations. In some runs the predator was slightly better (darker grey patterns), in others the prey was. In any case, these data showed that both

---

[2] IR-sensor activity is smaller when the robot faces a small dark object like another Khepera than when it faces a large bright surface like the walls

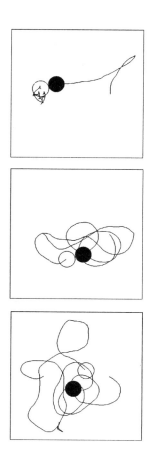

Figure 6: Behaviors of *adaptive-noise controllers*. Black disk is predator, white is prey. **Top**. Generation 20. **Center**. Generation 50. **Bottom**. Generation 80.

species employed behavioral strategies that were comparably challenging for the competitor. However, the fact that small patterns of change in the CIAO graphs were always perpendicular to the predator axis (both for the predator and the prey CIAO data) implied that performance changes were due to a behavioral change in the predator only. This could be also seen from the Ancestral Hamming Maps of figure 5. Here, the slow variation in fitness values during the first 20 generations is accompanied by a corresponding pattern of change in the genotype of the predator only. On the other hand, the genotype of the prey displays roughly the same amount of change along generations.

The hypothesis that the prey exploited noise to develop unpredictable controllers (that is, not improving much on initial random controllers) while the predator tried to develop more stable pursuit strategies was confirmed by the analysis of noise levels in the two species across generations. Similarly to what was done for the the fitness values, we compared at each generation population noise values and noise values of the best individual

between the two species. In all runs, the preys reported higher noise values than the predators, except for one run where the noise levels were roughly equal (the same run where the oscillation was observed). Two separate t-tests for checking differences in average noise level and in noise level of the best individuals for all evolutionary runs both displayed a significant difference ($p \ll 0.1$).

A qualitative analysis of behavioral patterns showed unpredictable manoeuvres for the prey and a not-so-smooth target-oriented navigation for the predator (figure 6). There were no detectable changes after generation 20. In all cases, the prey's trajectory was often changing while retaining sufficient obstacle-avoidance abilities (it sometimes stopped near a wall for a few instants and later moved away). The predator's behaviours were more predictable. In general, it was quite good at keeping the prey within the visual field, but its actions were not precise.

3.3 Directional-change controllers

Relative performance of the two species in this condition significantly differed from condition 1 (and also from condition 2), $\overline{R^3} = 72$ with standard deviation of the sample mean $\sigma = 15.39$, $p < 0.01$ for a two-tailed t-test of the difference of the means. In all the six evolutionary runs predators reported higher average and best fitness values than preys, except for short temporary oscillations (figure 7). Furthermore, in all runs, the average fitness of the predator population was more stable than that of the preys.

Although CIAO graphs revealed the presence of behavioral strategies specifically tuned to the behavior of the competitor, such as at generation 90 for the predator in the run plotted here in figure 7, this pattern was less marked than in condition 1. All CIAO graphs for all runs consistently displayed higher performance of the predator (darker grey levels). Ancestral Hamming Maps were not qualitatively different from previous conditions, except for a higher genetic variation between temporally adjacent generations.

More information can be gained by observing behavioral patterns of the two competitors during individual tournaments (figure 8). There is not much variation in the behavior of the predator. It always displays a very good tracking ability across generations: once the prey has been locked in its visual field, it quickly accelerates to maximum speed until contact. As a matter of fact, for the predator it is sufficient to get the sign of the synapses right. Then, independently of their initial random values, the synapses from active sensors will be increased causing an acceleration in the right direction. As compared to condition 1, where the predator tended to efficiently track in only one direction, here it can turn in both directions at equal speed. In condition 1 proper tracking in both directions would have required accu-

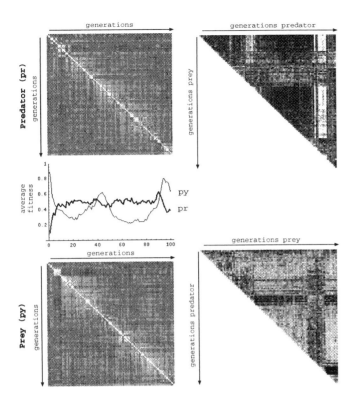

Figure 7: *Directional-change controllers*. **Left, center**: Average fitness across generations for predator (pr) and prey (py). **Left, top and bottom**: Ancestral Hamming Maps for predator and prey, respectively: see section 3 for explanation. **Right, top and bottom**: CIAO graphs for predator and prey. respectively: see section 3 for explanation.

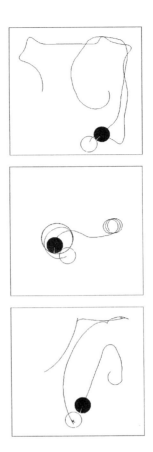

Figure 8: Behaviors of *directional-change controllers*. Black disk is predator, white is prey. **Top**. Generation 20. **Center**. Generation 70. **Bottom**. Generation 95.

rate settings of all synaptic strengths from visual inputs. Here, instead, since synapses are temporarily increased depending on active units [6, 8], individual adjustments of synapses take place when and where required depending on current sensory input. The trajectory in the center image of figure 8 shows another example of synaptic adjustment. Here, while the prey rotates always around the same circle, the predator performs three turns during which synaptic values from the visual units are gradually increased; at the fourth turn, the synaptic values will be sufficiently high to cause a straight pursuit (eventually, the prey will try to avoid the predator without success). Finally, the temporary drop in performance of the predator after generation 90 is due a more precise tracking combined with a slower motion (bottom image of figure 8). Such behavior was probably developed because the preys were also slower and more careful in avoiding obstacles (including the predator).

Although activity-dependent synaptic change are exploited by the far-sighted predator, not the same happens for the prey. Preys are faster than in condition 1 and 2, especially when turning near walls (where IR sensors become active and synapses temporarily strengthen), but they cannot increase their behavioral repertoire with respect to condition 1. Not even can they improve it because volatile changes of the synaptic values imply that most of the time they must re-develop on-the-fly appropriate strengths; although this can be well-suited for avoidance of static obstacles, it does not represent an advantage when facing another moving object such as the predator.

4 Discussion

Introducing protean controllers in co-evolutionary competition significantly affected various aspects of the system dynamics, both on the evolutionary and on the ontogenetic time-scale. On the evolutionary time-scale, noisy controllers ($c = 2$) caused a relaxation of the tightly coupled dynamics observed in the benchmark condition ($c = 1$). High behavioral variation during life of the competitors, especially in the case of preys, was such that only a sufficiently general behavioral strategy could pay off, both for the predator and for the prey. Co-evolutionary search here had higher probability of selecting individuals located in better zones of the fitness landscape, a well-known phenomenon in single-agent evolutionary systems with local variability [9, 12] Instantaneous fitness values reflected more closely behavioral progress, as in traditional single-agent static environments. On the other hand. directional-change controllers ($c = 3$) clearly favored dominance of one species – the predator– whose sensory-motor system profited most of non-random changes of synaptic values.

On the ontogenetic time scale, that is at the level of individual tournaments, the two species differentially exploited the two types of protean controllers. In condition 2, both species reported similar performances, but they differently exploited adaptive noise: preys employed higher noise levels to generate unpredictable and hard-to-track trajectories, whereas predators reduced noise level to maintain sufficient pursuit strategies. In condition 3, predators seemed to benefit from directional synaptic change to improve their pursuit abilities with respect to condition 1.

In order to check whether predators' superior performances in condition 3 were due to a real advantage of the predator rather than to some difficulties of the preys to cope with directional-change controllers, we performed two Master Tournaments. In a Master Tournament each individual is tested against each best competitor of *all* generations (see [7] for more details) and the resulting average fitness (in this case, over 100 tournaments) of each individual across generations is called Master fitness. The graph on the left of figure 9 shows the Master fitness for predators and preys co-evolved in condition 1 (run 1 displayed in figure 3), giving a relative performance $\overline{R} = -12$ (relative performance for the average fitness data of this run was $\overline{r_1^1} = -4$). The graph on the right of figure 9 instead shows the Master fitness for predators evolved in condition 3 (run 1 displayed in figure 7) against preys evolved in condition 1, giving a relative performance $\overline{R} = 42$ (relative performance for the average fitness data of this run was $\overline{r_1^3} = 50$). Had the advantage reported in section 3.3 been caused by underdeveloped preys rather than better predators, the Master Tournament between species evolved in different conditions should have generated opposite results.

5 Conclusion

The results reported in this paper provide initial experimental support to the arguments given in section 1 for the differential exploitation of protean behaviors in different co-evolving and competing species [11]. However, one should be careful before generalizing too much these results. Firstly, differential exploitation of sources of con-

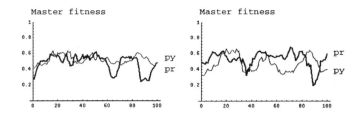

Figure 9: Master Tournament between species evolved in condition 1 (left) and Master Tournament between predator evolved in condition 3 and prey evolved in condition 1 (right).

troller variability here heavily depended on the sensory-motor systems of our species which were assumed to be different and unmodifiable. Secondly, the controller architecture could have been a limiting factor, being a simple perceptron with discrete-time dynamics: this might be a reason why in these experiments we had no evidence for the development of predictive behavioral strategies during life of each individual. Thirdly, the type of controller variability that we employed in these experiments was quite arbitrary, although specifically chosen to address the issue of random strategies against goal-directed strategies. It would be necessary to carry out further tests with different types of controller adaptation. Additionally, while still keeping the types of controllers employed in condition 2 and 3, it would be interesting to let each species evolve the most suitable controller among the two; for example, one could introduce an extra gene for each individual which specifies how the genotype should be decoded and observe whether there is a significant choice of type 2 for preys and type 3 for predators.

Finally, we think that competing co-evolutionary systems are an interesting testbed to study also other aspects of artificial evolution. One of these is genetic encoding, which here was deliberately kept as simple as possible. However, for co-evolution between different species to be a powerful engine of evolutionary progress, it would be advisable to employ a genetic encoding which takes better care of achieved progress, for example as in the work by Cliff and Miller [1].

Acknowledgments

D.F. thanks Francesco Mondada for providing the Khepera robots with the vision module and Inman Harvey for insightful comments on earlier parts of this work.

References

[1] D. Cliff and G. F. Miller. Tracking the red queen: Measurements of adaptive progress in co-evolutionary simulations. In F. Morán, A. Moreno,

J. J. Merelo, and P. Chacón, editors, *Advances in Artificial Life: Proceedings of the Third European Conference on Artificial Life*, pages 200–218. Springer Verlag, Berlin, 1995.

[2] D. Cliff and G. F. Miller. Co-evolution of Pursuit and Evasion II: Simulation Methods and Results. In P. Maes, M. Mataric, J-A. Meyer, J. Pollack, H. Roitblat, and S. Wilson, editors, *From Animals to Animats IV: Proceedings of the Fourth International Conference on Simulation of Adaptive Behavior*. MIT Press-Bradford Books, Cambridge, MA, 1996.

[3] R. Dawkins. *The Blind Watchmaker*. Longman, Essex, 1986.

[4] P. Driver and N. Humphries. *Protean behavior: The biology of unpredictability*. Oxford University Press, Oxford, 1988.

[5] D. Floreano and F. Mondada. Evolution of homing navigation in a real mobile robot. *IEEE Transactions on Systems, Man, and Cybernetics-Part B*, 26:396–407, 1996.

[6] D. Floreano and F. Mondada. Evolution of plastic neurocontrollers for situated agents. In P. Maes, M. Mataric, J-A. Meyer, J. Pollack, H. Roitblat, and S. Wilson, editors, *From Animals to Animats IV: Proceedings of the Fourth International Conference on Simulation of Adaptive Behavior*. MIT Press-Bradford Books, Cambridge, MA, 1996.

[7] D. Floreano and S. Nolfi. God save the red queen! competition in co-evolutionary robotics. In J. Koza, K. Deb, M. Dorigo, D. Fogel, M. Garzon, H. Iba, and R. L. Riolo, editors, *Proceedings of the 2nd International Conference on Genetic Programming*, Stanford University, 1997.

[8] D. Flotzinger. Evolving plastic neural network controllers for autonomous robots. Msc dissertation 9580131, COGS, University of Sussex at Brighton, 1996.

[9] G. E. Hinton and S. J. Nowlan. How learning can guide evolution. *Complex Systems*, 1:495–502, 1987.

[10] O. Miglino, H. H. Lund, and S. Nolfi. Evolving Mobile Robots in Simulated and Real Environments. *Artificial Life*, 2:417–434, 1996.

[11] G. F. Miller and D. Cliff. Protean behavior in dynamic games: Arguments for the co-evolution of pursuit-evasion tactics. In D. Cliff, P. Husbands, J. Meyer, and S. W. Wilson, editors, *From Animals to Animats III: Proceedings of the Third International Conference on Simulation of Adaptive Behavior*. MIT Press-Bradford Books, Cambridge, MA, 1994.

[12] S. Nolfi, J. L. Elman, and D. Parisi. Learning and evolution in neural networks. *Adaptive Behavior*, 3:5–28, 1994.

[13] T. S. Ray. An approach to the synthesis of life. In C.G. Langton, J.D. Farmer, S. Rasmussen, and C. Taylor, editors, *Artificial Life II: Proceedings Volume of Santa Fe Conference*, volume XI. Addison Wesley: series of the Santa Fe Institute Studies in the Sciences of Complexities, Redwood City, CA, 1992.

[14] C. W. Reynolds. Competition, Coevolution and the Game of Tag. In R. Brooks and P. Maes, editors, *Proceedings of the Fourth Workshop on Artificial Life*, pages 59–69, Boston, MA, 1994. MIT Press.

[15] K. Sims. Evolving 3D Morphology and Behavior by Competition. In R. Brooks and P. Maes, editors, *Proceedings of the Fourth Workshop on Artificial Life*, pages 28–39, Boston, MA, 1994. MIT Press.

[16] X. Yao. A review of evolutionary artificial neural networks. *International Journal of Intelligent Systems*, 4:203–222, 1993.

Temperature in Natural and Artificial Systems

Adrian Thompson

Centre for Computational Neuroscience and Robotics,
University of Sussex, Brighton BN1 9QH, UK.
adrianth@cogs.susx.ac.uk

Abstract

Recent experiments in evolutionary electronics have shown how artificial evolution can craft extremely efficient electronic circuits by manipulating a real physical silicon medium. Each individual circuit is physically instantiated in a reconfigurable chip (FPGA) for its fitness evaluation, so evolution can exploit all of the natural physical properties exhibited by the electronic medium, resulting in circuits well tailored to it. This can only be done properly by rigorously rejecting conventional design methods. Artificial evolution is then faced with a similar problem to that encountered in nature: how to construct a system from processes which all vary with temperature, such that the system can perform adequately over a wide range of temperatures? It is beneficial to do this in a more natural way than simply forbidding all analogue continuous-time dynamics, as conventional digital design does. Engineering proposals are formulated by analysing the correspondences between nature and evolutionary electronics — some of these are promising and surprising. There are wider implications for ALife, in that thermal considerations cannot be as easily ignored as 'implementation details' as might have been thought.

1 Introduction

It is now possible to allow artificial evolution to manipulate directly a real physical semiconductor medium to construct automatically electronic circuits that satisfy an engineering specification. Once preconceptions from conventional design methods are rigorously rejected, the silicon electronic medium can be exploited in a way that is truly natural to its properties, resulting in highly efficient circuits. Freely exploiting the physical properties of a medium has its pitfalls, and one is that the evolved circuit may be unable to operate over a sufficient range of temperatures to be of wide applicability. Natural evolution must have faced the same problem, and this paper aims to learn lessons from it. We shall see that there

are strong correspondences between the natural and electronic cases at every stage of the discussion, with highly suggestive consequences.

The motivation behind this research is to improve evolutionary electronics as an engineering technique. However, there are broader implications for ALife researchers, and these will be identified in the penultimate section. There is a lot of biology in this paper, but I am not a biologist. The biological information is taken from [1] except where indicated otherwise by citations, but any errors are my own responsibility.

The next section summarises a recent experiment in evolutionary electronics to illustrate the motivation for this research. We then consider the fundamentals of how temperature influences biological and silicon systems. The subsequent sections consider first how a system may *cope* with temperature change ('Temperature Compensation') and then how a system's internal temperature can be *stabilised* ('Thermal Regulation'). Both are effective methods of sustaining operationality in the face of changing external temperature, and they can be used together. Finally, some implications for ALife modelling are noted.

2 Motivation: Evolutionary Electronics

A Field-Programmable Gate Array (FPGA) is a Very-Large Scale Integration (VLSI) silicon chip. It consists of an undedicated array of components interspersed with wires of various lengths. Within the components are electronic switches which control their behaviour, and electronic switches also control how the inputs and outputs of the components connect to the wires. A particular setting of the switches defines which out of the vast range of possible electronic circuits is physically instantiated on the chip at any one time. Recent advances in FPGA technology make it possible to place the settings of the switches (and hence the physical circuit) directly under the control of an evolutionary algorithm — previously there were technical difficulties due to limitations of the chips [2]. With the newly introduced XC6216 device from Xilinx [3], the switch settings can be partially or completely reconfigured in a negligible amount of time, there is no limit on the number of reconfigurations, and the chip's architecture is such that it can never be internally damaged by any configuration. In this experiment, only a subset of the chip's capabilities was enabled: each component performed a single function of three inputs, and only nearest-neighbour connections were used.

The settings of the switches are determined by the contents of bits of RAM spread throughout the chip. This RAM can be written to as easily as conventional computer memory. Thus, any appropriate flavour of evolutionary algorithm can easily be implemented on a standard desktop computer and allowed to manipulate the physical circuit instantiated in silicon on the FPGA. Fitness evaluations can be the measurement of the performance of an evolved configuration as a real physical electronic circuit, behaving in real-time according to the laws of semiconductor physics. This means that evolution can be free to explore all possible configurations, and hence all possible behaviours in the repertoire of the FPGA. There is no need to constrain evolution to work only within the relatively small subset of circuits we know how to design, analyse or feasibly simulate. Instead, evolution can be allowed to explore beyond the scope of conventional design methodologies, exploiting richer architectures and dynamical behaviours, and using complex aspects of semiconductor physics.

In this spirit, the configuration bits of a 10×10 corner of the XC6216 FPGA were directly encoded as a linear bit-string genotype of 1800 bits, and allowed to evolve without constraint using a fairly conventional genetic algorithm. The individuals were evaluated one-at-a-time as configurations of a real FPGA chip. The task was a simple first-step towards signal-processing and pattern-recognition applications. A single input was driven with a sequence of audio tones of 1kHz and 10kHz frequency, presented in a random order. The target behaviour was for the single output immediately to go to a steady 5V level as soon as one frequency was present, and to go to 0V for the other one. Such a circuit might be used to demodulate binary data sent over a telephone line. The task might sound trivially easy until it is remembered that there are no external timing components: evolution must craft a continuous-time arbitrarily recurrent network of 100 components (each of which has an input⇒output time delay of only a few nanoseconds) to distinguish between input periods that are on a timescale five orders of magnitude slower. If achieved, this would be a significant feat, because this corner of the chip is only $1mm^2$ in area, and requires no external components.

Fig. 1 shows the progress of evolution. In the initial random population of 50 individuals (generation 0), all the circuits happened to be as bad as possible, for example maintaining a constant output voltage irrespective of the input. After 1400 generations, a promising partial solution is shown: the rich continuous-time analogue dynamics of the circuit are evident. The FPGA's com-

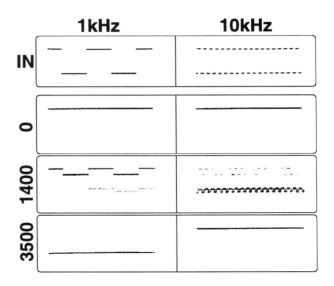

Figure 1: *The voltage waveforms of the two different tones presented to the input (top row), and of the corresponding output produced by the best of the population after 0, 1400 and 3500 generations (the three rows below). These are photographs of the oscilloscope screen, with the probes directly attached to the input pin and the output pin of the FPGA. See text for interpretation.*

ponents — intended to be used to perform operations of Boolean logic — are really just high-gain configurations of transistors, and in the absence of the constraints of a digital design methodology, this is just how evolution treats them. Finally, the best circuit of generation 3500 gives the desired behaviour, showing the 'digital-looking' output demanded by the fitness function, though it is certain that complex dynamics are still used internally.

The final circuit is shown in Fig. 2. Note the highly recurrent structure. It behaves in continuous-time as an unfolding of the laws of semiconductor physics: the chip is a dynamical system, not a computational one. The components shaded gray are part of the circuit's function even though they appear to be disconnected from it: they must be interacting by some subtle property of semiconductor physics such as electromagnetic coupling or interaction through the power-supply wiring. As a result of this rich unconstrained architecture, dynamics, and use of physical resources, the circuit is incredibly efficient: using just 32 cells it is one or two orders of magnitude smaller than one would expect from conventional methods. See [4] for full details of the experiment and the theory behind it. To many people, the experiment seems somewhat akin to the evolution of physical nervous systems in nature.

The circuit operates perfectly over the $\pm 5°C$ range of temperatures that the population experienced during evolution. However, the more the temperature deviates from this range, the more the circuit malfunctions. Conventional digital design, in forbidding the use

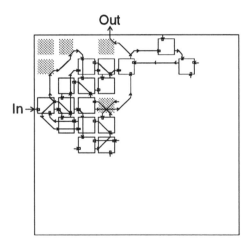

Figure 2: *The functional part of the final evolved circuit. The large boxes represent the components, the inputs of which are marked with small squares.*

of continuous-time analogue dynamics, can produce circuits with much greater ranges of operating temperature — at the expense of less efficient utilisation of the physical resources. How can evolution be allowed to naturally exploit the physical medium, and thus reap the benefits seen above, but yet produce circuits able to operate in a wide range of temperatures? Natural evolution must have faced the same problem: can we draw some inspiration from it? That is the purpose of this paper. To begin, the next section considers the roots of temperature's influence on biological and silicon systems.

3   The effect of Temperature upon Rate

The rate of chemical reactions increases with temperature. This is described by the Arrhenius relationship, which can be written in the form:

$$\ln \frac{k_2}{k_1} = \frac{\mu}{R} \left[\frac{1}{T_1} - \frac{1}{T_2} \right] \tag{1}$$

where T_1 and T_2 are the absolute temperatures corresponding to reaction velocities k_1 and k_2, R is the gas constant, and μ is the *critical thermal increment*: a constant characterising the particular reaction. When this relationship holds, a more friendly measure can be calculated: $Q_{10} = k_{t+10}/k_t$, where k_t is the rate at temperature t, and k_{t+10} is the rate at 10°C higher. So Q_{10} simply tells us by what factor a rate increases for a 10°C rise in temperature.

In biochemical processes, often composed of a complex pathway of many intermediate reactions, μ is only a constant over a limited temperature range, which might be smaller than that of the phenomenon under study. A change in temperature can change which of the steps in the pathway is the rate-limiting one, resulting in a sharp change in μ (and Q_{10}) at particular temperatures.

In practice, the interaction of several potentially rate-limiting processes (physical as well as chemical) can lead to gradual, rather than sharp, changes in μ and Q_{10} with temperature. Even for a single biochemical reaction, the rate increase with temperature falls off as temperature increases, presumably because of the destruction of enzymes on which they depend [5]. Nevertheless, the Arrhenius relationship holds for many biological phenomena under temperature ranges of interest, and is even reflected in behaviours such as the rate of creeping of ants, the chirping of crickets, the flashing of fireflies, the beating of cilia, and some respiratory and cardiac rhythms. 'The slope of the linear relationship between the log of the rate of most biological reactions and the reciprocal of absolute temperature is the Arrhenius μ divided by approximately 4.6, with μ defined by the limiting step.' [6, Chap. 37]. For thermochemical (enzymatic) reactions, Q_{10} in typically somewhere between 2 and 3 : they often go about twice as fast for every 10°C rise in temperature.

The temperature dependencies of *neural* systems also arise from physical, as well as chemical, origins; in semiconductors the processes are entirely physical. In general, the Q_{10} values associated with physical processes (such as for diffusion or conductivity), and also of those associated with photochemical reactions, are less than 1.5. The operation of both neurons and semiconductor devices is to a large extent based upon the movement of charge-carriers in an electric field (at a speed proportional to their *mobility*) and the interplay between this and the diffusion of those particles (at a speed proportional to their *diffusion constant*) in the concentration-gradient which is influenced by that movement. In neurons and semiconductors, the charge-carriers are different, and the processes establishing electric fields and concentration gradients are different, but the link between diffusion and the electric field is fundamental to both.

The Einstein relationship is crucial to this link: the diffusion constant is proportional to the mobility multiplied by the absolute temperature, so temperature appears in many of the fundamental equations of neurons and semiconductors (eg. the Nernst equation for equilibrium potentials at neuron membranes, and — via the Boltzmann distribution — basic equations in semiconductor physics) [7, 8]. The rest of this section will now give some examples of how these temperature dependencies are manifested in neural and electronic systems.

The refractory period for nerve impulses increases for lower temperatures [5]. Mammals (which have nerves capable of propagating impulses at speeds ranging all the way from $0.3 ms^{-1}$ to $100 ms^{-1}$) have a Q_{10} for the speed of nerve impulse propagation of around 1.7, with a lower bound of 5°C below which propagation ceases. In fact, the Q_{10} is higher at low temperatures: at high temperatures cell-membrane permeability changes become so fast that discharging of the cell membrane capacitance by fully activated permeability mechanisms begins to be rate-limiting. Conduction velocity in cold-blooded animals is less temperature-sensitive than in mammals. Conduction velocity can also change with acclimation[1] and seasons [7, Chap. 4] — see the next section.

As well as affecting the rate of action potential propagation, temperature influences the rate of neuron firing: 'The changes of action potential frequencies with temperature are associated, although not in a simple manner, with changes in resting potentials. Cooling reduces the resting potential (depolarization) and this leads to a rise in action potential frequencies; but certain nerve cells show a frequency increase when temperature is raised.' [9]

A similarly changeable situation prevails in VLSI chips such as the FPGAs used in evolutionary electronics. These devices are made in complementary metal-oxide semiconductor (CMOS) technology, where the rate-limiting factor is the time taken for a field-effect transistor's 'ON' resistance to charge or discharge the gate capacitances of the transistors connected to it and the parasitic capacitance of the interconnections. The overall outcome is that delays increase by about 0.3% per °C, which translates to a Q_{10} of 1.03. This sounds very good compared to the biological case, until we remember that electronic circuits are commonly expected to work with *no* observable change in performance over a very wide range of ambient temperatures — typically −40°C to 85°C or even 125°C.

Clearly, both biological evolution and evolutionary electronics has a challenging task in producing systems with adequate thermal stability. How does nature do it? The rest of the paper addresses this question, attempting to apply the findings to evolutionary electronics along the way, before finally commenting on the implications for ALife modelling studies. There are two complementary possibilities: the first is to produce a system that works even when the temperature changes, which I will call *compensation*. The second is to produce a system that *regulates* its internal temperature to be within limits it can cope with. Many animals do both.

4 Temperature Compensation

4.1 Cellular and Biochemical Compensation

If one were to go out in summer and measure the Q_{10} of some property of a cold-blooded animal one might infer that in winter that process will come to a complete standstill. Returning in winter to repeat the measurement, however, it may be found that the process is proceeding at the same rate as it did in summer. Many biologi-

cal processes display adaptation to temperature, coping with seasonal changes and different latitudes. How?

As temperature goes down, the primary thing to avoid or cope with is ice crystal formation — the crystals can cause mechanical damage to the cell membranes, and can have drastic effects on the vital osmotic and liquid balances as liquid water is removed. There are many wonderful ways in which this is achieved (eg. through supercooling [6, Chap. 21]). Of particular interest is the use of antifreeze substances; it appears that these can also prevent low-temperature changes in protein structure. In this way, important enzymes may be maintained in the active state even at low temperatures, partly escaping from the Arrhenius equation.

'Acclimation depends on exploitation of the accelerations and maintenance of the independence of the limitations of the Arrhenius equation.' [6, Chap. 37]. Inspection of the change in the rate-temperature curve before and after acclimation indicates that one, or most commonly both, of the following is responsible: (1) 'altered enzyme activity due to changes in concentration, pH, water activity, or relation among enzymes'; (2) 'a change in activation energy due to alteration of enzyme protein, a cofactor, or shift to alternate pathways.' [6, Chap. 37].

Thus, in response to a temperature change, the biochemical reaction pathway responsible for a particular function may be altered in mechanism to use reactions which are suited to the new conditions. It is conceivable that this strategy could be applied to silicon: the system could be composed of many alternative low-level mechanisms for each sub-function which automatically come into play as appropriate for the current temperature.

Antifreeze (and potentially all the above mechanisms) can be regulated by (possibly seasonal) patterns of neuroendocrine activity, as well as being directly influenced by temperature. Particular physiological processes can be indicated as being concerned with compensation by identifying temperature-dependent changes in the specific enzymes associated with them. Acetylcholinesterase activity points to nervous tissues or processes as the site of compensation or lethal collapse. It has long been known that heat-death in some animals is due to nervous-system failure with a loss of indispensable reflexes such as cardiac and respiratory rhythm. Other studies (eg. in fish) have indicated that the nervous system is also the locus most sensitive to cold.

These observations suggest that there is a useful role for the nervous system in partially controlling low-level biochemical adaptation. In the silicon scheme, then, perhaps some high-level controller should also influence the choice of fine-grained mechanisms to be invoked by the current temperature. However, that controller itself might demand particular thermal precautions, as in the case of the nervous system. Note that, using an FPGA capable of rapid partial reconfiguration, the al-

---

[1]The word 'acclimation' refers to the laboratory-equivalent of acclimatisation: temperature is manipulated, but other environmental factors which might simultaneously change in significant ways in the natural environment are held constant.

ternative mechanisms in the above scheme need not all be present on the silicon simultaneously: sub-circuits can be 'swapped' in and out of the chip as appropriate for the current temperature. Indeed, several entire systems could be evolved, each for a different temperature range, the entire circuit being swapped to cope with a temperature change. There is a biological analogy: 'The seasonal development of arthropods, particularly those with one generation per year, has usually evolved in such a way that only one specific stage is capable of hibernating successfully.' [6, Chap. 21]. Here, the genotype specifies several different structures, only one of which behaves appropriately in low temperatures (by hibernating).

4.2 Compensation in Behavioural Timescales

Numerous circadian (daily) rhythms have been documented in a wide range of behavioural and physiological variables.[2] For example, they play a role in thermal regulation, sleep, feeding and drinking behaviours, and endocrine, renal and reproductive function. In some cases the rhythm needs to be equivalent to an internal clock of considerable precision, for example it is widely believed that migratory birds use such a clock to correct for the sun's movement across the sky to allow it to be used as a compass. Rhythms on shorter timescales (eg. cardiac and respiratory patterns) and on the longer timescales of seasons and years are also important.

Some biological rhythms are directly derived from environmental cues, but others result from some sort of 'endogenous' oscillator in the animal. Such oscillators are capable of free-running in the absence of environmental cues but can also be entrained by multiple 'timegivers'[3] in the environment such as light-dark cycles, food-availability cycles, temperature cycles, and social and acoustic cues. 'Entrainment' means a gradual and ongoing resynchronisation to the environmental timegiver (rather than a sudden resetting). Ongoing interaction with timegivers can result in a different period of oscillation than the free-running period would be in the absence of cues. It has been shown that, apart from entrainment, circadian rhythms are not learnt phenomena, but are genetically specified.

In studies of the circadian rhythms of plants and insects, the Q_{10} of the free-running period's alteration with temperature has been found to be typically in the range 0.85–1.3, where something in the range 2–3 would be expected from consideration of the Arrhenius equation (see also [11, pp23–27]). This is in the absence of environmental timegivers, and appears to be the result of active compensation, rather than some inherent insensitivity in the mechanism. There is some evidence that the temperature compensating mechanism may not be an inherent feature of the oscillatory mechanism: certain *Neurospora*

mutants lack temperature compensation in a particular circadian rhythm that is otherwise normal [12].

How can such compensation be achieved? If the oscillation arises from the interaction of two or more processes, *each of which* is affected by temperature, then the interactions can be arranged so as to give an overall stability in period. For example, the period might depend on the products of a biochemical reaction which increases in rate with temperature; there could be a second reaction which inhibits the first one, and which also increases in rate with temperature. Another possibility is to take the net effect of processes having reciprocal temperature coefficients: this could even be applied to the mutual entrainment of multiple oscillators [13]. Note that even one-celled animals have temperature-independent endogenous rhythms (*ibid.*). Some progress has been made towards postulating neural bases for circadian rhythms, but this is still far from understood [12].

In an fascinating duality with the solar navigation of birds mentioned above, a prize of £20000 was offered in 1714 for the maker of a time-piece sufficiently accurate to enable longitude to be ascertained at sea. One of the problems was the variation with temperature of the lengths of pendulums and of balance-springs [14]. The solution was to use the net effect of two different metals having different thermal properties: this fits into the general scheme above. Presumably compensation schemes of an analogous nature can be built into electronics, or could arise through evolution given appropriate primitives and a selection pressure.

In evolutionary electronics, the thermal stability of internal timescales could also be achieved through interaction with external timegivers, as in entrainment. For example, if the 1kHz/10kHz discriminator is given a sequence of inputs consisting of both frequencies, then it is constantly being 'reminded' of what the two periods are: the inputs are themselves timegivers. The circuit need only say whether the current input corresponds to the higher or lower of the two frequencies it has received in the past. One way of doing this would be to use endogenous entrained oscillators, but other mechanisms are possible.

In applications where the inputs do not implicitly contain appropriate time cues, they could be augmented by an extra input which does. For example, an extra input could be driven by an external crystal oscillator (cheap, accurate, and temperature stable). This is superficially similar to the 'clock' used by digital designers to globally synchronise their circuits, with the subcircuits changing in lock-step on the beating of the clock. However, there is a fundamental difference: now the external oscillator is truly a timegiver, to be exploited by evolution in any way, and is *not* an enforced constraint on the system's dynamical behaviour. Evolution could totally ignore the clock input if it chose, or it could be used as a subtle in-

---

[2] The biology of circadian rhythms given here is taken from [10].
[3] Sometimes referred to as *zeitgebers*, even in English texts.

fluence on the circuit's dynamics. In this way, evolution remains free to explore rich architectures and dynamics beyond the scope of human design, but has appropriate resources to evolve thermal stability if there is a selection pressure for it.

I have suggested two mechanisms here (compensation and interaction with external timegivers) which could allow the evolution of temperature-stable circuits. In each case, though, there needs to be a selection pressure for evolution to favour temperature-stability. I propose to arrange for this by evaluating each individual circuit on several different FPGA chips in parallel, each being held at a different temperature (using Peltier-effect heat-pumps — see §5.1.2 — and hand-designed thermostatic control). An individual's fitness score will then reflect its ability to perform the desired behaviour in all of these different conditions.

5 Thermal Regulation

Having dealt with ways of *coping* with temperature variations, I now wish to consider the complementary strategy of stabilising internal temperature by some method of regulation. In order to do this, we first look at the means by which the internal temperature can be varied with respect to the ambience: these mechanisms are the 'actuators' of the thermal regulation control system. The control system itself will then be considered.

5.1 *Temperature-altering Mechanisms*

5.1.1 *Behavioural*

Faced with a sharp temperature change, many animals make an immediate behavioural response (seeking a more equitable environment). Placed in a temperature gradient, most cold-blooded animals will move about and gradually spend more time around a preferred temperature, which is a function both of the animal's species and of its thermal history. As temperature varies over the course of the day, behaviours include selecting suitable micro-habitats, basking, seeking shade, burrowing (which protects from both extremes of outside temperature), aggregation with conspecifics [15]; appropriate alternation between these can achieve a remarkably constant body temperature. On a longer timescale, temperature may alter the activity of endocrine organs and become a part of the complex stimulus of migration. Silicon systems controlling an autonomous mobile robot [16] might be at liberty to use such behaviours, but in general there is no escape for electronics from its given environment. There also seems to be no electronic counterpart for temperature-related activities such as nest-building, or the rather unique strategies of *Homo sapiens*. . . such as inventing air-conditioners [17].

5.1.2 *Heat Exchange*

Internal temperature can be controlled by regulating the amount of radiation, conduction and convection near the physical interface between body and environment (the *integument*). These can be altered by varying the area, orientation with respect to the sun and wind, posture with respect to the ground, colour, texture, reflectivity and thermal resistance of the exposed surfaces, and the use of insulation (hair, feathers, and layers of superficial tissue). Note that the integument does not necessarily have to be at the same temperature as the core of the body. Varying the integument's temperature not only directly influences the rate of heat transfer between body and environment (Fourier's law of heat flow [13]), but also indirectly affects the amount of convection in the air surrounding the body [6, Chap. 33](which is also dependent on posture).

The above applies to both the cooling and heating of the body; for cooling only, the evaporation of liquid (eg. water, saliva, sweat, or urine) from the body (skin, mouth, respiratory system) or the adjacent environment is extensively used by animals. 'Forced air' cooling is also used by panting, fluttering of the mouth and throat [18], or fanning with wings.

An important strategy in temperature regulation is to control the flow of blood between parts of the body at different temperatures; a typical example is the restriction of bloodflow between cold extremities and the core. Some animals have a specialised arrangement of blood vessels to perform *countercurrent heat exchange*, allowing parts of the body to be at different temperatures even when there is a considerable bloodflow between them. Examples include maintenance of the core at a higher temperature than the gills, legs, or tail; allowing particular organs to be held at a different temperature to the core (eg. testes), or to have their temperature regulated more precisely than the rest of the body (eg. brain).

The analogies with thermal management in present-day electronics are strong. The design procedure is typically as follows. Firstly, the designer calculates the power consumption ($\simeq$ heat generation) of the silicon chip, which is a flat thin slice of silicon of about $1cm^2$ area, stuck to the inside of a cavity inside a larger plastic or ceramic package (which allows for the mounting of the device on a circuit-board). For a particular packaging method, a 'thermal resistance from junction to ambient' is specified, where 'junction' refers to the transistors on the silicon. This allows the temperature of the silicon to be calculated for a given ambient air temperature. If the silicon would be too hot (the silicon being cold is not normally a problem), then either a different type of package is used or the heat transfer between the outside of the package (or *case*) and the ambient must be improved. The latter is done by mounting a *heatsink* onto the case using a paste of high thermal conductivity. The heatsink is usually a matt-black finned metal structure of large surface area, giving a very low thermal resistance to the ambience. Using the sum of the junction-to-case thermal resistance (also specified for the package) and the heatsink-to-ambient resistance, the silicon temperature can again be calculated, and a suitable heatsink selected.

Often forced-air cooling is used by mounting a fan on the heatsink or nearby to the package (sometimes there is just one fan blowing air through a large box of electronics), which effectively decreases the thermal resistance to the ambience [19]. A fluid other than air can also be used (water or freons; the latter are electrical insulators and can be allowed direct contact with the chip), and this fluid can be refrigerated rather than at ambient temperature: such methods are currently only used in rather exotic applications. Finally, it is possible to mount a *Peltier-effect heat-pump* [20] in the form of a wafer between the case and the heatsink. These electrically powered devices are used to pump heat from the case to the heatsink: the heatsink gets hotter with respect to the surrounding fluid, accelerating its heat-loss, and the case becomes cooler. Note that these devices can also operate in reverse to *heat* the case, and can be electronically controlled to maintain the silicon at a constant temperature: both are currently unusual.

The analogies with nature are obvious. The main difference is that silicon chips are normally just kept below a maximum temperature: we have seen that digital systems become slower with rising temperature. For conventional digital design methodologies, faster operation at low temperatures is not a problem. Another consideration is that the ageing mechanisms leading to device failure accelerate with temperature. Consequently, the amount of cooling is kept fixed at that necessary to guarantee a particular maximum temperature, and is not adaptive. A final difference is that evaporative cooling — extremely effective in nature — would be inconvenient (though theoretically possible) in electronic systems.

5.1.3 Heat Generation

In stabilising internal temperature, many animals (eg. insects, fish, birds, mammals) use the heat generated by all metabolizing tissues (*endothermy*). In many cases, this can be adaptively controlled (perhaps via the neuroendocrine system), not only by shivering or otherwise activating muscles, but also *non-shivering thermogenesis*. Some mammals even have a specialised thermogenic tissue (brown fat) for producing bursts of heat in response to cold stress: it serves no other function. 'The tissue is strategically localized in the neck and thoracic regions in relation to major blood vessels so that its heat is quickly transported to those organs (brain and heart) whose continuous high temperatures are vital...' [1].

The heat generated in the brain is a significant component of non-shivering thermogenesis, and a major part of this originates from neural activity; mostly arising from the metabolic processes needed to run the sodium-pump to restore ion concentrations after firing [7, Chap. 5]. There is a strong analogy with electronics here. Although there are research projects on reversible computing (using almost zero energy, thus generating almost no heat), current technologies are far less efficient than this. If used to perform digital operations, the CMOS FPGA chips used in evolutionary electronics generate heat at a rate proportional to the speed of logic switching (there is negligible heat generation when there is no activity in the circuit). This heat must be dissipated, as seen in the previous section.

In the type of unconstrained evolutionary electronics which motivates this paper, the circuit instantiated on the FPGA is a continuous-time dynamical analogue system, and is probably not 'doing' logic. Nevertheless, it is still true that the rate of heat generation rises with increasing frequency of activity in the circuit. This raises an interesting possibility — could a circuit evolve such that the heat produced by its activity maintains it at a preferred temperature? The circuit could potentially even *adapt* its levels of activity in response to a change in ambient temperature.

It turns out that there is *not* a known biological precedent for this: in contrast to an increase in tissue respiration of liver, heart, and skeletal muscle, the O_2 consumption of brain tissue remains constant during the development of non-shivering thermogenesis [6, Chap. 5]. Of course, the lack of a biological counterpart need not necessarily discount it in engineering systems. If there existed parts of the circuit (possibly distributed throughout a large system) which played no other role than to be highly active and generate heat to maintain vital subcircuits at a preferred temperature, then these would be analogous to brown fat in mammals. This is not an idle speculation, but a serious proposal: such thermogenic circuits could be built-in by hand, could be encouraged to evolve, or could be searched for in the analysis of a thermally stable evolved circuit.

5.2 Homeostatic Control Systems

Different species use different combinations of the temperature-altering mechanisms studied above, and according to different adaptive strategies, to maintain a relatively constant internal temperature. Species are often categorised as hot-blooded (homeotherms), cold-blooded (poikilotherms), endotherms, ectotherms, regulators, compensators, or conformers. These classifications of species are sometimes used inconsistently in the literature, and in ways potentially misleading for this paper, so I have avoided them until now. 'Homeotherm' means mammals and birds. The others — cold-blooded animals or *poikilotherms* — differ from homeotherms in lacking the central autonomic thermal controls (the hypothalamus in mammals, and the spinal cord in birds), the continuously high body temperatures, and the emphasis on thermoregulation as a balance between metabolic heat and insulation (in the form of feathers or fur). However, poikilotherms can use many of the mechanisms detailed above to maintain a remarkably constant body temperature in their natural environments [21, 22].

Both homeotherms and poikilotherms have biological stabilisation in the face of changing external temperature by homeostatic feed-back control mechanisms: in homeotherms it is the temperatures of particular parts of the body which are the controlled variables, whereas in poikilotherms the controlled variable might be, for example, metabolic rate [6, Chap. 5]. This does not necessarily imply a reduced involvement of the nervous system in the thermal regulation of poikilotherms. For example, adaptive responses in the thermal resistance of tissue in several poikilotherms have been found to be regulated by photoperiod (not by heat), indicating involvement of photoreceptors and the neuroendocrine system even in this compensatory adaptation [1].

The hypothalamic thermal control in mammals is reflexly activated by thermoreceptors of skin and mucous membranes, and by temperature change in the hypothalamus itself, or the blood circulating through it. Efferent nerves control muscles (eg. for panting or shivering), and, via other organs, the cutaneous blood vessels, the sweat glands, and the piloerector muscles (for raising hairs); the response via the endocrine system can also be on a much longer timescale, as we have seen. This does not mean that these things are solely under hypothalamic control, for example cutaneous vessels are also directly influenced by temperature.

Hypothalamic control, then, can be viewed as a discontinuous nonlinear negative-feedback control system, with a limited range of operation, aiming to maintain the temperature of various parts of the body at their particular set-points (which can be altered, eg. during exercise or by fever). Note that not all observations are easily explained from this viewpoint. See [23] for details of various control-theoretic models. They model response close to the set-points: further away, less-finely controlled emergency responses (such as massive shivering independent of skin temperature) come into play.

Mammals (derived from ancient poikilothermic reptiles) are often considered the most highly developed animals, breaking shackles of innate habits, and being able to adapt behaviour to changing circumstances. They are aided in both by the constancy of their internal environments [24]. Hoar notes that '...there is a good general correlation between the precision of temperature control and the complexity of behavioural organisation.' [1] There is a graded series from the poikilothermic reptiles

through the primitive mammals (monotremes — platypuses and spiny ant-eaters — and marsupials) to the Eutheria (placental mammals). 'Increasing complexity of organization (especially behavioural organization) makes homeothermy a necessity; or conversely, one may argue that complexity, both physiological and behavioural, becomes progressively more feasible as the internal environmental temperature, especially that of the nervous system, is stabilized.' [1]

These observations are tremendously suggestive for evolutionary electronics. Should we accept that the inclusion of a thermostatic control system is the price to be paid for an efficient complex 'electronic nervous system' able to operate in a wide range of ambient temperatures? For thermostatic regulation is indeed costly: in nature we even see animals prepared to give up activity altogether in order to abandon homeothermy when it becomes too costly to maintain (eg. hibernation). The cost of regulation depends on the degree to which conformity with the ambient temperature must be resisted: various trade-offs are found even within mammals [25]. In electronics, there would be the cost of the thermal sensors, the feedback controller, the actuators, and the energy required by these. Such a system is quite simple to build, however, and the components are only expensive in relation to the incredibly low cost of electronics currently achieved through economies of scale.

Thermal sensing might be done by measuring time-delays on the silicon (see §3), measuring the current through a slightly forward-biased electrostatic-discharge (ESD) protection diode (present around the edges of the silicon), or by mounting a thermocouple on the outside of the case. Use of both internal and surface thermosensors can enable more sophisticated control strategies [26]. A simple feedback controller is easy to construct using conventional electronic design principles, and a suitable actuator would be a Peltier-effect heat-pump used as described in §5.1.2 (or even the thermogenic subcircuits proposed in §5.1.3). All of this could be provided without having to try to evolve it, once one was convinced that thermostatic control was appropriate.

The energy consumption of thermostatic regulation could be prohibitive in many electronics applications. It is conceivable that in some situations the circuit could go into dormancy during periods of extreme ambient temperature when the costs of cooling/heating would outweigh the benefits of continued operation. As in animals, some minimal capabilities would have to remain, to 'wake up' in an emergency or when conditions are more comfortable, and to maintain functions that are indispensable (the equivalent of cardiac and respiratory rhythms in animals). It seems ludicrous to think of a hibernating circuit; however, some small-bodied animals (which can rapidly change body temperature) abandon homeothermy while asleep at night, and resume it during daytime. It is easy to think of applications where a piece of electronics could be allowed to do the same. Note that this idea can apply to both hot and cold extremes (in nature the summer equivalent of hibernation is estivation, and less profound forms of torpor also exist). Shutting-down of electronic sub-systems when they are not required is already widely used when power consumption is crucial, and indeed dormancy is also used by animals when food or water is scarce.

In an electronic system made of many parts, thermoregulation of the whole could emerge from the individual actions of the parts. There is a biological precedent for this: 'Colony activity resulting in some temperature control is common at least among some insects: avoidance and preference, shivering and quieting, fasting and feeding, varying metabolic water production, clustering and dispersal of swarms, nest placement and structure, opening and closing nest entrances, fetching water into the nest and fanning to ventilate and evaporatively cool it. Appropriate ones of these mechanisms are effective in maintaining quite narrow ranges.' [6, Chap. 37].

6 Implications for ALife Modelling

Part of the ALife enterprise is to use computer simulations as a tool in theoretical biology [27]. Animal behaviour, evolution, and neuroethology are studied. As is essential in any model, some of the complexity of the real system is left behind, and it might be thought that thermal considerations can safely be ignored as a 'mere implementation detail' with no impact on the essence of behaviour and evolution. It seems clear from the biological literature summarised here that this is not the case. Behavioural mechanisms for thermal regulation are ubiquitous and can be a significant component of an animal's lifestyle. This is especially the case when water economy, not considered above, is taken into account: to use evaporative cooling, one must have drunk sufficiently or be adjacent to an external liquid source.

We have even seen that thermal considerations can have an influence on the evolution of body size: small animals have a greater surface-area to volume ratio, which affects heat transfer with the environment [6, Chap. 32]. They also have smaller reserves of food, water, or energy (important for dormancy), but can easily seek thermal shelter by behaviours like burrowing [28]. Small animals can change their body temperature more rapidly than larger ones, so can suspend or resume thermoregulation relatively rapidly.

Thermal considerations can even influence macroevolution. Recently, physiological and morphological adaptations to climatic conditions in the house sparrow (*Passer domesticus*) in N. America have led to the differentiation of new sub-species living at distinct localities [15]. Such population dynamics cannot be understood without considering animals' responses to temperature.

It can be concluded that there is a wide range of biological phenomena within the scope of ALife which can only be fully understood with reference to animals' thermal responses.

7 Summary and Conclusion

Artificial evolution, when freely allowed to manipulate a physical silicon medium, does indeed share many of the same problems that natural evolution faces in crafting systems able to operate over a wide range of ambient temperatures. A number of engineering proposals have been constructed by analysing these correspondences.

In analogy to biochemical compensation, it was suggested that an electronic system could be composed of many subcircuits, and that there be alternatives for each subcircuit. For a particular subcircuit, the alternatives would operate over different ranges of temperature, and would automatically come into play as appropriate. All the alternative subcircuits need not reside on the silicon simultaneously: the fast reconfiguration of an FPGA could be used to 'swap' them in and out, possibly with the intervention of a high-level controller. Indeed, several whole systems could be evolved for different temperature ranges, and the system in its entirety swapped with another in response to a temperature change (there is even a biological counterpart for that). It was also seen how a system can stabilise its behavioural timescales by interaction with external timegivers, either implicit in the input, or explicitly supplied.

Temperature-altering mechanisms were discussed. The behavioural responses heavily relied upon by many animals are to a large extent not applicable in electronic applications other than autonomous mobile robotics. Several of the most important heat-exchange mechanisms found in nature are already in use in the electronics industry, with the exception of evaporative cooling, which seems inappropriate. The use of circuit activity adaptively to generate heat in analogy with thermogenic tissues in animals is highly promising, though there seems to be no precedent for the case where subcircuits with 'nervous' function also adapt their activity for thermal considerations.

The most radical suggestion to come from the biological literature was that precise homeostatic control of internal temperature is almost essential for a complex behavioural and physiological organisation. It is straightforward to arrange for this in electronic systems, but in the current climate of extreme low cost and low power consumption, the benefits will need to be great for commercial acceptance. Dormancy, and the use of collective regulation behaviours, are possibilities for reducing the power consumption of a homeostatically thermoregulated electronic system.

In conclusion, biology provides a wealth of new ideas for combining the new possibilities of extreme efficiency through the unconstrained exploitation of physical resources with an adequate thermal stability. Some of these are suitable for immediate inclusion into research programmes in evolutionary electronics. The fact that thermal considerations cannot be neglected as an inconsequential implementation detail is also worthy of note to ALife researchers interested in animal behaviour, evolution, and neuroethology.

ACKNOWLEDGEMENTS: This work is supported by Xilinx Inc., and the Centre for Computational Neuroscience & Robotics: many thanks to each. Thanks also to John Gray, Phil Husbands, Dave Cliff, Inman Harvey, and everyone.

References

[1] W. S. Hoar. *General and Comparative Physiology*. Prentice-Hall, 3rd edition, 1983.

[2] A. Thompson. Silicon evolution. In J. R. Koza et al., eds, *Genetic Programming 1996: Proc. 1st Annual Conf. (GP96)*, pp444–452. MIT Press, 1996.

[3] Xilinx, Inc. XC6200 Advanced product specification V1.0, June 1996. In *The Programmable Logic Data Book*. 1996. See http://www.xilinx.com.

[4] A. Thompson. An evolved circuit, intrinsic in silicon, entwined with physics. In Higuchi & Iwata, eds, *Proc. 1st Int. Conf. on Evolvable Systems (ICES'96)*, LNCS. Springer-Verlag, 1996. In press.

[5] W. B. Yapp. *An Introduction to Animal Physiology*. Oxford University Press, 1970.

[6] American Physiological Society. *Handbook of Physiology*. Section 4: Adaptation to the Environment. Waverly Press, 1964.

[7] American Physiological Society. *Handbook of Physiology*. Section 1: The Nervous System, Volume I: Cellular Biology of Neurons, Part 1. Waverly Press, 1977.

[8] C. A. Mead. *Analog VLSI and Neural Systems*. Addison Wesley, 1989.

[9] E. M. Pantelouris. *Introduction to Animal Physiology and Physiological Genetics*, vol. 32 of *Int. Series of monographs on pure and applied Biology. Division: zoology*. Permagon Press, 1967.

[10] M. C. Moore-Ede, F. M. Sulzman, and C. A. Fuller. *The Clocks That Time Us: Physiology of the Circadian Timing System*. Harvard University Press, 1982.

[11] J. E. Harker. *The Physiology of Diurnal Rhythms*. No. 13 in Cambridge monographs in experimental Biology. Cambridge University Press, 1964.

[12] C. Ladd Prosser, ed. *Neural and Integrative Animal Physiology*. Wiley-Liss, 1991.

[13] G. E. Folk Jr. *Textbook of Environmental Physiology*. Lea & Febiger, 2nd edition, 1974.

[14] H. A. Lloyd. Mechanical timekeepers. In *A History of Technology*, vol. III, chapter 24, pp648–675. Oxford University Press, 1957.

[15] H. Pohl. Thermal adaptation in the whole animal. In J. Bligh, J. L. Cloudsley-Thompson, and A. G. Macdonald, eds, *Environmental Physiology of Animals*, chapter 13, pp261–286. Blackwell Scientific Publications, 1976.

[16] A. Thompson. Evolving electronic robot controllers that exploit hardware resources. In F. Morán et al., eds, *Advances in Artificial Life: Proc. 3rd Eur. Conf. on Artificial Life (ECAL95)*, vol. 929 of *LNAI*, pp640–656. Springer-Verlag, 1995.

[17] T. H. Benzinger. The thermal homeostasis of man. In L. L. Langley, ed, *Homeostasis: Origins of the Concept*, Benchmark papers in Human Physiology, chapter 21, pp295–327. Dowden, Hutchison & Ross, 1973.

[18] G. A. Bartholomew, J. W. Hudson, and T. R. Howell. Body temperature, oxygen consumption, evaporative water loss, and heart rate in the Poor-will. In R. Ruibal, ed, *The Adaptation of Organisms*, Dickenson series on contemporary thought in Biological Science, pp15–25. Dickenson Publishing Company, 1967.

[19] R. W. Keyes. *The Physics of VLSI Systems*. Addison-Wesley, 1987.

[20] R. S. Components Ltd., PO Box 99, Corby, Northants NN17 9RS, UK. *Peltier effect heat pumps*, March 1988. Datasheet 7562.

[21] V. A. Pegel and V. A. Remorov. The heat-regulating mechanism and its development in poikilothermic animals. In J. W. S. Pringle, ed, *Essays on Physiological Evolution*. Permagon Press, 1965.

[22] D. W. Wood. *Principles of Animal Physiology*. Edward Arnold Ltd., 1983.

[23] S. Armstrong Talbot and Urs Gessner. *Systems Physiology*. John Wiley and Sons, 1973.

[24] Collins encyclopedia of animals. William Collins Sons, 1975.

[25] K. Schmidt-Nielsen, B. Schmidt-Nielsen, S. A. Jarnum, et al. Body temperature of the camel and its relation to water economy. In R. Ruibal, ed, *The Adaptation of Organisms*, Dickenson series on contemporary thought in Biological Science, pp26–42. Dickenson Publishing Company, Inc., 1967.

[26] G. Ström. Central nervous regulation of body temperature. In *Handbook of Physiology*, Section 1: Neurophysiology, Vol. II, chapter XLVI, pp1173–1196. Waverly Press, 1960. American Physiology Society.

[27] G. E. Miller. Artificial life as theoretical biology: how to do real science with computer simulation. CSRP 378, School of Cognitive and Computing Sciences, University of Sussex, 1995.

[28] M. S. Gordon, G. A. Bartholomew, A. D. Grinnell, et al. *Animal Physiology: Principles and adaptations*. Macmillan Publishing Co., 1982.

VLSE
Very Large Scale Evolution in Hardware.

J. S. McCaskill[◊], U. Tangen, J. Ackermann

Institute for Molecular Biotechnology,
Beutenbergstr. 11, Jena 07745, Germany
Email: jmccask@imb-jena.de
Homepage: http:/www.imb-jena.de
[◊]Communicating author to whom correspondence should be addressed.

Abstract

Programmable hardware is presented based on Field Programmable Gate Array technology which allows the implementation of a large spatial medium for the study of logical and physical models of evolution. In a first phase, a massively parallel computer was designed, NGEN, with configurable interface to a UNIX host workstation, broad band interconnect up to 3D (and sparse beyond 3D) and 144 tabula rasa processors (FPGAs) configurable down to the individual gate level[1]. This paper describes the implementation of a hierarchy of molecular evolution models, using a spatial mapping of the processor array and off chip memory, in an extension of the dataflow architectural concept. Starting with parallel random number generation and simple diffusion, the authors show how reactions, reactions in sequence space, reaction-diffusion systems, and evolving reaction-diffusion systems can be constructed in digital logic within a single framework. The evolution demands an individual level approach and large populations in the millions are realised through a careful dataflow conception between the FPGAs and off chip memory. Applications to predation, parasitism and cooperative evolution are outlined. Finally, the current status of development of a second generation VLSE computer, POLYP, with dynamical and autonomous reconfiguration possibilities is described. This work provides a link between pilot projects in evolvable hardware and simulations and experiments in molecular evolution. New results based on individual level simulations are presented for a cooperatively coupled amplification system with an *in vitro* biochemical experimental realisation (CATCH).

1. Introduction

Simple calculations and experiments in molecular evolution under rapidly evolving conditions show that a significant fraction of the population consists of unique individuals[2]. Evolution is a stochastic process requiring a massive computational effort when the sequence dependence of proliferation is taken into account. Work in our laboratory to construct *in vitro* model systems in which spatially resolved evolution can be studied in laboratory time-scales have resulted in molecular predator-prey[3] and cooperative systems[4] which allow the study of large populations, ca.

10^{12} individuals, and the investigations of key steps in the evolution of cooperation. To our knowledge these are the first such systems which allow evolutionary ecological studies *in vitro*. Furthermore, theoretical work has oulined the key importance of spatial isolation in the evolution of molecular cooperation, and two dimensional open biochemical reactors have been developed in microstructures for the investigation of these features in two dimensions[5]. Stochastic features of the reaction kinetics and the sequence dependence of the reaction rates (in particular, hybridisation) play a major role in these model systems. This experimental background to our work, prompted the step to a large computational facility with the above individual and stochastic properties. Parallel computation proved necessary, single parameter value simulations even for the continuous case with few components taking several days on a workstation (HP J280) for a 512x512 grid.

On the other hand, there is considerable interest in understanding the logical basis of evolution, in particular its seemingly open ended creativity, and the metaphor of programmable matter[6] has, following the seminal work of von Neumann[7], sought to analyse the logical basis of self-reproduction and evolution independently of the physical molecular realisation. Work on self-replicating cellular automata[8], Turing machines[9,10], stack machines[11], chemical lambda calculus[12], primitive assembler (e.g. Core-Wars[13], Tierra[14]) and others have helped to complement the detailed picture obtained from molecular biology within the context of logical possibility. Digital logic, if it can be (partially) reconfigured dynamically by the processes operating within it, opens a new world of electr5onic hardware evolution. While digital hardware evolution can be simulated (much more slowly) in software, the step to hardware opens new possibilities for the design of functioning devices by evolution and in particular for the evolution of devices which can evolve and operate interactively (on-line) in a real complex environment. For these reasons, we chose not to follow the classic computational paradigm of commercial parallel computation, but rather a shift of effort from negotiating with automatic parallel code producing compilers to the design of local processors which can process molecular data in a dataflow fashion. We have embraced the systolic algorithm methodology and created a

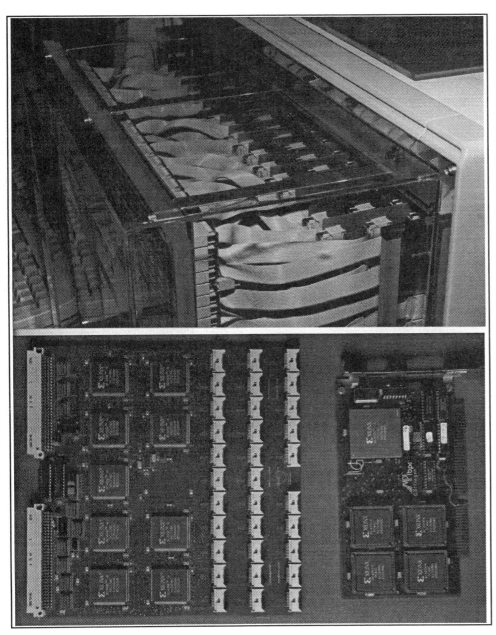

Fig 1: The VLSE Configurable Computer NGEN. The top figure shows the rack of 18 configurable processor boards with the broad band interconnect implemented via a frontplane in the foreground left. The lower figure shows the PCB design of the NGEN boards and a PC prototype predecessor. The back of the board is packed with 72 SRAM chips. The FPGAs are XC4008 chips which represented an optimum price-performance ratio at construction time.

a binary interaction which is processed systolically (i.e. bit serially and synchronously). A local automaton, the processor with local memory resources, is responsible for the processing. Strings are processed in a pipeline fashion, so that two biopolymers emerge from the processor as two others enter. Particular bit representations may be processed as if they corresponded to the absence of a biopolymer, so that this arrangement does not necessarily imply a constant population size. One example of processing which is pursued in this work involves the computation of the outcome of a competition between the two biopolymers depending on their sequences, leading to an output processing decision such as the copying of one of the biomolecules on both output channels.

computer architecture uniqely suited to the implementation of very large populations in programmable matter. These populations are too large to be distributed directly in the processors and require an extremely broad bandwidth and uninterrupted smooth flow of data between processors *via* an intelligent application of intermediate distributed SRAM resources.

The implementation of evolution in this hardware is based on binary encounters between biopolymers represented systolically as moving data binary strings. The representation may be chosen as the primary structure (sequence) of the biopolymers, an encoding of their folded structure or at a functional level a representation of the catalytic capabilities of the molecules. Two strings enter into

The VLSE machine NGEN was first brought into operation in May 1994 and completed with a dedicated high bandwidth front plane and variable clock card in 1995. A picture of the 18 processor cards plus UNIX frontend workstation in a 21 slot 1800W VME-bus chassis is shown in Fig. 1. Details of the hardware may be found in Ref 1. Both the local processors and their interconnections are configured in the FPGAs afresh for each simulation. Furthermore, simulations with functional gates with logical function rewritten by strings within the population are considered in later applications. Finally, a new VLSE computer, POLYP[15], is introduced which utilises rapid partial reconfiguration of its FPGAs and allows a further major step towards on-line evolving hardware.

2. Parallel random number generator for configurable hardware

Stochastic implementations of evolution on an individual level require random bits for the random walks of individuals, for reaction probabilities, for mutation and the choice between various such elementary processing steps. Conventional random number generation is not efficient in field programmable gate arrays, where a fundamentally parallel solution can be found. A digital circuit is mainly built up of two different resources: firstly the logical elements processing information and secondly the routing resources connecting the logic elements of the circuit. Because both resources are limited, their use has to be taken into account in the calculation of the costs of random number generation.

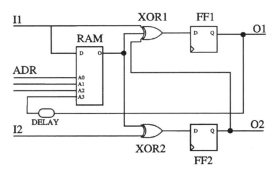

Fig. 2 Logical unit of parallel random number generator. Chains of simple units can be used for the parallel generation of pseudo-random numbers. Each processor unit receives two input bits, I1 and I2, and has two random bits as ouput, O1 and O2. One of the inputs (I1) is written in a 16-bit RAM element. The RAM output is XORed (XOR2) with input I2 and the result is stored in the flip-flop FF2. The bit previously stored in FF2 is XORed (XOR1) with input I1 and the RAM output. The result is stored in the flip-flop FF1. The lower three bits of the RAM addressing are provided by a global 3-bit counter. This unit fits in one configurable logic block of a Xilinx XC4000 series FPGA.

The above figure shows a basic unit found to generate highest quality random numbers[16] (according to the Grassberger self avoiding walk test, amongst others) when connected in linear chains. The latter topology is spartan in terms of the use of interconnect resources, both intra- and inter FPGA, and has found to be sufficient to remove correlations. The topology of the connections between the units in the chain plays an important role for the quality of the random number generator. Compared with linear feedback shift register approaches and cellular automata, the RNG described in Fig. 2 presents an efficient combination of delay and exclusive-or function elements and behaves very well under statistical tests.

3. Parallel individual diffusion of combinatorial objects

Arguably the simplest representation of an evolvable entity with combinatorial complexity is in terms of a string of characters. Such a linear string has of course a special place in the artificial life literature, since von Neumann argued that a linear representation of structures was necessary for universal self-reproduction[7] prior to the unravelling of the structure of DNA. We use linear strings, without loss of generality binary strings, to represent individuals, and in our primary application to the molecular level regard the string as encoding a particular molecular species. The sequence dependence of reaction rates may then be used both for constructing given reaction mechanisms and studying their evolution (see below). Later we shall also consider the extension to internally structured individuals where their spatial extent cannot be ignored in the diffusive motion (section 9). Diffusion provides an important example of a random process of individual motion which induces homogeneous mixing in the long time limit, i.e. every individual can move to an arbitrary location within the space and more importantly every pair of individuals become neighbours at some time. This is an important property from an evolutionary perspective. Furthermore, as seen below the locality of motion in diffusion is important in the evolution of cooperative interaction modes.

Given sufficient processor resources to house all individuals, diffusion can be assembled from independent random interchange processes in the various dimensions of the problem. When individuals are linear strings moving in pipelined shift registers in logic, the simplest exchange process involves a crossover of the wires or channels which conduct two neighbouring strings. This crossover must be implemented dynamically and synchronously with the beginning and ends of the strings, otherwise they will be cut. Such a dynamical partial rewiring of an FPGA can be implemented using two multiplexers. In order to ensure independence of the competing exchange processes for an individual, e.g. with the left or right neighbour, the classic dynamical trick of separating the possible exchanges into two classes can be used (as in lattice polymer automata[17] or diffusive cellular automata[18]). Random bits from the RNG in section 2 are used to control the multiplexers.

In this work we concentrate on 2D simulations, but this is not a hardware limitation and we briefly outline an extension to three dimensions. The key problem is the extension to large population sizes: larger than can be contained directly in the FPGAs available. This reflects the fundamental packing density advantage of dedicated memory chips (e.g. the 8*8*32kbit SRAMs employed for each FPGA in NGEN). In the dataflow conception developed here and in[19], the strings are clocked into the FPGAs in a bit serial fashion continously from and to inline SRAMs residing on the interchip interconnect. The most straightforward approach to avoiding data bottlenecks in 2D is to have one dimension (which we denote as horizontal) strung out in a linear chain embedded in the FPGA array and the other (vertical) successively in the SRAMs addressed as a single large virtual shift register. In this way, the 2D medium is processed row by row by the FPGA. Vertical exchange operators require the interchange between two successive strings entering the FPGA. This may be achieved using the limited RAM resources of the FPGAs to construct small virtual shift registers, through which the strings are fed. Vertical exchange is then implemented via multiplexers between the entering and leaving bits of these shift registers. Implementation details and a discussion of alternatives and the absence of correlations in the random walks may be found in[19]. This implementation of 2D diffusion is used in the following sections.

The 40 Mbytes of high speed (15nsec) SRAM in NGEN allow populations in the millions of strings to be realised. For example an array of 2300*2000 64-bit strings can be realised. Operating at 8MHz, the entire population can be processed at the rate of 256 passes per second. Most of the work reported here was performed with half this array (i.e. 2304*1026) using half the available SRAM.

In three dimensions, a natural extension of the 2D strategy can be carried out because the NGEN frontplane realises its optimum bandwidth for a 2D processor topology. Instead of embedding a linear chain in the 2D processor array, a square processor array with 16 processors per chip is extended transparently to the entire 12*12 chip array to form the x-y planes of the 3D implementation. With 64-bit strings this leads to a 3D space of 48*48*1026, which is too asymmetric for most purposes. For the 2D exchange operators, the Margolus and Toffoli rotations[18] of 2*2 squares on alternating lattices can be constructed efficiently in FPGAs, or the one dimensional case may be generalised directly. In order to even up the dimensions of the space, the processor array can be used to contain just a portion (square or elongated rectangle in x dimension) of the (x-y) plane.

A continuous trajectory of data through this plane subset can be achieved if the dataflow is diagonal to the memory dimension (z-axis). The top side (y dimension) of the x-y subset in one pass becomes the bottom side in the next pass. The diffusion across the interface between two neighbouring slabs can be handled simply by a special treatment of the end processors or a strict alternation of probabilistic upwards or downwards transitions from pass to pass. Technical details of cubic three dimensional implementations with periodic boundary conditions will be reported elsewhere.

4. Chemical reactions and reactions in sequence space

Our approach to the development of a chemically active programmable medium is influenced strongly by the desire to allow reactions between a combinatorially complex set of molecules: a precondition for the study of emergent evolution at the molecular level. For this reason, and because of its inherent stochastic nature, we have adopted an individual moving data approach to chemical reactions. Kinetic equations are replaced by elementary reaction event probabilities, which depend on the local configuration of molecules. From the point of view of solution chemistry, it suffices to consider unimolecular and bimolecular reactions: genuine higher order reactions such as trimolecular reaction steps can be decomposed into bimolecular steps and must be seen as condensed descriptions of such extended variable schemes since trimolecular collisions in solution are rare events. In contrast with probabilistic cellular automata models, the complexity of the molecules occupying lattice cells requires the outcome of chemical reactions to be computed, being too complex in general to be specified by a lookup table. Furthermore, the products of neighbouring cells cannot be computed as independent probabilistic events: neither in the case of diffusion nor of bimolecular reactions.

Reaction probabilities, and diffusion rates can be specified compactly in a bit serial fashion in logic using local ROM resources on the FPGAs. A single channel 16-bit ROM for example, together with a few function generators and the random bits (see section two) can be assembled to compute random events with a predefined probability once every 16 bits. If these probabilities need to change in the course of simulation, local RAMs may be used instead. Since molecules are also processed bit serially, these locally computed probabilities keep pace with the required reaction processing. Rare events can instead also be generated globally and accessed by all processors in turn.

Replication is a special autocatalytic reaction, whose treatment is particularly suited to the systolic approach, particularly in conjunction with the side reactions of mutation and recombination. Indeed, one motivation for the digital logic approach expounded here was the realisation that processes of diffusion, replication, saturation, mutation and recombination can all be realised by means of a simple systolic switch (shown in Fig. 3) governing the flow of information in two bit-serial streams of data. Replication which is limited by available resources, as in the logistic equation for example, can be modelled by the simple bimolecular reaction $A + B \rightarrow 2A$ in which B is a resource or non-occupied space. This fundamentally bimolecular process also has the advantage of allowing frequency dependent effects to be addressed within a unified framework (see below). Within the framework of population genetics, it is similar to a Moran model of constrained population size.

402

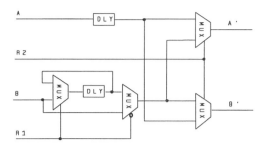

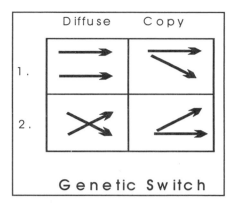

Fig. 3 Genetic Switch and logic implementation of diffusion as described in the text.

The sequence dependence of replication has been a major focus of study since the introduction of the quasispecies model. Since the eighties attention has shifted from the assignment of replication rates to sequences to models of their computation. RNA folding based models were introduced independently by McCaskill[2] and Fontana et.al.[20], and have been pursued intensively using dynamic programming algorithms. Kauffman introduced the N-k model[21] as a generalisation of spin-glass structure to allow sequence-dependencies of arbitrary correlation structure to be captured. In analogy with molecular folding and the conventional approach of sequence → structure → function, it is generally very convenient to decompose the computation of fitness into two steps:

1) folding with a complex dependence on sequence, which may be modelled as a mapping between sequence spaces, i.e. S→F(S)

2) local rate assignment and/or global averaging of local properties of the fold to compute fitness, i.e. F(S)→Rate

The important feature of this decomposition is that the complex (non-convex) features of the rate dependence on sequence are restricted to the first step. Simple averaging or summation is seen to be the usual second step when conventional models are decomposed in this fashion. The optimisation task is made difficult by the rugged sequence dependence of folding. Thuerk in particular investigated this phenomena[9] with iterative cellular automata implementing the folding. We have implemented a variety of models of this type, including random fitness and a stochastic version of the N-k model[21], in compact systolic algorithms for use with configurable hardware. The digital logic resources required are small enough that each local processor can

Fig 4. Spatial evolution on NGEN. The plot shows the local correlations in sequence in a simplest model of an evolving stochastic population. The replication probability dependence on sequence is the simple binary representation of numerical values for the sequences of length 64. The simulation of the large population, here of size 2304*1026, runs in seconds on NGEN because of the high update frequency (see text).

harbor digital logic for reaction rate computation from sequence. Particularly convenient and general is to replace summation in the second step by a probabilistic lookup using the folded sequence to determine the probability as in the implemetation of reaction rates above. An example of a spatial simulation on NGEN with such a fitness function is described in the following section (and in Fig. 4).

5. Reaction-diffusion and spatial evolution of individuals

Spatial correlations in sequences are a key feature of diffusive stochastic quasispecies models. The dependence of the error threshold and the local preservation of information on the interplay between diffusion rate and mutation rate for example is a practical and theoretical focus. Such issues gain added interest in the case of interactions (see below). The major influence of local diffusion on the dynamics of a population with sequence dependent replication rates is seen in Fig. 4. Of particular importance are the spatial correlation functions defined by:

$$c(r,t) = \int D(s(\vec{r}_1 + \vec{r}, t_1 + t), s(\vec{r}_1, t_1)) d\vec{r}_1 dt_1$$

where $D(s_1, s_2)$ is a measure of the distance between two sequences such as the Hamming distance.

The general treatment of sequence dependent rates of bimolecular replication reactions also benefits from the decomposition introduced in the previous section. The first step involves folding of the two partners, the second involves a decision as to which of the two sequences is replicated (as in the theory of evolutionary games). If this decision procedure induces a total ordering of the (folded) sequences, one expects the outcome to resemble the Darwinian optimisation of the quasispecies model. However, if the transitivity of the decision algorithm does not hold, as in R>P>B>R, then complex dynamics may ensue. If the resource (e.g. free space) is identified with the species B, then R and P behave as predator and prey species and the classic oscillations of the Lotka-Volterra family of models may be observed. An *in vitro* biochemical system showing predator-prey kinetics has been established[3,22], and so this type of simulation at the individual level will be subject to experimental evaluation.

6. Spatial evolution of cooperation

Following the early realisation that compartmentation was crucial to the evolution of molecular cooperation[23], difficulties with the coupling of compartmental replication with molecular replication were outlined[24]. Spatial isolation by distance had been prevalent as an alternative to island models of diversification in population biology, but not until the end of the eighties did theory[25] and experiments[26] for *in vitro* systems begin to address isolation by distance at the molecular level.

More recently, the discovery of self-replicating spot patterns, at first theoretically[27], in a model of Scott and Gray, related to the Selkov model for glycolytic oscillations, prompted

one of us[28] to propose a resource model of isothermal replication of RNA (and DNA) which also was shown to exhibit these concentration patterns. Essential for this behaviour is the explicit modelling of a resource with a higher diffusion coefficient than the amplifying species, and a non-linear concentration dependence of amplification which increases for higher concentrations before ultimately saturating through resource limitation. These patterns were shown[29], like spirals[25], to be effective at low mutation rates in maintaining cooperative replication in the presence of parasites.

In order to allow different diffusion rates in the large population simulations in configurable hardware, attention must be paid to avoid concentration effects. Because the active media must be used in a dense manner, even when dilute solutions are being implemented, a diffusional exchange between individuals with different mobilities introduces concentration dependencies which complicate the modelling process. A simple solution for the resource species is to place it on a separate lattice, by parcelling off one bit of each sequence describing the other biomolecules, and allowing additional diffusion of this bit position. An example of a stochastic individual level simulation of self-replicating spots, using this approach which allows evolution of the kinetic parameters, is shown in Fig. 5.

A bimolecular resolution of the Scott-Gray model was employed:

A+A→A'+A; A'+B→A+A; φ→B; A,A'→φ;

where A is the autocatalyst, B the resource and A' an activated autocatalyst, with the diffusion rate of the resource double that of the other species. φ is an empty placeholder. The kill rate k of the autocatalyst is modelled as sequence dependent according to a binary representation of annihilation probability, and provides an additive term to the physical dilution by the flow rate F. Already this sequence dependence, introducing a combinatorial family of autocatalysts A_i, has been used to rapidly scan through the parameter space using different sequences in the absence of mutation. Introducing mutation causes an optimization of the kill rate to the limiting flow rate term.

The major mutant of interest in such systems concern expoiters of the cooperative activation step. A variant of A which is primed by A but does not activate other molecules is a classic expoiter. The new question in this context is whether the spatial pattern formation automatically self-organizes to the self-replicating spot regime to convey resitance of the autocatalysts to such expoitation. A clean answer to this question requires a sequence-space analysis of an evolving popuation at the individual level, which has been implemented on NGEN. Classical simulations here are simply too time-consuming. The simpler phenomenom of exploiter suppression in the appropriate parameter regime of self-replicating spots has already been derived[28,29]. A similar

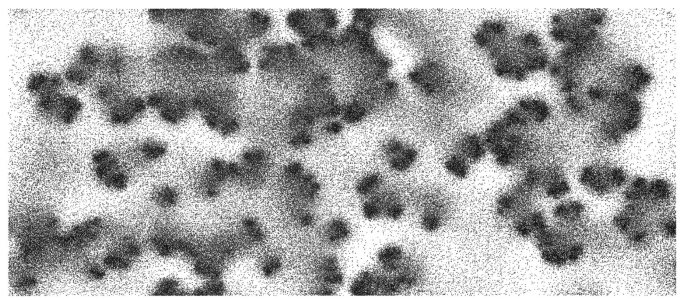

Fig. 5 Individual based stochastic simulation of self-replicating spot patterns according to the mechanism shown in eqn(1). The individuals are 63 bits in length and in this picture identical (a mutation rate of zero was used). The resource species is shown in white, the autocatalysts and empty space in black. Further details require a colour representation. The simulation was performed on NGEN using a 2304*1026 array.

result using partial differential equation modelling has been published recently[30]. Further details and results of the evolution of molecules in connection with self-replicating spot patterns will be reported elsewhere.

Recently an *in vitro* model system, CATCH[4], has been established which operates according to a cooperative kinetics and which should show self-replicating spots when placed in 2D flow reactor. Such experiments are underway. Further work is in progress to extend these seminal studies on the origin of molecular cooperation towards the classic high level cooperative features of modern molecular biology, such as the self-organisation of the genetic code. More generally, the evolution of complex functions divided into molecular modules and models with individuals possessing finite spatial extent are being investigated. This work will be reported elsewhere. In all these problems the availability of the configurable hardware tool NGEN makes new population levels and timescale accessible. We know of no other comparable effort in spatially resolved effort using configurable hardware.

7. Polyp

One challenge in conjunction with evolvable hardware in optimization scenarios is to obtain a microscopic feedback between processed information and the reconfiguration of the hardware. The reconfiguration of the logic in NGEN can only proceed at the whole chip level and is relatively slow, taking a few tenths of a second. A new generation of micro-configurable chips (Xilinx XC6200 FPGAs), in which the configuration data is individually addressable like SRAM, has been utilized to design a second generation VLSE computer, POLYP[15]. The Xilinx XC6200 FPGAs have already been used for analog evolution in hardware[31].

The hardware cards of POLYP are in 18 multilayer technology and wherever possible the parts are surface mounted. Four optical interface chips (Optobus) are connected via two crossbars to the eight agent FPGAs of type Xilinx XC6200. Two distributer FPGAs (XC4025) mediate the dynamic reconfiguration cycle and host communication of the agent FPGAs. These communicate with the host workstation via a control FPGA (XC4025) and an optimised design FPGA (XC4006) implementing the VME standard. Distributed SRAM is provided as in NGEN, and an additional direct broadband interconnect via two 160 pin connectors is provided. Further details may be found in[15].

Here we simply want to draw attention to the new possibilities of autonomous evolution control in this type of VLSE hardware as shown in Fig. 6. Two levels of hardware evolution can be considered, differing in the autonomy of the processing of the logical description. The description of the hardware logic involves the configuration bit sequence, or, since the configuration bits of POLYP can be written to as if they were addressable memories, an assembly of address-data pairs. Since the configuration data can also be read, the first approach involves extracting the current configuration data from one or more addresses and modifying either data or address before returning it to the chip. The entire dynamics of modification is then a fixed feature (implementable for example in the distributor FPGAs), and the reconfigurable logic does not have access to its own

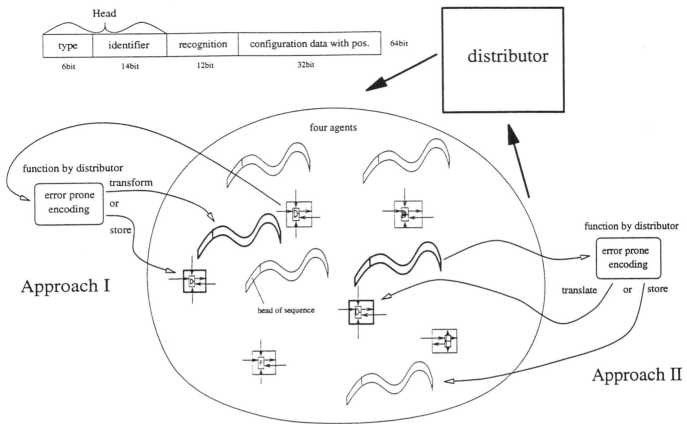

Figure 6: New opportunities for autonomous evolution in hardware on the second generation VLSE computer POLYP (see text). A similar version of this diagram was also reported in[15].

symbolic description. The second approach allows the configurable logic to process its own description, an external circuitry then causing the symbolic changes to modify the configurable logic. The latter may or may not involve mutational change. This is essentially the approach taken by biological systems, which process the information in their genome, resulting in a modified processing apparatus.

8. Outlook

The present paper has shown how configurable hardware may be used to construct very large scale evolving systems and tailored to a wide range of fundamental problems in evolution at the individual level. Further applications to practical optimisation and increasing molecular biological realism are expected. Indeed Breyer et.al. shows how a realistic model of *in vitro* cooperative evolution involving sequence dependent hybridisation in various registers may be achieved[32]. The primary goal of this work is not to achieve world peak performance in parallel simulation, although very creditable results have been achieved, but rather to show that the digital logic programmable media provides both a practical platform for realistic modelling and a new arena for artificial life modelling with its own criteria

of simplicity and inspiration of new types of models. Experience in the construction of evolving systems and models in distributed media will be crucial in the construction of hybrid evolware involving electronic and biochemical components. Microreactors, *in vitro* amplification systems and programmable logic may provide the basis for such a development.

Acknowledgement

Our thanks go to Thomas Maeke, Udo Gemm, Karsten Mekelburg, Harald Chorongiewski, Ludger Schulte, Bernd Senf and Jens Breyer for assistance at various stages of the NGEN project. This work was supported in part by the German Ministry of Science and Education (BMBF), Grant No 0310799. It is dedicated to Manfred Eigen whose vision of evolution machines has inspired the authors.

References

[1] McCaskill, J. S., Maeke, T., Gemm, U., Schulte, L. and Tangen, U. "NGEN: A Massively Parallel Reconfigurable Computer for Biological Simulation: towards a Self-Organizing Computer" in press, Lec. Note. Comp. Sci, 1997.
[2] Eigen, M., McCaskill, J.S., Schuster, P. "The Molecular Quasispecies", Adv. Chem.Phys. 75:149-263 1989.
[3] Wlotzka, B. and McCaskill, J.S. "A molecular predator and its prey: coupled isothermal amplification of nucleci acids." Chemistry and Biology **4** 25-33 (1997).

[4] Ehricht, R., Ellinger T. and McCaskill, J.S. "Cooperative amplification of templates by cross-hybridisation (CATCH)" Eur. J.Biochem. **243** 358-364 (1997).

[5] Schmidt. K., Foerster, P., Bochmann, A. and McCaskill, J. S. "Microstructured Flow Reactors for Two-Dimensional Experiments" in 1st International Conference on Microreaction Technology, 23-25 Feb. 1997, Dechema e.V. Frankfurt, Germany.

[6] Langton C. G., "Artificial Life" The Proceedings of an Interdisciplinary Workshop on the Synthesis and Simulation of Living Systems (1989), Santa Fe Institute, Addison-Wesley.

[7] Von Neumann, J. "Self-reproducing Automata", ed. J. Burks 1958.

[8] Reggia, J.A. et.al. "Simple systems that exhibit self-directed replication" Science 259 1282-1287 (1993).

[9] McCaskill, J. S., "Polymer Chemistry on Tape: A Computational Model for Emergent Genetics", tech. rep., Max-Planck-Society, 1988.

[10] Thürk, M. "Ein Modell zur Selbstorganisation von Automatenalgorithmen zum Studium molekularer Evolution" Doktorarbeit Friedrich-Schiller-Univ. Jena (Informatik) 1993.

[11] Tangen U., Weberpals, H. "Simulating Biological Evolution on a Parallel Computer", Lecture Notes in computer Science, W. GOUTSCH, U. HARMS EDS., Springer Proc. **796** Vol 1 (1994) pp 238-243.

[12] Fontana, W. "Algorithmic Chemistry" (1990) Technical Report LA-UR 90-1959, Los Alamos Natl. Lab.

[13] Rasmussen, S. "Towards a Quantitative Theory of the Origin of Life" in Artificial Life, SFI Studies in the Sciences of Complexity, Ed. C. Langton (Addison Wesley, 1988).

[14] Ray, T. S. "An Approach to the Synthesis of Life" Artificial Life II eds. Langton C. G. et al. (1991) 371-408, Addison-Wesley.

[15] Tangen, U., Schulte, L. and McCaskill, J. S. "A parallel hardware evolvable computer POLYP", submitted, 1997.

[16] Ackermann, J., Böddeker, B., Breyer, J., Tangen, U. and McCaskill, J.S. "A minimum logic parallel pseudo-random number generator fro configurable hardware." submitted to IEEE Transactions on Parallel and Distributed Systems, 1996.

[17] Rasmussen, S., and Smith, J.R. "Lattice Polymer Automata" Ber. Bunsen. **98** 1185-1193 (1994).

[18] Toffoli, T. and Margolus, N. "Cellular Automata Machines" Cambridge MA: MIT Press, 1987

[19] McCaskill, J.S., Ackermann, J. and Breyer, J. "Efficient dataflow architectures for diffusion in chemistry and population dynamics" in preparation (1997).

[20] Fontana, W. and Schuster, P., Biophys. Chem. **26** 123 (1987).

[21] Kauffman, S. A. and Weinberger, E. "The N-k model of rugged fitness landscapes." J.Theor. Biol. **141** 211 (1989).

[22] Ackermann, J., Wlotzka B. and McCaskill, J.S. "*In vitro* DNA-based Predator-Prey System with Oscillatory Kinetics" submitted to Bull. Math. Biol. (1996).

[23] Eigen M. (1971). "Selforganisation of matter and the evolution of biological macro-molecules." *Naturwissenschaften* **58** 465-523.

[24] Bresch, C., Niesert, U. and Harnasch, D. (1980). "Hypercycles, parasites and packages." *J.Theor. Biol.* **85** 399-405.

[25] Boerljist, M.C. and Hogeweg P. (1995). "Spiral wave structure in prebiotic evolution: hypercycles stable against parasites." *Physica* **D88**, 29-39.

[26] Bauer G., Otten H. and McCaskill J.S. "Traveling waves of *in vitro* evolving RNA" Proc. Natl. Acad. Sci USA **86** 7937-7941 (1989).

[27] Pearson, J.E. (1993). "Complex patterns in a simple system." *Science* **261**, 189-192.

[28] McCaskill, J.S. "Ursprünge der molekularen Kooperation: Theorie und experi-ment." Inaugural lecture at the Friedrich Schiller University, 31. Mai 1994, printed by the Institut für Molekulare Biotechnologie, Jena.

[29] Böddeker, B. and McCaskill, J.S. " Self-replicating spots as a basis for the spatial stabilisation of catalytic function." J. Theor. Biol. submitted (1996).

[30] Cronhjort, M.B. and Blomberg, C. "Cluster compartment-alization may provide resistance to parasites for catalytic networks" Physica D **101** (1997) 289-298.

[31] Harvey, I. and Thompson, A. "Through the Labyrinth Evolution Finds a Way: A Silicon Ridge" Lect. Not. in Comp. Sci., 1996, in press

[32] Breyer J., Ackermann, J., Tangen, U. and McCaskill, J.S. "Modeling the evolution in cooperatively coupled *in vitro* amplification systems" Poster submitted to ECAL97.

Lossless Image Compression by Evolvable Hardware

Mehrdad Salami, Masaya Iwata and Tetsuya Higuchi

Electrotechnical Laboratory (ETL)

1-1-4 Umezono, Tsukuba, Ibaraki, 305, Japan

e-mail: m_salami@etl.go.jp

Abstract

We have investigated the possibility of applying Evolvable Hardware (EHW) to lossless image compression. EHW is a hardware that its configuration changes by an evolutionary algorithm. One of the successful methods in image compression is prediction coding which is based on pixel prediction function using neighbor pixels. Most of the algorithms in lossless image compression use fixed linear functions for pixel prediction. We have designed special hardware for the lossless image compression by classification of neighbor patterns and defining a set of functions. An evolutionary algorithm modifies each function depending on their local performance. By using functions included in EHW and changing them in real time an adaptive prediction system is established. Here we test the EHW system for pixel prediction and later we will apply it for error prediction to enhance the performance of compression. Simulation results for pixel prediction are compared with some common methods in image compression and a better performance is achieved.

1 Introduction

Over the last decade there was a great interest to employ evolutionary systems like EHW for real applications in engineering and computer science. Evolvable Hardware is hardware which is built on software-reconfigurable logic devices like PLD (Programmable Logic Device) or FPGA (Field Programmable Gate Array). The hardware architecture of EHW can be reconfigured by using a genetic learning to adapt to a new unknown environment. If hardware errors occur, or if new hardware functions are required, EHW can alter its hardware structure rapidly and accommodates such changes in real-time. A GA (Genetic Algorithm) program changes the architecture of EHW depending on input-output data from the application. Each configuration of EHW is represented as a bit string and the GA program operates on a population of these architecture bits. In reality this EHW architecture represents a variable function and the GA program adapts this function for the application.

Unfortunately these evolvable systems are slow in learning and require fast computing power because of the extensive search strategy in them. Using this kind of search, which is sometimes called population based search, has some advantages and disadvantages. From one point of view because of the extensive search strategy, their chance of finding global optimum is very high regardless of the difficulty of the problem. This factor is very important when there is no mathematical model or prior knowledge of a system. On the other hand slow operation is not acceptable for real time problems. For example, applying the evolutionary system to an ATM communication network working with the speed of 150MHz would be extremely difficult.

The global optimization of evolutionary algorithms can be used for solving static problems like parametric design of aircraft or schedule optimization [1]. In that type of problem the mathematical model is very complex and unknown, and evolutionary algorithms during optimization or tuning should learn the parametric model of the application and in the same time find the best parameters. If there is no time constraint for computation then we can say evolutionary algorithms are optimum global optimization methods.

After successful usage of evolutionary algorithms for static problems, the interest is shifted to dynamic problem like on-line control of a system. In the past few years we have seen many conferences on industrial application of evolutionary algorithms. Unfortunately, so far the success in this field is less than expected, especially with the existence of other soft computing methods like Neural Network and Fuzzy Logic that have existed in these fields for sometimes [2]. There are two main problems for evolutionary algorithms in this type of applications: 1) Large computation time is needed for evolutionary algorithms and 2) How to test the system in real time without interference with the system. Any system based on evolution should consider these two problems and properly handle them.

Most of algorithms for lossless image compression use a mechanism for pixel prediction. They normally use fixed linear or non-linear functions for the prediction. On the other hand each image has its characteristics and needs a unique function for prediction. Using only one function for all images will not produce the best results. EHW because of having variable functions is a good choice for pixel prediction in lossless image compression. First, it is implemented in the hardware and has proper processing power for image compression. Usually the size of image data is very large and needs to be handled by hardware schemes [3] for real time systems. Second, due to changes in architecture of EHW by evolution, it can adapt itself to a specific image and produces an appropriate function for each image. In this way adaptive function selection of EHW can enhance the performance of compression.

This paper attempts to implement an evolutionary approach for on-line lossless image compression. The hardware architecture that we used here is inspired from Configurable Logic Block (CLB) of Xilinx FPGA chips. Besides the hardware, there is an extra unit inside the block for changing the behavior of hardware and that is the source of evolution for the hardware. We will also address how this evolvable hardware eliminates two main problems of evolutionary systems.

The rest of this paper is as follow. At the beginning in Section 2 a simple EHW model will be explained. Section 3 explains the lossless image compression and how an image can be compressed using predictive coding. In the section 4 evolvable hardware will be explained in detail. Section 5 demonstrates how to add error prediction to improve the compression ratio. Section 6 shows simulation results of image compression by EHW and compares it with other methods.

2   Evolvable Hardware

Traditionally the evolvable hardware (EHW) is based on primitive gates such as AND-gate and OR-gate. An evolutionary algorithm finds the best hardware architecture for a particular problem. Most research on EHW, however, has the common problem that the evolved circuit size is small [4] and then this simple evolutionary hardware is not powerful enough for industrial applications.

To overcome this problem, a new evolvable hardware at function-level is proposed. This new EHW represents non-linear functions in hardware, and by an evolutionary strategy an adaptive real-time function optimization system can be realized. A new FPGA (Field Programmable Gate Array) architecture dedicated to evolvable function-level hardware is designed based on that model [5].

The FPGA model in Figure 1 represents function-level EHW. The FPGA model consists of 4 columns, each containing four Programmable Function Units (PFUs). Each PFU can implement one of the following six functions: an adder, a subtracter, a sine generator, a cosine generator, a multiplier, and a divider. The selection of the function to be implemented by a PFU is determined by chromosome genes given to the PFU. Constant generators are also included in each PFU. Columns are inter-

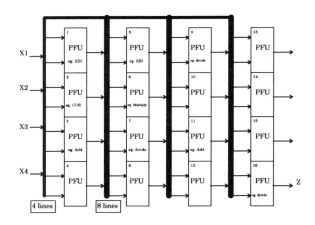

Figure 1: The FPGA model for function level evolution

connected by crossbar switches. The crossbars determine inputs to PFUs. This FPGA model assumes four inputs and one output. Data handled by FPGA are integer numbers.

This EHW can be used in many kinds of applications where hardware specifications are not known.

3   Lossless image compression

Digital transmission is a dominant means of communication for voice and image. It is expected to be flexible, reliable and cost effective, with the added potential for communication privacy and security through encryption. The cost of digital storage and transmission media are generally proportional to the amount of digital data that can be stored or transmitted. While the cost of such media decreases every year, the demand for their use increases at an even higher rate. Therefore there is a continuing need to minimize the number of bits necessary to transmit images while maintaining acceptable image quality.

Normally, images show a high degree of correlation among neighboring samples. A high degree of correlation implies a high degree of redundancy in the raw data. Therefore, if the degree of redundancy is removed, a more efficient and hence compressed coding of the signal is possible [6]. Image coding algorithms for lossless compression are usually based on one of two coding techniques: Transform Coding (TC) [7] or Prediction Coding (PC) [8]. The first method is based on block coding, where the input image is partitioned into blocks of pixels which are then encoded as separate entities. The second method is based on pixel prediction using neighboring pixels. The TC has a few practical problems such as selecting the size of block for different images and blocking effect for boundaries of blocks. Generally PC algorithms have better characteristics because they are free of block operation but on the other hand they are mathematically complex and require large computation time.

In a prediction system, there is an assumption that the appearance of data follows a mathematical model. If we have the right mathematical model then we can successfully predict what data will appear next. The inputs to the model are previous data or the status of the system and the output is the next data in the sequence.

The advantage of prediction is producing more compact data. For an 8 bits sample data, we need 8 bits to represent each data or sample. Suppose we have a good prediction system that successfully calculates the 4 most significant bits of the next symbol based on previous symbols. In that case we just need 4 bits to represent each symbol and it will reduce the size of data to half. The quality of the prediction model can be evaluated based on how close the model predicts data.

For one source of data it might not be difficult to build the mathematical model but for a wide range of source data it is not possible to apply one model. Image data is one of the most difficult types of data because it contains many sources of data and at each area of image one or more of them are active. Figure 2 shows a configuration for predictive based lossless image compression system.

The original image will be fed into a predictor system. For each pixel, the system reads the neighboring pixels and produces the predict value. The difference between original image and predicted one is the error image. The goal here is minimizing number of bits required for representing the error image.

Entropy is a means to calculate the minimum number of bits required for coding a stream of data. High entropy means higher number of bits are required to code the data. In prediction, input image normally has a high entropy and error image should have less entropy than original image. Less entropy for error image means less number of bits for coding and better compression rates.

Figure 3 shows the decoder system. It is very similar to

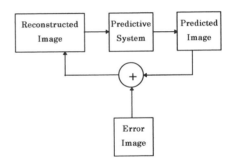

Figure 3: A decoder system

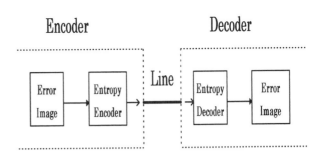

Figure 4: Including the entropy coding for a complete system

the encoder and the only difference is the source of data. In encoder the original image is represented and error will be produced but in decoder by using error image, the original image will be reconstructed. It is important to note that the complexity of encoder and decoder are similar.

For a complete system we need an entropy coding system for transmitting the error data (Figure 4). There are three major algorithms for entropy coding: Huffman coding, Arithmetic coding and LZW dictionary coding. The first two deliver better quality for image compression and the third one is adapted for text compression. We have to use one of them for transmitting the error data produced from encoding.

Prediction formula may be linear or non-linear [9]. In linear predictive coding, a gray level $g(i,j)$ is predicted by the linear combination of four pixel values as shown in Figure 5. The coefficients of the linear prediction are determined by adapting the least square method to the neighboring area of the pixel (i,j).

In a non-linear approach, a function f will be selected and optimized to predict pixel values. If the same neighbors as linear prediction are used then each pixel can be estimated as

$$\hat{g}(i,j) = f[g(i{-}1,j{-}1), g(i,j{-}1), g(i{-}1,j), g(i{+}1,j{-}1)]$$

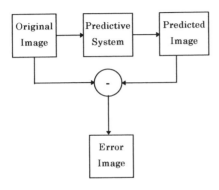

Figure 2: An encoder system

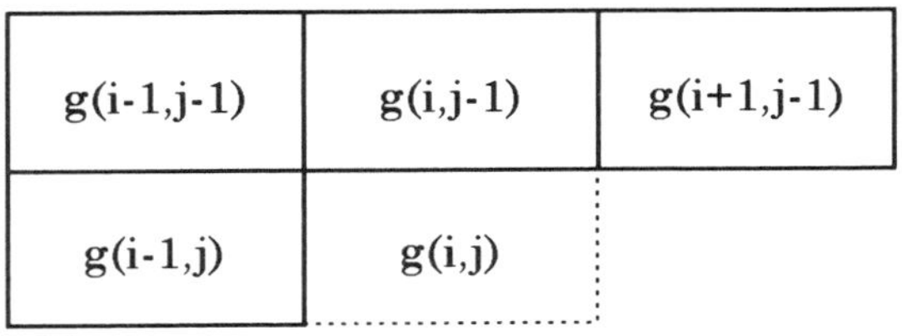

g(i-1,j-1)	g(i,j-1)	g(i+1,j-1)
g(i-1,j)	g(i,j)	

Figure 5: Prediction of pixel $g(i,j)$ from four neighbor pixels

where $\hat{g}(i,j)$ is the predict value for $g(i,j)$. JPEG (Joint Photographic Expert Group) uses a set of simple prediction formulas for lossless compression. The predictor function in JPEG combines the values of up to three neighboring samples ($g(i-1,j)$, $g(i,j-1)$ and $g(i-1,j-1)$) to form a prediction of $g(i,j)$ in Figure 5. This prediction is then subtracted from the actual value of $g(i,j)$, and the difference is encoded by entropy coding methods. Any one of the seven prediction functions listed in Table 1 can be used. Functions 1, 2 and 3 are used for one dimensional prediction and functions 4, 5,6 and 7 are two dimensional prediction [10].

Table 1: Prediction function for JPEG lossless coding

No.	Prediction Function f
1	$g(i-1,j)$
2	$g(i,j-1)$
3	$g(i-1,j-1)$
4	$g(i-1,j) + g(i,j-1) - g(i-1,j-1)$
5	$g(i-1,j) + (g(i,j-1) - g(i-1,j-1))/2$
6	$g(i,j-1) + (g(i-1,j) - g(i-1,j-1))/2$
7	$(g(i-1,j) + g(i,j-1))/2$

Most of the works so far in lossless image compression are based on linear functions, but this method is not always effective because it assumes the image obeys a linear model and the statistical properties of an image remain constant for the whole image [11]. In our work these two assumptions are removed and more flexible and effective algorithm based on EHW is applied.

4 EHW architecture for lossless image compression

Many systems in engineering like adaptive control, communication, robot navigation or data compression requires a prediction unit. This unit accepts previous data or the status of the system and predict the next data or action in the system.

Normally the prediction is performed by building the appropriate function. By knowing the type and the number of inputs and outputs a function can be optimized for a system. Selection of this function depends totally on the system. For linear systems, obviously the best function is a parametric linear combination of input, and with an interpolation algorithm the parameter can be determined. Unfortunately most real systems are non-linear and selection of the type of function is difficult even without considering the algorithm for optimizing it.

Selecting only one function for predicting data might be the easiest way for many systems. It would be easy to implement and obtain reasonable speed. On the other hand finding such a unique function for a non-linear system is very difficult if not impossible. Most of the previous function-level EHW are based on finding one prediction function by evolutionary algorithms and manipulating the function in real time [12]. These EHW systems are too dependent upon one function and this is why they need large computation time for evolution to a good result.

One solution for non-linear systems is to assume linear behavior for one area of system operation. Then we can define a set of linear functions to predict data for each area separately. For that purpose we need a classification unit to detect the status of the system and select one of the linear functions. This categorizing or classification can be separated from the functions itself. On the other hand this approach might not always work and depending upon the non-linearity of the problem in hand we might have poor results. There is another option to use a set of non-linear functions like in Radial Base Function (RBF) networks, but the problem is again how to separate the area to the region with sigmod behavior.

For Lossless Image Compression (LIC) classification is not very hard. The possible feature like sharp horizontal lines, horizontal lines, sharp vertical lines, vertical lines, 45 angle lines, 135 angle lines, curved lines and other type of lines should be classified and data for each class need to be prepared. On the other hand the difficult problem for LIC is function selection. As it mentioned before the appearance of data depends on many sources, some of them linear and some non-linear. Selecting one type of function, like in RBF, would not be useful and we need a combination of linear and non-linear functions. For the moment we will consider the architecture of EHW without considering the type of functions we want to implement. In the next section more explanation will be

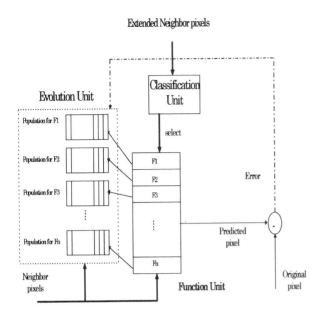

Figure 6: The proposed EHW model for pixel prediction

presented about function selection.

To make the problem easier for hardware it is better to separate the classification unit from the function unit. Figure 6 shows the EHW architecture for LIC application. It consists of three blocks. The first block is for classification inputs or selection functions, the second block is for implementing possible functions and the third one is responsible for evolution in hardware.

1 - Classification Unit

This unit accepts the neighboring pixels and depending on which pattern they represent, one of outputs will be activated. Normally it must classify the smooth region, sharp line in vertical and horizontal directions and other type of patterns.

The number of input-output for classification unit depends on application. For LIC, 11 integer inputs and 32 outputs seem sufficient. The 11 inputs are the neighbors of the current pixel (each 8 bits long) and each output is for recognition of one special pattern (Figure 7).

It is important to know why 11 inputs were used to describe the status or pattern. In Figure 4, only four neighboring pixels were used for prediction function, and that is like the status of the system. However, for classification we need one more previous state of the system. We then need another four neighbors for each neighbor of the current pixel. In totally, it will require knowing the value of seven more pixels as demonstrated in Figure 7.

The classification unit does not need to be changed

during processing and can be trained using off-line data only. This unit must be trained for classification of all possible patterns. There is no need to change the architecture of this unit during real time operation because, for example, when it can recognize a sharp horizontal line then the situation where the line occurs will never change. We can make this unit work better by presenting more patterns in off-line training. If off-line training is enough and we present sufficient data then we can fix this unit for real time operation.

2 - Function Unit

This unit receives the output from the classification unit and activates one of n possible functions for prediction. This unit also receives the neighbor pixels as input for the function. The output of this unit is the predicted pixel value.

Unlike the classification unit which is fixed for compressing different images, the function unit changes in real time depending on local characteristics of data. These basic functions can be found by off-line training data. In on-line operation for each function there is a population of functions, and after fitness evaluation of these functions for a certain period of time the best function will be selected as the active function. All the subsequent output data will be produced based on that function. Using the fitness calculated for all functions, the next generation will be created and fitness for new generation will be calculated again. During fitness evaluation of the current generation the best function from the previous generation will produce output data and the evolutionary algorithm will not delay the actual stream of data.

By separating these functions, in fact we make the problem much easier, so that we can solve it with limited time and hardware. The cost we paid for this simplification is that we cannot guarantee finding the best function all the time. We have to pay this price as long as there is restriction of time and hardware for any problem.

The number of functions is depend on application, but

g(i-2,j-2)	g(i-1,j-2)	g(i,j-2)	g(i+1,j-2)	g(i+2,j-2)
g(i-2,j-1)	g(i-1,j-1)	g(i,j-1)	g(i+1,j-1)	
g(i-2,j)	g(i-1,j)	g(i,j)		

Figure 7: The extended neighboring pixels for predicting pixel at $g(i, j)$

it is equal to the number of outputs from the classification unit. The type of function is also important and depends on the application. Some applications require linear functions and some non-linear functions.

3 - Evolution Unit

This unit is responsible for including adaptive behavior in the system. It accepts the neighboring pixels and for evolution it also needs the error of the past pixel predictions. This unit also controls which function is active in the function unit. It includes an evolutionary algorithm like GAs for each function. It has a population of functions and calculates the fitness of them based on the returned error values. After a certain time it downloads the best function into the function unit and generates a new population for fitness calculation.

Normally each function in the function unit is implemented in hardware and for speed purposes all individuals in the population must be implemented in hardware too. For each individual in the population there is a hardware unit controlled by a memory location which is called architecture bit. The architecture bit controls the operation of a hardware unit and can be changed by an evolutionary algorithm to create a new generation. It will guarantee speed requirement for LIC and eliminate the first problem of evolutionary systems.

For fitness calculation all individual in the population can calculate their fitness in parallel. When an error return to the evolution unit, it updates the fitness value of each individual by few integer operations and the fitness of an individual gradually forms. After a certain amount of time the best individual will be shifted to the function unit and a new population will be created.

In this model, if we forget evolution then the system will work perfectly in minimum time by selecting the best function and calculating the output based on that function. In most evolutionary systems there is a large delay because of evolution in the system, but here evolution is happening in background and not interfering with the actual operation of system. It will eliminate the second problem of evolutionary systems. By selecting the best functions for LIC from off-line training and evolution of the system for finding a better function in on-line operation, we can make sure this system at least produce similar performance as other algorithms for LIC.

The EHW configuration in Figure 6 is very similar to CLB configuration in FPGA Xilinx chips (Figure 8). The CLB unit is the core unit for logic calculation in Xilinx FPGA chips. They can be programmed to operate as a specific logic function. The EHW has some similarity and differences with CLBs. They are similar because they both use a function unit and selection unit. The main difference is that EHW uses an evolutionary algorithm for changing the functions but CLB can only be programmed externally. Besides this there are minor

differences such as a CLB unit can only be used for digital operations but EHW can also be programmed for integer operations. Although multiple CLB units can be used for integer operations but we need many connections between CLBs which results the slow integer operations. The proposed EHW configuration has the potential of being applied to other applications where a prediction unit is necessary such as in adaptive control systems.

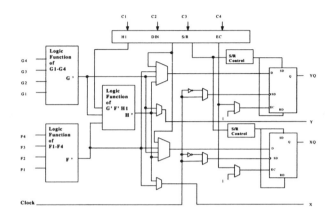

Figure 8: Simplified schematic of a CLB in Xilinx FPGA chip [13].

5 Error prediction

In the raw image there are many type of dependency between neighboring pixels, and with a mathematical modeling of the image these dependencies can be removed. Some of these dependencies are linear and some are non-linear. Removing these dependencies can be separated into two phases by prediction system: 1)using linear prediction functions and 2) applying non-linear prediction formula.

Normally the first phase of prediction in LIC is linear prediction of pixel values. Most of the methods for prediction (like JPEG) have only simple linear prediction which is efficient and easy to implement. In EHW approach for LIC we used a set of linear functions for this phase.

It has been seen that after pixel prediction a lot of dependencies still exist between neighboring pixels [14] and hence it needs another stage of prediction and this time based on error image. This stage is more difficult than the first stage because it involves non-linear function prediction.

For error prediction we can still use the same configuration of EHW in Figure 6 but the kind of functions and classification would be changed. Figure 9 shows the final

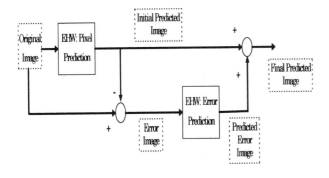

Figure 9: Full pixel prediction including error prediction in encoder

system for pixel prediction including error prediction.

The figure shows the process for encoding but in decoding the flow of data is reversed and the first EHW predicts the error and the second one predicts the pixel.

So far we have developed only the first part of this configuration for pixel prediction. Simulation results in the next section are based solely upon pixel prediction.

6 Simulation results

The system described was used to generate compressed data for digital images. In the first stage we tried to simulate only the first part of our system for pixel prediction. As it mentioned before for pixel prediction we need only linear functions. According to Figure 5 the inputs to these linear functions are four neighbor pixel values.

$$\hat{g}(i,j) = c1 * g(i-1, j-1) + c2 * g(i, j-1) + \\ c3 * g(i-1, j) + c4 * g(i-1, j-1)$$

where $\hat{g}(i,j)$ is the predict value for $g(i,j)$. The four constant value $c1..c4$ will be selected and updated by the evolution unit. Each parameter is represented by 8 bits and a GA was used for selecting the best set of parameters for each function. The function unit consists of 32 functions (n=32), which means the classification unit is designed to detect 32 different patterns and activate one of the functions.

We also need a procedure for updating the functions used by the evolution unit. At each time only one function is active in the function unit and this produces the output. However the evolution unit can replace it with a better function from the population. The population size for each function in the evolution unit is 30. After predicting a pixel value by an active function all in-

dividuals in evolution unit evaluate their predict value against the original pixel value and calculate the error. Only one error value is not enough for fitness and we need around 100 error values to make sure enough data is presented to calculate fitness. After the 100 cycles of the selection of a function, the genetic algorithm in evolution unit replaces the active function with the best individual in the population and produces a new population. In this mechanism we cannot define the maximum number of generations because it depends on image size and how many times each pattern will be selected. We used the integer representation for each individual in the population, two points crossover (pcross=0.6), mutation (pmut=0.01), roulette wheel selection, linear scaling and overlapping populations for genetic algorithms.

We have compared the performance of image compression of EHW with three other algorithms. The first one is JPEG which is described in Section 3. We select the best function out of seven possible functions for the compression. The second one is LOCO (LOw COmplexity) [15] which emphasizes low complexity for the compression system. The third one is called CALIC (Context-based Adaptive Lossless Image Codec) [16] which is one of the best algorithms for lossless image compression. It is important to mention that the second and third algorithms include context based error prediction, but here we only used their algorithm for pixel prediction. The JPEG algorithm consists of only pixel prediction.

For the experiment we used the JPEG image test set to compare the three algorithms with EHW. These are generally smooth natural images. The size of all images is 512 by 512 pixels with 256 grey levels for each pixel. Image data encoded and decoded in raster scan order in a single pass. In Table 2, we compare the pixel prediction performance of EHW with LOCO, JPEG and CALIC. Compression ratios are given in bits/pixel for the error of each image.

Table 2: Lossless compression of 9 test images for different algorithms (bit / pixel)

Image	LOCO	JPEG	CALIC	EHW
Lena	4.838	4.773	4.767	4.757
peppers	5.316	5.043	4.931	4.975
baboon	6.590	6.447	6.784	6.454
golhill	5.195	5.263	5.263	5.197
zelda	4.479	4.405	4.4	4.357
boat	4.866	4.944	4.891	4.824
barb	5.625	5.445	5.636	5.437
girl	3.753	3.841	3.73	3.858
yacht	3.978	4.048	4.3	4.1
Average	4.94	4.912	4.96	4.884

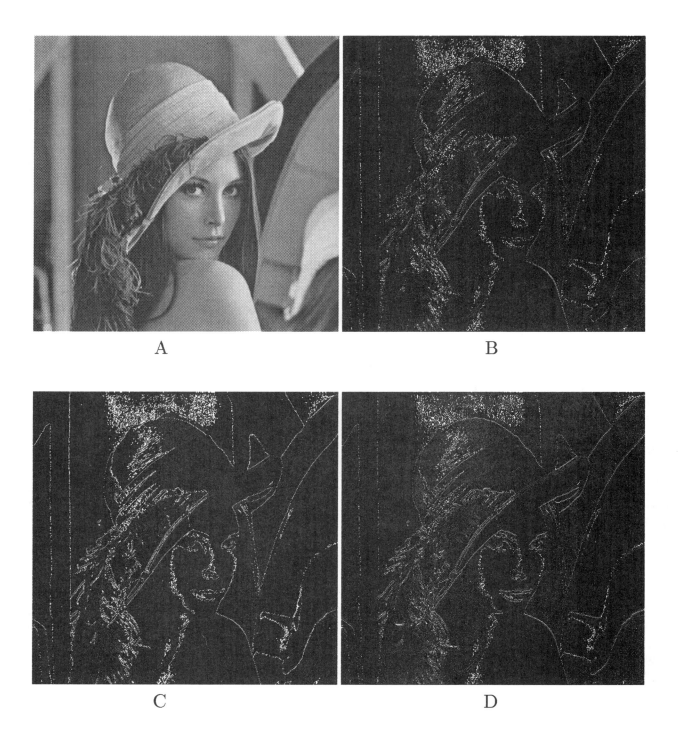

Figure 10: Comparison between LOCO, CALIC and EHW for pixel prediction. A) Original Lena image. B) Error image from LOCO pixel prediction (entropy=4.838 bit / pixel). C) Error image from CALIC pixel prediction (entropy=4.767 bit / pixel). D) Error image from EHW pixel prediction (entropy=4.757 bit / pixel)

According to the table, the EHW on average produces slightly better performance and creates better pixel prediction function. From the table we can see in some cases JPEG, CALIC or LOCO produce better results but they have the disadvantage that they use fixed functions for prediction. On the other hand EHW changes the prediction function and finds the appropriate function for each image dynamically. Only in two cases EHW did produce better results, but because of change in function on average it produces the best performance. It shows that the strategy for finding better functions and changing them during compression is successful.

To demonstrate the difference in compression performance we bring the error image for one of test images. Figure 10 shows the original image of Lena picture and three error images from LOCO, CALIC and EHW. The error image is the difference between original and predicted image. The black area means zero error value and white area means large error in prediction. From the picture we can see that in CALIC the white areas in error image are more clear than other two error images. If we look at the white lines in the error images we can see the lines are continuous in CALIC but in LOCO they are not continuous but still recognizable. For EHW the whiteness of lines is reduced compared to other methods and they are less recognizable. The entropy for the EHW error image is less than other two methods and it shows EHW prediction method is better than the methods used by other two algorithms.

7 Discussions

The previous section shows that EHW has a good capability for lossless image compression and the simulation results predict a better performance compared with some methods for image compression. However, the results are only based on pixel prediction and for a complete system we need to include error prediction. In error prediction other methods use a fixed algorithm or function for prediction but with EHW, we can search for this error function or change the algorithm depending upon previous data similar to pixel prediction.

The compression ratio is not the only factor to compare two methods in image compression. We also need to evaluate the cost of implementation and the speed of operations. As it mentioned in the section 4, the evolution unit will not interfere with the operation of the function unit and that means the prediction time in EHW is the same as if we use fixed functions. However we need to add extra time for the GA operations in the EHW configuration which is happening not very frequently. We can also consider to run the GA operations in parallel with the function unit.

Unfortunately the cost of the EHW system for lossless image compression will be more than other systems using fixed functions because of the evolution unit. Fortu-

nately we can always justify higher cost if we gain something from EHW configuration and that is robustness or reliability in compression. The EHW compression technique is more robust than other methods because of adaptive function selection. We can always find a set of images that a fixed function method has a poor performance for compression. On the other hand the performance of the EHW configuration for compression is independent of the test images.

For the next stage of research we want to apply EHW for error prediction. Error prediction is more difficult than pixel prediction because it uses non-linear functions, and finding these non-linear functions for EHW would be more difficult. We also want to implement the first part of this EHW system for pixel prediction in hardware and probably after completing the error prediction everything will be implemented in hardware.

8 Conclusions

This paper shows that the EHW can be applied to lossless image compression and the results of simulations demonstrate good performance of EHW in prediction. In other methods the function for pixel prediction is fixed and that limits the performance of compression. On the other hand EHW, by evolving the function during compression process, searches and selects a function depending on the characteristic of the image. We demonstrate adaptive function selection of EHW can be applied to real time applications. We also showed how the new EHW configuration eliminates some of difficulties in the evolutionary systems. In comparison of EHW method with some common methods in lossless image compression we found that the EHW produces higher compression ratio for a set of standard test images.

9 Acknowledgment

This work was supported in part by the NEDO (New Energy and Development Organization), and by the RWCP (Real World Computing Partnership).

References

[1] Davis L., "Handbook of Genetic Algorithms", Van Nostrand Reinhold, New York, 1991.

[2] Wang Li-Xin, "Adaptive Fuzzy Systems and Control", Prentice Hall Inc., New Jersey, 1994.

[3] Sayood K., "Introduction to Data Compression", Morgan Kaufmann Inc., San Francisco, 1996.

[4] Higuchi T. et al., "Evolvable Hardware", in *Massively Parallel Artificial Intelligence*, edited by Kitano H. and Hendler J., pp. 398-421, MIT Press, 1994.

[5] Murakawa M. et al., "Hardware Evolution at Function Level", Proceeding of Parallel Problem Solving from Nature (PPSN) 1996.

[6] Li J., and Manikopoulos C.N., "Nonlinear Prediction in Image Coding with DPCM", Electronics Letters, Vol. 26, No. 17, August 1990, pp. 1357-1359.

[7] Clarke R.J., "Transform Coding of Images", Academic Press, London, 1985.

[8] Gersho A., and Gray R.M., "Vector Quantization and Signal Compression", Kluwer Academic Publishers, Boston, 1995.

[9] Tekalp A.M., Kaufman H., and Woods J.W., "Fast Recursive Estimation of the Parameters of a Space-Varying Autoregressive Image Model", IEEE Transactions on Acoustics, Speech and Signal Processing, Vol. ASSP-33, No. 2, April 1985, pp. 469-472.

[10] Wallace G.K., "The JPEG Still Picture Compression Standards", Communication of ACM, Vol. 34, No. 4, April 1991, pp. 30-44.

[11] Dukhovich I.J., "A DPCM System Based on a Composite Image Model", IEEE Transactions on Communications, Vol. 31, No. 8, April 1983, pp. 1003-1017.

[12] Salami M., Murakawa M. and Higuchi T., "Data Compression based on Evolvable Hardware", Proceeding of the International Conference on Evolvable Systems (ICES96), Tsukuba, Japan, 1996, pp. 153-163.

[13] Xilinx Inc., "The Programmable Logic Data Book", Xilinx Incorporated, San Jose, California, 1994.

[14] Wu X., "Context Selection and Quantization for Lossless Image Coding", Proceeding of Data compression Conference 1995 (DC95), IEEE Computer Society Press, 1995, p. 453.

[15] Weinberger X, Seroussi G and Sapiro G., "LOCO-I: a Low Complexity, Context-Based Lossless Image Compression Algorithm", Proceeding of Data compression Conference 1996 (DC96), IEEE Computer Society Press, 1996, pp. 140-149.

[16] Wu X., "An Algorithmic Study on Lossless Image Compression", Proceeding of Data compression Conference 1996 (DC96), IEEE Computer Society Press, 1996, pp. 150-159.

A Colony of Ant-like Agents for Partitioning in VLSI Technology

Pascale Kuntz[1], Paul Layzell[2] and Dominique Snyers[1]
[1]Ecole Nationale Supérieure des Télécommunications de Bretagne
BP 832, 29285 Brest Cedex, France
Fax: (33) 2 98 00 10 30
Email: Pascale.Kuntz@enst-bretagne.fr
[2]Centre for Computational Neuroscience and Robotics
University of Sussex - Falmer - Brighton - England
Email: paulla@cogs.susx.ac.uk

Abstract

Inspired by entomologists' findings on the ability of ant colonies to cluster together similar objects in the absence of any centralised control, we present an original distributed algorithm to reveal interesting structural properties in the vertex sets of large graphs, represented on a two dimensional grid. We define a measure of dissimilarity which leads to the clustering of highly interconnected vertices into separate classes, which can then be partitioned using classical heuristics. The algorithm relies purely on local interactions between a set of ant-like agents and their environment and achieves excellent results for a wide range of graphs where the number of classes need not be known *a priori*. Whilst this article is geared to applications in VLSI technology, our algorithm is suitable for many other domains where networks of relationships can be modelled by graphs.

1 Introduction

Many engineers and researchers from a wide variety of domains are confronted with increasingly large networks of relationships. Their analysis invariably leads to inextricable computations that make preliminary stages of segmentation absolutely necessary. Examples of such networks can be found in fields as diverse as neuroscience and telecommunications, but the domain which has arguably produced the largest number of publications on this problem is that of Computer Aided Design (CAD). VLSI (Very Large Scale Integration) circuits are very often too complex to be designed or analysed on a global basis. Hence partitioning lies at the root of numerous CAD problems, notably (e.g. [6] [21], [24]):

- pagination, in which networks are divided up so that they can be represented legibly using automatic line-tracing software over several standard sized pages;

- logical tests carried out during the manufacture of integrated circuits to ensure reliability. The classical method of testing a small circuit composed of logic gates is to apply successively each binary configuration possible at its inputs. The subsequent output states then permit verification that the gates are functioning correctly. For large circuits, such an exhaustive approach is impractical, and an alternative method is to decompose them into testable subcircuits of smaller size;

- automatic circuit placement and routing, which consists of arranging the circuit components on a surface, and linking them using conductive strips, or routes. This fundamental phase in circuit design is a complex process which must cope with different objective functions (minimizing area taken by components, minimizing total route length, ...) and numerous various constraints (avoiding overlap of layout cells and route congestion, satisfying topological requirements imposed by the technology, ...).

In the following sections, we discuss the difficulties involved in graph partitioning using conventional methods, and explain an alternative approach of transforming the partitioning problem into one of clustering. We then describe how clustering in ant societies has been both observed and modelled, and adapt recent models to cluster graph vertices by defining a measure of dissimilarity on the vertex set when embedded onto a two dimensional grid. After discussing parameters relevant to the new model, we evaluate the algorithm on a series of graphs well known in VLSI literature. Finally we introduce two measures to assess quantitatively the global performance of the algorithm.

1.1 Graph Partitioning

When solving partitioning problems, it is usual to assign to the circuit in question a graph $G = (V, E)$ where V

is the set of vertices and E the set of edges, such that each edge connects two vertices. The vertices of V symbolise the different elements (transistors, gates or more complicated subcircuits called blocks, for VLSI circuits) and the edges of E symbolise the physical connections between these elements. Both vertices and edges can be weighted; such weights reflecting respectively for example the area taken up by a component and the multiplicity or importance of a wiring connection. Recent years have seen the appearance of circuits described by hypergraphs. Certain publications propose partitioning algorithms which are directly applicable to hypergraphs, while others suggest prior transformation of hypergraphs into graphs ([21]). We confine ourselves here to the case of graphs G for which the edges can be given positive weights, and are concerned with partitions of the set V of the graph's vertices, i.e. of the elements obtained by removal of the edges.

Most of the graph partitioning problems are known to be $\mathcal{NP}$-complete (eg. [12], [23]). Even the polynomial algorithms for the easier problem of partitioning when the number of partition components is known in advance run in $O(|V|^{k^2})$ steps ([13]); this complexity remains too high for real applications.

The complexity of these problems and the growing importance of their associated applications have stimulated the development of heuristics to tackle them anyway. Indeed, the use of heuristics allows optimal solutions to be approached in a reasonable computation time, albeit without necessarily ensuring optimality (e.g. [10], [18], [17]). Many such heuristics however exhibit a great sensitivity to the choice of the initial partition and the probability of getting trapped in local optima seems to dramatically increase with the size of the graph.

1.2   Graph Clustering

In an attempt to surmount such limitations, a new approach has emerged in the last few years. Its basic underlying idea is to transform the combinatorial partitioning problem into one of a clustering nature by constructing some bijective mapping between the graph vertices and points in a geometric space, generally $\Re^p$. Various mapping criteria have been proposed in the literature, all tending to transfer certain properties of the graphs (weight, density, ...) onto the new geometric object (e.g. [3], [21], [15]).

This paper presents a new mapping scheme based on the definition of a particular dissimilarity measure between graph vertices. Such a dissimilarity allows the adjacency between graph vertices to be taken into account. This new algorithm embeds the graphs on a two dimensional grid by placing the vertices on grid points which are separated by a distance corresponding to the given dissimilarity measure between graph vertices. The dissimilarity used here is the city-block distance. After a

satisfactory embedding has been achieved, classical clustering algorithms can regroup the neighbouring vertices on the grid into the same graph partition component.

There is currently no exact algorithm for solving the isometric embedding problem of placing elements into geometric space when the elements are only known by the matrix of city-block distances between pairs. Moreover, the associated heuristics published in the literature seem to be limited to the embedding of 50-100 elements (e.g. [16]). Our heuristic was able to embed graphs of at least 500 vertices with little trouble.

1.3   Clustering in Ant Societies

The algorithm presented here originates from the findings of entomologists who, on observing societies of ants, have remarked that larvae and food are not scattered randomly about the nest, but in fact are sorted into homogenous piles. Deneubourg *et al.* ([8], [5]) proposed a behavioral model where the spatial structure of the nest emerges as a result of simple, local interactions without the need for any centralised control or global representation of the environment. In this model, the environment is a two dimensional grid upon which is scattered a set of objects, each having random initial positions, and comparable with each other by an equivalence relationship. Each ant is modelled by an agent which is able to to move on the grid, and displace the objects according to probabilistic rules necessitating only local environmental information. The combined actions of a set of these agents lead to the grouping in the same spatial region of objects belonging to the same class of equivalence. This model has been applied with success in robotics to demonstrate the possibility of accomplishing complex tasks quickly, using several simple robots instead of a single complex one ([1]). Gutowitz ([14]) and Lumer and Faieta ([22]) have recently extended the model, the latter extending it to work with objects which are comparable according to a measure of dissimilarity; Lumer's algorithm forms one or more spatial groups such that similar objects belong to the same group, and dissimilar ones belong to different groups, each group being spatially distant from one another. In contrast to multidimensional scaling methods, this is a distributed algorithm, in the sense that no global optimisation criterion is calculated; only local optimisations (by the agents) are carried out. Analysis of computer simulations shows that the representation achieved preserves the order between small and large values of dissimilarity. This approach was originally tested using Euclidean distances. We extend it here to the representation of a graph with a view to its partitioning, by defining a dissimilarity on a set of the graph's vertices.

2   A New Graph Embedding Algorithm

We take a dissimilarity d as being defined on the set V of graph vertices. The grid on which the graph is represented is denoted by Γ.

2.1   The Ant Embedding Algorithm

We present an adaptation of the principles of Lumer and Faieta's algorithm based on the behavioural model of the ant colony proposed by Deneubourg *et al.* The model is a set A of ant-like agents whose environment is a two-dimensional grid. The smallest distance that an agent can travel is thus one grid position, or element. The graph is represented in the agents' environment by objects scattered upon the grid, each of which corresponds to one of the graph's vertices. The agents have no information about the objects (such as corresponding vertex number, or the cluster that the vertex is supposed to belong to); all they can do is determine how dissimilar two objects are from one another. We hereafter refer to these objects as vertices and denote the embedded vertex on the grid by v_i, and $\Pi_t(v_i)$ denotes the position of vertex v_i on the grid at t. Agents are able to move around the grid, pick up, carry, and drop vertices. However they are not permitted to move onto a grid position already occupied by another agent, nor are they allowed to drop a vertex onto a position occupied by another vertex. At the grid boundaries, agents are reflected. Each agent has a short-term memory containing the last m vertices it has carried together with their new positions at the instant of dropping.

Initially, vertices and agents are laid out at random positions on the grid. The algorithm then proceeds in discrete time steps, t. At each t, an agent of A is selected at random. If a vertex lies on its position the Agent can pick it up, likewise it can drop a vertex at that position if it is currently carrying one. If the agent is empty-handed, it then moves r grid positions in a random direction, otherwise it moves r grid positions in a probabilistic manner towards the position of the most similar vertex in its memory to the one it is carrying. The act of picking up a vertex and transporting it to its new position may take several time steps. Since a different agent is selected at each t, a number of agents and vertices may be in the process of moving at any one time, resulting in an effective parallel operation.

The decision whether or not to manipulate a vertex is carried out in a probabilistic fashion and is dependent purely on data available in the local neighbourhood. The probability $p_{pick}(v_i)$ that an agent will pick up a vertex v_i increases the more v_i is isolated, i.e. where the number of similar vertices in the immediate neighbourhood is small. By contrast, the probability $p_{drop}(v_i)$ that an agent will drop a vertex v_i increases with the number of similar vertices in the immediate neighbourhood. These probabilities are defined by

$$p_{pick}(v_i) = \left(\frac{k_p}{k_p + f(v_i)} \right)^2$$

and

$$p_{drop}(v_i) = \left(\frac{f(v_i)}{k_d + f(v_i)} \right)^2$$

with k_p and k_d constants

The local density function f represents an estimation of the density of similar vertices in the v_i neighbourhood, defined here by an area Σ of $\sigma \times \sigma$ grid elements in which v_i lies at the centre

$$f(v_i) = \begin{cases} \frac{1}{\sigma^2} \sum_{v_i ; \Pi_t(v_i) \in \Sigma} \left(1 - \frac{d(v_i, v_j)}{\alpha} \right) & \text{if } f(v_i) > 0, \\ 0 & \text{otherwise} \end{cases}$$

where $d(v_i, v_j)$ is the dissimilarity between v_i and v_j.

The maximum value of f is reached when all the elements of Σ are occupied with vertices v_j such that $d(v_i, v_j) = 0$, in which case $f(v_i) = 1$. Note that while f can never be negative, the same is not true for the expression within the sum. A highly dissimilar vertex to v_i is less desirable in Σ than an unoccupied position, hence the constant α scales the dissimilarities so that dissimilar vertices will lead to a reduction in the overall value of f. This aspect ultimately leads to visible separation of classified vertex clusters on the grid since any area containing both similar and dissimilar vertices will yield a low value of f, resulting in the displacement of any vertex within.

The appendix contains a formal version of the description above, in order to further aid researchers wishing to reproduce and/or modify the algorithm.

2.2   Dissimilarity on the Vertex Set

In embedding the abstract graph in a metric space E the aim is to explicitly convey through the subsequent geometric representation, the relationships of interdependence between the graph's vertices upon which an efficient partition is based. Here, these relationships are transferred into the new representation by means of a dissimilarity d, the representation in E having to preserve a certain isometry with respect to d. Generally speaking, the choice of the dissimilarity is a function of both the information available on the graph, and any constraints imposed by the desired application. The information may be of various natures: it may concern, in the case of electronic circuits, for example, the physical properties of the circuit components or electrical network on which the graph is modelled (e.g. [19]), or it may concern the topological characteristics of the abstract graph ([2]). We deal with the latter case: here, the dissimilarity between any two vertices of G is calculated from the simple description of relationships of adjacency between the vertices of V. Let $\rho(v_i)$ denote the set of vertices of V which are adjacent to the vertex v_i, and include v_i:

$$\rho(v_i) = \{v_j \in V; \{v_i, v_j\} \in E\} \cup \{v_i\}$$

We propose the use of a dissimilarity which has been applied to problems of pagination ([7]) . It reflects properties of local density: the larger the number of neighbours two vertices share, the more similar they are; the smaller the number of distinct neighbours they have, the more similar they become. This dissimilarity measure therefore, is aimed at regrouping in the same class those vertices having a large number of common neighbours and few distinct neighbours:

$$d(v_i, v_j) = \frac{|\rho(v_i) \Delta \rho(v_j)|}{|\rho(v_i)| + |\rho(v_j)|}$$

where Δ designates the symmetric difference (union minus intersection). In describing the graph by its adjacency matrix, d can be recognised as the Czekanowski - Dice coefficient which was originally defined to evaluate differences between binary data in ecology ([9]). Its geometric properties have been studied by several authors (e.g. [2], [4]); d is city-block distance.

3 Computational Experiments

3.1 Choice of Parameters

The performances of the algorithm depend on a set of independent parameters which concern the probabilities of placement/displacement, the local density function, the algorithm's distributed character with the number of agents and the size of the grid for graph representation. Nevertheless performances are robust in the sense that stable results are achieved for a wide range of parameter settings. Their respective efficient values are given below.

- **Probabilities of placement/displacement:** The constants k_p and k_d determine the extent to which the probabilities $p_{pick}(v_i)$ and $p_{drop}(v_i)$ depend on the local density function f. Numerical experimentations have revealed that they affect the speed with which clustering is achieved rather than the quality of clustering, with the exception of large values leading to unstable clusters for small class cardinalities (≤ 20). For the runs described below, they were set within the range 0.03 to 0.1.

- **Local density function:** since the algorithm relies on local interactions alone, the local neighbourhood size Σ should be kept small, i.e. 3×3 or 5×5. The constant $\alpha \in [0, 1]$ has, as described in § 2.1, the dual role of scaling dissimilarities so that close vertices end up in the same cluster, and ensuring a good separation between clusters. If $\alpha = Max\{d(v_i, v_j); v_j \in \Sigma\}$ then $f(v_i)$ yields relatively high values even for areas

containing a mixture of vertices with both low and high dissimilarity to v_i. This leads to poor separation of the classified clusters: such areas would form in practice around a vertex with intermediate values of dissimilarity, usually around the cluster boundaries. The high value of $f(v_i)$ associated with this area "attracts" more and more dissimilar vertices, resulting eventually in all the clusters lying in the same part of the grid, with little or no separation between them. If α is small then the algorithm tends to produce many, small classes. The most appropriate values for α were found by experimentation to lie in the range $[0.8, 1[$.

- **Agent parameters:** the number of agents should be fairly small with respect to the number of vertices n. A large number results in the displacement of too many vertices at any one time which disturb local optimisations: n should exceed the number of agents by approximately an order of magnitude. The agents' memory size m is small to avoid the memory facility acting as a sort of global map, the most appropriate values for m lying in the range $[10, 20]$. Finally the pace size i.e. r grid elements by which an agent moves at each t should be small but not necessarily unity, experimentation revealing that a pace of around 5 elements is most efficient.

- **Grid size:** the quantity of grid positions should exceed the quantity of graph vertices, n, by roughly an order of magnitude. Smaller grids inhibit class separation, since they do not have sufficient unoccupied positions, whereas larger grids, due to the increased search space involved, require more time steps to achieve classification.

Two slight modifications have been added in order to speed up the basic algorithm. 1) At each t, agents not carrying vertices can be transported instantaneously to the position of a vertex selected at random, to avoid aimless wandering in empty search space. 2) Agents can drop vertices onto grid positions adjacent to their own if their position is already occupied by another vertex. Note also that although the computational time was not our main interest here, due to the relatively simple computation involved, it is as low as 10 or 15 minutes on a 486 Personal Computer with significant graphical output overhead for a graph containing 500 vertices.

3.2 Results on Probabilistic Graphs

To evaluate the performances of the algorithm we consider a well-known class in VLSI layout of probabilistic graphs with an "expected structure" (Garbers and al. 1990). Let us denote by $G_{GAR}(k, nc, p_{int}, p_{ext})$ a graph containing k clusters of nc vertices each, where the probability of an edge v_i, v_j is p_{int} if v_i and v_j belong to the

421

same cluster (i.e. if $i \equiv j \pmod{nc}$), and p_{ext} otherwise, all edges being chosen independently. Figure 1 shows the representation of $G_{GAR}(4, 25, 0.167, 0.0032)$ after 200000 iterations of the algorithm; four compact and well separated clusters containing vertices 1-25, 26-50, 51-75, and 76 -100 are easily distinguishable, reflecting the expected underlying structure of the graph.

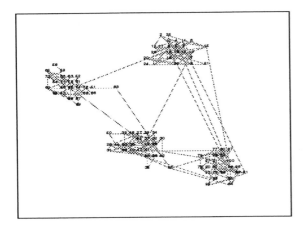

Figure 1: Graph $G_{GAR}(4, 25, 0.167, 0.0032)$ representation

The algorithm has been successively applied to graphs $G_{GAR}(k, nc, p_{int}, p_{ext})$ containing up to 500 vertices, with a variety of class sizes from $nc = 10$ to 50, with $p_{int} = O(nc - 1/2)$. In all cases, the expected classes are reflected on the grid by easily identifiable clusters as can be seen, for example, on Figure 2.

3.3 Quantitative evaluation

Clustering is achieved by interactions on a local scale, hence no global criterion is required. In order to evaluate the global success of the algorithm quantitatively, and in order to explain its operation, we introduce two measures which reflect the visual state of the grid representation as the algorithm proceeds.

3.3.1 Spatial entropy

Let $\Gamma_1, ..., \Gamma_r$ be a partition of the grid Γ in r sub-grids of same size (usually called grain from physics). The spatial entropy associated with this partition is defined by

$$-\sum_{i=1}^{r} p_t(\Gamma_i) log(p_t(\Gamma_i))$$

where $p_t(\Gamma_i)$ the proportion of vertices on Γ_i at time t. This measure reaches its minimum value 0 when their exists a sub-grid Γ_i containing all the vertices, and its maximum value 1 in case of uniform distribution $p_t(\Gamma_1) = ... = p_t(\Gamma_r) = 1/r$. It is used to reveal the

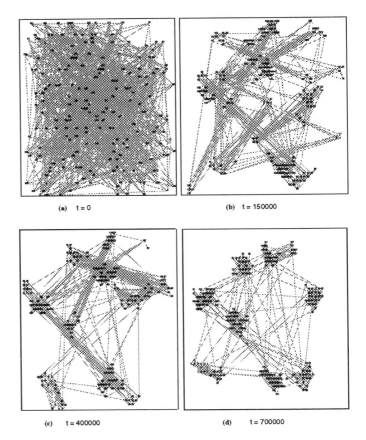

Figure 2: Graph $G_{GAR}(8, 25, 0.25, 0.0032)$ representation

existence of a structuration of the vertices on the space: the evolution from the initial random distribution of vertices, to their placement in compact clusters translates into a reduction of the overall spatial entropy.

Figure 3(a) depicts the variation of the spatial entropy for different grain sizes (3×3 and 6×6) for a graph $G_{GAR}(8, 25, 0.25, 0.0032)$. The large rapid decrease corresponds to a rapid initial clustering. Isolated vertices are quickly moved to locations of high local density (i.e. close to the positions of other vertices with which they are highly linked) and a number of clusters are quickly established, each containing vertices of the same expected class (Figure 2(b)). However the quantity of clusters at this stage greatly exceeds k. Small clusters are unstable, since the surrounding empty grid locations lead to relatively small values of f. Hence vertices within these clusters are moved to join other clusters, resulting in fewer, larger clusters, as shown in Figure 2(c). The entropy measurement shows this phase quite clearly - while spatial entropy with grain size 3×3 stabilises, the entropy measurement for 6×6 grains continues to fall. Finally, stochastic fluctuations at the borders of clusters lead to the domination of one cluster over others corresponding to the same class and resulting in one cluster per expected class. This is the desired representation (Figure 2(d)).

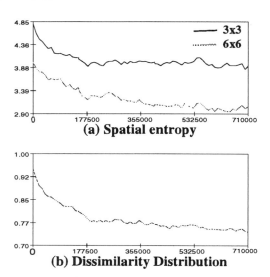

Figure 3: Graph $G_{GAR}(8, 25, 0.25, 0.0032)$

3.3.2 Local Distribution of Dissimilarity Values

While the spatial entropy measure reflects the organisation of the vertices into clusters, it does not indicate whether vertices are placed into the correct classes or not. Using the probabilistic graphs described above, we know a priori the class size and the class each vertex is expected to belong to. The allocation errors due to the probability p_{int} are small enough to be ignored here as shown by Garbers and al. ([11]). To verify the good partitioning of vertices into classes we study the evolution of the sum for each vertex v_i of the dissimilarities between v_i and its nearest neighbours -for the city-block distance- on the grid

$$\frac{1}{K_t} \sum_{v_i \in \Gamma} \sum_{v_j \in N_t(v_i)} d(v_i, v_j)$$

with $N_t(v_i)$ the set of the $(nc - 1)$ nearest neighbours of v_i minus the number of vertices of its class which are being displaced by agents at t. The sum is normalised by dividing by the total number K_t of dissimilarity calculations. The minimum value is reached when the nc nearest neighbours to every vertex all belong to the same class. Hence this measure reflects not only that vertices are placed in the "correct" cluster, but also whether cluster separation is good. Figure 3(b) illustrates its time variation for the graph described above: the rapid initial clustering corresponds to the curve's large initial gradient while the the subsequent agglomeration of the numerous small clusters corresponds to a slower rate of decrease.

Figures 4 and 5 both give the variation of the spatial entropy and the local distribution of dissimilarity values for several graphs $G_{GAR}(k, nc, p_{int}, p_{ext})$ described in § 3.2 ; the curves confirm the good visual results noticed previously. Figure 6 shows the embedding of a 500 vertex graph on a 52 × 52 grid. In order to compare with a family of graphs well-known in VLSI literature we have only presented here experiments with classes of equal sizes. Nevertheless the algorithm was also applied to graphs containing a priori various vertex classes and the results were as good as for equivalent cardinalities ([20]). The only problem appears for graphs containing one or more big subgraphs with a lot of links; instead of grouping all the vertices of such a set in a same class it tends to create different smaller classes.

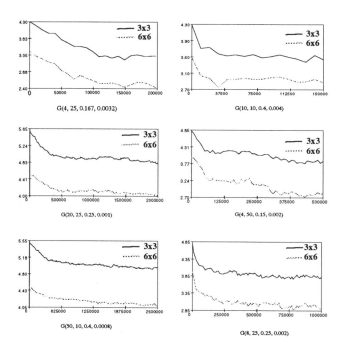

Figure 4: Variations of spatial entropy for different probabilistic graphs G_{Gar}

4 Discussion

The algorithm presented here has been shown to perform well on large probabilistic graphs for which the optimal partition is known in advance and on which the spatial entropy and the local distribution of dissimilarity can be used to evaluate the solution quality. Work is currently under development to compare this algorithm with others for the partitioning problem on real VLSI data. This comparison however, requires the choice of a classification algorithm for regrouping the graph vertices into common partition components.

Research is also actively pursued on the application of this heuristic to the isometric embedding problem in clas-

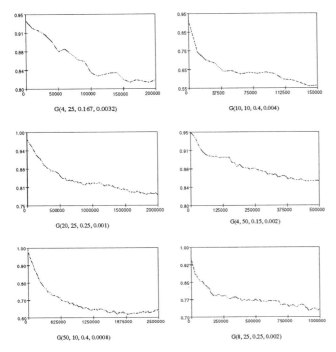

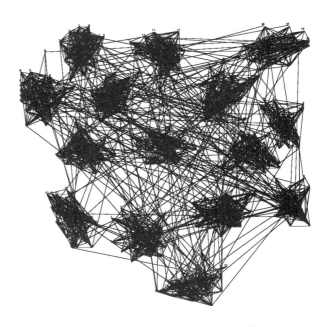

Figure 5: Variations of local distribution of d for different probabilistic graphs G_{Gar}

Figure 6: Graph $G_{GAR}(15, 36, 0.35, 0.002)$ representation at $t = 1000000$

sification. Its ability to deal with graphs of larger dimension than the ones usually dealt with by other heuristics from the literature has been shown (Figures 5 and 6).

Appendix: Formal description of the algorithm

In the following, Let $\Pi_t(a_h)$ and $\Pi_t(v_i)$ denote respectively the positions of agent a_h and vertex v_i on the grid, Γ at each discrete time step t. $\delta = \delta_1 + \delta_2$ denotes the city-block distance on Γ, where δ_1 (resp. δ_2) is the projection on the x-axis (resp. the y-axis). At each t, the state $s_t(a_h)$ of the agent a_h is defined by its position and either the vertex it is currently displacing, or 0 if it is not displacing any vertex: $s_t(a_h) = (\Pi_t(a_h),\ v_i)$ or $s_t(a_h) = (\Pi_t(a_h),\ 0)$.

Every agent a_h is assigned a tabu list $list(a_h)$ containing m pairs $(v_i, \Pi(v_i))$, corresponding to the last m vertices v_i displaced by a_h and their new positions $\Pi(v_i)$ at the instant of placement. This list is hence analagous to each agent possessing a short-term memory. The displacement of a new vertex v_j is carried out by a random walk (described below) with a heavy bias in the direction of the closest vertex in $list(a_h)$, in terms of dissimilarity d, to v_j. The algorithm proceeds at each discrete time step t in three phases :

1. **Select a_h at random from A.**

2. **Displace vertices:**
    If $s_t(a_h) = (\Pi_t(a_h),\ v_i)$ then

   - drop v_i in $\Pi_t(a_h)$ (i.e. $\Pi_{t+1}(v_i) = \Pi_t(a_h)$)
     with probability $p_{drop}(v_i)$.
   If v_i dropped in $\Pi_t(a_h)$ then
       - increment $list(a_h)$ by $(v_i, \Pi_{t+1}(v_i))$
   Else If $s_t(a_h) = (\Pi_t(a_h), 0)$ and $\exists v_i \in V$ s.t. $\Pi_t(v_i) = \Pi_t(a_h)$ then
       - pick up v_i (i.e. $s_{t+1(a_h)} = (\Pi_{t+1}(a_h),\ v_i)$) with
         probability $p_{pick}(v_i)$
   If v_i picked up then
       - choose $v_i^\star \in list(a_h)$ s.t $d(\Pi_t(a_h), \Pi(v^\star)) = Min\{d(\Pi_t(a_h), \Pi(v_j)); v_j \in list(a_h)\}$
       - set $\delta_h = 0$ and $\delta_h^\star = \delta_{h1}^\star + \delta_{h2}^\star$ (i.e
         $\delta_h^\star = \delta_1(\Pi_t(a_h), \Pi(v^\star)) + \delta_2(\Pi_t(a_h), \Pi(v^\star))$)

3. **Displace agents:**
    If $s_t(a_h) = (\Pi_t(a_h), 0)$ then
   - displace a_h by r grid elements in a random
     direction.
   Else If $s_t(a_h) = (\Pi_t(a_h),\ v_i)$ then
     If $\delta_h \leq \delta_h^\star$ then
         - displace a_h by r grid elements in the
           direction $v^\star$ along x-axis with probability
           $(1 - p_r)\left(\frac{\delta_{h1}^\star}{\delta_{h1}^\star + \delta_{h2}^\star}\right)$
         if a_h not displaced then
             displace a_h by r grid elements in the
             direction $v^\star$ along y-axis
         - set $\delta_h = \delta_h + \delta(\Pi_t(a_h), \Pi_{t+1}(a_h))$
     Else
     - displace a_h by r grid elements in a random
       direction.

The probability p_r introduces a small noise to cope

with certain configurations which would otherwise engender blockages, i.e. where agents prevent each other from moving. p_r was set to 0.05 for all runs.

References

[1] R. BECKERS, O.E. HOLLAND, and J.L. DENEUBOURG. From local actions to global tasks : stigmergy and collective robotics. In *Artificial Life IV*, pages 181–189. MIT Press, 1994.

[2] F. BUCKLEY and F. HARARY. *Distance in graphs*. Addison-Wesley, Toronto, 1990.

[3] T.N. BUI, S. CHAUDHURI, F.T. LEIGHTON, and M SIPSER. Graph bisection algorithms with good average case behavior. *Combinatorica*, 7(2):171–191, 1987.

[4] F. CAILLIEZ and P. KUNTZ. Contribution to the study of the metric and euclidian structures of dissimilarity. *Psychometrika*, 61(2):241–253, June 1996.

[5] E. COFFMAN, P. COURTOIS, E. GILBERT, and P. PIRET. A distributed clustering process. *Journal of Applied Probability*, 28:737–750, 1991.

[6] M. DAVIS-MORADKHAN. The problem of partitioning the nodes of a graph and its applications in VLSI technology : an overview. Laboratoire de Méthodologie et Architecture des Systèmes Informatiques MASI90.08, Université Pierre et Marie Curie, Paris, 1990.

[7] H. de FRAYSSEIX and P. KUNTZ. Pagination of large-scale networks ; embedding a graph in $\Re^n$ for effective partitioning. *Algorithms Review*, 2(3):105–112, 1992.

[8] J.L. DENEUBOURG, S. GOSS, N. FRANKS, A. SENDOVA-FRANKS, C. DETRAIN, and L. CHRETIEN. The dynamics of collective sorting : robot-like ants and ant-like robot. In *1st Int. Conf. on Simulation of Adaptative Behaviour : From Animals to Animats*, pages 356–363, Paris, 1990.

[9] L.R. DICE. Measures of the amount of ecologic association between species. *Ecologie*, 26:297–302, 1945.

[10] C.M. FIDUCCIA and M. MATTHEYSES. A linear time heuristic for improving network partitions. In *Proc. of the ACM/IEEE 19th Design Automation Conference*, pages 175–181, 1982.

[11] J. GARBERS, H.J. PROMEL, and A. STEGER. Finding clusters in VLSI circuits. In *IEEE Int. Conf. on Computer-Aided Design*, pages 520–523, 1990.

[12] M.R. GAREY, D.S. JOHNSON, and L. STOCKMEYER. Some simplified $\mathcal{NP}$-complete graph problems. *Theoretical Computer Science*, 1:237–267, 76.

[13] O. GOLDSCHMIDT and D.S. HOCHBAUM. A polynomial algorithm for the k-cut problem. School of business administration, University of California, Berkely, CA, 1987.

[14] H. GUTOWITZ. Complexity-seeking ants. In J.L. Deneubourg, G. Nicolis, and H. Bersini, editors, *Self Organization & Life, from simple rules to global complexity: Proc. of the second European Conference on Artificial Life*, Brussels, 1993.

[15] L. HAGEN and A.B. KAHNG. A new approach to effective circuit clustering. In *IEEE International Conference on Computer-Aided Design*, pages 422–427, Santa Clara, 1992.

[16] L. HUBERT and P. ARABIE. Multidimensional scaling in the city-block metric; a combinatorial approach. *Journal of Classification*, 9:211–236, 1992.

[17] B. KERNIGHAN and S. LIN. An efficient heuristic procedure for partitioning graphs. *Bell System Technical Journal*, 49:291–307, 1970.

[18] B. KRISHNAMURTHY. An improved min-cut algorithm for partitioning VLSI networks. *IEEE Trans. on Computer*, C-33(5):438–446, 1984.

[19] P. LAGOGNOTTE. The different electrical distances (in French). *Revue Générale de l'Electricité*, 7:5–10, 1991.

[20] P. LAYZELL. A new way to represent dissimilarities on a grid. Technical report, Ecole Nationale Supérieure des Télécommunications de Bretagne, Brest, France, 1995.

[21] T. LENGAUERT. *Combinatorial algorithms for integrated circuit layout*. John Wiley, London, 1990.

[22] E. LUMER and B. FAIETA. Diversity and adaptation in populations of clustering ants. In *Third Conf. on Simulation of Adaptative Behaviour*, pages 499–508, Brighton, 1994. MIT Press.

[23] D.W. MATULA and F. SHAHROKHI. The maximum concurrent flow problem and sparset cuts. Technical report, Southern Methodist University, USA, 1986.

[24] S.M. SAIT and H. YOUSSEF. *VLSI physical design automation : Theory and practice*. IEEE Press and Mc Graw-Hill, 1995.

Evolutionary Signal Processing:
A Preliminary Report

Tony Hirst

HCRL, Department of Psychology,
Gardiner Bldg, Open University, Walton Hall,
Milton Keynes, MK7 6AA

mailto: a.j.hirst@open.ac.uk, http://socsci.open.ac.uk/~monty

Abstract

The notion of Evolutionary Signal Processing in temporal and 'spatial' domains is introduced both theoretically and experimentally. Analytical results from quantitative genetics suggest that in a sinusoidally fluctuating fitness environment, the population mean phenotype tracks the optimum phenotype with a well defined attenuation and phase lag. I show that in the continuous model of (Lande, 1996) [1], evolution acts as a low pass analogue filter and in the discrete, non-overlapping generational model of (Charlesworth, 1993) [2] evolution acts as a band pass non-recursive digital filter. Results from a genetic algorithm experiment illustrate that these theoretical biology/signal processing models are applicable in the evolutionary computation domain. In addition to the filtering of continuous signals, evolutionary operators that are capable of transforming evaluation and fitness landscapes are likened to spatial image processing filters.

1 Introduction

Signals are quantities that convey information [3]. Signal processing relates to a set of techniques that allow the manipulation of signals and is frequently encountered in the guise of *filters* which are broadly defined as systems whose output signal differs from the input signal in a well defined way. A more useful definition is of a frequency selective system that attenuates certain frequency components whilst passing others unchanged. This applies to both temporal and spatial (typically image processing) domains.

In this paper, I will argue that it is possible to treat evolution as a filter of temporal signals. Traditional quantitative genetics discusses evolving systems in terms of optimal phenotypes, population mean phenotypes and measures of selection strength and genetic variance. By treating the optimum phenotype at any given time as the input signal to the evolutionary system, and the population mean phenotype as the system output, it is possible to characterise the *transfer function* of the evolutionary system. I shall draw on such transfer functions derived in quantitative genetics analyses [1][2] and liken them to those of signal processing filters as derived for use by engineers [3]. Preliminary results from an ongoing genetic algorithm (GA) study [4][5] offer support for the notion of evolutionary filters.

I shall also suggest that landscape transforming operators [6] may be likened to spatial filters acting on the evaluation or selective value landscape, equating the image mask with a suitably defined operator, or search space, neighbourhood [7].

2 Filtering Temporal Signals

The first part of this report covers the filtering of temporally varying signals. If there is a way of putting the evolutionary transfer function into the form of a traditional filter transfer function, relating genetic variance and selection strength parameters to the design parameters of a particular filter, it will be possible to use the knowledge of filter design to tune the evolutionary parameters so as to obtain the required filter characteristics. Since the 'output' of the evolutionary filter is given by the mean of the population, this represents population level filtering.

In this initial study, I shall consider only sinusoidally varying environments. It lies to further work to generalise the theoretical approach through the Fourier analysis of rather more complex optimal signals. First, I consider the continuous 'steady state' model of [1]. Second, the discrete, generational model of [2]. To maintain consistency in notation, simple substitution of symbols in some referenced equations has been followed.

2.1 A Continuous Model Realises an Analogue, Butterworth Filter

Now, from [1], a continuous sinusoidally varying evolutionary signal (optimal phenotype) given by:

$$f(t) = A \sin \omega t \qquad (1a)$$

is tracked by the (continuous) mean expressed signal,

$$g(t) \approx \zeta A \sin(\omega t - \beta) \qquad (1b)$$

realising the transformation function:

$$h(t) = g(t)/f(t) \qquad (1c)$$

where

$$\zeta = \frac{\gamma \sigma^2}{\sqrt{\gamma^2 \sigma^4 + \omega^2}} \qquad (2a)$$

and

$$\beta = \cos^{-1} \zeta \qquad (2b)$$

for additive genetic variance, σ; strength, γ, of (weak) stabilising selection towards $f(t)$; and system 'gain', ζ.

In electronic filter design, the filter characteristics given by the transfer function, $h(t)$, are often transformed from the time domain to the frequency domain through a Fourier transform, to give the relation $H(j\omega) = G(j\omega)/F(j\omega)$.

The gain (squared) of an analogue, low pass Butterworth filter, is now given by [3], equation (5.73) as:

$$|H(j\omega)|^2 = \frac{1}{1+\left(\frac{\omega}{\omega_c}\right)^{2n}} \quad (3)$$

where n is the degree of the filter, ω_c the cutoff frequency.

Inspection of these two independently used equations, (2a) (squared) and (3), shows them to be of the same form, since by rearranging (2a) the amplitude squared function of the evolutionary filter is seen to be given by:

$$|H(j\omega)|^2 = \zeta^2 = \frac{1}{1+\frac{\omega^2}{\gamma^2\sigma^4}} \quad (4)$$

which corresponds to a first order filter, $n = 1$, with cutoff $\gamma\sigma^2$. Note the gain never exceeds 1 (i.e. evolution is acting as a *passive* filter), and equals 1 for $\omega = 0$. The typical gain and phase responses of this system are given in figures 1a and 1b.

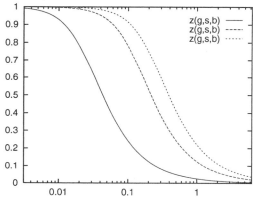

Figure 1a: Gain squared versus frequency, $b = \omega$, in radians per generation, for several $\gamma\sigma^2$, (see equation (2a)).

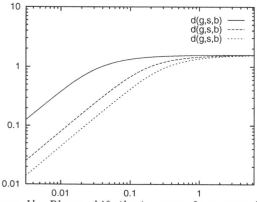

Figure 1b: Phase shift (lag) versus frequency, $b = \omega$, in radians per generation, for several $\gamma\sigma^2$, for equation (2b).

In this example, then, evolution is acting as a *low pass filter*, with a low cut-off frequency arising from the low genotypic variation (i.e. the evolutionary process only passes signals with a long period). In addition, the filter is maximally flat in the pass- and stop-bands.

2.2 Discrete, Non-Overlapping Generations

In his treatment of the evolution of recombination, [2] presents a theory one would expect to be rather more in accord with GA experiments, specifically the tracking of a sinusoidally varying environment with *discrete* generations (equations (5) to (8a) below are taken from this source).

As in the continuous case, two measures of variation are required: the additive genetic variance, V_g, and a quantity $V_s = V_e + 1/S$, where V_e is a the environmental variance (arbitrarily set to 1) and S is the strength of selection. V_g is itself a function of V_s and the generational variance due to mutation (and hence the mutation rate). Further, letting:

$$k = V_g/(V_g + V_s) \quad (5a)$$
and $$V = V_g/V_s \quad (5b)$$
so for small V, $k \approx V$ (5c)

In a fluctuating environment, with constant equilibrium values for V_s and V_g, and optimal phenotype $f(n)$ in generation n, the mean phenotype in generation n, $g(n)$, is given by:

$$g(n) = (1-k)^n g(0) + k\sum_{i=1}^{n}(1-k)^{i-1}f(n-i) \quad (6a)$$

$$\approx k\sum_{i=1}^{n}(1-k)^{i-1}f(n-i) \quad (6b)$$

approximating for large n and small k. Note that by taking these approximations, the current mean is only a function of the previous optimum, and *not* the previous mean. One reason for developing the ongoing experimental work reported in section 3, below, is to check the range over which the many approximations used in deriving this expression are likely to be valid.

In a sinusoidally varying environment:
$$f(n) = A\cos(\omega n) \quad (7a)$$
where $$\omega = \frac{2\pi}{T} \quad (7b)$$

For a low amplitude/period ratio, the solution is approximated by an integral with solution:

$$g(n) \approx \frac{2\pi ATV\sin(2\pi(n-1)/T)}{V^2T^2+4\pi^2} \quad (8a)$$

$$\approx \frac{A\omega V\sin(\omega(n-1))}{\omega^2+V^2} \quad (8b)$$

As in the previous continuous case, it is now possible to appeal to filter theory to try to understand the mean expression in those terms.

The gain squared term and phase shift, ψ, of the 'filter' are given by:

$$|H(j\omega)|^2 \approx \left(\frac{V}{\omega} + \frac{\omega}{V}\right)^{-2} \qquad (9a)$$

and

$$\psi(\omega) = -\omega + \frac{\pi}{2} \qquad (9b)$$

The phase shift (not shown) is a linear function of the environmental frequency with an additional constant shift of 90 degrees (not 180 degrees as Charlesworth states). This contrasts with the continuous result for which the phase change was also a function of the selection strength and genetic variance (i.e. V in this case).

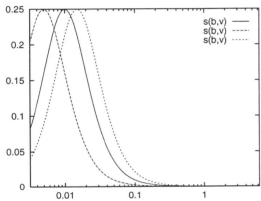

Figure 2: Gain squared versus frequency ($b = \omega$ in radians per generation) for several V for equation (9).

Plotting the gain term in figure 2 gives a characteristic typical of a band pass filter. The maximum value the gain (squared) term can take is simply 0.5 (0.25) and is located at:

$$\frac{d|H(j\omega)|^2}{d\omega} = \frac{d\left(2 + V^2\omega^{-2} + \omega^2 V^{-2}\right)}{d\omega} = 0 \quad (10a)$$

and so $\omega V^{-2} - \omega^{-3}V^2 = 0 \qquad (10b)$

giving $\omega = V$.

Further, taking the 3dB point (gain squared = 0.5, and which specifies the filter cut-off frequency), to be 3dB down on the maximum possible gain of 0.5 (i.e. for half the maximum gain squared (0.125 rather than 0.5)), the two cut-off points are located at the solution of:

$$\omega^2 - 2\sqrt{2}V\omega + V^2 = 0 \qquad (11a)$$

i.e. $\omega = V\left(\sqrt{2} \pm 1\right) \qquad (11b)$

What this means in evolutionary terms is that not only does the population fail to track high frequency signals, but also drifts away from tracking 'biologically stationary' optima where the environmental period is large. Although this may at first seem unreasonable, if one considers a case of high mutation and weak selection then it is likely that the mutation selection balance will allow individual population members to drift quite some distance from the optimum.

2.3 The Evolutionary Implementation of a Digital Filter

In terms of electronic filter design, what can we say about the transfer function? Firstly, I consider the characteristics of the signal being tracked and the signal being passed. In the above treatment, the input to the system is a continuous environmental signal, and the analogue filter analysis seems to hold. In a simple generational analysis, or simulation, populations are evaluated on the basis of an instantaneous sample of the environmental state. The filter is thus acting on a *discrete-time* or *sampled data* signal and as such is likely to be classed as a *digital filter*. The transfer function of a digital filter may be realised either recursively or non-recursively, as follows:

> For a system with input sequence $\{f(n)\}$ and output sequence $\{g(n)\}$:
> - a recursive filter obtains $g(n)$ as a function of $\{g(n-1), g(n-2),...; f(n), f(n-1),...\}$;
> - a non-recursive filters derives $g(n)$ as a function of $\{f(n), f(n-1),...\}$.

Now, the expression for $g(n)$ in equation (6a) is a function of $\{f(n-i)\}$ but not $\{g(n-j)\}$, $i, j > 0$. In this sense, the filter is a non-recursive filter, although unusual in that $g(n)$ is not a function of $f(n)$[1]. The phase characteristic, equation (9b), is typical of an antimetric (i.e. asymmetric) finite impulse response (FIR) filter, (which tend to be implemented *non-recursively*) given by Baher [3], equation (8.108), as:

$$\psi(\omega) = -\frac{\omega NT}{2} + \frac{\pi}{2} \qquad (12)$$

where ω is the environmental frequency, $\psi(\omega)$ is the phase response and N is the 'depth' of the filter (i.e. $f(n-0)...f(n-N)$ samples are used in finding $g(n)$, so strictly we require $N = n$) and T is the sampling period (in our case, $T = 1$ generation). If it is possible to equate (9b) and (12), this fixes $N = 2$ and hence (6b) would be a summation over $i = 0$ to 2. Given the approximation of (6a) to (6b), it is not unreasonable to expect that for higher values of i, little extra is contributed to the summation realising $g(n)$ from earlier generations.

Secondly, how is the evolutionary filter being realised? The evaluation-selection process takes two types of argument (as well as the selection type, strength etc. parameters) - the population under selection, and the current optimal phenotype, $f(t)$. The output population mean phenotype then corresponds to $g(t)$. The current population, let us call it $p(t)$, is derived through selective transmission of the previous population, $p(t-1)$, that is, as a function of the previous population, $p(t) = st(p(t-1))$. In this sense, the evolutionary filter may be realising a recursive design, since $g(t)$ (the mean expression of the population) is a function of $p(t)$ and hence of $p(t-1)$ (which supervenes $g(t-1)$). It lies to further work to clarify the actual architecture of the evolutionary filter, at least as it is modeled by genetic algorithms.

---

[1] If within generation learning is allowed [4,5,8,9], then $g(n)$ *may* be a function of the current environmental state, $f(n)$.

2.4 Consequences of Plasticity and the Transmission of Acquired Characteristics

Treatments of learning and culture [5], in which a distinction is made between genotype and expressed phenotype, may be modeled by changes in selection strength and genetic variation, with the following effect on cut-off frequencies:

- with individual learning, there are essentially two filters in operation, one providing an output phenotypic mean, the other the directly evaluated genotypic mean. The large amounts of phenotypic variation provide a high cut-off frequency for the phenotypic mean and so mean phenotypic tracking of rapidly fluctuating environments is possible; the reduction in selection pressure on the genetic basis of selected phenotypes lowers the cut off frequency of the 'genetic filter' and so rapid fluctuations of the optimum are not mirrored by the genotypic mean.

- in a cultural or social learning system (e.g. [8, 9]), the distinction between phenotype and genotype is essentially removed, in that traits acquired through learning in one generation may be transmitted directly to the next, although there is a single generation lag between the mean acquired trait and the mean inherited trait. The net effect of high phenotypic variance of the 'virtual population' induced through learning [5, 6], which under the inheritance of acquired characteristics translates to low genetic variance under strong selection (as individuals learn, then transmit, the same 'Good Tricks'), serves to set the single filter cut off frequency to an intermediate value.

What this means is that the evolutionary system has a low cut off frequency and only passes slowly changing signals. Cultural algorithms have an intermediate cut-off frequency and adaptive plasticity alone has a high cut off frequency, although all are low pass filters. [8] and [9] offer theoretical results demonstrating these properties, and the genetic algorithm model of [4] and [5] provides experimental support. The instability of systems where the environmental period is 1 or 2 generations [9] may be related to the sampling theorem which states that the sampling frequency should be at least twice the cut off frequency; this deserves further study.

3 Genetic Algorithm Study

In this experiment, I shall utilise an evaluation function originally owing to Cobb [10], that requires the tracking of a sinusoidally varying optimum that changes *between* generations :

$$f_t(p) = (p - e_t)^2 \quad (13a)$$

$$e_t = 1.0 + \sin(\alpha \times Generation) \quad (13b)$$

where p is a 32 bit Gray coded phenotypic individual over the range [0.0, 2.0], e_t gives an environmental state that varies sinusoidally over time, with rate parameter, α. Table 1 gives the generational period for the values of α considered.

Rate	0.001	0.01	0.05	0.1	0.5
Period	6283	628	126	63	13

Table 1: Period of environmental sinusoid in generations for the applied range of rates, α.

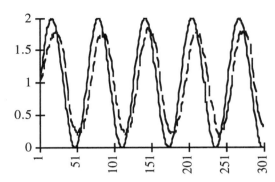

Figure 3a: Single typical run of population mean versus optimal signal; $\alpha = 0.1$, mutation rate fixed at 0.045/bit.

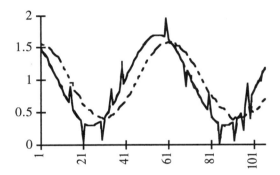

Figure 3b: Tracking a noisy sinusoid. Low amplitude, high frequency noise is filtered out by the population mean.

Previously reported results using this function (e.g. [10]) have concentrated on the ability of the *best* population member at any one time to track the environmental state. In this section, I shall be rather more interested to see how the population *as a whole* tracks the environment, specifically by monitoring population mean fitnesses.

In the experiment that follows, two phases may be identified in the evolutionary dynamic (no data shown) - firstly, a lead in period of search from the initially random population; secondly, the equilibrium dynamic. The initial phase may be likened to the initial 'settling time' of the system.

All experiments were carried out using a modified version of Genesis 5.0. Unless otherwise specified: tabulated results represent the mean of 10 runs; population size was 200; the mutation rate was set at 0.045 per bit; two point crossover was applied at a rate of 0.6 to individuals selected using linear ranking selection with rank minimum 0.5 (the rank minimum is used to set the strength of selection applied against individuals ordered by fitness rank: the lower the rank minimum, the greater the range of selective values over the population and the stronger the selection pressure against less fit individuals; see, for example, [11]).

Figure 3a demonstrates how the population mean does indeed track the optimum, with the population mean attenuated compared to the optimal signal and definitely lagging the optimum. In Cobb's study, high mutation rates were required to optimise the evaluation of the *best* population member. However, a high mutation rate renders the population as a whole unstable and the population mean fitness suffers. Experiments with an evolvable mutation rate (initially reported in [4], and in more detail in [5]) suggest that the evolutionary process optimises mean fitness rather than peak fitness (as one would expect, table 2) and a relatively *low* mutation rate is up to this task for a wide range of α. This is not to say that group selection is acting, only that mean fitness increases as a result of *individual* selection.

In figure 3b, noise in the optimum is filtered out by the population. It remains to further work to identify the signal/noise ratios that result in acceptable tracking performance given a noisy signal.

The frequency response of this particular evolutionary system (characterised by the recombination parameters and the selection function) is given in tabular form in table 3. Note the low pass filter response as one would expect from the previous analysis. Note how the evaluation measures (online (time averaged mean) and offline (time averaged best) fitness) suffer for increasingly fluctuating environments.

In accord with [1], changes in gain and lag result from altering the genetic variance, as regulated by the mutation rate. So for example, in table 4, lag is decreased by a slight increase in the mutation rate, although only by a generation or so, and increases slightly more for a decrease in rate of similar magnitude. For larger changes in the mutation rate, tracking properties of the population are altered and useful direct comparison becomes difficult. The amplitude of the mean expressed phenotype is similarly a decreasing function for increasing mutation rate, although the effect on mean tracking ability is the converse to that of the lag. That is, as mutation rate increases, whilst the lag between mean phenotype and the environmental target is reduced, the attenuation of the mean increases (i.e. there is a *worse* fit between the time delayed environmental signal and the mean value).

As with mutation rates, so with selection pressure, parameterised by the rank minimum value: by reducing the selection pressure, the effectiveness of a population's mean phenotypic tracking worsens and phase lag and attenuation both increase, as demonstrated in table 5.

It was mentioned that there were two distinct phases in each run of the GA - a lead in, searching phase, and an equilibrium phase. Recalling Charlesworth [2], one of the assumptions he made for equation (6b) that the number of generations, n, was large. It may be that through experiment, a more accurate estimate of the minimal value of n, for which the approximation holds, may be achieved.

m-rate/bit	0.015	0.030	0.045	0.060	0.075
Online fitness	0.49	0.55	0.56	0.55	0.53
Offline fitness	2.51	3.11	3.54	3.81	4.06

Table 2: *Online and offline fitness versus fixed mutation rate in the vicinity of the evolved rate for* $\alpha = 0.1$.

α	0.001	0.01	0.05	0.1	0.5
Online fitness	1.72	1.24	0.91	0.53	0.23
Offline fitness	6.11	4.75	3.39	2.78	1.62
peak to peak	2.0	1.99	1.82	1.70	0.28
mean lag	-	~8	7.43	7.01	3.89
lag sd	-	N/A	0.44	0.29	0.71

Table 3: *Gain and lag for a simple GA with mutation rate 0.02/bit, showing a low pass filter characteristic over* α.

m-rate/bit	0.015	0.030	0.045	0.060	0.075
peak to peak	1.71	1.64	1.56	1.45	1.38
mean lag	7.70	6.39	5.74	5.15	4.80
lag sd	0.44	0.38	0.32	0.27	0.36

Table 4: *regime SGA - selection rank minimum fixed at 0.5; alpha 0.1; discard first cross after origin start; change mutation rate from 0.035 to 0.055 through 0.045.*

rank min.	0.1	0.3	0.5	0.7	0.9
peak to peak	1.75	1.68	1.56	1.29	0.59
mean lag	4.00	4.80	5.74	7.28	8.75
lag sd	0.27	0.28	0.32	0.21	0.99

Table 5: *regime SGA - mutation rate fixed at 0.045; alpha 0.1; discard first cross after origin start; relax selection, parameterised by rank minimum, from 0.1 to 0.9 step size 0.2.*

4 Filtering 'Spatial' Signals: "Landscape Processing"

In this section, I shall briefly introduce the notion of *landscape processing*, which applies the metaphor of image processing to evaluation landscapes i.e. the landscapes corresponding to values conferred to individuals by an evaluation function ('fitness' function).

In [6] and [5], I suggested that the structure of landscapes and neighbourhoods respectively is induced by the evolutionary and plasticity operators. For example, the exactly one bitflip mutation neighbourhood of an individual length L bits comprises the L Hamming 1 neighbours of the individual. In this section, I will suggest how plasticity and fault induction [5] may be used to 'filter' an evaluation landscape. The argument is informally presented, and relies on a simplistic two dimensional representation of the search space. The evaluation landscape is visualised as a contour map, with thick contours signifying low fitness and fine contours high fitness, as in figure 4a.

It is now possible to consider filtering the 'evaluation image' in a manner akin to image processing techniques. Such methods often make use of a 3 x 3 pixel 'mask' (the Moore neighbourhood in cellular automata terms) to generate the next state of the central pixel following filtering. The mask is passed over each image pixel in turn to filter the whole image. A low pass filter corresponds to the mask shown in figure 4b. The central pixel, after filtering, is set to the mean prefiltered value of the pixel itself and its 8 nearest neighbours. This is similar to an individual being evaluated according to the mean evaluation over the whole of a suitably defined plasticity neighbourhood. White noise ('speckles') is often removed from an image through a *median filter*, in which the central pixel is given the median value of those taken over the mask.

In hybrid GA's that employ within generation local search such as steepest ascent learning corresponds to setting the focal 'pixel' to the *highest* value in the neighbourhood induced by local search, thus smearing any noise present, rather than removing it. Fault induction using steepest descent compares directly with using the *lowest* neighbourhood value (and 'blurring' of the image). Filtering through plasticity implements smoothing of the landscape by an individual and is thus individual level filtering.

Evaluation surfaces may be further transformed by the use of particular selection functions [6]. For example, whatever the population size, if the population is constrained such that no 2 individuals are allowed to be the same, and weak truncation selection is applied (so most individuals get a chance at reproduction) the evaluation surface is significantly smoothed. Since the selection function determines the range of allowable selective values over the population, selection function transformations of the

Figure 4a: An idealised 'landscape image'. Thick lines represent contours of low 'fitness', fine lines high 'fitness', over a search space structured by the genetic operators.

1	1	1
1	1	1
1	1	1

Figure 4b: An image mask as used in a low pass filter.

evaluation surface .are examples of population level spatial filtering.

5 Conclusion and Comments on Future Work

I have introduced the notion of Evolutionary Signal Processing, in which the evolutionary system and the landscape transformation operators that may be applied are treated as examples of temporal and spatial filters respectively. In doing so, I have raised at least as many questions as I have answered, and I shall try to address these now as suggestions for further work.

The techniques of Evolutionary Signal Processing may prove fruitful in a number of areas:

- the transfer of ideas and techniques between the disciplines of signal processing, quantitative genetics and evolutionary computation;
- the analysis of GA's as applied to the optimal tracking of temporally fluctuating systems;
- the transformation of fitness landscapes through local search operators defined in a manner akin to image processing masks.

In the first case, it may be possible to utilise the bias metric, (that is, the mean proportion of dominant alleles in a population taken over all loci), as a measure of the genetic variance in a more quantitative analysis of the GA model; equally useful would be a relationship between 'theoretical' variance and actual (evolved) equilibrium mutation rate. By using this knowledge to suitably define the evolutionary filter, one may track components below a certain (known) frequency, cutting out all higher frequency noise. It is likely that adaptive filtering (i.e. adaptive tracking of a dominant frequency) will be achieved through allowing the genetic variance (i.e. mutation rate) to evolve, subject to certain constraints on the signal/noise ratio.

By using plasticity, the two cut off frequencies (one for the phenotypic mean, the other for the genotypic mean) enable a form of tunable band pass filtering: by compensating the lag and lower frequency gain between the two evolved means, it may be possible to extract signals in the band between the two cut off frequencies by subtracting one mean from the suitably delayed and amplified other.

Although not considered in this report, it may be possible that a steady state GA with a small tournament size will approximate the analogue filter characteristics (i.e. 'continuous time' rather than discrete generations) even more closely. In a rapidly fluctuating environment, signal information is preserved through keeping 'generational time' down to a minimum (i.e. just the time it takes to evaluate the tournament participants). Sampling of the individuals for selection purposes should involve some sort of least recently used metric, perhaps competing least recently and most recently generated individuals. Where the tournament size equals the population size, M, the state of the population resembles $\{f'(n), f'(n-1), \ldots, f'(n-M)\}$ where $f'(n)$ represents the fittest individual of the current population and hence the population's best estimate at $f(n)$. This is close in spirit to the signal processing algorithms discussed above and deserves further study.

Other necessary GA work includes the accurate identification of cut off frequencies and selection pressures, along with an appropriate measure of genetic variation as mentioned previously. This will in turn allow for a more a detailed probing of the theoretical models.

Finally, landscape processing suggests another area of research, specifically the filtering of arbitrarily complex (local) landscapes into ones rather more suited to evolutionary search and optimisation, through the application of local search. Work by Happel and Stadler [12] on decomposing landscapes is the first step towards filtering the whole of those landscapes (i.e. the identification of landscape components that may then be removed or otherwise taken into account through operator design or guiding the search, for example).

Acknowledgments

Thanks to an anonymous reviewer for their comments on an earlier version of this paper.

References

[1] Lande, R, & Shannon, S. (1996) "The Role of Genetic Variation in Adaptation and Population Persistence in a Changing Environment." *Evolution* 50(1):434-437.

[2] Charlesworth, B. (1993) "Directional Selection and the Evolution of Sexual Recombination." *Genetical Research* 61:205-224.

[3] Baher, H. (1990) *Analog & Digital Signal Processing*. John Wiley & Sons Ltd.

[4] Hirst, AJ. (to appear) "Plasticity and Culture in Cyclically Fluctuating Environments." In *Proc. AISB97 Evolutionary Computation Workshop*, ed. D Corne & J Shapiro, LNCS, Springer Verlag.

[5] Hirst, AJ. (in prep) The Interaction of Evolution, Plasticity and Inheritance in Genetic Algorithms. PhD Thesis Dept. of Psychology, Open University.

[6] Hirst, AJ. (to appear) "On the Structure and Transformation of Landscapes." In *Proc. AISB97 Evolutionary Computation Workshop*, ed. D Corne & J Shapiro, LNCS, Springer Verlag.

[7] Hirst, AJ. (1996) "Search Space Neighbourhoods as an Illustrative Device." In Proceedings of *WSC1*, pp.49-54.

[8] Boyd, R, & Richerson, PJ. (1988) "An Evolutionary Model of Social Learning: the Effects of Spatial and Temporal Variation." *Social Learning: Psychological and Biological Perspectives*. Ed. TR Zentall & BG Galef Jr. Lawrence Erlbaum Associates. pp. 29-48.

[9] Feldman, MW, Aoki, K, & Kumm, J. (1996) Individual versus Social Learning: Evolutionary Analysis in a Fluctuating Environment. Working Paper 96-05-30, Santa Fe Institute.

[10] Cobb, HG. (1990) An Investigation into the Use of Hypermutation as an Adaptive Operator in Genetic Algorithms Having Continuous, Time-Dependent Nonstationary Environments. Navy Center for Applied Research in AI. December 11, 1990.

[11] Blickle, T, & Thiele, L. (1995) A Comparison of Selection Schemes Used in Genetic Algorithms. TIK-Report Nr.11, December 1995 v2, Swiss Federal Institute of Technology.

[12] Happel, R, & Stadler, PF. (1995) Canonical Approximation of Fitness Landscapes. Working Paper 95-07-068, Sante Fe Institute.

COMMUNICATION, COOPERATION
AND COLLECTIVE BEHAVIOR

Too many love songs: Sexual selection and the evolution of communication

Gregory M. Werner and Peter M. Todd
Center for Adaptive Behavior and Cognition
Max Planck Institute for Psychological Research
Leopoldstrasse 24, 80802 Munich Germany
gwerner@, ptodd@mpipf-muenchen.mpg.de

Abstract

Communication signals in many animal species (including humans) show a surprising amount of variety both across time and at any one instant in a population. Traditional accounts and simulation models of the evolution of communication offer little explanation of this diversity. Sexual selection of signals used to attract mates, and the coevolving preferences used to judge those signals, can instead provide a convincing mechanism. Here we demonstrate that a wide variety of "songs" can evolve when male organisms sing their songs to females who judge each male's output and decide whether or not to mate with him based on their own coevolved aesthetics. Evolved variety and rate of innovation are greatest when females combine inherited song preferences with a desire to be surprised. If females choose mates from a small pool of candidates, diversity and rate of change are also increased. Such diversity of communication signals may have implications for the evolution of brains as well.

1   Introduction

Why are there so many love songs on the radio? To the sometimes slight extent that they do, why do these songs change from year to year? Why do birds bother to sing so many notes? What would be the disadvantage of just a single long, loud blast? In short, why is there so much diversity in communication signals, both within and between generations?

In species with highly evolved, elaborate communication systems, there is often a great diversity of signals used within a given population, and between populations (including successive generations and recently-diverged species) over time. Humans of course have an unmatched capacity to generate novel signals (Pinker, 1994). Many songbirds have repertoires of dozens of distinct song types, a few species can sing hundreds of different songs, and the brown thrasher checks in with a remarkable repertoire size of over 2000 (Catchpole & Slater, 1995). Moreover, any one male of a given songbird species will typically sing a different repertoire from other conspecific males. Moving from air to ocean, cephalopods (particularly cuttlefishes, octopuses, and squids) also use a surprising variety of signal types, with some species using as many as 35 different displays in a wide range of combinations and sequences (Hanlon & Messenger, 1996). In all of these cases, the reason for extensive signal diversity remains a mystery: Catchpole and Slater (1995, p. 187) say that "At first sight, the diversity of modes of singing amongst birds is so great that it defies explanation," while Hanlon and Messenger (1996, p. 131), feeling that birds are easier to understand than their favorite animals, wonder, "does the great variety of signals [in cephalopods] serve as a measure of the signaller's fitness, as in bird song?"

Traditional reasons given for the evolution of communication cannot provide the whole answer to the questions surrounding signal diversity. If communication is viewed as a means of transferring veridical information from one organism to another (see Hauser, 1996), we would expect repeated communications of the same information (by one individual or within a population) to be performed in a similar manner to avoid misinterpretation by the receiver. In the particular case of accurate species identification for mating purposes, there should also be little variation between signals of conspecifics. If communication is seen instead as a way to manipulate the behavior of another organism (which can include non-veridical deceit–see Dawkins & Krebs, 1978), the signal used in any particular case should be the single one found to be most effective. And if communication is considered a means of altruistically benefiting one's genetic relatives (Ackley & Littman, 1994), we would expect convergence onto stable (but possibly family-specific) ways to help one another.

What then can drive the evolution of a large variety of elaborate communication signals? In this paper, we explore a particularly powerful force that can engender such diversity: sexual selection acting via coevolving mate preferences and traits. Specifically, we develop a simulation model that demonstrates how, when communicative signals are used by males to attract females as mates, sexual selection can drive the evolution of a variety of male songs and female song preferences. However, this evolution is likely to stagnate unless the females choose songs based not just on their evolved preferences, but also on a desire to be surprised by what they hear. Loosely speaking, when females can be bored by the same old song, males must strive to provide the females with something new in order to assure their own mating success. As a consequence, a variety of male songs evolves, both within a single generation, and across successive generations over time. (To explain the rapid cultural cycles of human love songs, we must resort to learning—see section 4—but here we show that evolution alone can generate these other major sources of signal diversity.)

In the next section, we consider past approaches to modeling the evolution of communication, and show how our current perspective can more readily explain the appearance and maintenance of signal diversity. Our simulation method here is an extension of our previous work on sexual selection, from a simple two-dimensional phenotype space to a multidimensional behavioral trait (a signal). In section 3, we describe how this method of modeling sexual selection is applied to simple songs and preferences, and show the results in terms of evolved song variation. We conclude with a consideration of the implications of sexual selection for the evolution of communication, and indicate the further directions in which this research itself can evolve.

2 Past approaches to modeling the evolution of communication

2.1 Communication for mutual benefit or manipulation

As indicated in the previous section, many functions have been proposed for evolved communication systems, and the most prevalent of these have been modeled recently using the techniques of individual-based evolutionary simulations. While none of the earlier models aimed specifically at exploring the mystery of signal diversity, their results do provide hints towards the explanation that we develop here, as we will show in this section. (Non-individual-based models, such as theoretical population genetics models, do not give us much insight into the evolution of diversity, because of the strong mathematically-required restrictions they place on the possible evolved signals.)

In most earlier simulations of the evolution of communication, the function of communicating has been taken to be the dissemination of information that will benefit the survival prospects of either the sender or the sender's

relatives. One of the first such studies was MacLennan's (1990, 1992) series of synthetic ethology experiments, which investigated the ways in which meaningful signals could arise in a breeding population of "simorgs." Meaningful signals in this case are those that tell an organism how to behave in response to an unknown aspect of the environment, so as to increase its chances of survival.

To allow such informative signals to evolve, MacLennan divides up his artificial world into local environments and restricts direct knowledge of each local environment to a single simorg, thereby "permit[ting] some simorgs to 'see' things that others cannot; otherwise there would be no advantage in communicating" (MacLennan, 1992, p. 639). Both signaller and receiver benefit in terms of a fitness gain if they successfully transmit information about a local environment. This is in marked contrast to the use of signals as a way of attracting other organisms (as potential mates), rather than informing them—in our simulation, there is nothing to "see" but the signal itself.

MacLennan is interested in the grounding of meaningful symbols through their attachment to states of the world. But it is this very process of grounding that ties the signals down and prevents them from evolving into more various and elaborate forms over time. By freeing signals from any concrete reference, other than the fact that a particular organism is able to produce that signal, sexual selection allows them to change continuously and fairly rapidly over time. (MacLennan's early simulations used only 8 world states and correspondingly only 8 possible signals, hardly allowing the evolution of much variety; but the number of signals used would always be tied down by the number of world states in his environment. When learning was added, individual signals often took on more than one meaning, indicating greater communication variety within the population, but even this diversity was static over time.)

Ackley and Littman (1994) explored altruism as a possible function of communication. In their simulation, local populations of organisms could evolve to signal one another about the common features of their local environment, again under the assumption that not every organism could see every feature. In contrast to MacLennan's world, the signallers in Ackley and Littman's model did not receive any fitness benefit from their selfless act of shouting—only the receivers would benefit. But since the receivers, all living nearby, were also all likely to be closely genetically related to the signaller, and since local populations competed with their neighboring populations through the occasional exchange of offspring, shouting out the right signals could benefit the signaller's genetic representation through kin selection.

Again, the pressure in this world to be informative all but eliminated any opportunity to be interesting or novel—the evolved signals were short and simple, and largely homogeneous within any given local environment.

They varied to a certain degree between localities, of course, at least early in any simulation run; but as more and more successful signalling strategies evolved at the local level, they could spread to take over the entire global world as well through the low-level migration process. Thus early diversity would evolve to stable homogeneity in most cases. Some variety could still emerge over time, as parasites periodically evolved to take advantage of current communication patterns and quickly spread across the world, only to be replaced at a later date by a new strain of altruistic communicators resistant to that breed of parasitism.

This kind of coevolutionary change between parasites and hosts resembles that which occurs in our sexual selection simulations between males and females, but at a much slower time scale, and without engendering the same kind of within-generation signal diversity. Note that in Nature, parasite-host coevolution may occur faster than male-female coevolution because of the rapid generation turnover in parasites, and indeed parasite-host coevolution may be the reason for the phenotypic variety created by sexual recombination. While this form of coevolution can possibly affect the evolution of signals that indicate parasite load (Hamilton & Zuk, 1982), it seems less likely that parasite selection pressure could directly foster the signal diversity within populations or across generations that is our main interest here.

Much closer to our current concerns is (perhaps not surprisingly) an earlier simulation created by the first author: Werner and Dyer's (1992) evolution of signals generated by females to guide blind males towards them for mating. The communication in this case functioned to allow reproduction between the roving males and the stationary, signalling females they succeeded in finding; thus we can say that this communication evolved via sexual selection rather than natural selection (as in MacLennan's case, or kin selection in Ackley & Littman's system). We could even say that the females' signals are evolving to be attractive to the males, and that the males are deciding which females are singing the most attractive songs (by "following" the songs they hear and mating with whichever one is most effective in literally attracting them).

As a consequence of this form of sexual selection, we can see the beginnings of signal diversity in this simulation: signal "dialects" appeared in some runs, leading Werner and Dyer to speculate that these "communication protocols could provide a natural way of establishing genetic barriers that spontaneously emerge" (Werner & Dyer, 1992, p. 685) and lead to distinct coexisting species. But these spontaneous breeding barriers emerge only slowly in the rather diffuse sexual selection operating in this model; in the simulations we report here, we greatly increase the power of sexual selection by allowing individuals to sample several potential mates, rather

than the few that a male might stumble across in Werner and Dyer's original setup. And this early simulation, like MacLennan's, does not generate diversity across time: once the population settles on a particular signal protocol, it wavers little from that solution.

2.2 Communication for mate attraction

To generate signal diversity both across time and at any given instant–that is, both diachronically and synchronically–we must somehow combine the power of Werner and Dyer's simulation to generate a variety of signals within one generation (albeit in a limited fashion) with the ability of Ackley and Littman's model to engender signal change from one generation to the next (albeit at a slow pace). Sexual selection through mate choice allows the former, leading a population to adopt a variety of sub-species signalling protocols (see Todd & Miller, 1991, for a simulation model of this effect for simple phenotypic traits). We need some force to push a population out of its attained stable pattern of speciation, though, the role that parasites played in Ackley and Littman's world. In sexual selection, this can be achieved through directional mate preferences (Kirkpatrick, 1987; Miller & Todd, 1993, 1995), which for example cause females always to look for brighter, or more colorful, or more ornamented males, and thereby push a population to continue evolving. For the evolution of communication, as we will see, this constant striving force can be effected through neophilia: females always looking for signals that are novel and unexpected.

Sexual selection has been implicated in the evolution of communication signals, particularly birdsong, ever since Darwin's (1871) introduction of the concept and his original proposal for the role of female choice in the evolution of elaborate male song (see Catchpole & Slater, 1995, chapter 7). In ethology, much research has been devoted in particular to the diversity-related issue of male song repertoire size in songbirds, seeking to identify the function of song variety at the individual level (as opposed to the population or multi-generation level that we address here; see Catchpole & Slater, 1995, chapter 8). The idea that female mate choice based on preferences for novelty in male song could lead to larger male song repertoires can be traced back to Hartshorn (1973) (following Darwin's lead a century earlier). It has more recently been argued by Searcy (1992; see also Hauser, 1996) based on the notion of dishabituation–that is, females exposed to the same song repeatedly will habituate to it (become bored) and respond less, but if a male can sing her different songs, this will cause dishabituation and increase her likelihood to respond to his overtures. This learning-based hypothesis remains contentious (Catchpole & Slater, 1995, pp. 179-182); here we avoid the question of the effect of learning on individual male repertoires, and instead focus on the corresponding mystery of the evolution of differences *between* individual males' song output.

This "good taste" hypothesis, that males who can sing many songs are simply more attractive to the tastes of females, stands in contrast to the "good genes" models of the evolution of large song repertoires. These latter theories propose instead that the number of songs a male sings is an indication of some underlying aspect of his genetic quality, for instance his strength, or longevity, or parasite resistance (Hamilton & Zuk, 1982), or food-finding ability (because singing takes a lot of energy; see Hauser, 1996, and Andersson, 1994, for discussion of these and other possible signs of quality). But the overall impression from a number of studies is that support for these "good genes" models for the evolution of song variety is equivocal at best (Hauser, 1996; Andersson, 1994; Catchpole & Slater, 1995).

Our simulations reported here support the "good taste" explanation for the diversity of song, extending the unit of analysis from the single singing male to a whole population evolving over time. (While we restrict each male to a single song at present, we could modify the simulation to see how the variety in each individual song repertoire can evolve as well.) The males in our model have nothing to offer (and nothing to be judged upon) other than the pretty song they sing, and females choose them solely because of that song and the hope that their own (male) offspring will sing as well and attract more mates as a consequence (the "sexy son" effect, which can lead to runaway sexual selection for particular traits and the preferences for those traits–see Weatherhead & Robertson, 1979; Andersson, 1994).

3 Coevolving hopeful singers and music critics

In our first attempt to evolve communication signal diversity, we coevolved artificial neural network "males" who produced rhythmic "songs" along with picky neural network "females" who judged those songs and used them to decide whom to mate with. In females, the neural network mapped inputs from an "ear" to output units that indicated her decision to mate or abstain. In males, the circuitry produced a sequence of sounds in response to the presence of a female. When this model was run, the male neural networks produced complex output patterns, typically containing several concurrent, not-quite-repeating patterns. These songs changed dramatically over evolutionary time, driven by the preferences of the female networks–but the patterns proved to be very difficult to analyze for complexity, diversity, or change. It was clear that the songs were evolving, but not clear how. It was time to call in more rudimentary musicians.

Each of the "dumbed-down" males we next turned to has genes that directly encode the notes of his song (rather than a song-generating network). Each male song

(and hence genotype) consists of 32 notes, each of which can be a single pitch selected from a two-octave (24 pitch) range. Females' genes now encode a transition matrix which is used to rate transitions from one note to another in male songs. This matrix is an N-by-N table, where N is the number of possible pitches the males can produce (24 in these experiments). Each entry in this table represents the female's expectation of the probability of one pitch following another in a song. For instance, entry {4, 11} (or C-G in our two-octave case) in a particular female's table captures how often she thinks pitch 11 will follow pitch 4, on average, in male songs. Given these expectations, females can decide how well they like a particular song in different ways, as we will see in the next subsection. Whatever method she uses, as she listens to a male, the female considers the transition from the previous note's pitch to the current note's pitch for each note in a song, gives each transition a score based on her transition table, and sums those scores to come up with her final evaluation of the male and his serenade.

Each female listens to the songs of a certain number of males who are randomly selected to be in her "courting choir." All females hear the same number of males, and the size of the courting choir–that is, a female's sample size–is specified for each evolutionary run. After listening to all the males in her potential-mate choir, the female selects the one that she most preferred (i.e. the one with the highest score) as her mate. This female choice process ensures that all females will have exactly one mate, but males can have a range of mates from 0 (if his song is unpopular with everyone) to something close to the courting choir size (if he has a platinum hit that is selected by all the females who listen to him). Each female has one child per generation created via crossover and mutation with her chosen male mate. This temporarily puts the population at about 50% above a specified "carrying capacity" (target population size). We then kill off approximately a third of the individuals, bringing the population back to a predetermined carrying capacity. This whole process is repeated for some desired number of generations.

3.1 Different ways females can rate their mates

We employed three different methods for scoring the male songs using these tables. In the first method, the female simply scores each transition as it occurs in the song by immediately looking up how much she expected that particular transition and adding it to the running total score for the song. Thus, those songs that contain more of the individual transitions that the female expects (for example, songs with many C-G transitions, if she expects C's to be followed by G's very often) will be scored higher by her, and she will prefer to mate with the males who sing these songs. We call this the *local transition preference* scoring method.

In the second method, the female listens to a whole song first, counting the number of each type of transition that occurs in the song (for example, she might tally up G's following C's four times in the song, and other notes following C's two times). Then from these counts she constructs a transition matrix for that particular individual song (for example, with an entry of .66 for the C-G transition, because that is what occurred two-thirds of the time after a C in this song). Finally, she compares that song's transition table with her expected (preferred) transition table, and the closer the two tables match (on an entry-by-entry basis), the higher score and preference she gives to that song.

Thus this method means that a female will prefer songs that match the overall statistical pattern of transitions in her transition table. We call this the *global transition preference* scoring method. Continuing with our example, if the female has a value of .75 stored in her own transition table for the C-G transition, she will like songs most that have a C-G transition exactly three-fourths of the time (along with other C-x transitions, where x is any note other than G, for the other quarter of the time that C appears). In contrast, with local transition scoring, she would prefer C-G transitions after every C, because they give a higher local score than any other transition from C.

The third scoring method produced females that enjoy being surprised. The female listens to each transition in the song individually as in the first method, looks up how much she expected that transition, and subtracts this probability value from the probability she attached to the transition she most expected to hear. Consider our female from the previous paragraph again. Whenever she hears a C in a male's song, she most expects a G to follow it (75% of the time). Imagine she instead hears a C-E transition in a song. This transition is a surprise to her, because it violates the C-G transition expectation–and so she likes this song more as a consequence.

But how much of a surprise was this note, and how much does it increase her preference for this song? To find out, the female critic first looks up the C-E transition in her table, and finds she expected that transition 15% of the time. Thus, this C-E transition was not a complete surprise, since she had some previous expectation for it, but it was a reasonably large one. We quantify the surprise level with a score of .75-.15=.6 for that transition (that is, prob(C-G) - prob(C-E)). This expected-minus-actual-transition-probability score is summed up for all the transitions in the current song, and the final sum registers how much surprise the female experienced, and therefore how much she preferred that song. Not surprisingly, we call this the *surprise preference* scoring method. Note that it will not result in the males singing random songs–in order to get a high surprise score, a song must first build up expectations, by making transi-

tions to notes that have highly expected notes following them, and then violate those expectations, by not using the highly expected note. Thus there is a constant tug-of-war between doing what is expected and what is unexpected in each song.

The first two preference scoring methods can be considered forms of non-directional mate preferences: evolved male songs that match evolved female expectations most precisely (either locally or globally) will receive the most mating interest. The third surprise preference scoring method, however, is a type of direction mate preference. Rather than rewarding male songs that match female expectations, surprising songs that are some ways off from the evolved female transition tables in song space will be sought after. Thus we expected to see less movement through song space for the local and global transition preferences (though possibly more speciation), and more constant change when surprise preferences were used.

We also expected that surprise scoring would create greater diversity within any given generation than would preferences based on matching local or global expectations, because there are more ways to violate expectations (causing surprise) than to meet them. Note that this is different from the kinds of directional preferences we have previously considered (Miller & Todd, 1993), where only a single preferred direction was indicated (e.g. a greener vs. a bluer patch of plumage). In those cases, the population could evolve to all head in one direction in phenotype space; here, the population will be more likely to scatter in many directions in phenotype space. (This is similar to apostatic selection for multiple phenotypes caused by pressure to evade easy detection predators–see Driver & Humphries, 1988.) But this is not an unreasonable effect to expect, because it can be a direct outcome of low-level dishabituation or novelty-seeking processes.

We varied two additional parameters beyond the female preference scoring method, to test their effects on the evolved diversity of songs. First, we controlled the number of males a female listens to before selecting a mate–that is, the size of her courting choir (2 or 20). This parameter is essentially a "volume knob" on the overall impact of sexual selection in the simulation–if females can only sample one male, then there is no sexual selection taking place, while the greater number of males she can listen to before choosing a mate, the stronger will be the selective force of her preferences. We expected that smaller sample sizes would lead to greater diversity than larger sample sizes, but that larger sample sizes might support a number of distinct "species" of songs. Smaller samples should, on average, give males a better chance of reproducing even if their song is not close to what is desired by females, because each male in a female's small sample set faces less competition than if she sampled a large number of males. On the other hand, we believed that large sample sizes would quickly draw males close to what was desired by females, but that the preferences could aggregate in distinct clusters. So while smaller samples could lead to a larger spread around a central average preference, larger samples could lead to more than one tight cluster (i.e., distinct species). Finally, the greater selection pressure on males caused by larger sample sizes should mean that there will be more rapid change in male songs across generations as well.

The last parameter we considered was whether female expectation transition tables were fixed across time (that is, female offspring contain exact copies of their mother's transition table) or allowed to coevolve with the male songs. We expected that coevolving preferences would allow more change (or diversity) in songs over time because the targets for the males would themselves be moving. In a system without coevolution, male songs will tend to converge on the female preferences and stay there, providing little evolutionary movement. Sexual selection via coevolving traits and preferences is the whole premise of our argument in this paper, so this comparison is a crucial one.

3.2 Resulting song change over time

We ran populations of 1000 individuals for 1000 generations in 12 different conditions: all combinations of 3 preference scoring methods, 2 sample sizes, and fixed vs. coevolving preferences. In each case, we initiated the males (i.e., their songs) randomly, and the first generation of female transition tables were set with probabilities calculated from a collection of simple folk-tune melodies. This way we could ensure that female preferences in our simulations at least started out with some resemblance to human melodic preferences; however, once evolution started moving the preferences and songs around, any hope of the population's aesthetics matching human aesthetics would quickly be lost. Thus, we could not listen to the system and readily judge its progress; we had to resort to more objective measures (further motivating the simplified form of song and preference representation described in the previous section).

To measure evolving song change over time–diachronic diversity–we use a "progress chart" technique modified from Cliff and Miller's (1995) work on measuring coevolutionary progress in pursuit-evasion games. This "ancestral distance map" (Cliff & Miller use Hamming distance) plots generations G in time from left to right (from generation G=0 to G=1000), and generations G' backwards in time (relative to each generation G) from top to bottom (from generation G'=G-1 to generation G'=G-999). At each point (G, G') in the triangular region so formed, we plot the difference between the modal male song (i.e. the most common note at each of the 32 positions) at generation G and that at generation G', with difference measured as the number of positions where the

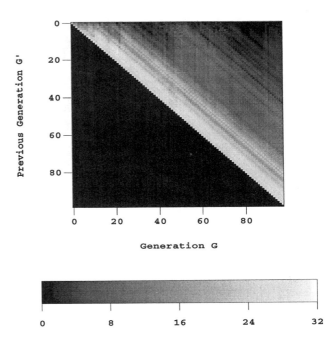

Figure 1: Change in modal song from current generation G (left to right) to all previous generations G' (from G-1 at top to G-999 at bottom). Here a coevolving surprise-preference sample-size-2 population shows continuous rapid change over time.

two songs differ. This difference score, from 0 to 32, is indicated by the darkness of the plotted point, with greater differences mapping onto lighter points. (See Figure 1.)

The top row of points in this type of plot shows the difference between the modal song at any particular generation and the modal song of the previous generation, while the rightmost column of points shows the difference between the modal song at generation G=1000 and the modal songs of all generations before that (from G'=999 at the top, to G'=1 at the bottom). The faster the population evolves and the modal song changes over time, the more of this plot will be filled with points registering the maximum difference of 32–that is, the bigger the light-colored regions will be.

Using this technique, we compared the rate of change of population modal songs over time for our 13 different conditions. Our results mostly matched our expectations, but there was a surprise: listening to only 2 males yielded much faster evolutionary change than choosing from 20 males. This was the largest effect on rate of change, and goes against the selection pressure argument we put forth in the previous section. Instead, this effect could occur because with bigger sample sizes, traits could match preferences much more closely, and so little movement of either would be necessitated over time; in addition, because both parents are more closely matched with a bigger sample size, their offspring will also resem-

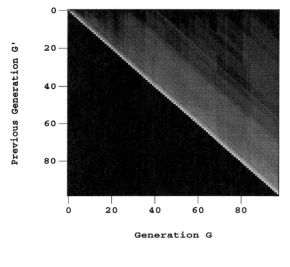

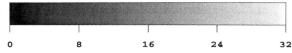

Figure 2: Change in modal song for a non-coevolving global-preference sample-size-20 population, showing little change over time.

ble them more closely, further slowing down change from one generation to the next.

Surprise scoring yielded greater change than either global or local transition scoring. Local scoring, in fact, made the population converge rather rapidly to the locally-preferred song transitions, so that male songs often degenerated to repetition of a single note or alternation between two notes. (This also gave these runs very low within-generation synchronic diversity scores, so we did not analyze this type of preference further.) Finally, coevolution led to faster change than fixed female preferences, at least when surprise scoring was used–the situation is less clear with global transition scoring, which we are investigating further.

We can easily visualize the difference between rate of change in the fastest case and its parametric "opposite" (i.e. changing all the parameters), which is one of the slowest cases, by plotting their progress charts. In Figure 1, we show modal song change for a coevolving surprise-scoring small-sample (i.e. sample-size 2) population. The relatively small region of dark points, indicating small changes between past and present generations, is dominated by a large light region, indicating large changes over time. (Remember that the maximum possible difference between any two modal melodies is 32, so the nearly-white region indicates that the something close to the maximum number of changed positions has been reached–more change is still occurring in that region, but our distance measure has hit ceiling and does

not reflect the further movement.) In Figure 2, we plot the chart for a fixed-preference global-transition-scoring large-sample (20) population. Here the differences between present and past modal songs are mostly small (dark points), meaning that little change has occurred over time. The light band along the diagonal indicates that there was a lot of change in the first few generations, as the initially random male songs were most strongly winnowed down, but after that little more transpired.

3.3   Resulting song diversity within populations

To measure the synchronic diversity of songs within a population at any particular generation, we computed the set of differences (again 0-32) between every pair of males' songs in the population. This set of differences could be plotted as a histogram for any given generation, with highly converged, low-diversity populations having histograms skewed toward low values, and unconverged, high-diversity populations having histograms skewed towards high values. Furthermore, populations with two or more distinct "species" of songs will show up as multiple peaks in the histogram (representing the distributions of between-species and within-species distances). To explore how this within-generation diversity changes across generations, we change each histogram into a one-dimensional density plot by essentially viewing it "from overhead" and representing high regions in the histogram with dark points in the plot. Then we can line up these one-dimensional density plots next to each other, generation by generation, to make a two-dimensional plot of the changing synchronic diversity in the population over time (see Figure 3). Now we have a plot with generation G along one dimension, and distance between each male song and the modal song along the other dimension, with the darkness of each point indicating the number of males who are that different from the population's current modal song.

We used this visualization method to compare the evolving synchronic diversity of songs in populations in 8 conditions (leaving out the degenerate hyper-converged local transition score populations). Again our expectations were mostly met, and again the largest effect came from the size of the female's sample set. Sampling 2 males preserved diversity in the population to a much greater degree than sampling 20 males; in the former case, most males retained 10-20 different notes from the modal song after 1000 generations, while in the latter, most males had only one or two notes different. Coevolution yielded greater synchronic diversity than fixed female preferences, but to a lesser degree than sample size (e.g. about 18 notes different from the modal song for the coevolving surprise sample-2 population versus about 11 notes different for the fixed surprise sample-2 population after 1000 generations). The preference scoring method (surprise versus global transition scoring) showed little

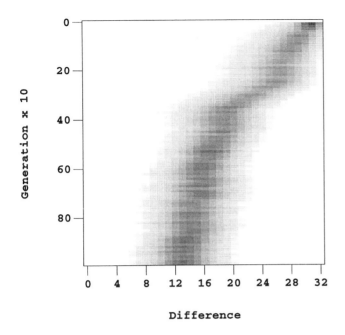

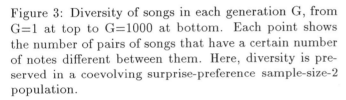

Figure 3: Diversity of songs in each generation G, from G=1 at top to G=1000 at bottom. Each point shows the number of pairs of songs that have a certain number of notes different between them. Here, diversity is preserved in a coevolving surprise-preference sample-size-2 population.

consistent effect on within-generation diversity, however.

We show the difference between the case with the greatest synchronic diversity and its parametric opposite with one of the lowest diversities in Figures 3 and 4 respectively. Figure 3 displays the song diversity in a coevolving surprise-scoring sample-2 population over time, starting at generation 0 at the top of the graph and proceeding to generation 1000 at the bottom. Diversity starts out maximal in the early generations (when the random initial male songs were all very far from the modal song), and declines somewhat over time. But even after 1000 generations, most male songs have about 20 notes out of 32 that are different from their population's modal song. In contrast, the fixed global-transition-scoring sample-20 population in Figure 4 converges from its initial diversity to population-wide homogeneity very rapidly. Within 150 generations, most males sing songs that are only slight (3-position) variations on the population modal song, and this clustering even gets slightly tighter over time. But this tight clustering from the large sample-size, when combined with the directional-selection effects of surprise preferences, can lead new song "species" to emerge and differentiate from each other over time. Figure 5 shows this effect, indicating that diversity across the whole population can be replaced by diversity between subpopulations.

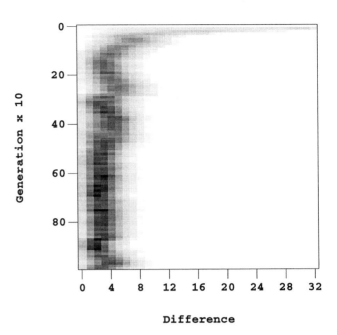

Figure 4: Diversity of songs in a non-coevolving global-preference sample-size-20 population, showing loss of diversity over time.

4 Implications and further work

What does all this mean? Without sexual selection, as we saw in section 2, simulation models have evolved little diversity in communication signals. When instead we replace natural selection with sexual selection, signal diversity within and across generations blossoms. Our simulations here lend strong support for the role of coevolving songs and directional (surprise-based) preferences in maintaining diversity over time (Figure 3), and in continuously altering that diversity as time goes by (Figure 1). With non-coevolving, non-directional preferences, progress is slower (Figure 2) and diversity collapses (Figure 4). The number of mates sampled is the selective-force amplifier for these effects: small sample sizes promote diversity and change, while large sample sizes encourage fulfilled desires and, counterintuitively, population conformity.

It is interesting to compare this sample size effect to that seen with tournament selection in standard genetic algorithms (as analyzed in Goldberg & Deb, 1991): there, the larger the set of competing individuals, the greater is the selection pressure and speed of evolution. The difference is that in tournament selection, individuals are being selected by a fixed global fitness function applying across all tournaments, while in our female choice situation, each competition is decided by a different female and her individual preferences. Thus holding many large tournaments will find the best individuals in the whole population according to some single criterion, and

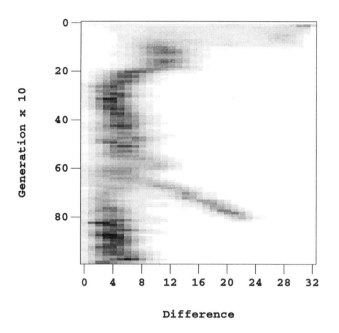

Figure 5: Diversity of songs in a coevolving surprise-preference sample-size-20 population, showing evolution of two tightly-clustered song "species" between generations 600 and 800.

the population as a whole can move quickly to the optimum. But correspondingly large mate-sample sets in the form of sexual selection incorporated here find the best individuals for each idiosyncratic female preference, leading to little cohesive population movement.

Overall, then, we have shown that sexual selection via coevolving male-generated mate-attracting signals and female-operated mate-assessing directional preferences can lead to the maintenance and continual turnover of signal diversity over time. But we have not yet satisfactorily answered the question of where such signal diversity comes from in the first place—why don't we just have *one* love song at a time, changing from year to year? In other words, how can we ever progress from one song to many? Our simulation does not yet address this question: we have started with an initial population of many different male songs, and seen how that diversity changes over time. What we need to do next is to start with a population of males who all sing the same song initially, and see how the different female choice configurations we have described here alter *that* population. We suspect that, once again, coevolving surprise-based preferences with small sample sizes will first diversify the population, and then continue to alter that diversity across successive generations. (We can also start out with a converged female population all sharing the same preferences for song traits, here in terms of note transitions, which are *not* present in the initial male population, and

see how male song evolution adapts to those preferences over time. This situation matches the idea of pre-existing sensory biases on the part of females, which can drive the evolution of new male traits, rather than the traits and preferences both emerging over time together.)

Another issue we are beginning to explore is how to create the female expectations in the first place: where should their transition tables come from? In our current system, females inherit their transition tables from their mother and father (after the females in the initial generation were loaded with transition expectations computed from real song examples, as mentioned in section 4.2). Because of this, "surprising" note transitions can only be surprising relative to a particular female's inherited expectations. But certainly for humans, and for other animals as well, expectations are built up through experience and learning within one's lifetime (see Bharucha & Todd, 1989). So instead we can let a female learn expectations about note transitions based on a set of songs from her current generation, or from the previous generation, as if she has heard those songs and picked up knowledge of her "culture" from them. Then she will be surprised when she hears something new that toys with these learned expectations, building them up and then violating them. We expect that using learning to create the note transition expectations, rather than evolving them, will allow the population to "change its tune" even more rapidly than the cases we have described in this paper, because the expectations will be able to shift just as rapidly as the songs themselves–learning operates faster than selection. Thus, love songs this year may be different from the love songs of yesteryear because, in part, everyone listening to them gets bored, and selects instead for novelty and surprise.

Furthermore, we could allow learning in the females to occur at an even faster time-scale, so that instead of habituating to songs heard too many times last week, each female could habituate to notes and phrases heard too many times within the current male's song. In this case, females would seek novelty and expectation-violation *within* each song they hear. To sing preferred songs, males will have to balance the amount of repetition and newness in one song just right. We expect that this will lead to increased complexity of the internal structure of the songs themselves (not just of the population of songs), allowing us to explore the other great mystery about elaborate communication signals.

One final question must be considered: So what? Why is it important to understand the sources of diversity in communication signals? Isn't that just the way the cultural world is, full of all sorts of inexplicable variety? The answer is no, that cannot be just the way the world is. The diversity of signals does not come for free: to be able to generate and evaluate this range of possibilities, there must be correspondingly extensive behavioral mechanisms as well. So the evolution of communication signal diversity must be linked to the evolution of brains and behavior more generally. Indeed, Miller (1993) has proposed that the very size and structure of the hyper-encephalized human brain has been most strongly (and most recently) shaped by a process of runaway sexual selection, new neural circuits being added by the pressure to produce and evaluate ever more elaborate mate-attracting cultural displays, including music and language. If this is true, our vast cultural diversity reflects the very essence of our evolved, sexually-selected human nature, and we should expect the never-ending flow of ever-changing love songs to be with us for a long time to come.

5 References

Ackley, D.H., and Littman, M.L. (1994). Altruism in the evolution of communication. In R.A. Brooks and P. Maes (Eds.), *Artificial Life V* (pp. 40-48). Cambridge, MA: MIT Press/Bradford Books.

Andersson, M. (1994). *Sexual selection.* Princeton, NJ: Princeton University Press.

Bharucha, J.J., and Todd, P.M. (1989). Modeling the perception of tonal structure with neural nets. *Computer Music Journal, 13(4),* 44-53.

Catchpole, C.K., and Slater, P.J.B. (1995). *Bird song: Biological themes and variations.* Cambridge, UK: Cambridge University Press.

Cliff, D., and Miller, G.F. (1995). Tracking the Red Queen: Measurements of adaptive progress in co-evolutionary simulations. In F. Moran, A. Moreno, J.J. Merelo and P. Cachon (Eds.), *Advances in artificial life: Proceedings of the Third European Conference on Artificial Life* (pp. 200-218). Lecture Notes in Artificial Intelligence 929. Berlin: Springer-Verlag.

Darwin, C. (1871). *The descent of man and selection in relation to sex.* London: John Murray.

Driver, P.M., and Humphries, D.A. (1988). *Protean behavior: The biology of unpredictability.* Oxford, UK: Oxford University Press.

Goldberg, D.E., and Deb, K. (1991). A comparative analysis of selection schemes used in genetic algorithms. In G. Rawlins (Ed.), *Foundations of genetic algorithms.* San Mateo, CA: Morgan Kaufman.

Hamilton, W.D., and Zuk, M. (1982). Heritable true fitness and bright birds: A role for parasites? *Science, 218,* 384-387.

Hanlon, R.T., and Messenger, J.B. (1996). *Cephalopod behavior.* Cambridge, UK: Cambridge University Press.

Hartshorn, C. (1973). *Born to sing.* New York: Harper & Row.

Hauser, M. (1996). *The evolution of communication.* Cambridge, MA: MIT Press/Bradford Books.

Kirkpatrick, M. (1987). The evolutionary forces acting on female preferences in polygynous animals. In J.W.

Bradbury and M.B. Andersson (Eds.), *Sexual selection: Testing the alternatives* (pp. 67-82). New York: Wiley.

Krebs, J.R., and Dawkins, R. (1984). Animal signals: Mind-reading and manipulation. In J.R. Krebs and N.B. Davies (Eds.), *Behavioral ecology* (pp. 380-402). Sunderland, MA: Sinauer Associates.

MacLennan, B.J. (1990). *Evolution of communication in a population of simple machines.* Technical report CS-90-99, Computer Science Department, University of Tennessee, Knoxville TN.

MacLennan, B.J. (1992). Synthetic Ethology: An Approach to the Study of Communication. In C. Langton, C. Taylor, J. D. Farmer, and S. Rasmussen (Eds.), *Artificial Life II* (pp. 631-658). Reading, MA: Addison-Wesley.

Miller, G.F. (1993). *Evolution of the human brain through runaway sexual selection: The mind as a protean courtship device.* Unpublished PhD thesis, Stanford University Department of Psychology. (Available through UMI Microfilms.)

Miller, G.F., and Todd, P.M. (1993). Evolutionary wanderlust: Sexual selection with directional mate preferences. In J. A. Meyer, H. L. Roitblat, and S. W. Wilson (Eds.), *From Animals to Animats 2: Proceedings of the Second International Conference on Simulation of Adaptive Behavior* (pp. 21-30) Cambridge, MA: MIT Press/Bradford Books.

Miller, G.F., and Todd, P.M. (1995). The role of mate choice in biocomputation: Sexual selection as a process of search, optimization, and diversification. In W. Banzhaf and F.H. Eeckman (Eds.), *Evolution and biocomputation: Computational models of evolution. Lecture notes in computer science 899* (pp. 169-204). Berlin: Springer-Verlag.

Pinker, S. (1994). *The language instinct.* New York: Morrow.

Searcy, W.A. (1992). Song repertoire and mate choice in birds. *American Zoologist, 32,* 71-80.

Todd, P.M., and Miller, G.F. (1991). On the sympatric origin of species: Mercurial mating in the Quicksilver model. In R.K. Belew and L.B. Booker (Eds.), *Proceedings of the Fourth International Conference on Genetic Algorithms* (pp. 547-554). San Mateo, CA: Morgan Kaufman.

Weatherhead, P.J., and Roberston, R.J. (1979). Offspring quality and the polygyny threshold: The "sexy son" hypothesis. *American Naturalist, 113,* 201-208.

Werner, G.M., and Dyer, M.G. (1992). Evolution of Communication in Artificial Organisms. In C. Langton, C. Taylor, J. D. Farmer, and S. Rasmussen (Eds.), *Artificial Life II* (pp. 659-687). Reading, MA: Addison-Wesley.

The Truth Is Out There:
the Evolution of Reliability in Aggressive Communication Systems

Peter de Bourcier[1] and Michael Wheeler[2]

1. CyberLife Technology Ltd, Quern House, Mill Court, Cambridge, CB2 5LD, UK
Phone: +44 1223 844894, Fax: +44 1223 844918, e-mail: peter@cyberlife.co.uk
2. Dept. of Experimental Psychology, University of Oxford, South Parks Road, Oxford, OX1 3UD, UK
Phone: +44 1865 271417, Fax: +44 1865 310447, e-mail: michaelw@psy.ox.ac.uk

Abstract

This paper reports on our ongoing research in which we employ an artificial life methodology to study the evolution of communication. We perform experiments using synthetic ecologies in which artificial autonomous agents (animats) with evolved signalling and receiving tactics are in competition over food. Synthetic ecologies permit an investigative strategy in which one relaxes certain restrictive assumptions that, in the interests of formal tractability, are made in mathematical models of biological communication. The experiments described here are examples of that investigative strategy. Motivated by suggestions from recent biological signalling theory, we allow individuals to pay attention to multiple sources of information about a potential opponent. Our results indicate that if signals are unreliable, then individuals will evolve to use another source of information which is guaranteed to be reliable (if such a source exists), and the strategy of paying attention to signals will be selected against. However, if we place an indirect fitness cost on the receiving tactic of obtaining guaranteed-to-be-reliable information, then, as this cost rises, it becomes adaptive and evolutionarily stable for receivers to pay attention to unreliable signals.

1 Introduction

In conflict situations, should we expect animals to produce reliable signals of their aggressive intentions, or should we expect cheats to prosper? If we should expect aggressive signals to evolve to be reliable, what evolutionary factors enforce that reliability? If we should expect aggressive signals to evolve to be unreliable, should aggressive communication systems persist at all in nature? For some time now we have been examining these sorts of questions through the methods and techniques of artificial life (henceforth 'A-Life'). (See [6, 7, 34] for our previous studies.) This ongoing research takes place within a theoretical framework that we call Synthetic Behavioural Ecology (henceforth 'SBE'). We carry out experiments in simple (although not trivial) synthetic ecologies, with the specific goal of making a contribution to the scientific understanding of how ecological context influences the adaptive consequences of behaviour. The term 'synthetic behavioural ecology' is designed to suggest a theoretical link between our approach and behavioural ecology, the sub-discipline of biology in which researchers aim to identify the functional roles that particular, ecologically embedded behaviour patterns play in contributing to Darwinian fitness. Of course, SBE is also closely related to certain other approaches within the artificial life community (e.g., [16, 31]).

It seems plausible that studies using well-constructed synthetic ecologies may, in time, help to bridge an explanatory gap that exists between real-world adaptive behaviour in natural environments and idealised mathematical models of that behaviour. Synthetic ecologies will always be idealisations of any natural ecology; but, unlike their natural counterparts, synthetic ecologies permit the precise variation of the key parameters affecting the observed behaviour, and the easy repeatability of experiments (cf. [16]). The relationship between synthetic ecologies and the mathematical models to which theoretical biologists are accustomed (see section 2) is less straightforward. Mathematical models are undoubtedly powerful theoretical tools. In particular, they allow biologists to make assumptions and arguments explicit. And there seems little doubt that synthetic ecologies do not afford the transparent formal rigour that mathematical models often achieve. However, as the formal modellers themselves sometimes observe, the biological realism of mathematical models, and therefore their usefulness to empirical research on animal behaviour, can sometimes be rather limited [11]. In part at least, this situation occurs because, in order to make those models mathematically tractable, certain restrictive assumptions have to be made (see section 3). Our thought is that SBE is potentially useful precisely because it provides a platform for experimentation which sits somewhere between field biology and formal mathematical modelling. Synthetic ecologies permit an investigative strategy in which the experimenter systematically relaxes the restrictive assumptions made in mathematical models. Miller recommends a similar strategy:

A powerful way of using A-Life simulations is to take an existing formal model from theoretical biology and relax the assumptions (preferably one at a time) that were required to make the mathematics tractable. The results of such a simulation are then directly comparable to the results of the existing formal model, and will be comprehensible and relevant for biologists. [22, p.10]

2 Biological Theory: Quality, Cost, and Reliability

Consider the following real-life scenario: The reproductive success of a red deer stag depends on its fighting ability. The stronger the stag, the larger its harem, and the more opportunities it will have to pass on its genes. Contests between stags in the annual autumn competition can be a dangerous business. Between 20 and 30 percent of stags become permanently injured at some point during their lives, and nearly all stags endure minor injuries. However, despite the image of violent conflict that such statistics suggest, all-out fights are comparatively rare. Why is this? The first reason is that it pays a stag to avoid those fights that it is likely to lose. The second is that fights are often seriously damaging to the victor as well as the vanquished. Thus there has been a selection pressure for settling contests by display rather than fighting, and the red deer world has witnessed the evolution of the distinctive (and adaptive) phenomena of roaring and parallel walking. In a typical confrontation, the harem holder and the challenger begin their contest by roaring at each other. If the holder roars at a faster rate than the challenger, then the challenger usually withdraws. If roaring fails to decide the issue, the two stags commence a parallel walking display which allows further assessment. Only if this second phase behaviour still fails to settle the contest does a serious fight occur [5].

For the student of adaptive behaviour interested in communication, there are some important lessons to be learned from this classic example of an animal contest. Most strikingly, the signalling system in operation is guaranteed to be honest. (An honest signal is one that reliably reflects the underlying quality of the signaller [30].) Honesty is ensured because the stag's signals are *biologically* correlated with the phenotypic traits that determine its ability to win a fight (e.g., size or physical condition). Such traits are known as the animal's *resource holding potential* or RHP [26], and signals which are biologically correlated with RHP are called *assessment signals* [19]. Roaring is a reliable signal of fighting ability, because, to roar at a fast rate, and to continue such roaring for what can sometimes be a protracted period, a stag must be physically strong. A weaker stag is simply unable to pay the costs of roaring at higher rates, so it cannot fool the opposition into treating it as stronger than it, in fact, is.

According to Zahavi's *handicap principle* [35], this idea - that high signalling costs increase the reliability of the signals made - is a fundamental principle of biological signalling systems. Zahavi reasons as follows: Biological signals will evolve only if (a) there is information about a potential signaller that a potential receiver wants and (b) it is in the potential signaller's interests to supply that information. Thus the information carried by signals must be reliable enough to warrant a receiver's attention, and unreliable signals will be selected out. However, if the signaller has to make an investment in its signals (where 'investment' means the cost in fitness that the animal incurs through, say, energy loss or risk of predation, as a result of making the signal) the reliability of signals will increase. A signal which is, for example, wasteful of energy is, as a consequence of that wastefulness, reliably predictive of the possession of energy. So not only is it the case that the costliness of signals guarantees their honesty, it is also the case that signals *will evolve to be costly and, therefore, to be honest*.

The handicap principle is still controversial within biology, and has received a number of different interpretations (see, for example, 3, 10, 13, 28). In his influential ESS-model of the way in which the handicap principle could operate in mating displays, Grafen [10] suggests a *strategic choice* interpretation, in which signallers of different qualities will signal at different levels that reveal true quality, because each signaller 'chooses' to endure a level of handicap appropriate to his or her quality. High quality individuals produce higher signals, and thus endure bigger handicaps, than low quality individuals. Grafen shows that for the strategic choice handicap to evolve, (i) higher signals must cost more, and (ii) the costs involved must be differential, in the sense that a specific signal must be proportionally more costly to a weak individual than to a strong individual. This is the interpretation of the handicap principle which we will adopt in what follows.

Despite all this talk of honesty, it seems that some animal signals are susceptible to exploitation by cheats. For example, when in foraging flocks, birds of several species sometimes give hawk alarms when there are no predatory hawks present. Other birds who hear the signal often flee, an event which permits the signaller to gain better access to the available food [24]. This is a clear case of *qualitative* deception. But deception may also be *quantitative* [12], and since a paradigmatic context for quantitative deception is aggressive signalling - the focus of this paper - let's consider the case of an animal which signals the intention to intensify an already-existing conflict situation, when, in fact, that animal would not be prepared to escalate the conflict to that higher level. It seems that such quantitative cheats - creatures who consistently signalled higher levels of aggressive intent than they in fact possessed - would tend to be more successful than honest signallers when confronting 'trusting' opponents in signalling contests. Thus they would take over the population. To put this point another way, the honest signalling of aggressive intentions appears not to be an *evolutionarily stable strategy* (or ESS). (An ESS is a strategy which, when adopted by most members of a population, means that that population cannot be invaded by a rare alternative strategy [18]. At the ESS fitness is maximised in the sense that individuals not adopting the ESS do worse [25].)

At first sight, then, it seems that signals of aggressive intentions ought to be unreliable. Following a line of argument which is consistent with Zahavi-esque reasoning, one might conclude from this that animals should not be expected to signal aggressive intentions at all, because, eventually, it would pay receivers to ignore such signals in favour of other sources of information, and the entire strategy of signalling aggressive intentions would be selected against [14, 17]. However, there is ample evidence from animal communication systems that some animals, such as male African elephants [27] and male Pere David's deer [33] do signal aggressive intent. Of course, the handicap principle itself might explain this phenomenon. For example, Enquist [8] uses a modification of the hawk-dove game [18] to demonstrate that if signals of aggressive intentions are costly and the costs are differential in the sense identified above, then the signalling of aggressive intentions is an ESS. So the handicap principle might well operate to secure the reliability of communication systems in which aggressive intentions are signalled. And if signals of aggressive intentions are reliable, then, all things being equal, such signals will not be selected-out.

Despite the undoubted theoretical significance of Enquist's result, in both of the examples of aggressive signalling just cited (African elephants and Pere David's deer), there are common circumstances in which low quality males appear to signal higher levels of aggressive intent than they, in fact, possess. This strategy enables the cheats to achieve a temporary domination of better quality males, which, in turn, permits them to enjoy increased mating success. In other words, these signalling systems are unreliable, yet they persist. Perhaps, as Harper suggests [12], receivers will evolve to ignore deceptive signals altogether only when those signals are qualitatively, rather than quantitatively, incorrect. Quantitatively incorrect signals still carry some information. A threat display - even one which has been exaggerated - is not a submission display.

Things get more complicated still once one gives due theoretical weight to the fact that the behavioural response of a receiving animal will be the result not of an incoming signal alone, but of that signal plus the degree of importance which the receiver gives to that signal. Receiver tactics will thus be an important factor in the evolution of communication systems. Hence 'receiver psychology' is increasingly discussed in the animal behaviour literature (e.g., [20, 30]). And that is not all that happens on the receiver-side of communication. Receivers, as well as signallers, often face fitness costs [30]. For example, receivers assessing the quality of potential mates who signal to them will often pay fitness costs in terms of the time taken over assessment, time that could be spent on other activities. And notice that in the case of red-deer roaring discussed earlier, a challenger has to bear the cost of roaring at an honest level himself, in order to elicit a signal from the harem-holder. Other receiver costs might include risks of predation and disease transmission. On this evidence Stamp Dawkins and Guilford conclude that "the receiver's ideal signal (one that is costly to give, and so gives an honest indication of quality, but costs nothing to receive) will be a rare commodity" [30, p.866]. They go on to argue that receiver costs will have important evolutionary consequences for communication systems. If signallers and receivers pay high costs for reliable signalling, then it may be to the mutual benefit of both to adopt a signalling system which is less costly and (therefore) not guaranteed to be reliable. Such signalling systems, involving so-called 'conventional' signals (signals in which the necessary connection between cost and honesty has been lost), may be established when, for example, (i) animals recognise each other as individuals (so that the full costs of assessment are avoided through memory of previous assessments), or (ii) animals recognise each other as members of categories of signallers who have been encountered previously. Once receiver costs are factored into our understanding, it seems much more likely that unreliable signalling systems which permit some level of cheating can be evolutionarily stable. If, on average, the fitness benefit to receivers from paying the costs of honest assessment is outweighed by the benefit from (a) conventional signalling coupled to (b) the occasional probing of signallers to impose costs on cheats, then unreliable signals may well persist [30].

What all this tells us is that the current biological theory of aggressive signalling, as rich as it undoubtedly is, contains gaps, shortfalls, and unanswered questions. In the SBE experiments described in the remainder of this paper, we endeavour to address two outstanding issues: multiple sources of information and the cost of finding out the truth.

3 The New Experiments: Rationale

We noted earlier that existing ESS-models often make certain restrictive assumptions that can reduce their usefulness to empirical studies. We suggested also that synthetic ecologies permit an investigative strategy in which these restrictive assumptions are systematically relaxed. The study of biological communication provides a context ripe for the application of this strategy. Although ESS-models are powerful mathematical tools for investigating the logic of animal signalling systems, even state-of-the-art models are limited, in that they do not allow for multiple receivers of one signal [11]. Relatedly, information flow is almost always assumed to be one-way; that is, there is a signaller and a receiver, and no scope for the same individual to be both a signaller and a receiver simultaneously. Our early SBE-models [6, 7, 34] demonstrated that the general logic of the handicap principle can carry over to multi-agent signalling systems in which these two restrictive assumptions are relaxed, systems which allow both for two-way information flow and for an individual signal to be picked up by many receivers. The synthetic ecology that we use in the experiments described here preserves these features. It also takes further the strategy of relaxing restrictive assumptions.

The sequential assessment game of Enquist and Leimar [9] is one ESS model which relaxes the assumption that information flow in signalling contests is one-way. However, even this highly sophisticated model embodies a third restrictive assumption, which is that contestants have no way of 'choosing' between different sources of information. They have access to direct information about an opponent's strength, but not to signalling information [11]. This is not a limitation of the sequential assessment game alone. As far as we know, situations in which combinations of signalling information and 'direct perception' of quality[1] might be used by an animal in aggressive confrontations have yet to be explored in detail by any concrete ESS-model, although Grafen and Johnstone have made some tentative suggestions about how such a model might be developed [11]. They suggest that an individual in an ESS-game might possess a number of registers, each of which contains a real number representing such values as an estimate of an opponent's strength based on recent evidence, or an estimate of an opponent's willingness to escalate a conflict. The best use to which such a register might be put by a particular individual depends on how other individuals are using their registers.

In the first experiment described below, we extend our model by making it possible for receivers to evolve to use one or the other of, or a combination of, signalling information and direct information about true quality. This extension was inspired primarily by recent discussions in biological signalling theory (such as Grafen and Johnstone's). However, it is also suggested by the path that our own work has taken. In our earliest SBE models [6, 34], the strategy of receivers was effectively fixed, such that the level of threat which a receiver registered was determined solely by the values of incoming aggressive signals. However, as stressed earlier, to understand communication systems, we need to consider not only the strategies of signallers, but also the strategies of receivers.

Hence we introduced the concurrent evolution of individual signalling and receiving strategies [7]. The results from this more complex ecological scenario suggested the following hypothesis (see [7, pp.766-71]): Where the fitness costs of signalling are low, signallers will tend to produce signals indicating levels of aggression well in excess of actual aggression. If there is no alternative source of relevant information, receivers may still pay heed to those signals. Where the fitness costs of signalling are high, the pressure on signallers to reduce the level of signalling may still lead to communication systems in which signals are not direct reflections of quality, in that signallers may tend to produce signals indicating levels of aggression lower than actual aggression. However, if receivers evolve to give a high degree of importance to those signals, the effect would be to compensate for the actual values of the signals. As receivers, individuals would still behave just as if signals were direct reflections of aggression (so they would benefit from not being drawn into costly conflicts); as signallers, individuals would benefit from the low level of signalling. Given this result, the obvious next move, carried out as our first experiment, is to give receivers the potential to respond to an alternative source of information about the quality of prospective opponents (a source that is guaranteed to be reliable), and to investigate the effects that the existence of such a source has, at various costs of signalling, on the evolution of the communication system.

The second experiment described below extends the model again, this time to connect our work directly with the recent biological literature on receiver costs (as discussed in section 2). In all of our previous synthetic ecologies, the costs of communication were borne entirely by signalling. In section 6 we describe what happens when an indirect fitness cost is placed on the strategy of finding out about the true RHP of potential opponents.

4 Experimental Model

A number of mobile animats (all with equal energy levels) and a number of stationary food particles (all with equal energy values) are distributed randomly throughout a two-dimensional world. This world is 1000 by 1000 units square (each animat being round and 12 units in diameter). Space is continuous, and the edges of the world are barriers to movement. When an animat lands on a food particle, the animat's energy level is incremented by the energy value of that particle, and the particle is deemed to have been 'eaten'. The food resource is replenished by new food particles which are added (with a random distribution) at each time-step; but the resource is also 'capped,' so that food is never more plentiful than at the beginning of the run.

Each animat has two highly idealised sensory modalities, which, for convenience, we label 'vision' and 'olfaction'. The visual system is based on a 36-pixel eye providing information in a full 360 degree radius around the animat,

---

[1] Direct in the sense that information about the quality of a potential opponent is not obtained from signals produced by that opponent.

with an arbitrarily imposed maximum range of 165 units. Each pixel returns a value corresponding to the proportion of that pixel's receptive field containing other animats. The olfactory system is sensitive to food. Its principles are similar to those of the visual system, the only differences being that the olfactory range is only 35 units, and food particles are treated as point sources.

Although animats receive energy from food, they also lose energy in various ways. A small existence-cost is deducted at each time-step, and animats also lose energy for fighting, moving, signalling, and reproducing (see below). If an animat's energy level sinks to 0, it is removed from the world; so food-finding is essential to survival. To encourage foraging, each animat has a hunger level (a disposition to move towards food) which changes in a way inversely proportional to its energy level.

What we think of as fights take place when animats touch. Fighting animats suffer large energy reductions. It is therefore plausible to regard an animat's energy level as a measure of its RHP. It is a characteristic of RHP that having a high RHP will generally be costly in contexts other than fighting. For example, being large may well be a sign of high RHP, but it also costs the animal in terms of growth and maintenance [12]. To reflect this fact, we impose a cost in energy to making a movement, such that each movement an animat makes results in a reduction in energy proportional to the amount of energy that the animat has. A movement made by an animat whose energy-level is near the maximum possible (see below) costs twice as much as a movement made by an animat who is on the verge of death.

If one is to be serious about evolutionary-functional explanations of animal contests, then aggression cannot be thought of as an end in itself or as a 'spontaneous appetite' [15], such that, in the absence of the performance of aggressive acts, the tendency to behave aggressively increases with time. Rather, aggressive behaviour needs to be conceptualised as a form of adaptive behaviour, with an adaptive purpose, such as to win or to defend a resource (see, e.g., [1, 8, 32]). In our synthetic ecological context, the food supply is limited and foraging is essential for survival. In effect animats are in competition for the available resources. Therefore it benefits an individual to inhabit an area which is not being foraged by other animats. It is here that aggressive movements play their adaptive role. We define an aggressive movement as a movement in which a first animat moves directly towards a second (which makes sense because fights occur when animats touch). Aggressive signals (indications of the apparent tendency that a signaller has to move directly towards a receiver) are calculated using the RHP (energy level) of the signaller (as explained below). Although aggressive behaviour is reactively triggered by the presence of other animats within visual range (so animats do not plan aggressive responses with the explicit goal of preserving an

exclusive foraging area) nevertheless aggressive behaviour does help an individual to 'defend' just such an area, precisely by driving away approaching animats. Hence aggressive movements serve the adaptive purpose of helping an individual to defend a resource, even though that purpose is not internally represented as an explicit goal in the mechanisms controlling that individual's aggressive behaviour.

Each member of the population has three evolved strategies which, along with that individual's dynamically changing hunger and energy levels, determine its behaviour.

Signalling strategy: Animats signal whenever at least one other animat is within visual range. Signals are produced in accordance with the calculation $S = E.C$, where S is the value of the signal made, E is that individual's current energy level (RHP), and C is an individual-specific constant, in the range 0-2. A C of 0 is equivalent to not making any signal, a C of 1 results in the value of actual RHP being used as the signal value, and a C of 2 results in the value of actual RHP being doubled and the subsequent value being used as the signal value. So the higher the value of C adopted by an individual, the higher the level of aggressive exaggeration in that individual's signals. Given this, an animat which evolves to have a very high value of C can be thought of as a bluffer whose strategy is to indicate a higher level of aggressive intent (stronger disposition to approach another animat) than it, in fact, has. An animat which evolves to have a very low value of C can be thought of as a different kind of bluffer, one whose strategy is to produce what are, in effect, suppressed signals of aggressive intent (indicating a weaker disposition to approach another animat than that individual, in fact, has). (See section 7 for a discussion of this interpretation of the level of exaggeration.)

Aggressive signals are displays for which a signalling animat has to pay, via a deduction in energy. (This is an appropriate tax since an animat's energy level is effectively equivalent to its RHP. The ways in which costs are paid in natural environments may be more complex, although the notion of an 'appropriate link' still seems to apply [29].) At the beginning of a run, the units of energy deducted per unit of aggressive signal are set by the experimenter. Thus the absolute amount of energy deducted increases with the values of aggressive signals. In this way, the cost of signalling is differential, in the sense required by the handicap principle, because, given a specific signal made by a high-energy individual, it will cost a low-energy individual proportionally more to produce that same signal.

Receiving strategy: Animats receive the signals of any other animats within visual range. The effect that a signal has on the behaviour of a receiving animat is a function of that animat's receiving strategy. This strategy is determined by an individual-specific constant, K that 'weights' incoming signals, in order to calculate a threat value. So $T = R.K$, where T is the threat, R is the incoming signal, and K is an individual-specific constant, in the range 0-2. A K of 0 would result in that individual ignoring incoming signals; a K of 1 means that the value of the incoming signal itself is used as the threat value; and a K of 2 results in incoming signals being doubled and the subsequent value being used as the threat value. So the higher the value of K, the higher the degree of importance that an individual is giving to incoming signals.

Sensitivity to RHP: A receiving animat is also sensitive, to some degree, to the energy level (RHP) of any animat within visual/signalling range. This sensitivity is determined by an individual-specific constant, P that 'weights' any energy value picked up, in order to calculate what we call 'assessed RHP'. The higher the value of P, the more sensitive the behaviour of an individual is to the RHP of other animats. So $W = H.P$, where W is assessed RHP, H is the visible animat's actual energy level (RHP), and P is an individual-specific constant, in the range 0-2. A P of 0 would result in that individual ignoring another animat's RHP; a P of 1 means that that RHP value itself is used as assessed RHP; and a P of 2 results in that RHP value being doubled and the subsequent value being used as assessed RHP.

At each time-step, the direction in which each animat will move (one of 36 possible directions) is calculated using the following equation:

$$P(d) = \frac{h.s(d) + e.v(d) + t(o).v(o) + w(o).v(o) + c}{\Sigma[i=1..n]\,(h.s(d_i) + e.v(d_i) + t(o_i).v(o_i) + w(o_i).v(o_i) + c)}$$

where $p(d)$ is the probability that the particular animat will move in the direction d; n is the number of possible directions of movement; h is the animat's hunger level; $s(d)$ is the value returned by the olfactory system in direction d; e is the animat's energy level; $v(d)$ is the value returned by the visual system for direction d; o is the opposite direction to d; $t(o)$ is the threat that the animat perceives from other animats from the opposite direction to d; $w(o)$ is the RHP assessment value for animats from the opposite direction to d; $v(o)$ is the value returned by the visual system in the opposite direction to d; and c is a small constant which prevents zero probabilities.

Each of the three evolved strategies is encoded in 8 bits of a 24 bit genotype. So the genotype as a whole specifies the set of strategies adopted by the particular individual in question. This is analogous to Grafen and Johnstone's notion of a register (see section 2 above). At the beginning of a run, a random population of genotypes is created, producing a random distribution of signalling strategies, receiving strategies, and RHP-sensitivities. When an animat achieves a pre-defined (high) energy level, it will asexually reproduce. The selection pressures imposed by the ecological context mean that different strategies (or different combinations of strategies) will have different fitness consequences, because only those individuals adopting adaptively fit strategies will have a high probability of becoming strong enough, in energy terms, to reproduce.

The result of reproduction is a single offspring placed randomly in the world. This only child is given the same initial energy level as each member of the population had at the start of the run, and the corresponding amount of energy is deducted from the parent. The parent's genotype is copied over to the offspring, but there is a small probability that a genetic mutation will take place (a 0.05 chance that a bit-flip mutation will occur as each bit is copied). So it is possible that the child will adopt different strategies to its parent.

The values of the various parameters for the synthetic ecology were set (largely as a result of trial and error) as follows: initial supply of food = 1200 particles; initial size of population = 30; initial energy level = 300; energy level at which reproduction takes place = 1000; energy value of 1 particle of food = 45; rate of food replenishment = a maximum of 16 particles per time step; maximum supply of food at any one time = 1200; existence-cost = 1; movement-cost = 1; cost of fighting = 50 units of energy per time step of fight; constant preventing zero probabilities = 1.

5 Experiment 1

As described earlier, the first of our new experiments was designed to investigate what would happen to the communication system, if receivers had available a guaranteed-to-be-reliable source of information about the RHP of potential opponents. Because we had recently carried out certain modifications to our experimental model we began the experiment by running the simulation with sensitivity to RHP suppressed, in order to confirm that the results of such runs were qualitatively identical to the results of our previous experiments in which individuals had no direct sensitivity to RHP [7]. We shall not discuss these preliminary results in detail, but we can report that we observed no qualitative divergence from our earlier results (as summarised in section 3 above).

We then enabled the capacity for animats to be sensitive to RHP, and ran the simulation many times, setting various values for the cost of signalling. To expose the trends in behaviour, we partitioned the total population into four sub-populations on the basis of signalling strategy, four sub-populations on the basis of receiving strategy, and four sub-populations on the basis of RHP sensitivity. The signalling groups were identified by ranges in the evolved value of the individual-specific signalling-constant, C (Group 1: 0-0.5, Group 2: 0.5-1, Group 3: 1-1.5, Group 4: 1.5-2). The receiving groups were identified by ranges in the evolved value of the individual-specific receiving-constant, K (Group 1: 0-0.5, Group 2: 0.5-1, Group 3: 1-1.5, Group 4: 1.5-2). Finally the RHP sensitivity groups were identified by ranges in the evolved value of the individual-specific RHP sensitivity-constant, *P* (Group 1: 0-0.5, Group 2: 0.5-1, Group 3: 1-1.5, Group 4: 1.5-2). The total energy present in each sub-population (a reasonable guide to adaptive success) was then recorded against time. Each sub-population, at any one time, included all individuals adopting a strategy from the appropriate band, including any offspring. To explain the nature of the observed behaviour, we shall describe the results of several, entirely typical, individual runs.

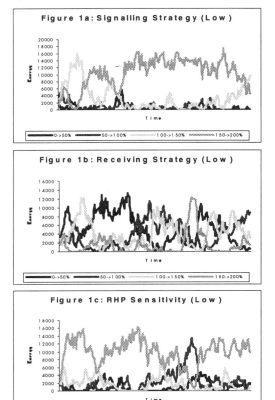

Initially, the cost of signalling was set to be low (0.0001 units of energy deducted per unit of aggressive signal). Figure 1a shows that, under this condition, high exaggeration was the most successful signalling policy (the dominant signalling group for most of the run was group 4). Figure 1b demonstrates that the population adopted various unstable mixes of receiving strategies, with different strategies dominant at different times. Finally, figure 1c shows that the group adopting the highest sensitivity to RHP (group 4) was dominant. Thus, with a low cost of signalling, individuals had evolved to pay attention to the direct, accurate source of information about RHP, rather than to the highly exaggerated aggressive signals. (Since receivers paid little attention to signals, one might wonder why it is that, in this low cost case, signallers maintained the policy of producing exaggerated signals. The answer seems to be that, when the cost of signalling is so low, there is virtually no disadvantage to continuing to

signal, and a signaller producing high-value signals might even experience the odd benefit, due to the fact that mutants giving a high degree of importance to incoming signals are occasionally born into the world.)

The cost of signalling was then increased to 0.1 units of energy deducted per unit of aggressive signal produced. Such high costs introduce a strong selective pressure for individuals to produce low-valued (i.e., suppressed) signals, in order to avoid a crippling level of investment in signalling. Figure 2a shows that, under these conditions,

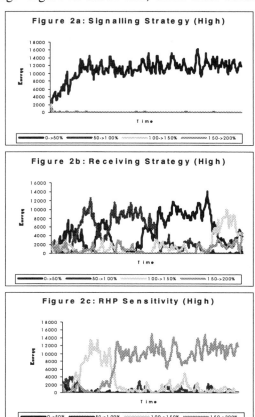

signalling group 1 (the group producing the lowest valued signals) were indeed dominant. For most of the run, the receiving population gave a relatively low degree of importance to these signals (in figure 2b, groups 1 and 2 are, for the most part, dominant). However, sensitivity to RHP was again high (group 4 is dominant).

Taken together, the results of these low and high cost scenarios suggest that if (i) signals are being exaggerated or suppressed, and (ii) there is a source of direct and (therefore) reliable information about RHP, then individuals will evolve to use that information, and the strategy of paying attention to signals will be selected against.

6 Experiment 2

Thus far, the costs in our synthetic ecology had been imposed solely on signalling. In order to relax this restrictive assumption, we proceeded to place a fitness cost on the strategy of finding out about the true RHP of potential opponents. In essence this is a variation on the idea of receiver costs. We assumed (i) that signals are cost-free to receive (although possibly costly to produce), but (ii) that it was possible, although costly, for receivers to find out the true RHP of signallers. In natural ecologies these conditions might be met if, for example, (i) receivers could perceive an aggressive signal whilst maintaining a safe distance from the signaller, but (ii) receivers could find out about the true RHP of that signaller by approaching or probing it in some way, thereby incurring costs by risking attack, predation, or disease. Respecting this line of reasoning, we implemented this new cost in our synthetic ecology by making it the case that the maximum distance at which an individual could perceive signals was twice that at which it could directly perceive RHP. Thus to gain direct access to RHP information, an individual had to bear the cost of an increased risk of attack by a strong opponent.

1b). Instead of an unstable and changing mix of receiving strategies, we observed that a high degree of importance was consistently given to the exaggerated signals (group 4 was dominant for most of the run). Figure 3c shows that sensitivity to RHP had declined considerably in comparison with the situation in the first experiment. Group 4, the group most sensitive to RHP, became the least successful of these groups.

When the cost of signalling was increased, the values of signals, once again, became suppressed in comparison with the low cost signalling case (see the dominance of groups 1 and 2 in figure 4a). Figure 4b shows that a high degree of importance was given to these suppressed signals (group 4 was the dominant receiving strategy). Figure 4c indicates that sensitivity to RHP was, overall, marginally lower than in the scenario described by figures 2a-2c, in which the cost of signalling was high, but access to direct information about RHP did not bear the indirect cost. (Compare the eventual stable dominance of group 4 in figure 2c with the

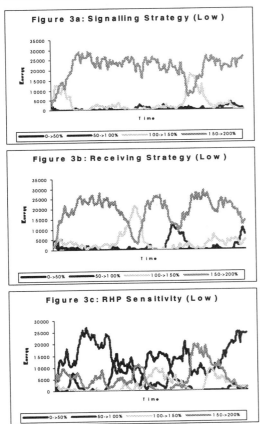

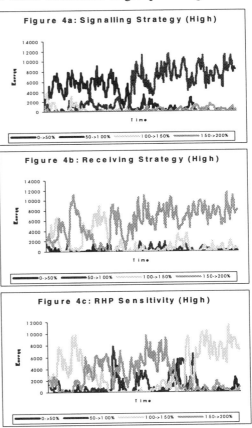

We ran the simulation in the same low and high cost scenarios as used in the previous experiment, recording the energy present in the various signalling, receiving, and RHP-sensitive sub-populations. Figure 3a shows that with the cost of signalling set to be low, the strategy of producing highly exaggerated signals was, once again, the most adaptive (group 4 was dominant). However, the results for the receiving strategies (figure 3b) were in marked contrast to those for the previous experiment (figure

alternating dominance between group 3 and group 4 in figure 4c.)

So, in the synthetic ecology used in our experiments, when it became risky - and hence costly - to access direct information about RHP, the population (in both the low and the high cost signalling scenarios) (i) reverted to the strategy of paying attention to potentially unreliable aggressive signals, and (ii) evolved to be less sensitive to RHP (considerably less sensitive, in the case of low cost signalling, and marginally less sensitive, in the case of high cost signalling). Overall our results suggest that even where a guaranteed-to-be-reliable direct source of information about RHP is available, it is by no means assured that that source of information will be exploited. If there are costs involved in using that source, then it can become adaptive to pay attention to potentially unreliable aggressive signals rather than, or perhaps as well as, that source.

7 Discussion and Conclusions

One might conceivably raise a worry about the interpretation which we have placed on the signalling system. We have used the term 'bluffer' to describe individuals who calculate the values of their signals by either exaggerating or suppressing the values of their energy variables, in the fashion described in section 4. Exaggerated or suppressed signals are, on our chosen interpretation, inaccurate guides to RHP. However, someone might, with some justification, challenge this interpretation, on the grounds that receiver strategies have to be taken into account when judging the reliability or otherwise of such signals. For example, a stable situation in which signallers had evolved to give exaggerated signals, but receivers had evolved give a low weighting to those signals would, on our chosen interpretation, count as an example of an unreliable signalling system. However, one could argue that that scenario ought to count as not merely stable, but reliable. Because the system is stable, it seems that receivers must be consistently and adaptively using signals as guides to behaviour. We are, in some ways, sympathetic to this line of reasoning, and it is worth commenting briefly on the implications of adopting such an interpretation. It seems that on any useful interpretation, reliability must presuppose stability. In our first experiment there is no doubt that, in both the signalling scenarios, the signalling system is relatively unstable when compared with sensitivity to RHP (compare, in particular, figure 1b with figure 1c, and figure 2b with figure 2c). Similarly, in the second experiment, there is no doubt that, in both the signalling scenarios, sensitivity to RHP is relatively unstable when compared with the signalling system (compare, in particular figure 3b with figure 3c, and figure 4b with figure 4c). Thus in our view, if one concentrates on the fundamental message of this paper, then adopting the alternative interpretation would not undermine our results. It seems also that it would be a relatively straightforward modification to adjust the way in which signal-values are calculated, in order to deflect any worries of the sort aired. We intend to investigate the effect of just such a modification in our future work.

There are two related ways in which the results reported here might be of theoretical interest: First, they lend support to a particular view in biology, by showing that that view has theoretical purchase in ecological contexts which are not easily studied using the formal machinery of mathematical modelling. To decide whether or not one ought to expect an observed biological aggressive communication system to be reliable, one should endeavour to identify how the various costs in the ecological context in question are distributed amongst the various strategies available to individuals. If costs are not borne by signallers alone, then stable unreliability may be not merely possible, but likely. It seems that this principle will apply not only to aggressive communication systems, but also to mate-signalling systems, and to other signalling systems as well. Second, we have pursued further the investigative strategy of using A-Life-style synthetic ecologies to relax certain restrictive assumptions made in formal mathematical models. Our results suggest that this investigative strategy is a potentially fruitful one.

Acknowledgements

Peter de Bourcier is an employee of CyberLife Technology Ltd. Michael Wheeler is supported by a Junior Research Fellowship at Christ Church, Oxford, with additional assistance from the McDonnell-Pew Centre for Cognitive Neuroscience, Oxford. Many thanks to Seth Bullock for invaluable discussions, and to two anonymous referees for helpful comments.

References

[1] J. Archer. *The Behavioural Biology of Aggression*. Cambridge University Press, Cambridge, 1988.

[2] R. Brooks and P. Maes, editors. *Artificial Life IV: Proceedings of the Fourth International Workshop on the Synthesis and Simulation of Living Systems*, Cambridge, Mass. and London, England, 1994. MIT Press / Bradford Books.

[3] S. Bullock. An exploration of signalling behaviour by both analytic and simulation means for both discrete and continuous models. This Volume. 1997.

[4] D. Cliff, P. Husbands, J.-A. Meyer, and S.W. Wilson, editors. *From Animals to Animats 3: Proceedings of the Third International Conference on Simulation of Adaptive Behavior*, Cambridge, Mass., 1994. MIT Press / Bradford Books.

[5] T.H. Clutton-Brock and S.D. Albon. The roaring of red deer and the evolution of honest advertisement. *Behaviour*, 69:145-170, 1979.

[6] P. de Bourcier and M. Wheeler. Signalling and territorial aggression: An investigation by means of synthetic behavioural ecology. In [4], 463-72, 1994.

[7] P. de Bourcier and M. Wheeler. Aggressive signaling meets adaptive receiving: further experiments in synthetic behavioural ecology. In [23], 760-71, 1995.

[8] M. Enquist. Communication during aggressive interactions with particular reference to variation in choice of behaviour. *Animal Behaviour*, 33:1152-1161, 1985.

[9] M. Enquist and O. Leimar. The evolution of fatal fighting. *Animal Behaviour*, 39:1-9, 1990.

[10] A. Grafen. Biological signals as handicaps. *Journal of Theoretical Biology*, 144:517-546, 1990.

[11] A. Grafen and R.A. Johnstone. Why we need ESS signalling theory. *Philosophical Transactions of the Royal Society: Biological Sciences*, 340:245-250, 1993.

[12] D.G.C. Harper. Communication. In J. R. Krebs and N. B. Davies, editors, *Behavioural Ecology - An Evolutionary Approach*, chapter 12, pages 374-397. Blackwell Scientific, Oxford, 3rd edition, 1991.

[13] P.L. Hurd. Communication in discrete action-response games. *Journal of Theoretical Biology*, 174:217-22, 1995.

[14] J. R. Krebs and N. B. Davies. *An Introduction to Behavioural Ecology*. Blackwell Scientific, Oxford, 2nd edition, 1987.

[15] K. Lorenz. *On Aggression*. Methuen, London, 1966.

[16] B. MacLennan and G. Burghardt. Synthetic ethology and the evolution of cooperative communication. *Adaptive Behavior*, 2(2):161-188, 1994.

[17] J. Maynard Smith. Do animals convey information about their intentions? *Journal of Theoretical Biology*, 97:1-5, 1982.

[18] J. Maynard Smith. *Evolution and the Theory of Games*. Cambridge University Press, Cambridge, 1982.

[19] J. Maynard Smith and G.A. Parker. The logic of asymmetric contests. *Animal Behaviour*, 24:159-175, 1976.

[20] P.K. McGregor. Signalling in territorial systems: a context for individual identification, ranging and eavesdropping. *Philosophical Transactions of the Royal Society: Biological Sciences*, 340:237-244, 1993.

[21] J.-A. Meyer and S.W. Wilson, editors. *From Animals to Animats: Proceedings of the First International Conference on Simulation of Adaptive Behavior*, Cambridge, Mass., 1991. MIT Press / Bradford Books.

[22] G.F. Miller. *Artificial life as theoretical biology: how to do real science with computer simulation*. Cognitive Science Research Paper 378, University of Sussex, 1995.

[23] F. Moran, A. Moreno, J.J. Merelo, and P. Chacon, editors. *Advances in Artificial Life: Proceedings of the Third European Conference on Artificial Life*, Berlin and Heidelberg, 1995. Springer-Verlag.

[24] C. A. Munn. Birds that 'cry wolf'. *Nature*, 319:143-5, 1986.

[25] G. A. Parker and J. Maynard Smith. Optimality theory in evolutionary biology. *Nature*, 348:27-33, 1990.

[26] G.A. Parker. Assessment strategy and the evolution of fighting behaviour. *Journal of Theoretical Biology*, 47:223-243, 1974.

[27] J. H. Poole. Announcing intent: Aggressive state of musth in African elephants. *Animal Behaviour*, 37:140-52, 1988.

[28] J. Maynard Smith. Mini review: Sexual selection, handicaps, and true fitness. *Journal of Theoretical Biology*, 115:1-8, 1985.

[29] M. Stamp Dawkins. Are there general principles of signal design? *Philosophical Transactions of the Royal Society: Biological Sciences*, 340:251-255, 1993.

[30] M. Stamp Dawkins and T. Guilford. The corruption of honest signalling. *Animal Behaviour*, 41(5):865-73, 1991.

[31] I.J.A. te Boekhorst and P. Hogeweg. Effects of tree size on travelband formation in orang-utans: Data analysis suggested by a model study. In [2], 119-29, 1994.

[32] F. Toates and P. Jensen. Ethological and psychological models of motivation - towards a synthesis. In [21], 194-203, 1991.

[33] C. Wemmer, L. R. Collins, B. B. Beck, and B. Rettberg. The ethogram. In B. B. Beck and C. Wemmer, editors, *The Biology and Management of an Extinct Species: Pere David's Deer*, pages 91-121. Noyes, New Jersey, 1983.

[34] M. Wheeler and P. de Bourcier. How not to murder your neighbor: using synthetic behavioral ecology to study aggressive signaling. *Adaptive Behavior*, 3:3:273-309, 1995.

[35] A. Zahavi. Mate selection - a selection for a handicap. *Journal of Theoretical Biology*, 53:205-214, 1975.

An exploration of signalling behaviour by both analytic and simulation means for both discrete and continuous models

Seth Bullock
Evolutionary and Adaptive Systems
School of Cognitive and Computing Sciences
University of Sussex, Brighton BN1 9QH
sethb@cogs.susx.ac.uk

Abstract

Hurd's (1995) model of a discrete action-response game, in which the interests of signallers and receivers conflict, is extended to address games in which, as well as signal cost varying with signaller quality, the value of an observer's response to a signal is also dependent on signaller quality. It is shown analytically that non-handicap signalling equilibria exist for such a model.

Using a distributed Genetic Algorithm (GA) to simulate the evolution of the model over time, the model's sensitivity to initial conditions is explored, and an investigation into the attainability of the analytically derived Evolutionarily Stable Strategies (ESSs) is undertaken. It is discovered that the system is capable of attaining signalling equilibria in addition to those derived via analytic techniques, and that these additional equilibria are consistent with the definition of conventional signalling.

Grafen's (1990) proof of Zahavi's handicap principle is generalised in an analogous manner, and it is demonstrated analytically that non-handicap signalling equilibria also exist for this continuous model of honest signalling.

1 Introduction

In the wake of the fall of group selectionist thought during the mid-sixties, theoretical biologists were left with many problems which had previously been comfortably dealt with through some appeal to the worth of behaviours at a group level. The existence of stable signalling systems was one such problem. Although it was feared that the selfish actions of individuals might compromise the stability of natural signalling systems, such systems appeared to be the frequent products of evolution. In the mid-seventies Zahavi (1975, 1977) proposed that the stability of such signalling systems may be maintained by a 'handicap principle' i.e., that the differential costs paid by signallers of differing quality ensure that honest advertisement is an Evolutionarily Stable Strategy (ESS). The reasoning runs something like this...

"If signallers differ in some variable of interest to an observer (let's call it quality), observers will be selected to take advantage of any honest indicator of this quality. A signal made as an advertisement of quality will necessarily incur some cost. If, for any signal, high quality signallers suffer less production costs than low quality signallers, then signallers are able to demonstrate their true quality through advertising more strongly than their poorer competitors. Once this strategy is adopted by the signalling population, the signal is an honest indicator of underlying quality. It cannot be invaded by cheats because to signal more strongly than your quality dictates results in a production cost which is not compensated for by the observer response."

However, a parallel argument runs something like this...

"If signallers differ in some variable of interest to an observer (let's call it need), observers will be selected to take advantage of any honest indicator of this need. A positive response made to an advertisement of need will necessarily induce some benefit. If, for any observer response, high need signallers gain more benefit than low need signallers, then signallers are able to demonstrate their true need through advertising more strongly than their less needy competitors. Once this strategy is adopted by the signalling population, the signal is an honest indicator of underlying need. It cannot be invaded by cheats because to signal more strongly than your need dictates can only result in a response which is not worth enough to compensate the increased production cost."

Notice that whilst the former argument (e.g., Enquist, 1985; Grafen, 1990; Hurd, 1995) assumes differential costs (i.e., that signaller quality might, to some extent, affect the cost of signal production), the latter does not, and that whilst the latter argument (e.g., Godfray, 1991) assumes differential benefits (i.e., that signaller quality might, to some extent, affect the worth of an observer's response), the former does not.

The former argument might be used to support claims that stotting gazelles are honestly informing predators of their ability to outrun a potential pursuer (e.g., Grafen, 1990). Similarly, the latter argument might be used to support claims that begging nestlings are honestly informing their parents of their need for food items.

Godfray (1991) has provided just such an argument for offspring begging calls. He demonstrates that honest signals of offspring need may be ensured by the facts that (i) signals are costly (he assumes that signal costs are constant across offspring irrespective of their need), and that (ii) the worth of parental resources increases with offspring need (i.e., differential benefits but no differential costs). In Godfray's model, parents are selected for responding positively to offspring with high need.

Grafen (1990) considers a similar situation, but with differing assumptions. He suggests that honest signals of offspring quality might be ensured by the facts that (i) parental resources are valuable (he assumes that either resource value is constant across offspring irrespective of their quality, or that resource value increases with offspring quality), and that (ii) the cost of signalling decreases with offspring quality (i.e., differential costs and constrained differential benefits). In Grafen's model, parents are selected for responding positively to offspring with high quality.

In the following sections a simple discrete game, originally due to Hurd (1995), is extended to explore the effects upon signalling equilibria of including, within a signalling model, the impact of both differential costs and differential benefits upon signaller fitness. Section 2 will detail the basic game and the simple extension to it. Section 3 will describe an implementation of the model as an iterative genetic algorithm simulation. Section 4 will consider Grafen's (1990) model, and the relation between its results and those of Hurd's (1995) model. It will be concluded that ensuring Zahavi's two handicap conditions is neither necessary nor sufficient for the existence of an honest communication ESS.

2 A Discrete Signalling Game

Hurd (1995) described a game in which a Signaller (S) is privy to some secret (either High or Low) which is of interest to an Observer (O). S makes a signal (East or West) to O. O, in return, makes a response (Up or Down) of interest to S. The game is schematised in Figure 1.

A signalling strategy determines which signal to make

in each of the two states. There are exactly four such strategies. Similarly a response strategy determines which response to give to each signal. There are four such response strategies (see Table 1). Under Enquist's (1985) definition of communication, only four of the 16 possible signal-strategy/response-strategy pairs constitute communication, as only these four prescribe different signals in response to different Signaller states, and different Observer responses to these different signals. This is represented schematically in Table 2.

The fitness consequences of moves in this discrete action-response game will follow those defined by Hurd (1995). In addition, and in contrast, to Hurd's model, we will assume that the value, to a Signaller, of an Observer's response to a signal is *not* independent of the Signaller's initial state.

Signaller fitness, w_S, is calculated as the cost of signalling subtracted from the benefit derived from the Observer response. The former term is defined as a function, c, of the Signaller's initial state, I (either High or Low), and the signalling action, A (either East or West), whilst the latter is defined as a function, v, of the Signaller's initial state, and the Observer's response, R (either Up or Down),

$$w_S = v(I, R) - c(I, A).$$

Similarly, Observer fitness, w_O, is calculated as a function, f, of the state of the Signaller, and the Observer response,

$$w_O = f(I, R).$$

The fitness consequences of each of the eight possible signalling scenarios are depicted in Figure 1.

Hurd defined the payoffs in order that the interests of S and O conflicted. Observers benefit from responding Up to High-state Signallers, and Down to Low-state Signallers,

$$w_O(H, U) > w_O(H, D),$$

$$w_O(L, U) < w_O(L, D),$$

whilst Signallers benefit from eliciting an Up, rather than a Down, response from Observers,

$$v(H, U) > v(H, D),$$

$$v(L, U) > v(L, D).$$

After Hurd, we define the relative value of an Up response for each class of Signaller as

$$V_H = v(H, U) - v(H, D) > 0,$$

$$V_L = v(L, U) - v(L, D) > 0.$$

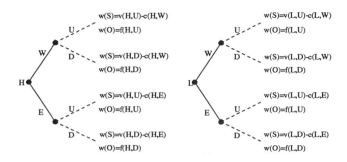

Figure 1: Decision trees and fitness consequences for a discrete action-response game. Initially, a Signaller (S) finds itself in one of two possible states (H or L) depicted by the two leftmost nodes of the decision trees. S makes one of two possible signals (E or W) depicted by a labelled solid line. Subsequently an Observer (O), naive as to the state of S, but informed by S's signal, makes one of two possible responses (U or D) depicted by a labelled dashed line. The fitness consequences of each of the eight possible interactions are depicted at the terminal node of each branch of the two decision trees. See text for further clarification.

Signalling Strategies and Response Strategies				
Bit Pattern	Signalling Strategy		Response Strategy	
(0,0)	S(East,East)	Cynic	O(Down,Down)	Mean
(0,1)	S(East,West)	Honest	O(Down,Up)	Believer
(1,0)	S(West,East)	Liar	O(Up,Down)	Non-Believer
(1,1)	S(West,West)	Bluffer	O(Up,Up)	Generous

Table 1: Each of the four possible Signalling Strategies, depicted in the form S(what to do if state is Low, what to do if state is High), and four possible Response Strategies, depicted as O(what to do if S plays East, what to do if S plays West), with their associated bit-pattern and descriptive. See Section 3 for the rationale underlying the allocation of descriptive terms to strategies.

Signalling Strategy-Response Strategy Pairs				
	Response Strategy			
Signalling Strategy	O(Up,Up)	O(Up,Down)	O(Down,Up)	O(Down,Down)
S(East,East)	.	.	.	.
S(East,West)	.	x	x	. .
S(West,East)	.	x	x	.
S(West,West)	.	.	.	.

Table 2: Each of the four possible Signalling Strategies and Response Strategies are shown. The four Signalling-Strategy/Response-Strategy pairs which constitute communication (*sensu* Enquist, 1985) are denoted 'x' whilst non-communicative pairings are denoted with a period.

Similarly, we define the relative cost of signalling West for both classes of Signaller,

$$C_H = c(H, W) - c(H, E),$$

$$C_L = c(L, W) - c(L, E).$$

In order that S(E,W) be the unique, best response to O(D,U) (the communication Signalling-Strategy/Response-Strategy pair arbitrarily chosen by Hurd as a candidate ESS), it must be the case that,

$$v(H, U) - c(H, W) > v(H, D) - c(H, E),$$

$$v(L, D) - c(L, E) > v(L, U) - c(L, W).$$

By substitution, it follows that,

$$V_H > C_H,$$

$$V_L < C_L.$$

It is plain that Hurd's result, $C_L > V > C_H$, is the special case inequality resulting from the substitution of $V = V_H = V_L$, i.e., the assumption that "V is equal for all signallers"(Hurd, 1995, p.219). Hurd depicts his special case graphically (see Figure 2a). He points out that signalling equilibria exist in part of the region of the graph defined by $C_H \leq 0$, which he interprets as indicating that 'handicap' signals need not be costly for High-state Signallers at equilibria, and indeed may be chosen preferentially by High-state Signallers. He also points out that despite the fact that all signalling equilibria satisfy the inequality $C_L > C_H$, signalling equilibria do not exist in certain areas of the graph satisfying this inequality, i.e., that $C_L > C_H$ is necessary but not sufficient for communication to be stable.

However, under conditions, modelled here, in which $V_L \neq V_H$, it can be shown that Zahavi's handicap principle is neither necessary nor sufficient for the existence of signalling equilibria (see Figure 2b and c). When the value of a beneficial response is greater for Low-state Signallers than High-state Signallers (i.e., $V_L > V_H$, see Figure 2b) signalling equilibria lie above the line $C_L = C_H$, but when the value of a beneficial response is higher for High-state Signallers (i.e., $V_L < V_H$, see Figure 2c) signalling equilibria may lie below the line defined by this inequality.

3 An Iterative Simulation of a Discrete Signalling Game

Simulations are sometimes presented as 'artificial worlds' worthy of investigation for their own sake; "Communication evolved within this world", "Different classes of parasite evolved within this world", "Mean fitness increased within this population when tools were introduced". However, this practice is theoretically bankrupt, and thus such statements have no scientific currency.

The 'creator' of artificial worlds is confused if she feels that she mimics the naturalist in simply observing her subject matter under various conditions. True naturalism takes place within an overarching theoretical framework, marshalling observations in order to support, or challenge, current biological theory. In contrast, the observations made of an artificial world constructed within no such framework can neither challenge, nor support, any theory with application wider than the artificial world itself. Such observations can serve no theoretician whose interests reach further than a full understanding of a specific artificial world. The extent to which the facts revealed by such observations constitute new knowledge is simply the extent to which the creator of an artificial world initially failed to understand it.

In baldly comparing and contrasting an artificial world with the real thing, the creators of such artificial worlds are attempting to both have their cake and eat it. However, there is no cake to be had in any appeal to 'interesting' similarities between the artificial world and the natural world, nor is there any cake to be eaten in drawing attention to 'interesting' contrasts between them. Unless such parallels were previously hypothesised to exist, they are either merely accidental (and thus not interesting), or merely purposed (and thus not interesting).

Within experimental scientific paradigms, no project is validly undertaken without an explicit hypothesis in mind; an explicit hypothesis requiring a theoretical framework, a reasonably rigorous vocabulary, etc., etc. Under such a paradigm, theory precedes experiment, informing and validating experimental design. The simulation becomes a means of testing hypotheses, of exploring the consequences of theories, of revealing the implications of a scientific position. The gathering of observations ceases to be an aimless whim, becoming a process with a goal wider than merely understanding a specific simulation. For an experimental scientist, the collection of observations is not valuable in and of itself, as certain simulation designers would seem to have us believe, but is only valuable with respect to hypotheses within a theoretical framework. It is in this light that the simulation presented within this section is intended to be viewed.

Whilst the analysis presented in the previous section reveals which areas of the parameter space admit of honest evolutionarily stable strategies (ESSs), it makes no claims concerning admissible trajectories in the state space occupied by a population of signallers and receivers playing a particular version of this discrete action-response game. In addition, the analysis above makes no attempt to describe the behaviour of systems which fail to attain an honest signalling ESS. Simulation-based paradigms seem perfectly placed to step into this breach, and indeed seem ill-prepared for any other scientific enterprise (de Bourcier & Wheeler, 1994; Miller, 1995; Noble, 1997).

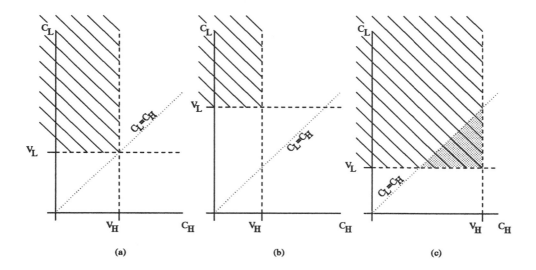

Figure 2: In each graph a pair of cost parameters (C_H, C_L) specifies a point in the plane of all possible versions of the discrete action-response game for a particular pair of value parameters (V_H, V_L) which divide the space into four quadrants. Graphs depict *(a)* Hurd's (1995) result in which $V_H = V_L$, *(b)* a scenario in which $V_H < V_L$, and *(c)* a scenario in which $V_H > V_L$. In each graph the diagonal hatching corresponds to (C_H, C_L) parameter values which afford stable communication equilibria, the line $C_L = C_H$ divides the space into two areas, the upper of which is predicted, under Zahavi's model, to contain handicap equilibria, whilst the lower is predicted to offer no communication equilibria. The shaded area in *(c)* highlights non-handicap parameter values in which (*contra* Zahavi) stable signalling may occur.

Therefore, in order to discover empirically whether signalling equilibria are attainable by a population initially behaving 'randomly', and to explore the behaviour of the system prior to (potentially) achieving an honest signalling ESS, an iterative simulation approach was undertaken[1].

A population of signallers/receivers was distributed across a 25-by-25 grid world. Each cell in the grid contained one signaller and one receiver. Each signaller was allocated a discrete internal state (either High or Low) at random[2]. In addition, each signaller inherited one of the four possible signalling strategies (represented as a two-bit binary number) from its parent. Similarly each

receiver inherited one of the four possible response strategies (again represented as a two-bit binary number) from its parent (see Table 1). The fitnesses of signallers and receivers were calculated as shown in Figure 1, each signaller interacting once with the receiver sharing its cell.

Once each signaller and receiver had been assessed the whole population was updated synchronously. The location of a parent was chosen using a normal probability distribution with standard deviation 0.75 centred on the location of the offspring's cell. Six potential parents were chosen for each offspring signaller. An offspring signaller inherited its signalling strategy from the fittest of these six. Similarly, an offspring receiver inherited its response strategy from the fittest of six receivers chosen from the previous generation in the same manner. A mutation rate of one bit in one hundred ensured that offspring sometimes inherited a strategy which differed from that of their parents. Populations were simulated for 500 generations in this manner, during which time the proportions of signallers playing each of the four possible signalling strategies, and the proportions of receivers playing each of the four possible response strategies, were recorded.

In order to fully specify a simulation run, several parameter values must be decided upon. The costs of signalling each of the two possible signals (East or West) must be specified for each of the two possible signaller

---

[1]Copies of the code, and a version of this paper with colour figures, are available from the W[3] URL:
`http://www.cogs.susx.ac.uk/users/sethb/eca197.html`

[2]i.e., the internal trait was non-heritable. This is in accordance with many models of signalling evolution (e.g., Hurd, 1995; Grafen, 1990). Models in which the advertised trait, in addition to the advertising strategy, is itself heritable encounter a problem known within evolutionary theory as the lek paradox. A full account of this problem is beyond the scope of this paper (interested readers are directed to Kirkpatrick & Ryan, 1991; Pomiankowski & Møller, 1995). Briefly, in simple models of signal evolution involving a heritable advertised trait, the variability of the trait across the population tends to decrease over evolutionary time. As the variation in the trait falls observers find any signal which distinguishes between signallers with differing traits less and less informative. As a consequence signalling (which involves some cost to the signaller and, possibly, the observer) tends to die out.

states (High or Low). Similarly, the benefit of obtaining each of the two possible responses (Up or Down) must be specified for each of the two possible signaller states. Finally the value to the receiver of making each of the two possible responses must be specified for each of the two possible signaller states.

The fitness consequences of receiver responses *for the receiver* were fixed at 40 for responding Up to a High-state signaller, or Down to a Low-state signaller, and zero otherwise.

The cost of signalling East for both Low-state signallers and High-state signallers was fixed at zero. All 576 possible pairs drawn from the set {10.0, 12.5, 15.0, ..., 70.0} were explored as costs of signalling West for High-state signallers, and signalling West for Low-state signallers.

The value *to a signaller* of a Down response was fixed at zero for both High- and Low-state signallers. The value *to a signaller* of a receiver response Up was drawn from the set {(40,40), (50,30), (30,50)} where the figures in parentheses denote (value to Low-state signaller, value to High-state signaller). These three pairs can be represented by Figures 2a, 2b, and 2c respectively.

These parameter values allow the exploration of cost parameters lying in each of the four quadrants for each of the three classes of scenario depicted in Figure 2.

The rationale underlying the choice of labels used throughout the results section to describe the possible strategies (see Table 1) reflects the costs and benefits descried above. Signalling East is a costless action and is thus the default signalling behaviour, whereas signalling West is costly and will be regarded as a positive action in comparison. Thus a signaller which always signals West will be dubbed a 'Bluffer', and one which signals West only when High state will be described as 'Honest' in that a positive signal is being used to advertise a positive (High) trait. Similarly, as obtaining a Down response is not beneficial to signallers, receivers which always respond Down will be termed 'Mean' in comparison to 'Generous' strategists which always respond Up.

The initial conditions imposed upon the populations were also varied. Populations initially with random behaviour (strategies drawn at random from the strategy set), were compared to populations initially converged at an Honest signalling strategy and Believing response strategy, and populations initially converged at a Cynical signalling strategy and Mean response strategy. These three classes of initial conditions will hence forward be referred to as 'Random', 'Honest', and 'Cynical' initial conditions, respectively.

3.1 Results

For each setting of the value parameters, a pair of cost parameters was taken to specify a system lying within one of four quadrants defined by the two inequalities

$$V_H > C_H,$$

$$V_L < C_L.$$

From the analysis carried out in Section 2, systems residing in the top-left quadrant of parameter space (hereafter Quadrant 1) satisfy the conditions for the existence of an honest signalling ESS. Systems residing in the top-right quadrant (hereafter Quadrant 2) cannot support honest communication as the costs of signalling are too great for both High- and Low-state signallers. Systems residing in the bottom-left quadrant (hereafter Quadrant 3) cannot support honest communication as the costs of signalling are bearable for signallers of Low state allowing them to mimic High-state signallers. Systems residing in the bottom-right quadrant (hereafter Quadrant 4) cannot support honest signalling as High-state signallers cannot afford to signal, whilst Low-state signallers can.

Five classes of behaviour were exhibited by the system. Stereotypical examples of trajectories through strategy space for four of these classes are presented in Figure 3, whilst their distribution across parameter space is represented by Figure 4. Trajectory (*a*): *Honesty* is produced only by systems with Quadrant 1 parameters; populations converge on Honesty and Belief. This class of behaviour corresponds to the honest signalling ESS predicted in Section 2. Although this ESS existed for all games within Quadrant 1 (i.e. from Honest initial conditions, no simulation ever deviated from Honesty), simulations from Random initial conditions, with parameters for which the inequality $V_H > V_L$ held, often failed to reach it.

Trajectory (*b*): *Conventional Cheating* is found only for games in which $V_H > V_L$. For such games, this class of trajectory accounts for all behaviour within Quadrants 2, and 4, some of the behaviour within Quadrant 3, and (for simulations from Random initial conditions) some of the behaviour within Quadrant 1; signalling populations converge on Cynic with a fluctuating proportion of Liars, whilst receiver populations converge on Non-Believers with a fluctuating proportion of Generous strategists. This class of behaviour is a non-signalling scenario suffering a low level of Liars which exploit Generous strategists (by signalling West when Low state). As the frequency of Lying rises the fitness of Generous strategists falls and they are replaced by Non-Believers, but as the frequency of Liars falls the fitness of Generous strategists rises and they replace Non-Believers. This pair of processes ensures that the populations never settle, and continually cycle due to the intransitive dominance hierarchy instantiated by the signalling and receiving strategies. I term this class of behaviour *conventional* due to the fact that the behaviour is maintained by negative feedback interactions typical of conventional signalling scenarios.

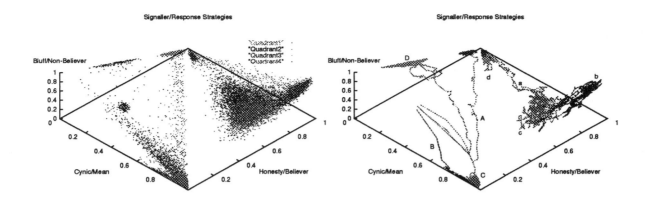

Figure 3: *Left plot:* Population evolution from Random initial conditions. The left and right sides of the plot contain four data sets. The left-side data set pertains to 20 populations of signallers, whilst the right-side data set pertains to 20 populations of receivers. Each data set represents points on state-space trajectories followed by evolving populations under parameters which fall into one of the four possible parameter quadrants. The co-ordinates of each point represent the proportion of signallers/receivers using each of the strategies denoted by the axis labels at instants sampled every 10 generations over 500 generations of evolution. The remaining fourth strategy is implicit in the graph (decreasing with distance from origin) as each strategy space has only three degrees of freedom, i.e., each population state-space is wedge shaped rather than cubic. Thus the density of points indicates the amount of evolutionary time populations spend in an area of strategy space. *Right plot:* Stereotypical trajectories through strategy-space for four of the five classes of system behaviour. Populations were evolved from Random initial conditions. Associated pairs of signaller and receiver trajectories are denoted by the same letter (upper case denotes signaller trajectories, lower case denotes receiver trajectories).

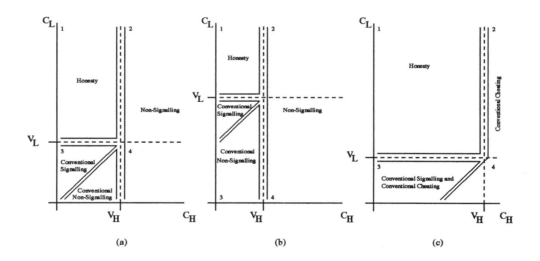

Figure 4: Graphs as per Figure 2 showing the classes of behaviour observed across the parameter space of the extended discrete action-response model. Honest behaviour is confined to the predicted quadrant of parameter space for all three graphs (although from Random initial conditions Conventional Cheating trajectories were observed within Quadrant 1 for simulations in which $V_H > V_L$). Non-Signalling trajectories account for the behaviour within Quadrants 2 and 4 (although Conventional Cheating trajectories are observed within Quadrants 2 and 4 for simulations in which $V_H > V_L$). Within Quadrant 3 two regions were observed separated by the line $V_L - C_L = V_H - C_H$. Conventional Signalling trajectories accounted for the region above this line, whilst Conventional Non-Signalling accounted for the region below it (although, for simulations in which $V_H > V_L$, Conventional Cheating trajectories were observed across the whole of Quadrant 3, whilst no Conventional Non-Signalling was observed).

Trajectory (*c*): *Non-Signalling* is found in Quadrants 2 and 4 for parameter values satisfying the inequality $V_H \leq V_L$; signalling populations converge on Cynic, whilst receiver populations wander in the centre of strategy space. Within this class of behaviour any strategy adopted by the receiver population can be exploited by the Low-state signallers, thus no clear response strategy emerges, and signallers cut their losses by refusing to signal.

Trajectory (*d*): *Conventional Signalling* is found only for parameter values lying within Quadrant 3, and satisfying the inequality $V_H - C_H > V_L - C_L$; signalling populations converge on a fluctuating mixture of Honesty and Bluffing, whilst receiver populations converge on Belief but maintain a significant, but very low (and fluctuating) frequency of both Mean and Generous strategists. This class of behaviour is a conventional signalling scenario suffering a degree of Bluffing strategists who exploit Believing receivers. In a manner similar to (*b*) above, the stability of this scenario is maintained through weak negative feedback interactions which induce cyclic trajectories typical of conventional signalling scenarios.

The fifth class of behaviour: *Conventional Non-Signalling* is also found only in Quadrant 3, under parameter values satisfying the inequalities $V_H - C_H < V_L - C_L$, and $V_H \leq V_L$; signalling populations converge on Cynic with regular insurgences of Bluffing strategists whilst receiver populations wander in the centre of strategy space with a slight over-representation of Believers. The invading Bluff strategy exploits the over-representation of Believing receivers, but is prevented from dominating the signaller population by negative feedback from the receiver population.

To summarise, several interesting, robust phenomena, which were opaque to the analysis carried out in Section 2 have been detailed. The behaviour of this very simple system varies from non-signalling equilibria, through scenarios in which stability is maintained through reciprocal fitness interactions which constitute the negative feedback indicative of conventional signalling(Maynard Smith & Harper, 1988, 1995), to honest signalling equilibria in which honesty is maintained though the interaction of differential costs and benefits. Further exploration of the system's behaviour will be necessary before the factors governing which mode of behaviour will evolve in a particular case are made explicit.

However, the discrete nature of the action-response game considered here, although attractively tractable, also risks lacking application to natural signalling through its very simplicity. Do the classes of behaviour exhibited in a discrete game such as the one considered above exist for more complex models? As a first step towards answering this question, an analysis of Grafen's (1990) model is undertaken in an effort to demonstrate that at least the results derived analytically in Section 2 will generalise to a continuous model.

4 A Continuous Signalling Model

Alan Grafen's (1990) model of Zahavi's handicap principle upheld Zahavi's contentions that in order for communication to be stable certain relationships between signal cost and signaller quality had to hold. Specifically, the criteria which Zahavi (1975, 1977) specifies are that (i) signals must be costly, and that (ii) for any given level of advertisement, signallers of low quality must suffer higher production costs than signallers of higher quality.

After defining signaller (male) fitness (*w*) as a function of three variables, the signaller's level of advertisement (*a*), the strength of observer (female) preference for advertising (*p*), and signaller quality (*q*), Grafen asserted that Zahavi's criteria could be formalised as conditions placed on various partial derivatives of the fitness function. First order derivatives were represented as *w* subscripted with a digit denoting the variable (*a*, *p*, or *q*) with respect to which the rate of change of fitness was being derived. Second order derivatives were similarly denoted by *w* subscripted with a pair of digits.

For example, the condition that signals must be costly (i.e., that, as advertising levels increase, fitness decreases) is maintained by the inequality, $w_1 < 0$,

$$\frac{\partial w}{\partial a} < 0.$$

That female preference is beneficial is similarly maintained by the inequality, $w_2 > 0$,

$$\frac{\partial w}{\partial p} > 0.$$

A further condition ensured that "better males do better by advertising more"(Grafen, 1990, p.520),

$$\frac{\partial w/\partial a}{\partial w/\partial p} \text{ is strictly increasing in q.} \qquad (1)$$

Grafen demonstrated that if the beneficial fitness consequence of female preference was independent of signaller quality ($w_{23} = 0$, which Hurd's (1995) model also assumes), or if the beneficial fitness consequences of the strength of female preference were greater for signallers of higher quality ($w_{23} > 0$), then that equation (1) holds can be ensured by the maintenance of the following inequality: $w_{13} > 0$ (i.e., that higher quality signallers pay lower advertising costs – Zahavi's second handicap criterion). Grafen proceeds to show that communication equilibria exist under these conditions.

Grafen then attempts to reverse this proof in order to show that *any* stable communication equilibria require that Zahavi's criteria hold, and thus that handicap equilibria are not merely "quirky possibilities"(Grafen, 1990, p.521).

4.1 General Solution

Condition (1) can be presented as

$$\frac{\partial(\frac{w_1}{w_2})}{\partial q} > 0$$

which, after application of the quotient rule, can be re-written as

$$\frac{w_{13}w_2 - w_1 w_{23}}{(w_2)^2} > 0.$$

The denominator is necessarily positive, and by assumption, w_1 is negative, whilst w_2 is positive. Thus, discarding the denominator, and dividing through by w_2 casts the general solution to equation (1) as

$$w_{13} + w_{23} * |\frac{w_1}{w_2}| > 0. \tag{2}$$

We will now explore the form that this inequality takes under each of the three classes of condition governing the manner in which the beneficial effects of signalling for the signaller are moderated by the signaller's quality; an analysis analogous to that carried out in Section 2 for the extension of Hurd's (1995) model.

First, under the condition in which the beneficial fitness consequence of female preference is independent of signaller quality (i.e., $w_{23} = 0$, analogous to Hurd's $V = V_H = V_L$), equation (2) reduces to $w_{13} > 0$. This is Grafen's result (i.e., Zahavi's second handicap criterion).

Under the condition in which the beneficial fitness consequences of female preference are higher for poorer quality signallers (i.e. $w_{23} < 0$), equation (2) reduces to,

$$w_{13} > |w_{23}| * |\frac{w_1}{w_2}|.$$

It is plain that, whilst this inequality *requires* that $w_{13} > 0$, it remains the case that the satisfaction of $w_{13} > 0$ is not *sufficient* for signalling to be stable. Lower quality signallers must not merely suffer higher advertising costs than their higher quality competitors, but must suffer advertising costs that are higher *by some amount large enough to balance any fitness benefits accrued through signalling.*

Conversely, under the condition explored by Grafen, in which the beneficial fitness consequences of female preference are higher for higher quality signallers (i.e., $w_{23} > 0$), equation (2) reduces to,

$$w_{13} > -w_{23} * |\frac{w_1}{w_2}|.$$

It is equally plain that whilst, as Grafen maintains, ensuring that $w_{13} > 0$ is *sufficient* to ensure a solution to this inequality, it is not *necessary*. This inequality admits of solutions in which $w_{13} < 0$, i.e. non-handicap equilibria exist.

4.2 Discussion

The partial differential equation denoted by w_{23} can be interpreted as governing the manner in which signaller quality might mediate the contribution to signaller fitness of observer responses. Grafen (1990) asserts that it is reasonable to assume that $w_{23} > 0$ in certain natural signalling scenarios (aggressive displays by harem defenders, begging nestlings, and stotting gazelles) which are paradigmatic of many (if not most) stable signalling systems.

However, consider a line of reasoning which might support the claim that Zahavi's second handicap criterion (that poor quality signallers must pay more for a certain signal than their higher quality competitors) is true of natural signallers. "Poor quality signallers", the reasoning runs, "pay higher signalling costs because, in proportion to their reserves, the energy expenditure, time expenditure etc., required for any signal is higher for poor quality signallers than for those of higher quality".

This line of reasoning has a corollary in the claim that "Poor quality individuals gain more from a particular observer response than their higher quality competitors because any resource gain would be greater proportionally for poor quality signallers than for those of higher quality". If this argument holds then typically (*contra* Grafen) $w_{23} < 0$.

This argument relies on what I shall call a 'relative' reading of Zahavi's second handicap criterion. Under this reading, although two signallers of differing quality use identical amounts of energy to produce a signal, the fitness consequences of making that signal differ as a result of the relative cost of signal production. From the perspective of a low quality signaller, the signal is *relatively* expensive, whereas from the perspective of a high quality signaller, it is *relatively* cheap. By relative I am referring to the energetic demands of signal production when compared to the signallers' energy resources. Such a reading allows one to construct the corollary above.

However, Zahavi's (1977) exposition of the second handicap criterion seems to promote a more 'absolute' account of signal costs. He claims that "it is reasonable to assume that high quality phenotypes and experienced individuals pay less for the cost of the same sized handicaps than low quality phenotypes" (p. 604). The thought here perhaps, is that the superior skills, metabolism, morphology, etc., of high quality phenotypes might just make signalling easier. This would result in a situation in which the absolute energetic expenditure required to make the same signal differs between signallers of differing quality. This absolute reading does not licence a corollary of the kind outlined above. In contrast, the benefit of an observer response might be considered to be best utilised by the same high quality individuals which find it easier to produce signals. For example, a particular worm might have a particular calorific value which could be best exploited by the metabolism of a large, fit, chick.

Such reasoning would support Grafen's (1990) contention that "the fitness gained by a marginal improvement in the parent's assessment of a chick is at least as great for big as for small chicks" (p. 527). However, a more 'relative' reading of signalling costs/benefits seems to motivate Godfray's (1991) model of offspring begging signals. He (directly reversing Grafen's assumption) assumes that "the benefits of [solicited parental] resources increase with [offspring] need". Yet, despite this contrast, Godfray reached the conclusion suggested by Grafen, that honest advertisement could be an ESS, and could be ensured by costly signalling.

The reason for this agreement is due to a second contrast between Grafen's appraisal of the begging scenario and that of Godfray's. Whereas Grafen assumes that the costs of signalling vary with need (with weaker signallers incurring higher production costs than their stronger competitors), Godfray assumes that they are constant. For Grafen differential signalling *costs* impose honesty, the associated signal benefits are either neutral with respect to need ($w_{23} = 0$), or favour the strong ($w_{23} > 0$). For Godfray, differential signalling *benefits* impose honesty through favouring the weak; the associated signalling costs are neutral with respect to need.

However, as was demonstrated in previous sections, once both costs *and* benefits are allowed to vary with signaller need, honesty can be seen to be maintained by a simple cost-benefit relationship. In the general case under consideration here, one cannot maintain that ensuring Zahavi's two handicap conditions is either necessary or sufficient for the existence of an honest communication ESS.

5 Conclusion

In summary, signalling equilibria were shown to exist under three conditions defined by Grafen (1990) using the inequalities, $w_{23} < 0$, $w_{23} = 0$, and $w_{23} > 0$, and also defined for the extension of Hurd's (1995) discrete action-response game explored here using the inequalities, $V_L < V_H$, $V_L = V_H$, and $V_L > V_H$. In concert these three classes of scenario were used to explore the effects of the benefits to signallers of their signalling behaviours, not merely the costs of such behaviours. Non-handicap signalling equilibria were shown to obtain under certain conditions. It was demonstrated that in order to show that a signalling system is stable, a relationship between signalling costs, signaller quality, *and* (*contra* Zahavi) signalling *benefits* must be shown to hold, *not* merely a relationship between signalling costs and signaller quality.

In addition to these analytically derived results, further exploration of Hurd's (1995) discrete action-response game was carried out utilising a simulation-based paradigm which allowed a qualitative account of

the system's dynamics to be formulated. As a result of this exploration, several interesting, robust phenomena, which were opaque to the analysis carried out in Section 2 were detailed. Amongst the phenomena described were classes of conventional signalling scenario. These stable signalling scenarios cannot be characterised as fixed points in the system's dynamics. They exist as higher dimensional attractors (e.g., limit cycles) in strategy space, and as such are not amenable to a simple ESS approach.

Further work, both analytic and simulation-based, must be undertaken before a full characterisation of the dynamics of these systems (both discrete and continuous) can be constructed, and the extent of their applicability to the evolution of natural signalling systems can be assessed.

Acknowledgements

Thanks to Guillaume Barreau, Ezequiel Di Paolo, Tim Guilford, John Maynard-Smith, Jason Noble, Danny Osorio, Marian Stamp Dawkins, Michael Wheeler, and Henrietta Wilson, for discussion concerning the issues raised here, and help with previous drafts of this paper.

References

de Bourcier, P., & Wheeler, M. (1994). Signalling and territorial agression: An investigation by means of synthetic behavioral ecology. In Cliff, D., Husbands, P., Meyer, J.-A., & Wilson, S. W. (Eds.), *From Animals to Animats 3: Proceedings of the Third International Conference on the Simulation of Adaptive Behaviour*, pp. 436 – 472. MIT Press.

Enquist, M. (1985). Communication during aggressive interactions with particular reference to variation in choice of behaviour. *Animal Behaviour, 33*, 1152 – 1161.

Godfray, H. C. J. (1991). Signalling of need by offspring to their parents. *Nature, 352*, 328 – 330.

Grafen, A. (1990). Biological signals as handicaps. *J. Theor. Biol., 144*, 517 – 546.

Hurd, P. L. (1995). Communication in discrete action-response games. *J. Theor. Biol., 174*, 217 – 222.

Kirkpatrick, M., & Ryan, M. J. (1991). The evolution of mating preferences and the paradox of the lek. *Nature, 350*, 33–38.

Maynard Smith, J., & Harper, D. (1988). The evolution of aggression: can evolution generate variability?. *Phil. Trans. Roy. Soc. Lond. B, 319*, 557–570.

Maynard Smith, J., & Harper, D. (1995). Animal signals: Models and terminology. *J. Theor. Biol., 177*, 305 – 311.

Miller, G. E. (1995). Artificial life as theoretical biology: how to do real science with computer simulation. CSRP 378, University of Sussex.

Noble, J. (1997). The scientific status of artificial life. Paper presented at the Fourth European Conference on Artificial Life (ECAL97), Brighton, UK, 28–31 July.

Pomiankowski, A., & Møller, A. P. (1995). A resolution of the lek paradox. *Proc.. R. Soc. Lond. B, 260*, 21–29.

Zahavi, A. (1975). Mate selection – a selection for a handicap. *J. Theor. Biol., 53*, 205 – 214.

Zahavi, A. (1977). The cost of honesty (further remarks on the handicap principle). *J. Theor. Biol., 67*, 603 – 605.

Social coordination and spatial organization: Steps towards the evolution of communication.

Ezequiel A. Di Paolo
School of Cognitive and Computing Sciences
University of Sussex, BRIGHTON BN1 9QH, U.K.
Fax: 44-1273-671320
ezequiel@cogs.susx.ac.uk

Abstract

Traditional characterizations of communication as a biological phenomenon are theoretically criticized, and an alternative understanding is presented in terms of recursive action coordination following works on cybernetics and autopoiesis. As first steps towards a study on the evolution of communication, two sets of computational experiments are presented, one dealing with non-recursive coordination and the other with coordination of recursive actions. In the first one coordinated activity evolves even in cases in which a game-theoretic analysis predicts the contrary. This is explained by studying the spatial organization in the distribution of agents. The second one shows the inappropriateness of the metaphor of communication as an exchange of information.

1 Introduction

The study of communication from an evolutionary perspective has received much attention lately. However, the view of communication traditionally advanced is far from theoretically unified and it is subject to much discussion and potential confusion, (see [17]).

I claim that this confusion is rooted in the way communication has been defined, partially as a consequence of using as primitives the same phenomena to be explained, (for instance, terms like "signal", "information", "reference", etc.). Two preconceptions in particular are disclosed and criticised here, together with their implications for the way the problem has been approached.

An alternative description of the phenomenon that avoids these criticisms is presented in terms of behavioral coordination as described by an observer. In order to support this view two sets of computational experiments were carried out, one dealing with simple (non-recursive) action coordination (presented and analysed in detail in sections 3 and 4) and the other with coordination of recursive (dialogic) action in the absence of hidden relevant information (section 5). The results obtained from these models show how coordinated activity can evolve in circumstances beyond the explanatory scope of the traditional theoretical framework.

The reader will notice that the limitations of game-theory and mathematical modelling appear as an underlying theme in section 3. Although, some conclusions are derived for the present piece of work, a full exploration of the methodological implications would deserve a separate treatment.

2 Theoretical considerations

Traditional studies on the evolution of communication in animal societies have, in general, approached the subject with too narrow a focus, characterizing the phenomenon with intuitive terms and *ad hoc* redefinitions. Evidence of this can be found in the presence of two important preconceptions in the theoretical understanding of communication. By preconceptions I do not necessarily mean *mis*conceptions. I am referring to those unspoken assumptions that are accepted as such and deserve no further discussion.

2.1 The role of selection

The first of these preconceptions has to do with the use of selective advantages as a necessary ingredient in *defining* communication. For instance, Wilson defines communication as the altering by one organism of the probability pattern of behavior in another organism in a manner adaptive to either one of them or to both [26]. Lewis and Gower define communication as "the transmission of signals between two or more organisms where selection has favoured both the production and reception of the signal(s)" [11]. Burghardt defines it as a behavior that is "likely to influence the receiver in a way that benefits, in a probabilistic manner, the signaller or some group of which it is a member" [6, 12]. Maynard-Smith and Harper define a signal "as an action or structure that increases the fitness of an individual by altering the behaviours of other organisms detecting it, and that has characteristics that have evolved because they have that effect" [17].

In these definitions communication is *characterized* in the same terms which are used to *explain* it, which is not only confusing, but methodologically very questionable as descriptions of phenomena and descriptions of the generative mechanism that give rise to such phenomena (explanations) belong necessarily to different domains. In other words, the question of how communication has come to exist is resolved *a priori* at the definition level, leaving no room for alternative/complementary mechanisms or their rebuttal, while at the same time providing a poor characterizations of the phenomenon. We do not *define* "wings" in terms of their selective advantages even if we may *explain* their presence in those terms.

Many biologists have appealed to these characterizations in order to rule out behaviors that intuitively do not constitute acts of communication but that would have to be included with the adoption of loose definitions such "an exchange of signals." However, the problem of poor characterization remains. Is an organism that has developed a mimetic character emitting a signal in order to confuse predator, as defended in [17]? Can we say that the predator acknowledges the signal by not receiving it? Such problems arise from deriving the logical conclusions of the idea of self-benefit in a description of the phenomenon that can be characterized independently of it. If we saw a group of animals committing collective suicide after a call given by one of them, we still would like to describe this as a case of communication. The fact that we rarely see such behaviors should perhaps be used to support selective *explanations*.

As I mentioned, one of the consequences of this mixing of descriptive and explanatory discourse is that complementary mechanisms that may play a role in explaining the evolution of communication, not necessarily in contradiction with natural selection, are out of the question. Even if such mechanisms played little or no role, the methodological problem would remain. By adopting the above definitions one is forced to ignore the *possibility* of such mechanisms as a genuine empirical question. If such mechanisms were found, one would be forced to adopt a theoretical framework that allows them.

2.2 Communication as information exchange

Another preconception about communication often found in the biology literature, is that it involves operationally the transmission of information from a sender to a receiver. This view implies that there is "something" that is being transmitted through some channel, although few researchers specify what it is. Hardly ever used in its technical sense [17], information is seen as a "thing" the pre-exists the activity we want to explain while, in fact, it is a consequence of that activity as seen by an observer, therefore it cannot play any operational role in its generation. Only after observing the activity are we able to speak about informational exchanges, and only in certain circumstances, (see [8, 19, 20, 24] for complete discussions on this point).

This metaphor has led many researchers to assume that a necessary condition for communication to arise is that not all relevant aspects of the environment are equally known to all the participants. It is interesting to see how this idea has influenced the computational approach to the problem, (see [12]). If all the relevant "information" is readily available to everyone, why "should" communication arise? In this view, communication can be understood only if there is some relevant feature of the environment whose conspicuousness has to be enhanced by a signal (such as a predator, or food), or if some internal state needs to be publicized.

2.3 Communication as coordinated activity in a consensual domain

Is it possible to *define* communication without appealing to concepts such as selective advantages or information? More importantly, can we work with such a definition? The understanding of communication that I will offer here is not new and it has been concurrently developed in different, though related, contexts including cybernetics [20, 24], autopoietic theory [13] and some branches of psychology and psychotherapy [4, 25]. Many philosophical perspectives also converge into similar, though not identical, views [3, 7, 10, 27]. Perhaps the most concise way of presenting this view is by using the language of autopoietic theory. It is, however, far beyond the scope of this section to give a thorough introduction to these concepts and the reader is referred to [14, 15] for a complete account of this important field.

Autopoiesis is a theory of the organization of living organisms as composite, autonomous unities. An autopoietic system is a dynamical system whose organization is maintained as a consequence of its own operation. Autopoietic systems in a given space produce their own components and boundaries and, as a result of the network of processes (of production, transformation and destruction) realized by the relations between these components, their organization is maintained dynamically. All living organisms are autopoietic systems that inhabit physical space. Autopoiesis is a property of the organization of the system; a given autopoietic organization is embodied in a particular *structure* or physical realization, and each state of such a system is determined *only* by that structure and a previous state. This seems almost trivial, but it is a fundamentally important point. It implies that any state of the system that we, as observers, can relate to a particular behavior when it is situated in an environment, is a direct result of the system's own structure and of its history. Thus, autopoietic systems are a subset of the larger set of operationally closed systems[1].

Any autopoietic system exists in a medium with which it interacts and, as a result of that interaction, its trajectory in state-space (its history) changes, although its operation as a dynamic system remains closed. As a structure-determined system, its structure determines its *domain of perturbations*, that is, what are the possible trajectories that can be triggered by interactions with the medium given a certain initial state without destroying the system. If the system undergoes changes of state that result in plastic changes of structure, and therefore changes in its domain of future perturbations, and all this happens without loss of its autopoiesis, then the system is said to undergo a process of *structural coupling* with the medium. If the medium is also a structurally plastic system then both systems may become structurally interlocked, mutually selecting their plastic changes, and thus defining a history of plastic interactions that for the organism is its *ontogeny*. As long as autopoiesis is maintained during this history, the organism is said to be adapted to the medium[2].

The process of structural coupling can not only account for changes in the individual during its lifetime, but also for phylogenic changes during evolution. *Phylogeny* is the result of the history of structural coupling of a series of autopoietic unities connected sequentially by reproduction during which adaptation is conserved. Selection acts negatively when, as a result of interactions with the medium, autopoiesis is lost, but it also acts through the process of structural coupling between medium and the organisms.

An organism undergoing a process of structural coupling with the medium may act recursively over its own states if the plastic deformations of the medium have been triggered by the organism's previous actions and at the same time these deformations will provoke future perturbations in the organism. In the particular case in which the medium includes another autopoietic system their individual ontogenies may become coupled. A domain of interlocked triggering of changes of state between the organisms participating in this network of co-ontogenies is established as long as the coupling subsists. This is called a *consensual domain*.

Behaviors in a consensual domain are mutually orienting behaviors. An observer can describe these behaviors as a case of coordinated activity. *Communication* is then defined as *the behavioral coordination that we can observe as a result of the interactions that occur in a consensual domain* [13, 15]. It is important to notice that by definition activity in a consensual domain is recursive, and we can distinguish it as coordinated activity, however, this

is not to be confused with the idea of recursion upon already existing coordinations. The latter enters as a further recursion which is identified as a defining characteristic of the phenomenon of "languaging" [13] which will not be addressed in this paper.

It is important to notice that all behaviors that arise from recursive actions in a consensual domain are included in this understanding of communication and not only those that can be described in semantic terms by an observer. Therefore, behaviors such as grooming, playing and the formation of hunting patterns *are* communicative behaviors. It is only through the history of structural coupling with the medium that a correspondence can be identified by an observer between situations in the medium and the behaviors which are coordinated and oriented in their presence as a result of communication. In these cases the observer may speak of certain actions as being signals that stand for a certain state of affairs or serve a certain function. However, a failure to find a semantic interpretation does not imply that the observed phenomenon is necessarily different in its essence. Even though more behaviors are embraced by it, our definition of communication is not a loose one. On the contrary, it is far more precise than traditional definitions, because it is based on operational considerations. While it is true that functional descriptions are very useful when we want to bracket complex operational details and view the phenomenon at different time scales, an operational description, if possible, is much preferred in the present context of model building.

3 Evolving non-recursive coordination

Let us consider the following game to be played by pairs of agents living in a shared environment. We will see an *agent* as an unity that is able to act in the environment. As a consequence of its actions, the agent receives certain payoff in a given currency that we may call *energy* and also spends a certain amount of its own accumulated currency. For most parts of this work agents will be seen as simple rather than composite unities, so that the focus will be more on global patterns of behavior rather than on the structural features of individual unities. When a certain level of energy is reached the agent is able to reproduce, and when this level falls below a certain minimum the agent dies. Energy can be accessed by the agents if they perform a correct action on an energy container or *food source*, of which there can be various types, each one of them requiring different actions in order to extract part or all of its energy. The total environmental energy contained in these sources is constantly renewed at a fixed rate.

There are two "components" to each agent's actions: the *effective component*, upon which the allocation of payoff is decided, and the *external manifestation* of the action, which is not directly relevant to the allocation of

---

[1] "Closed" is used here in the mathematical sense, see [1, 23].

[2] In slightly different terms Ashby arrives at a similar definition of adaptation in terms of stability and homeostasis: "... a form of behaviour is adaptive if it maintains the essential variables ... within physiological limits" [2, page 58].

payoffs. This means that for an agent to get a certain payoff the effective component of its action must match the action required by the particular food source it is dealing with. Behaviors that are required to get a certain amount of food in natural organisms, such as shaking the branch of a tree or digging the ground, can be thought of as the effective component, and the appearance of the movements implied in those behaviors to another organism as an example of one possible external manifestation of that behavior. Others may be sounds, gestures, etc. While in real cases it may be hard to decouple these two components in a single action, for simplicity's sake, we will suppose that, in this model, any effective component can be found with any external manifestation[3].

At each time step agents are selected to play the following game:

1. Each selected agent, who will play the *first role* (A_1), selects at random another different agent in its vicinity, who will play the *second role* (A_2).

2. A food source is randomly selected from A_1's vicinity.

3. A_1 perceives the type of the food source.

4. A_1 acts.

5. A_2 perceives the external manifestation of A_1's action, but not the type of food.

6. A_2 acts.

7. The payoff is distributed. If both agents perform the correct effective component the total amount of energy is equally distributed in halves. If only one of them performs the right action, that agent receives a proportion c of the total energy ($0.5 \leq c \leq 1$), the other receives no payoff and the rest of the energy remains in the food source.

The game is played indefinitely or until the population becomes extinct. All agents have the same chance of being picked as A_1. The possibility exists that effective components and external manifestations of actions may become correlated in such a way that agents playing the second role may "use" them as a prompt to act correctly over the food source even though they cannot perceive its type. However this may be against the immediate interest of the first player who may receive a smaller payoff. For convenience, I will speak of "signals" and "signalling" whenever I refer to the external manifestation of actions in the following paragraphs without attempting to make this a strict definition.

We can see that this game includes the feature of hidden information, as the agent playing the second role

is not able to see the food type that it is dealing with. In section 5 I show that the assumption that this is a necessity is invalid.

A game-theoretical dynamical analysis of a population of players of this game has been carried out for simplified conditions [8]. In order to make the model tractable geographical considerations were ignored so that agents can have access to any food source and play the game with any other agent in the population. Behavioral strategies were reduced to four possibilities without bias towards coordination. The results of this analysis show that an Evolutionarily Stable Strategy (ESS) exists in the total absence of coordinated activity. This means that a population consisting almost entirely of agents that behave selfishly and do not coordinate their activity cannot be invaded by any mutant population.

However, only a subset of initial conditions leads to this situation. For initial conditions outside this set the system does not evolve towards an equilibrium at all. The long term behavior is characterized by the presence of a periodic attractor in which the whole population oscillates indefinitely between periods of coordination and non-coordination, (Figure 1). Once within the regime, the system will remain in it permanently; therefore, the ESS state will never be reached. This sort of situation has been recognised as "an obvious weakness of the game-theoretic approach to evolution", [16, page 8]. Natural occurring examples of these cycles have been recently found in the mating strategies of the male side-blotched lizards [22]. In more general terms Zeeman showed that global convergence to an ESS is assured only in the absence of other attractors, which may exist and not be ESS's themselves [28].

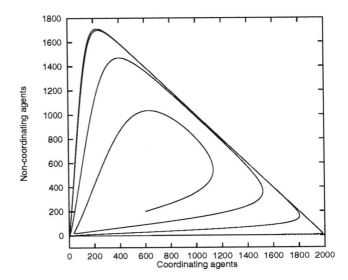

Figure 1: Periodic attractor (for 2 of the 4 species).

The game-theoretic dynamical analysis is important from a methodological viewpoint but not very conclu-

---

[3]This move leaves on one side an important area of research, namely the study of how signals or displays evolve out of pre-existing body structures and dispositions. Thanks to Jason Noble for pointing this out.

sive in terms of the processes leading to the evolution of coordinated activity. One immediate hypothesis is that spatiality may play an important role. Global accessibility does not represent interactions among real organisms fairly. In real life, neighbors tend to remain neighbors and the habitat of the offsprings tends to be the same habitat of the parents.

In order to account for these factors a computational model was developed in which the agents play the same game. Agents are situated in a toroidal grid (100 x 100) initially with a random distribution. In the same way a large number of food sources of different kinds is uniformly distributed in this grid. Neither the agents nor the food sources change positions with time. A neighborhood is defined as a square (10 x 10) centered around an agent, which represents the area the agent occupies during its lifetime. Agents play the game as described above, which means that they must perform a correct action depending on the type of food source they are dealing with in order to increase their energy level. There are around 100 food sources in an agent's neighborhood and only four different types of them. Each food source contains a certain amount of energy which is constantly being renewed at a fixed rate using a stochastic update rule. Agents will die if their energy level reaches zero. On the other hand, if the energy level increases, the agent will accumulate enough energy to reproduce. In this case a mate is selected from the neighborhood, and the offspring will occupy a randomly chosen position within the first parent's neighborhood, deriving its initial energy level from this parent. As the energy extracted from the agents in the form of costs does not return to the environment in reusable form, this scheme guarantees that the equivalent first and second law of thermodynamics are observed.

At each time step a number of agents equal to the size of the current population is randomly selected to perform the first role in the interactional game. The updating is performed asynchronously. A second player and a food source within the neighborhood of the first player are randomly selected. If no agent is found after a finite number of trials (about 10), the first player looses its chance to play the game, and the energy cost is discounted anyway.

The structure of agents is that of a state-less machine. The focus of this work will be on the global mechanisms that allow or constraint the evolution of coordinated activity as a first step towards an understanding of the evolution of communication. No claim will be made about the very important effects of ontogenic structural changes during the coordination of actions with other agents. Agents will be seen as simple unities most of the time. This is a strong simplification for a model which is partly based on concepts derived from autopoietic theory, however, I maintain that the framework provided by

this theory is still applicable for the design and understanding of the present and future studies.

The behavioral matrix is encoded in a haploid genome, represented by a bit-string. Offsprings receive their genome from the result of a uniform crossover operation on their parents genotypes, plus certain probability of mutation μ per place.

In this model there is no fitness function, neither are there any special rewards nor punishments for behaving in an specific way apart from the rules of the game. A problem derived from the use of this scheme is the lack of obvious measures of evolution. For our purposes, the simplest way to monitor the evolution of action coordination, is to look at changes in the average simultaneous success of the first and second players for the whole population.

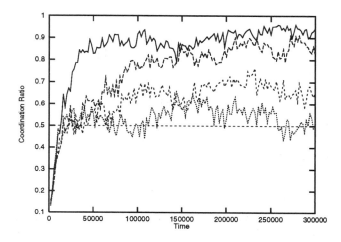

Figure 2: Coordination ratio for different values of c. The top (full) line between 90% and 100% corresponds to $c = 0.5$, the line between 80% and 90% to $c = 0.55$, the one between 60% and 70% to $c = 0.6$ and the one between 50% and 60% to $c = 0.65$. Values of c equal or greater than 0.7 reproduce the baseline case for this game.

In the simulation runs described here agents were able to perform 16 actions (4 effective components and 4 external manifestations). Only two of the effective components were actually relevant for the four food source types. A baseline case was run in order to understand what kind of activity evolved when agents weren't able to perceive each other reliably. In these runs, the external manifestation of the first player's action was replaced with a random signal when perceived by the second player. We may call the proportion of cases in which both players acted correctly simultaneously, the *coordination ratio*. This ratio stabilized at 50 % for random signals. Since no food type is predominant, the best "guess" a second agent can make given that there is no correlation between the "signal" it perceives and the particular type of food it is dealing with, is to perform any of the two relevant out of the four possible actions. For non-random signals any success in coordination of behaviors will be manifested as a greater coordination ratio than the one observed in the baseline case.

A study of the effect of parameter c on the coordination ratio was performed to see how the extra payoff against coordination affected the level of simultaneous success. Figure 2 shows the resulting evolution for different values of c in typical runs. We see that the proportion of coordinated activity for the whole population decreases as c is incremented from 0.5 to 0.7, and for greater values the baseline case is reproduced. This means that the level of coordination goes from almost perfect for $c = 0.5$ (neutral cost) to coordination by guessing when $c \cong 0.7$. No cycles are observed as in the mathematical model. The fact that for a certain range of costs *against* it, coordinated activity evolves anyway is in contradiction with the intuitions that can be gained from the mathematical model or from simplified selective arguments. Explanations for this phenomenon are found in the spatial organization of the system.

4   Spatial structures.

A simple inspection of the resulting data in all simulations shows that the individual history of coordination success can differ significantly from agent to agent and from the value of the coordination ratio at that time. For instance, groups of agents achieving 90 % of coordination success can coexist with other groups that achieve 60 % both in a stable state during the same simulation run. Even though an individual historical average is qualitatively different to an instantaneous population average, one would expect the resulting numbers not to differ much, especially if the coordination ratio has been stable for some time. This suggests that there may be some structure in the population that prevents the homogenizing effects of sexual reproduction.

4.1   Cluster formation and stability.

Figure 3 shows the spatial distribution after a short transient. Initially agents are distributed randomly across the whole environment. We can observe that the initial symmetry is broken and that agents show a tendency to aggregate into clusters. Symmetry breaking is caused by minor differences in the initial distribution of positions and is also due to the updating rules; so that some agents will be more successful than others just because they have a few more agents to interact with or have been called to act a few more times and, therefore, they have a slightly greater chance of accumulating enough energy for reproduction. As reproduction is also a local process and the position of the offspring does not differ much from the position of the the parents, there is a positive contribution to the same effect, namely the accumulation of agents in these particular areas.

Unfortunately, cluster formation mechanisms do not provide a satisfactory explanation of why clusters remain more or less stable structures as it is generally observed.

Tendency to expand. Figure 4 shows a qualitative model of a typical observed distribution of environmental energy and density of agents inside and in the vicinity of a cluster. It is easy to see that resources will be more frequently used in more populated areas towards the center of the cluster than on peripheral areas in which the population is more sparse, so that the amount of available energy will, on average, decrease towards the center as shown in the figure. Agents living in the periphery will have access to resources of greater quality, and the average energy gained per game played will be greater than that of agents in the center region. So, at first glance, peripheral agents would seem to be better off and have a better chance of having more offsprings, therefore the cluster would seem to experience a tendency towards *expansion*.

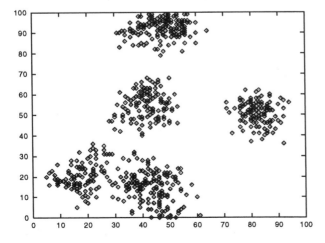

Figure 3: Distribution of the population in clusters.

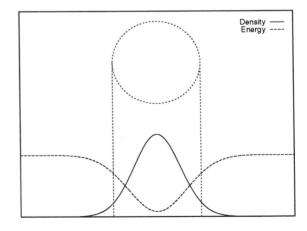

Figure 4: Energy and population distribution inside and around a cluster (circle).

Tendency to collapse. While all agents have the same probability of being *chosen* to play the first role in the game, the frequency with which an agent *actually* plays the game depends on the surrounding population density. The more densely populated the area, the higher the chance of finding a partner to play with. For this reason, agents living near the center of a cluster will play the game more frequently. Moreover, the probability of an agent playing the second role also depends on its position within the cluster. Given that the density distribution is not uniform, second players will be chosen more frequently from more populated regions. Agents in the center of a cluster will benefit from this effect in a cumulative way, and will, on average, play the second role more times than they play the first role. Conversely, agents living near the periphery will be chosen less frequently for playing the second role because their distribution is more sparse, and therefore, they will, on average, play the first role more times than the second role. The ratio (Second-role-frequency)/(First-role-frequency) for each agent has been observed to range from a minimum of 0.9 at the periphery to a maximum of 1.25 at the center of the cluster. In short, agents living in the populated areas near the center will 1) play the game more frequently than agents living in sparse areas and 2) they will perform the second role more frequently than the first one. So, in principle, they will stand a better chance of receiving more energy per unit of time. This provides the cluster with a tendency to *collapse*.

The equilibrium of both these tendencies determines the size of the quasi-stable cluster. Resulting clusters have been observed to have a typical radius of 1 up to 3 neighborhood sizes.

4.2 Why does action coordination evolve?

I said that clusters as quasi-stable structures result from an interplay of two opposing tendencies in the spatial organization that arise from the fact that conditions differ at the center and at the periphery of the cluster. The next obvious question that must be examined is if this difference of conditions has any effect on the evolution of coordinated activity.

Genetic homogeneity. Due to the nature of the cluster formation process and the homogenizing effect of sexual reproduction, clusters tend be inhabited by agents who are very similar genetically. Spatial homogeneity within a cluster will still be the case even when a new mutation appears. After a sufficiently long time (in practice not very long) there will be agents bearing the new mutation distributed across the whole cluster.

Conditions at the periphery of a cluster. Agents are subject to two qualitatively different "micro-environments" which emerge as a result of the spatial

organization[4]. We saw how agents living in the periphery have access to resources of better quality (Figure 4) and how these agents tend to play the second role less than they play the first one. Besides, they also tend to interact fewer times in absolute terms because of their sparse distribution. This means that, for these agents, to engage in coordinated activity is particularly costly because every time they do so they lose one of their fewer opportunities to obtain a greater absolute payoff.

Conditions at the center of a cluster. Agents inhabiting the center of a cluster have access to poorer, much more frequently used, resources, therefore the individual gain for not coordinating is not too high in absolute terms, though still positive. On the other hand, these agents tend to play the second role more times than they play the first one, which means that there may be cases (depending on the value of c) in which they will have a positive *individual* gain if they *do* coordinate their actions, simply because they will be acting as second players more frequently, provided that c is not too high. From a cost-benefit viewpoint, while it may pay a little extra to be a "deceiver", the situation may be that once a "deceiver" lineage starts to grow, it will pay more to reestablish coordination.

Selection. Ideally this situation would result in the existence of two distinct subpopulations, one of coordinating agents at the center of the cluster and one of non-coordinating agents at the periphery, but this is not possible due to the genetic homogeneity within a cluster. Given that the sizes of each subpopulation are comparable, and a newborn agent has comparable probabilities of being placed in any of the "two" regions, then there is no ground for selection to be very specific about which of the extreme behaviors to choose. Therefore, surviving agents will tend to be able to partially satisfy the conditions of both extreme micro-environments and, consequently, they will necessarily possess the ability to coordinate their actions up to a certain level.

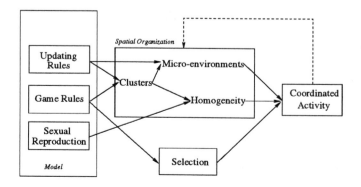

Figure 5: Explanatory mechanisms involved in the evolution of coordinated activity in the computational model.

---

[4]Or an environment presenting a continuum of variation to be more precise.

Thus, the evolution of coordinated activity in this model can be explained by the interplay of spatial organization and selective mechanisms. A diagram showing the relation between the components of this explanation can be seen in Figure 5.

It has been observed that the level of coordinated activity may have considerable variations from cluster to cluster in the same simulation run. Clusters can grow and, more rarely, shrink. These are interesting phenomena because they are related to the level of coordinated activity within the clusters. The following correlation has been consistently observed: *clusters with high level of success in coordination are larger in size and more populated than clusters with a lower level*. In general, the former can have a radius of up to 3 neighborhood sizes, while the latter have a radius of 1 neighborhood size or even less.

Why a particular cluster is small with a low level of coordinated activity while another is large with a high level of coordination must mainly be attributed to contingencies in their respective histories. We cannot look for general reasons because all agents evolve under the same general rules. All we can do is to describe, in terms of feedback mechanisms (see the dashed line in Figure 5), certain tendencies that appear once a cluster is already embarked in a particular historical path. What it is interesting is that this correlation can be deduced from the same explanatory mechanisms derived from the model in Figure 4, this is shown with some detail in [8].

Alternative explanations for the evolution of coordination could be attempted in terms of *kin selection*, but this would still require (at least some of) the mechanisms of spatial structuring to work, all of which should be "brought back" again in order to explain the cluster size/coordination correlation.

It must be remarked that these explanations are in fact simplifications of complex dynamical processes in which more ingredients than those mentioned may play an important part. For instance, I have followed a quasi-static approach, in which inertia has been unaccounted for. The complex effects arising from cluster interaction have also been ignored. The reason for this is that, interesting as these phenomena may be, they do not much further our understanding of how action coordination evolves due to the interplay of spatial organization and selection in this model.

5   Coordination of recursive actions

Coordination, as presented in the previous model, does not reflect the idea of ongoing mutual orientation of behaviors that is implied by the view of communication as arising from activity in a consensual domain. This sort of coordination is similar to that that can be observed between traffic lights and motorists, a simple traffic light system would operate independently of the actions of

the motorists, but not the other way around. Genuine consensual interactions could be expected, for instance, among drivers participating in a race. As the next logical step in the project, the previous model could be extended in order to approach a situation in which we may speak of a consensual domain. Strictly speaking, this will not be possible as long as the structure of the agents remains non-plastic, so this will not be yet a model of communication. However, the following modifications to the game can take us near this situation.

Instead of requiring an unique action, access to energy in the food sources requires the performance of a specific sequence of actions by both agents. Energy is released partially depending on an action being correct at the required step of the sequence. In this case the actions of *both* players depend on the perceived food type and the perceived external manifestation of the other agent in the previous step. This means that the second player has access to information about the food type. In spite of this, it is clear that the task the agents have to perform in not trivial. This game has a dialogic structure, the actions of an agent depend not only on the perceived food type but also on the previous actions of its partner, which recursively depend on the agent's previous actions. This provides a more realistic analogy with natural cases of coordinated behavior.

A simulation was run with four different types of food, two of them requiring a sequence of actions such as "A, B, C, D" where the first player must perform "A, C" alternating with the second player who must perform "B, D" and the two others requiring the sequence "C, D, A, B" which means that each agent must revert the order of its own actions. Payoffs are allocated after the first two actions, and then again after the last two actions in the same manner as in the previous game.

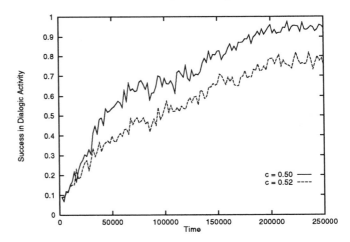

Figure 6: Evolution of dialogic coordinated activity for two values of c in two typical runs.

Figure 6 shows the evolution of dialogic activity (defined as the ratio of successfully produced sequences over the total number of games at each time step). We see that coordination of recursive actions evolves towards a high level. The same considerations about the spatial organization of the agents made for the first set of experiments still apply, and the level of dialogic activity has a dependency on c similar to that of the level of coordinated activity for those experiments.

These results show how agents coordinating their activity are able to perform tasks beyond their individual abilities. This particular game requires that both agents perform a sequence of actions (which depend on their role) in the presence of an external environmental feature that remains unchanged with time. Given that agents are state-less machines, this is something impossible for them to do individually. However, a couple of interacting agents can achieve an important level of success in this task, each one taking advantage of the presence of the other and "using" their interactions as the internal states they lack.

We see that a description of their behavior in terms of traditional notions of information is useless. If by information we mean information about features of the environment, we find that these are equally accessible to both participants, if we mean information about the state/intention of the agents, they haven't got any.

6   Conclusions

The first part of this paper was aimed at a methodological and conceptual criticism of the current approach to the question of the origin and evolution of communication. An analysis of the way the phenomenon is characterized in theoretical biology provided the necessary guidelines for identifying two important preconceptions prevalent in those studies, namely the use of selective advantages, elsewhere used only in explanatory discourse, at the definition level, and the loose use of the idea of communication as an informational exchange. A different understanding of communication was considered as a way of characterizing the phenomenon while avoiding the consequences identified with the inclusion of the previous preconceptions.

The computational model used for investigating the evolution of non-recursive coordination has demonstrated that coordinated activity can evolve even in those cases in which the static and dynamic mathematical models showed it would not. And the reason for this difference has been mainly the possibility that the computational model provides for studying the actions of selective mechanisms in the context of other concurrent processes such as spatial organization.

We observe clusters emerging as self-regulating spatial structures but to say that some complex structure "emerges" out of something simple is to locate the problem, not to solve it. That is why an explanation was advanced in terms of a qualitative model of the observed

distribution of population and energy in the region occupied by a cluster. In exploring certain issues arising from this model we were able to explain many of the observed phenomena like cluster quasi-stability, genetic homogeneity, etc., including the evolution of action coordination even in the presence of individual costs against it. It is apparent that spatial structures can provide a very strong influence on the outcome of an evolutionary process, resulting sometimes in far from intuitive characteristics (see also [5, 18]).

A broad analogy can be drawn between the position of an agent in a cluster in our model, and the degree of participation in a social organization for a natural organism. For instance, animals spending more time in social activities as a consequence of their developmental stage, or their social status, will be analogous to agents living in the center of a cluster. Such an analogy would suggest that many answers to the question of natural communication could be sought in the nature of group structure, and social hierarchies.

Interestingly, one of the correlations found in this study, the correspondence of cluster size and degree of coordinated activity, has a very suggestive parallel in primate societies: that of typical group size and relative neocortical size [21]. It has been suggested that language evolution has been deeply influenced by the growth in group size in humans as compared with other primates, and a functionalist explanation was advanced in terms of the role of language as a bonding mechanism in the maintenance of stability in large groups [9]. The way that the analogous correlation was explained within the present model has been rather different, more in terms of structural dynamics rather than functional adaptations, but the parallel is worth noting.

The following step towards an understanding of the evolution communication corresponds to a game in which agents act recursively, still without constituting a consensual domain in the strict sense. In this game, action coordination evolves non-trivially even when information is previously shared. This result also points to the relevance of social interactions in the evolution of cognitive capabilities, as agents in this simple model are able to perform actions not allowed by their structures at the individual level. It can be expected that the addition of plasticity to the structure of the agents will constitute an important further step.

The computational approach is particularly appropriate for the study of structures and concurrent processes in which the limitations of pure mathematical modelling are tested. In this case the addition of spatial considerations dramatically changed the results obtained by a simple cost-benefit selective analysis. This can be considered as a methodological warning sign, not only for the present project, but for many other projects in the study of biological phenomena.

Acknowledgements

Thanks to Phil Husbands, Inman Harvey and an anonymous reviewer for their helpful comments on previous versions of this work. The author is grateful to the *Consejo de Investigaciones Científicas y Técnicas de la República Argentina* and the Argentine Ministry of Education for their support.

References

[1] W. R. Ashby. *Introduction to Cybernetics.* Chapman and Hall, London, 2nd edition, 1956.

[2] W. R. Ashby. *Design for a Brain: The origin of adaptive behaviour.* Chapman and Hall, London, 2nd edition, 1960.

[3] J. L. Austin. *How to Do Things With Words. The William James Lectures delivered at Harvard University in 1955.* Oxford at the Claredon Press, 1962.

[4] G. Bateson. *Steps towards an Ecology of Mind: collected essays in anthropology, psychiatry, evolution and epistemology.* Intertext Aylesbure, 1972.

[5] M. C. Boerlijst and P. Hogeweg. Spiral wave structure in pre-biotic evolution: hypercycles stable against parasites. *Physica D*, 48:17 – 28, 1991.

[6] G. M. Burghardt. Defining 'communication'. In J. W. Johnson, Jr, D. G. Moulton, and A. Turk, editors, *Communication and Chemical Signals.* Appleton-Century-Crofts, New York, 1970.

[7] J. Dewey. *Experience and Nature.* Dover, 1958.

[8] E. A. Di Paolo. An investigation into the evolution of communicative behaviors. Cognitive Science Research Paper 445, School of Cognitive and Computing Sciences, University of Sussex, 1996.

[9] R. I. M. Dunbar. Co-evolution of neocortex size, group size and language in humans. *Brain and Behavioral Sciences*, 16:681 – 735, 1993.

[10] M. Heidegger. *Being and Time.* Harper and Row, New York, 1962. Trans. J. Macquarrie and E. Robinson.

[11] D. B. Lewis and M. D. Gower. *Biology of Communication.* Blackie, Glasgow, 1980.

[12] B. J. MacLennan and G. M. Burghardt. Synthetic ecology and the evolution of cooperative communication. *Adaptive Behavior*, 2(2):151–188, 1994.

[13] H. Maturana. Biology of language: The epistemology of reality. In G. A. Miller and E. Lennenberg, editors, *Psychology and Biology of Language and Thought. Essays in Honor of Eric Lennenberg*, pages 27–63. Academic Press Inc. New York, 1978.

[14] H. Maturana and F. J. Varela. *Autopoiesis and Cognition: The Realization of the Living.* D. Reidel Publishing, Dordrecht, Holland, 1980.

[15] H. Maturana and F. J. Varela. *The tree of knowledge: the biological roots of human understanding.* Shambhala, Boston, Mass, 1988.

[16] J. Maynard-Smith. *Evolution and the Theory of Games.* Cambridge University Press, 1982.

[17] J. Maynard-Smith and D. G. C. Harper. Animal signals: models and terminology. *Journal of Theoretical Biology*, 177:305–311, 1995.

[18] M. Oliphant. Evolving cooperation in the non-iterated Prisoner's Dilemma: the importance of spatial organization. In R. Brooks and P. Maes, editors, *Proceedings of Artificial Life IV.* MIT Press., 1994.

[19] S. Oyama. *The Ontogeny of Information.* Cambridge University Press, 1985.

[20] G. Pask. Developments in conversation theory - part 1. *International Journal of Man-Machine Studies*, 13:357 – 411, 1980.

[21] T. Sawaguchi and H. Kudo. Neocortical development and social structure in primates. *Primates*, 31:283 – 290, 1990.

[22] B. Sinervo and C. M. Lively. The rock-paper-scissors game and the evolution of alternative male strategies. *Nature*, 380:240, 1996.

[23] F. J. Varela. *Principles of Biological Autonomy.* Elsevier, North Holland, NY, 1979.

[24] H. von Foerster. The epistemology of communication. In K. Woodward, editor, *The Myths of Information: Technology and Post-industrial Culture.* Routledge, 1980.

[25] P. Watzlawick, J. H. Beavin, and D. D. Jackson. *Pragmatics of Human Communication: a Study of Interactional Patterns, Pathologies and Paradoxes.* Faber, 1968.

[26] E. O. Wilson. *Sociobiology: The new synthesis.* Belknap Press of Harvard University Press, Cambridge, Mass., 1975.

[27] L. Wittgenstein. *Philosophical Investigations.* Oxford: Basil Blackwell and Mott, 2nd edition, 1963.

[28] E. C. Zeeman. Population dynamics for game theory. In Z. Nitecki and E. Robinson, editors, *Global Theory of Dynamical Systems.* Springer Verlag, Berlin, 1980.

Grounding adaptive language games in robotic agents

Luc Steels (1,2) and Paul Vogt (1)
(1) VUB AI Laboratory, Pleinlaan 2, 1050 Brussels,
steels@arti.vub.ac.be, paul@arti.vub.ac.be
(2) SONY Computer Science Laboratory
6 Rue Amyot, Paris

Abstract

The paper addresses the question how a group of physically embodied robotic agents may originate meaning and language through adaptive language games. The main principles underlying the approach are sketched as well as the steps needed to implement these principles on physical agents. Some experimental results based on this implementation are presented.

1 Introduction

In the past five years, a large number of robotic agents, i.e. physical systems capable of sensori-motor control, have been built in order to investigate a bottom-up approach to artificial intelligence (see the overview in [8]). Important results have been achieved, particularly by using behavior-oriented architectures [14] and learning methods based on neural networks [6] or genetic algorithms [3]. Nevertheless, it is still largely an open question how these robots may reach sufficient complexity in order to qualify as cognitive agents. Most of the experiments have focused on 'low level' tasks like obstacle avoidance or navigation, and these have been difficult enough to preclude any work on cognitive tasks.

One approach for pushing ahead, taken for example in the COG project[1], is to increase the complexity of the robots themselves by adding many more sensory channels and many more degrees of freedom. Another approach, which we are exploring, is based on the hypothesis that communication, if not full-fledged language, is a necessary stepping stone towards cognitive intelligence. This implies that we cannot restrict ourselves to individual robots but must perform experiments how groups of robots may build up communication systems of increased complexity. In the spirit of the bottom-up approach, these communication systems must be developed by the robots themselves and not designed and programmed in by an external observer. They must also be grounded in the sensori-motor experiences of the robot as opposed to being disembodied, with the input given by a human experimenter and the output again interpreted by the human observer.

Some initial experiments have been reported in the Alife literature on how communication itself may arise to aid cooperation between agents [5],[15]. In this paper, we assume that there is already communication and focus instead on the grounding problem, as in [18]: How the evolving language is anchored into the sensory and motor data streams generated through normal behavior. We also address the problem of the origin of meaning: How the distinctions that the robots lexicalise may arise in the first place.

The work reported here builds further on earlier software experiments that show how agents may develop a shared vocabulary through a series of adaptive naming games [9] and how agents may generate distinctions to discriminate between objects in their environment [10],[12]. These papers can be consulted for formal descriptions of the mechanisms. This paper focuses in particular on how the software experiments have been carried to real robots.

The rest of the paper is in three parts. The first part explains the adaptive language games including the mechanisms that cause the build up of distinctions and of lexicons to express these distinctions. The second part discusses how adaptive language games have been mapped onto physical robots. The third part gives some results of concrete experiments. Conclusions and ideas for future research end the paper.

2 Adaptive Language Games

At the heart of our approach is the notion of a language game [17]. A language game involves two agents, a speaker and a hearer, as well as a context which consists of agents, objects and situations. Different kinds of language games can be played depending on the goals that the participating agents want to achieve. The game being pursued in the experiments reported here is for the speaker to identify an object in a certain context using linguistic means. We call this game the naming game. Initially extra-linguistic means, such as pointing, can be used to bootstrap the language. Other language games would allow the speaker to get the hearer to perform a certain action, to ask the hearer for more information, etc.

2.1 The basic scenario

To play a naming game both participants follow a specific scenario, which consists of the following six steps:

1. *Making Contact*: Two agents must make contact with each other. One assumes the role of speaker, the other of hearer. The agents are physically close together so that there is automatically a shared context.

2. *Topic identification*: Each agent perceives the surrounding environment through its sensors and identifies a set of objects which constitute the context. The speaking agent chooses one object in this context as the topic of the conversation. He then draws attention to this topic using extra-linguistic means, for example by pointing. The hearer thus also identifies the topic.

3. *Perception*: Each agent then categorises the sensory experience of the different objects in terms of features, and identifies a distinctive feature set which distinguishes the topic from the other objects in the context. It will often be the case that more than one distinctive feature set is appropriate.

4. *Encoding*: The speaker chooses one distinctive feature set (for example the smallest one) and encodes this into an expression. Encoding means that the smallest set of words, which expresses all the features in the distinctive feature set, is searched for in the lexicon.

5. *Decoding*: The hearer decodes the expression which means that he looks up all the words in his lexicon and reassembles a feature set covering all the words. Words are ambiguous in the lexicon (the same word may have different meanings), so that there is typically more than one possible feature set resulting from the decoding process.

6. *Feedback*: The hearer compares the decoded feature sets with the distinctive feature sets that he was expecting. If one of the distinctive feature sets is equal to the decoded feature set, the language games ends in success and the hearer gives a positive feedback. Otherwise the game ends in failure and the hearer signals failure.

This scenario assumes that (1) both agents have a perceptual apparatus for categorising sensory experiences and identifying distinctive feature sets and (2) a lexicon that associates features or feature sets with words and vice-versa. However we are precisely interested in the problem how (1) and (2) may originate. Initially the agents have no repertoire of perceptual distinctions and

no lexicon. They build these up as a side activity of each language game using the methods described in the following two subsections.

2.2 Originating distinctions

Each agent has a series of sensory-motor channels which are the direct output of sensors, the result of automatic low-level sensory processes, or the dynamically evolving contents of internal states such as left and right motor command streams. These sensory-motor channels are given by the hardware or low-level routines. For each channel there is a discrimination tree which divides the output of a channel into distinct regions. It is assumed that the discrimination trees are binary. Each end-node of a tree constitutes a feature. The feature is denoted by a string *agent-channel-region-subregion-subsubregion-* ..., as in a1-s0-0-1, which refers to a feature associated with channel s0 in agent a1. Initially there are no discrimination trees.

As part of the perception phase, the agent engages in a discrimination game. He categorises the sensori-motor states for each object based on his discrimination trees. The result is a set of features for each channel that contains active data, and this for each object. The different sets are then used to find the possible distinctive feature sets that distinguish the feature set of the topic from the feature sets of the other objects. If this fails, i.e. if no distinctive feature set can be built using the existing discrimination trees, a new distinction is created by a further subdivision of one of the end-nodes of a discrimination tree which was active in the categorisation process. The choice which of these nodes is expanded is arbitrary. The agent keeps track of which features are used and the success in discrimination. A forgetting process eliminates those end-nodes which turn out not to be useful.

Thus our approach is selectionist (as in [2]): There is a generator of diversity and a separate selectionist process which maintains or eliminates features from the feature population. Earlier software experiments [10] have shown that this method stabilises on a successful repertoire of discriminations. Moreover new objects, new sensori-motor channels, or new agents may at any time enter, causing the discrimination trees to be expanded and adapted as the need arises. Note that each agent builds up his own discrimination trees. There are similarities due to the fact that the agents operate in the same environment but this does not guarantee complete coherence. More coherence is reached when the lexicalisation of a feature is an additional selectionist criterion for its further survival, as discussed in more detail in [12].

2.3 Originating a lexicon

A lexicon consists of a set of word-meaning pairs, where the meaning consists of a feature set. Each agent has his own lexicon and an agent cannot directly inspect the lexicon of another one. Each agent maintains how often a word-meaning pair has been used and how successful it has been in its use. While encoding, a speaker will prefer word-meaning pairs that have been used more often and were more succesful in use.

A discrimination game results in a series of possible distinctive feature sets of which one is chosen by the speaker. This feature set is encoded by the speaker and then decoded by the hearer. Several things can go wrong in this process and each failure results in appropriate actions:

1. *The speaker does not have a word for a certain feature set.* In this case, the speaker is allowed to construct a new word (formed by a random combination drawn from a given prior alphabet) and associate that in his lexicon with the feature set. This happens with a low probability because a word may already exist in the population for this feature set.

2. *The hearer may lack a word used by the speaker.* In this case, the hearer can infer possible feature sets that might be meant by that word, based on the distinctive feature sets that he is expecting. In the simplest situation, there is only one feature necessary to distinguish the topic from the objects, so that the meaning is unequivocally known. It could also be that some words are known but not others. The meaning of the missing words must then be reconstructed from the remaining unknowns. Because there may be more than one distinctive feature set, it is inevitable that ambiguity creeps into the lexicon of the hearer. These ambiguities are weeded out by future use and success in use which determine what word-meaning pairs will become most common.

3. *Some of the feature sets decoded by the hearer do not match with the expected distinctive feature sets.* This means that there are some word-meaning pairs which are not shared by some of the agents. For the successful word-meaning pairs, both success and use is incremented, whereas for the others only the use is incremented, so that their future use diminishes.

4. *The feature set decoded by the hearer does not match with any of the expected distinctive feature sets.* In that case, the hearer extends the lexicon, using the same procedure as for situation 2 above.

Note that the approach is again selectionist. Agents create or infer word-meaning pairs. Which pairs 'survive' depends on use and success in use, and this is determined by how many agents have adopted the same word-meaning pairs. Typically we see a phase transition when one word starts to dominate for the expression of a particular meaning. This phase transition is due to the positive feedback loop inherent in the system: The more a word is used, the more success it will have in use and the more it will be used even more. Software simulations reported in [9] have shown that a group of agents indeed converges towards a common lexicon after a sufficient number of adaptive naming games. Moreover new agents may enter at any time, and due to the adaptive nature of the discrimination games, new features may enter the repertoire of possible meanings.

Given these results we now turn to the challenge of implementing these algorithms on physically embodied robots.

3 Physical implementation

As is well known by now, software simulations do not at all guarantee that the methods will also work in real world settings. Indeed, the problems encountered during the physical implementation of the language games have been enormous. Robots are basically parallel distributed computer systems which operate in real-time and whose communication links are very unreliable. We must therefore achieve overall reliability despite unreliable components and processes. Second we must have sufficiently robust and autonomous robots (also autonomous in terms of energy) to permit hundreds, and even thousands, of consecutive language games. Next, we must find equivalents of all the different steps in the scenario: Robots must be able to recognise each other, approach each other, and establish the necessary contact to start a language game. They must be able to point or in other ways draw attention to the topic. Their perceptual capabilities must be the basis of the discrimination games and finally they must realise the language games themselves. In addition, it remained to be seen whether the proposed discrimination mechanisms were adequate for handling the inherently noisy real world data coming from actual sensors and whether the lexicon would stabilise despite possible (and actual) failures at all steps of a game.

3.1 The robots and the ecosystem

The robots used in the experiments are Lego-vehicles built for our laboratory's experiments in self-sufficient robots (see figure 1) [7]. Each robot (size: 30 x 20 x 15 cm) has three infra-red sensors (mounted on the left-front, middle-front and right-front side), four infrared emitters (mounted on front, left, right, and back side), two visible light sensors (mounted on left- and right-front side), two modulated light sensors (mounted on left- and right-front side), various touch sensors mounted on all sides, and a battery sensor. There is a left and right motor. The overall processing capacity resides in a Mo-

Figure 1: The robots used in the experiment are Lego vehicles. which are autonomous with respect to sensing, actuating, computation, and energy.

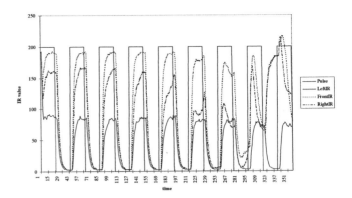

Figure 2: This figure and subsequent figures are taken from experiments with robots executing the language game scenario. The y-axis represents values of sensors, the x-axis time. The figure above shows the (square) pulsed infrared emission, and the detection by the three infrared sensors of the reflected light. The amount of reflection depends on how close surrounding obstacles are. Another robot is perceived when an out of phase infrared source appears, which happens here towards the end of the data set.

torala MC86332 micro controller with 128 kB ROM and 256 kB RAM located on a Vesta board. Its CPU is 16.78 MHz at 5V. The Vesta board is extended with a second board dedicated to low level sensory-motor processing and buffering [16].

The robots are programmed using a behavior-oriented architecture [7]. The sensors, actuators and internal states constitute continuous data streams and the behavior is based on continous dynamical systems implementing direct couplings between sensors and actuators. An example of such a coupling realises photo-taxis by minimising the difference between the left and right visible photosensors, as in Braitenberg vehicles. The couplings are modulated by motivational states. Thus the photo-taxis is modulated by a decreasing battery level, so that the robot drives towards the charging station when its energy resources are getting low.

The robots are equiped with a radio-link that is designed for communication among themselves at a reasonable speed, and for central monitoring of internal states. It is a module that extends the sensory-motor board. It has a build in power supply, a transmission and reception module, and an antenna. The module can transmit and receive messages up to 40 Kbit/s [16]. This radio-link is used for some of the extra-linguistic exchanges, as well as the linguistic communication itself. The radio-link is unreliable in the sense that it is not guaranteed that a message arrives, but when it arrives the message contains no errors.

The robots are located in an ecosystem which contains a charging station on which a visible light source is located. Robots can recharge their batteries by sliding into the charging station. There are also 'competitors' in the environment in the form of boxes in which a (modulated) light source is mounted. This light source takes energy from the global energy flowing into the ecosystem. Robots can dim a light by pushing against its box and thus assure that there is enough energy in the charging station. After being dimmed, the light source regenerates, thus requiring the robots to alternate between recharging and work. The biological motivation for this setup is explained in [4].

We now turn to the physical implementation of the different steps in the language game scenario. The objects that can be the topic of a conversation are: obstacles, the robot itself, other robots, the charging station, and the competitors.

3.2 Making Contact

The robot can be in three modes: Regular exploration, being the speaker, and being the hearer. Any robot which is in the first mode may at any time randomly decide to become a speaker, when he 'sees' another robot in the environment. The robots used in these experiments do not have vision. They can however recognise each other because each robot emits infrared as part of its obstacle avoidance behavior. This infrared light is modulated so that the infrared of one robot does not confuse the infrared of another one. A robot detects another one when there is an infrared source which is not his own (see figure 2).

478

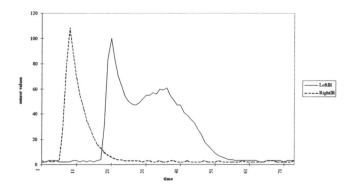

Figure 3: One robot perceives another robot (at the crossing of left and right infrared sensors) and then moves towards it. IR falls off again on approach because the emitters are placed below the receivers and less light is detected.

A robot which has adopted a speaker mode and which detects a possible hearer in the environment emits a request for entering into communication. On receiving this request, the other robot may switch from an exploration mode to a hearer mode. The hearer confirms that he wants to play a hearer role and halts while continuing to emit infrared. On receiving the confirmation, the speaker switches off its infrared and uses infrared-taxis to approach the hearer. Infrared-taxis means that the speaker moves up the infrared gradient as shown in figure 3. Movement stops when the gradient starts to fall off. The speaker broadcasts an "aligned" signal and turns on its infrared.

On receiving the alignment signal, the hearer also tries to position himself so that he faces the speaker. He turns off his own infrared emission and performs the infrared-orientation behavior while not moving forward. When maximum infrared is detected, the hearer emits in turn an "aligned" signal. The speaker turns off its infrared emission. The two robots are now in a situation as depicted in figure 4. They are facing each other and ready for starting a language game.

3.3 Topic Identification

The next problem is how both robots could get a shared perception of the environment. This has been handled as follows: The speaker and the hearer take turns in scanning the environment by making a 360 degree turn. During this scan all the sensory data are recorded giving a panoramic view as shown in figure 5. There is no direct sensing of the degree of turning. The robot recognises that he has turned 360 degrees when the same sensory data are perceived as at the start of turning. The time dimension is later used as a spatial dimension.

The next important issue is what counts as an object.

Figure 4: Two robots have approached each other and are now facing each other. Note the other objects in the environment surrounding the robots, which will be the subject of the conversation.

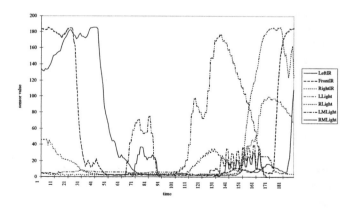

Figure 5: The result of a 360 degree scan for a single robot, in which data from 7 sensory input streams are recorded (no significant data appear on touch sensing or energy sensing).

The robot has no explicit notion of an object and no sophisticated visual sensing that could detect an object by matching it against a background for example. We notice that the robot is facing an object precisely at the point where two sensors of the same type (for example left and right visible light sensors) cross each other, simply because sensors come in pairs and are mounted on each side. Consequently these crossings are taken to be the positions of the object and the states of *all* sensory streams at those points will play a role in formulating a distinctive feature set to categorise the object. For example, another robot will not only be recognisable because he emits infrared light, but also because he reflects visible light, although less than the charging station.

Through this procedure, each robot constructs a series of objects and associated sensory data values. To this the robot adds himself as a possible topic of the conversation. The speaker then selects randomly one object from this list to be the topic of the conversation and proceeds by drawing the attention of the hearer to this object. This is again quite difficult to achieve because the robots have no physical device for pointing. We have opted for a procedure in which the speaker orients himself towards the topic. By convention, the speaker talks about himself when he does not engage in any movement for drawing attention to another object. The hearer can follow the turning and estimate the direction because each robot emits 4 infrared rays mounted on the front, left, back, and right side. Thus by counting the number of passing infrared rays, whose focal points are seen when left and right infrared is crossing, the quadrant in which the topic is located can be calculated (figure 5). For example, when three passing rays are measured, the speaker is pointing direction east which means that the topic is west of the hearer, i.e. to his left side.

Each of these various steps may (and does) go wrong. Sometimes one of the robots turns more than 360 degrees and loses track of its position. The hearer may not be able to detect well the turning of the speaker towards the topic and thus miss the topic. However the general success rate is high enough (about 75 %) to allow subsequent language games. At the moment we obtain 3 to 3,4 language games per minute.

3.4 Categorisation

As discussed in the previous subsection, the robots have a panoramic view of their environment and a list of objects with sensory states for each one. Moreover the topic of the conversation is now known by both robots. The next step is for each to derive a distinctive feature set which allows a discrimination of the topic from the other objects in the context. This proceeds along the lines outlined in section 2.1. The robots build up discrimination trees if there are not enough features to allow discrimination following the procedure describe in section 2.2.

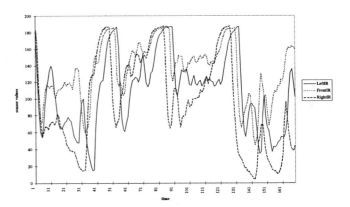

Figure 6: The speaker points towards the topic. The figure shows the infrared detection by the hearer. Each crossing of left and right IR sensors (beyond a certain threshold) indicates that one ray has passed. This happens around point 51, 85, and 131. Note that the data stream is also influenced by reflection from objects around the speaker and the hearer.

3.5 Encoding, Decoding and Feedback

The encoding and decoding steps proceed exactly as outlined earlier in section 2.3. The result of encoding is transmitted through the radio link. The robots use random combinations of letters to form new words when needed. Feedback is based on the same procedure as outlined in section 2.1: When the distinctive feature set decoded by the hearer matches with an expected feature set for the topic, the language game succeeds otherwise it fails. The hearer provides feedback by a signal through the radiolink.

4 Results

We have conducted different experiments with the present implementation. Each experiment consists of a series of language games. The results of one such experiment are now reported.

First we look at the discrimination games between two robots r1 and r2. An object is detected at time/position 176 with the values 9 for channel s0, 0 for s1 and 192 for s2. The discrimination ends in failure but leads to the construction of a new feature detector which expects a positive value for channel 0 (i.e. a value between 0 and 255).

```
Discrimination game by r2
Objects r2:
  o1 [176] [s0:9,s1:0,s2:192]
Topic r2: o1
Failure r2. No feature sets.
New feature detectors r2: r2-s0 [0,255]
```

Here is another discrimination game when the build up of discriminators is already further advanced. Two objects are seen o1 and o2, with both positive values for s0 and s2. This is not enough to discriminate so a new feature detector is created by further subdividing channel 2.

```
Discrimination game by r2
Objects r2:
  o1 [151] [s0:1,s1:0,s2:59]
  o2 [217] [s0:7,s1:0,s2:3]
Topic r2: o1
Feature sets r2:
  o1 {r2-s0,r2-s2}
  o2 {r2-s0,r2-s2}
Failure r2. No distinctive feature sets.
New feature detectors r2: r2-s2-0 [0,127.5]
    r2-s2-1 [127.5,255]
```

Here is a discrimination game involving three objects which is successful:

```
Discrimination game by r2
Objects r2:
  o1 [45] [s0:8,s1:0,s2:5]
  o2 [58] [s0:4,s1:156,s2:2]
  o3 [166] [s0:6,s1:0,s2:187]
Topic r2: o2
Feature sets r2:
  o1 {r2-s0,r2-s2-0}
  o2 {r2-s0,r2-s1,r2-s2-0}
  o3 {r2-s0,r2-s2-1}
Distinctive feature sets r2:
  {{r2-s1}}
Success r2.
```

The set of features of r2 at this point is as follows. Each feature is followed by the range on the channel and the score (use and success) of the feature.

```
r2-s0 [0,255] 125/3
  r2-s0-0 [0,127.5] 111/0
  r2-s0-1 [127.5,255] 92/0
r2-s1 [0,255] 125/11
  r2-s1-0 [0,127.5] 91/0
  r2-s1-1 [127.5,255] 72/0
r2-s2 [0,255] 136/14
  r2-s2-0 [0,127.5] 72/0
  r2-s2-1 [127.5,255] 120/5
```

When games continue, there is further refinement and the features that are most useful increase their use and success, as can be seen from figure 7.

We now look at the language games. An example of a complete successful language game (after 43 discrimination games and language games) is the following:

```
This is dialogue nr 43
Speaker: r2. Hearer: r1.
```

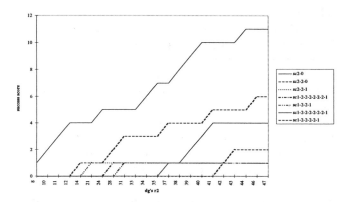

Figure 7: This figure plots in one robot the evolution in the success score of a feature over a period of 45 discrimination games. Features that are relevant in the environment gradually get a higher score.

```
Objects r2:
  o1: [138] [s0:2,s1:0,sc-2:183]
Topic r2: self
Distinctive feature sets r2:
  {{r2-self}}
Objects r1:
  o1: [9] [s0:1,s1:0,s2:186]
  o2: [185] [s0:2,s1:12,s2:188]
Topic r1: o1
Distinctive feature sets r1:
  {{r1-s0,r1-s2-2-2-2-2-1},
   {r1-s1,r1-s2-2-2-2-2-2-1},
   {r1-s0-0,r1-s2-2-2-2-2-1},
   {r1-s1-0,r1-s2-2-2-2-2-2-1},
   {r1-s2-2-2-2-2-1},
   {r1-s2-2-2-2-2-2-1}}
Encoded expression r2: (a b)
Decoded expression r1:
  {{r1-self},{r1-s2-1},{r1-s2-2-0},
   {r1-s2-2-2-2},{r1-s2-2-2-2-1},
   {r1-s0},{r1-s2-2-2-2-2-1},
   {r1-s2-2-2-2-2-1}}
Success
```

The game ends in success because the feature sets decoded by r1 match with one of the distinctive feature sets r1 was expecting. The lexicon of r1, r2 are at this point as follows. The meaning, the word and the score (use/success) is printed out:

```
The lexicon of r1:
r1-self == (a b) 10/1
r1-s2-1 == (a b) 1/1
r1-s2-2-0 == (a b) 3/1
r1-s2-2-2-2 == (a b) 0/0
r1-s2-2-2-2-2-1 == (a b) 0/0
r1-s0 == (a b) 0/0
```

```
r1-s2-2-2-2-2-2-1 == (a b) 1/1
r1-self == (a c) 0/0
r1-s1-2-2-0 == (a d) 0/0

The lexicon of r2
r2-self == (a b) 14/3
r2-s2 == (a b) 2/0
r2-s2-1 == (a b) 2/0
r2-s1-0 == (a b) 4/0
r2-s2-2-1 == (a b) 0/0
r2-s1-2-0 == (a b) 2/1
r2-s1-2-2-0 == (a c) 1/0
```

We see that r2 uses "(a b)" for itself and r1 has coupled the same word to features it uses for recognising r2. r2 has coupled features for r1 to "(a c)" and this is also the name r1 has adopted for itself. Finally "(a d)" is being used as name for the competitors (the boxes in which a modulated infrared is housed).

Overall there is now a context coherence of 88.5% (the agents recognise the same context). The agents successfully recognised each other as the topic 31% of the time. Recognition of other objects was still low after 45 games but increasing.

5   Conclusions

The paper reports on experiments with physically embodied robotic agents which are relevant for two fundamental questions in the origins of cognition, namely (1) how can a set of perceptual categories (a grounded ontology) arise in an agent without the assistance of others and without having been programmed in (in other words not innately provided), and (2) how can a group of distributed agents which each develop their own ontology through interaction with the environment nevertheless develop a shared vocabulary by which they can communicate about their environment.

The proposed solution centers around coupled adaptive discrimination games and adaptive language games. Agents engage in interactions with the environment or with others and change their internal structure in order to be more successful in the next game. Both systems are selectionist: Structure is created by random processes and eliminated based on selectionist criteria centering around use and success in use.

Although we feel that this experiment represents an important milestone, there are obviously many things which can and should be done next, and some of this work is already going on in our laboratory. First, we have done other software simumations showing how spatial categories may become lexicalised [11]. These experiments are currently being ported to physical robots. Second, we are doing experiments in which vision is the primary source of sensory experiences. One of these experiments is based on two robotic heads that are located

near the robotic ecosystem and give comments on the dynamically evolving scene they see before them. The use of vision allows for a much broader repertoire of objects and features and enables us to study how syntactic conventions may arise. The first results of this experiment are reported in [13]. Third, we are investigating other language games, including games where one robot attempts to entice the other robot to perform certain actions. It is clear to us that an exciting new area of bottom-up AI research is opening up and that through language and ontological development a possible road is opening up for evolving cognitive agents in a bottom-up fashion.

6   Acknowledgement

The experiments reported in this paper were conducted at the VUB AI Laboratory. Tony Belpaeme, Andreas Birk, Peter Stuer and Dany Vereertbrugghen have participated in creating and maintaining the robots and the ecosystem at the VUB AI Laboratory used in this experiment. Their contributions are supported by the Belgian government through an IUAP project (1990-1996). We are also indebted to Ruth Aylett from the university of Salford and a number of VUB undergraduate students, who performed the first attempts to develop a physical implementation of the language games.

Luc Steels developed the perception and language game algorithms. His research was financed by the Sony Computer Science Laboratory in Paris. Paul Vogt achieved the successful physical implementation as part of his masters thesis project for Cognitive Science and Engineering at the University of Groningen on a 'stage' at the VUB AI laboratory. This visit was financed by an EU Erasmus fellowship.

References

[1] Brooks, R. and L. Stein (1994) Building Brains for Bodies. Autonomous Robots (1) 7-25.

[2] Edelman, G.M. (1987) *Neural Darwinism: The Theory of Neuronal Group Selection.* New York: Basic Books.

[3] Husbands, P, I. Harvey, D. Cliff (1995) Circle in the Round: State Space attractors for Evolved Sighted robots. In: Steels, L. (ed.) (1995) The Biology and Technology of Intelligent Autonomas Agents. Nato ASI Series, vol 144. Springer Verlag, Berlin. pp. 222-257.

[4] McFarland, D. (1994) In: Proceedings of the third Simulation of Adaptive Behavior Conference. The MIT Press, Cambridge Ma.

[5] MacLennan, B. (1991) Synthetic Ethology: An Approach to the Study of Communication. In: Langton,

C., et.al. (ed.) Artificial Life II. Addison-Wesley Pub. Co. Redwood City, Ca. p. 631-658.

[6] Pfeifer, R. (1996) Building Fungus Eaters: Design Principles of Autonomous Agents. In: Proceedings of Fourth International Conference on Simulation of Adaptive Behavior. The MIT Press, Cambridge Ma.

[7] Steels, L. (1994) The Artificial Life Roots of Artificial Intelligence. *Artificial Life Journal* 1(1), pp. 89-125.

[8] Steels, L. (1994) A case study in the behavior-oriented design of autonomous agents. In: Proceedings of the third Simulation of Adaptive Behavior Conference. The MIT Press, Cambridge Ma.

[9] Steels, L. (1996a) Emergent Adaptive Lexicons. In: Maes, P. (ed.) (1996) From Animals to Animats 4: Proceedings of the Fourth International Conference On Simulation of Adaptive Behavior, The MIT Press, Cambridge Ma.

[10] Steels, L. (1996b) Perceptually grounded meaning creation. In: Tokoro, M. (ed.) (1996) Proceedings of the International Conference on Multi-Agent Systems. AAAI Press, Menlo Park Ca. p. 338-344.

[11] Steels, L. (1996c) A self-organizing spatial vocabulary. Artificial Life Journal, **3**(2).

[12] Steels, L. (1997) Constructing and Sharing Perceptual Distinctions. In: van Someren, M. and G. Widmer (eds.) (1997) Proceedings of the European Conference on Machine Learning. Springer-Verlag, Berlin.

[13] Steels, L. (1997) The origins of syntax in visually grounded robotic agents. In: Polack, M. (ed.) Proceedings of IJCAI 97. AAAI Press, Menlo Park Ca.

[14] Steels, L. and R. Brooks (eds.) (1995) Building Situated Embodied Agents. The Alife route to AI. Lawrence Erlbaum Ass. New Haven.

[15] Werner, G. and M. Dyer (1991) Evolution of Communication in Artificial Organisms. In: Langton, C., et.al. (ed.) Artificial Life II. Addison-Wesley Pub. Co. Redwood City, Ca. p. 659-687.

[16] Vereertbrugghen, D. (1996) Design and Implementation of a Second Generation Sensor-Motor Control Unit for Mobile Robots. Licenciaatsverhandeling VUB Dept of Computer Science. 1996.

[17] Wittgenstein, L. (1974) Philosophical Investigations. Translated by G. Anscombe. Basil Blackwell, Oxford.

[18] Yanco, H. and L. Stein (1993) An Adaptive Communication Protocol for Cooperating Mobile Robots. In: Meyer, J-A, H.L. Roitblat, and S. Wilson (1993) From Animals to Animats 2. Proceedings of the Second International Conference on Simulation of Adaptive Behavior. The MIT Press, Cambridge Ma. p. 478-485

Usage-based Structuralization of Relationships between Words

Takashi Hashimoto

Lab. for Information Representation, FRP,
The Institute of Physical and Chemical Research (RIKEN)
2-1, Hirosawa, Wako, Saitama, 351-01, JAPAN
Tel: +81-48-467-9626, Fax: +81-48-462-9881
takashi@irl.riken.go.jp
http://www.bip.riken.go.jp/irl/takashi/

Abstract

The development of structure of relationships between words is studied with a constructive approach by means of artificial agents with grammar systems. The agents try to recognize given sentences in terms of their own grammar. A word's relationship to other words, which represents meanings of the word, is derived by analyzing the word's usage in sentences, and which is calculated via the mutual dependency between words and sentences. The agents differentiate recognized words into clusters in a space of relationships among words. The structures of clusters can be classified into several types. The dynamics of clusters such as merging, boundary expansions, structural changes are observed. These clusters and their dynamics have some relevance with linguistic categorization.

1 Introduction

Language can be seen as an evolutionary system. At the time of its origin, a successful language must consist of simple syntax, a small number of words, and very few abstractions. Human languages have been constructed through such processes as word formation, grammaticalization, or expression diversification. Our own communication has inherited, via evolutionary pathways, some of the features of animal communication [1]. Accordingly, it is important to study the evolutionary aspects of language from primitive communication systems. Even now language is changing. Pidgin and creole languages are increasing in their complexity, and new expressions are daily being added to every language. Language, in short, is an ever-changing system.

Evolutionary linguistics is a new candidate for potentially clarifying the origins and evolution of language [2]. It is important to note that the origins and evolution of language are typically expressed as such dynamically complex systems as emergence, self-organization, collec-

tive behavior, clustering, diversification, hierarchy formation, and so on.

A language system must have both adaptability and stability. If a language is too rigid, its users will not be able to formulate new expressions to describe diverse experiences, and if it is too unstable, no communication will be possible at all. Geeraerts explains this point as it pertains to categorization: "To prevent the categorical system from becoming chaotic, it should have a built-in tendency towards structural stability, but this stability should not become rigidity, lest the system stops being able to adapt itself to the ever-changing circumstances of the outside world [3]." Such dynamical stability and adaptability is often seen also in complex systems.

Constructive approaches are highly advantageous for understanding dynamically complex systems [4]. These approaches are also useful for studying evolutionary linguistics, because they are based on the notion that language is an emergent phenomena in interacting distributed agents. In contrast to conventional linguistics, which attempt to describe various language phenomena, the constructive approach builds models with elements having its own internal dynamics and interaction among them, and observe emergence of global order as language-like behavior. We insist, however, that only emergence of global order is not enough. Since language is an ever-changing system, models must show not only emergence but the dynamics of global order through the dynamics between elements. Perhaps the most important consideration in the modeling of evolutionary language system is the introduction of the dynamics of elements. Elements can change their internal states and their relationships to other elements. These underlying dynamics often model the dynamics of the global-level relationships.

In keeping with this approach, we previously presented a language game played between number of agents having different grammar systems [5, 6]. We found that evolution of syntactic structure and emergence of community sharing common usages of language. The common usages punctually change through evolution of individual grammars. In the present paper, we incorporate a semantic feature, the relationships among words, into the above work, and tracing the development of this feature so as to understand the development of semantic structures of language.

The most controversial problem in linguistics is defining the meanings of words. A lot of discussion has been devoted to this problem. For example, words can be taken as indicators of external objects; they can be represented by bundles of necessary and sufficient conditions; they can be done by normal form, that is vectors of several features [7]; they can be done by set of binary features. We insist that the meanings of words can best be represented by their interrelationships. As Cruse has written, "We can picture the meaning of a word as a pattern of affinities and disaffinities with all the other words in the language with which it is capable of contracting semantic relations in grammatical context [9]."

The meanings of words should thus be discussed in terms of how language is used [8]. In the present context, this means that a word's relation to other words should be derived by analyzing the word's usage in numerous sentences. It is often said that a word indicates (a class of) objects. For example, the word *cup* indicates an object, cup. However, form a usage-based viewpoint, we rather consider the whole sentence "A word *cup* indicates an object, cup" as one usage of the word itself. This sentence forms a part of the web of semantic interrelationships of the word *cup*, such as with the words *object* or *indicates*.

Relations between words can be characterized as either syntagmatic and paradigmatic. The syntagmatic relation is established by the association of words in a sentence: for instance, by the relation between the words *read* and *book* in the sentence *I read a book*. The paradigmatic relation represents a semantic similarity between two grammatically identical words: for instance, the relation between the words *book* and *magazine* in the sentences *I read a book* and *I read a magazine*. Paradigmatic relations can be grasped through syntagmatic relations. In the above examples, the sentence *I read a book* suggests the syntagmatic relation between the words *read* and *book* and the sentence *I read a magazine* the syntagmatic relation between *read* and *magazine*. Through the basis of their relations with the word *read*, the words *book* and *magazine* can also be related. Further relating, the two sentences, the words *I* and *a* can be related to *book* and *magazine*. But because since words are used in many different sentences, the web of relationships among them assumes different forms according to their usage.

We evaluate such interrelationships by gauging a word's similarity to all other words based on its usage in sentences. Similarity is an important concept with respect to categorization. Entities are categorized via their similarity with each other. Similarity is a graded and subjective notion. To calculate the similarity of words based on their usage in sentences, we adopt Karov and Edelman's algorithm [10], which allows for the similarities to be graded. Karov and Edelman stress the mutual dependency between words and sentences, i.e., that similar words are used in similar sentences and similar sentences are composed of similar words.

The rest of this paper is organized as follows. At first, we define an artificial agent with grammar systems and its modification instructions as well as the calculation algorithm of similarity among words. After showing the basic characteristics of the similarity formula, simulation results of agents with grammar modification are shown. This results in a classification of structures according to their word similarities, as well as a developmental pathway for the structures. Finally, we discuss relevance of the structures of word similarities and their dynamics with linguistic categorization.

2 Model

In this section we describe our model. We first define agents as grammar systems, then detail their sentence-recognition process. Next, we define a method of articulating a sequence of words in a *sentence*, that is a sequence of the symbols '0' and '1'. Next, the similarities among words are defined. Finely, instructions for modifying a grammar system are given.

2.1 Agent

An agent is defined as a grammar system,

$$G_i = (V_\mathrm{N}, V_\mathrm{T}, F_i, S), \qquad (1)$$

where V_N is a set of non-terminal symbols, V_T is a set of terminal symbols, F_i is a list of rewriting rules, S is a start symbol, and a suffix i is ID of an agent. In this paper we use $V_\mathrm{N} = \{S, A, B\}$, $V_\mathrm{T} = \{0, 1\}$ as non-terminal and terminal symbols, respectively. A rewriting rule is an ordered pair (α, β) which is written as $\alpha \to \beta$. Here, α is a symbol over V_N. And β is an arbitrary finite string of symbols over $V_N \cup V_T$ not including the same symbol with α. The type of grammar that an agent can have is a context-free or regular grammar here.

2.2 Recognition of Sentences

Agents that are defined as grammar systems try to speak and recognize sentences. During this recognition process, an agent tries to rewrite from a given sentence into the start symbol S by use of its own grammar. The sentence is checked against each rule in the rule list, beginning with the topmost rule, to determine whether it contains the element in the righthand side of each rule. If it does, then the leftmost sequence that is equivalent to the righthand side is rewritten as the lefthand side of the rule. If the agent has no applicable rule even if the rewritten sentence is not S, the rewritten sentence is put back one step and the searching and rewriting processes restart from the next rule of the applied rule in the agent's rule list. This process is recursively applied. If an agent can put a given sentence back to the symbol S within 500 rewriting steps, we say that the agent can recognize the word.

2.3 Articulation

We introduce a method of articulating a sequence of words in a sentence based on the parsing of that sentence. Agents have three types of rewriting rules:

$$N \rightarrow \text{sequence of } T\text{s}, \qquad (2)$$

$$N \rightarrow \text{sequence of } N\text{s}, \qquad (3)$$

$$N \rightarrow \text{sequence of } N\text{s and } T\text{s}, \qquad (4)$$

where N and T are a non-terminal and a terminal symbol, respectively. A *word* is a series of terminal symbols in Eqs. (2) and (4). A sentence is a sequence of terminal symbols. Each agent articulates sequences of words within sentences by parsing it.

For example, an agent with a rewriting rule list, $S \rightarrow A0B, A \rightarrow 10, B \rightarrow 11$, parses a sentence "10011" as

$$10011 \overset{A \leftarrow 10}{\Longrightarrow} A011 \overset{B \leftarrow 11}{\Longrightarrow} A0B \overset{S \leftarrow A0B}{\Longrightarrow} S$$

and articulates it as a sequence of words "10·0·11". A mark '·' is used for a separator between words. The parsing tree is depicted in Fig. 1(a).

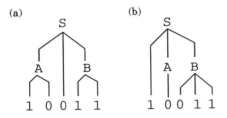

Figure 1: Two examples of a parsing tree.

The way of articulation of a given sentence depends on the rule list, which expresses the subjective aspect of similarity among words. The sentence in the above example, "10011," will be broken down into the word sequence "1·0·011" by an agent with the rewriting rule list, $S \rightarrow 1AB, A \rightarrow 0, B \rightarrow 011$, through the recognition process,

$$10011 \overset{A \leftarrow 0}{\Longrightarrow} 1A011 \overset{B \leftarrow 011}{\Longrightarrow} 1AB \overset{S \leftarrow 1AB}{\Longrightarrow} S,$$

the parsing tree of which is shown in Fig. 1(b).

2.4 Similarity and Affinity

Relationships between words are defined by the similarity of their usage in sentences. We use Karov and Edelman's definition [10] with some revisions. A key concept in this definition is that of the mutual dependency of words and sentences. That is, similar words appear in similar sentences and similar sentences are composed of similar words. We call a space of relationship among words *word-space*.

The similarities between words and between sentences are respectively defined by the following formulae:

$$sim_{n+1}(w_i, w_j) =
\begin{cases}
\sum_{s \ni w_i} weight(s, w_i) aff_n(s, w_j) & \text{if } i \neq j, \\
1.0 & \text{if } i = j,
\end{cases} \qquad (5)$$

and

$$sim_{n+1}(s_i, s_j) =
\begin{cases}
\sum_{w \in s_i} weight(w, s_i) aff_n(w, s_j) & \text{if } i \neq j, \\
1.0 & \text{if } i = j.
\end{cases} \qquad (6)$$

The functions $aff_n(s, w)$ and $aff_n(w, s)$ represent the affinity of a word for a sentence and that of a sentence for a word, respectively. They are defined as

$$aff_n(s, w) = \sum_{s' \ni w} weight(s', w) sim_n(s, s') , \qquad (7)$$

$$aff_n(w, s) = \sum_{w' \in s} weight(w', s) sim_n(w, w') . \qquad (8)$$

In the above four formulae, a suffix n indicates number of times to iterate, $w \in s$ means words included in a sentence s, and $s \ni w$ means sentences including a word w. The functions $weight(s, w)$ and $weight(w, s)$ are normalizing factors that decide what contribution each word and sentence will make toward affinity and similarity. They are given by

$$weight(s, w) = \frac{factor(s, w)}{\sum_{s' \ni w} factor(s', w)} , \qquad (9)$$

$$factor(s, w) = \frac{p(s)}{\#(s, w)} , \qquad (10)$$

$$weight(w, s) = \frac{factor(w, s)}{\sum_{w' \in s} factor(w', s)} , \qquad (11)$$

and

$$factor(w, s) = \frac{1}{p(w) lg(s)} . \qquad (12)$$

In Eqs. (10) and (12), $p(w)$ and $p(s)$ are the appearance probabilities of a word w and a sentence s, respectively;

$lg(s)$ is the length of a sentence s, which is defined by the number of words included in the sentence; and $\#(s, w)$ is the number of appearances of a sentence s including a word w. The more a word is used, the less informative it is, but the more a sentence is used , the greater its contribution. A word in a longer sentence is less important than one in a shorter sentence. If a word is absent in many sentences, its effect on similarity and affinity will be greater than that of ubiquitous used words.

At the initial iteration step ($n = 0$), the diagonal part of word similarity ($sim_0(w_i, w_i)$) is 1.0; the others are 0.0. Word-sentence affinity (Eq. (8)) at $n = 0$ is calculated from this initial word similarity matrix. Then, these four formulae are iteratively calculated as Eqs. (6) $\rightarrow$ (7) $\rightarrow$ (5) $\rightarrow$ (8).

2.5 Modification of Grammar

The grammar of an agent is modified in the course of time, depending on the usage at recognition processes. Modifications of the rule list are defined by the following three processes:

adding modification An altered rule of the mostly used rule at recognition processes is added to the end of the rule list.

replacing modification A randomly selected rule from the whole rule list is replaced with an altered rule.

deleting modification The least used rule is deleted from the rule list.

The times of use of each rule are counted only upon successful recognition of a path. Rules which are rewritten to erroneous recognition paths are not regarded as being used. These modifications are applied in probabilities m_{add}, m_{rep}, and m_{del}, respectively.

The ways of altering of a rule are as follows: 1) Replace a symbol of the left-hand of the rule with another non-terminal symbol. 2) Replace a symbol in the right-hand of the rule with another non-terminal or terminal symbol. 3) Insert a symbol in the right-hand side of the rule. 4) Delete a symbol from the right-hand of the rule. One of these alterations, as well as the point of insertion, replacement, or deletion in a rule, is randomly determined.

3   Characteristics of Word Similarity

We shall begin the analysis of our system with a consideration of the characteristics of word similarity. Similarity, straightforwardly understood from the earlier definition, has the following properties: Word similarity with the word itself is always 1.0; A word has higher similarity with a word in a frequent sentence than with one in a rare sentence; It has higher similarity with a word in a

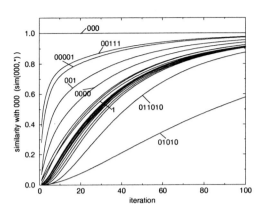

Figure 2: Transition of similarity of a word '000' with the other words per iteration of calculation of similarity and affinity. Iteration step vs. word similarity of a word '000' with the other words.

short sentence than with one in a long sentence; It has lower similarity with a word which is used with a frequent word in a sentence than with a word which is used with a rare word.

Words, even if they are not used in a sentence, can have similarity through their relation with other words. By a sentence "$w_1 \cdot w_2$," the word w_1 has similarity with the word w_2. Another sentence, "$w_2 \cdot w_3$," is the case for the similarity between the words w_2 and w_3. Despite the fact that no sentence uses w_1 and w_3 simultaneously, these two words come to have similarity through w_2 by iteration of the calculation algorithm. If the words have similar way of use within sentences, they are regarded as highly similar. With this feature of the algorithm we can take the paradigmatic relations between words into consideration.

Word and sentence similarity are non-decreasing functions of the iteration number n, if the weight functions, Eqs. (9) and (11), do not change in the course of iteration. Therefore, similarity converges to 1.0 after all.

The above characteristics are clearly seen in the following simulation, in which the grammar of agents is not modified in the course of simulation. Randomly generated sentences, in which the maximum number of symbols in a sentence is restricted to 8, are given to an agent until it recognizes 100 sentences. The similarity between all word-pairs is calculated after recognitions of 100 sentences. Since the appearance probabilities of each word and sentence are fixed after all recognitions, the weight functions do not change in the calculation.

An example of word similarity change per iteration is shown in Fig. 2 for a word '000'.[1] We can see mono-

---

[1] The rule list of the agent in this example is copied from a agent

tonically increasing curves of similarity, which will converge to 1.0. Similarity with the word itself, indicated by '000', is always 1.0 by definition. Similarities with words '00111' and '00001' rapidly increase in early iteration steps. Because these words are used in two-word sentences with the word '000' as "000·00111" (3 times) and "000·00001" (2 times), respectively, they have direct and strong relations. The difference between $sim(000, 00111)$ and $sim(000, 00001)$ depends on the times to be used. A word '0000' is used in a three-word sentence "000·0000·1" (2 times). Therefore the word '0000' has high similarity with '000'. In spite the use of '1' in the same sentence, the word has less similarity with '000' than similarity between the words '000' and '0000'. This is because the word '1' is used many more times (79 times) than the word '0000' (9 times).

Resemblance of usage of words in different sentences gives a high similarity value even when the words are not used in a sentence, as can be seen in the similarity between '000' and '001'. The word '001', which is not used with '000' in any sentence, is used only in sentences "001·00111," "001·00001" and "001·0000·1." But the respective usages of the words '000' and '001' resemble each other in these and the above listed sentences. Therefore $sim(000, 001)$ is a rather high value (Fig. 2).

4 Results of Simulation with Modification of Grammar

We describe the results of simulation with the rule modification processes which are introduced in §2.5. Sentences of at most 8 symbols are given to some agents. Similarity is calculated when the agent recognizes a given sentence. Thus the iteration step coincides with the number of recognized sentences. The modification occurs every 10 given sentences. Probabilities for rule modifications are $m_{add} = m_{rep} = m_{del} = 0.3$.

4.1 Dynamics of Word Similarity

Since similarity is calculated dynamically, the weight functions are not fixed in the course of iteration. Figure 3 is an example of transition of word similarity per each recognition. The initial rule list is the same as that for the agent depicted in the previous section.

In this case, the similarity functions are not non-decreasing. We can see more complex dynamics than that of without modification of grammar. Similarity with new words climbs from 0.0, while similarities with already appeared words are pulled down by the effect of the new words. Some words form clusters, as described in the next subsection. Similarities with words in a cluster show synchronized transition.

evolved in a simulation of our previous work [5, 6].

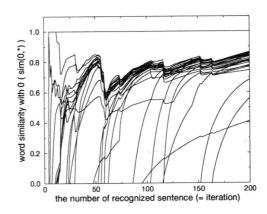

Figure 3: An example of transition of word similarity per each recognition. In this simulation, similarity is calculated per each recognition. Therefore the scale of horizontal axis coincides with the number of iteration. Rule list is modified per 10 given sentences. The initial rule list is the same as that in the example in the previous section. The similarity of a word '0' with other words is shown. X-axis is the number of recognized sentences (= iteration step), and Y-axis is word similarity.

4.2 Classification of Structure in Word-space

Words are clustered in word-space, the space of word similarity, according to having or not having similarity with each other. Various shapes of structures of cluster appear in the course of simulations. Their variety depends on the initial grammar of the agents. We classify structures in word-space into six types according to their shapes. Examples of simple structures of each type are shown in Fig. 4. Structures in word-space in actual simulations are compositions of some of these types.

The features of these graphs can be summarized by one of the following. (a) Words have no relation to other words; we call such words solitary words. (b) Words in a cluster have almost identical similarities with each other; we term this a flat cluster. (c) Words form a cluster, but similarity depends on words and gradually decays; we term this a gradual cluster. (d) Words are in a cluster but there are two peaks of similarity. Similarity from a word decays along one side but climbs along the opposite side; we term this a two-peak cluster. (e) There is a cluster having a stepwise structure. Words are thought to be divided in sub-clusters. (f) Words form plural, unrelated clusters.

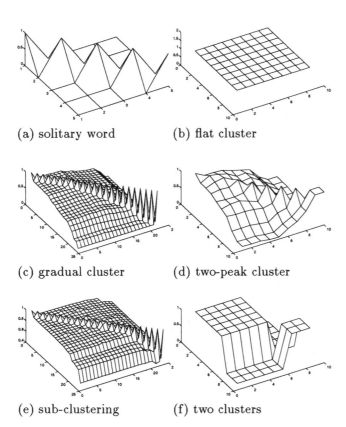

(a) solitary word   (b) flat cluster

(c) gradual cluster   (d) two-peak cluster

(e) sub-clustering   (f) two clusters

Figure 4: Examples of structures in word-space. Z-axis is word similarity defined by Eq. (5). Words are aligned in X- and Y- axes in descending order from a standard word appropriately selected to smoothly change similarities. We have six distinct types of structures. (a) Solitary word. No words have any similarity with the others. (b) Flat cluster. All words have almost identical similarity with the all other words. In these two cases, (a) and (b), the shape of clusters does not depend on the order of words in the X- and Y- axes. (c) Gradual cluster. Words are arranged in the X-axis in descending order of similarity with a standard word. In this case: '0' (standard word), '1', '11', $\cdots$, '111'. In case of gradual cluster, similarities of words with the last word in X-axis, '111', are also descent order. (d) Two-peak cluster. Words are arranged in the same manner as in (c). In this example: '11' (standard word), '0', $\cdots$, '0010'. In contrast with the gradual cluster, similarities of words with the last word in X-axis, '0010', are ascending order. (e) Sub-clustering. Words are again arranged in the same manner. In this example, '0' (standard word), '0000', $\cdots$, '00000'. Words are divided into two groups which have almost the same value of similarity with words in the same group. (f) Two clusters. There are two independent clusters in word-space.

4.3 Dynamics of Structure in Word-space

A general scenario of the development of structure in word-space is the following. At first an agent can recognize only a one-word sentence. It then develops the ability to recognize several sentences, but these all are one-word sentences, and therefore there are several solitary words in word-space. Then it becomes able to articulate sentences into plural words, which forms relations between words. Eventually words form gradual clusters in word-space. Such clusters change their structure through such processes as expansion of boundary or mergence of two clusters. Parallel to this development in word-space, the syntactic structure also develops from sequential, to branch, to loop structures.

Let us examine this scenario thoroughly by the example of two simulations. One is a simulation from the simplest grammar, namely from only one rewriting rule, which will show the developmental path in the early stage. The other is from a large grammar and will illustrate structural change in clusters.

4.3.1 Development in Early Stage

A simulation which is started from agents with only one rule as the initial grammar is taken to illustrate development in word-space at the early stage. We will be able to see typical pathways of development where sentences make relations between some solitary words and expand boundary of a cluster.[2]

An agent whose initial grammar has only a rule $S \rightarrow 1$ hears randomly generated sentences and tries to recognize them. Grammar of the agent changes in the course of simulation according to the modification method of grammar defined in §2.5.

Figure 5 shows increases in the whole number of recognized sentences, indicated by 'whole' in the graph and denoted N_r, and in the number of distinct sentences, indicated by 'distinct' in the graph and denoted N_k. We depict developmental pathways of structures in word-space by showing some snapshot figures of word-space in Fig. 6. Words articulated from recognized sentences are aligned as '0', '1', '01', '101', '10', '11', '011', '00' from 1 to 8 on the X and Y axes to clearly show structural changes in word-space.

The first sentence the agent can recognize is "1", and it is a one-word sentence. The shape in word-space is the simplest structure as Fig. 6(a), a solitary word structure classified in §4.2.

Since all sentences , which appear until N_g is 1580, namely "0","1", "01", "101", and "10", are recognized

---

[2]We should say it is an atypical example of simulation starting from small grammar. In case that the initial grammar is quite small, it is hard to develop to be able to recognize enough sentences to show particular structure in word-space. Since the modification ways introduced in §2.5 are rather weak in order to enlarge the set of recognizable sentences.

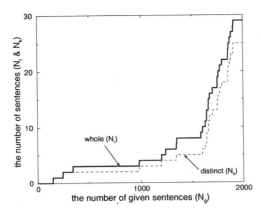

Figure 5: Transitions of the number of whole (N_r) and distinct (N_k) sentences which are recognized by an agent per each given sentence. The solid and dashed lines are the whole and distinct number of sentences recognized by an agent, respectively.

as one-word sentences, there are only solitary words in word-space (Fig. 6(b)).

From N_g of around 1580 to 1900, N_r of the developing agent is on a rapid increase phase as in Fig. 5. This phase begins when the agent gets an effective loop structure in its grammar. A set of recognizable sentences is enlarged by this loop structure. The fact that N_k also grows almost parallel to the line of N_r implies that the agent recognizes many new sentences.

In this rapid increase phase, many of the new sentences are no more than one-word in length. They make connections between solitary words. For example, a sentence "000111" first recognized at N_g is 1599 is articulated to "0·0·01·1·1". By this sentence solitary words '0', '1', and '01' are related and these three words form a gradual cluster (Fig. 6(c)). By the next recognized sentence, "0·0·101·1·1·1", a word '101' is incorporated into this cluster. As this manner, all five of the solitary words are related by $N_g = 1641$ (Fig. 6(d)).

The boundary of the cluster is extended through recognition of new sentences. A new word '11' is incorporated into the cluster at $N_g = 1747$ by a sentence "0·101·11" (Fig. 6(e)). At $N_g = 2853$ a sentence "0·0·0·1·011·1" expands the boundary to a new word '011' (Fig. 6(f)).

4.3.2 Development from Large Grammar

In this subsection, we exemplify a developmental path from an agent with many rules in its grammar. If an agent has the ability to recognize sentences to some extent at the initial point, it is likely to develop some structure in word-space. We will show a merging process of

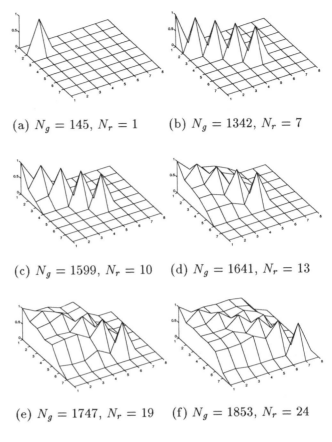

(a) $N_g = 145$, $N_r = 1$ (b) $N_g = 1342$, $N_r = 7$

(c) $N_g = 1599$, $N_r = 10$ (d) $N_g = 1641$, $N_r = 13$

(e) $N_g = 1747$, $N_r = 19$ (f) $N_g = 1853$, $N_r = 24$

Figure 6: Developmental path of structures in word-space of an agent from one rule as an initial grammar is shown. Z-axis is word similarity. Words are arranged in XY-plane to clearly show the clustering and its dynamics in word-space. That is, '0', '1', '01', '101', '10', '11', '011', '00' from 1 to 8. The symbols N_g and N_r in the equations under each graph are the number of given and recognized sentences, respectively.

clusters, a structural change from plural peak to nearly flat cluster, and a boundary expansion.

The agent in the following example is the same as that used in §3. There are 33 rules in the initial grammar of the agent. We would like to focus attention on a scenario of structural change in word-space. In the early period, there are two clusters and a solitary word (Fig. 7(a)). One cluster has a ragged surface and the other has a flat one. At $N_g = 74$, the former cluster develops two peaks. The latter expands its boundary and also becomes a two-peak cluster (Fig. 7(b)).

We can see a merging process of three clusters into a nearly flat cluster through the three-peak structure in Fig. 7(b) $\sim$ (f). A sentence "00·0101·1" connects two clusters mentioned above (Fig. 7(c)). This sentence does not contain a new word, but the usage of words in this sentence is quite new. The solitary word is included in the first cluster, and the three clusters begin to have stronger relations through more sentences (Fig. 7(d)). The connected cluster changes into a three-peak shape (Fig. 7(e)). But this three-peak structure does not endure for long before turning into a nearly flat cluster structure with an expanding boundary (Fig. 7(f)).

By recognizing new sentences, the cluster gets bigger and incorporates more solitary words (Fig. 7(g) and (h)). The similarity among old words loses its raggedness, but the new words have a smaller similarity at its boundary (Fig. 7(i)).

In the period of $N_g = 1680 \sim 1940$, the agent can recognize almost all words. This is because, by this time, the agent has one of the following two rule sets in its grammar:

$$S \to 0, A \to 1, A \to B, B \to S, S \to AA,$$

or

$$S \to 0, A \to 1, S \to AA, A \to S.$$

By this set of rules, all sentences except for a sentence "1" can be recognized. All sentences are broken break to combinations of the words '0' and '1' by this grammar, therefore no new word appears during this period. Consequently, the boundary of the cluster no longer expands, and the similarity among almost all words in the cluster finally approaches 1.0, which is the reflex of the convergence nature noted in §3, and which makes the structure of the cluster nearly flat, as in Fig. 7(j).

5 Discussion

5.1 Clustering as Categorization

We have shown clustering structures in §4. These clusterings can be regarded as categorizations of words by the agent, since words in a cluster have stronger relation with each other and less relations with words out of the cluster. Let us devote a little more space to discussing each types of structure classified in §4.2 from this point of view.

A solitary word is a word without any similarity to other words (Fig. 4(a)). Strictly speaking, we cannot say it is a cluster and also a category. Actually, we do not have a category with only one member in our knowledge system. There might be, however, such a simple structure of knowledge at the very beginning of our development.

All words in a flat cluster structure have almost identical similarity (Fig. 4(b)). Since its boundary is sharp, it is clear whether an entity is a member of the cluster or not. This type of cluster is like a category in which members are rigidly determined by *necessary and sufficient conditions* as scientific notions.

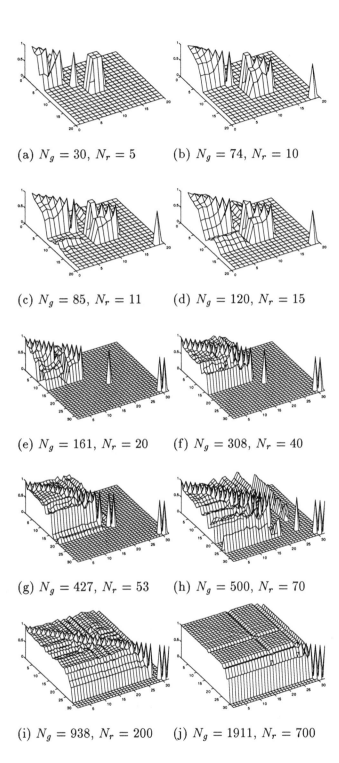

(a) $N_g = 30, N_r = 5$ (b) $N_g = 74, N_r = 10$

(c) $N_g = 85, N_r = 11$ (d) $N_g = 120, N_r = 15$

(e) $N_g = 161, N_r = 20$ (f) $N_g = 308, N_r = 40$

(g) $N_g = 427, N_r = 53$ (h) $N_g = 500, N_r = 70$

(i) $N_g = 938, N_r = 200$ (j) $N_g = 1911, N_r = 700$

Figure 7: Developmental path of structures in word-space is shown. Z-axis is word similarity. Words are arranged in XY-plane to clearly show clustering and its dynamics in word-space. The symbols N_g and N_r in the equations under each graph are the number of recognized and given sentences, respectively.

In contrast to the flat cluster, a gradual cluster has a graded change in similarity from large to small (Fig. 4(c)). This cluster has a peak. If we think of it as a category, a peak corresponds to the central member of a category. Words having small similarity with the central one are peripheral members of the category. This structure is like a *prototype category* [11, 12]. To what extent words are included in the category is matter of gradient.

The two-peak cluster (Fig. 4(d)) is an analogue of a category with two central members. It can be regarded as a *polysemous category*. All words in a single peak structure are characterized by how similar they are to a central member in the category. Whereas in the plural peak structure, such as in the case of two peaks, there are words which are similar to one central member but not to the other one, and there are words which have some degree of similarity to both central members of a category.

We can see the sub-clustering structure into two groups of words in a cluster (Fig. 4(e)). One is words with high similarity and the other is words with rather lower similarity. The two groups can be regarded as two subcategories within the category. This is the simplest case of a hierarchy of categories.

The structures of categories should change through various experiences. In our model, we have seen dynamics of clusters in word-space in §4.3.1 and §4.3.2. These dynamics are the expansion of boundaries, the establishing of connections between clusters, the incorporation of solitary words, and the structural changes from gradual or two-peak to flat cluster.

In the case of boundary expansions of clusters as in Fig. 6(d) ∼ (f) and Fig. 7(f) ∼ (i), the structure of the original clusters does not undergo large change. This satisfies the requirements for adaptability and stability of categorical system noted in §1 and shows resemblance, also in the context of dynamics, to the prototype category in its feature of flexibility, as expressed by Taylar when he says: "Prototype categories have a flexibility ··· in being able to accommodate new, hitherto unfamiliar data. ··· New entries and new experiences can be readily associated, perhaps as peripheral members, to a prototype category, without necessarily causing any fundamental restructuring of the category system [12]."

What, then, is the correspondence with a sentence making connection between clusters as shown in Fig. 7(c)? One candidate is metaphorical expression. A metaphor connects two semantic domains. For example, in the sentence *Sally is a block of ice*, the domains of the human and nonhuman or of the animate and non animate entities are connected.

But we cannot insist on this correspondence so strongly. Metaphor is not the only connection between two domains, although the basic logic of an original domain is applied to a destination domain by metaphor. Usually, the original domain is concrete and easy to conceptualize; on the other hand, the destination is abstract and hard to conceptualize [13]. But in our case, the two clusters are merely related, and we can discuss neither the mapping of logic between two categories nor which is abstract or concrete.

5.2   Future Problems

We plan to extend our model to a communication network system to discuss the emergence of a social structure among agents. In addition to this extension, we hope to address the following problems.

5.2.1   Convergence Nature of Word Similarity

The similarity among words and that of sentences by our definition has a non-decreasing nature. Therefore, by static calculation the similarities finally converges to 1.0, as shown in §3. This nature appears even in the dynamical calculation in §4, and structures in word-space tend to approach nearly flat clusters. This is partly because the set of vocabulary and symbols in our model is much smaller than that in an actual language system. To avoid this convergence, we should set some restrictions to calculate similarity.

5.2.2   Language Externals

We can show the dynamics of categorization and discuss the correspondences of our results with notion of prototype category, i. e., peaks in a cluster and prototype, or boundary expansion and flexibility. These correspondences will provide a clue to study the dynamics of categorization. But in order to investigate the problem more deeply, especially with respect to the prototype category, we should take into consideration not only interactions with other agent and entities within embedded environments but also interactions of the ability of language use with other cognitive and motor competence.

Our model might be highly structuralistic to talk over such cognitive linguistic notion as the prototype category. There is no external world of agent in our system and similarity and categorization are discussed based on language internal relations. Cognitive linguists say that effects from the language externals are important to the prototype categorization, as Taylor explains: "Prototype effects ··· arise from an interaction of core meaning with non-linguistic factors like perception and world knowledge, and can thus be assigned to other components of the mind [12]." How we incorporate such language external systems into our model is the next important problem.

6 Conclusion

We have proposed an evaluation of semantic relationship based on the relative similarity of language usages, and we have introduced a definition of similarity among words. We studied the development of structure in word similarity space in an artificial agent with a grammar system. Structures of cluster in word similarity space were classified into six groups: solitary word, flat cluster, gradual cluster, two-peak cluster, sub-clustering structure and plural clusters. The dynamics of the structures were found to consist of association of solitary words, boundary expansion, mergence of clusters, and structural change from gradual or two-peak cluster into flat structure. The relevance of these clustering and their dynamics with linguistic categorization was suggested.

Acknowledgment

This work is supported by the Special Postdoctoral Researchers Program at RIKEN. I am grateful to Associate Prof. Takashi Ikegami for his helpful comments and the encouragement. I would like to thank Prof. Shun-ichi Amari for his continual encouragement.

References

[1] Hauser, M. D., (1996), *The evolution of communication*, The MIT Press, Cambridge, MA

[2] Steels, L., (1997), Synthesising the origins of language and meaning using co-evolution, self-organisation and level formation, in *Evolution of Human Language*, Hurford, J (ed.), Edinburgh Univ. Press, Edinburgh

[3] Geeraerts, D., (1985), Cognitive restrictions on the structure of semantic change, in *Historical Semantics*, Fisiak, J (ed.), Mouton de Gruyter, Berlin, 127–153

[4] Kaneko, K. and Tsuda, I., (1994), Constructive complexity and artificial reality: an introduction, *Physica*, **D75**, 1–10

[5] Hashimoto, T. and Ikegami, T., (1995), Evolution of Symbolic Grammar Systems, *Advances in Artificial Life*, F. Morán et al. (eds.), Springer, Belrin, 812–823

[6] Hashimoto, T. and Ikegami, T., (1996), Emergence of net-grammar in communicating agents, *BioSystems*, **38**,1–14

[7] Putnum, H., (1975), The meaning of 'meaning', in *Mind, language and reality*, Cambridge University Press, New York, NY

[8] Wittgenstein, L., (1953), *Philosophische Untersuchungen*, Basil Blackwell

[9] Cruse, D. A., (1986), *Lexical Semantics*, Cambridge University Press, Cambridge

[10] Karov, Y. and Edelman, S., (1996), Similarity-based word sense disambiguation, Technical Report of Weizmann Institute, CS-TR 96-06

[11] Lakoff, G., (1987), *Women, Fire, and Dangerous Things*, Chicago , The University of Chicago Press

[12] Taylor, J. R., (1995), *Linguistic Categorization – Prototypes in Linguistic Theory*, Oxford, Oxford University Press

[13] Lakoff, G and Johnson, M., (1980), *Metaphors We Live By*, Chicago, The University of Chicago Press

Learning, Culture and Evolution in the Origin of Linguistic Constraints

Simon Kirby & James Hurford
Department of Linguistics
University of Edinburgh
Edinburgh
Scotland
simon@ling.ed.ac.uk

Abstract

This paper presents a computational model of language learning, transmission, and evolution. We contrast two explanations for the observed fit of language universals with language function that are prominent in the linguistics literature, and which appear to rely on very different explanatory mechanisms — innate constraints on the one hand, and parsing influenced language change on the other. We show using our model that both explanations can be subsumed under one mechanism of differential take up of competing forms in the language community and subsequent evolution of the learning mechanism to efficiently learn regularities in the input.

1   Introduction

One of the interesting challenges facing linguistics today is the explanation of the observed constraints on cross-linguistic variation.[1] Traditional linguistic typology (e.g. [14, 9, 16, 10]) as well as generative theories of language acquisition (e.g. [5, 15]) highlight the fact that the languages of the world appear to fall into a narrowly defined region of the space of logically possible languages. A language typology is a categorisation of some interesting subset of the dimensions along which languages can vary, and language universals are logical statements that relate orthogonal dimensions of such a typology. Although there is a lively debate about what these universal constraints on variation actually are, and what constitutes evidence for them [31], the greatest area of disagreement is clearly how to go about explaining the origins of these constraints [28]. The questions that this conflict of explanation gives rise to go to the heart of modern linguistics.

In this paper we will be examining one aspect of linguistic constraints: the appearance of design. Many attempts at explaining universals have pointed out their fit to the functions of language. Hawkins [17, 18] for example, attempts to explain a whole range of universals relating to word order in terms of the processing load on the human parser. Although this kind of research (known as functionalist explanations in linguistics) is important, we believe they leave the real problem unanswered – how exactly do functional pressures end up being expressed as cross-linguistic constraints on variation? Another influential strand of research (known as formal or innatist linguistics) treats language universals as the direct consequence of the structure of a domain specific language acquisition device (LAD) [5]. Although this bypasses the problem of how the constraints emerge, it fails to explain why the constraints appear to be designed for the purpose of making language easier to parse, for example.

In this paper we will argue that the obvious solution to this problem, namely that the LAD has evolved through natural selection to constrain languages to be functional, cannot work. This is true even though just such a constraining LAD would eventually led to a fitter population. Instead, we will show using a computational simulation of evolving and communicating language learners that a *linguistic* selection process means that languages themselves adapt over a historical (cultural) timescale. Surprisingly, this historical adaptation can *enable* or *bootstrap* the evolution of a functional LAD after all. What we are left with is a simple unified explanation of both innate *and* historically emergent constraints on cross-linguistic variation.

2   Phylogenetic functionalism

The Chomskyan LAD is assumed to alleviate the problems of learnability in natural language by severely constraining the search space for the language learner. The Principles and Parameters model, for example, can be thought of as a set of universal absolute constraints on linguistic variation (principles) and a set of finitely variable switches (parameters) that the learner varies in re-

---

[1] The authors would like to thank Ian Hodson, Bill Turkel, and Rob Clark for their helpful comments and assistance. Of course, they may well disagree with the contents of this paper. All correspondence should be addressed to the first author. This research was supported by ESRC grant R000236551 and by a visiting fellowship at the Collegium Budapest Institute of Advanced Study.

sponse to input data. The crucial input data to the learner in this view is *trigger experience* in that it triggers the setting of a particular parameter. The exact algorithm that governs parameter setting will be discussed below.

This theory of language acquisition is innatist since the learner is assumed to come equipped with knowledge about the target system at birth — specifically, the principles and the existence of parameters (although not the particular setting of those parameters). This means that language universals are directly explicable in terms of the constraints built into language learners from birth. If these universals look like they are designed to alleviate parsing pressures as Hawkins argues, then we are lead to the conclusion that the innate LAD must somehow be set up in such a way as to be *functional* or *adaptive* for the users of language. More precisely, the LAD in this view is set up in such a way that it constrains humans from acquiring languages that are dysfunctional in some way, for example by being hard to parse.

The remaining question is how the LAD came to be endowed with these functional constraints. Newmeyer [30] argues that the obvious answer is that the LAD has evolved through a process of natural selection. Fitter individuals are presumably those that are able to receive and transmit linguistic signals most efficiently, and hence it is unsurprising that LADs that lead to linguistic systems that are more communicatively efficient will be selected for. We will refer to this view as *phylogenetic functionalism*.

An example of the way phylogenetic functionalism works is given by the Subjacency Condition [33]:

Subjacency condition No rule can relate X, Y in the structure

$$\ldots X \ldots [\alpha \ldots [\beta \ldots Y \ldots$$
$$\text{or}$$
$$\ldots Y \ldots]\beta \ldots]\alpha \ldots X \ldots$$

where α, β are bounding nodes.

This is an example of a cross-linguistic universal principle that operates to constrain the distance over which a rule (typically movement of an element in a structure) can operate. The definition of *bounding node* is an example of a parameter, since it has been shown to vary from language to language within certain limits. In English, the bounding nodes are IP and NP which leads to the ungrammaticality of the sentences below in which *who* needs to be directly related to its trace over two intermediate bounding nodes:[2]

(1) *Paul phoned the singer who$_i$ we recorded $_{NP}$[the song which$_j$ $_{IP}$[t_i sang t_j]]

(2) *Who$_i$ did $_{IP}$[Paul tell you when$_j$ $_{IP}$[he had phoned $t_i t_j$]]

It has been pointed out that the subjacency condition tends to rule out sentences in which the distance between the *wh*-element and its co-indexed gap is long [3]. There is a pressure on the human parser to keep this distance at a minimum for reasons of memory load. The phylogenetic functionalist would say that this parsing pressure leads to the biological selection of a language acquisition device that had some way of eliminating the worst *wh*-extractions from the range of possible languages, hence the subjacency condition becomes part of our innate LAD.

3 Glossogenetic functionalism

An alternative explanation for the origin of particular language universals can be termed glossogenetic functionalism[3] [21, 23, 24, 20]. In this approach, the constraints on variation are not assumed to arise directly from the structure of our innate language learning mechanism. Instead, the universals emerge over a historical/cultural timescale from the process of language acquisition *and* use.

This type of explanation relies on the principle that language learner does not necessarily converge on the same grammatical system as the adults in the population. Crucially, the triggering experience that the learner uses will not accurately reflect the linguistic competence of the adults because it is filtered through the "arena of use" [20]. There are various pressures that operate during communication that will have a selective effect on the different linguistic variants that are being transmitted from generation to generation.

In earlier work [23, 25, 22] Kirby has shown that the selective effect of the parser in the cycle of acquisition and use can give rise to language universals of the sort that typologists observe cross-linguistically. It appears that languages adapt to aid their own survival over time. More correctly, proportions of competing variants in a language change over time through differential selection in the arena of use and this gives rise to a pattern of cross-linguistic variation that shows the characteristic "appearance of design" that we have been talking about. We will show an abstract version of this process at work in the simulation later in this paper, but for the moment it is worth having a look at a more concrete example that can be explained very simply in terms of glossogenetic functionalism.

---

[2]The details of this analysis are unimportant the crucial features of the Subjacency Condition are that it constrains the number of possible ways in which a "moved" element can be interpreted and it can be formulated in a universal fashion (as a principle) even though it varies from language to language (via different possible parameter settings).

[3]The term glossogenetic is used in contrast with the ontogenetic and phylogenetic timescales. It is the timescale over which languages change.

A well known language universal[4] relates to the ordering in the string of branching and non-branching constituents:

> **Branching Direction Theory** (BDT): . . . a pair of elements X and Y will employ the order XY significantly more often among VO languages than among OV languages if and only if X is a non-phrasal category and Y is a phrasal category." [11, p.89]

Hawkins [18] shows how a series of universals very similar to this one appear to be a response to parsing pressures. His theory of parsing complexity includes a measure of the distance between categories in the string which construct dominating tree structure. Simplifying somewhat, the longer the distance between non-branching nodes in a tree the higher the parsing complexity of that tree. The most efficient tree structures will be those which order non-branching nodes on the same side of branching nodes throughout the structure. The BDT states that languages which generate such tree structures will be more common than those that do not.

The glossogenetic functionalist would say that the parsing pressure for consistent branching direction leads to the *linguistic* selection in the arena of use of variant word orders that are consistent with the branching direction of the rest of the language over those that are inconsistent. So, if there are examples of prepositional phrases and postpositional phrases in the input data given to a learner with a language whose verb precedes its object, then the prepositional phrases are more likely to be parsed successfully. This eventually leads to the loss of the postpositional phrases in VO languages.

4   Elements of the model

In order to test the validity of the two types of functionalism outlined above and make explicit what exactly these theories involve, we have constructed a simple idea model that incorporates the necessary features to model all the processes that are involved in both approaches. Ultimately we wish to explore the different interactions between learning (using an algorithm with partial innate constraints), cultural transmission (through an arena of use involving linguistic selection), and biological evolution of the innate learning constraints (based on the communicative success of the individuals).

4.1   Representation of grammar

The representation of the mature grammatical competence of the individuals in the simulation is borrowed from a paper by Turkel [34] as are many of the other details of the implementation — Turkel's model is similar to the one presented in this simulation, but does not include any real cultural/linguistic transmission or a model of functional pressures.[5]

We simply encode a grammar as a string of 1s and 0s.[6] In the results reported here, every individual's competence is an 8 bit string. This leads to 256 *logically possible languages*. Of course, we expect to show that the actually occurring languages will not be evenly distributed in this space.

4.2   Representation of LAD

The LAD, again following Turkel who borrows from Clark [7], is coded in the genome as a string of genes each of which has three possible alleles: 0, 1 or ?. Wherever there is a 1 or 0 allele, the resulting LAD will only be able to acquire grammars with the same symbol in the corresponding position. These alleles can be seen as coding for different possible *principles*. The ? allele, on the other hand, corresponds to a *parameter*. The resulting LAD will be able to acquire grammars with either a 1 or a 0 in the same position as the ? in the genome.

The most constrained LAD, then, is one whose genotype consists of no ? genes. Such an LAD will only ever acquire one language. In fact, the LAD will not learn at all, since the language is fully innate. The least constrained LAD is one with solely ? genes — all parameters. Such an LAD could *in principle* learn any one of the 256 logically possible languages. In this extreme, there are no innate constraints on variation.

4.3   Utterances as triggers

As Clark and Roberts [8] do, we will treat each utterance in the simulation as a *trigger* for a particular subset of the set of possible grammars. To take a concrete example, the first Hungarian sentence below could potentially provide the learner with evidence that she is hearing a sentence produced from a language with locative case endings, but cannot even in principle trigger the setting of a pro-drop parameter (a parameter that specifies that subjects can be lacking in main clauses). The second sentence provides the opposite triggering experience.

(3) Én is   vagyok bárban
     I   also be(1SG) bar+in
     'I am in the bar too'

(4) Egy pohár sört   kérek
     a   glass beer+ACC want(1SG)
     'I want a glass of beer'

---

[4]This is a *statistical* language universal. It does not have the same *absolute* status as the Subjacency Condition, for example, but the universal is still a statistically significant statement about cross-linguistic distribution.

[5]Turkel's goal was to show the plausibility of a partial biologisation of learned parameter settings.

[6]This simple encoding scheme may seem unlike a typical grammar, but in the Principles and Paramaters framework, this encoding could be interpreted by a fixed function (provided by the LAD) as a grammar in the normal sense.

We accordingly code utterances as a string of 1s, 0s and *s. Each 1 or 0 potentially triggers the acquisition of a grammar with the same digit in the corresponding position. Each * carries no information about the 'target' grammar. With our example above, imagine that locative case-coding languages have a 1 in the first position of our grammar coding, and pro-drop languages have a 0 in the second position of the coding. The first sentence above would be represented as $< 1, *, \ldots >$. The second would be $< *, 0, \ldots >$.

In the simulation results reported here, the individuals produce utterances randomly which are consistent with their grammars and only provide evidence for one digit of their grammars. In other words, each trigger will have seven *s and one digit.

4.4   The Trigger Learning Algorithm

The next basic element of our model is an algorithm for parameter setting. An algorithm that has been discussed in the literature recently [32, 6, 35, 12] is the Trigger Learning Algorithm of Gibson and Wexler [13]. We employ this algorithm in our simulation for simplicity, but for the simulation runs presented here little relies on this choice. The reason for this, and general issues relating to parameter setting are discussed later.

The Trigger Learning Algorithm (TLA)   Given an initial set of values for n binary-valued parameters, the learner attempts to syntactically analyze the incoming sentence S. If S can be successfully analyzed, then the learner's hypothesis regarding the target grammar is left unchanged. If, however, the learner cannot analyze S, then the learner uniformly selects a parameter P (with probability $1/n$ for each parameter), changes the value associated with P, and tries to reprocess S using the new parameter value. If analysis is now possible, then the parameter value change is adopted. Otherwise, the original parameter value is retained.

4.5   Linguistic selection

So far we have made no reference to the role of communicative function in our model. All utterances in all languages have an equal status in the formulation given above. As mentioned earlier, Kirby [23] has modelled the role of communicative function in the cycle of acquisition and use as adjusting the probabilities of a variant being taken up as part of the learner's trigger experience. Robert Clark [6] shows how this idea of linguistic selection can be built into a modified version of the TLA.

In the original formulation of the TLA, a new parameter setting is only taken up if analysing the input is possible with the new setting and not with the old setting. In the simulations in this paper there is a certain probability (that can be varied from run to run) that the criteria for taking up a new parameter setting will

be based not on the absolute analysability of the trigger but on its parsability. The procedure on receiving a trigger is therefore:

Modified TLA   If the trigger is consistent with the learner's LAD:[7]

1. If the trigger can be analysed with the current grammar, score the parsability of the trigger with the current grammar.

2. Choose one parameter at random and flip its value.

3. If the trigger can be analysed with the new grammar, score the parsability of the trigger with the new grammar.

4. With a certain pre-defined frequency carry out linguistic selection (a), otherwise (b):

    (a) If the trigger can be analysed with the new grammar, and the new grammar's parsability score is higher than that of the current grammar, or the trigger cannot be analysed with the current grammar, adopt the new grammar.

    (b) If the trigger cannot be analysed with the current grammar, and the trigger can be analysed with the new grammar, adopt the new grammar.

5. Otherwise keep the current grammar.

4.6   Natural selection

In order to implement natural selection we need some way of assessing the communicative success of individuals *after* learning. We use the concept of a *critical period* [27, 26] during which learning occurs, which is followed by a period of continued language use, but no grammatical change. As a simplifying assumption we measure the communicative fitness of individuals after this critical period.

The fitness can be based on either the transmission ability of an individual, the reception ability of an individual, or a combination of both. Each individual is involved in a certain number of random communicative acts, for half of which he is the hearer and half the speaker. The individual's transmission ability is scored on the basis of how many of the utterances spoken were analysable by the hearer, and how parsable those utterances were. The individual's reception ability is scored similarly on the utterances heard. If speakers and hearers are drawn from the same linguistic community (see the next section for more details), then this procedure can be used to test both the success of learning, and the "functionality" of the individual's grammar.[8]

---

[7]This clause is here simply to save work, since it is possible that no combination of parameter settings will be able to analyse the trigger. In other words, the trigger is outwith the constraints imposed by the learner's LAD.

[8]Notice this looks similar to the linguistic selection in the previous section, but has no impact on the transmission of language from generation to generation.

Fitness measurement

1. For each utterance heard, with a certain pre-defined frequency carry out (a), otherwise (b):

   (a) If the utterance can be analysed, measure the utterance's parsability score, and with a probability proportional to that score increase reception fitness.

   (b) If the utterance can be analysed, increase reception fitness.

2. For each utterance produced, with a certain pre-defined frequency carry out (a), otherwise (b):

   (a) If the utterance can be analysed by the hearer, measure the utterance's parsability score, and with a probability proportional to that score increase transmission fitness.

   (b) If the utterance can be analysed by the hearer, increase transmission fitness.

5 Layout of the model

In the previous section we quickly reviewed the six central elements of the model: grammars, LADs, utterances, parameter setting, linguistic selection, and natural selection. Figure 1 shows how these various components fit together in our simulation.

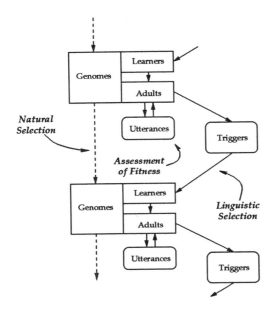

Figure 1: An overview of the simulation model.

On the right hand side of this diagram, we have the part of the model that deals with cultural transmission. Each generation of adults produces a set of triggers randomly in line with their grammars, and this acts as training data for the next generation of learners. In this way,

languages survive across generations, although there is not perfect transmission. Language change can occur through: failure to learn, linguistic selection in the modified TLA, and (as we shall see below) language contact.

The fitness of the adults is assessed as described above after learning has finished. This fitness assessment is used to select which individuals will mate to produce the next generation of learners. Rank selection is used — for the results presented here, the top 90 percent of the population have an equal chance of reproducing (the bottom 10 percent have no chance of reproducing). The new population of genomes is formed using one point crossover with a mutation probability of 0.001 per allele. At every generation, the entire population is replaced. Notice crucially the utterances that the adults produce are kept separate from the triggers that are given to the next generation. In a sense there are two "games" taking place in this model: an adult-to-child game which results in cultural transmission, and an adult-to-adult game that results in natural selection.

In order to model language change, it is important for the arena of use to be organised spatially [24, 29]. This is achieved in the simulation by organising the individuals in the population in a one-dimensional loop, as in figure 2. For the results reported, breeding is not spatially organised. It was found that organising *both* linguistic and genetic interaction spatially lead quickly to extreme genetic heterogeneity in the population. An investigation of this phenomenon is beyond the scope of this paper.

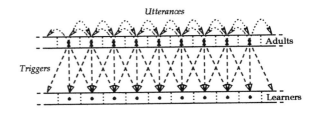

Figure 2: How the arena of use is spatially organised in the simulation.

6 Results

For the results in this section, the parsability scoring function is chosen arbitrarily to prefer 1s in the first 4 bits of the grammar. The score ranges from 0.0 to 1.0 proportional to the number of 1s. There are many ways of modelling the parsability of languages in the hypothetical 8 bit grammar space; this one is chosen here simply so that there are some specific parameter settings that lead to more parsable utterances and some that have no impact on parsability. Clearly, if the simulation is responding to functional pressures we should find the languages distribution at the end of the simulation to reflect the preference for grammars that start $< 1, 1, 1, 1, \ldots >$.

6.1 Natural selection for functional LADs

Firstly we wish to see if phylogenetic functionalism works. To do this we "turn on" natural selection, but "turn off" linguistic selection. In terms of the simulation, this means that the proportion of *triggers* that have their parsability scored in the TLA is zero, on the other hand parsability is measured for 10 percent of *utterances* in assessing fitness.[9] There are 100 individuals in the population, all of which start with a genome that is fully "plastic", in other words with no innate principles: $<?, ?, ?, ?, ?, ?, ?, ? >$. The critical period is set at 200 triggers.[10] The initial arena of use (the triggers fed to the first generation of learners) is completely random.

Figure 3 shows the average fitness of the population over time where each speaker produces 100 utterances in fitness testing, and is scored 1 for each successfully received utterance, and 1 for each successfully transmitted utterance. Figure 4 shows the average proportions of pa-

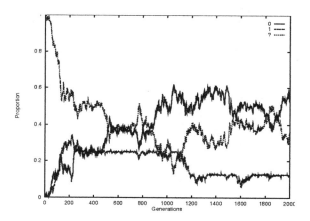

Figure 4: Average proportions of 0s, 1s and ?s in the LADs of the population.

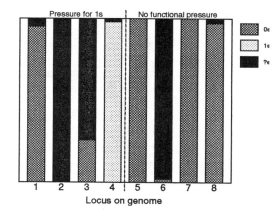

Figure 5: Average proportion of different alleles at the end of run. (The area of a bar is proportional to the number of those alleles in the population.)

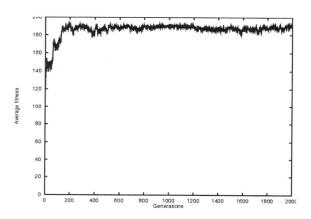

Figure 3: Average fitness against generations for typical run.

rameters and the two types of principle during the same run. This graph is typical for runs of the simulation with the initial conditions described. The final graph in figure 5 shows the proportions of the different alleles in the genomes at the end of the run — essentially the make up of the average LAD after evolution. This varied wildly from run to run.

It should be clear from these results that evolution has failed to respond to the functional pressure to have only 1s in the first four positions of the grammars. In

fact, the first grammatical parameter has been almost completely nativised as a '0' principle. This means that the individuals in the simulation simply cannot produce or parse optimal utterances. This explains why their fitness, although it increases initially never reaches the maximum possible 200. Similar results where also forthcoming when fitness was based solely on reception behaviour or transmission behaviour.

6.2 Linguistic selection for functional languages

For the next run of the simulation we enable linguistic selection in the TLA. As with the adult-to-adult utterances, we score the parsability of the adult-to-child triggers 10 percent of the time. Apart from the inclusion of linguistic selection during transmission of triggers, the

---

[9]Various degrees of parsability testing were tried. Different results only arise at the extremes of the range.

[10]Again, different values were tested, each giving a different degree of nativisation (see below). This value gives results in the middle of the range.

set up is identical to that in the previous section.

Figure 6 shows a space-time diagram of the languages that are present in the arena of use. The two languages that predominate after only 200 generations are $< 1, 1, 1, 1, 0, 0, 1, 1 >$ and $< 1, 1, 1, 1, 0, 1, 1, 1 >$. Both of these languages are optimally parsable. What

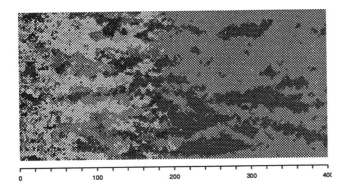

Figure 6: A space-time graph for the first 400 generations of the run. Each colour is assigned to one language type. Time runs horizontally left to right.

seems to be happening here is that languages are very rapidly evolving historically to become easier to parse. Even after only 57 generations, the main languages are $< 1, 1, 1, 1, 0, 0, 1, 1 >$, $< 1, 1, 1, 1, 0, 1, 1, 1 >$, $< 1, 1, 1, 1, 0, 0, 0, 1 >$ and $< 1, 1, 1, 1, 1, 0, 0, 1 >$. This looks like glossogenetic functionalism.

If we look at what is happening to the LADs in the same simulation run we see a different picture (figure 7). After 57 generations, only one of the parameters has been nativised as a principle. This makes it clear that it is linguistic, not natural, selection that is improving parsability. However, eventually the LADs do evolve, as more of the parameters become principles. The shape of the evolved LADs is shown in figure 8. The interesting feature of these results is that the LADs appear to have evolved to at least partially constrain learners to learn languages that are functional. This is exactly what is predicted by phylogenetic functionalism, but this result does not emerge without a prior *glossogenetic* evolution.

A natural selection pressure to communicate efficiently (either as a speaker or hearer) is not on its own enough to account for functional constraints on variation. In fact, it appears to lead to positively dysfunctional constraints on variation being built into the genome. The linguistic selection of triggers in the cultural transmission of language, on the other hand, accounts for the appearance of functional constraints very rapidly. It also, in combination with a natural selection pressure for communication, leads to a partial nativisation of these constraints in the LAD.

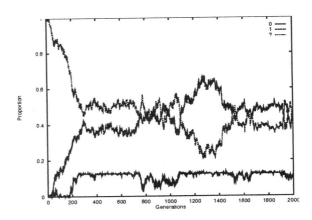

Figure 7: Average proportions of 0s, 1s and ?s in the LADs of the population with linguistic selection.

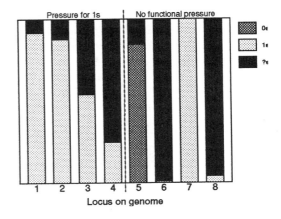

Figure 8: Average proportion of different alleles at the end of run in a population with linguistic selection.

7 Discussion

7.1 Why phylogenetic functionalism cannot work alone

It seems that phylogenetic functionalism, although an apparently obvious explanation for linguistic constraints, does not work alone. Evolution seems unable to optimise the innate constraints on learners in such a way that they are constrained to produce functional languages. Why might this be so?

The answer seems to lie in what selection pressures face a linguistic individual. If the pressure is to produce utterances that are potentially easy to parse, or to be able to analyse easily parsable utterances, then we would expect evolution to select the individual whose LAD reflects parsing pressures. However, an overriding concern for a communicating individual is to *correctly learn the language of her speech community.* Without a grammar that accurately reflects that of her peers, an individual will not be understood, nor be able to understand others, whatever the functionality of her grammar.

Consider the possible situations an individual with a mutated LAD might find himself in:

1. The individual may belong to a speech community that is speaking an optimal language. In this case, as long as the mutation does not constrain the individual in such a way that he cannot learn this language, there is no preferential selection for a more functional LAD over a less functional one.

2. The individual may belong to a speech community that is speaking a sub-optimal language. In this case, if the mutation produces a more functional LAD the individual is actually selected *against* because he will not be able to learn the language of his community.

In this rather simplified characterisation, then, there is no way that a mutation that increases the functionality of the LAD (in the sense that it constrains languages to be parsable) can give a direct fitness advantage to an individual. This is true even though the fittest population would be one where everyone possessed just such an LAD.

7.2   The Baldwin Effect

This result stands in contradiction to the fact that there *do* seem to be at least some functional innate linguistic constraints that humans are born with. The Subjacency Condition, reviewed earlier, appears to be one of them. There are also functional constraints on variation that are harder to account for in terms of innate constraints on learnability — the word order universals expressed in the Branching Direction Theory, for example. The results of the second simulation run seem to capture this *partial* innateness of functional constraints rather well. Why does adding linguistic selection make such a difference to the results?

The results show that even where there is no genetic change (i.e. the whole population is still completely plastic) the languages in the simulation converge on a (sub)set of optimal languages. Wherever there is linguistic variation in the input to a particular learner, for example when there are two languages in contact in the arena of use, there may be differential uptake of competing parameter settings. As Robert Clark [6] has proved, in this simple situation this will inevitably lead to languages becoming adapted to maximise their own transmission potential — in other words, more functional parameter settings survive.

Given a linguistic environment which is adapted glossogenetically to communicative function, the LADs in the population gradually evolve phylogenetically to mirror the existing constraints on variation. This is a clear example of the Baldwin Effect [1, 34, 19, 2] in opera-

tion. One of the predicted outcomes of the interaction of learning and evolution is that wherever there is a cost attached to learning (be it risk of making mistakes, or delay in knowledge acquisition), there will be a pressure to make innate those features of the learning task which are *predictable*. If the same parameter settings are consistently expressed in the trigger experience of generation after generation, there is no disadvantage to that parameter setting "becoming" a principle; it means less work for the learner. If, on the other hand, there are parameter settings that are highly variable glossogenetically, then there is a pressure for them to remain learnt by the population.

Notice that this pressure to nativise only exists where there is a disadvantage to learning. In our model this disadvantage is the risk of failing to converge on the correct grammar before the critical period. This is why, when the critical period is changed, the degree of eventual nativisation changed. Only when the critical period is extremely severe do we see a complete nativisation of the functional constraints. (See [26] for a model of how the critical period itself evolves.)

In summary, we have a two stage process:

1. From initially random initial conditions, linguistic selection leads to a glossogenetic adaptation of the languages in the arena of use. This results in observable constraints on variation, although the individuals are still completely plastic and so could potentially learn languages outwith these constraints.

2. This glossogenetic adaptation *enables* the phylogenetic adaptation of the LADs in the population through the Baldwin Effect. Over time, some of the regularities in the linguistic input become nativised. This means that at the end of this process, the constraints on variation "harden up" so that the individuals in the population could not even potentially learn the dysfunctional languages.

8   Extensions

The simulation in this paper is clearly a fairly abstract idea model — a first step towards explaining the complex interaction involved in the evolution of a learning mechanism for a shared culturally transmitted trait like language. In this section we briefly review the directions in which the model might be extended.

Diversity   One of the crucial aspects of the arena of use in the simulation is spatial organisation. One of the effects of this is to increase the sustainable level of diversity in the languages in the population. This is important because the evolving LADs are responding to regularities in the input, and without some variation in the input, there is simply a pressure to nativise a single language. The final degree of diversity is still low in the results shown in this paper, however. Within the model, this can be changed by altering the rate at which languages can spread sideways through the population. It would be interesting to experiment with some of the other features of the arena of use that Nettle [29] argues impact on the maintenance of diversity, such as social selection and varying competing functional pressures [24].

More complex functional constraints We have seen that only some of the parsing pressures get nativised, but the ones that do or do not seems to be arbitrary. It would be interesting if there was some way in which we could predict what sorts of functional pressure would be left to glossogenetic adaptation and what sorts would become part of the innate LAD. We have applied the model to a situation where the functionality of a particular parameter setting cannot be measured in isolation, but instead depends critically on other parameter settings. For example, the simulation has been tested on a situation where the optimal grammars are those where adjacent pairs of parameter settings are the same. In this regime, some optimal grammars would be: $< 1, 1, 0, 0, 0, 0, 1, 1 >$ or $< 0, 0, 1, 1, 0, 0, 1, 1 >$ and so on.

It turns out that although glossogenetic adaptation quickly gives us a pattern of variation which captures this functional pressure, there is no way for the Baldwin Effect to nativise it. There is no way of representing this pairing pattern in the LAD. It would require a representation with variables over parameter settings like: $< p_1, p_1, p_2, p_2, p_3, p_3, p_4, p_4 >$.

Interestingly, this kind of cross-parametric interdependence may be just the sort of thing that is going on with the branching direction universals. If we consider the order of head and modifier to be independently specifiable for each phrasal category in a grammar, then it might not be possible to capture in the LAD the parsing preference for consistent ordering across these categories. If this turned out to be true, then we might have an explanation why this word order universal is *statistical* rather than *absolute*. It exists as a constraint that emerges from the glossogenetic process rather than a constraint that is hard-wired into the genome.

The role of the parametric space The model as we have described it makes no direct reference to linguistic features — actual parameters, triggers, or functional pressures. We believe this is the correct first step in understanding the general processes involved, before moving on to more complex models. Briscoe [4] in a fascinating paper shows that it is possible to model the nativisation of more realistic-looking functional pressures. Simplifying somewhat, he models the LAD as a set of 11 parameters which, in combination with a particular syntactic theory (Generalised Categorial Universal Grammar), can generate strings of words which may act as triggers. Briscoe uses a particular theory of working memory to then assess the parsing cost of these triggers.

One of the interesting features of Briscoe's model — and others such as [32, 6] — is that the complexity of mapping from parameter settings to triggers leads to interesting unpredictable dynamics in the glossogenetic evolution of languages due to the ambiguity of some triggers and misconvergence by learners. This means that it is hard to tease apart the effect of the learning model and the functional pressures on the emerging universals. Of course, this is an important insight into the complexities of our object of study.

The problem is that we cannot make any specific predictions until we know more about the parametric space because as Robert Clark [6] shows, a small change in the details of the parameterisation lead to radically different end results. The status of the TLA is far from clear, however. A recent paper by Fodor [12] argues that the TLA is psychologically implausible, and instead suggests a theory of parameter setting that relies on single unambiguous triggers. This is not the place to explore Fodor's theory, suffice to say that some of the complexities introduced by misconvergence in non-trivial parameterisations may be ameliorated with different theories of acquisition.

9 Conclusion

We have shown that phylogenetic functionalism alone cannot work, but this does not mean that functional constraints cannot find their way into the innate Language Acquisition Device. Instead, we show that the introduction of linguistic (as opposed to natural) selection into a model of language acquisition, use, transmission, and evolution has profound effects on the evolutionary trajectory of learners. The very same mechanism (the differential filtering of triggers out of the learners input data due to parsing difficulty) can explain *both* historically emergent universals and innate constraints on variation.

In general, we have shown that for a culturally shared system like language, cultural evolution can bootstrap biological evolution. We are currently exploring the possibility that this kind of mechanism may be involved at an earlier stage of language evolution.

References

[1] J.M. Baldwin. A new factor in evolution. *American Naturalist*, 30:441–451, 1896.

[2] Richard Belew. Evolution, learning, and culture: computational metaphors for adaptive algorithms. *Complex Systems*, 4:11–49, 1990.

[3] R.C. Berwick and A.S. Weinberg. *The Grammatical Basis of Linguistic Performance: Language Use and Acquisition.* MIT Press, 1984.

[4] Ted Briscoe. Language acquisition: the bioprogram hypothesis and the Baldwin Effect. MS, Computer Laboratory, University of Cambridge, 1997.

[5] Noam Chomsky. *Knowledge of Language*. Praeger, 1986.

[6] Robert Clark. Internal and external factors affecting language change: A computational model. Master's thesis, University of Edinburgh, 1996.

[7] Robin Clark. The selection of syntactic knowledge. *Language Acquisition*, 2:85–149, 1992.

[8] Robin Clark and Ian Roberts. A computational model of language learnability and language change. *Linguistic Inquiry*, 24:299–345, 1993.

[9] Bernard Comrie. *Language Universals and Linguistic Typology*. Basil Blackwell, 1981.

[10] William Croft. *Typology and universals*. Cambridge University Press, Cambridge, 1990.

[11] Matthew Dryer. The Greenbergian word order correlations. *Language*, 68:81–138, 1992.

[12] Janet Fodor. Unambiguous triggers. *Linguistic Inquiry*, 1997. To appear.

[13] E. Gibson and K. Wexler. Triggers. *Linguistic Inquiry*, 25:407–454, 1994.

[14] Joseph Greenberg. Some universals of grammar with particular reference to the order of meaningful elements. In Joseph Greenberg, editor, *Universals of Language*, pages 73–113. MIT Press, 1963.

[15] Liliane Haegeman. *Introduction to Government and Binding Theory*. Blackwell, 1991.

[16] John A. Hawkins. Explaining language universals. In John A. Hawkins, editor, *Explaining Language Universals*. Basil Blackwell, 1988.

[17] John A. Hawkins. A parsing theory of word order universals. *Linguistic Inquiry*, 21:223–261, 1990.

[18] John A. Hawkins. *A performance theory of order and constituency*. Cambridge University Press, 1994.

[19] G. Hinton and S. Nowlan. How learning can guide evolution. *Complex Systems*, 1:495–502, 1987.

[20] James Hurford. *Language and Number: the Emergence of a Cognitive System*. Basil Blackwell, Cambridge, MA, 1987.

[21] Simon Kirby. Adaptive explanations for language universals: a model of Hawkins' performance theory. *Sprachtypologie und Universalienforschung*, 47:186–210, 1994.

[22] Simon Kirby. Constraints on constraints, or the limits of functional adaptation. To appear in: *Functionalism and Formalism*, 1996.

[23] Simon Kirby. *The Emergence of Universals: Function, Selection and Innateness*. University of Edinburgh, 1996. PhD thesis.

[24] Simon Kirby. Competing motivations and emergence: explaining implicational hierarchies. *Language Typology*, 1:5–32, 1997.

[25] Simon Kirby. Fitness and the selective adaptation of language. In J. Hurford, C. Knight, and M. Studdert-Kennedy, editors, *Evolution of Language: Social and cognitive bases for the emergence of phonology and syntax*. 1997. To appear.

[26] Simon Kirby and James Hurford. The evolution of incremental learning: Language, development and critical periods. Occasional Paper EOPL-97-2, Department of Linguistics, University of Edinburgh, Edinburgh, 1997.

[27] Eric H. Lenneberg. *Biological Foundations of Language*. Wiley, New York, 1967.

[28] Edith Moravcsik, editor. *Functionalism and formalism in linguistics: proceedings of the 23rd UWM linguistics symposium*. Benjamins, 1997. In preparation.

[29] Daniel Nettle. *The Evolution of Linguistic Diversity*. PhD thesis, University College London, 1996.

[30] Frederick J. Newmeyer. Functional explanation in linguistics and the origins of language. *Language and Communication*, 11:3–28, 1991.

[31] Frederick J. Newmeyer. *Language Form and Language Function*, chapter Langauge Typology and its Difficulties. 1997. In preparation.

[32] Partha Niyogi and Robert Berwick. The logical problem of language change. Technical Report AI Memo 1516 / CBCL Paper 115, MIT AI Laboratory and Center for Biological and Computational Learning, Department of Brain and Cognitive Sciences, 1995.

[33] H. Van Riemsdijk and E. Williams. *Introduction to the Theory of Grammar*. MIT Press, 1986.

[34] William Turkel. The learning-guided evolution of natural language. Manuscript, University of British Columbia, 1994.

[35] William Turkel. Noise-induced enhancement of parameter setting. Submitted to Linguistic Inquiry, 1997.

Generating Vowel Systems in a Population of Agents

Bart de Boer

VUB AI Laboratory

Pleinlaan 2

1050 BRUSSEL, BELGIUM

bartb@arti.vub.ac.be

Abstract:

In the sound systems of human languages remarkable universals are found. These universals can be explained by innate mechanisms, or by their function in human speech. This paper presents a functional explanation of certain universals of vowel systems using Alife-techniques.

It is based on language-like interactions between members of a population of individual agents. The agents start out empty, but have a "drive" to make (vowel) sounds to each other and to imitate these sounds. Through repeated "imitation games" and through modifications of their own sound system, based on the outcome of the imitation games, the agents reach coherence. The sound systems that arise have properties that are similar to those of human vowel systems.

Keywords: language origins, cultural evolution, phonological universals

1. Introduction

Alife techniques have been used to aid many fields of science, such as biology, ethology and psychology. In this paper alife techniques are applied to the field of linguistics. They are used to provide a functional explanation for a number of properties of the sound systems humans use for communication.

The human vocal tract is capable of producing an amazing number of different speech sounds. The UCLA Phonological Segment Inventory Database (UPSID, described in [14]) recognises 921 different speech sounds—652 consonants and 269 vowels—found in 451 languages. Still, the number of speech sounds (phonemes) used by any individual language is quite limited. According to Maddieson [14] the average lies between 20 and 37. The maximum number of phonemes of any language in the UPSID is 141 for the Khoisan language !Xũ, the minimum is 11 for the East-Papuan language Rotokas and the South-American language Múra-Pirahã [7,14]. Also, a number of remarkable universals can be found in the sound systems of languages. Some sounds, such as [a], [p] or [m] are much more frequent than others, such as [ɤ]*, [t͡ɬ']† or [ɴ]‡. Also the structure of sound systems is not random. If a language uses a certain

---

* Mid back unrounded vowel, found e.g. in Vietnamese.
† Dental ejective lateral affricate, found e.g in Navajo.
‡ Uvular nasal, found e.g. in Japanese.

voiced consonant (e.g. [d]), it will usually have the corresponding unvoiced consonant (e.g. [t]) as well. With vowels it is the same: a language will rather have a system consisting of, for example [i, e, a, o, u] than of [y, æ, a, ə, ɔ]. Apparently languages have symmetrical systems with sounds that are spread evenly, rather than random systems.

The traditional explanation for these phenomena is that humans use a number of *distinctive features* [8] for building up the system of speech sounds they use. A distinctive feature is a (usually binary) feature of speech sounds that can cause a difference in meaning between two words. An example is the voicing of consonants in English. The difference between the words "bed" and "bet" is that the last consonants of these words are voiced and voiceless, respectively. This causes a change in meaning, and therefore [voice] is considered a distinctive feature in English.

It is generally assumed [4,8] that these distinctive features are innate. According to this theory, all humans are born with the same set of distinctive features. When learning their mother tongue, they choose the set of distinctive features that this language uses, as well as the settings of the features for the individual sounds in the language. With the right set of distinctive features, the theory is quite able to predict the regularities that are found. It can also predict the sequence in which these sounds are learned. Furthermore it is able to explain that some sounds are rarer than other sounds by assuming that certain features and certain values for features are more *marked* than others.

Still, there are a number of fundamental problems with this theory. First of all, most proposed feature sets are not able to account for all the sounds that are found in the world's languages. Ladefoged and Maddieson [9, ch. 11] write: "The great variety of data that we have presented shows that the construction of an adequate theory of universal features is much more complex than hitherto thought." However, even if a feature-based theory would have sufficient features to account for all possible speech sounds, it would still not be able to account for the subtle, but important differences between sounds in different languages and dialects that every speaker of such a language uses and recognises. An example is the difference between English *coo*, French *cou* (neck), German *Kuh* (cow) and Dutch *koe* (cow), all of which would be described as a high back voiceless consonant, followed by a high back rounded vowel. Also the distinctive feature theory does not explain where distinctive features come from in the first place. There is a danger of circularity in deducing features from observations of regularities in language and then proposing these features as explanations of these regularities. As Lindblom et al. write: "...postulating segments and features as primitive categories of linguistic theory should be rejected..." [11, p. 187]

Another approach to explaining the structure of sound systems of human language is a functional one. Sound systems are explained by assuming that they are based on minimal articulatory and cognitive effort and maximal perceptual contrast. Especially in the area of vowel systems, this approach has been particularly successful. Liljencrants and Lindblom [10], Lindblom [13], Carré and Mrayati [3] and Boë et al. [2] showed, using computer simulations, that vowel systems can be explained by a maximisation of the acoustical contrast, while at the same time minimising the articulatory gestures that are needed. Observations of consonant systems of a wide range of languages [12] have obtained evidence that the same mechanisms are operating there. However no computer simulations to investigate these observations have been done yet because of the more complex articulatory and perceptual characteristics of consonants (for a simulation of simple syllables see Lindblom et al. [11]).

In the computer simulations of Liljencrants and Lindblom [10], Lindblom [13], and of Boë et al. [2], it is assumed that one can assign an energy function to vowel systems. This function has higher energy for systems with their vowels closer together and for systems that need more articulatory gestures. One then minimises this energy function for a given number of vowels.

Unfortunately, these computer simulations do not provide us with a mechanism that explains how this process takes place in human language. The only way in which vowel systems can change in human languages is by the interactions between—and the actions of—the users of the language. As no speaker has control over the language as a whole, this process must be considered an emergent property of language use. We can observe that a minimisation of the "energy" of vowel systems does take place in human language. However, we do not yet know by which actions of the individual speakers this minimisation is caused.

An attempt to model changing vowel systems in a population of communicating agents has been made by Berrah et al. [1], Glotin [5] and Glotin and Laboissiere [6]. They use an approach that combines learning and a technique which the authors call a "pseudo-genetic algorithm" [5, sect 4.4]. Their agents communicate using randomly initialised vowel systems with a fixed number of vowels. They communicate, change their vowel systems in a way that depends on the difference between their own vowels and those of the agent they spoke with. Then they calculate a fitness function that depends on the articulatory efforts they made. After a while a new generation of agents is calculated by procreating the fittest individuals, using selection and crossover. Their system produces vowel systems that look like human vowel systems. However, their system is not quite comparable to human speech communities, because of a number of assumptions they have made. First of all, their agents do not really learn a vowel system from scratch. The number of vowels, as well as the initial position of the vowels is coded in the agents' genes. The authors use this mechanism to efficiently explore the space of possible vowel systems. However, by precoding the number and position of the vowels, the authors disregard the process by which children acquire speech sounds from scratch. This process, however, is probably an important factor in determining the possible and stable shapes of sound systems. Simplifying this process away might therefore be an oversimplification. Their assumption also prevents the agents from adding or removing sounds from their vowel systems. Also, calculating a new population of agents requires that the *internal* states of the agents be crossed with each other. Glotin and Laboissiere[6] are aware that this is not realistic, but they nevertheless use it for exploring the possible vowel systems. A strong point of their is that it uses a very good speech synthesis model. Unfortunately, the computational complexity of this model makes it unsuitable for long simulations with lots of agents.

This paper proposes a system in which a population of agents learns vowel systems by observing and trying to imitate each other's speech sounds. The individual agents produce and perceive sounds under constraints that are meant to be similar to human ones. They manipulate their own sound systems in order to maximise the success in imitating the other agents. The system is based on Steels' ideas about the origins of language [16].

In the next two sections the architecture of the agents (section 2) and their interactions (section 3) are described. Also their relation to Steels' theory is described in somewhat more detail. In section 4 the results of a number of experiments are presented and in section 5 these results are discussed and related to other work in this area. Possible future work with the system is also suggested.

2. The Agents

Each agent in the system has its own list of vowels. This list is initially empty, and will be filled as the agents engage in interactions with other agents. The vowels are represented by the three main parameters that are used for describing vowels: tongue position, tongue height and lip rounding. The three parameters can have any value between zero and one. For tongue position, zero means front, and one means back. For tongue height, zero means low and one means high, and for lip rounding, zero means unrounded and one

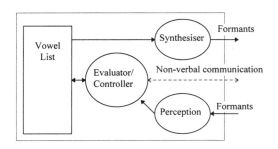

Figure 1: Agent architecture

means rounded. The agents are able to produce any "simple" vowel. The system is completely language-independent. No bias towards the vowel system of any language is present in the agents.

The vowels that are present in the agents are produced by a synthesiser and are recognised by a perception unit. A special control unit regulates the actions of the agents and the evaluation of vowels. The internal architecture of an agent is illustrated in figure 1.

The synthesiser is a simple articulatory synthesiser that is based on a second order interpolation of a number of artificially synthesised vowels. The input of the synthesiser consists of the three articulatory parameters and the output consists of the frequencies of the first four formants of the vowel associated with this particular articulation. The basic data for the formants have been taken from Vallée [18, pp. 162–164].

In the experiments a certain amount of noise has been added to the formant frequencies that are produced by the agents. The adding of noise consist of multiplying the formant frequencies by:

1) $1 \pm U(a)$,

in which $U(a)$ is a random variable uniformly distributed over $[-a, a]$, where a varies for different experiments. The addition of noise makes the games more natural. Similarly, in human speech it cannot be expected that sounds will always be produced and perceived accurately. The noise also makes it impossible for the agents to copy each other's phonemes perfectly, thereby forcing them to create sound systems in which the phonemes are not too close together, as well as opening the possibility of change and language evolution.

For each phoneme an agent creates, it generates the formants of an ideal articulation of this sound. This ideal articulation is called the *prototype vector* and it is stored together with the articulatory description of the phoneme. Every time an agent hears a sound, it calculates the distance between the prototype vectors of all the phonemes it knows and the formants of the sound it just heard. The phoneme with the prototype vector that is closest to the sound that was heard is considered to be the recognised phoneme. This whole process could in principle be implemented using neural networks, thereby increasing the biological plausibility.

The distance measure that is used to compare phonemes is of crucial importance to the form of the vowel systems that will be generated by the agents. In order to get natural vowel systems, and in order to be able to compare the results of the experiments with those of at least one other group, a distance measure that has been adapted from Boë et al. [2] was used in a slightly modified form. The distance measure takes into account that the human auditory system distinguishes vowels by their formant frequencies, lower formants having a greater influence, that it does not distinguish well between formants that are very close together and that it works in an essentially logarithmic manner.

For the distance function two weights need to be calculated:

$$2) \ w_1 = \frac{c - (F_3 - F_2)}{c}$$

$$3) \ w_2 = \frac{(F_4 - F_3) - (F_3 - F_2)}{F_4 - F_2}$$

Where w_1 and w_2 are the weights, F_1–F_4 are the formants in Bark[§] and c is a critical distance, set to 3.5 Bark.

The weighted sum of F_2, F_3 and F_4 which we will call F_2' will now be calculated as follows:

$$4) \ F_2' = \begin{cases} F_2, & \text{if } F_3 - F_2 > c \\ \dfrac{(2 - w_1)F_2 + w_1 F_3}{2}, & \text{if } F_3 - F_2 \leq c \wedge F_4\text{-}F_2 > c \\ \dfrac{w_2 F_2 + (2 - w_2)F_3}{2} - 1, & \text{if } F_4 - F_2 \leq c \wedge F_3 - F_2 < F_4 - F_3 \\ \dfrac{(2 + w_2)F_3 - w_2 F_4}{2} - 1, & \text{if } F_4 - F_2 \leq c \wedge F_3 - F_2 \geq F_4 - F_3 \end{cases}$$

The values of F_1 and F_2' for a number of vowels are shown in figure 2. We can see from this figure that the distribution of the vowels through the acoustic space is quite natural. However, as it is a two-dimensional projection of an essentially three-dimensional space, not all distances between all phonemes can be represented accurately. This is especially the case with the distinction rounded-unrounded. Unfortunately this is difficult to avoid in any system.

The distance between two vowels, a and b can now be calculated using a weighted Euclidean distance:

$$5) \ d = \sqrt{\left(F_1^a - F_1^b\right)^2 + \lambda\left(F_2^{a'} - F_2^{b'}\right)^2}$$

This again, in accordance with the work of Boë et al. [2]. The value of the parameter λ is chosen to be 0.5 for all experiments that will be described.

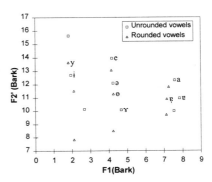

Figure 2: Vowels in F1-F2' space

With the articulator function and the perception function that have been described in this section, the agents can produce and perceive speech sounds in a way that is sufficiently human. This means that the results that are generated with these systems can at least to some extent be compared to the results of research into human sound systems.

3. The Imitation Game

The experiments presented in this work are concerned with the emergence of a coherent and useful phonology in a population of initially empty agents. In order to investigate how this can happen, the agents engage in exchanges of sounds, so-called imitation games**, the goal of which is to learn each other's speech sounds. If necessary, speech sounds are invented, in order to get the imitation games started, and also in order to introduce more possible sounds in the population.

The structure of the imitation games is based on Steels' ideas about the origins of language [16]. He considers language a cultural phenomenon that maintains coherence through self-organisation. Language is learnt by actively making hypotheses about the form of the language and by testing these in linguistic interactions, which he calls *language games*. Complexity arises through (cultural) evolution and co-evolution of linguistic structures. In his view, there is no need for innate mechanisms (a Language Acquisition Device) to explain the origin and the acquisition of language. According to Steels, the above mentioned mechanisms are able to explain both the historical origin as well as the acquisition of language.

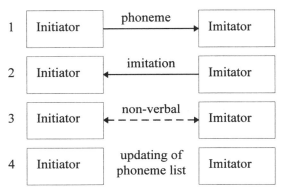

Figure 3: The imitation game

The basic rules of the imitation game that is played by two agents are very simple. Two agents are randomly selected from the population of agents. One of the agents, which we will call the *initiator*, selects one of its phonemes and says this to the other agent. The other agent, which we will call the *imitator*, interprets this sound in terms of its phonemes, and then produces the phoneme it thinks it has recognised. The other agent listens to this imitation, and also interprets it in terms of its phonemes. If the phoneme it recognises is the

_____

** Not to be confused with Suzuki and Kaneko's imitation games [17], which are completely different.

same as the one it just said, the imitation game is considered to be successful. If it is not equal, the game is unsuccessful. There follows a non-verbal communication, in which the imitator gets to know if its imitation was correct or not. The whole process is illustrated in figure 3.

For each phoneme in the phoneme list of both the initiator and the imitator, the number of times it is used and the number of times it was successful are kept. Every time a phoneme is uttered in a language game, its use count is increased. Every time it was successfully imitated, its success score is increased. If it was not successfully imitated, nothing happens to the success score. The quality of a phoneme is this success score divided by the number of times it was used.

Depending on the course of the language game, the initiator and imitator can change their repertoire of phonemes. The phoneme lists of the agents are initially empty, so at first the initiator has to choose a random articulator position, and use this as its first phoneme. If the phoneme list of the initiator is also empty, it tries to make an imitation of the sound it just heard, by saying sounds to itself, and using a hill-climbing heuristic in order to approach the sound it just heard. It then adds this imitation to its phoneme list.

If the initiator already has a list of phonemes, it picks one of these at random and utters it, or creates a new phoneme with a very small probability. If the imitator already has a list of phonemes, it picks the closest match (as described above) and uses this as imitation. If the imitation was successful, the imitator tries to shift the phoneme it said a bit closer to the sound it just heard, again using a hill-climbing heuristic. This in order to make the phoneme even better. If the imitation was not successful, and if the quality of the phoneme was low, the phoneme is also shifted, in order to try to improve the imitation. However, if the quality of the phoneme was high, the phoneme is not shifted, because its high score indicates that it is probably a good imitation of another phoneme. Therefore, we create a new phoneme (using again a hill-climbing heuristic) that sounds similar to the sound that had to be imitated.

Two other processes are going on. Firstly, phonemes that have low quality for a long time are removed from the phoneme list. With a certain probability, the initiator's phonemes that have a quality score that is below a certain threshold are removed. Secondly, phonemes that are too close together, are merged. Phonemes are considered too close together if they are so close together that they can be confused through the noise that is added to the formant frequencies. The phonemes are fused by taking the articulator position of the phoneme with the highest score as the new articulator position. The success and use counts of the new phoneme are calculated by adding the success and use counts of the old phonemes.

All the steps of the language game as have been described above, are both necessary within the system and could in principle be performed by humans. Without some of the steps outlined above the system does not function as well. If phonemes are not shifted closer together, they stay too far apart, they get confused and the number of phonemes can not be increased. If bad phonemes are not removed, they degrade the per performance. If similar phonemes are not merged, they tend to get confused and degrade the performance as well.

4. The Experiments

In this section we will present a number of experiments that have been conducted with the language games and the agents described above. The goal of the experiments was to investigate whether it was possible to develop a successful sound system in a population of initially empty (*tabula rasa*)

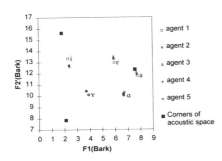

Figure 4: Sound systems of five agents

agents, and what form this sound system would take under different conditions of noise, and for different population sizes. The experiments that were conducted consisted of a predetermined number of iterated imitation games in a homogeneous population of agents.

The results of the first experiment are presented in figure 4. It shows the sound systems that were developed in a population of five agents after 1000 imitation games were played. The acoustic realisation of the phonemes was subject to 10% noise (a=0.1 in equation 1). It is clear from the clusters in the figure that the five agents share the same phonemes. The corresponding phonemes for the different agents are close together, while the phonemes within one agent are far apart. This is optimal for a sound system that is meant for communicating different sounds between agents. It can also be observed that the phonemes are spread through the available acoustic space in a way that is reminiscent of the way vowels of human languages are spread through acoustic space, even though the vowel system that was arrived at: [i,ɛ,a,ɑ,ɤ] probably does not appear in any human language.

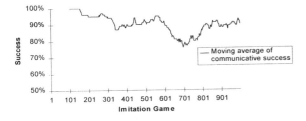

Figure 5: Success of agents with 10% noise

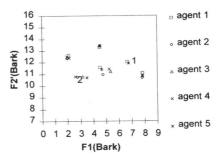

Figure 6: Sound systems in transition

The imitation success of the agents, as illustrated in figure 5 is constantly between 70% and 100%. The success starts at the 100% level in the beginning of the experiment, because at that time the agents only have one phoneme each and confusion is not possible. As soon as the agents start creating new phonemes, however, the success score drops, because phonemes are being confused. After a while, the agents succeed in making copies of the phonemes, and the success score returns to near 90%. The results shown are of the same run that resulted in the sound systems of figure 4, and are representative for the runs that are normally generated by the simulation.

If the amount of noise in the formant frequencies is increased, the area over which phonemes are "smeared" in acoustical space will also increase, and the number of phonemes that can coexist without confusion in the agents' vowel systems will decrease. We therefore expect smaller vowel systems and more variation within the realisation of individual vowels. This is illustrated in figure 7, which represents a typical sound system[††] of the agents after 5000 imitation games. This number is higher than in the previous experiment, as the agents apparently take longer to develop multiple phonemes if there is more noise. This is logical because newly generated phonemes have a higher chance of interfering with existing phonemes. Note that the realisation of a formant can be shifted as much as 2 Bark down or 1.5 Bark up by 30% noise, so any phoneme can be realised in a significant part of the acoustic space.

When one agent starts using a new phoneme, this can be

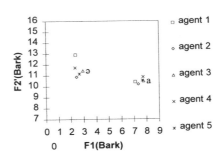

Figure 7: Sound systems with 30% noise

[††] The vowel system, consisting of /a/ and /ə/, coincidentally is similar to the vowel system of Oubykh, a West-Caucasian language.

508

Figure 8: score of twelve agent experiment

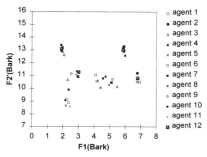

Figure 9: Phonemes of twelve agent experiment

adopted by the other agents in the population. First one agent invents a new phoneme at random. When it uses this phoneme in an imitation game, the imitation game is bound to fail. However, if a language game fails in an agent whose phonemes otherwise have a good quality score, a new phoneme will be generated that is like the phoneme that was just heard, as has been described in section 3. If this new phoneme does not interfere with the phonemes that are already present, it will be accepted by the population of agents, and will become successful as well. This process can be observed in figure 6. Here one of the agents, agent 1, seems not to have the phoneme marked with 2, that is otherwise shared by all other agents, but it does seem to have an extra phoneme, marked with 1, which it shares with one other agent, agent 5. Actually these two facts are unrelated. The phoneme marked with 2 is a phoneme that has been created by another agent than agent 1, some time before the moment at which figure 6 was made. Agent 1 has not yet had the opportunity to make a successful copy of this phoneme. The phoneme marked with 1, however, has been recently created by agent 1. The only agent that has had the opportunity to make a successful imitation of this phoneme is agent 5. It can be observed that new phonemes are created in gaps between existing phonemes in the acoustical space. Phonemes that are created outside such gaps will quickly be merged with the existing phonemes, or will interfere with existing phonemes, and be removed from the sound systems, because their quality scores will remain too low.

A last observation that will be made is what happens when the agent population is made larger. For this, experiments with 12[‡‡] agent have been conducted. The experiments were run for 3000 cycles and had 10% noise on the acoustic space. The success score of a typical experiment is shown in figure 8. We can see that the score stays above 80%, although it does seem to be decreasing a bit over time. This is undoubtedly due to the increasing number of phonemes in the population of agents. But there does not seem to be a big differences between figure 8 figure 5, which showed the success score of a population of five agents.

The phonemes of the twelve agents of this experiment after 3000 imitation games are shown figure 9. We can observe that there are four to six clusters of phonemes. Three of these are compact and unambiguous. Another cluster, which can be found between 4 and 6 Bark on the F1 axis and

around 11 Bark on the F2' scale is also unambiguous, but much more dispersed. This cluster is quite close to another diffuse cluster, which can be found between 2 and 3 Bark on the F1 scale and 9 and 12 Bark on the F2' scale. This cluster could also be considered as two separate clusters, as some agents (for example agents 6, 10 and 11) have two phonemes near the densest points in this cluster, whereas other agents (3 and 7) have only one phoneme in the centre of this cluster. This could indicate that the cluster represents a phoneme in the process of splitting. More research is needed, however, in order to make this clear.

In any case, it does not seem that the increase in the number of agents influences the success of the imitation very much. Of course, there is bound to be some influence, as an agent will play games with more other agents, so that its phonemes get shifted in more different directions and therefore converge less quickly to a common point. The fact that the number of agents does not greatly influence the success of imitation is promising, as for realistic experiments the number of agents has to be much larger than the five or twelve used in the present experiments. Fortunately, the simulations are not computationally intensive, so it should be possible to increase the number of agents to about a hundred times the number of agents that were used in the experiments presented here.

5. Conclusions and Future Work

The results of the experiments show that it is possible to generate realistic vowel systems in a distributed population of agents that try to imitate each other under constraints. No innate features that determine the form of the vowel systems were needed, nor does it appear to be necessary for the agents to inspect each other's internal state.

The experiments have also shown that the generated vowel systems are not static. They are constantly changing as a result of the invention of new phonemes, the shifting of existing phonemes due to noisy production, and the deletion and merging of phonemes. This is a phenomenon that is also found in natural language, albeit in a less extreme way than in our system. The agents in our system are probably not conservative enough. However, the observed changes seem to indicate that sound change in human language can be explained by the mechanisms that have been proposed in this paper. Previous attempts to explain vowel systems on functional grounds [1,2,3,5,6,10,13,18] have always resulted

---

[‡‡] The number of 12 agents was chosen because this is the number Berrah et al.[1] use in their experiments.

in static systems and could therefore not account for language change. Especially the fact that the agents actively imitate each other seems to be important, as this makes it possible for newly invented phonemes to become successful. In Berrah et al,'s system [1,5,6], for example, introducing a new phoneme would lead to its immediate rejection, as no matching phonemes would be found in the other agents. This would lead to a lower fitness of the agent that invented the phoneme, and thus both the agent as well as the phoneme would eventually disappear from the population. Only simultaneous invention of a new phoneme in multiple agents would make it possible for a new phoneme to be accepted.

Apparently the shape of vowel systems can be explained by considering them as the result of a self-organising process consisting of interactions (imitation games) in a population of independent agents that each change their local phonological knowledge according to the outcome of these interactions. Of course, this situation is a gross simplification of the way humans learn the sounds of their language. However, it does give an indication that we do not have to resort directly to innate mechanisms for explaining phonological phenomena.

These observations agree quite well with the observations that Steels [15,16] has made in trying to apply the ideas of self-organisation to other parts of language, notably lexicon formation. It appears that for more parts of language it is not necessary to invoke innate mechanisms, but that they can be explained by self-organising processes.

In the immediate future the system can be extended in several ways. Because of its dynamic nature, it can easily be extended to accommodate a changing population of agents. One could, for example, add and remove agents from the population, and see how this influences the dynamics. These agents can be made to differ in "age" so that older agents are more conservative than younger ones. An interesting question would then be whether this conservatism would stabilise the population. One could also investigate how the influx of new, empty agents would influence the stability of the population.

Another modification of the system would be to investigate more complex sounds. Investigating only vowels is easy, but also quite unrealistic if one wants to learn things about human language. One possible extension would be to investigate consonant-vowel syllables, as have already been investigated in a static system by Lindblom et al. [11]. For this, one would have to add constraints on articulation, as well as constraints on perception.

Considering (the phonology of) language as an emergent phenomenon of the interaction of language users allows us to use the tools of the study of artificial life and dynamic systems for the study of language. It opens up a new perspective that can make it easier to explain a number of phenomena that can nowadays only be explained by postulating innate mechanisms.

6. Acknowledgements

The work presented here has been done in part at the AI-lab of the Vrije Universiteit Brussel in Brussels, Belgium and in part at the Sony Computer science laboratory in Paris, France. It forms part of ongoing research project into the origins of language. It was financed by the Belgian federal government FKFO project on emergent functionality (FKFO contract no. G.0014.95) and the IUAP 'Construct' project (no. 20). I thank Luc Steels, Edwin de Jong and Dolores Cañamero for valuable suggestions on– and discussion of the ideas that are fundamental to the work and Hervé Glotin for personally explaining his Alife-work on phonology.

7. References

1. Berrah, Ahmed-Reda, Hervé Glotin, Rafael Laboissière, Pierre Bessière and Louis-Jean Boë,(1996) From Form to Formation of Phonetic Structures: An evolutionary computing perspective, in: Terry Fogarty and Gilles Venturini, eds. *ICML '96 workshop on Evolutionary Computing and Machine Learning*, Bari, pp. 23–29

2. Boë, Louis-Jean, Jean-Luc Schwartz and Nathalie Vallée(1995), The Prediction of Vowel Systems: perceptual Contrast and Stability, in: Eric Keller (ed.), *Fundamentals of Speech Synthesis and Speech Recognition*, John Wiley, pp. 185–213

3. Carré, René and Mohamad Mrayati, Vowel transitions, vowel systems, and the Distinctive Region Model, in: C. Sorin et al. (eds.) *Levels in Speech Communication: Relations and Interactions*, Elevier pp. 73–89

4. Chomsky, Noam and Morris Halle (1968) *The sound pattern of English*, MIT Press, Cambridge, Mass.

5. Glotin, Hervé, (1995) *La Vie Artificielle d'une société de robots parlants: émergence et changement du code phonétique*. DEA sciences cognitives-Institut National Polytechnique de Grenoble

6. Glotin, Hervé, Rafael Laboissière(1996) Emergence du code phonétique dans une societe de robots parlants. *Actes de la Conférence de Rochebrune 1996 : du Collectif au social*, Ecole Nationale Supérieure des Télécommunications - Paris

7. Grimes, Barbara F. (ed.)(1996) *Ethnologue: Languages of the World, 13th edition*, SIL.

8. Jakobson, Roman and Morris Halle (1956) *Fundamentals of Language*, the Hague: Mouton & Co.

9. Ladefoged, Peter and Ian Maddieson (1996) *The Sounds of the World's Languages*, Blackwell.

10. Liljencrants, L. and Björn Lindblom (1972) Numerical simulations of vowel quality systems: The role of perceptual contrast, *Language* **48** pp. 839–862.

11. Lindblom, Björn, Peter MacNeilage and Michael Studdert-Kennedy(1984), Self-organizing processes and the explanation of language universals, in: Brian Butterworth, Bernard Comrie and Östen Dahl (eds.) *Explanations for language universals*, Walter de Gruyter & Co. pp. 181–203

12. Lindblom, Björn and Ian Maddieson (1988), Phonetic Universals in Consonant Systems, in: Hyman, Larry M. and Charles N. Li (eds.) *Language, Speech and Mind*, pp. 62–78.

13. Lindblom, Björn(1996), Systemic constraints and adaptive change in the formation of sound structure, in: James R. Hurford, Michael Studdert-Kennedy and Chris Knight, *Evolution of Language: Social and Cognitive Bases for the Emergence of Phonology and Syntax*

14. Maddieson, Ian,(1984) *Patterns of sounds*, Cambridge University Press.

15. Steels, Luc (1996) The Spontaneous Self-organization of an Adaptive Language, in: S. Muggleton (ed.) *Machine Intelligence* **15**.

16. Steels, Luc (1997) Synthesising the origins of language and meaning using co-evolution, self-organisation and level formation, in: J. Hurford (ed.) *Evolution of Human Language*, Edinburgh: Edinburgh University Press.

17. Suzuki, Junji, Kunihiko Kaneko,(1994) Imitation Games, in: *Physica D* 75 pp. 328–342

18. Vallée, Nathalie, (1994) *Systèmes vocaliques: de la typologie aux prédictions*, Thèse préparée au sein de l'Institut de la Communication Parlée (Grenoble-URA C.N.R.S. no 368)

Cooperation Without Genes, Games Or Cognition.

Charlotte K. Hemelrijk

AI Lab, Department of Computer Science, University of Zürich,
Winterthurerstr 190, CH-8057 Zürich, Switzerland, Fax 0041-1-363
00 35, Email: hemelrij@ifi.unizh.ch.

Abstract

In this paper I describe how the spatial dynamics of autocatalytic interactions among entities in a virtual world led to a type of co-operation that typically would be studied from a game theoretical perspective. The entities were very simple and completely identical at the start of the simulation. They just aggregated and performed aggressive interactions in which winning was self-reinforcing. Patterns of reciprocation emerged at the level of the group, particularly in loose assemblages. These patterns appeared not to be due to global spatial structures as I have suggested before (Hemelrijk, 1996ab), but arose from local series of Tit-for-Tat like interactions. These involved pairs of individuals that 'collaborated' by taking turns in chasing away a third entity. Runs with varying parameter values showed that particularly those entities that were designed to be more aggressive, were more prone to co-operate. The processes responsible for the Tit-for-Tat like patterns are outlined. It is suggested that similar epiphenomena may contribute to co-operation found in real animals (such as reciprocation of support in primates, communal predator inspection by fish and co-operative hunting by lions). The explanatory value of game theoretical approaches to co-operation in real animals, such as the Prisoner's Dilemma is questioned. Firstly, because in that paradigm the ability to co-operate is attributed to a quality of the individual (be it in terms of genes or cognition) and arises from pay-off rationalisation, secondly because co-operation (or its absence) is studied in isolation, separate from other behavioural acts.

1 Introduction

Problems surrounding the evolution of co-operation are commonly studied using the Prisoner's Dilemma as a metaphor. In this game, individuals have the choice to either co-operate or defect. Costs and benefits of both options depend on the behaviour of the partner and are a priori defined. Many extensions of the Prisoner's Dilemma have been studied, such as iterated versions (Axelrod and Hamilton, 1981), versions involving more individuals (Eshel and Cavalli-Sforza, 1982) and games on a spatial grid (Axelrod, 1984; Nowak and May, 1992). A strategy that appeared to survive against a large array of alternatives is Tit-for-Tat, in which each of the two players copies the preceding behavioural act of its partner (Axelrod and Hamilton, 1981). Tit-for-Tat has become the prototypical co-operative strategy in both theoretical (e.g. Nowak and Sigmund, 1992,1993) and empirical studies of animal behaviour (e.g. Milinski, 1987; Dugatkin, 1988)

Evolutionary biologists often use game theory in the form of so-called Evolutionarily Stable Strategies. This approach is illuminating, because it shows how the fitness of individuals adopting a given behaviour is conditional on the relative frequency of those playing alternative strategies (Maynard Smith, 1983). A drawback is that in these games the problem under study is projected as a - genetically encoded - quality of the individuals (e.g. their identity as co-operators or defectors). Furthermore, possible links with other aspects of behaviour are not considered: the occurrence of co-operation is exclusively studied within the duality of co-operating or not.

Cognitive scientists also view co-operation as a quality of the individuals, but in this case it concerns specific mental abilities. For instance, when engaged in complex polyades (i.e. conflicts involving more than two opponents) primates are believed to reciprocate and exchange social favours. This exchange is assumed to be completely under individual control: participants are thought to keep track of the number of acts received and given and to have a motivation to pay in return (de Waal and Luttrell, 1988). The ability for such complex behaviour is attributed to the large cognitive capacities of the subjects (Byrne & Whiten, 1988).

An alternative perspective to the strongly rationalistic approach of evolutionary biologists and cognitive scientists outlined above is adhered in 'New Artificial Intelligence' (e.g. Pfeifer and Verschure, 1995). Its proponents advocate that seemingly complex behaviour may be achieved without pre-programmed internal control (in the form of genes or minds) and global knowledge (such as keeping records). Experiments with robots have demonstrated that co-operative behaviour which looks complex and sophisticated to an observer can be nothing more than the result of straightforward, simple interactions between agents and their local environment (Maris & te Boekhorst, 1996). Along the same lines, Deneubourg and Goss (1989) have shown that apparently 'clever decisions' in ants may emerge from self-reinforcing interactions. Therefore, any study trying to explain the complexity of social behaviour should at the same time ask what part of it must be coded explicitly as capacities of the individuals and what part is determined by interactions between individuals.

To gauge the complexity generating effects of inter-individual interactions, I investigated the 'social organisation' of a group of simple, artificial agents by means of an individual-oriented model. In particular, I studied how co-operation in a virtual world may arise as a self-organised phenomenon (Hemelrijk, 1996b). The set-up was inspired by the work of Hogeweg (1988). Using an individual-oriented model, she found that self-reinforcing dominance interactions between aggregating entities led to a social-spatial structure with dominants in the centre and subordinates at the periphery. This incited me to find out whether reciprocation of 'support' in dominance displays ('fights') - as recorded in a number of animal species and especially primates (Harcourt and de Waal, 1992) - may emerge as a side-effect of the type of dynamics studied by Hogeweg. If so, this would imply that such seemingly strategic behaviour may come about without a tendency to help or keep records of acts given and received (Hemelrijk, 1996ab).

Because 'help in fights' and its reciprocation was indeed recorded in such a model, I expected that it would originate from the same global spatial-social structure as described by Hogeweg (Hemelrijk, 1996b). In the present paper, I have tested this hypothesis and will show it to be incorrect. Reciprocation at the group level appeared instead to be due to bouts in which two 'collaborators' took turns in mutually supporting each other by chasing a third entity ahead. In their appearance these bouts resemble series of Tit-for-Tat, although none of the assumptions of such a strategic game were build into the model. In the discussion, I will therefore question the value of a game theoretical approach even when individuals display behaviour that appears to justify its application. Finally, I will relate these findings to examples of co-operation in real animals and will derive some new, counter-intuitive hypotheses concerning the occurrence of co-operation.

2 Methods

In this section I will outline how reciprocity is defined and measured and present a description of the model.

2.1 Operationalisation of reciprocity

At a group level, reciprocity can be approached in two ways, namely according to a model based on acting by one and reacting by another individual (the 'actor-reactor' model) or on acting and receiving by the same individual (the 'actor-receiver' model). In most studies the 'actor-reactor' model is tacitly assumed. It implies that actors direct relatively more acts to those reactors that perform relatively more acts to them in return compared to what these reactors give to other actors. For instance, individual A gives most to the animal that also directs more to A in return than to any other individual in the group. Drawbacks of this model are that complete reciprocation appears impossible for an odd group size and that it is very hard to protect oneself against deception (Hemelrijk, 1990a). For instance, to make sure that the most preferred partner gives more to ego than to others, ego has to trace how often this partner directs acts to all others. In general, individuals therefore have to keep track of all acts directed among all other individuals. To collect such global information is time-consuming and requires extensive cognitive abilities.

Under the 'actor-receiver' model, however, these problems do not arise: here, individuals give relatively more often to those from whom they receive more frequently in return. In this case, the required knowledge is much more 'local', since agents must tune their acts to what they receive from others, but do not have to bother about interactions among others. In addition, complete reciprocation is possible in both even and odd group sizes (Hemelrijk, 1990a).

To test for 'actor-receiver' reciprocation among all pairs of group-members, a specially devised statistic (τ_{Kr}) has been developed (Hemelrijk, 1990ab). This statistic measures the correlation between the corresponding rows of two social interaction matrices and the method reckons with the statistical dependency due to recurrent observations on the same individual (Hubert, 1987). The τ_{Kr}-value for the correlation between a matrix for 'given' acts and 'received' acts is thus a measure for the degree of reciprocation within a group.

2.2 The Model

The model is individual-oriented and event-driven (see Hogeweg & Hesper 1979; Hogeweg, 1988; Villa, 1992; Judson, 1994). The modelling environment (written in object-pascal, Borland Pascal 7.0) consists of three parts:

* the 'world' (toroid) with its interacting agents,

* its visualization,

* special entities that collect and analyze data on what happens in the 'world' (cf. the 'recorders' and 'reporters' of Hogeweg, 1988).

The 'world' consists of a regular lattice of 200 by 200 square cells. Each cell can be occupied by only one entity. In conformity with most primate studies on reciprocation, I will confine myself to small populations of 5-10 individuals. Agents are able to move in one of eight directions. They have an angle of vision of 120 degrees and their maximum perception distance (MaxView) is 50 cells. Agents group and perform dominance interactions according to the sets of rules that will be described below.

2.2.1 Grouping rules

In the primatological literature, two opposing forces affecting group structure are postulated: on the one hand animals are attracted to one another, because being in a group provides safety. On the other hand, aggregation implies competition for resources and this drives animals apart.

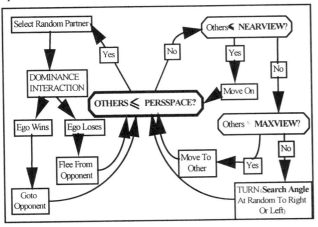

Figure 1. Flow chart for the behavioral rules of the entities

The forces leading to aggregation and spacing are realised in the model by the following set of rules (cf. Hogeweg, 1988; figure 1):

- If an agent sees another within a critical distance (parameter PerSpace), it performs a dominance interaction with that entity. In case several agents are within PerSpace, the interaction partner is chosen at random. If the agent wins the interaction, it moves towards its opponent, otherwise it moves away.

- If nobody is in its PerSpace, but an agent perceives others within a distance of NearView (eight cells), it continues to move on in its original direction.

- If an agent detects others outside NearView, but within its maximum range of vision (= MaxView), it moves towards them.

- If an agent does not perceive any other agent within maxView, it searches for group members by making a turn over an angle (x) at random to the right or left (= SearchAngle).

2.2.2 Perception of dominance

A number of hypotheses about how dominance rank is perceived by others are entertained by various authors (Hemelrijk, 1996a). The most simple one is that the others' capacity to win is directly perceived from external cues, such as pheromones in social insects. In many species, however, dominance may not be recognised externally. The capacities of others may then be estimated on the basis of an individuals' former encounters with a partner. Such a representation asks for more 'cognition' and was used in Hogeweg's SKINNIES (1988). Agents endowed with direct and estimated rank perception will be called Perceivers and Estimators respectively. The effects of both types of dominance perception will be compared in this paper.

2.2.3 Dominance interactions.

Interactions between agents with direct perception of dominance ranks (i.e. Perceivers) are modelled after Hogeweg & Hesper (1983) as follows:

1. Each entity has a variable DOM (representing the capacity to win a hierarchical interaction).

2. After meeting one another in their PerSpace, entities display and observe each others DOM. This represents an active display and only through such a display the partner obtains information about the DOM value of its opponent. Subsequent winning and losing is determined as follows by chance and values of DOM:

$$w_i = \begin{bmatrix} 1 & \dfrac{DOM_i}{DOM_i + DOM_j} > RND(0,1) \\ 0 & else \end{bmatrix} \quad (1)$$

where w_i is the outcome of a dominance interaction initiated by agent i (1=winning, 0=losing). In other words, if the dominance ratio of the interacting agents is larger than a random number (drawn from a uniform distribution), then agent i wins, else it looses.

3. Updating of the dominance values is done by increasing the dominance value of the winner and decreasing that of the loser:

$$DOM_i := DOM_i + \left(w_i - \dfrac{DOM_i}{DOM_i + DOM_j} \right) * STPDOM$$

$$DOM_j := DOM_j - \left(w_i - \dfrac{DOM_i}{DOM_i + DOM_j} \right) * STPDOM$$

$$(2)$$

The consequence of this system is that it behaves as a damped positive feedback: winning by the higher ranking agent reinforces their relative DOM-values only slightly, whereas winning by the lower ranking gives rise to a relatively large change in DOM. To keep DOM values positive, their minimum value was arbitrarily put at 0.01. STPDOM is a scaling factor and set at 0.5.

4. Winning includes chasing the opponent, who responds by fleeing in the opposite direction (under a small random angle).

In the case of indirect rank perception, the agents (i.e. Estimators) have to recognise others individually and to remember their personal experience with each partner. Dominance interactions are defined similarly as in the SKINNIES of Hogeweg (1988):

1. If an entity meets another in its PerSpace, it first consults its memory to establish whether it might win or loose a potential dominance interaction with that partner. Hereto, it performs the same dominance interaction as described in (1) and (2), but now based on the mental impressions it has of its own dominance rank and that of the other. If it looses this 'mental battle', it moves away while updating the impression of its own rank and that of the partner. If it wins, it updates and initiates a 'real' fight. Thus, unlike the Perceivers, the Estimators 'decide' whether or not to attack.

2. If it wins, a 'real' fight is initiated by displaying its expectancy to win as its updated relative dominance rank ($=D_i$) and the partner displays in return ($=D_j$). That is:

$$D_i = \frac{DOM_{i,i}}{DOM_{i,i} + DOM_{i,j}}$$

$$D_j = \frac{DOM_{j,j}}{DOM_{j,j} + DOM_{j,i}}$$

Thus entities display their 'self-confidence'. Note that this self-confidence varies depending on the experience ego has with a particular partner. The variability of the display is not a strategic option (such as dishonest signalling in a typical game-theoretic setting), but a direct consequence of behavioural constraints.

3. Winning is decided as in (1), using D_i and D_j instead of DOM_i and DOM_j.

4. Updating of the experiences of each of both entities is done similar to (2), but involves four representations:

$$DOM_{i,i} := DOM_{i,i} + \left(w_i - \frac{DOM_{i,i}}{DOM_{i,i} + DOM_{i,j}} \right) * STPDOM$$

$$DOM_{i,j} := DOM_{i,j} - \left(w_i - \frac{DOM_{i,i}}{DOM_{i,i} + DOM_{i,j}} \right) * STPDOM$$

for agent i. Updating for agent j is obtained by replacing $DOM_{i,.}$ by $DOM_{j,.}$.

From now on, the initiation of a dominance interaction will be called 'attack' for short.

2.2.4. Timing regime

Since parallel simulations cannot be run on most computers, a timing regime regulating the sequence of the activation, has to be included. The type of timing regime influences the results of a simulation. A biologically plausible timing regime must be locally controlled, i.e. by other entities and not by a monitor (e.g. Goss & Deneubourg, 1988). In the timing regime used here, each entity draws a random waiting time from a uniform distribution. The entity with the shortest waiting time is activated first. The decay of waiting time is the same for each entity. However, if a dominance interaction occurs within NearView of an agent, the waiting time of this agent is reduced stronger.

2.3 Experimental setup and Data collection

I have created cohesive and dispersed groupings by changing the values of two parameters, PerSpace and SearchAngle (Hemelrijk, 1996b). The parameter combination of perSpace of 2 and searchAngle of 90°, led to cohesive groups. To produce dispersed groupings, I doubled the PerSpace to 4 and halved the SearchAngle 45°. In addition, I studied the effects of all other combinations of high and low PerSpace and SearchAngle (i.e. perSpace, SearchAngle: 2,45; 4,90).

Per type of entity (Perceiver, Estimator) and grouping (Cohesive, Loose) five runs were done for each of three population sizes (N = 5, 8 and 10) giving a total of 60 experiments. For the remaining parameter combinations three runs were performed per type of entity for population size 8 (totalling 12 experiments). From the start of each run, every change of spatial position and heading direction of each entity was recorded. After stabilisation of the dominance ranks (which typically occurred around 1000*N activation), data were collected for the next 500*N activation. Every 10*N activation the distance between agents was calculated. Dominance interactions were continuously monitored and the following features were recorded: 1) the identity of the attacker and its opponent; 2) their updated DOM-values and 3) cases of triadic interactions that resemble 'support' (i.e. cases in which a third entity happened to attack one of two agents that were involved in a fight one time step before).

2.4 Data analysis

The degree with which group members reciprocate support is expressed by τ_{Kr}-values of the corresponding Kr matrix correlation (Hemelrijk, 1990ab).

To characterise the spatial distribution of the entities, I used circular statistics (Mardia, 1972). For each scan the centrality of each individual was calculated by drawing a unit circle around ego and projecting the direction of each other group member (as seen by ego) as a point on the circumference of that circle. Connecting these points with the origin gives vectors, whose average length measures the degree in which the position of group members relative to ego is clumped; longer mean vectors reflect more directedness and indicate lower centrality.

3 Results

3.1 Further analysis of former hypotheses.

In the model, reciprocation at a group level occurred in about 50% of the runs. In agreement with my former results (Hemelrijk, 1996b), the degree of reciprocation did not differ between Perceivers and Estimators, but was stronger in dispersed than in cohesive groups. My explanation for this has been that overall reciprocity emerged from a stable spatial-social structure. In conformity with the findings of Hogeweg (1988), I expected that dominants would occupy the centre and subordinates the periphery. This would imply that higher ranking entities encounter others more often than lower ranked ones. Because the probability of support is proportional to the encounter rate, the dominants should therefore also support others more often than subordinates. Following the same reasoning, each entity in turn was anticipated to encounter and support especially dominants, thus leading to reciprocation.

In assemblages with relatively permanent subgroups, I furthermore expected that this spatial heterogeneity made individuals direct more acts to and receive more acts from members of their own subgroup than from members of other subgroups. I speculated that this additional cause of reciprocation would explain the higher degree of reciprocation in loose groups. One way to test this idea is by statistically controlling for the effects of inter-individual distances: this should eliminate the effects of spatial heterogeneity and hence remove the extra source of reciprocity.

Although this is still an interesting hypothesis to be tested in differently constructed models and in real social groups, the data analysis did not support it as an explanation for the patterns found in this particular artificial world. Firstly, even after partialling out proximity (by means of the partial Kr Test, see Hemelrijk, 1990b), reciprocation remained stronger in loose than in cohesive groups. Secondly, I was unable to confirm that dominants tended to occur in the centre of a cohesive group: being more evenly surrounded at all sides by others was correlated with dominance only in 6.7 % of the runs. Furthermore, these correlation coefficients were not related to overall reciprocity (Kendall Rank correlation: Estimators, $\tau = -0.22$, $p = 0.25$; Perceivers: $\tau = 0.17$, $p = 0.40$).

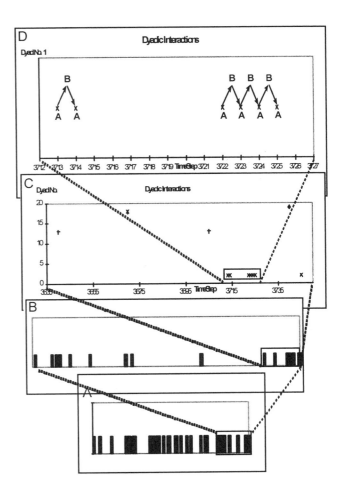

Figure 2. Distribution of acts of support during a period of stabilized ranks in a run of eight Estimators (PerSpace = 4, SearchAngle = 45°). A) Support interactions in the complete period. B) Enlargement of the window in A, showing the hierarchical clustering of support in time. C) Interactions annotated for each dyad in the enlarged window of B. C) Alternating acts of support (represented by an arrow) within one specific dyad.

3.2 Alternative explanations.

To explain my findings another course had to be taken. In my previous explanation I did not consider the temporal distribution of support and herewith, implicitly presumed it to be random. Inspection of the time series of support revealed that this assumption was incorrect: acts of support were clustered in time and organised in bouts (figure 2). Furthermore, in some bouts members of a dyad supported each other directly in turn, herewith immediately 'paying back' the 'help' they received. The frequency with which this occurred deviated significant from a random model (figure 4). Such bouts of 'immediate' reciprocation should be clearly distinguished from 'overall' reciprocation (which is measured at a group level by the τ_{Kr}-value). In general, strings of immediate reciprocation involved two partners that collectively chased away a third entity. In essence, immediate reciprocation arose because by fleeing from one partner, the victim ended up in the PerSpace of the other.

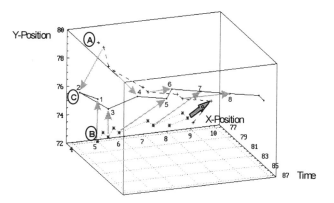

Figure 3. Series of events in one bout of immediate reciprocations of support among two Estimators (population size 8, PerSpace 4, SearchAngle 45°). Arrows represent acts of attack, the accompanying numbers indicate time steps. Note that at the ninth time step (thick arrow), one of the supporters becomes the new victim.

What happens during immediate reciprocation is illustrated for a specific case in figure 3. In the first time step, entity B attacks its victim, C. By fleeing in the opposite direction with a small random error, C ends up in the PerSpace of A, whereupon A is activated and displays against C (second time step). Herewith, A supports B. By escaping from A, C again is caught in the PerSpace of B. In the mean time, the dominance interaction between A and C has activated B who by now attacks C once more (third time step) etcetera. This particular bout ended at the ninth step when the spatial configuration became such that B displayed against its 'ally' A. Because B lost this interaction and was chased by A, the former 'collaborators' moved away from C and herewith terminated the string of events.

Because of these mutually reinforced interactions, the number of immediate reciprocations making up a bout deviated from those expected from a random model (e.g. a geometric distribution, see figure 4). In turn, the number of immediate reciprocations, as a percentage of the total support frequency appeared to be the major determinant of overall reciprocity at a group level (figure 5). By tracing the conditions that affect the occurrence of immediate reciprocations, we should be able to find out why overall reciprocation in loose groups is higher than in cohesive groups. It should be recognised that in this world the degree of cohesiveness was brought about by particular combinations of the values for PerSpace and SearchAngle: a small PerSpace (i.e. group members had to be very close before being attacked) and a large SearchAngle (implying that entities that got 'lost', quickly found back others)

promoted cohesiveness, whereas the opposite combination gave rise to loose groups.

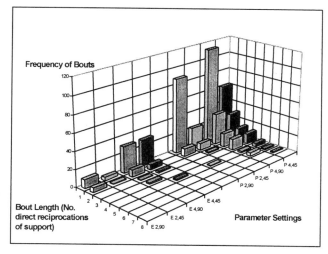

Figure 4. Frequency distribution of bouts of immediate reciprocations for different parameter combinations. Population size is 8. P = Perceiver, E = Estimator; the numbers 2 and 4 represent values of PerSpace, 45 and 90 stand for values of SearchAngle (in degrees). Loose groups are identified by the combination (PerSpace, SearchAngle = 4, 45), cohesive groups by (PerSpace, SearchAngle = 2, 90). Perceivers perform more immediate reciprocations than Estimators, but this is partly due to their higher frequency of dominance interactions (and hence frequency of support); remember that Perceivers attack anybody they encounter, whereas Estimators interact selectively. All distributions deviated significantly from a geometric series (following a test described by Haccou & Meelis, 1992), except those in low aggressive groups (P2,45; E2,45) and for Estimators in cohesive groups (and E2,90 and E4,90) whose sample sizes were too low for meaningful comparisons.

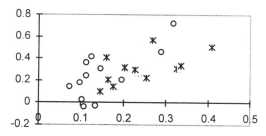

Reciprocation of support (τ_{Kr})

% Immediate Reciprocations of support

Figure 5. Relation between percentage of immediate reciprocation and the degree of overall reciprocation at a group level for population size of 8. (Perceivers (stars): Pearson correlation coefficient r = 0.58, n = 12, p<0.05 two-tailed; Estimators (open circles : n = 12, r = 0.72, p < 0.05 two-tailed).

Comparing different parameter settings within each type of entity, more immediate reciprocations and longer bouts were clearly associated with a larger PerSpace (figure 4). The impact of a large PerSpace can partly be attributed to the high frequency of support it brought about as a consequence of a high display rate. The thus enforced displacements increased inter-individual distances and hence reduced cohesiveness. A low degree of cohesion in itself sustained immediate reciprocity through limiting disturbances by others that might otherwise have broken off strings of alternating supports. In this way, a large PerSpace was the major prerequisite for the 'to-and-fro' mechanism of chasing a victim into each other's range of attack. A small SearchAngle also reduced cohesiveness, since entities had more difficulty to find back others. However, by decreasing cohesion, a small SearchAngle simultaneously lowered the frequency of support and with this the number of opportunities for immediate reciprocation dropped.

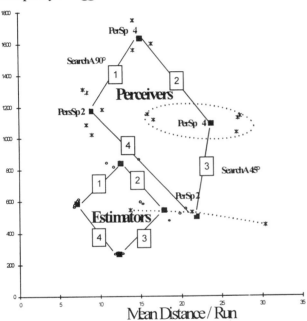

Frequency of Aggression / Run

Mean Distance / Run

Figure 6. The relation between mean distance, frequency of aggression per run, PerSpace and SearchAngle at a population size of 8. Values of individual runs are indicated by stars for Perceivers and by open circles for Estimators. Filled squares specify mean values per condition. For explanation of outlined numbers, see text.

From the above, it will be clear that the effects of the two parameters were not mutually exclusive. This is demonstrated in more detail in Figure 6. When PerSpace was increased from two to four (while keeping the SearchAngle high), not only the attack rate but - as a consequence - also the spacing among entities increased (step 1 in figure 6). If subsequently SearchAngle was reduced from 90° to 45° (while controlling for PerSpace) not only inter-individual distance increased but, as a result, also the attack frequency diminished (step 2 in figure 6). Turning down PerSpace (at the same SearchAngle)

reduced the occurrence of dominance interactions, spacing and hence inter-individual distances (step 3). Finally, the initial configuration was restored by increasing the SearchAngle again.

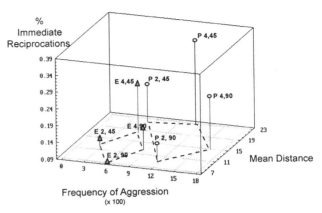

Figure 7. Relation between the percentage of direct reciprocation of support, mean distance and frequency of aggression for runs of population size 8. For abbreviations see figure 4.

In Figure 7 it is illustrated how these shifts in state in the aggression-distance space, were accompanied by corresponding changes in immediate reciprocation. It can be seen that the percentage of immediate reciprocation depends on both distance and aggression and that especially PerSpace was effective. This was so because a larger PerSpace brought about an increase in mean inter-individual distance as well as in the frequency of support. To a lesser extent, a lower SearchAngle generated the same effect. It also achieved more spacing but at the expense of a reduced frequency of support.

One problem that remains is how the difference in percentage of immediate reciprocation between Perceivers and Estimators came about. Furthermore, it is puzzling why this did not result in a distinction in reciprocation at a group level. This will be addressed in future research.

An overview of the results is presented in figure 8.

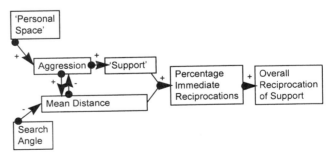

Figure 8. Summary of the main results.

3.2 Some anecdotes.

The results so far were based on thorough statistical analysis after systematic variation in parameters. However, a number of interesting observations that occurred too seldom for quantitative measurement remain worthwhile to report. Besides, anecdotes are of value to primatologists. Sometimes they use a large collection of anecdotes on certain behavioural sequences to evaluate underlying cognitive mechanisms (Whiten and Byrne, 1986).

A large PerSpace of 4 has statistically been shown to facilitate immediate reciprocation of support. This is further underpinned by the observation that only for high PersSpace I have witnessed repeated co-operation among more than two entities: In one run, three Perceivers took turns in pursuing a fourth entity.

Furthermore, an uninterrupted series of immediate reciprocation of support between two partners conforms the temporal structure of the Tit-for-Tat strategy (Axelrod and Hamilton, 1981). In the worlds of Estimators and of Perceivers such a series took the form of two entities 'co-operatively' chasing after a third. As described in the results, such sequences were sometimes broken off when one of the 'collaborators' started a dominance interaction with its 'ally' (see figure 3). This corresponds to 'defection' in the parlance of game theory. Also certain variations in the precise patterns of turn taking that have theoretical connotations in game theory were found. For instance, entities giving support once while being paid back twice (called 'Tit-for-Two Tats' in game theory) or the reverse, entities supporting twice before receiving one act ('Generous Tit-for-Tat'), emerged occasionally.

Regularly, a third entity approached a fight and attacked both opponents in succession. In primatological studies this is known as an 'impartial intervention' and suggested to have a pacifying function (de Waal, 1977).

In other cases, an entity that was opposed in a fight by a third one, shortly afterwards 'retaliated' this by opposing its enemy in return. This type of action has been classified as a 'revenge' by de Waal and Luttrell (1988).

4 Discussion

Through this model, I have shown that statistically significant reciprocation may emerge at a group level among entities that are in no way motivated to help, to pay in return or to keep track of records of acts (Hemelrijk, 1996ab). Furthermore, evidence was given that the degree of co-operation varied with the values of the parameters PerSpace (i.e. personal space) and SearchAngle (i.e. the angle over which 'lost' entities search to find back group members). The results warn against the use of intentional language and anthropomorphic interpretations, which implicitly assume sophisticated cognitive capacities. This is further underpinned by the 'anecdotes' that were abstracted from the behavioural records of the completely mindless entities that inhabited this artificial world.

The outcomes of this model also question the explanatory value of a game theoretical approach (in which anthropological labels are merely metaphors) to co-operation in real animals. More specifically, reciprocation

at a group level appeared to originate mainly from Tit-for-Tat like bouts of immediate reciprocation. These bouts emanated, however, without considering any particular costs or benefits associated with acts of co-operation and defection. Instead, these series were due to the intertwined effects of displaying dominance and social cohesion. By fleeing for a dominant, the looser sometimes ended up in the personal space of another, who subsequently drove it back in the attack range of the first opponent. This took the form of two (or more) partners chasing a communal victim ahead. This effect was stronger for more 'aggressive' entities (i.e. that were characterised by a larger PerSpace), because more aggression by chance led to more support and thus to more opportunities for reciprocation. Another consequence of higher display rates was that it spaced out group members; the resulting larger inter-individual distances in turn lowered the probability that sequences of co-operative acts were interrupted by others. An obvious requirement for immediate reciprocation was that personal space stretched further than the distance a fleeing looser covered in one time step. When this condition did not hold, very low frequencies of aggression, support and reciprocations resulted (data not shown).

Due to its self-organising propensity, the patterns that emerged from the model sometimes were counter-intuitive. For instance, at first sight it appeared rather bizarre to associate co-operation with a high aggressive tendency. To quote another example of the artificial world studied here: larger cognitive capacities (as present in Estimators compared to Perceivers) did not lead to more intricate patterns of social interactions. To explain these counter-intuitive results, one needs to think in terms of local processes, feedback, and multiple causality instead of the immediate cause-effect relationships or simplistic cost/benefit considerations. A last example concerns the finding that in the model reciprocation of aggression ('retaliation') was weaker than that of support (see also figures 6 and 7 in Hemelrijk, 1996b). The solution to this riddle was that in order to reciprocate attack, entities had to turn around fully (which they only did when they lost sight of group members ahead of them), whereas to reciprocate support they just had to move on in the same direction. In real animals, these spatial effects may be reflected in motivational dynamics: to reciprocate a received charge, a switch from fleeing to attacking has to be made. This probably asks for a more drastic change in internal regulation than the reciprocation of support, which merely involves the reiterated execution of an ongoing motivational state. This example also demonstrates how thinking about patterns in the artificial world may help us to think about mechanisms in the 'real' world.

Along similar lines the behaviour of Estimators and Perceivers mirrored a number of interesting instances of alleged co-operation in real animals. A case that comes to mind is the communal hunting by lions, where the fleeing distance of the prey diminishes until it is captured.

It also reminds of the support behaviour of captive male chimpanzees as observed by Hemelrijk & Ek (1991). These males appear to reciprocate support only during periods in which the dominance position of the alpha male is unclear. Unchecked by the interventions of an undisputed dominant, the males join up in fights against others and in this way end up reciprocating each other. A third example regards the alternating movements by two sticklebacks approaching a predator (supposedly to obtain information about its motivational state). Instead of interpreting these movements as an instance of Tit-for-Tat (as advocated by Milinski, 1987, and Dugatkin, 1988), Stephens et al. (1997) showed that this behaviour is better understood as a side-effect resulting from the joint effects of common orientation and social cohesion.

Despite the numerous experimental studies that have been done to confirm that animals play Tit-for-Tat, hardly any evidence for it has been accumulated (Noe & Hammerstein, 1995). This may be inherently due to fundamental problems with the game theoretical paradigm. Firstly, these theories are based on precisely defined costs and benefits. However, what constitutes a cost and what a benefit is in the eye of the beholder and they are probably immeasurable in most animals anyhow (Pusey & Packer, 1997). The individual-oriented approach presented here, by being free of arbitrarily defined costs and benefits, generates hypotheses that are more easily tested than those derived from game theoretical considerations. Secondly, the game theoretical approach reflects a problem under study as a quality of the individual, e.g. the conditional ability to co-operate or not. Moreover, these qualities are studied in isolation, i.e. the phenomenon to be explained is neither related to the way various behavioural activities of an individual animal are dynamically intertwined nor to the pattern generating potential of the (social) environment. In this respect game theory is very much like studying chess in order to learn more about intelligence, as has been fervently done in classical AI. However, it is precisely because of this rationalistic ideal that classical AI has faltered to explain even the most fundamental behavioural achievements. In this paper I have demonstrated the alternative option, i.e. how behavioural accomplishments can arise due to the dynamic interaction among different behavioural activities, the environment and other agents.

Acknowledgments

I am grateful to and Rolf Pfeifer and Bob Martin for continuous support. I like to thank René te Boekhorst for improving former versions of this paper. This work is supported by the Swiss National Science Foundation by a grant from the Marie Heim-Voegtlin Foundation.

References

Axelrod, R. 1984. *The evolution of cooperation*. New York: Basic Books.

Axelrod, R. and W. D. Hamilton 1981. The evolution of cooperation. *Science* **211**: 1390-1396.

Byrne, R. W. and A. Whiten 1988. *Machiavellian intelligence. Social expertise and the evolution of intellect in monkeys, apes, and humans*. Oxford, Clarendon Press.

Deneubourg, J. L. and S. Goss 1989. Collective patterns and decision-making. *Ethology, ecology and evolution* **1**: 295-311.

Dugatkin, L. A. 1988. Do guppies play tit for tat during predator inspection visits. *Behavioural Ecology and Sociobiology* **23**: 395-399.

Eshel, I. and L. L. Cavalli-Sforza 1982. Assortment of encounters and evolution of cooperativeness. *Poc. Natl. Acad. Sci. USA* **79**: 1331-1335.

Goss, S. and J. L. Deneubourg 1988. Autocatalysis as a source of synchronised rhytmical activity in social insects. *Insectes Sociaux* **35** (3): 310-315.

Haccou, P. and E. Meelis 1992. *Statistical analysis of behavioural data. An approach based on time-structured models*. Oxford: Oxford university press.

Harcourt, A. H. and F. B. M. de Waal, Ed. 1992. *Coalitions and alliances in humans and other animals*. New York, Oxford university press.

Hemelrijk, C. K. 1990a. Models of, tests for, reciprocity, unidirectionality and other social interaction patterns at a group level. *Anim. Behav.* **39**: 1013-1029.

Hemelrijk, C. K. 1990b. A matrix partial correlation test used in investigations of reciprocity and other social interaction patterns at a group level. *J. theor. Biol.* **143**: 405-420.

Hemelrijk, C. K. 1996a. Reciprocation in apes: from complex cognition to self-structuring. In: *Great ape societies*. L. F. M. W.C. McGrew T. Nishida, ed., pp. 185-195. Cambridge: Cambridge University Press.

Hemelrijk, C. K. 1996b. Dominance interactions, spatial dynamics and emergent reciprocaty in a virtual world. In: *From Animals to Animats 4: Proceedings of the fourth international conference on simulation of adaptive behavior*. M. J. M. P. Maes J-A Meyer, J Pollack, S. W. Wilson, ed., pp. 545-552. Cambridge, MA: The MIT Press/Bradford Books.

Hemelrijk, C. K. and A. Ek 1991. Reciprocity and interchange of grooming and 'support' in captive chimpanzees. *Anim. Behav.* **41**: 923-935.

Hogeweg, P. 1988. MIRROR beyond MIRROR, Puddles of LIFE. *Artificial life, SFI studies in the sciences of complexity*. Redwood City, California, Adisson-Wesley Publishing Company. 297-316.

Hogeweg, P. and B. Hesper 1979. Heterarchical, selfstructuring simulation systems: concepts and applications in biology. *Methodologies in systems modelling and simulation*. Amsterdam, North-Holland Publ. Co. 221-231.

Hogeweg, P. and B. Hesper 1983. The ontogeny of interaction structure in bumble bee colonies: a MIRROR model. *Behav. Ecol. Sociobiol.* **12**: 271-283.

Hubert, L. J. 1987. *Assignment methods in combinatorial data analysis*. New York and Basel, Marcel Dekker, inc.

Judson, O. P. 1994. The rise of the individual-based model in ecology. *Trends in ecology and evolution* **9**: 9-14

Mardia, K. V. 1972. *Statistics of directional data*. London and New York: Academic Press.

Maris, M. and R. te Boekhorst 1996. *Exploiting physical constraints: heap formation through behavioral error in a group of robots.* IEEE/RSJ International Conference on intelligent robots and systems IROS 1996, Senri Life Center, Osaka, Japan, **3**:1655-1661

Maynard Smith, J. 1983. *Evolution and theory of games*. Cambridge: Cambridge University Press.

Milinski, M. 1987. Tit for tat and the evolution of cooperation in sticklebacks. *Nature* **325**: 433-435.

Noe, R., Hammerstein, P. 1995. Biological markets. *TREE* **10**: 336-339.

Nowak, M. A. and R. M. May 1992. Evolutionary games and spatial chaos. *Nature* **359**: 826-829.

Nowak, M. A. and K. Sigmund 1992. Tit for Tat in heterogeneous populations. *Nature* **355**: 250-253.

Nowak, M. A. and K. Sigmund 1993. A strategy of win-stay, lose-shift that outperforms Tit-for-Tat in the Prisoner's Dilemma game. *Nature* **364**: 56-58.

Pfeifer, R. and P. Verschure 1995. The challenge of autonomous agents: Pitfalls and how to avoid them. In: *The artificial life route to artificial intelligence: building embodied, situated agents*. L. Steels and R. Brooks, ed., pp. 237-263. Hillsdale, New Jersey: Lawrence Erlbaum associates.

Pusey, A. and C. Packer 1997. The ecology of relationships. In: *Behavioural ecology. An evolutionary approach*. 4, J. R. Krebs Davies, N. B., ed., pp. 254-283. Oxford: Blackwell Scientific Publications.

Stephens, D. W., Anderson, J. P., Benson, K. E. 1997. On the spurious occurrence of Tit for Tat in pairs of predator-approaching fish. *Animal Behaviour* **53**: 113-131.

Villa, F. 1992. New computer architectures as tools for ecological thought. *Trends in ecology and evolution* **7**: 179-183.

Waal, F. B. M. de 1977. The organization of agonistic relations within two captive groups of Java-monkeys (*Macaca fascicularis*). *Z. Tierpsychology* **44**: 225-282.

Waal, F. B. M. de and L. M. Luttrell 1988. Mechanisms of social reciprocity in three primate species: symmetrical relationship characteristics or cognition ? *Ethology and Sociobiology* **9**: 101-118.

Whiten, A. and R. W. Byrne 1986. The St. Andrews catalogue of tactical deception on primates. *St. Andrews Psychological Report* **10**.

Interaction, Uncertainty, and the Evolution of Complexity.

Anil K Seth

Centre for Computational Neuroscience and Robotics
Innovations Centre, University of Sussex
Brighton BN1 9QG, UK
anils@cogs.sussex.ac.uk

'a starlit or a moonlit dome distains,
all that man is,
all mere complexities,
the fury and the mire of human veins.'

W.B. Yeats

Abstract

The evolution of complexity is investigated in the context of an 'iterated prisoner's dilemma' (IPD) co-evolutionary/game-theoretic ecology, populated by strategies determined by variable length genotypes. New evidence is found to support the dual hypotheses that both uncertainty, and interaction (by way of population stability), foster the evolution of progressively more complex entities. It is also argued that during periods of major evolutionary upheaval, complex entities suffer disproportionately and become less abundant in the population. The research is presented as an elaboration of the general principle that there is complexity in an organism by virtue of complexity in the environment, and has implications both for deepening understanding of the nature of biological evolution and for guiding the progress of artificial evolution.

1 Introduction

As Stephen Jay Gould [6] has consistently pointed out, the age of bacteria is not about to end anytime soon. Yet it can hardly be denied that over the course of biological evolution the complexity of the *most* complex things around has increased dramatically. It can indeed be said that in the earliest stages of life, there was nothing like the great variety of complex and wonderful creatures that now grace our world. Somewhere along the line complexity has evolved - not monotonically (witness the extinction of the dinosaurs), but it certainly has happened, and the mystery is *why*.

Two hypotheses are defended here. First, that *uncertainty* is a major drive for the evolution of complexity. The less predictable things are (up to a point), the more complex an organism needs to be in order to behave effectively. Thus complexity affords robustness in the face of noise, and as such, may be expected to evolve in noisy environments. This line of argument appeals to the general principle that there is complexity in the organism by virtue of complexity in the environment (see [1], for example); and noise, up to a point, makes an environment more complex.

The second hypothesis is that *social interaction* is a major drive for the evolution of complexity. Most explanations of this effect would follow the above general principle in arguing that interaction augments environmental complexity, and subsequently agent complexity. However the argument here is that socialisation confers population *stability* which, in turn, promotes complexity. These two arguments are not mutually exclusive and may well be complementary - it is just that the model deployed in this study is designed to investigate the latter. By drawing this distinction, this study begins to focus on more *mechanistic* explanations for the evolution of complexity, and may also begin to answer questions such as why some organisms are more complex than others.

These hypotheses are investigated through the analysis of the dynamics of co-evolutionary artificial ecologies developed to allow their constituents to evolve from being simple to being complex. These ecologies were constructed on the basis of the 'iterated prisoner's dilemma', with complexity and simplicity being charted by the 'memory' of the strategies deployed by the constituent agents to play this game. The model developed is the first to incorporate both variable length genotypes *and* partner choice mechanisms.

Following the evaluation of these two hypotheses, it was further observed that in unstable (not just uncertain) circumstances, complex entities are more fragile than simple ones, and become less predominant in a population. The description of this (not entirely surprising) behaviour was not an explicit goal of the research, but some *a posteriori* interpretations are presented in section 6.2.

The remainder of this paper is structured as follows.

Section 2 discusses the theoretical motivation of the research. Sections 3 and 4 examine the model and implementation employed, and section 5 presents sample results, which are discussed in section 6. Section 7 presents proposals for further research.

2 Theoretical Background

2.1 What is complexity?

The term 'complexity' is abundantly used, in spite of the absence of a comprehensive and concise definition. Indeed the definitions employed by most researchers simply appear to reflect the particular task or model involved. For example, for the biologist Bonner, complexity is simply the number of different cell types in an organism [4], but the philosopher Shea defines complexity in much more abstract terms as 'the number of parts and the irregularity of their arrangement' [17].

One problem is that complexity only makes intuitive sense when considered in relative terms. Therefore, to enjoy any kind of intuitively valid quantitative basis, it is best to restrict the application of the term to representations within *finitely presented languages* (such as the genotypes used in genetic algorithms, see [8]). This outlaws, for our purposes, the more expansive definitions prevalent in the philosophical literature.

A standard measure of complexity, applicable to finitely presented languages, is that of 'minimum description size'; otherwise known as 'Kolmogorov complexity'. This definition suggests that the complexity of a given expression is determined by its minimum length following compression, (still retaining all the original information). This certainly allows that mere duplications of expressions do not augment complexity, but it also implies that a purely random expression will necessarily be maximally 'complex', by virtue of having maximal information content. This is not ideal, as it precludes the possibility of expressions displaying internal structure being classed as more complex than random expressions. And the relationship of complexity to a particular language is just as important as the relationship to an observer - different languages may express information and be compressible in many different ways.

Thus there is no universally accepted definition of complexity, nor any single measure appropriate to evolutionary investigations. In the present project, we take the *memory* of an agent (as indicated by genotype length) as a measure of complexity, being quite aware that it is a definition not immediately applicable to other domains of inquiry. The justification for the use of this metric is that the evolution of longer memories implies (by virtue of the structure of the model) that more complex behavioural strategies are being deployed within the population. Dues are nevertheless paid to Kolmogorov complexity by employing the Lempel-Ziv compression al-

gorithm [10] to determine the information content of the genotypes. For the reasons given above this measure is no more valid than a direct measure of memory, but is included for the sakes of completeness and comparison.

2.2 Existing theoretical explanations for the evolution of complexity

It has often been assumed that neo-Darwinism provides a direct and satisfactory explanation for the evolution of complexity. But taken at face value, neo-Darwinism explains only how organisms come to be increasingly adapted to their particular environments or niches. Certainly, if an environment encapsulates an escalating 'predator-prey' situation then Darwinism can predict the evolution of more complex capacities by way of 'evolutionary arms races' (see e.g. [5]), but it is not clear that this kind of explanation can be extended to all instances of complexity evolution[1]. And just taking on board the general principle that organisms become complex through adapting to complex environments still leaves us in the dark over many questions. For example, why some things are more complex than others, what kinds of environmental complexities promote evolution, and how it is that organism complexity is vastly different from environmental complexity. More direct and satisfactory explanations are clearly required.

Bonner [4] describes a theory which argues that the evolution of 'gross phenotypical complexity' (such as the development of legs or lungs) can be attributed simply to organisms getting physically larger in order to exploit more areas of ecological niche space. Being larger requires being more internally complex in order to be self-sustaining, and canalization ensures that evolved internal complexity is retained should physical size reduce again over evolutionary time. More generally, it can be argued that greater structural complexity permits evolution to explore larger volumes of functional space, or even simply that, starting out simple, there is 'nowhere to go but up', and variation will more likely produce greater complexity than simplicity (but this has little to say about matters beyond the very simplest of organisms).

Other theorists have concentrated on trying to explain the evolution of neural/cognitive complexity, where physical size changes are not so important for their physical impact on the environment, as for their impact on extending the behavioural possibilities of the agent. A different class of theory has been developed to tackle this latter problem, many examples of which argue for various relationships between socialisation, language, and brain size, and as yet without any clear victor or objective methodology[2] (see e.g. [12]).

---

[1]Indeed, not all predator-prey situations *do* lead to arms races - for example, algae have hardly evolved sophisticated 'fish-avoidance mechanisms'.

[2]Ornstein, however, bucks the trend by suggesting that brain

The position adopted in the present paper is that a number of drives towards complexity undoubtedly existed, and may still exist. And since complexity is defined here in terms of 'behavioural' game-playing strategy, the present investigation falls more naturally into the context of neural/cognitive complexity rather than gross phenotypical complexity. However, since we are considering only general principles (neither the evolution of lungs nor the evolution of language), this is more an intuitive guide than a strict restraint. The dual hypotheses of noise and social stability as evolutionary motivational forces are therefore not to be considered as an exhaustive exploration of the subject, rather, as contributions to the aim of elaborating *just how* there is complexity in the organism in virtue of complexity in the environment.

2.3 Noise for robustness versus noise for complexity

Much emphasis has recently been placed on the importance of taking account of noise when evolving artificial systems in simulation - both for purposes of engendering real world robustness [15], and for disguising simulation inaccuracy [9]. The possibility of noise acting as a *driving force* for the evolution of complexity has, however, received much less attention, even though the concepts are closely related.

Lindgren [13] has used variable length genotype genetic algorithms ([8],[7]), to instantiate ecologies of agents interacting through the prisoner's dilemma. He demonstrated the evolution, in noisy environments, of increasingly complex agents, but he didn't rigorously address the possibility of a causal role for noise in the evolution of complexity, beyond suggesting:

> ...noise may disturb the actions performed by the players, which makes the problem of the optimal strategy more complicated. This increases the potential for having long transients showing evolutionary behaviour. [13], p.296.

Indeed, noise can be considered a good candidate for an evolutionary motivational force for the simple reason that uncertain environments are likely to punish very simple agents that rely on stability and regularity. Thus, if greater complexity can confer robustness against noise, we may expect to see evolution of complexity in noisy environments. In terms of our general principle, uncertainty could be considered as an important aspect of environmental complexity that leads to a corresponding complexity within the organism.

---

complexity evolved as a side-effect of some kind of neural air-conditioning mechanism during early hominid evolution in the hot African savannahs [16].

2.4 Partner selection and complexity

A general principle explanation would again have us believe that the inception of social interaction augments the complexity of the environments for the interacting agents, which then becomes reflected in the agents themselves. But this explanation, whilst conceptually attractive, is hard to assess in the context of the present paper because the actual mechanism for effecting social interaction is supplied, ready-made, to the agents[3]. Alternatively, it can be argued firstly that social interactions act to stabilise a population, by virtue of agents being able to choose suitable partners and refuse overtures from unsuitable agents. Then, secondly, echoing May [14], that this stability permits the evolution of complexity and an increase in population diversity. In this scenario, the very fact that non-trivial agent-agent interactions are happening at all provides the stimulus for evolution (with noise abetting this inherent tendency), and socially conferred stability provides a platform from which this evolution can really take off. Here we see how there might be mechanisms whereby different organisms may become differentially complex in similar environments, thanks to feedback mechanisms operating via processes such as social interaction.

3 Structure of the Model

3.1 The prisoner's dilemma

The prisoner's dilemma has long been established as a tool of great value in co-evolutionary investigations, [3],[11],[14],[20]. Essentially, it provides a framework for modelling non-trivial interactions between agents, where the maximisation of individual short term gain minimises the collective welfare, as illustrated by the following anecdote:

Imagine that you and an alleged accomplice have both been arrested, accused of a heinous crime. You are held in separate cells, and upon interrogation you can either *cooperate* by denying all knowledge, or *defect* by implicating your accomplice. You have no idea what your accomplice will do, but if you both cooperate, you will both be released (the reward, **R**), and if you both defect, then both of you will be jailed (the punishment, **P**). However, if you defect and she cooperates, then you will receive a payoff (the temptation, **T**) and she will go to jail for longer (the sucker, **S**). But if she defects and you cooperate, then you yourself are the sucker. The paradox is thus evident, - in a single meeting you will always do best to defect, in doing so either receiving the monetary payoff or avoiding being the sucker. But of course

---

[3]A worthy topic for future research would be to look at how 'social mechanisms' do evolve in social situations - the expanding literature on the evolution of communication is a useful step in this direction.

	player 2 cooperates	player 2 defects
player 1 cooperates	1:R=3 2:R=3	1:S=0 2:T=5
player 1 defects	1:T=5 2:S=0	1:P=1 2:P=1

Table 1: Prisoner's Dilemma Scoring Table

the logic is the same for your alleged accomplice, and if you both defect then you will both do worse than if you had both cooperated (see table 1). Note that the actual scores don't really matter so long as $T > R > P > S$ and $2R > T + S$.

Cooperation is thus unlikely to arise in a one-shot prisoner's dilemma, but if players can meet time and time again, and retain some memory of previous interactions, then cooperation on any given move does become a rational strategy. It is this 'iterated prisoner's dilemma' (IPD) that forms the core of the present study.

Many researchers have used genetic algorithms to evolve strategies to play the IPD (see e.g. [3],[11]), primarily for the purposes of investigating the evolution of cooperation. In these studies, as in the present model, the genotypes comprise of binary character strings representing policies for playing the IPD, with the length of the genotype determining the number of preceding moves (the game history) upon which each individual can base its strategy. Genotype length thus has a direct and valuable interpretation as 'memory'. It has been repeatedly demonstrated that cooperative strategies can and do arise and persist in artifical ecologies populated by these evolving strategies, [3]. In the present study, the evolution of cooperation *per se* is not of primary interest. Rather, cooperation within a population is taken as a useful metric of population *stability*, and the evolution of cooperating population provides a good platform for the subsequent investigation of the evolution of complexity.

3.2 Variable length genotypes and the iterated prisoner's dilemma

By introducing variable length genotypes (VLGs) into an IPD situation, Lindgren [13] demonstrated the evolution of longer and increasingly complex strategies (with longer memories) in noisy environments, (noise was introduced by invoking a certain probability for the opposite move to that specified by the genotype being made). In addition to the usual crossover and point mutations, Lindgren's strategies could also undergo *splitting* and *doubling* mutations, which incremented or decremented the potential memory (and hence potential complexity) of the strategy in question by one game iteration.

The present study employs splitting and doubling mutations in the same way as Lindgren in order to provide a quantitative method for following the evolution of

complexity[4]. This method is particularly attractive because the phenotypical strategy is not directly affected by a doubling mutation. By itself, an increase in memory doesn't change behaviour. Changes will only occur if the extra memory is subsequently used (through further mutations/crossover in the new genotype segment) to discriminate between possible courses of action (cooperation and defection in the current context). Thus, evolution of longer memories cannot simply be ascribed to some phenotypical side-effect of having a longer genotype, and must be attributed to some employment of the extra potential (or memory) provided; thus a more complex strategy.

3.3 Preferential partner selection

In real life, we normally exercise considerable discretion about who we interact with, rather than being forced to interact with everyone. This principle of partner selection allows new dimensions of emergent behavioural structure to develop, and has been introduced into a number of IPD models.

Stanley et al. ([19],[2],[18]) have published a series of papers looking at the formation of 'social networks' in an IPD context with choice and refusal permitted. Agents choose and refuse with reference to continuously updated expected payoffs that each agent maintains for every other agent in the population (they call this an IPD/CR mechanism). They demonstrate that cooperation is evolved rapidly under these conditions, and they discuss the emergence of a variety of metastable networks displaying distinct patterns of cooperativity.

The present study employs an IPD/CR mechanism similar to that developed by Stanley et al., but the innovation finds an original application in investigating the evolution of complexity, through the changes marked out by variable length genotypes.

4 Implementation

4.1 Genotype encoding scheme

At the heart of each individual in the ecology is a genotype, consisting of a string of c's and d's, determining the strategy of the individual for playing the IPD. The longer the genotype, the more it can be influenced by the history of the game, thus the longer the 'memory' of the individual.

Fig 1 illustrates how the genotype can code for a particular strategy. Each time a previous move in the game history (between two particular agents) is considered,

---

[4]VLGs have been considered to be very important in the evolution of complex entities by a number of researchers (see e.g. the SAGA genetic algorithm of Harvey [7]). This affirms the principle that in ALife GAs are not employed to solve a particular problem, but instead provide a substrate for open-ended evolution.

half of the genotype is (temporarily) thrown away (the non-shaded area in fig 1) - one half if the move had been cooperative, or the other if it had been a defection. In this way, the genotype in fig 1 (of length 16) can therefore encode a strategy with a memory of 4 prior interactions (after cutting a string of 16 characters in half 4 times, you are left with just a single character). The black square in fig 1 indicates which allele would be accessed for a [c,d,c,d] history.

However, the genotype must be made longer in order to specify the initial moves up until the memory limit. The genotype in fig 1 would require an extra 9 alleles to code for the initial 3 moves before the final 16 alleles can be used. The maximum genotype length employed is 127 alleles, providing a maximum memory of 6 iterations, although extensions to maximum memories of *any* integer value could be easily implemented.

Each time an iteration of the game is played, the moves made are stored in a history array so that they can be accessed by the strategies the next time the two players meet. This therefore constitutes the bones of the model; the agents interact by way of the IPD and their strategies can be influenced to different (and evolvable degrees) by what has happened in the past.

4.2 Code structure overview

The flow of the program is essentially very simple, as illustrated by the following pseudocode:

```
randomly initialise population
FOR EACH generation
    FOR EACH iteration
        if choice & refusal is enabled
            members choose and refuse partners
        else
            everyone chooses everyone (except self)
        one round of IPD is played (with or
                            without noise)
        history array and various scores are
                            updated
    ENDFOREACH
    new generation is created through breeding
                using a tournament GA
    every so often population statistics are
        calculated, and presented with graphics
ENDFOREACH
```

Noise is implemented in the same way as in the models of Lindgren [13]. That is, a certain probability (in this study, 1 percent)[5] is set with which the actual move made during an IPD interaction is opposite to that specified by the genotype.

---

[5]Preliminary experiments indicated that with much greater noise levels (above 5 percent), population cooperation evolved far too infrequently to sustain further study.

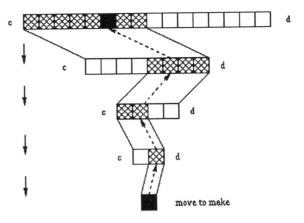

Figure 1: *genotype encoding scheme.*

4.3 Breeding procedures

A simple generational, tournament style GA is used, and the first part of the breeding procedure is to sort the population in order of fitness, which is a simple reflection of average score over all the IPD games played. If required, these fitnesses are adjusted so that longer genotypes, all else being equal, score less than short genotypes (a cost on complexity - see section 5.3).

Importantly, following crossover, splitting or duplication mutations can occur, with consequences for the memory of the new individuals. Duplication copies the latter half of the genotype twice again onto its own end, thereby preserving an appropriate section for initial move specification and also incrementing the memory by one. The actual strategy implemented by the genotype won't change after a memory increase - only further alterations through crossover or point mutation in the new genotype section can achieve this. Splitting the genotype reduces the memory by one, and of course, this mutation may well directly inflict a strategy change, if the discarded alleles were previously being used to dictate a more complex strategy utilising the full memory potential.

The crossover rate was set at 0.95, and all mutation rates were set at 0.005 (per bit for point mutations).

4.4 Preferential partner selection

If partner choice is allowed, then it proceeds on the basis that each member of the population maintains an 'expectation value' for every other member, reflecting the expected outcome of a round of prisoner's dilemma. This value, set initially to 3.0 (mutual cooperation) is allowed to alter on the basis of experience, as illustrated by the pseudocode overleaf, (based on [19]).

```
FOR EACH population member
    sort remainder on basis of expectation
    select the most preferable (up to a quota)
        and make offers; recipients thus form
        a list of offers
ENDFOREACH

FOR EACH population member
    FOR EACH offer received
        IF the offer is tolerable
            play one iteration and update
                scores and expectations
        ELSE
            refuse the offer (update expectation
                of refusee)
    ENDFOREACH
ENDFOREACH

FOR EACH member that has not played any games
    update fitness with 'wallflower' payoff
```

Given a standard IPD payoff matrix (as in table 1), the extra payoffs employed here are usually 1.0 for a refusal, and 1.6 for a 'wallflower'. The tolerance limit, below which refusals will take place, is usually set to be the same as the wallflower payoff, thus 1.6.

The expectations are updated according to the following equation (based on [19]):

$$exp[i+1] = \gamma.exp[i] + (1-\gamma).payoff$$

where 'γ' is a memory weight, and *'payoff'* represents whatever payoff (IPD or otherwise) is awarded.

This mechanism is an example of reinforcement learning, and over the course of a generation, the population members will develop distinct expectations of others based on the outcomes from early iterations. This will guide their offers in the future, and allow networks of social interactions to develop.

4.5 Statistics

The progress of the model was charted with a number of statistical measures. Average score (on the IPD) was used to implement breeding. Average memory was the complexity metric, and average cooperativity (and hence performance) was taken to indicate population stability.

Population diversity (the average Hamming distance between each possible genotype pair) was also calculated, as was the average Kolmogorov complexity of the population. In the results section, however, memory is presented as the sole complexity metric, since Kolmogorov complexity was not calculated for all cases, and correlated very strongly with memory in those cases when it was known.

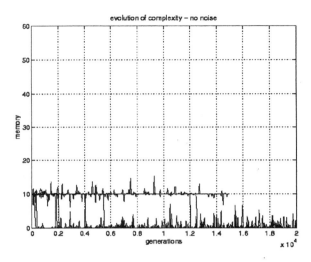

Figure 2: *evolution of complexity without noise.*

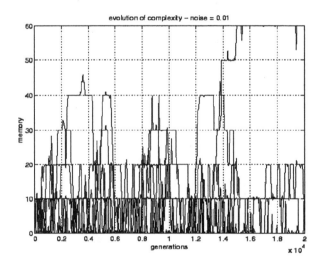

Figure 3: *evolution of complexity with noise.*

5 Results

5.1 Preliminary experiments

In general, the model was successful in evolving cooperative populations in non-noisy environments with or without partner choice, thus replicating the findings of Axelrod [3] and providing an adequate platform for further investigation. Further preliminary experiments looked at how strategies with *fixed* memories dealt with uncertain conditions, with results indicating that more complex strategies (of memory 6) were more robust and led to greater overall levels of cooperation than simple strategies (of memory 1). This provided some hope that complexity would therefore evolve in noisy environments.

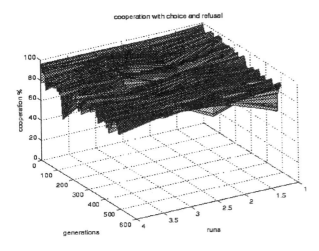

Figure 4: *cooperation with partner choice.*

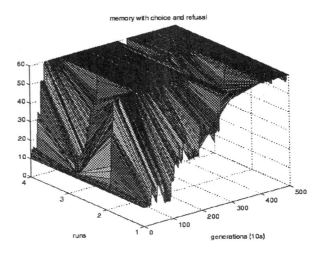

Figure 6: *evolution of complexity with partner choice.*

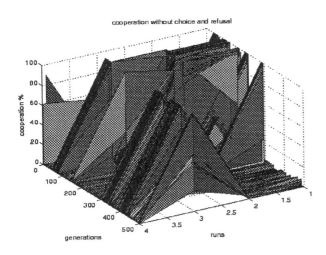

Figure 5: *cooperation without partner choice.*

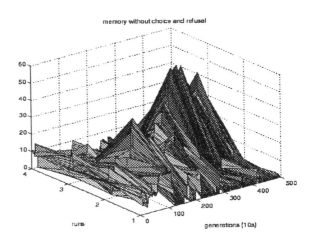

Figure 7: *evolution of complexity without partner choice.*

5.2 *Results* without *partner choice; noise kick-starts complexity*

Ecosystems were initially populated with 30 strategies of memory one, playing 20 rounds of IPD each generation (everyone playing everyone else), and were allowed to evolve over 20,000 generations. Fig 2 illustrates that, without noise, there is no tendency whatsoever for any kind of complexity to evolve, but fig 3 illustrates that, with noise, complexity does evolve, (12 runs are superimposed on these graphs). Not always, or even often, to the maximum. And not monotonically either. But the difference is clear; noise does promote complexity.

Also of interest is the observation that the evolving populations rarely sustain mixtures of complexities - this is particularly clear in fig 2 in which populations either completely comprise of memory 1 or memory 0 strate-

gies, but never both. And changes in population complexity occur very swiftly between stable, homogenously complex states - as can be seen in fig 3.

5.3 *Results* with *partner choice; interaction promotes complexity*

With the addition of the partner choice mechanism (and without noise), it is intially striking that the ecology evolves to full cooperation very quickly indeed, and is very stable over time, (the initial populations again consisted of 30 memory 1 strategies playing 20 IPD rounds each generation).

Fig 4 demonstrates that under partner choice, the level of cooperation (and population performance) achieved rises very quickly to near 100 percent and stays there. Without partner choice (fig 5), the evolved cooperation

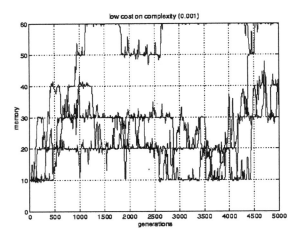

Figure 8: *a low cost on complexity.*

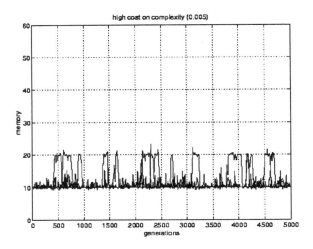

Figure 9: *a high cost on complexity.*

is much less stable and spends considerable time at zero. The case is similar for the evolution of complexity, as measured by memory. Fig 6 illustrates that, under partner choice, the initially simple memory 1 strategies evolve very quickly to a maximum memory of 6 and remain there. But without partner choice (fig 7), evolved complexity remains, almost without exception, at the initial level of 1 or lower. Thus, interaction (through partner choice) does promote stability and complexity.

5.4 A cost on complexity

Given that complexity evolves in an IPD/CR situation without any encouragement from noise, a series of experiments were performed with a *fitness cost* imposed on the possession of a long genotype. This fitness cost was compared over two values - high (0.5 percent) and low (0.1 percent). The values refer to the fitness percentage deducted per 'memory unit', and were kept low so that a long genotype which had scored well in the ecology would not score worse than a short genotype that performed poorly. It was only desired to assess the *ceteris paribus* effect of a cost on complexity.

Fig 9 overlays the results from 8 runs and illustrates that with a high cost, the evolution of complexity is abolished. With a low cost, (fig 8), this is not the case and, although complexity does not evolve with the rapidity and stability observed in the cost free cases, it certainly does evolve to a significant extent.

These experiments indicate that complexity is of sufficient value to an agent to offset a small incurred fitness cost, if not a large tariff. As a follow-up experiment, it was hypothesised that in ecologies where the 'cost barrier' precluded the evolution of complexity, the introduction of environmental noise might be able to kickstart the process and so allow complexity to develop after all.

A cost of 0.25 percent per memory unit was imposed,

and 12 runs were performed without noise, and 12 with 1 percent noise. Fig 10 and fig 11 clearly illustrate the beneficial influence of noise/uncertainty in the evolution of complexity.

5.5 Correlation between noise and complexity

A further interesting phenomenon observed in these experiments is the correlation observed between cooperation (or performance) and evolved complexity, (an effect that is only observable when both factors are sufficiently mobile). Two examples are presented here, fig 12 looking back at a non-partner-choice situation, with a rather high mutation rate (5 percent), and fig 13 looking at several superimposed runs with a high cost on complexity (0.5 percent) in a partner-choice situation. In both of these situations there are factors (high mutation, high cost) mitigating against long term stability of the population. Possible reasons for this correlation will be addressed below, in section 6.2.

6 Discussion

6.1 The evolution of complexity

It has been shown that both environmental uncertainty (noise) and social interaction can jointly promote the evolution of complexity.

In the case of noise, the suggestion is that since complexity confers robustness against noise (amongst other things), complex strategies will have a selective advantage over simple strategies in uncertain environments. The inherent uncertainty in the natural world may thus have been one of the catalysts for the evolution of the complexity of living organisms.

In the case of social interaction, the population stability evoked through partner choice is held to be in-

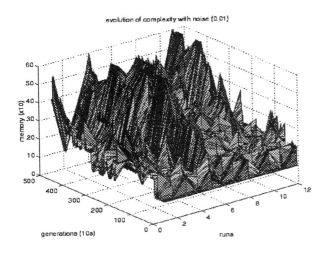

Figure 10: *evolution of complexity with noise, and a medium cost on complexity.*

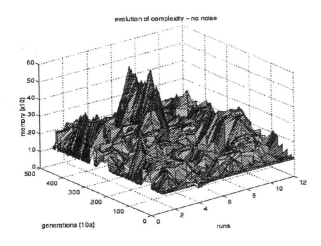

Figure 11: *evolution of complexity without noise, and a medium cost on complexity.*

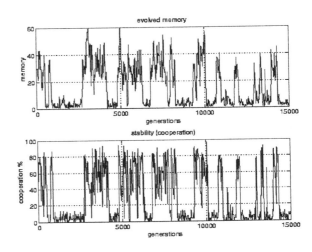

Figure 12: *correlation between complexity and stability (high mutation).*

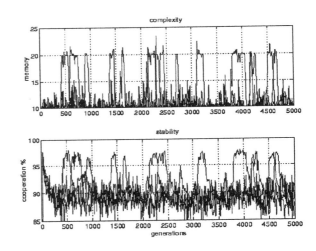

Figure 13: *correlation between complexity and stability (high cost).*

strumental in allowing complexity to evolve. It is argued here that there is a pre-existing drive towards complexity based on the fact that the mode of interaction through the IPD is non-trivial and so more complex strategies have the potential to do better[6]. But this potential is best exploited in stable circumstances, and can be augmented by the presence of environmental noise. The evolution of complexity through social interaction is a process that may not be available to all evolving organisms, suggesting that differential complexity may exist in the world thanks to there being different drives towards complexity, not all of which are (or have been) available

to all organisms.

These conclusions are presented as an elaboration on the overly general principle that 'there is complexity in the organism in virtue of complexity in the environment', (see [1]). This research begins to answer more specific questions about what *kinds* of complexity in the environment may promote organism complexity, and by what mechanisms. This has implications not only for understanding how complexity has evolved the way it has - why bacteria still flourish but now in a world also populated by human beings - but also for practioners of artificial evolution who wish to understand how to manipulate evolutionary forces in order to evolve artificial agents of increasing complexity, interest, and utility.

---

[6]A good example would be the tit-for-tat strategy, which is highly stable in non-noisy environments (see [3]), but which breaks down into mutual defection very quickly with the introduction of noise.

6.2 A correlation between stability and complexity

In unstable cirumstances, complexity correlates strongly with population stability - an observation that makes good sense in the context of stability promoting complexity. The argument here is that although complexity delivers robustness against environmental noise, it incurs brittleness in the face of large scale ecological change (ie. population instability). This may be because with greater complexity, there is more potential to exploit in becoming appropriate for the ecological niche in question - even if that niche presents some uncertainty. However, should the nature of the niche change dramatically, the specialisations of the complex entity are more than likely to prove disadvantageous. No such problem for the simple entity, which will have to undergo a much smaller genotypic change in order to suit the new niche (to a less adapted extent).

It is suggested that this phenomenon can be discerned in natural history, where complex organisms have suffered disproportionately during the huge ecological upheavals of the extinction events[7].

7 Future work

One obvious challenge would be to analyse the actual strategies that are deployed by the agents, to find out what kinds of complexities are being selected for. This would clearly deliver a deeper understanding of the nature and behaviour of the model.

As this project has been an exploratory study, the hypotheses presented would benefit from a more exhaustive testing and analysis process. A meta-study could combine the results across many different implementations, perhaps employing a variety of paradigms for founding the ecology (not just the IPD). This approach may also help in developing models that demonstrate evolved symbiosis between complex and simple organisms (bringing us back to our starting point - the age of bacteria is not over yet!).

A spatial element to the interaction of agents could be introduced, posing the question - would complexity evolve and thrive in isolated pockets before spreading across a population? And the mechanism for partner choice should be allowed to evolve as well, instead of being 'handed' to the agents in a ready-made form.

Acknowledgements

This work owes a great deal to my supervisors Phil Husbands and Inman Harvey, to my reviewers, and also to Tony White of Nortel Ltd. Financial support was provided by the EPSRC and by Nortel Ltd.

[7]The story told here is not going to be the only one. It is also undoubtedly important that the faster generational turnover of simple organisms abets their adaptation to changing ecologies.

References

[1] W.R. Ashby. *Design for a brain: The origin of adaptive behaviour.* Chapman Hall, 1952.

[2] D. Ashlock, M.D Smucker, E.A. Stanley, and L. Tesfatsion. Preferential partner selection in an evolutionary study of prisoner's dilemma. Economics report 35, Iowa State University, 1994.

[3] R. Axelrod. *The Evolution of Cooperation.* New York : Basic Books, 1984.

[4] J.T Bonner. *The Evolution of Complexity by means of natural selection.* Princeton University Press, 1988.

[5] R. Dawkins. *The Blind Watchmaker.* Longman, 1986.

[6] S.J. Gould. *Wonderful Life.* Penguin, 1989.

[7] I.R. Harvey. *The Artificial Evolution of Adaptive Behaviour.* PhD thesis, Sussex University, 1995.

[8] J.H. Holland. *Adaptation in Natural and Artificial Systems (2nd ed).* Cambridge, MA : MIT Press, 1992.

[9] N. Jakobi, P. Husbands, and I.R. Harvey. Noise and the reality gap: the use of simulation in evolutionary robotics. In F. Moran, A. Moreno, J.J. Merelo, and P. Chacon, editors, *Advances in artificial life; third european conference in artificial life.* Springer-Verlag, 1995.

[10] F. Kasper and H. Schuster. Easily calculable measures for the complexity of spatio-temporal patterns. *Physical Review A*, 36(2):842–848, 1987.

[11] C. Langton. *Artificial Life; an Overview.* MIT : Bradford Books, 1995.

[12] R. Leakey. *The origin of humankind.* Weidenfeld and Nicholson, 1995.

[13] K. Lindgren. Evolutionary phenomena in simple dynamics. In C. Langton, J.D. Farmer, S. Rasmussen, and C. Taylor, editors, *Artificial Life II.* Addison-Wesley, 1991.

[14] R. May. *Stability and Complexity in model ecosystems.* Princeton University Press, Princeton, NJ, 1973.

[15] J.M. Orbell, K. Runde, and H. Morikawa. The robustness of cognitively simple judgements in ecologies of ipd games. *Biosystems*, 37:81–97, 1996.

[16] R. Ornstein. *The Evolution of Consciousness.* Touchstone, 1991.

[17] M.C. Shea. Complexity and evolution: what everybody knows. *Biol. Phil.*, 6(3):303–324, 1991.

[18] M.D. Smucker, E.A. Stanley, and D. Ashlock. Analyzing social network structures in the iterated prisoner's dilemma with choice and refusal. Technical report cs-tr-94-1259, University of Wisonsin-Madison, Dept of Computer Science, 1994.

[19] E.A. Stanley, D. Ashlock D., and M.D. Smucker. Iterated prisoner's dilemma with choice and refusal of partners: Evolutionary results. In F. Moran, A. Moreno, J.J. Merelo, and P. Chacon, editors, *Advances in Artificial Life : Lecture Notes in Artificial Intelligence.* Springer-Verlag, 1995.

[20] M. Taylor. *Anarchy and Cooperation.* Wiley Press, 1976.

Stochastic simulation of ants that forage by expectation

C. Anderson, P. G. Blackwell & C. Cannings

School of Mathematics and Statistics
University of Sheffield, Sheffield, U.K.
e-mail: stp95ca@sheffield.ac.uk
Internet: http://www.shef.ac.uk/~ms/staff/blackwell/

Abstract

Stochastic simulation has been used to create an artificial colony of ants in order to study ant foraging strategies and the links between individual activity and the colony's self-organised behaviour. The ants, which forage by expectation, use a deterministic mathematical model developed by Ollason (1980, *Theor. Pop. Biol.* **18**: 44-56; 1987, *Theor. Pop. Biol.* **31**: 13-32). Results indicate that ants which have either too high an expectation of patch quality and reject good quality patches thus increasing their travel costs, and those who have too low an expectation and thus feed at poor quality patches, can be shown to be acting in a sub-optimal manner.

1 Introduction

Ants exhibit fascinating and complex social behaviour. They are able to co-operate and work together, and in essence act as if each were a 'super-organism' [11]. They forage for food individually and can only make locally based decisions yet are able to exploit even unpredictable environments efficiently and adapt as the environment changes. This is achieved through interaction between individuals by way of communication (direct and indirect) and between individuals and the environment through scramble or contest competition for food and other resources.

The emergence of patterns at the level of the society, resulting from interaction between the individuals and the environment within insect societies, is an example of self-organisation and emergent behaviour. Although the foraging rules of individuals may be simple, the emergent behaviour may exhibit very complex dynamics.

The great challenge in this area is to understand the relationship between the individual's activity and the emergent behaviour observed as one cannot be readily predicted from the other.

2 Ollason's learning model

2.1 Introduction

Ollason [16, 17] has published a deterministic mathematical model for hunting by expectation in which the behaviour converges to that predicted by the Marginal Value Theorem[1] [3]. However, it requires no omniscience, sampling or numerical analysis of multivariable functions. The only two requirements are that firstly the foragers remember and secondly that they stay feeding at a patch only as long as they are feeding faster than they remember doing. The model can determine not only how long to spend at a patch but whether to feed at a patch at all by checking a simple inequality.

The results of the model appear to conform fairly well with various empirical data (*e.g.* ducks [12], great tits [6]) and Ollason himself uses it to investigate ideal-free [9] behaviour of foraging *Formica aquilonia* ants [14].

However, as it stands the model predicts the behaviour of grazers, moving from one patch to another, without satiation or learning. *Formica* ants which are mostly honeydew feeders have a crop which they fill before returning to the nest and there is strong empirical evidence of learning and site-fidelity [5, 21]. This formed the motivation for the current work; to simulate a colony of ants feeding from a small number of constantly regenerating patches, using Ollason's model as the decision making process, and with various additions (see 2.3), such as giving the ants crops to make the simulation more realistic and to investigate the effects of these changes on the behaviour of the model.

2.2 The model

Ollason's model goes as follows: If $c_i(t)$ is the current size of patch i at time t with regeneration rate a_i being fed upon by randomly searching ants with individual

---

[1]Marginal Value Theorem: a predator in a patchy environment should leave the current patch when the marginal capture rate in the patch drops to the average capture rate for the habitat.

exploitation rates v_j totalling V_i then

$$\frac{dc_i(t)}{dt} = a_i - V_i c_i(t) \qquad (1)$$

which when solved gives

$$c_i(t) = \frac{a_i}{V_i}\left(1 - e^{-V_i t}\right) + c_i(0)e^{-V_i t} \qquad (2)$$

if there are foragers present and $c_i(0) + a_i t$ otherwise. Each ant has a memory with remembrance $m_j(t)$ (amount currently begin remembered - its expectation). Remembrance is being lost at a rate proportional to $m_j(t)$ determined by parameter K. If K is large the memory extends further into the past than with a smaller value of K. As the ant feeds, it remembers at its current feeding rate which exponentially decreases as food becomes scarcer. A hydraulic analogue of this is shown in Figure 1.

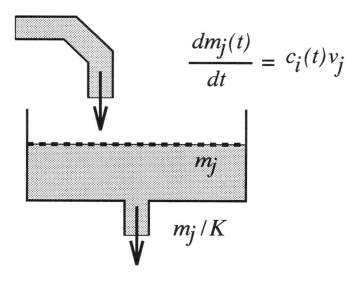

$$\frac{dm_j(t)}{dt} = c_i(t)v_j$$

$$m_j / K$$

Figure 1: hydraulic analogue of the model

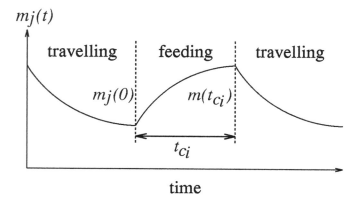

$$m_j(t)$$

travelling · feeding · travelling

$$m_j(0)$$ $$m(t_{c_i})$$

$$t_{c_i}$$

time

Figure 2: Diagrammatic profile of remembrance changes during feeding and travelling

The rate of change of remembrance is defined as

$$\frac{dm_j(t)}{dt} = c_i(t)v_j - \frac{m_j(t)}{K} \qquad (3)$$

where $c_i(t)v_j$ is the instantaneous rate of feeding.

Equations 2 and 3 are combined and solved to obtain remembrance $m_j(t)$ of ant j at time t given remembrance at time 0,

$$m_j(t)e^{\frac{t}{K}} = \frac{K a_i v_j}{V_i}\left(e^{\frac{t}{K}} - 1\right) + m_j(0) +$$
$$e^{t\left(\frac{1}{K} - V_i\right)}\frac{K v_j\left(c_i(t) - \frac{a_i}{V_i}\right)}{K V_i - 1} \qquad (4)$$

(This can be simplified if all n ants at a patch have the same exploitation rate as $V_i = \sum_{j=1}^{n} v_j = n v_j$)

An ant stays at the patch until $dm_j(t)/dt \leq 0$ (see Figure 2). This is given by

$$t_{c_i} = \frac{-K}{KV_i - 1}\ln\left\{\frac{\left(\frac{m_j(0)}{K} - \frac{v_j a_i}{V_i}\right)(KV_i - 1)}{KV_i\left(c_i(0)v_j - \frac{v_j a_i}{V_i}\right)} + \frac{1}{KV_i}\right\} \qquad (5)$$

The amount of food obtained by an individual with exploitation rate v_j in time t is

$$v_j\left\{\left(\frac{c_i(t)}{V_i} - \frac{a_i}{V_i^2}\right)\left(1 - e^{-V_i t}\right) + \frac{a_i t}{V_i}\right\} \qquad (6)$$

2.3 Additions to the model

Section 2.1 sets out the motivation for making additions to the model to make it more appropriate for simulating a colony of ants. This section goes into these additions in more detail.

1. Nest
   A nest was included in the simulation in contrast to Ollason's simulated colony of itinerant ants. As there must be some maximum distance to which ants from one colony will forage, due to the increased risks of predation, energetic considerations or interspecific/intercolony competition, a nest was simulated at the centre of a disc on which the patches were distributed (either randomly or equally spaced at a distance of half the radius from the nest). Trails exist between each nest-patch and patch-patch combination.

2. Crop
   Formica spp., amongst others, have a crop, part of the gut used to store liquid food such as honeydew during foraging which they fill (or partly fill) before returning to the nest. Consequently, the ants are

unable to feed continuously as in Ollason's model. Each ant was given a crop which they attempted to fill in a foraging trip before returning to the nest and emptying it into the 'social stomach' of the nest.

3. Returning to the nest

Each ant attempted to completely fill its crop before returning to the nest. However it was decided that there were certain situations in which it would be 'sensible' for the the ants to return to the nest without being fully replete.

The first is that if the patches are widely dispersed and an individual ant leaves a patch but has a nearly full crop (such as 95% full), it may not be sensible to travel to another patch, incurring energetic costs during travelling without the certainty of food upon arrival. In this situation an ant may return home. This is included in the simulation as a 'cropfill level' parameter.

Secondly, the ants are feeding from a small set of known patches (2 in this paper) rather than continuously along a trapline. Thus, if the regeneration rate of food in the environment is very low and the patches continually fall below an ant's expectations m_0, then it is futile to carry on travelling between the patches, rejecting the patches each time (and for real ants, incurring energetic costs). If they have rejected each of the patches during a foraging trip (and they only choose new patches to visit out of those they haven't rejected during the current foraging trip), then the ants return home, and spend some time in the nest before embarking on another foraging trip.

4. Initial remembrance

As foraging is much reduced during nightfall (e.g. [19]) and individuals may switch tasks in a real colony, it may be some time before an incoming forager starts out on its next trip. If their remembrance is continuously decreasing when not feeding then they will arrive at the first patch of their next trip with a low expectation. However, real ants must have some positive minimum expectation, at least sufficient to cover the energetic costs of their basal metabolic rate, searching and travelling. Therefore, in the simulations, each ant has an initial remembrance when arriving at the first patch of a foraging trip. As the nest↔patch travel times were constant this is equivalent to an (higher) initial remembrance when leaving the nest. Remembrance thus only declines during travelling between patches and not when travelling back to, or whilst in, the nest or travelling to the first patch.

5. Exponential time spent in nest

As the amount of time ants spend in the nest after a foraging trip is unlikely to be a constant due to task switching and natural variation and that the time

intervals between outgoing *F. rufa* foragers has been shown to form a Poisson stream (Table 1 of [13]), then the time spent in the nest for each simulated ant is from an exponential distribution with mean λ.

6. Biases

Formica spp. have been shown to exhibit site fidelity and to learn about their environment (e.g. [5, 15, 21]). As Ollason's model requires the foragers to have a memory, then it seems reasonable that they use this memory to remember which patch has been most productive for them in the past, i.e. learn about the environment, and to take this experience into account when deciding which patch to travel to.

Thus each ant has its own individual set of biases to each of the patches. For example in a two patch system if its biases are 75% to patch A and 25% to patch B then it is 3 times more likely to set out for patch A than patch B from the nest when starting a new foraging trip.

Initially, the ant's biases are a vector of normalised[2] reciprocal nest-patch distances. When an ant returns from a trip, it updates its biases based upon one of two criteria, either the amount of food it obtained at each patch during the last foraging trip or the amount of time spent at each patch. A normalised vector of the amount of food obtained, or time spent at, each patch is added to the current vector of biases for the patches and the resulting vector renormalised. Thus the ants exhibit learning and increase the likelihood of setting out to productive patches.

3 Simulation

A stochastic simulation program was written in 'C' based on a continuous time, event based, queueing paradigm. Although based on a deterministic mathematical model, stochasticity occurs in the probabilistic decisions of patch choice and the exponentially distributed times spent in the nest.

3.1 Parameterisation

Parameters were estimated for a single wood ant species *Formica rufa* L.. The majority of parameters were estimated or calculated using published data although some calculations do require some assumptions (indicated).

1. Colony size: based on data in [1, 2, 4, 13] colony (foraging population) size was set estimated as 100,000 and used for subsequent calculations. However, due to computational time constraints, a colony of only 100 ants was simulated with regeneration rate of

---

[2]normalised in the sense that the sum of the elements in the vector (which are always positive) is 1. The sum of all the elements is taken and each element in the vector divided by that sum.

patches suitably scaled (see 5. below). It is appreciated that such scaling down may possibly change the dynamics of the foraging behaviour. However, Gordon [10] found that in a similar species $F.\ polyctena$, which has similar sized colonies, that foragers tend to specialise on one of the foraging trunk trails and that experimentally depleted trails were not compensated for. Thus, local foraging populations may be smaller than the colony's total number of foragers. Also, at present there is no communication between the simulated ants, only learning, a blueprint which is characteristic of smaller colonies [1].

2. Trail length: 1000cm approximated from data in Skinner [19]

3. Running speed: 1cm/s from figure 6 of Holt [13]

4. Crop size : 6.27mg wet weight from Skinner [20]

5. Regeneration rate: from data in Skinner [20] calculations show a food influx of 98mg/s. Assuming this is for a population of 100,000 workers, require 98 x 100/100000 mg/s honeydew production for a colony of 100 foragers. With a 2 patch system we thus require 0.05 mg/patch/s.

6. Exploitation rate: there does not appear to be any published data for $Formica\ rufa$ but Dreisig (Table 2 of [7]) calculates an ingestion rate of 0.096 mg/min = 0.0016 mg/s for $F.\ pratensis$ and 0.02 mg/min = 0.0005 mg/s for $F.\ fusca$.
Thus the value used of 0.001 is at least likely to be within the right order of magnitude.

3.2 Standard parameter set

Table 1 was used as the 'standard' parameter set for the simulations. Simulations were run using this standard set with any changes indicated.

4 Results

4.1 Introduction

Simulations were run using the standard parameter set (see 3.2) with changes as indicated. Each point on the graphs (unless indicated otherwise) is the result of a single 10,000 iteration simulation.
Many of the y-axes are corrected for the total amount of time 'processed' during the 10,000 iteration simulation. The reason is that continuous time in the simulation is processed at different rates dependent upon the amount of intracolony-interference.
Optimality criteria for foraging strategies can be defined in a number of ways. For instance, optimality could be defined on the criterion of food influx, $i.e.$ maximising patch exploitation (proportion of available food taken)

Integers	
Number of iterations	10000
Output starting at iteration	4000
Output finishing at iteration	10000
Outputting every # iterations	1
Colony size, n	100
Number of patches	2

Reals	
Remembrance loss rate constant, K	256.0
Rate of leaving nest at start of simulation	0.32
Regeneration rate of patches, a_i	0.05
Distance of patches from nest	1000
Size of crop	6.27
Running speed	1.0
Exploitation rate, v_j	0.001
Initial remembrance, $m_j(0)$	100
Maximum feeding time per unit of food	Large
Acceptable cropfill level	95%
Mean time spent in nest, λ	100

Biases updated based upon food obtained
Patches regularly spaced

Table 1: The standard parameter set

and rate of which food items come into the nest. However, it could also be based upon the criterion of effort, the amount of time spent obtaining the food as each foraging trip is associated with an amount of time spent in the nest and so minimising trip length will maxmise the colony's proportion of time spent non-foraging. Both are considered in this paper.

4.2 Initial remembrance

Figures 3 and 4 show the effect of changing the initial remembrance for a range of regeneration rates.
When initial remembrances are low, the ants have low expectations when arriving at a patch and are likely to accept the patch irrespective of its quality. So, at low regeneration rates, ants with low initial remembrances (expectations) are spending a greater proportion of their time feeding. Ants with higher expectations however reject the poor patches and move on to other patches or return to the nest and spend a greater proportion of their time in the nest. However, when the influx of food to the nest is considered (Fig. 4) all are removing the food from the patches at the rate it is generated. Thus, those ants with low initial remembrances are acting in a suboptimal fashion based upon the criterion of effort.
At the other extreme, at high regeneration rates and when expectations are very high (500), an ant is likely to reject a patch even when the quality is good. It then travels to another patch during which its expectation decays exponentially and so it is then likely to accept the new patch. However due to the increased travel costs,

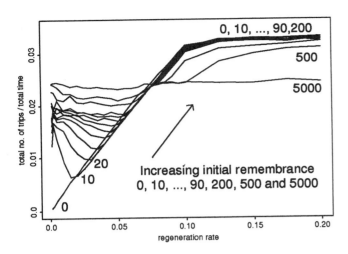

Figure 3: Mean number of trips for various initial re-membrances (0, 10, ..., 90, 200 and 500)

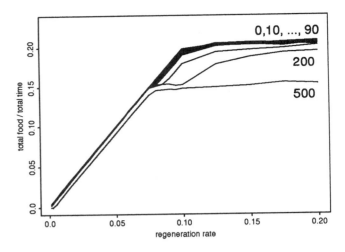

Figure 4: Food influx to nest for various initial remembrances (0, 10, ..., 90, 200 and 500)

these ants are unable to make as many trips as ants with lower expectations and from Fig. 4 can be shown to acting in a sub-optimal manner based on the criterion of food influx.

For this parameter set, there appears to be an optimal initial remembrance of approximately 90 where the ants are discerning enough at low regeneration rates to reject the patches yet at high regeneration rates do not waste time by rejecting good patches and extending their travelling times.

4.3 Remembrance loss rate constant, K

Figures 5, 6 and 7 show the effect of varying K, the remembrance loss rate constant parameter. It can be seen that having a small value of K, that is a short memory only considering events in the recent past is a disadvantage. It has the same effect as a high initial remembrance so the ants with small K reject patches and don't feed when it is worthwhile them doing so.

However, it can also be shown that very high values of K are disadvantageous. This is a consequence of Ollason's model. Ants leave the patch when $dm_j(t)/dt = c_i v_j - m_j(t)/K$ (eqn. 3) becomes negative. When K is large, this negative component is small and thus the ants stay longer at the patch. Figure 5 shows that there is an optimal range of K between 256 and 2048 *for a constant regenerating environment with this particular set of parameter settings* where the number of trips is maximised. This is optimal behaviour as each foraging trip is associated with an amount of time spent in the nest and so the ants are fully exploiting the environment (Fig. 4) but with the greatest proportion of their time spent non-foraging.

The relationships seen in Fig. 6 when the number of trips

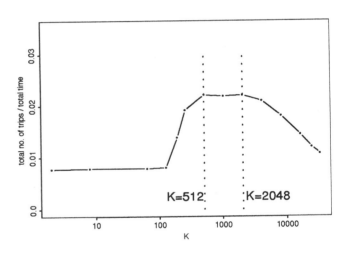

Figure 5: Number of trips against remembrance loss rate constant, K (log scale). Standard parameters with regeneration rate of 0.025

initially decreases and then increases with increasing regeneration rate, particularly at high values of K, is due to unimodality in the relationship between intra-colony interference and regeneration rate. As regeneration rate increases more ants decide to feed at the patches and the mean number feeding increases. However, as regeneration rate increases so does the ants's instantaneous rate of feeding and thus they spend a shorter time at the patch to obtain their food thus decreasing intra-colony interference. As regeneration rate approaches zero, the different curves will converge on a common point, equivalent to colony size / (travel time + mean time in nest). In this instance it is 100 / (3000/1 + 100) = 0.032.

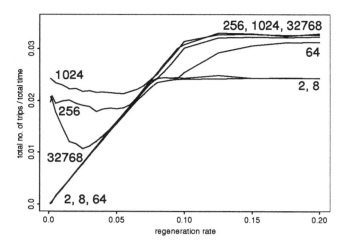

Figure 6: Number of trips for various values of remembrance loss rate constant, K, against regeneration rate

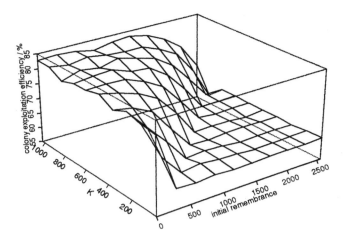

Figure 8: Colony's exploitation efficiency against various initial remembrance and K combinations. (Standard parameters with colony size of 40)

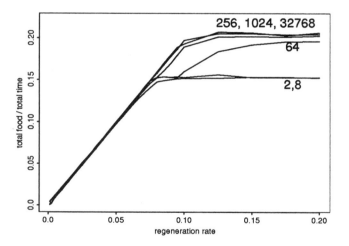

Figure 7: Food influx to nest for various values of remembrance loss rate constant, K, against regeneration rate

4.4 Relationship between initial remembrance and K

Figure 8 shows the effect on the colony's exploitation efficiency, that is food influx rate / total regeneration rate for various initial remembrance and K values.

It can clearly be seen that the surface plot can be divided into two sub-surfaces. The upper surface represents a set of parameter combinations in which the ants are working at their maximum capacity of about 83% efficiency for this reduced colony (to exaggerate the effect for purposes of illustration). The lower sub-surface represents ants with a lower overall efficiency with a high initial remembrance to memory loss ratio ($m_j(0) : K$) with a

clear linear relationship between the two along the transition line. The reason is that $dm_j(t)/dt$ is defined by $c_i(t)v_j - m_j(t)/K$ (eqn. 3) so high values of $m_j(t)/K$ through high $m_j(t)$ and/or low K make the ants more likely to reject the patches or feed for short periods.

As this is a two patch simulation, these ants are travelling from the nest to the first patch and either rejecting the patch because of their high initial remembrance or feeding for only a short time because of their short memories. They then travel to the other patch, their remembrance exponentially declining making them more likely to accept the second patch, feed for a short while or reject it and so on. The effect is that because they are too discriminating or feed for too short a time at each patch, they spend a greater proportion of their time travelling than the ants on the upper sub-surface.

4.5 Colony size

It is intuitively plausible that as the colony size increases, the overall efficiency of the colony (ability to fully exploit the environment) tends to 100%. However, it is interesting to question whether there an optimal number of foragers (or range) for each environment such that a larger colony is counter-productive as there is greater intra-colony interference at the patches and below which the environment may not be fully exploited? It can be seen from Figure 9 that this is indeed the case. As colony size increases, the exploitation efficiency increases roughly linearly until it reaches (and remains at) 100% at a colony of 70 ants and above. However, the percentage of successful trips[3] which remains at 100% up until a

---

[3] A successful trip is defined as one where an ant returns to the nest with some food in its crop.

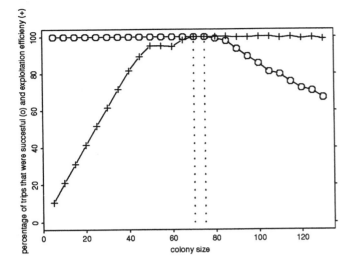

Figure 9: Colony's exploitation efficiency (+), *i.e.* proportion of available food taken by the colony and percentage of trips that were successful (o) against colony size.

colony size of 75 then shows a roughly linear decrease as intra-colony interference increases. Therefore, there is an optimal range of colony size for this parameter set of between 70 and 75 ants (the region between the two dotted lines) where the environment is fully exploited and thus the colony's success is maximised and where individual success is also maximised.

5 Discussion and further work

This paper shows some of the preliminary results of stochastic simulation program written to aid the study of self-organisation and emergent behaviour in foraging ants in an environment of constantly regenerating patches using Ollason's model [16, 17] for the foraging decisions made at the patches and with some ecologically reasonable additions.

Results from section 4.2 indicate that there are disadvantages to both high and low initial expectations but based upon different criteria. However due to the unique 'unselfishness' of social insect colonies, food influx is far more likely to be the optimising criterion than effort especially as foragers can be considered to be a disposable caste [18] and that there may be an excess of foragers waiting to be recruited [21].

Figure 9 shows an interesting relationship between individual and colony success with increasing colony size. It is unlikely that a colony will be able to measure overall colony success as they will not have perfect information about their environment. However it is more plausible that they could assess individual success and allocate foragers through recruitment in a self-organised manner until individual success is some figure less than 100%.

It would be expected that real colonies lie to the right of the optimal range to allow foragers to be recruited to new patches in a fluctuating environment.

Current work centres on the colony as a self-organising system using Ollason's model solely as a 'black-box' decision making process with the ants individually employing simple rules to modify their own behaviour. One such example is self-modification of the amount of time spent in the nest (*i.e.* non-foraging) after a foraging trip. Using only the individual's success and a very simple rule, a behaviour emerges at the level of the colony in which it is able to dynamically allocate near-optimal numbers of ants foraging at one time *and* respond to environmental fluctuations. Another example of the self-organising ability in this simulation setup is the ability of the ants to learn which are the most productive patches and develop site-fidelity (section 2.3). Work is in progress to study the development of site-fidelity in individuals and in the colony as a whole and to understand the underlying mechanisms at work as the environment changes and the ants respond to those changes.

With this simulation setup, there is huge scope for future work and the preliminary results have raised many interesting questions. Although constantly regenerating patches are realistic for certain types of food items, such as honeydew, wood ants also require protein and feed off small insects (including aphids). Their population dynamics are better described by logistic growth[4]. Thus it would be interesting to look at various patch types and combinations such as logistic, ephemeral and exhaustible. Also, most species of ants communicate in some form, either indirectly through olfaction of pheromone (hormone) trails or directly through physical contact. It would be easy to include pheromone trails and recruitment in the simulation program to complement other studies (*e.g.* [8, 23]) and would be very instructive for our understanding of ant foraging.

A Variables and constants used in the model

subscript i	number of patch
subscript j	number of ant
t	time
$c_i(t)$	size of patch i at time t
$m_j(t)$	remembrance of ant j at time t
t_{c_i}	time spent at patch i before leaving
v_j	exploitation rate of ant j
V_i	sum of exploitation rates of all ants at patch i
K	remembrance rate loss constant
a_i	regeneration rate of patch i

---

[4] $\frac{dN}{dt} = rN(1 - \frac{N}{\mathcal{K}})$ where N is population's size, $\mathcal{K}$ its carrying capacity, r the rate of population growth and t time

References

[1] Beckers, R., Goss, S., Deneubourg, J.L. & Pasteels, J.M.(1989) Colony size, communication and ant foraging strategy. *Psyche* **96**: 239-256.

[2] Brian, M.V. (1977) The Ants. The New Naturalist.

[3] Charnov, E.L. (1976) Optimal foraging, the Marginal Value Theorem. *Theoretical Population Biology* **9**: 129-136.

[4] Collingwood, C.A. (1979) The Formicidae (Hymenoptera) of Fennoscandinavia & Denmark. *Faune Entomologica Scandinavica.* Vol 8. Scandinavian Sciences Press.

[5] Cosens, D. & Toussaint, N. (1985) An experimental study of the foraging strategy of the wood ant *Formica aquilonia. Animal Behaviour* **33**: 541-552.

[6] Cowie, R.J. (1977) Optimal foraging in great tits *(Parus major). Nature* **268**: 137-139.

[7] Dreisig, H. (1988) Foraging rate of ants collecting honeydew or extrafloral nectar, and some possible constraints. *Ecological Entomology* **13**: 143-154.

[8] Fletcher, R.P., Cannings, C. & Blackwell, P.G. (1995) Modelling foraging behaviour of ant colonies. *Advances in Artificial Life: Third European Conference on Artificial Life, Granada, Spain, June 1995; Proceedings* edited by F. Morán, A. Moreno, J.J. Merelo, P.Chacón. Volume 929 of *Lecture Notes in Artificial Intelligence*, Springer Verlag.

[9] Fretwell, S.D. & Lucas, H.L. (1970) On territorial behaviour and other factors influencing habitat distribution in birds. I. Theoretical development. *Acta Biotheoretica* **19**: 16-36.

[10] Gordon, D.M., Rosengren, R. & Sundström, L. (1992) The allocation of foragers in red wood ants. *Ecological Entomology* **17**: 114-120

[11] Hölldobler, B. & Wilson, E.O. (1990) The Ants. Springer-Verlag, Berlin.

[12] Harper, D.G.C. (1962) Competitive foraging in mallards: Ideal free ducks. *Animal Behaviour* **30**: 575-584.

[13] Holt, S.J. (1955) On the foraging activity of the wood ant. *Animal Ecology* **24** (1): 1-33.

[14] Lamb, A.E. & Ollason, J.G. (1993) Foraging wood-ants *Formica aquilonia* Yarrow (Hymenoptera: Formicidae) tend to adopt the ideal free distribution. *Behavioural Processes* **28**: 189-198.

[15] Lamb, A.E. & Ollason, J.G. (1994) Site fidelity in foraging wood-ants *Formica aquilonia* Yarrow and its influence on the distribution of foragers in a regenerating environment. *Behavioural Processes* **31**: 309-322.

[16] Ollason, J.G. (1980) Learning to forage - optimally? *Theoretical Population Biology* **18**: 44-56.

[17] Ollason, J.G. (1987) Learning to forage in a regenerating patchy environment : can it fail to be optimal? *Theoretical Population Biology* **31**: 13-32.

[18] Porter, S.D. & Jorgenson, C.D. (1981) Foragers of the ant, *Pogonomyrmex owyheei*: a disposable caste? *Behavioural Ecology and Socoiobiology* **9** (4): 247-256.

[19] Skinner, G.J. (1980) Territory, trail structure and activity patterns in the wood-ant, *Formica rufa* (Hymenoptera : Formicidae) in limestone woodland in North-West England. *Journal of Animal Ecology* **49**: 381-394.

[20] Skinner, G.J. (1980) The feeding habits of the wood-ant, *Formica rufa* (Hymenoptera: Formicidae), in limestone woodland in North-West England. *Journal of Animal Ecology* **49**: 417-433.

[21] Sundström, L. (1993) Foraging responses of *Formica truncorum* (Hymenoptera; Formicidae); exploiting stable vs spatially and temporally variable resources. *Insectes Sociaux* **40**: 147-161.

[22] Veena, T. & Ganeshaiah, K.N. (1991) Non-random search pattern of ants foraging on honeydew of aphids on cashew inflorescences. *Animal Behaviour* **41**: 7-15.

[23] Watmough. J. & Edelstein-Keshet, L. (1995) Modelling the formation of trail networks by foraging ants. *Journal of Theoretical Biology* **176**: 357-371.

CHORUSING AND CONTROLLED CLUSTERING FOR MINIMAL MOBILE AGENTS

Owen Holland, Chris Melhuish, and Steve Hoddell
Intelligent Autonomous Systems Engineering Laboratory, Faculty of Engineering,
University of the West of England, Coldharbour Lane, Bristol BS16 1QY, UK
email: o-hollan/cr-melhu@uwe.ac.uk

ABSTRACT

This paper examines some strategies for controlling the sizes of clusters of simple mobile agents. The basic method is loosely modelled on the signalling behaviour of species such as crickets, frogs, and fireflies, where males attract females by making periodic calls or light flashes. A characteristic of such behaviour is that groups of animals broadcast their signals in synchrony, forming a chorus. In this paper, synchrony is used in conjunction with random deviations from synchrony in order to enable each individual to estimate the size of the group over a period of time. By arranging for an individual to approach a group which is below some required size, and leave a group which is above that size, cluster size can be controlled. Two types of controlled clustering are examined: seeded clustering, where a group is required to form at a particular spot, and unseeded clustering, where there is no preferred site. Results from simulations are presented. For seeded clustering, they show reasonable performance for low levels of noise, breaking down as noise levels are increased; for unseeded clustering, effective control is only achieved with almost no noise, and with a heavily modified algorithm.

1 Introduction

Multi-agent and multi-robot systems can often be divided into two broad categories: those using symbolic representations and explicit communication; and those using behaviour based techniques and implicit communication 'through the world'. For those developing the second type of system, there is usually some attraction towards minimalism, and a tendency to explore the use of behavioural strategies known to be used by biological systems such as social insects. The system described in this paper is both minimalist, and inspired by the collective behaviour of biological systems. A discussion of the relationships between minimalism, biological inspiration, collective behaviour, and the construction and application of multi-robot systems may be found in (Holland & Melhuish [1997].

1.2 Aggregation and the control of group size

Aggregation was identified early on as one of the primitives of swarm systems and collective behaviour (Mataric [1992]). We distinguish two extreme forms: pseudoswarming, in which each individual moves towards a given point using information which is independent of the locations of other agents; and true swarming, in which an individual's movements are wholly determined by the locations of other agents. (Holland & Melhuish [1996b]). Combinations of these types are frequent: leaf cutter ants are at first attracted by the vibrations made by an ant which has found a suitable leaf, but once close enough to detect the leaf are attracted by the leaf itself; robots attracted to an infra-red source can change course to avoid one another.

The control of group size has received little attention. It may be required for a number of reasons. For example, if a localised resource is sufficient for only a limited number of agents, there is little point in attracting extra agents to the resource. Again, it has been established by at least two sets of robot experiments (Beckers et al [1994]; Fontan & Mataric [1996]) that there may be an optimum number of robots for carrying out a given task under given circumstances; in such cases, the control of the size of the group undertaking the task may be critical to achieving the task quickly or efficiently.

The aim of this work is to find a suitable method for regulating the size of a group of agents. The basic idea is that each agent should individually derive an estimate for the size of any group of which it is effectively a member, and should then either approach the centre or focus of the group if the estimated group size is less than or equal to some internal parameter expressing the 'desired' group size, or should move away from the centre or focus if the estimated group size is too large. If the group is required to form at a particular point, then we assume that at that point sits a beacon which emits some omnidirectional field with a strength which reduces with distance from the beacon. Motion away from the group can therefore be arranged by moving away from the beacon. We call this seeded clustering. (The agents do not need to be able to sense the orientation of the beacon directly; the method of klinokinesis can be used - see Holland & Melhuish [1996a]).Where there is no requirement to cluster in a particular location, no beacon is available as a guide for movement, and so some signal must be derived from sensing or picking up signals from the other agents in the cluster. We call this unseeded clustering, and it is a much more difficult and complex problem.

A very simple method of achieving seeded clustering is to arrange for the agents to reduce the intensity of the attractive signal by the merely passive fact of their presence. This was used by Kube and Zhang [1992] in an early study of aggregation; robots were attracted to a lighted box in an arena, but robots reaching the box blocked the light from the view of the other robots, resulting in no more robots being attracted to the box once there were enough there to completely block the light. This use of passive properties is an attractive and neat solution, but works only when the number of agents required just happens to be the number obtained; it is difficult to tune, and is a rather precise function of the nature of the environment, task, and agents, so it cannot be extended to serve as a general method. Active properties offer more potential generality, and we have adopted the following set of constraints: the agents will be able to transmit and receive some actively broadcast signal, omnidirectionally transmitted and detected, and decreasing in intensity with some function of distance; and each agent will be assumed to contain some internal parameter which indicates the size of group required.

Some strategies satisfying this restriction can be ruled out after some quite general considerations. One factor of interest is the power of the signal. (For an insightful study of many aspects of signalling in animals, including power, see Endler [1993]). Since the method of regulation is constrained to be active, each broadcast by a agent will use power, so in the interests of economy some means of reducing the power would be useful. Further, the range will be a function of the broadcast power; a long range would require a high power handling capacity, which is likely to use more structural resources than a lower power arrangement. An intermittent broadcast at high power will achieve range, at the cost of losing temporal granularity; this intermittent high power need not require the capacity for high power generation, as some accumulator mechanism can be used to store energy which is suddenly released to give a high instantaneous power, just as the flea winds its legs up over a period of time and releases them to make a leap. We therefore decided to explore the use of an intermittent signal, and ruled out looking at the summation of constantly transmitted signals, for example from agents within a certain distance of the source.

The simplest intermittent signal is the equivalent of a click. It is characteristic of a click that two clicks will never overlap. If we assume that the intensity of a click must exceed some threshold in order to be registered by an agent, this means that the range over which a click can be detected will be fixed at some maximum. In contrast, a longer signal which overlaps other such signals can be expected to summate, and so will typically be detectable at a greater distance than a single signal, other things being equal. Although it would have been quite simple to devise a clicking mechanism - for example, clicking when close to the source, leakily integrating the time series of clicks, and

moving away from the source if the integrated quantity was higher than the group size threshold - this would have a fixed maximum range of action from the source. It is desirable that the message that the group is already large enough (or too large) should be detectable at the largest possible range, and so it was decided to investigate signals which were brief (saving power) but which could gain in range by being superimposed. This train of thought led us to study reports of natural systems which used such brief repeated signals. There are many such systems in nature; the best known are probably the sound choruses of crickets and frogs, and the light flashes of fireflies.

1.3 Chorusing in crickets, fireflies, and frogs

There is a large and fascinating literature on chorusing in crickets, fireflies, and frogs; particularly useful and accessible texts are: Greenfield [1994]; Sebeok [1977]; Ryan et al [1981]; Ewing [1989]; and Alexander [1975]. The outstanding characteristic for us was that most of the creatures which chorus, or broadcast intermittent signals in synchrony, appear to use a similar mechanism for synchronisation. Greenfield calls this mechanism 'the basic phase delay interactive algorithm'; essentially, a sawtooth pacemaker which produces a chirp when it rises to its maximum level is reset to the basal level by the perception of a chirp from another animal. If both animals have the same pacemaker period, they will be in synchrony on the subsequent chirp of the interrupting animal. There are of course many variations on this theme, including alternating rather than synchronous chirping, but most chorusing appears to follow this rule. The function of chorusing can be very varied, and is not always clear. One clear function is that of increasing the range of a group signal while retaining the temporal features which enable it to be identified and discriminated from other signals using the same modality. The role of the signal itself may be to attract females for mating, or to confuse predators by making signal localisation difficult. However, we have found no mention of chorusing being used to regulate group size.

2 Methods for estimating the size of an agent cluster

Our first idea for estimating group size was to take the local summed intensity of calls as the representation of group size. Unfortunately, assuming an inverse square law for the fall off of intensity with distance, this varied too strongly with distance to be useful. The second idea was slightly more contrived, but seemed to take advantage of the intermittent structure of the calls. We reasoned that, if all the members of a group were in perfect synchrony at the onset of one chirp, then in any real system there might be some stochastic variation in the subsequent individual start times for the next chirp. If this were 'corrected' by the basic phase delay interactive algorithm, then the next chirp would again be subject to some variation in individual start times, and so on. If all individuals had the same distribution of chirp periodicity (modelled by a fixed refractory period plus a random interval) then each individual in a group of n could be expected to be the first to chirp on a proportion $(1/n)$ of occasions. If a group size of p was required, it would only be necessary for each agent to have an internal representation of $(1/p)$; if it detected that it was the first to chirp on a proportion of occasions less than $(1/p)$, the group must have more than p members, and so the agent should select the behaviour of heading away from the group. Of course, the resolution required to control large group sizes would probably be prohibitive, but this looked a promising enough mechanism for controlling small groups.

The proposed mechanism depends on bringing neighbouring agents into synchrony. Since our system required agents to make correct decisions rapidly, it was not thought appropriate to use the basic phase delay interactive algorithm, because this never allows a chirp to be brought forward, but instead works by delaying chirps. Instead, we proposed that an agent able to chirp (i.e. not in a refractory state) would always be induced to chirp immediately it detected another agent's chirp. If one of a group of agents were to chirp, then all other agents not in refractory states would chirp at the next instant; this would provide the fastest possible synchronisation.

3 The λ mechanism: simulation details

The simulations use a circular arena 1200 units in diameter, with a source of attraction at the centre. Each agent has two directionally sensitive 'eyes', one on each side of, and at 60° to, the agent's longitudinal axis; the eyes each have a 120° field of view, and the intensity of the source of attraction detected by each eye falls off as the inverse square of the distance from the source to the eye. The environment and the eyes themselves also contribute Gaussian noise to the eyes' readings. Each agent also has a chirp transmitter and receiver; both are omnidirectional, and the detected intensity of a chirp declines with the inverse square of distance. There is a fixed threshold for the detection of any chirp energy.

In the first simulations, it became clear that the algorithm worked to some extent, but that certain modifications would be beneficial. The first change was to limit the chirping to agents within a certain distance of the source; agents outside that distance would synchronise their internal timers to received chirps, but would not themselves emit chirps. We called this mode of operation 'silent mode'. If this was not done, then randomly formed groups of agents at a distance from the source appeared to be able to disrupt the behaviour of the group close to the source.

Another factor noticed in early simulations was the effect of adding some background noise to the reception of chirps.

It can act in two ways: it can produce what has become known as stochastic resonance, occasionally enhancing subthreshold chirp signals so that they are registered, and so adding information to behaviour; on the other hand, large amounts of noise can reach the threshold, introducing spurious chirps and so adding noise to behaviour. Any systematic study should therefore include such noise to allow these factors to operate.

The agent can exhibit two related types of movement in relation to the source, each expressed in simple rules. In both, the first step is to compare the sensed source intensities in the left (L) and right (R) eyes. In the first, the attractive behaviour, the rule is:

If L > R rotate left 60° and move 4 units
else   **rotate right 60° and move 4 units**

This deliberately crude and noisy taxis rapidly brings an agent close to the source and keeps it there. In the second, repulsive behaviour, the rule is:

If L > R rotate right 60° and move 4 units
else   **rotate left 60° and move 4 units**

This will rapidly move an agent away from the source towards the periphery.

At any time, the rule to use is determined by the group size estimator, or λ mechanism. λ is the estimate of the reciprocal of the group size ($1/n$ for a group size n). It is compared with $\tau(\lambda)$, the reciprocal of the target group size. If $\lambda < \tau(\lambda)$, the repulsive rule is used; otherwise, the attractive rule is used.

The parameters of the chirping cycle and λ mechanism are as follows. Each agent has a refractory period (R) of 20 time ticks, during which it cannot chirp. It then passes into the latent period (L). L lasts a maximum of 20 time ticks, and, if no chirp is previously detected from another agent, the agent will start to chirp on one of these time ticks preselected randomly with equal probability. If a chirp from another agent is detected before the time for the spontaneous chirp, the agent will chirp on the next time tick. The chirp period (C) lasts for 6 time ticks. A chirp is transmitted only when the agent is within a radius of 50 units of the source. λ is estimated as the ratio of the number of unstimulated chirps produced to the total number of chirps produced in the previous 500 time ticks.

The simulations presented here examine the performance of the algorithm in an environment containing 15 agents which are initially distributed randomly throughout the arena. Five target group sizes are used (2, 4, 6, 8, and 10) and two conditions of background noise for the chirp mechanism (0% and 3% of maximum intensity). Ten trials were run under each condition. A trial is scored by noting the number of agents within 50 units of the source after 80,000 time ticks. The results are shown in Figure 1.

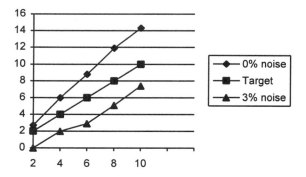

Figure 1: mean terminal group size

Qualitative observations of the agents under all conditions were unsurprising. On start up, those agents closest to the source reach it first, form the target group size, and then form a group larger than the target. The group expands a little until some agents are lost, and then a state of flux ensues, with agents being exchanged between the group close to the source, and a highly mobile cloud of agents slightly further away. While sometimes a definite annulus of agents can be seen surrounding the central group, it is not generally visible.

One clear problem is that the agents far away from the source are moving almost randomly, because the low intensity of the source at that distance is swamped by the Gaussian noise in the environment and in the eyes, and so the agents cannot move reliably either towards or away from the source, regardless of the rule they are supposed to be obeying..

As can be seen from Figure 1, the 0% noise condition produces groups rather larger than the target, and the 3% noise produces groups rather smaller than the target. Two conclusions can be drawn from this: setting $\tau(\lambda) = (1/n)$ does not produce accurate group sizes even with no noise, and so $\tau(\lambda)$ should be determined empirically, unless a better mathematical model is formulated; and $\tau(\lambda)$ must be adjusted to take account of any background noise which might affect chirp reception. Nevertheless, the mechanism has been shown to be capable of regulating group size in a systematic way, and so is probably worth investigating further.

These early indications of promise led to an examination of ways in which the performance could be improved while remaining within the limits imposed by the philosophy of minimalism. The first change was to replace the unweighted

moving-average computation of $\tau(\lambda)$ with a time-weighted average, which would allow more recent data to be weighted more heavily. For convenience, we changed the factor of interest to the count of the number of first chirps by other agents heard between successive first chirps of the agent in question. On average, the count will be one less than the number of agents in the group, and so a suitable estimate of group size (γ) is (chirp count + 1). In order to produce a time weighted average, the new estimate of this statistic, γ_t, is formed from the previous estimate γ_{t-1} by setting $\gamma_t = a\gamma + (1-a) \gamma_{t-1}$. (For $a=1$, this of course reduces to using the estimate γ, which is actually a simplification when compared to the λ mechanism.)

The logic of using a chorusing strategy had been rooted in the effects of summation in extending the distance at which a (combined) signal could be sensed and distinguished from noise. To check that this actually delivered some benefit, we also modified the λ mechanism so that summation did not increase range - that each agent transmitted the analogue of a click over a fixed range. We called this the κ mechanism.

4 Seeded clustering - comparing λ, κ, and γ

In early trials with both the λ and the γ mechanisms, we noticed that 'full' clusters which appeared stable could be completely destabilised by the approach of a single extra agent. Close examination revealed that this was due to the fact that the arrival of such an agent would cause most or all of the agents in the cluster to begin moving away from the beacon, because they had registered that the cluster was too large. This widening of the cluster would continue until one or more agents (usually several) had moved out of range of the others; the cluster would then begin to collapse again, possibly still including the intruder, and the process of expansion and contraction might continue for several cycles. It would obviously be desirable to make it possible for the intruder or intruders to be repelled or expelled, in preference to individuals already in the cluster.

Two methods were tried. The first was derived from the well-known strategy of orthokinesis, used by many single celled organisms to preferentially exploit regions of higher food concentration. If the speed of movement of an organism moving at random is a decreasing function of food concentration, then the time the organism will spend in a given region will increase with the region's food concentration. In our version, the agent step length was made a function of the sensed beacon strength (which decreases with distance); this means that agents on the outer edges of a cluster are much more volatile than those close to the centre. It also produces much more tightly grouped clusters, which in turn increases the distance between an intruder and the cluster at the time when the intruder's effects are felt. The second method was a silent mode: any agent within a radius of 25 units of the beacon was silent if at the previous step it had calculated that it was in a cluster which was too large. Such an agent should be leaving the cluster, and, by not chirping, it should prevent other cluster members from also deciding that they should leave the cluster.

5 Results for seeded clustering using λ, κ, and γ

The first set of experiments was designed to compare the basic λ, γ, and κ mechanisms, for a range of cluster demand sizes, and in both noise-free and noisy environments. Silent modes and orthokinesis were used. The variation in step length for orthokinesis was calculated as follows:

$$\text{step length } \sigma = \max\sigma\left\{1-\left(\frac{\max[LorR]}{\max input}\right)\right\}$$

where L, R are the inputs to the left and right sensors, and maxinput is the maximum possible input to either sensor (the input at the beacon site).

The factors of interest were the number of agents clustered around the beacon, and the mean distance from the beacon of those agents outside the cluster. Since stable clusters, when formed, would always fit within a circle of radius 25 units around the beacon, the cluster size was defined as the number within that radius, and any agents outside that radius were defined as being outside the cluster. (In the simulations described in section 3, the cluster radius was taken as 50 units; the reduction to 25 improves spatial resolution, and makes it less likely that an agent leaving the cluster is accidentally counted as a cluster member.) This simplified what might otherwise have been a formidable task of analysis. The (Gaussian) noise levels at the agents' beacon sensors were given mean levels of 0%, 3%, and 6% of the maximum beacon strength. Ten trials were made for each combination of noise level, mechanism type, and cluster demand size. The results are shown in Figs 2 - 4.

One possible problem with using the same fixed population size throughout is that we cannot be sure we are studying the effects of (target) cluster sizes, because the (target) number of non-cluster agents also varies systematically. However, since we are using silent modes, it is generally true that non-cluster agents do not affect cluster agents, and so we would not expect the number of non-cluster agents to affect our recorded outcomes to any degree. Additional simulations have confirmed this.

Figure 2a shows that, for no noise, all three mechanisms are able to control cluster size effectively, with the κ mechanism coming closest to the nominal cluster size. However, Figure 2b reveals the advantage of using the chorusing mechanism, as both the λ and γ mechanisms are

able to separate the non-cluster agents from the cluster by up to 168 units, whereas the κ mechanism achieves only around 40 units.

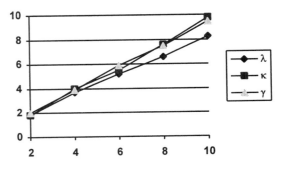

Fig 2a: Mean cluster size - 0% noise

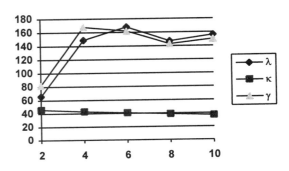

Fig 2b: Mean distance of non-cluster agents - 0% noise

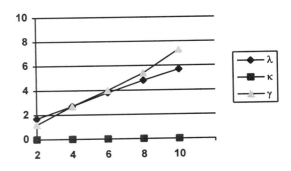

Fig 3a: Mean cluster size - 3% noise

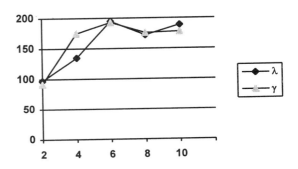

Fig 3b: Mean distance of non-cluster agents - 3% noise

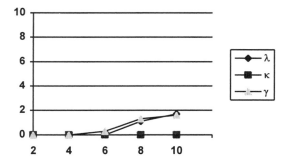

Fig 4a: Mean cluster size - 6% noise

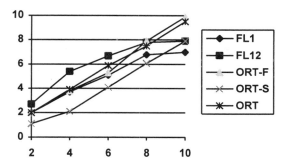

Fig 5: Mean cluster size - 0% noise

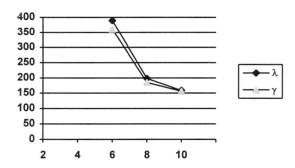

Fig 4b: Mean distance of non-cluster agents - 6% noise

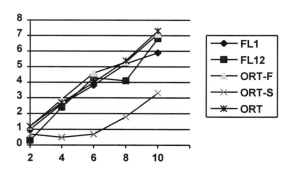

Fig 6: Mean cluster size - 3% noise

Figure 3a shows that even 3% of noise causes the κ mechanism to fail completely. The λ and γ mechanisms are still able to produce cluster sizes which, although lower than the nominal demand size, are still well differentiated from the higher and lower cluster sizes. Figure 3b shows that both mechanisms achieve large and similar separations between non-cluster and cluster agents - up to 195 units. Figure 4a shows the effective breakdown of all mechanisms, with both the λ and γ mechanisms producing clusters well below the demand size, with the non-cluster agents separated from the cluster agents by very large distances. On the basis of these results, we decided that further development would be confined to the γ mechanism alone.

6 Effects of orthokinesis, silent modes, and time-weighted filters on γ mechanism

A further set of experiments examined the effects of orthokinesis, silent modes, and time-weighted filters on the γ mechanism. All parameters were as for the previous set of experiments. The variations studied were: no orthokinesis, with two fixed step sizes of 1 unit (FL1) and 12 units (FL12); orthokinesis with no time-weighted filter, or $a=0$ (ORT-F); and orthokinesis with no silent mode (ORT-S). Results for these are shown in Figs 5 - 7 along with results for orthokinesis with filter and silent mode (ORT).

From Fig 5, it appears that the strategies which do not use orthokinesis (FL1 and FL12) may run out of resolution for the higher demand cluster sizes. All of the orthokinesis strategies perform adequately, with ORT and ORT-F producing cluster sizes closest to the nominal size.

Fig 6 shows the effects of 3% noise on performance. ORT-S is badly affected; ORT and ORT-F are somewhat degraded, but still have plenty of resolution. This confirmed that the silent mode is important for coping with noise, and that the time weighting introduced by filtering is of little or no consequence. FL1 and FL12 are still reasonable performers.

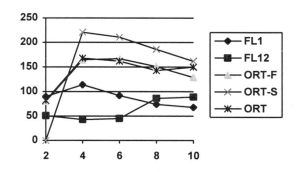

Fig 7: Mean distance of non-cluster agents - 0% noise

Figure 7 shows the increased separation obtained by using the ORT strategy with a silent mode when compared with fixed step length strategies. Although the separation achieved by ORT-S appears high, it predominantly reflects a failure to attract additional agents into the beacon area in the first place, and is a poor overall choice.

Figure 10 (at end of paper) shows some representative screen shots of the evolution of a seeded clustering sequence.

7 Unseeded controlled clustering

In the case of unseeded clustering, there is no beacon to use as a reference for direction of movement. The agents can therefore be simplified, because they do not require any beacon sensors. However, this means that the only source of information is the sensing of the chorusing inputs, and this might be thought to present a severe problem because the signal itself is intermittent, and the chorusing input sensor is omnidirectional. The solution to this problem is simply to use a two step klinokinesis mechanism as described in (Holland & Melhuish [1996]}.

Klinokinesis is the name given to various methods of achieving movement up or down a spatial gradient of stimulation by altering the rate and/or direction of turning as a function of the size and/or sign of some input which does not itself carry any directional information. Schöne [1980] describes an inverse klinokinesis (gradient ascent) in several types of bacteria: "Randomly distributed turnings, or jerks, interrupt the straight or slightly curved pathway of the bacterium so that it tumbles back and forth. When the bacterium enters a higher concentration of stimulant, the frequency of jerks decreases. As a consequence, the animal swims longer stretches in this direction. The sum of all the inter-jerk stretches results in a translocation up the gradient".

This technique of klinokinesis allows an agent to move up or down a gradient without being able to sense the gradient direction. The instantaneous strength of the chorusing field is all that is required, and this is already present in the agent. If the agents are in a localised cluster, then there will be a gradient of chorus signal strength which decreases with distance from the cluster; an agent which is some way from the cluster will therefore be able to move towards or away from the cluster by using klinokinesis in this field.

Early trials of unseeded clustering using the γ mechanism and klinokinesis were only intermittently successful. Even when all agents were started at the same location, the clusters which formed were not stable even over relatively short time periods. We reasoned that analogues of the additional techniques used in seeded clustering might help;

however, devising suitable implementations was not straightforward. To implement a silent mode, a measure of distance from the focus of a cluster is required, but none was directly available. In theory, it would have been possible to combine the estimate of cluster size with the sensed intensity of the chorusing signal to derive a function giving distance from the cluster, but this smacked of computational complexity and was not investigated. A simple, though partial, method is to arrange for agents to be silent when carrying out the 'moving away' behaviour; when they reach a point where they are sufficiently far from any complete cluster to stop moving away from any such cluster, they will start to chirp again. This also satisfies the requirement that agents far from the centre of any cluster should chirp, because if they do not, there can be no process of aggregation from an initially low density distribution.

The addition of a silent mode improved matters, but performance could still be very poor. A possible source was the reduced reliability of the cluster size detection mechanism in the unseeded clustering situation. Because the agents themselves are asynchronous and have stochastic elements, each agent makes frequent errors in estimating group size. An agent on its way out of a cluster could suddenly register a cluster size well below the target size, and would immediately head for the centre again, chirping and disrupting the cluster. This could be countered to some extent by tuning the filter parameter *a*, but proved a persistent source of disturbance. An additional, but inelegant and theoretically unjustifiable 'hack' was to give each agent a type of momentum, which ensured that an agent estimating a cluster size greater than the target size would head away from the cluster for a minimum of eight steps - 4,000 time steps - before being able to change course. This was usually sufficient to remove it far enough from the cluster to avoid disrupting the cluster. However, the ultimate aim is to tune the basic mechanism and parameters so that adequate performance is achieved without this supplementary method.

Observation of the time course of unseeded clustering revealed a problem very similar to that noted by (Holland & Melhuish [1996b]) in their study of uncontrolled aggregation in these swarms of simple agents. If an initial population is dispersed over the arena, a number of small groups will form quite quickly, and each will typically be much smaller than the target size if the target size is moderately large - six or more. For a group to increase its membership, it must come within range of another group. However, since there is no factor present which will drive separate clusters together until they are within some critical distance, the only mobility process operating is a kind of stochastic drift. The larger the cluster, the smaller the rate of drift. This can result in many millions of time steps being

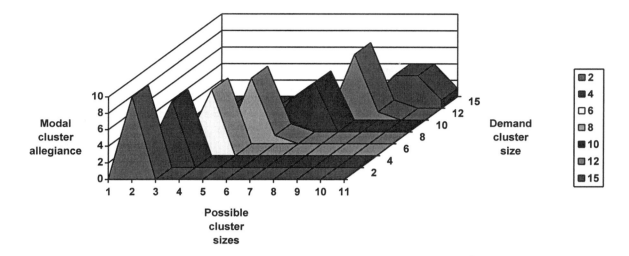

Figure 8   **Unseeded clustering: distribution of modal cluster allegiances**

required for a cluster of the target size to be formed by the collision of smaller clusters.

A possible amelioration of this affect can be achieved by using an adaptation of the variable step length technique which is used for orthokinesis. Each agent possesses an estimate of the size of any cluster of which it is part, and a parameter which corresponds to the target cluster size. By making step length increase with increasing difference between these two factors, agents in smaller clusters become relatively more mobile than larger but still 'incomplete' clusters. This has two beneficial effects: the agents in smaller clusters become more dispersed than those in larger clusters, and they also move faster as a group than larger clusters. Two initially widely separated complete clusters are therefore far less likely to collide than two widely separated and very incomplete clusters; and because of the greater spatial separation of the agents in smaller incomplete clusters, large incomplete clusters will be able to attract only the nearest agent(s) of passing or approaching small clusters, enabling them to become complete and repel the remaining agents while they are still at a distance. This mechanism is called 'error driven step variation'.

Possibly the most disappointing aspect of the performance of these unseeded clustering algorithms is their susceptibility to noise. We have not yet determined the cause of this, but we suspect that it may be due to the combination of the intermittency of the chorused signal, which is the only source of directional information for the agents, and the two-step gradient ascent algorithm which depends on the sign of the difference between two successive samples taken at discrete times. It may be possible to isolate the reason for the problem by providing the agents with better information for gradient ascent, possibly using some auxiliary data source giving an accurate and continuous gradient, and seeing if this improves noise tolerance to the levels of the seeded clustering algorithms. Fig 8 shows the effectiveness of the seedless clustering algorithm in its present state of development, using the silent mode, momentum, and error driven step variation. The noise level was set very close to zero (0.01%); the small amount of noise is technically useful for ensuring that no two sensor readings are ever equal. Agents were started at the centre of the arena; this is preferred to starting them at random positions because it reduces the early losses of agents at the absorbing boundaries, and shortens the time required for each run. When started in this way, all agents are in a single cluster which is much larger than the demand cluster size, and so they all move away from the centre in a sort of 'big bang'; once they are sufficiently dispersed, this general movement ceases and local interactions take over. This technique ensures that a number of small groups of various sizes are formed at a reasonable distance from one anther and from the periphery. From random starting positions, it can take a great deal of computational time to form reasonably large clusters; this method results in significant time savings. Ten trials were run for each demand cluster size, and measurements of agent positions were taken after one million time steps. The agents were grouped into clusters by the simple procedure of declaring any agents within a certain minimum distance of one another to be in the same cluster.

Analysing and displaying the results presents some problems. The mean cluster size is no longer a good measure, because in a situation where the demand size is 12, a perfect outcome might be a cluster of 12 and a cluster of 3, giving a mean size of 7.5 for a perfect result. Taking the largest cluster size is also unsatisfactory; for example, with a target size of 3, a distribution of 4, 3, 3, 3, 1, 1, would be inadequately described by 4. We therefore decided to use the cluster size in which agents were most frequently found, which we called the modal cluster allegiance. The graph of Figure 8 shows the distribution of modal cluster allegiances across the ten trials for each demand cluster size, and reveals the performance of the algorithm to be reasonably successful.

Figure 11 (at end of paper) shows some representative screen shots of the evolution of an unseeded clustering sequence.

8 Transferring the mechanism to a multirobot system

One axiom of behaviour based robotics has not changed in the last twelve years: simulation is never adequate, and ideas should be tested on a real robot system at the first opportunity. One of the research platforms at the IAS Lab is the Ubot, a 10-inch diameter autonomous mobile robot with differential drive, closed loop motor control, and a Motorola 68332 processor. Fifteen of these are under construction; they will be used in a variety of collective robot projects.

A chirping mechanism has been developed, and is shown in Figure 9 mounted on a Ubot. It consists of a Polaroid ultrasonic transducer mounted horizontally, facing down onto a shaped diffuser. When the transducer transmits, the diffuser reflects the highly directional pulse through a right angle to form an omnidirectional pulse parallel to the floor; when it receives, it gathers pulses from other robots and guides them to the transducer for reception. This arrangement works satisfactorily on the bench. Infra-red

transmitters and receivers with an effective range of 4m have also been developed; these will be used as beacons and beacon sensors in seeded clustering experiments. These technologies, and the seeded and unseeded clustering algorithms described in this paper, will shortly be evaluated on a group of Ubots. We are not expecting immediate success even with the seeded algorithms, because the noise levels of all signals will almost certainly be at least as high (3% to 6%) as the levels leading to failure in simulation.

6 Conclusions

We have shown in simulation that it is possible to use the biologically inspired principle of synchronous chorusing for the control of group size in very simple multiple mobile agent systems. Several related algorithms give reasonable

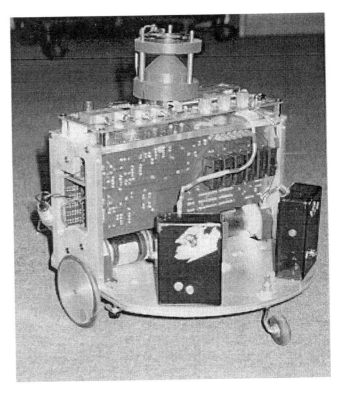

Figure 9: a Ubot with the prototype chirp mechanism

performance when the group is required to form at a particular point which is the source of a signal attenuating with distance (seeded clustering); performance is disrupted by noise levels of 6%. When there is no focal point (unseeded clustering) the algorithms require significant and perhaps unjustifiable modification before any useful degree of control is obtained; performance is disrupted by even small amounts of noise.

Acknowledgment

This work was partially funded by Royal Mail Strategic Headquarters.

References

Alexander R.D. [1975] Natural selection and specialised chorusing behaviour in acoustical insects. *Insects, Science, and Society*, ed. D. Pimentel, Academic Press

Beckers R., Holland O.E., and Deneubourg J-L. [1994], From local actions to global tasks: stigmergy and collective robotics, in R. Brooks and P. Maes, eds, Artificial Life IV, Proceedings of the Fourth International Workshop on the synthesis and simulation of living systems, MIT Press

Endler J.A. [1993] Some general comments on the evolution and design of animal communication systems. *Phil. Trans. Roy. Soc. London B* 340, 215-225

Ewing A.W. [1989] *Arthropod Bioacoustics: Neurobiology and Behaviour*. Edinburgh University Press

Fontan M.S. & Mataric M.J. [1996] A study of territoriality: the role of critical mass in adaptive task division. Fourth International Conference on the Simulation of Adaptive Behaviour

Greenfield M.D. [1994] Synchronous and alternating choruses in Insects and Anurans: common mechanisms and diverse functions. *Amer. Zool.* 34: 605-615

Holland O.E. & Melhuish C.R. [1996a] Some adaptive movements of animats with single symmetrical sensors. Fourth International Conference on the Simulation of Adaptive Behaviour

Holland O.E. & Melhuish C.R. [1996b] Getting the most from the least: lessons for the nanoscale from minimal mobile agents. Artificial Life 5, Nara, Japan

Holland O.E. & Melhuish C.R. (1997) An interactive method for controlling group size in multiple mobile robot systems. International Conference on Advanced Robotics, Monterey

Kube C.R. and Zhang H. [1992], Collective robot intelligence, in 'From animals to animats: Second International Conference on Simulation of Adaptive Behaviour', pp. 460-468

Mataric M.J. [1992], Designing emergent behaviours: from local interactions to collective intelligence, in 'From animals to animats: Second International Conference on Simulation of Adaptive Behaviour'

Ryan M.J., Tuttle M.D. & Taft L.K. [1981] The costs and benefits of frog chorusing behaviour. *Behaviour Ecology and Sociobiology* 8: 273-278

Schöne H. [1980] *Spatial orientation: the spatial control of behaviour in animals and man*. Princeton University Press.

Sebeok T.A.(Ed) [1977] How animals communicate

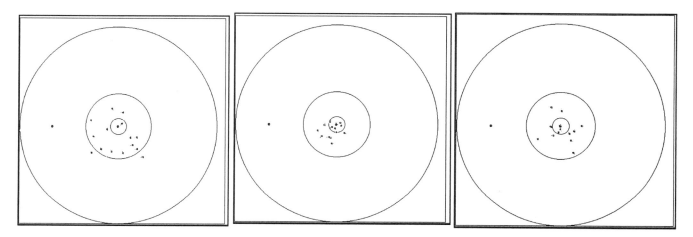

Figure 10: Stages in the development of seeded clustering (demand cluster size 4). The inner circle defines the cluster boundary (radius 25 units). Left: shortly after the start. Centre: after 10,000 time steps there are 8 agents in the cluster. Right: after 50,000 time steps there are 5 agents in the cluster.

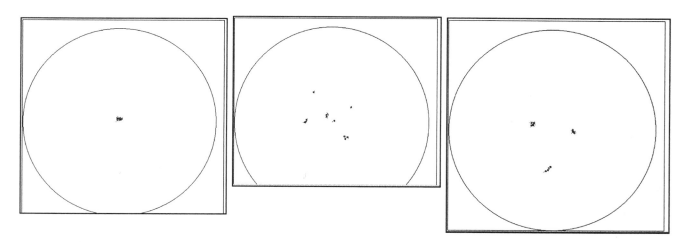

Figure 11: Stages in the development of unseeded clustering (demand cluster size 10). Left: all agents are started at the centre. Centre: after 250,000 time steps the cluster sizes are 6, 3, 3, 1, 1, 1. Right: at the end of the run, the cluster sizes are 6, 5, and 4.

ARTIFICIAL WORLDS

Studying Evolution with Self-Replicating Computer Programs

Tim Taylor and John Hallam
Department of Artificial Intelligence, University of Edinburgh
5 Forrest Hill, Edinburgh EH1 2QL, U.K.
{timt, john}@dai.ed.ac.uk

Abstract

A critical discussion is presented on the use of self-replicating program systems as tools for the formulation of generalised theories of evolution. Results generated by such systems must be treated with caution, but, if used properly, they can offer us unprecedented opportunities for empirical, comparative studies. A new system called Cosmos is introduced, which is based upon Ray's Tierra [15]. The major difference between Cosmos and previous systems is that individual self-replicating programs in Cosmos are modelled (in a very simplified fashion) on *cellular* organisms. Previous systems have generally used simpler self-replicators. The hope is that Cosmos may be better able to address questions concerning the sudden emergence of complex multicellular biological organisms during the Cambrian explosion. Results of initial exploratory runs are presented, which are somewhat different to those of similar runs on Tierra. These differences were expected, and indicate the sensitivity of such systems to the precise details of the language in which the self-replicating programs are written. With the strengths and weaknesses of the methodology in mind, some directions for future research with Cosmos are discussed.

1 Self-Replicating Program Systems as a Methodology for Studying Evolution

Within the last decade, computers have become powerful and affordable enough to enable a number of research groups to study the evolution of life in a new way. Rather than following the traditional approach of trying to capture properties of whole populations in mathematical models, the new approach models a large number of *individual* self-replicating entities which are competing against each other for resources required for replication. This is achieved by creating a computer which can run a large number of self-replicating programs in parallel[1].

Tom Ray pioneered this approach with his Tierra system [15, 16]. Since then, a number of other systems have also been developed, including Avida, developed by Chris Adami and Titus Brown [2], Computer Zoo, written by Jakob Skipper [18], and John Koza's system of self-replicating LISP-like programs [8].

Using such a methodology to study evolutionary systems is attractive for a number of reasons. For example, as the self-replicators are being modelled individually rather than as populations, the simulation respects the fact that a gene does not work in isolation. Rather, it is part of a large ensemble of genes which must all work together with some degree of cooperation in order for the individual organism which carries them to replicate and thus propagate the genes collectively [6]. Only through explicitly modelling individual organisms may we begin to understand the complex interactions between genes and organisms, and how these interactions affect the dynamics of the evolutionary process. In addition, by including an analogy to the process of development of multicellular organisms from single cells[2], this methodology provides a tool for investigating the interplay between such generative processes and an organism's genes—a question which is currently the subject of considerable debate (e.g. [6, 7, 14]).

In fact, systems which use self-replicating programs are not merely *simulations*. As the programs replicate *themselves* (with genetic novelty being introduced by mutations and the flawed execution of instructions), rather than being selected and copied according to an externally defined fitness function (as in genetic algorithms), they *recreate* the conditions necessary for evolution. Such systems can therefore be called *synthetic life* or *artificial life*[3], rather than just simulations.

Every computer-based self-replicating program system therefore provides a new instance of evolution. This

---

[1]In practice, a virtual computer is created (i.e. implemented in software), with parallelism simulated by time-slicing between the programs. Similar approaches are also being employed to investigate related subjects such as the *spontaneous emergence* of self-replicating programs (e.g. [8, 13]), although it is unclear what this work can tell us about the emergence of biological life.

[2]For example, by modelling organisms as *parallel* programs which can dynamically create additional processes.

[3]The term 'artificial life' is now used in a wide variety of situations, but we would argue that only systems based upon *self*-replicating entities are deserving of the term in the strong sense.

leads the way to a field of empirical study we have previously been unable to explore, namely *comparative evolution*. This refers both to comparisons *between* different instances of evolutionary systems (including biological evolution), and also to comparisons *within* a single system. The latter involves investigating the sensitivity of the system to initial conditions, parameters, etc. by running it many times over under slightly different conditions—a strategy which is not, of course, possible in the case of biological evolution.

When studying a population of organisms which are the end-product of an evolutionary process, we generally want to disentangle the relative contributions of three factors to the final state of the system:

1. Features due to chance events/historical accident.

2. Features due to the particular components of the system and to the laws governing their interaction.

3. Features which may be general to a wide class of evolutionary systems.

Through empirical studies of comparative evolution, the hope is that we can begin to investigate each of these factors, and move towards a truly general theory of genetic auto-adaptive systems (to use a term suggested in [1] to cover both biological evolution and self-replicating program systems).

When studying the performance of a genetic auto-adaptive system it is important to consider the relative contributions of each of the three factors. For example, runs on Tierra often result in the evolution of 'parasite' programs which cannot replicate by themselves, but utilise the code of neighbouring programs to perform this task [15]. At first glance, this is an exciting and unexpected result. However, when Tierra's mechanisms for template-driven branching are considered, where the flow of control in a program can jump just as easily to a point on a nearby program as it can to somewhere on the same program, the fact that parasites emerge becomes a little less surprising. The fact that we observe parasitic behaviour in nature and in Tierra might lead one to suppose that this may be a common feature of genetic auto-adaptive systems. However, on closer inspection it would appear that the emergence of parasites in Tierra owes much to the particular design of the language.

Parasites and symbiosis also emerged in Computer Zoo, but there too, Skipper came to the conclusion that "the concept of remote execution seems to be essential to the evolution [of parasitic behaviour]" [18].

A number of researchers have voiced their concern about the extent to which self-replicating program systems can really help us in our understanding of biological evolution. Mathematical biologist Robert May has said that, although he finds this work stimulating, he has "slight reservations about the extent to which the conclusions are perhaps inadvertently built into the program",

as well as doubts about the robustness of the findings[4]. These are justified concerns, but they can be partially allayed by using carefully designed comparative studies [3]. In this way, by manipulating individual factors and noting effects on measured variables, the relative contributions of factors to the behaviour of the system can be investigated.

Indeed, several within-system comparative studies have been published for Avida (e.g. [1]) and Tierra [16][5]. However, just looking at differences *within* a system may not be enough to satisfy critics of this methodology. There will always be questions of how close an analogy is being drawn to biology, and of what stage of biological evolution the system is trying to recreate. Problems arise in these areas because there is a conflict between trying to model the physics and chemistry of the real world, and creating an efficient and "natural" representation for the logical/informational world of the computer. The complexity of the physical/chemical natural world must usually be greatly simplified in a computational model, and many aspects of this complexity are ignored completely.

The extent to which such questions matter depends upon whether one is really trying to model biological life, or rather trying to create artificial life in an appropriate form for the digital medium. To the extent that the former is true, it must be asked how important are the simplifications and omissions of the model to the performance of the system.

These issues again highlight the need for comparative studies, not only within systems, but also *between* them. The greater variety of genetic auto-adaptive systems we have access to, the more we can learn about how important the particular components of a system, and the laws governing their interactions, are to the behaviour of that system. Unfortunately, because of the impossibility of exactly modelling the complexities of physical and chemical systems, it is still the case that, at least in the near future, self-replicating computer systems will be more similar to each other than they are to biological evolution. Therefore, we may still not be able to learn much about biological evolution at this stage using such a methodology. However, this should not prevent us from exploring these systems, as gross simplifications must be made in the initial stages of any branch of scientific enquiry.

2 Motivations for Building a New Genetic Auto-Adaptive System

There are a number of reasons why the new system has been created. The first is simply because, as just men-

---

[4]From [4], Chapter 8.

[5]This study looked at the effects of using each of four different instruction sets. A more informative experiment would consider the effects of individual instructions within an instruction set.

tioned, the more such systems we have, the more we can learn about evolution. This is especially true if the systems are somewhat different to each other.

A second reason was to attempt to pitch the analogy at a somewhat later stage of biological evolution. One of the original aims of Tierra was

> "to parallel the second major event in the history of life, the origin of diversity [the Cambrian explosion, 600 million years ago]. Rather than attempting to create prebiotic conditions from which life may emerge, this approach involves engineering over the early history of life to design complex evolvable organisms, and then attempting to create the conditions that will set off a spontaneous evolutionary process of increasing diversity and complexity of organisms. This work represents a first step in this direction, creating an artificial world which may roughly parallel the RNA world of self-replicating molecules (still falling far short of the Cambrian explosion)" Tom Ray [15].

The system described in this paper is called Cosmos[6]. It has been designed to model (in a very simplified fashion) some of the features of cellular organisms, such as gene regulation, an evolvable mapping between genotype and phenotype, energy storage, inter-cellular communication and inter-organism communication. The hope is that Cosmos may be better able to address questions concerning the sudden emergence of complex multicellular organisms during the Cambrian explosion, in the face of selective pressures which should normally force evolving systems in the direction of smaller and simpler organisms. This is a question that has interested ecologists for a long time.

It is a commonly held belief that once evolution hits upon multicellularity, the emergence of complex organisms is an inevitable result. We may therefore wish to ask questions such as: How easy is it for evolution to hit upon multicellularity? What are the initial advantages for organisms that adopt multicellularity over those that do not? What conditions are required for multicellular organisms to emerge?

On the other hand, mathematical models of ecosystems suggest that, in general, increased complexity makes for diminished community stability [11]. As there are many cases where Nature appears to maintain ecosystem stability despite the complexity of the ecosystem, there is therefore also a need to "elucidate the devious strategies which make for stability in enduring natural systems" ([11] p.174).

The creation of the Cosmos system not only required various new features to be added to the basic Tierra

design, but also required a number of existing features to be modified to fit the new analogy. The main innovations of Cosmos are described in Section 3, but the reasons for changing existing features of Tierra are as follows:

- It has already been said that programs in Tierra can directly execute the code of neighbouring programs. This could be argued to be analogous to certain processes in a (hypothetical) system of self-replicating RNA molecules. However, as Cosmos programs are supposed to be analogous to *cellular* organisms, they should not be able to directly execute the genetic code of other organisms. There is clearly still a need to allow organisms in Cosmos some method of communication and/or interaction, but this should preferably be somewhat more indirect.

- In Tierra, CPU time is the analogy for energy in a biological system. At each timeslice, every program is allowed to execute a certain number of instructions, depending only on the size of the program being executed. In a sense, the programs are getting energy 'for free', in that there is no notion of a program having to *capture* and *store* energy, and then *convert* the energy into useful work (executing an instruction). Cellular biological organisms certainly do have to concern themselves with such issues, so the idea of energy (CPU time) as a *commodity* which must be captured, stored and converted to useful work is incorporated into the design of Cosmos.

- As a consequence of Tierran programs being given energy for free, a somewhat arbitrary mechanism has to be introduced to decide which programs get killed off when the available memory in the system starts to fill up. The 'reaper queue' performs this function— programs are placed at the bottom of the queue when they are born, and programs at the top of the queue get killed off when more memory is required. Programs can move up the queue if they cause error conditions when run, and they can move down the queue if they successfully execute difficult combinations of instructions, "but, in general, the probability of death increases with age" [15]. The reaper queue effectively imposes an upper limit on the lifespan of programs. While at first glance this may seem like a sensible mechanism, there is no *a priori* reason for assuming that there should be a fixed maximum lifespan for all members of an evolving system. Indeed, in nature we see great diversity in the duration of organism life-cycles. The typical lifespan for members of a species is presumably a compromise between factors such as an individual's longevity, its fecundity, and the evolvability of the lineage. In Cosmos, the chance of an organism dying depends upon how much energy it has stored within it (as explained in Section 3).

---

[6]Cosmos is an acronym for "COmpetitive Self-replicating Multicellular Organisms in Software".

This mechanism imposes no fundamental limits on the lifespan of organisms.

This final point raises a more fundamental question. In any population of self-replicating entities which are competing against each other for resources required for replication (e.g. energy and materials), there are three factors which determine the rate at which any particular type of replicator will spread throughout the population [6]. These are the life-span or *longevity* of the replicator, the rate at which it replicates (its *fecundity*), and the number of errors in makes while producing copies of itself (its *copy-fidelity*). In Tierra, evolution can change the fecundity of a program by making it shorter or longer (a shorter program can be copied quicker than a longer one, all other things being equal). However, the reaper queue mechanism means that programs have minimal control over their longevity. Tierran programs also have no control over their copy-fidelity, as this is determined by global parameters of the system. The design of Tierra therefore restricts programs to evolve along the 'fecundity axis', with longevity and copy-fidelity being more or less fixed. Cosmos has been designed to allow organisms to also evolve along these other two axes.

There is an additional advantage in requiring programs to capture energy (potential CPU time) from the environment and store it for future use: each program becomes a potential resource of energy for other programs. There is therefore the potential for predator programs to evolve which prey on the energy resources of other programs, and for an exploitative coevolutionary arms race to emerge [12]. If such a process occurs, organisms on a number of different trophic levels might emerge in the system. Such conditions are undoubtedly of great importance in the evolution of complex organisms. In fact, it has even been proposed [19] that the Cambrian explosion was *caused* by the appearance of the first organisms that ate other organisms (heterotrophs).

3 Novel Features of the Cosmos System

The Cosmos system is explained in detail in [20]. It is written in an object-oriented style that allows it to be easily modified and expanded. The general design philosophy has been to make the system as flexible as possible and to try to model as many features of cellular organisms and their physical/chemical environment as possible, at least in a very abstract way, so as not to constrain the system's evolutionary potential. In addition, care was taken to ensure that all features of the system could be implemented in a computationally efficient way.

The general mode of operation is the same as Tierra, in that it simulates the parallel execution of a large number of self-replicating programs written in a low level language that has been designed to be robust under muta-

tion. Variety between programs is introduced by two methods: a *mutation* operator, whereby any bit of any program in the system can be flipped (with a constant, low probability), and *flawed execution of instructions*, whereby an instruction, which would normally be executed once, might instead by execute twice or not at all (the rate at which this happens is again very low, but is an evolvable property of an individual program).

Cosmos uses a different instruction set to Tierra. Most Tierran instructions have equivalents in Cosmos, but additional instructions are included to provide the different functionality described below (and in Section 2).

As already mentioned, a primary motivation for building Cosmos was to address questions concerning the sudden emergence of complex multicellular organisms in the Cambrian period. In Cosmos, parallel programs are considered as the analogy of multicellular biological organisms. The same analogy has been used for studying multicellularity in Tierra [17, 21, 22]. (Using this analogy, the process of development from a fertilised egg cell to an adult organism is equivalent to the formation of a parallel computer program from an initially serial program by the dynamic creation of parallel processes as the program runs.)

Therefore, Cosmos has been designed with mechanisms to allow for parallel programs with inter-process communication and analogies for genetic regulation and energy transfer between cells. The main features which differ from some or all previous systems are as follows:

3.1 Cellularity

Each program within Cosmos is an *Organism* object. An organism contains one or more *Cell* objects. Each Cell object represents a single process, so that an Organism with one Cell is a serial program, and an Organism with multiple Cells is a parallel program. A Cell contains a bit string—the *Genome*, which gets translated to the executable code of the process. A Cell also contains a number of other objects, including: *Nucleus Working Memory* for writing a copy of the Genome for replication; *Communications Working Memory* for composing arbitrary messages; a *Regulator Store* containing promoters and repressors which dictate which sections of the Genome are translated; a buffer for receiving incoming messages; an 'Energy Token' Store; four 16 bit registers and a stack.

When a Cell issues a `divide` command, the contents of the Nucleus Working Memory are written to the Genome of a new Cell object in a new Organism object. Most of the other structures of the new Cell are initially empty, but half of the parent Energy Token Store is transferred to the child, as is half of the contents of the Regulator Store.

The process by which a Cell dynamically creates a parallel process (another Cell) within the same Organism is exactly the same, except it is initiated by a `split` command rather than a `divide`.

Other points to mention are that when a Cell splits, it can specify a preferred location for its offspring in relation to itself (which is important for intercellular gene control and energy transfer, explained later), and, once created, a Cell can migrate to a new location within the Organism. There is also an experimental parameter which defines the energy *cost* of multicellularity (i.e. at each timeslice, a certain number of energy tokens are deducted from each Cell in a multicellular Organism, proportional to how many neighbouring Cells it touches).

It is worth highlighting a few consequences of this design. As mentioned previously, some experiments have already been conducted on evolving parallel programs in Tierra [17, 21, 22]. (This work will be referred to as *Parallel Tierra*.) Parallel Tierra uses a shared memory approach to parallelism, and, although it is theoretically capable of supporting MIMD (Multiple Instruction, Multiple Data) programs (i.e. differentiated multicellular organisms), it has so far only demonstrated the evolution of SIMD (Single Instruction, Multiple Data) programs. In contrast, Cosmos uses a distributed memory model of parallelism, and the regulator system that it employs (explained later) should promote the emergence of MIMD programs. In addition, unlike in Parallel Tierra, each cell within a multicellular organism in Cosmos actually contains a separate copy of the genome. Although this may appear to be unnecessary, it has a number of possible advantages. For example, the process of cell splitting (organism growth by the creation of parallel processes) is virtually identical to that of cell division (creating a new organism). This means that it is far easier for evolution to experiment with multicellular organisms, as little change is required from the basic self-replicating algorithm to produce an organism that grows rather than divides. Cosmos is therefore better suited for looking at the initial *emergence* of multicellular organisms from unicellular ones[7], and the conditions under which successively more complex multicellular organisms might evolve. Any satisfactory account of the evolution of multicellular organisms must proceed in a stepwise manner such as this. As Richard Dawkins notes in [5], "[a] complex developmental sequence has to have evolved from an earlier developmental sequence which was slightly less complex" (p.258), so "[t]he Darwinian must begin by seeking immediate benefits to genes promoting this kind of life cycle, at the expense of their alleles" (p.263). Another consequence of the design is that all cells within an organism can potentially divide to produce a new organism. In other words, they are all potentially germ-line cells[8]—no *a priori* assumptions are made as to which cells are germ-line and which are not.

---

[7] In contrast, in the work reported on Parallel Tierra, the initial ancestor program has itself been parallel rather than serial.

[8] Unlike in Parallel Tierra where only one process is capable of producing a new organism.

3.2 Communication

Cosmos uses a very flexible method for allowing programs to broadcast and receive messages to and from other programs. Basically, any cell can compose an arbitrary bit string in its Communications Working Memory, and then transmit this message to the environment. Other cells (which could belong to the same organism or a different one) can then issue a command to pick up specified types of environmental messages which are being transmitted from cells in their locality. This mechanism is an attempt to allow programs to develop arbitrary channels of communication in much the same way that biological organisms can communicate arbitrary messages using media such as light and sound.

There is a further twist to this mechanism—if certain conditions are matched for a received message, it will be treated as equivalent to the host code (i.e. it may be executed like a section of the program). In this way, genetic material may also be transferred between programs. Again, the general design philosophy has been to allow the evolutionary process some of the freedoms enjoyed by biological organisms and to prevent it from being unduly constrained. The analogy to the biological case is tenuous, but the fact that we are working with a logical/information medium, rather than a physical/chemical medium, must be respected. Whatever the details of the design, the important point is to provide that organisms with *some* forms of communication, as we are only now beginning to realise the great importance of communication in biological organisms even as simple as bacteria [9].

3.3 A $2\frac{1}{2}$D Environment

One of the problems that has been observed with the process of evolution in Tierra is that it suffers from premature convergence due to global interactions between cells [2]. Adami and Brown sought to overcome this problem in Avida by giving each of the cells a location on a two dimensional toroidal grid. Cells can only interact with other cells occupying nearby grid positions, thereby slowing down the rate of propagation of evolutionary changes throughout the total population and promoting heterogeneity (biodiversity). In Cosmos, programs live on a 2D grid, where each cell occupies a specific grid position. Each organism is flat—that is, each of its cells must be located at a different position on the grid. Within a multicellular organism, individual cells can only pass regulators and energy tokens to neighbouring cells with which they are in physical contact. Cells from different organisms can, however, share a grid position and thus compete for energy. The system is therefore $2\frac{1}{2}$D, but is still computationally easy to manage. Organisms can move around the grid if their cells execute the appropriate instructions.

As well as promoting biodiversity, this design means that the organisms live in a Euclidean space which is at least partially comparable to the 3D space of biological organisms.

3.4 Energy Tokens

At the beginning of each timeslice, a number of *energy tokens* are distributed across the environment. Each cell must issue an *et_collect* command to pick up tokens from its current location. These tokens get added to the cell's Energy Token Store. When it is that cell's turn to execute some instructions, energy tokens are deducted from its store for each instruction it executes. If the level of the store falls below a certain threshold, the cell dies.

There is a (high) limit on the total number of cells that may exist on a single Cosmos system. If this limit is reached, memory is released by killing off cells stochastically, where the chance that a cell is killed is inversely proportional to the level of its Energy Token Store. However, the total number of cells in the system can also be effectively controlled via the quantity of energy tokens that are pumped into the environment at each timeslice. By reducing this quantity, it is possible to reach a situation where this global culling is never required, because the rate at which cells are dying through lack of energy equals the rate at which new cells are being produced.

It could be argued that this mechanism is to some extent equivalent to the 'reaper queue' of Tierra—that 'illegal instructions' are just being replaced by 'amount of energy' as the factor which governs how long a cell survives. However, the current method has the advantages of not imposing a maximum age limit on cells, and of allowing the possibility of the development of trophic levels within the population of organisms, as mentioned in Section 2.

An additional feature concerning energy tokens is that, in a multicellular organism, a cell can send energy tokens to neighbouring cells with which it is in physical contact. This feature was included to allow for the possibility of the evolution of organisms which possess specialised energy collecting cells which distribute energy to the rest of the organism.

3.5 Indirect Mapping from Genotype to Program Instructions

The genome of a cell in Cosmos is literally represented as a string of bits, which gets translated into instructions using a 'genetic code' stored in the cell. In other words, in contrast to any other system of this type, there is an indirect mapping between genotype and phenotype[9].

It has been argued that the mapping from genotype to phenotype determines the *phenotypic variability* of a

---

[9]Where 'phenotype' in this case refers to the executable program.

species, and therefore its *evolvability* [23]. Cosmos can be used to investigate such issues. For example, it is easy to test the effect of different mapping schemes on the behaviour of the system. Also, it can easily be configured so that each cell owns its own map of the genetic code, which can therefore evolve along with the rest of the cell.

3.6 Regulation of the Genome

The flow of control when reading a genome is governed by the presence of *Regulators*. These come in two forms, *promoters* and *repressors*. Both types are associated with a short bit string which determines to which parts of a genome they may bind. Promoters define the sites at which translation of the genome may begin, and repressors define sites at which translation stops. There are two ways that regulators can enter (or leave) a cell— they can either be produced (or destroyed) by the cell itself through the execution of specific commands in the instruction set, or, in the case of multicellular organisms, they can be passed from one cell to a neighbouring cell within the organism. In this way, a complex regulatory network can emerge. This mechanism was designed in an attempt to loosely model gene regulation in biological cells. It is hoped that such a system might promote the emergence of cell differentiation via gene control in multicellular organisms. Another consequence of this mechanism is that, as the genome and the regulators work at the level of individual bits, different promoters are not restricted to binding to the genome in the same reading frame. In other words, if, for example, one promoter binds to the genome five bit positions down from a second promoter, and each instruction is encoded in six bits, the first bit of the first instruction translated by the first promoter is actually the last bit of the first instruction translated by the second. The promoters are working in different reading frames, and will translate the genome into completely different programs. This can also happen in biological systems, where it has been observed that some species actually encode multiple instructions on the same section of the genome by using shifted reading frames (e.g. [10] p.144).

4 Observations from Preliminary Runs

In this section, some observations from the very first exploratory runs of Cosmos are described. The purpose of these was to quickly ascertain the basic behaviour of the evolving programs, and to check that the system worked correctly over a number of long runs, before commencing work on more carefully designed, more specific, comparative experiments.

Three long runs have been conducted, each using similar parameter settings, but with different schedules of energy token distribution across the environment. The parameter settings for the runs are listing in the Ap-

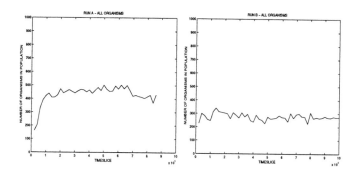

Figure 1: Number of Organisms plotted against Time in Run A (left) and Run B (right). See text for details.

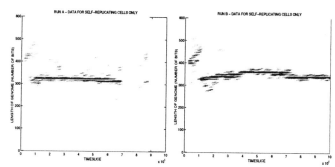

Figure 2: Length of Genomes plotted against Time in Run A (left) and Run B (right). See text for details.

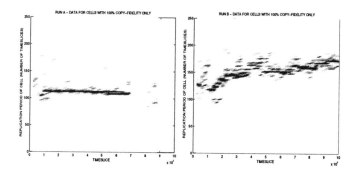

Figure 3: Cell Replication Periods plotted against Time in Run A (left) and Run B (right). See text for details.

pendix. In the light of the discussion in Section 1 it is stressed that the scientific significance of these observations, by themselves, is minimal, as they are not carefully constructed comparative experiments. Most importantly, each experiment has so far only been run once, so conclusions cannot be drawn as to the generality of the observed results across a wide range of random number seeds.

For this reason, the runs are not analysed in great detail. However, they are described primarily to demonstrate that the behaviour of the system is somewhat different to Tierra. This was expected, and emphasises the fact that an important factor governing the behaviour of these systems is the specific design of the language in which the programs are written, and the rules governing how they interact with their environment.

In these runs, a grid size of 50 x 50 was used. The grid was initially inoculated with 900 identical ancestor programs, evenly distributed across an area of 30 x 30 positions in the centre of the grid. The ancestors perform more or less the same actions as does the Tierran ancestor described in [15]—the general procedure is to first calculate (by template matching) the start and end points of the genome in memory; then to copy instructions one at a time from the beginning of the genome to the end into the Nucleus Working Memory (this section of the program will be referred to as the 'copy loop'); and finally to issue a *divide* instruction to create a new organism object with a genome constructed from the contents of the Nucleus Working Memory. At each timeslice, each cell in the population was allowed to execute 10 instructions (if it had enough Energy Tokens). Each run lasted for about 1 million timeslices[10].

Comparing the results of the runs across a number of measures, Runs B and C gave qualitatively similar results, but these were fairly different to the results of

Run A. Because of the similarity between B and C, the following discussion will describe Runs A and B only. In none of these initial runs did multicellular organisms evolve in significant, sustained numbers. For this reason (i.e. the majority of organisms were single-celled), the terms 'organism' and 'cell' are used more or less interchangeably in the following discussion.

The runs only differed in one respect (apart from the random number seed)—the way in which energy tokens were distributed around the environment at the start of each timeslice[11].

In Run A the distribution was even, i.e. every grid position was given the same number of energy tokens. Ten tokens were deposited at each position at each timeslice, which could enable a cell to execute ten instructions. Therefore, as long as there is only one cell at a given position, that cell can obtain sufficient energy from the environment to survive indefinitely, without having to move around in search of more energy tokens.

In Run B, the grid was divided into five bands of 10 x 50 positions for the purposes of energy token distribution. Grid positions in the leftmost band received 8 energy tokens per timeslice, and each band to the right of this received one more token per timeslice (so the middle

---

[10] As there were, on average, about 300-400 cells in the population throughout the runs (Figure 1), the system therefore executed about (300 or 400)x10x1000000, or 3-4 billion individual instructions, during the run. This took approximately 100 hours of processor time on a Sun Sparc 4 workstation.

[11] Also, Runs A and C lasted for 1 million timeslices, whereas Run B, running on a slower machine, was terminated after 880,000 timeslices.

band received 10, and the rightmost band received 12). The total number of energy tokens deposited in the environment at each timeslice was the same as in Run A, but in Run B grid positions in the two leftmost bands received fewer tokens than average, and those to the right received more than average. The particular distribution used meant that 60% of the grid positions received sufficient (or more than sufficient) energy tokens to support a single cell, but 40% received insufficient energy.

Figure 1 shows how the number of cells in the system varied over time. Although the upper limit on the number of cells in the system was set at 2500, most of the 900 ancestral programs died off almost immediately in both runs. This was due to overcrowding, as each grid position can only support a single cell. When a cell divides, its offspring is placed at a random nearby grid position, so the environment can only support populations where there is some space between individual organisms (at least in the case where these organisms are immobile). In Run A, the population size stabilised at around 450 organisms (at least until timeslice 700,000), and in Run B it stabilised at around 260-270 organisms. (The fact that Run B supported about 60% of the number of organisms supported by Run A is a consequence of the different energy token distributions, mentioned previously.)

Figure 2 shows how the length of genomes in the population varies over time[12]. (The length of the initial ancestor program is 396 bits, i.e. 66 6-bit instructions.) One difference between the behaviour of Cosmos in these runs and that reported for runs on other systems [15, 16, 22, 21, 18] is the fact that in Cosmos, at each timeslice, all of the genomes are of roughly the same size—there are no parasites or symbiotes of much shorter length (as are often observed in the other systems). This result was, of course, expected, as Cosmos does not allow cells to execute the code of other cells.

There are a few more points of interest about Figure 2. In both runs, over the first 50,000 to 100,000 timeslices, there was a tendency for program length to *increase*, and there is considerable diversity in the lengths of programs in the population at any given time. This increase in program length is accompanied by a decrease in fecundity—the programs are replicating at a slower rate (Figure 3). This is a surprising result, as, recalling the discussion at the end of Section 2, one would ordinarily expect programs in such a system to evolve in the direction of *higher* fecundity (at least, this is the general behaviour observed in runs of Tierra). A closer look at how the programs changed during this period reveals that extra *et_collect* instructions were being inserted into the programs' copy

loops. The *decrease* in a program's overall fitness due to the increase in program length that results from the addition of extra instructions is evidently more than compensated by the *increase* in fitness due to the collection of more energy from the environment (the more stored energy a program has, the less likely it is to die[13]).

However, at around about 100,000 timeslices (slightly earlier in Run A, later in Run C), there is an abrupt change to organisms of much shorter length. This occurs when a mutation creates a program without many of the initial instructions which are concerned with the calculation of the size of the genome, which actually turn out to be redundant due to various details of the memory addressing scheme used and the particular actions of some of the instructions. Once this transition has occurred, the length of the programs remains fairly stable throughout the rest of the run. Although this general pattern was observed in all three runs, the actual lengths of programs after the transition were slightly different in each case—in Run A the programs settled in the range of roughly 310-320 bits, in Run B it was 330-350 bits, and in Run C, 270-290 bits. It is also known that it is possible to write considerably shorter self-replicating programs (a self-replicator of length 126 bits has been hand-written by one of the authors [TJT]), yet in each of these runs there was no gradual decrease in length once the initial transition was made. This observation emphasises the fact that some fairly significant details of the results (in this case the lengths of the programs at the end of the run) depend upon chance events (in this case the particular mutation that caused the initial transition to shorter programs). The population certainly does not march inevitably to some sort of global optimum state.

One more point about Run A (left side of Figures 2 and 3) is that, roughly between timeslices 700,000 and 850,000, the population completely lacked any individual organisms that were able to make exact copies of themselves. A closer look at the programs that were around during this period shows that they generally retained most of the code required for self-replication, but with minor errors that prevented them from replicating correctly. Importantly, however, they still generally contained a loop (the copy loop inherited from their ancestors) with many *et_collect* instructions within it, so the programs generally had high energy levels and were therefore unlikely to be killed off. The total number of organisms in the population was slightly depressed during this period (Figure 1), but not by a great amount. At around timeslice 850,000 a mutation occurred which reintroduced faithful self-replicators into the population.

Figure 3 shows how the length of time between successive replications of a cell (i.e. the speed with which

---

[12]In this figure, at each timeslice data is only included for *self-replicating* cells, i.e. those which had made at least one faithful copy of themselves by that time. In this figure, and also in Figure 3, the darkness of the plot at any given point corresponds to the number of cells taking that ordinate value at that timeslice.

[13]The time of death of individual organisms was not recorded for these runs, so graphs of organism longevity against time (which might be expected to rise if this explanation is correct) cannot be plotted. This will be corrected in future runs.

a cell replicates) varies over time[14]. Whereas in Run A (left side of Figure 3) the replication period is fairly static after 100,000 timeslices throughout the rest of the run, in Run B (right side of Figure 3) and in Run C, there was a fairly gradual *increase* in replication period (i.e. a *decrease* in fecundity) over the run. This occurred despite the fact, as mentioned earlier, that the fecundity of organisms might be expected to increase over time in systems such as this, and also despite the fact that the *length* of the programs remained fairly constant during the run. Again, inspection of the programs over this period shows that there was a gradual accumulation of *et_collect* instructions within the copy loop. As the length of the programs remained fairly constant, it appears that most of these new *et_collect*'s came about by the mutation of existing (apparently redundant) instructions in the programs. There was a small trend for an increase in the number of instructions contained in the copy loop over time (the new instructions generally being even more *et_collect*'s), which accounts for the gradual increase in replication period.

5 Conclusions and Directions for Future Research

The results of these initial exploratory runs of the system demonstrate, if nothing else, that Cosmos behaves somewhat differently to systems such as Tierra and Avida. This was expected, because of the differences in design highlighted in Sections 2 and 3. The results also provide encouraging signs that Cosmos is capable of displaying diverse behaviours under different conditions, and that in many cases the programs do not seem to be simply evolving in the direction of increased fecundity (as is the usual observation in other systems of this type). Much of the interesting behaviour of the results reported seems to be due to the fact that energy is a commodity to be collected and used. As the organisms are responsible for energy collection, they have some control over their expected lifespan (their longevity), which is certainly also the case in the evolution of biological organisms. Programs in Cosmos also have some control over their copy-fidelity, as the rate at which flaws occur as a program runs is also an evolvable parameter of each program. Future experiments on Cosmos will look in detail at the general nature of the relationship between replicator longevity, fecundity and copy-fidelity in evolving populations.

A series of more detailed and careful experiments with Cosmos is shortly to begin. One important question to consider right at the start is how much of the behaviour of the system is due to chance events. In other words, how much do results vary when running the system a number of times under exactly the same conditions (except for a different random number seed)? It is vital to have some idea of this variability in order to know how many trials should be conducted for each set of parameter settings in future experiments. The role of chance events in determining the behaviour of the system may have been particularly influential in the runs reported in this paper, as the fairly small population sizes will have promoted genetic drift. Tests will be run to gauge the magnitude of this effect.

Experimentation will then concentrate on the investigation of a number of theories which have been proposed to explain the initial emergence of multicellular biological organisms. In addition to Stanley's theory [19] of the evolution of heterotrophs as the prime cause of the Cambrian explosion, developmental biologist Lewis Wolpert has suggested that multicellular organisms might originally have emerged in conditions where food was sparsely distributed in the environment[15]. When no food was available, a multicellular organism would be able to begin eating its own cells to survive until environmental food was available again. Cosmos may be easily configured to test such a scenario.

Experiments are also planned to investigate the sensitivity of the system to the genotype-phenotype mapping, for reasons mentioned in Section 3. At present, there are 61 instructions in the Cosmos instruction set, and these are encoded using 6 bits (giving a total of 64 different possibilities). There is therefore virtually no redundancy in the encoding, in contrast to the biological genetic code which encodes 20 amino acids with 64 possible codons. In one set of experiments, a reduced instruction set will be investigated, which consists of just 21 primary units which can be encoded on the genome. The full functionality of the existing system is maintained by allowing the primary units to form compound instructions. This is somewhat analogous to the way in which biological genomes encode just 20 amino acids, which, when decoded, are then assembled into a vast array of useful proteins.

Some exploratory runs were conducted with a much shorter ancestor than was used in the experiments reported in Section 4. The outcome of these runs was that very little evolution happened at all. It appears to be necessary to inoculate the system with an ancestor that contains a certain amount of redundancy (as was apparently contained in the longer ancestor used in Section 4). Indeed, this was also found to be true in Avida, for which it has been reported that "redundancy has emerged as a necessary requirement for successful evolution" [1]. This may be even more true of Cosmos, as it attempts to model cellular organisms at the verge of a Cambrian ex-

---

[14]In this figure, at each timeslice data is only included for self-replicating cells with 100% copy-fidelity (i.e. those that had only ever produced *exact* copies of themselves). This restriction is due to the way in which the replication rate figures were collected, and will be corrected in future runs.

[15]This theory, which he named 'cannibalistic altruism', was discussed during a recent talk by Wolpert at the Royal Museum of Scotland, Edinburgh, on 20 February 1997.

plosion of complexity and diversity. It could be that supplying the ancestral cells with just a self-replication algorithm in the genome is not enough. Many of the necessary genetic regulatory networks involved in the Cambrian explosion of biological organisms conceivably already existed before the Cambrian period, so that the rapid evolution of the organisms was triggered by coming across ways to regulate these networks and adjusting the degree of pleiotropy between their phenotypic effects. To facilitate the emergence of complex organisms in Cosmos, it may be that the ancestral genome not only has to be large, but must also be composed of a number of discrete functional units. Ideas such as these are discussed in a general context by Wagner and Altenberg in [23].

Throughout this paper, the issue of the importance of remote execution of code for the evolution of parasites has been raised a number of times. Experiments will be conducted on Cosmos in which cells *can* read and execute the genomes of other cells in the system. These conditions would be expected to encourage the evolution of parasites (i.e. to replicate the results observed in Tierra, Avida and Computer Zoo).

As a closing remark, the Cosmos system has been designed and developed over the course of a year or so. When re-reading Ray's original description of Tierra [15] recently, it was of interest to note that in the final section, "Extending the Model", Ray suggests a number of ways in which Tierra could be extended. These include

1. Making instructions expensive.

2. Modifying the way CPU time is allocated.

3. Separation of the genotype from the phenotype.

The incorporation of each of these features in Cosmos came about through largely independent lines of thought (Ray's suggestions having been initially overlooked), but it is satisfying to note that there is some agreement on how to extend such systems.

Acknowledgements

Tim Taylor would like to thank Tom Ray and Kurt Thearling for their comments on the system as it was being developed. He gratefully acknowledges support from EPSRC grant number 95306471. The facilities used for this work were provided by the University of Edinburgh.

References

[1] C Adami. Learning and complexity in genetic auto-adaptive systems. *Physica D*, 80(1-2):154–170, 1995.

[2] C Adami and CT Brown. Evolutionary learning in the 2D artificial life system 'Avida'. In R Brooks and P Maes, editors, *Artificial Life IV*, pages 377–381. The MIT Press, 1994.

[3] PR Cohen. *Empirical Methods for Artificial Intelligence*. MIT Press, 1995.

[4] P Coveney and R Highfield. *Frontiers of Complexity: The Search for Order in a Chaotic World*. Faber and Faber, 1995.

[5] R Dawkins. *The Extended Phenotype*. WH Freeman, Oxford, 1982.

[6] R Dawkins. *The Selfish Gene*. Oxford University Press, Oxford, 2nd edition, 1989.

[7] BC Goodwin. *How the Leopard Changed its Spots: The Evolution of Complexity*. Weidenfeld and Nicolson, London, 1994.

[8] JR Koza. Artificial life: Spontaneous emergence of self-replicating and evolutionary self-improving computer programs. In C Langton, editor, *Artificial Life III*, pages 225–262. Addison-Wesley, 1994.

[9] R Losick and D Kaiser. Why and how bacteria communicate. *Scientific American*, 276(2):52–57, February 1997.

[10] REF Matthews. *Plant Virology*. Academic Press, San Diego, CA, 3rd edition, 1991.

[11] RM May. *Stability and Complexity in Model Ecosystems*. Princeton University Press, 2nd edition, 1974.

[12] J Maynard Smith. *Evolutionary Genetics*. Oxford University Press, 1989.

[13] AN Pargellis. The spontaneous generation of digital 'life'. *Physica D*, 91:86–96, 1996.

[14] RA Raff. *The Shape of Life: Genes, Development and the Evolution of Animal Form*. University of Chicago Press, 1997.

[15] TS Ray. An approach to the synthesis of life. In Langton, Taylor, Farmer, and Rasmussen, editors, *Artificial Life II*, pages 371–408. Addison-Wesley, Redwood City, CA, 1991.

[16] TS Ray. Evolution, complexity, entropy and artificial reality. *Physica D*, 75:239–263, 1994.

[17] TS Ray. An evolutionary approach to synthetic biology: Zen and the art of creating life. *Artificial Life*, 1(2):195–226, 1994.

[18] J Skipper. The computer zoo—evolution in a box. In FJ Varela and P Bourgine, editors, *Toward a Practice of Autonomous Systems: Proceedings of the First European Conference on Artificial Life*, pages 355–364, Cambridge, MA, 1992. MIT Press.

[19] SM Stanley. An ecological theory for the sudden origin of multicellular life in the late Precambrian. *Proc. Nat. Acad. Sci.*, 70:1486–1489, 1973.

[20] TJ Taylor. The COSMOS artificial life system. Technical report, Department of Artificial Intelligence, University of Edinburgh. In Preparation.

[21] K Thearling. Evolution, entropy and parallel computation. In W Porod, editor, *Proceedings of the Workshop on Physics and Computation (PhysComp94)*, Los Alamitos, November 1994. IEEE Press.

[22] K Thearling and TS Ray. Evolving multi-cellular artificial life. In R Brooks and P Maes, editors, *Artificial Life IV*, pages 283–288. The MIT Press, 1994.

[23] GP Wagner and L Altenberg. Complex adaptations and the evolution of evolvability. *Evolution*, 50(3):967–976, 1996.

Appendix - Parameter Settings for Runs Reported in Section 4

Size of Grid = 50 x 50, Max Cells Per Process = 2500, Max Cells Per Org = 16, Ancestor type: LA1, Inoculation scheme: 30 x 30, Overlap Type = Overlap, Distribution Type = [Runs A&B:Land, Run C:Mixed], Distribution Max Delta = [Run A:0.0, Runs B&C:0.2], Energy Sharing Type = Shared, Apply Flaws = true, Default Flaw Rate = 10, Mutation rate = 1 in 100000 per 5 timeslices, MulticellularityPenaltyFactor = 1.0, EnergyTokenStoreLowerThreshold = 1, NumOfEnergyToksPerGridPosPerSweep = 10, NumOfEnergyToksPerCollect = 10, MaxEnergyTokensPerCell = 500, MaxEnergyTokensPerGridPos = 200, NumOfInstructionsPerTimeSlice = 10.

Self-replication in a 2D von Neumann architecture

Florent de Dinechin

IRISA, campus de Beaulieu, Rennes, France

fdupont@irisa.fr

Abstract

This paper introduces new tools for the experimental study of the evolution of living systems. It borrows the main ideas developed by T. Ray in his evolution simulator Tierra, but addresses the main weakness of this system, the linear topology of its memory which is induced by *addressing by template*. We define an execution model in a *two dimensional* (2D) memory, in which sequential programs are stored on "threads" in the memory plane, and *jump* instruction are replaced with physical thread connection. We present an implementation of this 2D execution model and give examples of programs, including a self-replicating one. Then the use of this model for simulating evolution is discussed.

1 Introduction

In trying to define a science of life which is more universal than what we may observe on Earth, fundamental biologists rely more and more on abstract models and computer simulations. Such models, often termed *artificial life* [4], may address several research fields. The first is the study of the fundamental laws of *metabolism,* i.e. the energetic aspects of living systems [5]. The second one is to study the *emergence* of macroscopic behaviors from the interaction of microscopic entities [10]. A third aim of artificial life, which motivates this paper, is a better understanding of the *evolution* process: its purpose is to provide an artificial framework allowing us to carry out *experiments* about evolution, instead of the mere *observation* of our own terrestrial evolution process. Such experiments are needed to abstract the universal laws of evolution from the casual contingencies of the history of the earth.

The first steps in this direction were the cellular automata (CA) of von Neumann [14], who only studied self-replication. Among other, Langton [3] and Sipper [11] also addressed the question of evolution. Meanwhile Rasmussen et al. [7, 6] showed that a completely different model, inspired from computer architecture, could also be used in this domain. These ideas inspired T. Ray's Tierra simulator [8] providing the most spectacular simulations of evolution to date. In this model, the world

is a computer memory, and the living beings are self-replicating computer programs, subject to mutation and death mechanisms inspired from biological life. Experiments using this system sometimes lead to the effective evolution of initial self-replicating programs towards more and more efficient and more and more complex ones. This simulator was also used and extended to study adaptation and learning in such "living" systems [1].

However we see weaknesses in Tierra as a tool for the study of artificial life. The first is the poor topology of the substrate – a linear memory – which prevents the apparition of complex interactions between more than two neighboring creatures. This topology is a consequence of one of the key features of the Tierra virtual computer, the fact that memory locations are addressed by their content *(by template)* instead of their address like in conventional computers. As a consequence, a *centralized* operating system is needed for memory allocation, to overcome this poor topology. Although it obviously doesn't prevent evolution from occurring, it is very different from what we know of Earth life, where all the interactions are local in a three dimensional space. As this question of locality is crucial in the study of self-organizing behavior, we fear that Tierra may be unable to simulate one of the major events in terrestrial evolution, the apparition of *multicellularity*.

A richer topology allowing one to truly exploit locality is thus needed. *Two dimensional* CA are much older than Tierra itself, however they are badly suited to the study of evolution: they are too *brittle*, which means that a small change in a "living" (able to self-replicate) organization has a very low probability of preserving this ability. The purpose of this paper is therefore to provide a bridge between cellular automata and the Tierra model, inheriting the topology of the first and the resistance to mutation of the latter.

This question has already been addressed, e.g. in the Computer Zoo [12] and Avida [2] systems. Both, however, separate a 1D space where the instructions are stored (à la von Neumann) and execute themselves, and a 2D "physical" space. Our system is both simpler and closer to the real world, as there is only one space where the programs both run and interact. This space is a memory shared by all the programs, as in Tierra, but this memory has a 2D topology. The von Neumann execution model in 2D memory which we introduce is of little practical use in computer science, but we feel it addresses a need in the field of artificial life.

The remainder of this paper is organized as follows: the following section discusses the topology of memory accesses in conventional computers and in the Tierra virtual computer, then introduces the notion of 2D memory. Section 3 describes a virtual processor designed on top of this notion, with some example programs. Then section 4 discusses the use of this virtual processor to study the evolution of programs "living" in this 2D memory. Finally we draw conclusions from these initial experiments.

2 Memory topology

2.1 The von Neumann model

In computer science, the fact that the memory is monodimensional, i.e. that its address space is linear, has been a constant since the the very beginning: the Turing machine, an abstract model used to study the very foundations of computing, is based on a linear ribbon on which the data are written. The other example is the architectural model on which most general-purpose computers have been based, which is also due to von Neumann [13]. It consists basically of a processor communicating with a memory. A memory location is accessed by its address which is an integer. There are two operations possible on this memory: store a data at a given address, or read the data at a given address. We say that the memory is monodimensional because its address space (the set of the integers) is a monodimensional Euclidean space.

The processor contains a register usually called *program counter* or PC, and indefinitely executes the same cycle: read the program instruction stored at the address held by PC, decode it, execute it, add 1 to PC, and start again. The set of possible instructions may be very simple or very complex, but it always contains some instructions to read and write data at a given address in memory.

Now to define a topology of the memory we have to define a notion of *distance* between two memory locations. From a computational point of view, the relevant distance is is not the distance between their addresses, but rather the time it takes to access a memory location from a read or write instruction stored in another memory location. In the von Neumann model, this access time to a data is independent from both memory locations[1]. Therefore there is no need for more complex address spaces: if the logical topology of the memory is linear, the practical topology is such that each memory location is a direct neighbor to each other in terms of access time. This is how the linear memory may be inter-

preted for example as a two dimensional picture, without any complexity overhead.

2.2 The Tierra virtual computer is not a von Neumann computer

Ray himself made a similar analysis [9], but this analysis doesn't hold for his own work: in the simplified computer model used in the Tierra simulator, there is no absolute address space. During memory operations (and also jmp instructions) the memory location to access isn't defined by its *address*, but by its *content* (called in this case a *template*). A local search must be performed, from the PC location, to find this template. Thus read/write/jump topology is actually 1D. Note that, in compensation, the instruction mal allocating the memory for a daughter program has no such restriction: the daughter is allocated anywhere in the soup. Thus mother/daughter topology is unrestricted, and therefore inconsistent with the read/write/jump topology.

In the 2D systems designed so far (to our knowledge Czoo [12] and Avida [2]) this inconsistency is even worse: read/write/jump operations happen in some 1D program space, while cell interactions happen partly in this program space, partly in some 2D "physical" space which is distinct from the previous. This works as far as evolution is concerned, and actually it is somehow similar to the 1D DNA program in the 3D living cells of the biological world. We intend, however, to simulate the most basic level of "chemistry": cells and cellularity may appear in the run of the simulation but we don't want to impose them by an external controller.

Our motivation is therefore to reconcile the program space and the physical space (as in cellular automata and real world chemistry) and build a model in which reads, writes, jumps, as well as daughter creation and other cell-cell interaction, obey the same Euclidean 2D topology. This unified space will be termed a *2D memory*.

2.3 Two dimensional memory

The definition of a 2D memory is very straightforward: the address of a memory location is a couple of integers instead of a single integer. This couple may be viewed as the coordinates of the location in a plane.

It is more difficult to define what a *program* is in such 2D memory: in the von Neumann model, a program is a set of consecutive memory locations holding instructions. The order of execution of the instructions in time reflects their order in the linear memory (only special jump/goto/branch instructions break this order). The execution of a program in 2D memory raises a new question: which, of the 4 neighbors of an instruction, is the instruction to be performed next? In other terms, how do we map the (linear) time onto our bidimensional memory?

---

[1]In current actual computers this is no longer true: there is a hierarchy in the memory access times which exploits a notion of locality. This doesn't affect our argument.

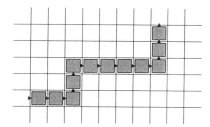

Figure 1: A program thread in 2D memory

We have studied two possible approaches. The first is to store, in each memory location and in addition to its data, an arrow pointing to the "next" memory location, which is one of its neighbours: up, right, down or left for instance. A program is then a sequence of instructions according to this succession relationship: when one looks at the memory, a program appears as a thread in this memory (Fig.1). The interesting thing is that the notion of *loops*, implemented in linear memory using a sequence of instruction including a *jump* instruction, actually appears as a loop in 2D. There is no need for a jump instruction, the thread simply drives to itself. Moreover, what programmers call "loop nests" actually appears as nests (Fig.2). In this figure, the instructions labelled F are *fork* instructions, which have two possible successors depending on the state of a flag.

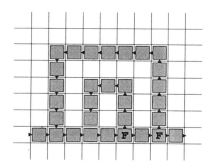

Figure 2: A loop nest in 2D memory

What we implemented – and will present in the remainder of this paper – is a slightly more complex model, such that the programs are *invariant by rotation*. To ensure this property, no absolute orientation is stored in the memory. Instead, the PC (within the processor) holds this absolute direction along with the address of the location it points. The memory locations only hold a *relative change* to this direction for the next instruction: keep the direction (F for "forward"), turn right (R), or turn left (L). The behavior of the PC is thus similar to the head of a Logo turtle, as shown by Fig 3.

To clarify things, here is the basic cycle corresponding to the von Neumann cycle: *read* the instruction pointed to by the PC, *execute* this instruction, *move the PC* to the next instruction (which is given by the PC orienta-

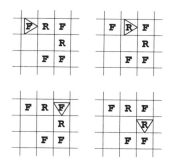

Figure 3: Execution of a 2D program

tion), *rotate* the PC according to the direction change (which is contained in this instruction), and start again. Figure 3 shows four of these basic cycles. The arrow is the PC orientation, and the instructions are not given, only their direction change. Notice that the head (the PC) first moves, then (possibly) rotates.

It is obvious that this execution model has the same expressive power as usual sequential computers: one may easily translate a sequential program into our model, by copying all the non-*jump* instructions on a thread and implementing the *jump* instructions as parallel threads of *no operation* instructions. Our first example will illustrate that.

We now present our implementation of this execution model, in a simple virtual processor whith a very restricted instruction set.

3 Ziemia

Our implementation is aimed at simulating evolution more than performing general-purpose computations. We assume that the reader is familiar with the Tierra virtual computer [8], from which we tried to keep the main features, in particular the small number of instructions. Another feature we borrowed from Tierra is the name, as Ziemia means "earth" in Polish.

One important difference between Ziemia and Tierra is that in our virtual computer, the only data manipulated are instructions: the Tierra language allows numerical computations, that is manipulating data (numbers) which are not present in the soup by themselves. Our model is closer to biology (if one admits that the only data manipulated by the DNA is amino-acids), but our main motivation was to keep the instruction set as small as possible. Performing computations is of course still possible, as our first example will show.

3.1 The Ziemia virtual processor

A virtual processor consists of three address registers called P (the PC), X and Y (each holding an address and a direction), two data register called A and B (each holding an instruction and a direction change), and a flag used with some conditional instructions. In addition, the processor possesses two stacks, one for data and one for addresses.

A memory location holds a byte, in which two bits code the direction change, one bit is used for memory management, and five code the instructions. There are therefore at most 32 different instructions, out of which 6 are currently unused.

The following array briefly describes the current instruction set:

Np0	No Operation 0
Np1	No Operation 1
LdA	Load A: A ← (P)
A=B	A ← B
X=P	X ← P
X=Y	X ← Y
SXY	Swap X and Y
SAB	Swap A and B
RdA	Read A: A ← (X); flag set if (X) was Frk
WrA	Write A: (X) ← A
Flw	X follows the arrow it points
PsX	Push X on address stack; if full, set flag
PsA	Push A on instr. stack; if full, set flag
PpX	Pop X from addr stack; if empty, set flag
PpA	Pop A from instr. stack; if empty, set flag
APp	Discard top of addr. stack; if empty, set flag
IPp	Discard top of instr. stack; if empty, set flag
A?B	Set flag if A=B
X?Y	Set flag if X=Y
Run	Creates a new process whose P ← X
New	X = random addr. in the neighborhood of P
Frk	Fork: if flag set, move as usual, otherwise go forward
MvF	Move X forward
MvR	Move X right
MvB	Move X backward
MvL	Move X left

3.2 Implementation and example

We implemented a simulator for this virtual computer. We also had to write a 2D program editor which is very different from a text editor used to edit usual programs. This editor integrates a step-by-step debugger, which we used to write and test simple programs such as that of Fig.4. This figure is a screen dump of this editor: at each memory location it shows the instruction and the direction change stored there.

The program of Fig.4 performs the sum of two integers. It implements the usual binary addition, using the stack to store the carry bit. The threads composing this program are clearly visible. It is entered at the upmost LdA instruction (surrounded by two upwards arrows). The address register X must point to the least significant bit

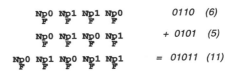

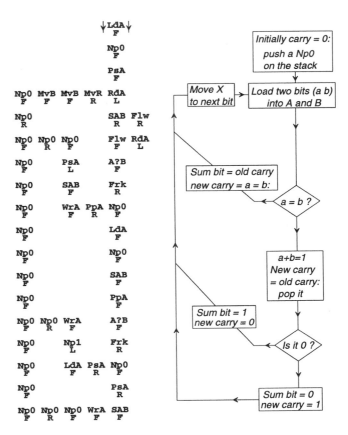

Figure 4: Binary addition in Ziemia

of one of the numbers (written in binary using Np0 and Np1) as on the figure. The execution of this program mimics the flow chart given in the same figure. The interested reader should refer to Fig. 3 to step through the program.

4 Simulating evolution with Ziemia?

We programmed a complete system in the philosophy of the Tierra simulator: several processors share the memory and execute different programs. The operating system shares the simulation time between the processors, and maintains a count of the errors they make during their execution. Using this data, it removes the less successful processors from the simulation, leaving their code. In addition, several types of mutations may be applied to the system. We only implemented "cosmic ray" mutations, that is low-frequency random bit-flipping in the memory[2].

4.1 Self-replication

We injected, in an initially blank memory, an ancestor which is the self-replicating program given in Fig.5. It consists of several threads (a thread starts with a Frk instruction), some of them form loops. The whole program loops on itself, starting bottom left (the boxed X=P instruction) with a smaller loop which copies a thread from the mother program (pointed to by register X) to the daughter program (pointed to by register Y). Each time this copy loop encounters a Frk instruction, it pushes on the address stack the corresponding location so as to come back to it later when it has finished copying the current thread. In this program we chose to end each thread with a Np1 instruction: the copy loop thus stops when it encounters this instruction, and pops the next thread to copy from the address stack. If this stack is empty the copy is terminated, and a Run instruction is performed on the daughter program, creating a new processor for it.

In our experiments, a growing population of this ancestor program is easily observed, but to date no significant evolution occurred. Depending on the scheme by which

---

[2]In Tierra experiments, other kinds of mutations (such as copy flaws) change little to the global evolution. We assume for a start the generality of this result.

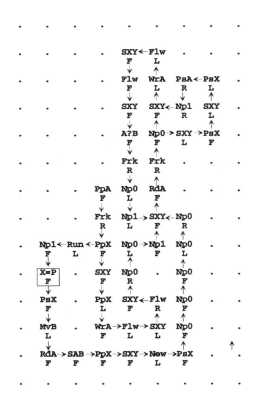

Figure 5: Self-replicating program

programs are killed when the memory is saturated, it is possible to have a stable population of this program which resists mutations up to a certain rate. However, mutations do not seem to create new "living" programs: we observe new program loops with a sometimes complex behaviour (as the 2D memory is mapped on a computer screen we observe the apparition of various new repetitive patterns) but these mutants, being unable to self-replicate, are eventually killed by the system. Sometimes they invade the memory and make life impossible even for the ancestor, resulting in the extinction of the simulation, a phenomenon already described by Ray.

Very few experiments have been carried out yet, but they have shown that our system is too *brittle* to support an evolution process. The rest of this paper studies this brittleness issue.

4.2 Addressing by template versus physical branching

A major difference between Tierra and Ziemia is the absence of addressing by template, replaced, as we already showed, with physical branching (see Fig.4 and 5). Addressing by template – a feature of Tierra borrowed from biology – is actually the basis of the evolution in the Tierra and Avida systems: the first significant mutations leading to new self-replicating creatures are modifications of the templates. For example, parasites, whose program don't contain any copy loop, are obtained by modifying the template structure of the Tierra ancestor to spare this copy loop.

We believe that physical branching could play the same role as addressing by template: in a memory saturated with dead code, a wandering PC due to some mutation has a high probability of encountering an "interesting" program thread, just the same way as in Tierra a mutated jmp instruction has a high probability of encountering the mutated template somewhere in the soup. In a 2D topology, however, this probability is (very roughly) squared, which increases brittleness. Besides, the probability that this PC comes back to its initial thread is very low, much lower than in the 1D case. This is the main reason why a mutant doesn't live.

We are considering various possible answers to this problem. The idea is to tie somehow a wandering PC to its initial program loop, for example by extending the instruction set with a *fork and push* instruction to be used in conjunction with a *return* instruction, in a way similar to the sequential subroutine call of Tierra. Another possibility is to introduce copy flaw mutations that preserve the threads.

4.3 Cellularity

The other fundamental difference between Ziemia and Tierra is the existence, in Tierra, of a *private* memory space for each program, a segment of memory which is readable by all but on which only itself has the right to write. This private space is compared, in the Tierra metaphor, to the inside of a living cell protected by a semi-permeable membrane.

The drawback of this private space option is to rely on a centralized management system. Besides it is very difficult, for topological reasons, to design an equivalent in the 2D case. We therefore used a simpler scheme: each memory location contains one bit telling whether it is "alive" or "dead". All the processes have the right to write on "dead" locations, and none has the right to write to "alive" locations. A memory location is set "alive" each time it is accessed for reading or writing. The system periodically and randomly sets blocks of memory "dead". Thus, as long as a process is running, its code is kept "alive". Once the process is removed, its code remains flagged "alive" for a while, but is eventually set "dead" by the system.

The strong point of this approach is that there is no *centralized* cellularity: read/write access right is determined locally (another approach, more memory expensive, is to store at each memory location an identity number of the only processor which has the right to write there). To achieve our goals we will try and avoid a centralized cellularity mechanism, although we feel it is one of the key features making evolution possible in Tierra.

5   Conclusions

The work presented in this paper has two clearly distinct aspects. The first, concerning the domain of computer science, is the definition of a sequential execution model in bidimensional memory, validated by an implementation which allowed us to write several programs in this model. This work is interesting in itself, mostly because the absence of *jump* instruction makes structured programming mandatory and spatially explicit (see the loop nest and adder examples). This would be enough to try and use it as a programming model for parallel processing, but alas, to our knowledge, it is totally unrealistic from a technological point of view.

The other aspect is more specifically the use of this model to simulate evolution process in a world where, like in the real one, the physical space and the functional space are interdependent, and the interactions are local. So far we were able to exhibit a self-replicating program which is slightly more complicated than Tierra's ancestor, but much simpler – and hopefully less brittle – than a self-replicating 2D cellular automata. However evolvability is unsuccessful so far: preserving a high-level property such as self-replication is a known difficult problem. We have identified weaknesses of our model and proposed some solutions which remain to be explored. We are confident in the model : the 2D topology in itself shouldn't be an obstacle to evolution, since biological life evolved

in a 3-D world, and Tierra in a 1-D one. Trying to solve the current problems will help us learn more about the underlying mechanisms and conditions of evolution.

References

[1] Chris Adami. Learning and complexity in genetic auto-adaptive systems. *Physica D*, 80:154, 1995.

[2] Chris Adami and C. Titus Brown. Evolutionary learning in the 2D artificial life system 'Avida'. In *Artificial Life IV*. MIT Press, July 1994.

[3] C.G. Langton. Self-reproduction in cellular automata. *Physica D*, 10(1-2):135–144, 1984.

[4] C.G. Langton and K. Kelley. Toward artificial life. *Whole Earth Review*, 58:74–79, 1988.

[5] F. Morán, A. Moreno, E. Minch, and F. Montero. Further steps towards a realistic description of the essence of life. In *Nara Fifth International Conference on Artificial Life*, May 1996.

[6] S. Rasmussen, C. Knudsen, and R. Feldberg. Dynamics of programmable matter. In *Artificial Life II*, Redwood City, 1992. Addison Wesley.

[7] S. Rasmussen, C. Knudsen, R. Feldberg, and M. Hindsholm. The Coreworld: emergence and evolution of cooperative structures in a computational chemistry. *Physica D*, 42:111–134, 1996.

[8] T.S Ray. An approach to the synthesis of life. In *Artificial Life II*, Redwood City, 1992. Addison Wesley. See also : *Evolution and Optimization of Digital Organisms,* included in the freeware Tierra distribution.

[9] T.S Ray. Artificial life. In W. Gilbert and G. T. Valentini, editors, *From Atoms To Mind*. In press, 1997.

[10] C.W. Reynolds. Flocks, herds, and schools: A distributed behavioral model. *Computer Graphics: Proceedings of SIGGRAPH '87*, 21(4):25–34, July 1987.

[11] Moshe Sipper. Co-evolving non-uniform cellular automata to perform computations. *Physica D*, 92:193–208, 1996.

[12] Jakob Skipper. The Computer Zoo – evolution in a box. In *European Conference on Artificial Life*, 1991.

[13] J. von Neumann. First draft of a report on the EDVAC. Technical report, University of Pennsylvania, 1945.

[14] J. von Neumann. *Theory of Self-Reproducing Automata.* University of Illinois Press, Urbana, 1966.

The Garden of Chances:
an Integrated Approach to Abstract Painting and Reactive DAI

Guillaume Hutzler—Bernard Gortais—Alexis Drogoul

LAFORIA/IBP/CNRS - Université Paris VI
4, Place Jussieu, case 169
75252 Paris Cedex 05

" Simple extrapolations of interactive art can embellish the behavioral model to include inputs from the weather, time of day (...). Or, with more fantasy, we can imagine a future of the visual arts populated with (...) caustic canvases (...) that get to know their future owners, who in turn get to know and love them "

N. Negroponte

Abstract

Following our development experience with an artistic application using multi-agent techniques —*The Garden of Chances*— we elaborate in this paper a comparative study of abstract painting and reactive Distributed Artificial Intelligence (DAI). More specifically, we underline the interest of reactive DAI as a tool for artists, while showing how abstract art reformulates the recurrent problematics of emergence and interpretation, providing us with a new basis for approaching Artificial Life and reactive DAI. We also suggest new research directions in the field of data visualization using artistic paradigms.

1. Introduction

Since the very first developments of computer science, art has taken significant interest in the use of computers for the generation of colored images in a more or less automated manner [Leavitt 76]. This early interest has gradually developed until becoming what is now called *computer art*. Appropriating (and sometimes actively participating to) every computer science breakthrough, computer art has attracted both artists and computer scientists, stimulating mutual interactions between the two communities ([Cohen 79, 88], [Gips and Stiny 75], [Todd and Latham 92]). The project *The Garden of Chances* (*GoC* in short) that we present in this paper has been developed in a deliberate attempt to associate abstract art and reactive Distributed Artificial Intelligence (DAI) in an interdisciplinary investigation of the issues of emergence and interpretation.

As an artistic project, the *GoC* proposes to make the link between real and imaginary worlds. In this paradigm, weather data of a given place are used to give life to graphical worlds of two-dimensional colored shapes. On the one hand, colors provide the spectator with a poetical representation of the climatic atmosphere of the place. On the other hand, shapes are generated and animated as metaphorical equivalents of plants in a garden. On the technical side, the *GoC* has been designed as a reactive multi-agent system, relying on biological simulation techniques explored within the MANTA project [Drogoul 93].

This interdisciplinary approach allows us to discuss a comparative analysis of abstract painting and reactive DAI, with regards to the processes of design and evaluation. Based on this analysis, we propose to address in a novel way the Artificial Life issues of emergence and interpretation. Regarding emergence, the purpose is to isolate, at the level of individual behaviors, mechanisms likely to produce some specific temporal and spatial structuring of space at the global level. Regarding interpretation, we propose to associate aesthetic criteria with more pragmatic notions of organization and function, enriching the problematics of functional meaning with that of aesthetic meaning. We claim that these interactions between art and science to be very profitable for both fields. While DAI supplies the artist with tools to experiment new modalities for painting, the artist provides DAI with interesting new prospects in the study and the visualization of complex systems.

The paper is organized as follows: in Section 2, we describe the *GoC* project, both in its artistic and technical aspects; in Section 3, we develop a comparative analysis between abstract painting and reactive DAI, and we suggest future research directions.

2. The Artistic Project: *The Garden of Chances*

The *GoC* project is based on a metaphorical link between real and artificial worlds. This makes it very close to the Artificial Life paradigm, with the notable difference that it does not aim at reproducing or simulating a given reality, but only at providing a poetical representation of it. This approach is further developed in Section 2.1 along with the description of the artistic project. The implementation choices that have been made in order to satisfy the project requirements are then explained in Section 2.2. We finally discuss the first results obtained in Section 2.3.

2.1. The Artistic Paradigm

The philosophy underlying the artistic work is to let the automatic generation of images be directed by a real time incoming of real world data. This has led to the development of a first computer artwork called *Quel temps fait-il au Caplan? (What's the weather like in Caplan?)*. In this project, weather data coming in hourly from *MétéoFrance* stations were used to suggest the climatic atmosphere of a given spot (actually a small place in Britain) by means of color variations inside an almost fixed abstract image. To put it naively, rather warm tints were used when the temperature was high, dark tints when clouds appeared to be numerous, etc. In addition to meteorological parameters, the system also took astronomical ones (season and time of the day) into account, which eventually allowed very subtle variations. When functioning continuously all year long, the animation makes the computer screen become a kind of artificial window, giving access to a very strange world, both real and poetic.

The *GoC* is basically designed with the same principles, namely using real data for the creation of mixed worlds, imaginary landscapes anchored in real world. In addition to colors modulations, the weather data are used to give life to a set of two-dimensional shapes, so as to create a metaphorical representation of a real garden. Thus, each graphical creature is able to grow up like a plant, benefiting from the presence of light and rain, competing against similar or other hostile shapes, reproducing and dying like any living creature. By so doing, the goal is definitely not to produce accurate simulations of natural ecosystems nor realistic pictures of vegetation. The focus is rather put on enabling the artist to experiment with lots of different abstract worlds until he obtains some imaginary ecosystem fitting his aesthetic sensitivity. The graphical space doesn't have the passiveness of coordinate systems anymore; we rather consider it as an active principle giving birth to worlds, as the raw material from which everything is created.

2.2. The Computer Realization

In agreement with artistic requirements, the system has been implemented as a programmable platform, allowing the artist to undertake a true artistic research. Capitalizing on our experience with biological simulation systems ([Drogoul 93]), we designed it as a genuine vegetal simulation platform, supplying growth, reproduction, and interaction mechanisms similar to those observed in plants. Indeed, we believe the difference between metaphorical and simulated ecosystems only resides in the perspective adopted during the experimentation process.

2.2.1. General Description

The core of the platform is a multi-agent system, associating plants to agents evolving in a simulated environment. Both the agents and the environment are characterized by sets of **parameters** that define their health condition at any given time. The evolution of these parameters is defined through **laws** which establish links and mutual interactions between them. In addition, agents may activate one or more **behaviors** at any time. Finally, agents will be represented on the screen by colored shapes, which won't have necessarily something to do with plants but may be freely designed by the artist. A given still image will thus be close to his painting work, while the dynamics of the whole system will more closely rely on the artificial side of the project, i.e. the simulation of natural processes of vegetal growth.

2.2.2. Agents and Environment

Parameters constitute the basis for the representation of both agents and the environment. Actually, four types of parameters have been defined in order to describe the simulated world.

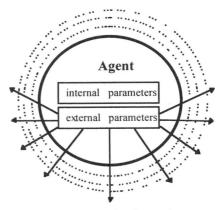

Figure 1 - Agent's internal and external parameters

Agents are characterized by internal and external parameters as shown in Figure 1. Internal parameters describe the resources of the agent (water, glucose, etc. with the vegetal metaphor, or any other quantifiable resource). By contrast, external parameters represent any substance or information that the agent may propagate around him (chemical substances that plants release in the soil or the atmosphere, signals, etc.).

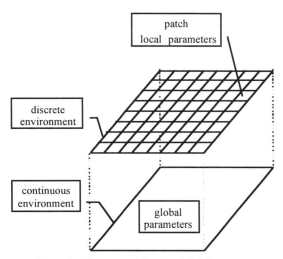

Figure 2 - Environment's local and global parameters

The environment is characterized by local and global parameters as shown in Figure 2. Local parameters correspond to variables whose value and evolution can be defined in a local way, i.e. for each square of the grid covering the environment (substances present in the soil, water or mineral materials for example). On the contrary, global parameters represent variables which have a nearly uniform action on the whole environment (meteorological variables, real world data, etc.).

2.2.3. Laws and Behaviors

Starting from parameters, we define laws and behaviors, describing the relationships linking the evolution of a set of parameters to another set of parameters. This allows us to describe how some parameters evolve (slow decrease of the energy of an agent to sustain its metabolism, etc.) and to specify the interactions between the agents (chemical aggressions, etc.), between an agent and its environment (water drawn from the soil to feed a plant, etc.), and even between different levels of the environment (supply of underground waters by the rain, etc.).

To put it more formally, one can define, for each law, a set of influences and/or preconditions in relation with the value of some parameters. They constitute the triggering conditions of the law. The evaluation of these conditions results in a value and/or a vector which in turn determines how the law modifies the target parameters. This feedback on parameters is done using fixed or proportional effects. In addition to laws, behaviors give agents the ability to undertake a particular action (to grow, move, reproduce, die). Figure 3 illustrates these general principles.

Laws and behaviors are managed by a scheduler that activate them with a given periodicity. According to the vegetal model, every potentially activable law and behavior can be triggered concurrently during a single timestep, even if several laws and/or behaviors are associated with the same

agent. A simulated plant can thus simultaneously execute different operations such as drawing water from the soil, realizing photosynthesis, growing, releasing chemical substances, etc.

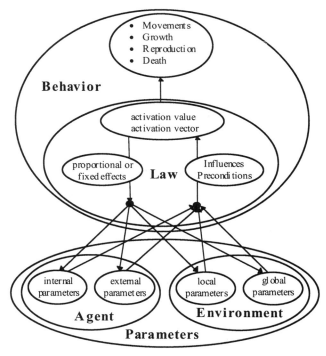

Figure 3 - Relationships between parameters through laws and behaviors

2.2.5. User Programming of the System

The whole system can be programmed and the parameters set from a unique configuration file. Any element of a simulation (agents, parameters, laws, behaviors, and even shapes and colors) can be defined using a simple script language. This file can be edited and modified using various specialized editors.

The artist has thus the possibility to specify a simulation-artwork in a comprehensive fashion through the definition of the different families of agents that may populate it (parameters, shape, color, etc.), and of the mutual interactions between agents of these families (laws and behaviors).

2.3. A First Evaluation of the *GoC*

Figure 4 is an example of the aspect of the screen at a given time, i.e. a still black and white snapshot of the animated colored images. Set aside aesthetic and artistic discussions, the scientific evaluation of the quality of such a system proposing a metaphorical visualization of real data, would have to be done under two complementary points of view :

Figure 4 - "The Garden of Chances" snapshot

- what can the spectator say about the data that were used to generate the pictures ? In other words, does the representation used for visualizing the data make sense for the spectator ?
- if the current representation doesn't make sense for him, how easy is it for the spectator to make the system evolve until it finally fits his sensitivity ?

Since the *GoC* has originally been developed in an artistic perspective, experimental protocols have yet to be designed in order to scientifically address these issues. The *GoC* would surely prove not so well adapted for the visualization of any kind of data. We feel however that this artistic approach to both complex systems and data visualization may provide us with new paradigms for the visualization of complex data. Indeed, as we explain it in next section, abstract painting may be analyzed in the complex systems framework, therefore shedding a new light on the standard problematics of organization and interpretation. Real world data for their part, be they meteorological, economical or of another type, cannot be simply understood without considering the complex interactions between a great number of variables. Finally, abstract painting has acquired for more than eighty years a valuable experience on the communication with human spectators through graphical metaphors.

After developing these points further in the following section, we will show how they should be integrated in a single effort to make complex interacting data accessible to direct visual perception.

3. Abstract Painting and Reactive DAI: a Comparative Analysis

Traditionally associated with W. Kandinsky, the birth of abstract painting has radically transformed the painting community, by upsetting some of the most fundamental conceptions of the field. More specifically, artwork creation and evaluation processes were approached from a totally new point of view. Similarly, reactive DAI raises the issues of emergence and interpretation in new terms as compared to cognitive DAI and mainstream AI.

By going beyond a simple "art versus science" classification, we intend to underline the similarities shared by abstract painting and reactive DAI in several respects. We show in particular that the creative processes of abstract painting make it an "emergent" art. Furthermore, it appears that interpretation issues in reactive DAI are reformulating questions raised by abstract painting since its foundation.

3.1. Abstract Painting as an "Emergent" Art

As opposed to what may suggest its "fixed" aspect, painting is a dynamic art, through both creative processes and artwork evaluation processes. "*The work of art is born of the movement, is itself fixed movement and is perceived in movement.*" [Klee 85] Besides, if we think of an artwork as a set of graphical elements, abstract painting can be thought of as a visual research in which the artist guides the evolution of a complex system of interacting shapes and colors.

3.1.1. The Creative Process

In this context, we pretend to approach artistic creative processes as an organizational work within a complex system of graphical entities.

In this work, the painter's attention is alternatively directed toward the organization of the system as a whole or on a specific entity. A line, a shape, a color, bear a distinct meaning in themselves, but are especially meaningful with reference to each other, generating tension and movement. In music, some notes or chords create tensions that must be resolved so that the piece can end. Similarly in painting, some shapes and colors create tensions that must be resolved by the addition of adequate new colored shapes. A shape requires the addition of a new one, which in turn requires a third one like a counterpoint, in a creative dynamics in which the artist is guided as much by the gestated work as by its own will. The work asserts itself upon the artist as much as the artist asserts himself upon the work. We therefore speak of "emergent painting". Finally, some dynamic equilibrium must be found in order to end the creative process, in which tensions calm down without disappearing. "The composition norm is the entirety constituted by the coordinated functioning of the organs, the autonomous whole endowed with an immobile activity or an active immobility" [Klee 85].

3.1.2. The Aesthetic Meaning

The creative process looks very much like a graphical improvisation in which the painter is constantly evaluating the aesthetic meaning of the gestating work. To this end, he establishes a continuous feedback-loop between creation and evaluation, between emergence and meaning interpretation. Regarding evaluation and interpretation, the painter gets confronted to a double problem, which is specific to abstract art. Due to the transition towards abstraction, painting has abandoned real world references, which hitherto made it easier for a painting to make sense. With abstract painting, the meaning is not given anymore in an explicit manner to the spectator. By contrast, the later has to project his own meaning in the artwork, which he does in relation with its personal experiences. "Finally, the artwork only appears as we think it contains some message" (François Morellet, painter). Furthermore, a graphical entity can only make sense when considered in relation with other graphical entities, replaced in the context of the whole artwork. A global approach is therefore necessary to appreciate abstract painting artworks.

3.1.3. The Artistic Answer

While introducing this new problematics in art, Kandinsky tried to develop a new methodology that would take them into account. The purpose was to make abstract art understandable by elaborating a language of its own, on the model of music which had developed syntactic and grammatical rules. Painting for its part could only elaborate on the basis of heterogeneous composition rules, and Kandinsky proposed to put together a complete scientific theory of painting from the very basic graphical element (the point) up to high-level semantic notions.

In this process, Kandinsky borrowed the methods of experimental psychology in the study of visual perception, since it was meant to understand how the painter could communicate with the spectator on an emotional ground through colored signs and shapes. After isolating systematically the emotional impact of colors [Kandinsky 89] and shapes [Kandinsky 91], he moved on to study the reciprocal effects of graphical elements on one another.

Although scientific, Kandinsky's approach is still based on some particular artistic sensitivity and can not pretend to universality in painting. Although quite complete, it doesn't exhaust the subject, doesn't exclude other conceptions ([Moles 66], [Chacron 80]), and most importantly, doesn't restrain creation within a rigid framework ("Rules are only the necessary ground for a flowering" [Klee 85]). Computer science and DAI now offer new tools for artists to undertake similar researches [Cayla 95] and the *GoC* pretends to be such a tool. It has to be underlined however that it stands apart by closely associating artistic and computer science researches.

3.2. Reactive DAI, as an "Artistic" Science

Regarding the problematics of the interpretation of the activity of a set of agents, reactive DAI is confronted to the same difficulties as the painter evaluating an artwork. In both fields, the difficulty does arise of a signification which is neither fully objective nor fully subjective but lies somewhere in the middle. The signification of an abstract artwork is not in the artwork itself nor in the eye of the viewer, but gets created by the confrontation of both. Similarly, the signification associated with a multi-agent system is not self-contained in the agents, but is not completely subjective either ("Intelligence is in the eye of the observer" [Brooks 91]). Some signification emerges because the system has some properties that are recognized to be important by a human observer. In both cases, some bi-directional flow has to get established between the observer and the studied object, be it an artwork or a multi-agent system.

Trying to understand this convergent approach, it appears that reactive DAI has abandoned the human reference of AI (cf. the Turing test) the same way as abstract painting has abandoned the real world reference of figurative painting. New metaphors such as animal or vegetal societies have become necessary in order to understand and interpret the dynamics of reactive multi-agent systems. It is yet possible to imagine interaction modalities that don't exist in natural systems. That's the philosophy of cellular automata in

Artificial Life and we lack appropriate metaphors to analyze the resulting structures and organizations.

3.3. The *GoC* Revisited

We propose in this section to reexamine the *GoC* in the light of the comparative analysis we developed in the previous section. In particular, we show how we may take advantage of the convergent approaches of abstract painting and reactive DAI. By formalizing the interactions between the two fields, it would make it possible to help both the artist in the conception of artistic animations and the computer scientist in the visualization of complex systems. By combining the two, new paradigms could be explored for complex data visualization.

3.3.1. *GoC* and Emergence of Meaning

With reactive DAI, the artist gets confronted to the difficulties that are peculiar to researches involving auto-organizational and emergent phenomena ([Cariani 90], [Mataric 93]). After experimenting several evolutionary processes to generate and animate the constituent graphical elements of its image, the artist comes to think about the conception of those processes in order to get a particular spatial and temporal dynamics. Those problematics, concerned with form and structure, spatial as well as temporal, are typical of Artificial Life ([Prusinkiewicz 94], [Fleischer et Barr 94]), but are raised in an artistic context, in which they are inescapable. For that reason, researches that have been done in order to set up the foundations of a scientific theory of painting can constitute a potential source of understanding of the structuring processes of a complex system.

We intend to focus more specifically on two problematics, linked to the creation of an artwork by the artist with the help of the system (or by the system with the help the artist):

- To begin with, we propose to study existing links between the growth and interaction mechanisms programmed at the individual level, and the spatial and temporal dynamics observed at the global level. In a long-term view, the purpose is to think about a typology of suck links between individual and global levels. With this perspective, the idea is to consider several architectures proposed in the field of reactive DAI with an artistic perspective, that is by analyzing the visual outputs of the system with respect to previously formalized rules concerning colors, shapes, artistic composition in short. Many examples taken from natural systems such as embryogenesis, ecosystems regulation, and so on may also be explored with the same point of view. In this process, both the knowledge of the artist and methodological tools specific to multi-agent systems are necessary to extract the relevant information in each case. A specific methodology such as "Cassiopeia" [Collinot

et al. 96], which aims at analyzing and designing complex systems based on structural and organizational features, is necessary in order to establish a formal framework in the process of analyzing multi-agent architectures. The painter for his part brings his artistic knowledge which gives a new light to standard problematics.

- Second, it has to be determined how the environment can influence the evolution of those morphogenesis processes. "Environment" is understood in a very wide acceptation since it covers the topology of the physical environment in which agents live, as well as possible perturbations exerted on the system, be they accidental or intentional. In the artistic field, the purpose may be to understand how the artist could interact directly with the system in order to make it evolve toward a satisfying look and dynamics. Or, by inverting the point of view, to understand how the system could adapt to the viewer (and user) in order to satisfy his aesthetic preferences.

3.3.2. *GoC* and Interpretation of Meaning

When he is either painting or experimenting various dynamics with the *GoC*, the painter constantly evaluates on the resulting work. This evaluation appears to be very similar in both activities, set aside the dynamic characteristics of the *GoC*, which makes it a musical as well as graphical composition. In the reactive DAI context, by contrast, we are more inclined to think about the evolution of a whole system in structural, organizational and functional terms [Steels 91].

In his painting activity, the artist is familiar with the evaluation of abstract artworks, which can be considered as complex systems of colored shapes interacting according to ill-defined modalities. However, the artist succeeds in extracting aesthetic signification from this jumble of colors and shapes, by a global treatment of the graphical space. The idea is to associate these notions of aesthetic signification to more classical ones of function, structure or organization. The long-term purpose is to integrate both conceptions in the single framework of the *GoC*, in a wider vision:

- One of the main interests of the typology evoked in the previous section would be to make to enable the recognition of structural or functional characteristics of a complex system by the observation of the system from an artistic point of view. To this end, it has to be studied how aesthetic criteria may be associated to the notions of interaction, structure, organization or even function during the analysis of complex systems. Once again, we postulate that we have a lot to learn from the collaboration with the painter concerning these problematics.

- Conversely, it is very important to understand how data may be transmitted to the observer by the mediation of image. In the *GoC*, several weather data are integrated in the generation of a single image (in fact a succession of images) in order to provide the observer with an immediate perception of complex data. By understanding how images may be interpreted as a structured organization, we may also improve the transmission of complex, interacting data.

3.3.3. Adapting to the User

Based on the research conducted on emergence and interpretation, we propose to make the *GoC* system much easier for the user to manipulate. Indeed, the artist undertaking visual researches or the user trying to find an adequate representation for his data are obliged to adapt to the system in order to obtain satisfying results. Even if they finally succeed in getting these results fitting their aesthetic sensitivity, they have to think in the same terms as the system (parameters, laws, etc.), which is completely unnatural. Consequently, the purpose is to ban those notions in order to establish a direct interaction between the system and the spectator. There are naturally several requirements that the system should satisfy to be able to answer adequately to the user's actions.

On the first hand, the system must be able to get knowledge about what it is currently doing, and must have some control over its evolution. On the other hand, it must be able to interpret and learn what the user is wanting it to do, and to spontaneously evolve towards what it "thinks" the user would like it to be.

This is only possible if we know how to relate the local level (the system level) and the global level (the user level) and vice versa. We thus advocate a formalizing work on this issue, which we pretend would be most profitable in the context of an interdisciplinary research associating artists with computer scientists.

4. Conclusion

When conducting this comparative analysis between abstract painting and reactive DAI, we did not advocate a fusion of the two fields. Art and science have slowly diverged, since the XVIIth century when they were integrated in culture until today where indifference is the most common attitude. This does not mean however that the two may not communicate. We showed with the *Garden of Chances* that interactions between art and science were potentially very fertile, for both communities. Indeed, while DAI supplies the artist with tools to experiment with novel painting modalities, the artist brings DAI completely novel prospects in the study of complex systems and for the visualization of complex data.

Thus, we described with the *Garden of Chances* a unifying framework allowing one to see complex systems from both structural and functional viewpoints, but also from an aesthetic viewpoint, each of them shedding a new light on each other, thereby constituting a fertile source of inspiration.

5. Bibliography

[Brooks 91] BROOKS R. A., "Intelligence Without Reason", in Proceedings of IJCAI'91, Sydney, Morgan-Kaufmann, pp. 569-595, 1991.

[Cariani 90] CARIANI P., "Emergence and Artificial Life", in *Artificial Life II*, , Ed. C. Langton, Addison-Wesley, London, 1990.

[Cayla 95] CAYLA E., "TAPIS-BULLES1 - Prototype d'une approche multi-agents des formes et des couleurs", in 3èmes Journées Francophones IAD & SMA, Chambéry-St Badolph, pp. 375-386, 1995.

[Chacron 80] CHACRON J., *Esthétique mathématique - Théorie de la peinture*, Editions Scientifiques de l'Art, Amiens, 1980.

[Cohen 79] COHEN H., "What is an Image", in Proceedings of IJCAI'79, Tokyo, Morgan-Kaufmann, pp. 1028-1057, 1979.

[Cohen 88] COHEN H., "How to Draw Three People in a Botanical Garden", in Proceedings of AAAI'88, St Paul, pp. 846-855, 1988.

[Collinot et al. 96] COLLINOT A., DROGOUL A. et BENHAMOU P., "Agent Oriented Design of a Soccer Robot Team", International Conference on Multi-Agent Systems, Japan, December 1996.

[Drogoul 93] DROGOUL A., De la simulation multi-agents à la résolution collective de problèmes: une étude de l'émergence de structures d'organisation dans les systèmes multi-agents, Thèse de Doctorat, Université Paris VI, 1993.

[Ferber 95] FERBER J., *Les systèmes Multi-agents*, Interéditions, Paris, 1995.

[Fleischer et Barr 94] FLEISCHER K. et BARR A. H., "A Simulation Testbed for the Study of MultiCellular Development: The Multiple Mechanisms of Morphogenesis", in *Artificial Life III*, Addison-Wesley, London, 1994.

[Gips et Stiny 75] GIPS J. et STINY G., "Artificial Intelligence and Aesthetics", in Advance Papers of IJCAI'75, Tbilisi, Morgan-Kaufmann, pp. 907-911, 1975.

[Kandinsky 89] KANDINSKY W., *Du spirituel dans l'art et dans la peinture en particulier*, Gallimard, Paris, 1989.

[Kandinsky 91] KANDINSKY W., *Point et ligne sur plan - Contribution à l'analyse des éléments de la peinture*, Gallimard, Paris, 1991.

[Klee 77] KLEE P., *Histoire naturelle infinie - Ecrits sur l'art II*, Dessain et Tolra, Paris, 1977.

[Klee 85] KLEE P., *Théorie de l'art moderne*, Denoël, Paris, 1985.

[Leavitt 1976] LEAVITT R. ed., *Artist and Computer*, Harmony Books, New York, 1976.

[Mataric 93] MATARIC M. J., "Designing Emergent Behaviors: From Local Interactions to Collective Intelligence", in *From Animals to Animats II*, MIT Press, Cambridge, pp. 432- 441, 1993.

[Minsky 93] MINSKY M., "The Future Merging of Science, Art and Psychology", Applied Artificial Intelligence, Vol. 7, No 1, 1993, pp. 87-108, January-March.

[Moles 66] MOLES A. A., *Information Theory and Esthetic Perception*, University of Illinois Press, Urbana, 1966.

[Prusinkiewicz 94] PRUSINKIEWICZ P., "Visual Models of Morphogenesis", in Artificial Life, Volume I, Nb 1/2, MIT Press, pp. 61-74, Fall 1993/Winter 1994.

[Steels 91] STEELS L., "Towards a Theory of Emergent Functionality", in From Animals to Animats, MIT Press, Cambridge, 1991.

[Todd et Latham 92] TODD S. et LATHAM W., "Artificial Life or Surreal Art?", in *Towards a Practice of Autonomous Systems*, Ed. F.J. Varela et P. Bourgine, MIT Press, Cambridge, PP. 504-513, 1992.

An Adaptive Approach for Reactive Actor Design

Daria E. Bergen[*]
The Naval Research Laboratory
bergen@enews.nrl.navy.mil

James K. Hahn[†]
The George Washington University
hahn@seas.gwu.edu

Peter Bock[†]
The George Washington University
pbock@seas.gwu.edu

Abstract

To address the complex and dynamic conditions of a virtual environment, computer animation researchers are applying methods similar to the ones used in artificial life to create reactive actors. A reactive actor is a control entity whose behavior is based on the sensory information it receives from the environment. The system presented within this paper, RAVE (Reactive Actors in Virtual Environments), demonstrates the successful use of a reinforcement learning model to automatically generate controllers for typical 2D navigational tasks. This is an improvement to existing methods because it requires no programming, can be used for a variety of tasks, and the control algorithms adapt during run-time. Collective Learning Systems (CLS) theory is integrated with a hierarchical controller to create control modules that quickly converge on optimal navigational strategies. Five different worlds are created to train and evaluate the actors. Performance metrics and results are presented for three different navigational tasks: obstacle avoidance (*avoid*), heading towards a goal object (*goto*), and moving away from a threat (*retreat*).

CR Categories: G.3 [Probability and Statistics]: Probabilistic Algorithms; I.2.6 [Artificial Intelligence]: Learning; I.3.7 [Computer Graphics]: Three-Dimensional Graphics and Realism - Animation, Virtual Reality.

Additional Keyword: Behavioral Modeling, Collective Behavior, Virtual Actors, Learning Automaton.

1.0   Introduction

Designing motion control algorithms for characters within virtual environments presents new challenges for computer animation researchers. A virtual environment differs from a classical frame based animation system mainly in its non-deterministic nature. Kinematic methods, such as key framing, are not effective due to the unpredictable movement of the user. Unlike creating a one minute motion sequence for a computer generated scene, the motion generated for a virtual environment must be valid for an unspecified length of time. To address these complex and dynamic conditions, actors should respond to events within the environment as they occur and not simply follow pre-specified scripts.

A *reactive actor* is a control entity that autonomously chooses its behavior based on information it receives from the environment and its internal state. Within the field of computer animation, there has long been an interest in the creation of autonomous actors (Magnenat-Thalmann & Thalmann, 1991; Zeltzer, 1985), and advancements in virtual environment technology makes improvement to methods for virtual actor creation and control both timely and crucial.

The objective of this work is to develop an adaptive control technique to improve the creation and run-time control of reactive actors. The system presented within this paper, RAVE (Reactive Actors in Virtual Environments), demonstrates the successful use of a reinforcement learning model to automatically generate controllers for typical 2D navigational tasks. Collective Learning Systems (CLS) theory is integrated with a hierarchical controller to create control modules that quickly converge on optimal navigational strategies. This model can also be used for adaptation, during run-time, to cope with changing environment conditions. In reactive actor design, adaptation has previously been explored only as a pre-processing step. This work demonstrates why learning, during run-time, is a useful and necessary component.

2.0   Problem Domain

Traditionally, a combination of hierarchical control and procedural methods have been used in reactive actor design (Blumberg & Galyean, 1995; Perlin & Goldberg, 1996; Tu & Terzopoulos, 1994; Zeltzer, 1985). Hierarchical approaches are chosen because they lead to reusable, extendible, and responsive control models. A generic hierarchical model is presented in Figure 1. The left column lists the associated level of control abstraction (Zeltzer, 1985), and the right enumerates the input to each subsystem. In brief, sensors receive world information and possibly task level commands from the animator. The reasoning engine interprets the sensory information and selects an appropriate task from the actor's motion repertoire. The functional control units invoke procedural control units to achieve their goals. Finally, the procedural control units update effectors which cause some attribute(s) of the actor to change.

Researchers in the fields of Artificial Life (Langton, 1994) and Adaptive Behavior (Maes, 1992) are also interested in designing autonomous beings. There are many similarities between the design of autonomous agents and the design of autonomous actors, particularly in the low-level architectural design. At a high level, however, the focus is less similar. Within the field of computer animation, the essence is the story. Animators are interested in generating characters that are expressive and have consistent personalities. While a certain level of autonomy is desired, the animator must also be able to direct the actor at various levels and during different stages of design.

Given this as the high level research goal, one can identify at least six major research areas in reactive actor design. Finding the balance between *autonomy* and *directability* is the first essential component. Questions concerning when, where, and how much autonomy is necessary and when, where, and how an animator will direct an autonomous actor remain to be answered (Blumberg & Galyean, 1995). Methods for creating *expressive motion*

---

[*] The Naval Research Laboratory, 4555 Overlook Ave. SW, Code 5707, Washington, DC 20375
[†] The George Washington University, Department of EE&CS, 801 22nd Street NW, Washington, DC 20052

(Perlin, 1995) are still being explored. The actor should exhibit a consistent personality and the animator should be able to influence its personality directly and indirectly. *Task decomposition* is another important area. Determining exactly how an animator breaks down a complex task into primitive modules remains to be solved. *Behavior arbitration* involves combining the primitive tasks to create complex behavior. Issues in behavior selection, smooth transitioning between tasks, and methods for avoiding "dithering" (Blumberg, 1994) must be addressed. Finally, the exact roles of *learning and evolutionary methods* within the design of the control units must be identified. Are they mutually exclusive design decisions, or can they compliment each other in the creation and control phases?

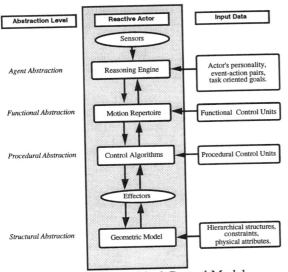

Figure 1: Hierarchical Control Model

A subset of these research problems is addressed within this work. A bottom-up approach is taken, and the individual control units within the actor's motion repertoire are the focus of this paper. Specifically, the problem of designing and controlling a motion repertoire for obstacle avoidance and 2D navigation is investigated. Issues concerning the evaluation of motion characteristics and the role of learning in control module creation are examined.

3.0 Related Work

Motion repertoires for navigational tasks have been defined procedurally with standard program languages (Reynolds, 1987; Sun & Green, 1993; Tu & Terzopoulos, 1994) and with dataflow networks (Wilhelms & Skinner, 1990). Programming expertise is required when a procedural method is used and creating algorithmic descriptions for each primitive task can be tedious and time consuming. Reynolds's seminal work in behavioral modeling (Reynolds, 1987) was initially presented as a means of reducing the tedium associated with scripting the paths of many actors. This general model has been modified slightly over time but remains the standard method for obstacle avoidance and low-level navigation.

Evolutionary techniques and standard search methods have been used to automatically generate task level modules for articulated figure motion (Gritz & Hahn, 1995; Ngo & Marks, 1993; Sims, 1994; van de Panne & Fuime, 1993). The results achieved are impressive and the motion generated

with these models is believable and enjoyable to watch. However, the adaptation of the control modules has strictly been applied as a preprocessing step. Researchers have not explored issues related to run-time adaptation. Evolutionary methods are useful for globally exploring large search spaces but not for a localize search. Since animators also desire a variety in behavior, evolutionary techniques are ideal for exploring the entire controller space and finding a specific style of motion. They fail to offer assistance, however, when minor modifications to a control algorithm are needed. Alternative methods must be used when incremental improvements or run-time adaptation is desired.

The system presented within this paper uses an adaptive machine learning methodology to automatically generate functional control units for typical 2D navigational tasks. This is an enhancement to existing methods used for navigation because it requires no programming, can be used for a variety of tasks, and the control algorithms adapt during run-time. The method has been used for obstacle avoidance, movement towards a goal, and movement away from a threat.

4.0 RAVE Architecture

An overview of the RAVE architecture is presented in Figure 2. As with other reactive systems, sensory information is extracted from the world, passed to the actor, and used to determine the actor's behavior. The uniqueness of RAVE lies in the design of the motion critic sub-system and the addition of an adaptive learning module.

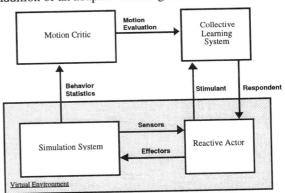

Figure 2: RAVE Architecture

4.1 Sensors and Effectors

Within the literature, two alternative approaches to synthetic vision have been explored; object (or symbolic) based (Reynolds, 1988) and image based (Horswill, 1992) vision models have both been used. RAVE uses a symbolic vision sensor. This was chosen over an image based approach for a number of reasons. One advantage is that exact information can be conveyed to the actor; algorithms for determining object type, velocity, distance, and color are not necessary. Computing symbolic features also requires little additional overhead since many object attributes are already kept in a database for rendering purposes. Finally, a symbolic approach can be easily extended. Additional features can be incorporated quickly by appending attributes to the sensory input stream.

Within this work, three vision channels provide information about the closest object in the left, middle, and right field of view (FOV); object type, distance, and direction information are provided. Parameters for the vision module include the angle for each field of view triangle (α, β, and ψ) and the length of the vision range (v). See Figure 3.

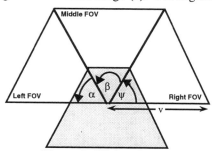

Figure 3: Vision Sensor

Moving towards a goal or away from a threat requires additional information. The bearing sensor is used to receive azimuth and distance information about a goal or threat object. The user can vary the desired range (d) and the sensing range (r). The desired range will determine how close to a goal or how far from a threat the actor should be. The sensing range determines at what range the actor can differentiate distances. For example, the bearing sensor in Figure 4 would return a value of "NW and beyond sensing range".

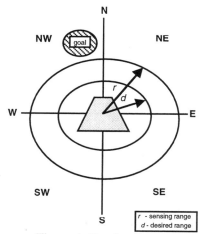

Figure 4: Bearing Sensor

An actor is represented with a position vector (**p**) and an azimuth (θ). Each actor travels at a constant speed in the direction of its heading vector (**h**). The effector modifies the heading vector by requesting a change in θ. This turns the actor to the left or to the right.

4.2 Motion Critic

The motion critic receives behavioral statistics from the simulation system and assesses the quality of the motion. The criteria used to evaluate the motion may remain constant or vary over time. The assessment is sent to the Collective Learning Systems (CLS) as an evaluation.

Computing an evaluation requires assigning a quantitative measurement to the motion sequence. This is not always straightforward task. For example, one valid measurement for obstacle avoidance would be to count the number of collisions that occur. The actor would receive a positive evaluation (reward) for a small number of collisions and a negative evaluation (punishment) for a large number of collisions. Using this as the only criterion, however, could create an actor that moves in a circular pattern. This may or may not be the behavior the designer had in mind. An

evaluation that combines the number of collisions and the distance traveled would create different results. Examples of various evaluation policies are presented within §5.5. Varying the evaluation policy is one method of controlling the resulting motion.

4.3 Collective Learning System

Collective Learning System Theory (Bock, 1993) is an adaptive machine learning methodology inspired by learning automata theory (Narendra & Thathachar, 1974; Samuel, 1959; Tsetlin, 1962) and related to classical automata theory and statistical analysis. A collective learning automaton (CLA) is a finite state machine that modifies its internal structure, learning the appropriate state transitions, as a result of its interaction with the environment. An overview of a collective learning automaton is presented in Figure 5.

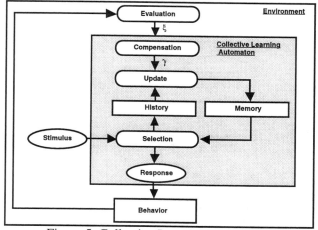

Figure 5: Collective Learning Automaton

The CLA receives evaluations from the environment and adjusts its behavior as a function of the rewards and punishments it receives. The environment does not evaluate the CLA after every interaction; a sequence of stimulus-response pairs are saved in a history structure (η) and evaluated together at the end of a stage. The length of a stage is determined by a system parameter, collection length (l). The evaluation (ξ) is received by the compensation function which provides a method for the CLA to adjusts its view of the evaluation. The compensation function converts ξ into a compensated value (γ) that is used by the update process. The update process uses γ to either increase or decrease the probability of a stimulus-response pair from happening again.

The selection process occurs at every timestep. The stimulus received from the environment is used to access the CLA's state transition matrix (Figure 6). This matrix consists of column vectors of all possible stimuli $<\phi_1, \phi_2, ..., \phi_n>$ and associated with each stimulus is a tuple of valid responses $<\omega_1, \omega_2, ..., \omega_m>$. A weight ($w_{ij}$) is stored with each stimulus-response pair. This weight is used by the selection process to determine the approach response for a given stimulus.

CLS theory was chosen for this application because it converges quickly, and updates to memory can be performed in real-time. This model also gives the animator the ability to make small modifications to the behavior of the actor; he can control the motion by modifying the evaluation function or by adjusting the learning parameters. Finally, another appealing aspect of this model is that once the controller has converged, rules which were learned can be extracted if desired.

Stimulus (Φ)

Response (Ω)	ϕ_1	ϕ_2	$\cdots$	ϕ_n
ω_1	w_{11}	w_{12}	$\cdots$	w_{1n}
ω_2	w_{21}	w_{22}	$\cdots$	w_{2n}
$\vdots$	$\vdots$	$\vdots$	$\ddots$	$\vdots$
ω_m	w_{m1}	w_{m2}	$\cdots$	w_{mn}

Figure 6: State Transition Matrix (STM)

4.4 Run-time Loop

At every timestep, the objects within the actor's vision field are determined and used to select a response. The stimuli-response pair is saved in a history file and processed at the end of the stage. The response is used to update the actor's position and heading. Collision detection is performed at the new location to ensure the move is valid. If the response results in a collision, forward motion is prevented, and the actor is placed at its previous location. At the end of the stage, the motion sequence is evaluated, compensated, and subsequently used to update the actor's STM. The following is pseudo-code of the run-time loop for a learning reactive actor:

```
while simulation is running do
    for k = 1 to collection length do
        draw world;
        φᵢ = process input stimuli;
        ωⱼ = select response(φᵢ);
        save stimuli-response(φᵢ,ωⱼ,ηₖ);
        p' = update position(ωⱼ);
        check for collisions;
        if (a collision occurred) p' = p;
        calculate behavior statistics;
    endfor
    ξ = evaluate motion for stage;
    γ = compensate evaluation(ξ);
    update STM (γ,η);
endwhile
```

4.5 Performance Metrics

In order to measure the performance of the control modules, a number of metrics were designed to monitor the actor's ability to learn. These metrics are similar to the evaluation functions used by the motion critic. They are scaled to the range of [0,100] with 100 representing perfect performance. The following "scores" are used to verify RAVE's ability to automatically generate three navigational tasks: obstacle avoidance (*avoid*), heading towards a goal object (*goto*), and moving away from a threat (*retreat*).

During the run of each experiment, the statistics collected depend on the navigational task being learned. For the *avoid* task, the minimize-collisions (S_{minc}) and the maximize-distance (S_{maxd}) scores are collected. For the *goto*

task, the time-in-goal-region score (S_{in}) determines how long the actor stays within the desired goal region. Conversely, the time-outside-threat-region score (S_{out}) indicates how well the actor is staying away from a threat. The experiments are subdivided into contests which last for 1800 timesteps (see §6.0). The scores for each contest are computed as follows:

$$S_{minc} = 100\left[1 - \frac{C_c}{C_{cmax}}\right]$$

$$S_{maxd} = 100\left[\frac{D_c}{D_{cmax}}\right]$$

$$S_{in} = 100\left[\frac{T_{in}}{TS_c - TT}\right]$$

$$S_{out} = 100 - S_{in}$$

where C_c is the number of collisions that occurred during the contest; C_{cmax} is the maximum number of collisions that can occur; D_c is the distance traveled during the contest; D_{cmax} is the maximum distance an actor can travel during a contest; T_{in} is the number of timesteps the actor stays within the desired range; TS_c is the number of timesteps per contest; and TT is the travel time, the minimum time needed to travel to a goal or away from a threat region. Travel time is incorporated into the equation to account for the actors being placed at random locations at the beginning of each contest.

5.0 Technical Approach

Five different worlds were created for training the actors. Each world is 100x100 units and is bounded by walls. The four worlds used to train the actors for the *avoid* task are shown in Figure 7.

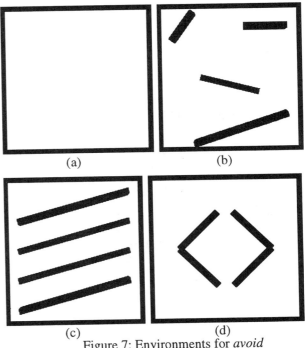

(a) (b)

(c) (d)

Figure 7: Environments for *avoid*
(a) Open Field, (b) Hidden Corners,
(c) Racing Lanes, (d) Courtyard

The Open Field world contains no obstacles within its boundaries. The Hidden Corners, Racing Lanes, and

Courtyard worlds have four internal wall obstacles. The angles and spacing between the walls were varied to create worlds with different characteristics. The Hidden Corners world contains wall obstacles oriented at angles of 53°, 0°, 14°, and 17°. Two dead-end passageways were created to observe how actors handled this situation. The Racing Lanes world was created to see whether a world with symmetry was easier to navigate. Each wall within this world is oriented at 14°. Finally, the Courtyard world was created to test the actor's ability to move through openings between walls. The walls are oriented at 45° angles, and the openings are 7 units wide.

The *goto* and *retreat* tasks used the same world (Figure 8). Five goals or threats were placed in the world, and the target object was changed every 5 contests. The hemispheres represent possible goals or threats within the world. Only one object was active at any given time. The desired range to stay next to the goal or away from the threat is depicted as a circle surround the object.

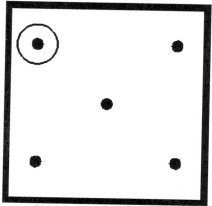

Figure 8: Environment for
goto & retreat

5.1 Sensor Implementation

The actors are one unit long, and each has a total vision field of 180°. The left, middle, and right FOVs were set to equal angles of 60°. For the *avoid* task, the vision range was 20 units; and for the *goto* and *retreat* tasks it was 10 units in length. Initial results were obtained with the actors traveling at a constant speed of 10 units per second.

In order to determine which objects are within the actor's FOV, objects are first culled against the bounding rectangle of the actor's entire vision field. Axis-aligned bounding boxes are computed for all objects and used for an initial overlap test. Exact intersection testing is needed only if these areas overlap. Since an interactive update rate is necessary, an exact edge-to-edge intersection test with the object's polygons is not performed; geometric footprints are used to simplify the calculation. Footprints are created by projecting the bounding rectangle onto the ground plane. The edges of the footprint are then checked against the field of view triangle.

5.2 Stimulus-Response

At the beginning of each timestep a stimulant key is created to access either the vision or bearing STM. The vision sensor returns which objects, if any, are within the actor's left, middle, and right FOV. The object type and distance from the actor are used to create an index to the actor's vision STM. Objects within the world are classified

into six categories; a 3-bit identifier is used as an object ID. The distance to the object is quantized into four values: very close, close, far, and very far. Distance is encoded with 2-bits. The object and distance encoding are listed in Table 1.

Object		
	Space (SPA)	000
	Obstacle Static (OBS)	001
	Obstacle Moving Towards (OBT)	010
	Obstacle Moving Away (OBA)	011
	Goal Static (GOS)	100
	Threat Static (THS)	101
Distance	Very Close	00
	Close	01
	Far	10
	Very Far	11

Table 1: Object and Distance Encoding

The distance range is quantized in a linear manner and the distance bits (dbits) are set as follows:

$$dbits = \begin{cases} 00 & \text{if } distance \leq \frac{1}{4}v \\ 01 & \text{if } \frac{1}{4}v < distance \leq \frac{1}{2}v \\ 10 & \text{if } \frac{1}{2}v < distance \leq \frac{3}{4}v \\ 11 & \text{otherwise} \end{cases}$$

where *distance* is the distance from the actor to the object and v is the length of the vision range. The object ID and distance code for the left, middle, and right FOV are concatenated to form a 15-bits key. The stimulant is used to retrieve the respondent tuple from the vision STM (Figure 9).

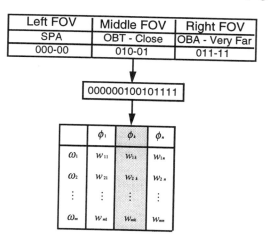

Figure 9: Sensors to STM Index

The stimulant for the bearing STM is calculated in a similar manner. The bearing sensor returns the azimuth and distance from the goal or threat object. The azimuth is quantized into eight values: N, NW, W, SW, S, SE, E, and NE. This value is encoded with a 4-bit identifier. The distance from the object is again quantized and encoded with 2-bits. The distance encoding is different for the bearing sensor:

$$dbits = \begin{cases} 00 \text{ if } distance \leq d \\ 01 \text{ if } d < distance \leq \dfrac{d+r}{2} \\ 10 \text{ if } \dfrac{d+r}{2} < distance \leq r \\ 11 \text{ otherwise} \end{cases}$$

where *distance* is the distance from the actor to the goal or threat; d is the desire range; and r is the sensing range. The azimuth and distance code are concatenated to form a 6-bit stimulant key.

The response for both STMs consists of a heading adjustment in the range of [+45°, -45°]. For the result presented within this paper the response range, $\Phi = \{+45°, +30°, +20°, +10°, 0°, -10°, -20° -30°, -45°\}$.

5.3 Evaluation and Compensation

At the end of every stage, actors receive an evaluation, ξ, in the range of [-1,1]. The actors are evaluated when a collision occurs and after every 20 timesteps. With this parameter setting, actors receive an evaluation approximately every second, assuming 20 frames per second (fps).

To train the actors for the *avoid* task, and to create behavior which minimizes the number of collisions, the evaluation ξ_{minc} is computed as follows:

$$\xi_{minc} = \begin{cases} \dfrac{TS_s}{l} \text{ if } C_s = 0 \\ -1 \text{ otherwise} \end{cases}$$

where TS_s is the number of timesteps without a collision and l is the collection length. As mentioned previously, one way of avoiding collisions is to travel in a circle. This is usually not the desired behavior, so an evaluation function was created to encourage straight movement. The evaluation function used to maximize distance traveled, (ξ_{maxd}), is computed as follows:

$$\xi_{maxd} = \begin{cases} \dfrac{D_s}{D_{smax}} \text{ if } D_s \geq \dfrac{3}{4} D_{smax} \\ -\dfrac{D_{smax} - D_s}{D_{smax}} \text{ otherwise} \end{cases}$$

where D_s is the distance traveled during the stage and D_{smax} is the maximum distance the actor can travel, in a straight line, during the stage.

A number of policies can be used to compute the final evaluation (ξ). Informal experiments where the average of ξ_{minc} and ξ_{maxd} was used, lead to poor performance. Stages where the actor avoided all obstacles were not rewarded appropriately when the distance criteria was not met. Conversely, the actor was rewarded for mediocre collision avoidance when it was able to travel a great distance, while bumping into things. A dynamic evaluation function was ultimately used; the actor was trained to first avoid obstacles and then encouraged to maximize its distance traveled. The final evaluation function used for the *avoid* task is:

$$\xi = \begin{cases} \xi_{minc} \text{ if } \xi_{minc} < 1 \\ \xi_{maxd} \text{ otherwise} \end{cases}$$

For the *goto* task, in order to move towards a goal region, the actor must minimize its distance from the goal object. The evaluation function used to decrease the distance from the goal (ξ_{dd}) is:

$$\xi_{dd} = \begin{cases} \dfrac{\Delta D_{towards}}{D_{smax}} \text{ if } D_{se} > r \\ 1 \text{ otherwise} \end{cases}$$

where $\Delta D_{towards} = D_{ss} - D_{se}$; D_{ss} is the distance from the goal at the start of the stage; and D_{se} is the distance from the goal at the end of the stage. For this task, the actor was trained to first avoid obstacles and then to decrease its distance from the goal until it was inside the goal region. Once inside the goal region, the actor should minimize its change in distance from the goal. This evaluation ($\xi_{min\Delta d}$) encourages the actor to circle the goal:

$$\xi_{min\Delta d} = 1 - 2\left[\frac{\Delta D}{D_{smax}}\right]$$

where $\Delta D = |D_{ss} - D_{se}|$. The final evaluation function used for the *goto* task is:

$$\xi = \begin{cases} \xi_{minc} \text{ if } \xi_{minc} < 1 \\ \xi_{dd} \text{ if } D_{se} \geq r \\ \xi_{min\Delta d} \text{ if } \xi_{min\Delta d} < 1 \\ \xi_{maxd} \text{ otherwise} \end{cases}$$

Finally, for the *retreat* task, the objective is to train the actors to stay away from the threatening object. The evaluation for this task (ξ_{id}) encourages the actor to increase the distance between itself and the threat object.

$$\xi_{id} = \begin{cases} \dfrac{\Delta D_{away}}{D_{smax}} \text{ if } D_{se} < r \\ 1 \text{ otherwise} \end{cases}$$

where $\Delta D_{away} = D_{se} - D_{ss}$. The dynamic evaluation function used for *retreat* trains the actor to first avoid collisions, then maximize its distance from the threat, and once outside the threat region, maximize its distance traveled. The final evaluation function used for the *goto* task is as follows:

$$\xi = \begin{cases} \xi_{minc} \text{ if } \xi_{minc} < 1 \\ \xi_{id} \text{ if } D_{se} < r \\ \xi_{maxd} \text{ otherwise} \end{cases}$$

For all initial experiments $\gamma = \xi$; evaluations were used directly in the update function. Investigating the affects of the compensation function on the "personality" of the actor is an area that will be explored in future work.

5.4 Update Function

The compensation value (γ) is applied to the weights of the stimulus-response pairs within the history structure (η). The update function increases or decreases the strength of the stimulus-response pair in the actor's vision or bearing STM. Again, a number a policies can be used. An elementary update function simply adds γ to the initial weight:

$$w'_{ij} = \max(\gamma + w_{ij}, w_c) \text{ if } \gamma \geq 0$$

$$w'_{ij} = \min(\gamma + w_{ij}, w_f) \text{ otherwise}$$

where w_{ij} is the weight associated with stimulus i and response j; w_c is the weight ceiling; and w_f is the weight floor. This update policy works well when the environment is static or changes very little. During informal experimentation, it was found that this method is not appropriate for this application. The actor could learn a sub-optimal navigational strategies early in the match, and when it was in a region of the world where the strategy was not appropriate (i.e. a sharper turn was necessary), it would need to "unlearned" erroneous information. Discovery and extinction factors are used within the update function to adjust for situations like this. When using the discovery and extinction values, the increase or decrease in weight is proportional to the distance from the weight floor or ceiling. With this policy, sub-optimal strategies quickly lose their strength and new responses will be tried. The update policy used for this work is as follows:

$$w'_{ij} = \delta(w_c - w_{ij})(\gamma + w_{ij}) \text{ if } \gamma \geq 0$$

$$w'_{ij} = \varepsilon(w_{ij} - w_f)(\gamma + w_{ij}) \text{ otherwise}$$

where δ is the discovery factor and ε is the extinction factor.

5.5 Selection Function

The selection policy used is MTDS/RA [Maximum Thresholded Deterministic Selection with Random Arbitration] (Bock, 1993). The bounded weights within the respondent tuple are mapped to pseudo-probabilities and the respondent with the largest probability, within a threshold value, is selected. If two or more respondents fall within the selection range, a respondent within the range is randomly picked.

5.6 Behavior Arbitration

For the *goto* and *retreat* tasks, a heuristic is used to determine how to alternate between collision avoidance using the vision STM and directed movement using the bearing STM. If an object is within the actor's vision field, a pending collision is assumed, and the vision STM is used to circumvent the collision. If no pending collisions are identified, the bearing STM is used to provide the actor with information concerning the goal or threat object. Table 2 provides a summary of the various environment parameters used in this work.

6.0 Results

A total of twelve experiments were run to test the performance of RAVE. Scores (§4.5) were computed at the end of every contest and a total of 50 contests were executed for each experiment. To provide them with an opportunity to learn a variety of navigational strategies, the actors were randomly placed at a new position and heading at the beginning of every contest.

Size of World	100x100 units
Number of Actors	1 to 5
Number of Wall Obstacles	4 to 8
Number of [Goals | Threats]	5
Switch [Goal | Threat]	after 5 contests
Speed of Actor	10 units per sec
Vision Range (v)	10 or 20 units
Left FOV Angle (α)	60°
Right FOV Angle (β)	60°
Middle FOV Angle (ψ)	60°
Sensing Range (r)	30 units
Desired Range (d)	10 units

Table 2: Environment Conditions

To validate the *avoid* task, actors were trained in the four worlds described in §5.0. One set of experiments was run with only one actor and another set with a total of five actors in the world. All actors were adaptive, and each had its own memory structure. Figure 10 demonstrates typical navigational strategies which were learned; the path the actor took through the environment is traced, and the S represents the start of the path. Actors were able to converge to an optimal strategy quickly, and the graphs in Figure 12 demonstrate near perfect collision avoidance occurring as early as contest number 5 (after 9000 timesteps). It took a longer period of time to learn to navigate the worlds with internal wall obstacles. The periodic decline in performance, shown in Figure 12b, represents contests where the actor was placed at a new location and needed to learn how to navigate that particular area of the world.

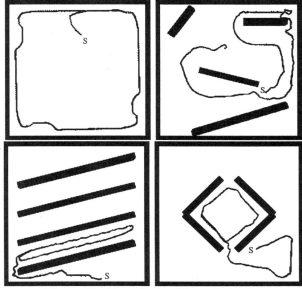

Figure 10: Obstacle Avoidance Behavior

For the *goto* task, one world was used. Again, one experiment was run with only one actor and another with five actors in total. Figure 11a provides an example of a typical goto strategy which was learned. The graphs in Figure 13 plots the performance metrics for this task. Figure 13a was an experiment performed with only one actor within the world, and Figure 13b demonstrates the results when five actors were within the world. Remaining within the desired range to the goal is more difficult when other actors are present. Collision avoidance takes precedence over staying within the desired range, and the lower scores in the S_{in} score represent times when the actor needed to stay outside the region to avoid a collision.

The world used to verify the *retreat* task was similar, except that the goal objects are now treated as threats. Again, one experiment was run with only one actor and another with five actors. A screen shot of a path taken when retreating from a threat is shown in Figure 11b, and the performance metrics are presented in Figure 14. Again, the actors were trained to avoid collisions, leave the threatening area, and once outside the range of the threat, maximum their distance traveled.

Stage	20 Timestep
Contest	90 Stages
Match	50 Contests

Table 3: Experiment Parameters

Experiments were run on a SGI Indigo[2] Extreme with a 150Mhz R4000 MIPS RISC processor and 64MB of RAM. RAVE can be run interactively or in batch mode. When run interactively, with a 200x200 display window, 72 fps can be achieved while the actors are learning. A contest takes approximately 25 seconds, and a match can be completed within 21 minutes. In batch mode, a contest takes 5 seconds, and a match is finished in 4 minutes.

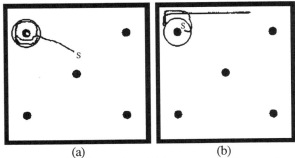

| (a) | (b) |

Figure 11: Examples of (a) *goto* and (b) *retreat*

7.0   Conclusions

This adaptive methodology for reactive actor design and control can be used to aid in the building and controlling of reactive actors. The robustness of functional control units is improved when an adaptive approach is used, because the actors can modify their behavior during run-time. The usefulness of this approach was demonstrated with three different navigational tasks: *avoid*, *goto*, and *retreat*. Evaluation functions for assessing the quality of the motion and performance metrics for monitoring the actor's motions were designed.

8.0   Future Work

RAVE will be extended to include additional tasks within the motion repertoire. It is hoped that a comprehensive set of navigational tasks can be designed so that all types of navigational movement can be easily created. Additional experiments will be performed to explore the robustness of RAVE. The design of a complexity metric which assigns a numeric value to the difficulty of navigating through a specific virtual world would provide a quantitative measurement for comparing reactive models. Finally, additional experiments are needed to determine how various evaluation functions and learning parameters affect the characteristics of the resulting motion.

Acknowledgments

This work was funded in part by the Tactical Electronic Warfare Division (TEWD) of the Naval Research Laboratory and by the Office of Naval Research.

References

Blumberg, B. (1994). Action-Selection in Hamsterdam: Lessons from Ethology. In J.-A. Meyer, H. L. Roitblat, & S. Wilson W. (Eds.), From Animals to Animats: Proceedings of the Third International Conference on Simulation of Adaptive Behàvior (SAB94) Cambridge, MA: MIT Press.

Blumberg, B. M., & Galyean, T. A. (1995). Multi-Level Direction of Autonomous Creatures for Real-Time Virtual Environments. SIGGRAPH'95, 47-54.

Bock, P. (1993). The Emergence of Artificial Cognition: An Introduction to Collective Learning. River Edge, NJ: World Scientific.

Gritz, L., & Hahn, J. K. (1995). Genetic Programming for Articulated Figure Motion. Journal of Visualization and Computer Animation, 6, 129-142.

Horswill, I. (1992). A simple, cheap, and robust visual navigation system. In J. A. Meyer, H. L. Roitblat, & S. Wilson W. (Eds.), From Animals to Animats 2: Proceedings of the Second International Conference on Simulation of Adaptive Behavior (SAB92) (pp. 129-136). Cambridge, MA: MIT Press.

Langton, C. G. (Ed.). (1994). Artificial Life IV: Proceedings of the Workshop on Artificial Life. Cambridge, MA: MIT Press.

Maes, P. (1992). Behavior-Based Artificial Intelligence. In J. A. Meyer, H. L. Roitblat, & S. W. Wilson (Eds.), From Animals to Animats 2: Proceedings of the Second International Conference on Simulation of Adaptive Behavior (SAB92) (pp. 2-10). Cambridge, MA: MIT Press.

Magnenat-Thalmann, N., & Thalmann, D. (1991). Synthetic Actors in Computer-Generated 3D Films. New York: Springer-Verlag.

Narendra, K. S., & Thathachar, M. A. L. (1974). Learning Automata - A Survey. IEEE Transactions on Systems, Man, and Cybernetics, 14, 323-334.

Ngo, J. T., & Marks, J. (1993). Spacetime Constraints Revisited. SIGGRAPH'93, 343-350.

Perlin, K. (1995). Real Time Responsive Animation with Personality. IEEE Transactions on Visualization and Computer Graphics, 1(1).

Perlin, K., & Goldberg, A. (1996). Improv: A System for Scripting Interactive Actors in Virtual Worlds. SIGGRAPH96, 205-216.

Reynolds, C. W. (1987). Flocks, Herds, and Schools: A Distributed Behavioral Model. SIGGRAPH'87, 25-34.

Reynolds, C. W. (1988). Not Bumping Into Things. In Physically Based Modeling Coursenotes Atlanta, Georgia: SIGGRAPH'88.

Samuel, A. L. (1959). Some studies in machine learning using the game of checkers. IBM Journal of Research and Development, 3, 211-229.

Sims, K. (1994). Evolving Virtual Creatures. SIGGRAPH'94, 15-22.

Sun, H., & Green, M. (1993). The Use of Relations for Motion Control in an Environment With Multiple Moving Objects. Graphics Interface'93, 209-218.

Tsetlin, M. L. (1962). On the Behavior of Finite Automata in Random Media. Automation and Remote Control, 22, 1210-1219.

Tu, X., & Terzopoulos, D. (1994). Artificial Fishes: Physics, Locomotion, Perception, Behavior. SIGGRAPH'94, 43-50.

van de Panne, M., & Fuime, E. (1993). Sensor-Actuator Networks. SIGGRAPH'93, 335-342.

Wilhelms, J., & Skinner, R. (1990). A "Notion" for Interactive Behavioral Animation Control. IEEE Computer Graphics and Applications, May 1990, 14-22.

Zeltzer, D. (1985). Towards an integrated view of 3-D computer animation. The Visual Computer, 1(4), 249-259.

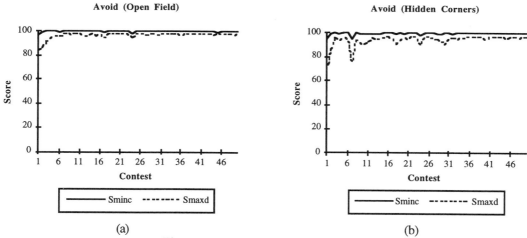

Figure 12: *Avoid* Performance Metrics

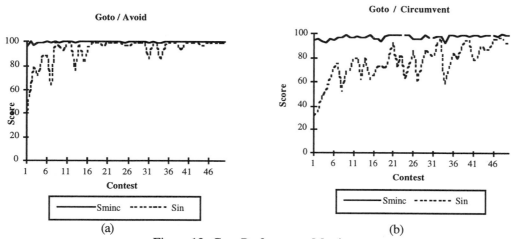

Figure 13: *Goto* Performance Metrics

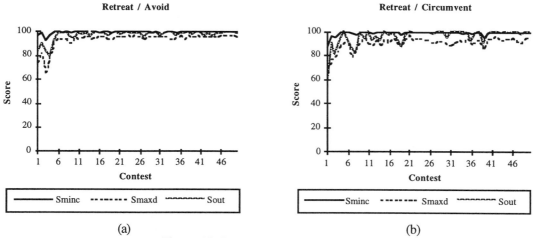

Figure 14: *Retreat* Performance Metrics

AUTHOR INDEX